TABLE 2

Real Gross National Product (billions of 1982 dollars, except as noted)

Year	Gross National Product	Personal Consumption Expenditures	Gross Private Domestic Investment	Net Exports of Goods and Services	Government Purchases of Goods and Services	Product (Percent Change from Preceding Period)	Gross National Product Deflator (Price Index)
1929	709.6	471.4	139.2	4.7	94.2		14.6
1933	498.5	378.7	22.7	−1.4	98.5	−2.1	11.2
1939	716.6	480.5	86.0	6.1	144.1	7.9	12.7
1940	772.9	502.6	111.8	8.2	150.2	7.8	13.0
1941	909.4	531.1	138.8	3.9	235.6	17.7	13.8
1942	1,080.3	527.6	76.7	−7.7	483.7	18.8	14.7
1943	1,276.2	539.9	50.4	−23.0	708.9	18.1	15.1
1944	1,380.6	557.1	56.4	−23.8	790.8	8.2	15.3
1945	1,354.8	592.7	76.5	−18.9	704.5	−1.9	15.7
1946	1,096.9	665.0	178.1	27.0	236.9	−19.0	19.4
1947	1,066.7	666.6	177.9	42.4	179.8	−2.8	22.1
1948	1,108.7	681.8	208.2	19.2	199.5	3.9	23.6
1949	1,109.0	695.4	168.8	18.8	226.0	.0	23.5
1950	1,203.7	733.2	234.9	4.7	230.8	8.5	23.9
1951	1,328.2	748.7	235.2	14.6	329.7	10.3	25.1
1952	1,380.0	771.4	211.8	6.9	389.9	3.9	25.5
1953	1,435.3	802.5	216.6	−2.7	419.0	4.0	25.9
1954	1,416.2	822.7	212.6	2.5	378.4	−1.3	26.3
1955	1,494.9	873.8	259.8	.0	361.3	5.6	27.2
1956	1,525.6	899.8	257.8	4.3	363.7	2.1	28.1
1957	1,551.1	919.7	243.4	7.0	381.1	1.7	29.1
1958	1,539.2	932.9	221.4	−10.3	395.3	−.8	29.7
1959	1,629.1	979.4	270.3	−18.2	397.7	5.8	30.4
1960	1,665.3	1,005.1	260.5	−4.0	403.7	2.2	30.9
1961	1,708.7	1,025.2	259.1	−2.7	427.1	2.6	31.2
1962	1,799.4	1,069.0	288.6	−7.5	449.4	5.3	31.9
1963	1,873.3	1,108.4	307.1	−1.9	459.8	4.1	32.4
1964	1,973.3	1,170.6	325.9	5.9	470.8	5.3	32.9
1965	2,087.6	1,236.4	367.0	−2.7	487.0	5.8	33.8
1966	2,208.3	1,298.9	390.5	−13.7	532.6	5.8	35.0
1967	2,271.4	1,337.7	374.4	−16.9	576.2	2.9	35.9
1968	2,365.6	1,405.9	391.8	−29.7	597.6	4.1	37.7
1969	2,423.3	1,456.7	410.3	−34.9	591.2	2.4	39.8
1970	2,416.2	1,492.0	381.5	−30.0	572.6	−.3	42.0
1971	2,484.8	1,538.8	419.3	−39.8	566.5	2.8	44.4
1972	2,608.5	1,621.9	465.4	−49.4	570.7	5.0	46.5
1973	2,744.1	1,689.6	520.8	−31.5	565.3	5.2	49.5
1974	2,729.3	1,674.0	481.3	.8	573.2	−.5	54.0
1975	2,695.0	1,711.9	383.3	18.9	580.9	−1.3	59.3
1976	2,826.7	1,803.9	453.5	−11.0	580.3	4.9	63.1
1977	2,968.6	1,883.8	521.3	−35.5	589.1	4.7	67.3
1978	3,115.2	1,961.0	576.9	−26.8	604.1	5.3	72.2
1979	3,192.4	2,004.4	575.2	3.6	609.1	2.5	78.6
1980	3,187.1	2,000.4	509.3	57.0	620.5	−.2	85.7
1981	3,248.8	2,024.2	545.5	49.4	629.7	1.9	94.0
1982	3,166.0	2,050.7	447.3	26.3	641.7	−2.5	100.0
1983	3,279.1	2,146.0	504.0	−19.9	649.0	3.6	103.9
1984	3,501.4	2,249.3	658.4	−84.0	677.7	6.8	107.7
1985	3,618.7	2,354.8	637.0	−104.3	731.2	3.4	110.9
1986	3,717.9	2,446.4	639.6	−129.7	761.6	2.7	113.8
1987	3,845.3	2,515.8	669.0	−118.5	779.1	3.4	117.4
1988	4,016.9	2,606.5	705.7	−75.9	780.5	4.5	121.3
1989	4,117.7	2,656.8	716.9	−54.1	798.1	2.5	126.3
1990	4,155.8	2,682.2	690.3	−37.5	820.8	.9	131.5

Source: *Economic Report of the President, 1991*, Tables B-2 and B-3.

· ECONOMICS

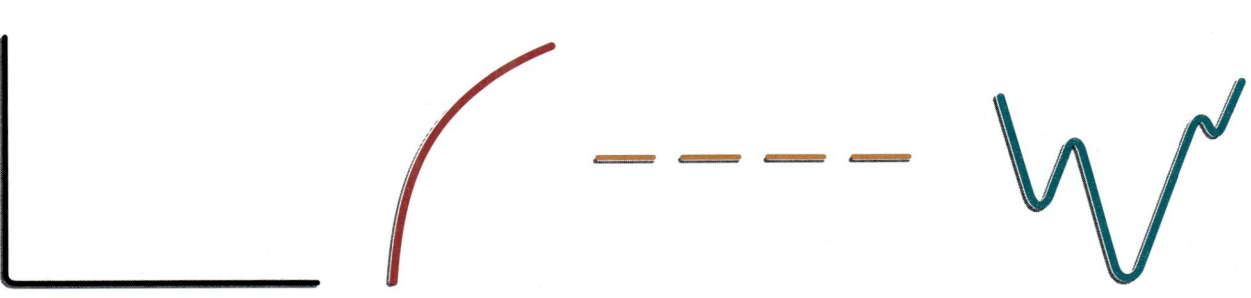

Alan E. **Dillingham** · Neil T. **Skaggs** · J. Lon **Carlson**

ILLINOIS STATE UNIVERSITY

ECONOMICS
Individual Choice and Its Consequences

ALLYN AND BACON

Boston \ London · Toronto \ Sydney · Tokyo \ Singapore

Executive Editor: Rich Wohl
Developmental Editor: Allen Workman
Series Editorial Assistant: Cheryl Ten Eick
Cover Administrator: Linda Dickinson
Composition Buyer: Linda Cox
Manufacturing Buyer: Louise Richardson
Editorial-Production Services: Leslie Olney
Art Coordinator: Grace Sheldrick
Copy Editor: Karen Stone
Text Designer: Melinda Grosser for *silk*
Cover Designer: SRZS Designs
Editorial-Production Administrator: Peter Petraitis

Copyright © 1992 by Allyn and Bacon
A Division of Simon & Schuster, Inc.
160 Gould Street
Needham Heights, Massachusetts 02194

All rights reserved. No part of the material protected by this copyright notice may be reproduced or utilized in any form or by any means, electronic or mechanical, including photocopying, recording, or by any information storage and retrieval system, without the written permission of the copyright owner.

ISBN: 0-205-13012-7

Printed in the United States of America.

10 9 8 7 6 5 4 3 2 1   96 95 94 93 92 91

To
my children, Blythe and Shane,
for the joy they have added to my life
and to
my parents, John and Carole,
for their support and friendship

To
Barb and the Girls
Caroline, Becky Jo, Meredith, and Lindsey
for all the times they've had to ''wait until tomorrow''

To
my wife, Brenda,
for all her patience, encouragement, and support

CONTENTS

Preface 0

PART I
Basic Economic Principles

CHAPTER 1
Economic Thinking 1

What Is Economics? 2

The Fundamental Premise of Economics 3

What Are Economic Problems? 4
- Using the Fundamental Premise to Identify Economic Problems 4
- How to Be Your Own Private Economist 5

Basic Economic Choices 6

An Illustration of Concepts: The Production Possibilities Frontier 7
- Make Graphs Work for You 7
- Production Possibilities Frontier 8
- The Drive to Satisfy More Wants 13

DOES IT MAKE ECONOMIC SENSE? How Much Is a Life Worth? 14

Economics as Science 16
- Scientific Process 17

WHY THE DISAGREEMENT? Parson Malthus's Doomsday Model 18
- Social Goals and the Progress of Science 19

Summary 21

Questions for Thought 22

APPENDIX TO CHAPTER 1
Graphical Analysis 24

CHAPTER 2
Mutually Beneficial Exchange 32

Choice and Value 34
   Individual Choice 34
   Costs and Benefits 35
Economic Efficiency 35
   Efficiency as a Goal 36
Gains from Exchange 37
   Comparative Advantage at "Walden Pond" 38
   Comparative Advantage and International Trade 40
WHY THE DISAGREEMENT? A Reunited Germany: Too Much Free Trade? 44
   Gains from Trade: Costs and Benefits. . . Again 46
Costs of Exchange 46
   Transactions Costs 46
DOES IT MAKE ECONOMIC SENSE? Buying a Lemon: A Case of Inadequate Information 47
   Potential Costs of Specialization 48
   Trade Can Make Some People Worse Off 48
   Individual versus Group Well-Being 49
Summary 50
Questions for Thought 51

CHAPTER 3
The Market Mechanism: Supply and Demand 54

The Market as a Rationing Device 56
   Scarcity Implies Choices 56
   Rationing Mechanisms and Behavior 57
   The Market Mechanism: Mutually Beneficial Exchange 58
Consumption Decisions: Demand 58
   Budget-Constrained Choice 59
   Negatively Sloped Demand Curve 59
   Factors Shifting the Demand Curve 61
   From Individual Demand to Market Demand 63
Production Decisions: Supply 65
   Firms Are Profit Seekers 65
   Positively Sloped Supply Curve 65
   Factors Shifting the Supply Curve 67
   From Individual Firm Supply to Market Supply 70
The Market Mechanism at Work: Equilibrium 71
   Individual Choice and Competition 71
   Market Equilibrium 73
   Price as a Signal of Altered Alternatives: Response to Change 75
   Change in Demand 76
   Change in Supply 77
   Change in Demand and Supply 79

WHY THE DISAGREEMENT? Profiteering by Oil Companies 80
DOES IT MAKE ECONOMIC SENSE? Speculators and Market Stability 84
   Market Adjustments as Responses to Changed Alternatives 86
Summary 86
Questions for Thought 87

CHAPTER 4
Economic Efficiency: A Measure of Market Performance 90

Gains from Trade 92

Economic Efficiency of Market Equilibrium 92
- Social Benefits from the Demand Curve 92
- Social Costs from the Supply Curve 94
- Society's Net Gain: Costs and Benefits. . . Again 94

THE ECONOMIST'S TOOL KIT
Relationship Between Total and Marginal 96
- Conditions for Efficient Market Outcomes Are Restrictive 100
- Market Failure 102

Market Disequilibrium Generates Market Inefficiency 102
- Price below Equilibrium 103
- Price above Equilibrium 103

Price Controls Introduce Economic Inefficiencies 105
- Price Ceilings and Floors 105
- Rental Housing 105
- Agricultural Products 107

Why Would Society Choose to Be Inefficient? 109

DOES IT MAKE ECONOMIC SENSE?
Government Purchases of Entire Dairy Herds 110
- Other Social Goals 110
- Income Redistribution 113
- Efficiency–Equity Tradeoffs 113

WHY THE DISAGREEMENT?
The Distribution of Benefits from Farm Programs 114
- Why Is Economic Efficiency So Important to Economists? 115
- Inefficient Markets and Government Intervention 116

Summary 116

Questions for Thought 118

CHAPTER 5
Decision Making in an Imperfect World 120

The Market Mechanism Is a Decision-Making Device 122
- Decentralized, but Interdependent, Decision Making 122
- How Markets Resolve Society's Three Economic Problems 123
- The Invisible Hand 124

Problems for the Market 124
- Lack of Competition 125
- Presence of Externalities 126
- Existence of Public Goods 130

DOES IT MAKE ECONOMIC SENSE?
Restrictions on Cigarette Smoking 132
- Lack of Economic Stability 134

Opportunities for Collective Action 135
- The Economics of Public Choice 135

WHY THE DISAGREEMENT?
Captured Regulators 140

Summary 142

Questions for Thought 143

PART II
Microeconomics

CHAPTER 6
The Elasticity of Demand 146

Changes in Price and Quantity Demanded 148
- Consumer Responsiveness to Price Changes 148
- Calculating the Coefficient of Price Elasticity 150
- Elastic versus Inelastic Demand 152

THE ECONOMIST'S TOOL KIT
Point Elasticity 154
- Consumer Response to Price Reexamined: Elasticity and Total Revenue 155

DOES IT MAKE ECONOMIC SENSE?
The Incidence of a Tax 158

Determinants of Price Elasticity of Demand 160
- Available Substitutes 160
- Cost of the Good Relative to Total Income 162
- Time and the Availability of Substitutes 162

WHY THE DISAGREEMENT?
The Problem of Illegal Drugs 163

Other Measures of Elasticity 164

Summary 165

Questions for Thought 166

CHAPTER 7
The Theory of Consumer Behavior 168

The Consumer Choice Problem 170

Measuring Consumer Utility 171
- Total versus Marginal Utility 171
- Diminishing Marginal Utility 173

Maximizing Consumer Utility: Costs and Benefits. . . Again 173
- Marginal Utility versus Price 173

DOES IT MAKE ECONOMIC SENSE?
The Paradox of Value 174

Consumer Demand Curves 177
- Demand and Utility Maximization 177
- Income and Substitution Effects 178

Consumer Decision Making in Practice 179
- Transactions Costs in the Theory of Demand 180

WHY THE DISAGREEMENT?
The Poverty Programs Controversy 182

Summary 183

Questions for Thought 184

APPENDIX TO CHAPTER 7
Indifference Curves Analysis 185

Overview 185
- The Utility Function and Indifference Curves 185
- Indifference Curves and the Marginal Rate of Substitution 186
- The Budget Constraint 186
- Utility Maximization 188
- Deriving the Demand Curve 189

CHAPTER 8
Entrepreneurial Behavior 192

The Entrepreneurial Challenge 194

Ways to Categorize Firms 195
- Industries 195
- Legal Structure 197
- Market Structure 201

The Firm's Objective: Profit 202
- Definition of Profit 202
- Economic Profit Is Not Accounting Profit 203

WHY THE DISAGREEMENT?
Do Firms Maximize Economic Profits? 204
- Profitability of American Business 205

Framework for Decision Making: Costs and Benefits. . . Again 207

DOES IT MAKE ECONOMIC SENSE?
How Can *USA Today* Keep Operating with No Profit in Seven Years? 209

Technology and Production Costs 210

Summary 211

Questions for Thought 212

CONTENTS xi

CHAPTER 9
Production Costs, Revenues, and Profit Maximization 214

The Short-Run Production Process 216
    Production Function 216
    The Firm's Cost Functions 218

THE ECONOMIST'S TOOL KIT
Average–Marginal Relationships: A Hint 224
    Short-Run Cost Functions 224

Long-Run Production Costs 227

WHY THE DISAGREEMENT?
Excess Capacity in the Electric Utility Industry 228
    Long-Run Cost Minimization 228
    Long-Run Average Cost 231
    Economies of Scale 232

DOES IT MAKE ECONOMIC SENSE?
A New Round of Container-Ship Construction 233

Firm Output and Revenue 234
    Price-Taking Firms 234
    Price-Searching Firms 235

Short-Run Profit Maximization 237
    Profit Maximization for the Price-Taking Firm 237
    Profit Maximization for the Price-Searching Firm 238

Supply Decisions in a Dynamic Economy 239

Summary 240

Questions for Thought 241

APPENDIX TO CHAPTER 9
Isoquants, Input Prices, and Least-Cost Production 243

Overview 243
    The Production Function and Isoquants 243
    Isoquants and the Marginal Rate of Technical Rate of Technical Substitution 244
    The Isocost Line 244
    Least-Cost Production 246
    The Effect of a Change in Relative Input Prices 247

CHAPTER 10
The Perfect Competition Model 248

Characteristics of a Perfectly Competitive Market 250

Determination of Profit. . . Or Loss 251
    To Produce or Not to Produce 253
    Sunk Costs Again 254

DOES IT MAKE ECONOMIC SENSE?
Government Bailout of the Farm Credit System 256

Short-Run Supply Curve for the Price-Taking Firm 256

Perfect Competition and Rational Behavior 258

The Dynamics of the Market Mechanism: Long-Run Equilibrium 258
    Demand Changes in Perfectly Competitive Markets 259
    Long-Run Supply 262
    Consumer Sovereignty 264

Production Costs and Efficiency 265
    Economic Efficiency in the Long Run 265
    Cost Changes in Perfectly Competitive Markets 266

General Equilibrium in the Economy 270

WHY THE DISAGREEMENT?
Restrictions on Free Trade 272

Costs and Benefits Again: The Invisible Hand of the Market 273
- Perfectly Competitive Markets Allocate Resources Efficiently 273
- Economic Efficiency Is Achieved Through an Invisible Hand 273

The Perfectly Competitive Model in the Science of Economics 274
- The Economic Problem and Economic Efficiency 274
- Perfect Competition is a Reference Point 275
- A Close Approximation to Perfect Competition 275
- Imperfect Information and Mobility 275

Summary 278

Questions for Thought 279

CHAPTER 11
Small Firm Behavior: The Imperfect Competition Model 280

Real People, Space, and Time 282
- Costly Information and Mobility 282
- Heterogeneous Consumer Tastes 283

Monopolistic Competition 283
- Short-Run Profit Maximization 284

Long-Run Equilibrium Position 287
- Market Forces Eliminate Economic Profits 287
- Efficiency Implications 289

DOES IT MAKE ECONOMIC SENSE?
Shakeouts in the Fast Food Industry 289

Competitive Pressure 291
- The Incentive to Escape Competition 291
- Product Differentiation 292
- Government Regulation 293

WHY THE DISAGREEMENT?
Taxi Decontrol 294

Summary 295

Questions for Thought 296

CHAPTER 12
Large Firm Behavior: The Imperfect Competition Model 298

Resource Immobility and Competitive Pressure 300
- Barriers to Entry 300
- Long-Run Economic Profits 302

Monopoly 303
- Short-Run and Long-Run Profit Maximization 304
- Efficiency Implications 306
- Natural Monopoly 307

WHY THE DISAGREEMENT?
Local Phone Service—How Much Should It Cost? 312

Oligopoly 312
- General Characteristics 313
- Short-Run Profit Maximization: Competition Among Rivals 315

THE ECONOMIST'S TOOL KIT
Game Theory and the Prisoner's Dilemma 316

Alternatives to Competition 318
- Collusion Among Rivals 318
- Successful Collusion 320
- Government Regulation and Cartel-Like Behavior 321
- Mergers 322

Oligopoly: Economic Profits and Efficiency 323
- Economic Profits 323
- Economic Efficiency 323

DOES IT MAKE ECONOMIC SENSE?
With a Monopoly on Natural Gas, Why Advertise? 324

Summary 325

Questions for Thought 326

CHAPTER 13
The Regulation of Business Behavior: Policy in Transition 328

Lack of Competition and Market Outcomes 330

    Lack of Competition Causes Inefficiency 330

    Can Market Failure Be Corrected? 330

Collective Decision-Making Options 331

    Definition of Property Rights 331

    Government Ownership of Business 331

    Establishment and Enforcement of Rules for a Competitive Environment 333

    Regulation of Firm Behavior 337

WHY THE DISAGREEMENT? Should We Reregulate the Cable Television Industry? 338

The Deregulation of Business Behavior 340

    A Brief Review of Significant Deregulation Developments 340

The Case for Deregulation 342

    Regulation Influences the Form of Competition 342

    Regulation Redistributes Income Deliberately or Arbitrarily 343

    Regulation Can Reduce Competition and Efficiency: The Establishment of Cartel-Like Conditions 346

Airline Deregulation: A Case Study 347

DOES IT MAKE ECONOMIC SENSE? Additional Deregulation of the Air Transportation Industry 349

The Market Mechanism in Action 350

    Deregulation Spurs the Market On 350

Summary 351

Questions for Thought 352

CHAPTER 14
The Theory of Resource Markets 354

Determinants of Resource Prices 356

The Firm's Demand for Resources 356

    Marginal Physical Product 357

    Product Price and Marginal Revenue Product 358

    Marginal Resource Cost and the Demand Schedule for Labor 360

Market Demand for Resources 361

Price Elasticity of Demand for Resources 363

Determinants of Resource Price Elasticity 364

    Price Elasticity in the Short Run 364

    Price Elasticity in the Long Run 365

DOES IT MAKE ECONOMIC SENSE? Management, Unions, and Trade Policy 366

Supply of Resources 366

    Resource Supply in the Short Run 367

    Resource Supply in the Long Run 369

WHY THE DISAGREEMENT? The Tin Cartel: Doomed to Fail? 370

    The Labor Supply Schedule: Costs and Benefits. . . Again 373

Equilibrium in the Resource Market 374

Summary 377

Questions for Thought 378

CHAPTER 15
The Market for Labor 380

Significance of Labor in the Economy 382

The Labor Market as an Abstraction 383
- A Labor Market for Each Skill 383

The Aggregate Labor Market: Wage and Employment Determination 383

Explaining Observed Wage Differences 385
- Equalizing Wage Differences 386
- Nonequalizing Wage Differences 389

DOES IT MAKE ECONOMIC SENSE? Market Wages: Professional Sports versus Education 390
- Disequilibrium Wage Differences 392

Investment in Education: Costs and Benefits. . . Again 392

Discrimination in the Labor Market 394

WHY THE DISAGREEMENT? Wage Setting by Comparable Worth 396

Noncompetitive Labor Markets 396

Long-Term Employment Contracts 399

Summary 400

Questions for Thought 401

CHAPTER 16
Trade Unions and Collective Bargaining 402

The Purpose of Labor Unions 404

DOES IT MAKE ECONOMIC SENSE? Are Strikes Logical? 406

American Unionism: Structure and Membership 408

Union Membership in the United States: Growth and Decline 409
- Labor Unions Prior to the 1930s 409
- Organized Labor's Golden Years: 1935 to 1955 410
- Stagnation and Decline: 1955 to the Present 411

The Goals of Labor Unions 413
- A Public Choice Model of Union Decision Making 414

A Model of Unions' Impact on Wages and Employment 415

Policies to Increase Union Power 416
- Policies to Alter the Demand Curve 417
- Policies to Prevent Undercutting the Union Wage 417

WHY THE DISAGREEMENT? Increasing the Minimum Wage 418

Unions and Wages: The Evidence 420

The Effects of Unions: Monopsony 421

Unions and Economic Welfare: A Broader View 421

Summary 422

Questions for Thought 423

CHAPTER 17
The Capital Market 424

Consumption or Investment: Costs and Benefits. . . Again 426

The Investment Decision 427

Demand for Capital 427
- Present Value of a Future Sum 428
- The Computer Investment 429
- Demand Curve for Capital 429

WHY THE DISAGREEMENT? Private versus Social Discount Rates 430

Investment Benefits 431
- Reduced Costs 431

DOES IT MAKE ECONOMIC SENSE? Labor Opposition to Technological Change 433
- New Products 434
- Productivity Growth 434

THE ECONOMIST'S TOOL KIT An Unemployment Measure for Capital 435

Investment Costs: The Interest Rate 436
- The Rate of Interest and the Return to Capital 438
- Why Do Interest Rates Differ? 439
- Financial Markets and Intermediaries 440

Summary 440

Questions for Thought 441

CHAPTER 18
Income Equality and Poverty 442

The Distribution of Income in the United States 444
- Family Income as a Measure of Well-Being 447
- Distribution of Lifetime Incomes 448
- Income Differences by Family Characteristics 450
- Marginal Productivity Theory and Income Distribution 453
- Income Redistribution 454

Poverty in the United States 455
- Is the Incidence of Poverty Overstated? 457
- Causes of Poverty 458

WHY THE DISAGREEMENT?
Should Welfare be Workfare? 458

Income Redistribution and Antipoverty Policy 462
- Antipoverty Policies 463

DOES IT MAKE ECONOMIC SENSE?
Diverging Poverty Rates 464

Summary 466

Questions for Thought 467

CHAPTER 19
Externalities, Public Goods, and Common-Property Resources: Problems for the Market Mechanism 468

Conditions That Lead to Inefficient Market Outcomes 470
- Property Rights Revisited 470
- The Coase Theorem 471

Externalities 473
- External Costs 473
- External Benefits 475
- Policy Prescriptions 476

External Costs and Environmental Pollution 477
- When is Pollution a Social Problem? 477
- The Opportunity Cost of Improved Environmental Quality 478
- Optimal Amount of Environmental Quality: Balancing Benefits and Costs 478

DOES IT MAKE ECONOMIC SENSE?
The Benefits and Costs of Reducing Pollution from Wood-Burning Stoves 480
- Pollution-Control Policies 480

WHY THE DISAGREEMENT?
Reauthorization of the Clean Air Act 485

Public Goods 486
- Determining the Optimal Quantity of Public Goods 486
- The Problem of Free Riders 488
- Policy Prescriptions 488

Common-Property Resources 489
- Policy Prescription 490

Cost of Information 490
- Decisions Made in Ignorance 490
- Efficiency Considerations 491
- Equity Considerations 492
- Policy Prescriptions 492

Opportunities for Collective Action 492
- The Challenge of Good Public Policy 492
- The Complications of Political Behavior 493

Summary 493

Questions for Thought 494

xvi CONTENTS

PART III
Macroeconomics

CHAPTER 20
Public Choice 496

Behavior of Elected Legislatures 498
- What Do Elected Officials Maximize? 498
- Voter Behavior 498
- Outcomes in Political Markets 500
- Political Power and Legislative Outcomes 501

Bureaucracy 504
- What Do Bureaucrats Maximize? 504
- Nature of Bureaus 504
- Evidence 505

DOES IT MAKE ECONOMIC SENSE?
Fighting Fires for Profit 506

Constitutional Economics 507

WHY THE DISAGREEMENT?
The Firemen First Principle 508
- Freedom and Leviathan 509
- Benefits of Restraint 510

So What's the Bottom Line? 511

Summary 511

Questions for Thought 512

CHAPTER 21
From Individual Choice to Macroeconomics 514

The Economic Choice Problem 516
- Sources of Funds 516
- Uses of Funds 517

Individual Choice and the Budget Constraint 517
- An Example 518
- The General Case 520

Market Demands and Supplies 520
- Interdependence of Markets 521

Aggregation Across Markets 522
- Gross National Product 523

Measuring Production when Prices Are Changing 526

WHY THE DISAGREEMENT?
Social Welfare and Real GNP 526
- Price Indexes 528

THE ECONOMIST'S TOOL KIT
Price Indexes 529

DOES IT MAKE ECONOMIC SENSE?
Are GNP Comparisons Among Nations Worth Making? 530

Summary 532

Questions for Thought 532

APPENDIX TO CHAPTER 21
National Income and Product Accounts 534

CHAPTER 22
Overview of Macroeconomics 536

The Macroeconomic System 538
- Circular Flow 538
- Income and Expenditure Categories 539
- Expanded Circular Flow Model 540

DOES IT MAKE ECONOMIC SENSE?
Say's Law of Markets 542

Recent Behavior of the U.S. Economy 543
- Output and Prices 543
- Employment and Unemployment 546
- The Twin Deficits 548
- Macroeconomic Goals 549
- Complex Issues Require Sophisticated Analysis 550

The Macroeconomic Framework 550
- Goods and Services Market 550
- Labor Market 551
- Credit Market 551
- Money Market 552
- Putting It All Together 553

WHY THE DISAGREEMENT?
Is Macroeconomics Possible? 553

Summary 554

Questions for Thought 554

CHAPTER 23
Aggregate Demand for Goods and Services 556

Consumption Demand 558
- Interdependence of Consumption Demand and Labor Supply 558
- Income and Consumption: Keynesian Theory 558
- Empirical Evidence on Consumption 560
- Theory of Consumption 563

DOES IT MAKE ECONOMIC SENSE?
Borrowing to Sustain Consumption 566
- Durable Consumer Goods 567
- Income Taxes, Transfer Payments, and Consumption 569

WHY THE DISAGREEMENT?
Temporary Tax Changes 570

Investment Demand 570
- Real versus Financial Investment 570
- Gross and Net Investment 571
- Common Sense of Net Investment 572
- Investment Demand Curve 572
- Factors Affecting Investment Demand 574
- Inventory Investment 575
- Instability of Investment Spending 576

Government Demand for Goods and Services 578

Net Exports 578

Aggregate Demand for Goods and Services 579
- Factors Affecting Aggregate Demand 579
- Aggregate Demand Curve 580
- Shifting the AD Curve 582

Summary 583

Questions for Thought 584

APPENDIX TO CHAPTER 23
The Present Value Approach to Investment Decisions 586

CHAPTER 24
Aggregate Supply of Goods and Services 588

Labor Market 590
- Aggregate Supply of Labor 590
- Aggregate Demand for Labor 592
- Labor Market Equilibrium 594

WHY THE DISAGREEMENT?
Immigration: Good or Bad for the United States? 596

Natural Output Level 599
- Factors Determining the Natural Output Level 599

DOES IT MAKE ECONOMIC SENSE?
Are We Running Out of Resources? 600

Aggregate Supply 603
- Sticky Wages, Employment Changes, and Short-Run Aggregate Supply 603
- Wage Adjustment, SRAS Shifts, and Long-Run Aggregate Supply 608
- Stability of the SRAS Curve 609

Summary 610

Questions for Thought 610

APPENDIX TO CHAPTER 24
Microfoundations of the Labor Market 612
- Labor Supply Theory 612
- Labor Demand Theory 614

CHAPTER 25
The Long-Run Model: The Economy with Flexible Prices 618

Long-Run Aggregate Equilibrium 620
- The Model in Motion: Aggregate Demand Changes 621
- The Model in Motion: Aggregate Supply Changes 624

DOES IT MAKE ECONOMIC SENSE? Growing Wealth and Declining Happiness 625

The Long-Run Model and Actual Economic Behavior 626
- Output Growth 627

THE ECONOMIST'S TOOL KIT Growth Rates 629
- Role of Government in Promoting Growth 632

WHY THE DISAGREEMENT? Does the United States Have a Savings Crisis? 634
- Theoretical Models and Reality 635
- Price-Level Growth 637

Summary 641

Questions for Thought 642

CHAPTER 26
The Short-Run Model: The Economy with Wage and Price Rigidities 644

Sticky Wages and Output Movements 646

Expectations Formation 647
- Adaptive Expectations 648
- Rational Expectations 649

THE ECONOMIST'S TOOL KIT Adaptive Expectations 650
- Are Rational Expectations Reasonable? 651

DOES IT MAKE ECONOMIC SENSE? Possibility of a Vertical SRAS Curve 653
- Problem of Output Persistence 654
- Contracts and Persistence 655

Working with the Short-Run Model 656
- Aggregate Demand Changes 657
- Aggregate Supply Changes 659

THE ECONOMIST'S TOOL KIT The Expenditure Multiplier 660
- The 1960s: Aggregate Demand on the Move 661
- The 1970s: The Migration of SRAS 664
- The 1980s: Reversing the Inflationary Spiral 665

An Overview of Stabilization Theory 667
- The Stabilization Problem 667
- Stabilization Policy 668

WHY THE DISAGREEMENT? Responding to Oil Price Shocks 670
- A Word of Caution 672

Summary 673

Questions for Thought 673

APPENDIX TO CHAPTER 26 Price Adjustment Process 675
- Factors Limiting Price Flexibility 675
- Cost-Based Pricing and the Transmission of Inflation 676

CONTENTS xix

CHAPTER 27
Money: What It Is and Why People Hold It 682

Nature of Money 684
- Barter 684
- Efficiency of Indirect Trade 685
- Characteristics of a Medium of Exchange 686
- Functions Served by Money 687

The U.S. Money Supply 688
- Basic Definitions 688
- Evolution of the U.S. Money Supply 689

DOES IT MAKE ECONOMIC SENSE?
Could New Money Rescue the Soviet Economy? 692

Theory of Money Demand 693
- Income: The Primary Determinant of Money Demand 693
- Role of Opportunity Cost 694
- Credit Cards and Money Demand 696

Aggregate Demand and Changes in Money Demand 696
- Effects through the Budget Constraint 697
- Effects through the Interest Rate 698
- Money Supply Definitions, Money Demand, and Monetary Policy 700

WHY THE DISAGREEMENT?
Stable Money Supply Growth 702

Summary 706

Questions for Thought 706

CHAPTER 28
The Banking System, the Federal Reserve, and Monetary Policy 708

Financial Intermediation 710

Federal Reserve System 711
- A Brief History of the Federal Reserve System 711
- Structure and Functions of the Federal Reserve System 714

How Money Is Created 716
- Multiplier Process 717
- Relaxing Assumptions: The Effect on the Multiplier 720
- Monetary Base: The Raw Material for the System 720
- An Empirical Note: Growth of Money and the Monetary Base 721

Monetary Policy: Tools and Strategy 723
- Mechanics of Open Market Operations 723
- Discount Rate 725
- Reserve Requirements 726

DOES IT MAKE ECONOMIC SENSE?
Eliminating Reserve Requirements 726
- Strategy of Monetary Policy 727

WHY THE DISAGREEMENT?
Should the Federal Reserve System Be Independent? 730
- Policy in a Political Environment: The Place of the Federal Reserve in the Governmental System 731

Effect of Changes in the Money Supply on Aggregate Demand 731

Summary 733

Questions for Thought 734

APPENDIX TO CHAPTER 28
The Savings and Loan Crisis 736
- Background 736
- Deregulation 737
- Moral Hazard 738
- Legislative Action 738

CHAPTER 29
The Credit Market 740

The Interest Rate Is the Price of—What? 742
- Money and Credit: What's the Difference? 742
- Loans and Bonds 743
- Bond Prices and Interest Rates 744

Which One Is *the* Interest Rate? 745

Credit Market Model 746
- Demand for Credit 746
- Supply of Credit 750

Using the Credit Market Model 753
- Interest Rate Determination 753
- Working with the Model 753

WHY THE DISAGREEMENT?
Those Dangerous Foreign Savers 755
- Nominal and Real Interest Rates 758

Linking the Two Interest Rate Models 759

DOES IT MAKE ECONOMIC SENSE?
Can the Federal Reserve Control Interest Rates? 762

Summary 764

Questions for Thought 764

APPENDIX TO CHAPTER 29
Interest Rates and Bond Prices 766

CHAPTER 30
Government Finance and Fiscal Policy 768

Recent Trends in Government Finance 770

Fiscal Policy 772
- Government Spending and Aggregate Demand 772
- Government Spending and Aggregate Supply 774
- Taxation and Aggregate Demand 776
- Taxes and Aggregate Supply 778

Budget Deficits and Borrowing 780

WHY THE DISAGREEMENT?
Paying for Social Security 782
- A Historical Look at Deficits 782
- Actual and High Employment Deficits 784
- Effect of Deficits on the Credit Market 785
- Effect of Deficits on Aggregate Demand 786

DOES IT MAKE ECONOMIC SENSE?
Ricardian Equivalence Principle 788
- Effect of Deficits on Aggregate Supply 789

Countercyclical Fiscal Policy versus Balanced Budgets 790
- Do Governments Always Grow? 791
- The Idea of a Balanced Budget Amendment 791

Government Debt 793
- How Large Is the National Debt? 793
- Is the Debt a Burden on Future Generations? 795
- Other Possible Negative Effects of the Debt 796
- Monetizing the Debt: Inflation and the Budget 796

Summary 797

Questions for Thought 798

CHAPTER 31
Labor Market Rigidities and Unemployment 800

Labor Demand, Labor Supply, and Unemployment 802

Aggregate Unemployment 804
   Flow Model of Unemployment 804

DOES IT MAKE ECONOMIC SENSE?
Average Unemployment Duration and the Long-Term Unemployed 806
   Categories of Unemployment 808

WHY THE DISAGREEMENT?
Path to a Career or Just a Dead-End Job? 810
   Natural Rate of Unemployment 810

Explaining the Existence of Unemployment 812
   Shortcomings of the Simple Labor Demand–Supply Model 813
   Two Complementary Theories of Unemployment 815

Unemployment Policy 825
   Unemployment Is Really a Variety of Problems 825
   Cyclical Unemployment: Aggregate Demand Policy 826
   Frictional and Structural Unemployment: Aggregate Supply Policy 826

Summary 827

Questions for Thought 828

CHAPTER 32
Cyclical Behavior: Theory and Evidence 830

Charting the Business Cycle 832

What Causes Business Cycles? 835
   Keynesian View: Investment Instability 835

WHY THE DISAGREEMENT?
Has the Economy Really Become More Stable? 836
   Monetarist View: Money Supply Instability 841
   New Classical Modifications of Monetarist Theory 844
   New Keynesian Economics 845
   A Look at the Empirical Evidence 846
   What Causes Some Recessions to Turn into Depressions? 858

DOES IT MAKE ECONOMIC SENSE?
Is the Business Cycle Disappearing? 861

What Type of Stabilization Policy Might Be Successful? 862

Summary 863

Questions for Thought 864

CHAPTER 33
Monetary Policy: A Further Treatment 866

Monetary Transmission Mechanism 868

Theory of Monetary Policy 869
   Keynesian View of the Economy 870
   Keynesian Theory of Countercyclical Policy 870
   Monetarist View of the Economy 871
   Monetarist Theory of Monetary Policy 872

Critique of the Theories of Monetary Policy 875
   Has Monetary Policy Been Stabilizing? 875
   Why Hasn't Countercyclical Policy Worked Better? 880

DOES IT MAKE ECONOMIC SENSE?
A Return to the Gold Standard? 888
   Would a Policy Rule Improve Monetary Policy? 889

WHY THE DISAGREEMENT?
Would a Constant Money Supply Growth Rate Have Caused a Depression in the Early 1980s? 892

Summary 893

Questions for Thought 894

xxii ■ CONTENTS

CHAPTER 34
Fiscal Policy: A Further Treatment 896

Countercyclical Fiscal Policy in Theory and Practice 898

    Theory 898

WHY THE DISAGREEMENT?
Pro-Growth or Just Pro-Rich? The Debate Over Cutting the Capital Gains Tax 902

    Practice 902

    Fiscal Policy Since World War II 908

DOES IT MAKE ECONOMIC SENSE?
Is the Economy Depression Proof? 912

How Powerful Is Fiscal Policy? 913

    Crowding out (or in) in the Short Run and the Long 913

    Composition of Government Spending 915

    Measuring the Effect of Fiscal Policy 917

National Industrial Policy 919

Summary 923

Questions for Thought 924

PART IV
The International Economy

CHAPTER 35
International Trade 926

Theory of Trade 928

    Comparative Advantage: An Example 928

    Terms of Trade 930

    Price Equalization and Gains from Trade 931

    Gains from Trade: A Technical Analysis 933

    Costs of Adjusting to International Trade 934

Changing the Terms of Trade 936

    Tariffs and Quotas 936

    Arguments in Favor of Tariffs 938

DOES IT MAKE ECONOMIC SENSE?
Protectionism and Domestic Employment 940

    Using Trade Theory to Estimate the Cost of the Voluntary Import Agreement on Japanese Automobiles 942

Exports, Imports, and the Balance of Trade 944

    Trends in International Trade 944

    What Does the United States Trade? 945

WHY THE DISAGREEMENT?
Is Japan a Boon or a Threat to the U.S. Economy? 948

Summary 949

Questions for Thought 950

CHAPTER 36
International Finance and the Open-Economy Model 952

Balance of Payments 954

Determining the Exchange Rate 957
- Demand for a Currency 957
- Supply of a Currency 958
- Exchange Rate 959

Fixed and Flexible Exchange Rates 960
- Purchasing Power Parity 961
- Policies to Hold an Exchange Rate Fixed 962
- A Middle Course: The Dirty Float 965

DOES IT MAKE ECONOMIC SENSE?
Bolshoi Mac, or Why Does McDonald's Want Rubles Anyway? 966

Open-Economy Macroeconomics 967
- Flexible Exchange Rate System 967
- Fixed Exchange Rate System 970
- Comparing Flexible and Fixed Exchange Rate Systems 972
- Government Budget Deficits in a Flexible Exchange Rate System 973

WHY THE DISAGREEMENT?
Selling America 974

Summary 975

Questions for Thought 976

CHAPTER 37
Comparative Economic Systems: Theory and Evidence 978

Major Problems Facing Any Economy 980

Market and Socialist Responses to the Major Economic Problems 980
- What, and How Much, to Produce 980
- How to Produce the Desired Goods 982
- How Output Is Distributed 982

Comparing Market and Socialist Economies 983
- What, and How Much, to Produce 983
- How to Produce the Desired Goods 984
- How Output Is Distributed 984

A Continuum of Market Types 985
- State Ownership of the Means of Production 985
- State Planning of the Economy 986
- Income Distribution and Welfare 986
- Mix and Match: Multiple Dimensions of Modern Economies 987

A Quick Look at Some Representative Economies 988
- A Command Economy: The USSR 988
- Poland: Shock Therapy for a Command Economy 991

WHY THE DISAGREEMENT?
Slicing the Socialist Pie 992
- Market Socialism: Yugoslavia 996
- Government Planning in a Market Economy: France 997
- A Welfare State: Sweden 998
- The Free Market at Work: Hong Kong 999

DOES IT MAKE ECONOMIC SENSE?
Is the U.S. Social-Welfare Effort Superior to the Swedish? 1000
- What Are We to Conclude? 1000

Summary 1001

Questions for Thought 1002

Glossary 1004

Index 1017

PREFACE

The discipline of economics as practiced by economists has changed considerably over the past two decades. Although this is particularly evident in the area of macroeconomics, it can also be seen in modern microeconomic analysis. The changes in economics reflect both changes in the economic problems being confronted and changes in economic theory itself. As an example of the former, consider the attention devoted by the news media to the incentive effects and supply-side implications of economic policy. As examples of the latter, note the search for sound microeconomic underpinnings of macroeconomics and the development of the theory of contestable markets.

As has always been the case, changes in the topics economists discuss and in the way economists approach problems first appear in technical journals, then in upper-level textbooks, and finally — after a considerable lag — in principles texts. For some years now the many advances in economic reasoning that emerged from the tumultuous 1970s have been filtering into principles texts. Although *Economics: Individual Choice and Its Consequences* is not the only recent text to incorporate a significant number of the new advances, these new advances more clearly define the content of *Economics* than of most competing texts. In *Economics*, content and pedagogy go hand in hand to present students with a relevant and modern treatment of economic principles.

Too often textbooks present current issues or the latest theoretical developments within a framework designed to highlight a different set of issues, making it difficult for students to understand the importance of the topic. Furthermore, too many textbooks continue to include topics of doubtful relevance simply because those topics "have always been taught." Students are thus doubly harmed, by not receiving the clearest presentation of relevant material and by being forced to comprehend material bearing little relationship to the economic problems dominating current discussions.

Economics is unique in its approach to both content and pedagogy. The wide variety of topics discussed are tied together by constant attention to the unifying concepts that underlie all facets of economic analysis. Detailed information on the content innovations of *Economics* is included in the preface of the Annotated Instructor's Edition.

Learning Aids

We believe that the most important learning aid in the *Economics* package is the organization of the text itself. In addition to the organization of the text, learning aids include the following:

1. **Chapter overviews** give a bird's eye view of what is coming in each chapter.
2. **Learning objectives** follow each chapter overview and highlight the most important themes in that chapter.
3. **Extended examples** demonstrate the relevance of economic theory to real world events.
4. **Why the Disagreement?** boxes in every chapter present opposing sides on current hot topics of economic policy. The economic interests of both parties are explained by showing the underlying economic model and how it applies to the point of disagreement.
5. **Does It Make Economic Sense?** boxes in every chapter illustrate how economic theory, applied properly, can explain what on the surface appears to be behavior that contradicts economic principles.
6. **The Economist's Tool Kit** boxes appear in selected chapters and discuss specialized economic techniques or data.
7. **Margin definitions** of key terms run throughout every chapter.
8. **Section Recaps** appear in the margin and summarize the major points of each section of the text.
9. **Chapter Summaries** briefly recount each chapter's main arguments.
10. **Questions for Thought** conclude each chapter and are arranged in three categories: **knowledge** questions, **application** questions, and **synthesis** questions. They are designed to test understanding of the material, and to prepare for exams.
11. **Glossary** of key terms at the end of the text provides a quick and handy reference for review.
12 **Carefully selected and designed graphs** are used throughout the text. Three features of these graphs that are especially useful:

    - Pedgogical use of color has successive curves in a lighter shade than preceding curves, make movements of those curves easy to follow.
    - Highlight boxes within graphs concisely explain the concept of the graph right next to the graph itself.
    - A complete caption for each graph helps interpret and explain the graph in clear and simple terms.

Supplements

An innovative and complete supplements package includes:

1. A unique Annotated Instructor's Edition
2. A test bank (in print and computerized form)
3. A student Study Guide
4. Transparency overlays
5. Software
6. CNN videos
7. A CNN Video User's Guide

Detailed information on each of these supplements can be found in the preface of the Annotated Instructor's Edition.

Available Formats

Economics: Individual Choice and Its Consequences can be ordered in any of three versions: a hardback text that includes both microeconomics and macroeconomics, a paperback volume on microeconomics, and a paperback volume on macroeconomics. The following table indicates the content of each version.

Combined text	Micro text	Macro text
Part I Basic Economic Principles	*Part I*	*Part I*
1. Economic Thinking	1	1
2. Mutually Beneficial Exchange	2	2
3. The Market Mechanism: Supply and Demand	3	3
4. Economic Efficiency: A Measure of Market Performance	4	4
5. Decision Making in an Imperfect World	5	5
Part II Microeconomics	*Part II*	
6. The Elasticity of Demand	6	
7. The Theory of Consumer Behavior	7	
8. Entrepreneurial Behavior	8	
9. Production Costs, Revenues, and Profit Maximization	9	
10. The Perfect Competition Model	10	
11. Small Firm Behavior: The Imperfect Competition Model	11	
12. Large Firm Behavior: The Imperfect Competition Model	12	
13. The Regulation of Business Behavior: Policy in Transition	13	
14. The Theory of Resource Markets	14	
15. The Market for Labor	15	
16. Trade Unions and Collective Bargaining	16	
17. The Capital Market	17	
18. Income Inequality and Poverty	18	*(continued)*

Combined text	Micro text	Macro text
Part II Microeconomics	*Part II*	
19. Externalities, Public Goods, and Common-Property Resources: Problems for the Market Mechanism	19	
20. Public Choice	20	
Part III Macroeconomics		*Part II*
21. From Individual Choice to Macroeconomics		6
22. Overview of Macroeconomics		7
23. Aggregate Demand for Goods and Services		8
24. Aggregate Supply of Goods and Services		9
25. The Long-Run Model: The Economy with Flexible Prices		10
26. The Short-Run Model: The Economy with Wage and Price Rigidities		11
27. Money: What It Is and Why People Hold It		12
28. The Banking System, The Federal Reserve, and Monetary Policy		13
29. The Credit Market		14
30. Government Finance and Fiscal Policy		15
31. Labor Market Rigidities and Unemployment		16
32. Cyclical Behavior: Theory and Evidence		17
33. Monetary Policy: A Further Treatment		18
34. Fiscal Policy: A Further Treatment		19
Part IV The International Economy	*Part III*	*Part III*
35. International Trade	21	20
36. International Finance and the Open-Economy Model		21
37. Comparative Economic Systems: Theory and Evidence		22

Acknowledgements

We owe a debt of greater or lesser size to a large number of people, including colleagues, student assistants, reviewers, marketing research participants, focus group participants, production personnel, and family and friends. All played an important role in developing and refining this project over several years. A number of colleagues (at ISU and elsewhere) contributed to the text by reading and commenting on various portions of it or by discussing troublesome issues with us. Those particularly deserving mention include Mark Walbert, Stu Dorsey, Mike Nelson, Dan Rich, Bob Roth, Ray Cohn, Tony Ostrosky, Mark Wohar, Carla Tighe, Dean Hiebert, Mat Morey, and Karl McDermott. The Economics Department secretaries, Judy Robbins and Monica Martindale, often went beyond the pale in helping us mail manuscripts, galley proofs, and other materials on the spur of the moment.

A number of student assistants provided valuable services of various kinds. They include Scott Cooley, Deb Foderberg, Tim Kelley, Doug Preble, Joe Ryan, Cathy Schmidt, Bintao Shi, and Jim Webber. The students who used earlier drafts of the manuscript as their text also deserve thanks.

The list of reviewers that follows is lengthy. We are grateful to all of the reviewers for the effort they put into this project. We especially want to thank a handful of reviewers who went above and beyond the call of duty in the work they did on multiple drafts of the text: Bill Even, Albert Gutowsky, George Hoffer, Rebecca Morton, Ed Price, and Jim Stephenson.

James Stephenson
Iowa State University

Dennis P. Leyden
University of North Carolina-Greensboro

Thomas Hatcher
Fordham University

Louis Pisciottoli
California State University — Fresno

Wofgang Mayer
University of Cincinnati

John Isbister
Merrill College

Martha Williams
Kent State University

Pamela J. Brown
California State University — Northridge

Patricia Graham
University of Northern Colorado

Albert Gutowsky
California State University — Sacramento

George Hoffer
Virginia Commonwealth University

Alfred Lubell
SUNY — Oneonta

Rebecca Summary
Southeast Missouri University

Jean Gauger
Arizona State University

Dennis Jansen
Indiana University

William Even
Miami University

Kathleen Brook
New Mexico State University

Edward Price
Oklahoma State University

Richard McHugh
University of Missouri

Loraine Donaldson
Georgia State University

Norman Obst
Michigan State University

Win Fields
Miami University

Rebecca Morton
Nicholls State University

John Garen
University of Kentucky

Elchanan Cohn
University of Southern California

Vincent H. Smith
Montana State University

Glenn R. Hueckel
Purdue University

Anthony Bryski
Mercer University

A. Edward Day
University of Central Florida

Robert Carson
SUNY — Oneonta

Peter Frevert
University of Kansas

Andrew Barnett
Auburn University

Nancy Jianakoplos
Michigan State University

Lawrence Brunner
Central Michigan University

Philip Sorensen
Florida State University

James Walker
Indiana University

Don Williams
Kent State University

Robert Berry
Miami University

LuAnn Duffus
California State University — Hayward

Charles Fischer
Pittsburg State University

Richard Rosenberg
Pennsylvania State University

Paul Trescott
Southern Illinois University

James P. LeSage
Bowling Green State University

Michael Kuplik
University of Montana

Arthur Diamond
University of Nebraska-Omaha

Janet West
University of Nebraska

Paul Coomes
University of Louisville

Mark Wheeler
Bowling Green State University

T. Norman VanCott
Ball State University

Mary Jean Rivers
Seattle University

W. Charles Sawyer
University of Southern Mississippi

William B. Green
Sam Houston State University

Gary Sellers
University of Akron

Thomas Cosimano
Texas A&M University

Mark Plant
University of California — Los Angeles

Mark Berger
University of Kentucky

Frank A. Scott, Jr.
University of Kentucky

Michael Nieswiadoney
University of North Texas

Eleanor Snellings
Virginia Commonwealth University

Gary Gigliotti
Rutgers University

Joseph Rezny
St. Louis Community College

Dermot Gately
New York University

William Metz
Macomb Community College

Vincent Panzone
College of DuPage

Richard Fryman
Southern Illinois University

Stephen Happel
Arizona State University

William Weber
Eastern Illinois University

Philip Klein
Pennsylvania State University

We owe special thanks to Larry Gwinn for co-authoring the student study guide and to Dennis Jansen for developing the test bank.

A large number of economists answered one or more of our questionnaires. We thank the following respondents:

Ian Bain
University of Minnesota

John H. Beck
Case Western Reserve University

Jim Bradley
University of South Carolina

Everett Campbell
Moorehead State College

Phillip Caruso
Western Michigan University

John Conant
Indiana State University

Steven R. Cox
Arizona State University

D. Allen Dalton
Boise State College

Loraine Donaldson
Georgia State University

O. Homer Erekson
Miami University

Nancy Fox
New York University

Pauline Fox
Southeast Missouri State University

R.M. Friedman
California State University — Northridge

John R. Garrett
University of Tennessee at Chattanooga

Robert Gassler
Ursinus College

Howard Giles
Murray State College

Paul W. Grieves
Western Illinois University

Richard C. Healy
University of Lowell

Whitney Hicks
University of Missouri

G.E. Hoffer
Virginia Commonwealth University

Randall Holcombe
Auburn University

Thomas Ireland
University of Missouri

Mark Jelavich
Northwest Missouri State

Cynthia Jones
University of North Carolina — Charlotte

Richard Kecha
University of Wisconsin — Parkside

Bob Kirk
Indiana University — Purdue University at Indianapolis

A.M. Lubell
SUNY — Oneonta

Bernard Malamud
University of Nevada — Las Vegas

Paul Natke
Central Michigan University

Kenneth Newotny
New Mexico State University

Bette Polkinghorn
California State University — Sacramento

E.O. Price
Oklahoma State University

Rex Pulley
Arkansas State University

Susan Randolph
University of Connecticut

Mike Reed
University of Nevada — Reno

Mary E. Rieder
Winona State College

Lyon Robert
Temple University

Richard Rosenberg
Pennsylvania State University

William Schaniel
West Georgia College

Stephen Shmansre
California State University — Hayward

Robert R. Sharp
Eastern Kentucky University

Robert Shellborne
Ohio University

Calvin Sieber
University of Iowa

Eleanor Snellings
Virginia Commonwealth University

We also appreciate the ideas and insights about supplement packages provided by participants in our focus group. They were:

J. Roberto R. Garrido
Unversity of Philippines — Los Banos in Laguna

Vivek Ghosal
Miami University of Ohio

Mary Ann Hendryson
Western Washington University

Radha Murthy
California State University — Fullerton

Susan George
Texas A&M University

Jorge Gonzales
Trinity University — Texas

Arvind Jaggi
Franklin & Marshall College

A host of people have worked on the production of the book. Deserving of special mention is Karen Stone, whose work as copy editor was superb. Grace Sheldrick did an excellent job copyediting the artwork, and the illustrators at Precision Graphics in Champaign, Illinois — especially Nancy Krueger, who did most of the illustrations — produced some beautiful work. Staff members at Allyn & Bacon who have contributed greatly to the book include Allen Workman, Peter Petraitis, Leslie Olney, and Mary Beth Finch. Our largest debt is owed to our editor, Rich Wohl, who has been with us for the duration of the project. Rich has been a fountain of ideas and suggestions (some accepted gladly, others with resistance) and has kept this project going through the good times and the bad. There would have been no completed text without his considerable efforts.

Finally, the place of honor at the end goes to our families and friends, who have suffered with us and rejoiced with us, but most of all, who have stuck by us and have never stopped asking, "Is the book finished yet?" — even when we wished they would.

ECONOMICS

OVERVIEW

Our civilization is founded on the accomplishments of our ancestors. Through hard work, determination, and sacrifice, generations of ordinary people built up a quite extraordinary social system. They literally constructed society, at no small cost to themselves. As we go about our daily affairs in the last decade of the twentieth century we seldom pause to consider this basic human enterprise. We are caught up in educating ourselves, raising our families, pursuing careers, and generally enjoying the fruits of our labors and those of generations that preceded us. Much of the world's population enjoys a higher standard of material well-being than ever before. We have developed mechanisms of social cooperation that reconcile the rights and goals of individuals with those of societies. We have gained a measure of control over our environment. We have succeeded in extending the time one can expect to spend on earth. We are even routinely exploring the universe.

This impressive record of human accomplishment, which has given us life as we know and enjoy it today, has not altered a fundamental characteristic of human existence: *Achievement requires sacrifice*. Economics focuses on this fact. Economics is concerned with the decision-making process confronting people who are forced to make costly choices. This chapter introduces the subject of economics, identifies the basic nature of economics, and presents the economic decision-making framework.

Economic Thinking

CHAPTER 1

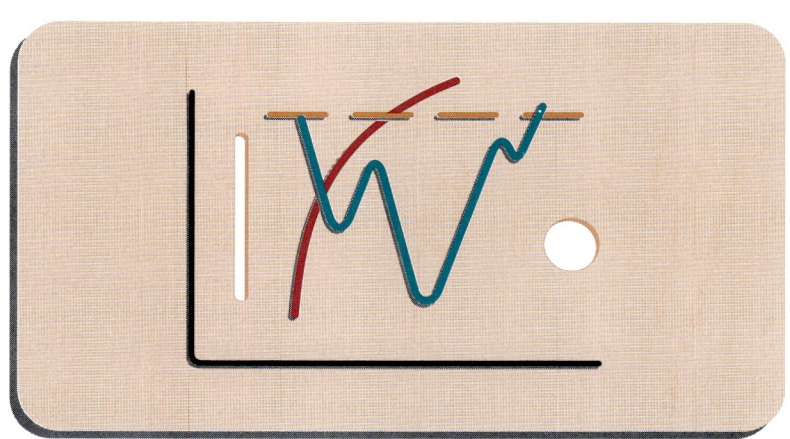

Learning Objectives

After reading and studying this chapter, you will be able to:

1. Define economics.
2. Use the basic economic problem of scarcity to explain the Fundamental Premise of Economics.
3. Use the production possibilities frontier model to illustrate the concepts of scarcity, choice, and opportunity cost by applying the model to individual and social choice problems.
4. Identify the economic dimension of decisions, problems, or policies.
5. Explain the basic process of science, a process shared by economics.

What Is Economics?

Most people can tell you that economists work in banks, or for corporations, or in academia, or for the government. If you ask people to identify economic problems, they invariably name such social problems as inflation, unemployment, trade deficits, health care costs, and government deficits. The public even turns some economists into media figures who receive the kind of attention usually reserved for heads of state, artists, and movie and TV stars. However, this familiarity with economic issues and economists does not extend to an understanding of the discipline itself. People are stymied by a request to define economics. This book explains the fundamental nature of economics and demonstrates the widespread usefulness of the economic approach by developing the basic principles of economics and applying them to a variety of individual and social problems. We begin by defining economics.

The traditional definition of economics found in dictionaries or in economics textbooks is something like this: **Economics** is the study of how individuals and societies *decide* to use scarce *resources* to produce goods and services and distribute them for *consumption*. Note that the word *decide* is as important to the definition of economics as the "economic" terms *resources* and *consumption*. Economics is about deciding or choosing among alternatives. Choice is a key element in all economic problems. Thus, throughout the book we will focus on the process of making choices. At this point we want to stress the fact that the end goal of economic decision making is current or future consumption.

People satisfy their wants by consuming goods and services. They are nourished by food and water. They clothe themselves and seek shelter. Human wants extend far beyond these basic survival needs, but regardless of the specific want, consumption is the act of satisfying a want.

A productive **resource** is a raw material (a natural substance) or a man-made good that is used in the production of other goods or services. Such resources are also called **factors of production**, since they are used as **inputs** into the production process. Factors of production include land (defined broadly to include all natural resources), labor, capital (man-made tools of production and the technology embodied in them and *human capital*, the skills and knowledge embodied in a person), and entrepreneurial ability (the ability to organize and plan production and develop new products). Resources are required to produce the goods and services with which wants are satisfied.

Resources are *scarce* in the sense that they are available in limited quantities, while human wants tend to be unlimited. Since not all wants can be satisfied with existing resources, choice is necessary: Individuals and societies must decide on the uses to which limited resources will be put. It is not possible for all people to satisfy all their wants. *In a world of scarce resources, it is impossible to avoid making choices.*

The necessity of choosing one alternative over others led John Maynard Keynes, perhaps the dominant figure in twentieth-century economics, to focus on the process of choosing as the central element in economics. He said that economics is "... a method ... *of thinking which helps its possessor to draw correct conclusions."* Economics is a way of thinking that helps individuals and societies make decisions consistent with improved well-being. You should keep in mind this focus on economics as a way of thinking as you embark on the study of economics. Notice the emphasis: Economics is more an approach to

---

Economics
The study of how people decide to use scarce resources to produce goods and services and distribute them for consumption.

Resource
A raw material or produced good available for use in the production of other goods and services

Factor of production (input)
A resource used in production.

decision making or problem solving than an established set of answers to questions or solutions to problems.

Combining Keynes's emphasis on thinking with our earlier discussion of the necessity of choice, we arrive at a succinct definition of economics: *Economics is a general framework for decision making when resources are scarce.*

The Fundamental Premise of Economics

We have seen that scarce resources force people to make choices. People cannot have all the goods and services they want, so they must decide which to acquire and which to do without. Choosing to acquire more of one good means having less of another. Choosing to buy a car may mean no movies and pizzas for the next year (or two or three). Such a choice is costly, since many people really enjoy movies and pizzas. The cost of choosing one good or service over others is the value of the most desirable alternative given up. Economists call this broad concept **opportunity cost**.

How do people go about making necessary, but costly, choices? Economics is based on the assumption that people behave rationally, that is, that individuals are **rational decision makers**. This assumption implies that people can and do make choices that they believe will make them better off. The assumption of rationality does not imply that people never behave emotionally or act on a whim. Sometimes people buy things on the spur of the moment. Later they might regret the purchase. Such an action may be irrational, but most people learn from such disappointments. Economists believe that rational decisions predominate and that the assumption of rationality enables us to explain a great deal of human behavior.

Going one step further, the assumption of rationality implies nothing about what an individual likes or dislikes. A person's preference for heavy metal rock music over Mozart or his preference for hot dogs over prime rib implies nothing about his rationality. A person who prefers hot dogs to prime rib behaves rationally by purchasing hot dogs. *Rationality means that people are capable of establishing goals and of acting in a manner consistent with the achievement of those goals.* People are purposeful, making decisions that benefit themselves. Goals vary from person to person and across societies, but people act in ways that they believe are beneficial to themselves.

Combining the fact that scarcity implies costly choice with the assumption of rationality enables us to formulate a proposition that we shall call the Fundamental Premise of Economics: *In all decision making, individuals choose the alternative for which they believe the net gains to be the greatest.* Virtually all economic theory and analysis is built upon this premise. The conclusions of every chapter in this book are based on it.

An extremely important implication follows from the Fundamental Premise: When decisions are costly, *incentives matter*. The Fundamental Premise asserts that people attempt to obtain the maximum benefit possible from the choices they make. This is equivalent to saying that they seek to achieve their goals at the minimum cost. To accomplish this they must pay attention to costs and benefits. Changes in costs and benefits alter the incentives for people to make particular choices by altering the gains from different alternatives. When the benefits of an alternative increase and its costs remain the same, the incentive to choose that alternative increases. It is now more attractive

Opportunity cost
The value of the most desirable alternative given up when choosing an option.

Rational decision maker
Someone capable of setting goals and acting purposefully toward achieving those goals.

because the net gain from choosing the alternative has increased. When the perceived benefits of a college education increase, more people go to college. On the other hand, as the costs of a particular alternative increase, fewer people choose the now less-attractive alternative. The number of drivers who exceed the speed limit depends upon the cost of speeding. When the law is enforced by radar monitoring, fewer drivers speed. The use of radar raises the expected cost of speeding. In short, in attempting to achieve the greatest gain possible from a set of alternatives, *individuals economize.*

The Fundamental Premise of Economics is a powerful tool for understanding, predicting, and even altering human behavior. We demonstrate its power throughout this text by applying it to diverse individual and social problems.

What Are Economic Problems?

An attempt to identify economic problems is one way of suggesting the benefits that might be derived from a study of economics. Nearly everyone recognizes that such issues as unemployment, competition from foreign imports, government deficits, rising health care costs, and failing family farms are economic problems. However, fewer people are able to pinpoint the element that links these diverse problems together. The Fundamental Premise of Economics can be used to isolate the economic element in these and other problems.

Using the Fundamental Premise to Identify Economic Problems

Economics is a general framework for decision making when resources are scarce. The common element in the list of problems just presented is the decision-making framework. Consider unemployment. Society would like to avoid unemployment because of the lost output and the cost to unemployed workers and their families associated with unemployment. To achieve full employment we first must understand why the economy generates unemployment. We also want to know the full effects of actions taken to achieve full employment. Policies designed to push the economy to full employment might cause other problems. For instance, in the past when some full employment policies were pursued, inflation developed. Since there are good reasons for preferring stable prices, such full employment policies were costly. Economists search for less-costly ways to maintain full employment.

Another issue receiving attention in the news media is foreign import competition. We read about so-called unfair competition and about the jobs, even entire industries, lost to foreign imports. Do foreign imports really generate so much unemployment? Why does government permit them if they impose such costs on us? Are any benefits gained from the inflow of imports? This problem is a good example of the Fundamental Premise at work. Consumers want to obtain the most goods and services possible with their limited incomes. Foreign goods are attractive to consumers when they are cheaper or better than available American goods. Thus, imports do offer us (as consumers) benefits: lower product prices or better products. However, imports reduce sales of domestic products, causing some domestic industries to shrink and unemployment to rise, at least for a time. Are we better or worse off with such trade? The economic decision-making framework, with its concern for making the best use of scarce resources, fits this problem nicely. (Incidentally, economists generally believe free trade is beneficial to society.)

These examples illustrate the common element in the list of traditional economic problems and policies. The key is an effort to solve a problem or achieve a goal in a way that is least costly to society. Thus, the scope of economics is really very broad. Since economics is a framework for making sound decisions, it has wide applicability. If decision makers face a resource constraint, their decisions have an economic dimension. Economics can benefit individuals (and societies) facing a wide array of decisions and problems. Some less traditional issues on which economic analysis sheds light include the following:

- criminal justice
- product safety
- marriage and divorce
- environmental quality
- technological innovation
- allocation of time
- highway safety
- education decisions
- sexual behavior
- athletic competition
- university problems
- student behavior

The economics of some of these topics is explored in this text. We challenge you to apply the Fundamental Premise of Economics to these "unusual" problems or issues as a way to practice using economics to understand human behavior.

How to Be Your Own Private Economist

This book examines the decision making of individuals in a wide variety of roles: as consumers, producers, resources owners, taxpayers, policymakers, and politicians. Our basic premise is that individuals — in all these various roles — seek to achieve goals and resolve problems in a manner that makes them better off. The book's title comes from this basic premise. We are interested in the reasons people make the decisions they make and the consequences of those decisions for the decision maker and others.

The primary objective of the text is to demonstrate the *economic way of thinking* as well as to help you understand this beneficial decision-making framework. In essence, we want to help you to become your own economist by helping you to come to the best decision possible *given your goals*. To help you do this we provide a set of general questions that economists try to answer for all kinds of decisions.

Questions for Use in Decision Making

1. What is the decision maker's goal?
   a. How will achievement of the goal make the decision maker better off?
   b. What is the relationship of this goal to other goals?
2. What are the constraints on the decision maker?
   a. Can the constraints be altered by the expenditure of resources?
   b. Would such an action be worthwhile for this decision?

3. What are the decision maker's alternatives?
    a. What are the advantages (benefits) and disadvantages (costs) of each alternative?
        (1) to the decision maker?
        (2) to others or society?
4. What is the best alternative? Why?
    a. For the decision maker?
    b. For others or society?
5. What is the observed behavior or action of the decision maker?

You can use these questions to your benefit in the following way: When you read a passage that examines a particular decision maker and decision, recall these questions. Identify the manner in which these general questions have been posed and answered for each specific decision. Sometimes the questions can be used in reverse order. We might want to explain some observed action or decision. Referring repeatedly to these questions will help you tie together different parts of the text and see the forest as well as the trees.

Basic Economic Choices

Scarcity necessitates choices of many different types. As individuals we must decide how to use the resources that we have: our intellectual and physical assets, our material wealth, and our time. Do I want to be a concert pianist or a chemical engineer? As a student, do I want to maintain a perfect 4.0 grade point average or do I want a more active social and extracurricular life? Should I buy a car? Should I save more and spend less?

Businesses face choices because of limited resources as well. Should a new product line be added? How many units should be produced this month? Should workers be hired or laid off? Should the firm invest in a new production technology? Should one firm buy another company it has been watching, or agree to be purchased by an interested third company?

Societies are faced with innumerable complex social choices. How much of society's resources should be devoted to national defense? Should government spending be increased or decreased? How much individual liberty will be permitted? Should the government try to control the economy? How will society choose which goods to produce? What criteria will be used to distribute the goods produced?

Such decisions as these—about what to produce, how to produce it, and how to distribute the goods produced—are made every day by individuals in their roles as consumers, producers, resource owners, and citizens. The nature of the decisions varies widely, but all decisions have a common element: A decision is required because resources are scarce; each choice entails an opportunity cost. Choosing one alternative means forgoing another. The true cost of a decision is the value of the opportunity given up because of the decision.

The opportunity cost of becoming a concert pianist is the value of the opportunities given up to become a skilled pianist. The years of training devoted to piano and the money spent on lessons could have been used to do other things. The opportunity cost of buying a car is the value of other goods and services that cannot be purchased because one's income and savings go to pay for the car. The opportunity cost of saving is the satisfaction forgone by consuming less now. The opportunity cost of attending an economics lecture is the highest-valued alternative use of the time that one spends in class.

What is the opportunity cost incurred by a business when it adds a new product? When an automobile company develops a new model, it spends some of its profits developing the new car rather than using them to improve current models or paying higher dividends to stockholders. The firm's engineers spend time developing and refining the new model rather than working on making existing models safer, more fuel efficient, or more durable. Introducing a new model may mean the company cannot afford to refit factories producing other models with robotics technology that would lower production costs. The firm forgoes a number of alternatives when it chooses to introduce a new car line.

Social choices also have opportunity costs. The opportunity cost of national defense is the nonmilitary production forgone to provide a defense for the country. The opportunity cost of a war is the human and nonhuman resources expended in the war effort. These resources have valuable alternative uses. The cost to society of redistributing income (taking income from one group of individuals and giving it to another) includes both the resources that must be devoted to managing the redistribution program (resources which have alternative uses) and any lost output that might result if taxing one group and providing income grants to another causes either group to work less.

In a world of scarcity, the ability to identify true opportunity costs is very valuable. One of the most important objectives of studying economics is to acquire this skill. The chapters that follow repeatedly raise the question, What are the true costs of choosing an alternative? The next section develops our first graphical model to illustrate the basic concepts of scarcity, choice, and opportunity cost.

An Illustration of Concepts: The Production Possibilities Frontier

Scarce resources limit the extent to which individuals or societies can satisfy their wants and achieve their goals. In this section we illustrate constrained choice making and the opportunity costs associated with such choices. We develop a tool to illustrate the concepts of scarcity, choice, and opportunity cost. Before plunging into the analysis of these issues, however, a brief word of advice and encouragement about graphical analysis is in order.

Make Graphs Work for You

Graphical analysis is used extensively in economics courses and books; this book is no exception. It is full of graphs for very good reasons. Graphical analysis is used to help explain the principles of economics. Graphs are intended to be an aid to learning. However, many economics students seem to be confused by graphs, making it more, rather than less, difficult to understand economic thinking.

A story can be told, an argument made, or an idea explained in various ways. Information can be conveyed verbally, mathematically, or graphically. Simple pictures can be used as well. This book uses a combination of approaches. For instance, the concept of a production possibilities frontier is developed in writing and with graphs. The graphs illustrate the concept. You should concentrate on understanding the connection between the graphs and the written explanation, avoiding the tendency to memorize graphs. If you understand a concept well enough, you should also understand the graphical illustration. Try to develop graphical illustrations of concepts on your own. Working with graphs is a good way to *practice* economics.

Graphs serve a dual purpose in economics. First, they convey a large amount of information at a glance. Graphs conveniently illustrate the relationships between variables. Second, graphs serve as an aid to economic reasoning. By correctly shifting the lines in a graph, a student can produce the outcome that results from a change in an economic variable. Understanding how to work with graphs is not a substitute for thinking correctly about the problem at hand, but such understanding can guide correct thinking.

Graphs are expressions of mathematical relationships. The benefits of using graphs are increased by a sound understanding of basic algebra. An appendix on graphical analysis appears at the end of this chapter. It serves as a review and refresher for readers who are uncomfortable with graphs or who want to review the basic mathematics of graphical analysis. *If, in reading the remainder of the chapter, you feel unsure about what a graph means or how it is used, you should read the appendix before continuing.*

Production Possibilities Frontier

In this section we develop a useful graphical framework and use it to illustrate the implications of scarcity and choice with three examples.

Individual Choice   Consider a problem that all college students face: the allocation of time. People have only twenty-four hours a day at their disposal. Full-time students must eat, sleep, study, and possibly work. They also spend time in various social and extracurricular activities. Consider a college student named Sarah. Assume that Sarah spends eight hours each day in such activities as eating, sleeping, and bathing. She is left with sixteen hours a day to either study or participate in other college activities.

Here is the basic economic problem: Sarah has limited resources. This example considers only one resource: time. Because time is limited, Sarah cannot do all she would like to do. She has sixteen hours a day to allocate to various activities of value to her. She must make some choices. Lumping her time use into two categories simplifies the problem: Sarah either studies or participates in other activities. The daily time that she spends studying cannot be spent doing something else and vice versa. Sarah faces a tradeoff.

Graphing her **resource constraint** illustrates Sarah's problem. Refer to Figure 1 (a). Sarah's problem is how to allocate time to two different alternative activities. Only sixteen hours are available each day for both activities. On the graph, hours of study time are measured along the vertical axis and hours of other activities along the horizontal axis. Sarah could choose to spend sixteen hours a day studying. If she did, no time would be available for other activities, and she would be at point A. Or, she could spend all her time on other activities and no time studying. She would then be at point I. If she chose to spend some time on both activities, she would be at some point between A and I, such as B or F or G.

Resource constraint Maximum quantity of resources available for use in production or consumption.

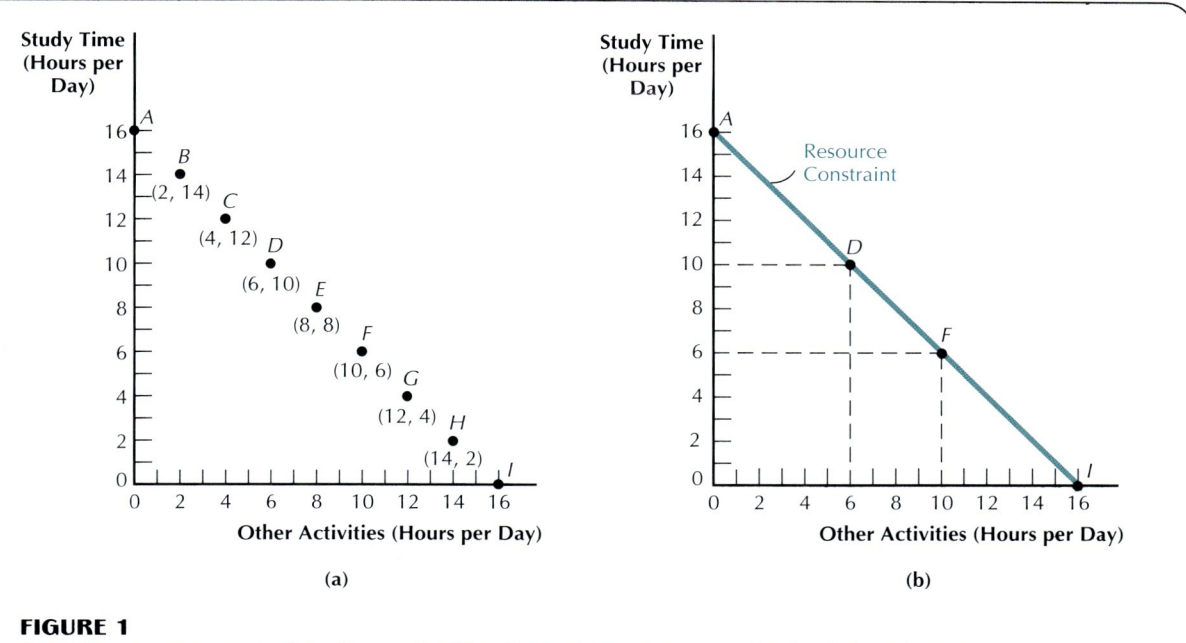

FIGURE 1
Sarah's resource constraint. The availability of only sixteen hours per day to study or to pursue other activities forces Sarah to make choices. She can choose any combination of study and other activities on her resource constraint. In drawing this resource constraint, we assume that Sarah has exactly sixteen hours per day to allocate.

Sarah can allocate her available time however she chooses. Her resource constraint is identified more clearly in Figure 1 (b). The line AI connects all combinations of hours that total sixteen. Sarah could choose any combination of points (or hours) on the line AI, but because she has exactly sixteen hours available, no combination of hours off the line AI is possible. Sarah is constrained by her sixteen hours a day.

Figure 1 (b) also illustrates the implications of Sarah's time constraint. If Sarah chooses to study ten hours a day, she will have available only six hours for other activities (point D). She can increase the time available for other activities only if she reduces the time devoted to studying. If Sarah spends ten hours a day on other activities, she can devote only six hours to study. The opportunity cost of four more hours of other activities (moving from point D to point F) is the value she attaches to four hours of study time.

This simplified example of the allocation decisions caused by a scarce resource demonstrates that choices caused by scarcity have opportunity costs associated with them. The assumption that Sarah devotes exactly sixteen hours to two particular kinds of activities simplifies the problem. However, other sacrifices are open to Sarah if she decides to study more without eliminating any of her other activities. By reducing the time she spends sleeping and eating, Sarah would have more than sixteen hours to devote to study or other activities. Graphically, the resource constraint would shift outward. Total time devoted to studying and other activities would increase. (Lack of sleep and proper nourishment might also prove costly, however.)

Social Choice People make literally hundreds of decisions like Sarah's each day. Although many decisions are not very complicated or significant, many are extremely important. The impact of scarce resources and the cost of choices forced on people by scarcity are great. Sarah's problem introduced these basic economic concepts and illustrated the use of graphical analysis in a simple fashion. An example faced annually by the U.S. government illustrates a traditional and fundamental social choice.

Every society must decide which goods and services it will produce. An important choice for most national governments is determining the share of national resources that will be set aside for military uses or national defense. Because resources are limited, the more resources a country devotes to defense, the fewer it has available for nondefense or civilian consumption. Some countries devote as much as half of all spending to military purposes; other countries spend as little as one percent of income on defense.

With a given stock of resources, the output — goods and services — an economy can produce in a period of time is limited. The limit can be represented by a production possibilities frontier. A **production possibilities frontier (PPF)** shows all the possible combinations of two goods that can be produced if currently available resources are fully employed using the available technology. The frontier for a hypothetical country choosing between military and nonmilitary (consumer) goods is illustrated in Figure 2. (Of course, not all nonmilitary goods are consumer goods — factories, for example — but we will ignore this complication for now.) The production of military goods is measured on the vertical axis, and consumer goods production is measured on the horizontal axis. Note that, while Figure 1 showed a *resource constraint,* Figure 2 shows *production possibilities.* The focus has shifted from the resources themselves to what can be produced with the resources.

The output of military and consumer goods is limited to the quantity combinations lying on or beneath the production possibilities frontier AG. OA military goods can be produced if no consumer goods are produced, and if no military goods are produced, OG consumer goods can be produced. With the existing stock of resources and level of technology, combinations of military and consumer goods beyond the frontier are unattainable.

The first thing you might have noticed about the production possibilities frontier in Figure 2 is its shape. While the resource constraint in Figure 1 was a straight line (linear), the PPF in Figure 2 is concave from below (bowed away from the origin between A and G). There are sound economic reasons for these shapes. When Sarah spent one more hour studying, she automatically spent one less hour on other activities. When we focus on resources, a one-to-one tradeoff exists. This tradeoff never varies, so the resource constraint is linear.

The PPF is drawn concave because not all resources are equally useful in producing military and consumer goods. Some resources have rather specialized uses. They are not very productive when transferred to other uses. For example, suppose the United States were at point A in Figure 2. All resources are devoted to producing military goods. How much would military production fall if some resources were transferred to consumer goods production? The answer depends on *which* resources are used. If the resources that contribute least to military production, such as the labor of skilled furniture makers or clothing designers, were transferred to the production of consumer goods, military production would fall very little. However, these resources might con-

Production possibilities frontier (PPF)
All the maximum possible combinations of two goods that can be produced with available resources.

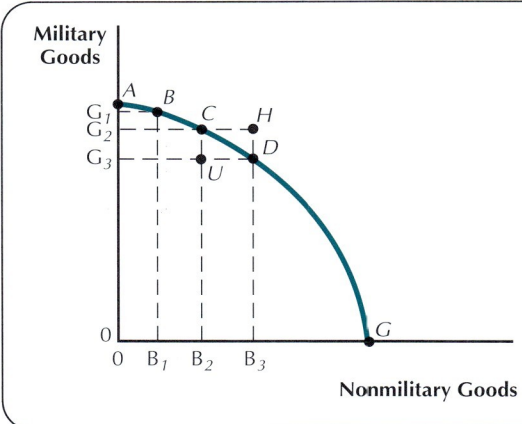

FIGURE 2
Production possibilities frontier for military and nonmilitary goods. Given the resources available to society, only points on or within the PPF are attainable. At point U, some resources are unemployed. Point H is unattainable.

tribute greatly to consumer goods production. In moving from point A to point B on the production possibilities frontier, very few weapons are given up to acquire a substantial quantity of furniture and clothing. The shape of the PPF is implied by the Fundamental Premise of Economics: To be on the PPF, society must produce military and nonmilitary goods in a manner yielding the greatest net gains.

If additional quantities of consumer goods equal in size to OB_1 are desired, their opportunity cost increases. The quantity of military goods given up to acquire more consumer goods increases as consumer goods production rises, because resources less specialized to consumer goods production are now being transferred away from military goods production. As consumer goods production expands, metal that could have been used to produce tanks is used to make automobiles. The farther out along the consumer goods axis we move, the greater the opportunity cost of additional units of consumer goods. More and more military goods must be forgone, because resources better suited to military production are now being used to produce consumer goods. By the time we reach point G, very few additional consumer goods are being produced with the last resources shifted from military to nonmilitary production. The tendency for the opportunity cost of producing a good to rise as more and more of the good is produced is known as the *law of increasing opportunity cost.*

If the economy's resources are fully employed, some combination of military and nonmilitary goods on the production possibilities frontier will be produced. In this case, a decision to have more military goods or more consumer goods is costly. Suppose the economy is producing at point C, and society decides to produce more consumer goods. It must sacrifice some military production. Because of its resource constraint, it cannot move to point H; it must reduce its production of military goods, moving along the frontier to a new combination such as point D. Consumer goods production increases from B_2 to B_3, but this increased output is paid for by a reduction in military production from G_2 to G_3. The opportunity cost of more consumer goods is fewer military goods.

Note that if resources are not fully employed, that is, if society is not producing on the frontier, output of either military or consumer goods can be increased without giving up any of the other type of goods. If society is initially at point U below the frontier, unemployed resources exist. Some valuable resources are not being utilized in any type of production. By employing these idle resources, the production of military goods or consumer goods or both can be increased without reducing the output of any goods.

Another Example: Environmental Quality The PPF model can be used to investigate less traditional issues such as the cost of environmental quality. The decision to have more or less environmental quality is analogous to the military and consumer goods decision. Environmental quality is an economic good; it is costly to produce. A decision to have more environmental quality is also a decision to have less of other goods and services, since resources must be shifted from the production of other goods to the protection of the environment. This decision can be illustrated with a production possibilities frontier, as in Figure 3. The frontier AG represents the combinations of environmental quality and other goods and services that can be produced with the nation's stock of resources. When resources are fully employed, the economy is located somewhere on the production possibilities frontier. If the economy is on the frontier, increased environmental quality requires the sacrifice of some other goods. The reduced output of other goods is the cost of improved environmental quality. (If the economy is inside the PPF, it is possible to increase environmental quality without producing fewer other goods.)

As in the military and consumer goods case, the opportunity cost of increasing the production of environmental quality depends on the amount already being produced. (The same is true for other goods and services.) The opportunity cost of additional units of environmental quality increases as environmental quality rises, because it is inexpensive to improve environmental quality when it is very bad (by using sand and charcoal to filter water, for

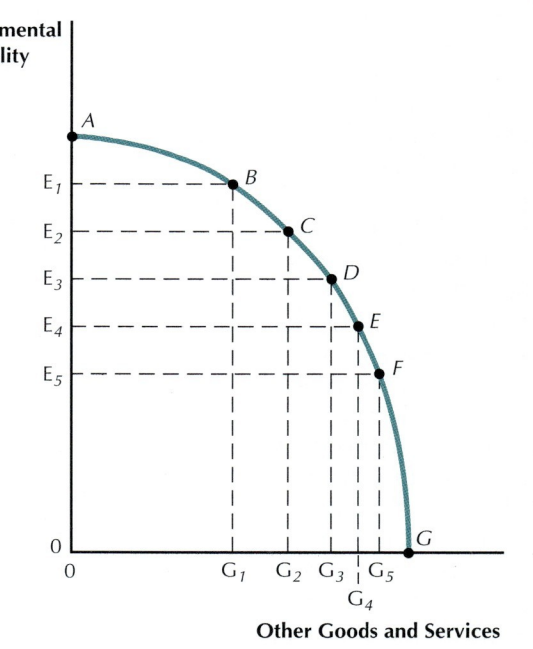

FIGURE 3
Production possibilities frontier for environmental quality and other goods. As the level of environmental quality increases, larger and larger quantities of other goods must be given up to improve the environment even further.

example) but very expensive to eliminate small traces of pollutants. The cleaner the environment becomes, the more costly further improvements are. This is but another application of the law of increasing opportunity cost.

The discussion of the cost of environmental quality has omitted from consideration some important issues of *social choice* and *distribution,* just as did the military and consumer goods example. How does society choose the combination of environmental quality and other goods that is best? Which combination leads to the highest level of well-being for society? Related questions center on which members of society receive the benefits from consuming more environmental quality or more other goods, and who pays for these goods. These complex and important issues are explored in Chapters 2 through 5.

The Drive to Satisfy More Wants

The production possibilities frontier presents a vivid illustration of the constraint imposed by scarce resources. Since not all wants can be satisfied, people attempt to use available resources to their best advantage. The Fundamental Premise of Economics embodies this human reaction to resource constraints. People seek to get as much as they can from their limited resources.

Production possibilities frontier analysis illustrates the costliness of unemployed resources. Even when resources — factories, machines, people — are not idle, not all wants can be satisfied. Some goals must be sacrificed to achieve others. When resources are underutilized, some wants that could be satisfied are not. Opportunities are wasted. Full employment of resources is an important economic goal.

The drive to satisfy more individual or social wants extends beyond attempting to operate on the production possibilities frontier. If the PPF can be pushed outward, more wants can be satisfied. By obtaining more resources or by using existing resources to produce more goods and services, societies can push their production possibilities frontiers outward.

Increasing the Stock of Resources   Societies obtain additional future resources by using existing resources to produce them. This process is called **investment**. Some resources that could be used to satisfy current wants instead are used to produce more factories or machines or training facilities or to explore for more mineral deposits in order to expand the society's future resource base. The factories, machines, transportation systems, and other produced goods that are themselves used to produce other goods and services are called the **capital stock**. Thus, investment is often referred to as **capital formation**. Resources are also devoted to education and training designed to increase the intellectual and technical capabilities of the population. The quality of the labor force depends on society's investment in human capital.

When a society increases its resources, its production possibilities rise. Investment in productive resources loosens the resource constraint, enabling people to enjoy more of all goods. Investment is not a costless activity, however. Resources devoted to the production of hydraulic drill presses or the planting of pine forests or the training of engineers are unavailable to satisfy consumer wants. The opportunity cost of an investment good is the highest-valued collection of consumption goods forgone when resources are devoted to investment. Increasing future resources requires society to give up some current consumption.

SECTION RECAP
Economic choice is costly. If the economy is operating on its PPF, acquiring more of one good means giving up more of another good. A PPF illustrates this tradeoff. A PPF shows the maximum quantities of two goods that an economy can produce at any particular time.

Investment
The use of existing resources to create additional future resources.

Capital stock
The factories, machines, and other goods used to produce more goods and services.

Capital formation
Investment in productive capital stock.

Does It Make **Economic Sense?**

How Much Is a Life Worth?

Most people recoil from the thought of attaching a dollar value to human life. Such a response is very human. None of us likes to imagine that lives are being treated indifferently by businesses, governments, or other organizations. However, in a world of scarce resources people are unable to have all the goods they might like — and safety is a good. Thus, we must ask if the safety-at-any-cost attitude is reasonable. Does it make economic sense?

The choice between any two economic goods (or groups of goods) can be presented in the form of a production possibilities frontier. In the case of safety, the frontier is concave, because the opportunity cost of additional units of safety rises as the world becomes safer. If risk is to be completely eliminated, society must be willing to forgo immense quantities of other goods and services. However, even this statement is inaccurate, because safety has multiple dimensions. For example, eliminating cancer-causing pollution from water may force us to accept greater cancer risk from air pollution. Pollutants that had previously been disposed of in rivers or lakes will now be disposed of in other ways, including by burning. Waste byproducts can be totally eliminated only by halting production.

Consider a couple of examples. Federal regulations limit to ten parts per million (of air breathed by workers) the amount of the chemical benzene to which workers in benzene production facilities can be exposed. The Occupational Safety and Health Administration (OSHA) sought new regulations reducing the permissible benzene levels to one part per million. The best estimate of the cost of the program was $267 million in capital expenditures, $124 million in first-year operating expenses, and $74 million per year in operating expenses thereafter. The estimated benefits of the new standards were one life saved every three years. Thus, an expenditure of $539 million to save the first life and continuing expenditures of $222 million per life saved would be necessary.*

To a dying worker's family $222 million might not seem excessive. However, we must ask how many lives could be saved if this much were spent on less-costly safety systems. For example, studies of highway safety have concluded that the installation of such safety devices as signposts that break away on impact and paved shoulders on the side of roads would save lives at a cost of far less than $1 million per life. Thus, $222 million would save hundreds of lives if used to make highways safer.

A highway example further illustrates the opportunity cost of safety standards. In 1967, interstate highway safety design standards were made stricter. The intent was to reduce the number of lives lost in interstate highway accidents. Undoubtedly the stricter standards saved lives. However, the cost of interstate highway construction was increased substantially, reducing the number of miles of new interstate highways states could afford to build. The fact that fewer miles of interstate highways were built meant that more people had to drive on noninterstate roads than if the stricter standards had not been passed. However, the old pre-1967 interstates were safer than noninterstate highways. It has been estimated that the lives lost because fewer miles of interstate highways were built exceeded the lives saved by the stricter interstate standards. In other words, costs exceeded benefits.

If the costs of completely eliminating certain kinds of risk are so high, why do people support such stringent standards? Several possible reasons exist.

1. Some people simply do not understand that tradeoffs exist. That is, they do not recognize the opportunity costs of their proposals — including the lives lost because costly regulations in some areas prevent less-costly actions in others.

2. Professionals often have expertise in one area and little knowledge of other areas. They tend to concentrate on what they understand. For example, some engineers understand safety but not opportunity cost, and they tend to ignore the latter.

3. Some people have a blind faith in technology. Although it is true that technological innovation can shift the production possibilities frontier outward, enabling society to enjoy more safety without giving up more alternative goods, legislating stricter standards does not guarantee that technological improvements will occur. Typically, meeting stricter standards is costly.

---

*Some of the examples cited here are drawn from Steven E. Rhoads, *The Economist's View of the World* (Cambridge, U.K.: Cambridge University Press, 1985), Chapter 2. This book provides excellent examples of how basic economic concepts can be applied to real-world issues.

Figure 4 illustrates the investment decision. At the present time two countries, we'll call them Avalon and Bataria, face a decision. They can devote their resources to two alternative uses, either current consumption or investment (capital formation). The production possibilities frontier in Figure 4 (a) indicates that the two countries have identical stocks of resources at present. However, they make different decisions about how to use their current resources. Avalon chooses to forgo a large amount of current consumption to devote a relatively large share of its resources to capital formation. On the other hand, Bataria decides to consume most of its current resource stock, devoting only a small fraction of its resources to investment.

Figure 4 (b) shows the future outcome of this consumption-versus-investment decision. Because Avalon devoted more of its existing resources to the creation of capital equipment, its future resource base has grown larger than Bataria's. Avalon's PPF lies to the right of Bataria's. In the future, options will be available to Avalon that will be unavailable to Bataria. When facing the consumption-versus-investment decision, Avalon will have the luxury of both consuming and investing more than Bataria. This is possible only because Avalon chose to make a larger sacrifice in terms of forgone consumption in an earlier period.

Investment is the primary way societies increase their stocks of resources and satisfy more wants over time. Investment takes many forms. A firm uses its existing resources to build new plants and add new equipment. Individuals forgo current consumption to educate themselves. Nations forgo current governmental services to build more social capital, such as highways, for the future. Both firms and governments use resources in an effort to develop ways to produce more goods and services with the existing stock of resources. Improved technology enables societies to make better use of resources.

Getting More through Technological Change Technology is an important determinant of the output that can be produced with a given stock of resources. **Technology** is the application of knowledge about the physical and natural world to the production of goods and services. It determines the kind and quantity of inputs necessary to produce a good or service as well as the kind and quality of goods available. Technological advances permit economies to produce both higher-quality new products and old products at lower cost.

Technology
The application of knowledge about the world to the production of goods and services.

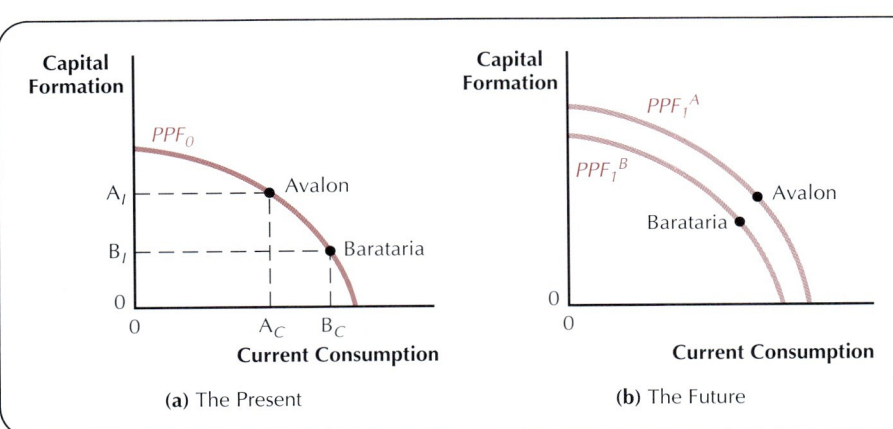

FIGURE 4
Investment decision. *(a) The Present (b) The Future.* Investment in capital formation enables a society to produce and consume more in the future. Avalon chooses to allocate a greater proportion of its resources in the present to capital formation than does Bataria (a). Choosing to consume less in the present will give Avalon future alternatives unavailable to Bataria (b).

Thus, an improvement in technology shifts the PPF out to the right just as an increase in the stock of resources does.

The benefits of technological change have been readily apparent since the Middle Ages. Improved technologies are in large part responsible for the remarkable increases in the standard of living experienced by much of the world's population. Many new ideas arise quite by accident, the fruit of someone's imagination and creativity. However, the benefits of such advances are so great that most societies devote significant quantities of resources to the pursuit of technological advancement. People give up some current consumption to support the research, experimentation, exploration, and development that can lead to technological change.

Escaping the Frontier through Specialization and Trade   Individuals and nations have different **resource endowments** (stocks of resources). Individuals vary in terms of intelligence, physical skills, imagination, and interpersonal skills. Nations have different endowments of natural resources. Some countries have a great deal of land relative to other inputs. Other countries have rich mineral resources and little farm land. Resource differences mean that the opportunity cost of performing certain services or producing certain kinds of goods varies across individuals and countries.

Differences in resource endowments generate opportunities for individuals and countries to escape their resource constraints by specializing in low-opportunity-cost activities and trading for other goods and services that are relatively costly for them to produce. If two countries have different resource endowments and agree to trade, each can escape its production possibilities frontier by specializing and trading.

Chapter 2 discusses the principle of mutually beneficial trade in detail. Trade is treated at length in a separate chapter because it is such an important vehicle for escaping individual resource constraints and satisfying more wants with the limited resources available.

Economics as Science

Science is the systematic study of how the world works. It represents an attempt to determine cause and effect—to understand the likely consequences of particular events. The Nobel laureate George Stigler classified economics as a science when he said, "The central task of an empirical science such as economics is to provide general understanding of events in the real world."[1] Economists seek to understand how the world works just as physicists or biologists do, though the particular objects of study differ markedly among these scientific disciplines.

Science develops when people interested in a particular set of problems interact with one another in an attempt to solve those problems. Once again quoting Professor Stigler, "A science requires for its very existence a set of fundamental and durable problems."[2] Only when problems persist for extended periods can they be addressed systematically. This parallels ordinary life. We behave "scientifically" in response to problems with which we are

---

Resource endowment
The stock of resources available to a person or nation.

SECTION RECAP
The desire to acquire more goods and services leads societies to invest in capital goods and technological development in an attempt to push their PPFs outward. It also leads to specialization and trade, which enables individuals and economies to escape their PPFs.

Science
The systematic study of how the world works.

---

[1] George Stigler, "Nobel Lecture: The Process and Progress of Economics," *Journal of Political Economy* 91 (August 1983), p. 533.
[2] "Nobel Lecture," p. 533.

familiar by reacting in the ways that have proved best. For example, we react to driving on icy streets by slowing down, braking gently, and turning gradually. These responses have proved best. However, drivers in northern regions who face icy streets every winter tend to respond much more systematically than do drivers in southern states who rarely encounter ice. So it is with science. Enduring problems are addressed systematically, and better solutions are developed as experience grows.

Scientific Process

The manner in which science proceeds is not difficult to understand. The development of a particular science begins with the observation of regularities. Observers attempt to explain the regularities by developing generalizations — called *theories* — about the causes of the observed regularities. The theories link cause and effect. The ancient Greek astronomer Ptolemy observed the regular movements of the sun, moon, stars, and planets and developed a theory of the relationship of the heavenly bodies. Ptolemy's system placed the earth at the center of the universe. From his theory *testable implications* — called *hypotheses* — could be developed. If the universe was ordered as Ptolemy asserted, then certain patterns *had to occur*. The fact that some of these patterns did *not* occur led later astronomers to look for a superior explanation of the behavior of the cosmos.

Theory
A set of generalizations purporting to explain observed regularities.

Hypothesis
An implication of a theory that can (in principle) be shown to be true or false.

The Polish astronomer Nicolaus Copernicus developed the theory that the earth turns on its axis and with the other planets revolves around the sun. Because the Copernican theory could explain the movement of the heavenly bodies much more accurately than the Ptolemaic theory, Copernican theory won out. However, Copernicus stated his theory some *fourteen hundred years* after Ptolemy articulated his. For over a thousand years the Ptolemaic system, which astronomers knew to be flawed, was the dominant theory. Why? Because until Copernicus developed his theory, no one put forth a better explanation than Ptolemy's. This illustrates an important fact about the scientific process: *Even a poor theory beats no theory at all.* More generally, a theory with known flaws is preferred to alternative theories with more flaws. Humans operate on the basis of generalizations, and relatively poor generalizations are better than none at all.

Copernicus was able to advance beyond Ptolemy in part because he "stood on Ptolemy's shoulders." Copernicus addressed the same problems as had Ptolemy, and he could use the shortcomings of Ptolemy's system as a basis for developing his own ideas. Similarly, economists today address the same issues that Adam Smith, generally regarded as the first scientific economist, addressed over two hundred years ago. The basic theory of markets developed by Smith still exists today, though in a modified form. Modern economic theory addresses issues Smith would never have thought about tackling. but the basic insight into the economic process is the same now as in 1776 when Smith published *An Inquiry into the Nature and Causes of the Wealth of Nations.* Smith noted that rational self-interested behavior, instead of producing chaos, usually produces social coordination. Economists are still concerned with how this process of social coordination works and why it sometimes breaks down. Because many of the basic economic problems have never changed, progress in understanding economic behavior can take place. One generation of economists can learn from the mistakes and successes of preceding generations.

Model
A simplified representation of reality that focuses attention on the issues the scientist wishes to examine.

Scientific Models   Scientific theories are usually expressed in terms of **models**. A model is a simplified representation of reality that abstracts from nonessential features while concentrating on essential features. Models come in all forms, many of which are very familiar. Department stores use mannequins to display clothes, thus enabling us to imagine how good the clothes would look on us. The mannequins are models of real people, though they lack any of the internal organs necessary to life. To carry out their purpose, it is only necessary that mannequins look like humans on the outside.

Scientists study the effect of automobile crashes on passengers by placing crash dummies in cars and running the cars into concrete block walls. The crash dummies are also models of people, though they have few if any external features. For their purpose, looking real is unnecessary. What is important is that they measure the effect of an auto crash on the human body.

Scientific models come in many forms: maps, graphs, pictures, mathematical equations. Each model is an attempt to represent the problem being addressed in as simple and manageable a way as possible. Reality is too complex to be understood without simplification. Scientists, including economists, use models as aids in locating the important linkages producing observed behavior. We have already encountered one economic model—the production

---

Why the Disagreement?

Parson Malthus's Doomsday Model

Of all the resources available to produce goods and services for human consumption, no other is so valuable as human effort. Without human ingenuity and inventiveness there would be no production process. The economist Julian Simon recently called the human mind "the ultimate resource," an opinion that is not new. Over 200 years ago English social thinkers were attempting to develop policies to encourage more rapid population growth. They believed that the wealth of England would increase more rapidly if more human resources were available.

Just as a social consensus in favor of policies to increase population growth seemed to be developing, an English minister-turned-political-economist named Thomas Malthus published an *Essay on Population*, which argued that mankind was doomed to misery through overpopulation. Malthus maintained that rapid population growth was a serious social problem, rather than a source of wealth. His arguments created a furor in his own time and are still discussed today. Given their lasting influence, we should ask, Why the disagreement over population growth?

The standard arguments in favor of rapid population growth circulating in the late eighteenth century were long on optimism and short on analysis. Many of the leading proponents of population growth were *utopians*, who believed that progress was inevitable. They foresaw a future when all social problems would fade away in the face of a rapidly rising standard of living. But such progress seemed hampered by a static population, and the opinion almost universally held by English social thinkers was that the population had not grown in over a century. (In fact, the English population had been growing rapidly, but until the census of 1801, data showing this growth were not available.)

Malthus approached the issue differently. He attempted to carefully examine the implications of population growth. Using available evidence on the rate at which population grew, Malthus concluded that over time the world's population would increase geometrically, or as he put it, ". . . the human species would increase as the numbers 1, 2, 4, 8, 16, 32, 64, 128. . . ." What struck him was the way population seemed to grow easily and rapidly, especially compared to the increase in land available for food production. Malthus believed that increasing the amount of cultivable land was very difficult. He argued that land

possibilities frontier model. It abstracts from nearly all the detail of the economy, but it enables us to see that all choices constrained by scarce resources entail costs. Since this was the purpose of the model, it worked well.

Social Goals and the Progress of Science

As noted, science is based on the existence of a set of durable problems. Scientists attack problems of interest to them. Over time, however, society's ideas about what constitutes interesting problems change. Thus, the basic attitudes and goals of society affect the progress of science. Science is not only affected by social values, however; it also affects them by raising new issues or concerns that alter the way we think about our world.

Some examples are instructive. Scientists working with the theory of atomic physics developed nuclear fission. This discovery was first used in atomic bombs, and today the United States and the Soviet Union both have vast arsenals of nuclear weapons. Concern that these weapons could some day be used changed the face of politics in the United States. Presidential, senatorial, and congressional candidates were forced to develop positions on nuclear weapons control. Similarly, but more positively, developments in the treatment

---

would increase only arithmetically (that is, 1, 2, 3, 4, 5, 6). Based on these assumptions, Malthus concluded that population growth would quickly outstrip growth in the supply of food, dooming the world's population to misery: wars, disease, famine. Food shortages would cause these miseries to recur again and again to keep the population and food supply in balance.

When Malthus published his arguments and conclusions in 1798, his readers were overwhelmed by his pessimism. Malthus's policy prescriptions were no less dismal than his basic argument. Since the rate of population growth was the problem, he believed society should take steps to discourage population growth. Although he suggested that "moral restraint" would be helpful in restricting the number of births, he was not optimistic that such restraint would actually occur. He opposed government policies to improve the plight of the poor, because he felt that doing so would worsen the future population–food supply imbalance.

Malthus was one of the first economists to face up to the implications of scarcity. The world was not encouraged by his findings. Neither Malthus nor the English population could foresee the technological progress that would affect both sides of his equation: the ability to dramatically increase food production on existing land and the ability to effectively control fertility.

Although Malthus's model did not produce accurate forecasts of actual population and food trends, it was important because it moved the population issue into the realm of scientific discussion. Malthus presented several testable generalizations about the interaction of population and food supply. As data on population growth and the factors affecting it have been collected, Malthus's hypotheses have been tested. In general, they have been rejected. Although food shortages and famine exist in various parts of the world today, these problems are due to wars and political instability rather than to an inability to grow enough food to feed the population. However, other generalizations about population trends have replaced Malthusian hypotheses, and new generalizations are being developed and tested. Through this process of hypothesis generation and testing, knowledge advances. By changing the terms of the discussion, Malthus contributed to the advance of economic science.

of cancer and other diseases have altered the way we react to these diseases. Government faces political pressure from groups who think more should be spent on research and prevention of cancer. In both examples, scientific progress — *increased understanding of how the world works* — has led to a change in social attitudes.

Social goals also affect science. As scientific research into laser technology has made high-powered laser weaponry seem feasible, some politicians have called for intensive research in that area. Federal funding for the Strategic Defense Initiative, popularly known as Star Wars, has spurred development of lasers powerful enough to destroy incoming missiles. Whether such advanced laser technology can be developed is uncertain, but the desire to have such defensive weapons has affected the scientific process. Similarly, the rapid spread of the AIDS virus has led to a surge of research in that area. A major social goal is finding a cure for the disease, and science is being enlisted in the service of this social goal. In the social area, the poor performance of American school children in comparison to those in other countries has led to research on how students learn.

Positive and Normative Issues The scientists seeking an antibody to the AIDS virus are practicing **positive science**. Positive science is the study of how the world works. Either an antibody fights the AIDS virus, or it does not. It is a question of fact. On the other hand, the belief that society should use more of its scarce resources to find a cure for AIDS is a **normative position**. Heart disease claims far more lives each year than does AIDS, so it is not obvious to everyone that scarce medical research dollars should be allocated to AIDS research rather than to researching heart disease. Similarly, determining how children learn is a positive issue; deciding what they should be taught is normative. Normative issues are not questions of fact but of values or beliefs. Such issues cannot be settled by positive scientific analysis.

Although positive and normative issues are conceptually distinct, the two often tend to blend together. Scientists study important problems, but what is considered important is a normative issue. AIDS research is being expanded because many people believe it *should* be. Limits are placed on biogenetic engineering because some people fear the unknown consequences of altering genes and believe we *should* be very cautious in such research.

Economics is as subject to the overlapping of positive and normative issues as any other science. Major economic problems have arisen that have caused the course of economic research to change. The Great Depression of the 1930s, when over one fourth of all American workers were without jobs, caused a shift in the focus of economic research. Previously, little attention had been paid to analyzing how unemployment might be overcome. In the 1930s this became a major problem to be addressed and remains so to this day. The inflation of the 1970s similarly affected economic thinking, spurring research into the causes and consequences of rapid price increases.

Normative values held apart from any social problems can also affect the course of research. Economists are concerned with the working of **markets** — the institutions that coordinate the activities of buyers and sellers. Understanding the causes of **market failure** — the breakdown of coordination — is important to many economists (including the authors of this text) because markets are *believed to be* desirable. Why? Because properly functioning markets are not under the control of any particular individual or group. Markets coordinate

Positive science
The study of how the world works; an examination of what is (rather than what should be).

Normative position
Based on a set of values; expresses what should be (rather than what is).

Markets
Institutions and arrangements that coordinate the activities of buyers and sellers.

Market failure
The breakdown of market coordination.

economic activity in an impersonal manner, allowing maximum scope for individual choice. People can, within the limits of their resource constraints, make their own consumption and production decisions, deciding what is best for themselves.

Despite the overlapping of normative and positive issues, the two often are separable. Many economic issues are matters of fact: Does or does not a particular consequence result from a particular cause? As is the case in other sciences, however, many hypotheses are difficult, if not impossible, to test. Economists attempt to resolve issues that cannot be directly tested by examining the predictions of theoretical models, statistically estimating how one thing affects another, and examining the historical record for clues to the relationship between economic variables. Even then many issues are not resolvable, so that one's *beliefs* about how the world works are important in determining how one interprets economic behavior.

> **SECTION RECAP**
> Science progresses as people systematically study a set of durable problems. Science progresses through the development of theories and the testing of hypotheses implied by the theories. The questions studied by scientists are shaped by the values of society, just as the results of scientific research shape society's values.

Summary

Economics is the study of how individuals and societies **decide** to use **scarce resources** to produce goods and services and **distribute** them for **consumption**. The **basic economic problem** is the scarcity of resources relative to human wants. Since all individuals, groups, and societies face this constraint, their decision making is similar in that they all attempt to achieve as much as possible with their available resources. We call this notion the **Fundamental Premise of Economics:** In all decision making, individuals choose the alternative for which they believe the net gains are the greatest.

Economics has much broader application than is commonly thought. Since economics is a method of thinking that helps one make decisions consistent with improved well-being, it can be profitably employed whenever a decision maker faces a resource constraint. The same basic set of questions applies to a wide variety of decisions. Learning to use economic thinking is easier if this basic set of questions is kept in mind as different decisions are analyzed.

Scarcity necessitates choice. If resources were not scarce, we could all have everything we want. Since we cannot have everything, we must make choices. The costs of a choice are forgone opportunities. The true cost of a decision is the value of the opportunity given up because of the decision. The key to good decision making is the ability to identify the true **opportunity costs** of a choice.

The basic concepts of scarcity, choice, and opportunity cost are illustrated with a **production possibilities frontier** model. The model reveals the costs of choices made when resources are fully employed. The model also separates all attainable choices from those that are unattainable because of the resource constraint.

The shape of the production possibilities frontier reflects the nature of the opportunity costs in a decision. When opportunity costs are constant regardless of the quantities of goods produced, the PPF is linear. When opportunity costs increase as additional units of a good are produced, the PPF is concave.

A society can increase its stock of resources by (1) investing current resources in capital formation, (2) achieving technological progress which increases output from a stock of resources, and (3) trading with others on the basis of least-cost production.

Economics is a (social) **science.** Economists seek to develop generalizations about observed economic phenomena in order to explain, predict and possibly control the economic environment. Science develops when people systematically study fundamental and durable problems. One generation of scientists builds on the knowledge of the preceding generation. Social values affect and are affected by scientific research. What society believes is important, a **normative** value, becomes the subject of scientific research. This research attempts to determine how the world works — a **positive** question, a question of fact.

Scientific theories are usually presented as **models** — simplifications of the relationships among a set of variables. Models are built for specific purposes, omitting aspects of the real world irrelevant for those purposes. The production possibilities frontier model concentrates on the costliness of choice under resource constraints.

Questions for Thought

Knowledge Questions

1. What is the opportunity cost of your college education?
2. Is it rational to get a college education? Do the benefits outweigh the costs? How are benefits and costs calculated?
3. What is a scientific model?
4. Think of the decisions you have made in the last week. Which ones were economic decisions? What made them economic decisions? Explain.

Application Questions

5. Consider the production possibilities for the country New Coolidge. Its citizens produce two goods, garlic and wool, according to the following production possibilities schedule:

New Coolidge

Garlic	Wool
0	450
150	375
300	300
450	225
600	150
750	75
900	0

What is the opportunity cost of a unit of wool (in terms of garlic)? Is the opportunity cost of producing wool constant or increasing? If the economy is initially producing and consuming 450 units of garlic and 225 units of wool, what will be the cost of increasing wool production to 375 units? Why would New Coolidge decide to make such a change?

6. Choose a recent article in the *Wall Street Journal* (or other newspaper) on an economic policy or problem. Identify the different viewpoints and disagreements. Which ones are scientific? Normative?
7. What is the opportunity cost of consuming: (1) a cup of coffee, (2) a cigarette, (3) a marijuana cigarette? What is the opportunity cost of an hour of work for a college student? What determines the cost?

8. Roger has been placed on a strict diet: 1500 calories per day. Without exceeding his calorie limit, Roger must eat a balanced diet. Demonstrate that Roger's problem is essentially an economic problem.

Synthesis Questions

9. List at least three ways that society can reduce the litter of drink cans and bottles. Which alternative would be most effective? Are there any disadvantages with this scheme? Which alternative would be least effective? Does this alternative have any advantages?
10. Think of some models that you use to anticipate the events of a day. Which ones explain why the events occur? Which ones help you control events?
11. We all own things that break or malfunction. What factors influence our decision to repair something ourselves or to hire someone to fix it or to replace it?
12. Suppose you are thinking of becoming a distance runner. What economic decision must you first make? Explain. What must you know and do to become a successful distance runner?

Appendix to CHAPTER 1

Graphical Analysis

Graphs present numerical or mathematical information in a convenient, readable form — for those who know how to read them. This appendix provides a brief review of a few of the basics of graphical analysis.

When confronting a graph, the first thing you should ask is, What's measured along the axes? Economists use graphs to display all sorts of relationships. A huge variety of variables can be measured along the axes. Be sure you know what is being measured. Next note the units of measurement. Economic variables may be measured in dollars, or physical units, or percentage points, or other ways. Some of these variables may have a time dimension. For example, a graph might plot *annual* expenditures on color television sets on one axis. It is important to recognize the time dimension involved.

The graphs in this book are either one or two dimensional. A one-dimensional graph plots data in one direction only. The most common form of one-dimensional graph is a *bar chart*. Figure 5 is an example of a bar chart. It shows the level of spending in the United States on gasoline and oil for the years 1983 through 1986. Expenditures, measured in dollars, are plotted along the vertical axis (the *y-axis*). Nothing is measured along the horizontal (*x*) axis; the spending bars are simply lined up side by side.

Most of the graphs in this book are two dimensional; they measure variables along two axes. The simplest form of two-dimensional graph is a *scatter diagram*. It is used

FIGURE 5
Bar chart of spending on gas and oil. The bar chart shows that consumer spending on gasoline and oil was approximately constant at just over $90 billion annually from 1983 through 1985 and that it fell significantly in 1986. Source: *Economic Report of the President, 1986*, Table B-14.

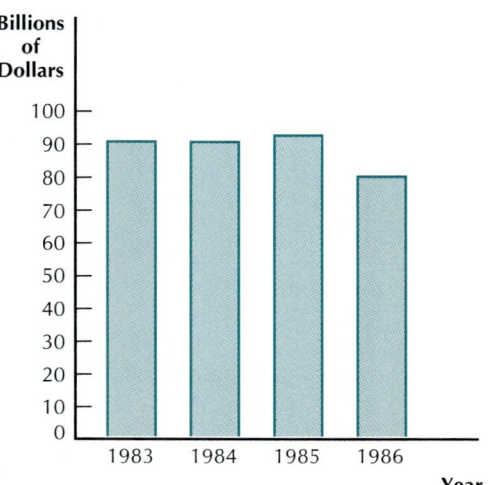

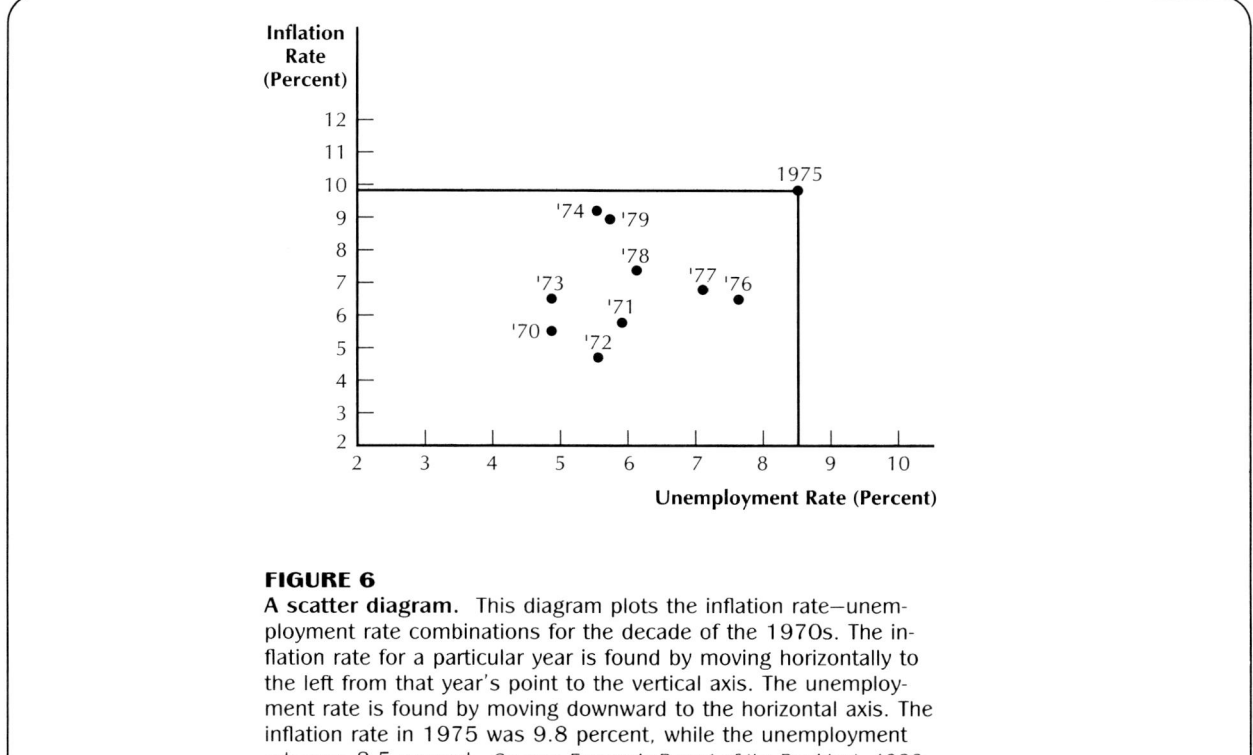

FIGURE 6
A scatter diagram. This diagram plots the inflation rate–unemployment rate combinations for the decade of the 1970s. The inflation rate for a particular year is found by moving horizontally to the left from that year's point to the vertical axis. The unemployment rate is found by moving downward to the horizontal axis. The inflation rate in 1975 was 9.8 percent, while the unemployment rate was 8.5 percent. Source: *Economic Report of the President, 1986*, Tables B-3 and B-35.

to show the relationship between two variables. Figure 6 provides an example of a scatter diagram. It shows the inflation rate–unemployment rate combinations for each year during the 1970s. The inflation rate is measured in percentage points along the *y*-axis. The unemployment rate is measured in percentage points along the *x*-axis.

Note that each point on a scatter diagram conveys two bits of information. Consider the point labelled "1975" in Figure 6. It tells us that the inflation rate in 1975 was 9.8 percent, while the unemployment rate was 8.5 percent. The other nine points on the diagram provide the same information for the other nine years in the decade.

Scatter diagrams provide a convenient way to display the relationship between two variables. *Time series* graphs are a convenient way to show the behavior of a variable over time. In a time series graph, time is plotted along the *x*-axis and the variable (or variables) of interest along the *y*-axis. Figure 7 shows how a time series graph can be used to present information. It plots the behavior of consumer spending on motor vehicles and parts for the decade 1976–1985. Spending is measured in billions of dollars *per year*. Each point tells us how much was spent in a particular year.

While time series graphs seem straightforward, they can be deceptive. You must be careful to note the units in which the plotted variable is measured. By varying the units of measurement, or by shrinking or stretching the units along the axes, the time series behavior of a variable can be made to *appear* to change. Figure 8 illustrates this. It duplicates the plot of spending on motor vehicles and parts shown in Figure 7. However, in Figure 8 we stretch the units of measurement by focusing on the range of spending values actually experienced during the 1976–1985 period.

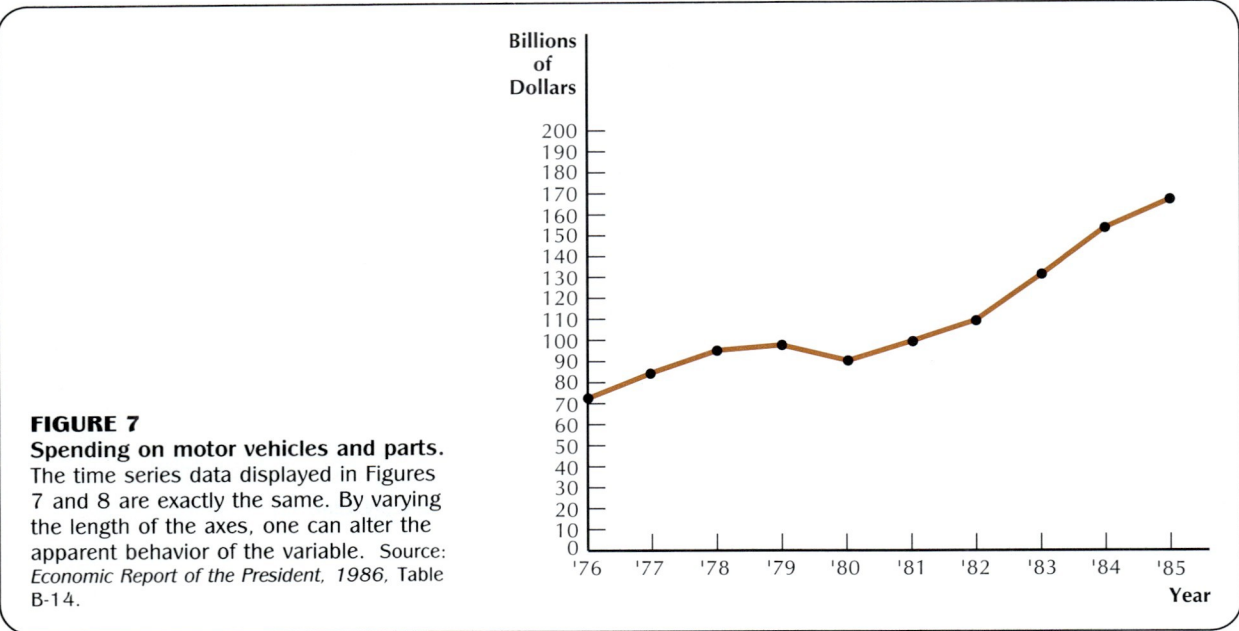

FIGURE 7
Spending on motor vehicles and parts.
The time series data displayed in Figures 7 and 8 are exactly the same. By varying the length of the axes, one can alter the apparent behavior of the variable. Source: *Economic Report of the President, 1986,* Table B-14.

Many of the graphs in this book — indeed, most of them — do not plot actual data. Rather, they illustrate theoretical relationships. It is the *relationship between variables* that is important in such graphs. This relationship is mathematical; the graph summarizes it in simple form.

Chapter 1 develops one graph of this type — the production possibilities frontier (PPF). PPFs illustrate the maximum quantity of two goods that can be produced from

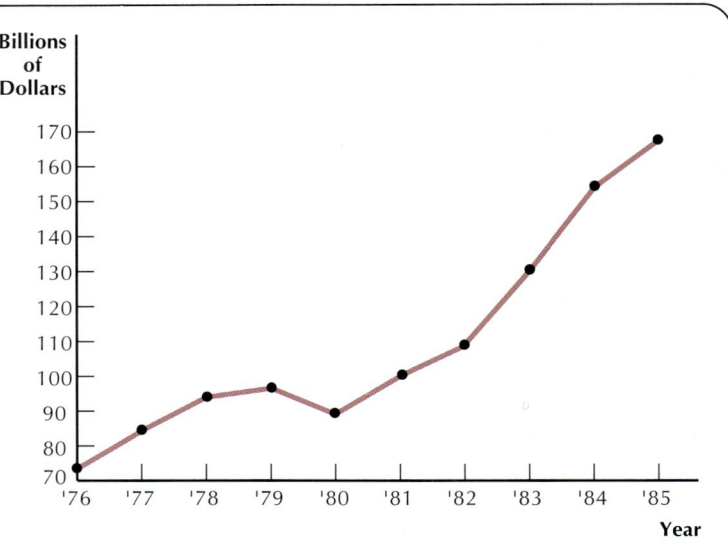

FIGURE 8
Spending on motor vehicles and parts.
Shrinking the horizontal axis and focusing on a smaller range of values on the vertical axis makes the year-to-year changes in spending appear much larger than in Figure 7.

a given stock of resources. Since a linear PPF is simpler mathematically than a curved PPF, we will examine a linear PPF first. Consider PPF_1 in Figure 9. It shows the tradeoff facing a farmer who can produce corn or soybeans on his land. Both corn and beans are measured in bushels per year. PPF_1 shows that by devoting all his cropland (and other resources) to corn production, he can produce a maximum of 6000 bushels in a year. If he devotes all his resources to soybean production, he can grow 2000 bushels of beans. By allocating some land to the production of corn and some to beans, he can trade off corn for beans along the PPF.

This PPF illustrates an algebraic relationship. The equation of PPF_1 can be derived easily. Suppose soybean production is zero. Then the farmer produces 6000 bushels of corn. If soybean production rises to 1000 bushels, corn production *falls* by 3000 bushels. For every bushel of beans produced, corn production declines by three bushels. Thus, the equation for PPF_1 can be written:

$$CORN = 6000 - (3 \times BEANS)$$

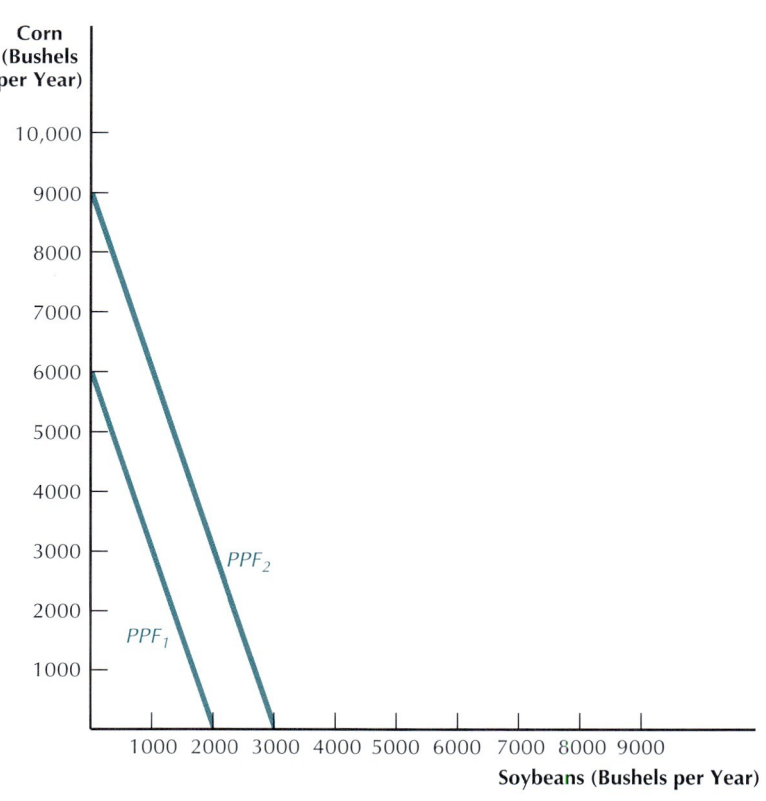

FIGURE 9
Linear production possibilities frontiers. The equation for PPF_1 is $CORN = 6000 - 3(BEANS)$. The equation for PPF_2 differs only in that the intercept term rises to 9000. The two PPFs are parallel, so their slopes are the same.

In terms of conventional *x*s and *y*s, it would read:

$$y = 6000 - 3x$$

The *y*-intercept of the equation (obtained by setting *x* to zero) is 6000. The *slope* of PPF$_1$ is -3. Slope measures the change in the *y* variable per one unit increase in the *x* variable. In this case, *y falls* by three units when *x rises* by one unit, so the slope is negative.

Suppose the farmer were given some additional land and equipment. Then he could produce more of both corn and soybeans. His PPF would shift outward to PPF$_2$. The equation describing PPF$_2$ differs from the equation for PPF$_1$ in only one respect: Its intercept term is larger. The rate at which corn can be traded off for beans (represented by the slope) does not change. The equation for PPF$_2$ is $y = 9000 - 3x$.

The slope of a straight line is constant. The slope of a curved line changes as one moves along the line. Figure 10 shows a curved production possibilities frontier. We can see immediately that the slope of the PPF is negative everywhere; when soybean production rises (along the *x*-axis), corn production falls (along the *y*-axis). But the *amount* by which corn production declines when soybean production rises by one bushel depends upon where on the PPF the farmer is operating.

Consider the movement from point A to point B. The slope of *a straight line* drawn from A to B is $-750/675 = -1.11$. (Corn production falls by 750 bushels, while

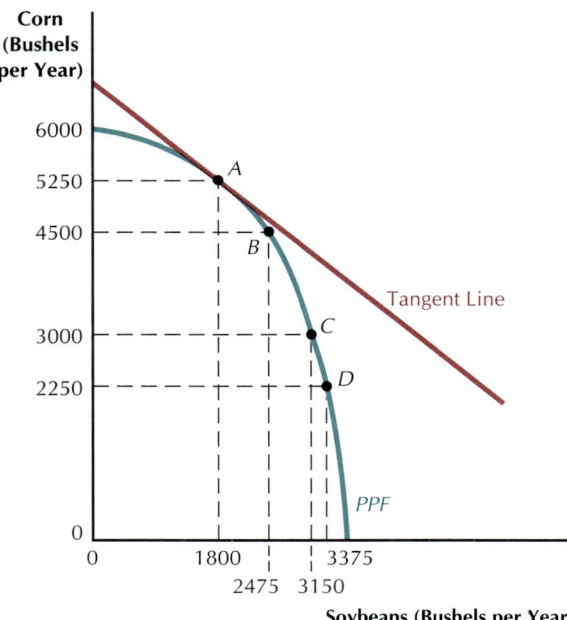

FIGURE 10
Curved production possibilities frontier. The slope of a curved PPF changes as you move along the curve. The slope at point A is measured by finding the slope of a line tangent to the PPF at A.

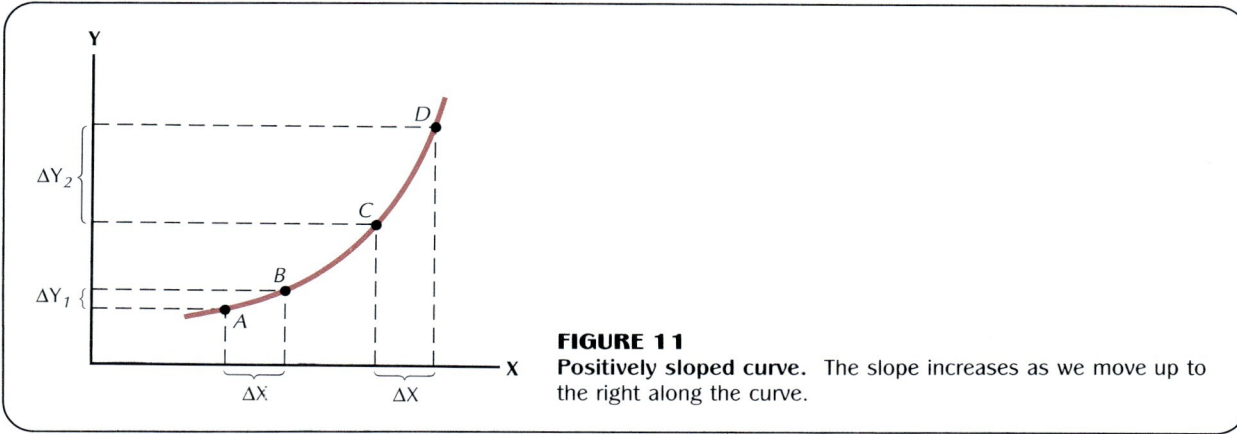

FIGURE 11
Positively sloped curve. The slope increases as we move up to the right along the curve.

soybean production rises by 675.) The slope of a straight line from C to D is $-750/225 = -3.33$. As noted, the slope changes as we move along a curve.

We find the slope of a curve at a particular point by drawing a straight line *tangent to the curve* at the relevant point. Then we measure the slope of the straight line. A tangent line touches the curve *only* at one point. The slope of the line tangent to point A in Figure 10 is -0.77. The slope of the tangent to point B (not shown) is -1.8.

Figure 11 illustrates a positively sloped curve. As in the case of the concave PPF, as one moves along the curve its slope changes. The slope between points A and B is smaller than the slope between points C and D, because the change in y between A and B is smaller than the change in y between C and D, although the change in x is the same between each pair of points.

The area under a curve is sometimes of interest in economic analysis. Deriving the area under a linear curve is not difficult. Suppose we want to determine the area under the curve in Figure 12. Since the area is a triangle, we apply the equation for the area of a triangle: ½ (length × width). Measuring the length along the x axis and the width along the y axis, we calculate the area to be ½ (50 × 10) = 250.

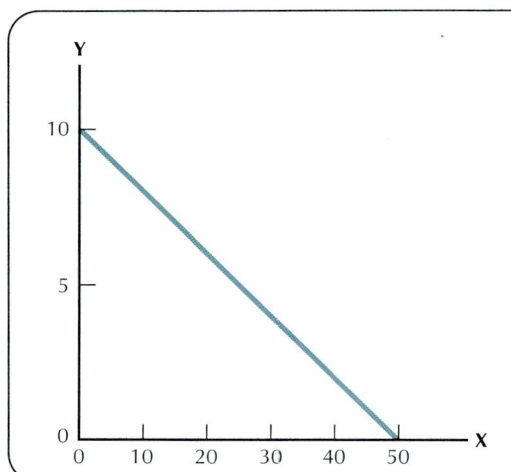

FIGURE 12
Area under a curve. The formula for a triangular area is ½(length × width). The area under this curve is ½(50 × 10) = 250.

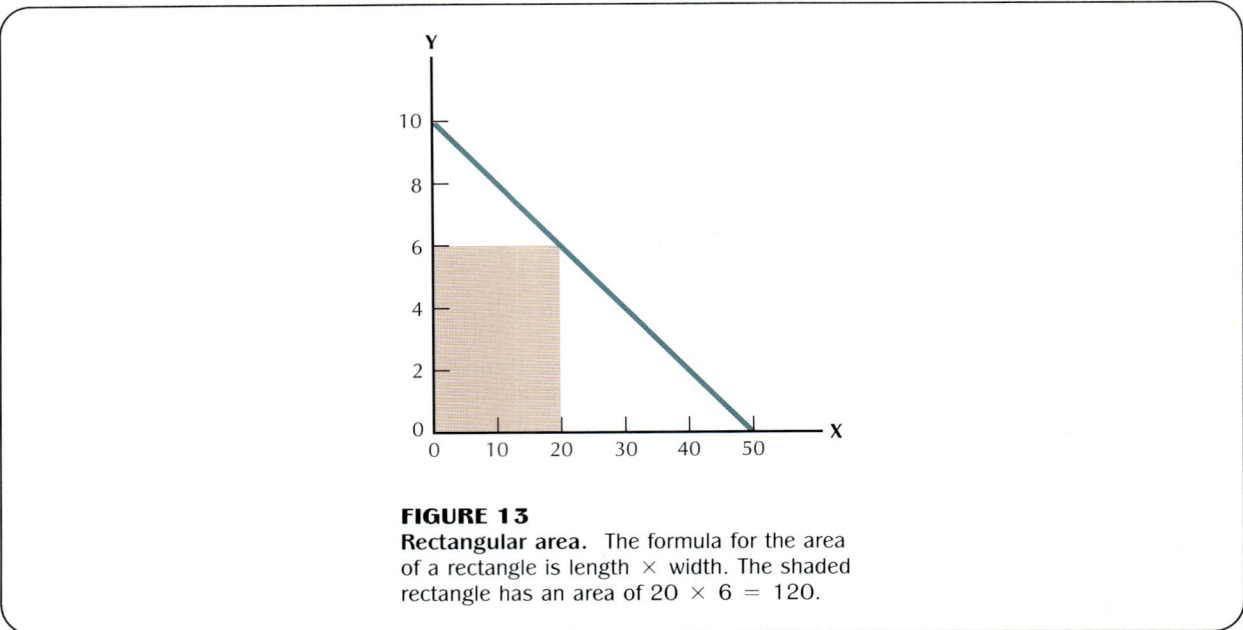

FIGURE 13
Rectangular area. The formula for the area of a rectangle is length × width. The shaded rectangle has an area of 20 × 6 = 120.

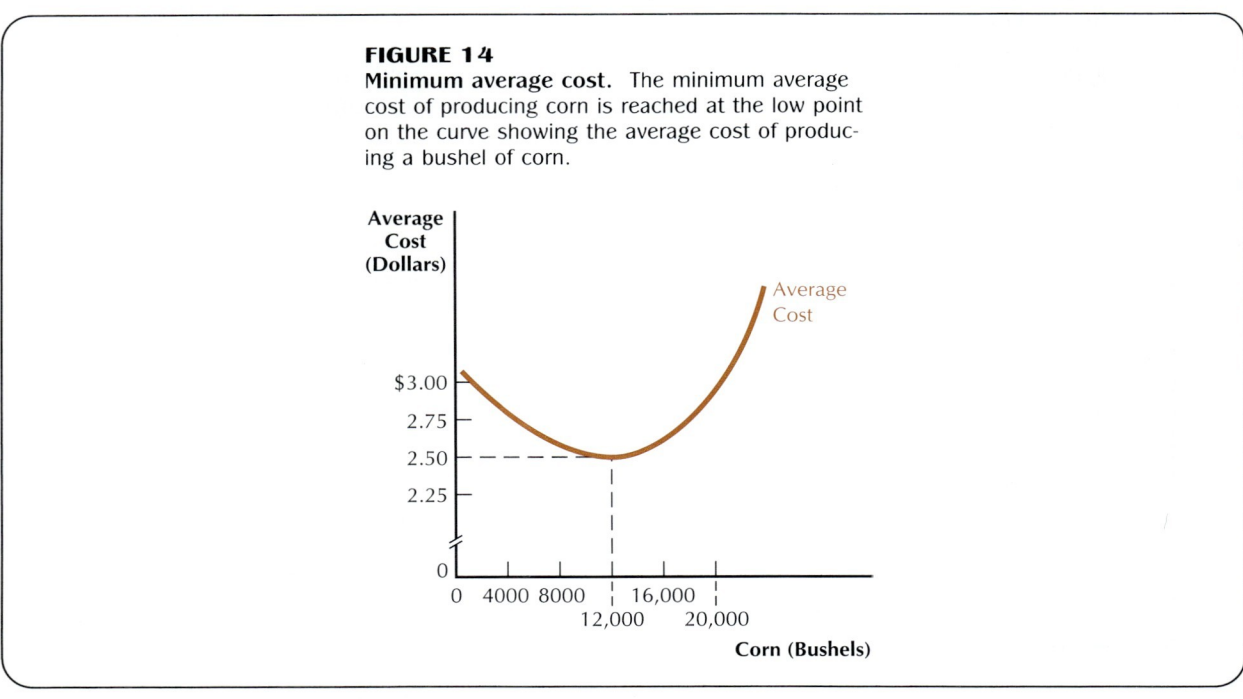

FIGURE 14
Minimum average cost. The minimum average cost of producing corn is reached at the low point on the curve showing the average cost of producing a bushel of corn.

Another calculation frequently called for in microeconomics is even simpler. Suppose we want to calculate the area under the curve in Figure 13 up to $x = 20$ and $y = 6$. This area is a rectangle, the area of which is calculated according to the formula $A = $ length $\times$ width. In this case, the area is $20 \times 6 = 120$. Many times the size of an irregularly shaped area can be calculated by dividing the area into triangles and rectangles, calculating the area of each, and summing the areas.

Sometimes the minimum or maximum value on a curve is important. Figure 14 illustrates the relationship between the average cost of producing a bushel of corn and the quantity of corn being produced. At $Q = 12{,}000$ bushels the average cost of producing a bushel of corn reaches its minimum. A curve turned upside down relative to the cost curve in Figure 14 could be used to show the maximum value attained by a variable.

You will learn more about graphs as you work your way through this book. These basics should help you get started. The most important thing to remember is that all the graphs in the text convey information. Concentrate on understanding their message, rather than just remembering what they look like.

OVERVIEW

Chapter 1 introduced the discipline of economics by identifying a simple, basic proposition upon which all economic theory is based: People make choices in a manner consistent with improvement of their well-being. We discussed the behavioral implications of this fundamental premise, as well as the scope of the economics discipline. Chapter 2 extends this introductory discussion of economics by illustrating the

Mutually Beneficial Exchange

notion of value and how it influences decisions. We consider more formally the concept of efficiency and its relationship to value. Finally, we illustrate these concepts with two examples of voluntary exchange. The purpose of the examples is to show how the Fundamental Premise of Economics is applied in a variety of contexts and to demonstrate the motivation for exchange between people and between economies.

CHAPTER 2

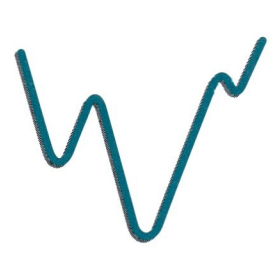

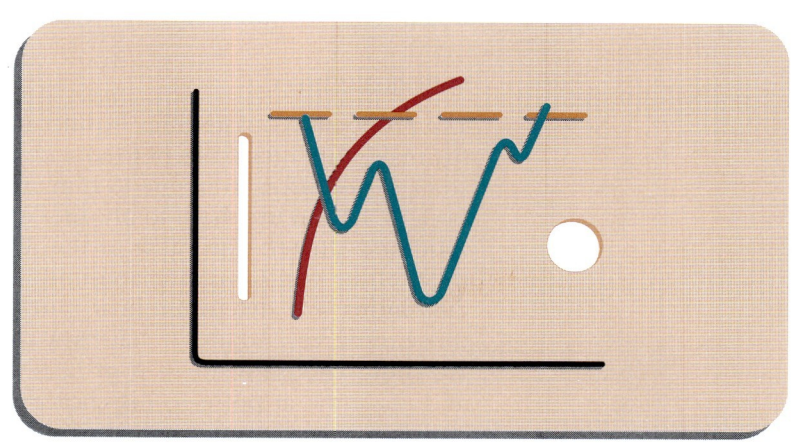

Learning Objectives

After reading and studying this chapter, you will be able to:

1. Define the notion of value.
2. Define *economic efficiency* and explain how it is related to *productive efficiency*.
3. Explain how the concept of economic efficiency is related to the Fundamental Premise of Economics.
4. Explain the principle of comparative advantage.
5. Use the production possibilities frontier model to explain a country's gains from specialization and trade.
6. Identify and explain the costs of trade and exchange.
7. Distinguish between the individual and social perspectives on a problem.

Choice and Value

People seek to satisfy as many wants as the scarce resources available to them will permit. This is true even though the preferences of different people differ widely. Social customs, ethnic traditions, and religious values all affect people's preferences, though the individuality of people from similar backgrounds is often obvious. Different people also differ greatly in their resource endowments—the physical and financial assets, labor skills, and intellectual and physical abilities they possess. There are many talented basketball players, but only one Michael Jordan. Similarly, income varies widely. In 1988 per capita (per person) income was $19,840 in the United States, but only $330 in China and $650 in Senegal.

Despite the variety of wants and resource constraints, all individuals seek to maximize the net benefits, or value, they derive from their incomes. However, the differences in preferences and resources imply that the specific way in which individuals go about maximizing the value of their resources varies greatly. An example using the production possibilities frontier model illustrates this phenomenon.

Individual Choice

The production possibilities frontier in Figure 1 belongs to Adam. It illustrates the maximum quantities of food and shelter that he can produce with the total stock of resources available to him. The resources are valuable to Adam only because he can use them to produce and consume something of value to him: food and shelter. The value of the resources derives from the uses to which they can be put. Given the amount of resources available and the production conditions that determine how much food or shelter can be produced with those resources, Adam can have any combination of food and shelter on PPF_1. He could choose to be at A or B, for example. If Adam chooses to produce and consume at point A, his choice indicates that this combination of food and shelter is more satisfying to him than any other combination of food and shelter on PPF_1. That is, Adam prefers point A to any other point on PPF_1.

Another person, Barbara, with the same resource constraint might prefer the combination at B in Figure 1. She prefers more shelter and less food than Adam. Adam and Barbara value food and shelter differently. The valuation of goods and services is subjective; it reflects differences in tastes and goals. This notion of valuation is normative; we cannot appeal to other facts or objective criteria to argue that either Adam or Barbara is somehow right and the other is wrong. An individual's valuation of a good is reflected in his actions. Adam could choose to produce and consume at point B, but he opts for A because he prefers that combination. Since Barbara prefers B to A, she uses her resources differently than Adam uses his.

Now, suppose that, rather than having resources that could be used to produce either food or shelter, Adam simply is given 25 units of food and 75 units of shelter (combination B). (The units of measurement are arbitrary.) We already have noted that Adam prefers combination A, though A's resource cost is the same as B's. If Adam were given the opportunity to trade some shelter for some food, he could increase his satisfaction. Suppose Barbara is given combination A. Then they could make themselves better off by trading. If Adam traded 25 units of shelter to Barbara for 15 units of food, they would both benefit. (Graphically, they would change places on the PPF; Adam would

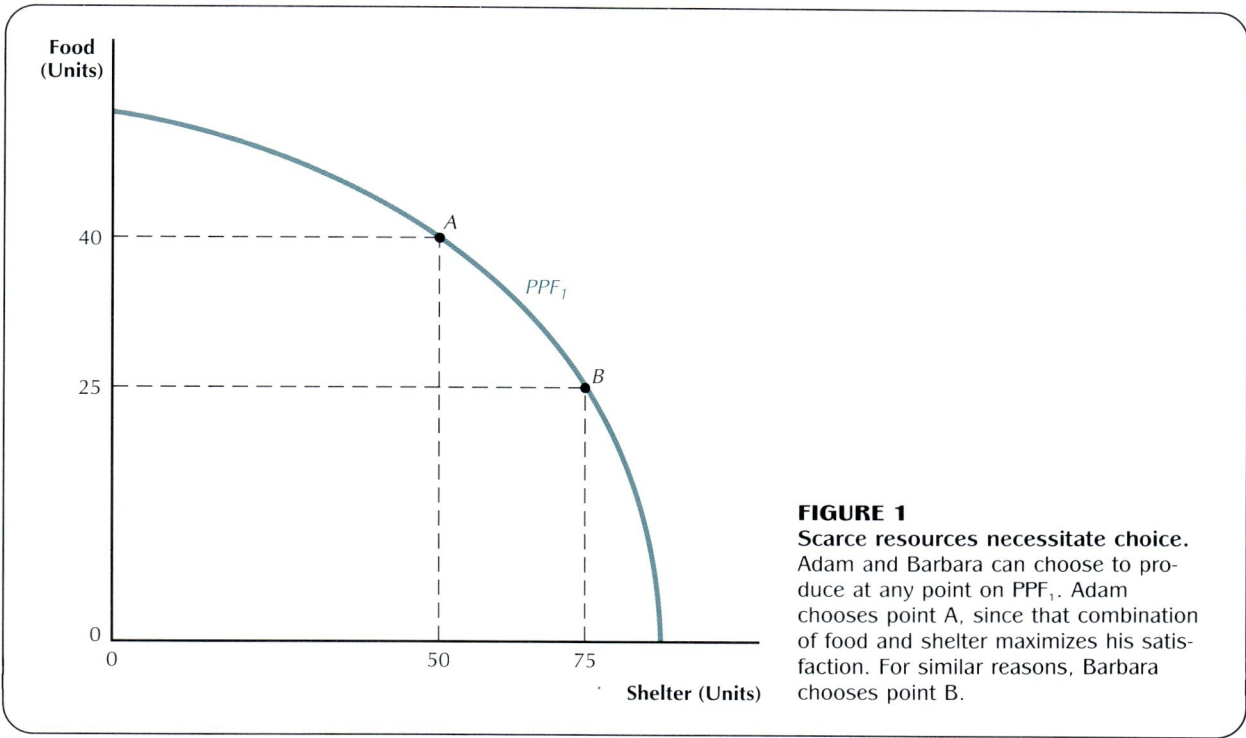

FIGURE 1
Scarce resources necessitate choice.
Adam and Barbara can choose to produce at any point on PPF_1. Adam chooses point A, since that combination of food and shelter maximizes his satisfaction. For similar reasons, Barbara chooses point B.

go to point A, Barbara to point B.) Each would reach the food–shelter combination on the PPF that he or she most preferred.

This example illustrates an important point. Satisfaction is achieved not by possessing resources, but by consuming the goods or services produced with them. The value an individual attaches to a stock of resources depends on the satisfaction derived from them. Individuals seek to make themselves as well off as they can by using resources to satisfy their particular wants. Resources are valuable only to the extent that they can be used to achieve an objective. If possessing resources were the end of economic behavior, everyone would be indifferent between points on the same PPF, because a PPF represents what can be produced with a *given* resource endowment.

Costs and Benefits

As we emphasized in Chapter 1, the fact that resources are limited implies that choices are costly. A decision to have more of one good is a decision to have less of another. The preferences and goals of individuals determine the values associated with alternatives and therefore influence the economic decisions individuals make. Thus, the benefits and costs of an alternative are specific to individuals or groups and are, to some extent, determined subjectively.

Economic Efficiency

Early in Chapter 1 we defined the Fundamental Premise of Economics: In all decision making, individuals choose the alternatives which they believe will produce the greatest net gains. The **net gain** of an action is the difference

Net gain
Difference between benefits received and costs incurred.

Economic efficiency
Obtaining the maximum net gain from an action.

Productive efficiency
Operating on the production possibilities frontier; producing without wasting resources.

Allocative efficiency
Using resources to produce goods with the highest possible value.

between the benefits received and the costs incurred. Benefits and costs reflect the subjective valuations of individual decision makers. An economically efficient choice is one that maximizes this net gain. **Economic efficiency** means obtaining the maximum benefits for a given cost or minimizing the cost of a given benefit. In other words, economic efficiency is getting the most satisfaction out of available resources.

We can illustrate the concept of economic efficiency by referring to the choice of a point on a production possibilities frontier. PPF_1 in Figure 1 illustrates the maximum combinations of food and shelter that Adam can produce with his given stock of resources. If Adam utilizes his resources as productively as possible, not wasting any of them, he can produce any combination of food and shelter on PPF_1. Operating on the production possibilities frontier requires **productive efficiency**. No resources are wasted; the maximum amount of output is obtained from the available inputs.

However, not all points on PPF_1 are equally satisfactory to Adam. Although the resource cost to Adam of all combinations on PPF_1 is the same, his satisfaction is maximized at point A. If Adam were to use his resources to produce and consume at any point other than point A, such as at point B, he would not maximize his benefits. Thus, *economic efficiency requires not only productive efficiency (no waste) but also* **allocative efficiency** — *the allocation of resources to their highest-valued uses*. Only at point A does Adam maximize the difference between the benefits and costs of production and consumption.

Efficiency as a Goal

Individuals and societies have many different goals. The unhampered pursuit of individual satisfaction may not be compatible with some other goals. For

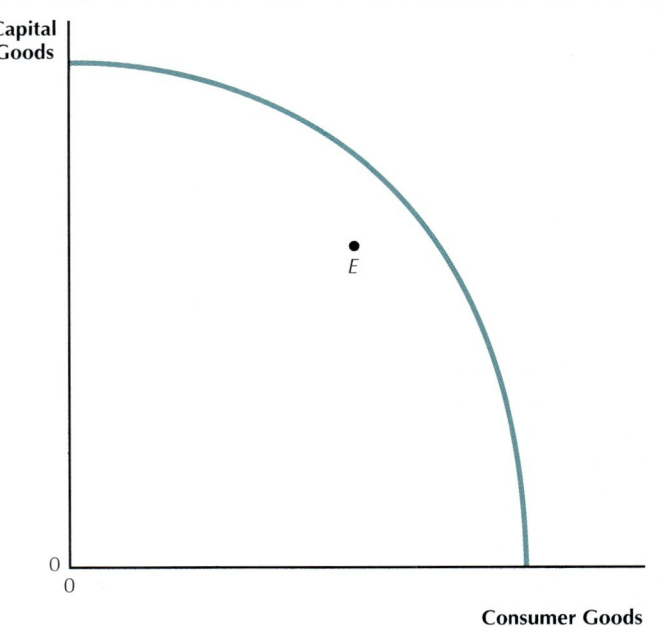

FIGURE 2
Efficiency–equity tradeoff. Income redistribution programs designed to promote social equity may reduce the level of production, moving the economy inside its production possibilities frontier.

example, society may choose to guarantee a minimum income level for all members of society. To do this, it may have to redistribute income from wealthier members of society to poorer ones through government taxation and spending programs. Such redistribution may reduce the level of satisfaction wealthy people are able to attain (while increasing the satisfaction of poorer people), and may even reduce the level of production of the economy, moving the economy inside its production possibilities frontier to a point such as E in Figure 2. In such a case, the goal of social equity dominates the goal of economic efficiency.

However, *within the constraints imposed by other social goals*, individuals and societies attempt to achieve economic efficiency. To do otherwise would be to waste scarce resources. Within the limits set by a concern for equity or liberty or economic growth or whatever other goals society might have, individuals and societies strive for economic efficiency — the proper allocation of resources in a productively efficient manner. Since economics contributes greatly to our understanding of how economic efficiency can be achieved, discussions of efficiency absorb most of our attention in this book. To a large extent the job of an economist is to determine how specified goals can be achieved as efficiently as possible.

SECTION RECAP
Economic efficiency combines both productive efficiency (producing without waste, on the PPF) with allocative efficiency (allocating resources to their most highly valued uses).

Gains from Exchange

Within the constraints imposed by other individual or social goals, people attempt to act in an economically efficient manner, that is, to obtain the greatest satisfaction possible out of available resources. This was the objective of Adam in his individual production and consumption of food and shelter and is the objective of all those people who interact with large numbers of other people in their daily economic activities. The large majority of people in the world fit into the latter category; very few people are, or want to be, totally self-sufficient.

Why are so few people self-sufficient? The Fundamental Premise of Economics asserts that people choose to do what is most beneficial for themselves. If the Premise is true (and we believe it is), then most people must believe that economic interaction, specifically the voluntary exchange of goods and services, makes them better off than they could be without trading.

Refer back to Figure 1. Adam maximizes his **utility** (the standard economic term for consumer satisfaction) subject to the amount of resources available to him by producing and consuming at point A. He cannot do as well producing and consuming at any other point on PPF_1. If he is to be made better off, then he must move to a point *beyond* his production possibilities frontier. This is exactly what voluntary exchange enables individuals — or societies — to do. By specializing in production and trading for other desired goods, individuals are able to push their *joint* production possibilities outward.

Utility
Economic term for consumer satisfaction.

The remainder of the chapter investigates the nature of voluntary trade. It shows how trade can result in mutual gain for the traders by developing two different examples of trade and exchange. Each example demonstrates that an individual (or a society) can make himself (or itself) better off by consuming at a point beyond his (or its) *individual* production possibilities frontier, by engaging in mutually beneficial trade. The examples illustrate different ways in which exchange can improve economic welfare. In the first example, an exchange allows two people to produce the same output with less effort. In the second example, two countries are able to increase the quantity of goods available for consumption by specializing and trading with one another.

Comparative Advantage at "Walden Pond"

The first illustration of the benefits of exchange involves two men, Henry and Jack, who have retired to the isolated countryside to live in solitude and simplicity, much as Henry David Thoreau did at Walden Pond. They want to use their time for thinking, writing, and communing with nature. Each has a cabin on the edge of a large stream at the base of a small wooded hill, which separates the cabins. They discover one another one day at the stream, where both are fishing. They spend their days fishing, foraging for wild vegetables, and enjoying quiet contemplation. Neither of them enjoys fishing or foraging as activities; rather, they fish and forage to provide themselves with food.

Evening visits and conversations reveal the following interesting patterns. Henry spends much of his day foraging and fishing. It takes him four hours a day to catch enough fish for his daily diet; he also spends two hours a day searching for wild vegetables. Although Jack has exactly the same daily diet, it takes him only an hour and a half each in foraging and fishing to get the same daily foodstuffs for which Henry works six hours a day. Jack is both a better fisherman and a better forager than Henry; he has an **absolute advantage** in both activities.

Absolute advantage Ability to produce a good at a lower resource cost than other producers.

These productivity differences cause Jack and Henry to wonder if there is a way for them to trade tasks and get the same work done in less time. In fact, there is. Suppose Jack fishes for both of them, while Henry forages for both. Then the total time spent on fishing and foraging is reduced from nine hours a day to seven. Jack spends three hours each day catching fish for both men, and Henry spends four hours foraging for wild vegetables. This time-saving trade raises several questions, the first of which is how the trade reduces total work time.

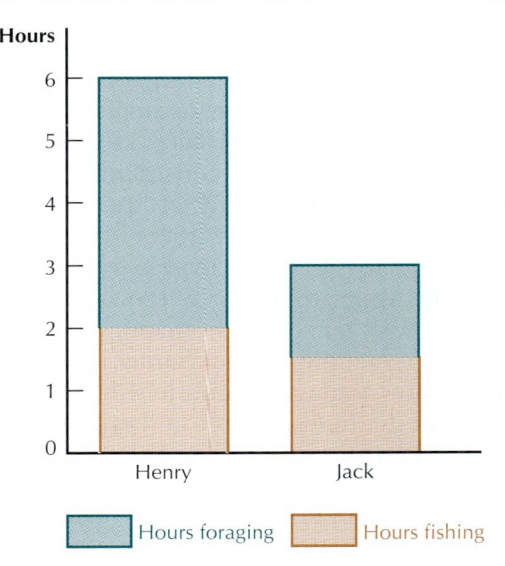

FIGURE 3
Daily work at "Walden Pond". Working independently, Henry requires six hours per day to catch his daily fish and collect his daily vegetables. Jack requires only three hours to obtain the same amount of food.

TABLE 1
"Walden Pond" opportunity costs

Relative Costs of Activity	Henry	Jack
Opportunity cost of one day's fish in terms of servings of vegetables	2.0	1.0
Opportunity cost of one daily serving of vegetables in terms of daily servings of fish	0.5	1.0

Henry and Jack are able to reduce the time it takes to produce their vegetables and fish by *specializing* in activities for which each is the least-cost producer and then *trading* the fruits of their labors. In what sense is Jack the least-cost producer of fish? *Cost must be measured in terms of alternatives forgone.* In the time it takes for Jack to catch his desired quantity of fish, he could have found and picked his daily vegetables. The opportunity cost to Jack of his daily diet of fish is one daily serving of vegetables. It takes him an hour and a half to complete either activity. Henry must give up two daily servings of vegetables to catch his daily provision of fish. He requires four hours to catch his daily fish, but only two hours to gather his vegetables. Thus, Jack gives up less than Henry to get a day's fish. Figure 3 and Table 1 present the opportunity cost data in convenient form.

While Jack is the least-cost producer of fish, Henry is the least-cost forager; he gives up only half a day's serving of fish to gather his vegetables. Jack gives up one day's serving of fish to find his vegetables. Jack is the least-cost fish producer relative to Henry, and Henry is the least-cost producer of vegetables relative to Jack.

Suppose the two men agree to specialize in production and trade goods. Jack catches fish for both men, while Henry gathers vegetables for both. By specializing and trading, they are able to reduce the total time required to produce two daily servings of fish and two daily servings of vegetables. Figure 4 shows the time spent fishing and foraging with and without trade. If each man both fishes and forages, the total daily time required to complete the activities is nine hours (six for Henry plus three for Jack). If Jack specializes in fishing, while Henry forages, the total time requirement falls to seven hours. If they attempted to specialize in the wrong goods, producing their relatively high-opportunity-cost goods, the total time required to complete their daily activities would rise to eleven hours.

When each one specializes in that activity for which he is least-cost producer, Henry and Jack are able to minimize the total cost of a day's worth of food for each of them. By specializing and trading, they have reduced the opportunity cost of a day's food, even though Jack has an absolute advantage in both activities (he can complete either activity in less time than Henry can). The gains come from exploiting comparative advantage. The principle of **comparative advantage** says that *total output is greatest when each good is produced by its least-opportunity cost producer.* This principle applies to groups of individuals, to nations, and to the world economy.

How the gains from an exchange are distributed is another important issue. Notice that the specialization and exchange required to reduce the total time requirement to seven hours also distributes the entire two-hour savings to

Comparative advantage Ability to produce a good at a lower opportunity cost than other producers.

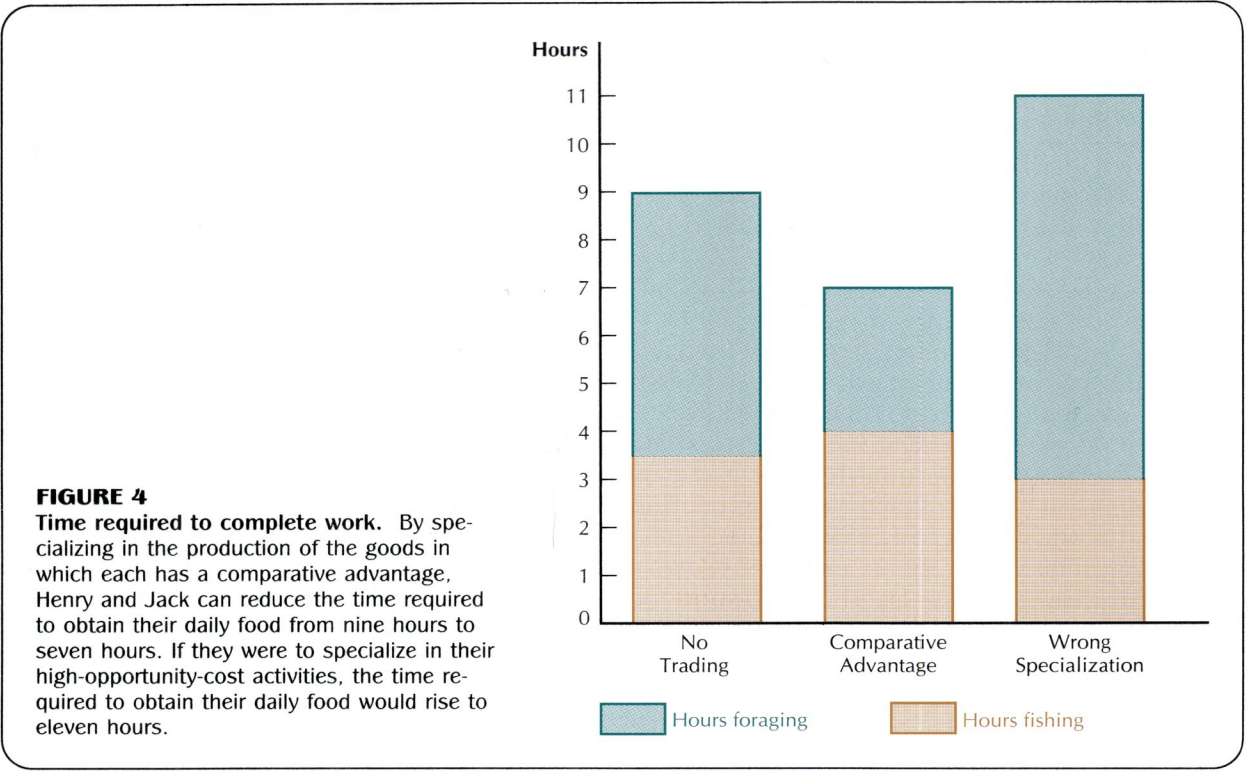

FIGURE 4
Time required to complete work. By specializing in the production of the goods in which each has a comparative advantage, Henry and Jack can reduce the time required to obtain their daily food from nine hours to seven hours. If they were to specialize in their high-opportunity-cost activities, the time required to obtain their daily food would rise to eleven hours.

SECTION RECAP
Specializing in low-opportunity-cost production activities and trading with others reduces the total cost of producing a given quantity of goods.

Henry, who now works four hours rather than six, while Jack continues to work three hours as he did before specializing. What kind of exchange would save time for both Henry and Jack? Henry would have to forage for both and do some fishing. For example, Henry might gather vegetables for both and then catch a third of his daily fish. That would leave Jack with responsibility for one and two-thirds servings of fish. Henry would spend four hours foraging and an hour and a third fishing. Jack would spend two and a half hours fishing. To get both tasks done, trading one day's serving of vegetables for two thirds of a serving of fish, they would spend a total of seven hours and fifty minutes, saving over an hour in total, with the savings split roughly equally.

Comparative Advantage and International Trade

The second example of comparative advantage and exchange examines trade between countries. Such trade is motivated by the same kind of gains that motivated Henry and Jack to cooperate for time savings. Countries trade when they can make themselves better off. This basis for trade may seem strange to you, since news reports frequently suggest that a country is harmed, rather than helped, by trade with other countries. In fact, Congress regularly considers measures to protect domestic firms from foreign competition. A variety of protectionist measures restricts the quantity of imports that can enter the United States. Does trade really improve an economy's well-being?

The basis for international trade is the principle of comparative advantage. Trade between two countries arises when it is mutually beneficial. International trade permits countries to consume more goods and services than they could without trade. That is, it permits countries to escape their individual resource constraints.

Let's consider a simple example of trade in two goods, shoes and wheat, between two countries, the United States and South Korea. Each country can produce both shoes and wheat, and initially they do not trade. Both countries produce wheat and shoes and consume what they produce. The production and consumption options for each country are given by their respective production possibilities frontiers, depicted in Figure 5 and Table 2. South Korea can produce 150,000 pairs of shoes and no wheat or 50,000 tons of wheat and no shoes, or any (linear) combination of the two goods on its PPF. The United States can produce 150,000 pairs of shoes and no wheat or 150,000 tons of wheat and no shoes. (Linear PPFs are used for simplicity.)

Several possible production–consumption combinations are identified in Table 2. For example, South Koreans could choose to produce and consume 150,000 pairs of shoes and no wheat or 120,000 pairs of shoes and 10,000 tons of wheat, or any of the other combinations shown. Assume that in the absence of trade South Koreans choose to annually produce and consume the combination of 50,000 pairs of shoes and 33,333 tons of wheat. The United

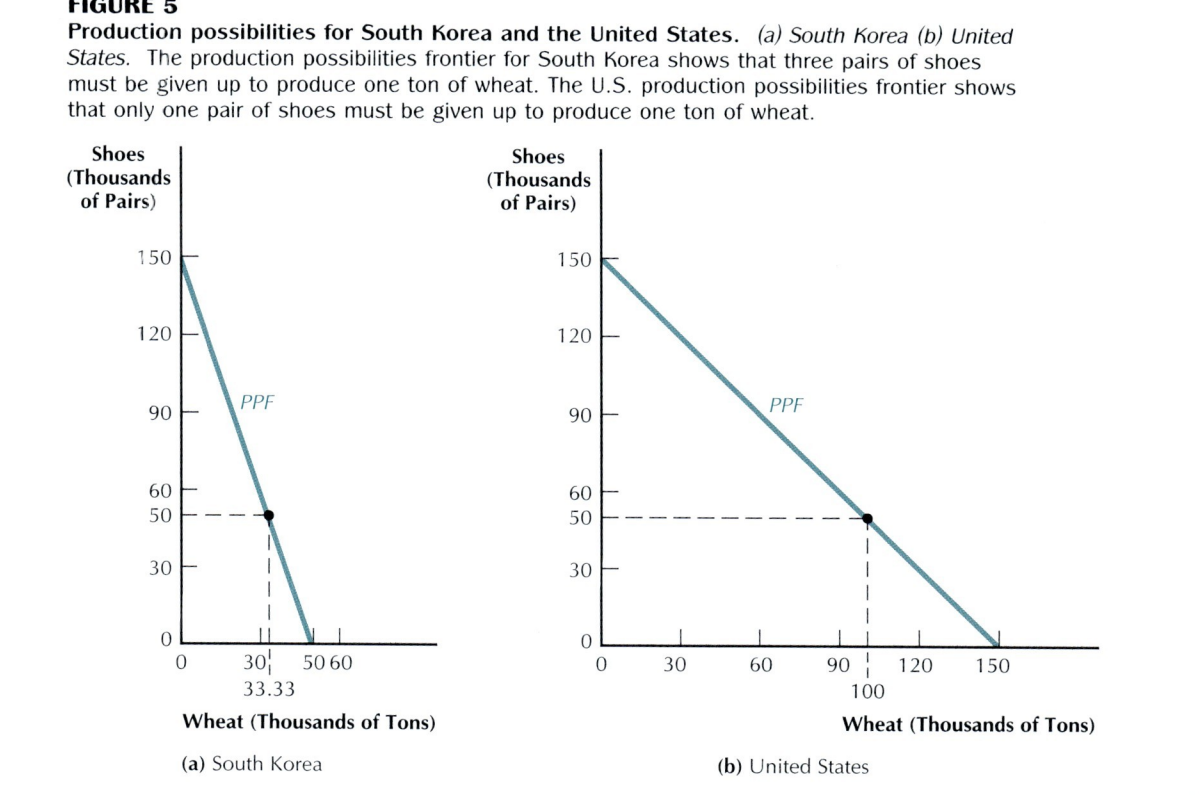

FIGURE 5
Production possibilities for South Korea and the United States. *(a) South Korea (b) United States.* The production possibilities frontier for South Korea shows that three pairs of shoes must be given up to produce one ton of wheat. The U.S. production possibilities frontier shows that only one pair of shoes must be given up to produce one ton of wheat.

(a) South Korea

(b) United States

TABLE 2
South Korean and U.S. production possibilities

South Korea		United States	
Shoes	Wheat	Shoes	Wheat
150	0	150	0
120	10	120	30
90	20	90	60
60	30	60	90
* 50	33⅓	* 50	100
30	40	30	120
0	50	0	150

Shoes are measured in thousands of pairs, wheat in thousands of tons.
Note: * indicates pretrade positions of the two countries.

States, on the other hand, can produce 150,000 pairs of shoes and no wheat or 150,000 tons of wheat and no shoes or any linear combination thereof. Before trade the United States chooses to produce and consume 50,000 pairs of shoes and 100,000 tons of wheat.

South Korea and the United States can both benefit from trade because of their different resource endowments and consequent differences in relative opportunity costs. Table 3 identifies these costs. To produce an additional 1000 tons of wheat, South Koreans must give up 3000 pairs of shoes. For example, in moving from the combination 150,000 pairs of shoes and no wheat to the combination 120,000 pairs of shoes and 10,000 tons of wheat, the South Koreans must give up 3000 pairs of shoes for each 1000 tons of wheat produced. The United States gives up only 1,000 pairs of shoes per 1000 tons of wheat. Therefore, the United States is the least-cost producer of wheat: It gives up less than South Korea does to get additional wheat.

To obtain an additional 1000 pairs of shoes, South Korea only gives up 333 tons of wheat (10,000 tons of wheat for 30,000 pairs of shoes), while the United States must sacrifice 1000 tons of wheat for 1000 pairs of shoes. Thus, South Korea is the least-cost producer of shoes relative to the United States. South Korea has a comparative advantage in shoes, and the United States has

TABLE 3
Opportunity cost of producing wheat and shoes

	South Korea	United States
Cost of 1000 tons of wheat (thousands of pairs of shoes given up)	3	1
Cost of 1000 pairs of shoes (thousands of tons of wheat given up)	⅓	1

a comparative advantage in wheat. South Korea and the United States can gain from trade.

Americans are willing to trade wheat for shoes any time they can obtain 1000 pairs for less than 1000 tons of wheat. For instance, a trade of 500 tons of wheat for 1000 pairs of shoes would make U.S. consumers better off. On the other hand, South Koreans would trade 1000 pairs of shoes any time they could get more than 333 tons of wheat for them. Thus, an exchange of 1000 pairs of shoes for 500 tons of wheat also would benefit South Korean consumers.

If the United States specializes in the production of the good in which it has a comparative advantage (wheat) and South Korea specializes in the production of the good in which it has a comparative advantage (shoes), the two countries can trade and make themselves better off. By specializing in production and trading at a ratio between one ton of wheat for one pair of shoes and one ton of wheat for three pairs of shoes, both South Korea and the United States could achieve wheat and shoe consumption levels beyond their respective production possibilities frontiers. At a ratio of, for example, one ton of wheat for two pairs of shoes, both nations benefit from trading.

Figure 6 illustrates graphically the result of specialization and trade. South Korea specializes in shoe production, producing 150,000 pairs of shoes and no wheat, point A on its PPF. The United States specializes in wheat production, producing 150,000 tons of wheat and no shoes, point A' on its PPF. South Korea continues to consume 50,000 pairs of shoes annually, so it has 100,000

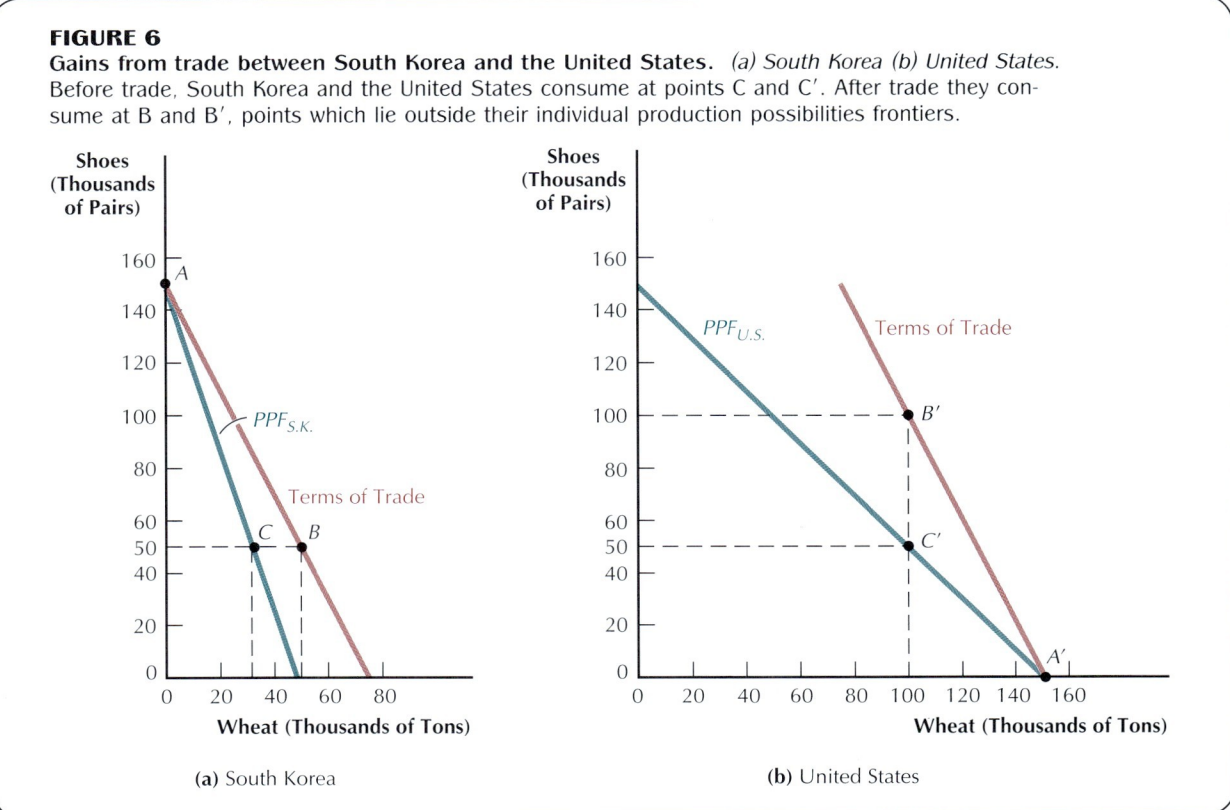

FIGURE 6
Gains from trade between South Korea and the United States. *(a) South Korea (b) United States.* Before trade, South Korea and the United States consume at points C and C'. After trade they consume at B and B', points which lie outside their individual production possibilities frontiers.

(a) South Korea

(b) United States

pairs to trade to the United States for wheat. The United States continues to consume 100,000 tons of wheat, so it has 50,000 tons available for trade.

The two nations exchange goods at a ratio of two pairs of shoes for a ton of wheat. South Korea obtains 50,000 tons of wheat in exchange for its 100,000 pairs of shoes. After trade South Korea consumes 50,000 pairs of shoes and 50,000 tons of wheat annually, a net increase of 16,667 tons of wheat. This is represented by point B, a point beyond the South Korean production possibilities frontier. The United States consumes 100,000 tons of wheat and 100,000 pairs of shoes, a net increase of 50,000 pairs of shoes. Point B' lies beyond the U.S. production possibilities frontier. Without sacrificing more shoes, South Koreans are able to consume more wheat. Likewise, Americans are able to consume more shoes without sacrificing more wheat.

Specialization and trade allows each nation to reduce the opportunity cost of the good it acquires in trade. By trading, South Korea is able to acquire one ton of wheat for two pairs of shoes; producing its own wheat requires giving up three pairs of shoes. The United States gains by reducing the opportunity cost of shoe consumption from one ton of wheat per pair of shoes to one-half ton of wheat per pair. In fact, South Koreans would gain by trading at any ratio lower than three pairs of shoes per ton of wheat. Americans would gain at any ratio higher than one pair of shoes per ton of wheat. Thus, any

Why the **Disagreement?**

A Reunited Germany: Too Much Free Trade?

For more than two centuries, economists have argued that free trade between economies benefits the people of both nations. History confirms the argument: First Great Britain, then the United States, and later Japan and West Germany became economic powers by pursuing policies of (mostly) free trade. Nations such as South Korea, Taiwan, and Singapore currently are using international trade as a means to achieve prosperity. Given the excellent historical record of free-trading countries and the success enjoyed by West Germany from the early 1950s to the present, it is not surprising to find that many Germans—including Chancellor Helmut Kohl—viewed the reunification of East and West Germany as an opportunity to leap forward economically, through the institution of *totally* free trade. If free trade between two distinct nations is good, unifying two economies should be great.

Not all Germans were delighted by the idea of a rapid reunification of the two economies, however. It is not surprising that some Germans would oppose reunification. After all, a large number of bureaucrats in the old East German government stood to lose their jobs. But the apprehension spread well beyond such officials. Concern among East Germans was so widespread that one European newspaper was prompted to write: "When you read the lamentations of the East German papers one would believe that they were going to be reunited with Pakistan or Bangladesh and the collective wealth was going to be distributed evenly."* Many West Germans also argued against rapid integration of the two economies. Why the disagreement?

Uniting two economies differs from free trade between distinct economies in one very important respect: In a unified economy, workers are free to move anywhere in search of better employment; in two distinct economies, labor mobility is much more limited. The fact that unification enabled East Germans to move freely to the West meant that, upon unification, firms in the East would be forced to offer wages and benefits comparable to those in the West. Failure to do so would lead to a mass emigration of East German workers to the West in search of better employment. The problem for East

trading ratio between one pair of shoes per ton of wheat and three pairs of shoes per ton of wheat benefits both countries. *For trade to be mutually beneficial, the trading ratio (commonly called the* terms of trade*) need only lie between the two countries' individual opportunity cost ratios.*

After trade South Korea no longer produces wheat, nor does the United States produce shoes. Specialization eliminated one industry—and its employment opportunities—in each country. However, the other industry expanded—increased its employment—because of trade. It is this aspect of trade, the specialization of production, that prompts calls for protection. Although shoe firms go out of business in the United States, and shoe industry jobs vanish, the wheat industry expands, and new jobs are created. In the process, total output in South Korea and the United States increases. Trade based on comparative advantage allows more output to be produced from the stock of resources in the two countries. Greater economic efficiency is achieved.

Resource reallocations and employment changes can cause problems in an economy, at least in the short run. In addition, complete specialization makes South Korea and the United States dependent upon one another, a situation that carries some risks for both countries. Both of these important issues are considered in detail in the chapter on international trade.

Terms of trade
The ratio at which two goods are traded for one another.

SECTION RECAP

By specializing in the production of goods in which a nation has a comparative advantage and trading with other nations, a country can escape its production possibilities frontier.

German firms was that four decades of communist rule had left them with antiquated, inefficient factories that use far more labor, energy, and raw materials to produce goods than do West German firms. The inefficiency of the East German firms meant that the only way they could hope to compete with West German firms was to pay their workers very low wages. However, unification eliminated that option.

Unification created some sticky problems for West Germans as well. The West German government was committed to reunification from the time Germany was split apart after World War II. As part of that commitment, West Germany automatically granted citizenship and full social welfare benefits to anyone immigrating from East Germany. If large numbers of East Germans were to immigrate, the cost to West German taxpayers would be immense. Ironically, the only way to prevent them from immigrating was either to provide welfare benefits to all Easterners without forcing them to move or by subsidizing the wages of East German workers, thereby removing the incentive to collect welfare benefits. (The cost of subsidizing East Germany led many West Germans to label the new states of unified Germany collectively *Fass ohne Boden (FOB)*, German for "barrel without bottom.")**

Nearly everyone believes that the reunification of Germany will ultimately benefit both East and West Germans. The disagreement over reunifying the two economies was about how rapidly reunification should occur. Proponents of rapid reunification argued that gradualism would only increase the expense, since a complete overhaul of the East German economy was needed. Opponents could offer no persuasive arguments that gradualism would be less expensive. Ultimately, the economic arguments became moot, as political pressures forced a rapid reunification. West Germans will continue to pay a high economic price for reunification until the capital stock in the East can be brought up to the standards of market economies. When that occurs, however, unified Germany will be easily the largest economy in Europe and a true economic superpower.

*Quoted in "Gloom in the East Weighs on Bonn," *Insight,* September 3, 1990, p. 37.
**See "East Whaddyamacallit," *The Economist,* October 20, 1990, p. 60.

Gains from Trade: Costs and Benefits . . . Again

Both of the preceding examples of exchange demonstrated that both parties to voluntary trade gain. In the case of individual exchange we saw that individuals pursuing their self-interest were able to make themselves better off—without making anyone worse off. Henry and Jack were able to reduce the time required for a given amount of production. In the case of international trade, the total production and consumption of the two trading nations increased. If the gains from international trade were allocated properly, no one in either South Korea or the United States need consume less, and some (or all) could consume more.

The principle of comparative advantage lies behind these gains. This principle presents a simple, yet powerful rule for achieving the objective of welfare maximization: Give up that which is less valuable in return for something that is more valuable. Specialize in producing those goods for which you have a comparative advantage, and trade for other goods of value to you. Doing so enables individuals or nations to use their resources in a way that increases their value.

Alternatives play a very important role in the nature and extent of trade and exchange. Alternatives determine the gains from trade. What matters are relative benefits and costs. For instance, Jack was an efficient fisherman relative to Henry. Or to put it another way, Jack specialized in fishing because Henry was relatively bad at it. If by chance Henry could have caught the daily requirement of fish in one hour rather than four, Jack would have been the relatively inefficient fisherman. In the second example, the United States is a relatively inefficient shoe producer because it is such an efficient wheat producer. The actions taken to improve one's welfare depend upon the alternatives available. When alternatives change, relative costs and benefits change, and other actions may become more beneficial.

Costs of Exchange

Our discussion of the benefits of specialization and exchange raises several important issues. We have emphasized the benefits of voluntary exchange because these gains are the motivation for much of the economic activity that occurs throughout the world. However, the stress on gains from exchange is not intended to ignore problems that can accompany trade and exchange.

Transactions Costs

Trade cannot be carried out without cost. Resources are consumed in acquiring information about trading opportunities, working out trade agreements, and transporting goods. Such **transactions costs** reduce or possibly eliminate the gains that could be realized if trade were costless. If transactions costs are equal to or greater than the gains from trading, trade will not take place.

Because transactions costs reduce the gains from trading, society benefits when people discover ways to reduce transactions costs. The development of the internal combustion engine and its use in motor vehicles reduced transportation costs tremendously and enabled exchange to expand. Nearly a century before the automobile, the development of steam locomotives and the technology to make steel rails had reduced costs in a similar fashion. Modern

Transactions costs
Costs of trading, including costs of acquiring information, working out trade agreements, and transporting goods.

Does It Make **Economic Sense?**

Buying a "Lemon": A Case of Inadequate Information?

Approximately 25 percent of U.S. workers earn their incomes by helping people buy and sell things. Clerks in retail stores, salespeople of various types, wholesale distributors, brokers, and dealers all make a living by transferring goods from producers to consumers. To the casual observer, they appear to produce little or nothing, yet they are paid for acting as go-betweens. Can the existence of so many nonproductive workers be justified? Does it make economic sense?

People who are trying to maximize their net gains from trade will attempt to avoid paying for things they do not need. If the assistance of sales clerks and goods brokers is worthless, why would people use their services? Such a line of reasoning suggests that the host of middlemen who engage in trade must produce something of value. But what?

Different middlemen produce different things. Retail clerks help customers save time and effort by quickly locating desired items. Wholesale distributors reduce the cost of goods to retailers by specializing in moving goods from producers to retailers. Some middlemen provide consumers with information on product quality or location. Inadequate information can result in costly mistakes, so quality information about goods is potentially very valuable.

As an example of a market specialist producing valuable information about product quality, consider the used car dealer. Economist George Akerlof has noted that the presence of *asymmetric information* in a market can make mutually beneficial trading an impossibility.*

Asymmetric information arises when the person selling a used car has good information about the car's quality while a prospective buyer has little information about it and limited ability to determine it. Certainly, a prospective buyer can examine the car carefully, inside and out, and can take it for a test drive, but severe problems may remain undiscovered. Many serious mechanical problems can be camouflaged temporarily. Furthermore, if the prospective buyer does not personally know the seller, the seller's assurance that the car is sound is not worth much. If the car is a lemon, the seller can gain by advertising it as a good car and selling it for more than it is really worth.

Under such circumstances, people who want to sell used cars that *are* in good shape find that no one will pay them what their cars are really worth. Since prospective buyers realize that they may be buying a lemon, they are unwilling to pay what a good used car is really worth. After all, it might be a lemon. Furthermore, people who would like to sell high-quality used cars do not sell them because of the low prices they are offered. The only people willing to sell used cars are the owners of lemons! Consequently, many potentially beneficial trades do not occur.

Used car dealers are able to partially overcome the problem of asymmetric information. If the people who become used car dealers are better than most people at distinguishing lemons from good cars, they may be willing to pay more for a car they believe to be of good quality than an ordinary prospective buyer would pay.

Thus, the sellers of good-quality used cars may find it beneficial to sell their cars to dealers. Used car dealers who develop reputations for honesty can obtain higher prices for the used cars they sell than individual sellers can. Prospective buyers trust the quality evaluations of honest dealers and are willing to pay more for cars sold by such dealers.

How does a used car dealer develop a reputation for honesty? First and foremost, the dealer must attempt to be honest and must stand behind the cars he or she sells. Often used car dealers offer limited warranties that cover major repairs on their cars for thirty days or 1000 miles. Dealers may also join such organizations as the Better Business Bureau, an agency that records consumer complaints about businesses. Dealers can point to an absence of complaints as evidence of their honesty. Dealers who also sell new cars advertise the quality of their used cars through such labels as "OK Used Cars" (Chevrolet), "A-1 Used Cars" (Ford), and "Select Used Cars" (Chrysler).

By overcoming to some degree the problem of asymmetric information, used car dealers benefit both buyers and sellers of used cars. The dealers collect part of the gains by selling their cars for more than they paid for them. Used car dealers earn their incomes by producing valuable information. Using the services of such middlemen does make economic sense.

---

*George Akerlof, "The Market for 'Lemons': Quality Uncertainty and the Market Mechanism," *Quarterly Journal of Economics* (August 1970), pp. 488–500.

computer technology has revolutionized the financial sector of the economy. Information — and money — move from place to place in seconds, enabling exchange to proceed in a manner unimagined fifty years ago.

Transactions costs represent a use of society's resources, just as production costs do. When transactions costs are lowered, more resources are available for other uses. The production possibilities frontier moves outward.

Potential Costs of Specialization

When we think of specialization, assembly line jobs often come to mind. Tasks are broken down into different steps, and workers are assigned only one repetitive task. Such jobs are often monotonous, offering little or no opportunity to exercise initiative and requiring a machine-controlled work pace. An example of such a job is that of boiled-egg peeler. Restaurants often find it less costly to buy boiled, peeled eggs from a supplier than to cook and prepare the eggs themselves. Firms specializing in the sale of precooked, peeled eggs employ workers to peel the eggs by hand.[1] A peeler peels the egg, inspects it and sorts it into one of several categories. Workers are expected to peel at least twenty eggs a minute.

Such specialization reduces the cost of producing goods and services. However, specialized jobs can generate boredom, alienation, and emptiness in the lives of workers. Do individuals really benefit from this kind of work?

The gains from specialization and trade cannot be measured by some narrowly defined, objective measure, such as increased output. The gains from an exchange are measured in terms of value to the parties to the exchange. Workers who voluntarily accept a job, such as that of egg peeler, are trading their time and effort, and their willingness to put up with possibly unattractive working conditions, for the benefits of employment, such as wages and fringe benefits. For many people, an assembly line job would not be beneficial; they would not accept such a job. For such people, the costs of the job are greater than the benefits, since they have alternative opportunities that are more attractive. For other workers, this job may be the best opportunity available. Higher output is the reward for specialization, but the cost of this reward might be boredom. In general, an exchange is based on all factors that matter to individuals, either as benefits or as costs.

Trade Can Make Some People Worse Off

We have stressed the gains that accrue to those participating in voluntary exchange. According to the principle of comparative advantage, economic efficiency is achieved when goods and services are produced by the people with the lowest opportunity costs. Specialization and trade on the basis of comparative advantage does not always make *everyone* better off, however. Following the principle of comparative advantage can quickly make some people worse off.

The pressure put on many locally owned stores in small towns by the opening of a Wal-Mart store provides an excellent example of how changing trade patterns — based on changes in comparative advantage — can impose costs on some. Because of its large volume purchases, Wal-Mart can buy most goods

---

[1]The job is explained in "Boiled-Egg Peelers Aim for Perfection, and That's No Yolk," *The Wall Street Journal,* July 9, 1985.

at a cheaper price than small stores. The savings are passed along to consumers in the form of lower prices. However, the owners of small stores often cannot match the low Wal-Mart prices. They lose business and eventually close. Thus, although the opening of a Wal-Mart store benefits consumers in small towns and rural areas, it usually harms the owners of small stores. It is not surprising that such businesspeople often band together to oppose the opening of a Wal-Mart in their town.

Individual versus Group Well-Being

The Wal-Mart example poses an important question for society. When one individual or group is harmed and another benefits by an action, how are the benefits and costs to be weighed? An international trade example illustrates the general problem. Over the last twenty-five years, foreign car manufacturers have accounted for an increasing share of annual car sales in the United States. From 1965 to 1989 the share of U.S. auto sales accounted for by foreign cars rose from 6 percent to about 33 percent. This trend caused the domestic auto manufacturing industry to reduce employment by about 15 percent. The auto industry and its workers have argued that the foreign competition is unfair and that they should be protected from it by restrictions on imports. Although millions of consumers have gained by being able to buy the cars they liked best at lower prices — foreign cars — thousands of auto workers have lost their jobs. Should society protect them?

In answering this question we must recognize that two views always exist on such an issue: an individual view and a social perspective. Although we cannot ignore the individual view, it is the social perspective to which we must pay attention if we are interested in society's overall welfare. The individual view of this problem varies depending upon the individuals concerned. Consumers are better off as a result of the foreign competition; they get cheaper, and often better, automobiles. Displaced auto workers are clearly worse off. Unemployed auto workers lose good jobs and the attractive lifestyles built around them. With the arrival of lower-cost foreign producers, a valuable employment opportunity is lost. Is society better or worse off?

The social perspective acknowledges that some individuals are better off and others worse off as a result of the imports. What is the net gain to society from the foreign trade in automobiles? Do the benefits outweigh the costs? The evidence suggests that trade is indeed beneficial. Two major studies of the impact of foreign competition on the auto industry and the restrictions placed on such competition found that the cost to consumers of protecting the domestic automobile industry in the 1980s has been three to four times as great as the benefits to auto workers, as measured by worker compensation. Put another way, if society had wanted to protect auto worker incomes, it would have been only one fourth to one third as costly to consumers to have simply paid higher taxes to support displaced auto workers at their previous income levels, rather than paying the higher automobile prices resulting from restricting trade.[2]

---

[2]Similar conclusions are reached by Robert W. Crandall, "Import Quotas and the Automobile Industry: The Costs of Protectionism," *The Brookings Review* 2, No. 4 (Summer 1984), pp. 8–16; and Charles Collyns and Steven Dunaway, "The Cost of Trade Restraints: The Case of Japanese Automobile Exports to the United States," *IMF Staff Papers* 34, No. 1 (March 1987), pp. 150–175.

Society is composed of many people. Taking the social perspective amounts to making a decision about what is best for these people, not just in the present, but also over long periods of time. Individuals acting in concert as society must determine the limits of both individual and social rights. For example, society might determine that no individual has the right to take another's property by force or coercion but that it is perfectly acceptable to reduce another person's income by performing better than that person in the marketplace. In such a case, society determines whether the *processes* by which individuals seek to maximize their satisfaction are acceptable, without determining the *outcomes* of those processes. In other cases, society may choose to determine outcomes, as when a minimum standard of living is guaranteed by the government (acting on behalf of society).

The people of a society must also determine the limits of social rights. The more rights granted to government, the fewer rights left for individuals. For example, when society chooses to use government to make a high level of services available to all citizens, it also chooses to limit the rights of individuals to the enjoyment of the income produced by their own labor. Government services must be financed, so individual incomes will be taxed. The higher the level of government services, the higher the level of taxation. Individual actions to maximize satisfaction thus are limited by social goals.

Both individual and social perspectives exist on almost all issues. Efficient social decisions are made within the constraints imposed by the social perspective, which in democratic societies reflects the values and goals of the people comprising society. Costs and benefits are associated with almost every decision in a world of limited resources. Although we cannot avoid some costs, we want to avoid making decisions that generate costs greater than the accompanying benefits. When social decisions are made, the individuals who incur the costs are often different from those who reap the benefits. Only if we choose alternatives that generate net benefits do we have the opportunity and the resources to help those who bear the burden of an efficient decision.

SECTION RECAP
Specialization and trade can harm producers who do not have a comparative advantage. Therefore, individuals often oppose free trade, even when the net gains to society from such trade are large.

Summary

Scarcity forces individuals and societies to make choices. The preferences, goals, and resource endowments of people and societies vary widely, but behavior is similar. Individuals seek to maximize the consumption value of their resources. The diversity in preferences and resource endowments leads to a wide variety of choices by individuals attempting to maximize the value of their resources.

A valuable use of resources is defined by the individual; it reflects the preferences and goals of the individual. **Value** is determined subjectively. **Economic efficiency** implies getting the most satisfaction from available resources—maximizing the difference between the benefits and costs of alternatives. This general notion of efficiency pervades economic analysis. Specific applications appear throughout the remainder of the text.

Economic efficiency is enhanced when individuals engage in **mutually beneficial exchange.** The basis for these exchanges is the principle of **comparative advantage.** Since tastes and resource endowments differ across individuals and societies, two individuals can gain by exchanging less-valued goods or resources for more highly valued goods or resources. What one person values highly may be of little value to another person.

Comparative advantage is concerned with **relative opportunity costs.** Output is maximized and economic efficiency is achieved when each good is produced by the low-opportunity-cost producer. Gains from specialization and trade exist when resource endowments differ. The pattern of trade and exchange based on comparative advantage depends fundamentally on the alternatives available to individuals and nations. Available alternatives determine the low-opportunity-cost options. When alternatives change, the pattern of specialization and trade changes.

Society must reconcile patterns of exchange that impose costs on some and confer benefits on others. The interaction among people and nations motivated by the principle of comparative advantage requires individuals and groups to choose appropriate decision-making techniques. The people comprising society must decide what limits to place on individual rights, as well as what limits to impose on government acting as society's agent. Such decisions determine which exchanges and what terms of trade are permitted.

Two perspectives exist on virtually every issue: an individual perspective and a social one. Individuals are assumed to follow their own self-interest. That which makes an individual better off does not necessarily make everyone in society better off. If society decides to prohibit some economic activities, the decision itself makes some individuals better off and others worse off. A social decision is efficient when the value of the benefits generated exceeds the value of the costs imposed. A significant attribute of economic analysis is that it focuses on the social perspective.

Chapter 3 begins to consider in some detail the issues just raised. It pays particular attention to the identification and analysis of decision-making techniques that reconcile the pursuit of individual economic efficiency with economic efficiency for society.

Questions for Thought

Knowledge Questions

1. What is the difference between productive efficiency and economic efficiency?
2. What is the *principle of comparative advantage?* How is economic efficiency improved by following this principle?
3. Under what circumstances is a trading ratio beneficial to both parties to a potential exchange?
4. Before the 1970s, houses in the midwest were built with very little insulation, a construction method considered efficient at the time. By 1980, it was considered inefficient. Why?

Application Questions

5. It takes two and a half hours to travel by bus to Chicago's O'Hare Airport from Bloomington, Illinois, but only thirty minutes by plane. The bus fare is $20 and

the air fare is $50. If the value of your time is $10 an hour, would you travel by bus or plane? At $15 an hour? At $20 an hour?
6. Professor Anderson is a respected economist who runs a thriving research and consulting firm whose services are demanded throughout the state. Because of his abilities, Professor Anderson commands a wage rate of $40 an hour for his services. He is also an excellent computer programmer. In fact, he can program twice as fast as the graduate student programmers he hires for $7.50 an hour. Should he do his own programming? Explain.
7. The average size of a farm in the United States is about 450 acres and is worked by two or three people. The same number of people work a farm of less than an acre in parts of Asia. What role do relative prices play in determining the land–labor mix for agricultural production? Which of these two farm sizes is more efficient?
8. When repairs on a car are necessary, some people do the work themselves. Others who know just as much about automobiles hire an auto mechanic to do the work. What factors influence this decision?
9. Idaho and California produce oranges and potatoes. The production possibilities frontiers for both states are given below. What is the opportunity cost of potatoes in California? In Idaho? What is the opportunity cost of oranges in California? In Idaho? Who has the comparative advantage in orange growing? In potato growing? Would they both gain from trade with one another if they traded at a ratio of 100 pounds of potatoes for 300 pounds of oranges?

California		Idaho	
Oranges	Potatoes	Oranges	Potatoes
(in hundreds of lbs.)		(in hundreds of lbs.)	
0	60	0	150
50	50	50	125
100	40	100	100
150	30	150	75
200	20	200	50
250	10	250	25
300	0	300	0

Synthesis Questions

10. Meredith and Lindsey have much in common. Each is married, their husbands both have the same income, they each have two children whose ages are the same. However, Meredith has a full-time job, while Lindsey works at home, devoting her time and effort there. What would cause them to choose these different careers? Explain.
11. During the energy crisis of the 1970s, the federal government gave much thought to rationing gasoline usage. Economists argued that the efficiency of a gasoline rationing plan allotting an equal number of gasoline coupons to each private automobile would be enhanced if auto owners were permitted to buy and sell the coupons from one another. Explain why the opportunity to trade coupons would improve economic efficiency.
12. Consumers trade part of their incomes for agricultural products like flour and milk. These exchanges are motivated by the drive for economic efficiency. How does a government program that raises the price of wheat and milk affect these trades between consumers and farmers (through retailers)?

13. Should a society permit unrestricted mutually beneficial trading in the following goods and services?

    medical care
    drinking water
    land
    public transportation
    private transportation
    liquor
    marijuana

Explain.

OVERVIEW

The scarcity of resources, and of the goods and services produced with resources, forces every society to adopt some mechanism to ration goods and services to uses and users. Many possible rationing mechanisms exist. Some rationing mechanisms rely on a few people, following a plan, to make economic choices for society, while others give wide latitude to individual choice in allocating resources and goods and services. If individual choices are not to produce economic chaos, however, they must be reconciled to one another in some manner. The market mechanism provides a means of reconciling millions of individual choices when these choices are constrained by scarce resources.

The market is a term applied to the processes that coordinate the wishes of consumers who demand goods and services and producers who supply goods and services. By affecting the prices of goods and services, the forces of consumer demand and producer supply interact to bring order to an economic system that is controlled by no single planner. Individuals pursuing their own interests also serve the interests of society by helping to satisfy the wants of others.

Since the U.S. economy relies heavily on markets to coordinate economic activ-

The Market Mechanism: Supply and Demand

ity, we deal with market behavior in every chapter. We use the market model to address a wide variety of problems, all having a common element: people making choices under resource constraints. Thus, it is important to understand the basic market model presented in this chapter.

The attention given to market processes should not obscure the fact that not all market solutions are socially desirable. Under certain conditions, market processes may not produce economically efficient outcomes. At other times, efficient market outcomes may not meet society's standards of equity or fairness, as when some people are unable to earn enough income to live at a socially acceptable level. In such instances, other decision-making mechanisms may augment or replace the market even in an economy that relies on markets to coordinate most economic decisions.

CHAPTER 3

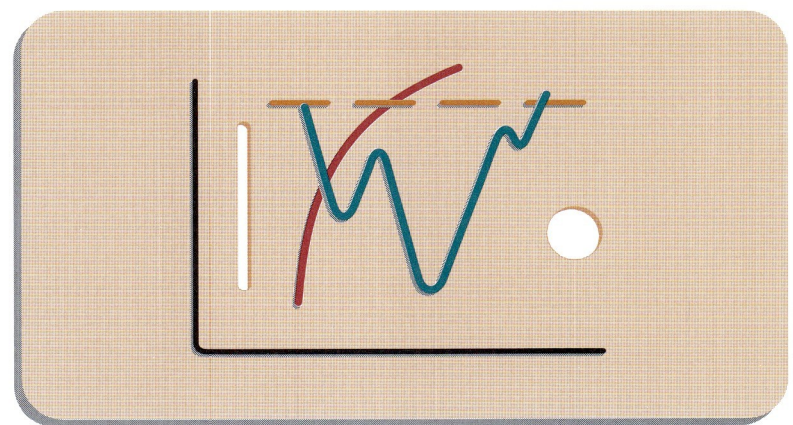

We begin the chapter with a discussion of the general rationing problem caused by scarce resources. A number of potential decision-making criteria are discussed. We then proceed to the definition of a market, the development of the concepts of demand and supply, and an exploration of the process by which demand and supply interact to determine equilibrium in the market.

Learning Objectives

After reading and studying this chapter, you will be able to:

1. Distinguish between centralized and decentralized decision making.
2. Understand how markets ration goods to consumers and producers.
3. Explain why the laws of demand and supply are important to economists.
4. Distinguish between a change in demand (or supply) and a change in quantity demanded (or quantity supplied).
5. Describe how market clearing is achieved in a free market economy.
6. Explain how a specific change in demand or supply alters prices and amounts produced and consumed.

The Market as a Rationing Device

Resource scarcity implies that not all wants can be satisfied. Thus, societies must develop ways of reconciling the competing claims of individuals and groups. In this chapter we explore the nature of this basic social problem and analyze in depth one particular mechanism for reconciling competing claims — the market.

Scarcity Implies Choices

Every economy must answer three basic questions:

1. What will be produced?
2. How will it be produced?
3. For whom will it be produced?

Since most resources can be used to produce a variety of goods or services, the economy must somehow determine which of the many possible goods and services will actually be produced. For example, consider the many possible uses of steel. Somehow the economy must determine how much steel to produce and how to use that quantity. Should the steel go into automobiles, or bridges, or metal buildings, or industrial machines? The economy must have a mechanism to determine which goods will be produced and to allocate resources to the production of the goods and services people actually prefer. An economy that produces lots of goods nobody wants has failed to properly allocate its resources.

The allocation decision is closely related to the decisions of how to produce goods and how to distribute the goods that have been produced. Most goods can be produced in more than one way. An economy that uses its resources efficiently (that is, doesn't waste resources) can produce more goods and services than an economy that produces inefficiently. Once produced, the goods must be distributed in some manner to the people who ultimately consume them.

The rules an economy uses to ration goods to ultimate consumers heavily influence how resources are allocated. Different economic systems have vastly different rationing mechanisms. Some economies ration resources and products by relying almost entirely on markets to reconcile individual choices. In such **market economies** individuals own most property and have the freedom to make decisions concerning how to use their property. Although not a pure market economy, the U.S. economy is dominated by market activity. At the opposite extreme are **command economies**, in which decision making is centralized in the hands of a few powerful planners and individuals have limited economic choices. The Soviet and Chinese economies are largely of this type, although the use of markets is increasing in both.

Most economies lie between the extremes of free markets and complete government direction. Sweden is an example of a **mixed economy** — an economy in which economic decision making is shared by market participants and government. Even in the United States the government plays an important role in the economy. However, the market is used to a much greater extent in the United States than in Sweden, where the government provides most basic economic services, such as housing, health care, and education. To finance these services, the Swedish government claims more than half the income of

---

Market economy
An economy in which individuals own most property and make most decisions about its use; decisions are coordinated through markets.

Command economy
An economy in which decision making is centralized in the hands of a few planners.

Mixed economy
An economy in which economic decision making is shared by individuals and government.

Swedish citizens through various forms of taxation, while total taxes in the United States claim about one third of total income.

In a democratic society, the economic decision-making system is based on the people's values and goals, which are shaped by the society's particular history and its political and moral philosophy. Social differences lead to economic differences. Thus, it is not surprising that even in democratic societies we see a wide variety of economic arrangements.

Rationing Mechanisms and Behavior

Since scarce goods must be rationed, *some* rationing mechanism is always in use. The rationing mechanism actually chosen may reflect either philosophical, social, and cultural values, or the views of a powerful ruling elite. However they are chosen, once in place, rationing mechanisms affect the behavior of members of society. Competition for goods and services exists in every society, since competition results from scarcity. However, the form competition takes depends to a large extent on the rationing mechanism used by a society.

The rationing mechanism used in market economies is price, or willingness to pay. Goods are rationed to those who are willing (and able) to pay the most. In a market economy, competition largely takes the form of attempting to acquire wealth, because wealth enhances a person's ability to acquire goods and services on the basis of willingness to pay. Income becomes an important measure of one's power and position in society.

Other rationing mechanisms produce different types of competitive behavior. One simple rationing device used in some economies is rationing by queue. People line up to buy meat or bread or tickets for sporting events. Competition takes a different form when goods are rationed to those who stand in line. People who are best able or most willing to wait in line the longest are able to obtain the most resources, having outbid other individuals who are unwilling to pay as much in terms of time spent in line.

Political criteria are often used to ration goods. Political leaders may attempt to effect a desired income distribution or may simply override the market to achieve other aims, such as military conquest. Sets of rules, some quite arbitrary, are used to allocate resources. The rules reflect the power of some individual or group or society's values. For instance, racial or ethnic preference or membership in a party can be a rationing criterion. When affiliation with a political party is an important rationing criterion, people compete for goods by attempting to advance politically.

Often a combination of rationing devices is used in a single economy. Access to a college education in the United States is based in part on willingness to pay and academic performance, and students bid to enter college on these bases. Market exchanges often require waiting in line as well as willingness to pay the market price. Employers hire new employees on the basis of past performance, general knowledge, and even appearance, and job seekers compete on these criteria. To borrow money one must demonstrate creditworthiness and some financial security. Potential borrowers compete for borrowed funds by establishing good credit ratings, sources of collateral with which a loan can be secured, and an income stream that will enable the borrower to repay the loan.

When analyzing the strengths and weaknesses of the market as a rationing device, it is important to remember that *some rationing device is always in use.*

The fact that the market does not perform as well as one might hope in a particular instance is not grounds for replacing it unless some other rationing mechanism is likely to produce better results.

The Market Mechanism: Mutually Beneficial Exchange

When decision making is left to individuals, the basic economic questions (what? how? for whom?) are answered by the free interaction of individuals in society. People are free to arrange and negotiate mutually beneficial exchanges. Of course, society defines property ownership rights and the kinds of exchanges that are allowed through some social decision-making process. The government establishes the rules of the game and allows individuals to make their own decisions within the framework of those rules. Since the decisions made by individuals reflect the rules governing market exchange, the particular set of rules adopted by government is important.

As we argued in Chapter 2, all voluntary trades reflect the attempt to trade something of lesser value for something of greater value. Markets arose in response to this desire. If individuals are to obtain the maximum benefit from exchanging goods and services, they must know what their alternatives are. They seek to make the best trade they can, but they are able to do this only if they know the available trading opportunities: who has goods for trade, what kind of goods are being offered, and what terms of trade are acceptable. Acquiring such information is costly. To make a beneficial trade decision, one must commit time, effort, and resources to the task. Markets developed to economize on such transactions costs.

Although a market can be a physical location, not all markets operate in one place. People buy vegetables at a produce market, brokers sell common stocks on the New York Stock Exchange, feedlot owners buy cattle at an auction barn, and people borrow (buy) and lend (sell) loanable funds at banks and thrift institutions. In each of these examples a market exists in both a physical and an abstract sense. Buyers and sellers meet at a specific geographic location to interact, establishing a **market price** and determining the quantity of the good exchanged. However, a market need not have a specific geographic location. The *market* is the *process* by which buyers and sellers determine the terms of trade. Although purchases of new cars or fast food take place at specific locations, the markets for new cars and fast food—as well as the markets for cattle and loanable funds—encompass transactions occurring in many places at once. Market participants are aware of market prices, trends in prices, and other market-related information, and they tie geographically separated markets together by searching for the most beneficial trades.

The precise manner in which the market mechanism operates to establish a market price and determine the quantity exchanged is very important for understanding the benefits and limitations of market decision making. The remainder of the chapter explores the functioning of the market mechanism.

Consumption Decisions: Demand

People satisfy wants by purchasing and consuming goods and services. The decisions that individuals and families make as consumers have an important impact not only on their own welfare but also on the economic well-being of others.

Market price
Price established by the interaction of consumers demanding a good and producers supplying the good.

SECTION RECAP
Scarce resources force societies to ration goods. Some rationing mechanism is always in use. The market rations goods by allocating them to those who are able and willing to pay the most for them.

Budget-Constrained Choice

Limited incomes force consumers to make choices. Choosing one good or service forces them to give up other desirable goods and services. Thus, consumers attempt to acquire the goods and services that provide them with the maximum satisfaction. This is the Fundamental Premise of Economics applied to consumption decisions.

How does an individual decide which goods to buy and which to give up? A consumer cannot simply buy those goods that yield the most satisfaction, because different goods have different opportunity costs. A new car yields much more satisfaction than a candy bar, but its opportunity cost is thousands of times higher. A consumer must pay attention not only to the benefits of a good, but also to the opportunity cost of the good.

Changes in the market price of a good alter the opportunity cost of consuming the good. When the price of a good increases, a consumer must make a greater sacrifice to obtain the good. The increased cost makes the good less attractive to consumers, who *economize* on the now more-costly good by reducing their purchases of the good and switching to other less costly ways of satisfying their wants.

Negatively Sloped Demand Curve

The relationship between the consumption of a good and its price is so predictable that economists have dubbed it the **law of demand**: The quantity of a good consumed is negatively related to the price of the good, holding constant other factors that influence consumers' willingness or ability to pay for the good. A higher price reduces consumption and a lower price encourages consumption.

Consider a teenager's demand for root beer. The law of demand says that as the price of a can of root beer rises, the number of cans Shane (the teenager) will purchase falls. That is, *holding other factors besides price constant*, the quantity of root beer demanded by Shane at any particular price falls as the price rises. The Latin phrase *ceteris paribus*, meaning "other things being equal," is usually substituted in economic writing for the phrase *other factors held constant.*

Table 1 shows Shane's *demand schedule* for root beer. The demand schedule shows the maximum quantity of cans demanded per week at various prices, assuming all other factors affecting Shane's demand for root beer to be constant. The demand schedule is graphed in Figure 1.

Shane's demand schedule displays the negative relationship between price and quantity demanded summarized by the law of demand. This negative relationship exists because Shane experiences *declining marginal benefits* from consuming root beer. The **marginal benefit** of a can of root beer is the added satisfaction Shane derives from consuming *one additional* can. As Shane acquires more cans of root beer, the marginal benefit of each *additional* can falls. Shane values the first few cans of root beer more highly than additional cans. He is willing to pay 70¢ per can to consume three cans each week. However, the benefit he receives from drinking root beer declines with each additional can he drinks, so the price of a can of root beer would have to fall to induce him to buy more than three cans. Should the price decline to 65¢ per can, Shane would be willing to buy an additional three cans (for a total of six) per week. *Shane's demand schedule for root beer is a marginal benefit schedule.*

Law of demand
The quantity demanded of a good is negatively related to its price, holding constant other factors that affect demand.

Ceteris paribus
A Latin phrase meaning "other things being equal."

Marginal benefit
The satisfaction derived from consuming an additional unit of a good.

TABLE 1
Shane's demand for root beer

Price (per can)	Quantity Demanded Weekly (number of cans)
$0.40	21
0.45	18
0.50	15
0.55	12
0.60	9
0.65	6
0.70	3
0.75	0

Note the terminology used in this example. The term *demand* applies to the entire demand schedule or to the demand curve that depicts the schedule. *Demand* refers to a relationship between price and quantity demanded. The entire schedule of prices and quantities demanded listed in Table 1 represents Shane's demand for root beer. The term *quantity demanded* refers to a particular number of cans demanded at a particular price. Given a price, quantity demanded can be read from the demand schedule or curve. At a price of 65¢ per can, Shane's quantity demanded of root beer is six cans per week. Since the popular media often misuse these terms, referring to particular quantities as "the demand for good X," you should be aware of the precise definitions.

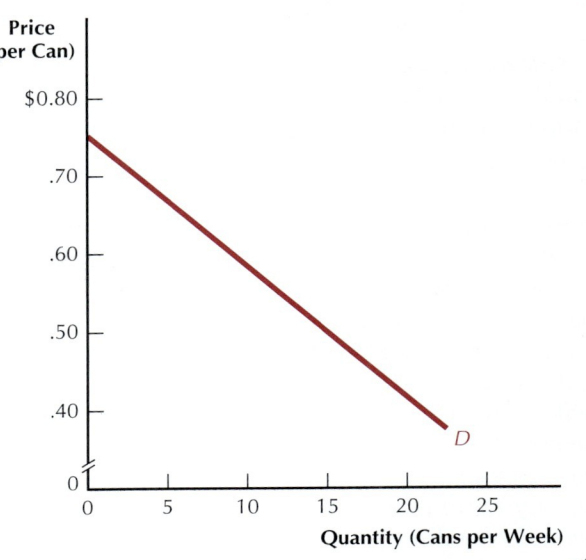

FIGURE 1
Shane's demand for root beer. The demand schedule presented in Table 1 can be graphed as a demand curve, as shown here. All factors affecting Shane's demand for root beer other than the price of root beer itself are assumed constant when drawing the demand curve.

Factors Shifting the Demand Curve

The demand schedule in Table 1 and the demand curve in Figure 1 illustrate the importance of opportunity cost (price) as a determinant of the quantity of a good demanded (willingly consumed). However, the demand for goods and services is also influenced by factors other than price. Consumer income, the prices of other goods and services, consumer tastes, and consumer expectations all affect the quantity of a good consumers desire to purchase. We can summarize these influences on quantity demanded in the following equation:

$$Q_d = f(P, \text{Income, Other Prices, Tastes, Expectations})$$

The equation says that quantity demanded (Q_d) is a function of (depends on) the good's price (P), income, other prices, tastes, and expectations. The mathematical notation f( ) read "is a function of," tells us what factors affect quantity demanded.

When we draw a demand curve we assume that all factors affecting quantity demanded except price remain constant. Only the good's own price is allowed to vary: Demand is the relationship between quantity demanded and market price, *ceteris paribus*. When one of the other factors changes, the quantity demanded at any particular price changes, and the demand schedule (curve) shifts.

Income Income changes alter the budget constraint facing consumers, causing them to change their demands for goods and services. An increase in income usually causes demand for a good to increase. For instance, people tend to eat out more often as their income increases. An increase in income causes the demand for restaurant meals to increase, *ceteris paribus*. Returning to our previous example, an increase in income might cause Shane to increase his demand for root beer. With a higher income, Shane might be willing to buy more cans of root beer at every market price. Table 2 illustrates the impact of increased income on Shane's demand for root beer: The demand schedule shifts from D_1 to D_2. Figure 2 (a) illustrates the rightward shift in demand. Goods whose demand increases when income increases are called *normal goods*.

An increase in income causes the demand for some goods to decrease. Consumers often substitute more expensive but more preferred goods for less expensive, less attractive goods as their incomes increase. For example, Shane might decrease his demand for peanut butter sandwiches as his income rises, choosing to substitute hamburgers and pizza for peanut butter sandwiches. The demand for hamburgers and pizza increases and the demand for peanut butter sandwiches decreases as income rises. In this case peanut butter is an *inferior good.* If an increase in income were to cause the demand for peanut butter sandwiches to decrease, we would observe a reduction in the quantity demanded at every market price. Table 2 and Figure 2 (b) illustrate a decrease in demand for peanut butter sandwiches; the demand curve shifts to the left, from D_1 to D_3.

Prices of Other Goods The demand for a good such as root beer is influenced by the prices of other goods as well as its own price. Often consumers can choose among several alternatives — or **substitutes** — to satisfy a particular want. People switch from chicken or pork to beef when beef prices fall relative to poultry and pork prices. They rent more movie videos as movie theater prices

Substitutes Goods that are alternatives to one another in consumption.

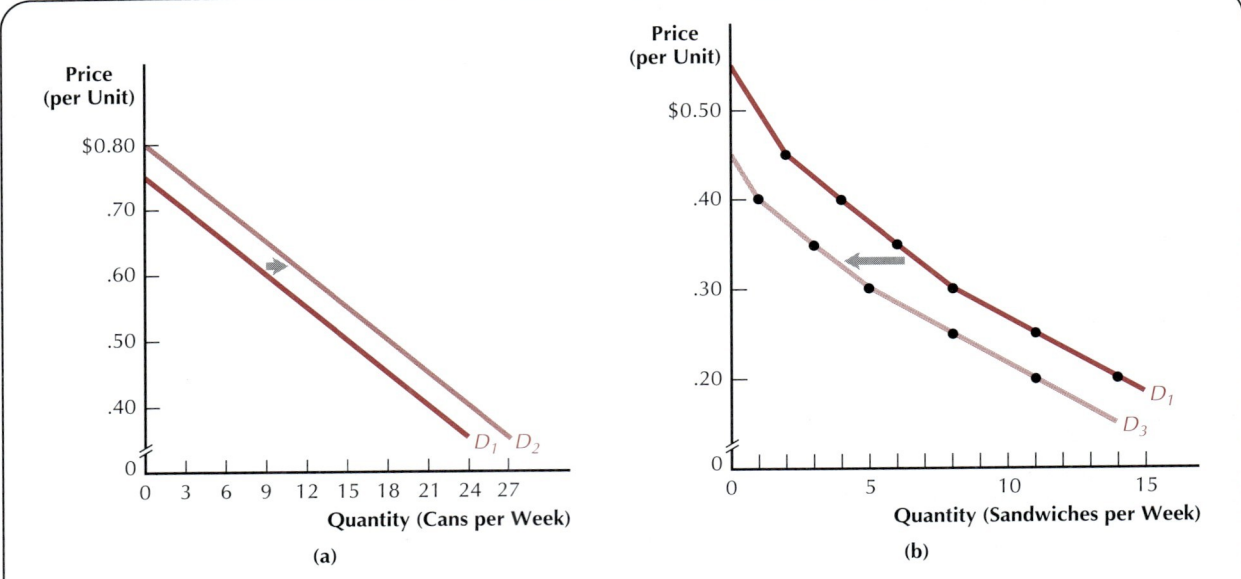

FIGURE 2
Effect of income increase on demand. An increase in income causes Shane to demand more root beer at every price (a). Root beer is a normal good. The same income increase causes Shane to demand fewer peanut butter sandwiches (b). Peanut butter sandwiches are an inferior good.

rise. They fly instead of taking the bus or train when air fares fall relative to bus and train fares.

The demand for a good decreases when the price of a substitute falls and increases when the price of a substitute rises. Thus, a decrease in Pepsi-Cola prices causes a decrease in the demand for root beer, and an increase in movie theater prices causes an increase in demand for movie videos. The demand

TABLE 2

Effect of income changes on Shane's demand

Root Beer			Peanut Butter Sandwiches		
Price	Q Demanded (Original Income)	Q Demanded (Higher Income)	Price	Q Demanded (Original Income)	Q Demanded (Higher Income)
.40	21	24	.20	14	11
.45	18	21	.25	11	8
.50	15	18	.30	8	5
.55	12	15	.35	6	3
.60	9	12	.40	4	1
.65	6	9	.45	2	0
.70	3	6	.50	1	0
.75	0	3	.55	0	0

for a good is positively related to the prices of substitute goods: The demand for the good (root beer) increases as the substitute good (Pepsi) becomes more expensive. At every root beer price, a larger quantity of root beer is demanded.

Consumers value some goods more highly when they are consumed along with other **complementary goods**. Examples include bread and butter, automobiles and gasoline, and cassette players and cassettes. The demand change caused by an increase in the price of a complementary good is the opposite of the change caused by an increase in the price of a substitute. When the price of cassette players rises, the demand for cassettes decreases. Fewer consumers purchase cassette players, so fewer cassettes are demanded at any cassette price. When the price of a complementary good (cassette players) rises, the demand for a good (cassettes) falls.

Complementary goods Goods that produce more consumer satisfaction when consumed together than when consumed separately.

Consumer Tastes A demand schedule tells us the maximum amount consumers are willing to give up to acquire various quantities of a good. The willingness to sacrifice to consume a good is determined by consumer tastes. Any change in consumer tastes causes demand to change. Tastes are revealed by what we consume. Today, U.S. consumers purchase more whole wheat bread and less white bread than twenty years ago. People eat less beef and more chicken now. Since such changes in tastes change the quantities of goods consumers are willing to buy at any market price, changes in tastes cause demands to increase and decrease. Increased preferences for whole wheat bread cause the demand for whole wheat bread to increase, and the corresponding shift in tastes away from white bread causes a decrease in the demand for white bread.

Expectations The decision to buy goods today is influenced both by current prices and incomes and by expected future prices and incomes. An early freeze in Brazil that destroys the coffee crop causes consumers to anticipate increased coffee prices. As a result, some coffee drinkers buy more coffee today than they would in the absence of the expected price increase. (Today's demand for coffee increases.) Similarly, an expected income increase can cause a family's *current* demand for furniture to increase. Altered expectations cause the current relationship between quantity demanded and market price to change.

From Individual Demand to Market Demand

The total market demand for a good depends on both the factors influencing individual demand and on the number of consumers in the market. Market demand reflects the demand of many individuals. A *market demand curve* is the horizontal sum of all individual demand curves for a good. Table 3 derives the market demand for root beer under the assumption that only two consumers exist. The market demand schedule is the summation of the individual quantities demanded by Shane and Blythe at every price. For example, at a price of 40¢ per can, Blythe demands twelve cans of root beer per week, while Shane demands twenty-one cans per week. Market quantity demanded equals the sum of the individual quantities demanded: 33 = 12 + 21. The market demand curve is shown in Figure 3, along with the individual demand curves.

This example helps to explain the role of advertising in the business world. If the makers of Barq's Root Beer can persuade more consumers to drink Barq's, the quantity of Barq's demanded will increase at every price. Advertising attempts to affect consumer tastes, persuading people to try a product they don't

SECTION RECAP
A demand curve shows the maximum quantities of a good consumers are willing to purchase at various prices. All factors affecting demand except the good's own price are held constant when deriving a demand curve. A change *(continued)*

TABLE 3
Deriving market demand

Price	Shane's Quantity Demanded	+	Blythe's Quantity Demanded	=	Market Quantity Demanded
.40	21		12		33
.45	18		10		28
.50	15		8		23
.55	12		6		18
.60	9		4		13
.65	6		2		8
.70	3		0		3
.75	0		0		0

SECTION RECAP
(continued)
in the good's price alters quantity demanded along the demand curve. A change in any factor affecting demand other than price shifts the demand curve.

use or to consume more of products they already use. By influencing the preferences of current consumers and by attracting new consumers, advertising shifts the market demand curve to the right. At every price a larger quantity of the good is demanded.

Market demand depends on the same factors as individual demand (price, income, other prices, tastes, and expectations). An increase in a good's price moves us up along the market demand curve. Changes in consumer income, the prices of substitutes or complements, tastes, and expectations affect market demand just as they affect individual demand.

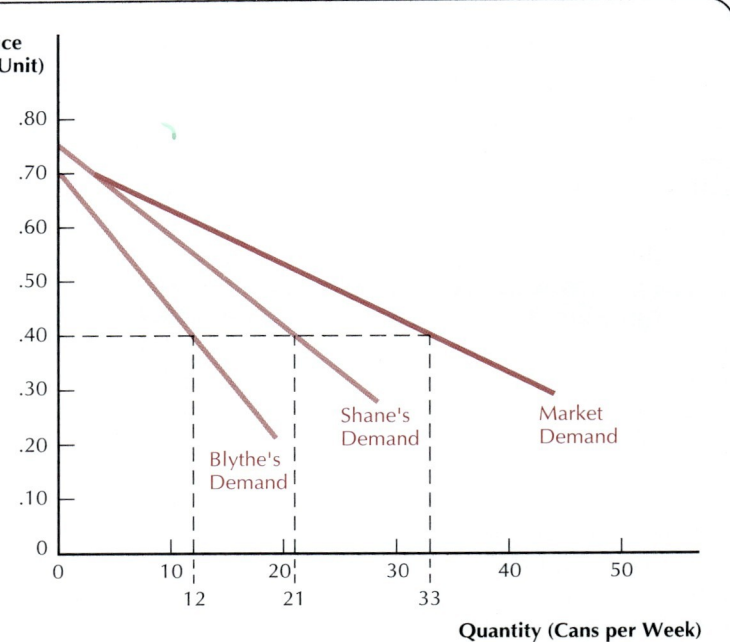

FIGURE 3
Market demand for root beer. Market demand is derived by adding individual quantities demanded at each price.

Production Decisions: Supply

This section considers the decisions of firms, or producers, and develops the law of supply. When considering the consumer side of the market we emphasized the relationship between quantities demanded and the opportunity cost of consumption, market price. Consumers compare the benefits they obtain from consumption to the price of the good (determined in the market) in making decisions about the kinds and quantities of goods to consume. We now turn to production or supply decisions. How do producers decide which goods to produce and in what quantities to produce them? Market price also plays an important role in these decisions.

Firms Are Profit Seekers

Business enterprises — *firms* — are formed by entrepreneurs seeking to maximize income by producing and selling goods or services. In many ways firms are as unique as individuals. They produce different kinds of products and have different management philosophies. However, all firms are alike in that they have one primary objective: They are in business to make a profit. **Profit** is the difference between revenue and the opportunity cost of production. Producers attempt to earn a profit by purchasing factors of production — *inputs* — and using them to produce a good or service for sale to consumers. The opportunity cost of production is composed of two elements: (1) the total cost of inputs used in production, and (2) the profits forgone when firms choose not to produce other products (that is, the value of the best alternatives given up).

Profit
Difference between revenue and the opportunity cost of production.

Positively Sloped Supply Curve

Just as demand curves reflect the marginal benefits consumers derive from consuming goods and services, so supply curves reflect the marginal costs incurred by firms in the production of goods and services. Firms are willing to supply goods and services to the market only if they expect to receive a price that covers the marginal cost of production. The cost in question is opportunity cost. **Marginal cost** is the highest-valued opportunity forgone by a firm to produce an *additional* unit of output.

A firm producing with a *fixed capital stock* — a fixed amount of factory or office space and a fixed number of machines — typically experiences an increase in marginal cost as production expands. Additional units of output are more costly to produce than previously produced units. Marginal cost rises as firms expand production under conditions of fixed capital because additional inputs are less productive. Firms will produce at higher output levels (and at higher marginal cost levels) only if they receive a higher price for their products. Firms will only produce quantities of output for which price equals or exceeds marginal cost.

Marginal cost
The value of the best alternative given up to produce an additional unit of a good.

Consider the example of root beer production. Factories must use special machines to fill and seal the cans and bottles of root beer and then package them in six-packs, twelve-packs, and cases. The finished packaged root beer must then be shipped by truck to buyers. To expand production, the firm must purchase more inputs and either require workers to work overtime or hire more workers. If overtime is required, workers must perform their tasks for ten or twelve hours per day rather than eight. The firm must pay the workers a higher wage rate for overtime work, thus increasing the labor cost of the additional output. Furthermore, since the workers are tired after eight hours of work, they may make more mistakes during the overtime period, thus ruining more materials than usual. This raises the input cost of additional output.

If the production level is increased further, the firm must hire more workers. Adding additional workers to a fixed number of machines and factory space usually reduces worker productivity. Workers get in each other's way, production bottlenecks force some workers to waste time waiting for other workers to catch up, and more workers are needed for such tasks as inventory control and moving supplies around the factory. If firms choose to circumvent such overcrowding problems by establishing a second or third work shift, they usually must pay workers more to work odd hours. Furthermore, running machines around the clock leaves no time for maintenance, so that production has to be shut down just to service the machines.

Finally, if output is greater than the shipping capacity of the producing firms' trucks, firms will be forced to find alternative means of transporting root beer to their buyers. These alternatives will be costlier than using the firms' trucks. (If they were not costlier, firms would be using them instead of operating their own trucks.) Hence, higher transportation costs also affect the marginal opportunity cost of output.

Under such conditions, firms will produce additional units of output only if the price of output covers the marginal cost of production. Consider Table 4 and Figure 4, which display the marginal cost schedule and curve for the root beer firm. The marginal cost of the two-millionth can produced during a week is 40¢. The firm is willing to produce two million cans of root beer each week only if the price offered for root beer is at least 40¢ per can. The marginal cost of the three-millionth can is 42¢. Only if the price offered is at least 42¢ will the firm expand its production from two million to three million cans per week. As the price of root beer rises, the firm is willing to produce additional units. Given the price of root beer we can see how many cans the firm is willing to produce by looking at the firm's marginal cost schedule. When the market

TABLE 4

Root beer firm's supply curve

Quantity Supplied (Millions of cans)	Marginal Cost (Dollars per can)
2	.40
3	.42
4	.46
5	.52
6	.60
7	.70
8	.82

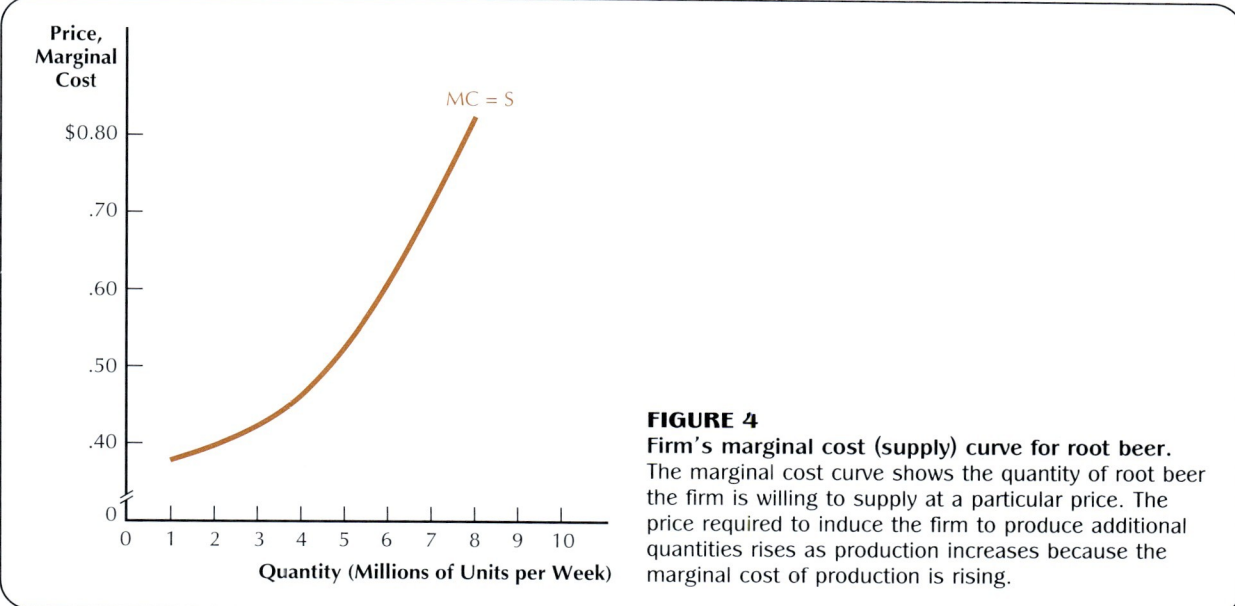

FIGURE 4
Firm's marginal cost (supply) curve for root beer.
The marginal cost curve shows the quantity of root beer the firm is willing to supply at a particular price. The price required to induce the firm to produce additional quantities rises as production increases because the marginal cost of production is rising.

price equals the firm's marginal cost of production for a particular output level, the firm will supply that output level to the market. Since a supply curve tells us the maximum quantity a firm is willing to supply at various prices, *the firm's marginal cost curve is its supply curve.*

Since marginal cost typically rises with output when capital is fixed, we can state the **law of supply** under conditions of fixed capital as follows: The quantity willingly supplied during a specified period of time is positively related to market price, *ceteris paribus*. A higher price gives producers the incentive to increase production.

The period during which a firm's capital stock is fixed is called the **short run**. During the short run, firms can buy more material inputs and hire more labor, but they do not have time to expand their plant (factory or office space) and equipment. The length of the short run varies depending upon what firms are producing. The time required for an accounting firm to acquire new office space, computers, and file cabinets may be very short, while the time needed to construct a new electrical power plant may be several years. Whatever the length of time required to expand its capital stock, most firms can produce larger outputs more efficiently with more capital. Thus, in the **long run** when firms have time to adjust the amount of capital used in production, production costs may fall. The discussion in the remainder of this chapter focuses on production in the short run (when capital is fixed).

Law of supply
The quantity supplied of a good is positively related to its price, holding constant other factors that affect supply.

Short run
The period of time during which at least one factor of production is fixed in quantity.

Long run
A period of time sufficient for a firm to vary the quantities of all factors of production.

Factors Shifting the Supply Curve

Although price is a powerful influence on firm output, it is not the only factor influencing production decisions. Even in the short run, the quantity supplied is affected by such other factors as the prices of inputs, the technology, and the prices of other goods that a firm could or does produce. Using functional notation, we can say that:

$$Q_s = f(P, \text{Input Prices, Technology, Other Output Prices})$$

where f stands for "is a function of" (depends on). We will examine the factors affecting supply decisions in turn.

Input Prices Input prices are the prices firms pay to obtain factors of production. Wages and payments for fringe benefits constitute the price of labor. Rent is the payment for the use of land and equipment that is not purchased. Firms pay interest on borrowed financial capital. An increase in input prices increases the cost of production, shifting the marginal cost (supply) curve up and to the left from S_1 to S_2 in Table 5 and Figure 5 (a). Since at every market price the firm is now willing to produce fewer cans of root beer, an increase in input prices decreases supply. A decline in input prices lowers marginal cost and increases supply, as illustrated by the shift from S_1 to S_3 in Figure 5 (b).

Technology The state of technology determines the kind and quantity of inputs necessary to produce a given quantity of a good or service. When a firm uses the best available technology, it can produce a unit of a good at the lowest possible cost (productive efficiency). An advance or improvement in technology is the development of new means of producing a good using a smaller quantity of inputs than was previously possible. For example, advances in the technology of computer chip manufacturing have led to drastic reductions in the cost of producing computers. Technological innovation also results in the development of new products that are less costly to produce than the products they replace. Thus, technological change lowers production costs and increases supply. If a technological improvement were to lower the cost of producing root beer, the root beer supply curve would shift to the right, as shown in Figure 5 (b).

TABLE 5

Effect of changes in input prices on supply

	Quantity Supplied (Millions of Units)		
Price	Original	After Input Price Increase	After Input Price Decrease
.40	2	1	3
.42	3	2	4
.46	4	3	5
.52	5	4	6
.60	6	5	7
.70	7	6	8
.82	8	7	9

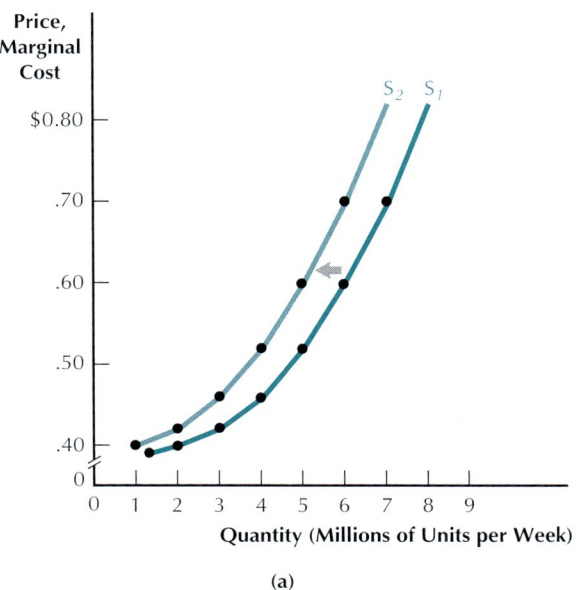

(a)

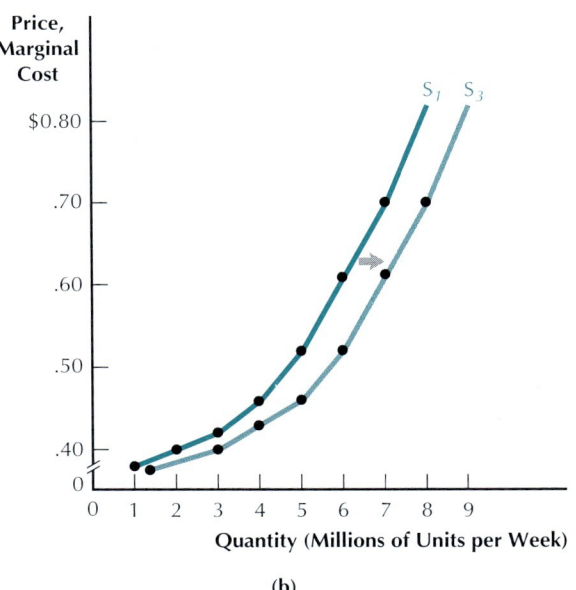

(b)

FIGURE 5
Input prices and supply shifts. An increase in input prices increases the marginal cost of production, shifting the supply curve up and to the left (a). A decrease in input prices reduces marginal cost, shifting the supply curve down and to the right (b).

Other Output Prices Firms are not permanently committed to the production of particular goods. Rising prices for other goods may cause firms to switch to the production of different goods. For example, if the price of fruit drinks were to rise sharply, root beer bottlers might switch from bottling soda pop to bottling fruit drinks. The increased price of fruit drinks increases the bottlers' opportunity cost of bottling root beer—more potential profit is given up by continuing to bottle soda pop. Thus, an increase in fruit drink prices could lead to a reduction in the supply of root beer as bottlers switch from producing pop to producing fruit drinks.

Other output prices can affect the supply of certain products in another way. Some products can be produced only in combination with other products. For example, an increase in the price of beef, which increases the quantity of beef supplied to the market, automatically increases the supply of hides, from which leather products are made. That is, increased beef prices cause the supply of leather curve to shift to the right.

From Individual Firm Supply to Market Supply

The number of suppliers affects supply just as the number of consumers affects demand. The *market supply curve* is the horizontal sum of all individual firm supply curves. A market supply curve is constructed from firm supply curves by adding up the quantities that each firm willingly supplies at each market price. This exercise is illustrated in Table 6 and Figure 6.

In this simple example only two firms, Sweet Tooth, Inc., and Root Beer Unlimited, Ltd., produce and sell root beer in a particular area. Their supply schedules are given in Table 6 and the corresponding supply curves are shown in Figure 6. To derive the market supply curve, add the quantities that the two firms are willing to supply at each market price and plot them against various prices, as in Figure 6. For example, if the price of root beer were 60¢ per can, Root Beer Unlimited would produce five million cans per week and Sweet Tooth, Inc., would produce six million cans per week, jointly supplying the market with 11 million cans per week. If other suppliers were to enter the

---

SECTION RECAP
A supply curve shows the maximum quantities of a good firms are willing to supply at various prices. A supply curve slopes positively because marginal cost increases as output increases in the short run. All factors affecting supply decisions except product price are held constant *(continued)*

TABLE 6
Deriving market supply of root beer

Price	Sweet Tooth, Inc. Quantity Supplied*	+	Root Beer Unlimited, Ltd. Quantity Supplied*	=	Market Quantity Supplied*
.40	2		0.5		2.5
.42	3		2.0		5.0
.46	4		3.25		7.25
.52	5		4.25		9.25
.60	6		5.0		11.0
.70	7		5.75		12.75
.82	8		6.5		14.5

*In millions of units.

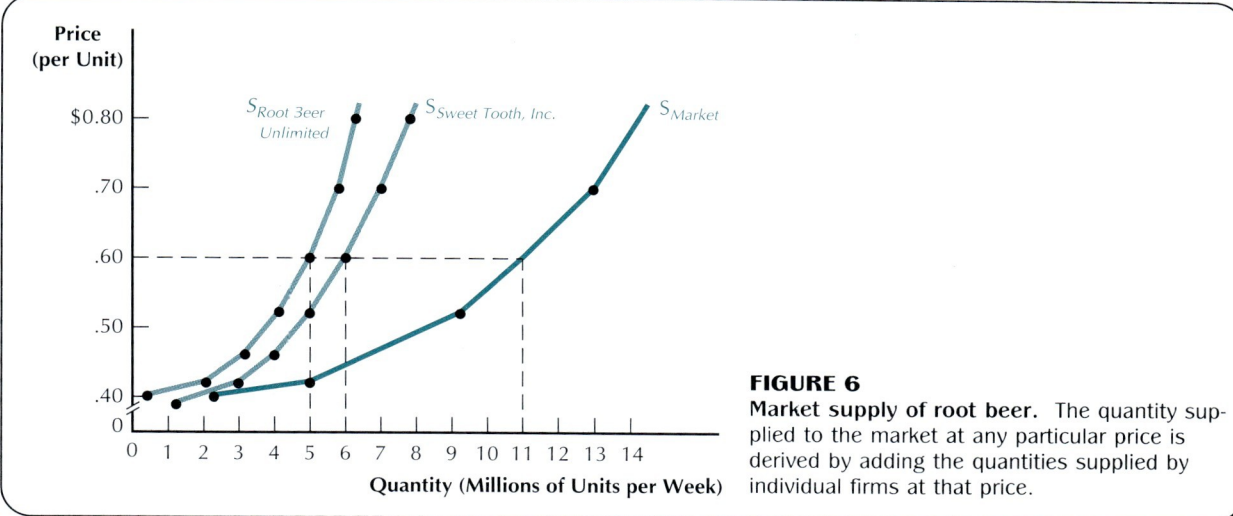

FIGURE 6
Market supply of root beer. The quantity supplied to the market at any particular price is derived by adding the quantities supplied by individual firms at that price.

market, the market supply curve would shift further to the right. Additional quantities would be supplied at every market price. If the number of suppliers were to decrease, because, for example, a firm goes out of business, market supply would decrease. A smaller quantity would be available at every market price.

In summary, an increase in input prices or in the prices of alternative outputs causes the supply of a good to decrease. The **supply curve shifts to the left as marginal (opportunity) costs rise. An** improvement in technology or an increase in the number of suppliers producing a good increases supply, shifting the supply curve to the right.

> **SECTION RECAP**
> *(continued)*
> when deriving a supply curve. A change in a good's price alters quantity supplied along the supply curve. A change in any other factor affecting supply shifts the supply curve.

The Market Mechanism at Work: Equilibrium

The market mechanism is the process by which buyers and sellers, acting in their own interests, establish a market price and determine the quantity of a good exchanged in a market.

Individual Choice and Competition

Buyers and sellers voluntarily engage in market transactions. Buyers (consumers) attempt to improve their well-being by obtaining goods and services for consumption at the lowest possible prices. Sellers (producers) seek to earn profits by selling goods and services at the highest possible prices. However, in a competitive market neither buyers nor sellers can control the market price. Furthermore, both buyers and sellers must have good information about relevant alternatives, and they must be able to purchase or sell in a variety of geographically separated markets if the market outcome is to be efficient. If buyers or sellers do not possess good information about product quality or the existence of other traders, potentially beneficial exchanges will not be made. If buyers are unable to shop outside a particular geographic area, sellers in that area may be able to raise prices above their competitive levels, to the detriment of consumers. A market that satisfies these characteristics — many buyers and sellers, good information, and trader mobility — and in which relatively homogeneous (identical or nearly identical) goods are traded is said to be *competitive*. In such a market, price is determined by the interaction of buyers and sellers, and the competitive process of price determination establishes market equilibrium.

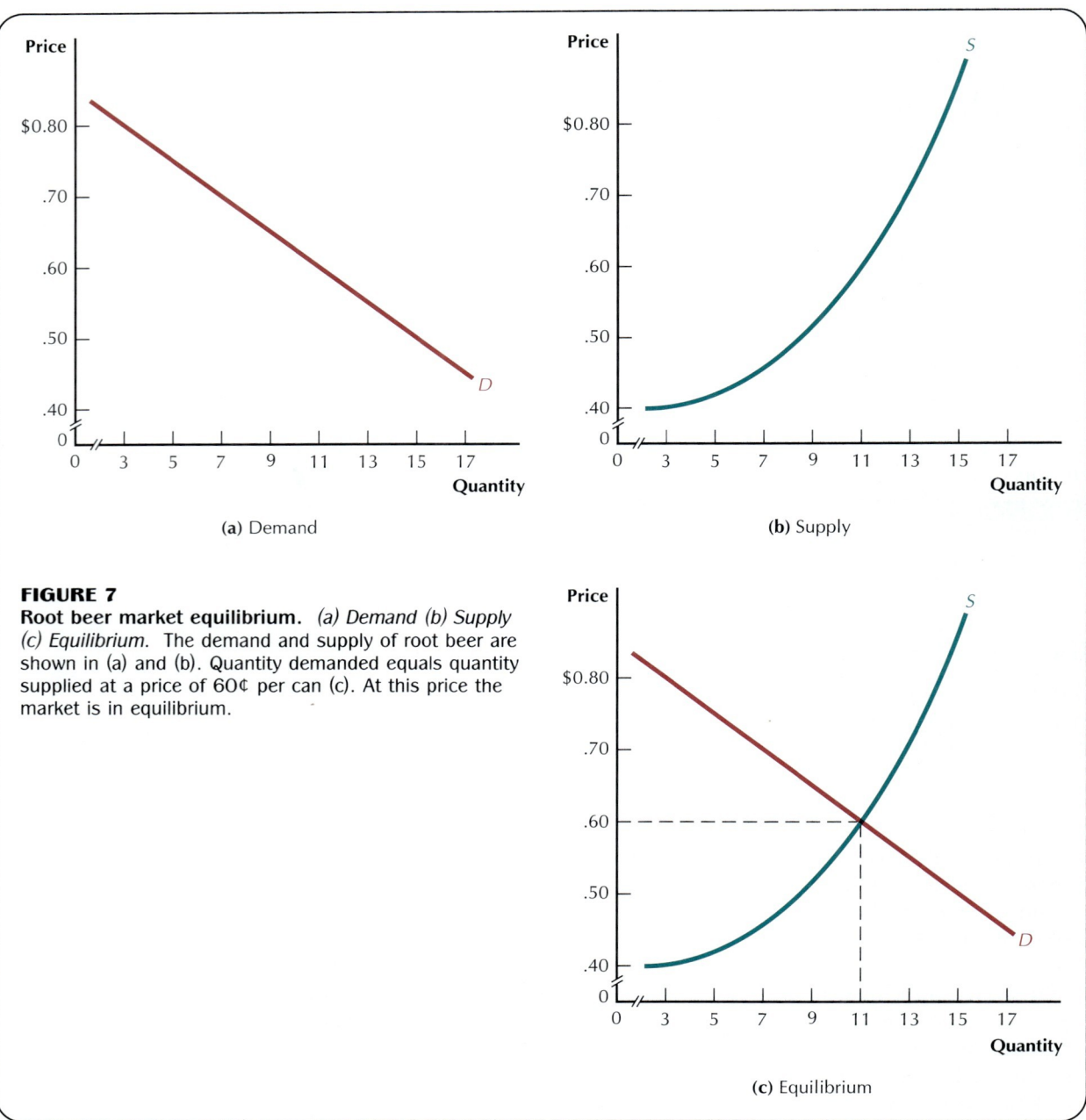

FIGURE 7
Root beer market equilibrium. *(a) Demand (b) Supply (c) Equilibrium.* The demand and supply of root beer are shown in (a) and (b). Quantity demanded equals quantity supplied at a price of 60¢ per can (c). At this price the market is in equilibrium.

Market Equilibrium

Demand and supply determine price and quantity exchanged in the market. A price–output **equilibrium** is established in a market when demand and supply factors are balanced so that there is no pressure for the outcome to change. An *equilibrium price* is a market price from which there is no tendency to change. So long as the forces affecting supply and demand remain the same, the equilibrium price remains unchanged.

Given the laws of demand and supply, only one equilibrium price–output combination exists. All other price–output combinations are **disequilibrium** combinations; they cannot be maintained because forces in the market push price and output toward the equilibrium combination. These forces originate in the competition among buyers and sellers. The process by which market equilibrium is established can be illustrated using the root beer market example.

Figures 7 (a) and 7 (b) show demand and supply schedules for root beer. The demand and supply curves are combined in Figure 7 (c). Notice that the demand and supply curves intersect at only one point, where price equals 60¢ per can and output equals 11 million cans. Sixty cents is an equilibrium price, because at this price the quantity willingly demanded each week by consumers just equals the quantity willingly supplied by producers (11 million cans). At a price of 60¢ per can, market forces do not push the price higher or lower.

If the price of root beer were not equal to 60¢ a can, market forces would push the market price toward the equilibrium level. Consider Figure 8 (a), which reproduces Figure 7 (c). If the market price of root beer were 50¢ per can, the quantity of root beer demanded by consumers would exceed the quantity supplied by producers. The demand schedule shows that consumers are willing to purchase 15 million cans of root beer weekly at 50¢ per can. The supply curve shows that producers are willing to supply only 8.6 million cans of root beer at this price. Consumers are not able to purchase all the root beer they want at a price of 50¢ per can. An **excess demand** or **shortage** exists at a price of 50¢ per can.

Consumers will quickly purchase the available quantity of root beer. Those consumers who shop a day or two after the root beer has been delivered to stores will find the shelves empty, all the root beer having been purchased by shoppers who arrived earlier. Retailers, noticing that their stocks of root beer are being purchased faster than they are being delivered, will increase their orders from producers. As their stocks of root beer are depleted, producers will ration root beer to stores by increasing the price at which they sell the drinks. They also will increase production.

Retailers will raise the price they charge for root beer because they are paying a higher price. At the higher price, consumers reduce the quantity they demand. For example, at a price of 55¢ a can, quantity supplied increases to 10 million cans per week, while quantity demanded falls to 13 million. Increasing the price to 55¢ reduces but does not eliminate the shortage of root beer. Since quantity demanded still exceeds quantity supplied, consumers will continue to bid up the price of root beer by purchasing all that is available. Stores will continue to increase their orders for root beer, and root beer suppliers will respond to the signal that consumers want more by increasing quantity supplied *at a higher price*. So long as quantity demanded exceeds quantity supplied, the price will continue to rise. When the price reaches the point at which quantity demanded and supplied are equal, a price of 60¢ in

Equilibrium
A price–output combination at which there is no pressure for either price or output to change.

Disequilibrium
Any price–output combination at which market forces are acting to change price or quantity.

Shortage (excess demand)
Quantity demanded exceeds quantity supplied at a particular price.

74 ■ CHAPTER 3 THE MARKET MECHANISM: SUPPLY AND DEMAND

(a) Excess Demand

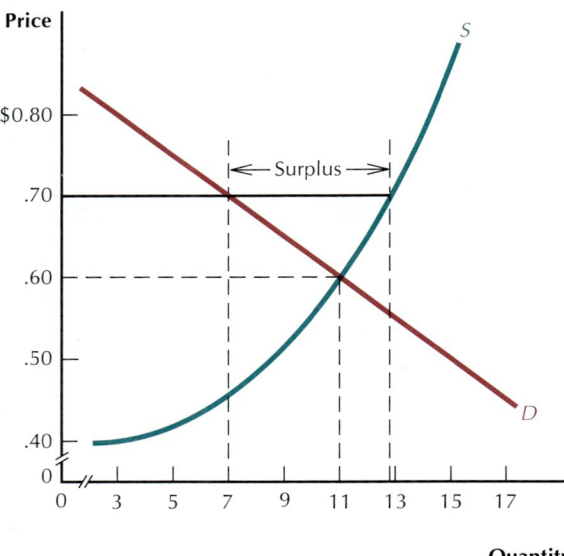

(b) Excess Supply

FIGURE 8
Excess demand and excess supply. *(a) Excess Demand.* A price below the equilibrium level generates excess demand. At a price of 50¢ per can, the quantity demanded (15 million cans) exceeds the quantity supplied (8.6 million cans), creating a shortage. *(b) Excess Supply.* A price above the equilibrium level generates excess supply. At a price of 70¢ per can, the quantity supplied (12.75 million cans) exceeds the quantity demanded (7 million cans), creating a surplus.

this case, the shortage is eliminated, as is the pressure for producers to increase the price.

While a price below the equilibrium price causes a shortage and sets in motion forces that push the price up, a price above equilibrium causes a **surplus** or **excess supply** that pushes the price down. A surplus exists when the quantity willingly supplied at a particular price exceeds the quantity willingly demanded. Figure 8 (b) illustrates the effect of a surplus. At a price of 70¢ per can, the quantity of root beer demanded is less than the quantity supplied. In particular, a price of 70¢ causes a surplus of 5.75 million cans. Retailers find their root beer inventories growing, and they reduce the size of their orders from producers. Producers, competing against one another to sell root beer, begin to lower their prices to encourage purchases. They produce and sell less at the lower prices, and consumers increase quantities consumed at the lower price. The surplus shrinks, but so long as quantity supplied exceeds quantity demanded, downward pressure on the price exists. At lower prices, retailers notice that consumers are increasing their purchases so that store inventories of root beer are shrinking. Competition among producers drives the price down to the equilibrium level, where quantity supplied equals quantity demanded.

Surplus (excess supply) Quantity supplied exceeds quantity demanded at a particular price.

Price as a Signal of Altered Alternatives: Response to Change

The market mechanism rations scarce goods and services based on the costs of production (supply) and the benefits of consumption (demand). Buyers and sellers jointly determine the price at which a good is exchanged and the quantity that is exchanged, but in a competitive market no buyer or seller can individually influence the market outcome. The set of prices of goods and services existing at a point in time constitutes an opportunity set for buyers and sellers that influences their consumption and production decisions.

Consumers attempt to maximize satisfaction from a given expenditure on consumer goods. The existing set of prices defines their opportunities. While the benefits of consumption are determined by consumers themselves, they must take the cost of consumption as given. Consumers do not control market prices. When market prices change, consumers' opportunities change. Consumers react by altering the quantities of goods they buy.

Producers seek to maximize profits from the production and sale of goods. The set of existing market prices determines the revenue that producers can expect to receive from product sales. Producers can influence costs, through the choice of inputs and technologies, but in a competitive market individual producers have no control over the market price. Any producer choosing to charge a price either above or below the market price loses profits. If market prices change, the set of profitable opportunities changes. Firms respond to the new alternatives by producing more or less of a product, by discontinuing production of an old product, or by initiating production of a new product. Production changes reflect changed alternatives.

Thus, market price is an important element in consumption and production decisions. A change in price signals to market participants that conditions have changed. Market participants respond to these signals by altering their behavior as the market moves to a new equilibrium. Although the notion of market equilibrium is important, it should not be overemphasized. Understanding economics requires understanding the human behavior that causes a market to move from one equilibrium to another equilibrium. This *process of adjustment* is most important. The economy is characterized by change. The market mechanism works precisely because it responds to new developments through adjustments in market price.

Change in Demand

A *change in demand* is represented by a shift in the demand curve to the left or right. When one of the factors affecting demand other than the good's own price changes, the demand curve shifts, establishing a new market equilibrium. Suppose that people's tastes for tea increase. What happens in the tea market? Consumers are willing to buy more tea than they purchased previously at any market price. The demand for tea increases (shifts to the right). The process of moving to a new price–output equilibrium is illustrated in four steps in Figure 9. The initial equilibrium in the tea market is depicted in Figure 9 (a). The equilibrium price is P_e^0 and the equilibrium quantity is Q_e^0. The change in tastes causes the demand curve for tea to shift to the right from D_0 to D_1 in Figure 9 (b). The maximum quantity of tea consumers are willing to demand is now greater at every price.

The change in demand sets in motion a number of changes, leading to a new equilibrium price and quantity in the tea market. Panel (c) depicts these changes. The increase in demand causes a shortage at the original equilibrium price, P_e^0. The quantity demanded, Q_d, exceeds the quantity supplied, Q_e^0. P_e^0 is now a *disequilibrium price*. The excess demand leads to a rapid depletion of grocers' inventories of tea. Grocers increase their orders of tea from producers, but producers are able to supply more tea only at higher prices. Grocers pass the higher prices along to consumers. As the price of tea is bid up, the quantity demanded falls (along the new demand curve, D_1) and the quantity supplied increases (along the original supply curve). A new equilibrium, E', is established in the tea market, as depicted in Figure 9 (d). Both the new price, P_e^1, and the new quantity, Q_e^1, are higher than the original price and quantity exchanged.

Note that the distinction between a change in *demand* (or *supply*) and a change in *quantity demanded* (or *supplied*) is important in the analysis of a market change such as an increase in demand for tea. Increased preferences for tea cause a *change in demand:* The demand curve shifts to the right. The increase in demand raises the price of tea, and as the price of tea rises the *quantity of tea supplied* to the market increases along the supply curve from the old price, P_e^0, to the new price, P_e^1. A change in demand (supply) is represented by a shift in the demand (supply) curve. A change in quantity supplied (demanded) is represented by a movement along the supply (demand) curve.

Any change in demand caused by changes in income, tastes, expectations, or the prices of substitutes or complements changes the market equilibrium. An increase in demand causes market price and quantity to rise, while a decrease in demand causes the market price and quantity to fall.

SECTION RECAP
Ceteris paribus, an increase in demand increases both price and quantity. A decrease in demand decreases both price and quantity.

Change in Supply

A *change in supply* is represented by a shift in the supply curve to the left or right. When one of the factors affecting supply other than the good's own price

THE MARKET MECHANISM AT WORK: EQUILIBRIUM 77

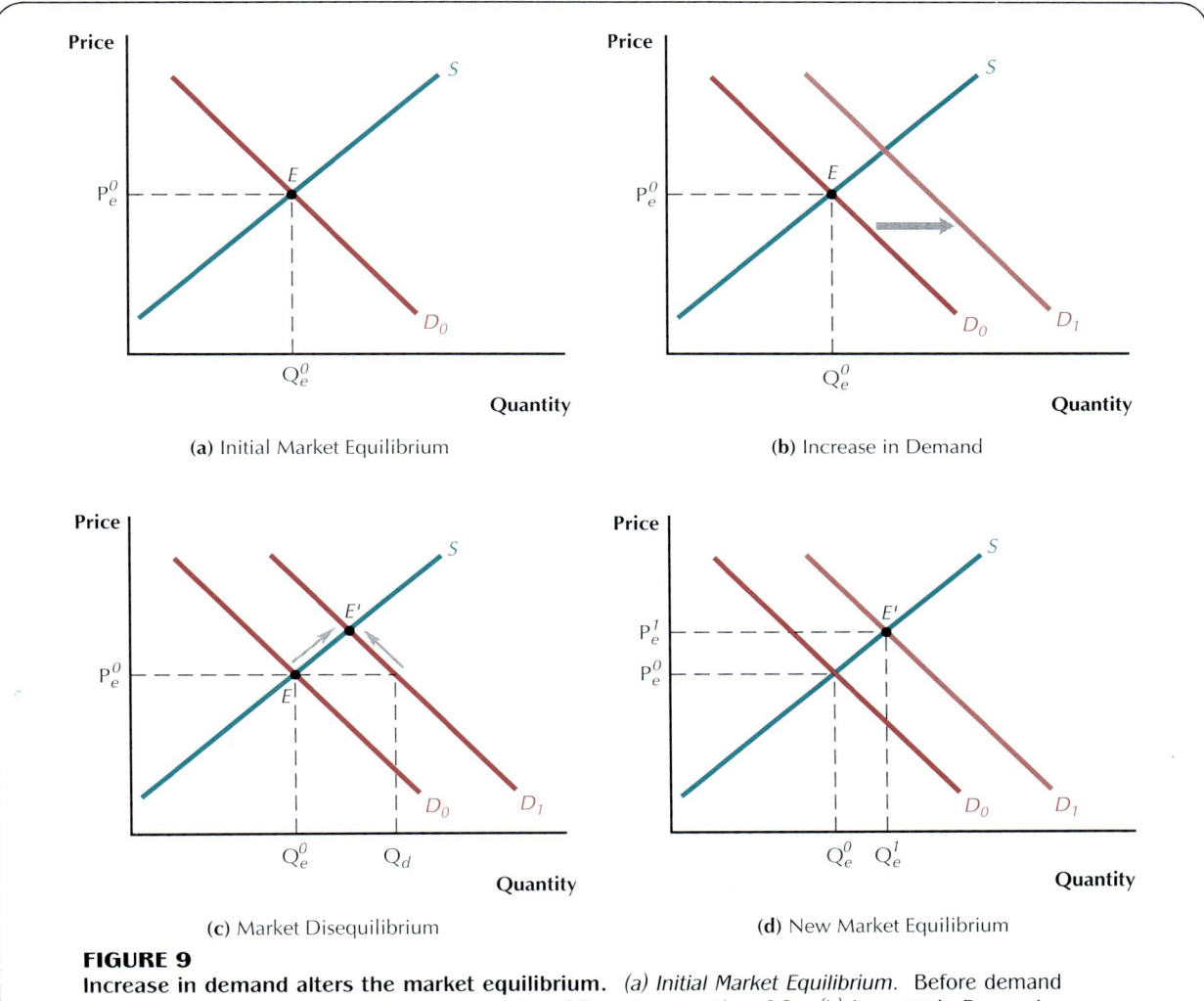

FIGURE 9
Increase in demand alters the market equilibrium. *(a) Initial Market Equilibrium.* Before demand changes, the market is in equilibrium at a price of P_e^0 and a quantity of Q_e^0. *(b) Increase in Demand.* When one of the factors influencing demand changes, causing demand to increase, the demand curve shifts to the right to D_1. At any price, the quantity demanded on D_1 is greater than the quantity demanded on D_0. *(c) Market Disequilibrium.* The increase in demand generates a disequilibrium at the initial price, P_e^0: Quantity demanded, Q_d, exceeds quantity supplied, Q_e^0. The shortage prompts consumers to bid up the price. Quantity supplied increases along S and quantity demanded decreases along D_1.
(d) New Market Equilibrium. The price rises to P_e^1, the new equilibrium price. The equilibrium quantity traded is Q_e^1. The increase in demand increases both the equilibrium price and quantity.

changes, the supply curve shifts, establishing a new market equilibrium. Two examples illustrate the process leading to a new market equilibrium when supply changes.

Suppose that an early frost in Brazil destroys the coffee crop. The market supply of coffee decreases as a result. Figure 10 illustrates the effect of the frost on the coffee market. The coffee market equilibrium before the early frost is illustrated in Figure 10 (a). The frost reduces the quantity of coffee available

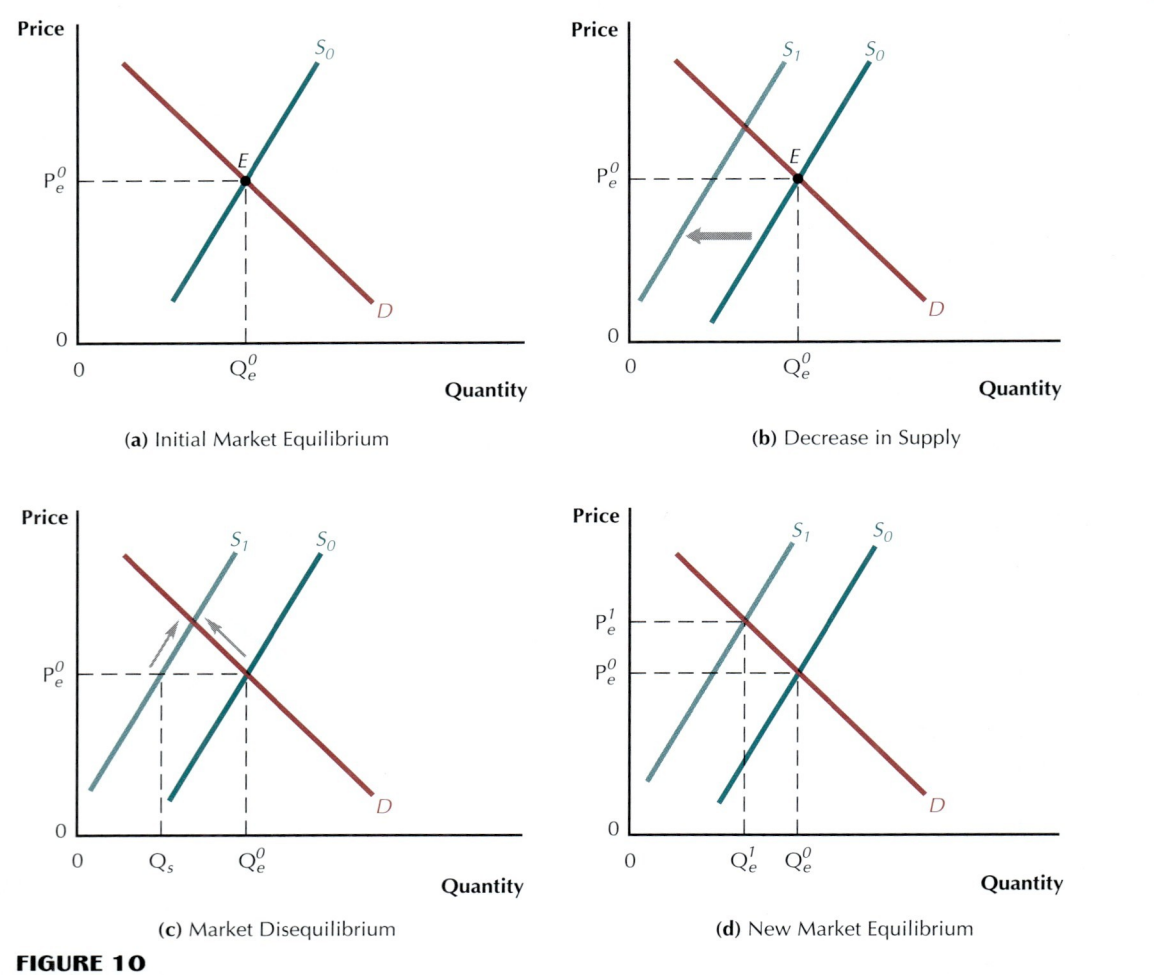

FIGURE 10
Decrease in supply alters market equilibrium. *(a) Initial Market Equilibrium.* Before supply changes, the market is in equilibrium at a price of P_e^0 and a quantity of Q_e^0. *(b) Decrease in Supply.* When one of the factors influencing supply changes, causing supply to decrease, the supply curve shifts to the left to S_1. At any price the quantity supplied along S_1 is less than the quantity supplied along S_0. *(c) Market Disequilibrium.* The decrease in supply causes a disequilibrium at the initial price, P_e^0: Quantity demanded, Q_e^0, exceeds quantity supplied, Q_s. The shortage prompts consumers to bid up the price. Quantity supplied increases along S_1 and quantity demanded decreases along D. *(d) New Market Equilibrium.* The price rises to its new equilibrium level, P_e^1. The equilibrium quantity traded falls to Q_e^1. The decrease in supply increases equilibrium price and decreases equilibrium quantity.

at any market price; it is as if the bad weather causes a large increase in the costs of production. Supply decreases and the coffee supply curve shifts to the left, to S_1 in Figure 10 (b). The change in supply causes a market disequilibrium at the original price, generating forces that push the market toward a new equilibrium.

The process of moving to a new equilibrium is illustrated in Figure 10 (c). At the original market price, P_e^0, excess demand now exists: The quantity demanded, Q_e^0, exceeds the quantity willingly supplied, Q_s. Consumers experience this shortage in the form of empty shelves in grocery stores. Producers ration their coffee supplies to retailers by raising the price they charge. Grocers pass the price increase along to consumers. By paying the higher price, the consumers who value coffee more highly bid the available coffee away from other consumers who value it less highly. As the price rises, the quantity of coffee demanded decreases along the demand curve. The price rise also causes an increase in quantity supplied along the new supply curve, S_1. These changes, caused by the rising price, gradually eliminate the shortage of coffee. A new equilibrium price is established when the quantity demanded again equals the quantity supplied, at a higher price. The equilibrium quantity exchanged in the market falls from Q_e^0 to Q_e^1 [Figure 10 (d)].

As this example clearly demonstrates, a decrease in supply increases market price and decreases market output. An increase in supply leads to a decrease in the equilibrium market price and an increase in output. To further illustrate the effects of a supply increase, consider the television market. Assume that technological improvements reduce the cost of producing television sets. What happens?

The pattern of changes is similar to the pattern in preceding examples. Technological change enables producers to produce TV sets at lower cost. The decrease in costs means that producers are willing to supply more TV sets than before at any market price. Thus, the supply curve shifts to the right. The rightward shift of the supply curve creates an excess supply (surplus) at the original equilibrium price, generating pressure for price adjustment. Producers, competing to sell the now less-costly TV sets, cut the market price in an effort to sell more sets. As the price falls, two effects are observed. First, the quantity willingly supplied decreases along the new supply curve. Second, the reduced price causes the quantity demanded to increase along the original demand curve. As the price falls, the surplus shrinks. At the new equilibrium price the quantity supplied just equals the quantity demanded. The increase in supply, caused by the technological advance, reduces the equilibrium price and increases quantity.

A change in input prices also causes a change in supply. Input prices influence supply through their effect on production costs. An increase in input prices increases costs, decreasing supply. Decreased input prices reduce costs and increase supply.

SECTION RECAP
Ceteris paribus, an increase in supply decreases price and increases quantity. A decrease in supply increases price and decreases quantity.

Change in Demand and Supply

The preceding examples demonstrated the way in which a market returns to equilibrium after it is disturbed by a change in demand *or* supply. Disequilibrium generates clear-cut responses by buyers and sellers, and their actions reestablish market equilibrium at a new price–quantity combination. When only demand or supply changes, the direction of change in price and quantity is clear.

What happens in a market when both supply and demand change? The answer is not so obvious. However, a little analysis allows us to identify the information needed to predict the price and quantity effects of a change in both demand and supply. Consider again the root beer market. What happens in this market when both supply and demand increase?

Why the **Disagreement?**

Profiteering by Oil Companies

Since 1973 the world has experienced three major increases in the price of crude oil. In 1973 and again in 1979 the Organization of Petroleum Exporting Countries (OPEC) sharply restricted the supply of oil in order to push the price higher. In 1990 the invasion of Kuwait by Iraqi forces reduced the world oil supply, as virtually all countries joined a worldwide boycott of oil from Iraq or Kuwait. The price of crude petroleum — and the price of gasoline at the pump — shot upward.

It is not surprising to find that a restriction in the supply of crude oil leads to an increase in the price of gasoline, since crude oil is overwhelmingly the major input in the production of gasoline. As we have seen, and as Figure 11 shows, a sharp increase in the price of an input (oil) shifts the supply curve of a product (gasoline) to the left. If demand is constant, the equilibrium price rises. Economists see this as a natural response to higher production costs. However, a large number of Americans, including some prominent politicians, see the issue differently. In the 1970s, Congress passed a windfall profits tax, which transferred most of the oil company revenues earned from higher gasoline prices to the federal government. The price jump

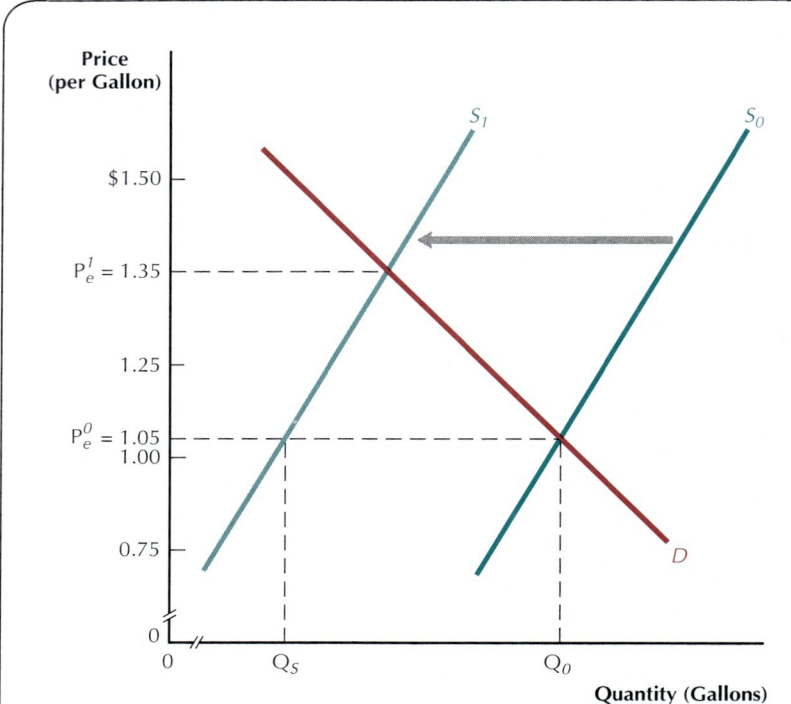

FIGURE 11
Decreased supply of gasoline. An increase in the price of crude oil, the most important input in the production of gasoline, decreases the supply of gasoline. The equilibrium price rises from $1.05 to $1.35 per gallon. If a government policy holds the market price below $1.35, a shortage develops; quantity demanded (Q_0) exceeds quantity supplied (Q_s).

Suppose a fall in the price of sugar decreases the cost of producing root beer. Supply increases; the supply curve shifts to the right. Figure 12 (a) illustrates the original and new equilibrium positions. An increase in supply, *ceteris paribus*, causes equilibrium price to fall to P_s and quantity exchanged to increase to Q_s. But what happens to price and quantity when demand also increases? If consumers' preferences for root beer increase, the demand curve shifts to the right, as in Figure 12 (b), increasing the market price to P_d and the equilibrium output to Q_d.

in 1990 inspired Senator Robert Packwood of Oregon to propose reinstating the windfall profits tax and led Illinois Senator Paul Simon to submit a bill calling for heavy fines for oil companies that profiteered by charging higher gasoline prices. The senators obviously have a very different view of the world than most economists. Why the disagreement? The idea that seems to underlie proposals for penalizing oil companies for increasing prices is that oil companies should not benefit from an artificially restricted oil supply. Since oil is traded in a world market, the price of any given grade of oil is the same around the world, except for differing transportation costs. When the world price of oil rises, the value of the oil owned by American companies also increases. The oil used to produce gasoline costs American companies more, but the oil companies also receive the benefits of higher crude oil prices for the oil they pump from wells in the United States. Since the oil companies have done nothing to deserve higher prices (and higher profits) for their domestic oil, they should not be allowed to benefit from the higher prices.

To an economist, such reasoning is highly suspect. A number of objections immediately pop into mind. First, if the government forces oil companies to hold the price of gasoline below its equilibrium value, a shortage will develop. Figure 11 illustrates this. In the face of higher oil prices, the equilibrium price of gasoline rises to $1.35 per gallon. If the government were to force oil companies to hold the price at the level prevailing before the supply reduction, $1.05, a shortage would develop. The quantity demanded at a price of $1.05 per gallon exceeds the quantity supplied. Not all the consumers wanting to purchase gasoline at $1.05 per gallon can obtain all the gasoline they want. How is the available gasoline to be rationed? In the 1970s, the rationing device was waiting in line. In some areas, drivers were forced to wait in line for hours to buy small quantities of gasoline. Sometimes the people who valued gasoline most highly—and were willing to pay for it—were unable to obtain enough gasoline to run their businesses.

A second objection to artificially holding down gasoline prices is the impact such a policy has on the incentive of oil companies to search for new sources of oil. In effect the government is saying, "If the price of oil falls, the price of gasoline must come down, but if the price of oil rises, gasoline prices cannot follow." In an era when calls for energy sufficiency are being heard more and more frequently, such a policy seems counterproductive. Oil companies have no incentive to engage in costly, high-risk efforts to drill for more oil in the United States if they cannot benefit from higher oil prices.

Finally, oil companies seem to be singled out for disapproval when they behave in the same way producers in other industries behave. When frigid weather destroyed fruit and vegetable crops throughout most of Texas and Florida in December 1989, the prices of fresh fruits and vegetables soared. Growers in southernmost Texas and Florida, as well as growers in California and Mexico, profited immensely from the higher prices. These growers did nothing to earn the higher prices they received; they simply sold their produce at the market price. Similarly, every time a drought hits the Grain Belt, farmers in areas that receive rain benefit. Yet they are not charged with profiteering.

In the oil market, as in any other market, a policy that prevents price from moving to its equilibrium level has unintended consequences. In the oil market, the unintended consequences could prove harmful to U.S. consumers both at the time price controls are imposed and later when less oil is available.

What are the combined effects on market price and quantity of an increase in both supply and demand? Quantity exchanged unambiguously increases—both a supply increase and a demand increase have a positive effect on the quantity exchanged. These changes reinforce one another, causing an even greater increase in equilibrium quantity. The price effect of a simultaneous increase in supply and demand is ambiguous, however. An increase in supply tends to depress market price, but an increase in demand pushes price up. The two forces counteract one another. Price might increase, decrease, or stay the

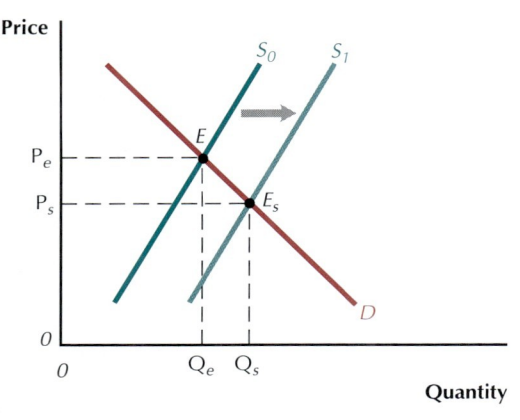

(a) Increase in Supply

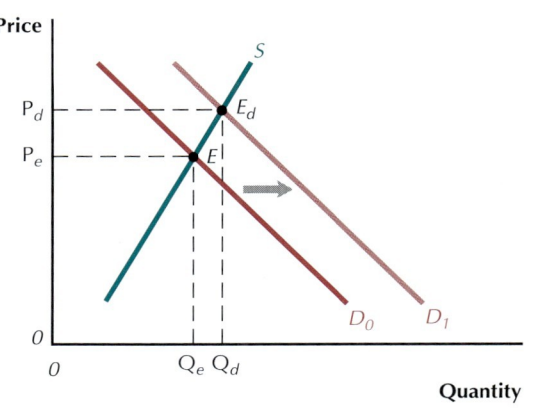

(b) Increase in Demand

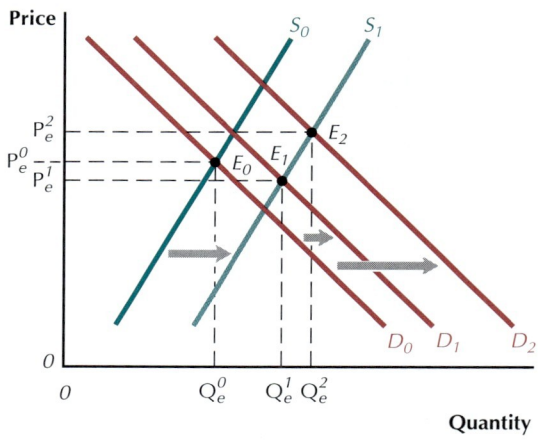

(c) Increase in Both Supply and Demand

FIGURE 12
Effect of an increase in both supply and demand.
(a) Increase in Supply. The supply curve shifts from S_0 to S_1, reducing equilibrium price from P_e to P_s and increasing equilibrium quantity from Q_e to Q_s. *(b) Increase in Demand.* The demand curve shifts from D_0 to D_1, increasing equilibrium price from P_e to P_d and equilibrium quantity from Q_e to Q_d. *(c) Increase in Both Supply and Demand.* The supply curve shifts from S_0 to S_1 and the demand curve shifts from D_0 to either D_1 or D_2. Since both curves shift to the right, equilibrium quantity unambiguously increases. The direction of change in equilibrium price is less obvious, because the price effects of the two shifts offset each other. If the supply shift is larger than the demand shift, as when demand increases to D_1, price falls. If the supply shift is smaller than the demand shift, as when demand increases to D_2, price rises.

same. In Figure 12 (c), the change in supply and the change in demand are superimposed on the same graph. If demand increases to D_1, the equilibrium price falls by a small amount, from P_e^0 to P_e^1. However, if demand increases by a larger amount, to D_2, the equilibrium price increases to P_e^2. If the demand and supply curves had shifted to the right by exactly the same amount (measured by horizontal distance), the price would not have changed.

The movement from P_e^0 to P_e^1 is representative of developments in many new product markets. After the product is introduced, both supply and demand increase. Costs of production fall as producers develop more efficient production techniques. Consumers increase their demand for the product as they become more familiar with it and identify the full range of benefits derived from the product. When pocket calculators were first introduced, basic units sold for well over $100. At that time annual sales were only fraction of today's sales. In the past fifteen years the costs of producing calculators have fallen

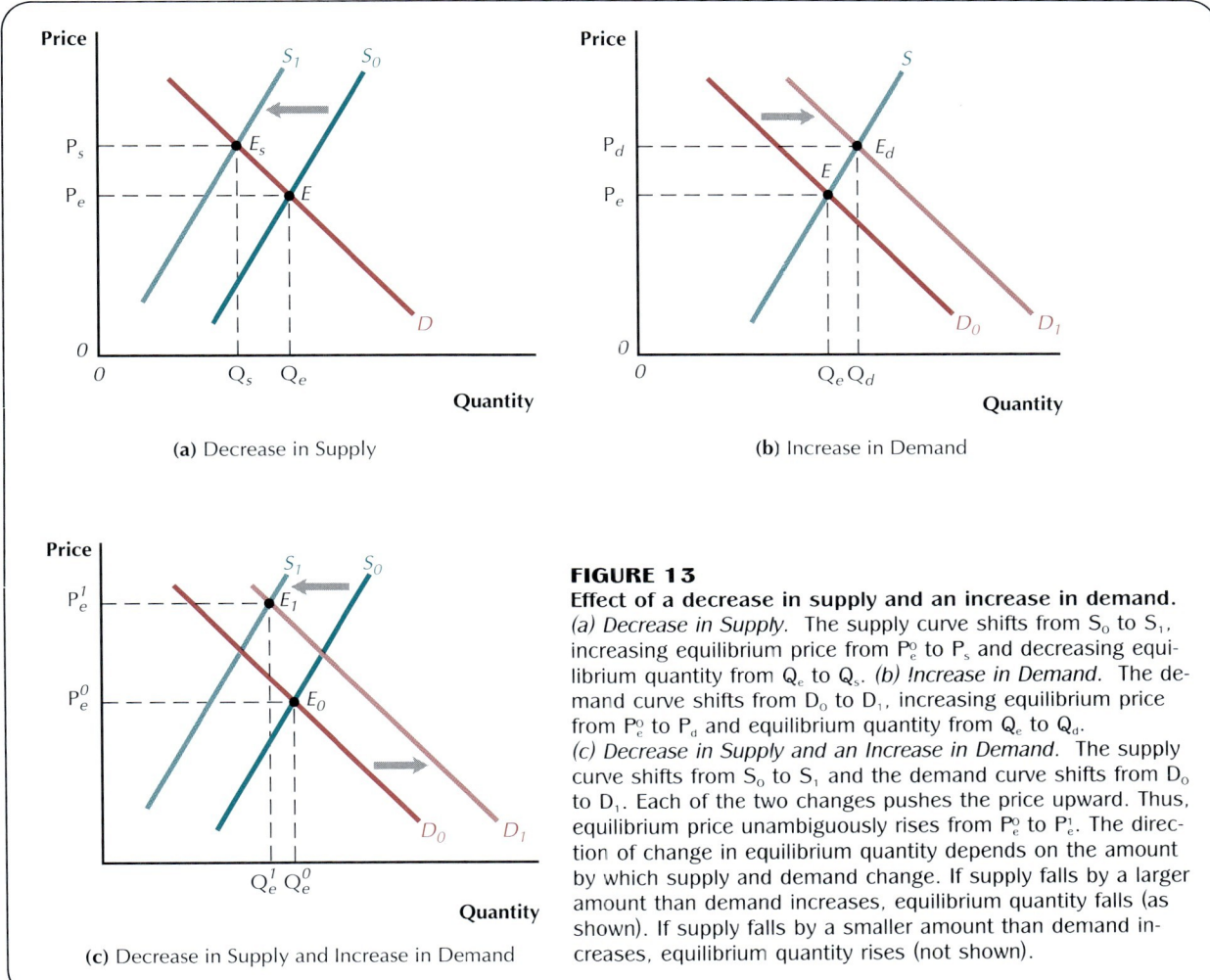

FIGURE 13
Effect of a decrease in supply and an increase in demand.
(a) Decrease in Supply. The supply curve shifts from S_0 to S_1, increasing equilibrium price from P_e^0 to P_s and decreasing equilibrium quantity from Q_e to Q_s. *(b) Increase in Demand.* The demand curve shifts from D_0 to D_1, increasing equilibrium price from P_e^0 to P_d and equilibrium quantity from Q_e to Q_d.
(c) Decrease in Supply and an Increase in Demand. The supply curve shifts from S_0 to S_1 and the demand curve shifts from D_0 to D_1. Each of the two changes pushes the price upward. Thus, equilibrium price unambiguously rises from P_e^0 to P_e^1. The direction of change in equilibrium quantity depends on the amount by which supply and demand change. If supply falls by a larger amount than demand increases, equilibrium quantity falls (as shown). If supply falls by a smaller amount than demand increases, equilibrium quantity rises (not shown).

further and faster than calculator demand has increased. Thus, we have experienced a steady decline in price while the quantity of calculators sold has increased.

Other combinations of changes in demand and supply can produce more unusual results. Suppose the supply of oats were decreased by widespread crop failure. Consider what would happen if such a development were combined with a sudden increase in demand caused by reports that oat bran is a very healthful food (consumer preferences for oats increase).

The effect of a combined decrease in supply and increase in demand is illustrated in Figure 13. The supply decrease causes equilibrium price to rise and quantity to fall, as in Figure 13 (a). Meanwhile, consumers are demanding greater quantities of oats at all prices, as shown in Figure 13 (b). Price and quantity exchanged would both increase in the absence of any decrease in supply.

GRAPH GUIDE 7: OVERLAY TRANSPARENCY #5. Pages 1 and 2 show the initial equilibrium and the effect of a decrease in supply. Pages 3 and 4 show how the effect of a simultaneous increase in demand on equilibrium quantity can vary.

Does It Make Economic Sense?

Can Speculators Add to Market Stability?

Speculation — the word itself seems almost unsavory. The bane of market economies, in the eyes of many, is the supposedly excessive amount of buying and selling done for purely speculative reasons. Speculators buy not to consume, but to earn a quick profit when (and if) prices move in the direction they expect them to move. A speculator buys and sells goods or financial assets in the hope of making a profit from price movements. A speculator might buy wheat and hold it in the expectation that the price of wheat will rise in the near future. If the speculator is right, he profits by selling at a higher price than he bought. If he is wrong, he loses.

Either way, the speculator apparently produces nothing; whatever gains or losses the speculator realizes seem to be economically irrelevant.

Perhaps, however, speculators are not really irrelevant; perhaps they are positively harmful. Speculators are often blamed for price fluctuations in markets as diverse as basic commodities (such as wheat) and foreign currencies (such as the Japanese yen). Many people believe that speculators create market instability in their quest for speculative profits. Yet economists argue to the contrary — that speculation can actually stabilize markets. Does this make economic sense?

Speculation is, by definition, risky. Speculators buy and sell based on what they *expect* to happen in the future. Thus, speculation can be profitable or unprofitable — and stabilizing or destabilizing. As an example of stabilizing speculation, consider the actions of commodity speculators who expect a poor grain crop in a particular year. Based on the best weather forecasts available, speculators conclude that rainfall is likely to be very light throughout the Grain Belt. They expect the drought to decrease the supply of grain significantly, driving the price of grain higher, as in Figure 14 (a). Acting on their expectations, the speculators demand grain before the drought and consequent crop failure have materialized. The speculative buying drives grain prices up *before supply decreases*. Figure 14 (b) illustrates this, as demand increases along the initial supply curve. Both price and quan-

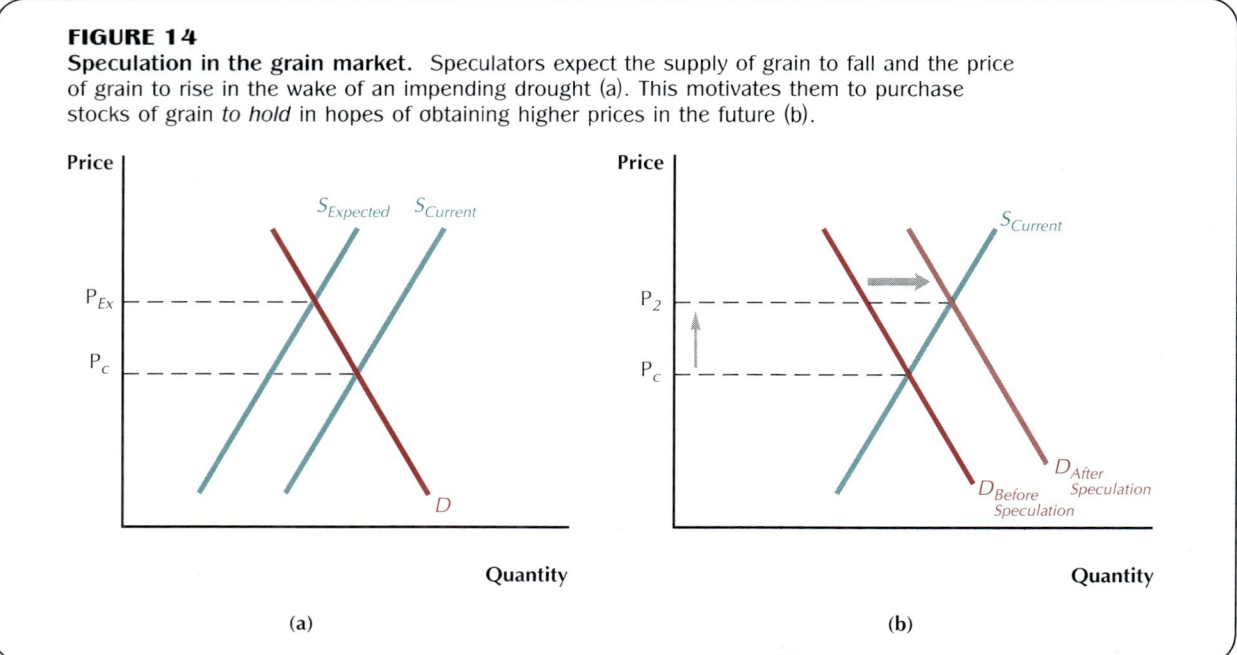

FIGURE 14
Speculation in the grain market. Speculators expect the supply of grain to fall and the price of grain to rise in the wake of an impending drought (a). This motivates them to purchase stocks of grain *to hold* in hopes of obtaining higher prices in the future (b).

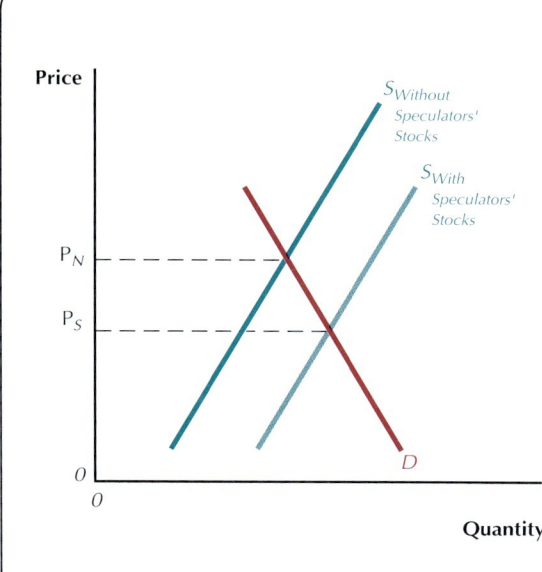

FIGURE 15
Grain market after the drought. The drought pushes the price of grain upward, but the sale of stocks bought by speculators before the drought limits the price increase. Instead of rising to P_N, the price rises only to P_s.

tity rise, although the initial quantity of grain actually being consumed does not increase. Demand rises because speculators want to *buy and hold* grain until the price rises. Grain consumers now face a higher price than before, so they purchase and consume less grain than before the speculative demand increase.

If the speculators are correct and grain supply is reduced by drought, the speculators profit from their activity. Grain consumers also may benefit. As the supply of grain falls and the market price of grain rises, speculators begin to supply their accumulated stocks to the market. This adds to the postdrought supply of grain, as shown in Figure 15. Without speculation, the price would rise to P_N. The stocks accumulated by speculators are added to the total supply of grain after the drought, holding the price down to P_s. Consumers gain by paying lower prices than they would have paid in the absence of speculation.

In this case, the speculative activity raises the price of grain somewhat before the drought and lowers it somewhat after the drought, relative to what the price would be in the absence of speculation. The overall effect is to reduce the size and instability of price movements. Actual speculation in commodities makes use of more complex types of contracts than described in this example, but the effect of successful speculation is much the same.

We should acknowledge that speculation can be destabilizing. If speculators bet on a drought but plenty of rain falls, they will force the market price up unnecessarily. The subsequent decline in the price of grain will be larger than necessary. Speculators do not gain from such destabilizing behavior, however. They take losses on their grain holdings if the market price does not rise above their purchase price. It is also possible in some markets for speculators to profit by temporarily driving the price far above its market level. If they are able to sell their stocks at the artificially high prices, the speculators can make huge profits while leaving other market participants to take losses when the price returns to its market level. Such anticompetitive behavior lies well outside the realm of beneficial speculation.

SECTION RECAP
An increase in both demand and supply increases quantity, but has an indeterminate effect on price. A decrease in both demand and supply decreases quantity, but has an indeterminate effect on price. An increase in demand and a decrease in supply increases price but has an indeterminate effect on quantity. A decrease in demand and an increase in supply decreases price, but has an indeterminate effect on quantity.

The combination of decreased supply and increased demand produces the result illustrated in Figure 13 (c). Both the supply decrease and the demand increase put upward pressure on the price of oats, so the equilibrium price unambiguously rises. However, the reduced supply puts downward pressure on quantity, while the increased demand tends to increase quantity. The effect on the equilibrium quantity exchanged is ambiguous. If the supply shift is stronger, quantity exchanged falls; if the demand shift is stronger, quantity exchanged rises. As shown in Figure 13 (c), the supply shift is stronger: Equilibrium price rises and equilibrium quantity falls.

When both supply and demand in a market change simultaneously, the impact on price and quantity depends on the net effect of supply and demand changes. As a consequence, we must know the magnitude of the supply and demand changes to predict the direction of change in *both* price and quantity.

Market Adjustments as Responses to Changed Alternatives

When the market is used to ration goods and services, market price plays a very important role. It provides information used by all buyers and sellers in making economic decisions. When any factor that affects supply or demand changes, market price changes. The change in price is a signal that conditions in the market have changed. Price changes alter the alternatives of consumers and producers, inducing them to alter their decisions. Seeking to maintain the satisfaction they derive from consumption, consumers respond to price changes by adjusting their purchases of goods and services. Seeking to maximize profits, producers respond to price changes by altering their production plans and output levels.

A new equilibrium market price reflects the effects of both the initial change in market conditions and consumer and producer responses. The key to understanding how the market allocates goods and resources is understanding how consumers and producers respond to price movements.

Summary

Scarcity of resources necessitates the **rationing** of goods to users. Every society must develop ways to reconcile competing claims on limited resources. Societies must decide **what to produce, how to produce it,** and **to whom it will be distributed.** These decisions can be made in centralized or decentralized ways. **Centralized decision making** occurs when government makes the important economic decisions. A **decentralized economy** is characterized by individual decision making. Such an economy typically relies on markets as the rationing device. Other rationing criteria exist. The choice of criteria affects only the nature of competition for scarce goods; competition itself results from scarcity.

A **market** is a process by which individuals freely negotiate the terms of exchange for goods and services. Market transactions are **mutually beneficial exchanges** with two sides: demand and supply.

On the **demand** side, consumers seek to maximize the satisfaction they derive from consuming goods and services. The quantity of a good purchased depends upon a number of factors, including price. The **law of demand** says that price and quantity demanded are inversely related. Other factors that affect demand include consumer income, tastes, expectations, the prices of other goods, and the number of consumers. When these factors change, the relationship between price and quantity demanded changes. This is called a **change in demand.**

On the **supply** side, firms produce goods and services to sell to consumers for a profit. The higher the market price, *ceteris paribus*, the greater the opportunity for profit. Thus, the **law of supply** states that a positive relationship exists between market price and quantities willingly supplied to the market. Other factors affecting the supply relationship include input prices, technology, other output prices, and the number of suppliers. Changes in these factors cause a **change in supply.**

The interaction of consumers and suppliers establishes a **market equilibrium** price at which quantity supplied equals quantity demanded. At any other price the market is in disequilibrium and pressures exist for the price to move toward the equilibrium price. These pressures arise from the behavior of consumers and producers adjusting their consumption and production to the market price.

A change in demand or supply shifts the demand or supply curve, creating a disequilibrium at the initial market price. The excess demand or supply causes consumers or producers to respond by bidding price up or down. As the price changes, quantities demanded and supplied change. Adjustments continue until quantity demanded again equals quantity supplied at a new equilibrium price.

The supply and demand, or market, model developed in this chapter is a specific application of the Fundamental Premise of Economics. The model has wide applicability, as subsequent chapters demonstrate.

Questions for Thought

Knowledge Questions

1. Explain the difference between centralized and decentralized decision making. Give an example of each kind of decision making in the U.S. economy.
2. How do universities typically ration the following goods and services?

    dormitory rooms
    athletic scholarships
    library books
    parking spaces
    textbooks
    football tickets

3. Explain the difference between scarcity and shortage.
4. What is the *law of demand?* Under what conditions is this law an accurate description of actual behavior?

Application Questions

5. "Health insurance that covers 100 percent of all medical expenditures encourages consumption of health services." Using a demand curve, justify this statement.
6. The demand and supply functions for sweatshirts (the basic grey kind) are as follows:
   a. Graph the demand and supply functions for sweatshirts and find (approximately) the equilibrium price and quantity.
   b. What effect will an increase in the price of gym shoes (a complement) have on the equilibrium price and quantity of sweatshirts, *ceteris paribus?* Explain the effect using your graph.
   c. What effect will a wage increase for workers in the sweatshirt industry have on the equilibrium price and quantity of sweatshirts, *cet. par.?* Explain the effect using your graph.

Demand		Supply	
Price	Quantity Demanded (per period)	Price	Quantity Supplied (per period)
$6	5,000	$6	8,002
5	6,000	5	7,335
4	7,000	4	6,668
3	8,000	3	6,001
2	9,000	2	5,334

7. "In the past five years the average price of our Chevrolets has risen about 6 percent a year and each year we have sold 10 percent more cars than the previous year." How can this car dealer sell more cars as the price of the cars increases?
8. Using a change in supply and/or demand, explain the following phenomena:
   a. Afternoon movie prices are lower than evening prices.
   b. Winter hotel rates in Florida are higher than summer rates.
   c. Corn prices are higher in years of drought.
9. Is the ticket price for rock concerts typically set at the equilibrium level? Is it set above or below equilibrium? How is the disequilibrium eliminated?

Synthesis Questions

10. What factors influence the price of these goods: pork, toothpicks, condominiums, microcomputers. Which of these goods tend to experience both price increases and decreases? Which ones tend to decrease over time? Do any of the goods experience very little price fluctuation? Explain each response.
11. Explain what happens in the wheat market when a surplus exists. What happens to price and quantity? Why? Does the automobile market adjust to a surplus any differently? Explain.
12. The equations for the demand and supply functions in question 6 are as follows:

$$Q_d = 11,000 - 1,000P$$

$$Q_s = 4,000 + 667P$$

Solve for the equilibrium price and quantity. (Hint: at equilibrium, quantity supplied equals quantity demanded).

Suppose the supply function changes to:

$$Q_s = 1,000 + 667P$$

Does supply increase or decrease? What is the new equilibrium price and quantity?

OVERVIEW

In this chapter we combine the concepts of mutually beneficial trade and economic efficiency introduced in Chapter 2 with the supply and demand model presented in Chapter 3. We examine how, under well-defined conditions, a market equilibrium established by the interaction of supply and demand leads to economic efficiency. A graphical model of an efficient market equilibrium is developed, and the conditions that ensure the efficiency of market equilibrium are discussed. We demonstrate that market intervention, through price floors and ceilings, leads to inefficient market outcomes. We conclude the chapter with a discussion of situations in which a society might choose to be inefficient.

Economic Efficiency: A Measure of Market Performance

CHAPTER 4

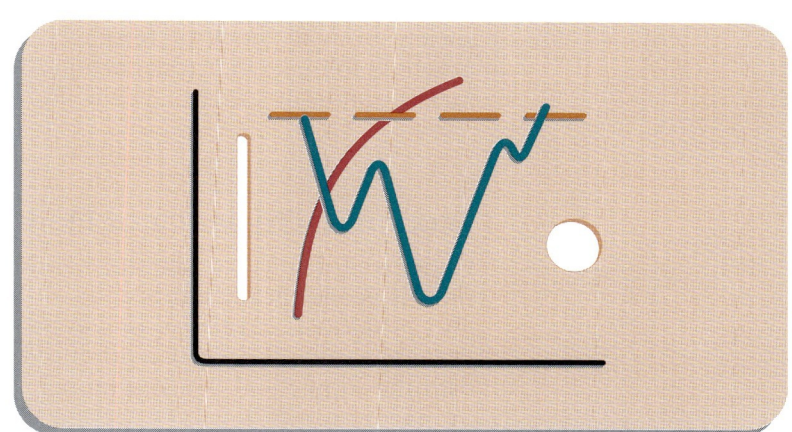

Learning Objectives

After reading and studying this chapter, you will be able to:

1. Determine the social benefits of consumption from the demand curve and the social costs of production from the supply curve.
2. Identify the social net gain from producing and consuming a good.
3. State the conditions necessary for a market equilibrium to be efficient, explain why it is efficient, and graphically illustrate your explanation.
4. Define and illustrate consumers' surplus and producers' surplus.
5. Explain why a price ceiling or floor causes market inefficiency.
6. Discuss why society might decide to pursue an economically inefficient policy.

Gains from Trade

Individuals and societies seek to obtain as much as they can from the limited resources they possess. Chapter 2 presented some examples of one way to increase the value of one's resources: mutually beneficial trade. People trade with one another, giving up something of lesser value for something of greater value. Market transactions, explained in Chapter 3, are one form of mutually beneficial exchange. Consumers sacrifice income that could be used to buy other things to buy goods or services whose consumption yields more satisfaction to them. Producers sell to consumers when they can profit by the sale. Both parties to such voluntary exchanges are better off as a result of the exchange.

Economic efficiency is one benchmark against which the gains from market trades can be measured. Recall from Chapter 2 that *economic efficiency is the achievement of the maximum difference between benefits and costs.* When market decision making is employed to answer the three basic economic questions—what, how, and for whom to produce—society has the potential for achieving economic efficiency: generating the greatest net gain (benefits less costs) to society from its stock of resources. Thus, market decision making has the potential to make individual actions based on self-interest consistent with the maximization of society's well-being.

Economic Efficiency of Market Equilibrium

Under well-defined conditions, which are discussed shortly, a market equilibrium is economically efficient. *In an efficient market, trading at the equilibrium price produces as large a net gain as possible for society, given consumer tastes and production costs.* The net gain produced by an efficient market can be illustrated with the supply and demand model.

Social Benefits from the Demand Curve

When we graph an individual's demand curve, we plot the maximum quantities of a good the person is willing to buy at various prices. When the price is very high, the quantity demanded is low; the consumer finds it beneficial to consume very few units of the good. As the price of the good falls, the consumer demands additional units of the good. At a lower price, the consumer gains by buying more of the good, because the marginal benefit of an additional unit of the good exceeds the (lower) price. The consumer purchases additional units of the good until the marginal benefit from consuming the good equals its price. Thus, the good's price measures the marginal benefit of the last unit of the good purchased. For example, if a person is willing to buy four pounds of oranges per week at a price of 60¢ a pound, the marginal benefit of the last pound of oranges purchased is 60¢. If the marginal benefit were less than 60¢, the final pound of oranges would not be purchased. Thus, the individual's demand curve provides us with a measure of the benefits the individual enjoys from the consumption of a good.

The market demand curve can also be used to measure the total benefits to *society* of consuming a particular good. To illustrate this, consider the demand for top-quality ground beef. The ground beef demand curve in Figure 1 (a) reveals that at a price of $3 per pound U.S. consumers are willing to buy

ECONOMIC EFFICIENCY OF MARKET EQUILIBRIUM   93

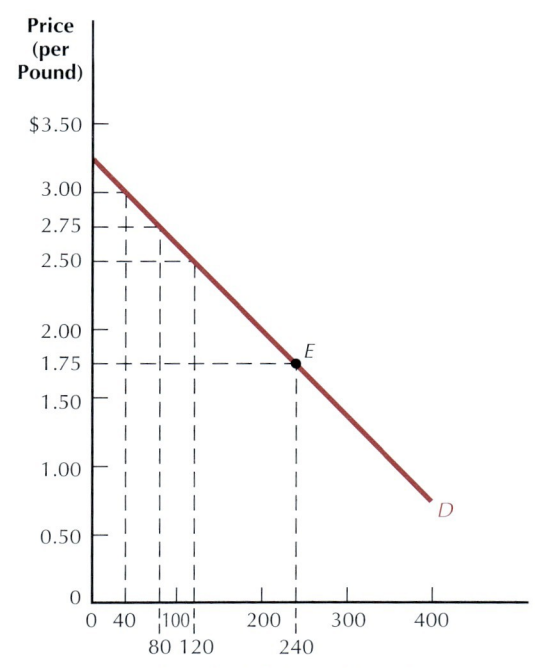

(a)

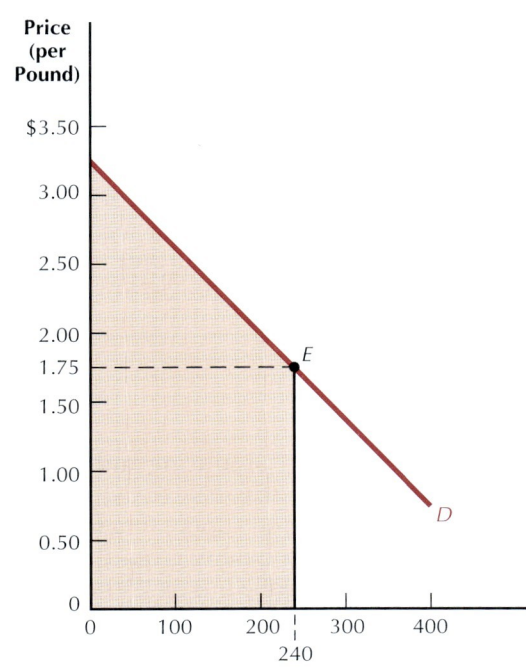

(b)

FIGURE 1
Benefits of consumption of ground beef. (a) The demand curve shows consumers' willingness to pay for each quantity of ground beef. The amount consumers are willing to pay is a measure of the marginal benefit of consuming a particular quantity of ground beef. (b) The total benefits from consuming a particular quantity of ground beef can be calculated by adding up the willingness to pay for each pound. The total willingness to pay for 240 million pounds of ground beef is represented by the shaded area under the demand curve.

up to 40 million pounds of ground beef per month. If the price were $2.75 per pound, they would like another 40 million pounds; at a price of $2.50 per pound, yet another 40 million pounds; and at a price of $1.75 per pound an additional 120 million pounds (for a total of 240 million pounds of ground beef).

The demand curve shows us the benefit to consumers of each additional million pounds of ground beef. The vertical distance from the quantity axis to the demand curve measures the marginal benefit to consumers of a particular quantity of ground beef. By adding up the benefit of each additional million pounds, from the first million to the 240th million, we can derive the total benefit to consumers from consuming 240 million pounds of ground beef. Graphically, this amounts to adding up the area under the demand curve, up to 240 million pounds. Thus, the total social benefits derived from the consumption of 240 million pounds of ground beef equal the shaded area under the demand curve in Figure 1 (b).

Social Costs from the Supply Curve

The supply curve tells us the quantity willingly supplied at each market price. The supply curve reflects the marginal cost of production. Producers seeking to maximize profits will supply a unit of output only if the marginal benefit (the price received) equals or exceeds the marginal cost of production. The supply curve reveals the minimum price at which a producer will sell a unit of output. This price must be just equal to the marginal cost of production.

Consider the supply curve of top quality ground beef in Figure 2 (a). Producers are willing to supply 60 million pounds at a price of $1 per pound. At a price of $1.50 per pound they will supply an additional 120 million pounds, and another 60 million pounds will be produced if the price rises to $1.75 per pound. At a price of $1.75, a total of 240 million pounds of ground beef is produced each month. The supply curve identifies the price that is necessary to get each pound of ground beef produced. This price represents the marginal cost of each pound. Adding up the prices at which each million pounds is produced, up to 240 million pounds, yields the total social cost of producing 240 million pounds of ground beef. The shaded area under the supply curve between zero and 240 million pounds in Figure 2 (b) represents total social cost.

Society's Net Gain: Costs and Benefits . . . Again

Having examined separately the benefits and costs of producing and consuming ground beef, we now look at the net gain (benefits less costs) from the ground beef market. In Figure 3 the market demand and supply functions have been graphed together. The equilibrium price of top quality ground beef, the price at which quantity demanded equals quantity supplied, is $1.75 per pound. At that price the quantity exchanged in the market is 240 million pounds per month.

The equilibrium market outcome is efficient when the marginal benefit to consumers of the last unit purchased equals the marginal cost to producers of

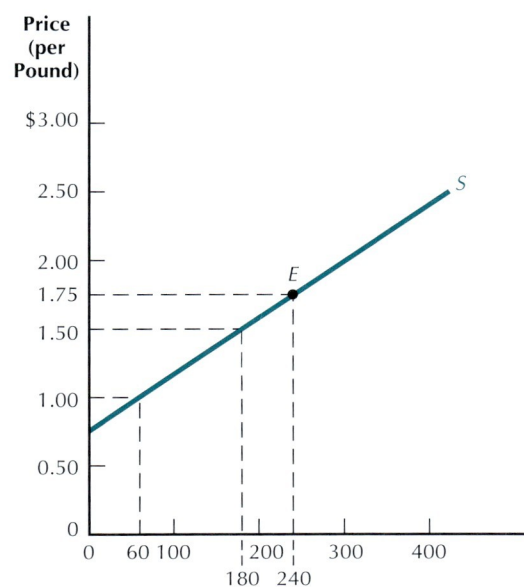

(a)

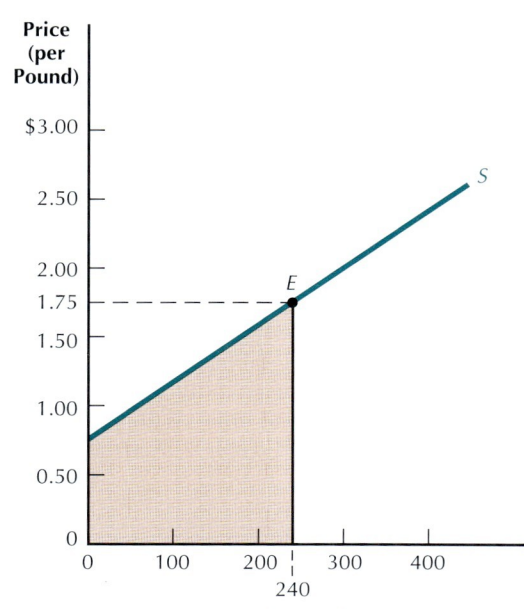

(b)

FIGURE 2
Costs of production of ground beef. (a) The supply curve shows producers' willingness to supply any particular quantity of ground beef. A pound of ground beef is supplied only if its price is equal to or greater than its marginal cost of production. The supply curve *is* the short-run marginal cost curve. (b) The total social cost of producing a given quantity of ground beef can be derived from the supply curve. The cost of producing 240 million pounds of ground beef is represented by the shaded area under the supply curve.

TABLE 1
Costs of producing picnic tables

Number of Tables	Total Cost	Marginal Cost
0	0	
		$50
1	$50	
		60
2	110	
		70
3	180	
		80
4	260	

Relationship between Total and Marginal

Economists continually make comparisons at the margin, examining the change in one variable in response to a unit change in another variable. Since the efficiency of market equilibrium is most easily demonstrated when the relationships between marginal value and total value and marginal cost and total cost are understood, we will examine the relationship between total and marginal more closely.

Table 1 presents a hypothetical cost schedule for a small firm producing picnic tables. Column 2 indicates that the total cost of production rises as more picnic tables are constructed. Column 3 derives the marginal cost of producing each additional picnic table. The marginal cost of a particular table is simply the addition to total cost incurred in the production of that table. For example, the marginal cost of the third picnic table is the difference between the total cost of producing three tables and the total cost of producing two tables: MC = $180 − 110 = $70.

Since marginal cost equals the change in total cost caused by producing an additional picnic table, the total cost of any particular number of tables equals the sum of the marginal costs of producing that number of tables. For example, the total cost of producing three tables is $180. The sum of the marginal costs of producing the first three tables is $50 + 60 + 70 = $180. *The sum of marginal costs equals total cost.*

The same principle applies to marginal benefits and total benefits enjoyed by consumers. The total benefits from consuming a particular quantity of a good equals the sum of the benefits enjoyed from consuming additional units of the good up to that quantity, in other words the sum of marginal benefits. Table 2 illustrates this.

The Economist's **Tool Kit**

TABLE 2
Benefits from buying and using picnic tables

Number of Tables	Total Benefit	Marginal Benefit
0	0	
		$200
1	$200	
		160
2	360	
		120
3	480	
		80
4	560	

Suppose consumers are willing to pay $200 to buy one picnic table. The marginal benefit of the first table is $200. Consumers are willing to pay $160 to acquire a second table, $120 for a third table, and $80 for a fourth. The total benefits of purchasing and using four picnic tables equals the sum of the marginal benefits: $560.

In mathematical terms, marginal cost equals the change in total cost divided by the change in the number of units produced:

$$MC = \Delta TC/\Delta Q$$

To derive an accurate estimate of marginal cost, the change in quantity produced should be small (for example, one unit rather than 100 units). Marginal benefit equals the change in total benefit divided by the change in the number of units consumed:

$$MB = \Delta TB/\Delta Q$$

Again, the change in quantity should be small.

supplying that unit. Such is the case at point E in Figure 3. To the left of point E the marginal benefit of an additional pound of ground beef exceeds its marginal cost. To the right of point E the marginal cost of an additional pound exceeds its marginal benefit. Marginal benefit equals marginal cost at point E. Society's net benefit from the production and consumption of ground beef is maximized by producing and consuming 240 million pounds of ground beef per month.

Figure 3 illustrates this. In Figure 3 (a) the social benefits of consumption are represented by the shaded area (light and dark) under the demand curve and the social costs are represented by the darker shaded area under the supply curve. For any given level of output up to 240 million pounds, the benefits of consumption exceed the costs of production. As output increases, the benefits of *additional* consumption decrease and the costs of *additional* production increase. The benefits of the 240 millionth pound just equal the costs of production. Beyond 240 million pounds marginal costs exceed marginal benefits, since beyond that output level the supply curve lies above the demand curve.

The *net gain* from producing and consuming 240 million pounds of ground beef is the difference between total social benefits and total social costs. The net gain from the ground beef market appears in Figure 3 (a) as the lightly shaded area under the demand curve but above the supply curve, the triangular area labeled ABE in the figure. This area pictures the gains to society from producing and consuming 240 million pounds of ground beef (sold at $1.75 a pound).

The net gains from exchange illustrated in Figure 3 (a) are enjoyed by two distinct groups, consumers and producers. Demand and supply analysis enables us to identify how the gains are distributed between the two groups.

Consumers' surplus
The difference between the value of a good to consumers and the amount consumers paid to acquire the good.

Consumers' Surplus   When society gains from an activity, both the size of the gain and how it is distributed to members of society are of interest. When the activity in question is the production, exchange, and consumption of a good or service via the market mechanism, a straightforward way exists to identify the share of the gain that accrues to consumers and the share that goes to producers. Figure 3 (b) compares what consumers are willing to pay to what they actually pay for ground beef. The demand curve tells us what they are *willing to pay*. The market price of $1.75 is what they *actually pay* for each of the 240 million pounds of ground beef. The difference between what consumers are willing to pay and what they actually pay is **consumers' surplus**. In this example, consumers' surplus is the lightly shaded triangle P_eBE. This area pictures the consumers' share of society's net gain from producing and consuming top quality ground beef.

Total consumers' surplus is the summation of individual consumer's surplus. Suppose Vinita would be willing to pay up to $2 for a pound of ground beef. If the market price is only $1.75 per pound, she is required to pay less for a pound of ground beef than it is worth to her. She consumes ground beef worth $2 to her but pays only $1.75 for it. The difference, 25¢, is a measure of the consumer's surplus Vinita enjoys from the transaction.

Other consumers value ground beef differently than Vinita does. Dave would be willing to pay $2.25 for a pound of ground beef, so he enjoys

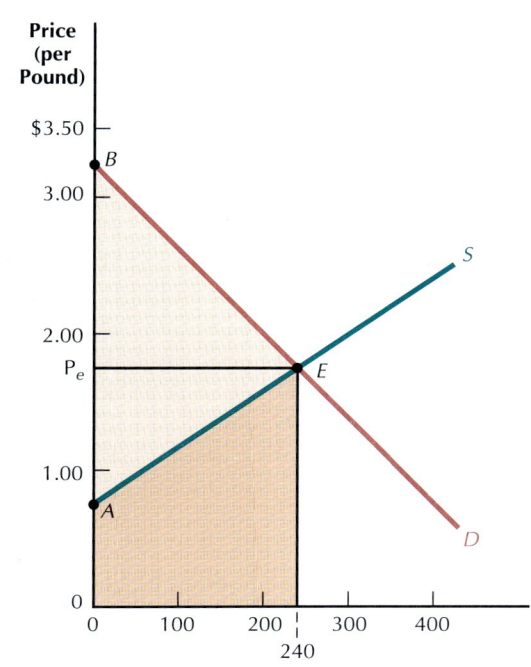

(a)

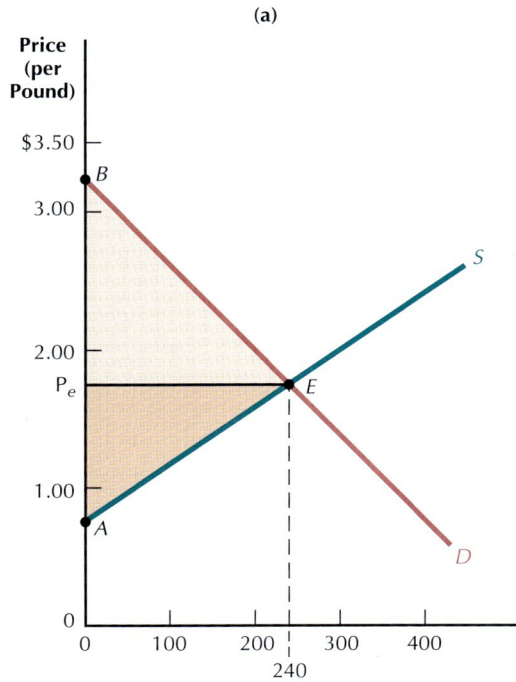

(b)

FIGURE 3
Net gain from producing and consuming ground beef.
(a) The net gain from producing 240 million pounds of ground beef is the difference between total benefits and total cost. The benefits and costs of production are taken from Figure 1 (b) and 2 (b). The difference, the lightly shaded triangle ABE, is the social net gain. (b) The net gain is divided between consumers and producers. The net gain of consumers, the lightly shaded triangle P_eBE, represents what consumers were willing to pay minus what they actually paid. The net gain to producers, the darker triangle AP_eE, is the difference between what producers receive and total production cost.

consumer's surplus of 50¢, but Lisa would be willing to pay no more than $1.75 for a pound of ground beef, so she obtains no consumer's surplus from buying a pound. The ground beef is worth exactly what she must pay for it.

Total consumers' surplus is the sum of the consumer's surplus enjoyed by each individual consumer who buys ground beef at a price of $1.75 per pound. It is a measure of how much more consumers would have been willing to pay for 240 million pounds of ground beef than they actually paid.

Producers' Surplus The share of society's net gain accruing to producers is the difference between the price at which producers would have willingly produced and sold each pound of ground beef and the price at which they actually sold each pound. This difference is called **producers' surplus**. For any given quantity of ground beef the supply curve tells us the price at which producers would be willing to produce and sell the ground beef. The market price ($1.75) is the price at which each pound of ground beef actually sells. For every pound produced and sold — except the very last pound — producers would have been willing to sell at a price below the market price. The sum of the difference between market price and supply price for each pound of ground beef sold constitutes the producers' surplus associated with the ground beef market equilibrium. The darkly shaded triangle AP_eE in Figure 3 (b) illustrates producers' surplus.

Producers' surplus
The difference between the revenue received by producers for a good and the opportunity cost of producing the good.

Conditions for Efficient Market Outcomes Are Restrictive

The market is an attractive rationing mechanism because, under certain conditions, it produces efficient outcomes while allowing decentralized decision making, thus solving society's basic economic problems while preserving considerable individual freedom. In economic markets the preferences of consumers and the costs of producers work through demand and supply to determine an equilibrium market price. This price rations the available quantity of goods on the basis of ability and willingness to pay.

A market equilibrium is economically efficient only if the demand curve reflects true social benefits and the supply curve reflects true social costs. A number of situations exist in which the demand or supply curve might not represent true social benefits or costs. Although economists disagree among themselves about the exact conditions required for economic efficiency, three conditions are generally agreed upon: Competition exists, all social benefits and social costs are incorporated into decision making, and the economy is relatively stable. These three conditions were implicitly assumed to hold in the discussion of market equilibrium and efficiency in Chapter 3 and in this chapter, though they sometimes fail to hold in real-world economies.[1]

---

[1] It should be noted that an efficient market outcome may be regarded as inequitable. If the initial distribution of wealth is very unequal — perhaps a few people are very wealthy and many are very poor — efficient markets will result in outcomes that are still unequal. Society may choose to intervene to adjust the initial distribution.

Competition Exists The efficient operation of a market hinges on the presence of competition. By **competition**, an economist means a situation in which neither individual buyers nor individual sellers are able to influence the market price. In practice this means that the number of buyers and sellers is large enough to prevent one buyer or seller from affecting the market outcome. The presence of competition makes pursuit of private gain consistent with social well-being. Individuals cannot use their market power to transfer wealth from other market participants to themselves. For example, if one producer dominates a market, that producer can force the market price above the competitive equilibrium level by restricting the quantity of goods supplied to the market. In such a case, goods are not produced even though their marginal social benefits exceed their marginal social costs. The market outcome is inefficient.

Competition
A situation in which no individual buyer or seller is able to influence the market price.

All Social Costs and Benefits Are Incorporated in Decision Making Consumers make consumption decisions based on the benefits derived from consuming goods. Producers make supply decisions based on production costs. Economic efficiency presumes that all social benefits and costs are incorporated in the process that establishes market equilibrium. If some of the benefits of consumption go to people who do not pay for the goods or some of the costs of production are borne by someone other than producers, demand and supply do not reflect true social benefits and costs.

The emission of pollutants into the air or water by firms provides an example of a divergence between private costs and social costs. If no antipollution laws exist, firms will treat the air and public waterways as free pollution-disposal resources. Although the cost to firms of polluting is zero, members of society pay through poorer health, and the attending higher medical bills, and through a lower quality of life. Because firms do not consider the true social costs of their activities in this instance, they tend to overproduce goods and underproduce environmental quality. The market outcome is inefficient.

Stability of the Economy Economic stability has several dimensions. At the most basic level, there is the requirement of stable rules of the game governing activity in an economy. In particular, efficiently operating economies must have a stable system of **property rights**—legal rights to own and use property as the owners see fit within the limits prescribed by law. In the absence of firmly established property rights, people are unwilling to innovate and invest or even to work harder than necessary. (The low productivity of collective farms in the Soviet Union is an example of this. Since workers who produce a lot have been paid no more than workers who produce little, workers have had little incentive to work hard.) If property rights are not respected, people realize that any economic goods they manage to accumulate might be taken away from them. People will engage in risky, innovative activities—the kinds of activities that drive a dynamic economy—only if they believe they will get to enjoy the benefits of their activities.

Property rights
Legal right to own and use property as the owner sees fit, within limits prescribed by law.

A second kind of stability relates to the monetary system. Most market trades are carried out using money as a **medium of exchange**—an asset generally acceptable in exchange for other goods and services. The general

Medium of exchange
An asset generally acceptable in exchange and used to make most purchases.

Value of money
Quantity of goods and services a unit of money will buy.

SECTION RECAP
The price–output equilibrium produced by a competitive market in which demand reflects all social benefits and supply reflects all social costs is efficient; it maximizes the net gains to society from producing and exchanging goods. When competition is absent, or when demand and supply in a market do not incorporate all social benefits and costs, the market outcome is inefficient.

acceptability of money facilitates trading, thus enabling extensive specialization in production to take place. Producers do not have to worry about being able to trade the products they produce for all the many products they want to consume. They simply sell their products for money and use the money to buy other goods and services.

An economy operates efficiently only if the monetary system is relatively stable. Uncertainty about the value of money in the present or in the near future can lead to serious inefficiencies as people fail to make beneficial exchanges because they fear the effects of monetary instability. Large changes in the **value of money**—what a unit of money will buy—can ruin some people while enriching others. Society as a whole suffers from such instability. Thus, governments have long regarded control of the value of money as a government right (though it is a right that has been abused repeatedly through the centuries).

Instability in the total flow of spending on goods and services in the economy can also reduce economic efficiency. If the flow of household spending in product markets declines sharply, the income received by producing firms falls. Lower incomes force firms to reduce their expenditures for productive inputs. Resources, including labor, are unemployed; the economy operates on the interior of its production possibilities frontier. Unemployed workers, lacking income, must reduce their purchases of goods and services. Thus, many potentially beneficial exchanges are foregone.

Market Failure

When any one of the three conditions is not met, the market fails in the sense that the market outcome is economically inefficient. Market failure implies that society, through government, has the *opportunity* to improve its well-being by intervening in the market or by using some nonmarket rationing device to allocate resources. Government intervention does not guarantee a social outcome superior to the market outcome, but the potential for improvement exists. Chapter 5 is concerned with when and how government should intervene to overcome market failures. Much of the rest of this book is devoted to two issues: (1) examining how markets work, so that the sources of market failure can be determined and possible solutions proposed, and (2) examining government economic policies to assess how well they have performed and how they might be improved. In the remainder of this chapter we assume that the conditions for market efficiency are met in order to examine how intervention in efficient markets leads to socially inefficient results.

Market Disequilibrium Generates Market Inefficiency

In a state of disequilibrium, the market price does not equate quantity demanded and quantity supplied. The resulting market outcome is inefficient. This section examines the social net gain from the ground beef market when the market price is below or above equilibrium. Comparing the net gain of each of these outcomes to that of the equilibrium case demonstrates the inefficiency associated with market disequilibrium, as well as demonstrating the fact that *competitive markets maximize net social gains*. This demonstration sets the stage for a discussion of the efficiency effects of **price floors** — laws or regulations that hold the market price above its equilibrium level — and **price ceilings** — laws or regulations that hold the market price below its equilibrium level. The general discussion is then applied to agricultural policies designed to keep market prices above equilibrium and to rent controls designed to keep apartment rents below equilibrium levels.

Price floor
A law or regulation holding the market price above its equilibrium level.

Price ceiling
A law or regulation holding the market price below its equilibrium level.

Price below Equilibrium

When market price is below its equilibrium level, a shortage develops — quantity demanded exceeds quantity supplied. Consider the situation illustrated in Figure 4 (a). When the price is $1.50, only 180 million pounds of ground beef are produced and sold, while 280 million pounds are demanded. Note that at 180 million pounds the marginal benefits of consuming more ground beef exceed the marginal costs of production. However, producers do not supply more ground beef because the marginal cost of supplying more than 180 million pounds exceeds the price of $1.50. When output for which benefits exceed costs is not produced, potential gains from trading are lost. The below-equilibrium price of $1.50 reduces the net social benefit from ground beef consumption by an amount equivalent to the darkly shaded triangle, FCE.

Price above Equilibrium

Market prices above equilibrium also cause market inefficiency. Producers supply quantities whose marginal cost exceeds their marginal benefit to consumers, thus reducing net social benefit. Suppose the price of ground beef is $2.25 a pound as in Figure 4 (b). At that price 360 million pounds of ground beef are produced, while only 160 million are demanded. A surplus of ground beef is created by the above-equilibrium price. Note that beyond the equilibrium quantity of 240 million pounds the costs of production (measured by the area under the supply curve) exceed the benefits of consumption (measured by the area under the demand curve). Output whose production costs exceed consumption benefits is produced. Too many resources are allocated to beef production. If the surplus ground beef is distributed to consumers, the net gain at the equilibrium price, ABE, is reduced by the loss (the darkly shaded triangle) EGF. If all or part of the surplus is destroyed, the loss is larger because consumers obtain no benefits from the surplus that is destroyed.

These two cases illustrate the uniqueness of market equilibrium: *At the equilibrium price only those units of output for which the marginal benefits equal or exceed the marginal costs are produced.* The net gain from production and consumption is maximized at this price. At any other price producers either (a) fail to produce output for which the benefits exceed the costs (underallocate

SECTION RECAP
The net gains to society are reduced when the market price is held either above or below its equilibrium level.

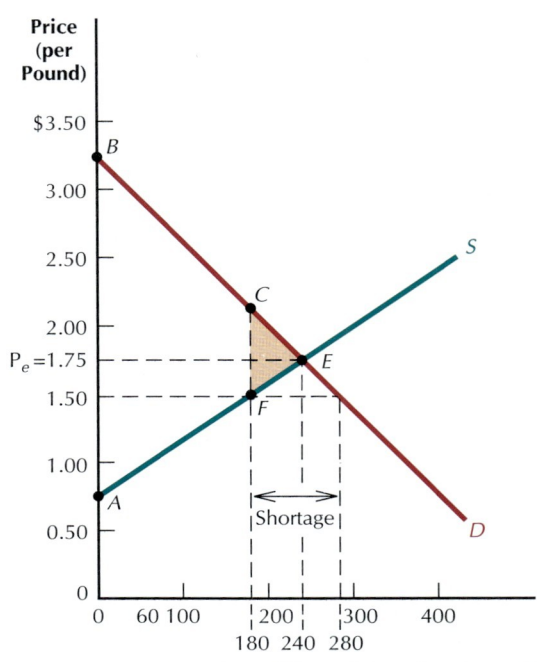

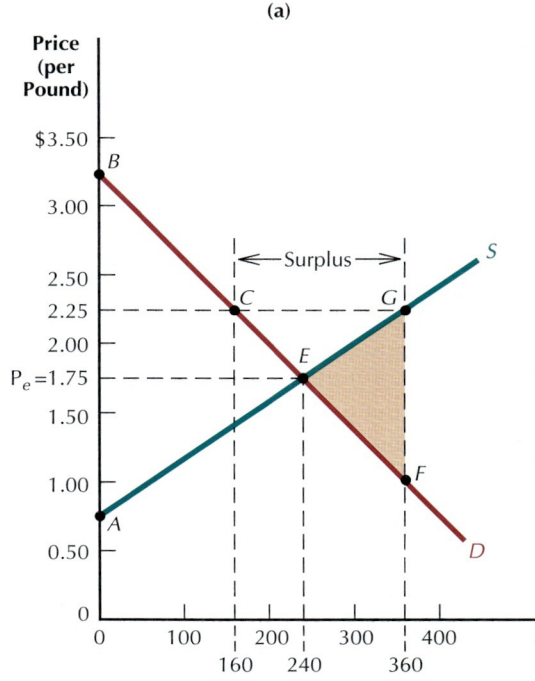

FIGURE 4
Disequilibrium prices cause inefficiency. (a) A below-equilibrium price causes a shortage: 280 million pounds are demanded but only 180 million pounds are supplied. Output for which the benefits exceed the costs is not produced. Social net gain is reduced by the shaded triangle FCE. (b) An above-equilibrium price causes a surplus: 360 million pounds are supplied but only 160 million pounds are demanded. The last 120 million pounds generate greater costs than benefits. Social net gain is reduced by a minimum of the shaded triangle EGF.

resources), or (b) produce output for which costs exceed benefits (overallocate resources).

Price Controls Introduce Economic Inefficiencies

Price controls—floors or ceilings—prevent markets from moving to equilibrium. Efforts to intervene in markets to control prices are not uncommon. Governments often attempt to regulate prices through decrees or legislation, declaring that prices in some markets are too high or too low. Consumers sometimes successfully lobby their governments to hold the price of housing or fuel below the equilibrium level. On the other hand, businesses often lobby government to hold prices above equilibrium levels on products they produce or to prevent so-called unfair competition. Numerous examples of such market intervention in the U.S. economy have been documented.

Price Ceilings and Floors

A price ceiling prevents a price from rising above a certain level. In the mid-1970s, a price ceiling was placed on the retail price of gasoline. The price of some natural gas sold in interstate markets was limited by a price ceiling until 1989. A price floor prevents the market price from falling below a certain level. Since the 1930s the United States has had a minimum wage law establishing a price floor in the labor market. Employers cannot legally pay workers covered by the law less than the minimum wage.

When consumers and producers are free to trade, their actions establish a market equilibrium price that equates quantity demanded and quantity supplied. The market's rationing and allocating function is carried out by price adjustments in response to changes in factors that affect supply and demand. A price floor or ceiling prevents the market price from moving to the equilibrium level, thus disrupting this rationing and allocating function. Two examples illustrate this.

Rental Housing

Several U.S. cities, including New York and Berkeley, California, have rent control laws. These laws establish maximum rents that landlords can charge. Such laws were enacted because of the widespread belief that apartment rents were too high. Proponents of rent control (typically tenant groups) generally argue that shelter is a basic need and that society should not allow its price to be so high that families cannot afford decent housing. Opponents (landlords and economists) argue that rent controls fail to provide affordable housing to the poor, instead creating a host of problems not encountered when the price of housing is allowed to move freely.

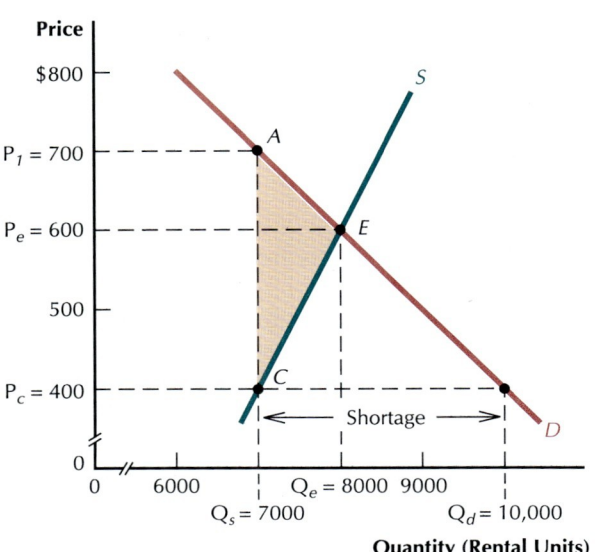

FIGURE 5
Effect of rent controls on the rental housing market. A rent control law establishes a price ceiling at P_c. Since P_c lies below the equilibrium price, P_e, a shortage of housing develops. At P_c, quantity demanded of $Q_d = 10{,}000$ units exceeds quantity supplied of $Q_s = 7000$ units. The rent control law prevents price from rising and eliminating the market disequilibrium and forces landlords to ration rental units by some other means. The net loss to society of the rent control law is represented by the shaded triangle CAE.

The equilibrium price established in the rental housing market reflects the interaction of supply and demand. When a price ceiling is established below the equilibrium price, the market price cannot rise to the equilibrium level.[2] The effect of a price ceiling is illustrated in Figure 5. In the absence of intervention in this particular market, the equilibrium price for rental housing would be $P_e = \$600$ per month and the equilibrium quantity exchanged would be $Q_e = 8000$ units rented. However, a rent control law establishing $P_C = \$400$ per month as the maximum rent prevents the market from reaching equilibrium. At the maximum legal price of $400 the quantity willingly de-

---

[2]A price ceiling is effective only if it is *below* the equilibrium price. If the price ceiling in Figure 5 were $P_1 = \$700$ per month instead of $400 per month, it would not affect the market outcome. Excess supply exists at a price of $700, and market forces would push the price down to its equilibrium level.

manded, 10,000 units, exceeds the quantity willingly supplied, 7000 units. The price ceiling generates excess demand for, or a shortage of, housing. In the absence of the price ceiling, consumers of housing would bid the price up, but the ceiling prevents the price from rising. Not all people who are willing to pay $600 per month for housing are able to obtain it.

When the price mechanism is not used to ration available housing, other rationing criteria arise. People who want rental housing must now look harder and spend more resources in the search. When an apartment is advertised for rent, many people respond. Apartment seekers try to be the first person to call the landlord. They might pay someone to help in finding an apartment or for information about upcoming vacancies. Or, prospective renters might offer bribes to landlords. Notice that, at $Q_s = 7000$ units in Figure 5, the price renters are willing to pay for rental housing ($700) exceeds the ceiling price. All or part of the difference could be offered as a bribe to a landlord and the renter would still benefit from the exchange.

In these circumstances, landlords can choose to rent to whomever they please, using any criteria they like when choosing tenants. Some landlords might choose to practice racial discrimination. Some will charge fees for services usually included in the rent or for such necessities as keys. Realizing a shortage of housing exists, landlords have the incentive to allow the quality of housing to deteriorate. Lower-quality housing is less costly to maintain, thus enabling landlords to earn a profit even at the below-equilibrium rental price.

Although rent control laws lower the market price of housing, the total cost to renters may not fall. In addition, such laws create other problems: a shortage of housing, rationing of housing according to arbitrary criteria such as race or sex, bribery, and deterioration in the quality of housing. In cities that have maintained rent control laws for several decades, abandoned apartment buildings are common. When the condition of apartments becomes so bad that they can no longer be rented out, landlords board up the buildings and abandon them. The removal of apartments from the market worsens the housing shortage.

Price ceilings are also economically inefficient. The shaded triangle CAE in Figure 5 represents the net loss to society resulting from the price ceiling. Some socially beneficial trades are eliminated by the ceiling. Some consumers are willing to pay a price higher than both the ceiling price for rental housing and the marginal cost of providing the housing. Although both consumers and producers would benefit from trading, the price ceiling prohibits these mutually beneficial exchanges from taking place. As shown in Figure 5, the monthly loss in social welfare generated by rent control is $150,000 (the area of the triangle CAE = ½ × $300 × 1000).

Agricultural Products

The prices of agricultural products, such as wheat, corn, cotton, and dairy products, have fallen over time relative to the prices of most other goods. Technological advances in genetics, pesticides, fertilizers, and farm implements have reduced the marginal costs of production and increased the supply of agricultural products. Since large-scale operations are able to use modern techniques and materials more efficiently than smaller farms, many small farms have been caught in a cost–price squeeze: Their costs have not fallen as fast as the prices of their products. In an attempt to raise agricultural prices and incomes the government long ago imposed price floors in various agricultural product markets.

The wheat market is a good example. The government maintains a support price, or price floor, for wheat. Figure 6 illustrates the effect of such a policy. In the absence of the price floor the wheat market would be in equilibrium at a market price of P_e = \$3.20 per bushel and quantity traded of Q_e = 1800 million bushels. The support price is designed to keep the wheat price above

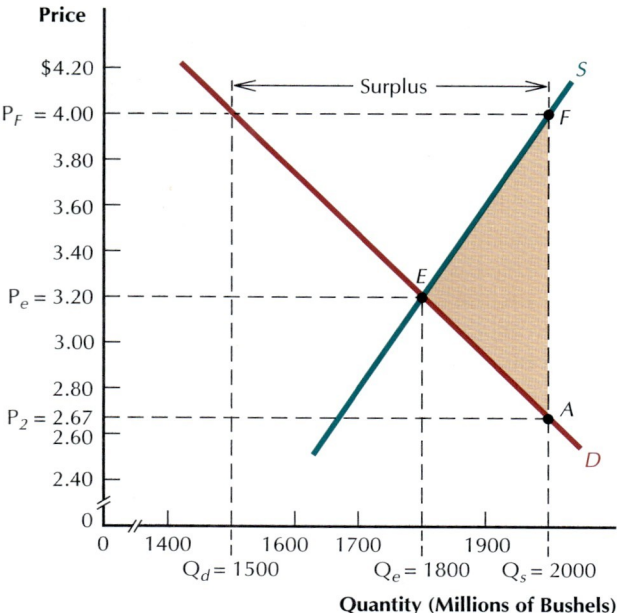

FIGURE 6
Effect of a price floor on the wheat market. An agricultural price support program establishes a price floor at P_f. Since P_f lies above the equilibrium price, P_e, it generates a surplus of wheat. At P_F, the quantity supplied of Q_s = 2000 bushels exceeds the quantity demanded of Q_d = 1500 bushels. The government stands ready to purchase the surplus wheat, since consumers will not buy it. If the government distributes the surplus wheat to those who value it most highly, the net social loss from the program is represented by the shaded triangle EFA. If the government destroys all or part of the surplus, the net social loss is even larger.

a certain level. This particular price floor is called a support price because, when necessary, the government takes action to support the price at $P_F = \$4$ per bushel. At the support price a surplus of wheat exists: The quantity supplied, $Q_s = 2000$ million bushels, exceeds the quantity demanded, $Q_d = 1500$ million bushels. In the absence of the price support policy, the price per bushel would fall from $P_F = \$4$ to $P_e = \$3.20$.[3]

At the support price, farmers grow more wheat than consumers are willing to buy. The government maintains a price of $4 per bushel by being a consumer of last resort. At the support price consumers are willing to buy only 1500 million bushels of wheat. To ensure that the market price stays at least as high as $4, the government must purchase the surplus wheat produced at the support price. Wheat farmers benefit from the guaranteed minimum price for wheat, but consumers pay a higher price for the wheat they purchase, as well as higher taxes to provide funds for the government purchase of surplus wheat. In addition, taxpayers must provide the funds to store and ultimately dispose of the grain. As in the case of rent control, the support program creates a number of problems that outweigh the benefits received by the favored group.

Price floors are also economically inefficient. Consumers improve their well-being by trading something of lesser value for something of greater value. Consumers exchange their income for wheat only when the wheat they obtain in return is more valuable to them than what they could have purchased with the income. The wheat price support causes wheat to be produced that would not be purchased voluntarily by consumers, that is, whose marginal cost exceeds its marginal value to consumers. If the surplus wheat is distributed to consumers, the net loss to society from the wheat price support program is represented in Figure 6 by the shaded triangle EFA, which in this example equals $133 million ($½ \times \$1.33 \times 200$ million). If the surplus wheat is destroyed, the loss is much larger than EFA, since consumers are paying for the surplus production through higher prices and taxes but are enjoying no benefits from it. In fact, the Department of Agriculture estimated that the wheat price support system cost American taxpayers alone over $1.8 billion in 1988.[4]

SECTION RECAP
Rent control laws hold the price of rental units below the equilibrium level. A shortage results, and the quality of rental housing deteriorates. Wheat price supports hold the price of wheat above the equilibrium level. A surplus results, and taxpayers and consumers lose more than producers gain.

Why Would Society Choose to Be Inefficient?

An economy is efficient when it uses all of its resources to produce at minimum cost those goods and services of most value to consumers. Since resources are scarce, it is costly to be inefficient; society goes without something it could have had. But societies have many, sometimes conflicting, goals, and efficient use of resources is only one of them.

---

[3] A price floor is effective only when it is established above the equilibrium price. If the price support were set at P_2 in Figure 6, competition between consumers of wheat would push the price up to P_e.
[4] *Statistical Abstract of the United States, 1990*, Table No. 1126, p. 649.

Does It Make Economic Sense?

Government Purchases of Entire Dairy Herds

The Food Security Act of 1985 provided for the government purchase of whole dairy herds from dairy farmers. Cattle purchased under the program were to be exported or slaughtered. Officials expected the implementation of the act to result in the slaughter of 1.5 million dairy cattle by August 1987. (In fact the program was shelved because of enforcement problems.) The program was established to help reduce a huge surplus of dairy products that government price support programs helped to create. Price support programs have become very expensive. For example, in the 1980s the government annually spent over $2 billion on dairy price support purchases. Does it make economic sense for the government to purchase and slaughter millions of dairy cattle?

Whether the whole herd buyout program makes sense depends upon one's point of view. People who believe that government should support the incomes of dairy farmers argue that the program makes sense in the context of the history of dairy policy. The program is simply the latest in a series of government interventions in the dairy market to increase prices and the incomes of dairy farmers. A system of price supports has held the market price above the equilibrium price since 1949. The price supports have led to increased production.

The Food and Agriculture Act of 1977 increased price supports substantially, and dairy farmers responded by sharply increasing production. By 1983 the government was attempting to reduce output by taxing dairymen who received price support payments but did not reduce production. The attempt failed. Later that year the government began to pay farmers for every pound reduction of milk output below their previous output levels. The government also helped organize a massive promotion and advertising program to encourage increased milk consumption.

Despite such policies, surpluses grew. By 1985 the government owned huge surplus stocks of dairy products: 153 million pounds of butter, 662 million pounds of cheese, and 993 million pounds of nonfat dry milk. (By the end of 1988 the government had 5.7 billion pounds of dairy products in storage.) The government cannot sell surplus stocks, because doing so would reduce market prices. The government's only options are to destroy the surplus stocks or give them away to people who otherwise would not purchase dairy products. Huge quantities of surplus dairy products have been given away under various programs.

The whole herd buyout program is a logical policy in the context of this policy history. Since government price supports and government-supported research into milk

Other Social Goals

In the United States the market mechanism is used to coordinate many individual decisions, in large part because it is consistent with two major goals: efficiency and individual liberty. However, intervention in a market or replacement of market decision making with some form of collective decision making is common when the market outcome is inconsistent with other social objectives. Ethical standards of fairness and justice lead us to refuse to trade some goods in markets. For example, people are selected for human organ transplants on criteria other than ability to pay, and slavery — the sale and purchase of human beings — is forbidden.

production have been so important to the dairy industry for four decades, many government officials and politicians argue that ending supports would be excessively harmful to dairy farmers; the industry is dependent on the government's help. This puts the government in an uncomfortable position: It is difficult, if not impossible, to reduce price supports or production without hurting the industry.

Viewed from the economic perspective developed in this book, the dairy support program does not make sense. The basic problem is that consumers are unwilling to pay a price that makes milk production at current levels profitable. Farmers produce output whose marginal costs exceed marginal benefits. As a consequence of the program, dairy prices are higher than they otherwise would be and taxpayers must pay higher taxes.

Programs such as the herd buyout program often do not achieve their primary objective — reduced surpluses — because of the actions of people who do not participate in the programs. For example, when some farmers sell out to the government, others who remain in business may profitably expand their own herds, offsetting the expected decrease in output. Furthermore, market intervention often creates problems in other markets. A successful buyout program would increase the number of cattle being slaughtered, depressing the market price of beef, making cattlemen worse off. Government concern about the possible effects on beef prices led lawmakers to place restrictions on the number of dairy cattle that could be slaughtered and to require the U.S. military to step up its purchases of beef, increasing the demand for beef and supporting beef prices.

Such programs as the whole herd buyout plan would be unnecessary if dairy prices were not maintained at artificially high levels by government policies. None of these dairy programs makes sense on economic efficiency grounds. The buyout plan was designed to reduce government expenditures on the dairy programs, while continuing the price and income support programs that created the problem.

A society can pursue any number of goals. The goal of economic efficiency has been discussed at some length, and other important goals are familiar. Individuals seek to improve their material standard of living. *Economic growth* is the means by which a society's overall standard of living is increased. Societies also place a high value on *national security. Individual liberty* and *equity* concerns are also important. Different cultures have different notions of fairness and justice, and these views shape the means by which decisions are made as well as the importance attached to various social goals.

Many decisions are made through collective means, including some through the political decision-making process. Criteria other than willingness to pay and economic efficiency are important in political decision making. National security is not left to the private market. (Chapter 5 discusses why these decisions are made collectively.) The government purchases goods and services for national defense, but the production and sale of such goods is not subject to the same forces as is the sale of goods and services exchanged in a market. (This is one reason why we often read about problems between the government and its contractors.) Government concerns about national security influence many other economic policy decisions. Some people even argue that the various agricultural programs are justified on national security grounds, an argument used to defend protection of other domestic industries from foreign competition.

Agricultural employment has shrunk so much that it now accounts for less than 3 percent of U.S. jobs. It could conceivably get even smaller if further productivity gains occur or U.S. consumers buy more agricultural products from other countries. Should we allow this vital industry to become so small? An adequate and secure food supply is important to society. If the United States were to become engaged in a major war and outside sources of food were suddenly cut off, we would be at a disadvantage if our domestic industry could not adequately respond to demand. Thus, some supporters of American agriculture argue that the inefficiency associated with agricultural programs is justified as part of the cost of our national security.

Noneconomic criteria often dominate political decision making. Twentieth-century American society has its roots in agriculture. The United States was a rural society as recently as the early twentieth century. Many people value the tradition of the family farm. In a market context, tradition may carry little weight, but in a political context, it might be important enough to persuade voters to support legislation that seems to help maintain the well-being of those citizens still on the farm, even though it is economically inefficient.

Another element of the farm problem receives a great deal of attention in the political setting but much less in the market context. Economic losses are a signal to owners of resources that profitable opportunities in an industry are shrinking. Losses prompt resources to leave the industry, reducing supply and pushing up price. Resource mobility is important to the competitive functioning of markets. Our market model implicitly assumed that the movement of resources in and out of markets is costless. However, resource mobility is not costless. When a firm goes out of business, the firm's owners often suffer losses. The firm's workers are unemployed and must look for new jobs. Such developments may impose hardships, at least temporarily, on individuals and families.

In a market context, adjustment costs are simply part of the price paid for the functioning of a healthy market and the efficiencies gained from the market. In a political decision-making context, however, such human costs may be accorded more importance. In the case of agriculture, mobility costs are high. People who have grown up on a farm, who are only familiar with a rural life, must change their way of life. They must look for employment elsewhere, and frequently they must move to a city. The costs of such a fundamental change in lifestyle can be very important in political decision making. Politicians may opt for policies that are inefficient economically because they want to reduce emotional and social costs.

Conflicting social goals make it difficult for government decisions to be satisfactory with respect to all social goals. In fact, most such decisions are compromises. Licensing health care practitioners may reduce competition and efficiency, but it improves the quality of health care for society. Requiring the use of seat belts restricts individual freedom, but is also saves lives. A random-lottery military draft is an inefficient way to obtain human resources for the military, but it may be consistent with society's notion of selfless service to one's country. The government might respond to an international political development by eliminating trade with another country. By its action the government sacrifices some economic efficiency to achieve a political objective.

Income Redistribution

One of the three basic economic questions that all societies must answer is, For whom are society's goods and services produced? In a pure market economy, access to goods and services is determined by the resources one possesses. Markets ration goods to those willing to pay the most, and market outcomes are efficient, *given the existing distribution of income.* This point is an important one to remember. There is no efficient income distribution. Although a particular income distribution affects the outcomes of market transactions by affecting the structure of demand, it does not determine whether the market outcomes are efficient or not.

The distribution of income generated by a market economy may not be consistent with society's sense of a fair or just distribution of income. Since a fair distribution of economic well-being is an important goal for most societies, they may choose to redistribute income in an attempt to achieve more equitable distributions. Although Americans value individual liberty, the U.S. government taxes workers to provide Social Security income to retirees. Some liberty is sacrificed to achieve the redistribution of income. We are willing to let a family's income be determined by the efforts of its members — and luck — only so long as the family is not too unfortunate. Employed workers are taxed to provide income to unemployed workers. Society provides a minimal income guarantee to low-income single-parent families with young children. Such programs both satisfy notions of fairness and promote social stability.

A wide array of policies and programs designed to redistribute income from some groups to other groups exists. What people in a society consider to be the best income distribution for that society depends on the people's sense of fairness and equity; it is determined by normative considerations. In some societies income is distributed very equally, but in others it is distributed very unequally. Religious and ethical values have an important part to play in the economy, since they are important determinants of a society's goals and values.

Efficiency—Equity Tradeoffs

Although economic efficiency is independent of the initial distribution of resources in an economy, policies designed to redistribute income usually affect

Why the Disagreement?

The Distribution of Benefits from Farm Programs

The principles underlying current agricultural programs have not changed for fifty years, although these programs have been controversial since their inception. Disagreements flare up each time agricultural legislation is reconsidered and revised, a process recently occurring about every five years. Everyone involved in the legislative process understands that U.S. agricultural policies are inefficient. However, a majority of legislators believes that the distributional benefits of the farm programs outweigh the costs of inefficient production. A vocal minority strenuously disagrees. Why the disagreement?

Without a doubt, the income redistribution aspects of farm policies underlie the longevity of the programs. Using farm programs as a way to redistribute income is legitimate, however, only if these programs are effective vehicles for achieving the income redistribution goal. Let us assume that the specific objective of these policies is to provide income support to those farmers whose incomes are being eroded by the divergent trends in farm income and farm costs, especially those farmers who are financially distressed and are finding it difficult to generate enough income to finance their indebtedness. With these objectives in mind, two important questions arise: Who pays for the programs? Who benefits from the programs?

The answer to the first question is well known. The burden of agricultural programs falls on consumers (who pay higher food prices) and taxpayers. The burden falls disproportionately on low-income consumers, because they spend a larger share of their income on food than do higher-income consumers.

Are the programs' beneficiaries financially troubled farmers? Unfortunately, the answer is, Not in general. Consider the following evidence. Farms vary widely in size and in annual sales. Many farms are smaller than 100 acres and annually market less than $2,500 in products. Other farms consist of more than 5,000 acres and have annual sales in excess of $500,000. The financial well-being of the

the efficiency of markets to some degree. By distorting the demands of consumers or the supplies of producers, redistributional policies drive the market price and output away from the equilibrium levels that would exist in the absence of intervention. Both consumers and producers lose. Some redistributional policies have only minor effects on the efficiency of markets, while others impose huge costs on society by reducing efficiency dramatically. Thus, if income redistribution is a social goal, it is important to design redistributional programs so that their negative effects on efficiency are minimized. Redistributional policies that reduce efficiency by an unnecessarily large amount make society poorer by eliminating the production of goods and services that could be used to satisfy wants.

Examples of redistributional policies that appear to have large negative effects on economic efficiency are not hard to find in the United States or abroad. For example, in Germany unemployment insurance benefits are so generous that many unemployed workers remain unemployed for many months or even years. They refuse to accept jobs (to supply labor services) because the alternative of paid leisure is so attractive. This problem exists to a lesser degree in the United States as well. Another example of inefficiency created

farm, its net income, and the value of government payments vary by farm size as well.

If we rank farms by the annual value of their sales and look at various measures of well-being or profitability, we see dramatic differences. We also see the impact of the government support programs. The 14 percent of all farms with annual sales in excess of $100,000 account for 48 percent of all farm acreage and 76 percent of all farm sales. (All figures are based on 1987 data.) *These farms also receive nearly 58 percent of all government payments to farmers,* an average annual payment of $18,787. The one-half percent of all farms with the highest sales (about 11,000 farms) receive 3.2 percent of all government payments, the average payment being $27,636. (In 1986, one farmer got a check for $12 million!) By contrast, the 76 percent of farms with the lowest sales, about 1.8 million farms, generate almost 24 percent of farm sales and receive only 42.4 percent of government payments. The average payment to these farmers was $2,280 in 1987.

When the General Accounting Office examined the debt position of farmers receiving government payments, it found a pattern similar to the one above: Two thirds of government payments go to those farmers with the fewest financial problems and the largest net worth.

The evidence suggests that agricultural programs do not work very well as income redistribution programs. They are financed primarily by the less well-to-do, and they distribute government payments primarily to relatively well-to-do farmers.

---

by a redistributional policy was the diversion of resources from productive uses into tax shelters that took place before the reduction of income tax rates in the 1980s. Wealthy individuals, who faced marginal income tax rates (that is, tax rates on the last dollars of income earned) in excess of 50 percent, often preferred to invest in nonproductive ventures that exploited tax loopholes rather than investing in productive market activity. The U.S. government not only lost billions of dollars of tax revenue, but also the economy suffered because valuable resources were misallocated to nonproductive uses.

Since what constitutes a fair income distribution is more a matter of values than of analysis, economists have little if any comparative advantage in discussions of what the income distribution *should be.* However, once an income distribution goal has been set, economic analysis can contribute greatly to the achievement of that goal at a minimum cost to society.

Why Is Economic Efficiency So Important to Economists?

The topic of economic efficiency receives more attention than any other topic in Part I of this text and provides the motivation for much of the analysis in the remainder of the book. Why do economists devote so much attention to this particular social goal and relatively little to the other goals mentioned in this chapter? The reason for paying so much attention to economic efficiency is probably clear by now, but it bears repeating. Being economically efficient is the logical response to the basic economic problem of scarce resources relative to human wants. Economic inefficiency implies that society is failing to satisfy some wants that could be satisfied at no social cost.

The extent to which society is successful at achieving economic efficiency affects the achievement of other objectives. An efficient economy has more income to redistribute, should it choose to do so, than does an inefficient economy. Efficient environmental policies minimize the cost of protecting the air and water. An efficient economy promotes economic growth and the resulting increases in living standards. Other social goals may reduce the level of economic efficiency that could be achieved if efficiency were the *only* social goal, but that does not mean that the economy should not be as efficient as possible within the constraints imposed by other social goals.

Inefficient Markets and Government Intervention

SECTION RECAP
Societies have many goals besides efficiency. Some of these goals may conflict with the goal of efficiency, leading governments to adopt inefficient policies. Still, given the other goals adopted by government, being as efficient as possible is important, since being inefficient needlessly reduces social welfare.

This chapter has examined agricultural markets and policies as a vehicle for explaining and illustrating the notion of economic efficiency. Although agricultural policies generally have been poor policies from the perspective of economic efficiency, they have persisted for over fifty years in basically the same form.[5] The reason for the persistence of inefficient agricultural policies must be that they satisfy, to some degree, other social goals — equity, national defense, preserving tradition. Has the cost been worth it? Society — and its policymakers — must address this question, since it is clear that government intervention in otherwise competitive markets has been quite costly.

Government intervention in markets less perfect than agricultural markets may be far less costly and more beneficial to society. When markets do not meet the conditions necessary for efficient market outcomes, government intervention may be able to improve efficiency while simultaneously addressing other social goals. Chapter 5 considers in some detail the potential benefits from government intervention in imperfect markets.

Summary

Economic efficiency is defined as the achievement of the maximum difference between benefits and costs. Under well-defined conditions the equilibrium achieved through market decision making is economically efficient.

---

[5] It should be noted that, even in the face of massive government intervention, market forces dominate in the long run. The size of the agricultural sector has dwindled steadily throughout this century.

Since a demand curve tells us how much consumers are willing to pay for each quantity of a good, we can calculate the total benefits from consuming a given quantity of a good by adding up the amount consumers are willing to pay for each additional unit. Similarly, the supply curve tells us the marginal cost of producing each unit of a good. The social cost of producing a given quantity of a good is calculated by adding up the marginal opportunity cost of producing each unit of output.

The **net social gain** from producing and consuming a good can be derived from market demand and supply by subtracting the cost of production from the benefits of consumption. The difference is the net gain to society. The net gain is greatest when the market price and quantity exchanged are the equilibrium price and quantity.

The net gain from an activity can be divided into **consumers' surplus** and **producers' surplus.** Consumers' surplus is the difference between what consumers would have been willing to pay to consume a given quantity of the good and what they actually had to pay. Producers' surplus is the difference between the price producers actually received for a good and the minimum price for which they would have produced and sold the good.

At least three conditions must be met for markets to operate efficiently. First, markets must be **competitive.** No single buyer or seller can use market power to affect the market price. Second, **private costs and benefits must equal social costs and benefits.** Third, the economy must be **stable** enough to permit people to engage in beneficial trades.

Disequilibrium market prices are inefficient relative to the equilibrium price. A market price below equilibrium leads to a **shortage.** Output for which the marginal benefits of consumption exceed the marginal costs of production is not produced. Resources are underallocated to this market, and mutually beneficial exchanges are not made.

A disequilibrium market price above equilibrium leads to a **surplus;** more output is produced than is consumed. Output for which the marginal production costs exceed marginal consumption benefits is produced. Resources are overallocated to this market.

Price floors and ceilings introduce inefficiency into market outcomes because they establish market prices above or below the equilibrium price. In the United States a system of price floors has long been used to support agricultural prices and to stabilize and enhance farm incomes.

The United States has maintained and expanded an array of programs that are clearly inefficient in an attempt to achieve other social goals. Economic efficiency is only one among many potentially conflicting goals. The desire to achieve an **equitable income distribution** often leads societies to alter the distribution of income generated by the market. In addition, once the government has intervened in a market, political decision making becomes an important influence. Political decision making is subject to different forces than market decision making.

Questions for Thought

Knowledge Questions

1. Explain why and how the benefits of consuming a given quantity of a good can be calculated from the demand curve.

2. When the market price is above the equilibrium price, as is the case with a price floor, resources are overallocated to the market. Explain what overallocation means.

3. Explain the concepts of consumers' and producers' surplus.

4. Why is economic efficiency important even in an economy that chooses to engage in massive income redistribution?

Application Questions

5. In Figure 3 point A is at a price of $0.75 and point B is at a price of $3.25. Calculate the net gain in dollars from producing and consuming 240 million pounds of ground beef. (Hint: Remember the area of a triangle is equal to ½ × base × height.)

6. Describe the consumer's surplus that you gain when you purchase and consume one unit of a particular good.

7. Figure 4 (b) illustrates the impact of a $2.25 price floor on ground beef. What changes in demand or supply would make the price floor completely ineffective? Explain.

8. In Figure 4 (b) point F is at a price of $1 and point G is at a price of $2.25. What is the net loss to society of an above-equilibrium price *if the surplus production is distributed to those who value it most highly?* What can you say about the net loss to society if the surplus production is destroyed?

Synthesis Questions

9. Suppose that a rent control law is being considered for your college town. The law would keep apartment rents below present equilibrium levels.
   a. Who would favor the law? Who would oppose it? Why?
   b. How would your strategies for finding and renting an apartment be altered by the law?
   c. How would the behavior and policies of landlords be altered?
   d. Draw a graph, illustrating the inefficiency of this law.
   e. Can you think of an alternative policy that might address the problem of high rents, yet be less inefficient? Explain.

10. Suppose the social cost of production in a market exceeds the private cost of production (perhaps because firms ignore the social costs of pollution).
    a. Where does the social supply curve lie relative to the private market supply curve?

b. Draw a graph showing the excess social costs of operating at the free market equilibrium level.
c. Suppose the government imposes a tax on the good in question, increasing private production costs. Is such a tax inefficient *under these circumstances?* Explain your answer.

11. Explain why the efficiency of an economy is independent of the income distribution existing in the economy.

OVERVIEW

Our discussion of economic principles has covered a lot of territory. Chapter 1 examined the basic economic problem of scarcity, discussing the implications of this problem for decision making. Chapter 2 considered specialization and exchange as the best means for meeting the wants of societies in the face of limited resources. Chapter 3 continued this discussion in more specific terms by discussing the market as the mechanism for specialization and exchange. By intentionally ignoring some real-world complications we developed a simple model of supply and demand that illustrates the gains associated with free trade. Chapter 4 used the market model to illustrate more formally the efficiency of market outcomes and the inefficiency that can accompany market intervention. We were careful to note that market outcomes are efficient only under well-defined conditions. Chapter 4 also considered social goals that might conflict with efficiency.

Decision Making in an Imperfect World

In this chapter we look more closely at situations in which all the conditions necessary for economically efficient market outcomes are not met. When one or more of the conditions are not met, an opportunity exists for nonmarket decision making to improve on the market outcome. We discuss the kind of government decision making that might improve upon the market outcome. However, it is important to remember that government action does not ensure an improvement on the market outcome. Some potentially serious problems are associated with government decision making just as with market decision making. We identify and discuss several important potential problems with government action.

CHAPTER 5

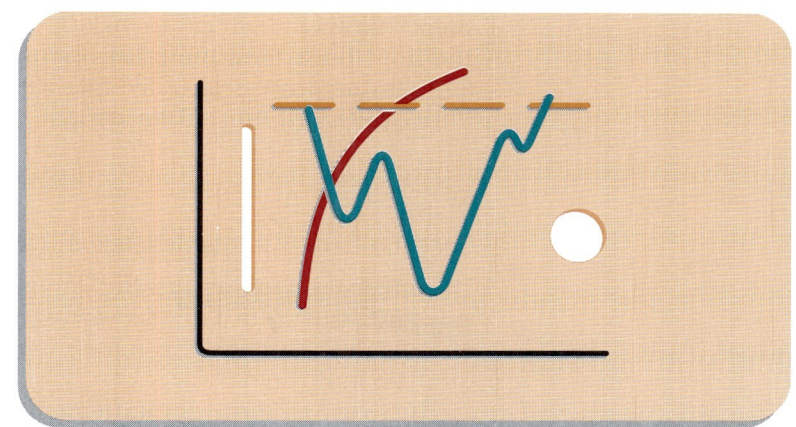

The topics discussed in this chapter serve as a guide and outline to the major economic issues developed and discussed throughout the remainder of the text.

Learning Objectives

After reading and studying this chapter, you will be able to:

1. List and explain four conditions that can cause market outcomes to be inefficient.
2. Define externality.
3. Explain the free rider problem.
4. Provide three basic reasons why government action may not improve upon market outcomes.
5. Apply basic economic principles to political behavior and explain the implications of this analysis for government decision making.

The Market Mechanism Is a Decision-Making Device

A modern economy is an exceedingly complicated machine for getting things done. The number of different goods and services produced in an economy is difficult to imagine. Consider, for instance, the range of products available in a single grocery or hardware store, much less a shopping mall. How do people decide to produce all those products? What prompts individuals and companies to invent and develop the new products that are introduced each year? How do companies determine all the different jobs to be performed and then get people to do them? In the United States more than a hundred million people go to work each day at different jobs in hundreds of thousands of companies scattered all across the country. What ensures that enough clothes, computers, pencils, colas, office buildings, parks, books, and tomatoes are produced? What guarantees that there will be enough welders, programmers, salespersons, physicians, plumbers, secretaries, musicians, engineers, hairstylists, and farmers to produce all these different goods?

The answer to all these questions seems a bit shocking. A market economy simply allows individuals to make their own decisions about what to consume and how to use time and other resources. All of these questions are answered through the process of individual decision making. In fact, decentralization works quite well most of the time.

Decentralized, But Interdependent, Decision Making

Decentralized decision making is possible because of the coordination provided by markets. In a market economy an individual's decisions are not made in isolation. Through the interaction of supply and demand, markets coordinate individual choices.

It is easy to forget the extreme interdependence of our decisions. When Harry decides to buy a new compact disc, he goes to the music store and plunks down the $14 price of the disc. This is, of course, exactly the way most day-to-day purchases are made. It is useful to consider this simple decision more carefully, however. Harry's decision to purchase the $14 disc was influenced by the decisions of millions of other people: consumers, producers, and resource owners. The price was determined by both demand and supply. The demand for compact discs depends on consumer tastes for CDs and all other products, as well as the incomes of consumers. The supply of discs depends on the cost of resources necessary to manufacture discs, and the cost of these resources depends on the outcomes of other markets. Technology influences the cost of producing the discs and other products as well as the kinds of other products available. All of these forces influence the determination of a price for compact discs. When any of these many factors changes, the price of CDs is affected, and Harry's consumption decision may be altered—which in turn affects the decisions of many other people.

Markets not only coordinate individual decisions, they actually promote specialization and interdependence. Economic decisions have to do with exchanges—mutually beneficial exchanges. Harry trades $14 of money income for a compact disc because it is more valuable to him than anything else he could obtain with $14. The music store sells the CD for $14 because its owner is better off without the CD and with the money income. These mutually beneficial exchanges are made on the basis of comparative advantage.

Trade on the basis of comparative advantage increases economic well-being and encourages specialization. The gain from a trade is the difference between the value of what is given up and the value of what is acquired in trade. When people specialize in activities in which they have the lowest opportunity cost and trade for economic goods for which they have relatively high opportunity costs, the benefits of trade increase. Markets facilitate trade and specialization. One of the reasons that modern economies are so complex is the extensive specialization brought about by trading. The complexity of a modern economy masks these simple, but fundamental, patterns of specialization and interdependence.

How Markets Resolve Society's Three Economic Problems

In performing its rationing and allocating functions, the market mechanism resolves society's three basic economic problems.

What Is Produced? In a market system, consumers are free to consume those goods and services that they find most beneficial to them. Consumers buy goods for which the consumption benefits exceed the costs. Producers have an incentive to produce those goods that are most valuable to consumers, because producers benefit the most by satisfying consumer wants. In a market economy, consumers are sovereign. They vote with their dollars. Willingness to pay is reflected in higher prices, which attract more producers and lead to increased supplies.

How Are Goods Produced? Because prices moderate consumption and producers must compete for consumer dollars, producers have an incentive to keep costs down. If a producer is inefficient in production, a competitor will be able to produce the good at lower cost and attract customers away. There exists a strong incentive to be efficient in production, to use the best available technology, and to look for an even better technology for tomorrow.

For Whom Are Goods Produced? The goods and services produced in a market economy are rationed to those consumers willing and able to pay the highest price. Ability to pay is determined by one's income, which in turn reflects the quantity of resources owned and supplied to the market. Those who supply more resources and who supply those resources to the most highly valued uses have higher incomes. Since income determines one's command over other goods and services, the incentive to supply resources to their most productive employment opportunities is strong.

In a market economy, the distribution of income is unequal. High-income and low-income consumers bid for available goods and services. High-income individuals are able to buy more goods and services, but low-income consumers make offers sufficient to acquire goods in many markets. Not only ability to pay, but also willingness to pay, determine who gets available economic goods.

The Invisible Hand

The most important attribute of the market system is that through market exchanges the decentralized, independent decisions of individuals are coordinated in a systematic and beneficial way. Individuals make decisions in their own self-interest, seeking to improve their economic well-being. When decisions are coordinated through the market mechanism, the rational, self-interested responses of economic agents to changes in prices have unintended beneficial impacts on the economy. This is the rationing and allocating function that the market performs. If more people prefer to buy compact discs rather than cassette tapes, they will bid CD prices up. The higher price will attract profit-seeking businesses, which will produce increased quantities of compact discs. The increased supply moderates the increase in CD prices. Tape prices and quantities fall as consumers purchase more CDs and fewer tapes. No single planner directs that these changes be made. Individuals, acting in their own self-interest, bring about the changes.

The most important, and to many the most amazing, attribute of market decision making is that, under well-defined conditions and with a minimum of government involvement, the market achieves economic efficiency for society. When individuals are left alone and allowed to pursue their own private well-being, they unwittingly increase society's well-being. This beneficial social effect of the pursuit of individual self-interest was labeled the *invisible hand* by Adam Smith, the father of modern economics. In *An Inquiry into the Nature and Causes of the Wealth of Nations* (1776) he described it this way:

> As every individual . . . endeavors as much as he can . . . to [maximize his own economic well-being], every individual necessarily labors to render the annual revenue of the society as great as he can. He generally, indeed, neither intends to promote the public interest, nor knows how much he is promoting it. . . . he intends only his own gain, and he is in this . . . led as if by an invisible hand to promote an end which was no part of his intention.

SECTION RECAP
Prices coordinate the interdependent decisions of millions of consumers and producers in a market economy. The market system allows individuals to make their own decisions, within the constraints imposed by resources and consumer preferences, thus maximizing individual liberty.

This invisible hand is the most attractive attribute of the market mechanism: The individual pursuit of self-interest is consistent with society's achievement of economic efficiency. However, the invisible hand works to the benefit of society only if markets operate in a reasonably efficient manner. Market failure can lead to a sharp divergence between private and social benefits. The next two sections consider major causes of market failure and how society might act to overcome these failures through government policies.

Problems for the Market

In this section we examine in some detail four circumstances in which the market mechanism fails to generate an economically efficient outcome: (1) lack of competition, (2) the presence of externalities, (3) the existence of public goods, and (4) the lack of economic stability. The causes of the problems are identified and possible corrective actions that could be taken by the government are discussed. The four cases account for many of the major economic problems that a society faces and for much of the debate and controversy surrounding economic policy.

Lack of Competition

The beneficial effects of the market mechanism derive from the presence of competition among economic decision makers. Competition limits the gains that accrue to people acting in their own self-interest. Consumers want to obtain the benefits of consumption at as low a price as possible, but the bids of other consumers for the same goods limit gains from consumption. Producers want to maximize profits, but the price they charge is limited by the competition of other firms seeking to sell to the same consumers. Competition makes earning profits more difficult.

In a world of scarce resources, benefits (consumption goods, profits) can be obtained only at a cost. Everyone would like to obtain benefits at as low a cost as possible. Thus, an incentive exists for both consumers and producers to attempt to minimize the competition they face, thereby obtaining desired goods at a lower cost. By reducing competition, consumers may be able to buy at a lower price or producers may be able to sell at a higher price.

Firms can benefit from a reduction in the competition they face by charging higher prices and thus earning larger profits. Firms can avoid competition in a number of ways, including becoming large enough to prevent competitors from entering the market, and colluding with other sellers. When large firms employ mass production techniques to produce output, the investment in capital equipment can be enormous. The cost of constructing huge, expensive production facilities can discourage other firms from competing in the market. Firms also sometimes **collude** — agree to sell output at a specified price. If all firms agree, competition among them is effectively eliminated.[1]

The effect of reduced competition is reduced output and higher prices. By restricting the quantity of goods supplied to the market, noncompetitive firms force the market price up. Consumers pay higher prices per unit for a smaller quantity of goods and lose the benefits of consuming some goods whose marginal social benefits exceed their marginal social costs.

In a modern economy a number of markets exist with firms that are large relative to the size of the market. The presence of relatively large firms usually means fewer firms in an industry. Examples of industries dominated by a few large firms are electrical equipment manufacturing, paper and paper products manufacturing, and the steel, auto, and computer hardware industries. The smaller the number of competitors, the easier it is to organize and maintain a collusive agreement. Thus, the potential for market inefficiency due to lack

Collude
Agree to sell output only at an above-equilibrium price.

---

[1] Though a proponent of free markets, Adam Smith was well aware of the harmful effects of collusion. Once again quoting from *The Wealth of Nations:* "People of the same trade seldom meet together, even for merriment and diversion, but the conversation ends in a conspiracy against the publick, or in some contrivance to raise prices."

of competition is high. In this setting, the potential exists for government action to improve upon the market outcome by penalizing collusion and taking other actions designed to reduce prices and increase output.

If government action is to reduce the inefficiency associated with a lack of competition, the specific market circumstances leading to reduced competition must be specified and government policies that address these circumstances must be developed. One of the major concerns of **microeconomics**—the study of consumer and firm behavior in individual markets—is how the structure of markets affects competition.

> **Microeconomics**
> Study of consumer and firm behavior in individual markets.

Presence of Externalities

When making decisions, people pay attention to the benefits they enjoy and the costs they must bear. Our discussion of market decision making and supply and demand has implicitly assumed that the private costs and benefits motivating individuals equal the social (private and public) costs and benefits of their actions. We assumed that the price paid by a consumer reflects the social cost of producing the good, and that the private benefits from consumption and production equal the social benefits.

However, situations exist in which the costs or benefits of consumption and production activities are experienced by others without their consent. When a nonsmoker sits next to a smoker and breathes cigarette smoke, the nonsmoker's well-being is affected by the smoker's consumption behavior. The nonsmoker bears a cost because the smoker enjoys cigarettes. Commuters who drive during rush hours in large urban areas impose costs on other commuters by contributing to traffic congestion. Lost time and greater risk of accidents add to the normal costs of driving (such as fuel and wear and tear on the car).

Consider one more simple example. Suppose Sandi lives in a house in an old neighborhood in town, and one by one her neighbors begin to improve their homes by adding aluminum siding, renovating their plumbing and wiring, and landscaping their yards. Although Sandi makes none of these costly improvements, her house becomes more valuable, because it is now in a nicer neighborhood. The value of Sandi's house is increased by the actions of her neighbors. They incurred costs to improve their homes, and Sandi benefited from their expenditures at no cost to herself.

These examples are instances of **externalities**, market exchanges that impose costs or bestow benefits on people who do not participate in an exchange. Externalities are often called **spillover effects**, because the actions of producers or consumers spill over into the lives of other people. An **external cost** is a cost imposed by a market transaction on individuals who are not party to the transaction. Environmental pollution is an external cost associated with many different market transactions. When a manufacturer emits pollutants into the air or water, he avoids the cost of eliminating the pollutants, thus selling his product to consumers at a lower price than would otherwise be possible. However, others in society, including individuals who do not buy or benefit from the manufacturer's products, suffer the cost of the pollution. An **external benefit** is a benefit generated by a market transaction that accrues to individuals

> **Externalities (spillover effects)**
> Market exchanges that generate costs or benefits for people not directly involved in the exchanges.
>
> **External cost**
> Cost of a market transaction imposed on someone other than the parties to the transaction.
>
> **External benefit**
> Gain from a market transaction going to an individual other than the purchaser of the good.

who are not party to the transaction. In the example above, Sandi gained economic benefits from the actions of her neighbors although she incurred no costs to obtain those benefits.

In market transactions in which social and private benefits and costs are equal, no externalities exist; all costs and benefits are included in the decision making of market participants. An externality causes social benefits or costs to exceed private benefits or costs. Since market participants pay attention only to the benefits and costs they experience, some benefits or costs are omitted from decision making. When externalities are generated by a market transaction, the market equilibrium outcome is not efficient.

The problems that externalities cause for the market mechanism are illustrated in Figure 1. Figure 1 (a) shows the effects of external costs on the market outcome. Assume that the suppliers in this market emit water pollutants in the process of producing their product. In making production decisions they are free to ignore the social costs of pollution. Thus, the production costs they incur are less than the social costs of producing the output. The difference between social and private costs is illustrated with two supply curves. Supply curve S_{Priv} reflects the private costs to producers and interacts with demand, D, to determine the market equilibrium price and output, P_2 and Q_2. But S_{Soc} is the true supply curve, reflecting the cost to society of producing output. At every output level social costs exceed private costs. If there were no external costs, that is, if producers were forced to pay all social costs when producing the product, the market equilibrium would be at E_2 instead of E_1, at a higher price and lower output level.

Figure 1 (b) illustrates the inefficiency resulting from external costs. External costs cause society to overallocate resources to the production of the good. When the external costs are ignored by market participants, society produces output for which the social costs of production exceed the benefits, the increment to output $Q_2 - Q_1$. In the absence of external costs, the social gain from production would be ABE_2, the difference between social benefits and social costs. But since some costs are ignored in the market, firms produce output that reduces the net gain by the amount E_2CE_1 — the amount by which the total social costs of producing the output between Q_1 and Q_2 exceeds the social benefits from its consumption. Too much output is produced in markets with external costs.

External benefits cause economic inefficiency, but in a different manner than external costs. When social benefits exceed private benefits, resources are underallocated to the market and too little output is produced. Consider the benefits of vaccinating for contagious diseases. When a person is vaccinated against a disease such as measles, other people who associate with the vaccinated individual benefit from the vaccination. The probability that the individual's family, friends, and work associates will catch measles is reduced. Thus, the social benefit from a vaccination exceeds the private benefit.

Figure 2 (a) depicts this problem. Consumer demand is captured by D_{Priv}, which reflects the private benefits of vaccination against a contagious disease. Since external benefits exist, social benefits exceed private benefits. Demand curve D_{Soc} reflects social benefits — the benefits to vaccinated and unvaccinated people from vaccinations. The vertical difference between the two demand curves is a measure of the external benefits of vaccination received by

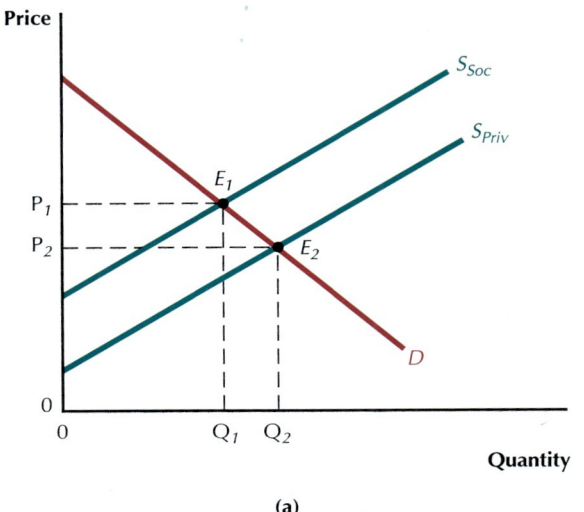

(a)

FIGURE 1
External costs. (a) When private and social costs diverge, external costs exist. Producers fail to take into account all social costs. They behave as if the supply curve is S_{Priv} rather than the true social supply curve S_{Soc}. The result is an equilibrium at E_2 rather than at E_1: External costs lead to lower market prices and higher output. (b) For a market outcome to be efficient, a good should be produced until the marginal benefits from consumption equal the marginal social costs of production. A market with external costs violates this rule. At Q_1, marginal social benefits equal marginal social costs. The net gain to society is ABE_1. However, external costs cause resources to be overallocated to this market; production expands to Q_2 units. Each additional unit between Q_1 and Q_2 generates social costs in excess of social benefits. The net gain to society from the production and consumption of the good is reduced by an amount equivalent to the area E_2CE_1.

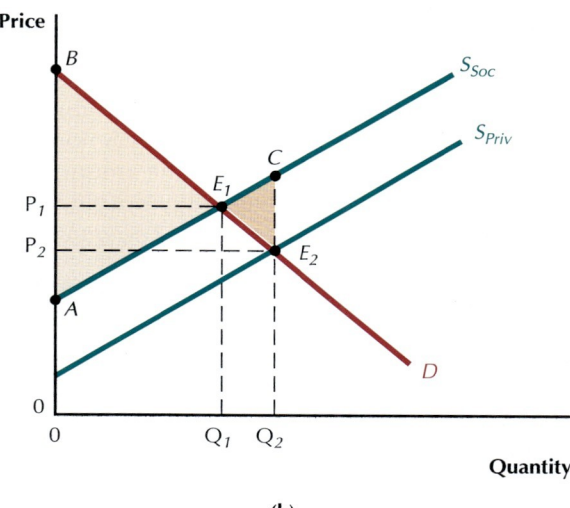

(b)

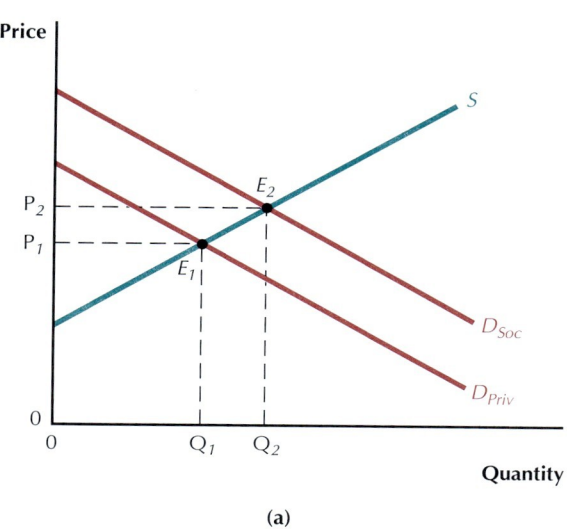

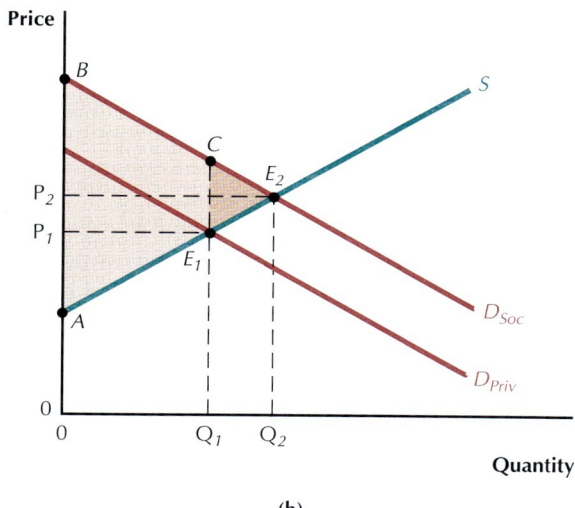

FIGURE 2
External benefits. (a) External benefits arise when private and social benefits diverge. In this example D_{Soc} represents true social benefits and D_{Priv} represents only private benefits. Consumers in this market pay attention only to private benefits. Thus, the market equilibrium is at E_1. Market price and output are reduced by the presence of external benefits. (b) The omission of social benefits from private decision making causes the output produced and consumed to fall short of the efficient level. With external benefits, society produces and consumes only Q_1 units. However, the benefits of producing additional units of output exceed the costs until output level Q_2 is reached. Expanding production to Q_2 would increase the net social gain from producing and consuming the good by an amount equivalent to the area E_1CE_2.

unvaccinated people who are less likely to contract a contagious disease because other people have been vaccinated for it. Market equilibrium is determined by the interaction of consumers and producers, both of whom act only upon private benefits and costs. The result is an equilibrium at E_1. However, additional output beyond the Q_1 level generates social benefits in excess of costs. Society benefits from the production of additional units of output (more vaccinations) up to output level Q_2. These units are not produced because the external benefits are ignored by market participants. Consequently, resources are underallocated to the market. The net gain to society is measured by $ABCE_1$ in Figure 2 (b). The gain could be increased by E_1CE_2 if the external benefits were taken into account and output increased to Q_2, since social benefits exceed social costs for all the vaccinations between Q_1 and Q_2.

When externalities exist, appropriate government actions can improve upon market outcomes. Government action that internalizes externalities by making private benefits and costs reflect social benefits and costs has the potential for moving the market outcome closer to the economically efficient level. Governments might intervene in the market through taxes or subsidies, enact some sort of regulatory policy, or assign ownership rights for previously public property to specific people or organizations. While such actions are potentially beneficial, in practice making the appropriate corrections through government action is difficult.

Existence of Public Goods

Our study of the production and consumption of economic goods and services has thus far implicitly assumed that all goods and services are **private goods**, goods whose use by one person (in consumption or production) means that less is available for use by others. When a person buys a gallon of gasoline or a pizza, less gasoline and fewer pizzas are available for consumption by others. Markets do a good job of allocating resources when economic goods have this characteristic of privateness.

Private good
A good whose use by one person reduces its availability for use by other people.

Some goods are not private goods, however. Some economic goods can be consumed by more than one person without reducing the quantities of the good available for use by other people who cannot be excluded from enjoying the benefits of the goods. Such goods are called **public goods**. The maintenance of city streets and highways is a public good. Once the potholes have been filled, everyone who drives on the roads benefits from the maintenance work, and one person's trip on the road does not reduce the supply of good roads available for others to use (ignoring congestion problems). National defense is another excellent example of a public good. When a nation establishes a given level of defense capability, it is consumed by all citizens. The consumption of defense by one person does not reduce the amount available for consumption by others. An idea or a technique is a public good. When someone discovers the biochemical process within the human body that causes cancer cells to develop and multiply, that understanding can be put to work to prevent cancer. The new understanding of the causes of cancer is a public good. The ideas are available for use by everyone, and the use of the ideas to save one

Public good
A good whose use by one person does not reduce its availability for use by other people.

person from cancer does not prevent the ideas from being used to save other people.

How does society decide the quantity of public goods to produce and who should pay for them? In the case of private goods, the market mechanism provides good answers to these questions. Private goods are produced when the benefits exceed the costs, and those consumers who value the goods the most — measured by willingness to pay — pay for the goods and consume them. However, the market mechanism is of little help in answering these same questions for public goods.

Unless consumers can be excluded from the consumption of public goods, they will not reveal their true willingness to pay for public goods. They have an incentive to **free ride** on other consumers. Consumers know that once national defense is provided, all will benefit regardless of how much any individual is willing to pay. National defense cannot be provided to only a select few who pay for it. If it is provided to one person, it is provided to everyone. Thus, individuals have an incentive to act as if the public good is of little or no value to them in the hope that they will enjoy the benefits of the good without having to bear the costs of providing it — the **free rider problem**.

Under such conditions, the market mechanism fails as an efficient rationing device. Consumers will not voluntarily pay an amount equal to the true benefits they receive from the public good. Instead, they act as if the value of the good is much less than it really is. Under such conditions, it might be impossible for any private producer to supply the public good profitably, and if some private producers could make a profit, the market equilibrium output would generally be far less than the economically efficient output level. When public goods are provided by the market, resources are underallocated to the activity.

Public goods present a serious problem for markets. A more centralized decision-making process through some kind of government action is generally necessary to ensure that public goods are provided in quantities that approach efficient levels. The federal government provides national defense and collects taxes to pay the costs. Federal, state, and local governments tax their constituents to generate funds to construct and maintain roads. Note that sometimes governments can identify the primary beneficiaries of public goods and force them to pay the costs of providing the public goods. Many states have toll roads that are paid for only by the people who travel the roads. The federal government funds much of its highway construction by means of fuel taxes. Governments also provide direct research support and copyright and patent protection to those individuals who expend resources developing ideas of value to society, thus enabling researchers and inventors to benefit from the provision of public goods and increasing the supply of such goods.

In the area of public goods, the opportunities for socially beneficial government action are great. However, difficult problems still must be resolved for government action to produce efficient outcomes. A key problem is the determination of the economically efficient quantities of public goods to be produced. In addition, when public goods or services are produced in the public sector, or are produced by only one or two private producers who do not face competitive pressures, it is difficult to ensure that they are produced efficiently.

Free ride
To consume without paying an appropriate price.

Free rider problem
Incentive for consumers of public goods to understate the true value of the good to them in order to reduce the amount they must pay to consume it.

Does It Make Economic Sense?

Restrictions on Cigarette Smoking

Recent years have witnessed a growing concern about the long-run health consequences of cigarette smoking, which has resulted in increased regulations governing smoking. The federal government regulates smoking on airlines, trains, and buses. Smoking is no longer permitted on commercial airline flights of less than six hours. Some cities have banned smoking in public places. In 1986, San Francisco adopted a relatively comprehensive ban, and in 1988, New York City enacted smoking restrictions. Many firms have also adopted policies that substantially restrict the locations in which their employees are permitted to smoke, and the number of firms with such policies is growing. Do bans on smoking make economic sense?

By treating cigarette smoking as an economic good, we can use economic tools to analyze the problem. Cigarette smoking produces an external cost. Many nonsmokers dislike breathing cigarette smoke. In addition, growing evidence indicates that nonsmokers who breathe cigarette smoke suffer adverse long-term health consequences. Figure 3 illustrates the problem for society. Cigarette consumers and producers are able to ignore the external costs of smok-

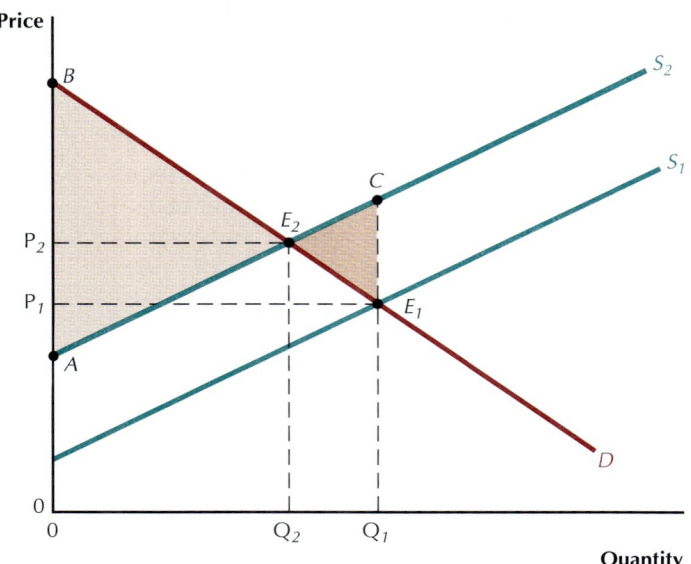

FIGURE 3
Market for cigarettes. When nonsmokers breathe the smoke of cigarette smokers, they bear an external cost of smoking. If the full social costs of smoking were borne by smokers the quantity of smoking would be reduced and society would be better off. Ignoring external costs, the cigarette supply curve is S_1. The social supply curve, which includes external costs, is S_2. At the market price of P_1 the quantity of smoking (Q_1) is inefficient, since the social costs of each additional pack of cigarettes smoked beyond Q_2 exceed the social benefits. The net social gain from smoking, ABE_2, is reduced by the amount E_2CE_1. Policies designed to reduce smoking or restrict where smoking can occur can move society closer to Q_2, thus generating a net social gain.

ing. As a result, the cigarette market equilibrium is E_1, with a lower price and higher output level than the socially optimal equilibrium that incorporates all social costs of smoking (E_2). This outcome is inefficient because resources are overallocated to smoking. The additional cigarette output $Q_1 - Q_2$ generates costs in excess of benefits.

Society would benefit if cigarette output were reduced to Q_2. The problem is how to achieve this market adjustment. Can market methods be used or is government action necessary? The government could simply ban all smoking. This strategy seems unlikely to succeed given the number of people who smoke. Because the benefits consumers enjoy from smoking exceed the social costs in some situations, society is better off in an efficiency sense if it allows smoking. A ban would cost society the net gain from Q_2 cigarettes. Such a ban could also be viewed as restricting individual freedom.

At the other extreme, market methods could be used to incorporate the omitted external costs into the decision making of cigarette consumers. If cigarette smokers were forced to compensate nonsmokers who breathe their smoke, the externality would be eliminated. The cost of smoking would rise, and less smoking would occur. However, this solution is exceedingly impractical because people consume a common property that is owned only by society at large—the air around us. (Cigarette smoke would not be a problem if each person had a private air supply.) It is difficult to imagine the chaos and the costs that would be generated by a system that requires each cigarette smoker to negotiate a payment to every nonsmoker exposed to secondhand smoke.

The policies being adopted to deal with the smoking problem represent a compromise designed to achieve a feasible solution that moves society closer to the social equilibrium represented by Q_2. The adopted policies attempt to deal with the worst aspects of the externality, yet preserve some individual liberty for everyone. The bans have been adopted for situations in which smoke presents the worst problems for nonsmokers, such as in airline cabins. The bans usually provide arrangements whereby both smokers and nonsmokers have designated areas to which they can retreat to avoid offending others.

Lack of Economic Stability

A nation's government plays a vitally important role in the functioning of its economy. While this point is obvious for countries with centralized decision making, such as the Soviet Union or China, it is equally true of decentralized, market economies. In market economies, an important function of the government is to establish the rules of the game. A market economy functions through mutually beneficial exchange, which depends on the assignment of private property rights — private ownership of economic goods. Individuals must have a legal right to the goods or services they produce or purchase. Governments establish the systems by which ownership is defined and enforced.

The absence of secure property rights sharply reduces the incentive for individuals to invest and take risks in the hope of increasing their personal wealth. The entrepreneurship that drives dynamic market economies is likely to be absent. Instead, people are tempted to simply get by, since any excess goods and services beyond their immediate needs might be confiscated at any time. Long-range planning and the economic benefits that accompany it — saving, capital accumulation, and economic growth — depend on a system of stable property rights.

Governments also seek to promote a different kind of stability — macroeconomic stability — over shorter periods of time. As explained in Chapter 4, the uncertainty that accompanies monetary instability reduces economic efficiency. Market participants make more mistakes than they do in an environment of stable prices, and the amount of long-term contracting undertaken is reduced. Some potentially beneficial exchanges are never made. Economic research has shown that a strong connection exists between the growth and variability of the money supply and the growth and variability of prices. Since national governments partially control the monetary system through regulation of banks and other financial institutions and through direct intervention in the system by government-controlled **central banks**, the responsibility for maintaining monetary stability falls on government.

Monetary policy — government control of the money supply as a means of influencing the overall level of economic activity — affects output and employment as well as prices. The process through which money affects the level of employment of society's resources is complex and is a major concern of **macroeconomics** — the study of the behavior of the economy as a whole. However, the fact that monetary policy does affect employment is undisputed. Since economic efficiency hinges on the full employment of society's resources, government is again responsible to some degree for maintaining conditions favorable to the efficient use of resources.

Monetary policy is not the only tool of government stabilization policy. Governments also use **fiscal policy** — the power to tax and spend — as a tool to affect the level of macroeconomic activity. Through judicious use of its policy tools, government can to some degree smooth out *business cycles* — the periods of rapid expansion or contraction of economic activity that characterize market economies. Unfortunately, wide disagreement among economists exists as to what judicious use of policy tools is. This makes macroeconomics a somewhat unsettled, but very lively, area.

Central bank
Governmental agency that controls a nation's money supply.

Monetary policy
Government control of the money supply as a means of influencing the level of economic activity.

Macroeconomics
Study of the behavior of the whole economy.

Fiscal policy
Use of government powers to tax and spend to affect the level of economic activity.

SECTION RECAP
The outcomes produced by markets are not efficient if there is a lack of competition, if externalities cause private and social costs and benefits to diverge, if many goods are public goods, or if the economy is unstable because of a weak system of property rights or macroeconomic instability.

Opportunities for Collective Action

Centralized decision making addresses the same problems as market decision making. Society seeks to solve basic economic problems: what, how, and for whom to produce goods and services with the use of scarce resources. Government action may be a good alternative or supplement to market action when one or more of the four problems described above exists. When government action is taken in these instances, the primary objective is to do a better job of tackling the "what" and "how" questions facing society. Government does a better job by improving upon the economic efficiency of the market outcome. Governments tackle the "for whom" question when they enact laws that alter the distribution of resources or income in society. Although economic efficiency is of concern when considering changes in the distribution of income, society's notions of equity or fairness often outweigh efficiency considerations, as we saw in Chapter 4.

Although government decision making offers an opportunity to improve on market outcomes when the market fails, government action does *not* ensure an improved outcome. A government solution could conceivably make the situation worse. For example, a governmental program to reduce pollution could be too costly: Pollution might be reduced, but at a cost in terms of forgone output that far exceeds the benefits of reduced pollution. Or government efforts to manage the level of economic activity might turn out to be destabilizing, making inflation or unemployment worse than it was before the government intervention. Or government regulation of firms might reduce competition among firms instead of increasing it.

Some government economic activities fail to improve on the market solution simply because policymakers do not have enough information to accomplish what they seek to do. Many examples of such governmental failures exist. Governments that have attempted to replace the market with governmentally determined allocation of resources have found that the information required to efficiently allocate resources is simply too great for central planners to comprehend. Inefficiency has resulted. Other governments have engaged in active management of the macroeconomy in an attempt to maximize economic growth and stabilize employment. Often such activism has led to disappointing results—inflation, instability, and low growth rates. The complexity of the macroeconomy is so great that even policies designed by the brightest policymakers have had unintended consequences.

Government policies may prove to be less than optimal for another reason. Politicians and government officials sometimes have incentives to implement policies that fail to maximize net social benefits. The next section applies economic principles to the study of political behavior, an endeavor known as the **economics of public choice**.

Economics of public choice
Application of economic principles to the study of political behavior.

The Economics of Public Choice

Economic analysis is based on the assumption that individuals choose among alternatives on the basis of expected net gain to themselves. The relative benefits and costs of an action determine whether it is chosen or not. The same general principle of economic decision making can be applied to political behavior. How do voters choose a candidate for whom to vote? They vote for the candidate who appears to support those programs and policies that will most benefit themselves. Politicians are elected if they appear to satisfy the preferences of a majority of the voters better than alternative candidates. Knowing this, candidates tend to support policies favored by a majority of their constituents. The point here is straightforward: In their roles as voters and politicians, individuals behave in a manner consistent with improving their well-being, just as they do in their roles as consumers and producers.

Economists have been applying basic economic principles to the study of political behavior for over three decades. The purpose of public choice analysis is to evaluate public decision making on the same terms as market decision making. We have already reviewed the conditions under which decentralized market decision making reconciles the pursuit of individual self-interest with the achievement of maximum social welfare. By analyzing public decision making in the same way, we seek to establish conditions under which such decision making leads to maximum social welfare as well.

The first question that public choice theory must address is very basic: Assuming that individuals pursue their self-interest, do forces exist that harmonize the interests of public decision makers with the social welfare? If the political marketplace is really competitive — potential candidates do not face extraordinary barriers when attempting to run for office, voters have good information on the positions of candidates and the actual voting records of incumbents, potential voters actually vote — elected officials will find it beneficial to represent the interests of their constituents. However, if such competition is absent, elected officials may benefit more by pursuing their private interests than by promoting the interests of society as a whole. In this case, public decision making may produce results that are both inefficient and inequitable. Unfortunately, a number of unique characteristics of the public choice process may bias the decisions of government officials against pursuing socially optimal policies. We consider potential problems first on the voter, or demand, side of the political marketplace, and then on the politician, or supply, side.

Voters as Consumers In a representative democracy, individual citizens elect representatives to make public decisions for them. They vote for the candidates who they believe will best represent their interests. In turn, the political well-being of candidates depends in large part on their ability to satisfy the wishes of those they seek to represent. Political officeholders are agents of voters. When voters cast their ballots in support of a particular candidate, they expect that candidate to work to provide public goods and services desired by the voters. Voters are like consumers, using their political ballots to obtain desired public goods and services through their elected representatives.

Although consumers in markets and voters seeking to satisfy wants through the public sector are both motivated by individual self-interest, they face different constraints on their ability to acquire valuable goods and services. We mention three important differences.

Individual Voters Cannot Unbundle Goods and Services. Because voters must support one person to represent them on a wide variety of public matters, they cannot vote for only those public goods and government policies they want.

They must vote for one candidate who will support a number of different government policies, some of which inevitably run counter to the wishes of some of the candidate's supporters. By voting for one candidate, voters opt for one bundle of goods instead of another. With one vote individuals express their preferences on a wide range of government-provided goods and policies, such as national defense, support for higher education, welfare policy, and support for space exploration. Voters are able to register their preferences only weakly, compared to consumers who are buying private goods or services.

Furthermore, a politician must support the majority view or not be reelected. There is an element of compulsion in public sector action that is absent in the market. Private consumers purchase and consume only the goods of most value to them; they do not purchase goods they dislike. However, voters who hold minority views are provided with public goods and government policies they may dislike.

Individual Voters Can Get a Free Lunch but Society Cannot. In the private sector all economic goods are costly. Consumers must sacrifice some of one good to obtain another. In less formal terms, *there's no such thing as a free lunch.* However, this fundamental rule does not apply to individual voters. A new government policy may benefit some voters at the expense of others. It is possible for governmental action to confer benefits on some voters at no cost to them. Rational individuals understand this possibility and support government actions that benefit them personally. People support tax laws that reduce their taxes—but someone must pay for government services. Senior citizens tend to support expanded Medicare benefits. Those of us in higher education tend to support increased funding for student loans and scholarships. Nearly everyone has some favorite public service that produces private benefits far in excess of individual costs.

Of course, society cannot get something for nothing. A governmental action that confers benefits on one group of voters must be paid for by someone else. Increased Medicare benefits make senior citizens better off at the expense of other members of society who must pay higher taxes or go without other government services. More generous loans and scholarships to college students help them finance their educations and increase the demand for the services of university faculty, but this increased support must be paid for by other taxpayers. An individual or group of individuals may be able to escape the resource constraint through some kind of government action, but society certainly cannot escape it.

The Costs of Being Informed May Exceed the Perceived Benefits. If voters are to make choices that maximize their benefits, they must have good information about the candidates running for office. Poorly informed voters may vote for candidates who support positions quite different from those held by the voters. However, acquiring information about a politician's position on the full range of issues decided by the political process is costly. Time, effort, and perhaps money are required to collect the information needed to understand the issues confronting political decision makers. The expected benefits from collecting such information may be small for two reasons: (1) Individual voters gain or lose very little from many political decisions, and (2) a single voter is not likely to be able to change the outcome of the political decision-making process even if fully informed. When the costs of acquiring information exceed the expected benefits from having the information, voters may choose to remain ignorant of the issues being addressed by their elected representatives. Thus, the complaints frequently encountered in newspapers about uninformed voters often miss the point that it may be rational to be uninformed.

Since it is much less costly to choose a candidate by watching television news programs and advertisements and reading news coverage of speeches than it is to investigate detailed positions on a number of issues, many voters obtain their information about candidates secondhand. Political parties, or other kinds of labels, are shortcuts to identifying a candidate's position on issues.[2] Voters may also follow the advice given in particular newspapers or magazines because they find themselves in general agreement with the views of the editors.

Once elected representatives are in office, voters tend to ignore how they vote on most issues. Rarely do voters attempt to persuade their representatives to change their positions on political issues. For many people the perceived benefits of such investments are not large enough to outweigh the costs. Such an attitude may lead to the adoption of legislation that benefits a few at the expense of many.

The problem with the view that ignorance of the political process is rational is that the majority of voters may ultimately lose control of government to a minority who aggressively work to ensure passage of legislation favoring them. The proper functioning of an elected representative government depends on the existence of an informed electorate. To the extent that the electorate is uninformed about the issues confronting public decision makers, the public decision-making process tends to be dominated by special-interest groups that forcefully pursue legislation beneficial to their members, even if the legislation is harmful to society as a whole. The ultimate result of rational ignorance, then, may be the conversion of representative government into a political contest among interest groups seeking to use government for their own private ends, whatever the social consequences.

SECTION RECAP
Political markets may fail to produce socially beneficial outcomes because voters must vote for a bundle of governmentally provided goods, rather than for individual goods; some voters may attempt to transfer wealth from other voters; and voters may be uninformed about the positions adopted by their representatives.

Politicians as Suppliers   Political candidates and politicians, like other decision makers, are motivated by self-interest. They seek to supply, or produce, the public sector goods, services, and policies demanded by their constituents. The motivation for a private sector firm is profits. The motivation for a politician is reelection. Politicians respond to their constituents because they want to be reelected.[3]

At first glance such an incentive structure for politicians may seem reassuring in the sense that one can expect politicians to be responsive to the

---

[2]Labels such as "environmentalist" or "pro-life" can convey substantial information about the positions candidates will adopt as legislators, since voting in opposition to such labels is easy to detect. Voters who feel betrayed can then punish their legislator by voting for his opponent in the next primary or general election. Thus, adopting specific labels constrains the voting patterns of legislators.

[3]Some public choice studies have assumed that politicians are income maximizers who seek to use their political powers to increase their incomes as much as possible. Maximizing reelection chances and maximizing income produce different behavior in some instances. We will examine only the reelection assumption in this text.

voters. Producer response to the dollar votes of consumers is part of the process that makes markets good rationing devices: Consumers get what they are willing to pay for. In a truly competitive political market, elected representatives would have powerful incentives to represent the wishes of their constituents on many, if not most, issues. Unfortunately, the problems on the demand (or voter) side of the political market, combined with some additional problems on the supply (or politician) side, imply that the desire of politicians to be reelected and their responsiveness to voters is not necessarily consistent with achievement of overall social welfare. Two important biases can affect the decision making of politicians.

The Power of Special Interests. The equal distribution of votes in a democracy (one person, one vote) does not ensure that political power is equally distributed. A **special-interest group** is a well defined, usually relatively small, group of individuals whose economic well-being is jointly determined and significantly influenced by particular economic events, policies, or laws. Examples of special-interest groups include firms in various industries (such as oil, auto, steel, computer, or agriculture) or groups of industries (such as the National Association of Manufacturers or the Chamber of Commerce); occupational groups (American Medical Association, trade unions, American Bar Association, or other professional organizations); or special-interest organizations (such as the National Rifle Association and Common Cause).

Special-interest group Cohesive group of individuals with a common interest in some economic or social issue.

Under certain circumstances special-interest groups can wield disproportionate influence in political decisions. Since these groups stand to gain substantial private benefits from favorable political decisions, they are willing to provide substantial support to politicians who in turn support their causes. If the benefits of a particular piece of legislation accrue to a special-interest group, while the costs of the legislation are spread over a large number of individual taxpayers, a strong incentive exists for politicians to accept the special-interest group's assistance and support its preferred position. When the costs are spread over a large number of voters, the cost to each individual is small. Thus, voters have little incentive to be informed on the issue or to expend resources to oppose the special-interest group's actions.[4]

An example illustrates the interest group problem. In 1980, U.S. auto makers appealed for protection from Japanese imports. A year later, President Reagan announced a voluntary export restraint agreement with Japan that limited the number of cars Japanese auto makers could export to the United States each year. The result was substantially increased benefits (profits) for domestic manufacturers and higher prices for automobiles sold in the United States.[5] United States auto makers and auto workers benefited from the quota

---

[4]Donald Wittman has argued that special-interest groups do not wield as much power as most people think, because even small costs imposed on many voters can cost an incumbent dearly in the next election. If even a small percentage of voters change their votes because of the costs imposed on them by the incumbent, the incumbent could lose. See "Why Democracies Produce Efficient Results," *Journal of Political Economy* 97 (December 1989), pp. 1395–1424. Of course, Wittman's argument assumes that incumbents do not have other advantages that give them market power, which itself is an arguable proposition.

[5]Charles Collyns and Steven Dunaway, economists at the International Monetary Fund, estimated that the voluntary export restraint added over $1600 to the average price of a new automobile in 1984. "The Cost of Trade Restraints: The Case of Japanese Automobile Exports to the United States," IMF *Staff Papers* 34 (March 1987), pp. 150–175.

Why the Disagreement?

Captured Regulators

In modern industrial economies, many markets do not meet the stringent conditions for perfect competition. Some markets are dominated by three or four producers; in others, brand names give particular producers market power. Whatever the imperfection, consumers can suffer by being forced to pay prices higher than the competitive level. Such an outcome has led both economists and noneconomists to call for greater government regulation of markets as diverse as trucking and cable television. Other people, who admit that many markets are far from perfect, strongly oppose increased government regulation, noting that some of the worst abuses of market power have come in heavily regulated industries, such as banking and defense contracting. Why the disagreement? One source of disagreement is concern about how regulators actually behave. Specifying how regulators *should* behave is often fairly simple. In the real world, however, regulators do not always behave as they should. Economists have understood one reason for suboptimal regulatory behavior for several decades: Many regulatory bodies are captured by the industries they are supposed to regulate. A regulatory body is captured whenever the regulated industry itself comes to dominate the regulatory agenda. Instead of limiting the market power of producers, the regulatory agency uses its powers to limit competition, thereby making life easier (and probably more profitable) for the firms in the industry. An industry achieves dominance over regulators through several means. In many instances, regulatory bodies rely on regulated firms for the information needed to regulate the industry. A working relationship between the regulator and the regulated can develop, whereby regulatory agencies find their job made easier if they do not treat regulated firms too harshly.

Another way firms influence regulators is through legislative lobbying or direct political control over regulations. Firms often make large campaign contributions to legislators, who then support the industry's position in regulatory hearings. A recent example of such lobbying came to light in 1988 when the savings and loan crisis fi-

(restriction on imports). The costs of the quota were spread over a large number of consumers who had only one thing in common: They purchased automobiles. Although the cost increase for each purchaser was not small, the benefits enjoyed by the owners and employees of U.S. automobile companies were huge by comparison.

Shortsightedness of Political Decision Making. Another important bias in political decision making arises in the timing of the receipt of benefits and payment of the costs of political actions. Since the politician's objective is to be elected (and then be reelected) and since most terms in office last only a few years, political decision making tends to be shortsighted. Political action is biased toward those laws and policies that generate benefits now and postpone costs until later. If voters are shortsighted, valuing today's benefits more highly than tomorrow's costs, politicians can benefit by promoting policies that produce immediate benefits, even if the long-term costs exceed the long-term benefits. Unfortunately, the best economic policy may be the one that imposes costs today and yields benefits tomorrow.

nally became too serious to be ignored any longer. Investigators discovered that the Federal Home Loan Bank Board, the regulatory agency governing savings and loan institutions, had attempted to close several insolvent (bankrupt) savings and loan institutions in the mid-1980s. They were defeated in their attempt by political pressure from a number of powerful politicians, including then-Speaker of the House Jim Wright of Texas. Speaker Wright and the other legislators involved all had close connections with the savings and loan industry.

Local governments often tightly regulate the activities of taxi cab companies and street vendors. By limiting entry into such businesses, city councils restrict the supply of transportation and fast food, driving up prices and increasing the profits of firms lucky enough to have licenses to operate.

Regulated firms also capture regulators by providing jobs for regulatory experts who leave their agencies. Many regulators go on to become executives in regulated firms. (Many employees of regulated firms also work for regulatory agencies at some point in their careers.) Since the length of service of a regulator is often rather short, regulators are understandably concerned about their future job prospects. Such a concern can lead them to treat regulated firms too kindly at times.

When a regulatory agency has been captured, consumers or taxpayers pay the price. Regulations support high prices and limit competition, rather than protecting the consumer's interests. Indeed, much of the impetus for deregulation came from dissatisfaction with the behavior of regulatory agencies. In many industries, deregulation proved to be a boon for consumers. When the trucking industry was deregulated, shipping rates dropped sharply. When the airline industry was deregulated, air fares fell. Firms in those industries had been benefiting greatly from the enforced absence of competition. The disagreement over regulation concerns issues other than regulatory capture, but the widespread evidence of poor regulatory behavior is a major element of the case against government regulation.

Examples of shortsighted political behavior are not hard to find. The savings and loan crisis provides a recent example. In the early 1980s hundreds of the nation's savings and loan associations (S&Ls) were *insolvent* — the value of their liabilities (what they owed) exceeded the value of their assets (what they owned). Rather than taking immediate action to close the insolvent institutions, the agency regulating S&Ls, the Federal Home Loan Bank Board (FHLBB), lowered its regulatory standards. Neither Congress nor the Reagan administration objected to the reduction in standards. They wanted to avoid the cost of closing insolvent S&Ls and seemed to hope that the problem would cure itself; if left alone, insolvent S&Ls might once again become profitable. The lower standards permitted the FHLBB to allow many insolvent S&Ls to continue to operate. Losses mounted throughout the 1980s, and the eventual cost to the government (and taxpayers) of the S&L bailout will probably be at least twenty times what the cost would have been in the early 1980s.

SECTION RECAP
Politicians may fail to represent the interests of their constituents because of special-interest group influences or shortsightedness.

Political Self-Interest versus Society's Economic Well-Being This brief discussion of the economics of public choice serves two purposes. It provides another illustration of human behavior in the context of scarce resources. We have examined political behavior as a response to the incentives that individuals face as voters and as politicians. This approach to governmental decision making is a powerful tool for anticipating the actual expected benefits of government decision making. Public choice analysis also leads us to conclude that a number of rather powerful forces can cause government action to fail. These forces influence individual behavior in such a manner that governmental decision making can fail to improve upon more decentralized decision-making approaches. Understanding these forces enables us, as citizens of a democracy, to calculate the true social benefits of turning decisions over to the political process.

Summary

The market mechanism is an amazingly effective device for rationing and allocating resources. Markets permit complex modern societies to function relatively well with very little centralized direction by coordinating individual decisions. Under well-defined conditions market economies achieve economic efficiency.

Four factors can prevent these conditions from being met: (1) lack of competition in markets, (2) the existence of externalities, (3) the existence of public goods, and (4) economic instability. Any of these factors can cause market outcomes to be inefficient. **Lack of competition** raises prices and reduces output. **External costs** cause resources to be overallocated to markets, prices to be too low, and output to be too high; **external benefits** cause an underallocation of resources to the market, with both price and output falling below efficient levels.

Public goods permit individuals to attempt to **free ride** on others, by understating the value of the goods to them. The result is an underallocation of resources and low price and output relative to the efficient outcome. **Economic instability** can cause a number of problems that lead to reduced economic efficiency.

When these factors exist, government decision making may be able to improve upon the market outcome. The government might intervene in the market or simply shift the decision making from the private to the public sector. However, it is important to stress that government action does not necessarily improve upon a market outcome. Government action can fail, too.

The situations that cause problems for markets can also cause problems for government decision making. Government action can fail because society simply does not have enough information or understanding to resolve the problem. In this case government action has no clear advantage over the market approach.

Rational political behavior can prevent government action from improving upon the market mechanism. The incentives that voters and politicians face can cause government action to be biased against efficiency. The **economics of public choice** demonstrates that voters are often rationally ignorant, that special interest groups can wield political power in their favor and at the expense of others, and that political decisions are biased towards immediate, short-run action, which may not be the most efficient solution to a problem.

Questions for Thought

Knowledge Questions

1. Distinguish between a private and a public good.

2. Distinguish between microeconomics and macroeconomics. Why is an understanding of microeconomics important to the study of macroeconomics?

3. Define externality.

4. What are the goals of a politician?

5. Is it possible to be rationally ignorant? What impact does such behavior have on society?

Application Questions

6. In a market economy consumers and producers act in their own self-interest. How does competition ensure that their actions promote social welfare?

7. List five situations leading to externalities. Are they external benefits or costs? Has society attempted to solve any of these five problems? How?

8. Explain why an economic incentive to litter exists. Is litter more of a problem (a) in movie theaters, (b) along highways, or (c) in your neighborhood? Why?

9. Are the following goods private or public?

    a city park
    national defense
    garbage collection
    fire protection
    postal service

10. Do you know the name of your Congressional representative? Does he or she favor:
    a. subsidies to agricultural producers?
    b. student loans for higher education?
    c. restrictions on Japanese imports?
    How might these policies benefit or harm a college student?

Synthesis Questions

11. In recent years the Soviet Union has adopted the use of the market in many situations in order to improve the performance of its economy. This change is a drastic one for a communist government that has for many years refused to adopt decentralized decision making, calling it inconsistent with its political and social values. What does this recent change tell us about the Soviet Union's economic goals in the 1990s?
12. The distribution of income is not a factor determining the achievement of economic efficiency in an economy. Can you explain why? Can you explain how income redistribution policies might introduce some economic inefficiency?

OVERVIEW

In Chapter 3 we established the relationship between the price of a good and the quantity demanded—the law of demand. The fact that the demand curve is downward sloping means that consumers will buy more of a good when the price falls and less when the price rises. But how much more (or less)? Just how responsive are consumers to price changes? Our objective in this chapter is to develop a quantitative measure of the

The Elasticity of Demand

sensitivity of quantity demanded to a change in market price. This measure of responsiveness is called the *price elasticity of demand*. We will see that, depending on the price elasticity of demand, changes in price can cause the total amount of money spent on a good to increase, decrease, or stay the same.

Elasticity of demand depends on a number of different factors, including the number of available substitutes, the time period under consideration, and the relationship between the price of a good and total income. It is important to understand how each of

these factors influences elasticity. This understanding enables producers and policymakers to predict such things as how a change in price will influence total spending on a good, what kind of impact a tax imposed on a good will have on its sales, and who will bear the burden of a tax.

CHAPTER 6

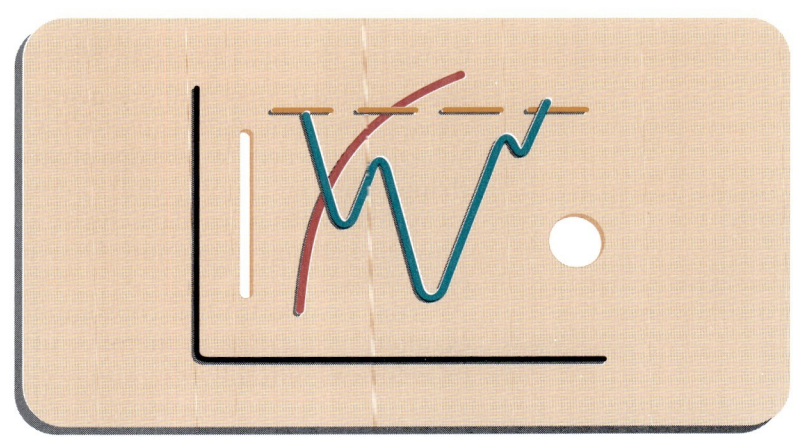

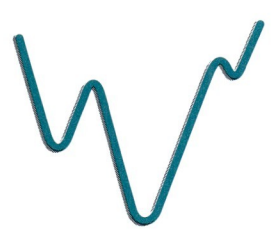

This chapter also examines the responsiveness of quantity demanded to other factors that influence consumer demand, such as income and the price of related goods. The concept of the elasticity of supply is also briefly considered.

Learning Objectives

After reading and studying this chapter, you will be able to:

1. Define the general concepts of elasticity and price elasticity of demand.
2. Identify the major factors that influence price elasticity of demand.
3. Calculate the price elasticity of demand and distinguish between elastic and inelastic demand.
4. Explain how total revenue (expenditures), price changes, and the price elasticity of demand are related.
5. Identify and describe other measures of elasticity of demand.

Changes in Price and Quantity Demanded

In Chapter 3 we answered an important first question about consumer behavior: What is the general relationship between changes in price and changes in the quantity demanded? We now turn to an extremely important second question about the relationship between price and quantities demanded: How much of a change in quantity demanded do we expect to see when the price of a good changes by a given amount?

Figure 1 shows three different demand curves, D_1, D_2, and D_3, which each represent the demand for a different good. At price P_0, the quantity demanded is the same for each demand curve. In addition, a price decrease to P_1 causes quantity demanded to increase in each of the three cases because the demand curves are all negatively sloped. However, although quantity demanded increases in all three cases, the *amount* of the increase differs for each demand curve. How can the differences in consumer responses associated with each demand curve be measured, and why are the responses different?

Consumer Responsiveness to Price Changes

The knowledge that quantity demanded decreases when price rises and increases when price falls is useful for understanding and predicting consumer behavior. However, knowledge of the specific extent of such responses to price changes is even more useful. Consumer responsiveness to price changes is measured by the **price elasticity of demand**, which describes the relationship between a change in quantity demanded of a good or service and a change in price.

Your own individual consumption responses to price changes vary. For example, an increase in the price of pizzas from $8 to $24 might cause you to reduce significantly the number of pizzas you purchase in a given time

Price elasticity of demand
The relationship between a change in quantity demanded of a good or service and a change in price.

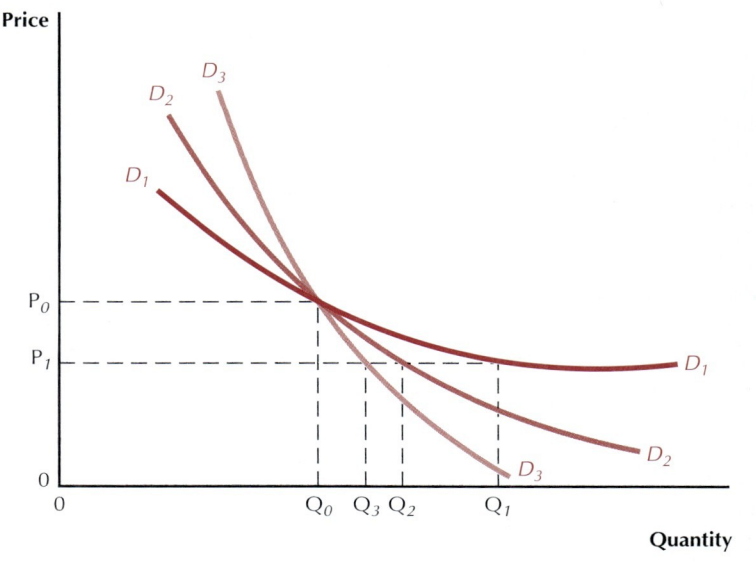

FIGURE 1
Responsiveness of quantity demanded to a change in price. This figure shows that for the three demand curves, D_1, D_2, and D_3, the quantity demanded at price P_0 is the same. A price decrease to P_1 causes quantity demanded to increase, but the extent of the increase in quantity demanded differs for each demand curve. The responsiveness of quantity demanded to a change in price is measured by the price elasticity of demand.

TABLE 1
Consumer response to price changes

	(A)	(B)	(C)	(D)	(E)
Good Consumed	Price Increase	Decrease in Daily Consumption	% Δ in Price	% Δ in Quantity Demanded	The Ratio (D)/(C)
Coffee	25¢/cup	1,000 cups	100%	25%	0.25
Fresh Peas	50¢/lb.	200 lbs.	33%	90%	2.73
Televisions	$75/set	40 sets	25%	25%	1.00

period. The same would probably be true for a tripling of the price of Big Macs. On the other hand, a tripling of the price of course notebooks might have virtually no impact on the quantity that you consume. Because there is variation in an individual's response to changes in the prices of two or more different goods, and in the responses of different individuals to a change in price of a particular good, we need a method for measuring the change in quantity demanded *relative* to the size of the price change. A relative measure is needed because changes in different measures are being compared. In the case of movements along a demand curve, a change in dollar price is being compared to a change in physical units of a good.

Economists measure the relative changes in quantity demanded and price by comparing the *percentage* change in quantity demanded to the *percentage* change in price. The resulting ratio is called the **coefficient of elasticity** (e_d), or:

$$e_d = -\frac{\% \text{ change in quantity demanded}}{\% \text{ change in price}}$$

An important qualification must be stated regarding the preceding formula. Note that according to our formula, e_d is negative. Technically, a price elasticity of demand estimate is the ratio of a positive and a negative number. Thus, the ratio has a negative sign. This negative value arises because demand curves are negatively sloped. However, since the ratio is always negative, usually the negative sign is dropped from use. We will observe this practice in the remainder of the chapter.

Why is the coefficient of elasticity calculated using percentages rather than absolute changes? To answer this question, suppose we are interested in the responses of consumers in a medium-sized city to price changes for three different goods. The three goods, the price changes, and the resulting changes in quantity demanded are given in Table 1. Note that in columns (A) and (B) both price changes and quantity changes are in absolute terms. For example, when the price of coffee rises by 25¢, daily coffee consumption falls by 1000 cups. A small absolute change in price causes a large absolute decrease in coffee consumption. However, the opposite occurs for TV sets. Can we make a concrete judgment about the sensitivity of consumers to price changes for these two goods based on absolute changes in price and quantity? No, we cannot.

Coefficient of elasticity
The ratio of the percentage change in quantity demanded to the percentage change in price.

150 CHAPTER 6 THE ELASTICITY OF DEMAND

Information on absolute changes in price and quantity is inadequate for making judgments about consumer responses to price changes. Assessing consumers' sensitivity to price changes requires information on the size of the price change *relative* to the price of the product and on the size of the change in quantity demanded *relative* to the total quantity demanded. This information is also provided in Table 1. Note that columns (C) and (D) provide a different type of information from that found in columns (A) and (B). In particular, columns (C) and (D) tell us the percentage increase in price and the resulting percentage change in quantity demanded for each of the three goods. In column (E) the price elasticity of demand has been calculated using the definition above.

The percentages reported in columns (C) and (D) of Table 1 provide useful information with respect to the sensitivity of quantity demanded to changes in price. The coffee price increase represents a doubling of price. However, this relatively large increase in price caused only a 25 percent reduction in the quantity of coffee consumed each day. This price–quantity change yields an elasticity coefficient of 0.25. (The elasticity coefficient is a pure number; there are no units attached to it.) On the other hand, the pea price increase is just 33 percent, but it induced a reduction in quantity demanded of 90 percent. The price elasticity of demand for peas is 2.73.

The elasticity coefficient is useful for comparing consumers' responses to the price changes of different goods. A given percentage price change of 10 percent affects the quantity of fresh peas demanded by much more than the quantity of coffee demanded. Based on the information in Table 1, a 10 percent increase in price would cause coffee consumers to decrease the quantity demanded of coffee by 2.5 percent. However, the same 10 percent increase in the price of peas would cause the quantity demanded of peas to fall by 27.3 percent. Coffee consumers clearly are less sensitive to price changes than are pea consumers.

Using the elasticity coefficients in column (E) of Table 1, the three goods in our example can be ranked according to the responsiveness of consumers to price changes. Consumers are least sensitive to coffee price changes and most sensitive to changes in the price of fresh peas. Their sensitivity to TV price changes lies somewhere between that of the other two goods. What differences in coffee, fresh peas, and TV sets or in consumers' tastes for these goods can explain this particular ranking? This question and its answer are discussed at length below. However, we must first resolve a potential problem in the calculation of elasticity coefficients.

SECTION RECAP
For a movement along a demand curve, price elasticity of demand measures the percentage change in quantity demanded *relative* to the percentage change in price. The resulting ratio is a pure number that measures the sensitivity of quantity demanded to price changes.

Calculating the Coefficient of Price Elasticity

Calculating elasticity can be thought of as a two-step process. The first step involves calculating the percentage changes in price and quantity demanded from information on the old and new prices and quantities. In the second step, the ratio of the percentage change in quantity to the percentage change in price is calculated.

One potential source of confusion in the calculation of elasticity must be identified and resolved. The problem is how to calculate the percentage changes in price and quantity. The elasticity calculations in Table 2 illustrate this problem. The formula for the coefficient of elasticity can be rewritten as:

$$e_d = \frac{\frac{\text{change in quantity}}{\text{quantity}}}{\frac{\text{change in price}}{\text{price}}}$$

However, when we actually calculate an elasticity coefficient with this formula, we face a complication: Should the changes in price and quantity be divided by the initial price and quantity or by the new price and quantity? Columns (C) and (D) in Table 2 indicate that this decision can have an important impact on the elasticity calculation. Column (C) contains the calculated elasticity for the price and quantity changes in the illustration above using the initial price and quantity. Column (D) contains the same calculation using the new price and quantity. As indicated by the comparison of columns (C) and (D), depending upon the specific price and quantity amounts and the size of the changes relative to these amounts, one can get dramatically different elasticity estimates.

Since the objective of the elasticity calculation is to obtain a specific measure of the sensitivity of consumers — measured by quantity responses — to price changes, it is important that we adopt one method for elasticity calculations and that it be used consistently. *For discrete price changes the most appropriate method of calculating the elasticity coefficient uses the average of the two prices and*

TABLE 2
The price elasticity calculation

	(A)	(B)	Elasticity		
			(C)	(D)	(E)
	Price	Quantity	Initial Price and Quantity	New Price and Quantity	Average Price and Quantity
Coffee			0.25	0.67	0.43
Old	25¢	4000			
New	50¢	3000			
Change	25¢	1000			
Peas			2.70	36.36	5.74
Old	$1.50	222			
New	$2.00	22			
Change	$0.50	200			
TV Sets			1.00	1.67	1.29
Old	$300	160			
New	$375	120			
Change	$ 75	40			

the two quantities. This method has been used to calculate the elasticities in Column (E) of Table 2. Notice that use of the average price and quantity generates elasticity estimates that lie between the estimates derived using either the old or the new price and quantity. The average price and quantity give us a single estimate of the price sensitivity of consumers over the range of prices between the old and new price. The following formula employs the average price and quantity to calculate price elasticity:

$$e_d = \frac{\dfrac{\text{old Q} - \text{new Q}}{\dfrac{\text{old Q} + \text{new Q}}{2}}}{\dfrac{\text{old P} - \text{new P}}{\dfrac{\text{old P} + \text{new P}}{2}}}$$

This formula can be reduced to:

$$e_d = \frac{\Delta Q}{\Delta P} \cdot \frac{\text{old P} + \text{new P}}{\text{old Q} + \text{new Q}}$$

Use of this formula will eliminate any question about the appropriate procedure and thus allow us to concentrate on the implications of the estimate rather than the validity of the estimate.

Elastic versus Inelastic Demand

According to the elasticity estimates in Table 3, coffee consumers are relatively insensitive and pea consumers are relatively sensitive to price changes. Mathematically, the absolute value of the coefficient of elasticity ranges from zero to infinity.

At one extreme, quantity demanded may be totally insensitive to a change in price—consumers purchase the same quantity of the good no matter how high or low price is. In this case the percentage change in quantity demanded is zero, regardless of the value of the percentage change in price, and therefore the coefficient of elasticity is equal to zero.[1] In such a case demand is said to be **perfectly inelastic**. A perfectly inelastic demand curve is pictured in Figure 2 (a). An individual addicted to a drug or alcohol might have a demand curve for the addictive good that is perfectly inelastic, at least over a wide range of prices. The same is true of individuals who require specific medications, such as insulin, to maintain their health.

At the other extreme is **perfectly elastic demand**. When demand is perfectly elastic the value of the coefficient of elasticity is infinity. A perfectly elastic demand curve is shown in Figure 2 (b). Consumers will purchase all the available quantity at one price but purchase none at a higher price and infinite amounts at any lower price. A good example of such a demand curve is the demand curve for an individual farmer's corn or wheat. The farmer faces a perfectly elastic demand curve because he can sell any amount he grows at the market price, but no one will offer more than the market price and he will not sell for less than the market price.

SECTION RECAP
In order to be consistent in our measurement of price elasticity of demand over different ranges on a demand curve, the percentage changes in price and quantity demanded are based on the *average* of the old and new values for price and quantity demanded.

Perfectly inelastic demand The percentage change in quantity demanded is zero, regardless of the value of the percentage change in price; the coefficient of elasticity equals zero.

Perfectly elastic demand The percentage change in quantity demanded is infinite for a price decrease, regardless of the value of the percentage change in price; the coefficient of elasticity equals infinity.

---

[1] Recall that, by definition, a ratio in which the numerator takes the value of zero is equal to zero.

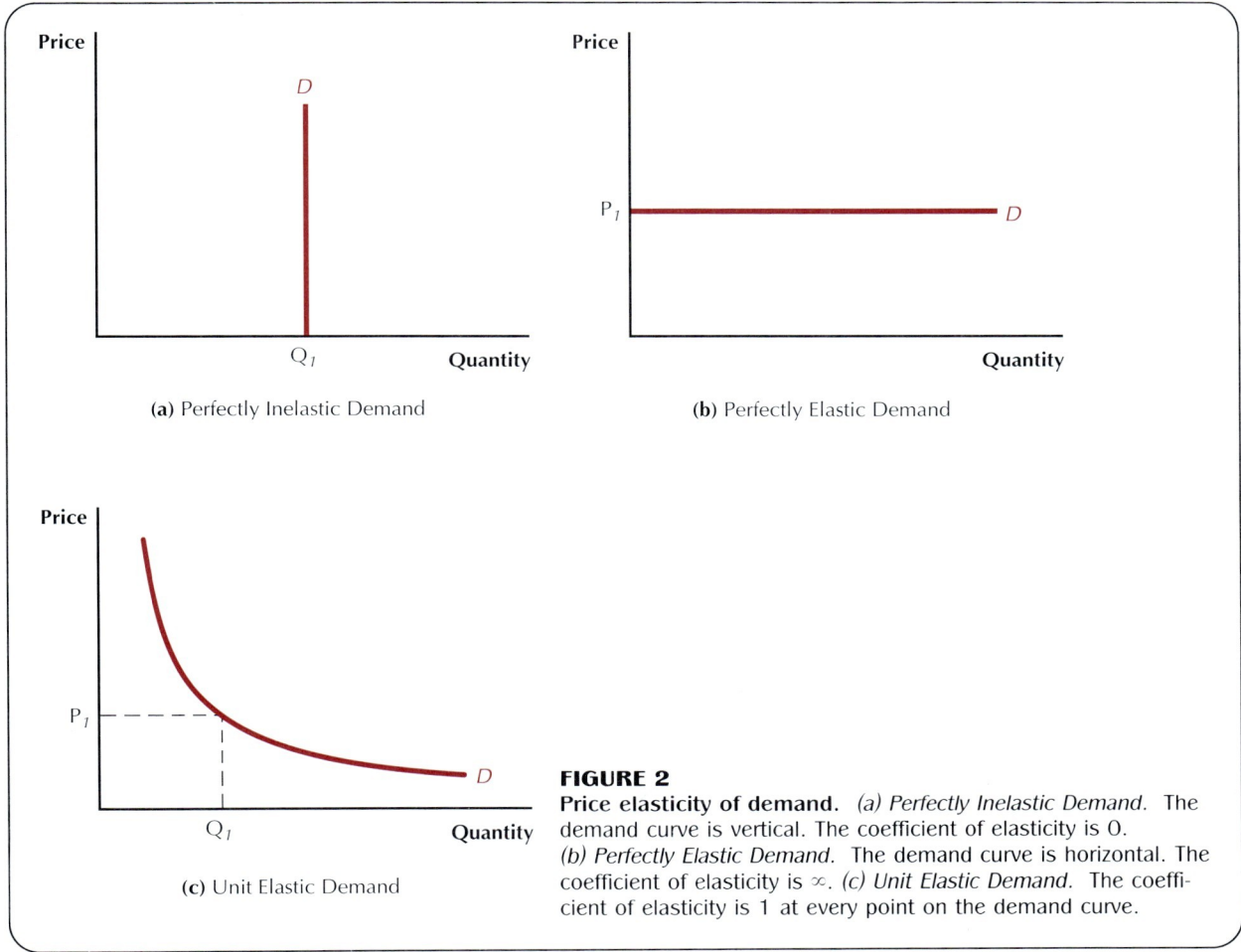

FIGURE 2
Price elasticity of demand. *(a) Perfectly Inelastic Demand.* The demand curve is vertical. The coefficient of elasticity is 0. *(b) Perfectly Elastic Demand.* The demand curve is horizontal. The coefficient of elasticity is ∞. *(c) Unit Elastic Demand.* The coefficient of elasticity is 1 at every point on the demand curve.

A third unique elasticity coefficient divides all other elasticity coefficients into one of two categories: inelastic and elastic. When the percentage change in quantity demanded is equal to the percentage change in price the coefficient of elasticity is equal to one. In this case demand is **unitary elastic**.[2] A unitary elastic demand curve is depicted in Figure 2 (c). The elasticity definition implies that an entire demand curve can have unitary elasticity only if for any price change the percentage change in quantity demanded is equal to the percentage change in price.

When the elasticity coefficient is between zero and one, demand is **inelastic**. Consumers are relatively insensitive to price changes. Examples of goods and services for which demand is inelastic include electricity, clothing, and medical care. When the elasticity coefficient is greater than one, demand is

Unitary elastic demand
The percentage change in quantity demanded is exactly equal to the percentage change in price; the coefficient of elasticity equals one.

Inelastic demand
Quantity demanded is relatively unresponsive to a change in price; the coefficient of elasticity is greater than zero but less than one.

[2] A demand curve that is unitary elastic is represented by an equilateral hyperbola of the form:
$$x = \frac{a}{y^M}$$
where x is quantity, y is price and M = 1.

154 ■ CHAPTER 6   THE ELASTICITY OF DEMAND

Arc elasticity
The price elasticity of demand between any two points on a demand curve.

Point elasticity of demand
Price elasticity at a single point on a demand curve.

Point Elasticity

In our discussion of the price elasticity of demand, we have focused on the calculation of **arc elasticity** — the elasticity between two points on a demand curve. However, it is also possible to calculate the price elasticity of demand at a single point on the demand curve. This value is referred to as the **point elasticity of demand**. The formula for calculating the point elasticity of demand is derived from the same premise as the arc elasticity of demand. Recall that elasticity is measured as:

$$\frac{\% \Delta Q}{\% \Delta P}$$

This can be rewritten as:

$$\frac{\Delta Q/Q}{\Delta P/P} = \frac{P}{Q} \cdot \frac{\Delta Q}{\Delta P}$$

For a linear (straight line) demand curve of the form:

$$Q = a - bP$$

in which b represents the slope of the demand curve, that is, $b = \Delta Q/\Delta P$. For a

The Economist's *Tool Kit*

Elastic demand
Quantity demanded is relatively responsive to a change in price; the coefficient of elasticity is greater than one.

SECTION RECAP
Price elasticity of demand is not the same as the slope of the demand curve. In general, elasticity varies along the demand curve. When the percentage change in quantity demanded is greater than the percentage change in price, demand is elastic. When the percentage change in quantity de- *(continued)*

elastic. Consumers are relatively sensitive to price changes. Examples of goods and services for which demand is elastic include china and glassware and restaurant meals.

The Difference between Price Elasticity and Slope   An understanding of the technical side of price elasticity of demand is enhanced by a very important consideration. Elasticity is not the same thing as slope.[3] A slope calculation incorporates only information about the extent of change in one variable as the other variable changes. An elasticity coefficient incorporates both the value of the two variables, price and quantity, at a particular point, and information about the extent of change in quantity demanded as price changes.

For a demand curve that is a straight line, the slope is constant; the slope does not change as we move along the demand curve. However, for the same demand curve, elasticity varies depending upon the particular range of the demand curve in question. Consider, for example, the linear demand curve for office visits per year to a medical clinic depicted in Figure 3. Since it is linear, the demand curve has a constant slope. In this example, the slope is equal to (−)0.01. However, the price elasticity of demand varies along the demand curve. Two price changes are identified in Figure 3. One change shows an increase in price from $18 to $19 per office visit and the other change shows an increase in the price of an office visit from $5 to $6.

Since the demand function is linear, the change in quantity demanded must be the same for equivalent price changes: a $1 increase in the price of an office visit reduces the number of visits by 100 (per year). However, the

---

[3]A demand function is a functional relationship between two variables (price and quantity), and therefore we can calculate the slope of the curve representing the function.

given combination of P and Q on the demand curve, denoted P* and Q*, point elasticity is calculated as:

$$\frac{P^*}{Q^*} \cdot b$$

This last formula further emphasizes the difference between the price elasticity of demand and slope. Note that the calculation of the point elasticity requires both the slope of the demand curve and the values of price and quantity for the point in question on the demand curve. Examination of this last formula also highlights the relationship between point elasticity and arc elasticity. In particular, arc elasticity incorporates the average of the old and new values of price and quantity when calculating elasticity over a range on a demand curve. P* and Q* are simply the mathematical limits of the averages of the old and new prices and quantities as the differences between the old and new values approach zero.

Point elasticity is useful when we are interested in the effects on quantity demanded of very small changes in price. However, in many situations, that is, when price changes are substantial, arc elasticity provides more useful information.

---

price elasticity of demand for the two price changes is quite different. The $18 to $19 price range has an elasticity coefficient of 0.44 associated with it, while the $5 to $6 price range has an elasticity coefficient of 0.11. The demand curve has a constant slope, but its elasticity is greater at the higher price (between A and B) than at the lower price (between C and D).

Consumer Response to Price Reexamined: Elasticity and Total Revenue

The law of demand says that when the price of a good changes, the quantity consumed (or sold) changes in the opposite direction. Consequently, a price change can cause total spending on a good to increase or decrease. Stated differently, *in almost all cases a price change will cause the amount of total revenue received from the sale of a good to change.* Total revenue from a good is the product of its market price, P, and the quantity, Q, of the good consumed, or P × Q. The price elasticity of demand allows us to determine the specific relationship between price changes and changes in total revenue.

A price increase with no change in quantity consumed will cause an increase in total expenditures and hence total revenues. However, as we have already seen, according to the law of demand a price increase leads to a reduction in the quantity demanded. Thus, a price increase tends to increase total revenue because price goes up, but total revenue tends to fall because quantity demanded decreases. The net effect of a price change on total revenue is determined by the size of the change in price relative to the size of the change in quantity demanded.

When demand is inelastic the percentage change in quantity demanded is smaller than the percentage change in price. This means that the change in

SECTION RECAP
(continued)
manded is less than the percentage change in price, demand is inelastic.

Total revenue
The product of a good's market price and the quantity of the good purchased.

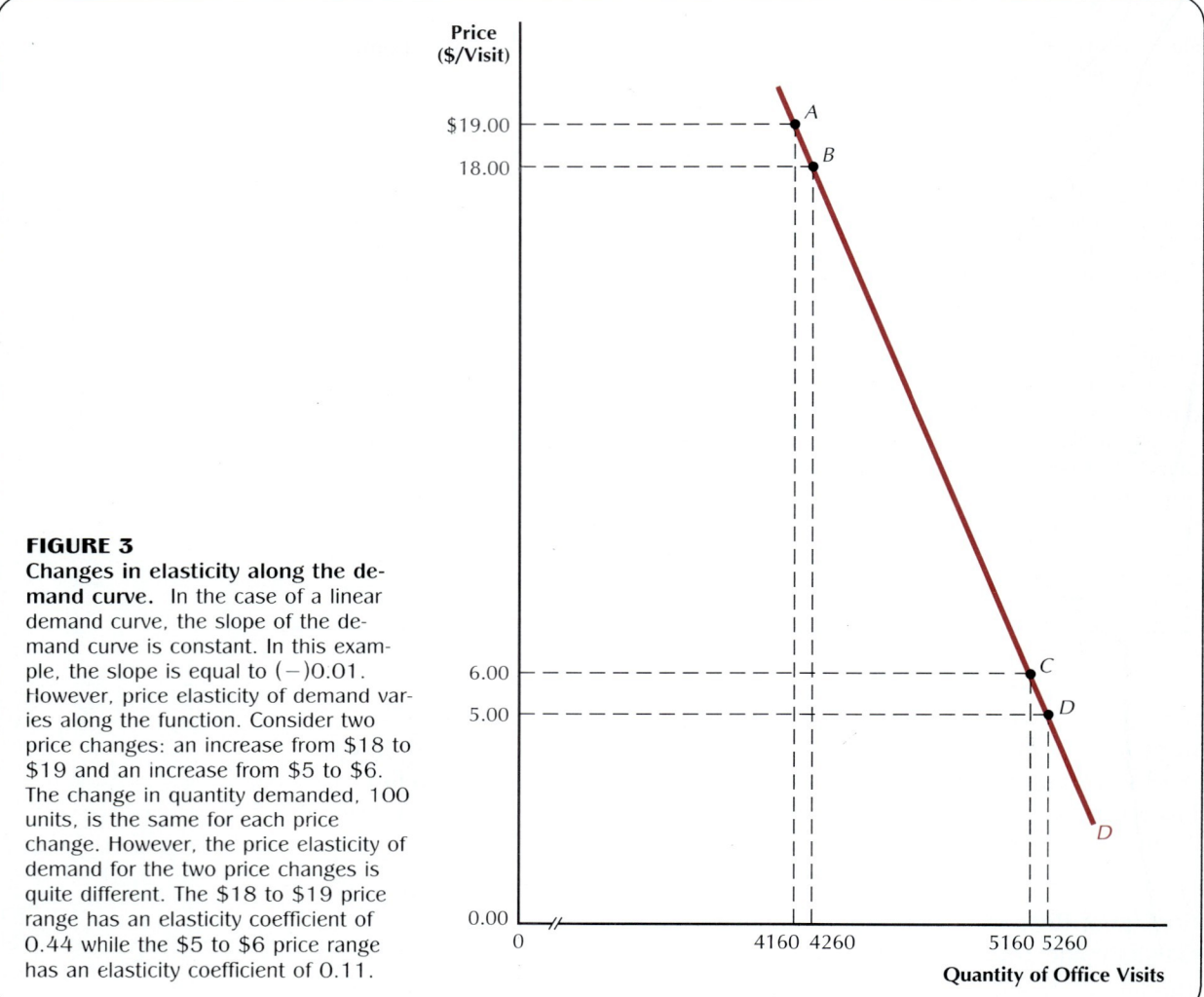

FIGURE 3
Changes in elasticity along the demand curve. In the case of a linear demand curve, the slope of the demand curve is constant. In this example, the slope is equal to (−)0.01. However, price elasticity of demand varies along the function. Consider two price changes: an increase from $18 to $19 and an increase from $5 to $6. The change in quantity demanded, 100 units, is the same for each price change. However, the price elasticity of demand for the two price changes is quite different. The $18 to $19 price range has an elasticity coefficient of 0.44 while the $5 to $6 price range has an elasticity coefficient of 0.11.

price has the greater effect on total revenue. Consequently, *when demand is inelastic total revenue moves in the same direction as price, and in the opposite direction of quantity demanded.* This result is illustrated by reference to Figure 3. Between points A and B, and C and D, demand is price inelastic. As such, when price falls from $19 (point A) to $18 (point B), total revenue declines from $79,040 ($19 × 4160) to $76,680 ($18 × 4260). In a similar fashion, when price falls from $6 (point C) to $5 (point D), total revenue falls from $30,960 to $26,300.

On the other hand, when demand is elastic the percentage change in quantity demanded is larger than the percentage change in price. This means that the change in quantity demanded has a greater effect on total revenue than the change in price. Consequently, *when demand is elastic total revenue moves in the opposite direction of price, and the same direction as quantity demanded.*

With unitary elasticity the percentage change in quantity demanded exactly offsets the percentage change in price. Thus, *when demand is unit elastic a price*

TABLE 3
The relationship between elasticity, changes in price, and changes in total revenue

Demand is:	Elasticity Coefficient	Relationship between Change in Price and Change in Total Revenue
Inelastic	0 to 1	Price increases, total revenue increases Price decreases, total revenue decreases
Unit Elastic	1	Price increases } no change in Price decreases } total revenue
Elastic	> 1	Price increases, total revenue decreases Price decreases, total revenue increases

change has no effect on total revenue. The relationships between price elasticity, price changes and total revenue changes are summarized in Table 3.

The relationship between elasticity, price changes, and changes in total revenue highlights a very important fact: Higher prices do not always mean an increase in total revenue. The impact of a price change on total revenue depends upon the price elasticity of demand for the product. This relationship implies that an understanding of consumer sensitivity to price is important to firms attempting to maximize profits.

Table 4 contains information on price, quantity demanded, and total revenue for a linear (straight line) demand curve. As the table indicates, when price falls from $18 to $10, quantity demanded and total revenue both increase. Hence, over this range, demand is elastic. However, as price falls from $10 to $0, quantity demanded increases but total revenue falls. Over this range, demand is inelastic.

As an illustration of the implications of the relationship between the price elasticity of demand and total revenues, consider the case of legalized gambling. In many states, including Illinois, New York, and California, gambling is an important source of tax revenues. In addition, there is a strong temptation on

SECTION RECAP
Price elasticity of demand, price changes, and changes in total revenue are related. When demand is elastic, a price increase will result in a decrease in total revenues. When demand is inelastic, a price increase will cause total revenues to rise. If demand is unit elastic, a change in price will leave total revenues unchanged.

TABLE 4
Price changes, total revenue, and elasticity: an illustration

Price	Quantity Demanded	Total Revenue	Elasticity
$18	1	$18	
16	2	32	5.67
14	3	42	3
12	4	48	1.86
10	5	50	1.22
8	6	48	0.82
6	7	42	0.54
4	8	32	0.33
2	9	18	0.18

Does It Make Economic Sense?

The Incidence of a Tax

In 1983 the federal excise tax on gasoline was increased by 5¢ from 4¢ to 9¢ a gallon. At the same time, about twenty states increased their state taxes on gasoline. The tax hikes were proposed as conservation and fund-raising measures. (The last big OPEC oil price increase was in 1979, and most developed countries were still struggling to adjust to the much higher price of energy at this time.) The excise tax is paid by suppliers; that is, the government collects the tax from them. The tax increase, it was argued, would reduce gasoline consumption because suppliers would pass the tax on to consumers. Newspaper accounts of the proposed tax increase and consumer reactions to it clearly suggested that consumers expected to bear the full burden of the tax. Does this expectation make economic sense? It depends upon the price elasticity of demand for gasoline.

In Figure 4, the supply curve labeled S_B is the gasoline supply curve before the tax increase. Suppose the total tax increase was 6¢ a gallon (5¢ federal, 1¢ state). The imposition of a tax shifts the supply curve up vertically by the amount of the tax (6¢) because suppliers must get an additional 6¢ a gallon to receive the same price as they received before the tax for any quantity of gasoline supplied. S_A is the supply curve after the tax increase. The vertical distance between the two supply curves is 6¢—the amount of the tax.

The initial price of gas was about $1.22 a gallon in 1982 (for leaded regular). If consumers had paid all of the tax increase, the price of gas would have had to rise to $1.28 a gallon. However, as Figure 4 indicates, the new equilibrium price rose to less than $1.28; it was at about $1.27 in 1983. The increase in market price (in this case from $1.22 to $1.27) is the part of the tax paid by consumers. In this example, consumers paid 5¢ of a 6¢ tax, or about 83 percent of the tax. Suppliers paid the other 17 percent. The extent to which a tax can be passed on to consumers depends upon the consumers' quantity response to price changes. When demand is inelastic, as it is for gasoline, consumers absorb most of a tax increase. However, suppliers pay at least part of the tax unless demand is perfectly inelastic. (If the demand curve in Figure 4 were vertical, the price would have increased by exactly 6¢, the full amount of the tax increase.) On the other hand, consumers do not bear as much of the tax burden on goods for which demand is very elastic. Suppliers cannot shift the burden to consumers because an elastic demand means that consumers have alternatives; they will substitute other goods for the good being taxed.

The long-run demand for gasoline is less inelastic than the short-run demand (about 0.7 compared to 0.2). Thus, over time as drivers are able to make more adjustments, the overall burden of the tax increase is shifted back somewhat toward suppliers. Over the long run, consumers pay a smaller share of the tax than they do in the short run.

The trend in average gas prices since 1982 indicates that factors

---

the part of lawmakers to place a high tax rate on gambling, both because of the potential revenues it could generate and because such so-called sin taxes are politically attractive. However, the price elasticity of demand for gambling has been estimated to be approximately 1.59, indicating that demand is relatively elastic.[4] This estimate suggests that states might actually increase their total tax revenue by decreasing tax rates (which affect the price of gambling) and thereby increasing the total amount of revenue to which the tax rate is applied.

Price Discrimination Have you ever tried to figure out the strategy behind the rather complicated pricing of airline tickets? For travel between two points

---

[4]D.B. Suits, "The Elasticity of Demand for Gambling," *Quarterly Journal of Economics* Vol. 94, pp. 155–162.

CHANGES IN PRICE AND QUANTITY DEMANDED ■ 159

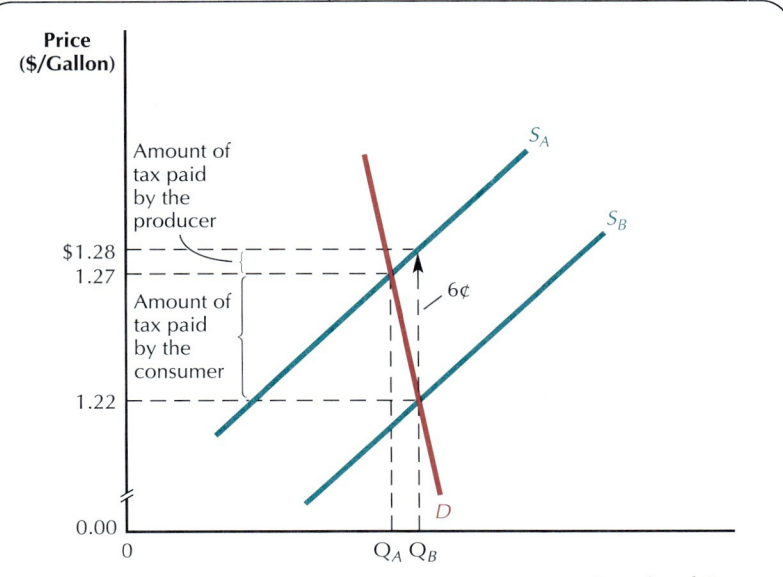

FIGURE 4
Elasticity of demand and the incidence of a tax. In this figure, the supply curve labeled S_B is the supply curve for gasoline before the tax increase of 6¢ a gallon. The imposition of the tax shifts the supply curve up vertically by the amount of the tax (6¢) to S_A. The pretax price of gas was $1.22 a gallon. If consumers paid all the tax increase, the gas price would rise to $1.28 a gallon. However, because demand is not perfectly inelastic, the new equilibrium price is less than $1.28; it is $1.27. The increase in market price of 5¢ is the part of the tax that consumers pay. Suppliers pay the remainder of the tax, 1¢.

other than taxes have also been at work in the gasoline market. By 1984 the average price of a gallon of leaded regular was down to $1.13. By the end of 1989 the average price had fallen below 95¢ in many areas of the country, suggesting that other major developments offset the effect of higher taxes on gasoline prices. The advent of the crisis in the Persian Gulf in August 1990 reversed this trend. During August and September, gas prices rose more than 30 percent in the United States. And prices were increased further when the federal excise tax on gasoline was increased by an additional 5¢ per gallon in December 1990. Nevertheless, the increase in the price of gas did not keep pace with the increase in the price of crude oil and the increase in taxes that occurred during the same period.

such as Chicago and San Francisco there is a variety of fares, and the lowest fare might be less than half the highest fare — even though the cost of carrying an additional passenger is the same regardless of the fare charged. The fare for which you are eligible depends on factors such as how long you plan to stay, how early you make your reservation, and which day of the week you travel. The pricing of airline tickets is an example of **price discrimination**, the practice of charging different customers different prices for the same good or service when price differences are not justified on the basis of cost differences. Firms attempt to price discriminate because willingness to pay for a service and price elasticity vary across consumers and because raising the price to some customers and lowering it for others can increase total revenue.

Some people, such as many businesspeople who must travel on short notice, have an inelastic demand for air travel. Other people, such those who are taking trips for pleasure or who have the opportunity to plan a trip well

Price discrimination
The practice of charging different prices to different consumers of the same good or service.

in advance, have an elastic demand. An airline can take advantage of these differences if it can identify each of the different groups. If the firm raises air fares for those whose demand is inelastic, it increases total revenue. Moreover, the firm can lower fares for those with elastic demand and raise total revenues further!

The variety of air fares available for flights to the same location is an example of price discrimination. There are many other examples of firms charging different prices to consumers whose elasticities of demand differ. For example, a variety of businesses charge lower prices to children and senior citizens. Restaurants, movie theaters, and other public transportation companies also practice this kind of price discrimination.

Price discrimination is based on the fact that certain groups are more sensitive to prices and, therefore, reduced prices have a much bigger impact on the quantity consumed by those groups. In the case of children, requiring them to pay the regular price for a meal or a ticket would simply make it too expensive for many families to dine out or go to the movies. Consequently, firms that do not price discriminate lose sales not only to children, but also to their parents, who might otherwise purchase the good or service. In the case of senior citizens, many people are on low, fixed incomes which in turn restricts quantity demanded. A reduction in price for certain groups — price discrimination — increases the total quantity demanded without requiring the firm to reduce price on the previous units sold.

Determinants of Price Elasticity of Demand

We now return to an important question that was raised but not answered when we first introduced the concept of elasticity. What factors influence the price elasticity of demand for a good or service? Elasticity of demand varies widely — across different goods, and across consumers of the same good. Economists have estimated price elasticities of demand for many goods. Estimated elasticities for selected products and services are presented in Table 5. The products have been grouped according to whether demand is generally inelastic or elastic. Can this extensive variation in elasticity be explained? What are the attributes of the products, or the consumers, that account for these differences?

Available Substitutes

The most important influence on price elasticity of demand is the availability of substitutes for a good. When substitutes for a good or service exist, a consumer has consumption alternatives. Depending on how close these substitutes are, even a small price increase can prompt consumers to switch to one of the alternatives. The estimated elasticity for fresh peas (in Table 3) suggests that, as a group, consumers are quite sensitive to changes in the price of fresh peas. This sensitivity arises because of the many close substitutes for fresh peas: frozen peas, canned peas, other fresh vegetables, and other canned or frozen vegetables.

There are many other goods for which the price elasticity of demand is relatively high. There are a number of close substitutes in the fast food market — McDonald's, Burger King, Taco Bell, and Kentucky Fried Chicken, just to name a few. Consumers are sensitive to a change in the price of a given product in

TABLE 5

Selected estimates of price elasticity of demand

Good or Service	Price Elasticity
Owner-occupied housing	0.04
Electricity	0.13
Bread	0.15
Water	0.20
Clothing and shoes	0.20
Medical care	0.31
Eggs	0.32
Auto repair	0.40
Newspapers and magazines	0.42
Beef	0.64
Tires	0.86
Movies	0.87
China and glassware	1.55
Restaurant meals	2.27

Sources: H. S. Houthakker and Lester D. Taylor, *Consumer Demand in the United States: Analyses and Projections*, 2d ed. Cambridge, MA: Harvard University Press, 1970; and P. S. George and G. A. King, *Consumer Demand for Food Commodities in the United States with Projections for 1980*, Berkeley, CA: University of California, 1971.

this market due to the wide variety of available substitutes. In a similar manner, the price elasticity of demand for new Chrysler automobiles is quite high because of the close substitutes available — used Chryslers and other new and used cars (as well as other means of transportation such as trucks or buses).

The inelastic demand category includes such goods as cigarettes and coffee. Consumers are relatively insensitive to price changes for these goods because they *perceive* few, if any, close substitutes. In some objective sense, a wide variety of liquid refreshments are good substitutes for coffee: tea, water, milk, soft drinks. However, for coffee drinkers who drink coffee because of its caffeine content, there are few good substitutes. For these consumers, coffee price increases have only a small effect on consumption. Cigarette smoking is addictive; thus, smokers are insensitive to cigarette price changes. To smokers, no good alternatives exist. Returning to our air travel example, trips taken on short notice are motivated by the need to get somewhere quickly. There are no close substitutes for air travel for such trips. Consequently, the demand for this kind of air travel is quite inelastic. What matters in determining price elasticity of demand is the consumer's perception of the available substitutes.

The availability of substitutes also depends on the definition of the product or service category. Generally, price elasticity of demand is greater for the more narrowly defined categories of goods or services. We can talk about autos, or new autos, or new Chrysler autos, or new Chrysler LeBaron autos. The price elasticity of demand for these groups increases as the category becomes more narrowly defined because the range of available substitutes increases. The demand for salt is very inelastic; it has few substitutes. The demand for Morton salt is less inelastic because other brands of salt are available. Even less inelastic (more elastic) is the demand for Morton salt at a particular grocery store. Alternatives include Morton salt sold at other stores.

Cost of the Good Relative to Total Income

Another influence on price elasticity of demand is the size of the expenditure on a good relative to the consumer's total income. The price of white bread is relatively low and, furthermore, its price is an insignificant fraction of most individual or family incomes. If the price of a loaf of white bread doubled, it would have almost no impact on quantities consumed. (Even at the doubled price a household would now spend perhaps $5 or less every week on white bread.) On the other hand, as Table 5 indicates, an increase in the price of restaurant meals, which command a relatively larger percentage of a household's income, would lead to a significant reduction in the quantity demanded. The same is true of such big-ticket items as compact disc players, TV sets, home computers, and VCRs. As such, there is a positive relationship between the cost of a good relative to total income and the price elasticity of demand.

Time and the Availability of Substitutes

Time can affect price elasticity of demand in two ways. Often the adjustments that consumers wish to make in response to price changes take time. The full adjustment to a price change can take a relatively long time. Consequently, the longer the period of time available for adjustment, the more elastic is demand for the good or service.

For example, the full response to an increase in the price of fresh vegetables takes little time. There is no difference in the short-run and long-run price elasticities for vegetables. The adjustment to an increase in the price of heating fuel takes much longer, as all homeowners discovered in the 1970s and early 1980s. A relatively rapid increase in the price of fuel oil and then natural gas eventually caused marked consumer adjustments. However, in the short run, consumers had few alternatives. They turned down their thermostats, substituting a colder house and more clothing for fuel consumption. In addition, many consumers purchased portable space heaters. They also improved the seals around windows and doors.

Over a longer period of time consumers had additional alternatives: installation of storm doors and windows, added insulation, and even more efficient heating systems. Wood-burning stoves also became popular due to the relatively low cost of firewood. With even more time consumers were able to consider buying new houses with energy-saving features including solar heat, or even "earth homes" that are partially underground. The initial reduction in the quantity of fuel used was relatively small, but the adjustment continued over time. The long-run price elasticity of the demand for energy is greater than the short-run elasticity.

Some consumption activities have a time dimension. If we want to fly to New York City this week for an important meeting, we will be relatively insensitive to air fare changes. Our demand will be relatively inelastic since there are few good alternatives to air travel if we really want to travel 2,000 miles and still work four days this week. On the other hand, if we plan to fly to the

Why the **Disagreement?**

The Problem of Illegal Drugs

Society has long viewed the use of illegal drugs such as heroin and cocaine to be detrimental to social welfare. Criminal activities such as robbery, theft, and murder are considered by many to be a direct result of drug abuse. To reduce the problems associated with the use of illegal drugs, law enforcement agencies have concentrated on attempting to eliminate, or at least reduce, the available supply. In addition, to reduce supply and demand, stiff penalties have been enacted for people convicted of selling or using drugs. However, an increasing number of individuals have questioned the effectiveness of this approach and have instead argued for the legalization of many drugs. Why is there such fundamental disagreement over policy in this area?

The arguments for each of the respective policies can be couched in economic terms. On the supply side of the market, when shipments of drugs are intercepted before they reach the street, supply is reduced. In addition, severe penalties for convicted drug dealers raise the expected costs of doing business and thereby reduce the incentive to enter the market as a supplier. On the other hand, penalties for drug users (consumers) reduce the expected benefits of consumption, decreasing the demand for drugs. The overall result of a decrease in the supply of and demand for drugs should be a reduction in the use of illegal drugs and an increase in social welfare.

Proponents of the legalization, or decriminalization, of drugs argue that, in fact, increased penalties for selling and buying drugs do not affect the market significantly. They maintain that the demand for illegal drugs is relatively inelastic because drugs are addictive. As such, supply reductions that drive up the price simply result in an increase in criminal activity such as robbery and theft as users scramble to obtain the means to support their drug habits. Furthermore, higher drug prices create an incentive for new suppliers to enter the market in pursuit of larger profits.

Proponents of legalization assume that the legalization of otherwise illegal drugs would increase the drug supply and reduce the profitability of the industry for the criminal element. This is because the high profits associated with drug dealing would disappear with the introduction of additional suppliers and the resulting decrease in prices. It is also argued that, subsequent to legalization, the government could tax the sale of these drugs. The relatively inelastic demand would ensure a steady flow of tax revenues which could then be used to fund efforts to monitor the industry and pay the costs of programs designed to help drug addicts. Finally, it is argued that legalization would free up law enforcement resources currently committed to trying to reduce the supply of drugs. These resources could be used in other areas of law enforcement.

Clearly, economic analysis provides only part of the analysis relevant to formulating sound social policy in this area. Moreover, the arguments that have been noted here only consider the effects of policy in the market for illegal drugs. The implications of effects such as spillovers into other markets resulting from a possible increase in the level of drug abuse have not been addressed. However, this discussion does demonstrate how economic analysis can be used to shed some light on the effects that a particular policy can generate.

West Coast for a vacation next year, we will be more sensitive to air fare changes because we have more alternatives to choose from over the course of a year, including a change in the specific date of the vacation or the possibility of taking the train or driving our own car.

In contrast to the previous examples, we demand consumer durables, like TV sets, stereo systems, refrigerators, washing machines, or cars, for the services they provide over a period of time. Because these purchases can be moved up or delayed in time, their price elasticity is greater in the short run than in the long run. It is again a question of alternatives. For these products consumers have more flexibility in the short run. In late 1988, domestic auto manufacturers offered discounts to buyers, the most dramatic of which was zero-interest-rate financing on car loans. This effective reduction in car prices caused

SECTION RECAP
Availability of substitutes, the cost of a good relative to total income, and the time period in question all affect the price elasticity of demand for a good or service. In general, an increase in any one of these factors will cause the price elasticity of *(continued)*

SECTION RECAP
(continued)
demand to increase. However, for goods such as consumer durables, elasticity is greater in the short run than in the long run.

an increase in sales. However, while the auto industry was pleased with the response, many economists argued that the impact was illusory. They maintained that consumers had simply moved up their auto purchases and that 1989 sales would be reduced by the early buying. Consumers are much more sensitive to auto prices in the short run than in the long run.

Other Measures of Elasticity

The concept of elasticity is general. It is the percentage change in one variable that is caused by a percentage change in another variable. If a change in X causes a change in Y, we would define the elasticity of Y with respect to X as the ratio of the percentage change in Y to the percentage change in X. Economists use this elasticity concept to measure not only the price elasticity of demand but also a variety of other relationships. Three of these other elasticity measures are defined below.

Income elasticity of demand
A measure of the responsiveness of quantity demanded to a change in income.

Income Elasticity of Demand The **income elasticity of demand** shows how responsive consumer demand for a good or service is to a change in income. The income elasticity of demand (e_Y) is calculated as the percentage change in quantity demanded (holding price constant) that is induced by a percentage change in income, that is:

$$e_Y = \frac{\% \text{ change in quantity demanded}}{\% \text{ change in income}}$$

Income elasticity can be positive or negative since an increase in income can cause quantities consumed to increase (normal goods) or decrease (inferior goods).

As we saw in Chapter 3, increases in income cause people to consume more of most goods. For example, we would expect to observe an increase in the amount of dining out as a result of an increase in income. In a similar fashion, many families might purchase a second or third car as a result of an increase in income. The income elasticity of demand enables us to predict the amount by which demand will increase for a given increase in income. For normal goods such as those in the examples above, the income elasticity of demand is positive — a percentage increase in income leads to a percentage increase in demand.

Income elasticity of demand is negative for inferior goods — goods for which demand decreases as income increases. A percentage increase in income leads to a percentage decrease in demand. Macaroni and cheese is considered by many to be an inferior good. Consequently, when income increases, the demand for macaroni and cheese falls.

Cross price elasticity of demand
A measure of the responsiveness of the quantity demanded of one good to a percentage change in the price of another good.

Cross Price Elasticity of Demand Changes in the price of one good can also affect the demand for other goods. The extent of such an impact is measured by the **cross price elasticity of demand**: the ratio of the percentage change in quantity demanded of one good (holding its price constant) to the percentage change in the price of another good. The cross price elasticity of demand between two goods, X and Y, is calculated as:

$$e_{X,Y} = \frac{\% \text{ change in quantity demanded of good } X}{\% \text{ change in the price of good } Y}$$

Substitute goods have positive cross price elasticities, indicating a positive relationship between the quantity demanded of a good and the price of its substitutes. Complementary goods have negative cross price elasticities. The negative sign reflects the fact that when the price of a good rises (or falls), the quantity demanded of its complements moves in the opposite direction.

Cross price elasticities are of special interest to producers of close substitutes. For example, changes in the price of one breakfast cereal can affect the sales of other breakfast cereals. The producers of corn flakes would like to know, and they attempt to estimate, the cross price elasticity of demand for corn flakes with respect to the price of Wheaties. They are interested in how much the quantity demanded of corn flakes will increase (or decrease) when the price of Wheaties goes up (or down).

Producers are also interested in the cross price elasticities of complements. When OPEC imposed the oil embargo in 1974, and began to dramatically increase the price of oil, gasoline prices were quick to follow. As a result, consumers began to alter their demand for automobiles, increasing purchases of smaller, more fuel-efficient cars. Auto manufacturers can use estimates of the cross price elasticity between gasoline and fuel-efficient cars to predict increases in demand (as well as decreases in demand for less fuel-efficient autos) that would result.

Price Elasticity of Supply In this chapter the focus has been on the demand curve and thus price elasticity of demand. However, elasticity of supply is also an important measure of price response. The **price elasticity of supply** is the ratio of the percentage change in quantity supplied to the percentage change in market price. Determinants of supply elasticities are discussed in later chapters.

Price elasticity of supply A measure of the responsiveness of the quantity supplied to a percentage change in market price.

Summary

The **price elasticity of demand** is the ratio of the percentage change in quantity demanded to the percentage change in price. This measure captures the sensitivity of consumers to price changes. When consumers are relatively insensitive to price changes, demand is said to be **inelastic**—the elasticity coefficient is between zero and one. When consumers are relatively sensitive to price changes, demand is said to be **elastic**—the elasticity coefficient ranges from one to infinity.

Since the coefficient of elasticity is the ratio of percentage change in quantity to percentage change in price, it tells us the relationship between price changes and resulting changes in total revenue from a good. When the price of a good for which demand is inelastic increases, total expenditure on the good increases. For goods whose demand is elastic, a price increase causes total expenditure to fall.

Consumer responses to price changes, and therefore the price elasticity of demand, are heavily influenced by the availability of substitutes. Other factors that influence the price elasticity of demand include the percentage of total income accounted for by the good in question and the time period under consideration.

A number of other measures of elasticity can be calculated that provide additional insights into the responsiveness of demand. The **income elasticity of demand** measures the responsiveness of demand to changes in the level of income. The **cross price elasticity of demand** measures the responsiveness of demand for one good to changes in the prices of complements and substitutes.

Questions for Thought

Knowledge Questions

1. Define the price elasticity of demand. What does the price elasticity of demand measure?
2. Can you think of a good or service for which demand is generally elastic (or inelastic), but your own demand for the good is inelastic (or elastic)? How do you explain the difference?
3. What are some substitutes for a sofa, a movie seen at a movie theater, and an artificial heart? How much would an increase in the price of these goods affect the quantities that consumers purchase?
4. Summarize the relationship between elasticity, price changes, and changes in total revenue.

Application Questions

5. Salt was taxed for hundreds of years. In fact, at times French monarchs generated as much as 10 percent of their royal income from a salt tax. What attributes made salt a good commodity to tax?
6. The price of a good whose elasticity is 1.5 has just decreased by 10 percent. Will the quantity consumed increase or decrease? By what percent?
7. Calculate the price elasticity of demand for wheat in the two situations below:

The Wheat Market	Farmer Brown's Wheat
Old price, $3.40/bu.; old quantity, 2.5 billion bu.	Old price, $3.40/bu.; old quantity, 28,000 bu.
New price, $3.20/bu.; new quantity, 2.525 billion bu.	New price, $3.20/bu.; new quantity, 35,000 bu.

Can you account for the difference in elasticities?

8. In the ten years between 1971 and 1981, the price of gasoline increased by more than 350 percent, from an average of about 36¢ to about $1.31 per gallon. What happened to total household spending on gasoline during this period? Explain.

Synthesis Questions

9. The income elasticity of demand for margarine is negative. Describe the effect associated with an increase in the income of margarine consumers on the demand for butter.

10. If a university wishes to increase its tuition revenue, should it increase or decrease tuition rates? Why?
11. What effect does price discrimination have on the total amount of a particular good sold relative to the amount sold if only a single price were offered?
12. Assume that the demand curve for a particular good can be written in the form:

$$Q = 15 - 2P$$

Assuming that $P = 5$, calculate the point elasticity of demand. In addition, calculate the price elasticity of demand over the range $P = 5$ to $P = 7$. How do your estimates of the point and arc elasticity differ? Why?

OVERVIEW

In Part I, we introduced the basic economic problem of scarcity and the fundamental proposition that individuals seek to maximize their economic well-being. We demonstrated, through a variety of examples, that trade and exchange are motivated by the desire of individuals—consumers and producers—to improve their well-being. To achieve that end, individuals choose those alternatives for which the marginal net benefit—the difference between benefits and costs—is greatest.

The logic of individual choice and the concepts of scarcity, choice, and opportunity cost represent the foundation on which all economic theory is built. Beginning with this chapter, we examine these concepts from the viewpoints of the individual consumer, producer, and resource owner. In particular, we consider the specific choice problems of consumers (on the demand side of the market) and producers (on the supply side of the market), and show how they use the basic economic principles developed in Part I in their decision-making processes.

This chapter, which introduces the consumer choice problem, has two objectives. The first is to demonstrate how the Fundamental Premise of Economics can be applied to

The Theory of Consumer Behavior

CHAPTER 7

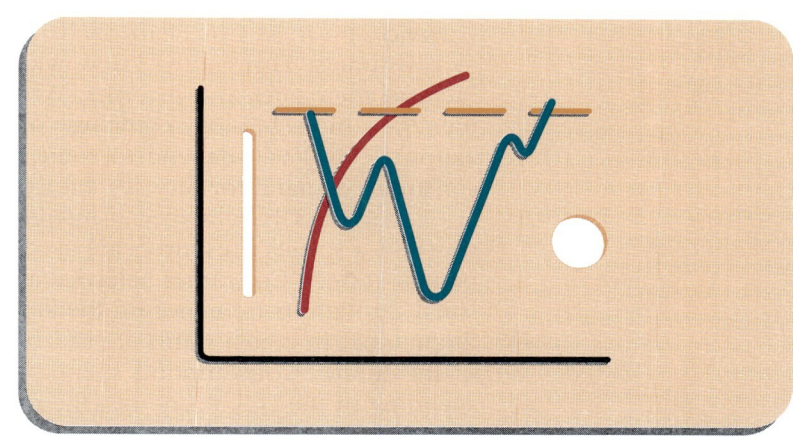

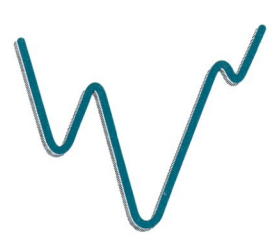

the consumption decisions of individuals. The second is to provide a rationale for the law of demand, which states that the market price and quantity demanded of a product are inversely related. We will see that the consumer's desire to maximize his or her well-being is in fact the reason for negatively sloped demand curves.

Learning Objectives

After reading and studying this chapter, you will be able to:

1. Explain the basic consumer choice problem.
2. Explain what the term *utility* refers to and distinguish between total and marginal utility.
3. Explain the consumer's utility-maximizing rule and its relationship to negatively sloped demand.
4. Explain how changes in relative prices result in downward-sloping demand curves.
5. Describe various types of transactions costs and their influence on the consumer's decision-making behavior in actual practice.

The Consumer Choice Problem

In the United States alone there are at least 225 million consumers. Each consumer makes many consumption decisions every day and literally thousands of decisions in a year. Although some of these decisions are made with considerable care, many are made on the spur of the moment. Some of the more important decisions include where to live, what kind of residence to occupy, what to wear, what to eat, how to get from place to place, and how to spend one's time. There are thousands of possible answers to these questions, and the variety of alternatives to choose from is truly bewildering.

Many of us are curious about why people make a particular consumption choice. Our curiosity often derives from the fact that someone we know has faced the same decision as we have, but has chosen a different alternative. For instance, you may own a sports car while your friends own compact economy cars or, in some cases, have no car at all. Why didn't these people buy the same type of car you did?

Other very good reasons exist for wanting to understand consumption behavior. Business firms earn their incomes by providing goods and services to consumers. Firms must know what appeals to consumers if they are to increase their sales and incomes. Whether you want to own a bicycle shop, manage a biotechnology company, or work in a health maintenance organization (HMO) will depend to some extent on information you have about consumer demand for bicycles, biotechnology, and health care.

Economists have a special interest in consumer behavior. To the extent possible, a society's resources are used to satisfy the wants of individual members of society. Consumer behavior affects the extent to which wants are satisfied through its influence on the kinds of goods produced in the economy, the manner in which wants are satisfied, and the stock of resources available in the future. Consumption spending accounts for about two thirds of all spending in the U.S. economy (the other third is accounted for by business, government, and foreigners). Consequently, changes in consumer spending can also contribute to changes in the price level and the level of unemployment in the economy. All of these issues are important to economists.

The key to understanding consumer behavior is to concentrate on the goal of consumption activity and the individual's resource constraints. In simple terms, welfare maximization for a consumer consists of purchasing a set of goods and services that yields maximum benefits. Economists use the term **utility** to denote the benefits, or satisfaction, derived from consuming an economic good. Utility is synonymous with benefits. The statement "I get no utility from watching that TV program," means only that I get no benefits from watching the program; it implies nothing at all about the general usefulness or worth of the program.

Consumers seek to maximize utility. However, all consumers have limited resources. This constraint is usually reflected in a limited amount of income.[1] We use our resources, or income, to acquire those goods and services we wish to consume. What rule do consumers use to select and purchase goods and services so that they maximize the utility derived from their limited income? The next two sections develop the answer to this question.

Utility
The benefits derived from consuming an economic good.

---

[1]Budget constraints were introduced in Chapter 3. The Appendix to this chapter presents a more technical discussion of the role of the budget constraint in the consumer's decision-making process.

Measuring Consumer Utility

Our previous analysis of consumer demand has already suggested the nature of consumer decision making. When making a choice among several alternatives, consumers pay careful attention to the benefits and costs associated with each possible choice. The question we address here is, How does a consumer measure the benefits from consumption? That is, how does a consumer *measure* utility?

Utility is not something that can be measured like the number of apples in a box or shares of stock in a company, or the weight of cattle or square footage of apartment floor space. Utility is subjective. Utility is a way of talking about the value an individual attaches to a good. A special dinner is valuable to you if it gives you satisfaction. We know it has value to you because you stand ready to sacrifice for it, as indicated by the price you are willing to pay. However, if you told your friends that you get 150 units of utility from this dinner, they would probably just stare at you quizzically and scratch their heads. Your measure of utility is subjective. It has meaning only to you.

Total versus Marginal Utility

In establishing a decision-making rule for consumers we must be careful to distinguish between the *total utility* derived from consuming a good and the **marginal utility** derived from consuming one more unit of the good. Both utility concepts are important, but for very different purposes. As the term suggests, for a single good or service, *total utility refers to the utility received from all units of the good or service consumed.* However, for decision-making purposes, it is important to pay attention to the marginal utility of consuming one more unit of the good. *Marginal utility is the additional benefit the consumer receives from consuming one more unit of the good or service.*

To illustrate the notions of total and marginal utility and the relationship between the two measures, consider Tom's consumption of hamburgers. In column (A) of Table 1, the number of hamburgers that Tom might consume

Marginal utility
The additional benefit the consumer receives from consuming one more unit of a good or service.

TABLE 1

Tom's utility from hamburger consumption

(A)	(B)	(C)
Number of Hamburgers (per week)	Total Utility (in units of utility)	Marginal Utility (in units of utility)
0	0	—
1	200	200
2	380	180
3	540	160
4	655	115
5	715	60
6	745	30
7	757	12
8	757	0

(per week) is listed. Column (B) contains the total utility that Tom derives from consuming a given quantity of hamburgers. Column (C) indicates the marginal utility derived from consuming each additional hamburger. Notice that utility is measured in units. Only Tom knows the significance of a unit of utility. All we know for sure is that more units (more hamburgers) are associated with greater total utility. The total utility column indicates that no utility is obtained when no hamburgers are consumed and that the total utility from hamburger consumption increases as the number of hamburgers eaten each week increases, up to at least seven hamburgers a week. When Tom eats five hamburgers a week, he gets 715 units of utility.

The marginal utility column (C) tells us the addition to total utility associated with the consumption of each additional hamburger. Notice that the marginal utility of any specific level of hamburger consumption is equal to the difference in total utility between that level and the previous one. For example, the marginal utility of the fourth hamburger is 115 units, which is the difference between a total utility of 655 units (for four hamburgers) and 540 units (for three hamburgers). In general, marginal utility is the addition to total utility derived from consuming one more unit of a good.

FIGURE 1
The law of diminishing marginal utility.
As illustrated in Figure 1 (a), total utility increases as hamburger consumption increases up to seven hamburgers a week. However, total utility increases at a decreasing rate because the marginal utility of each additional hamburger is getting smaller and smaller. The marginal utility function is plotted in Figure 1 (b). Note that the marginal utility curve is negatively sloped: As the quantity of hamburgers consumed increases, marginal utility decreases.

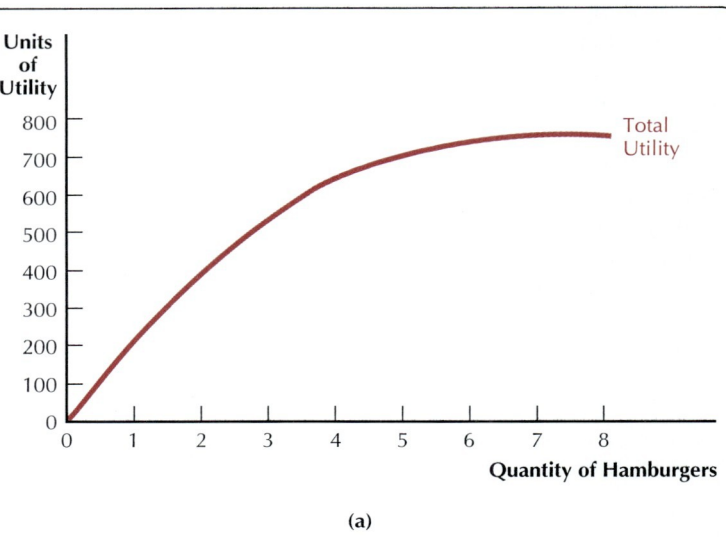

(a)

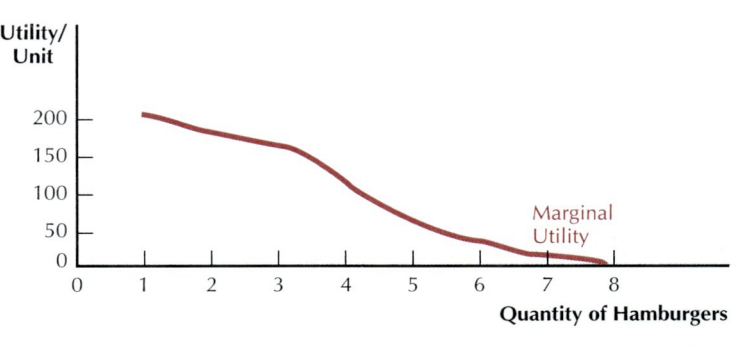

(b)

Diminishing Marginal Utility

Tom's hamburger habit also illustrates a very important principle of consumer behavior. This principle is the **law of diminishing marginal utility**: *as an individual consumes more and more of a good, the marginal utility of additional units eventually decreases.* This principle is illustrated in Figure 1 (b). The marginal utility function is negatively sloped: As the quantity of hamburgers consumed increases, marginal utility decreases. The total utility function is graphed in Figure 1 (a). Total utility increases as hamburger consumption increases up to seven hamburgers a week. Note, however, that total utility increases at a decreasing rate because the marginal utility of each additional hamburger is getting smaller and smaller.

The relationship between the quantity consumed and marginal utility is referred to as a *law* because economists accept it as a generalization about consumer preferences. Although you might be able to identify instances contrary to the law, these would be exceptions to usual consumer behavior. The generalization is useful for understanding and predicting consumer behavior most of the time.

The law of diminishing marginal utility is based on the premise that individuals have a hierarchy of wants that they wish to satisfy. The first unit(s) of a consumed good is (are) used to satisfy the most important wants, and later units are put to less valuable uses. For many people, the first cup of coffee in the morning is very valuable. Some people might even say that the first cup of coffee in the morning is a necessity. But these same people would admit that the second, third, and fourth cups are progressively less valuable.

The law of diminishing marginal utility is also a useful way of emphasizing the important difference between total utility and marginal utility. Water is an economic good for which we all have very valuable uses, yet its price per gallon is very low and we use it quite freely. It is a fact that a human cannot live for very long without water. However, much of our water consumption is for much less valuable uses, such as washing cars or watering lawns. The total utility derived from water consumption is quite high. But we consume so much water that the marginal utility of the last gallon consumed is very low.

Law of diminishing marginal utility
As an individual consumes more of a good, the marginal utility of additional units eventually decreases.

SECTION RECAP
In making consumption decisions, consumers focus on the marginal utility gained from consuming an additional unit of a good rather than the total utility from consumption.

Maximizing Consumer Utility: Costs and Benefits . . . Again

Having developed an understanding of the concept of marginal utility, we can now examine the rule consumers follow to maximize the total amount of utility gained from consumption of a combination of goods and services. However, to do this, we need to be able to directly compare the consumer's benefits from consumption with the opportunity cost of consumption. For most transactions in a market economy, the opportunity costs of consumption are measured in terms of market prices.

Marginal Utility versus Price

Thus far, we have concentrated on the total and marginal utility of a single good. However, consumers purchase many different goods. Also, most consumers are faced with a budget constraint that limits the amount of money

Does It Make Economic Sense?

The Paradox of Value

Over time, economists and others have observed that certain goods, such as precious gems and stones, command a very high price in the market, while other goods we would consider necessities, such as water, are sold at a very low price. This phenomenon is referred to as the *paradox of value*. When we think of price as the consumer's willingness to pay, a question immediately arises. Why are people willing to pay so much for something of seemingly little value to society, yet so little for a necessity? In other words, why are consumers' valuations of the two goods so seemingly incongruous? Does it make economic sense?

To understand the paradox of value requires the application of utility theory and supply and demand analysis. Utility is a measure of the benefit that a consumer receives from consuming a particular good or service. The theory of consumer behavior asserts that individuals are utility maximizers. However, due to budget constraints, consumers must make choices involving tradeoffs among the various goods they consume. Because of the budget constraint, as the consumption of a particular good increases, the opportunity cost of consuming the good, measured by the amount of other goods forgone, increases as well.

Stated differently, the value associated with additional units of the good declines.

Returning to the water–diamond paradox, the first glass of water we consume quenches our thirst and, for a given period of time, satisfies our physical need for water. One could argue that the benefit associated with the first glass of water — and therefore the value attached to it — is extremely large (think of someone who has been stranded in the desert). Additional glasses of water in the same time period yield considerably less benefit (are considerably less valuable). In the extreme, the value associated with the consumption of water could become negative. As the value of additional units of a good declines, so does our willingness to pay for additional units of the good.

A second characteristic of water that must be considered is its supply relative to demand. In most areas of the United States water is relatively abundant. Thus, the total supply of water is fixed. If we think in terms of a graphical analysis, this implies that the supply curve is vertical. However, because supply is large, the supply curve intersects the horizontal axis at a very high quantity. On the demand side, as people consume more water for different uses the value of additional units diminishes, and they move down the demand curve for water. Because supply is large relative to demand and the demand curve is downward sloping, the demand and supply curves for water intersect at a relatively low price.

Luxuries such as diamonds, on the other hand, are in short supply. Once again, the supply curve can be considered to be vertical. However, in this case the supply curve intersects the horizontal axis at a relatively low quantity. In addition, many people derive considerable utility from the possession of diamonds. Thus, willingness to pay is relatively high — at least for the first units of diamonds consumed. The combination of high willingness to pay and relatively limited supply results in an intersection of the supply and demand curves at a relatively high price.

Numerous other examples of the paradox of value exist. Consider the price paid for a top quality baseball player versus the average salary paid to grade school teachers, the price paid for caviar versus a loaf of bread, or the price paid for designer clothing versus discount store substitutes. In each case, the question of whether the price paid reflects the value of the good or service is a legitimate one. However, application of the concepts of utility and supply and demand sheds light on the seeming paradoxes.

Marginal utility per dollar (MU/P)
A ratio that measures the additional utility per additional dollar spent on a good or service.

the consumer can spend per time period. How do consumers decide how much they will buy to maximize their utility from the consumption of many different goods?

To achieve maximum utility from limited income, consumers compare the ratio of marginal utility (MU) to price (P) across all goods — that is, they compare the ratio MU/P for each good or service they buy. The ratio MU/P measures the additional utility per additional dollar spent on the good in question. In the simple case where an individual is consuming only two goods, A and B, the factors that must be considered are the individual's total income (or money available to spend), the prices of the two goods, and the marginal utility function for each good. An individual can consume more of each good so long as the total amount spent on the two goods is no greater than the individual's total income.

To see how an individual maximizes utility, consider the following example. Jane is a student at Brainbender University. She has $250 that she can spend each month and the only two goods that she purchases are sky diving jumps and compact discs (CDs). Jane's problem is deciding how to allocate her income between sky diving jumps, priced at $60 per unit, and CDs, priced at $10 per unit, in such a way that her total utility from consuming sky diving and CDs is maximized. Table 2 contains information on the total utility (TU), marginal utility (MU), and marginal utility per dollar spent (MU/P) for each unit of sky diving and CDs purchased.

Which combination of goods should Jane purchase? To answer this question, note that MU/P is 15 for the first CD, and MU/P is 2.08 for the first jump. Hence, Jane will buy the first CD at a cost of $10 because, per dollar spent, she gains more utility from the CD. In deciding on how to spend the remaining $240 ($250 − $10) the next choice is between the first jump, for which MU/P is 2.08, and the second CD, for which MU/P is 10. Note that Jane gains more marginal utility per dollar spent on the second CD than the first jump. Jane therefore will buy a second CD. The same is true when comparing the third, fourth, and fifth CDs to the first jump. In comparing the first jump to the sixth CD, however, the jump now yields greater marginal utility per dollar spent (2.08 > 1.75). Thus, Jane will now buy the first jump. Jane now has $140 left ($250 − $10 − $10 − $10 − $10 − $10 − $60).

In deciding which additional goods to buy, Jane will continue to compare MU/P for the next unit of each good. Jane's utility-maximizing combination

TABLE 2
Jane's utility from the consumption of sky diving jumps and compact discs

Jumps				Compact Discs			
Number of Units	TU_J	MU_J	MU_J/P_J	Number of Units	TU_{CD}	MU_{CD}	MU_{CD}/P_{CD}
0	0	—	—	0	0	—	—
1	125	125	2.08	1	150	150	15
2	225	100	1.67	2	250	100	10
3	315	90	1.5	3	325	75	7.5
4	390	75	1.25	4	350	25	2.5
5	450	60	1	5	372.5	22.5	2.25
6	495	45	0.75	6	390	17.5	1.75
				7	405	15	1.5
				8	415	10	1.0

Per-unit price of jumps = $60
Per-unit price of CDs = $10

of sky diving jumps and CDs is three jumps and seven CDs. With this combination, MU/P for the third jump is equal to 1.5, which is in turn equal to MU/P for the seventh CD. Jane has exhausted her income since (3 × $60) + (7 × $10) = $250. In addition, the total utility associated with this combination is 720. There is no other combination that Jane can afford that will yield greater total utilty from the consumption of sky diving jumps and CDs.

As the preceding example suggests, in the case of two goods an individual maximizes utility by purchasing the combination of goods A and B such that:

$$\frac{MU_A}{P_A} = \frac{MU_B}{P_B}$$

and all income is spent.[2] In words, this equation states that the marginal utility of the last dollar spent on good A is equal to the marginal utility of the last dollar spent on good B. In the case of more than two goods, the rule generalizes to:

$$\frac{MU_1}{P_1} = \frac{MU_2}{P_2} = \ldots = \frac{MU_n}{P_n}$$

Consumer decision-making rule
To maximize utility, consumers purchase a combination of goods such that the ratio of marginal utility to price is equal across all the goods consumed.

Consumer equilibrium
Achieved when the total utility from consuming a combination of goods and services is maximized.

where n represents the total number of different goods consumed. We can now state the **consumer decision-making rule**: *To maximize utility, consumers purchase goods and services in such a combination that the ratio of marginal utility to price is equal across all the goods and services consumed.* When a consumer maximizes total utility from consuming a combination of goods and services, **consumer equilibrium** is achieved.

The next question that arises is, How does the consumer use the utility-maximizing decision rule to get from a disequilibrium consumption level to an equilibrium one? Assume, based on the previous example, that Jane consumes four jumps and one CD. In this case, MU/P is equal to 1.25 for the last jump purchased, MU/P is equal to 10 for the last CD purchased, and total utility is 490. Clearly, this combination is inefficient. This inefficiency is indicated by the fact that:

$$\frac{MU_J}{P_J} < \frac{MU_{CD}}{P_{CD}}$$

SECTION RECAP
In deciding how to allocate one's income, the consumer compares the marginal utility to the price of each good consumed. By consuming goods such that the ratio MU/P is equal for the last unit of each good consumed, the consumer maximizes total utility.

If Jane reduces the number of jumps she purchases from four to three, she gives up 75 units of utility—the marginal utility of the fourth jump. However, the $60 that Jane saves by not purchasing the fourth jump can be used to purchase six additional CDs. The six additional CDs add 255 units of additional utility to Jane's total utility. Thus, Jane realizes a net gain of 180 (255 − 75) units in total utility. Jane is better off by consuming fewer jumps and more CDs. In making this adjustment, the MU of the last jump purchased increases and the MU of the last CD purchased decreases, causing the MU/P ratios to move toward equality.

Note that moving from disequilibrium to equilibrium increases one's utility. Consumers rank all purchases based on the marginal benefit–marginal cost ratio, MU/P. (Remember that the benefits are subjectively determined by the consumer.) They then make their purchases based on this ranking, always spending on the good whose next unit has the highest marginal benefit–marginal cost ratio. The ratio gives the consumer a measure of the benefits

[2]This example assumes that the individual derives no utility from savings.

per dollar of expenditure. Consumers seek the greatest possible gain from each dollar spent. They therefore buy goods and services in a manner that keeps these ratios equal at the margin across all goods and services.

Consumer Demand Curves

We have seen how consumers maximize their total utility from consumption. The next step is to consider the relationship between consumer choices and the shape of the demand curve. As the following discussion illustrates, economists have developed a multifaceted explanation for the downward-sloping demand curve presented in Chapter 3.

Demand and Utility Maximization

The rule for utility maximization is used to determine how much of each good a person will consume given a set of prices and a fixed amount of income. The question that arises now is, What if prices change? We can now use this rule to derive the demand curve for a particular good.

Referring again to Jane's decision problem, assume that the per-unit price of sky diving falls from \$60 to \$30. The effect of this decrease in price is illustrated in Table 3. Table 3 is the same as Table 2, with the exception that the fourth column, labeled MU_J/P_J has now changed, reflecting the change in the price of jumps. After the price change, the ratio MU_J/P_J is now larger for each jump, as indicated in Table 3. Using the rule for utility maximization, Jane will now purchase six jumps and seven CDs. With this combination, the marginal utility per last dollar spent on jumps is equal to the marginal utility

TABLE 3

The effect of a change in price on Jane's utility from the consumption of sky diving jumps and compact discs

Jumps				Compact Discs			
Number of Units	TU_J	MU_J	MU_J/P_J	Number of Units	TU_{CD}	MU_{CD}	MU_{CD}/P_{CD}
0	0	—	—	0	0	—	—
1	125	125	4.17	1	150	150	15
2	225	100	3.33	2	250	100	10
3	315	90	3.0	3	325	75	7.5
4	390	75	2.5	4	350	25	2.5
5	450	60	2	5	372.5	22.5	2.25
6	495	45	1.5	6	390	17.5	1.75
				7	405	15	1.5
				8	415	10	1.0

Per-unit price of jumps = \$30
Per-unit price of CDs = \$10

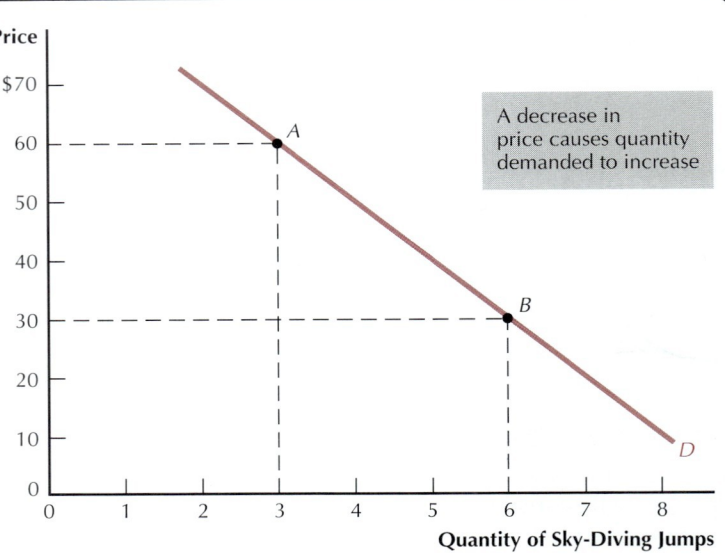

FIGURE 2
Utility maximization and the law of demand. If a consumer is originally maximizing her utility and then the price of a good decreases, the ratio MU/P is no longer equal across all goods. To once again maximize her utility, the consumer will purchase additional units of the good whose price has fallen. All else constant, a decrease in price has caused an increase in quantity demanded; the demand curve is downward sloping.

per last dollar spent on CDs, and Jane's income is exhausted (6 × $30 + 7 × $10 = $250). Note that, as a result of the decrease in the price of jumps, the number of jumps purchased by Jane has increased.

Jane's adjustment to the change in the price of jumps is illustrated graphically in Figure 2. When the price of jumps was $60 per unit, Jane purchased three jumps. This price–quantity combination is associated with point A in Figure 2. After the price decrease, from $60 to $30, the quantity demanded of jumps increased from three to six. Jane moved from point A to point B. Connecting points A and B yields a downward-sloping curve which is, in effect, Jane's demand curve for sky diving. It has been constructed by holding income and the prices of other goods constant and allowing only the quantity demanded to change as prices vary. Using the rule for utility maximization, we have shown that the demand curve for a normal good is downward sloping.

We have used the consumer's decision-making rule to derive the law of demand. In essence, we have applied the Fundamental Premise of Economics to the individual consumption decision. We have concentrated on relatively simple cases to highlight the fact that the theory of consumer behavior is just a specific case of the general welfare-maximizing behavior of rational individuals. Next, we consider the two component effects of price changes that result in downward-sloping demand curves.

Income and Substitution Effects

The following discussion explains in more detail the reasoning that causes economists to argue that demand curves are negatively sloped. A price change has two effects on a consumer's economic well-being and behavior. One effect is a substitution effect, the other an income effect.

The **substitution effect** is a response to a change in *relative* prices. The term *relative prices* refers to the price of one good measured as the amount of other goods that an equivalent amount of money would buy. For example, if

Substitution effect Consumers purchase more of a good whose price has fallen relative to the prices of its substitutes.

a cassette costs $6 and a CD costs $12, the relative price of a CD is two cassettes. According to the substitution effect, when the price of good A drops relative to the prices of other goods, consumers will substitute more of A for other relevant goods.

In the example involving sky diving and CDs, in which the price of a jump is $60 and the price of a CD is $10, the relative price of one jump is six CDs. A decrease in price makes a good less expensive relative to other goods. Moreover, the price decrease causes the MU/P ratio for the good in question to rise relative to the MU/P ratio for other goods. Thus, it is beneficial for the consumer to buy more of the good whose price has decreased. Total utility can be increased by substituting additional units of the good for other relatively more expensive goods. The decrease in price causes an increase in quantity demanded.

The **income effect** refers to the effect of a price change on the consumer's purchasing power, or real income. When the price of a good is reduced, the consumer can continue to buy the same quantities of goods as before. However, because the price of at least one good is now lower, the consumer has some income left over which can be used to buy additional units of the good whose price has fallen (as well as other goods). Once again, a decrease in price has led to an increase in quantity demanded: the essence of a downward-sloping demand curve.

In summary, according to the substitution and income effects, a decrease in the price of a normal good causes an increase in quantity demanded for two reasons. First, since the good is less expensive relative to other goods, the consumer substitutes the good for others. Second, the decrease in price causes real income, or purchasing power, to increase. This prompts the consumer to purchase additional quantities of normal goods. The two effects reinforce each other. If price had increased, the two effects would have worked together in the opposite direction, leading the consumer to buy less of the now more-expensive good.

Income effect
The increase in real purchasing power that results from a decrease in the price of a consumption good, *ceteris paribus*.

SECTION RECAP
The law of demand is a result of the substitution and income effects of a price change. In particular, if the price of a good falls, *ceteris paribus*, consumers will substitute more of the good for other, relatively more expensive goods. In addition, the decrease in price increases consumers' purchasing power, enabling them to increase their consumption of the good whose price has fallen, as well as other goods.

Consumer Decision Making in Practice

It is not atypical for someone to come away from his first reading of the theory of consumer behavior rolling his eyes skyward and muttering about "this ridiculous marginal utility per dollar business!" The theory of consumer behavior gives some people the impression that economists believe consumers are just microcomputers with arms and legs, but without souls, who spend three quarters of their time making careful calculations to ensure that utility is maximized and the other quarter of their time consuming the goods and services so carefully chosen. This impression is mistaken. Consumption is the objective of all economic activity. The benefits of consumption are the comfort, the joy, the excitement, the pure pleasure of satisfying one's wants. To maximize benefits, a rational consumer follows the decision-making rule established in this chapter: Consume goods and services in quantities such that MU/P is equal for all goods and services consumed.

This is not meant to suggest that whenever someone makes a decision concerning the consumption of a particular good that she explicitly considers the marginal utility of each unit consumed. Instead, what we are arguing is that whenever someone consumes what she considers to be the best combination of goods and services, she has implicitly set MU/P equal for all goods.

Transactions Costs in the Theory of Demand

The primary concern of economists is with the relationship between the opportunity cost of consumption and its benefits. We have generally assumed that the opportunity cost of consumption is captured in the market price of the good. In many instances, however, the market price of a good accounts for less than the full opportunity cost of consumption. The difference between the full opportunity cost and the market price is called the **transactions cost** of consumption. Although transactions costs take a variety of forms, they all have the same impact on consumer behavior—the cost of consumption is greater than the market price.

Transactions costs include all costs (except price) that are incurred in the process of purchasing and consuming a good or service. Waiting costs, taxes of different kinds (especially so-called nuisance taxes), contractual costs (which can be substantial when buying consumer durable goods), and the expected costs of risks assumed in consumption (for example, penalties if caught consuming illegal goods or services) are all examples of transactions costs. All these costs drive a wedge between the market price of a good and the true opportunity cost of consumption.

Time spent in making a transaction is a transaction cost. We typically do not think too much about this cost, but sometimes it is an important part of the opportunity cost of consumption. If a service station in town advertises its gasoline for 30¢ a gallon, it will attract considerable attention because this price is below the market price. Many people will attempt to take advantage of the offer. Consequently, although you can buy the gasoline for 30¢ a gallon, you may have to wait in line for a long time. Waiting is a transaction cost that will influence your gasoline consumption decision.[3]

The theory of consumer behavior we have developed in this chapter assumes that individuals are rational and informed and that transactions costs are zero. That is, for simplicity we have assumed away the frictions of the real world. While these frictions do not alter the consumer's decision-making rule (that is why we initially assumed them away), they do change the manner and sometimes the outcomes of the decisions we make. Let's consider three types of transactions costs or friction: (1) **information costs**, (2) **mobility costs**, and (3) **decision-making costs**.

Information Costs The assumption that consumers are fully informed decision makers implies that their consumption decisions are made with knowledge of all available consumption alternatives and prices. In actual practice, consumers may not be fully informed—for good reason. The acquisition of information is costly. For relatively inexpensive purchases, acquiring information on all alternatives may not be worth the additional cost. If you want to buy a personal stereo, such as a Sony Walkman, you might visit two stores and see five to ten different products. Additional visits to other stores might enable you to see a few more different stereos. However, the chances are low of saving a great deal of money as a result of the continued search for additional information. This possible gain must be weighed against the costs of additional store visits.

Transactions costs Any of the opportunity costs of consumption that are not incorporated in the market price of a good or service.

Information costs The costs incurred in gathering information to be used in making a consumption decision.

Mobility costs The expense, time, and effort spent traveling to a particular location to complete a transaction for a consumption good.

Decision-making costs The time, effort, and risk involved in making a consumption decision.

---

[3]Since a demand curve incorporates transactions costs, any change in transactions costs will change the cost of consumption and therefore the demand for the product. An increase in transactions costs reduces the gain from consumption and shifts the demand curve to the left. A decrease in such costs shifts the demand curve to the right.

On the other hand, consumers who are making major purchases, such as automobiles, houses, a college education, or consumer durables will spend considerable amounts of time and money collecting information. The potential gains from this process are substantial in this kind of purchase. Notice that these costs are transactions costs for the purchase. One reason we are a little uncomfortable with the theory of consumer behavior is that we know consumers are not fully informed. However, consumers use the same benefit–cost calculation that they use to make their consumption choices when deciding how much information to acquire.

Mobility Costs   A second cost associated with consumption decisions, but ignored so far, is mobility costs. It takes time to go from one place to another. Movement is costly. We expend resources directly on some transportation source such as a car or bus. In addition, time is a scarce good and therefore costly. Travel time requires a sacrifice. Thus, mobility costs can affect the outcome of consumption decisions. If we want to purchase a beverage for a small dinner party, we will purchase it from the least-cost supplier. However, time can be an important factor in the decision. If we decide to make the purchase only a half-hour before the party, the proximity of the supplier will be an important factor in the purchase decision. We may buy the beverage at a higher price than we know is available elsewhere because we can get it from a nearby location and therefore make the purchase in a shorter period of time.

In deciding how far to travel for the beverage, we had good, complete information and we opted for a higher-priced purchase. However, notice the decision-making process. We wanted a beverage for a party in thirty minutes. That is not the same kind of consumption purchase as a beverage for a party next week. Having the beverage fifteen minutes sooner is more valuable to us than the increased purchase price. Again we have used the consumer decision rule in a more complicated, but real world, context. The rule we followed was the one developed in this chapter. In fact, we used it in a very sophisticated way. We recognized that the full cost of the beverage included both the price of the beverage and the travel time to make the purchase. Remember that good decision making requires the identification of the true costs and benefits of each alternative.

Decision-Making Costs   The third type of cost involves the decisions themselves. One of the reasons that the MU/P rule bothers many people when they are first exposed to it is that it suggests that we spend an inordinate amount of time making decisions. In fact, you may have wondered at one point or another how a consumer could really use this rule and still have time to consume anything. This insight is an important one. The very process of decision making itself is costly; it takes time and effort and requires the expenditure of resources. Thus, we would expect these costs to affect consumption decisions to some extent. Do I really want this item enough to justify the required expenditure? This question is one we have all asked ourselves at one time or another.

Our uncertainty about the extent to which we will benefit from a consumption good makes the decision itself costly. This risk is much like the risk a businesswoman faces in deciding to start a business. She believes that she will be able to make a profit, but she is not guaranteed a profit. The risk that we assume in either of these decisions is the source of a decision-making cost. Consumers do make mistakes. They overestimate consumption benefits, or

Why the **Disagreement?**

The Poverty Programs Controversy

Programs to reduce poverty are probably the government's most controversial domestic programs. The debate over the appropriate extent of support provided and the structure of the programs is, it seems, never ending. Ever since Michael Harrington's book *Hunger in America* (1963) startled the country with a vivid depiction of poverty in the United States, and President Lyndon Johnson launched the War on Poverty in the 1960s, the country has been embroiled in a public debate of the relative benefits and costs of antipoverty programs. Although there have been repeated calls for welfare reform, the general structure of these programs has changed little since they were first established nearly thirty years ago, and total funding has increased substantially. Why have these programs generated so much disagreement?

Statistics suggest that it is not a general unwillingness to support worthwhile causes, including caring for the poor and destitute, that accounts for the emotional intensity of the debate. In 1985, Americans contributed an estimated $70 billion to private charitable and philanthropic organizations. However, it is important to note that a contribution to a private charitable organization, such as the Salvation Army or United Way, differs from support provided for a government poverty program in at least one important aspect — the contribution to the charity is voluntary, and support provided for government programs through the payment of taxes is not.

The proponents of relying primarily on voluntary contributions to fund antipoverty efforts believe that the net benefits associated with this approach outweigh the net benefits associated with government-sponsored programs. From an economic perspective, an individual chooses to donate to a charity just as he chooses to purchase a consumer good. He compares the benefits — the marginal utility of the donation — to the cost. In this case, the cost is the amount of the donation. The benefit from a donation is the satisfaction derived from the gift. Consumers have favorite charities or causes that are especially important to them. Alternatively, they might make a donation in their own names, obtaining both satisfaction from the use to which the donation is put and recognition for their support. A donation is made when the marginal utility of a dollar spent on a gift is higher than the marginal utility per dollar spent on the available consumption alternatives. Overall, there is a net gain — both the donor and the recipient gain from the charitable contribution.

Unlike charitable donations, tax payments to support poverty programs are not vountary. In addition, the taxpayer has very little control over the cause to which the taxes go. Thus, to some taxpayers these payments represent sacrifices — costs incurred — with little or no benefit in return. In effect, society requires them to make an exchange by which their own welfare is reduced rather than enhanced. Moreover, the beneficiaries of these tax payments are viewed as receiving resources — income or services — with little or no sacrifice. The resource constraints under which we all live make the idea of a free lunch attractive to everyone. Consequently, it should not be surprising that when one individual is required to sacrifice for someone else's benefit, dissatisfaction frequently surfaces.

On the other hand, proponents of government-sponsored antipoverty programs feel that the government is better equipped to address the problems of the needy than are private individuals and organizations. In this case it could be argued that the government is in a much better position to identify the individuals most in need of assistance. As such, there is less risk that truly needy individuals will be overlooked when aid is distributed. In addition, it could be argued that funneling funds through a single distribution point makes it possible to compare the benefits of providing assistance to alternative groups. This improves the likelihood that funds will be distributed where they are most highly valued. The result is that total utility is increased by having the government allocate funds to those individuals it identifies as having the greatest need.

Clearly, the arguments on both sides merit consideration. In addition, it is clear that no simple solution to the debate over the appropriate form of income redistribution will be forthcoming soon. However, application of the concept of utility theory helps explain why different individuals take the position they have on this issue.

they make purchases based on erroneous or incomplete information. However, in the long run their reaction to these mistakes is consistent with the theory of consumer behavior: When consumers become aware of the problem they correct the mistakes.

Decision-making costs do have an impact on consumer decisions. Although we have assumed that consumers maximize utility, we have provided no further information about the specific nature of this goal. For instance, are consumers maximizing lifetime utility when they make consumption decisions today or when they made them last year? This question is a difficult one to answer. In reality, the precise framework within which consumers attempt to maximize utility varies across consumers. Among consumers with similar incomes, some might live for today while others might essentially live for tomorrow. These orientations suggest different consumption patterns. The differences arise because of different values placed on goods available today versus goods available tomorrow.

None of these real-world complications voids the theory of consumer behavior. They simply change the manner in which the decision rule is used in actual practice.

> **SECTION RECAP**
> Transactions costs, such as information costs, mobility costs, and decision-making costs all affect consumer decision making by increasing the full opportunity cost incurred in consuming a particular good. However, they do not alter the consumer's decision-making rule.

Summary

In this chapter the fundamental proposition of economics has been applied to a specific set of decisions: the choices of individual consumers. The general problem is the basic economic problem of scarcity. Consumers derive **utility** from the consumption of economic goods and services. However, since consumers have limited resources or incomes, they must make consumption decisions by weighing the costs and benefits of each purchase to maximize the utility derived from their incomes.

Consumers choose goods and services in quantities that give them the greatest utility from each dollar of income they spend. The opportunity cost of consumption is measured by market prices, over which a consumer has no control. Consumers take prices as given. The benefits of consuming another unit of a good depend upon the consumer's taste for the good, the quantity of the good already consumed, and the consumption alternatives available to the consumer.

The rule for maximizing utility is for the consumer to adjust quantities consumed of all goods such that MU/P is equal for the last unit of all goods consumed. The result of utility-maximizing behavior is that the quantity willingly consumed is inversely related to market price: Demand curves are negatively sloped.

The **substitution effect** and the **income effect** provide two additional explanations for why demand curves are downward sloping. According to the substitution effect, consumers will consume additional quantities of a good when its price declines because the good is now less expensive relative to other, substitute goods. The income effect suggests that as the price of a good falls, a person's purchasing power increases, enabling her to purchase more of the good.

Questions for Thought

Knowledge Questions

1. What is the difference between marginal and total utility? Think of an example that illustrates the difference.
2. What is the difference between the cost of watching a baseball game on TV and going to one at the ball park? What is the difference in utility gained from each?
3. Assume that your income is fixed at its present level. Is there a way that you could change your pattern of expenditures and increase the satisfaction that you get from your income?
4. In your own words, how do the substitution effect and the income effect explain the downward-sloping demand curve?

Application Questions

5. Using Table 2, assume that the price of CDs increases to $65 per unit. What would the new utility-maximizing combination of jumps and CDs consist of? Once you have determined the new utility-maximizing combination of goods, use the old and new price–quantity combinations of CDs purchased to construct a demand curve for CDs. Is the demand curve downward sloping?
6. Use the rule for utility maximization to explain how an increase in the price of one good causes the demand for its substitute to increase.
7. Subsequent to the Iraqi invasion of Kuwait in August 1990 the price of a gallon of gas rose by more than 30 percent in most parts of the United States. Use the substitution and income effects to analyze the effects of this price change in the markets for gas and fuel-efficient cars.
8. Assume that an individual is currently using all of his income to consume two goods—X and Y. If the prices of X and Y are $3 and $8, respectively, and the MU of the last unit of good X is 8 while the MU of the last unit of Y is 15, is this individual maximizing his utility? If not, what should he do to increase utility?

Synthesis Questions

9. A local record store sells albums with quantity discounts. The first two albums are sold at their list price, but the third album is sold at a 10 percent discount and the fourth album at a 20 percent discount. Use the law of diminishing marginal utility to explain this pricing policy.
10. The development of the fast food industry is often attributed (in part) to the increased number of women, especially married women, working outside the home. Explain this argument. What is the full opportunity cost of a meal prepared at home?
11. The theory of consumer behavior asserts that individuals derive utility from consuming goods and services. Their limited incomes prevent them from satisfying all wants. Yet consumers typically do not spend all of their income. They save part of it. How can savings be consistent with utility-maximizing behavior?
12. Explain, in terms of changes in marginal utility, the effect of an increase in the transactions costs associated with a particular good on the demand for that good.

Appendix to CHAPTER 7

Indifference Curves Analysis

Overview

This appendix presents a more technical approach to the concepts of utility maximization and the law of demand. It is intended to provide additional insights into the derivations of the rule for utility maximization and the downward-sloping demand curve.

The Utility Function and Indifference Curves

The theory of consumer behavior assumes that for normal goods, consumers have a well-behaved set of preferences. In particular, we assume that more is preferred to less and that, holding total utility constant, the value of additional units of a good declines as more of it is consumed. The implication of these assumptions is that in the process of choosing between two goods and holding total utility constant, the amount of one good that a consumer is willing to give up to get one more unit of the other good becomes smaller and smaller. Alternatively, the consumer must receive larger and larger amounts of one good in exchange for each additional unit of the other good given up to still receive the same amount of total utility.

This concept is illustrated in Table 4, which identifies specific combinations of two goods, jeans and shirts, that yield the same level of utility for a representative consumer. As the table indicates, the additional amount of one good the consumer must consume to maintain a constant level of utility must increase as the amount of the other good consumed is decreased. For example, if the consumer reduces his consumption of jeans from nine units to five units, he must increase consumption of shirts by one unit; an average of .25 units for each unit of jeans given up. When consumption of jeans decreases from five units to two units, consumption of shirts must increase by three units, and so forth.

The information in Table 4 is also plotted in Figure 3. The resulting curve is called an **indifference curve**. It locates all the combinations of jeans and shirts that yield the same level of total utility. A consumer receives the same amount of total utility from any combination of goods on a given indifference curve. As such, the consumer is indifferent between the combination of jeans and shirts associated with point A and the combination associated with point B.

Indifference curve
All combinations of two goods, X and Y, that yield the same level of total utility.

TABLE 4

Alternative combinations of two goods that yield the same level of utility for a representative consumer

Utility	Amount of Jeans Consumed	Amount of Shirts Consumed
15	9	1
15	5	2
15	2	5
15	1	9

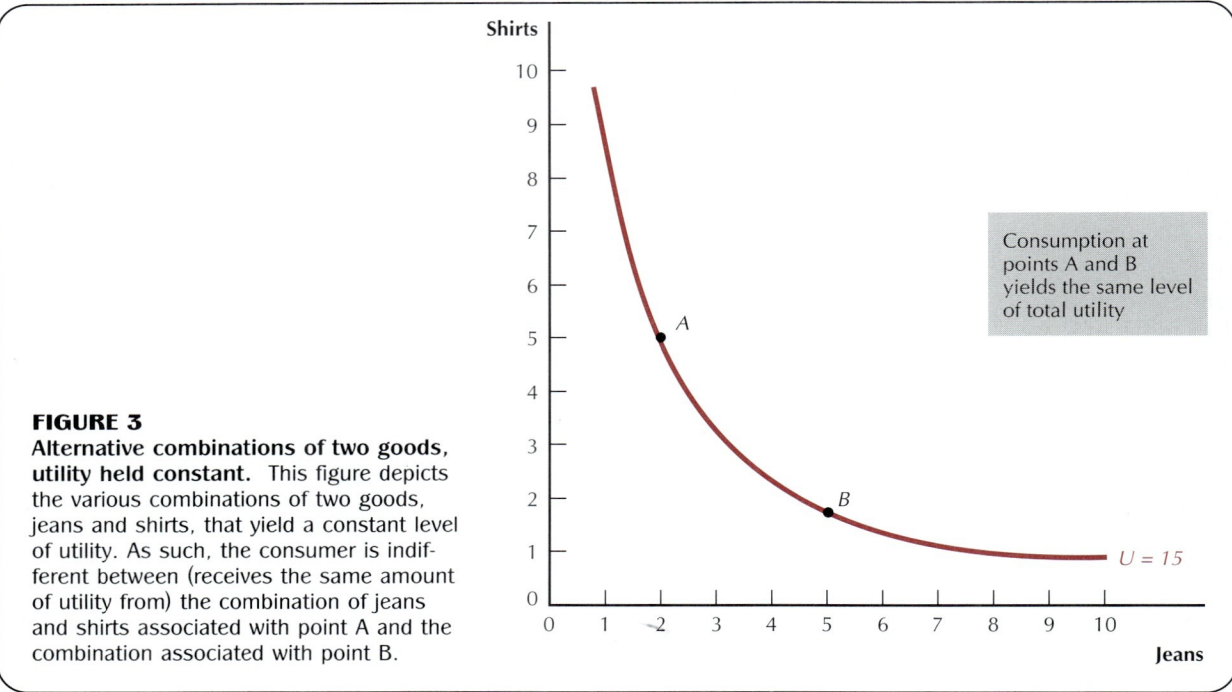

FIGURE 3
Alternative combinations of two goods, utility held constant. This figure depicts the various combinations of two goods, jeans and shirts, that yield a constant level of utility. As such, the consumer is indifferent between (receives the same amount of utility from) the combination of jeans and shirts associated with point A and the combination associated with point B.

Indifference Curves and the Marginal Rate of Substitution

Marginal rate of substitution
The ratio of the marginal utilities of two goods, holding total utility constant; the slope of the indifference curve.

Indifference curve map
A set of indifference curves, each of which is associated with a different level of total utility; moving up to the right (away from the origin) moves the consumer to higher levels of utility.

The rate at which a consumer is willing to exchange one good for another and still remain at the same level of total utility is known as the **marginal rate of substitution**, or MRS. The MRS between any two goods, X and Y, is equal to the ratio $-MU_X/MU_Y$ and it is the slope of the indifference curve. In most cases, the MRS is assumed to change as we alter the combination of the two goods consumed (holding total utility constant). In our example, the marginal rate of substitution of jeans for shirts is equal to the ratio $-MU_J/MU_S$.

Figure 4 depicts an **indifference curve map**. Each indifference curve, for example, the curve labelled U_1, locates all the combinations of jeans and shirts between which the consumer is indifferent. Note that the indifference curves are convex to the origin, that is, they are bowed in toward the origin. The slope of an indifference curve at any point is simply the MRS of jeans for shirts, $-MU_J/MU_S$.

Moving up to the right (away from the origin) moves the consumer to higher levels of utility. As such, U_3 is associated with a higher level of utility than U_2, and U_2 is associated with a higher level of utility than U_1. To maximize utility, a consumer will seek to consume a combination of goods that lies on the highest indifference curve possible.

The Budget Constraint

The consumer is constrained, however, by the amount of income available to him for consumption. In the simple case being considered here, where only two goods are being consumed, the budget constraint can be written mathematically as:

$$M \geq P_J J + P_S S$$

where M represents total income, and P_J and P_S are the prices of jeans and shirts,

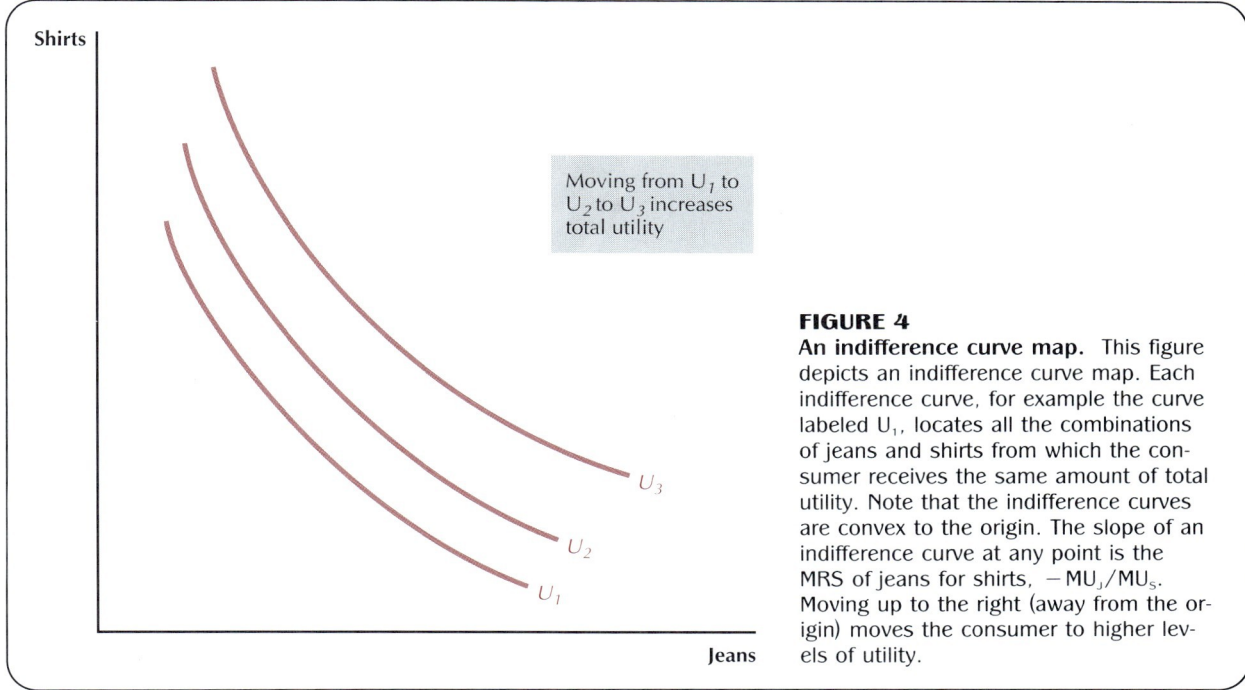

FIGURE 4
An indifference curve map. This figure depicts an indifference curve map. Each indifference curve, for example the curve labeled U_1, locates all the combinations of jeans and shirts from which the consumer receives the same amount of total utility. Note that the indifference curves are convex to the origin. The slope of an indifference curve at any point is the MRS of jeans for shirts, $-MU_J/MU_S$. Moving up to the right (away from the origin) moves the consumer to higher levels of utility.

respectively. The budget constraint simply states that total expenditures on X and Y must be less than or equal to available income.

A budget constraint has been graphed in Figure 5. The slope of the budget constraint is $-P_J/P_S$. The slope is found by solving the budget constraint for S, that is:

$$M = P_J J + P_S S$$
$$P_S S = M - P_J J$$
$$S = M/P_S - (P_J/P_S)J$$

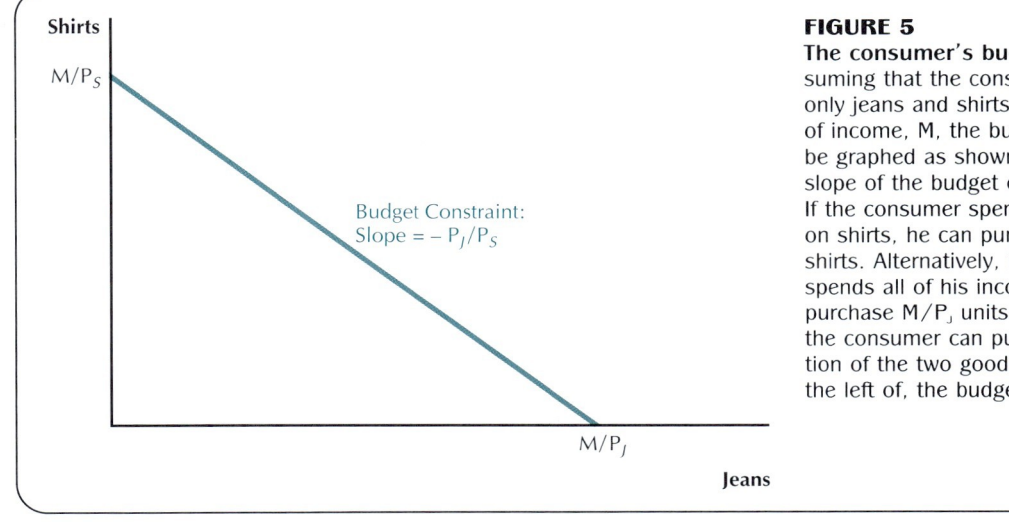

FIGURE 5
The consumer's budget constraint. Assuming that the consumer is purchasing only jeans and shirts with a fixed amount of income, M, the budget constraint can be graphed as shown in this figure. The slope of the budget constraint is $-P_J/P_S$. If the consumer spends all of his income on shirts, he can purchase M/P_S units of shirts. Alternatively, if the consumer spends all of his income on jeans, he can purchase M/P_J units of jeans. In addition, the consumer can purchase any combination of the two goods that lies on, or to the left of, the budget constraint.

FIGURE 6
Utility maximization in the case of two goods. The information in Figures 4 and 5 has been combined here to illustrate the utility-maximizing level of consumption. Utility is maximized by consuming the combination of goods associated with point C, J_C and S_C, respectively. At point C, the consumer's budget constraint is just tangent to indifference curve U_2, and the MRS of jeans for shirts is equal to the slope of the budget constraint. Points A and B are also attainable by the consumer, since each point lies on the consumer's budget constraint. However, if the consumer moves to any point other than C, such as A or B, he will automatically place himself on a lower indifference curve.

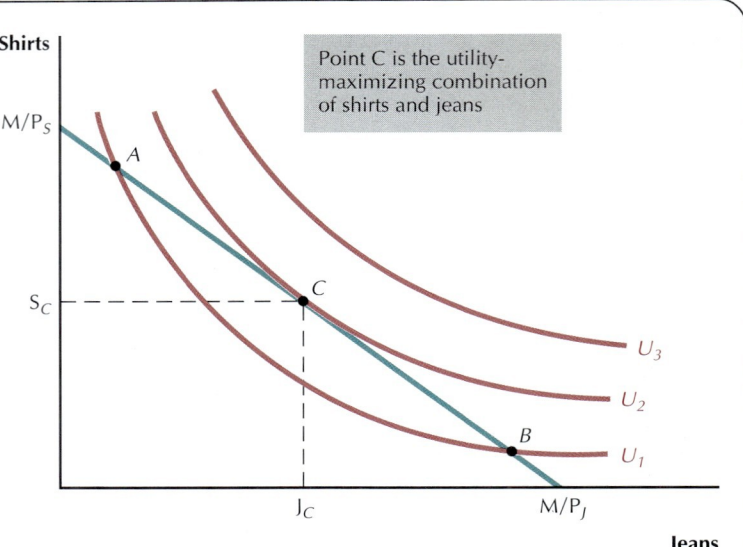

Point C is the utility-maximizing combination of shirts and jeans

Note that if the consumer spends all of his income on shirts, he can purchase M/P_S units of shirts. In a similar fashion, if the consumer spends all of his income on jeans, he can purchase M/P_J units of jeans. In addition, the consumer can purchase any combination of shirts and jeans that lies on, or to the left of, the budget constraint.

Utility Maximization

To maximize utility, the consumer will consume that combination of goods that lies on the highest indifference curve he can attain for a given budget constraint. The information in Figures 4 and 5 has been combined in Figure 6, which illustrates the utility-maximizing level of consumption for our consumer. Note that, as it is drawn, the consumer's budget constraint is just tangent to indifference curve U_2, at point C. The consumer will maximize his utility by consuming the combination of jeans and shirts associated with point C, J_C and S_C, respectively. At point C, the MRS of jeans for shirts is equal to the slope of the budget constraint, $-P_J/P_S$ or:

$$\frac{-MU_J}{MU_S} = \frac{-P_J}{P_S}$$

which can be rewritten as:

$$\frac{MU_J}{P_J} = \frac{MU_S}{P_S}$$

Note that this is simply the rule for utility maximization that we derived in the main part of the chapter.

To see why point C maximizes utility, consider points A and B. Both of these combinations of jeans and shirts are attainable by the consumer, since each point lies on the consumer's budget constraint. However, each of these points lies on indifference curve U_1, which is associated with a lower level of total utility than U_2. In fact, if the consumer moves to any other point (on or inside his budget constraint) except point C, he will automatically place himself on a lower indifference curve.

Deriving the Demand Curve

The indifference curve map and the budget constraint can also be used to derive the demand curve for a good. As an illustration, assume that the price of jeans increases from P_J to P'_J. This has the effect of causing the budget constraint to rotate in toward the origin as illustrated in Figure 7 (a). Note that the budget constraint still intersects the vertical axis at M/P_S. This is because the price of shirts and the level of income have not changed. Hence, the consumer can still purchase the same number of shirts as

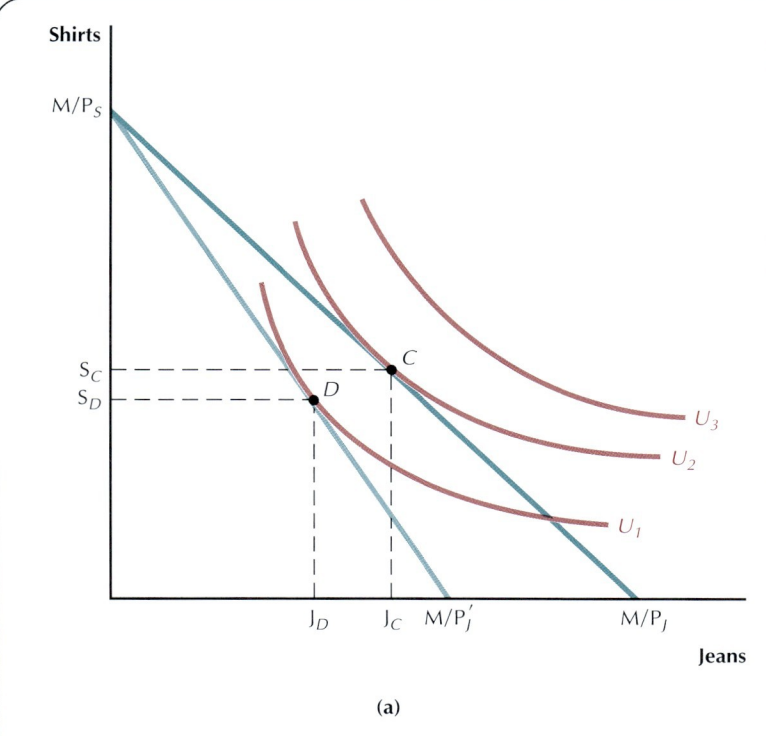

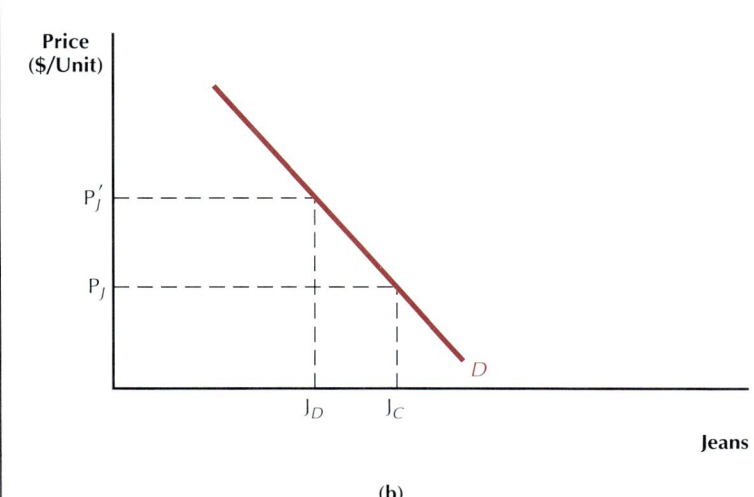

FIGURE 7
Deriving the demand curve for jeans. If the price of jeans increases from P_J to P'_J, the budget constraint will rotate as illustrated in Figure 7 (a). Because the price of shirts and the level of income have not changed, the consumer can still purchase the same amount of shirts as before. However, because the price of jeans has increased, the consumer now is able to purchase only M/P'_J units. Point D is the new utility-maximizing combination of jeans and shirts. The demand curve for jeans is derived in Figure 7 (b). At the initial price, P_J, the consumer purchased J_C units of jeans. Once the price of jeans increased to P'_J, the consumer reduced his purchases of jeans to J_D units. The demand curve for jeans is downward sloping.

before. However, because the price of jeans has increased, the consumer is able to purchase fewer pairs of jeans. As shown in Figure 7 (a), if the consumer were to spend all of his income on jeans, he could only purchase M/P'_J units.

Because the budget constraint has now rotated, it is tangent to a lower indifference curve, in this case U_1. Point D is now the utility-maximizing combination of jeans and shirts. The increase in the price of jeans has forced the consumer to a lower level of utility. In addition, the consumer is now consuming fewer units of jeans (as well as shirts).

The demand curve for jeans is derived in Figure 7 (b). At the initial price, P_J, the consumer purchased J_C units of jeans. Once the price of jeans increased to P'_J, the consumer reduced his purchases of jeans to J_D units. As we would expect, the demand curve for jeans is downward sloping, as shown in the figure.

The Substitution and Income Effects. Additional insights into the theory of demand can be seen by focusing on Figure 7 (a), which has been recreated in Figure 8. The increase in the price of jeans from P_J to P'_J caused purchases of jeans to fall from J_C to J_D. This reduction in jeans purchased can be broken down into two components: the **substitution effect** and the **income effect**.

Recall that the substitution effect states that when the price of a good increases, the consumer will consume less of the good and increase consumption of other, relatively less-expensive goods. The substitution effect is seen graphically when a line is constructed, parallel to the new budget constraint and just tangent to the original indifference curve. The dashed line that is tangent to U_2 at point E has been so con-

Substitution effect
Consumers purchase more of a good whose price has fallen relative to the prices of its substitutes.

Income effect
The increase in real purchasing power that results from a decrease in the price of a consumption good, *ceteris paribus*.

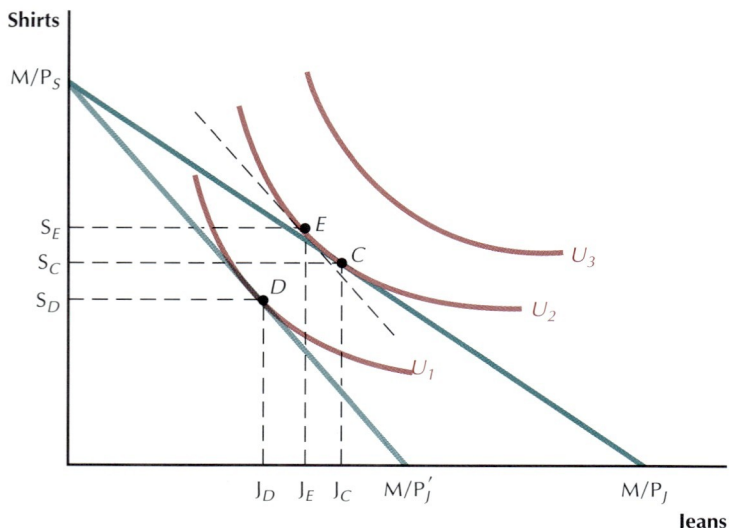

FIGURE 8
The substitution and income effects. The substitution effect is illustrated by constructing a line parallel to the new budget constraint and tangent to the original indifference curve, as shown by the dashed line tangent to U_2 at point E. J_E is the quantity of jeans that would be consumed after the price increase, holding utility constant. The income effect is shown by the movement from J_E to J_D. This is the amount by which consumption of jeans declines as a result of the reduction in purchasing power associated with the increase in the price of jeans. The substitution and income effects combine to cause the consumption of jeans to fall from J_C to J_D.

structed. The quantity of jeans associated with point E, J_E, is the amount of jeans that would be consumed after the price increase, but holding utility constant. Consumption of jeans has fallen by the amount $J_C - J_E$. (Note that consumption of shirts has increased).

The income effect is shown by the movement from J_E to J_D. This is the amount by which consumption of jeans declines as a result of the reduction in purchasing power associated with the increase in the price of jeans. Once again, the substitution and income effects combine to cause the consumption of jeans to fall from J_C to J_D.

OVERVIEW

In the previous chapter we saw that consumers choose the goods and services they consume by weighing the marginal benefits of consumption against the marginal costs, measured by market prices. In this chapter, we begin an equally close look at economic behavior on the supply side of the market: the decision making of firms.

Like consumers, firms are diverse in many dimensions.

Entrepreneurial Behavior

They vary in size, ranging from conglomerates with world-wide operations and thousands of employees to small one-person operations in local communities. They employ different production technologies and use different kinds of resources. They may produce basic commodities such as sand, lumber, corn, or oil, or they may produce exotic and unique products: Rolls-Royces, Cray computers, nuclear power plants, artificial hearts. However, just as we assume that all consumers have a common objective—utility maximization—we assume there is an element common to all firms: They are all in business to make a profit.

To analyze the behavior of the broad range of firms that exist, we need a means of categorizing firms.

Consequently, in this chapter we explore alternative methods for categorizing firms. Depending on how firms are categorized we can say more or less about how they behave when they attempt to maximize the amount of profit they earn.

In this chapter, we also carefully define the notion of profit. In addition, we devote attention to the time dimension of the decisions of firms, making an

CHAPTER 8

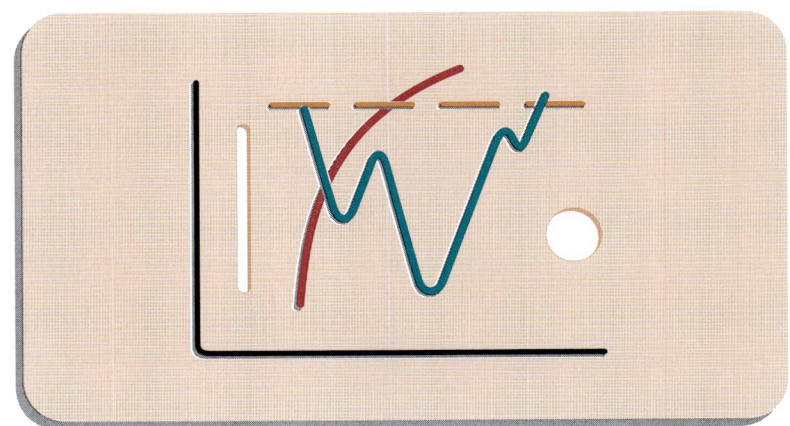

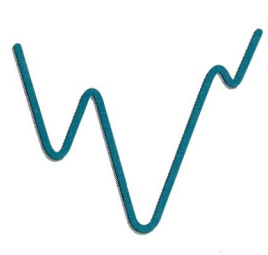

important distinction between short-run and long-run decisions. We also initiate a discussion of the determinants of production costs, which continues into the next chapter.

Learning Objectives

After reading and studying this chapter, you will be able to:

1. Describe three approaches that can be used to categorize the range of firms that operate in the U.S. economy.
2. Explain the advantages and disadvantages of the three legal forms of business organization.
3. Identify the major characteristics that distinguish the different types of market structures that exist in the economy.
4. Define normal profit and economic profit.
5. Explain the difference between economic profit and accounting profit.
6. Distinguish between a short-run and a long-run decision.

The Entrepreneurial Challenge

As the first step in our analysis of the behavior of firms we need to address the question, Why do firms exist? In brief, firms facilitate the efficient allocation and organization of productive resources. We have already seen how specialization can enable individuals to consume a greater amount of output than they could otherwise. Firms take advantage of the benefits of specialization by bringing together the inputs needed to produce a particular product. Within the firm, inputs such as capital and labor have specialized functions and each input contributes to the production of the firm's output. The problem for the firm is deciding the types and quantities of inputs it should purchase to achieve its objectives.

Generally speaking, the decision making of firms is quite like that of consumers. In both cases, the decision maker chooses among available alternatives to maximize well-being: Consumers maximize utility, firms maximize profit. This decision process requires that the decision maker—consumer or producer—evaluate the costs and benefits of each alternative. However, many supply decisions have an element of *riskiness* associated with them that is absent from most consumption decisions.

A business firm attempts to make a profit by purchasing resources, combining them in a way that yields a consumer good or service, and then selling the good or service at a price that is at least as great as the cost of production. The real problem for the firm is that there is never any guarantee that consumers will pay a high enough price and buy enough units of the good for the firm to earn a profit. The firm must make an educated guess about the expected demand for the product.

In addition, firms must incur costs before they earn revenues. Production takes time. Resources must be purchased and production facilities established before there is output to sell to consumers. The producer must be able to finance production during the time between the purchase of inputs and the sale of outputs. The firm incurs debts before it has a chance to sell its product and generate revenue. A firm's success is uncertain. Getting into business to sell a product is risky. One can win big or lose big!

It is this aspect of supply that makes entrepreneurship important. An **entrepreneur** is a person who organizes, manages, and assumes the risks of a business enterprise. In a market economy characterized by competition and resource mobility, this riskiness persists over time. Even an established and very profitable firm can become unprofitable and fail if its owners or managers do not continue to study consumer wants, seek product improvements or new products, look for new production technologies, and respond to changes in market conditions. All of these decisions involve some uncertainty and risk. Business success requires the continued willingness to assume risks.

Clearly, understanding how a firm's decision-making process works requires an understanding of many interrelated issues such as how output is produced, how costs are determined, and how much revenue the firm can expect to earn from a particular level of output. However, before we can begin to address these specific questions, we need to group firms together into broad categories so as to simplify our analysis.

Entrepreneur
A person who organizes, manages, and assumes the risks of a business enterprise.

SECTION RECAP
Like consumers, firms attempt to maximize their well-being, which is measured by profits. However, unlike most consumption decisions, production decisions involve an element of risk. Entrepreneurs assume the risks of a business enterprise.

Ways to Categorize Firms

Because we have such a rich diversity of firms in an economy, we can categorize them in a number of ways. In this section, we identify three different ways we can group firms.

Industries

Firms can be grouped according to the products they produce. These groupings are called **industries**. When we speak of the auto industry, the construction industry, the pharmaceutical industry, or the wholesale trade industry, we are referring to those firms that produce similar products: automobiles and trucks, residential and commercial buildings, drugs, or the distribution of goods from manufacturers to retailers. These industry groupings can be quite general, such as the manufacturing industry, or very specific, such as the lumber and wood products industry. Table 1 displays a list of general industry categories taken

Industry
A grouping of firms that produce a similar product.

TABLE 1

The standard industrial classification of businesses

Two-Digit Categories

Agricultural production — crops	Agriculture, Forestry, and Fishing
Agricultural production — livestock	
Agricultural services	
Forestry	
Fishing, hunting, and trapping	
Metal mining	Mining
Coal mining	
Oil and gas extraction	
Nonmetallic minerals, excluding fuels	
General building contractors	Construction
Heavy construction, excluding building	
Special trade contractors	
Food and kindred products	Manufacturing
Tobacco products	
Textile mill products	
Apparel and other textile products	
Lumber and wood products	
Furniture and fixtures	
Paper and allied products	
Printing and publishing	
Chemicals and allied products	
Petroleum and coal products	
Rubber and miscellaneous plastics products	
Leather and leather products	
Stone, clay, and glass products	
Primary metal industries	
Fabricated metal products	
Industrial machinery and equipment	
Electronic and other electric equipment	
Transportation equipment	
Instruments and related products	
Miscellaneous manufacturing industries	*(continued)*

TABLE 1

(Continued)

Two-Digit Categories

Railroad transportation	Transportation and Public Utilities
Local and interurban passenger transit	
U.S. Postal Service	
Water transportation	
Transportation by air	
Pipelines, excluding natural gas	
Transportation services	
Communications	
Electric, gas, and sanitary services	
Wholesale trade — durable goods	Wholesale Trade
Wholesale trade — nondurable goods	
Building materials and garden supplies	Retail Trade
General merchandise stores	
Food stores	
Automotive dealers and service stations	
Apparel and accessory stores	
Furniture and home furnishings stores	
Eating and drinking places	
Miscellaneous retail	
Depository institutions	Finance, Insurance, and Real Estate
Nondepository institutions	
Security and commodity brokers	
Insurance carriers	
Insurance agents, brokers, and service	
Real estate	
Holding and other investment offices	
Hotels and other lodging places	Services
Personal services	
Business services	
Auto repair, services, and parking	
Miscellaneous repair services	
Motion pictures	
Amusement and recreation services	
Health services	
Legal services	
Educational services	
Social services	
Museums, botanical, zoological gardens	
Membership organizations	
Engineering and management services	
Private households	
Services, not elsewhere classified	
Executive, legislative, and general	Public Administration
Justice, public order, and safety	
Finance, taxation, and monetary	
Administration of human resources	
Environmental quality and housing	
Administration of economic programs	
National security and international affairs	

Source: United States, Office of Management and Budget, *Standard Industrial Classification Manual*, 1987.

from an industry classification scheme adopted by the federal government. The major industry categories, listed on the right-hand side of the table, are comprised of more detailed industry categories, listed on the left-hand side of the table.

Firms within each of the industry categories are similar in many respects. They sell products in the same or related markets and thus face similar market conditions — changes in demand, new technological developments, competition from other sectors, or cost pressures. Within an industry, firms use generally similar production processes. The relative size of these industries reflects patterns of consumer tastes, the nature of society's resource endowment, the level of economic development, and other characteristics of the economy. For example, measured by levels of employment, the agricultural sector in the United States has been shrinking since the turn of the century, the manufacturing sector has stabilized at a level achieved in the 1960s, and the service and government sectors have grown considerably.

Legal Structure

Business firms also can be categorized according to one of three basic legal structures: sole proprietorship, partnership, and corporation. The firm's legal structure affects how much control its owners have over the business, the firm's access to financial resources, and the liability (legal responsibility) of the owners for the financial obligations of the firm. The characteristics of each legal form of business are discussed in turn.

Sole Proprietorship   The simplest form of business organization is one that is owned and operated by a single individual; thus it is called a **sole proprietorship**. The owners of these businesses are self employed. They have complete control over all business decisions and are personally responsible for all obligations assumed by the business. In a very real sense, the owner is the business. The business itself is not recognized as a legal entity separate from the owner. The owner is legally responsible for contracts entered into between the firm and other individuals or businesses. When legal action is taken against the firm, it is the owner who is sued.

Sole proprietorship
A business that is owned by a single person.

Sole proprietorships are numerous, but they tend to be small. Business situations in which we frequently encounter sole proprietorships include small retail operations such as ice cream stores and cleaning establishments, general contractors and builders, and real estate agents. In 1984, there were more than 11 million nonfarm sole proprietorships in existence. About four fifths of them had annual sales of less than $50,000, and only one percent had sales in excess of $500,000 annually.

Sole proprietorships tend to be small for very good reasons. While the sole proprietor has the important advantage of being in complete control of the business, she faces two severe limitations in this business form. First, the law makes no distinction between the owner and the business; the owner is personally liable for the financial obligations of the firm. This liability is unlimited; the owner's personal assets can be taken to satisfy the firm's creditors.

Second, proprietorships have limited access to the financial resources necessary for growth. It is costly for a firm to expand its production or to develop new or improved products. These costs are incurred before the firm is able to sell the additional or new products. Thus, the firm must have access to financial

Financial capital
The money firms acquire from lending institutions and individuals to finance production activities, including current production, expansion, product development, and so forth.

Partnership
A business that is owned by two or more people. Each partner is personally liable for all of the firm's obligations.

Corporation
A legal business entity that is owned by a group of individuals. The corporation can sue and be sued, but the liability of each owner is limited to the amount of money he or she has invested in the firm.

resources, referred to as **financial capital**, to finance these activities.[1] A sole proprietor's ability to raise financial capital to support growth of the business is limited. If the business is to remain a sole proprietorship, funds for research, development, and growth must be generated by the firm or borrowed. Borrowing opportunities are constrained by the characteristics of the business form; loans are secured by the personal assets of the owner. In summary, sole proprietorships tend to be very small businesses that are owned and managed by one person. Owners of these firms have limited access to financial capital and bear all the risks—including legal liability—of doing business.

Partnership   A **partnership** differs from a sole proprietorship in only one way: There are two or more joint owners of the business. Some of the more common examples of partnerships include many law and accounting firms, construction companies, consulting firms, and medical clinics. In a partnership, decision-making power is shared by the owners; each partner has the power to act for the partnership. Each partner is personally liable for the obligations of the firm, and the owners face unlimited liability for the firm's actions.

Because the assets of more than one person are available to secure loans, the partnership arrangement improves the firm's ability to raise financial capital for expansion of the business. However, the firm's decision making may be somewhat more complicated in a partnership than it is in a sole proprietorship, because ownership is shared. Dissolution of a partnership can be difficult and costly. Partners must find other individuals who are willing to purchase the firm. If new owners cannot be found, the firm's assets must be sold off.

One variation on the partnership as a form of business is the *limited partnership*. Under this kind of partnership there are two kinds of partners: general and limited partners. General partners are just like the partners of a simple partnership: they have full control of the business and bear unlimited personal liability for the firm's actions. On the other hand, a limited partner has no management control or responsibility and bears only limited liability for the firm's actions. A limited partnership is a means for acquiring additional financial resources for the firm. The ownership rights of limited partners are determined by the financial investment they make in the partnership. Their risk is limited to the investment they have made in the firm. If the firm fails, the most they lose is the amount of their investment.

In 1984, there were about 1.6 million partnerships, 60 percent of which had annual sales of less than $50,000. About 7 percent of all partnerships had sales in excess of $500,000. Partnerships tend to be larger than proprietorships, in part because of better access to resources for growth and expansion. Nevertheless, partnerships tend to be relatively small firms. In summary, partnerships tend to be somewhat larger than sole proprietorships and involve at least two owners. However, each owner is liable for all of the firm's actions, just as in the case of the sole proprietorship.

Corporation   The **corporation** is itself a legal entity and therefore is quite different from a sole proprietorship or partnership. A corporation has the legal powers and rights of an individual. A corporation can enter into legally enforceable contracts with individuals or other corporations. A corporation can

---

[1]Note the distinction between money or financial capital and real capital, which refers to resources such as buildings, roads, and machinery.

TABLE 2
Number and annual sales of firms by legal form of business organization, 1984

Size of Firm by Annual Sales	Number of Firms (thousands)				Annual Sales (billions)			
	Total	Sole Proprietors	Partnerships	Corporations	Total	Sole Proprietors	Partnerships	Corporations
Total	16,077	11,262	1,644	3,171	$7,782	$516	$318	$6,948
Percent Distribution	100.0	100.0	100.0	100.0	100.0	100.0	100.0	100.0
Under $50,000	68.5	80.7	61.9	28.4	1.4	18.8	1.9	0.1
$50,000–$499,999	24.8	18.2	31.2	44.9	7.9	53.7	17.0	4.1
Over $500,000	6.7	1.1	6.9	26.8	90.7	27.5	81.4	95.8

Source: U.S. Department of Commerce, Bureau of the Census, *Statistical Abstract of the United States*. Table 824.

sue and be sued for its actions. However, its owners cannot be sued. Thus, the owners of a corporation face *limited liability* — they are liable only to the extent of their investment in the firm.

Corporations must be licensed by a state and are governed by a charter that describes the structure of the corporation and its principal activities. As a general rule, the owners of the corporation select a board of directors and a chairperson who are responsible for overseeing the operations of the corporation. The board usually employs managers to make the firm's decisions and manage the firm's day-to-day business activities. Consequently, the owners of the corporation have only indirect control of the firm's decisions.

The corporation is the dominant form of business organization in the United States. In 1984, there were about three million corporations, a quarter of which had annual sales of less than $50,000. Another quarter had sales in excess of $500,000. However, a glance at Table 2 reveals a clearer picture of the importance of corporations in the economy. If we arbitrarily consider firms with sales in excess of $500,000 a year as large, then large firms account for only a small fraction (6.7 percent) of the total number of firms, but they account for 90 percent of annual sales. Furthermore, corporations are the largest firms. They alone account for 89 percent of total annual sales. (These figures would be basically the same if we defined large as sales in excess of $1 million a year.) Large firms are a fact of life in the U.S. economy and other developed economies, and most large firms are corporations.

Financial Capital for the Corporation. An important advantage of the corporate form of business organization, as compared to sole proprietorships and partnerships, is the corporation's ability to obtain financial capital. A corporation can acquire the funds to support its growth and expansion from three sources: (1) the sale of ownership shares in the business, (2) its own profits, and (3) borrowing from financial institutions or individuals. The extent to which a corporation relies on each source depends on the relative cost of each funding source.

Shares of stock
Certificates of ownership in a company. **Stockholders** are the owners of the firm.

Dividends
The amount of profit per share of stock outstanding that is paid to the firm's stockholders.

Retained earnings
Profit that the firm reinvests in the business to support activities such as research, product development, and expansion.

Bond
A note that promises to pay its holder a specified amount of interest plus the face amount of the bond at a specified point in the future.

Maturity
The length of time for which a bond is issued.

When a firm sells ownership shares of the company, it is said to sell **stock** in the company. The owners of the firm are then **stockholders**. Funds acquired through the sale of stock represent *equity capital* because the stockholders have an ownership stake in the company. Different kinds of stock exist, and each kind carries different ownership rights. The basic form of equity ownership is *common stock*. Common stockholders share in the control of the business and its profits and losses. However, they share in the control of the company only very indirectly, mainly by voting for or against the management team hired by the company and for or against very broad decisions or policies.

Firms decide how much of the profits are returned to stockholders. These returned profits are called **dividends** and are paid per share of stock outstanding. Typically firms pay out only part of their profits as dividends. Those profits retained by the firm, called **retained earnings**, are reinvested in the firm and support activities such as research, product development, and expansion. This part of the firm's profits can be indirectly beneficial to stockholders. If reinvested profits increase the value of the firm, the price of the firm's shares of stock will rise. Shareholders may then sell their holdings at a higher price than they paid for them. Often, rapidly growing firms will pay no dividends, reinvesting all profits in the business. Shareholders gain only from the increasing value of the company as reflected in its stock price.

Common stockholders share in the firm's losses, too. They receive their share of profits (their dividends) only after all the firm's creditors have been paid. If the firm fails, they lose their investment in the company, which, however, is the sole extent of their liability.

Firms also borrow financial capital. They typically borrow for short-term needs by obtaining loans from financial institutions, such as banks, thrift institutions, or insurance companies. Such loans are an important source of financial capital for proprietorships and partnerships. However, they are a relatively expensive source of funding. To reduce the cost of borrowing, corporations issue **bonds** to obtain most of their borrowed funds. A bond is a promissory note: The purchaser loans a fixed amount, called the principal, to the firm in return for its promise to pay the bondholder a fixed amount of interest each year and to repay the face amount of the note—the amount borrowed—at a specific time in the future. The length of time for which the bond is issued is called its **maturity**. The bond *matures* after this period of time has elapsed. At the date of maturity the company pays back the principal amount of the bond. Most of this borrowing is long term, and bonds are often issued for ten to thirty years. A bond is a contract between the issuing corporation and the bondholder. If the interest is not paid on time, the bondholder can legally force the firm to make the payment, even if the firm must liquidate its assets to do so.

When someone buys a hundred shares of common stock in a corporation, he or she purchases an ownership share for an indefinite period of time. When someone buys a thirty-year corporate bond, the company has thirty years before it must repay the principal. What if both of these individuals wanted to liquidate their respective investments after two years? The corporation would not buy the stock back, nor would it redeem the bond before the maturity date (except under exceptional circumstances). Each investor would have to find another individual willing to buy the stock or bond at an acceptable price.

When a corporation issues new shares of stock or new bonds, their prices are established in the *primary market* — the market for new stocks and bonds —

and are determined by the willingness of investors to buy the new stock or bonds. Stocks and bonds are generally referred to as **securities**. **Securities markets** are *secondary markets* in which existing shares of stock or bonds are bought or sold. It is in these markets that the price of an existing share of stock or a bond is determined by the market forces of supply and demand. The existence of these markets allows corporations to issue new shares of stock and new bonds at higher prices, because potential investors know they can sell their investments at any time.

In summary, corporations constitute the dominant legal form of business structure in the United States. Corporations have the advantage of being able to raise large amounts of financial capital through the sale of stocks and bonds. Owners of corporations enjoy limited liability; however, they have only indirect control over the decisions made by the firm.

Market Structure

A third approach to categorizing firms in the economy is based on the type of market in which a firm operates. **Market structure** (or *industry structure*) refers to the characteristics of output markets that influence the behavior of firms. These characteristics include the number of firms in the market, the size of the firms, and the variety of products produced by the firms. This chapter and the several that follow examine the economic behavior of firms, focusing on how their decision making and actions are influenced by these various characteristics.

These characteristics affect firm behavior because they determine the *degree of competition* in a market. If we think of the degree of competition as measured on a continuum, at one end we would have very competitive industries. A competitive industry is typically characterized by many small firms that produce a very similar product (where small is defined as share of the market output accounted for by each firm). Agriculture and retail trade are two broadly defined industries characterized by strong competition.

At the other extreme are industries comprised of only one firm. These industries are called *monopolies*. It is difficult to imagine a pure monopoly industry. Most industries have at least a few competing firms, and firms that produce similar, but not identical, products can be considered competitors for these so-called monopolies. One example of an unregulated monopoly industry is cable TV. There is only one supplier of the service—cable TV—in a given geographic region. Other examples of monopoly involve *regulated monopolies*. A regulated monopoly is a single firm that is given the legal right to be the only producer in an industry (usually in a limited geographic region). These firms are typically public utilities, such as electric power or natural gas companies.

Between the two extremes of competition and monopoly are all kinds of industries with varying degrees of competition. The extent of competition influences the pricing, output, and resource-utilization decisions of firms. Chapters 9 through 12 discuss the impact of market structure on the behavior of firms in much more detail. We introduce the notion of market structure now because it is an important way to categorize firms. As the concepts presented in the next few chapters are developed, market structure will take on even more importance as a factor in understanding the behavior of firms and the public regulation of the actions of firms.

Security
The physical evidence of ownership of debt, such as a stock certificate or promissory note.

Securities markets
Secondary markets in which existing shares of stock or bonds are bought and sold.

Market structure
The characteristics of output markets including the number of firms in the market, the size of the firms, and the variety of products produced by firms, that influence the behavior of firms.

SECTION RECAP

Firms can be categorized according to the industry in which they operate, their legal structure—proprietorship, partnership, or corporation—or on the basis of the type of market structure in which they operate. Of these, market structure focuses on the characteristics of output markets that influence the pricing and output behavior of firms, and hence is the basis for analyzing the economic decisions firms make.

The Firm's Objective: Profit

We have just detailed several ways to classify differences in firms: different products, different legal forms of organization, and varying degrees of competition. Although firms differ in various ways, they *all* have one thing in common: They are in business to make a profit. Profit is the incentive for production. *In our analysis of the behavior of firms, we assume that the firm's objective is to maximize profits.* Although profit plays a central role in the behavior of firms, it is an often misunderstood concept. Therefore, a careful explanation of the economist's definition of profit is necessary.

Definition of Profit

In general terms, **profit** is measured as the difference between total revenue and total cost. Total revenue and total cost are determined by how much output is supplied to the market and purchased by consumers. Supply decisions in turn depend upon the actual or anticipated benefits and costs of producing goods and services. The revenue generated by the sale of a firm's output constitutes the benefits of production and is determined by the demand curve for the firm's output. The **costs of production** are the full opportunity costs of all resources used in production of the firm's output.[2] However, accounting for the full opportunity costs of production is complicated.

When inputs are purchased in a market, their purchase prices are their opportunity costs. These costs are **explicit**. Hourly wages or monthly salaries are paid for labor. Machinery is purchased or rented. Raw materials are bought in markets. The cost of funds obtained from bond sales is determined by the interest rate paid to obtain the borrowed funds. Explicit costs involve the expenditure of funds by the firm to acquire the resource in question.

However, some resources used in production are not purchased in a market. In many instances, the firm owns resources that it may or may not use in the production process. Using these resources is costly so long as they have alternative uses. These costs are **implicit**; the firm does not pay an individual or another firm for the use of these resources. Implicit costs are measured by the value of the opportunity forgone when the resources are used in production.

There are many examples of implicit costs. For instance, when a firm uses retained earnings (profits that are not distributed to the firm's owners) to finance an expansion of its production facilities, it does not pay interest charges as it would have to if it had sold bonds or borrowed money to raise the needed funds. Nevertheless, it incurs a cost. Retained earnings could be invested in financial markets. The rate of interest that the retained earnings would earn in the market is the implicit cost of using these funds for expansion. It is a real cost incurred by the firm, and should be included in the firm's assessment of the costs and benefits of expansion.

The use of existing capital also generates implicit costs. A machine—capital—contributes to production until it wears out and is replaced. How do we determine the cost of using the machine to produce a specific quantity of output? The cost is the loss in the value of the machine due to its use in production.

Profit
The difference between total revenue and total cost.

Costs of production
The full opportunity costs of all resources used in the production of the firm's output.

Explicit costs
The out-of-pocket expenses incurred by a firm; they involve the expenditure of money to buy resources, raise financial capital, and so on.

Implicit costs
The opportunity costs of using resources that are already owned by the firm.

---

[2] Recall that the opportunity cost of a resource is the highest-valued alternative use of the resource.

This cost is called **depreciation**. Depreciation is another kind of implicit production cost.[3]

One of the most important resources in the production of goods and services is *entrepreneurial ability*, that difficult-to-define willingness to assume the risks associated with organizing and managing a firm. The owners of the firm contribute their entrepreneurial ability to the production process. In addition, the owners of the firm invest their own financial assets in the business. These funds have valuable alternative uses that the owners have forgone to be in business. The provision of these resources — risk taking and financial capital — is costly, and their owners will use them elsewhere unless they are compensated. These opportunity costs of production are also implicit costs.

The combined payments for risk taking and the financial capital of owners that is just sufficient to keep the entrepreneurs/owners in business is called **normal profit**. Normal profit is another implicit cost of production. If the firm's owners cannot earn a normal profit, this implies that their entrepreneurial abilities and financial assets have more valuable alternative uses. The firm's owners would therefore be better off to shut down and divert these resources to their higher-valued uses.

Now we are ready to define **economic profit**. As we have just shown, the total opportunity costs of production consist of the sum of all explicit and implicit costs. Economic profit is the difference between total revenue and the total opportunity costs of production:

Economic Profit = Total Revenue − Total Costs [including normal profit]

It is important to keep the distinction between economic profit and normal profit in mind. Normal profit is an implicit cost of production. Economic profit is the revenue earned by the firm in excess of its total (explicit plus implicit) costs of production.

When total revenues equal total costs, economic profit is zero. This situation is acceptable to the firm. All costs are paid, including payments to the entrepreneurs/owners for their contributions, and each input receives as payment the value of its opportunity cost — the highest payment the inputs would receive in the market (in the next-best alternative). If economic profit is positive, resources in the firm are receiving higher payments than can be received elsewhere. If economic profit is less than zero, the firm is experiencing losses. Resources in the firm are earning payments that are less than they would receive elsewhere.

Depreciation
The loss in the value of a piece of capital due to its use in production.

Normal profit
An implicit cost incurred by the firm; the amount of payment that is just sufficient to keep the entrepreneurs/owners in business.

Economic profit
The difference between total revenue and the total opportunity costs of production.

Economic Profit Is Not Accounting Profit

By now you have noticed that the economic definition of profit is different from the meaning of profit as it is used in everyday conversation. In everyday use, the term *profit* refers typically to the revenue left over after paying the bills. This definition is common terminology for profit as it is defined in an accounting sense. *Accounting profit is the difference between total revenue and explicit,*

Accounting profit
The difference between total revenue and explicit, or accounting, costs.

---

[3]Often, references to depreciation are references to the concept of accounting depreciation, and not true depreciation. For tax accounting purposes, the federal government has established a set of rules for depreciating different kinds of equipment and property. For example, a microcomputer is depreciated over three years according to federal tax rules. These accounting rules correspond only more or less to expected true depreciation.

Why the **Disagreement?**

Do Firms Maximize Economic Profits?

A central theme in this chapter is that firms maximize profits. In fact, our model of decision making by firms is based on this assumption. Without it, our predictions of firm behavior could be quite different than they are. Although this assumption is a common one among economists, some people, including some economists, believe that firms do not seek to maximize profits. They contend that firms have other objectives or that it is simply too difficult or costly for a firm to seriously attempt to maximize profits. Why the disagreement over firms' objectives?

Some analysts argue that corporations choose to maximize sales instead of profits. Corporations are run by a management team that must answer to the owners, but owner control of management is weak and indirect. Thus, management objectives rather than owner objectives are more important in understanding the behavior of firms, and managers tend to be more interested in sales volume than in profit levels. Sales, as opposed to profit levels, are important to managers because the size of the firm has such a big impact on the economic well-being of management. All of the benefits of being a manager—salary, fringes, power, prestige—are more directly related to the size of the firm than to profits. If profits are acceptable to the owners, then the firm will seek to maximize its sales.

Another argument against the assumption of profit maximization derives from the importance of corporations as a form of business. According to this argument, corporations do not maximize profits or, for that matter, anything else (such as sales). They are "satisficers" rather than "maximizers." Since corporations are large organizations managed by a large number of people, the decisions of firms are generally compromises between management groups with different responsibilities, objectives, and perspectives. Management by compromise makes it difficult for the firm to maximize anything. Decision making is slow, reactions to new situations take time, and outcomes reflect efforts to satisfy different groups within the firm as much as efforts to improve the firm's profits. This envi-

---

> **SECTION RECAP**
> Firms attempt to maximize economic profit, which is the difference between total revenues *(continued)*

or accounting, costs. The implicit costs of production, including normal profit, are omitted from an accountant's definition of profit.

Why the different definitions? The different meanings given to the notion of profit arise for good reasons. Economists are concerned with the true social cost of producing economic goods. *Normal profit is the minimum payment just sufficient to attract the firm's owner(s) into business, and consequently, preclude their employment elsewhere. Economic profit is the difference between total revenues and total opportunity costs in excess of normal profit.* The absence of normal profit will cause the owners of firms to exit the industry in search of more profitable employment opportunities for their entrepreneurial contributions.

Accountants are concerned with other problems. It is the accountant's responsibility to maintain systematic records of the financial transactions of businesses. To carry out this task, many accounting conventions, or rules, have been established to ensure that financial records are maintained similarly in all businesses. These conventions are required because some transactions, such as depreciation expenditures, are difficult to measure, and because regulations and tax laws require certain kinds of information.

The appropriate and systematic accounting of a firm's financial affairs is important to the owners and managers of the firm (they use this information to make decisions), to other businesses who buy from or sell to the firm, to the stockholders of the firm, and to various taxing authorities. Of foremost importance to all these groups is the financial viability of the firm. In an

ronment generates behavior that is designed to achieve satisfactory levels of profits or sales.

How do economists respond to these arguments against profit-maximizing behavior by firms? Generally, they defend profit maximization as the firm's primary objective. Several arguments support their defense. The first point is an important one: Firms come into existence to make a profit and they cease to exist if they are unsuccessful at it. An entrepreneur decides to risk scarce resources in anticipation of a gain. If the gain is not realized, the entrepreneur has made himself worse off. The failure to actively seek profit, even if one experiences losses along the way, is counter to the Fundamental Premise established in Chapter 1: In a world of scarcity, individuals act to make themselves better off.

A second argument concerns the possible effects of a firm's failure to maximize profits. In short, such firms are at risk of being taken over by another firm or group of individuals. Although takeovers can be initiated for a variety of reasons, one distinct possibility is the failure of the current management to maximize profits. This failure can lead to an undervaluation of the firm's assets. Outside individuals view such situations as a way to realize a quick gain. Hence, the threat of a takeover is another motivation for profit maximization.

A point raised in connection with consumer behavior is also relevant here. In reality, firms are more complex than we have assumed them to be. For instance, managers must make decisions that will have effects far into the future, even though they do not know what the future holds. Thus, their decision making is based on expectations that may or may not be realized. In addition, although we use as a model a firm that produces and sells one product, firms are constantly developing improved or new products, and many firms sell more than one product. Decisions about how to allocate resources among these competing ends are quite complex and are based on imperfect information. Thus, while firms seek to maximize profits, it may be difficult to discern their pursuit of profit even if maximizing profits is their objective.

accounting sense, profit is a residual, the part of total revenue that remains after explicit costs have been paid. This accounting profit includes both normal and economic profit. Owners of firms, as well as these other groups, are not concerned about the distinction made by economists; they simply prefer more profit to less.

Thus, the two definitions of profit arise because of two different interests. Economists are concerned with one set of problems and the business community with another. It is important to keep this distinction in mind as we analyze the behavior of firms. We note one more time: *Normal profit is a cost of production while economic profit is the difference between total revenue and total costs.*[4]

Profitability of American Business

We conclude this discussion of profits with several points on the quantitative magnitude of profits. Since the accounting definition of profit is the only widely available, systematic measure of profits, we will use this profit measure to describe the size and variation of profit levels in the U.S. economy. In addition, we will restrict our discussion to profits earned by corporations. This focus is

SECTION RECAP
(continued)
and total costs (explicit and implicit) including a normal profit. Economic profit differs from accounting profit to the extent that accounting profit does not account for implicit costs, including a normal profit.

---

[4]In the remainder of the text, when the term *profit* is used, unless otherwise specified, it refers to economic profit.

not only convenient in terms of the profit data available, but it is also a relatively accurate depiction of the size of all profits since, as we have already noted, corporations account for about 90 percent of all business sales in the United States.

Aggregate Profits The most useful way to describe profits is in relative terms. In 1985, corporate profits were $281 billion. It is difficult to assess this profit level unless we have a benchmark against which to compare it. **National income** is the total annual income paid to all owners of resources. Comparing corporate profits to national income tells us that in 1985, profits were 8.7 percent of national income. By comparison, the largest component of national income is compensation of employees (wages, salaries, and fringe benefits). In 1985, employee compensation was 73.5 percent of national income. Table 3 shows profits as a share of national income for the past twenty-five years. On average, profits have amounted to about 10 percent of national income during this period, although the profit share has been falling steadily.

Two other kinds of profit measures are given in Table 3 as well. Profits are calculated as a share of stockholder equity (the aggregate value of ownership shares), and as a share of annual sales. By comparing profits to stockholder equity we get a crude measure of the annual return on a dollar invested in the company. The profits–to–sales ratio is a measure of the profit earned per dollar of revenue earned by the firm. Corporate profits averaged about 12 percent of stockholder equity and less than 5 percent of sales during this period.

Variations in Profit Levels While the aggregate value of profits remains a fairly stable share of national income over time, profit levels vary by industry, and industry profits fluctuate widely from year to year. Profits as a share of sales are given for several manufacturing industries for two different years in Table

National income
The total annual income paid to all owners of resources. It is the sum of all wages, rent, interest, and profit.

TABLE 3

Corporate profits in the United States, 1961–1989

Year	Profits as Percentage of National Income	Profits as Percentage of Stockholder Equity*	Profits as Percentage of Annual Sales*
1961–65	12.7	10.7	4.9
1966–70	11.6	11.6	4.9
1971–75	9.5	11.9	4.6
1976–80	9.9	14.7	5.3
1981–85	7.8	11.2	4.1
1986	8.3	9.5	3.7
1987	8.1	12.8	4.9
1988	8.3	16.1	6.0
1989	7.0	14.4**	5.3**

*All manufacturing corporations.
**Average for the first three quarters of 1989.
Source: *Economic Report of the President, 1990*, Tables C-23 and C-91

TABLE 4

Corporate profits as percent of sales, and changes in annual profits: selected manufacturing industries

Manufacturing Industry	After Tax Profits as Percentage of Sales		Percentage Change in Level of Profits	
	1980	1986	1979–80	1986–87
All manufacturing	4.9	3.7	−11.9	30.0
Food and kindred products	3.4	3.3	5.2	5.7
Textile mill products	2.2	3.2	—	—
Paper and allied products	5.1	4.2	—	—
Printing and publishing	5.5	6.0	—	—
Chemicals and allied products	7.1	6.6	−25.0	35.8
Petroleum and coal products	7.7	5.1	39.6	116.7
Rubber and miscellaneous plastics	2.0	3.8	—	—
Stone, clay, and glass	4.2	3.6	—	—
Primary metals industry	4.1	−0.6	−25.0	133.3
Fabricated metals	4.2	3.9	−17.3	17.1
Machinery, excluding electrical	6.5	5.8	−14.1	43.6
Electrical machinery	5.0	4.4	−9.6	16.3
Transportation equipment	−0.3	5.2	−153.0	−3.4
Instruments	9.3	7.0	—	—

Source: *Economic Report of the President*, annual issues

4. The variation in profits across industries and years is evident. Data in the last two columns of Table 4 demonstrate this volatility. These two columns give the percentage change in profit levels between 1979 and 1980 and between 1986 and 1987, respectively. For the entire manufacturing sector, profits declined by almost 12 percent between 1979 and 1980; at the same time some industries, petroleum and coal for instance, experienced profit increases. Large differences are evident in the percentage decline in profits across industries. Automobile industry profits fell by 150 percent. Between 1986 and 1987, profits generally increased, but again there was wide variation in the increases across industry categories. Profit levels are volatile because profit is a relatively small residual; it is the difference between revenues and costs, and on average is only about 5 percent of revenues. *Thus, small changes in revenues or costs can cause large relative changes in profits.*

Framework for Decision Making: Costs and Benefits . . . Again

We have identified profit maximization as the firm's goal, and have now defined the notion of economic profit that we will use throughout our analysis of the behavior of firms. The firm makes myriad decisions in its effort to maximize profits. It must choose a product to produce and sell. It must decide upon a particular production technology to use to produce the good or service. After the firm is in business, it must make output and price decisions and be ready to make decisions of all kinds in response to changes in the market. In all of these decisions, the firm has a range of alternatives to choose from. One of the most important determinants of the alternatives available to a firm in its decision making is the time dimension of the decision.

For convenience we will distinguish between long-run and short-run decisions and will use this important distinction throughout the rest of the book. A **long-run decision** for a firm is a planning decision. In the long run, a firm is free to vary all its inputs. The decisions to enter a new business or build a new plant are long-run decisions. The choice of a least-cost combination of *all* inputs, or the technology that embodies this combination, is a long-run decision. (We note that the period of time over which available technologies change may be considered the "very long run.") Long-run decisions are based on expectations about future prices and costs. The decision maker is free to consider a wide range of alternatives and faces few constraints.

A **short-run decision**, on the other hand, is a constrained decision. A firm's short-run decisions center on how to use existing plant and equipment efficiently. In the short run, at least one of the firm's input levels is fixed. For example, in the short run the firm's production technology and its stock of capital equipment are fixed. The firm's short-run profit-maximizing decision is to choose an output level (and levels of inputs that can be varied in the short run) that maximizes profit.

Note that the firm also attempts to minimize the costs of production in the short run. The difference between least-cost production in the short run and the long run lies in the fact that in the short run, the firm is not free to vary all of its inputs — at least one input is fixed in amount. As a consequence, the least-cost combination of inputs for the short run may differ from the long-run least-cost combination.

The short run is not a chronological period of time but rather is defined by the firm's production technology. For example, it may take an electrical utility five or more years to vary all of its inputs. It takes a long time to build a new power-generating plant. (It has taken from ten to twenty years to build some nuclear power plants.) On the other hand, an entrepreneur in retail trade may be able to vary all of his inputs within a six-month period. A retail store can be built from scratch and stocked for business in a matter of months. This implies that the short run is approximately five years in the electrical utility industry but only six months in retail trade. The nature of the firm's business determines the length of the short run.

This distinction between short run and long run is a general one. It can be used to characterize all kinds of decisions, not just those made by firms, although that is the use to which it will be put in the next few chapters. Before a semester begins, you decide whether to work or go to school or which courses to take. If you decide to go to school and enroll in five classes, you may consider dropping one of the courses during the semester. The decision to take five courses in this semester was a long-run, planning decision; the decision to drop a course is a short-run decision that is influenced by the fact that you are enrolled in four other courses. The decision to buy a car is a long-run decision based on the expected benefits and costs of the car. The decision

---

Long-run decision
A planning decision. In the long run, all inputs are variable, including the amount of capital stock employed by the firm.

Short-run decision
A constrained decision. In the short run, the amount of at least one of the inputs employed by the firm is fixed.

Does It Make **Economic Sense?**

How Can *USA Today* Keep Operating with No Profit in Seven Years?

In 1982, Gannett Co., a company that owns many local newspapers in the United States, launched a national daily newspaper called *USA Today*. It suffered losses each year of operation, accumulating operating losses in excess of $250 million by mid-1989. While it did earn a monthly profit for the first time in early 1987, it showed an annual loss in 1987 and again in 1988. Moreover, these loss figures underestimate the true loss generated by the paper. These figures exclude the costs of literally hundreds of person-years of work from reporters, editors, and other personnel that *USA Today* borrowed from other Gannett papers. These figures also omit the capital expenditures on plant and equipment for the paper. Does it make economic sense to continue to publish *USA Today* in the face of years of losses?

For Gannett, the answer to this question has continued to be "yes!" The decision to initiate a new newspaper, a national daily, was a long-run decision made by the Gannett Co. management. It is a new product for which only imperfect substitutes, such as *The New York Times* or *The Wall Street Journal*, exist. Gannett decided to start the paper based on its expectations concerning the potential for success — the potential for profits over time. Gannett believed that a newspaper like *USA Today* could become a profitable business, but it would take time. Costs were expected to exceed revenues for a number of years because circulation of the paper was expected to grow slowly, causing subscription and advertising revenue to grow slowly. On the other hand, initial costs would be high. Actual revenue and cost experience for the paper have been close to initial projections.

The short-run problems for the managers of *USA Today* have been to minimize the losses, but continue to make the expenditures that would contribute to growth in the paper's popularity. An ever-present decision in a business experiencing steady losses is "Should we halt production and shut down the business or continue production in the face of losses?" This decision must be made (or reassessed) based on changing expectations about future revenues and costs, not the losses previously suffered. Past losses are sunk costs; decisions today will not alter those losses. The relevant questions are about the future. Are revenues growing as anticipated? Are costs in line with projections? Do we still believe the paper can be profitable given more time and work? Does Gannett have a more profitable use for the financial capital it is using to cover the yearly losses?

Gannett continues to believe in the long-run profitability of *USA Today*. From the outset it was a risky decision. Whether it will turn out to have been a profitable decision in the long run remains to be seen.

---

about how much to use the car — once you have purchased it — is a short-run decision. The constraint is the particular car that you own.

Sunk Costs We have argued that decisions should be based on the true opportunity costs of different alternatives. Sometimes, however, it is difficult to distinguish between the true opportunity costs of an action and costs that have already been incurred — **sunk costs**. Historical costs are sunk costs because they have been paid in the past and a decision today will not alter them. Thus, *sunk costs are irrelevant to today's decision making and should be ignored*. When a firm is deciding whether to produce another unit of its output, it should consider only the extra costs of the unit such as those for materials and labor. The cost of an existing machine used to produce the unit should be ignored. The firm owns the machine, and its cost is not altered by producing one more unit (ignoring depreciation).

Sunk cost
A cost that has been incurred in the past that can no longer be recovered. Sunk costs are irrelevant for current decisions.

What about other decisions? Should the tuition cost of a course be considered when trying to decide whether you should drop the course? No, unless you will get a tuition refund. The tuition cost was incurred in the past when you made the long-run decision and, after any refund period has expired, dropping the course will not change that cost. What matters for this decision is the future costs incurred and benefits received by continuing in the course. Tuition has become a sunk cost.

What costs do you consider when trying to decide whether to drive your car or fly from San Diego to Chicago? Only the cost of driving your car versus the cost of the air fare is relevant. The cost of driving your car includes only those costs actually incurred for this trip. The cost of the car purchase is sunk and therefore irrelevant. However, a drive of this length does reduce the value of the car because of wear and tear on the car. This change in value, called *economic depreciation*, is a true opportunity cost of the trip and should be considered in this decision. In addition, do not forget to include the opportunity cost of your time. It takes longer to drive than it does to fly.

In the next chapter, we will see very explicitly how profit-maximizing firms ignore sunk costs in their short-run decisions. Remember that only the true costs of an action or decision should be included in the decision-making process. Sunk costs should be ignored. Good economic decision making is forward thinking.

SECTION RECAP
Long-run decisions are planning decisions, since all inputs are variable in the long run. In the short run, at least one input is fixed. Hence, short-run decisions are constrained to focus on how to use existing fixed inputs efficiently. In either case, sunk costs are nonrecoverable and should therefore be ignored in the decision-making process.

Technology and Production Costs

The cost of production is the full opportunity cost of all resources used in producing a good or service. Cost is determined by two factors: input prices (including implicit costs) and technology. The prices of inputs used in production are determined by the market forces of supply and demand. Technology determines the kind and quantity of resources necessary to produce a good or service. A variety of technologies that employ different kinds and combinations of inputs may be available for producing a given good. Some require more labor relative to capital and other inputs — **labor-intensive production**. Others use more capital relative to labor and other inputs — **capital-intensive production**. The technologies also may differ according to the desired output per period of time. The long-run problem for the firm is to choose the production technology that minimizes the costs of production, given the kinds of inputs required for production, relative input prices, expected product price, and expected levels of production per period of time.

Technology plays a key role in determining the overall level of economic well-being in society. It is the constraint that determines the minimum level of cost that can be achieved in the accomplishment of a specific objective, for example, the production of one hundred automobiles. Technological change reduces costs by permitting society to achieve the same level and quality of output with less costly or fewer inputs. Technological change creates new production processes that allow us to produce new goods and services of more

Labor-intensive production
Use more labor relative to capital and other inputs.

Capital-intensive production
Use more capital relative to labor and other inputs.

value than existing goods and services. Over time technological change lowers the minimum level of costs that can be achieved in the economy.

Summary

This chapter provides an introduction to the behavior of decision makers on the supply side of the market and a broad description of the business sector in the United States. The three legal forms of business are **sole proprietorships, partnerships,** and **corporations.** The first two forms are simple organizational arrangements that make it easy for anyone to start a business. For legal purposes the owners and the business are one and the same entity. Owners of these businesses have strong management control but face unlimited liability as well as serious limits in financing business growth.

The corporation is by far the dominant form of business, accounting for almost 90 percent of all business sales. Corporations are separate legal entities, limiting the owners' liability. The corporation has a range of options for raising capital, including the sale of common stock, the issuance of bonds, and borrowing from financial institutions.

Market structure refers to characteristics of output markets that influence the behavior of firms through their impact on the degree of competition the firm faces. Industries with many small firms tend to be very competitive, while industries with only a few firms tend to be less competitive. When the industry is comprised of only one firm, called a **monopoly,** the firm faces little competition.

Firms are in business to make a profit. While firms differ in many respects, we assume that they all seek to maximize profits. **Normal profit** is a part of the opportunity cost of production. It is the payment that is just sufficient to motivate the entrepreneur to assume the risks of supply.

Economic profit is the difference between total revenue and the total opportunity cost of production, which includes normal profit. When a firm is earning zero economic profit, all factors of production are receiving payments equal to their highest-valued employment opportunity. When economic profit is greater than zero, resources are earning more than their next-highest-valued earnings opportunity. Economic profit is not equivalent to accounting profit. Accounting profit omits normal profit and other implicit costs of production.

A **short-run** decision concerns how to use existing plant and equipment efficiently. In the short run, at least one input employed by the firm is fixed and cannot be varied. On the other hand, a **long-run** decision is a planning decision. The firm can vary all of its inputs. The choice of a least-cost combination of inputs for an expected level of output is a long-run decision.

A **sunk cost** is not a true opportunity cost of an action. It is a cost that has already been incurred and cannot be altered by a future decision. Sunk costs are ignored in economic decision making.

The opportunity costs of production are determined by two factors: input prices and technology. Input prices reflect the value of resources in alternative employment opportunities. Technology determines the kind and quantity of resources necessary to produce a good or service.

Questions for Thought

Knowledge Questions

1. Explain the difference between a partnership and a corporation.

2. Explain the difference (to the firm) between common stock and corporate bonds.

3. Why is the stock market a secondary market?

4. Why is normal profit considered a cost of production?

Application Questions

5. When demand for a firm's product increases, the firm can take a number of steps to increase quantities supplied to the market. Some are listed below. Rank them by how quickly the firm can implement them. Explain your ranking. Which actions are short run and which are long run?
   a. Begin a second production shift by hiring more workers.
   b. Build a second production line in the existing plant.
   c. Buy more materials and increase the rate of production per day.
   d. Deplete product inventories.
   e. Build a second manufacturing plant.

6. When the price of gasoline doubled, consumers' short-run response was to reduce the amount of driving they did. What are some possible long-run responses? Why are they long run?

7. Suppose I purchase a car for full-time use in my pizza business. The purchase price is $12,000. After using the car for three years, I sell it to a car dealer for $5,000. What is economic depreciation on the car over this three-year period? Explain. How is this cost different from depreciation figured for the Internal Revenue Service?

8. Assume that you have been offered a job that pays $40,000 per year. In addition, you have the opportunity to start your own business. The revenues are expected to be $100,000 per year and explicit costs will be $62,000. Which employment option would you choose and why?

Synthesis Questions

9. Suppose that you have signed a twelve-month lease on an apartment for $200 a month, anticipating that you will be in school this coming summer as well as this academic year. However, you have obtained a summer job elsewhere. What is the minimum amount of rent for which you would be willing to sublet your apartment rather than let it sit empty for the summer? Explain your reasoning.

10. Suppose one firm controls all bauxite (an ore from which aluminum is made) in the world. Is this firm a monopolist? Explain. (Hint: Do close substitutes for aluminum exist?)

11. Assume that you have been offered the opportunity to invest in a new business and that you have a choice between forming a partnership and becoming a limited partner. Which option would you choose and why?

Production Costs, Revenues, and Profit Maximization

OVERVIEW

In Chapter 8 we defined production costs as the total opportunity costs of production. We also distinguished between economic profit, normal profit, and accounting profit, highlighting normal profit as one component of costs. The distinction between short-run and long-run decisions was also introduced.

This chapter presents a more formal, technical treatment of the supply decisions of firms by building the first of several simple, abstract models of the behavior of the firm. The short-run profit-maximizing behavior of the firm is the focus of this chapter. The relationships that are established in this chapter form the basis of the analyses in Chapters 10–13.

The short-run problem for a firm is to determine the output level that maximizes profits. To calculate the amount of profit associated with any output level, it is necessary to identify the relationships between inputs and outputs on the cost side, and outputs and prices on the revenue side. On the cost side, we will define and use both average and marginal cost. On the revenue side we will define and use both average and marginal revenue. The firm's short-run profit-maximizing rule is then determined. One of the important conclusions of this chapter is that, regardless of the markets in which they operate, all firms use the same rule to maximize profits.

CHAPTER 9

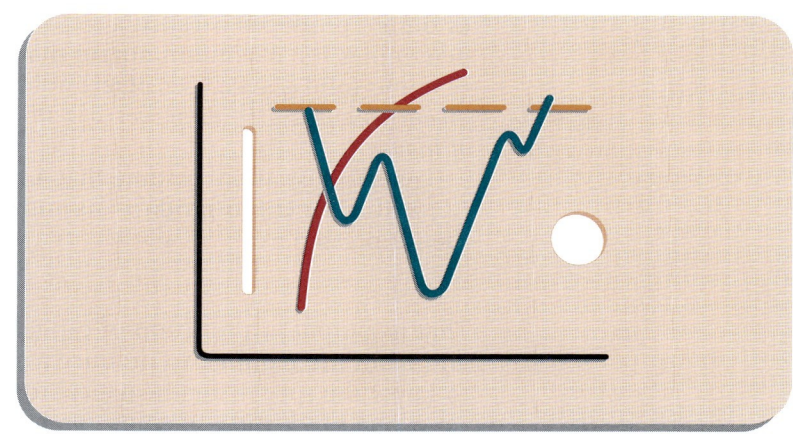

Issues related to the firm's long-run decision-making process are also introduced in this chapter. Since firms can vary all inputs in the long run, the long-run objective of a firm is to employ all resources in the combination and amount that minimize costs.

Learning Objectives

After reading and studying this chapter, you will be able to:

1. Explain what a production function is.
2. Explain why short-run marginal cost increases.
3. Distinguish between marginal and average product functions, and marginal and average cost functions.
4. Describe the firm's long-run cost-minimization rule and use it to explain the firm's responses to input price changes.
5. Describe how economies of scale affect the size of the firms in an industry.
6. Explain the differences between a price-taking and a price-searching firm.
7. Explain how firms identify the short-run profit-maximizing level of output.

The Short-Run Production Process

A firm exists to earn a profit. It attempts to accomplish this objective by purchasing raw materials, labor, and other inputs, combining these inputs in a manner determined by existing technology to produce an output, and then selling this output to consumers at a price that is at least as high as the cost of producing the good. The firm's costs are determined by the prices of the inputs it must purchase, the particular technology employed in production, and any implicit opportunity costs. The technology determines the kind and quantity of inputs required to produce the good.

Production Function

To understand the short-run relationship between output and costs, we must first understand the physical process of production. The technical relationship between the quantity of inputs required to produce a good and the quantity of output produced is called a **production function**. The production function determines the maximum output that can be produced from a given quantity of inputs (and a given level of technology). Thus, *the production function embodies productive efficiency — the process of getting the maximum output from a given quantity of inputs.*

Production function Determines the maximum output that can be produced from a given quantity of inputs (and a given level of technology).

As an illustration, assume that a production process requires only capital (K) and labor (L) to produce output (Q). The general production function is then expressed as:

$$Q = f(K, L)$$

That is, output is a function of capital and labor. To know how much capital and labor are required to produce a given amount of output, we would have to know the specific mathematical form of the production function. In many cases, the production function for an actual firm may be so complex that it is very difficult to characterize mathematically. However, the general principles of production and cost that are explained in this chapter with a simple two-input production function apply even to firms with very complex production processes.

In the short run, the firm employs at least one input that is fixed in amount; it cannot vary the quantity of this input. Capital is usually fixed in the short run. Mathematically, we can express this condition as:

$$K = \bar{K}$$

where the bar indicates that capital is constant or fixed in amount. Thus, the short-run production function becomes:

$$Q = f(\bar{K}, L)$$

or simply:

$$Q = f(L)$$

In the short run, the firm's level of output is determined by the quantity of labor employed with a fixed stock of capital equipment. (Dropping $\bar{K}$ in the second equation simply reflects the fact that for this production function, a change in L is the only source of a change in Q.)

TABLE 1
Short-run production function for snow removal

Units of Labor Per Day	Measures of Daily Productivity		
	Total Output	Marginal Product	Average Product
0	—	—	—
1	20	20	20.0
2	45	25	22.5
3	73	28	24.3
*4	99	26	24.8
5	121	22	24.2
6	136	15	22.7
7	141	5	20.1

Capital units = 3
*Diminishing marginal returns are incurred with the fourth unit of labor.

A simple example of a short-run production function for snow removal in a parking lot is given in Table 1. In this example, output is measured as cubic yards of snow removed per minute. The short-run production function is illustrated in the first two columns of the table. The first column shows the amount of labor employed. The second column shows how much output is produced for each amount of labor (assuming a fixed stock of capital, in this case, three snowplows).[1] Notice the output pattern. As more and more labor is added to the production process, output increases, but ultimately it increases by smaller and smaller amounts.

The change in output associated with an additional unit of the variable input (labor in this example) is called its **marginal physical product** (MP), and can be written, in the case of labor (L), as:

$$MPL = \frac{\Delta Q}{\Delta L}$$

where the delta (Δ) is read as *change in*. The marginal product of the variable input is important in the firm's decision-making process. It tells the firm how much additional output will be produced by adding one more unit of the input to the production process. The third column of Table 1 shows the marginal product associated with each unit of labor. Note that the marginal product of labor rises from 20 units to 28 units as we employ the first 3 units of labor. However, beginning with the fourth unit of labor, marginal product begins to decline, falling to 5 units of output for the seventh unit of labor.

This pattern of diminishing marginal productivity for the variable input occurs in every short-run production function. It is the **law of diminishing returns** in production. *Diminishing returns occur in the short run because more*

Marginal physical product
The change in total output resulting from the employment of an additional unit of a variable input.

Law of diminishing marginal returns
At some point, the marginal physical product of an input begins to decline.

---
[1]For simplicity we have chosen to present this production function as a schedule, relating output quantities to different levels of the variable input. The production function could also be written as a mathematical equation from which such a schedule could be derived.

and more of one input is being added to a production process with at least one fixed input. The amount of additional output that can be produced in this case is physically limited by the amount of the fixed input. In Table 1, the law of diminishing marginal returns occurs between the third and fourth units of labor employed.

To better understand this concept, note that the firm in our example has three machines — snowplows — that produce the firm's output — snow removal. At least one worker must operate the plows. Additional workers will increase output. One or two additional workers can increase output significantly. Each worker is able to spend more time operating machines and less time running between them. As we add more than three workers, however, fewer ways exist for them to increase output. They can operate the plows while other workers rest or they can take care of all the other tasks while three workers only operate the plows. However, as more and more workers are added, less and less additional output is produced. At some point, an additional worker might actually reduce output by simply getting in the way and reducing the productivity of other workers.

Suppose we are growing mushrooms in a cave that has one acre of growing space. In the short run, we are stuck with that one acre. We can add more workers, more fertilizer, or more of any other input in the mushroom-growing production process and increase output. However, as we add more and more of these variable inputs, additions to output begin to decline. What we can get out of one acre of land (in a cave or not) is limited. Diminishing marginal productivity occurs in the short run because at least one input cannot be varied.

A concept closely related to marginal product is average product. The **average product of a variable input (AP)** is defined as output per unit of the variable input. In the case where labor is the variable input:

$$APL = \frac{Q}{L}$$

Average productivity for each unit of labor is in the fourth column of Table 1.

All three measures of output, or productivity, are graphed as functions of the labor input in Figures 1 (a) and (b). In Figure 1 (a) we have drawn the production function. Output increases as more units of labor are added, but the rate of increase in output decreases with additional units of labor. The marginal product of labor and the average product of labor are illustrated in Figure 1 (b). Initially, both marginal product and average product increase as units of labor are increased. However, the marginal product of labor begins to decline when diminishing marginal productivity sets in. This occurs at point B in Figure 1 (b). The average product of labor continues to rise until marginal product and average product are equal. Once marginal product falls below average product, at point C in Figure 1 (b), average product begins to decline as well. This relationship is also shown numerically in Table 1.

The Firm's Cost Functions

The production function is one important determinant of production costs. It determines the kind and quantity of inputs required for a given level of output. The other determinant of costs is input prices. The firm pays the market price for each input that it purchases to use in production. Therefore, for any given level of output, the **total cost** of production (TC) is just the sum of the costs (price times the quantity) of each input used in the production process.

Average product of a variable input
The amount of output per unit of the variable input employed.

SECTION RECAP
In a constant-cost industry, long-run supply is perfectly elastic; a change in demand does not affect the long-run equilibrium market price. In an increasing-cost industry, the long-run supply curve is upward sloping; an increase in demand leads to an increase in the long-run equilibrium market price.

Total cost
The sum of the costs of each input (fixed and variable) used in production.

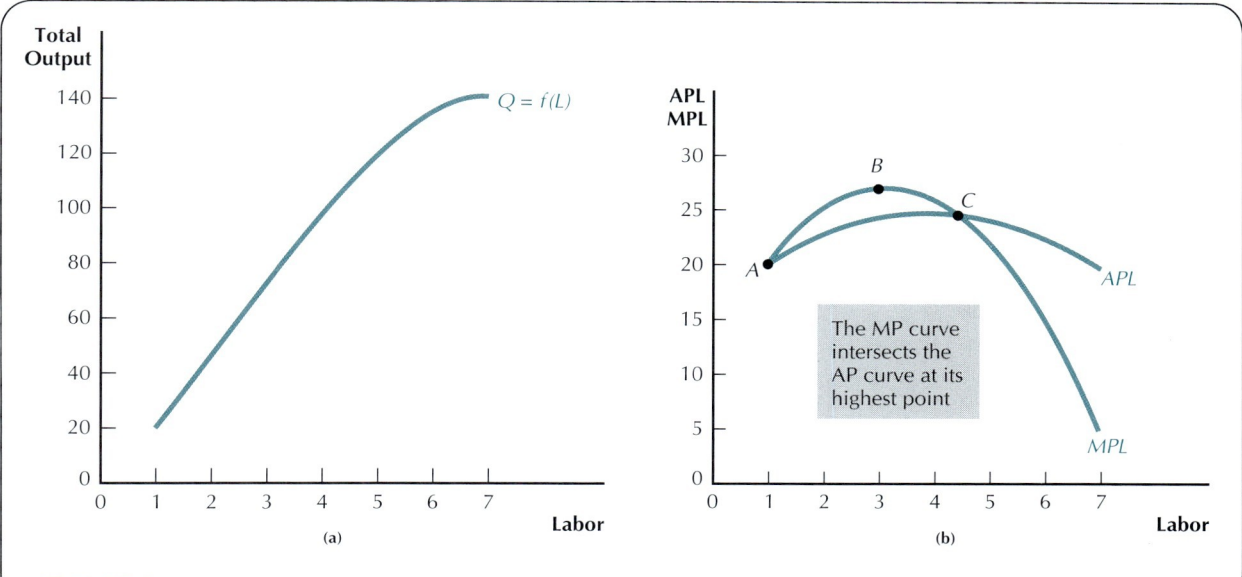

FIGURE 1
The short-run production function, average product (AP), and marginal product (MP). The production function illustrated in Figure 1 (a) is drawn assuming a fixed amount of capital and only one variable input, labor. As the amount of labor increases, output increases as well, but ultimately it increases by smaller and smaller amounts. The average product (AP) and marginal product (MP) functions are graphed in Figure 1 (b). When MP is greater than AP, AP is rising and the MP curve intersects the AP curve at its maximum (point C).

In the short run, at least one input is fixed and other inputs are variable. **Fixed cost** does not vary with output. Total fixed cost (TFC) is the sum of all costs that do not vary with output. In our example, the fixed cost is the cost of capital. Other examples of fixed costs include overhead expenses, the building in which the firm is located, and the entrepreneur's opportunity costs. In the short run, fixed costs are sunk costs. They are incurred regardless of the level of output. Thus, in making short-run output decisions, fixed costs are ignored. **Variable cost** varies directly with the quantity of output produced. Total variable cost (TVC) is the sum of all costs that vary directly with the quantity of output produced. Examples of variable costs include some labor costs, the costs of raw materials, and the cost of energy used in the production process. Because all costs are either fixed or variable, it is the case that:

$$TC = TFC + TVC$$

Fixed cost
Any cost that does not vary with output. In the short run, fixed costs are sunk.

Variable cost
Any cost that varies directly with the quantity of output produced.

The cost functions for the production function example in Table 1 — the snowplow operation — are calculated in Table 2 and graphed in Figure 2. The cost figures in Table 2 are calculated on the assumption that the price of a unit of labor is $30, the price of capital per unit per day is $25, and the amount of capital is fixed at 3 units (the snowplows). Since more output is produced only with more inputs, total cost increases as output increases.

In the short run, the change in total cost resulting from a change in the level of output is equal to the change in total variable cost. Total fixed cost, by definition, is constant with respect to output changes. In our example, the

TABLE 2
Short-run cost functions for snow removal

Total Output	Fixed Cost	Total Variable Cost	Total Cost
0	75	0	75
20	75	30	105
45	75	60	135
73	75	90	165
99	75	120	195
121	75	150	225
136	75	180	255
141	75	210	285
Capital units = 3 (snowplows)	Capital price per day per unit = $25		Labor price per day = $30

cost associated with the three snowplows does not change, regardless of the amount of snow that is removed. However, as we add more or less labor, total cost and total variable cost increase or decrease accordingly. Total cost and total variable cost differ by the amount of total fixed costs.

The shape of the total cost function is determined by the production function. Notice that total cost begins to rise rapidly beyond an output level of 120

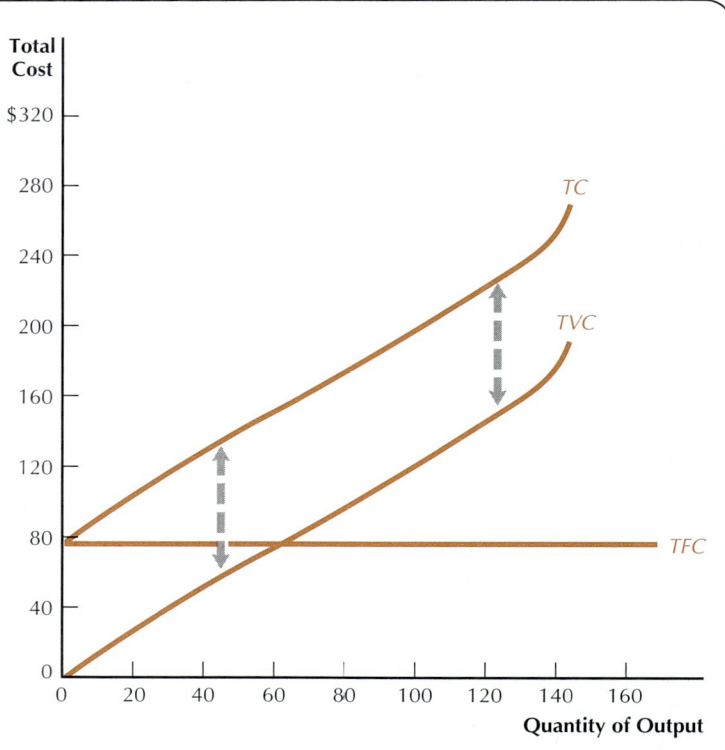

FIGURE 2
Total cost functions. This figure illustrates the total cost functions in Table 2. The price of labor is $30 per unit, the price of capital is $25 per unit, and capital is fixed at 3 units. Because fixed costs do not vary with the level of output, total fixed cost (TFC) appears as a horizontal line at $75. Total costs (TC) and total variable costs (TVC) increase with the level of output. The vertical difference between TC and TVC is TFC.

units. This rapid increase is caused by the diminishing marginal productivity of the labor input. We are paying the same price for each additional worker, but each additional worker is adding less and less output to production. Thus, the cost of each additional unit of output begins to rise rapidly. We see this influence more clearly in other measures of cost.

Two other kinds of cost measures are important for the firm's decision making—average cost and marginal cost. We can define three different average cost functions, one for each of the total cost functions noted above.

1. **Average total cost** (ATC) is total cost per unit of output:

$$ATC = \frac{TC}{Q}$$

This cost measure is also popularly referred to as *unit cost* of production, the average total cost of a unit of output.

2. **Average variable cost** (AVC) is total variable cost per unit of output:

$$AVC = \frac{TVC}{Q}$$

3. **Average fixed cost** (AFC) is total fixed cost per unit of output:

$$AFC = \frac{TFC}{Q}$$

Fixed costs are constant in the short run. Therefore, as output increases, average fixed cost steadily declines. Furthermore, since:

$$TC = TVC + TFC$$

it is also true that:

$$ATC = AVC + AFC$$

Thus, we need only work with two of these functions and we can always derive the third one. We will use average total cost and average variable cost explicitly in our analysis of the firm's supply decisions. However, remember that we can always calculate average fixed cost since average fixed cost equals average total cost minus average variable cost.

The other cost function that is very important in the firm's decision-making process is **marginal cost** (MC)—the addition to total cost associated with the production of an additional unit of output:

$$MC = \frac{\Delta TC}{\Delta Q}$$

The marginal cost of a unit of output is the additional cost the firm incurs by producing that one unit of output.

The average and marginal cost functions calculated for the total cost functions in Table 2 are presented in Table 3 and are graphed in Figure 3. In Figure 3, each cost function tells us the value of that particular cost measure at each level of output. For example, to find marginal cost, average variable cost, average fixed cost, and average total cost for 45 units of output, draw a vertical line at 45 units on the output scale (horizontal axis). The point at which the vertical line intersects each cost function is the cost at that output level. Cost is read off the vertical axis. Compare the values for the four cost functions at 45 units of output on the graph in Figure 3 with the values in Table 3.

Average total cost
Total cost per unit of output.

Average variable cost
Total variable cost per unit of output.

Average fixed cost
Total fixed cost per unit of output.

SECTION RECAP

Total costs are the sum of total fixed costs and total variable costs. Fixed costs are associated with the fixed inputs to the production process. Variable costs are associated with the variable inputs to the production process.

Marginal cost
The addition to total cost associated with the production of an additional unit of output.

TABLE 3
Short-run production and cost functions

Units of Labor Per Day	Measures of Daily Productivity			Total Costs ($)			Average Cost ($/unit)			Marginal Costs
	Total Output	Marginal Product	Average Product	Fixed	Variable	Total	Fixed	Variable	Total	
0	—	—	—	75	—	75	—	—	—	—
1	20	20	20.0	75	30	105	3.75	1.50	5.25	1.50
2	45	25	22.5	75	60	135	1.67	1.33	3.00	1.20
3	73	28	24.3	75	90	165	1.03	1.23	2.26	1.07
4	99	26	24.8	75	120	195	0.76	1.21	1.97	1.15
5	121	22	24.2	75	150	225	0.62	1.24	1.86	1.36
6	136	15	22.7	75	180	255	0.55	1.32	1.88	2.00
7	141	5	20.1	75	210	285	0.53	1.49	2.02	6.00

Capital units: 3   Capital Price per day per unit: $25   Labor price per day: $30

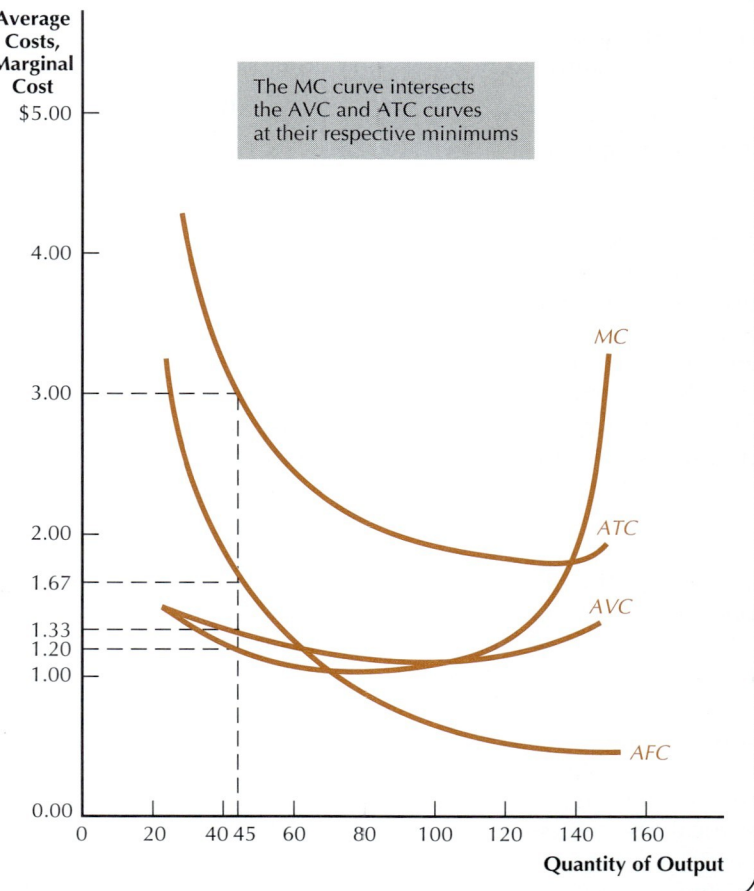

FIGURE 3
The firm's short-run cost functions: AFC, AVC, ATC, and MC. This figure illustrates the firm's average and marginal cost curves. Costs are read off the graph by drawing a vertical line at the level of output of interest. For 45 units of output, AFC = $1.67, AVC = $1.33, ATC = $3, and MC = $1.20. AFC is equal to the vertical difference between ATC and AVC.

The MC curve intersects the AVC and ATC curves at their respective minimums

Average fixed cost is calculated and graphed in Figure 3. It is downward sloping because as output increases, the amount of fixed cost per unit of output declines. As we noted above, we can always derive average fixed cost from average total cost and average variable cost and, in the short run, fixed costs are ignored. Therefore, we will devote no further attention to average fixed cost in this chapter.

The other cost functions—average total cost, average variable cost, and marginal cost—are U-shaped; they initially decrease as output increases and then begin to increase with further increases in output. This general pattern is a result of the law of diminishing marginal returns in the production function.

Consider first the marginal cost curve. It is a mirror image of the marginal product curve. As illustrated in Table 3, when marginal product rises, marginal cost falls; when marginal product falls, marginal cost rises. (Note in Table 3 that when 3 units of labor are employed, marginal product is at its maximum and marginal cost is at its minimum.) Additional workers are hired at a constant price per worker, but these additional workers initially add more and then later add less to total output. Since marginal product ultimately decreases in the short run, marginal cost ultimately increases. *Short-run rising marginal cost is caused by diminishing marginal productivity.*

What about the shape of the average variable cost curve? It is a mirror image of the average product curve. The initial increase in marginal product causes average product to rise; in other words, the initial decrease in marginal cost causes average variable cost to fall. However, at some output level, between 73 and 100 units in our example, marginal product begins to fall, thus marginal cost begins to rise. The increasing cost of production at the margin eventually pulls average variable cost up. This occurs at the level of output where marginal cost begins to exceed average variable cost.

The U-shape of the average total cost function is also the result of the behavior of marginal cost. In addition, average total cost and average variable cost differ only by the amount of average fixed cost. At any output level, the vertical distance between the average total cost and average variable cost functions is equal to average fixed cost. (Or stated in mathematical terms again: ATC − AVC = AFC.) Thus, as output increases, and average fixed cost declines, the vertical distance between average total cost and average variable cost gets smaller.

Marginal cost—the cost of an additional unit of output—may differ from average cost. If it is higher than the average, it will cause the average to rise; if it is lower than the average, it will cause the average to fall. As a consequence of this relationship between the margin and the average, the marginal cost curve cuts the average total cost curve at the minimum point of the latter. This is so because, so long as marginal cost is less than average total cost, average total cost will fall. But the moment marginal cost exceeds average total cost, average total cost will rise. The same is true of the relationship between marginal cost and average variable cost.

The average–marginal relationship holds for any variable, be it exam scores, costs, revenues, productivity, or whatever. What happens at the margin is the crucial issue in decision making. It tells us the consequence of a specific action. The average, on the other hand, describes what has happened in total. It reflects not only the change at the margin, but also the accumulated value of all the previous units of the variable in question.

SECTION RECAP
Increasing short-run marginal cost is a result of diminishing marginal productivity. In turn, MC determines the shape of the average total cost and average variable cost functions. As long as marginal cost is less than ATC (AVC), ATC (AVC) will decline. When MC exceeds ATC (AVC), ATC (AVC) will begin to rise.

Average–Marginal Relationships: A Hint

It is worthwhile to stop and consider the relationship between an average and a marginal function in more general terms. In this chapter we have examined average and marginal productivity as well as average and marginal cost. At other places in the book we will be using other average and marginal concepts. The relationship between average and marginal productivity, average and marginal cost, or average and marginal anything is a mathematical one. A more familiar example illustrates the relationship.

Suppose your grade in your economics course is to be determined by your average score on nine different exams. Table 4 contains your score on each exam, your total points and your course average. On the first exam you score 100 points. Having taken only one exam, your average score is 100 points. On the second exam, you score 85 points (this is the marginal number of points), and this reduces your average grade to 92.5 points $[(100 + 85)/2]$. The third exam reduces your average further: You score 70 points and your average falls to 85 points $[(70 + 85 + 100)/3]$. When you realize that this trend will give you a low semester grade, you work harder and your exam scores begin to climb. On the next two exams you score 75 and then 80 points, respectively. Although your average continues to fall, (calculate the average for the five exams to see that this is so) it falls more slowly. On the sixth exam your score of 85 points actually causes your average point total to rise for the first time. Your later exam scores are higher, pulling your semester average up even farther.

Notice two very important points:

1. Your average score reflects your total exam performance. It is a record of your performance on all previous exams. It tells us nothing about how you will do on the next exam. The same relationship holds for average and marginal costs. Average cost

The Economist's *Tool Kit*

Short-Run Cost Functions

The short-run cost functions capture the relationship between output and costs — variously defined — in the short run. Given a set of cost functions for a firm, we can determine the change in costs — total, average, or marginal — associated with a particular change in output. Some general patterns in costs are illustrated by the representative set of short-run cost functions in Figure 4. These cost functions have the same general shape as those in our example.[2] In addition, the marginal cost curve intersects both the average variable cost curve and the average total cost curve at their respective minimum points. This relationship holds for all short-run production processes. Mathematically, marginal cost will always intersect the average cost functions at their minimum points.

Short-run capacity
The level of output at which the average total cost of production is minimized.

Short-Run Capacity of the Firm. The **short-run capacity** of a firm is defined as the level of output at which average total cost is at a minimum. It is an optimal level of output in the sense that average total cost is minimized. In Figure 4

---

[2]Note that the average fixed cost curve has been omitted from the graph.

TABLE 4
Relationship between marginal and average exam scores

Exam Number	Marginal Exam Grade	Total Exam Points	Average Exam Score
1	100	100	100.0
2	85	185	92.5
3	70	255	85.0
4	75	330	82.5
5	80	410	82.0
6	85	495	82.5
7	90	585	83.6
8	95	680	85.0
9	100	780	86.7

tells us the cost of producing a given quantity of output. It does not tell us the cost of the next unit of output.

2. Your marginal test scores affect your average score. Your score on the next exam, the marginal exam, or your score on the last exam tell us about your current performance. The marginal scores affect the average. If your score on the next exam is above your average, it will cause the average to rise. If it is equal to the average, the average will not change. If it is lower than the average, it will cause the average to decline.

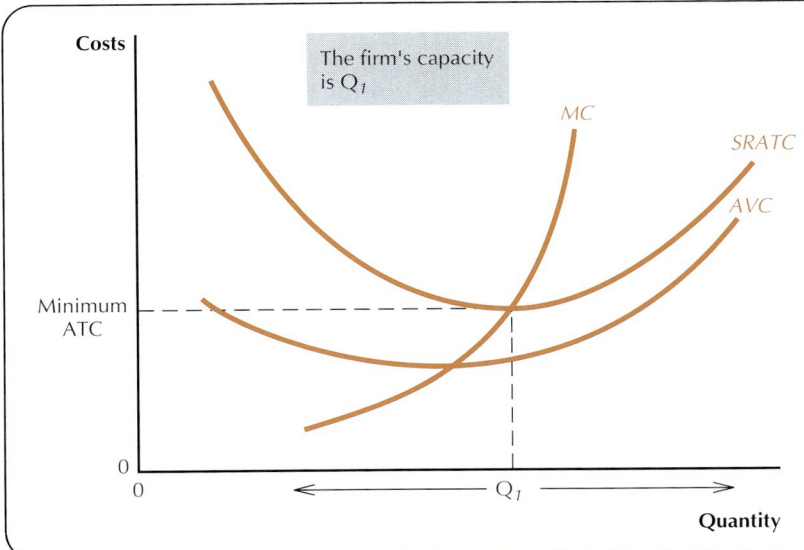

FIGURE 4
Representative short-run cost functions. The cost functions illustrated here are representative of the short-run costs incurred by many firms. The short-run ATC and AVC curves are U-shaped. In addition, the MC curve intersects the ATC and AVC curves at their respective minimums. As long as MC is less than ATC and AVC, respectively, ATC and AVC are each declining. However, when MC exceeds AVC, AVC begins to increase. The same is true for ATC.

the short-run average total cost function (which has been labelled SRATC to avoid any confusion between the short run and the long run) reaches a minimum at Q_1. Hence, Q_1 is the short-run capacity of the firm. Note that if output is less than or greater than Q_1, average total cost is higher.

When a firm produces at an output level below its capacity, it is *underutilizing* its existing plant and equipment. For example, referring to Figure 4, when output is less than Q_1, the firm is producing below capacity. In this case, average total cost is high because of the firm's high average fixed cost. Recall that fixed costs are usually associated with the firm's capital. By expanding output to Q_1, the firm makes more efficient use of its capital stock, and average fixed costs and average total costs decline.

On the other hand, when a firm produces a level of output that exceeds its capacity, it is *overutilizing* its plant and equipment. Referring once again to Figure 4, if output exceeds Q_1 the firm's average total cost rises because of high marginal costs. At output levels above Q_1 diminishing marginal productivity has pushed marginal costs above average total cost. In the snowplow example, capacity is exceeded when the sixth worker is hired (see Table 3).

The U-shaped pattern of short-run average costs is one reason why the choice of a production technology is important to the firm. The firm wants to keep costs as low as possible. In addition, it wants to use a short-run production technology that will allow it to produce at the capacity output level. To do this, the firm must correctly anticipate the volume of its sales. If it anticipates sales of 1 million units a month but only has sales of 250,000, it is stuck with excess capacity and high average total costs in the short run. On the other hand, firms can suffer from underestimating sales. If sales are 1.5 million units a month, the firm's capacity is being overutilized and average total costs are high for another reason. The high output level is associated with low marginal productivity of the variable inputs, raising marginal cost and average total cost.

Determinants of Short-Run Costs. At the beginning of the chapter we said that short-run costs are determined by the production function and input prices. This causal relationship can now be illustrated using the cost functions we have developed. Figure 5 illustrates two sets of cost functions, $SRATC_1$ and MC_1, and $SRATC_2$ and MC_2. Costs increase when the prices of variable inputs increase or the production function changes so that more variable inputs are required to produce the same amount of output. If either of these changes occurs, the cost functions shift up, for example from $SRATC_1$ to $SRATC_2$. Costs decrease when the prices of variable inputs are reduced or the production function changes so that fewer variable inputs are required to produce the same amount of output. If either of these changes occurs, the cost functions shift down, for example from $SRATC_2$ to $SRATC_1$. (Note that because these changes affect variable costs, the average variable cost curve shifts as well.)

Another determinant of costs is taxes. One of the costs of doing business is paying the taxes that have been levied on business firms by governments. Thus, taxes are part of the costs of production. A tax increase raises costs; a tax decrease lowers costs. Assume, for example, that a firm's costs are characterized by MC_1 and $SRATC_1$ in Figure 5. If a tax is placed on each unit of the good produced, it causes both the marginal cost and average total cost curves to shift up vertically (by the amount of the tax) to MC_2 and $SRATC_2$, respectively.

SECTION RECAP
When a firm operates at capacity in the short run it is utilizing its fixed inputs efficiently. Changes in the prices of variable *(continued)*

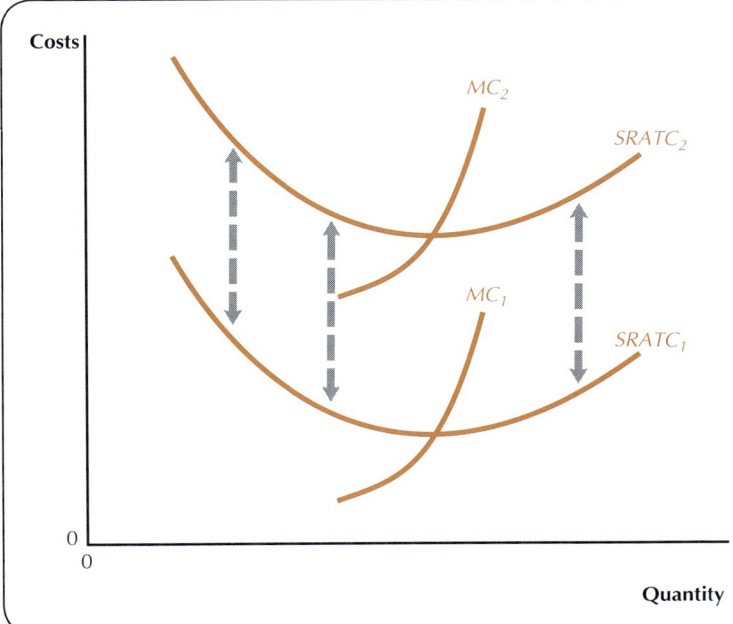

FIGURE 5
Changes in short-run costs. This figure illustrates two sets of cost functions, SRATC$_1$ and MC$_1$, and SRATC$_2$ and MC$_2$. Costs increase when input prices increase or the production function changes so that more inputs are required to produce the same amount of output. If either of these changes occurs, the cost functions shift up, for example from SRATC$_1$ to SRATC$_2$. If costs decrease, the cost functions shift down, for example from SRATC$_2$ to SRATC$_1$.

This section has described and explained the short-run relationship between output and costs. To establish the firm's short-run decision rule for maximizing profits, we still need to develop the firm's output–revenue relationship. Before considering the demand side of the market, however, we continue our discussion of production costs by taking a brief look at the firm's long-run decision-making process.

SECTION RECAP
(continued)
inputs or the production function can cause the firm's short-run cost functions to shift up or down.

Long-Run Production Costs

The firm's long-run decisions are planning decisions. Decisions to start a new business firm, to alter the firm's capacity, or to go out of business are all long-run decisions. In making long-run decisions, the firm faces fewer constraints than it does in the short run because it is free to vary all of its inputs. *In the long run, all inputs are variable.* On the other hand, the firm faces more uncertainty when making long-run decisions because these decisions are based, by necessity, on *anticipated* production costs and product demand.

A firm enters a particular market or industry to earn profits. It attempts to maximize long-run profits by choosing a short-run production technology that minimizes costs. This decision is a challenging one because the firm has to predict future product demand, technological developments, and changes in input prices. Our discussion of capacity utilization has already illustrated the importance of correctly anticipating demand. Once a production process has been chosen, the firm is stuck with it in the short run. If the firm has erred in anticipating product demand, it will experience higher production costs (and reduced profitability) due to either overutilization or underutilization of the firm's capacity. For this reason we want to pay careful attention to the firm's long-run choice of a production technology.

Why the Disagreement?

Excess Capacity in the Electric Utility Industry

Over the past fifteen years a number of electric utility companies began construction of nuclear power plants to meet the anticipated demand from their customers. However, utility companies' efforts to pass on the construction costs of these plants to consumers have met with considerable resistance. Aside from the issue of the degree of safety associated with this type of electric power generation, many individuals have questioned whether these plants are really needed. They have argued that, in many cases, the production capacity of the utility far exceeds demand. Utilities, on the other hand, have argued that this excess capacity is justified. Why the disagreement?

Part of the answer to this question lies in the fact that utilities have a responsibility known as the *obligation to serve*. According to the obligation to serve, utilities must maintain sufficient generating capacity to provide service to all customers who demand it and are willing and able to pay for it. Utilities argue that, to be able to meet their obligation to serve, they must maintain excess generating capacity — capacity that exceeds the normal level of demand. The excess capacity serves as a backup in the event of a failure of one of the firm's regular generating units or when a generating unit requires regular maintenance. In addition, the excess capacity can be used to provide additional power when extreme weather conditions, such as a prolonged heat wave, cause a surge in demand for electrical power.

Utilities have also defended the recent expansion in generating capacity on the grounds that, because of the obligation to serve, the utility must predict what demand will be in five to ten years so that it can begin construction now on plants that will be necessary to meet future demand. The growth in demand that was predicted for the 1980s and 1990s was based on the growth of demand in the 1960s and 1970s. It only became apparent in the late 1980s that demand did not grow as rapidly as was predicted.

Critics respond that many utilities are maintaining a level of excess capacity that far exceeds the level necessary to ensure adequate service and enable utilities to meet their obligation to serve. Critics argue that the overexpansion by utilities has caused fixed costs to be much greater than they would be if the utilities had planned more carefully and developed a level of capacity more consistent with the level of demand for electricity. As we will discuss in Chapter 12, the price of electric service is regulated by government and is based on the utility's costs of production. As such, an increase in average costs often leads to higher prices for electricity. Critics maintain that because of the utilities' overexpansion, customers are being forced to pay a per-unit price that exceeds the price that would prevail if the utilities had behaved in a more efficient manner.

Many critics have also argued that utilities purposely overbuilt in an effort to earn additional profits. Briefly, utilities are allowed to charge a price that enables them to pay all of their fixed and variable costs that are determined to have been prudently incurred. The price is also set such that the utility has the potential to earn a profit, specified as a maximum percentage of total fixed costs. As fixed costs increase, it is argued, so do total profits.

It is easy to see why there is such disagreement over this issue. Utilities must meet their legally imposed obligations. At the same time, customers want electric service provided at the lowest cost possible. Both sides of the argument have merit. It is also obvious that the disagreement will not be resolved easily or quickly.

Long-Run Cost Minimization

Let's consider a simplified version of the complex long-run decision of a firm seeking to maximize profits. Suppose that the firm knows the annual output it will produce and the input prices it must pay for the resources it employs. To maximize profits, the firm must choose from among the available production technologies the one that minimizes its costs of production. The choice of a production technology, or a short-run production function, is the same as the choice of a cost-minimizing combination of inputs.

In a way, the firm's choice of input combinations is very similar to the consumer's choice of a utility-maximizing combination of consumer goods. Consumers want to get as much utility as they can for each dollar they spend on goods and services. In a like manner, the firm wants to get as much output as possible for each dollar that it expends on resources. What matters in the firm's decision is the productivity of the inputs and their costs. The firm compares the benefits of employing a particular input to its cost and then compares the gain from one input to the gain from another. We know from the previous sections that the benefit of an input to the firm is the input's contribution to output — its marginal product.

We can state the firm's decision rule for long-run cost minimization formally. Suppose again that there are only two inputs, capital and labor. For a given expenditure on capital and labor, the firm minimizes its production costs by employing capital and labor in quantities such that the marginal product of capital per dollar expended upon it is just equal to the marginal product of labor per dollar expended upon it:

$$\frac{MP_K}{P_K} = \frac{MP_L}{P_L}$$

Note that the form of this equation is very similar to the one for maximizing consumer utility. The reasoning that leads to the equation is similar as well. Unless this equation is satisfied, the firm can simply alter the ratio of capital and labor employed and increase output without increasing costs. For example, if the ratio of marginal product to price for capital exceeds that for labor, the firm can reallocate its expenditures from labor to capital (reducing its employment of labor and increasing its employment of capital with no change in total expenditures) and increase output because the firm gets more output from a dollar spent on capital than it does from a dollar spent on labor. When such a reallocation occurs, the two ratios converge because of diminishing marginal productivity. As the firm hires more capital, the marginal product of additional units of capital declines; as the firm reduces its employment of labor, the marginal product of the marginal unit of labor rises.

As an aid to better understanding this concept, consider the following numerical example. Assume that a firm can purchase labor for $9 per unit and capital for $7 per unit. In addition, the firm is faced with the production function in Table 5. Note that the firm can produce 150 units of output by

TABLE 5
A long-run production function using capital and labor

Labor	Total Product of Labor	Marginal Product of Labor	Capital	Total Product of Capital	Marginal Product of Capital
0	0	0	0	0	0
1	30	30	1	40	40
2	57	27	2	72	32
3	78	21	3	93	21
4	92	14	4	106	13
5	98	6	5	109	3

hiring 3 units of labor and 2 units of capital, or 2 units of labor and 3 units of capital. If the firm decides on the first combination (3L and 2K) the total cost of production is $41 [(3 × $9) + (2 × $7)]. However, it is also the case that:

$$\frac{MP_K}{P_K} = \frac{32}{7} > \frac{22}{9} = \frac{MP_L}{P_L}$$

which indicates that this is not the cost-minimizing combination of resources for producing 150 units of output. In fact, if the firm hires one less unit of labor and one more unit of capital (2L and 3K) it will still produce 150 units of output, but the total cost is now only $39 [(2 × $9) + (3 × $7)]. In addition:

$$\frac{MP_K}{P_K} = \frac{21}{7} = \frac{27}{9} = \frac{MP_L}{P_L}$$

The long-run cost minimization rule also suggests the firm's long-run response to changes in relative input prices. In the short run, an increase in the price of one or more inputs, *ceteris paribus*, leads to higher costs because the firm cannot substitute among all inputs in the short run. At least one input is fixed. However, in the long run, all inputs are variable. Consequently, if, for example, the price of labor rises relative to the price of capital, firms have an incentive to substitute capital for labor. Assuming that the firm is initially employing an efficient combination of labor and capital, if the price of labor does rise, the ratios of productivity per dollar are no longer equal:

$$\frac{MP_K}{P_K} > \frac{MP_L}{P_L}$$

The firm's cost-minimizing response is clear: Hire more of the now relatively cheaper input (capital) and reduce employment of the now relatively more expensive input (labor). The firm substitutes capital for labor until the marginal product–price ratios are once again equal.

Firms, like consumers, are sensitive to the prices of the goods and services they buy. When factor prices change, firms adjust their input purchases to get as much productivity as they can for each dollar spent. When the price of labor rises relative to the prices of other inputs, firms try to economize on labor by substituting other inputs for labor. For example, in some assembly work, auto manufacturers substitute robots for humans. The Coast Guard is automating its remaining manned lighthouses to reduce the cost of providing navigational assistance to ships. When the price of gold rises, dentists seek to employ alternative metal alloys in crowns and bridges. When the price of energy rose rapidly in the 1970s, firms substituted more capital or labor for energy in their production processes by employing more fuel-efficient equipment and adopting more labor-intensive technologies.

Substitution in production is generally a long-run process. None of the substitution examples just mentioned can be carried out in the short run. It takes time to make these kinds of changes, and the amount of time required varies widely, depending upon the nature of the production process. It takes years to substitute nuclear fuel for coal in the production of electricity, but only weeks or months to substitute bigger, more automated tractors for farm labor. In the short run, the firm's response to input price changes is limited to changes in output. However, in the long run, the firm has more options. It can vary its usage of all inputs by adopting a new production function with a different mix of inputs.

SECTION RECAP
In the long run, all inputs are variable. Hence, the firm's objective is to hire the combination of inputs for which marginal product divided by price is equal for the last unit of each input employed.

Long-Run Average Cost

In the long run, there is a least-cost combination of inputs for producing each level of output. If we express these least-cost input combinations in terms of average or unit cost, we can examine the relationship between long-run average cost and the level of expected or planned output. The function that relates long-run average cost (LRAC) to the planned output level is called the **long-run average cost curve**. A long-run average cost curve is illustrated in Figure 6.

The long-run average cost curve shows the cost of producing different levels of output when all inputs are allowed to vary. The long-run average cost curve can be considered a *cost frontier* because it separates the set of attainable levels of cost from those that are unattainable, given input prices and the present state of technology. Those points below the long-run average cost curve are unattainable cost levels. Those points above the curve are attainable.

The long-run average cost curve is often called a *planning curve* or *envelope curve*. This terminology reflects the fact that the long-run average cost function is not a cost function for a particular production technology. Instead, the long-run average cost function is derived from a set of short-run average total cost functions. As we move from left to right in Figure 6, the amount of capital associated with each short-run average total cost curve is increasing. Consider, for example, a retail firm's decision of how much floor space to occupy. Once the firm selects a certain amount of square footage, its capacity is fixed in the short run. A decision to expand the amount of floor space it employs is a long-run decision. Expanding to a larger size moves the firm to a new short-run average total cost function that is to the right of the previous one. In a similar manner, a decision by a manufacturing firm to add an additional assembly line is a long-run decision that would move it to a new short-run average total cost function.

Firms adopt a particular short-run function when they choose a short-run production technology to employ. The firm's long-run decision problem is to choose that combination of inputs and capacity that minimizes production costs. In Figure 6, a firm can produce Q_1 units of output with three different

Long-run average cost curve
The cost of producing different levels of output when all inputs are allowed to vary; it shows the effect on average total cost when the capacity of the firm is varied.

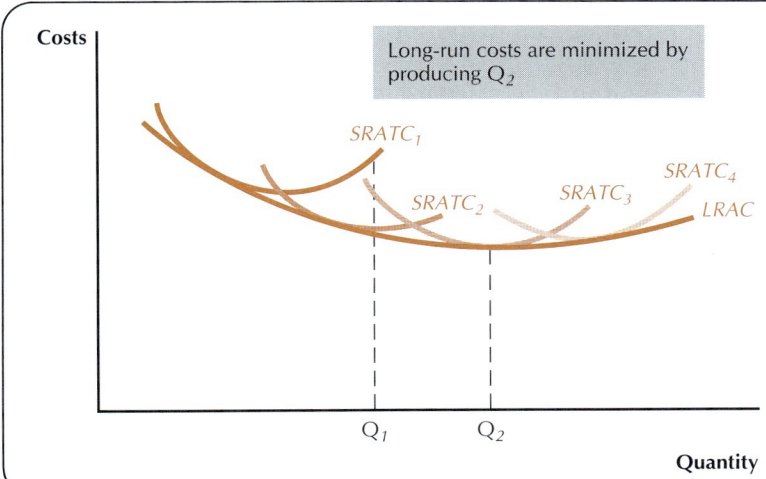

FIGURE 6
The long-run average cost curve. The long-run average cost curve (LRAC) shows the average cost of production when all inputs are allowed to vary. Each short-run average cost curve is drawn for a given level of the fixed input. As we move to the right, the amount of the fixed input is increasing. At output levels below Q_2, as capacity expands, LRAC declines due to economies of scale. As capacity expands beyond Q_2, however, LRAC begins to increase, due to diseconomies of scale.

short-run cost functions, but only one cost function, SRATC$_2$, minimizes the cost of producing Q$_1$ units of ouput.

Economies of Scale

What is the relationship between the planned output level and average total costs? The long-run average cost function in Figure 6 has been drawn such that average total costs decrease as planned output increases up to a point (Q$_2$) and then average total costs begin to increase with larger planned output levels. Since we are assuming that input prices are constant, the reduction in costs (the negatively sloped portion of the long-run average cost curve) must come about because output is increasing faster than the increase in costs as the scale (size) of operations increases. A firm is said to experience long-run **economies of scale** when average total costs fall as the scale of production increases.

Economies of scale arise because of specialization and substitution among inputs. With a larger scale of operations, firms can employ many inputs in more specialized, and usually more productive, ways. Capital equipment with very specialized functions can be employed when the expected volume of output is large. In addition, firms can take advantage of a greater division of labor, allowing workers to specialize in specific tasks. The division of labor itself can result in increased productivity. Moreover, the resulting increase in experience achieved by workers who specialize in certain tasks also increases productivity. The assembly line has become synonymous with mass production technologies. In assembly line production, the manufacturing process has been broken down into literally hundreds or thousands of separate, small steps performed by different workers.

The increased employment of capital relative to labor and other inputs is an important source of improved productivity as well. The cost of developing and adopting technologically advanced capital equipment is high. However, its cost per unit of output can be very low if the scale of production is large enough. A firm that expects to produce and sell a hundred hamburgers a week will employ less capital equipment and less specialized capital equipment than a firm expecting to produce ten thousand hamburgers weekly. The larger firm can reduce its average total costs by spending more on automated, specialized capital and less on labor. (Check out the difference in equipment in a McDonald's franchise and a local mom-and-pop hamburger stand—if you can find a mom-and-pop place!)

The shape of the long-run average cost curve in Figure 6 also suggests that a firm can become too big. At output levels beyond Q$_2$, economies of scale have been exhausted, and average total costs begin to rise as planned output increases. A firm that produces at a capacity level beyond Q$_2$ is experiencing **diseconomies of scale**. The explanation for diseconomies of scale is simply that the firm grows so large that it becomes increasingly difficult to manage. The difficulties encountered in managing such a large firm introduce inefficiencies into its operations. As an example, Ford produces its F-series pick-up truck at three separate plants. This is because the average total cost of producing all of the output at a single plant would be greater than the minimum average total cost of production at each of the three individual plants.

In some industries, average total costs are invariant with respect to the planned volume of output. This case is known as **constant economies of scale**

Economies of scale
An increase in the capacity of the firm results in a decrease in the average total cost of production.

Diseconomies of scale
An increase in the capacity of the firm results in an increase in the average total cost of production.

Constant economies of scale
An increase in the capacity of the firm has no effect on the average total cost of production.

Does It Make **Economic Sense?**

A New Round of Container-Ship Construction

The transportation of ocean freight was revolutionized over thirty years ago with the development of container ships. Freight is first packed into large metal container boxes about twenty feet long, and then the containers are loaded onto ships, transported to their destination, and unloaded from the ship. Trucks can transport the containers from the shipping firm to the dock and then from the dock to the receiving firm. The containerization of ocean shipping significantly reduced the cost of ocean freight.

In 1985, container-shipping prices fell by almost 50 percent as a result of relatively weak economic activity worldwide and a substantial increase in the number of container ships competing for the available freight business. As a result of the low prices, at least one shipping company with twelve super-size container ships went bankrupt. By the middle of 1987, shipping prices were rising again, although they had not regained their 1985 level. At the same time, shipping companies committed more than $1 billion toward a new round of giant container-ship construction. The ships that were planned for construction were almost twice as large as the average container ship in service in 1987. Many people in the shipping industry questioned the decision to add more capacity to the industry at a time when market prices were at such historically low levels. ("New Round of Giant-Ship Construction is Under Way," *Wall Street Journal*, June 16, 1987.) Given the state of the ocean shipping market at the time, it is reasonable to ask, Did this new ship construction make economic sense?

The decision to build new bigger ships is a long-run decision. Such decisions are based on anticipated future prices and costs. While existing prices play a role in long-run decisions, it is the expected future prices and costs that are most important. In 1987, shipping firms saw both additional benefits and cost reductions from adding to their shipping capacity. The demand for ocean shipping was increasing. Economic activity and international trade as a percentage of total output in economies worldwide was increasing, and shipping rates were being pushed up by the increase in demand. In addition, the ships planned for construction were expected to result in economies of scale for the firms. These large ships were designed with bigger engines and more fuel-efficient hull designs and would be able to carry more cargo and move it faster, resulting in cost savings. Reduced crew, docking and fuel costs were expected per ton of goods shipped on the new vessels.

In light of the shipping market situation that existed in 1987, a decision to expand capacity might seem strange, but long-run decisions are based on the expected future state of the market. Investment decisions such as the one considered here are risky. If freight prices failed to increase or the ship design did not result in the expected cost reductions, this investment could have turned unprofitable. On the other hand, waiting longer to make the decision could have been equally costly if the market strengthened—as expected—but a firm had not added these new ships to its fleet.

For a firm faced with constant economies of scale, the long-run average cost appears as a horizontal line.

The precise relationship between the scale of operations and average total cost will vary by industry and change over time as technology changes. The potential for significant economies of scale is greater in the production of electricity than in the manufacture of fine furniture. Technological change can increase or decrease economies of scale. New developments in papermaking technology may lead to smaller paper mills with average total costs as low as the large mills presently in use. It is interesting to note, however, that the new Japanese automobile assembly plants, which utilize the latest technology, have capacities that range from 220,000 to 270,000 units — the same as Henry Ford's 1920 Model-T plants.

SECTION RECAP

The long-run average total cost curve reflects the effects of increasing the scale (capacity) of the firm. Economies of scale are associated with decreasing long-run average total costs. Diseconomies of scale are associated with increasing long-run average total costs.

Firm Output and Revenue

The purpose of this chapter is to examine the relationship between costs, revenues, and profits for a firm. We have now solved one piece of the puzzle: the relationship between inputs, outputs, and the costs of production. We now turn to the next question: What is the relationship between output and revenue for the firm? Once this question is answered, we can address the issue of profit maximization.

The input–output–cost relationships established in the above sections apply to all firms, regardless of size or other characteristics.[3] However, a firm's output–revenue relationship is determined by the demand curve for its product. There are two broad categories of firms based on product demand curves, and these categories reflect the market structure in which the firm operates. Firms are either *price takers* or *price searchers*. The demand curve faced by a price-taking firm is perfectly elastic (horizontal). The demand curve faced by a price-searching firm is negatively sloped.

Price-Taking Firms

Price-taking firm
Takes the market price as given; the output decisions of the individual firm have no effect on market price.

A firm is a **price taker** when its output decision has no effect on market price. The firm takes the market price as given.[4] A price-taking firm's demand curve is illustrated in Figure 7 (b). Note that the industry demand curve, shown in Figure 7 (a), is downward sloping, but the firm's demand curve is perfectly elastic at the market equilibrium price, P_e, which is established by the interaction of market supply and demand. The firm can produce at any output level, for example Q_1 or Q_3, and will receive the same per-unit price for its product, P_e.

The revenue functions for a price-taking firm are defined as follows.

1. As we noted in Chapter 7, total revenue (TR) is simply the product of market price and the quantity of output produced:

$$TR = P \times Q$$

Average revenue
The amount of revenue per unit of output sold.

2. **Average revenue** (AR), also called unit revenue, is total revenue per unit of output:

$$AR = \frac{TR}{Q} = \frac{(P \times Q)}{Q} = P$$

Marginal revenue
The change in total revenue associated with a change in output.

3. **Marginal revenue** (MR) is the change in total revenue associated with a change in output:

$$MR = \frac{\Delta TR}{\Delta Q} = \frac{(P \times \Delta Q)}{\Delta Q} = P$$

For price takers, the addition to total revenue from an increase in output of one unit is just the market price. Consequently, average and marginal revenue are the same. Moreover, because the firm's output decisions do not affect market price, average revenue and marginal revenue are constant. Referring to Figure 7, the average revenue function and the marginal revenue function are shown by a horizontal line that intersects the vertical axis at P_e. As this example

---

[3]This statement holds for all firms that are price takers in the input markets.
[4]Price-taking firms are discussed in detail in Chapter 10.

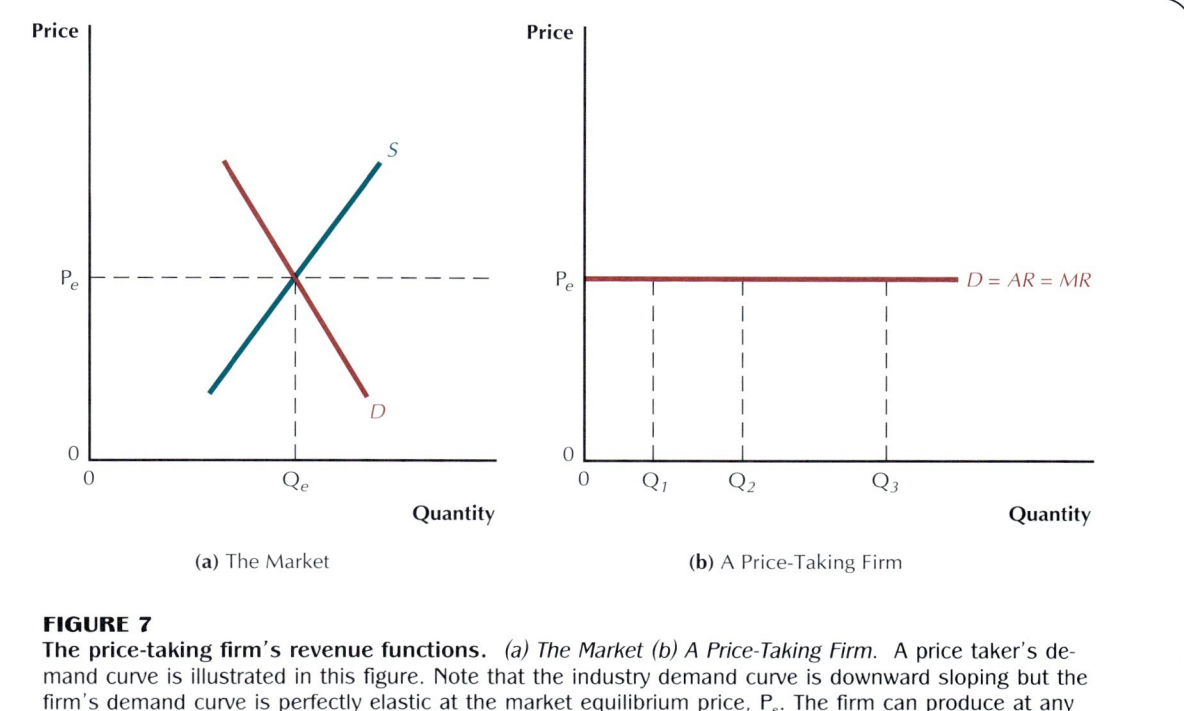

FIGURE 7
The price-taking firm's revenue functions. *(a) The Market (b) A Price-Taking Firm.* A price taker's demand curve is illustrated in this figure. Note that the industry demand curve is downward sloping but the firm's demand curve is perfectly elastic at the market equilibrium price, P_e. The firm can produce at any output level, for example Q_1 or Q_3, and will receive the same per unit price for its product, P_e. Consequently, P = MR = AR for the price-taking firm.

suggests, the price-taking firm's demand curve is also its average revenue curve and its marginal revenue curve.

Price-Searching Firms

A firm that has some degree of price-setting power is a **price searcher**. These firms face negatively sloped demand curves, and *search* for the profit-maximizing price–output combination. Price-searching firms operate in market structures characterized by some degree of imperfect competition.[5]

Because price-searching firms face negatively sloped demand curves, their revenue functions differ in some respects from those of the price taker. Like the price taker's, the price searcher's demand function is also its average revenue function because:

$$AR = \frac{TR}{Q} = \frac{(P \times Q)}{Q} = P$$

However, in contrast to the price-taking firm, the price searcher's marginal revenue function is different from its demand function (and average revenue function). Consequently, for all levels of output greater than one unit, price

Price-searching firm Has some degree of market power; the output decisions of a price searcher affect market price.

---
[5] These market structures are described in detail in Chapters 11 and 12.

and marginal revenue differ. Recall that:

$$MR = \frac{\Delta TR}{\Delta Q}$$

Price changes as output changes for the price searcher. As we move down the demand curve and output increases, price falls. Since price equals average revenue, average revenue also falls. Marginal revenue falls as well, but faster than average revenue—marginal revenue is less than price. When the price-searching firm sells one more unit of output, it gains revenue equal to the new lower market price for the extra unit sold. However, the previous units of output are now sold at the lower price as well, so the firm loses revenue on all the units that were previously sold at the higher price.

Table 6 illustrates the problem for the price-searching firm. Because it faces a negatively sloped demand curve, additional output can be sold only by lowering price. When price falls from $7 to $6.50, output increases by one unit. The additional output generates $6.50 in additional revenue. However, all units of output are sold at the $6.50 price. Before the output increase, three units were sold at $7 each. The price reduction caused revenue on these units to fall by $1.50 ($.50 × 3 units). Thus, the change in total revenue associated with an increase in output of one unit is $6.50 − $1.50 = $5.00, and:

$$MR = \frac{\Delta TR}{\Delta Q} = \frac{\$5}{1} = \$5$$

When price is $6.50, AR is $6.50 and MR is $5.

Both the average revenue and marginal revenue functions for the price-searching firm are graphed in Figure 8. As is shown in the graph, the marginal revenue function lies below the average revenue function. [In fact, when the demand curve is linear (a straight line), the marginal revenue curve is exactly twice as steep as the demand curve.] When demand is negatively sloped, marginal revenue falls as output increases. For price searchers, P = AR > MR.

The cost functions defined in this chapter apply to all firms, regardless of market structure. The marginal revenue functions are different for price-taking

SECTION RECAP
Price-taking firms take the market price as given. For the firm, price is invariant to the level of output; therefore, price and marginal revenue are equal. Price-searching firms face a downward-sloping demand curve; as they increase output, per-unit price declines. Consequently, at each output level, marginal revenue is less than price.

TABLE 6
Revenue functions for a price-searching firm

Output	Price	Total Revenue	Average Revenue	Marginal Revenue
1	8	8	8	8
2	7.5	15	7.5	7
3	7	21	7	6
4	6.5	26	6.5	5
5	6	30	6	4
6	5.5	33	5.5	3
7	5	35	5	2
8	4.5	36	4.5	1
9	4	36	4	0

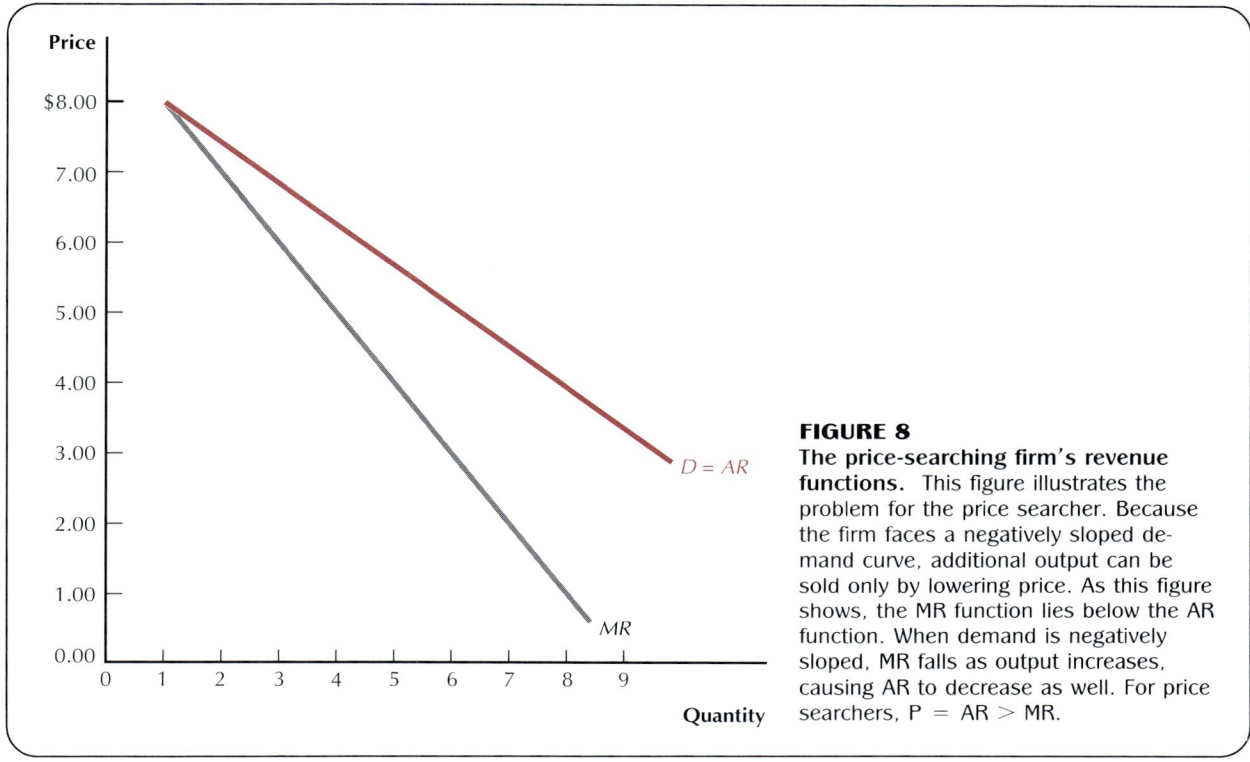

FIGURE 8
The price-searching firm's revenue functions. This figure illustrates the problem for the price searcher. Because the firm faces a negatively sloped demand curve, additional output can be sold only by lowering price. As this figure shows, the MR function lies below the AR function. When demand is negatively sloped, MR falls as output increases, causing AR to decrease as well. For price searchers, P = AR > MR.

and price-searching firms because the demand curves faced by these two kinds of firms are different. The remainder of this chapter focuses on the rule firms in any market structure use to maximize profits.

Short-Run Profit Maximization

Now we are ready to establish the firm's rule for maximizing profits (or minimizing losses) in the short run. It is very important to note that, in fact, this rule is the same regardless of whether the firm is a price taker (perfect competitor) or a price searcher. We consider the case for the price taker first.

Profit Maximization for the Price-Taking Firm

It is useful to begin by reviewing the short-run situation in which the price-taking firm finds itself. In the short run:

- at least one of the firm's inputs is fixed; thus, the firm faces rising marginal cost
- the firm takes input prices as given
- the firm takes market price as given; thus, marginal revenue is constant.

The short-run situation for the price-taking firm is illustrated graphically by putting the cost and revenue functions together, as in Figure 9. Now we are able to see the importance of the output–cost and output–revenue relation-

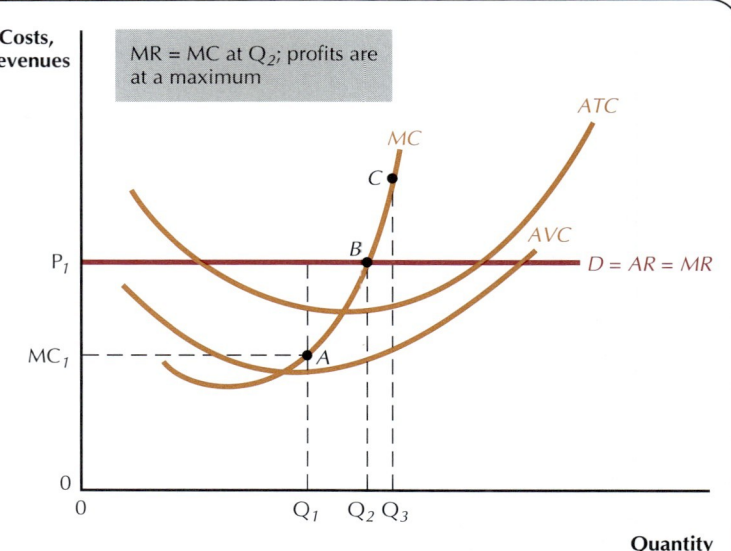

FIGURE 9
Determination of the profit-maximizing level of output: the case of the price-taking firm. The output level that maximizes the price-taking firm's short-run profits is found where marginal revenue and marginal cost are equal. At Q_1, marginal revenue exceeds marginal cost. MC at Q_1 is MC_1. As long as MR > MC, the firm increases profits by increasing production. At output level Q_2, MR equals MC (point B). For units of output beyond Q_2, for example output level Q_3, MC exceeds MR: Producing more than Q_2 units reduces profits.

ships. In the short run, the firm can control only one variable that affects costs or revenue: output. Therefore, *the short-run profit-maximizing decision for the price-taking firm is an output decision.*

The output level that maximizes the price-taking firm's short-run profits is found where marginal revenue and marginal cost are equal. To see that this is the case, consider the output levels identified in Figure 9. At Q_1, marginal revenue, which equals market price, P_1, exceeds marginal cost. Marginal cost at Q_1 is MC_1. If another unit of output is produced, it adds to total profit (the difference between total revenue and total cost) because marginal revenue is greater than marginal cost. In more general terms, the additional benefits of another unit of output — measured as marginal revenue — are greater than the additional costs — measured as marginal cost. As long as marginal revenue is greater than marginal cost, the firm increases profits by producing one more unit. However, as output increases, marginal cost rises. At output level Q_2, marginal revenue, or market price, is just equal to marginal cost (point B). For units of output beyond Q_2, such as Q_3, marginal cost exceeds marginal revenue: The cost incurred to produce an additional unit of output exceeds the benefit — the marginal revenue that is earned. Producing more than Q_2 units reduces profits. Thus, *the firm maximizes short-run profits by producing the output level at which MR = MC.*

Profit Maximization for the Price-Searching Firm

In the case of the price-searching firm, the demand curve faced by the firm is downward sloping. The short-run cost and revenue functions for a price-searching firm are illustrated in Figure 10. According to the rule for profit-maximization — produce the level of output at which MR = MC — the firm should produce Q_1 units of output and charge a price of P_1 if it wishes to maximize

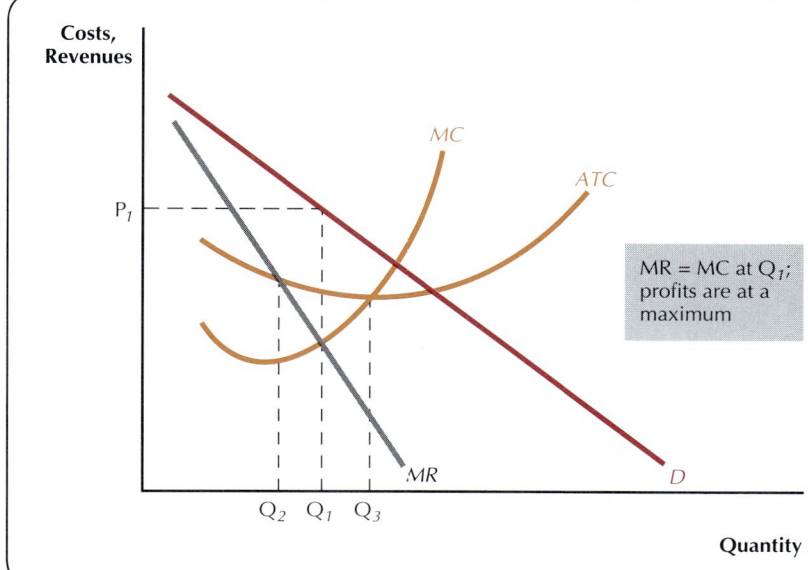

FIGURE 10
Determination of the profit-maximizing level of output: the case of the price-searching firm. The output level that maximizes the price-searching firm's short-run profits is found where marginal revenue and marginal cost are equal. At Q_2, marginal revenue exceeds marginal cost. If another unit of output is produced, it adds to total profit (the difference between total revenue and total cost) because MR > MC. So long as MR > MC, the firm increases profits by producing one more unit. At output level Q_1, MR is just equal to MC. For units of output beyond Q_1, for example output level Q_3, MC exceeds MR: Producing more than Q_1 units reduces profits.

profits. To see that this is, in fact, the profit-maximizing level of output, consider the output levels Q_2 and Q_3. At output level Q_2, marginal revenue is greater than marginal cost and the firm can add to its profit by increasing the level of output. In fact, this is true for all levels of output less than Q_1. On the other hand, if the firm decides to produce at Q_3, then it will be adding more to its costs than to its revenues since the addition to total cost, marginal cost, is greater than the addition to total revenue, marginal revenue. This is true for any level of output greater than Q_1. Hence we have shown that *price-searching firms also maximize profits by producing the level of output at which MR = MC*, just as in the case of the price taker.

Supply Decisions in a Dynamic Economy

In this chapter, we have derived a relatively simple decision rule for short-run profit maximization: Produce that level of output at which MR = MC. The decision rule was explained using an abstract picture of the firm's cost and revenue functions. Actually implementing this rule in a complex and dynamic economy is quite a challenge. Consumer demand, and therefore product prices, are changing all the time. Input markets are also dynamic; changes in supply and demand in these markets cause input prices to change. Technological developments alter production processes as well, making existing technologies less productively efficient than new ones.

To maintain their competitiveness and productive efficiency, firms must attempt to anticipate new developments and respond quickly to changes in market prices and cost conditions. While the firms' short-run options are limited to output changes, they must make these adjustments quickly to maximize

SECTION RECAP
In the case of both the price-taking firm and the price-searching firm, profits are maximized by producing the level of output at which MR = MC.

profits. In addition, these decisions are being made at the same time that firms are considering and making long-run decisions.

Summary

This chapter has examined the short-run profit-maximizing behavior of the firm. To determine short-run profits, we derive the relationship between output and short-run costs and between output and revenue for the firm. Costs are determined by input prices and the firm's **production function,** the technical relationship between the quantity of inputs employed and the level of output. In the short run, both input prices and the production function are assumed to be fixed.

Marginal physical product measures the change in output associated with a change in the quantity of a variable input employed in production. The marginal product of a variable input is subject to the **law of diminishing returns**—marginal productivity ultimately decreases as more and more units of the input are added to production.

The relationship between production costs and output is measured in various ways. **Average total cost,** or **unit cost,** is the cost per unit of output. We also distinguish between **average variable cost** and **average total cost. Marginal cost** is the change in total cost associated with a change in the level of output. The firm's short-run marginal costs ultimately increase because of diminishing marginal productivity. Average and marginal cost functions are generally U-shaped over the relevant range of output.

In the long run, all inputs are variable. The firm is choosing a set of inputs that minimizes its cost of producing an anticipated volume of output. Once the firm makes this choice it is back in a short-run position. The firm seeks to employ inputs in a combination such that the marginal physical productivity per dollar spent on each input is equal across all inputs. If the firm fails to achieve this position, it can increase output with no change in costs by simply reallocating its spending on inputs.

The **long-run average cost** curve is the locus of all points representing the least-cost input combination (measured by average total cost) for each output level. If the long-run average cost curve is downward sloping, there are **economies of scale** in the industry: The larger the expected volume of output for a firm, the lower are its average total costs. **Diseconomies of scale** imply rising average total costs as firm size increases.

The output–revenue relationship for a firm depends upon the shape of the firm's demand curve. A firm is a **price taker** if its demand curve is perfectly elastic or a **price searcher** if its demand curve is negatively sloped. Since price is invariant with respect to output for a price taker, revenue per unit of output (**average revenue**) and the change in revenue associated with a change in output (**marginal revenue**) are constant and equal to market price.

For a price searcher, price falls as output expands. Thus, average and marginal revenue fall as well, and marginal revenue is less than average revenue.

In the short run, firms seek to maximize profits by producing at the output level at which the difference between total cost and revenue is the greatest. That output level is the one at which marginal revenue equals marginal cost.

Questions for Thought

Knowledge Questions

1. Define the following terms: marginal product, average product, total cost, variable cost, fixed cost, marginal cost.
2. What firm or product market characteristics generate a perfectly elastic demand curve for the firm's output?
3. Distinguish between economies of scale, diseconomies of scale, and constant economies of scale.
4. List examples of firms that are more accurately described as price takers and price searchers, respectively.

Application Questions

5. A price-taking firm's short-run production function is:

Units of Labor per Day	Units of Output per Day
5	120
6	140
7	155
8	165
9	168

The price of labor is $20 per day. Ten units of capital are used each day, regardless of output level. The price of capital is $50 per unit.
   a. Calculate marginal product for each level of labor input.
   b. Calculate total, average, and marginal costs.
   c. Graph the average and marginal cost functions.
   d. If market price is $6.67, what is the profit-maximizing output level?
   e. Should the firm produce if the market price is $2? Explain.

6. Assume that a firm is faced with the following cost functions:

Output	Average Variable Cost	Average Total Cost
0	0	0
1	25	55
2	21.2	36.3
3	19.2	29.2
4	18.8	26.3
5	19.4	25.4
6	21.2	26.2

   a. Calculate marginal cost for each level of output.
   b. If the firm is a price taker and the market price is $22, how many units should the firm produce?

7. Use the firm's long-run cost-minimizing decision rule to explain the differences in the relative use of capital and labor in agriculture in the United States and the People's Republic of China.

8. Referring to Table 3, and assuming the firm is a price taker, determine the firm's profit maximizing level of output when the price is $1, $2, and $6, respectively.

Synthesis Questions

9. A sales manager is responsible for two sales representatives. One rep has had average monthly sales of $10,000 for the past six months. His sales in the last three months have been $10,000, $8,000, and $5,000, respectively. The other rep has averaged $5,000 monthly in the last six months, with monthly sales of $4,500, $5,500, and $6,500 in the last three months. With which sales rep should the sales manager spend more time? Why?
10. Explain overutilization of capital. What would prompt a firm to produce in this situation? Explain.
11. Marginal cost can be calculated as Wage/MP in the example in Table 2 and in question 5 above. Explain why $\Delta TC/MPP = Wage/MP$ in these examples.
12. Referring to Table 3, assume that a tax of $2 per unit is imposed on the firm's output. Recalculate the marginal cost, total cost, and average cost functions. Does the level of output at which average total cost and average variable cost are at a minimum change? Why or why not?

Appendix to CHAPTER 9

Isoquants, Input Prices, and Least-Cost Production

Overview

This appendix presents, at a more technical level, the relationship between the firm's production function, input prices, and the least-cost method of producing a given level of output. As you work through the explanations that follow, note the similarities between this analysis and the analysis of utility maximization found in the appendix to Chapter 7.

The Production Function and Isoquants

The firm's production function tells us how much output can be produced from a given level of inputs and a particular technology. Assume that we are looking at a production process that uses only two inputs — capital (K) and labor (L). Various combinations of the two inputs can be employed to produce a specific level of total output, that is, the inputs can be substituted for each other. However, according to the law of diminishing marginal productivity, additional units of each input yield increasingly smaller additions to total output, all else constant. The implication of this assumption is that, as the amount of one input employed is decreased by a particular increment, the additional amount of the other input that must be employed to continue producing the same level of output must increase.

This concept is illustrated in Table 7, which identifies specific combinations of the two inputs, K and L, that yield the same level of total output for the firm. As the table indicates, to maintain a constant level of total output, as the amount of one input employed, say capital, is decreased by one unit, the *additional* amount of the other input (labor) the firm employs must increase. For example, if the firm reduces the amount of capital employed from 5 units to 4 units, it must increase the employment of labor by 10 units. When employment of capital decreases from 4 units to 3 units, employment of labor must increase by 15 units, and so forth.

The information in Table 7 is also plotted in Figure 11. The resulting curve is called an *isoquant*, or *equal output curve*. It locates all the combinations of K and L that yield the same level of total output; that is, the firm produces the same quantity of total output from any combination of inputs on a given isoquant.

Isoquant
All the combinations of a set of inputs that yield the same level of total output.

TABLE 7

Alternative combinations of two inputs that yield the same level of total output for a representative firm

Total Output	Amount of K Employed	Amount of L Employed
300	5	10
300	4	20
300	3	35
300	2	55
300	1	90

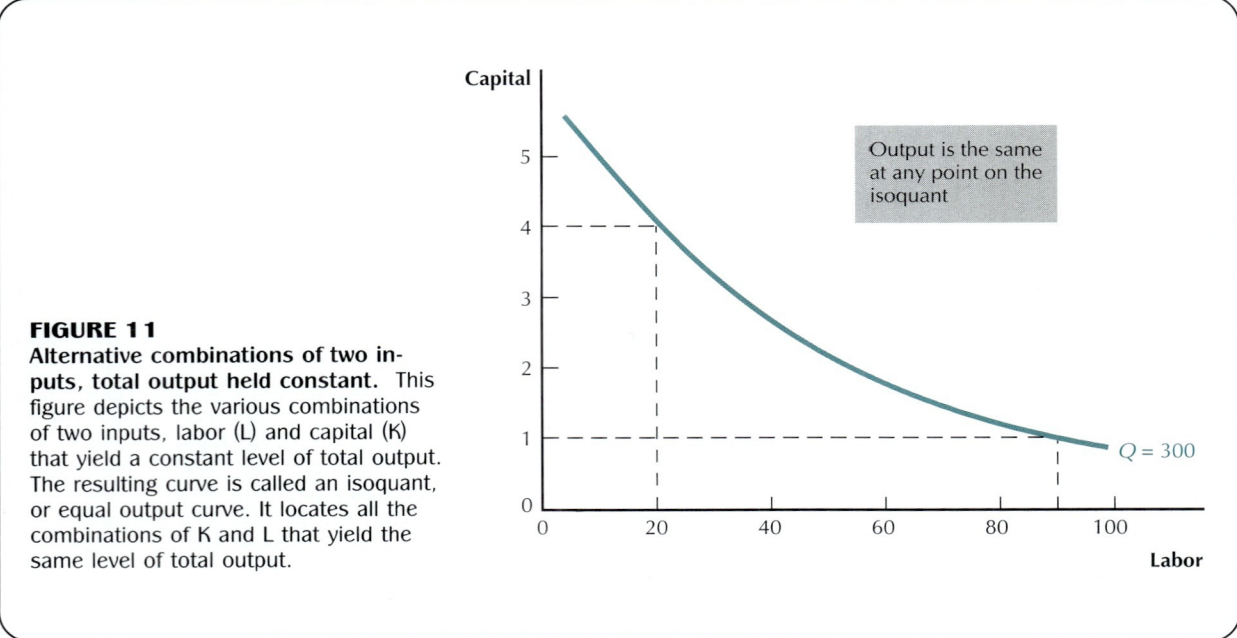

FIGURE 11
Alternative combinations of two inputs, total output held constant. This figure depicts the various combinations of two inputs, labor (L) and capital (K) that yield a constant level of total output. The resulting curve is called an isoquant, or equal output curve. It locates all the combinations of K and L that yield the same level of total output.

Isoquants and the Marginal Rate of Technical Substitution

The rate at which a firm can substitute one input for the other and still produce the same level of total output is known as the **marginal rate of technical substitution**, or MRTS. The MRTS between L and K is equal to the negative of the ratio of their marginal products, $-MP_L/MP_K$. In most cases, the MRTS is assumed to change as we alter the combination of the two inputs employed (holding total output constant).

Figure 12 depicts an **isoquant map**. Each isoquant—for example, the isoquant labeled Q_1—locates all of the combinations of the two inputs K and L that can be used to produce the same level of total output, Q_1. Note that the isoquants are convex to the origin; that is, they are bowed in toward the origin. This feature is due to the assumption of diminishing marginal productivity of each input. The slope of an isoquant at any point is simply the MRTS between L and K, $-MP_L/MP_K$. Moving up to the right (away from the origin) moves the firm to higher levels of total output. As such, Q_3 is associated with a higher level of total output than Q_2, and Q_2 is associated with a higher level of total output than Q_1.

The Isocost Line

The firm's objective is to produce a given level of output at least cost. The firm is constrained, however, by the prices of the inputs used in the production process. In the simple case where only two inputs are being used, the firm's total cost (TC) function is written as:

$$TC = P_L L + P_K K$$

where TC represents total cost, and P_L and P_K are the prices of labor and capital, respectively. The total cost function is used to derive a set of **isocost lines**, or *equal cost lines*. Each isocost line locates all the combinations of the two inputs that result in the same total cost.

A series of isocost lines has been graphed in Figure 13. Note that the isocost lines are parallel. The slope of each isocost line is $-P_L/P_K$. The slope is found by solving

Marginal rate of technical substitution
MRTS between two inputs, for example, labor (L) and capital (K), is equal to the negative of the ratio of their marginal products, or $-MP_L/MP_K$.

Isoquant map
All the output levels that can be produced with a set of inputs; moving up to the right (away from the origin) moves the firm to higher levels of total output.

Isocost line
All the combinations of two inputs that result in the same total cost.

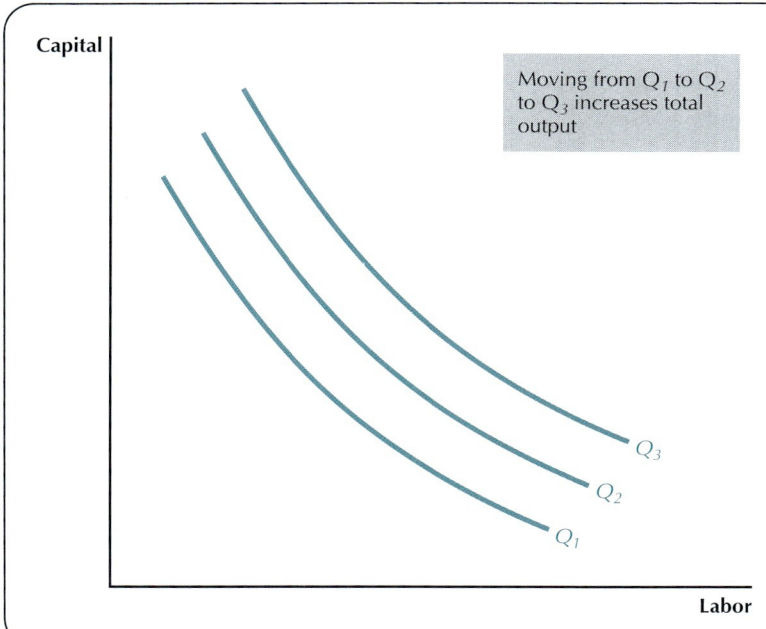

FIGURE 12
An isoquant map. This figure depicts an isoquant map. The isoquants are convex to the origin due to the assumption of diminishing marginal productivity of each input. The slope of each isoquant at any point is the MRTS between labor and capital, $-MP_L/MP_K$. Moving up to the right (away from the origin) moves the firm to higher levels of total output.

the total cost function for K and holding total cost constant, that is:

$$TC = P_L L + P_K K$$
$$P_K K = TC - P_L L$$
$$K = \frac{TC}{P_K} - \left(\frac{P_L}{P_K}\right) L$$

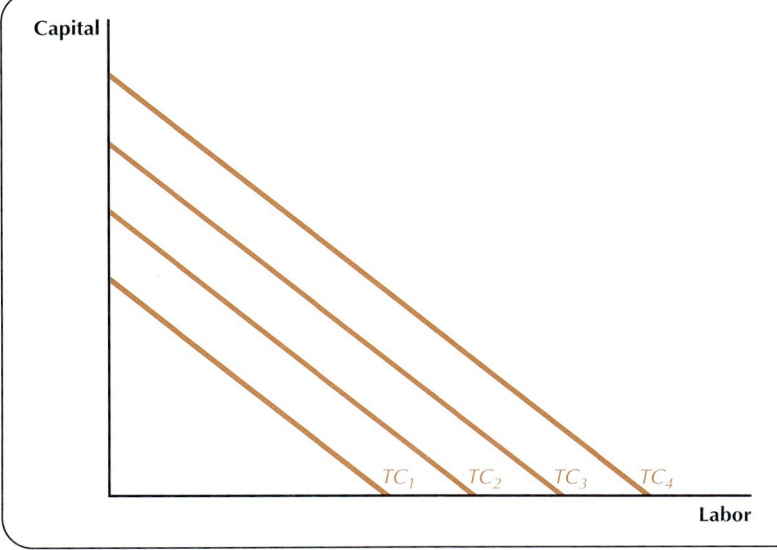

FIGURE 13
The isocost line. An isocost line locates all the combinations of the two inputs—labor and capital—that result in the same total cost. A series of isocost lines has been graphed in this figure. Note that the isocost lines are parallel. The slope of each isocost line is $-P_L/P_K$. As we move out to the right (away from the origin) the total cost associated with each isocost line increases.

Note that as we move up to the right, total costs are increasing—each isocost line is associated with a higher level of total costs.

Least-Cost Production

To produce a given level of output efficiently, the firm will employ that combination of resources that minimizes the total costs of production. The information in Figures 11 and 13 has been combined in Figure 14, which illustrates the cost-minimizing combination of resources for producing output level Q_1. The firm will minimize the costs of producing Q_1 units of output by employing the combination of inputs associated with point C, L_C and K_C. Note that, as it is drawn, the isocost line labeled TC_2 is just tangent to the isoquant labeled Q_1, at point C. Therefore, the two curves have the same slope at that point. Stated differently, the MRTS between L and K is equal to the slope of the isocost line, $-P_L/P_K$ or:

$$\frac{-MP_L}{MP_K} = \frac{-P_L}{P_K}$$

which can be rewritten as:

$$\frac{MP_L}{P_L} = \frac{MP_K}{P_K}$$

Note that this is simply the rule for least-cost production that we derived in the main part of the chapter.

To see why point C minimizes costs, consider points A and B. Both of these combinations of L and K could be employed to produce Q_2. However, each of these points lies on a higher isocost line than isocost line TC_2. Each of these isocost lines corresponds to a greater level of total costs. In fact, if the firm employs any combination of resources to produce Q_2 other than the combination associated with point C, it will automatically increase its total costs of production.

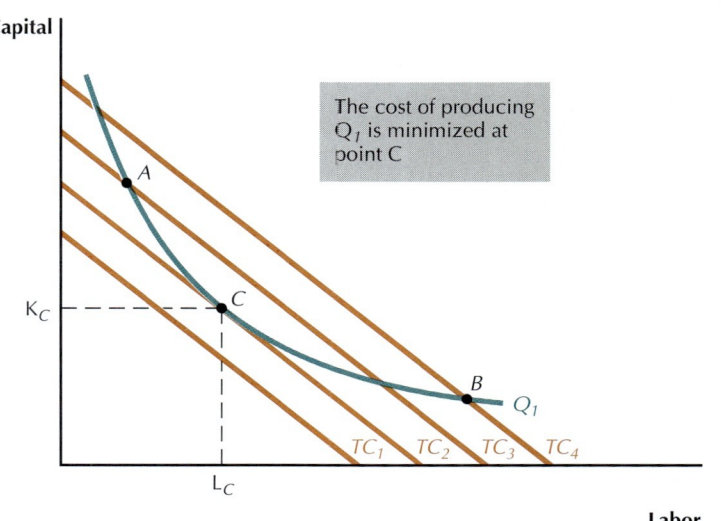

FIGURE 14
The least-cost input combination. The information in Figures 11 and 13 has been combined in this figure, which illustrates the cost-minimizing combination of resources for producing output level Q_1. The firm will minimize the costs of producing Q_1 units of output by employing the combination of inputs associated with point C, L_c and K_c. Note that at this point the MRTS between labor and capital is equal to the slope of the isocost line, $-P_L/P_K$. The combinations of labor and capital associated with points A and B could also be employed to produce Q_2. However, each of these points lies on a higher isocost line than isocost line TC_2 and therefore corresponds to a greater level of total costs.

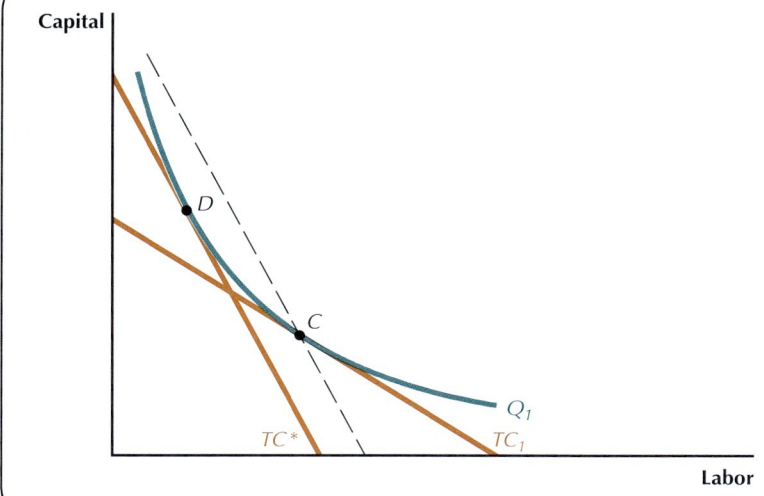

FIGURE 15
The effect of a change in relative input prices. Assume that the price of labor increased from P_L to P_L^*. This would have the effect of causing the isocost line to rotate and become steeper. Isocost line TC* reflects the increase in slope resulting from the increase in the price of labor to P_L^*. To once again produce Q_1 at least cost, the firm must substitute capital for labor. Failure to do so would put the firm on the higher isocost line that is shown by the dashed line passing through point C.

The Effect of a Change in Relative Input Prices

Assume that the price of labor increases from P_L to P_L^*. This would have the effect of causing the isocost line to rotate and become steeper, as illustrated in Figure 15. Isocost line TC* reflects the increase in slope resulting from the increase in the price of labor to P_L^*:

$$\frac{P_L^*}{P_K} > \frac{P_L}{P_K}$$

Also:

$$\frac{P_L^*}{P_K} > \frac{MP_L}{MP_K}$$

As Figure 15 indicates, to once again produce Q_1 at least cost, the firm must increase the amount of capital employed and decrease labor, that is, substitute capital for labor. Failure to do so would put the firm on a higher isocost line, which is shown by the dashed line passing through point C.

Once the firm substitutes capital for labor, and moves to point D, the condition for least cost production is once again met:

$$\frac{-MP_L}{MP_K} = \frac{-P_L^*}{P_K}$$

and:

$$\frac{MP_L}{P_L^*} = \frac{MP_K}{P_K}$$

OVERVIEW

In this chapter we develop the model of a perfectly competitive market. Although this model is a simplification of the kind of markets that we more generally observe in our own economy, it allows us to identify key factors that influence the behavior of profit-maximizing firms and determine the efficiency of market outcomes. As such, the perfect competition model serves as a benchmark by which we can evaluate market structures that more closely approximate those actually observed in our economy. These other market structures are considered in Chapters 11 and 12.

We begin the chapter with an examination of the basic characteristics of a perfectly competitive market. We then consider the short-run and long-run profit-maximizing behavior of the perfectly competitive firm. Several examples of competitive markets in action are used to highlight the role of competitive markets as rationing and allocating mechanisms. These examples vividly demonstrate the power of the consumer in a market economy and reveal the means by which perfectly competitive markets generate long-run economic efficiency.

The Perfect Competition Model

CHAPTER 10

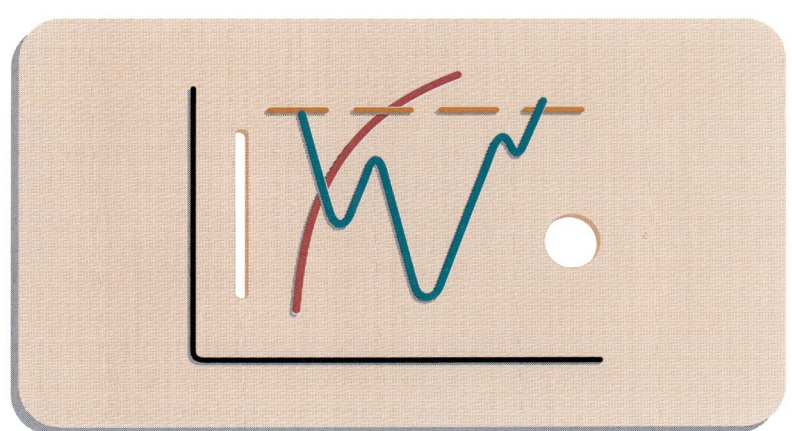

Learning Objectives

After reading and studying this chapter, you will be able to:

1. Describe the perfectly competitive market structure.
2. Determine the amount of profit associated with the profit-maximizing level of output for a firm.
3. Identify the perfectly competitive firm's short-run supply curve.
4. Explain how long-run market equilibrium is reestablished once it has been disturbed.
5. Construct the long-run supply curve for a constant-cost industry and an increasing-cost industry, respectively.
6. Explain how the model of a perfectly competitive market illustrates the concept of economic efficiency.

Characteristics of a Perfectly Competitive Market

Perfect competition
A large number of relatively small price-taking firms that produce a homogeneous product and for whom entry and exit are relatively costless.

The model of a **perfect competition** serves as a benchmark for analyzing how efficiently different market structures allocate society's scarce resources. As we will see below, a perfectly competitive market achieves an efficient allocation of resources. Consequently, we can use the results of this model to assess the degree of inefficiency associated with the outcomes in imperfectly competitive markets. The following conditions are assumed to characterize a perfectly competitive market.

1. Firms in the market are all small relative to the size of the market. A perfectly competitive market consists of a relatively large number of small firms; the output of each firm makes up only a very small proportion of total market output. Therefore, changes in a single firm's output level, even large changes, have little or no measurable effect on total market supply and therefore no influence on market price.[1] Good examples of perfectly competitive markets include agricultural markets, and some resource or raw materials markets. In the U.S. wheat market, for example, there is a very large number of wheat producers and each producer is responsible for a relatively small amount of total market output.

2. Firms in the market produce a homogeneous product. The firms in a perfectly competitive market produce and sell homogeneous (identical) products—each unit of market output is a perfect substitute for another unit. Consequently, buyers are indifferent between suppliers. Buyers of wheat are indifferent as to which wheat farmer produced the wheat they purchase. Farmer Jones' wheat is identical to Farmer Brown's wheat.[2]

3. The market is characterized by freedom of entry and exit. In a perfectly competitive market, there are no barriers to entry or exit. Resources are assumed to be mobile (they can be shifted into and out of the market costlessly) and as a consequence, firms can enter or leave a perfectly competitive market costlessly. If existing firms in the market are earning economic profits, new firms will be attracted and will enter the market. If existing firms are incurring economic losses, this will eventually drive at least some firms out of the market. In our wheat example, if wheat farmers incur losses, some farmers will switch to other crops. On the other hand, if wheat farmers earn economic profits, other farmers will switch to wheat in an effort to capture part of the profits.

SECTION RECAP
Perfectly competitive markets are characterized by a large number of small firms that produce a homogeneous product and by resource mobility. Perfectly competitive firms are price takers.

As a result of these characteristics, firms in a perfectly competitive market are price takers. The individual firm's output decision does not influence market price. Rather, market price is determined by the interaction of market demand and supply. The individual firm takes the market price as given in deciding how much output to produce. Wheat producers are price takers. The output decisions of individual wheat producers have no impact on the market price of wheat.

---

[1] In contrast, if one firm constituted half of market output, its output decisions would affect market supply and thereby alter market price.

[2] Actually there are several different kinds of wheat. But it is easy to grade wheat to determine what kind it is, and different prices are established for each kind. A market exists for each kind, and the markets are large enough that wheat farmers, regardless of the kind of wheat they grow, are price-taking firms.

Determination of Profit . . . Or Loss

The fact that a perfectly competitive firm is a price taker has important implications for the firm's decision-making process. In particular, because each firm is a price taker, the demand curve for the individual firm's product is perfectly elastic. The firm can produce as much output as it wants to and sell it at the market price. There is no incentive to lower price to increase sales. On the other hand, if the firm tries to raise its price above the market price, consumers will simply switch to one of the firm's competitors. Therefore, for the perfectly competitive firm, the problem of profit maximization is strictly an output decision.

In Chapter 9 we established the rule for determining the profit-maximizing output level—produce the level of output at which marginal revenue equals marginal cost.[3] Now we want to calculate the amount of economic profit or loss associated with a chosen output level.

Referring to Figure 1 (a), which illustrates demand and supply for a good produced in a perfectly competitive market, the equilibrium market price is P_1 and equilibrium market output is Q_M. The representative firm depicted in Figure 1 (b) takes P_1 as given. In Chapter 9 we showed that market price equals average revenue. In addition, we showed that, because the perfectly competitive firm is a price taker, the per-unit price of output is constant; marginal revenue is also equal to market price. Finally, because consumers are willing to pay the same price, P_1, for each unit of output the firm produces, the marginal revenue curve is also the firm's demand curve, or:

$$P = AR = MR = D$$

For the firm depicted in Figure 1, profits are maximized at Q_1, the output level at which marginal revenue equals marginal cost. (Note that Q_1 is a fraction of Q_M.) Having determined the profit-maximizing output level, total economic profit, or loss, can be calculated in the following manner.

1. Calculate total revenue. Total revenue is equal to price times quantity. Thus, at the profit-maximizing level of output, total revenue is:

   $$TR = P_1 \times Q_1$$

   The calculation of total revenue for the firm is illustrated in Figure 1 (b). It is the rectangle OP_1BQ_1.

2. Calculate total cost. The second step is to calculate total cost at output level Q_1. Since:

   $$ATC = \frac{TC}{Q}$$

   it is also true that:

   $$TC = ATC \times Q$$

   In Figure 1 (b), we see that at Q_1, average total cost is D, which is found by locating the point at which the vertical line from Q_1 intersects

---

[3] For a review of the derivation of the rule for determining the profit-maximizing level of output, see Chapter 9, p. 237.

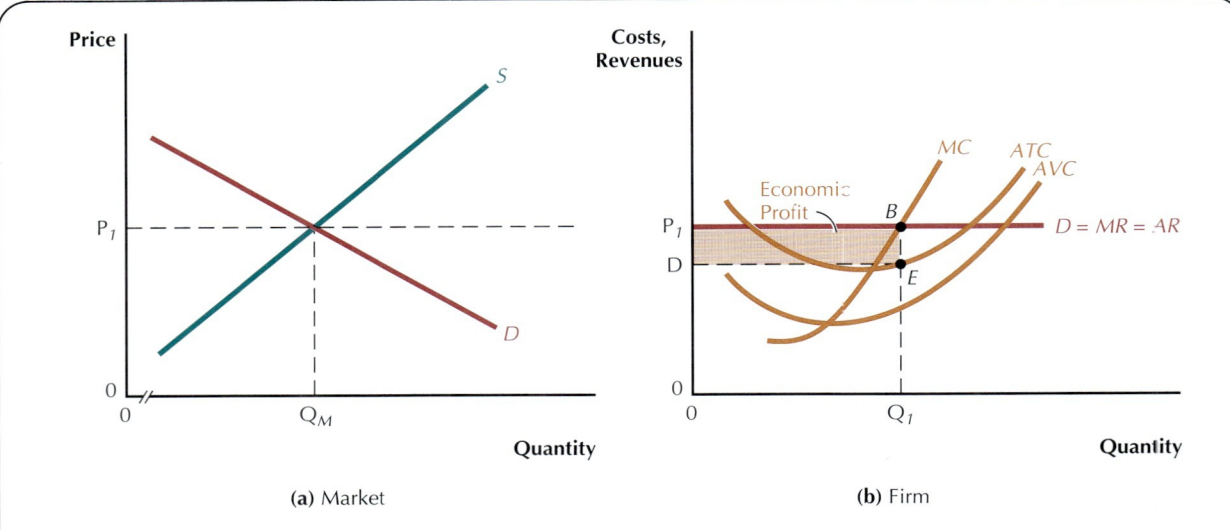

FIGURE 1
Determination of short-run profit: economic profit. *(a) Market (b) Firm.* In this example, the market price is P_1 and the profit-maximizing level of output is Q_1. Total revenue is equal to the rectangle OP_1BQ_1. Total cost is the rectangle, $ODEQ_1$. The economic profit earned by producing Q_1 units of output is the area DP_1BE.

the ATC curve. The total cost of producing Q_1 is therefore:

$$TC = D \times Q_1$$

which is the rectangle, $ODEQ_1$, in Figure 1 (b).

3. Calculate economic profit. Economic profit is the difference between total revenue and total cost. The economic profit earned by producing Q_1 units of output is the rectangle DP_1BE, in Figure 1 (b). Given market price P_1 this firm earns positive economic profit by producing at Q_1, the output level at which marginal revenue equals marginal cost. At any other output level, total profit is lower.

The profit-maximizing output level and amount of profit are determined for any market price in the manner described in the above example. Suppose, for example, that price falls from P_1 to P_2, as illustrated in Figure 2. Given this new market price, the profit-maximizing output level falls to Q_2 because marginal revenue equals marginal cost at this lower output level. Total revenue is now $Q_2 \times P_2$, or the rectangle OP_2FQ_2. Since average total cost at Q_2 is also P_2, total cost is $Q_2 \times P_2$, or the rectangle OP_2FQ_2. Thus, total revenue is equal to total cost, and economic profit equals zero. (Remember that normal profit is considered a cost of production; it is part of total costs.)

In Figure 2, the firm is earning zero economic profit. Notice that when price equals average total cost at the profit-maximizing level of output, as it does in this example, average total cost is at a minimum. At any market price below the minimum average total cost, the firm will suffer a loss. To see that this is the case, recall that price equals average revenue. If average revenue is less than average total cost, on average, the firm pays out more than it takes in on each unit of output produced.

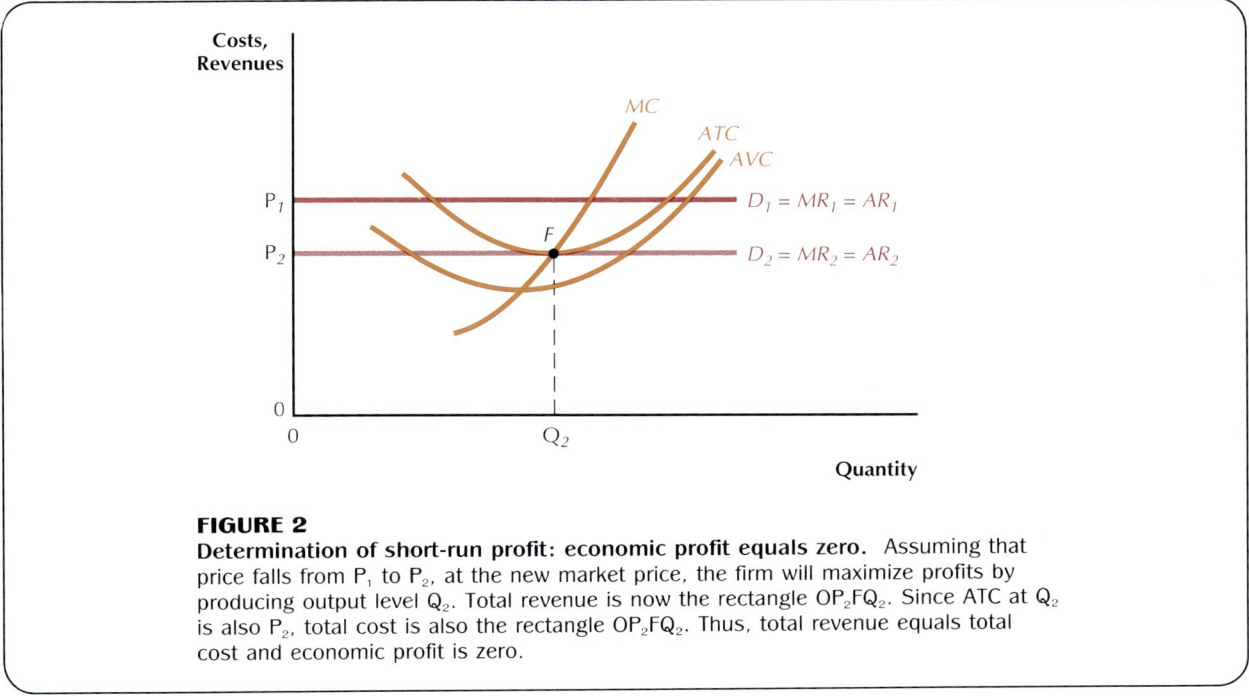

FIGURE 2
Determination of short-run profit: economic profit equals zero. Assuming that price falls from P_1 to P_2, at the new market price, the firm will maximize profits by producing output level Q_2. Total revenue is now the rectangle OP_2FQ_2. Since ATC at Q_2 is also P_2, total cost is also the rectangle OP_2FQ_2. Thus, total revenue equals total cost and economic profit is zero.

To Produce or Not to Produce

If market price equals minimum average total cost at the output level at which marginal revenue equals marginal cost, total revenue equals total cost and economic profit is zero. This price–output combination is called the **breakeven point** because at any price above minimum average total cost the firm earns economic profit and at any price below minimum average total cost the firm suffers losses. At the breakeven point economic profit equals zero.

In the short run, the perfectly competitive firm is an active business. Its objective is to maximize profits or minimize losses. In addition, its profits (or losses) are determined only by its production decision—how much output it produces. What should the firm do when price is less than average total cost and the firm is incurring losses? Again, the firm's only decision variable is output. Should it produce and, if so, how much should it produce to minimize losses?

When market price is less than average total cost but greater than average variable cost, the firm minimizes losses by continuing to produce the output level at which marginal revenue equals marginal cost. Such a situation is depicted in Figure 3. At the market price P_3, marginal revenue equals marginal cost when Q_3 units are produced. However, at that output level, price is less than average total cost. Total revenue is the area OP_3AQ_3 ($P_3 \times Q_3$). Total cost is the area $OGHQ_3$ ($H \times Q_3$). Since total cost is greater than total revenue, the firm suffers an economic loss equal to the area P_3GHA.

Why does the firm continue to produce at all when it is incurring losses? To answer this question, recall that total cost is the sum of both total fixed and total variable costs. If the firm does not produce at all, its losses are equal to its total fixed cost. However, so long as price is greater than average variable

Breakeven point
The level of output at which price equals average total cost and economic profit is therefore zero.

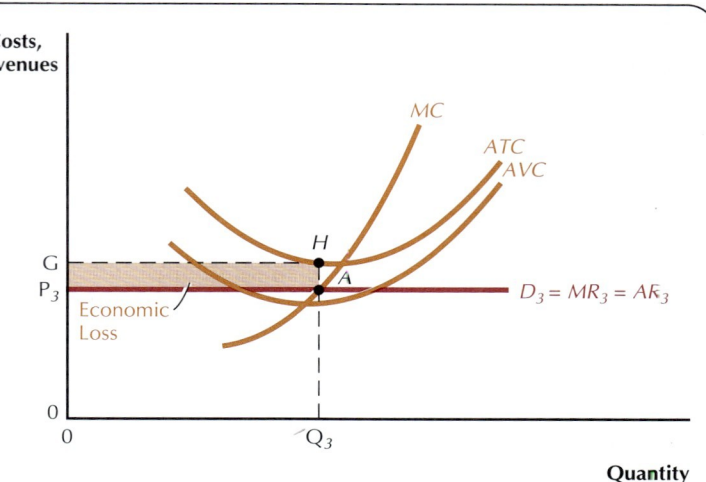

FIGURE 3
Short-run economic loss: price greater than AVC. When market price is less than ATC but greater than AVC, to minimize losses the firm produces the output level at which MR = MC. At the market price P_3, MR equals MC at Q_3, and at that output level $P_3 <$ ATC. Total revenue is the rectangle OP_3AQ_3. However, total cost is the area $OGHQ_3$. Since total cost is greater than total revenue, the firm suffers a loss in the amount of the area P_3GHA.

Shutdown point
The price level at which average variable cost is at a minimum. If price falls below this level, the firm minimizes losses by shutting down.

SECTION RECAP
So long as P > AVC at the profit-maximizing level of output, the firm minimizes losses by continuing to produce. If P < AVC at the profit-maximizing level of output, the firm minimizes losses by shutting down.

cost, the firm can generate revenues in excess of total variable cost. By producing at Q_3, the firm can pay all of its variable costs and have some revenue left to pay part of its fixed costs, thus reducing the losses it suffers in the short run. Consequently, *when price is less than average total costs but greater than average variable cost at the output level at which marginal revenue equals marginal cost, the firm minimizes its losses by continuing to produce.*

However, when market price falls below the minimum point on the average variable cost function, the firm minimizes losses by shutting down. The price at which marginal revenue, marginal cost, and minimum average variable cost are equal is called the **shutdown point**. At prices below the minimum average variable cost the firm is not generating enough revenue to pay all of its variable costs, let alone any fixed costs. At such a price, the minimum loss incurred is the fixed costs. Any production at all increases the loss to more than just fixed costs. Figure 4 illustrates the shutdown point. At a price equal to minimum average variable cost, in this case, P_4:

$$TR = P_4 \times Q_4 = TVC$$

If the firm produces Q_4, its loss is exactly equal to its total fixed costs, or the rectangle P_4XYZ. At any price below P_4, the loss from production would increase—the firm would incur losses equal to its fixed costs *plus* part of its variable costs. Thus, *at prices below minimum average variable cost the loss-minimizing output level is zero output—no production.*

Sunk Costs Again

In the short run, fixed costs are sunk costs and are ignored in the firm's decision-making process. We have just seen this in our analysis of short-run profit-maximizing behavior. However, our approach to the firm's short-run profit-maximizing decision may seem a bit strange to those who work in business or have studied business. You may be thinking, But the firm has to pay its fixed costs first, then worry about its variable costs. How can it ignore its fixed

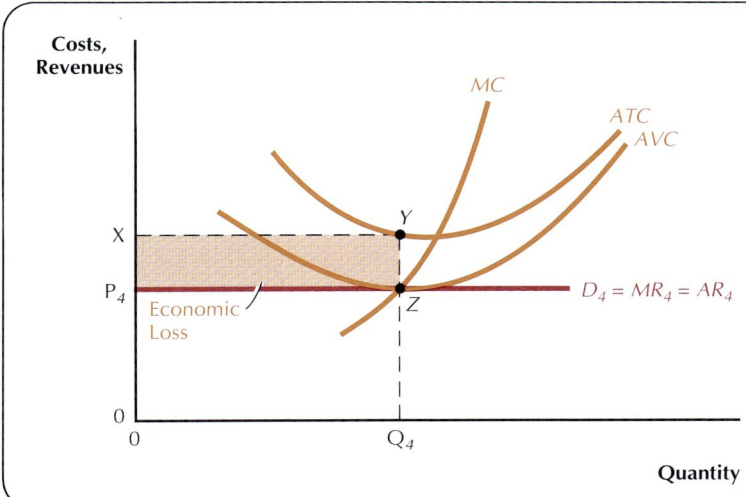

FIGURE 4
The shutdown point. When price falls below minimum AVC, the firm shuts down. It cannot generate enough revenue to pay all of its variable costs, let alone any fixed costs. At a price equal to minimum AVC, in this case P_4, TR = $P_4 \times Q_4$ = TVC. The firm's loss is equal to its TFC, the rectangle P_4XYZ. At any price below P_4, which is referred to as the shutdown point, if the firm continues to operate, the losses from production will increase. At prices below P_4 the loss-minimizing output level is zero output—no production.

costs? Of course, the firm does pay its fixed costs and in a broad, long-run sense it cannot ignore them.

The analysis of the firm's behavior has focused, thus far, on the short run. A firm incurs the obligations of its fixed costs when it decides to go into business. The decision to go into business is a long-run decision based on *anticipated* prices, revenues, and costs. However, once the firm is in business, it is operating in the short run. The price-taking firm has no control over market prices or its cost structure (determined by the production function) in the short run. Its short-run problem is how to maximize its welfare given that it is in business and has certain fixed-cost obligations.

Once in this short-run situation, how does the firm maximize its welfare? It produces additional output if the additional revenue exceeds the additional cost incurred. The cost of additional output is the cost of the variable inputs. If the revenue from production is at least as great as the variable costs incurred, the firm is better off producing output. Any additional revenue in excess of variable costs can be used to pay off part of the firm's fixed costs. However, if the revenue generated by producing output is less than the additional costs of production (the variable costs), the firm is better off shutting down. If the firm continued to produce, it would pay not only all of its fixed costs out of its pocket, but some variable costs as well. The profit-maximizing firm pays attention to the actual costs and benefits of a decision. In the short run, when deciding on what level of output to produce, fixed costs are sunk costs and they are ignored.

This does not imply, however, that losses are totally ignored. When a firm incurs short-run losses, it has important long-run decisions to make. It will continue to incur losses only if it believes that demand for its product will rise in the future, thus pushing up the market price. The firm also must be able to finance its short-run losses. To some extent, these decisions are related. If the firm must borrow to cover its short-run losses, its accessibility to lenders will depend in part on the lenders' beliefs about the firm's expected future profitability.

Does It Make Economic Sense?

Government Bailout of the Farm Credit System

Over the time period between 1985 and 1987, the Farm Credit System—which was created to facilitate the provision of credit to farmers for the purchase of land, equipment, and seed—lost approximately $5 billion in loan defaults. The defaults occurred primarily because low crop prices prevented farmers from paying off loans for farm land. The problem was compounded by a decrease in land prices that made it impossible for farmers to pay off the debt by selling their land. In turn, the growing losses of the Credit System made it more difficult to raise funds through bond sales, thus threatening the supply of credit to an already weakened farm sector. As the financial health of the Farm Credit System deteriorated, calls for some kind of bailout plan arose. Support for a bailout plan was based on a number of arguments. A bailout of the farm credit system is consistent with many other government farm programs. In addition, society seems generally willing to provide special treatment to the farm population. Finally, concerns about the impact of additional agricultural problems on the overall economy seem to have influenced Congress. After considerable debate, Congress passed controversial legislation in December 1987 that provided for a $4 billion injection of new funds into the Farm Credit System and reorganized the system of credit banks that serve farmers. In light of the existing losses and the fact that the bailout plan was projected to cost taxpayers in excess of $1 billion* it is worth asking, Did additional support for the Farm Credit System make economic sense?

First, consider this financial crisis at the farm level. Farmers are price takers. No individual farmer can affect the price of his product, and agricultural product prices can vary considerably from year to year. For a growing season (even for several seasons)—the short run in agriculture—land is the fixed input for the farmer. The farmer decides upon an expected short-run output to produce in order to maximize short-run profits. (The output is "expected" because the farmer has only imperfect control over the relationship between inputs and output.) Prices fluctuate from year to year, but so long as the farmer's revenues are at least equal to his total costs over a period of several years, short-run losses are not a serious problem. In the good years, economic profit can be used to

Short-Run Supply Curve for the Price-Taking Firm

The decision rule for maximizing profits (and minimizing losses) says that the price-taking firm produces at the output level at which marginal revenue (which equals price) equals marginal cost so long as the market price exceeds average variable cost. If the firm's marginal cost function and the market price are known, we can determine the firm's output level.

The firm's marginal cost curve, above its intersection with the average variable cost curve, tells us the quantity of output supplied by the firm at every market price. Therefore, *the firm's marginal cost curve above the minimum of the average variable cost curve is the firm's short-run supply curve.* The short-run supply curve for a typical price-taking firm is illustrated in Figure 5. Given the firm's short-run cost functions and its decision rule to produce the output level at which marginal revenue equals marginal cost, changes in price from P_1 to P_4 trace out the short-run, positively sloped supply curve of the firm.

When supply curves were first introduced we said that they reflect the opportunity cost of production. Now we can see that point more clearly. The firm's supply curve is its marginal cost curve, which tells us the additional cost to the firm of producing each additional unit of output. The market short-run supply curve is the horizontal sum of these individual supply curves. That is, we sum up the quantity of output each firm is willing to produce at each price. The resulting price–quantity combinations constitute the market supply curve.

SECTION RECAP

The firm's short-run supply curve is its marginal cost curve above minimum AVC. The market short-run supply curve is the horizontal sum of the individual firms' supply curves.

catch up on mortgage payments for the land.

However, if annual losses occur over a period of consecutive years, the farmer runs into financial difficulties and may have to sell his land and equipment to pay his debts and then leave farming for some other kind of work. If the value of the farmer's land and equipment is insufficient to pay off the debts, the farmer may be forced into bankruptcy. The steep decline in land values and the decrease in farm prices in the early and mid-1980s did force many farmers into precisely this situation.

The bailout plan was opposed for several different reasons. Further aid to agriculture represents further government support to one particular sector of the economy and sets a precedent for increased government intervention in private markets. It was also argued that a bailout would provide additional support for farmers to remain in an industry already suffering from excess supply, and was therefore inefficient. Note that as farmers leave the industry, supply decreases, causing an increase in market price. Assuming resource mobility, exit would continue until price rose high enough that the remaining farmers could earn a normal profit. The bailout had the effect of reducing the incentive for resource owners to exit from agriculture. Losses in the farm sector suggest that those resources are more valuable in other markets. Finally, the bailout was opposed as simply too expensive. The federal government's continued deficits have created serious macroeconomic problems. The bailout plan made it that much more difficult to resolve the government's spending problems.

The economic arguments would appear to provide the most support for the position maintained by the opponents of the bailout. However, as the preceding discussion suggests, the motivation for this particular policy derived as much from considerations about what the government *ought* to be doing with regard to agricultural policy (a normative question) as it did from consideration of the relative economic costs and benefits (a positive question) of the plan. Economic analysis provides only one piece of information that policymakers use in their decision-making process. In the case of the Farm Credit System it is reasonable to conclude that other concerns played a dominant role.

*"Senate Approves $4 Billion in Aid to Farming Banks," *The New York Times*, December 5, 1987.

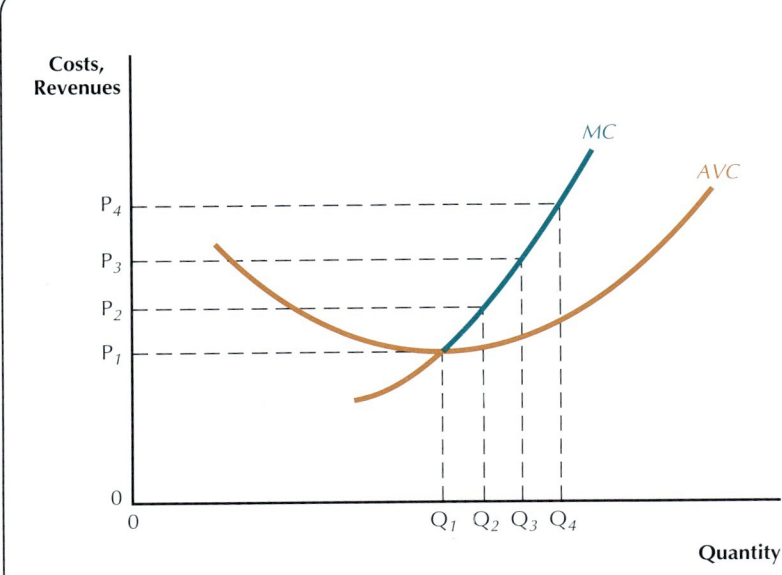

FIGURE 5
Short-run supply curve for a price-taking firm. The firm's MC function, above its intersection with the AVC function, determines the quantity of output supplied by the firm at each market price. Therefore, the firm's MC function above the AVC function intersection *is* the firm's short-run supply function.

Perfect Competition and Rational Behavior

Our next step is to take a close look at market decision making in action. We will see how the utility-maximizing behavior of individual consumers and the profit-maximizing behavior of individual producers generate the outcomes observed in markets. These market outcomes are also considered in terms of their broad economy-wide implications. It was argued in Chapter 4 that competition is an important prerequisite for economic efficiency. The focus now shifts to the characteristics of a perfectly competitive economy that constitute conditions for achieving economic efficiency.

Implicit in the definition of perfect competition is the assumption of costless information and mobility. In other words, it is assumed that economic decision makers are aware of all the alternatives available to them. They know the prices of all goods and inputs, and they are aware of differences in profit levels across markets. In addition, it is assumed that decision makers and resources can move from market to market in a costless fashion. If information and mobility are costless, individuals will acquire all information and therefore have perfect information. In addition, they will move when and where necessary at no cost to take advantage of opportunities — they are perfectly mobile.

We know that these assumptions are unrealistic. Information is costly to acquire and it is also costly to get around. However, these assumptions are simplifications that permit us to concentrate on the issues important in understanding how markets operate. Relaxing these assumptions does not alter the basic principles derived from this abstract economic model. In fact, after acquiring an understanding of this perfect market model, one can then use the model to deduce market developments that arise because of costly information and mobility.

As a preface to the following examples of competitive markets in action, it is useful to recall the Fundamental Premise of Economics and an important assumption about information and mobility. The Fundamental Premise is a basic assumption about human behavior. It says that individuals behave rationally — in making decisions people choose the alternative that maximizes their net gain from each decision. Consumers seek the best price for what they buy. Entrepreneurs seek out the most profitable business ventures. Individuals look for the highest-paying jobs. Investors search for the highest-yielding investment alternatives. This rational behavior is the force that drives markets to equilibrium.

The Dynamics of the Market Mechanism: Long-Run Equilibrium

Chapter 3 introduced supply and demand analysis and illustrated how markets work. We examined the process by which market equilibrium is disturbed by a change in some factor affecting supply or demand and then is reestablished by further changes in the market. Now we return to this equilibrium process with a better understanding of both consumer and producer behavior in competitive markets. We will again illustrate the disturbance of market equilibrium and the return to a new equilibrium. However, this time the process is examined in more detail by relying on the profit-maximizing behavior of price-taking firms and the assumptions just reviewed in the above section.

Demand Changes in Perfectly Competitive Markets

Consider a specific market: the market for wood pencils. Assume that all pencils produced in this industry are exactly alike. The industry produces a homogeneous product. For the purposes of our example, assume that pencils are all No. 2 yellow wooden pencils. If the industry is perfectly competitive, firms are price takers. The many individual firms in the industry each face a perfectly elastic demand curve and firms can enter and exit the market freely.

What happens in the pencil market when an increase in the demand for pencils disturbs the pencil market equilibrium? How is a new equilibrium reestablished and how does the new equilibrium compare to the original one? To answer these questions, consider Figure 6.

Initial Equilibrium Figure 6 (a) depicts the market for pencils, and Figure 6 (b) depicts the cost and marginal revenue curves for a representative firm. The market supply curve, S_1, is the horizontal sum of the individual firms' marginal cost curves. The market demand curve, D_1, is the horizontal sum of all the individual consumers' pencil demand curves. The market and the firms in the market are initially in equilibrium at a price of P_1. Market output is Q_{M1}.

The equilibrium price, determined by the interaction of supply and demand, is taken as given by each firm. Each firm sets its output level, Q_{F1} in Figure 6 (b), such that its marginal cost is equal to marginal revenue (the market price). Since at Q_{F1}, market price also equals the firm's short-run and long-run minimum average total (unit) cost, the firm's total revenue equals total cost and economic profit is zero. The market and each firm in the market are in long-run equilibrium—there is no pressure for market price to rise or fall. In addition, there is no incentive for firms to leave or enter the market. Existing firms are earning a normal profit. The fact that each firm is operating at the minimum of the long-run average cost curve indicates that firms are using the optimal plant size. New firms cannot enter and operate at lower cost than the firms currently operating in the market.

Increase in Demand Now assume that consumer demand for pencils increases. An increase in demand occurs when any factor affecting consumer demand changes in the appropriate direction. For example, the demand increase could be caused by an increased preference for pencils, an increase in the price of substitutes for pencils, or an increase in the income of pencil consumers. The increase in demand shifts market demand from D_1 to D_2 as shown in Figure 6 (c).

Short-Run Response to Increased Market Price The increase in market demand causes market price to increase from P_1 to P_2. Following the short-run profit-maximization rule, each firm responds to the higher market price by increasing output from Q_{F1} to Q_{F2}. [This increase in output is illustrated in Figure 6 (d).] As each firm increases its output, the quantity of pencils supplied to the market increases from Q_{M1} to Q_{M2}. In the market, a new short-run equilibrium is reached at P_2 and Q_{M2}. Note that the new higher market price is greater than the firm's average total cost at Q_{F2} units of output, as illustrated in Figure 6 (d). Consequently, each firm is now earning economic profit equal to the shaded rectangle DP_2BC. The increased willingness to pay for pencils has created short-run economic profits for existing firms.

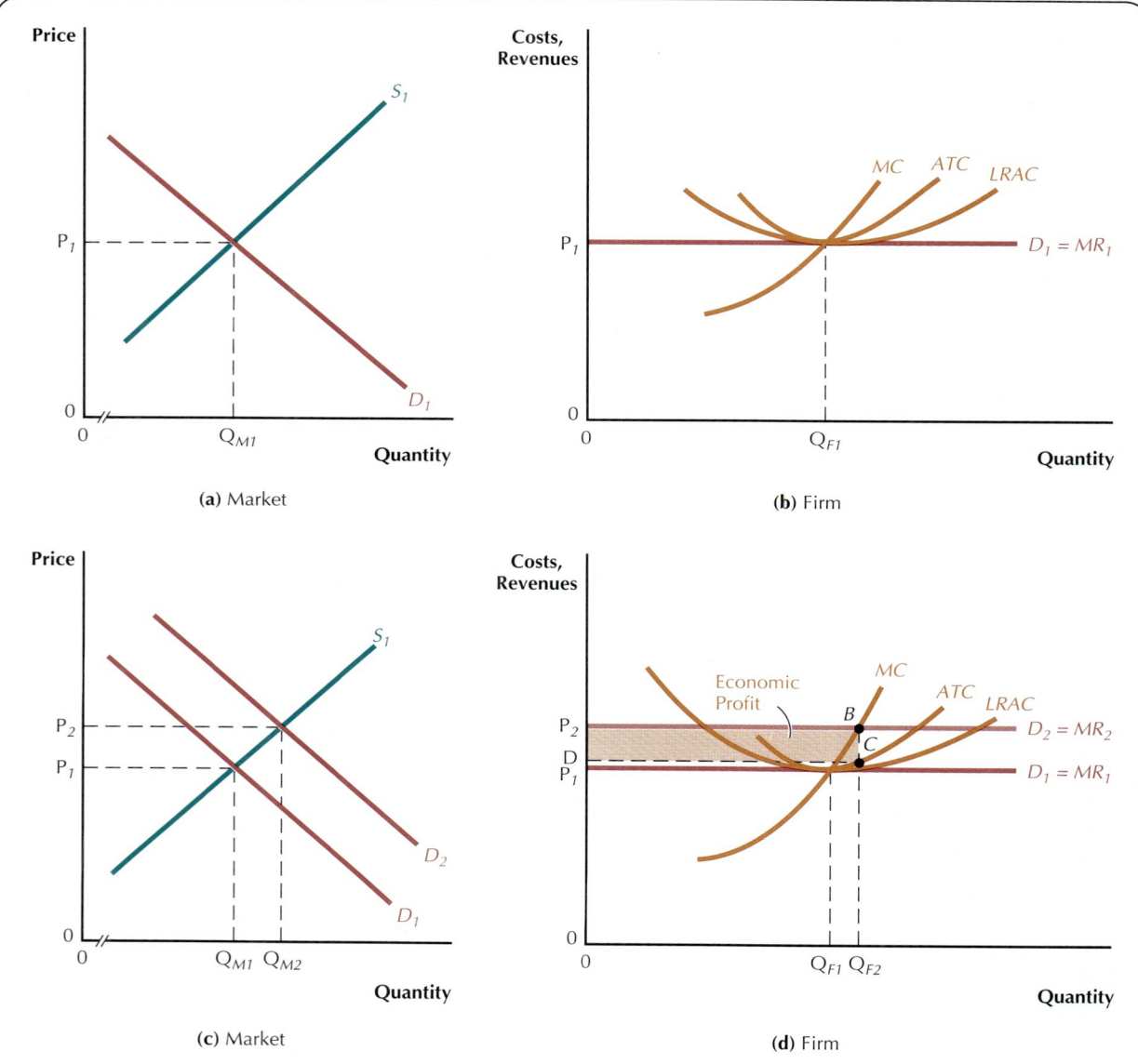

FIGURE 6
Short-run adjustment to a change in demand. *(a) Market (b) Firm (c) Market (d) Firm.* Figures 6 (a) and 6 (b) depict the market for pencils and the situation for an individual firm, respectively. Initially, equilibrium price is P_1, market output is Q_{M1}, the firm's output level is Q_{F1}, and economic profit is zero. As shown in 6(c), an increase in demand shifts market demand from D_1 to D_2 and market price increases from P_1 to P_2. Each firm increases output from Q_{f1} to Q_{f2} as illustrated in Figure 6(d) and the quantity supplied to the market increases from Q_{M1} to Q_{M2}. In the market, a new short-run equilibrium is reached at P_2 and Q_{M2}. Each firm is now earning economic profit equal to the rectangle DP_2BC.

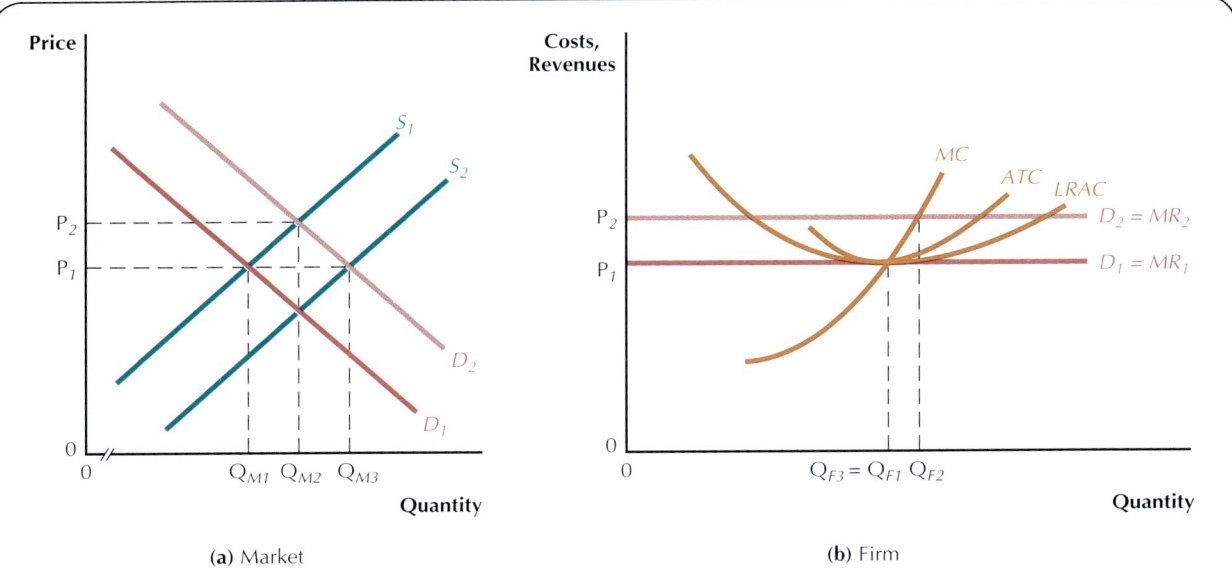

FIGURE 7
The long-run market adjustment. *(a) Market (b) Firm.* Over the long run, as new firms enter and existing firms increase production, market supply increases, shifting market supply from S_1 to S_2 in Figure 7 (a). Output increases, but market price also falls, reducing the incentive for entry into the market. Existing firms reduce production to maximize profits in the face of the now-declining price. As shown in Figure 7 (b), firm output eventually returns to Q_{F1}, price returns to P_1, and firms once again earn zero economic profit. The long-run market equilibrium price and quantity are P_1 and Q_{M3}.

Long-Run Market Adjustment The short-run increase in market price and the increased production and profits of existing firms are really only the beginning of the market adjustment to a new long-run equilibrium. As we have already noted, firms in this industry are now earning positive economic profits. However, these so-called excess profits over and above normal profits attract attention. Entrepreneurs notice the increased profits in the industry and are attracted to them. Additional resources are brought into the industry as new firms enter. The increase in the number of firms increases market supply and market output increases.

This long-run increase in supply is illustrated as a shift in market supply from S_1 to S_2 in Figure 7 (a). The increase in market supply causes output to increase, but this in turn causes market price to fall from P_2 back toward P_1. The decrease in market price erodes economic profits and reduces the incentive for additional firms to enter the market. In addition, existing firms reduce production to continue to maximize profits in the face of the now-declining price. As shown in Figure 7 (b), each firm's output eventually returns to Q_{F1} and price returns to P_1, a price at which the firms in the market earn zero economic profits.

New Long-Run Market Equilibrium Established The market has now returned to long-run equilibrium after the initial equilibrium was disturbed by the increase in pencil demand. Once all adjustments have occurred, the new long-run market equilibrium is at the old price P_1, but at a higher level of output, Q_{M3}. Firms are earning only normal profit and there is no pressure in the market for price to change.

Let's summarize what has happened in the pencil market. Consumers decided that pencils were more valuable than they were previously — they were willing to pay more for pencils. Consumers signaled this change in the value of pencils through their spending: They began to buy more pencils at the old equilibrium price, bidding up the price. As the market price rose, firms began to earn economic profits. The higher-than-normal profits attracted resources into the market from elsewhere in the economy. The resources were able to move because we assumed resource mobility. The increased number of firms, competing with one another, bid the market price down until all economic profits had been eliminated. At the new market equilibrium the economy produces more pencils than before, at the initial market price. At the new long-run equilibrium, pencils are produced at minimum unit cost and sold to consumers at a price that just equals the unit cost.

Decrease in Demand A decrease in market demand brings about opposite adjustments. If consumer demand for pencils decreases, firms which had been earning zero economic profits begin to incur losses because price, and hence marginal revenue, has declined. In the short run, firms respond by reducing output to once again equate marginal revenue with marginal cost. However, firms are now incurring economic losses. Consequently, further changes will occur over the long run.

The economic losses eventually drive some firms out of the industry. They move to other industries with better profit prospects. As firms depart the industry, market supply decreases, driving up market price. The rise in market price reduces and ultimately eliminates losses, prompting increased output from the remaining firms. A new long-run market equilibrium is established at the original market price, but at a reduced output level. There are fewer firms in the industry and they are earning no economic profit.

Again the market mechanism has performed its rationing and allocating function. If consumers value pencils less, they indicate this change by purchasing fewer pencils. The fall in market price generates losses for pencil firms. These losses signal entrepreneurs that too many resources are being employed in producing pencils and drive resources out of the pencil market and into some other, more profitable, industry. Finally, the pencil price remains the same in the long run, just equal to the cost of production.

Long-Run Supply

Constant-Cost Industries In our pencil market example, after all adjustments to the increase in the demand for pencils had taken place, the equilibrium market price returned to its original level of P_1. This type of industry is called a **constant-cost industry**. In this type of industry, input prices, and therefore short-run and long-run costs, remain constant when the level of output and the demand for resources (inputs) change. As a consequence, the optimal plant size is left unchanged.

SECTION RECAP
Assuming a perfectly competitive market is initially in long-run equilibrium, an increase (or decrease) in demand will result in economic profits (or losses) for existing firms. However, entry or exit by firms will eventually eliminate any short-run profits or losses.

Constant-cost industry
Input prices are invariant to the level of output, causing the long-run supply curve for the market to be horizontal.

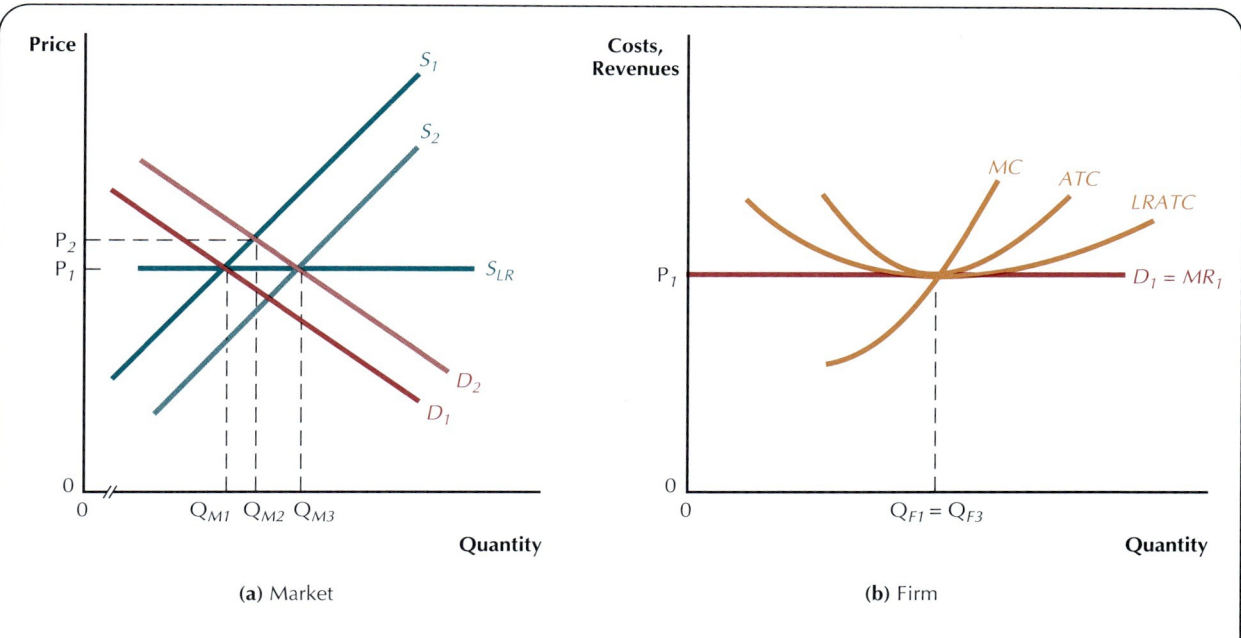

FIGURE 8
Long-run supply in a constant-cost industry. *(a) Market (b) Firm.* Figure 7 has been recreated in this figure. After all adjustments to the increase in the demand for pencils have taken place, the equilibrium market price is at its original level of P_1. In this type of industry, which is called a *constant-cost industry*, costs remain constant when the level of output and hence the demand for resources (inputs) change. The long-run supply curve for a constant-cost industry is horizontal (perfectly elastic), as shown by the heavy black line labeled S_{LR} in Figure 8 (a).

Figure 7 has been recreated in Figure 8. For the market depicted in Figure 8, the long-run supply curve is shown by the heavy black line labeled S_{LR} in Figure 8 (a). The long-run supply curve is found by constructing a line that connects the market equilibrium price–quantity combinations that exist before the change in demand and after the change in demand and all supply adjustments have occurred. *The long-run supply curve for a constant-cost industry is horizontal (perfectly elastic).*

Increasing-Cost Industries An industry in which an increase in the supply of a good puts upward pressure on input prices is called an **increasing-cost industry**. In this case, an increase in the demand for inputs causes input prices to rise — there is a movement up the supply curve of the input(s). An increasing-cost industry is illustrated in Figure 9. Assume that demand has increased as in our previous example, causing market price to rise from P_1 to P_2. As firms respond by increasing output and additional firms enter the market, market supply increases. However, because it is an increasing-cost industry, production costs are also increasing. The increase in costs is the result of increased demand for inputs whose supply is less than perfectly elastic. Consequently, the short-run and long-run cost curves in Figure 9 (b) begin to shift up as supply increases. In this case the new equilibrium price is P_3 and the equilibrium market quantity is Q_{M3}. Firms once again earn zero economic profit.

Increasing-cost industry Input prices are an increasing function of the level of output, causing the long-run supply curve for the market to be upward sloping.

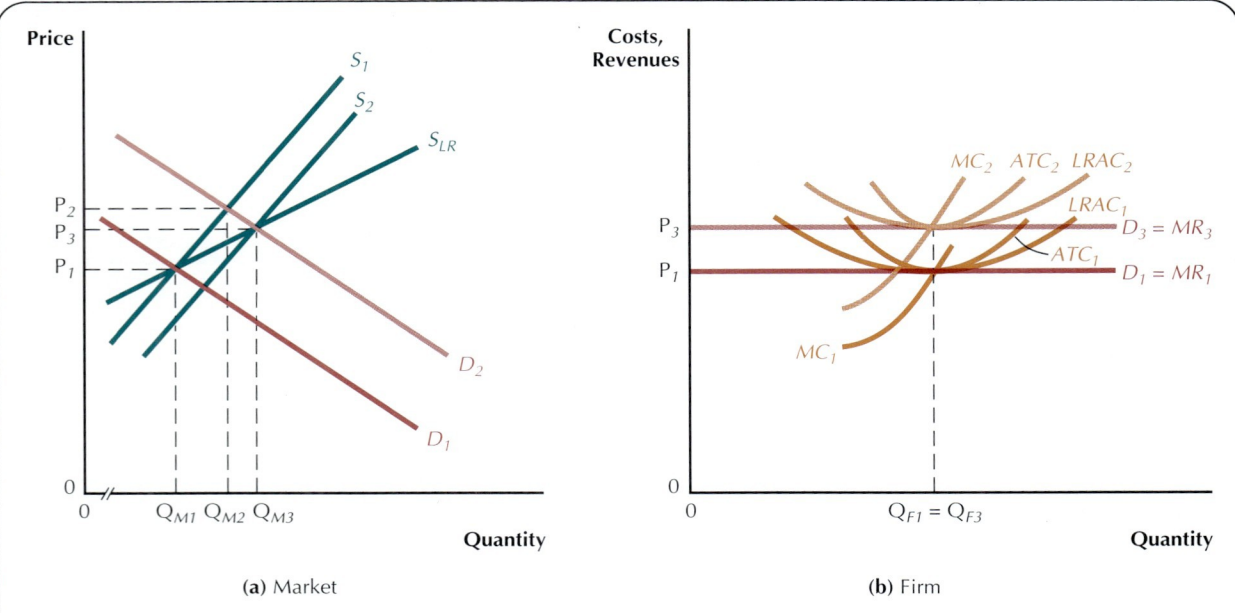

FIGURE 9
Long-run supply in an increasing cost industry. *(a) Market (b) Firm.* This figure illustrates the situation for an *increasing-cost industry*. In this case, an increase in the demand for inputs causes input prices, and therefore costs, to increase. Assuming that demand has increased, market price will rise from P_1 to P_2 (Figure 9 (a)), causing market supply to increase. However, production costs are also increasing. Consequently, the cost curves in Figure 9 (b) shift up as supply increases. The new long-run market equilibrium price is P_3, equilibrium quantity is Q_{M3}, and firms once again earn zero economic profit. In the case of an increasing-cost industry, the long-run supply curve, S_{LR}, is upward sloping.

Consumer sovereignty
The ability of consumers' preferences to influence the level of output in competitive markets.

Note that *in the case of an increasing cost industry, the long-run supply curve*, S_{LR}, *is upward sloping*. This reflects the fact that as output increases, costs are also increasing. Hence, over the long run, as supply increases, so does the price that a firm must receive to earn a normal profit.

Consumer Sovereignty

SECTION RECAP
In a constant-cost industry, long-run supply is perfectly elastic; a change in demand does not affect the long-run equilibrium market price. In an increasing-cost industry, the long-run supply curve is upward sloping; an increase in demand leads to an increase in the long-run equilibrium market price.

In the examples above, changes in consumer demand caused long-run changes in the market that were consistent with consumer prferences. More or fewer pencils were produced depending on whether consumers valued pencils more or less. Market sensitivity to consumer preferences is a general attribute of competitive markets: Markets respond when consumers express their preferences through their spending on goods and services. This power of consumers in competitive markets is called **consumer sovereignty**.

In a competitive market economy it is the consumer who decides what is produced. Consumers influence the price of economic goods through their willingness to pay for such goods. Consumers compete for goods by bidding up market prices. Higher prices mean increased opportunities for profit on the supply side of the market. Profit-maximizing producers seek out these opportunities by producing more of the goods valued highly by consumers. Changes in consumer preferences lead to changes in market prices. Producers respond to higher prices by reallocating resources to the production of the now more-valuable goods and away from production of less valuable goods.

Production Costs and Efficiency

One of the conditions necessary for efficient market outcomes is that markets be competitive. If we assume all other conditions — for example, perfect information and perfect mobility — are met, the long-run equilibrium output level of perfectly competitive firms is economically efficient.

Economic Efficiency in the Long Run

In the short run, every firm maximizes profits by producing the level of output at which marginal revenue equals marginal cost. Since the perfectly competitive firm's demand curve is perfectly elastic, price equals marginal revenue and the profit-maximization decision rule becomes:

$$P = MR = MC$$

We have also shown that the firm produces the level of output at which marginal revenue equals marginal cost in the long run as well. It is also the case in the long run that market price equals the minimum short-run and long-run average total cost of production, or:

$$P = MR = MC = \text{minimum ATC} = \text{minimum LRAC}$$

This unique level of output is ensured in the long run by the resource mobility that we assumed as an attribute of perfectly competitive markets. In the absence of freedom of entry and exit into a market, firms could earn economic profits in the long run. The market equilibrium price would then exceed the minimum average cost of production.

Because, in long-run equilibrium, price equals minimum short-run and long-run average total cost, firms are using the existing plant size as efficiently as possible. In addition, they are using the most efficient capacity, or scale of plant. The assumptions that characterize a perfectly competitive market ensure that firms will employ the efficient level of capacity in the long run. To see why, assume that firms are not operating at minimum long-run average cost. In this case, a new firm could enter the market with a more efficient plant size, that is, the plant size associated with minimum long-run average cost. The firm could then charge a price for its product that is lower than the price charged by existing firms but greater than its average total cost; thus the firm would earn economic profit. Buyers would switch to the lower-priced product and existing firms would incur economic losses. In the long run, the remaining firms would be forced to switch to the plant size associated with the minimum long-run average cost to avoid additional economic losses.

In addition to producing at minimum average cost in both the short run and the long run, perfectly competitive firms produce the level of output at which price equals marginal cost. This condition is referred to as **allocative efficiency**. When price equals marginal cost, the value to consumers, measured by price, of the last unit of the good purchased is just equal to the value of the additional resources, measured by marginal cost, used to produce it. If

---

SECTION RECAP
In the long run, perfectly competitive firms employ the efficient capacity; in other words, they operate at minimum LRAC. In addition, they are allocatively efficient, since P = MC for the last unit of output produced.

Allocative efficiency Results when output is produced to the level at which P = MC; the value of the variable inputs used to produce the last unit of output is equal to the value of the last unit of output produced.

price is less than marginal cost, too many resources are going into production of the good in question. The value of the resources used to produce the units of output for which price is less than marginal cost exceeds the value of those units of output. The opposite is true in the case in which price is greater than marginal cost.

The market outcome is economically efficient because firms have no price-setting power. In addition, freedom of market entry and exit ensure that competition will drive the price down to the mimimum average total cost of production in the long run.

Cost Changes in Perfectly Competitive Markets

We have considered how a competitive market adjusts to changes in demand. The question we now address is, What happens when the costs of production change?[4] Does the perfectly competitive market handle such changes as well as it does demand-side changes? The answer is yes. In fact, the supply-side changes are handled in a very similar fashion.

Increased Input Prices Suppose that the price of labor employed by pencil manufacturers rises. In the short run, this increased input price increases production costs. However, in the short run, firms are stuck with their existing production technology. They cannot substitute relatively less expensive inputs for the more expensive labor. Figure 10 illustrates the problem for pencil producers. The initial effect of the input price increase is depicted in Figures 10 (a) and (b). The long-run market equilibrium quantity, Q_{M1}, is disturbed by the increase in production costs. The short-run cost functions shift up from ATC_1 to ATC_2, and from MC_1 to MC_2 as shown in Figure 10 (b). As a result, the firm's short-run supply function decreases — each firm now supplies less output at each market price. The decrease in supply for each firm translates into a decrease in market supply, represented by the shift in market supply from S_1 to S_2 in Figure 10 (a).

Since these price-taking firms have no control over market price they reduce output to Q_{F2}, following their profit-maximizing decision rule. However, so long as market price remains at P_1, firms incur economic losses. The losses incurred by each firm are equal to the area P_1ABC. These losses cause a further adjustment to occur: Some firms also begin to leave the market. This causes the supply curve to shift further to the left, to S_3 in Figure 10 (a). Because the number of firms and output of the remaining firms have both declined, market output falls to Q_{M2} at the initial price of P_1.

With the decrease in market supply, there is a shortage of pencils at P_1 — quantity demanded exceeds quantity supplied by the amount $Q_{M1} - Q_{M2}$. Competing for the quantity of pencils available, consumers bid the market price up. Referring to Figure 10 (c), as the market price rises from P_1 to P_2 along S_3, the short-run losses incurred by the remaining firms in the industry are reduced. In their efforts to maximize profits, firms increase output as price rises.

---

[4]This discussion should not be confused with the analysis of an increasing-cost industry. In the latter, costs increase as a result of a change in the demand for inputs, which was caused by a change in demand for the product.

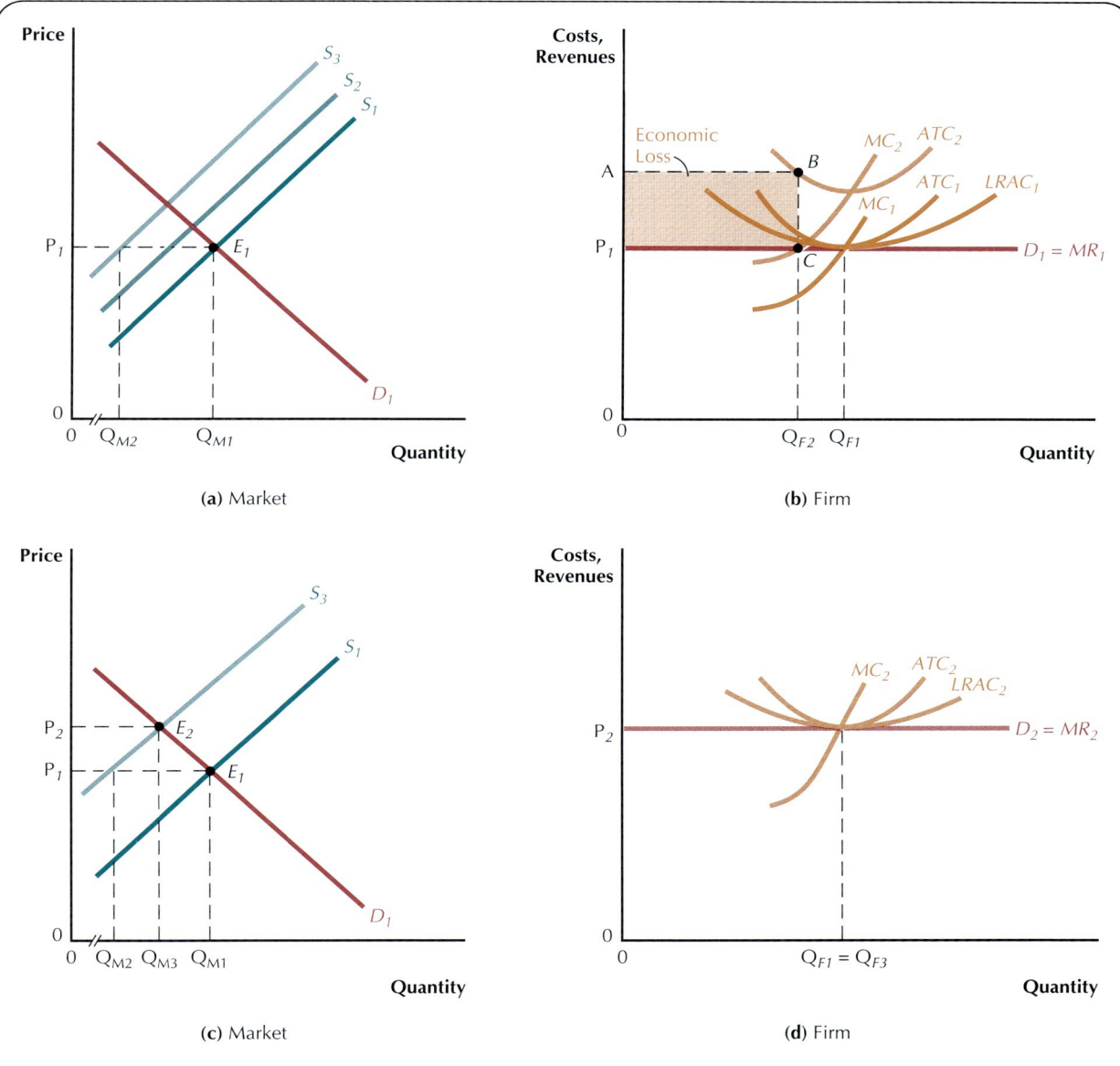

FIGURE 10
The effect of an increase in input prices. *(a) Market (b) Firm (c) Market (d) Firm.* This figure illustrates the effect of an increase in input prices. The increase in costs causes market supply to shift from S_1 to S_2 in Figure 10 (a). Firms reduce output to Q_{F2}, incurring economic losses equal to the area P_1ABC, which causes some firms to exit, shifting market supply to S_3. Market output falls to Q_{M2}. At the initial price of P_1 there is a shortage; thus consumers bid the market price up. Figure 10 (c) illustrates the new long-run market equilibrium, E_2. Market price, P_2, is higher and output, Q_{M3}, is reduced. As shown in Figure 10 (d), each firm is once again earning a normal profit since P = MC = minimum average cost.

Figure 10 (c) illustrates the new long-run equilibrium, E_2. Compared to the initial long-run equilibrium, E_1, market price (P_2) is higher and output (Q_{M3}) is reduced. The increased cost of producing pencils has been passed on to consumers through the higher market price. As shown in Figure 10 (d), the remaining firms are once again earning a normal profit since price equals marginal cost equals minimum average total cost.

Note that the increase in the market price of pencils is not the result of a direct action by firms. They are price takers and have no direct control over price. Rather, the decisions that they made as they sought to minimize their losses caused market supply to be reduced, and competition among consumers bid the market price up. Fewer pencils are produced at the new equilibrium because consumer demand is negatively sloped. Pencils are now more costly for society to produce. The market mechanism has translated these increased costs into higher pencil prices. The reduced quantity of pencils produced is rationed to those who value pencils the most.

The new equilibrium established at E_2 ignores another long-run process set in motion by the increased price of labor. In the short run, firms have no alternative but to absorb the higher costs and adjust output downward. However, over time, firms look for ways to offset the increased production costs. If firms were employing a cost-minimizing combination of inputs before the labor price increase, the price increase has caused them to be in long-run disequilibrium. Productivity per dollar spent on labor is now reduced. Firms therefore search for new input combinations to reduce costs. As they adjust their input mix by installing new production processes, to the extent that production costs are reduced, their short-run costs would shift down again. The extent to which less costly input combinations can be found depends upon the nature of the production process and the time available to make the adjustment. Generally, the potential for substitution is greater, the longer the period of time in question.

Technological Change   Production costs can also be altered by changes in technology. Generally, we think of technological change as an advance: New technologies lower costs or make possible the production of new products. In perfectly competitive markets, the cost savings from technological change are passed on to consumers in the form of lower prices. Figure 11 illustrates the process by which this occurs.

Referring to Figure 11 (a), at an initial long-run equilibrium position with a market price of P_1 and market output of Q_{M1}, firms are earning zero economic profit. As shown in Figure 11 (b), price equals marginal cost equals minimum average total cost and each firm is producing Q_{F1} units of output. Now assume there is an improvement in technology that increases the productivity of labor used to produce pencils. When the new technology is adopted by the firm, its short-run costs fall. As shown in Figure 11 (b), the firm's cost functions shift down from ATC_1 to ATC_2 and MC_1 to MC_2, shifting its supply function to the right.

With the new marginal cost function, MC_2, the firm sets output at Q_{F2}, where P_1 equals the new marginal cost. At output level Q_{F2} each firm is earning economic profits, shown by the area AP_1BC. However, these profits will not persist. The existence of economic profits causes new firms to enter the market.

Market price initially remains at P_1. However, as each price-taking firm increases its output and the number of firms in the market increases, market

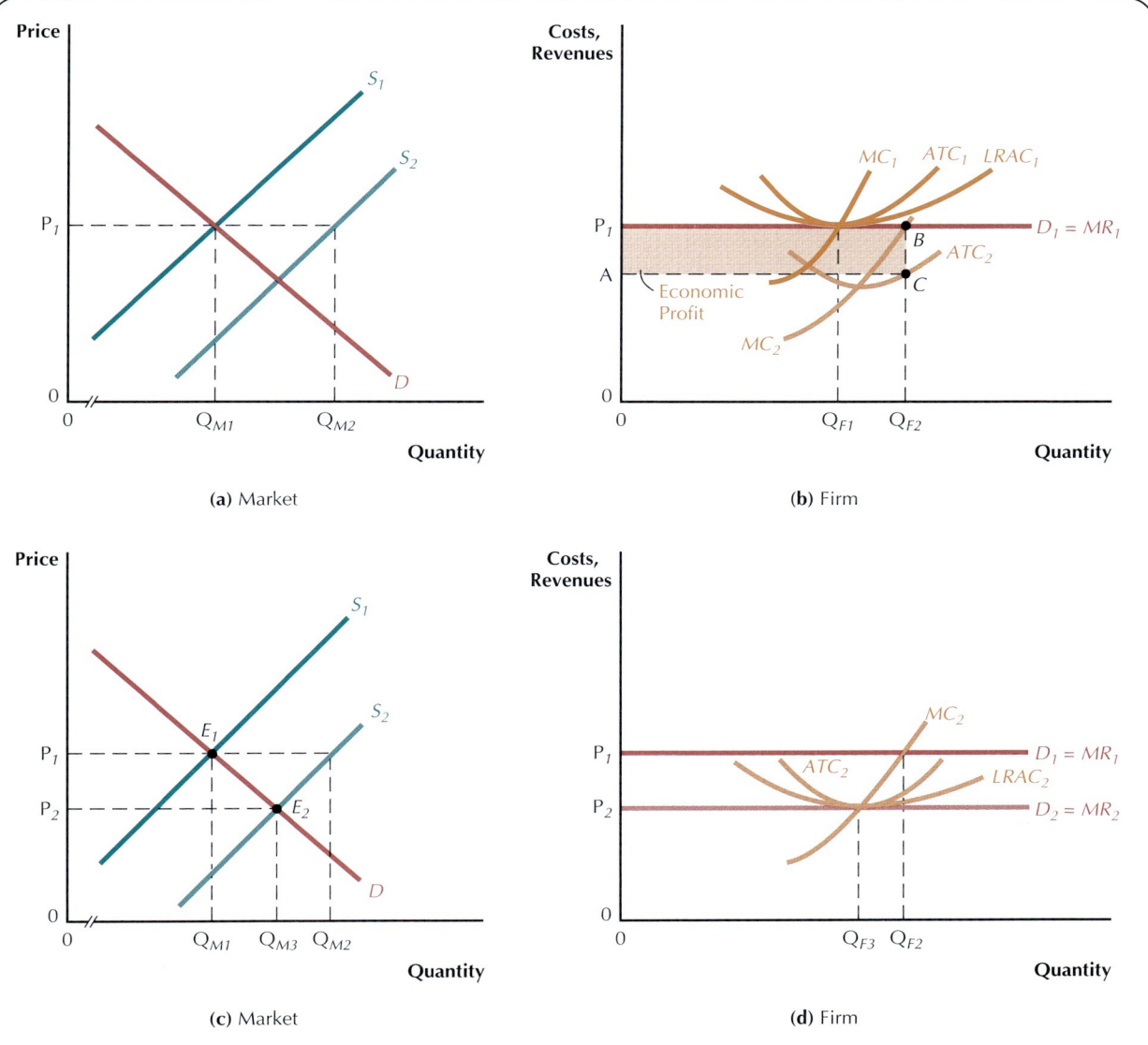

FIGURE 11
The effects of an improvement in technology. *(a) Market (b) Firm (c) Market (d) Firm.* Adoption of a new technology causes the firm's cost functions to shift down to ATC_2 and MC_2. Firms increase output to Q_{F2} and earn economic profit, shown by the area AP_1BC. Entry by new firms and increased output by existing firms causes market supply to shift to the right from S_1 to S_2 creating excess supply (Figure 11 (a)). As market price falls to P_2, each firm's output is decreased to Q_{F3} and economic profits are reduced to zero (Figure 11 (d)). Long-run equilibrium is reestablished at E_2 with an equilibrium price and quantity of P_2 and Q_{M3}, respectively (Figure 11 (c)).

supply shifts to the right from S_1 to S_2 in Figure 11 (a). At the new market output level of Q_{M2} the quantity supplied exceeds quantity demanded by the amount $Q_{M2} - Q_{M1}$, putting downward pressure on market price. Producers compete with one another to sell the excess supply. Market price is bid down. As market price falls, each firm's output is decreased and its profits are reduced.

A new long-run equilibrium is established at E_2 in Figure 11 (c). Market equilibrium price is reestablished at P_2 and the new equilibrium quantity is Q_{M3}. As shown in Figure 11 (d), market price has fallen to the level of the new lower minimum unit cost for each firm. As a result of entry by new firms, economic profits disappear. Firms once again earn only a normal profit. Competition has eroded the profits that arose from the technological innovation and the cost savings have been passed on to consumers. They now get pencils at a lower price and, as a result of the lower price, the equilibrium quantity of pencils consumed in the economy has increased.

SECTION RECAP
A change in production costs or technology will cause a change in the long-run market equilibrium price and level of output in a perfectly competitive market.

General Equilibrium in the Economy

This chapter has focused on the dynamics of the market mechanism, closely examining how the rational decision making of consumers and price-taking producers in competitive markets keeps markets moving toward equilibrium. Market equilibrium can be disturbed by many different factors — shifts in demand, changes in relative factor prices, and changes in technology, to name a few — but the market mechanism acts to reestablish a new equilibrium when such disturbances occur. We have illustrated these market dynamics by taking a close look at individual markets. However, we do not want to lose sight of the big picture.

All markets in an economy are tied together. A change in one market causes changes in other markets. The changes in these markets cause further changes. In a sense, everything depends upon everything else. This interrelatedness is illustrated in the *circular flow model* in Figure 12. A change in the pencil market will affect all other markets. If demand for pencils increases, more pencils will be produced at a higher pencil price. Since consumers have limited incomes, the increased spending on pencils must be balanced by decreased spending (decreased demand) for other goods. To produce more pencils, more labor is employed in the pencil industry. This additional labor must come from other industries.

An increase in the demand for labor pushes the price of labor up, and therefore the costs of producing other goods rise as well. These costs are translated into price increases by the resulting decrease in product supply. These price changes cause consumers to adjust their spending on consumer goods. In addition, the higher price of labor causes firms to try to substitute alternative inputs for labor. Thus, the demand for other inputs will increase, causing price changes in other input markets. These price changes will alter costs again, affecting product market supply.

Partial equilibrium analysis
Focuses on the conditions necessary for equilibrium in a particular market, independent of other markets in the economy.

General equilibrium analysis
Is concerned with the relationships across markets and the conditions necessary for equilibrium in all markets simultaneously.

These simple examples highlight the interrelatedness of all markets. When we focus on the equilibrium outcome in one particular market, we are concerned about a **partial equilibrium**. When we focus on the relationships across markets and the equilibrium conditions in all markets, we are concerned about **general equilibrium**. In this chapter, partial equilibrium analysis has been used to illustrate the characteristics of a perfectly competitive market economy

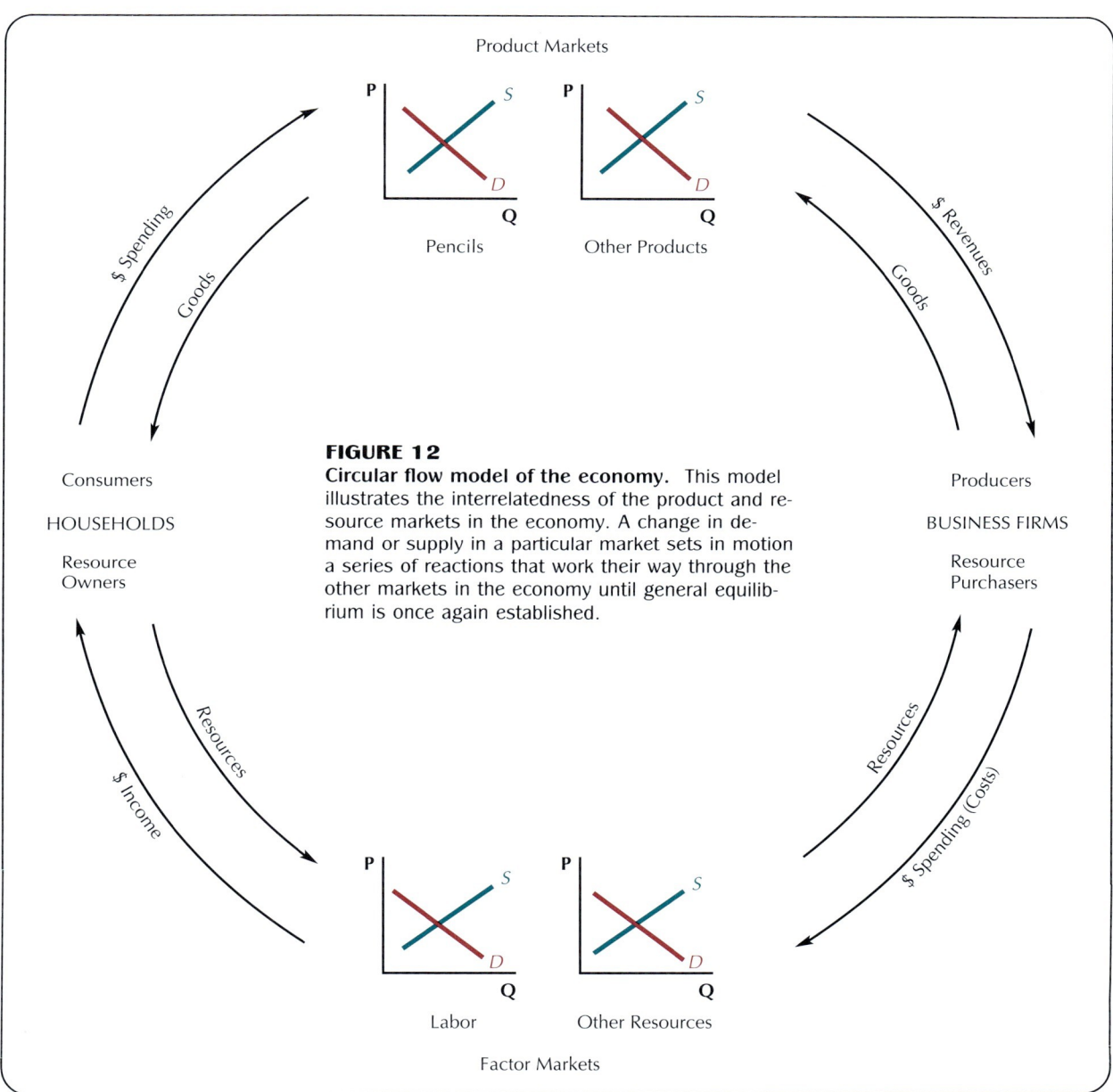

FIGURE 12
Circular flow model of the economy. This model illustrates the interrelatedness of the product and resource markets in the economy. A change in demand or supply in a particular market sets in motion a series of reactions that work their way through the other markets in the economy until general equilibrium is once again established.

that is in general equilibrium. *If all markets are perfectly competitive and are in long-run equilibrium, consumers are buying goods and services in the quantities that maximize their utility. The prices prevailing in the economy are equal to the minimum unit cost of production. Producers are earning only normal profits and consumers are getting the goods that are most valuable to them at exactly the social opportunity cost of producing them. The economy has achieved economic efficiency.*

Of equal importance, if a change occurs in any one market to disturb this economy-wide equilibrium, it sets in motion market forces that will reestablish a new equilibrium with different market prices and outputs, but with the same economic efficiency characteristics.

Why the **Disagreement?**

Restrictions on Free Trade

Over the past twenty years, U.S. demand for foreign-made autos has steadily increased. Japan's share of the U.S. auto market in 1990, including imports and models built in the United States, increased to approximately 28 percent. In response to this trend, U.S. auto makers—in particular, Ford and Chrysler—have consistently maintained that foreign competition adversely affects the domestic economy by taking away jobs from U.S. workers. To offset these job losses, these auto makers and the United Auto Workers union (UAW) frequently demand that trade restrictions, such as quotas, be imposed on autos imported from Japan. Partly in response to these demands, Japanese imports were capped in 1981. In 1991, Ford, Chrysler, and the UAW once again demanded that Japan be forced to reduce the number of autos it sells in the United States in order to preserve domestic jobs and protect the domestic auto industry.* However, many observers, including most economists, disagree with this strategy. They argue that it would be costly not only to Japanese auto makers, but to U.S. consumers and labor as well. In view of this controversy it is worth asking, Why the disagreement?

Proponents of trade restrictions argue that restrictions are necessary to protect domestic industries and jobs since imports reduce the demand for domestically produced autos. This decrease in demand results in unemployment, which leads to further reductions in demand for goods and services and pushes the economy toward recession. Proponents of trade restrictions also contend that the competition from imports is unfair because foreign producers enjoy much lower costs of production than do domestic competitors. Finally, many proponents argue that trade restrictions are necessary to ensure the self-sufficiency of the economy and to minimize the degree to which the United States becomes dependent on foreign-produced goods.

Opponents of trade restrictions contend that free trade is necessary to maximize social welfare. In particular, they point out that free trade provides a greater degree of competition and moves producers closer to the efficient level of production. As the number of foreign firms in the market increases, more of the pressures of competition are brought to bear on domestic producers. Firms in the market seek out the least-cost method of production in an effort to earn short-run economic profits, resulting in a more efficient use of resources. Competition also drives the equilibrium market price to its lowest possible level. Overall, free trade allows consumers to choose from a wider array of goods and this results in a higher level of consumer well-being.

To the extent that foreign competition is reduced, so is the pressure to minimize costs and therefore prices. In fact, the restrictions imposed on Japanese imports in 1981 resulted in a dramatic increase in the average price of a new car. Over the period from 1981 to 1989, the amount of time it took a family earning the median household income to earn enough money to buy a new car rose from 18.7 weeks to 24.7 weeks.

In the most recent debate, opponents of restrictions on the number of imported Japanese autos further argued that the adverse effects of restrictions would not be limited to domestic consumers. Citing the increase in the number of Japanese autos produced in the United States, critics point out that restrictions would also result in the loss of many domestic jobs. During the 1980s, Japan's share of the domestic car market, including imports and models built in the United States, rose from approximately 20 percent in 1985 to roughly 28 percent in 1990. However, over this same time period, the share of all autos sold in the United States that were built in Japan fell from roughly 20 percent to about 18 percent. Reducing the number of Japanese autos sold in the United States would result in fewer sales of both foreign-made and U.S.-made Japanese autos. This would in turn translate into fewer jobs for U.S. auto workers. There is no doubt that free trade can lead to a more efficient use of the world's resources or that the economies that engage in free trade experience an increase in the level of available consumption opportunities. However, it is also clear that free trade can have adverse effects on specific domestic industries. The debate over free trade involves the issue of economic efficiency as well as issues of fairness and the benefits to the individual versus the benefits to the economy as a whole. Viewed in this light, it is easy to see why this disagreement exists.

*J.B. White and J. Mitchell, "Detroit Rolls Out Old Ploy: Quotas," *The Wall Street Journal*, January 14, 1991, p. B1.

For simplicity we will continue to rely on partial equilibrium analysis to explain the decisions of economic agents and to examine the implications of those decisions for society. It is assumed that each market constitutes a small part of the total economy and that the effects of a change in one market on all other markets are small. However, keep in mind the interrelatedness of markets. The scarcity of resources causes economic decisions to have effects throughout the economy in addition to the immediate effects that are easily observed.

Costs and Benefits Again: The Invisible Hand of the Market

The power and efficiency of the market mechanism are captured in the dynamics of the market. It is the way that a market economy and, in particular, a perfectly competitive market economy, handles change that best illustrates the amazing power of the market. The merits of a perfectly competitive market economy are summarized in the two points discussed below.

Perfectly Competitive Markets Allocate Resources Efficiently

Goods and services are allocated to their highest-valued use. Consumers who value goods the most are willing to pay the highest price for them. Inputs are allocated to their highest-valued uses. The value of an input is determined by its use in production. Owners of inputs want to maximize the value of their resources — the firms bidding the most for inputs will be those firms responding most closely to consumer preferences.

Only goods for which consumer benefits exceed the opportunity cost of production are produced and those goods are produced at minimum opportunity cost. On the one hand, market competition is a cruel taskmaster. Competition keeps long-run market prices at the level of production costs. Only normal profits are earned in the long run. On the other hand, the market rewards increased productivity and lower costs. Producers have an incentive to minimize costs today and look for ways to reduce costs in the future in an effort to earn short-run economic profits. The cost savings from technological change are passed along to the consumer in the long run.

Economic Efficiency Is Achieved through an Invisible Hand

The market mechanism is a decentralized decision-making institution. No one individual or group of individuals directs the economy's decision making. Instead, individuals are left alone to pursue their own individual self-interest. Consumers seek to maximize utility, producers seek to maximize profit, and resource owners seek to maximize income. However, competition limits the harm that the self-interested action of one person can impose on others. In fact, competition between decision makers has the curious effect of preventing individual gain at the expense of others and promoting a cooperation between and specialization among individuals that ensures maximum social welfare. This effect is the *invisible hand* of which Adam Smith spoke. Each individual pursues his or her own self-interest and in doing so contributes to the achievement of maximum social welfare. Consumers seek the benefits of consumption at the lowest cost possible, but competition from other consumers limits their gains. Producers seek maximum profits, but competition among producers ensures that they only earn normal profits in the long run.

The Perfectly Competitive Market Model in the Science of Economics

It should be clear from the discussion in this chapter, as well as the treatment of markets and efficiency in chapters 3 through 5, that the perfectly competitive market model is a very special and important one in economics. At this point in your study of economics, the careful attention that is paid to the case of perfect competition may be somewhat puzzling. For this reason we end this chapter by devoting a few pages to the role of the perfectly competitive model in economic analysis.

The Economic Problem and Economic Efficiency

The basic economic problem for any society is one of scarce resources with which to satisfy unlimited individual wants. The central purpose of an economic system is to allocate resources and distribute economic goods in a manner that satisfies the greatest amount of wants. A perfectly competitive market economy is indeed such an economic system. Society obtains the maximum value from its stock of resources. One of modern society's major goals — satisfaction of the maximum amount of wants possible — is thereby achieved.

The perfectly competitive market model is a theoretical benchmark against which we evaluate other markets. We know that few actual markets approach perfect competition. However, by constructing a perfectly competitive market model we identify those characteristics of consumers, firms, resource owners, and market structures that are necessary for achieving an important social goal, economic efficiency. This theoretical framework can be used to examine actual market conditions, understand why actual market outcomes are not efficient, and develop policies to promote more competition and increase economic efficiency.

The perfectly competitive model is an attractive economic system to many societies, not only because of its efficiency properties, but also because it is consistent with another valued social goal — individual freedom. Recall that the value of any good is derived from the satisfaction it provides to individuals. Individuals express the value they attach to specific goods through their dollar votes. We measure this value by individual willingness to pay for a good. The value of a good to society is the sum of these individual valuations.

These individual votes are coordinated by the market mechanism. Resources are free to move to their best opportunities, and "best" is defined by resource owners. Individuals are free to pursue their own self-interest. The market mechanism coordinates these decisions, limits the power of any one decision maker, and provides incentives that make individual self-interest consistent with achievement of society's maximum economic well-being.

Perfect Competition Is a Reference Point

The perfectly competitive market model is built upon a handful of key assumptions reviewed earlier in the chapter. When these assumptions do not hold, market outcomes are altered—they diverge from the optimal outcomes of perfectly competitive markets. We investigate the characteristics and operations of actual markets by considering the impact that changing or relaxing these key assumptions has on long-run market equilibrium. We compare the characteristics of observed markets and their outcomes to the perfectly competitive model. For instance, the last section of this chapter discusses some of the implications of more realistic assumptions about the availability of information and mobility. In Chapter 11 it is assumed that firms are price searchers instead of price takers. In Chapter 12 we look at how restrictions on resource mobility affect market outcomes. The array of government policies designed to promote competition or replace the market mechanism in certain markets is considered in Chapters 11–13.

A Close Approximation to Perfect Competition

The model of perfect competition is an extremely simple and abstract view of a market economy. However, the simplifying assumptions that are made serve a very important purpose. We have established the conditions necessary for an economic system to fully achieve its primary goal. It is a powerful model that serves as a useful benchmark for us in many of the following chapters.

Unfortunately, such an abstract model can be misleading. Because of its simplicity it may appear to be of little use in understanding the economy. Our concentration on basic decision rules and simple examples may make the model seem even more unrealistic. Consider the example illustrating the firm's decision rule for short-run profit maximization as a case in point. It was assumed that there were only two inputs, capital and labor, employed in a well-defined production process. The important entrepreneurship input, which includes the skill employed in following a decision rule, was ignored. The firm's competition consisted of a large number of virtually identical firms producing identical products with identical production functions. The adjustments to changes in market price were explained as if they were almost automatic. This determinism and lack of ambiguity in the model can make it seem so far from reality that the important insights from the exercise are missed, or at least discounted. We hope you fight off this almost instinctive reaction. The discussion below is intended to help you.

Imperfect Information and Mobility

Consider a market economy that only approximates perfect competition. Assume that both information and mobility are not perfect, but that all firms are price takers. Because decision makers have limited information, they make many decisions based on *anticipated* future market conditions. In addition, costly mobility slows market responses and changes the structure of some markets. What implications do these changes have for the performance of the economy?

In effect, information and mobility become economic goods — they are costly to produce. The amount of information acquired by a decision maker will depend upon the expected benefits from having the information and the cost of acquiring it. If the purchase of information is thought of as any other good, the optimal amount of information is that amount at which the marginal cost is just equal to the marginal benefit. Consider the firm's behavior in this context. It might, for example, not know exactly how much output is produced by a given combination of inputs. It certainly cannot foretell the future. It does not know what future market prices for its product or its inputs will be. Furthermore, different firms may have different amounts of information and make different decisions based on available information.

By assuming that information is costly and that expectations are important, we have made firm decision making much more challenging. Entrepreneurial skill becomes important, and firms can make mistakes. For example, firms must choose a particular production technology and determine firm size based on the *expected* volume of output. With costly information the kinds of technologies and the size of firms will vary within the industry. Thus, different firms will be stuck with different unit costs in the short run. Competition will drive the market price down to the level of minimum unit costs — those firms with relatively high unit costs will be driven from the market. Only those firms with the lowest production costs will stay in the market over the long run.

When new technological advances occur, some firms are slower than others to adopt them. It is often unclear initially what the cost saving from such investments will be. However, competition in the market will penalize late action to adopt cost-saving technology. Those firms that act quickly will push costs lower, expand output, earn more short-run economic profit, and weaken the market position of higher-cost firms. Downward pressure on market price is a strong incentive to use the least-cost technology.

Now consider responses to market price changes. Price increases generate short-run economic profits, attracting the attention of entrepreneurs and resource owners. As firms expand and new firms come into the market, price is pushed down, eliminating economic profit. In a world of costly information and mobility, this adjustment process is slower and less smooth. When the market price rises, it is not known if this is a permanent or temporary change. If an existing firm believes the price increase is temporary and does not expand when other firms do, it forgoes economic profit that accrues to other firms. It is also possible for the market to overreact to an increase in price. In the long run, new firms enter the market in response to the price increase. The increased supply depresses market price so that the new equilibrium is at a higher market output level and a price below the short-run higher price.

It is also possible for too many new firms to come into the market. If an entrepreneur believes the price increase is permanent, starts up a new firm, and then discovers it was only a temporary increase, he will face losses. Moreover, supply can increase so much that market price will be depressed below the original price causing firms to experience losses. Refer to Figure 7 again. If too many firms enter the market in response to the price P_2 (at which existing firms are earning economic profits), supply will shift to the right, beyond S_2, and market price will fall below the long-run equilibrium price of P_1. The losses cause further adjustments — this time a reduction in market supply pushing the price back up to the long-run equilibrium level.

This pattern of oscillation around a new equilibrium position is attributable to incorrect expectations about the price change and to the time and expense of changes in capacity. Some entrepreneurs may interpret the increase in market price as a signal of further price increases, leading them to build too much capacity for the actual volume of sales. In addition, it takes time to make a long-run decision to start a business or add capacity. By the time some firms can make a decision and complete construction of production facilities, the increase in output from other new firms may have caused price to stabilize or begin to fall.

Costly mobility also implies that the movement of resources and the transportation of goods are costly. Resources are attracted to the most profitable alternatives. However, now the price differences between alternatives must be large enough to more than offset the costs of mobility. Resource owners are less sensitive to relative differences in prices. Firms must employ inputs to ship output to consumers. These transportation or mobility costs cause firms' production costs to vary. Therefore, regional or local markets with different equilibrium prices can exist in the long run. For example, farmers are price takers. However, the market price they receive for their output depends, in part, upon the costs of transporting it to the market. These price differences persist in the long run.

When we allow for imperfect information and mobility, our model of the economy begins to take on a closer resemblance to the economy that we observe. It is in a constant state of flux. Changes are occurring continuously all over the economy, and markets are adjusting constantly. The adjustments to change are not smooth. New firms are being organized every day while other firms are going out of business. Some markets are expanding while others are shrinking. New technologies and products are being introduced daily. Some firms seem poorly managed and fail in a short period of time, while other firms are well managed and seem to always be in the right place at the right time. The frictions of real life slow the dynamic process of adjustment to equilibrium. Long-run equilibrium may never be reached, but the economy is always moving toward it. The market mechanism establishes an incentive structure that rewards behavior consistent with the achievement of economic efficiency.

If the economy were filled with only price-taking firms, the overall economy would function much like the perfectly competitive market model. The market mechanism rewards firms for producing the goods that are the most valuable to consumers. The pursuit of economic profit drives producers to be responsive to consumers' preferences. Competition among firms erodes short-run profits, and firms produce output at minimum unit cost. In the long run, economic profit is zero. Consumers not only obtain goods they most value, they obtain them at a price equal to the social opportunity cost of production.

This chapter has laid the groundwork for a closer look at the complexities of a market economy and has established a reference point for evaluating economic performance. Perfect competition is a benchmark by which we evaluate other market structures. The next few chapters take a closer look at the economic implications of price-searching firms and the lack of resource mobility.

SECTION RECAP
The model of perfect competition serves as a benchmark to assess the efficiency of alternative market structures.

Summary

A firm earns economic profits when market price exceeds average total cost. Economic profit is zero when market price equals the minimum of average total (unit) cost. If price falls below the minimum average total cost, the firm will minimize losses by continuing to produce so long as market price exceeds average variable cost. If price is less than average variable cost, losses are minimized by shutting down and producing nothing.

The price-taking firm's short-run marginal cost curve (above its intersection with the average variable cost curve) is the firm's short-run supply curve because it reveals the level of output the firm will produce at every market price.

If a perfectly competitive market is initially at long-run equilibrium, firms are earning zero economic profits. A product price increase will cause existing firms to increase output and positive profits will be generated that will attract additional resources into the market in the long run. When supply increases, market price is bid down, economic profits are competed away, and the market returns to a new long-run equilibrium at which price equals marginal cost equals minimum ATC for all firms.

A change in costs causes a similar market adjustment. A decrease in costs causes unit cost to fall below the market price, generating economic profits. Firms expand output, following the marginal revenue equals marginal cost rule. The increased production at the initial market price leads to excess supply in the market. The market price gets bid down, profits are eroded, and a new long-run market equilibrium is established at a lower price and increased output level. Economic profit is again zero.

When perfectly competitive markets reach their long-run equilibrium, economic efficiency is achieved: Only those goods and services for which consumer willingness to pay exceeds the social opportunity cost of production are produced and consumed. In such an economy consumers are sovereign.

In addition, goods and services are produced at the minimum opportunity cost of production. Competition among producers and the mobility of resources between markets ensure that market price is always bid down to minimize unit cost in long-run equilibrium.

When all markets in a perfectly competitive economy are in long-run equilibrium, **general equilibrium** is achieved. In most of our analyses and examples we concentrate on only one or two markets, and thus a **partial equilibrium.** However, it is important to remember that market outcomes are interrelated. Developments in one market cause changes in many other markets. It is this complex interrelatedness across markets that makes the market mechanism such a powerful decentralized decision-making tool.

The perfectly competitive market is a simple, abstract market model. Careful attention is devoted to it because it serves as a starting point, or benchmark, for our analyses of other kinds of markets that more closely resemble the kind of markets we actually observe. By carefully studying this perfect market model we are better able to understand the way our economy actually operates and to design policies that can help us alter those market outcomes with which society is dissatisfied.

Questions for Thought

Knowledge Questions

1. Explain why fixed costs are sunk costs in the short run.
2. Distinguish between partial and general equilibrium.
3. What assumptions in the perfect competition model ensure that economic profit is zero in the long run? Explain.
4. What assumptions in the perfect competition model ensure that price equals the minimum average cost in the long run? Explain.

Application Questions

5. Scarce resources cause all market outcomes to be interrelated. Explain how a change in price affects another market in the four cases below:
   a. An increase in college tuition on the pizza market.
   b. An increase in the price of wheat on the pizza market.
   c. A decrease in the price of computers on the shirt market.
   d. An increase in the price of copper on the computer market.
6. Suppose that the market for raw cotton is perfectly competitive and that the development of synthetic fibers reduces the demand for cotton.
   a. What happens to the market price of cotton? What is the short-run response of cotton producers to the change in the price of cotton? Explain the sequence of events.
   b. What is the long-run response in the market? Assuming that the cotton market is a constant-cost industry, how do the new long-run equilibrium price and quantity compare to the initial equilibrium price and quantity?
   Illustrate, graphically, your answers to a and b.
7. When a price-taking firm earns zero economic profit, its short-run average total cost is at a minimum. Explain why and illustrate graphically.
8. Referring to Table 3 in Chapter 9, and assuming the firm is a price taker, determine the firm's profit-maximizing level of output and calculate the amount of profit (or loss) when the price is $1, $2, and $6. What are the approximate values of the firm's long-run equilibrium price and level of output?

Synthesis Questions

9. Referring to question 6 above, suppose that the government establishes a program to support the price of cotton by being the consumer of last resort to ensure that the price does not fall below the initial equilibrium. That is, the government simply buys any cotton consumers are not willing to purchase at the initial equilibrium price. What will happen in the cotton market when demand decreases? Explain how the new long-run equilibrium would differ from the one in question 6. What are the implications for economic efficiency?
10. Is consumer sovereignty a normative or positive concept? Explain why you answered as you did.
11. Explain why producers would like to restrict or eliminate competition from other firms.
12. Assume that the production technology changes for a good that is currently produced in a perfectly competitive market. In particular, the new technology is such that the marginal costs of production for a single firm decline over the entire range of the demand curve for the good in question. How would this affect the number of firms that operate in this market? Explain.

OVERVIEW

In Chapter 10 we developed the model of a perfectly competitive market. As was pointed out at the end of the chapter, this model is an abstraction. Very few, if any, actual markets meet all the characteristics of a perfectly competitive market. Nonetheless, the perfect competition model enables us to identify the conditions necessary for economic efficiency in product markets. With this knowledge, we can evaluate

Small Firm Behavior: The Imperfect Competition Model

the economic performance of actual markets that we observe in everyday life.

This chapter relaxes some of the assumptions of the perfect competition model and examines the resulting effects on economic efficiency. In effect, we are introducing some of the complexities of actual markets into our analysis. The model that results is one that more closely approximates many of the markets we observe. The implications of this model for efficiency are evaluated using perfect competition as the benchmark.

In this chapter we develop the model of *monopolistic competition*. Monopolistically competitive markets are characterized by many small firms, each of which possesses at least some degree of market power. Firms behave as price searchers. An important result of our analysis is that although competition ensures that monopolistically competitive firms earn zero long-run economic profits, nonetheless each firm produces output inefficiently. However, the fact that monopolistically competitive firms produce a differentiated product also means that consumers enjoy

a greater variety of choices with respect to specific goods and services than they would in a perfectly competitive market.

CHAPTER 11

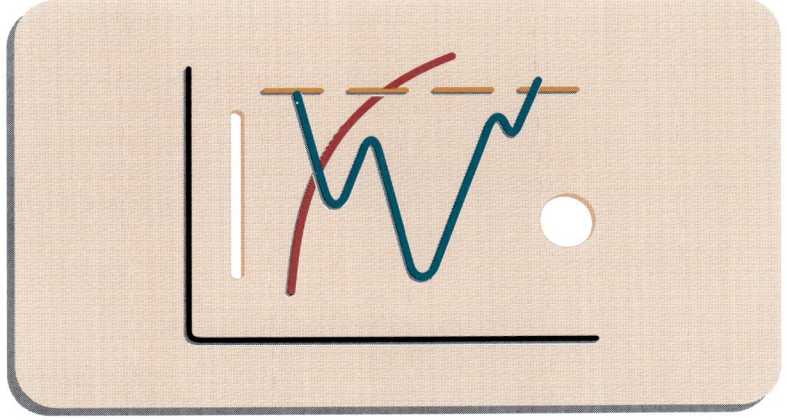

Learning Objectives

After reading and studying this chapter you will be able to:

1. Describe the basic characteristics of a monopolistically competitive market.
2. Describe the two major forms of product differentiation.
3. Explain how price and output are determined in a monopolistically competitive market in the short run.
4. Explain how monopolistically competitive markets move from short-run to long-run equilibrium.
5. Discuss the differences, in terms of efficiency, between perfectly competitive markets and monopolistically competitive markets.
6. Describe how government regulation can benefit firms in monopolistically competitive markets.

Real People, Space, and Time

We have already noted that very few markets are perfectly competitive. Many markets, such as the markets for groceries, gasoline, fast food, and clothing are characterized by a large number of firms that are small relative to the market they serve. However, firms within each of these markets usually charge a range of prices, rather than a single "market" price, for the goods or services they produce. In addition, the products offered are not homogeneous (as is the case in perfect competition). Instead, firms offer a wide variety of similar, but not identical, products and services. For instance, convenience stores such as 7-Eleven or Circle K offer many of the same products as major supermarkets, but provide the additional benefit of being close by, thus reducing travel time for many customers. In a similar manner, gas stations offer varied services and products, fast food restaurants offer different products (Big Mac versus Whopper) and clothing stores offer different brands and styles. In all of these examples, consumers have a range of prices and products to choose from.

Recall also that in the simple model of consumer choice behavior, and in the model of perfect competition, information and mobility are assumed to be costless. Decision makers — both consumers and producers — possess perfect information regarding the choices they must make. Also, as supply and demand conditions change in individual markets, resources are assumed to move between markets until equilibrium is once again reached. The fact that information and mobility are not costless and the observation that consumers have heterogeneous (varied) tastes explain why we observe the types of markets described above.

Costly Information and Mobility

Costly information and mobility have important and predictable implications for the structure of a market. Because resources are not perfectly mobile, different producers of the same good may end up paying different prices for what is essentially the same resource. Consequently, it is possible for different prices to exist for the same good across different locations. In addition, because information is costly, consumers (and resource owners) may not be aware of the fact that different prices exist for the same good. In either event, the result is that there is not a single equilibrium price for the good in question.

A look around us confirms the argument that, for many goods and services, there exists a set of prices, rather than one single price, even within the same city. A check at different supermarkets, convenience stores, and the corner mom-and-pop store will yield a range of prices for the same product. Why is this the case? One possibility is that consumers are not aware of all the prices being asked for a given item. This is a result, at least in part, of the fact that it takes time to observe all the prices for the good in question.

Finding the lowest price for a given product is costly; it takes time and effort. To the extent that time is spent gathering information on competing prices, that time cannot be spent doing anything else. Consequently, an efficient use of time requires the consideration of the opportunity cost of time spent in a specific endeavor.

In addition to the time spent looking for the lowest price for a given good or service, traveling to the location of the firm offering the lowest price also takes time. In many cases, a consumer may be aware that the lowest price for a particular good is charged at a firm across town, while the same good can be had for a slightly higher price from a firm that is much closer. In this case, the savings in travel costs associated with going to the nearby firm may outweigh the extra cost paid for the good. Consequently, it is the case that even if a product is homogeneous in respects other than location, firms may have some control over price. Interstate travelers know that gas stations located next to an interstate exchange on the outskirts of a city generally charge a higher price for a gallon of gas than firms located in the middle of town. While interstate travelers could drive to gas stations in the middle of town that may offer lower prices, the inconvenience and time spent may not be worth the savings in reduced prices.

Heterogeneous Consumer Tastes

Variations in consumers' tastes also affect product price and the range of products offered by firms by expanding the market for substitute goods and services. Firms respond to variations in consumers' tastes through **product differentiation** on the basis of one or more characteristics of the product. Product differentiation enables a firm to fill a niche in a particular market. To the extent that consumers attach different values to specific characteristics of a product or service, firms can charge different prices depending on the characteristics their product offers.

A relatively large number of gas stations operate in most cities. Moreover, a number of different brands of gasoline are often available in the same city, and even on adjoining street corners, suggesting a high degree of competition among firms. However, gas stations differ in terms of characteristics such as the ability of their gas to clean your carburetor, or the quality of the service they provide. Consequently, we frequently observe a range of prices for gasoline.

Fast food restaurants also offer differentiated products. Note that in this case product differentiation occurs on several levels. Some firms offer quicker service than others. Other firms specialize in different products—hamburgers versus chicken versus fish. Firms also differentiate their products on the basis of the quantity and type of inputs used—"one-third pound of all-U.S. beef." One result of this differentiation is that prices differ across firms.

In both of the above examples, product prices differ on the basis of consumers' tastes and preferences and consumers' valuations of the different characteristics each firm offers. However, it is also important to note that product differentiation can allow firms to satisfy a greater range of tastes and preferences than a homogeneous product could. In this sense, firms are simply responding to market forces.

We have talked about some specific kinds of complexities observed in consumer and firm behavior. The question we turn to next is, What impact do these phenomena have on the behavior of firms?

Product differentiation Variations in one or more characteristics of a good that are designed to distinguish the good from its competitors.

SECTION RECAP
For many goods, consumers are faced with a range of prices rather than a single price. Price differences can be the result of costly information and mobility, and product differentiation designed to satisfy heterogenous consumer tastes.

Monopolistic Competition

The world we have described above is clearly different from the world implied by perfect competition. A perfectly competitive market is characterized by a large number of small firms that produce a homogeneous product. As a result, each firm is a price taker and, in the long run, economic profit is equal to

Monopolistic competition
A market characterized by a large number of relatively small price-searching firms, resource mobility, and product differentiation.

zero. However, as we have just seen, in many instances markets are characterized by a large number of small firms that produce a heterogeneous product. In fact, as the examples cited above suggest, this type of market pervades our economy. This market structure is referred to as **monopolistic competition**.

Monopolistically competitive markets are similar to perfectly competitive markets in some respects — there is usually a large number of firms, each firm is small relative to the market, and resources are assumed to be mobile, that is, there is ease of entry and exit. However, these two markets differ in one important aspect — perfectly competitive firms produce a homogeneous product, and firms in a monopolistically competitive market produce differentiated products. As a result, monopolistically competitive firms are able to exercise some degree of control over price, regardless of the source of the product differentiation.

A *monopoly market*, which is discussed in detail in Chapter 12, consists of a single seller of a good or service. *The fact that sellers can differentiate their product on whatever basis is the monopoly element of monopolistic competition.* Because the monopolistically competitive firm somehow distinguishes its product from that of its competitors, it acts as a price searcher. However, because there are many close, if not perfect, substitutes for its product, the demand curve faced by the monopolistic competitor is affected by the decisions of other firms.

Because there are many small firms in a monopolistically competitive market, individual firms constantly face the threat of competition. The high degree of resource mobility in these markets increases this threat. The individual firm must therefore constantly strive to distinguish itself from its competitors in an effort to earn economic profits.

Short-Run Profit Maximization

Before analyzing the short-run behavior of a monopolistically competitive firm, we need to summarize the major characteristics of a monopolistically competitive market. They are:

1. A large number of small firms. Monopolistically competitive markets consist of a large number of firms. The output of each firm is relatively small compared to the market as a whole.

2. Ease of entry and exit. As in the case of perfect competition, ease of entry and exit is assumed in monopolistic competition — there is a high degree of resource mobility.

3. Product differentiation. The output of the firms in a monopolistically competitive market is differentiated. Products can be differentiated on the basis of one or more characteristics, including product quality, advertising claims, consumer perceptions, location, and availability. Product differentiation is the source of the monopoly element in these markets.

Like firms in a perfectly competitive market, monopolistically competitive firms seek to maximize profits. However, *unlike perfectly competitive firms, which are price takers, monopolistically competitive firms act as price searchers. As a result of product differentiation, monopolistically competitive firms face a downward-sloping demand curve.*

Perfectly competitive firms are price takers because price is the only factor that distinguishes one firm's output from that of the other firms—output is homogeneous. For firms to compete effectively, they cannot raise their price above the market-determined price (quantity demanded would fall to zero). Product differentiation enables the monopolistically competitive firm to alter the price it charges without losing all its customers. The decision to buy a particular product is based not only on price, but on the specific attributes of that product as well. However, the monopolistically competitive firm's price-setting power is not unlimited. Ease of entry and exit in the market and the large number of competitors limit the individual firm's ability to set price.

Figure 1 illustrates the short-run position faced by a monopolistically competitive firm. Note that the demand curve is downward sloping—the result of product differentiation. Because each firm is a price searcher, it seeks out the price–quantity combination that maximizes economic profits.

The cost curves in Figure 1 are of the standard form developed in Chapter 9. The average total cost curve is U-shaped, and marginal cost cuts the average total cost curve at its minimum point. (For expositional ease, the average variable cost curve is not shown.) In addition, the demand curve and the average revenue curve are the same. However, unlike the case of perfect competition, the marginal revenue (MR) curve is *not* the same as the firm's demand curve. As we saw in Chapter 9, when the demand curve is downward sloping, the marginal revenue curve lies below the demand curve.

The rule for profit maximization is that firms maximize profits (or minimize losses) by producing the level of output at which marginal revenue equals marginal cost. For the firm depicted in Figure 1, the profit-maximizing level of output is Q_1. The demand curve, D, indicates that the firm can charge a price of P_1 for each of the Q_1 units of output. The average total cost of producing Q_1 units is found by locating the point where the vertical line drawn at Q_1 intersects the average total cost curve and then reading the corresponding dollar

> **SECTION RECAP**
> Monopolistically competitive markets are characterized by a large number of firms that each produce a small share of total market output, and a high degree of resource mobility. Because firms sell a differentiated product, each firm acts as a price searcher.

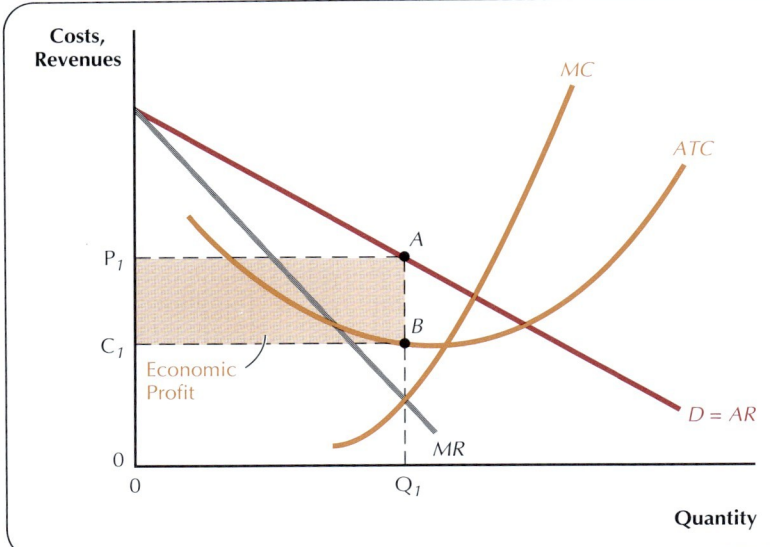

FIGURE 1
Short-run economic profits for a monopolistically competitive firm. This figure illustrates the short-run position faced by a monopolistically competitive firm. Using the MR = MC rule, the profit-maximizing level of output is Q_1. According to the demand curve, D, the firm can charge a price of P_1 for each of the Q_1 units of output. Total revenue is therefore equal to the rectangle OP_1AQ_1. Total cost is equal to the rectangle OC_1BQ_1. Thus, in the short run, this firm is earning an economic profit equal to the rectangle C_1P_1AB.

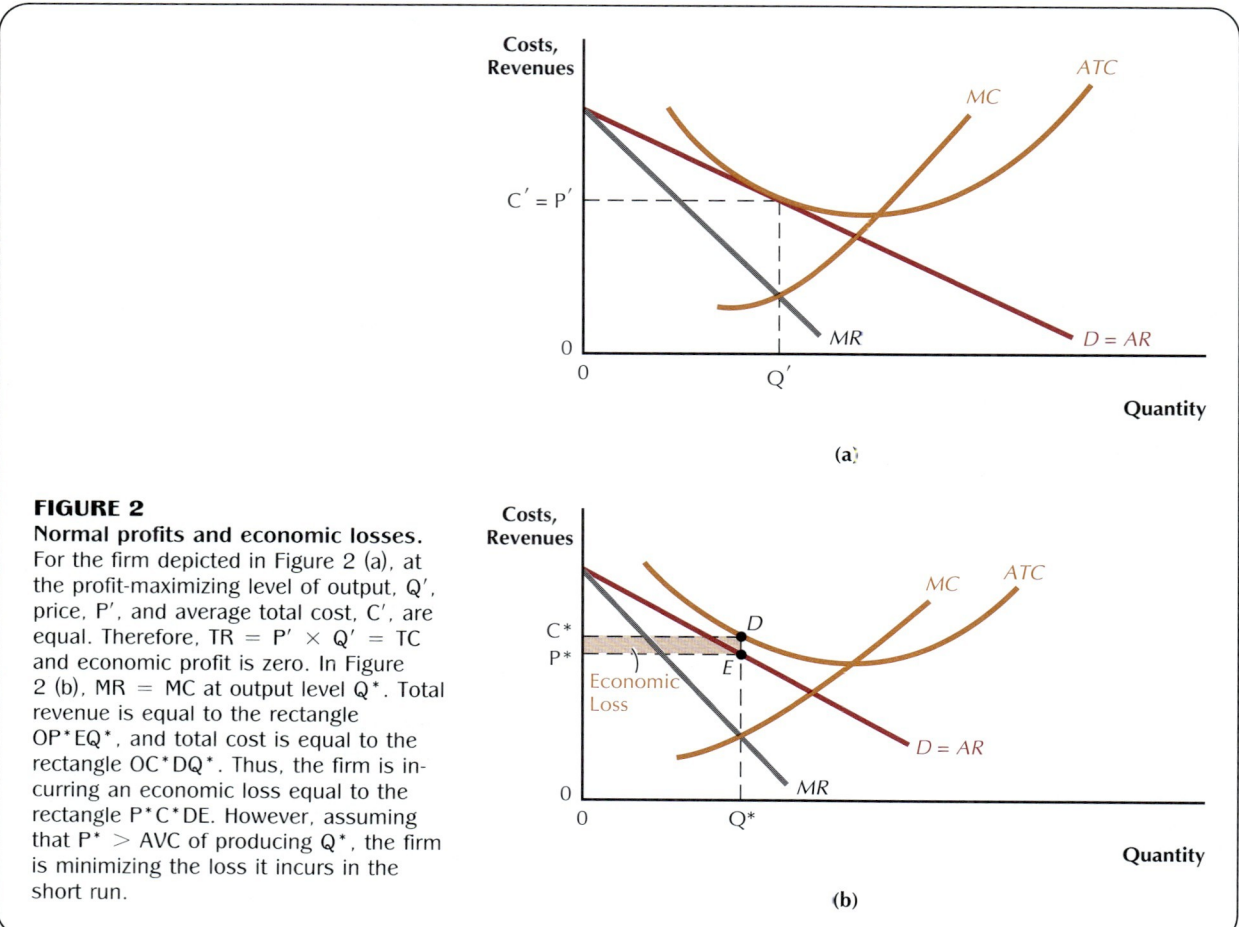

FIGURE 2
Normal profits and economic losses.
For the firm depicted in Figure 2 (a), at the profit-maximizing level of output, Q', price, P', and average total cost, C', are equal. Therefore, TR = P' × Q' = TC and economic profit is zero. In Figure 2 (b), MR = MC at output level Q*. Total revenue is equal to the rectangle OP*EQ*, and total cost is equal to the rectangle OC*DQ*. Thus, the firm is incurring an economic loss equal to the rectangle P*C*DE. However, assuming that P* > AVC of producing Q*, the firm is minimizing the loss it incurs in the short run.

amount off the vertical axis. Thus, in this case the average total cost of producing Q_1 units is C_1.

Recall that profit (or loss) is the difference between total revenue and total cost. For the firm in Figure 1, total revenue is equal to the rectangle OP_1AQ_1. Total cost is equal to the rectangle OC_1BQ_1. Thus, in the short run, this firm is earning economic profit equal to the rectangle C_1P_1AB.

In Figure 1, the firm is earning positive economic profit. However, it is also possible for firms in monopolistically competitive markets to earn economic profit equal to zero or incur economic loss in the short run. These situations are illustrated in Figure 2. The firm depicted in Figure 2 (a) is earning zero economic profit. Note that at the profit-maximizing level of output, Q', price, P', and average total cost, C', are equal. Therefore, total revenue is equal to total cost and economic profit is zero.

In Figure 2 (b), marginal revenue equals marginal cost at output level Q*. At this level of output, the price charged, P*, is less than average total cost, C*. Total revenue is equal to the rectangle OP*EQ*. Total cost is equal to the rectangle OC*DQ*. Thus, the firm is incurring an economic loss equal to the rectangle P*C*DE. However, assuming that P* is greater than average variable

---

SECTION RECAP
Monopolistically competitive firms maximize profits by producing the level of output at which MR = MC. They may earn economic profit or normal profit, or incur economic losses in the short run.

cost, by producing Q* the firm is minimizing the loss it incurs in the short run. (Recall that so long as the firm is earning a price that is greater than its average variable costs of production, it should continue to produce in the short run.)

Long-Run Equilibrium Position

In the long run, monopolistically competitive firms earn zero economic profits. The question we consider now is, How does the adjustment process (from the short run to the long run) work and how is this long-run equilibrium outcome characterized?

Market Forces Eliminate Economic Profits

Consider once again the case depicted in Figure 1 which has been recreated in Figure 3. In the short run, the firm is earning an economic profit. These profits act as a signal to other firms to enter the market in an effort to compete for these profits. (Recall that entry and exit are assumed to be relatively costless in a monopolistically competitive market.) The effect of the increase in the number of firms competing in the market can be analyzed as follows.

As new firms enter the market, the number of available substitutes for the good in question increases. In turn, the share of customers buying the output of any specific firm falls as some buyers switch to the newly offered products. Consequently, the demand for each firm's output decreases. Assuming the available pool of customers is constant, the demand curve faced by each individual firm shifts to the left. In addition, as the number of substitutes for a given good increases, the demand for any specific good becomes more elastic. These two effects are shown graphically by the demand curve labeled D' in

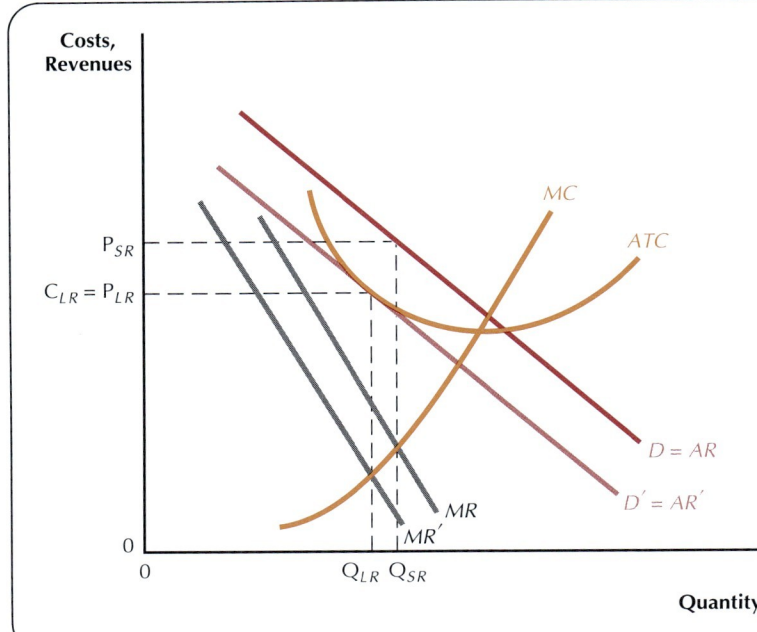

FIGURE 3
The adjustment to long-run equilibrium. In this figure, the firm is initially earning a short-run economic profit, which creates an incentive for other firms to enter the market. As the number of substitutes increases, the demand curve faced by the individual firm shifts to the left and becomes more elastic, as shown by the demand curve D'. In long-run equilibrium, the demand curve is tangent to the ATC curve at the level of output at which MR = MC. At output level Q_{LR}, TR = TC. Thus, the firm is earning zero economic profit. However, the firm is operating inefficiently; it could increase output and lower the average total cost of production.

Figure 3. Note that relative to the original demand curve D, D′ has shifted left. Firms continue to enter the market until firm demand falls to where price is equal to average total cost.

In long-run equilibrium, the demand curve faced by the firm is just tangent to the average total cost curve at the level of output at which marginal revenue equals marginal cost. In Figure 3, equilibrium occurs at the output level Q_{LR}. At this level of output, price, P_{LR}, equals average revenue which equals average total cost, C_{LR}, and therefore, total revenue equals total cost. Thus, the firm is earning zero economic profit.

However, because the demand curve is downward sloping, the point where it is tangent to (touches) the average total cost curve is to the left of the minimum average total (unit) cost of production — the firm is not operating at capacity. The firm is therefore operating at an inefficient level of output. The firm could increase output and lower its average total cost of production. However, doing so would force the firm to incur an economic loss. It is also the case that price is greater than marginal cost for the last unit produced.

In our example of the gas stations located at different points in the city, it is reasonable to assume that, to the extent that a particular firm is earning economic profit, this would attract other firms into the market. In particular, assuming that economic profits are being earned by existing sellers, we would expect to see an increase in the number of such firms operating close to the interstate exchanges. The level of output sold by each firm would fall and entry would continue until all existing economic profits had been competed away. In addition, it is likely that sellers would attempt to differentiate their products on the basis of particular characteristics such as service and possibly the sale of additional goods, such as refreshments.

As another example, consider the recent boom in the quick-service oil change business. A large number of firms specializing in this type of service have entered the market in a remarkably short period of time. This quick entry reflects the high degree of resource mobility in this particular market and the effect of existing profits on the incentive for new firms to enter. Firms in the market compete on the basis of price, location, and a variety of services in addition to simply changing the oil in a person's car.

In the fast food industry, firms are constantly offering new and different products to attract customers and earn economic profit. Competitors respond by offering similar products to retain their existing customers. These firms also compete on the basis of service. For example, it is now almost impossible to find a fast food restaurant that does not have a drive-up window.

In all of the above examples there is a common thread — firms will compete on any basis that makes a difference to consumers. The result of this intense competition is to constantly drive economic profits in the market to zero.

In summary, the two most important features of long-run equilibrium in monopolistically competitive markets are:

1. **In the long run, firms earn zero economic profit.** As the preceding analysis indicates, in the long run, firms in monopolistically competitive markets earn zero economic profit. Recall that for perfectly competitive markets, long-run economic profit equals zero as well.

2. **Long-run inefficiencies exist.** In the long run, firms produce at an average total cost that is greater than the minimum average total cost possible. Consequently, fixed inputs are used inefficiently. In addition, long-run price is

SECTION RECAP
Due to competition for economic profits and a high degree of resource mobility, in long-run equilibrium, monopolistically competitive firms earn zero economic profit.

greater than marginal cost (price is greater than marginal cost). Hence, resources are allocated inefficiently.

Efficiency Implications

From the perspective of economic efficiency, monopolistic competition compares unfavorably with perfect competition. When a perfectly competitive market is in equilibrium, price is equal to marginal cost and each firm in the market is operating at the minimum of its average total cost curve. Thus, the

---

Does It Make **Economic Sense?**

Shakeouts in the Fast Food Industry

The fast food industry offers consumers a wide range of choices. A drive through most cities and towns in the United States confirms that consumers are faced with a formidable array of different brand names and product types from which to choose. In addition, it is interesting to note the seeming regularity with which new firms enter the market in a particular area and existing firms offer new products.

It is also interesting to note the number of firms that go out of business in this industry and the rate at which products are dropped as new ones are added. This phenomenon is referred to as a *shakeout*. Shakeouts occur as a result of the intense competition for economic profits. If a new product line proves to be profitable for a firm, duplication by other firms is the usual result. Duplication leads to an increase in supply and the elimination of profits. Firms respond to the erosion of profits by developing new products.

Given the rate at which shakeouts occur in the fast food industry, the industry would appear to be characterized by excess supply, suggesting that firms in the industry earn little if any economic profits.

Given these observations, it is worth asking, does the type of behavior witnessed in the fast food industry make economic sense? Recall from our discussion of monopolistically competitive markets that firms are constantly striving for new ways to earn short-run economic profits. One of the primary means of achieving this objective is through product differentiation. In the market for fast food, there is substantial variety in the tastes of consumers. Children tend to prefer fun foods and are often drawn to products that capitalize on a currently popular theme such as a cartoon program or movie. Many adults, on the other hand, prefer foods that emphasize a healthy diet and good nutrition.

Tastes differ within groups as well. One adult may prefer salads while another prefers fish to beef. In addition, different individuals may have a preference for different types of sandwiches: bacon and cheese hamburger versus a ham and cheese sandwich versus a chicken sandwich. Different children, on the other hand, may have a preference for one fast food chain over another due to a particular commercial. (Note that adults are also subject to the persuasive elements of advertising.)

Firms are aware of the considerable divergence among tastes and preferences. They also know that, although a product may be selling well today, it is always possible that entry by a competitor will reduce the demand for their product. Firms in the fast food industry have responded to this threat by offering a wide variety of substitutes rather than a single product. In addition, firms are constantly developing new products designed to attract new customers and, they hope, increase profits. Ultimately the purpose of product innovation is to maximize the demand for fast food. Although the introduction of a new product might reduce the demand for one of their existing lines, firms expect that the increase in the number of new customers realized from the new product will more than offset any loss that occurs. However, this behavior also results in intense competition, which leads to frequent shakeouts in the industry.

The conclusion is that, from the firm's perspective, the type of behavior examined here makes economic sense. Although firms and products continue to come and go, the primary motivation is short-run profits. As long as firms are able to differentiate their products, and in so doing, retain existing customers and attract new ones, economic profits can be earned.

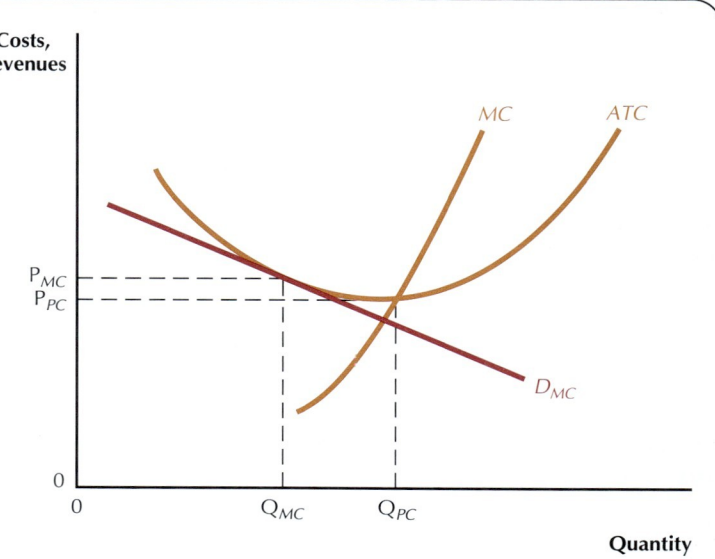

FIGURE 4
Equilibrium and efficiency: perfect competition versus monopolistic competition. In a perfectly competitive market, equilibrium output and price will be Q_{PC} and P_{PC}. If, on the other hand, the firm is operating in a monopolistically competitive market and faces the demand curve labeled D_{MC}, equilibrium output and price will be Q_{MC} and P_{MC}. However, the difference between the two sets of equilibria disappears as the demand curve faced by the monopolistically competitive firm becomes more elastic.

allocatively efficient level of output is produced and the firm is using its plant size as efficiently as possible.

As Figure 3 illustrates, however, the long-run price charged by the monopolistic competitor is greater than the marginal cost of production. Hence, *the monopolistically competitive firm is allocatively inefficient.* In other words, the value of the output produced, measured by price, is greater than the value of the additional resources used to produce the last unit of output, measured by marginal cost. Society would prefer more of the good in question.

We also noted that in equilibrium, production does not occur at the minimum point on the average total cost curve. As such, the monopolistically competitive firm is using its available plant size — its capacity — inefficiently. A smaller number of firms could produce the same total amount of output at a lower average total cost and still earn a normal profit by setting price equal to the minimum average total cost.

From the strict viewpoint of economic efficiency, monopolistic competition compares unfavorably with perfect competition. However, it is worth noting that, in many cases, the loss of efficiency may not be particularly great. Note that the more elastic is the demand curve faced by the monopolistic competitor, the closer will be equilibrium price and output for the monopolistically competitive firm and the perfectly competitive firm. In addition, the monopolistically competitive firm will move closer to the minimum of average total cost as the demand curve becomes more elastic.

This comparison is illustrated in Figure 4. If the market is perfectly competitive, equilibrium output and price will be Q_{PC} and P_{PC}. If, on the other hand, the firm is operating in a monopolistically competitive market and faces the demand curve labeled D_{MC}, equilibrium output and price will be Q_{MC} and P_{MC}, respectively. Equilibrium price is higher for the firm in monopolistic competition and equilibrium output is lower. However, the differences between the two sets of equilibria disappear as the demand curve faced by the monopolistically competitive firm becomes more elastic.

SECTION RECAP
In the long run, monopolistically competitive firms do not make efficient use
(continued)

In addition, monopolistic competition provides a benefit to consumers that is absent in the case of perfect competition — increased choice. As a result of product differentiation, consumers have a set of alternatives from which they can make their selections of what to consume. Thus, it is possible for a greater range of consumer tastes and preferences to be satisfied. As a consequence, the total amount of consumer satisfaction associated with the consumption of a particular good or service may be greater than it would be if the good were produced in a perfectly competitive market. The large number of monopolistically competitive markets in our economy is testament to the fact that consumers prefer a wide variety of choices.

> **SECTION RECAP**
> *(continued)*
> of their capacity. In addition, they produce an inefficient level of output. However, they offer consumers the benefit of increased choice relative to perfectly competitive markets.

Competitive Pressure

One of the most important similarities between firms in a perfectly competitive market and those operating in a monopolistically competitive market is the extent of competition. In both cases, firms are subjected to the constant pressure of competition. Each firm seeks to maximize profits. Yet firms have only limited control over the forces influencing profitability, and the amount of control depends upon the market structure in which the firm operates.

Since firms in a perfectly competitive market are price takers, their only control over profits lies on the cost side. Such firms can earn short-run economic profits by reducing average (unit) costs. However, the creation of these short-run economic profits simply increases the incentive for competition by other firms. In the long run, economic profits equal zero.

On the other hand, firms in a monopolistically competitive market are price searchers. Each firm faces a negatively sloped demand curve. Therefore, these firms have a degree of control over price as well as their costs, and can compete on the basis of price. Monopolistically competitive firms also rely heavily on **nonprice competition**, such as product differentiation and advertising, to gain more customers at any given price, and they work to keep reducing unit costs. Nonetheless, long-run market adjustments drive economic profit to zero.

> **Nonprice competition**
> Activities such as product differentiation and advertising, which are designed to increase the demand for a firm's output.

The Incentive to Escape Competition

The constant competitive pressure of profits creates an incentive for firms to try to escape competition. After all, it is competition that eventually eliminates any economic profits. Of course, the desire to avoid competition is not confined to profit-maximizing firms. Consider a student about to take an exam. Knowledge of the questions and answers on the exam, before the fact, would ensure the student of a high grade. In a sense, a high grade is not unlike economic profit for the firm. Note that this knowledge in effect relieves the student of the need to compete for the high grade. In a similar manner, resource owners would like to be able to sell their resources in markets free of competition. In this way, resource owners would be able to maximize the potential gains that could be realized from the sale of their resources.

There are two ways that firms can escape the pressures of competition. The first is to differentiate the product in such a way that there are no, or very few, substitutes for the product in question. As the number of available substitutes for a product or service declines, the pressure of competition is reduced.

The second approach involves the imposition of restrictions on the mobility of resources, in particular, restrictions on market entry. As resource mobility is reduced, once again, competitive pressures will decline.

Firms in monopolistically competitive markets have relied on both of these approaches to reduce competitive pressures. In many cases, firms have relied on a combination of these approaches.

Product Differentiation

We introduced the notion of product differentiation in the course of identifying the principal characteristics of a monopolistically competitive market. Product differentiation gives firms some control over product price. While product differentiation can be either real or imagined, it has the effect of distinguishing competitors from each other and creating what are essentially different markets for a particular good or service.

Real product differentiation occurs when similar products differ as a result of actual characteristics such as quality of inputs or location of the firm and the consequent availability of the product. For example, certain brands of bread claim that only the "choicest" ingredients are used. Other brands claim that all the ingredients are purely natural. In a similar fashion, different brands of blue jeans differ in price, at least in part due to the varying quality of the denim used to make them.

In our example of the gas stations located next to the interstate exchanges and in the middle of town, the same product was differentiated on the basis of convenience. Interstate drivers could travel a short distance and pay a higher price or travel a longer distance and pay a lower price. The seller simply takes advantage of the opportunity cost of travel time in setting price at each location.

In other cases, firms claim that their product is unique. For example, many fast food restaurants claim to use a specific method or secret ingredients in preparing the food items they serve. Kentucky Fried Chicken claims that its secret recipe of eleven different herbs and spices results in a fast food unlike any other. The objective of such devices is to eliminate competition from other producers. In any case, real product differentiation distinguishes a particular good from its competitors.

Imagined product differentiation is the result of efforts such as advertising or packaging that create the impression that two or more products are different when, in fact, they are composed of exactly the same inputs. Imagined product differentiation can also be the result of the individual's personal assessment of the good or service in question. Regardless of the type of differentiation employed, however, the result is that a consumer is willing to pay different prices for what is, at least to some degree, the same product.

In contrast to perfectly competitive markets, where advertising is virtually nonexistent, monopolistically competitive markets are characterized by extensive advertising. Many monopolistic competitors — gas stations, fast food chains, and clothing manufacturers, to name a few — rely heavily on advertising to distinguish their product from that of their competitors. The purpose of advertising is to highlight the differences among competing goods and services. Such advertising can be designed to inform consumers about real differences among competing products, or simply to persuade them. A considerable amount of advertising is also used to develop and maintain brand loyalty by creating an image of the type of people who consume a particular product.

Real product differentiation
Similar products differ as a result of actual characteristics such as quality of inputs or location of the firm.

Imagined product differentiation
The result of efforts such as advertising or packaging that create the impression that two or more products are different when, in fact, they are composed of the same inputs.

Proponents of advertising argue that it yields benefits to the consumer because it provides them with valuable information they can use in their decision-making process. However, critics of advertising argue that the primary purpose of advertising is simply to persuade rather than to inform. They also argue that advertising does little to alter the share of the market controlled by each firm in the market. Thus, advertising simply raises the costs of production and hence the price that is charged for each unit of output. Proponents of advertising respond to this criticism by arguing that advertising has the effect of increasing the level of output sold and, in so doing, moves firms down along their long-run average total cost curve, reducing the average total costs of production. Whether advertising is, in fact, beneficial is a matter of considerable debate, as the foregoing suggests. In any event, it is a tool that is heavily relied upon to differentiate products from one another.

Product differentiation is intended to reduce the price elasticity of demand. As demand becomes more price inelastic, the quantity demanded becomes less sensitive to price changes. This enhances the firm's ability to earn economic profits. More importantly, as demand becomes more price inelastic, it is easier to maintain economic profits over a period of time. Price inelasticity implies a lack of available substitutes.

Although product differentiation can benefit the firm in the short run, its long-run effectiveness is limited because of the continuous pressure exerted by competition. Although a firm may differentiate its product in the short run, competitors are constantly looking for ways to eliminate the source of the differentiation. In the case of real product differentiation, competitors are constantly seeking ways to copy or duplicate the product in question or produce a better product. In the case of advertising, firms are constantly competing with each other to persuade customers that their product is superior. The result is that the effects of a particular type of product differentiation rarely last long. Therefore, firms must be constantly looking for new ways to differentiate their product. It also provides the basis for reliance on a second means by which competition is reduced — government regulation.

SECTION RECAP
Product differentiation — whether real or imagined — is designed to increase short-run economic profits. Advertising may serve to highlight real product differences or may simply be designed to persuade customers that there are product differences that do not, in fact, exist.

Government Regulation

When people think of government regulation of a market or industry, they usually think in terms of efforts designed to promote competition or otherwise protect consumers. A large body of government legislation and regulation is designed to provide quality assurances for consumers. However, from an economic perspective, the effect of much of this regulation is to actually limit the amount of competition in particular markets.

There are many examples of restrictions on market entry. The requirement that a firm possess a license to sell alcohol is a classic example. In most areas, a bar, liquor store, restaurant, or other similar establishment cannot sell alcoholic beverages without a license. From society's perspective, the purpose of this restriction is to ensure that some measure of control is exercised over alcohol consumption. The growing emphasis on alcohol awareness and the threat posed to society by those who drink and drive is reflective of the benefits society associates with such restrictions. From an economic perspective, however, this has the effect of restricting the available supply and pushing price above what it would be in the absence of such a restriction.

Why the **Disagreement?**

Taxi Decontrol*

With the introduction of the Model-T Ford in the 1920s, the taxi business experienced a tremendous surge in supply. In effect, the cost of entry into the market was reduced substantially. However, the surge in supply resulted in cutthroat competition. In addition, the level of safety decreased as an increasing number of inept drivers entered the market. Customers were also increasingly faced with having to pay unreasonably high prices to dishonest drivers in situations where the customer was unaware of the true market price. Many cities throughout the country responded to this situation by regulating the local taxi industry. In many situations, strict limits were imposed on the number of taxis that could operate in a city and the fares that could be charged. Interestingly, although many of the limits on the number of permitted taxis were set in the 1930s, in many cities the same restrictions are still in place. For example, the number of cabs that can legally operate in New York City has been set at 11,787 since 1937. In addition, it was not until 1990 that Boston raised the limit, established in 1934, on the number of permitted taxis.

The failure to update restrictions on the number of permitted taxis, combined with population growth, has created a considerable amount of excess demand for taxi service in many cities, especially during periods of peak demand. In response to this problem, many cities have begun to consider either decontrolling their taxi market or, at least, easing restrictions on entry and rates for service in order to improve the level of service available to customers. However, such moves toward deregulation have met considerable resistance from the taxi industry, which argues that deregulation is not in the consumer's interest. Why the disagreement?

The principal argument by proponents of deregulation is rather straightforward. If restrictions were eased, competition would increase along with the number of taxis in the market. This increase in competition would move rates toward the economically efficient level and ensure that the quality of service is maintained at an acceptable level. In effect, competition would ensure that inefficient providers of taxi service are forced out of the business while providing a level of supply consistent with the demand for taxi service.

Proponents of deregulation also point out that restrictions on entry into the taxi industry create incentives for illegal behavior, such as black markets in taxi service. These markets are not subject to the safety regulations that have been designed to protect the welfare of

---

SECTION RECAP
Government regulation that restricts entry into a market in an effort to protect consumers' interests also has the effect of increasing the potential for existing firms to earn economic profits.

Establishments such as beauty parlors and barber shops, various medical practitioners, and taxi cab services must obtain a license to operate in many parts of the country. In many situations, the number of available licenses is limited. (See the box on taxi cab decontrol.) In addition, individuals who want to work in these jobs must pass a test or otherwise be certified first.

In each of the examples just noted, government has regulated otherwise competitive markets in an effort to ensure product quality and promote the interests of consumers. However, such regulation also promotes the interests of the firms left operating in the affected market. This is especially true in the case where regulation takes the form of restrictions on entry into the market. As a result of restricted entry, firms can charge a higher price than they would be able to in an unregulated setting.

Although regulation of monopolistically competitive markets is designed to protect the consumer and, in many cases, maintain product quality, it is often the case that producers realize long-term benefits as well. As Figures 1 and 3 illustrated, although it is possible for a monopolistically competitive firm to earn economic profits in the short run, over time those economic profits will be competed away. However, if entry is limited, as is the case in many regulated monopolistically competitive markets, economic profits can

consumers and the general public. Deregulation would eliminate the incentive for black markets and facilitate the maintenance of minimum safety standards.

Opponents of deregulation point to the experiences of cities that have attempted to eliminate restrictions on the taxi industry. Beginning in the 1980s, a number of cities, including Seattle and San Diego, began to lift restrictions on rates and entry into the taxi market. However, in both cases, subsequent to decontrol, ceilings were imposed on rates to prevent price gouging. In addition, San Diego reimposed restrictions on entry into the market.

Opponents of deregulation point out that many of the problems that arose subsequent to deregulation reflect the nature of the industry. For example, price gouging is rather easy when it comes to out-of-town customers who are unfamiliar with local rates and the distance that must be traveled to get from one point to another. This lack of information makes it nearly impossible to determine whether a reasonable rate is being charged for taxi service. Opponents also point out that open entry makes it very difficult to monitor the large number of independent taxis that are attracted into the market. To the extent that individual cab drivers exhibit behavior that reflects poorly on the city, this can damage the city's image and have adverse effects on its tourist industry. Finally, it is worth noting that in many cities the legal right to operate a taxi has, in and of itself, become a very valuable commodity. For example, in New York City a permit to operate a taxi was worth more than $130,000 in 1989. In Boston, a permit sold for $95,000 during the same time period. In San Diego, permit values rose to $15,000 subsequent to the reimposition of restrictions on entry. Obviously, the elimination of restrictions on entry would eliminate the value of these permits, resulting in a substantial economic loss for their owners who, not surprisingly, oppose deregulation.

The experiences of cities such as Seattle and San Diego would suggest that, at the least, the effects of deregulation in the taxi market are mixed. In addition, it appears that at least some form of regulation will be imposed on most taxi markets for the foreseeable future. This reflects the unique character of the taxi industry and the competing goals, protection of customers and the pursuit of economic profits, that guide the behavior of regulators and firms, respectively.

*This discussion is based on "Cab Decontrol is Hailed and Booed," *Insight*, Dec. 5, 1988.

persist over the long run. In addition, the price paid remains higher than it would be in the presence of increased competition. Thus, producers gain at the expense of consumers, who are left paying a higher price.

Summary

This chapter has examined a second form of market structure — **monopolistic competition.** Although monopolistic competition is similar to perfect competition in many respects — large number of relatively small firms, ease of entry and exit, and long-run economic profits equal to zero — there are some important differences. In particular, monopolistically competitive firms sell a product that is **differentiated.**

Product differentiation can be either **real** or **imagined.** Real product differentiation is the result of some difference in the quality of inputs used, the production process employed, or some similar attribute. Imagined product differentiation is generally the result of advertising. The result of product differentiation is that monopolistically competitive firms behave as price searchers as opposed to firms in perfect competition, which are price takers.

In the short run, monopolistically competitive firms can earn economic profits, break even, or incur a loss. However, over the long run, the presence of profits or losses and the associated entry into or exit from the market will force all firms to a situation where economic profit is equal to zero.

Compared to the perfectly competitive market, the long-run equilibrium in a monopolistically competitive market is inefficient. In particular, at the equilibrium level of output, price exceeds marginal cost and the firm is allocatively inefficient. In addition, firms are operating at a point to the left of the minimum of their average total cost curve.

Because competition increases the elasticity of demand for a product and reduces economic profits, monopolistically competitive firms attempt to reduce competition wherever possible. Two basic approaches are relied upon — product differentiation and government regulation.

Product differentiation has the effect of reducing the number of available substitutes for a particular good or service. As such, demand is less elastic and the firm is able to exercise greater control over the price charged and, consequently, profits.

Government regulation is usually employed in monopolistically competitive markets to limit the amount of competition. While the stated purpose of such regulation is to protect the consumer by maintaining product quality, regulated firms can also benefit. In particular, restrictions on entry into markets limit the available supply and can result in the realization of economic profits by existing firms over the long run.

Questions for Thought

Knowledge Questions

1. List and briefly describe the major characteristics of a monopolistically competitive market.
2. Briefly describe what is meant by the term product differentiation. What is the difference between real and imagined product differentiation?
3. What is the objective of regulation of monopolistically competitive markets?
4. Describe the basic similarities and differences between perfectly competitive and monopolistically competitive markets.

Application Questions

5. Assume that firms in a monopolistically competitive market are currently experiencing economic losses.
   a. Construct a graph that illustrates this situation.
   b. Verbally and graphically describe the adjustment in the market to long-run equilibrium.
6. Good X is produced in a monopolistically competitive market. In addition, each of the firms in the industry uses essentially the same technology. Competitors distinguish their individual products primarily on the basis of imagined product differentiation. Assume that one of the firms in the market discovers a new production process that substantially reduces the unit costs of production. Verbally and graphically analyze the effects of this discovery on long-run equilibrium in the market.

7. Graphically analyze the effect of government regulation that restricts entry of new firms into the market on the long-run equilibrium in a monopolistically competitive market.
8. Analyze, graphically and verbally, the short-run and long-run effects of an increase in demand for a good produced by a monopolistically competitive firm.

Synthesis Questions

9. Perfect competition results in the economically efficient level of output and price while monopolistic competition offers consumers a greater degree of choice among competing goods. Which market structure do you think better serves the interests of the consumer? Of society? Why?
10. Advertising is a central feature of monopolistic competition. However, viewpoints differ considerably with respect to the value of advertising. Use the Fundamental Premise of Economics to analyze the value of advertising. Does consideration of the Fundamental Premise tend to support the use of advertising?
11. Discuss the implications of perfect competition versus monopolistic competition as they relate to the concept of consumer utility. Which market structure do you think better serves the objective of utility maximization?
12. Regulation of seemingly competitive markets is supposedly intended to protect consumers. However, it is clear that in many instances one of the results of regulation is an increased price for the good in question. Can you think of an economic argument that would justify this increased price?

OVERVIEW

In the last chapter, we examined the pricing and output behavior of firms that operate in monopolistically competitive markets. We stressed the implications of this type of market structure for economic efficiency by comparing it to the perfect competition model. In this chapter we consider markets dominated by one or a few firms. Now we will be examining markets with potentially much less competition than is found in perfect competition.

Large Firm Behavior: The Imperfect Competition Model

Both perfect competition and monopolistic competition are market structures characterized by a large number of competing firms that are able to earn no long-run economic profit. Competition and resource mobility combine to eliminate any short-run economic profit. In contrast to these markets, many industries in the United States consist of only one or a few firms, each of which controls a large share of the total output in a market. Examples include electric and natural gas utilities in a geographic region and the automobile, flat glass, steel, petroleum, breakfast cereal, chewing gum, and cigarette industries.

Firms in industries such as those listed above may possess considerable market power because there is little resource mobility. Both the reasons for and the consequences of this lack of mobility are discussed in this chapter.

CHAPTER 12

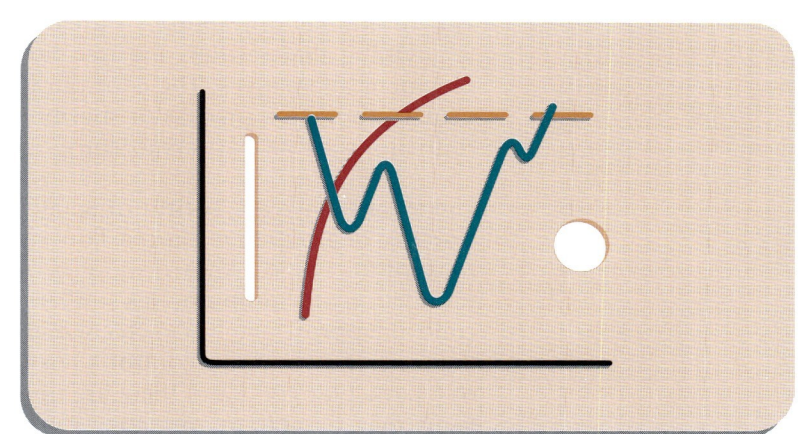

Learning Objectives

After reading and studying this chapter, you will be able to:

1. Describe the various types of barriers to entry into a market.
2. Explain the implications of resource immobility for long-run economic profits.
3. Describe the short-run and long-run equilibrium conditions for a monopolist and the implications for efficiency.
4. Describe the situation of a natural monopoly.
5. Describe the major characteristics of an oligopoly.
6. Explain the role of collusion in the price-setting behavior of oligopolistic firms, and discuss the major obstacles to successful collusion.

Resource Immobility and Competitive Pressure

As we have already seen, competition for economic profits reallocates resources to their most valued uses and leads to the efficient use of those resources. In the case of perfect competition, it serves to ensure that the price of the good is equal to the opportunity cost of production. Many markets in the U.S. economy, however, are characterized by a small number of large firms. The popular view is that such firms possess considerable market power and that there is an absence of competition. In this chapter we examine the origins of this type of market structure and the efficiency of outcomes in such markets. A key factor in competitive markets is resource mobility. If resources are immobile, the forces of competition are weakened, short-run economic profits can persist into the long run, and inefficiency can result.

Barriers to Entry

Barrier to entry
Anything that restricts the free flow of resources between profitable employment alternatives.

The immobility of resources is the result of **barriers to entry**. An entry barrier is anything that restricts the free flow of resources between profitable employment alternatives. The control of specific resources, the control of a particular production process or specific products, economies of scale, and legal restrictions are all barriers to entry.

Control of Resources A firm or small number of firms may gain control of a resource or group of resources. For example, ALCOA for a long time controlled most of the world's known supplies of bauxite, a raw material essential to the production of aluminum. In a similar fashion, the De Beers diamond syndicate controls approximately 85 percent of the world's diamond supply. To the extent that one or a few firms control a resource that is necessary for the production of a particular good and there are no good substitutes for this resource, these firms may be able to earn long-run economic profit. This is because other, new firms will be unable to enter the market and compete. Consequently, there will be no competition from new firms to bid product price down to unit cost.

Control of Production Processes and Products One or a few firms may have exclusive rights to a production process for a particular good. In this case, entry is restricted to the extent that alternative (substitute) production processes are not available. So long as potential competitors are unable to develop production processes that can be used to produce a comparable product, the existing firm, or firms, will be able to exercise considerable market power.

Patent
Issued by the government, it entitles its owner to exclusive rights to a production process for a period of seventeen years.

To protect its rights to a particular production process, a firm (or an individual) can apply for a **patent**. A patent entitles its owner to exclusive rights to the process for a period of seventeen years. Other firms are legally prohibited from using the production process during that time. A patent serves two purposes. On the one hand, it acts as an inducement to firms to develop new, and possibly more efficient, production processes in their pursuit of economic profits. The patent guarantees the firm that it will be able to enjoy the benefits of research and development and not have to share those benefits with its competitors for a period of time. On the other hand, patents limit the degree of competition that arises in a particular market. For many years Xerox held a patent on plain-paper copying and IBM held patents on tabulating machines.

These patents insulated their owners from competitive pressure for a period of time.

In addition to holding a patent on a production process, it is possible to hold a patent on a particular good. To the extent that there is a demand for the good, the owner of the patent is able to exercise considerable control over pricing and output in the market. Patents can therefore act as a significant barrier to the production of particular goods.

Patents prevent the production of exact duplicates of a good. They do not, however, restrict the production of substitutes. Guitar manufacturers in the United States have long held patents on specific models of guitars such as the Gibson Les Paul, the Fender Stratocaster, and the line of Martin acoustic guitars. However, in recent years a number of Japanese firms have successfully entered the guitar market with a series of models that are very similar to their U.S. counterparts. This example highlights the fact that in some situations patents may only be imperfect or weak barriers to entry. (It also illustrates once again the power of the desire for profits.)

Economies of Scale   In Chapter 9 we discussed the concept of economies of scale. Economies of scale occur when the long-run costs of production decrease as the scale of operation of a single firm increases. When economies of scale are substantial, it is possible for one or a few firms to control the market. Potential competitors who attempt to enter the market with a smaller scale of operation will incur higher average production costs than a larger, existing firm. Thus, the new firm cannot charge as low a price as the existing firm and remain profitable.

The existence of economies of scale implies that the costs of entry into the market may be substantial. A large scale of operation is usually associated with a high level of fixed costs, which are in turn the result of large capital requirements. The auto and steel industries exemplify this situation. In this case, entry is limited by the sheer magnitude of the financial requirements of entry into the market.

Legal Barriers   In some instances, the government may eliminate the potential for entry into a market through the granting of a *franchise* or a *license* to operate in a particular market. Electric, natural gas, water, and telephone companies, for example, are usually granted a franchise in a particular service territory. These firms are the sole producer of the good or service in question in that territory. However, as we shall see shortly, the pricing and output decisions of these firms are usually regulated in an effort to generate the economically efficient level of output. Cable television represents an exception to the rule. Throughout the country, a single provider of cable television is granted a license to serve a particular area. However, the pricing and output decisions of these firms are not regulated. In light of this fact, Congress, in 1989, began to debate the issue of whether the cable television industry should be regulated to better serve the public's interest.

As the preceding discussion suggests, barriers to entry are seldom perfect or permanent. Firms in all market structures respond to the incentive for additional profits. To this end, firms are constantly looking for new production techniques and alternative resources that will result in lower production costs and enable the firm to earn economic profits. In addition, legislative and

SECTION RECAP
Barriers to entry can limit the degree of competition in a market. Sources of barriers to entry include exclusive control of resources, patents, economies of scale, and legal barriers such as franchise agreements.

regulatory restrictions are constantly changing. When AT&T was broken up, the market for telecommunications equipment broadened considerably.

Long-Run Economic Profits

Markets dominated by a small number of firms differ from the market structures we have analyzed in earlier chapters in a very important way. In the long run, it is possible for firms in markets with one or a few firms to earn positive economic profits. This potential is the direct result of the entry barriers that restrict resource mobility in such markets.

Recall from our previous discussions that short-run economic profits attract additional resources into a market. As firms compete for short-run profits, additional resources are allocated to the production of a good, supply increases, price falls, and economic profits disappear. In addition, firms have an incentive to reduce their average total costs of production to the lowest point possible. However, if resources are immobile, the reallocation process is disrupted.

Figure 1 illustrates the situation faced by a firm that controls a significant share of a market in which resources are immobile. The firm is a price searcher and faces a downward-sloping demand curve. Profits are maximized by producing the level of output at which marginal revenue equals marginal cost — in this case, Q_1 — and charging the price P_1. The firm is earning economic profits equal to the rectangle $C_1 P_1 AB$. However, due to resource immobility, competitive forces do not erode profits. Consequently, these short-run economic profits can persist into the long run. Figure 1 depicts both the short-run and the long-run positions for the firm. Note that if resources were mobile, additional firms would enter the market and entry would continue until economic profits were driven to zero.

Because price is greater than marginal cost, the firm depicted in Figure 1 is producing a level of output that is allocatively inefficient, that is, it is too low. However, as we have already noted, many industries characterized by a

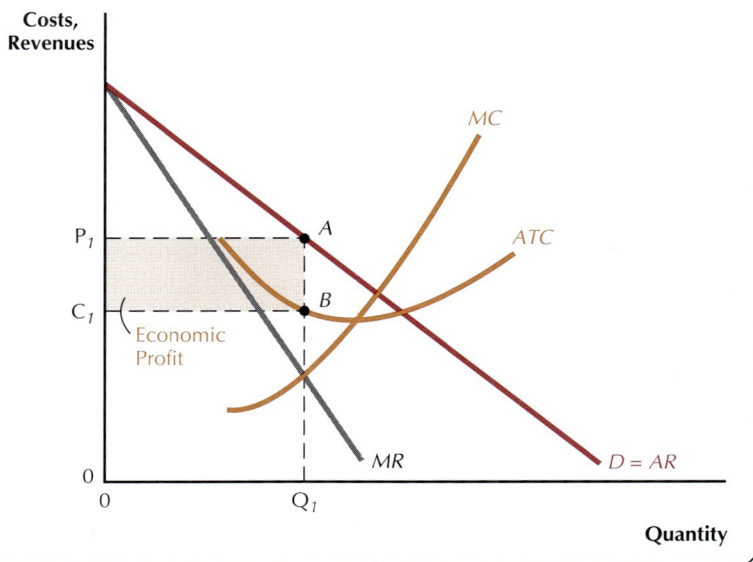

FIGURE 1
Short-run and long-run equilibrium for a price-searching firm. This figure illustrates the situation faced by a firm that controls a significant share of a market in which resources are immobile. Profits are maximized by producing Q_1 and charging the price P_1. Economic profits equal the rectangle $C_1 P_1 AB$. Due to resource immobility, these short-run economic profits can persist into the long run.

few firms that are large relative to the market are also characterized by economies of scale. Economies of scale imply that, in order to minimize the average (unit) costs of production, the industry should consist of only one or a few relatively large firms. However, the small number of firms is also associated with a lack of competition and therefore the benefits of competition. Consequently, we are often confronted with a tradeoff. In particular, one of the conditions that encourages an efficient level of output—a large number of competing firms—may result in unit costs that are higher than they would be otherwise. This tradeoff complicates the question of what to do when this type of market structure arises.

> **SECTION RECAP**
> Barriers to entry can enable firms to earn economic profit in the long run. When economies of scale are a factor, there is a tradeoff between the efficient level of output and efficient production.

Monopoly

Thus far, our analysis of markets dominated by one or a few firms has focused on the sources of market power. We now turn to the specific question of how prices and output levels are determined by firms in this type of market structure and the implications for economic efficiency. We begin with the case of **monopoly**, a market comprised of a single firm.

A firm is a monopolist if it is the only producer of a good for which no close substitutes exist. Familiar examples of monopolies include electric and natural gas utilities, local telephone companies, Amtrak rail service, and public transportation in a particular city. Note that in all of these examples there is a single provider of the particular good or service. If we think in more general terms—energy, communications, or transportation services—substitutes, although imperfect, do exist. Natural gas can be substituted for electric service in many uses, taxicabs and personal cars can be substituted for bus service, and telegrams can be substituted for phone calls. Nonetheless, there is only one producer of the specific good or service in each location.

> **Monopoly**
> A single firm that produces all the output in a particular market.

From a theoretical perspective, the monopoly model is the direct opposite of perfect competition. Recall that the perfect competition model enabled us to identify the conditions that characterize efficiency in production. In contrast, the monopoly model enables us to identify the effects on efficiency of the complete absence of competition.

The major characteristics of the monopoly market structure are summarized as follows:

1. **A single firm.** Monopoly implies the existence of a single firm in the market. Although imperfect substitutes for the good or service may exist, the monopolist is the only producer of the good. The monopoly may be defined geographically. There are a large number of electric utilities in the United States; however, there is only one provider of electricity in a specific geographic region. In a similar fashion, there is only one provider of natural gas or local telephone service in a particular geographic region.

2. **Barriers to entry.** Monopoly is the result of one or more barriers to entry. Consequently, the monopolist is able to operate in a relatively competition-free environment. This fact has important implications for the distinction between short-run equilibrium and long-run equilibrium for the monopolist.

Because the monopolist is the only firm in the market, it faces the market demand curve for the good. As a result, the monopolist is a price searcher.

> **SECTION RECAP**
> A monopoly market is characterized by a single firm and significant barriers to entry. A monopolist is a price searcher.

Like firms in any other market structure, the monopolist maximizes profits by producing the level of output at which marginal revenue equals marginal cost.

Short-Run and Long-Run Profit Maximization

Following the rule for profit maximization, firms in all market structures produce the level of output at which marginal revenue equals marginal cost. To this extent, the monopolist behaves in the same manner as monopolistically competitive and perfectly competitive firms, searching out the price that will maximize profits.

Short-Run Profit Maximization   Figure 2 illustrates the situation faced by a monopolist. Note that the monopolist depicted in Figure 2 faces the same type of cost curves faced by firms in the other market structures that we have analyzed. However, unlike the firms in the other market structures, the monopolist's demand curve is the market demand curve. Since the market demand curve is downward sloping, the monopolist's marginal revenue curve lies below the demand curve. Once again, the demand curve is also the average revenue curve.

To maximize profits, the monopolist produces the level of output at which marginal revenue equals marginal cost, Q_1. The monopolist's ability to set price is constrained only by the demand curve for the good or service. According to the demand curve in Figure 2, the highest price consumers will pay for Q_1 units of output, and therefore the highest price the monopolist can charge, is P_1.

Profits, once again, are calculated as the difference between total revenue and total cost. The average total cost of producing Q_1 units of output is C_1. Consequently, by producing Q_1 units of output and selling them at a per-unit

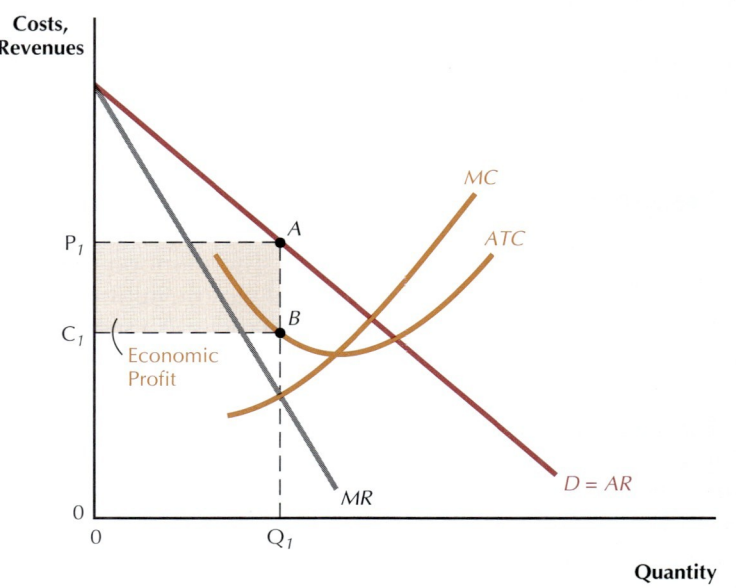

FIGURE 2
Short-run equilibrium for the monopolist: economic profits. To maximize profits, the monopolist produces the level of output at which MR = MC, that is, Q_1. According to the demand curve, the highest price that consumers will pay for Q_1 units of output is P_1. The average total cost of producing Q_1 units of output is C_1. Consequently, the monopolist is earning economic profits equal to the rectangle C_1P_1AB.

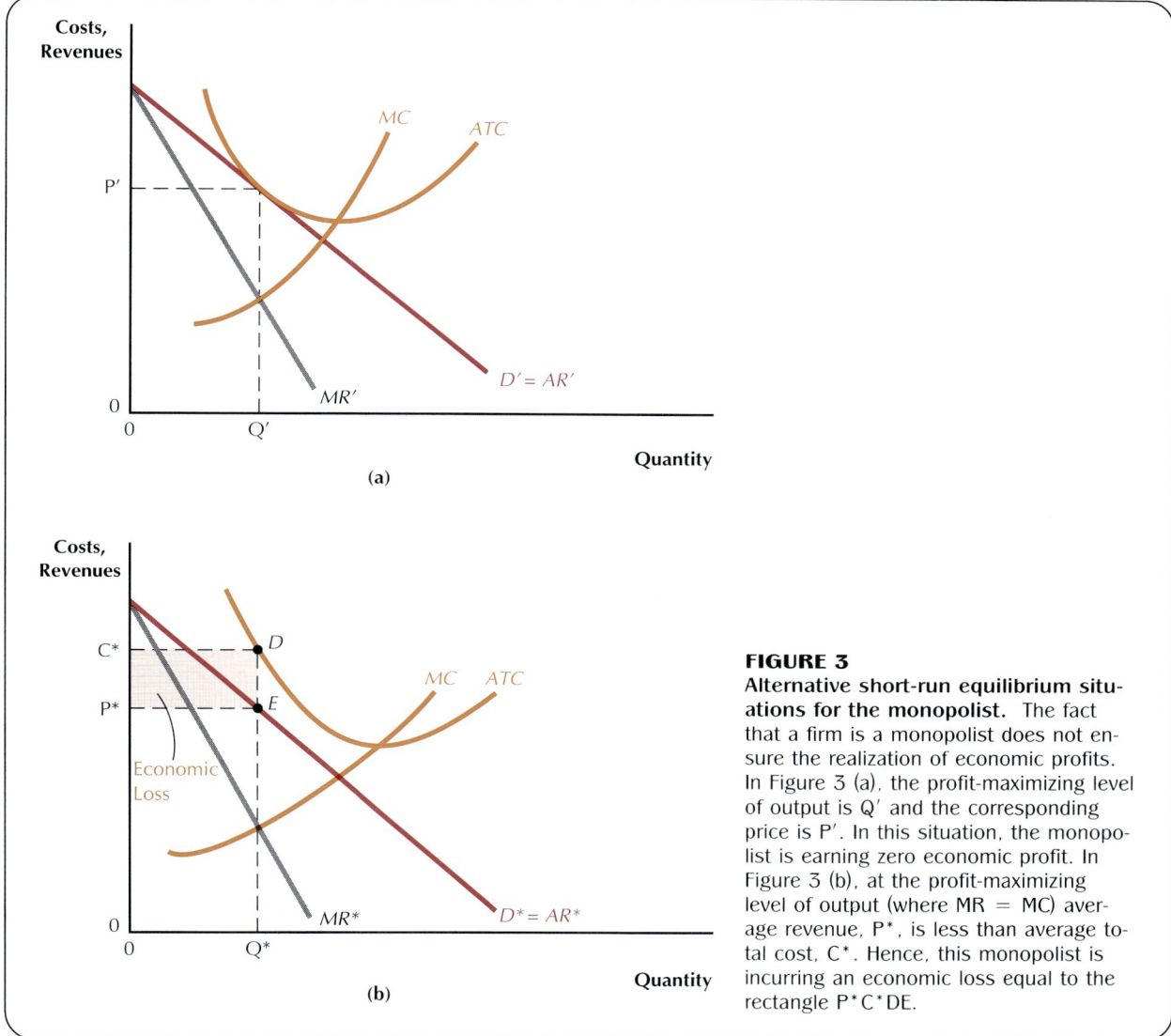

FIGURE 3
Alternative short-run equilibrium situations for the monopolist. The fact that a firm is a monopolist does not ensure the realization of economic profits. In Figure 3 (a), the profit-maximizing level of output is Q' and the corresponding price is P'. In this situation, the monopolist is earning zero economic profit. In Figure 3 (b), at the profit-maximizing level of output (where MR = MC) average revenue, P*, is less than average total cost, C*. Hence, this monopolist is incurring an economic loss equal to the rectangle P*C*DE.

price of P_1, the monopolist is earning economic profits equal to the rectangle C_1P_1AB.

In the situation depicted in Figure 2, the firm is earning an economic profit. However, the fact that a firm is a monopolist does not ensure the realization of economic profits. Remember that the monopolist's price-setting power is limited by the demand curve for the good. Consider, for example, Figure 3 (a). In this case the profit-maximizing level of output is Q' and the corresponding price is P'. At the profit-maximizing level of output the firm is earning zero economic profit.

Figure 3 (b) illustrates a case of economic loss for a monopolist. At the profit-maximizing level of output (where marginal revenue equals marginal cost), average revenue, P*, is less than average total cost, C*. Hence, this monopolist is incurring an economic loss equal to the rectangle P*C*DE.

SECTION RECAP

A monopolist has the potential to earn economic profit in both the short run and the long run. However, the fact that a firm is a monopolist does not guarantee economic profit (or even a normal profit).

Long-Run Profit Maximization For firms that operate in perfectly competitive and monopolistically competitive markets, long-run economic profits equal zero. This is the direct result of resource mobility. *The fact that resource immobility eliminates competition enables a monopolist who is earning economic profits in the short run to continue to do so in the long run, so long as demand and cost conditions remain unchanged. In addition, the monopolist has the potential to increase profits through technological innovation that reduces the costs of production.*

Long-run profits are not guaranteed, however. As we saw in Figure 3 (b), demand and cost conditions may actually result in a loss for the monopolist. Short-run economic profits persist into the long run only so long as there are no adverse changes in demand or cost conditions. In addition, for short-run economic profits to persist into the long run, the barriers to entry that gave rise to the monopoly must remain intact. If the firm's monopoly position is the result of a patent that expires, new firms may enter the industry. In a similar fashion, if new sources of scarce inputs are developed by potential competitors, the monopolist's position will be eroded. Technological change can also alter economies of scale. In the last decade we have witnessed a considerable increase in the number of competitors in the market for long-distance telephone service.

Efficiency Implications

An unrestricted monopoly market generates equilibrium market outcomes that are economically inefficient. Recall that in the case of perfect competition, firms acting in their own self-interest end up promoting society's welfare. In particular, perfectly competitive firms produce the allocatively efficient level of output, since price equals marginal cost for the last unit of output produced. Also, because each firm operates at the minimum of its long-run (and short-run) average cost curve, perfectly competitive firms use their capacity efficiently. However, a profit-maximizing monopolist will, in most cases, violate both of these conditions.

Figure 4 illustrates the demand and cost conditions for a particular good. Assuming that all the output is produced by a single firm, the profit-maximizing price and level of output are P_M and Q_M. If, instead, the industry were characterized by a high degree of competition, the marginal cost curve would represent the sum of the marginal cost curves of all the firms in the industry.[1] Price would be set equal to marginal cost, the level of output would be Q_C and the corresponding price would be P_C.

As we can see from Figure 4, left on its own the monopolist will produce a level of output that is too low (since $Q_M < Q_C$) and charge a price that is too high ($P_M > P_C$). Monopoly is allocatively inefficient because, at the profit-maximizing level of output, price is always greater than marginal cost. Hence, too few resources are allocated to the good in question. It is also the case in most instances that the monopolist does not operate at the minimum of its average total cost curve and is therefore does not make efficient use of its capacity.

One final note with respect to Figure 4 concerns the triangle ACF. This area represents consumer and producer surplus that would be realized if the market were perfectly competitive, but is lost if the market is served by an unrestricted monopolist. If the market were perfectly competitive, consumer

---

[1] This assumes that cost conditions are the same in both situations.

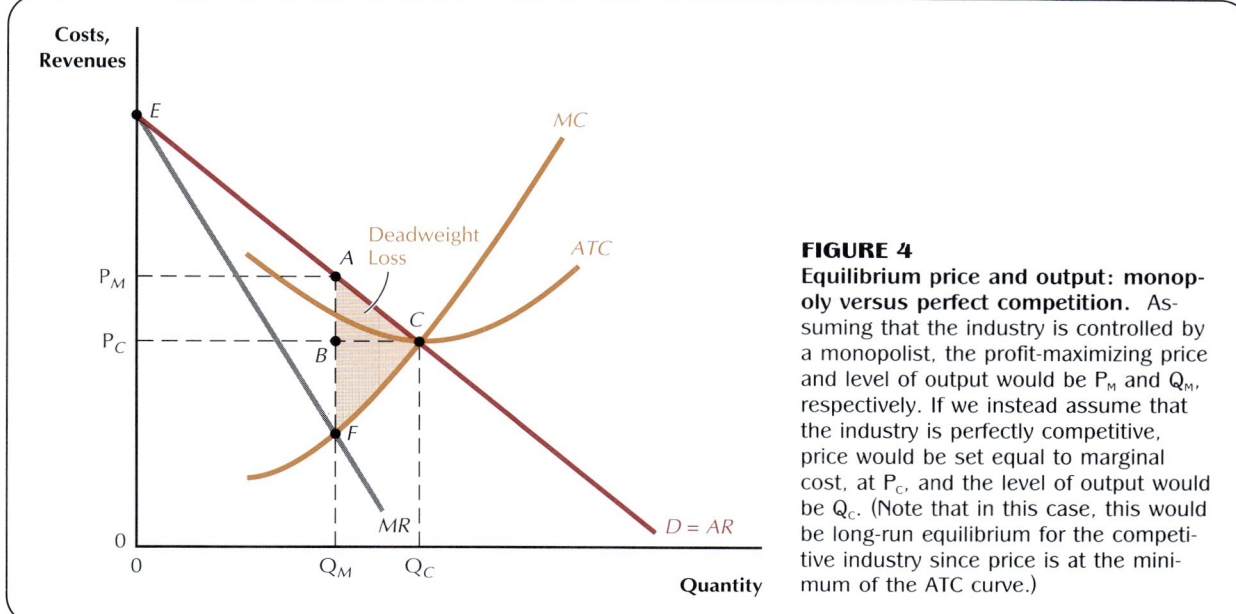

FIGURE 4
Equilibrium price and output: monopoly versus perfect competition. Assuming that the industry is controlled by a monopolist, the profit-maximizing price and level of output would be P_M and Q_M, respectively. If we instead assume that the industry is perfectly competitive, price would be set equal to marginal cost, at P_C, and the level of output would be Q_C. (Note that in this case, this would be long-run equilibrium for the competitive industry since price is at the minimum of the ATC curve.)

surplus would be equal to the area $P_C EC$. However, because the monopolist is able to restrict output and raise price, consumer surplus is reduced to the area $P_M EA$. The amount of consumer surplus represented by the area $P_C P_M AB$ is transferred to the monopolist in the form of producer surplus. The area ABC is lost consumer surplus. In a similar fashion, the triangle BCF represents lost producer surplus. The combined loss of producer and consumer surplus, shown by the triangle ACF, is referred to as a *deadweight loss*. It is a benefit that is lost to everyone — it is not captured by consumers or the firm. Deadweight loss is simply another cost of unrestricted monopoly.

SECTION RECAP
Unrestricted monopoly results in an inefficient level of output and use of resources. As a result, there is a deadweight loss incurred by society.

A natural monopoly is a special case of the monopoly market structure. A natural monopolist has a long-run average cost curve that is downward sloping over the relevant range of output. The most common examples of natural monopolies are regional electric and gas utilities and local telephone service. The key point with respect to a natural monopoly is that one firm can produce all of the output demanded in the market at a lower per-unit cost than can two or more firms.

Figure 5 illustrates the cost and demand conditions for a natural monopoly. The long-run average cost curve, labeled LRAC, and the long-run marginal cost curve, labeled LRMC, represent the long-run costs incurred by the monopolist. (Recall that long-run cost curves reflect the effect on average costs of allowing the plant size to vary.) For the firm illustrated in Figure 5, the long-run marginal cost curve lies below the long-run average cost curve. Recall that so long as marginal cost is less than average cost for a given level of output, average cost will decline. The demand curve represents total market demand for the good in question.

Natural monopoly
The long run average costs of production are decreasing over the relevant range of output.

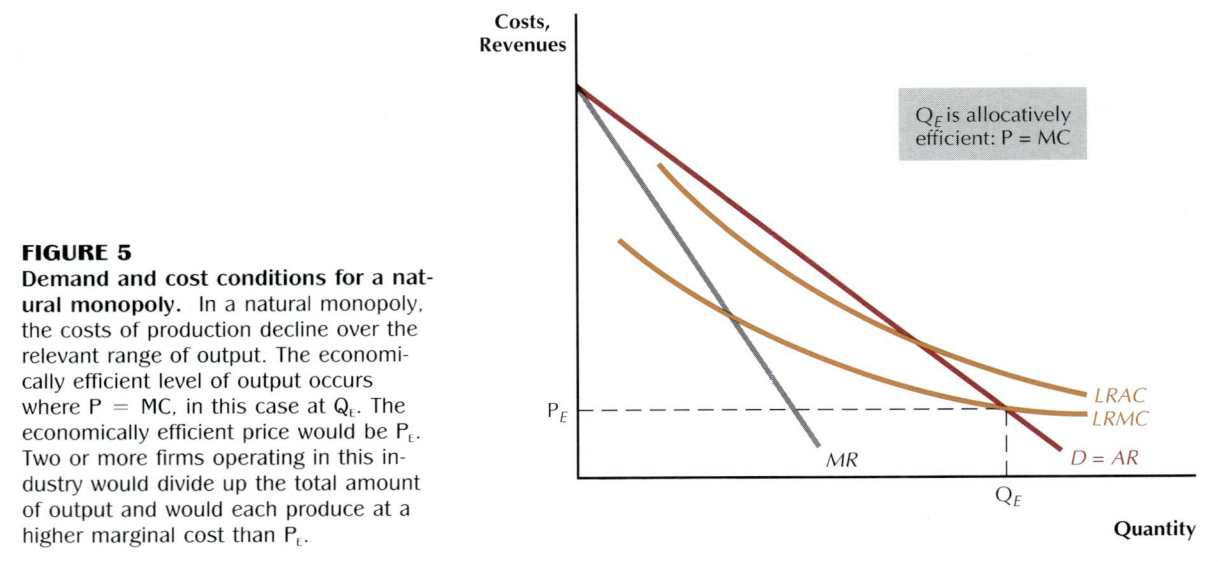

FIGURE 5
Demand and cost conditions for a natural monopoly. In a natural monopoly, the costs of production decline over the relevant range of output. The economically efficient level of output occurs where P = MC, in this case at Q_E. The economically efficient price would be P_E. Two or more firms operating in this industry would divide up the total amount of output and would each produce at a higher marginal cost than P_E.

In Figure 5, the demand curve intersects the long-run average cost curve to the left of the average cost curve's minimum. Consequently, one firm can produce all the output demanded in the market at a lower average per-unit cost than could two or more firms. More importantly, the marginal costs of production—both short run and long run—and therefore the amount of resources used to produce a given level of output are minimized by having a single producer. If two or more firms were to operate in the industry, the marginal cost of production would necessarily be higher than the marginal cost of production incurred by a single producer. This is because each firm would produce a level of output that is less than Q_E.

From the viewpoint of efficiency, *if a market is a natural monopoly, production by a single firm is preferred to a competitive market because average (unit) costs are minimized.* However, as we have already seen, in the absence of intervention in the market, the profit-maximizing monopolist will produce a level of output that is less than the economically efficient amounts. As illustrated in Figure 6, the price and level of output that correspond to point M on the demand curve represent the profit-maximizing price–output combination for an unregulated natural monopolist. However, the economically efficient level of output, which occurs where price equals marginal cost, is located at point E on the demand curve.

The efficiency problem is further complicated by the fact that if the monopolist is forced to produce the efficient level of output, the monopolist will incur a loss. In Figure 6, the efficient price and level of output are P_E and Q_E. However, the average total cost of producing Q_E units of output is C_E. Clearly, P_E is less than C_E. If the firm is forced to produce at point E, it would incur an economic loss represented by the rectangle $P_E C_E A E$ in Figure 6. A rational monopolist forced to produce this output level would simply cease production altogether.

SECTION RECAP
In a natural monopoly, production costs are minimized by allowing a single firm to produce all the output in the market. However, the unrestricted natural monopoly does not have an incentive to produce the allocatively efficient level of output.

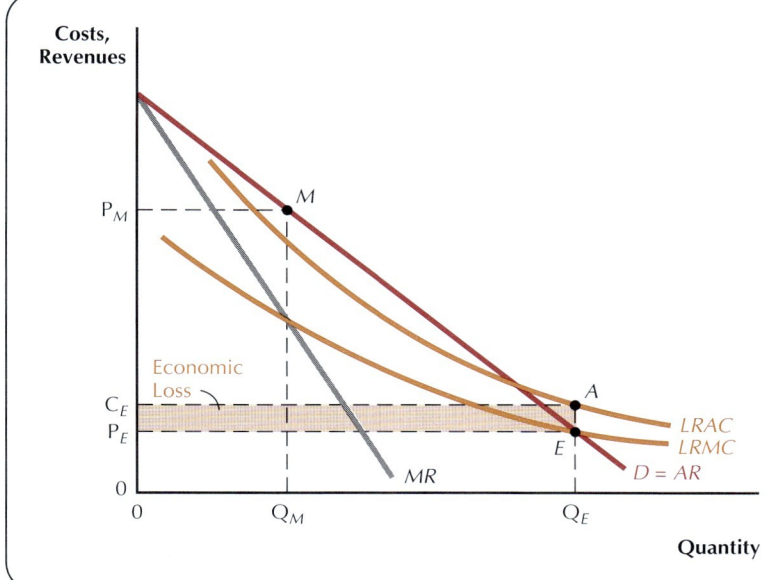

FIGURE 6
Natural monopoly and output. The profit-maximizing natural monopoly will produce the level of output at which MR = MC, in this case, at point M on the demand curve. The corresponding level of output is Q_M. If, instead, the monopolist were forced to produce the efficient level of output, production would occur at point E on the demand curve, and the price and level of output would be P_E and Q_E, respectively. However, the average cost of producing Q_E is C_E. Consequently, the monopolist would incur an economic loss equal to the shaded area.

Economic policymakers, therefore, face a dilemma. If the monopoly is prohibited and the industry is instead populated by many smaller competitive firms, the result is that output is produced inefficiently — output is produced at a higher average and marginal cost than if produced by a monopolist. Consequently, resources are wasted. Alternatively, if the monopolist is allowed to operate without restrictions, it will produce an inefficient level of output, since price is greater than marginal cost. Policymakers have responded to this dilemma by seeking to take advantage of the lower production costs while denying the monopolist its market power. Natural monopolies are allowed to operate, but in a regulated environment.

Regulation of Natural Monopoly The behavior of a regulated monopoly such as a public utility is usually governed by some form of regulatory commission. The major objectives of the commission are to ensure that costs are reasonably and prudently incurred and that the rates firms are allowed to charge are justified by the costs of production. In determining the price(s) that the regulated firm will be allowed to charge its customers, regulatory commissions generally rely on what is referred to as **rate-of-return regulation**. In this form of business regulation, prices are set at a level that will cover the costs of production and provide the firm's investors with a competitive rate of return on their investment.

The critical determinant of the actual rates that are charged under rate-of-return regulation is the **revenue requirement**. The revenue requirement is determined by the *rate of return*, the *rate base*, and *operating expenses*. The rate of return refers to the amount of profit the firm is allowed to earn, expressed as a percentage of the rate base. The rate base refers to the total costs of capital (less depreciation) to which the rate of return is applied. Operating expenses consist of the variable costs of production.

Rate-of-return regulation
Prices are set at a level that will cover the costs of production and provide the firm's investors with a competitive rate of return on their investment.

Revenue requirement
The amount of money a regulated firm such as a utility must earn to be able to cover its production costs and earn a normal profit.

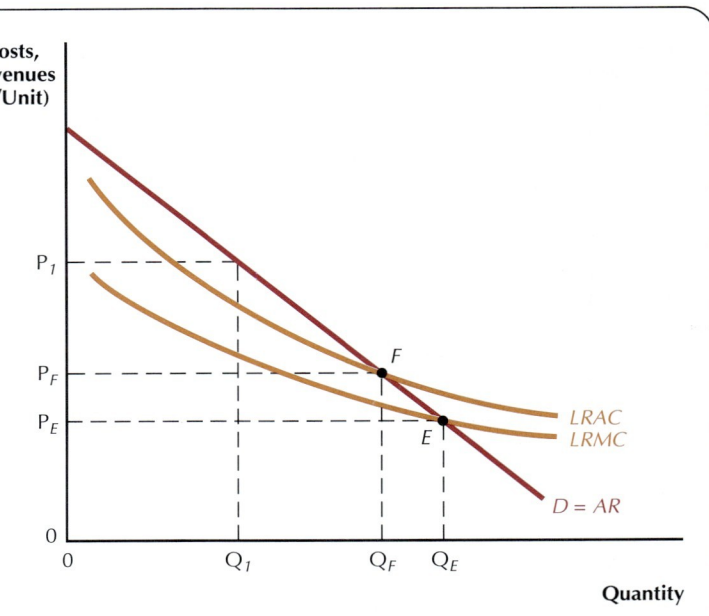

FIGURE 7
Rate-of-return regulation and the level of output. The LRAC curve is constructed to reflect the costs of production and a normal rate of return for the producer. If a single price is charged to all customers, equilibrium will occur at point F on the demand curve. The firm will earn a normal profit, since AC = AR. Block pricing could result in production at point E, the efficient level of production. With block pricing, different prices are charged for different levels of output. Excess profits earned on units of output to the left of Q_1 are used to offset the losses incurred on units of output between points Q_1 and Q_E.

Mathematically, we can write the revenue requirement as:

$$RR = ror(RB) + OE$$

where RR is the revenue requirement, *ror* is the rate of return, RB is the rate base and OE represents variable operating expenses. As an example, assume that the competitive rate of return for a particular electric utility is determined to be 10 percent, the rate base is equal to $10 million and operating expenses equal $2 million. Then, the firm would be allowed to collect $3 million [= (.1)10 million + 2 million] in total revenue over a given time period (usually one year). To generate this total amount of revenue, specific rate schemes must be developed and approved by the regulatory commission.

The objective of rate-of-return regulation is to encourage the efficient allocation of resources. However, one obvious problem associated with the rate-of-return approach to rate-setting is that there is a clear disincentive for regulated firms to control costs. As the rate base increases, the amount of profits a firm is allowed to earn will increase as well. While firms must be able to justify additional costs that they want to add into the rate base, it is often difficult for the staff of a regulatory commission to determine whether such costs are in fact justified.

Another problem with rate-of-return regulation is that although it results in an improvement over the unregulated monopoly, the resulting level of output nonetheless is inefficient. In Figure 7, the curve labeled D represents the demand for electric power in a given geographic region. The long-run marginal and average costs of production incurred by the electric utility are measured by the curves labeled LRMC and LRAC, respectively. As it is shown here, the long-run average cost curve has been constructed to reflect both the average costs of production and the rate of return, r*, that has been established by the governing regulatory body.[2] That is, we have simply incorporated the rate of return into long-run average cost.

The economically efficient level of electricity production occurs at point E on the demand curve. However, assuming that a single price is charged for each unit of output, the largest amount of output that the firm could produce and still earn a normal profit is Q_F. This level of output falls short of the efficient amount. However, note that a firm producing at point E would incur an economic loss.

One way to deal with this problem is through the application of **block pricing**. With block pricing, different units of output are sold at different prices. In effect, the sale of some units results in a rate of return in excess of r* while the sale of other units generates a rate of return below r*. These latter units correspond to the levels of output between Q_F and Q_E in Figure 7. The end result is that the pluses and minuses cancel out, and the firm earns an average rate of return equal to r* while the efficient level of output is produced.

A simple form of block pricing is illustrated in Figure 7. To ensure the efficient level of output, a price of P_E must be charged for the level of output Q_E. Assume that, in fact, this price is charged for the units between Q_1 and Q_E. Clearly, because price is less than average total cost, the firm incurs a loss on these units of output. However, to offset the loss, the firm could charge a price of P_1 for the units of output between 0 and Q_1. The sale of the first Q_1 units generates economic profits (since price is greater than average total cost), which can be used to offset the losses incurred on the $Q_E - Q_1$ units sold at the lower price.

Even in the case of block pricing, however, potential problems exist. Specifically, income redistribution occurs because different consumers end up paying different prices for the same product. Those individuals paying higher prices subsidize the purchases of consumers who enjoy the lower price. In our example, customers who consume the first Q_1 units pay an average per-unit price greater than average total cost while customers consuming the units between Q_1 and Q_E pay the lower price of P_E.

Price discrimination — the practice of charging different prices to different customers of the same good or service — is also utilized to affect the level of total output. In the case of electricity and natural gas, for instance, rates are often based on customer classifications — industrial, commercial, and residential — with customers in each class paying rates either above or below the actual cost of service. The fact that residential demand for electricity is more inelastic than commercial or industrial demand is used in the rate-setting process. This reflects the recognition that if rates are set too high for customers whose demand is more elastic, the customers will simply switch to relatively lower priced substitutes. This would in turn mean even higher rates for the remaining customers who must bear the costs of production.[3]

Block pricing
A pricing technique in which a regulated firm is allowed to sell blocks of output at different prices in order to simultaneously earn a normal profit and produce the efficient level of output.

Price discrimination
The practice of charging different prices to different buyers of the same good or service.

SECTION RECAP
The pricing and output decisions of natural monopolies are often regulated. Rate-of-return regulation combined with techniques such as block pricing and price discrimination is intended to simultaneously provide producers a fair rate of return and consumers an allocatively efficient level of output at a fair price.

---

[2]It should be noted that a normal rate of return is included in all the ATC curves throughout the text. However, in the case of rate-of-return regulation, the normal rate of return and the rate of return selected by the regulatory body may differ.

[3]Individual customer classes are often subdivided into different rate classes according to usage levels as well.

Why the **Disagreement?**

Local Phone Service — How Much Should It Cost?

Since AT&T agreed to break up and create separate companies to provide residential and long-distance service, the cost of residential phone service has steadily increased. The increase in residential rates has in turn raised serious questions about how those rates should be set. Many analysts, including some economists, have argued that local phone rates should be kept low, regardless of the cost incurred in providing this service. They maintain that universal service is a right to which everyone should be entitled. Others have argued that local phone rates should be based on the cost of service, irrespective of the resulting affordability of the service. Why the disagreement?

In fact, it is easy to see why this disagreement exists. For many years, the rate charged to residential customers in the telecommunications market was set below the cost of providing service to this group of customers. To compensate for the losses that resulted from this practice, the rates charged to long-distance customers were set above average cost. In effect, long-distance customers subsidized residential service. This type of pricing behavior is known as *cross subsidization*. Cross subsidization consists of the practice of charging different prices to different groups of customers and using profits from one group to cover the losses generated by another group. The effect of cross subsidization in the telecommunications market was to maintain relatively low and stable rates for residential customers. The increase in residential rates is largely the result of the loss of cross subsidies from long distance service that AT&T formerly used to hold down residential rates. The question that now confronts regulators and industry representatives alike is, How should rates be set in light of these changes? On the one hand, there is a legitimate concern that basic phone service should be available to all who desire it. The telephone has become almost a necessity for many people. Telephones provide an efficient means of communication that enables individuals to increase their total utility — not to mention productivity. In addition, phones provide a means of acquiring

---

Oligopoly
A small number of firms dominate the market; the economic well-being and behavior of the firms is mutually interdependent.

Mutual interdependence
One firm's actions influence the actions of other firms in a market.

Oligopoly

Like the model of perfect competition, the monopoly model provides us with useful insights. An important conclusion of the monopoly model is that, left unchecked, economic inefficiency — which results from an absolute lack of competition — may be substantial. We now modify the monopoly model to consider the market dominated by a few firms. This type of market structure is called oligopoly. The big corporations that we hear about daily and that together account for most of the output (in dollar terms) of the economy are oligopolists.

We want to examine the profit-maximizing behavior of oligopolists and the market outcomes associated with this behavior, just as we have analyzed the behavior of firms in other market structures. However, our treatment of oligopoly differs from our handling of the other three market structures in one important way. In the cases of perfect competition, monopolistic competition, and monopoly we were able to describe the equilibrium market outcomes in unambiguous terms. We will not be able to do that in the case of oligopolists because of the unique nature of oligopolistic markets. *In an oligopoly there are only a few rival firms whose economic well-being and behavior is mutually interdependent. One firm's actions influence the actions of other firms.* Consequently, market outcomes can be quite ambiguous. We will describe and explain the source of this interdependence among firms, the alternative outcomes we ex-

speedy assistance in the event of an emergency. Without the ability to phone for an ambulance, for example, it is likely that many more lives would be lost each year. Viewed from this perspective, universal service is an equity issue. Viewed from a different perspective, telephones enable individuals to acquire a wealth of information on topics ranging from products and prices to available job opportunities that would be considerably more costly to acquire by other means, such as physically visiting each location. In economic terms, many observers would argue that the benefits from universal service outweigh the costs incurred to provide it.

On the other hand, it has been pointed out that pricing telephone service below the marginal cost of production results in an inefficient allocation of resources. In particular, if the price of a good is set below marginal cost, too many resources will be allocated to production of this service (assuming that demand is completely met). One of the major objectives of breaking up AT&T was to eliminate inefficiencies that resulted from the regulation of the industry AT&T dominated. Pricing phone service below the marginal cost of production would simply perpetuate this inefficiency. In addition, pricing phone service below marginal cost would substantially undermine the firm's ability to earn a normal profit, raising the possibility that phone companies could be forced out of business. As such, other customers, such as commercial and industrial customers would have to pay a greater share of total costs in order to help maintain the financial viability of the phone company. However, this approach amounts to income redistribution and therefore raises another equity issue.

As the preceding arguments suggest, there is no simple solution to the problem. Regardless of which approach is ultimately chosen, some will be gainers and some will be losers. The only question is who the gainers and losers will be. Many state regulatory commissions are in the process of trying to deal with this difficult issue. Undoubtedly, the issues of equity and efficiency will be at the forefront in the ensuing debate.

pect to observe, and the features of the market environment that account for these different outcomes.

General Characteristics

Examples of oligopolies include the steel, auto, breakfast cereal, and chemical manufacturing industries. A small number of firms that serve a local market, such as three grocery stores in a large city, would be considered an oligopoly as well. Oligopolists may produce a homogeneous or a differentiated product. For example, firms in the steel or chemical industries may produce essentially the same product. Firms in the auto or breakfast food industries, on the other hand, produce differentiated products. The following is a summary of the major characteristics of oligopolistic markets.

1. **Small number of dominant firms.** Oligopolists are often large firms, each producing a significant portion of total market output. In some cases, a market may actually consist of hundreds of firms. However, to the extent that the market is dominated by one or a few firms, it is considered to be an oligopoly.
2. **Mutual interdependence.** Because the market is dominated by a few firms, the price and output decisions of one firm affect the profitability of the remaining firms in the market. Mutual interdependence is an

> **SECTION RECAP**
> Oligopolies are characterized by a small number of firms that produce a large share of market output, mutual interdependence among firms, and barriers to entry. Oligopolists are price searchers.

incentive to develop alternatives to price competition in the pursuit of economic profit.

3. **Barriers to entry.** Like monopoly markets, oligopoly markets are usually characterized by considerable resource immobility, especially economies of scale. Barriers to entry limit the threat of competition and facilitate the ability of firms to earn long-run economic profit.
4. **Homogeneous or differentiated product.** As the examples cited above indicate, the output of an oligopolistic market may be either homogeneous or differentiated.

Like monopolies, oligopolistic firms are price searchers. Firms that produce a differentiated product each face their own downward-sloping demand curve. For firms that produce a homogeneous product, mutual interdependence causes the individual firm's demand curve to be downward sloping.

Market Concentration The size of oligopolistic firms and the small number of firms in an industry have often led individuals to associate "bigness" and "fewness" with less competition and greater profits. The degree of concentration in an industry or market refers to the share of the total market output produced by one or more firms. A **concentration ratio** is a measure of industry concentration. For example, a four-firm concentration ratio is the percentage of sales in an industry accounted for by the four largest firms. Concentration ratios can also be constructed with respect to the amount of physical output, the amount of labor employed, and so forth. Four-firm and eight-firm (directly analogous to the four-firm measure) concentration ratios for selected industries are presented in Table 1.

> **Concentration ratio**
> A measure of market concentration, that is, the extent to which one or more firms control the level of production in an industry.

A high four-firm concentration ratio indicates that most of the sales or output (or whatever) in the industry are accounted for by the four largest firms. It also suggests the presence of barriers to entry into the market. However, it does not necessarily imply that there are only a few firms in the industry. Hence, it is possible to have an industry that is essentially oligopolistic, but in which the number of firms is large. For example, there were 723 firms operating in the photographic equipment and supplies industry in 1982. However, the four largest firms produced 74 percent of the output of the industry.

Historically, four-firm (and eight-firm) concentration ratios were relied upon to assess the degree of competition in an industry. More recently, the Herfindahl–Hirschman Index (HHI) has been used by the U.S. Justice Department to assess the degree of concentration in a particular industry.[4] It has been argued that the HHI provides a more accurate measure of the overall degree of concentration. This is because the HHI takes account of all the firms in the industry, rather just the top four or top eight. The HHI is calculated as the sum of the squares of the market shares (percentages) of each of the firms in the industry. The formula for the HHI is:

$$HHI = S_1^2 + S_2^2 + S_3^2 + \ldots + S_n^2$$

where S_1 through S_n are the market shares of each of the n firms.

> **SECTION RECAP**
> Measures of market concentration, such as concentration ratios and the Herfindahl–Hirschman Index are used to determine the extent to which an industry is dominated by one or a few firms.

Table 2 illustrates the effect that use of the HHI has on measures of concentration relative to the four-firm concentration ratio. According to guidelines

---

[4]Market concentration is one of the pieces of information used in determining whether a firm is in violation of the antitrust laws. See Chapter 13 for further discussion.

TABLE 1

Four-firm and eight-firm concentration ratios for selected industries, 1982

SIC Code	Industry	Four-Firm Concentration Ratio	Eight-Firm Concentration Ratio
2043	Cereal breakfast foods	86%	D
2066	Chocolate and cocoa products	75%	89%
2067	Chewing gum	95%	D
2284	Thread mills	61%	77%
2296	Tire cord and fabric	81%	99%
2322	Men's and boys' underwear	64%	81%
3211	Flat glass	85%	D
3333	Primary zinc	75%	100%
3353	Aluminum sheet, plate, and foil	74%	90%
3711	Motor vehicles and car bodies	92%	97%
3721	Aircraft	64%	81%
3996	Hard-surface floor coverings	99%	99+%

Note: D = Data withheld to avoid disclosing data for individual companies.
Source: U.S. Department of Commerce, 1982 Census of Manufactures, Subject Series, MC82-S-7, *Concentration Ratios in Manufacturing*; Washington, DC, 1986.

developed by the Justice Department, a market with an index of less than 1000 is unconcentrated, a market with an index between 1000 and 1800 is moderately concentrated, and a market with an index in excess of 1800 is highly concentrated.

Short-Run Profit Maximization: Competition Among Rivals

Unlike the other market structures we have analyzed—perfect competition, monopolistic competition, and monopoly—the profit-maximizing decision of an oligopolist is difficult to analyze graphically. This is a direct result of the

TABLE 2

A comparison of the four-firm concentration ratio and the Herfindahl–Hirschman Index

Industry Structure	Four-Firm Concentration Ratio	Herfindahl–Hirschman Index
Single firm	100	10,000
4 equal-sized firms	100	2,500
6 equal-sized firms	67	1,667
8 equal-sized firms	50	1,250
10 equal-sized firms	40	1,000

The Economist's Tool Kit

Game Theory and the Prisoner's Dilemma

The mutual interdependence of the firms in an oligopoly is similar to the problem faced by two individuals involved in a game. In chess, for example, one player's choice of which piece to move depends, in large part, on how she thinks her opponent will respond. In other games, such as cards, players must select strategies that they believe will yield the greatest payoff given their opponents' potential actions.

The study of game theory is devoted to the analysis of strategic behavior under uncertainty. In part, game theory allows one to identify the solution to a problem that achieves a particular goal. For example, one strategy is to behave so as to minimize the maximum loss that could be incurred in a particular situation. Alternatively, the player may wish to maximize the minimum gain possible.

One particular game, which closely resembles the situation faced by many oligopolistic firms, is known as the *prisoner's dilemma*. In its generic form, two individuals must select one of two behaviors. However, the payoff associated with each behavior depends upon what the other player does. As an illustration, consider the situation faced by two firms who comprise a market. Depending upon how each firm prices its output, each firm will earn varying levels of profit. The possible payoffs are shown in Table 3, which is referred to as a *payoff matrix*.

Table 3 indicates that if both firms charge a price of $10, each will earn $200 of profit (payoff 1). In addition, if both firms raise their price to $12, each firm's profits will increase to $250 (payoff 3). However, the individual firm's profits will be greatest if it holds its price constant and the other firm raises its price (payoffs 2a and 2b). Each firm must decide whether to charge $10 or $12 per unit. (This is the dilemma.) If firm A decides to charge $12 and firm B follows suit, both firms win. However, if firm B charges $10, firm A loses. So long as one firm believes that the other may lower its price, each firm maximizes its minimum payoff (profit) by charging a price of $10. In this situation, this is the equilibrium strategy.

mutual interdependence of the firms in the industry. In response to a decision by one firm to increase (or decrease) the price of its product, the other firms may alter their prices as well.

Because of this mutual interdependence, competition among firms may lead to reduced profits for everyone in the long run. To see that this is the case, consider the following example. Assume that an industry is made up of only two firms, A and B, each of which is initially operating at a profit-maximizing level of output (and is earning economic profits). Now assume that firm A lowers its price in an effort to increase its sales and profits. Initially, when firm A lowers its price it attracts customers away from firm B. So long as marginal revenue is greater than marginal cost for the additional units sold, firm A's profits increase in the short run at the expense of firm B. However, the price cut by firm A and the resulting increase in its profits creates an incentive for firm B to cut its price as well in an attempt to regain lost profits. If firm B responds to firm A's price reduction by lowering its price, each firm will produce roughly the same share of market output that it did initially. However, the price the firms receive for each unit of output will be lower. Assuming that average costs have remained the same, each firm's economic profits have declined.

TABLE 3
Payoff matrix for two competing firms

			Firm B Price			
			$10		$12	
Firm A	P r i c e	$10	$200, (A) (payoff 1)	$200 (B)	$300, (A) (payoff 2a)	$150 (B)
		$12	$150, (A) (payoff 2b)	$300 (B)	$250, (A) (payoff 3)	$250 (B)

Note that the situation in Table 3 is very similar to that faced by firms A and B in our previous example. In particular, if each firm originally sells its output at a per-unit price of $12 and either firm lowers its price, the eventual outcome will be a loss of profits for both firms—assuming the other firm follows suit. (Note that if the second firm does not follow suit, its profits will fall even further.) If instead, each firm is initially charging a per-unit price of $10, an increase in price by either firm will cause its profits to fall. The other firm will increase its profits by continuing to charge the original price of $10. Clearly, the actions of the firms are mutually interdependent.

Figures 8 (a) and 8 (b) illustrate the situation described above. Initially each firm is producing Q_1 units of output and charging a price of P_1. Because price (which equals average revenue) is greater than average total cost, each firm is earning an economic profit. If firm A lowers its price to P_2, it will attract buyers away from firm B and sell more output. Firm A is now operating at point 2 in Figure 8 (a). The decrease in price by firm A has the effect of shifting firm B's demand curve to the left, to D_2 in Figure 8 (b). Firm B is now selling less output at the original price of P_1. However, firm B will respond by lowering its price to P_2 to regain its lost customers. As firm B lowers its price, firm A's demand curve shifts left to D_2 in Figure 8 (a). Firm A's output falls back to Q_1. Once all adjustments have taken place, each firm's output level is unchanged, but price and profits have declined.

This action–reaction scenario suggests that competition among oligopolists may lead to reduced profits for each firm. Since competition makes each firm worse off, it is a no-win situation. This motivates firms to look for other strategies to increase economic profits. Not surprisingly, cooperation among firms is an attractive alternative.

It is in the interest of oligopolists to agree to work together to jointly set price and output in the market. If they do, the industry, in effect, becomes a

SECTION RECAP
As a result of mutual interdependence, oligopolistic firms that attempt to *(continued)*

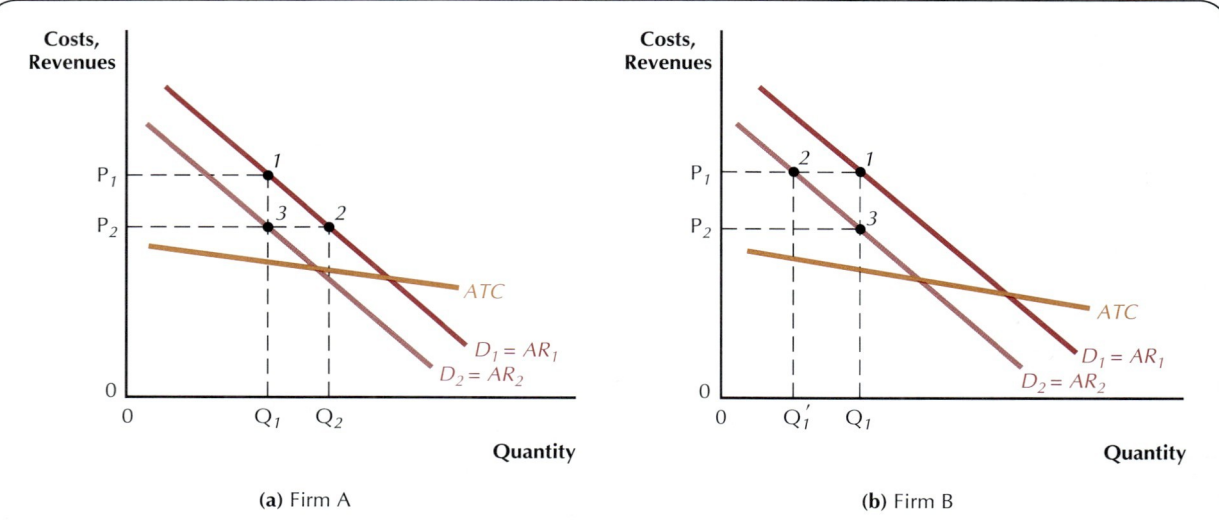

FIGURE 8
The interdependence of pricing decisions by firms in oligopoly. *(a) Firm A (b) Firm B.* Figures 8 (a) and 8 (b) illustrate the situation for two firms—A and B—that each produce Q_1 units of output and charge a price of P_1. Because $P = AR > ATC$, each firm is earning an economic profit. Assuming firm A lowers its price to P_2, it will attract buyers away from firm B and will move to point 2 in Figure 8 (a). The decrease in price by firm A has the effect of shifting firm B's demand curve to the left, to D_2 in Figure 8 (b). Firm B will respond by lowering its price to P_2 to regain its lost customers. As firm B lowers its price, firm A's demand curve shifts left to D_2 in Figure 8 (a) and firm A's output falls back to Q_1. Once all adjustments have taken place, each firm's output level is unchanged, but price and profits have declined.

SECTION RECAP
(continued)
compete on the basis of price will end up losing profits. This creates an incentive for firms to cooperate with one another.

shared monopoly. Consider again the situation of firms A and B. If the firms agree to divide up the market among themselves, each firm can produce the level of output that maximizes profits. Because they have agreed not to compete with each other on the basis of price, each firm can continue to earn economic profits over the long run, provided demand and cost conditions do not change. Entry barriers prevent competition from others and economic profits persist in the long run.

Alternatives to Competition
Collusion Among Rivals

We have assumed that the objective of all firms in all markets is to maximize profits. Yet we have learned that competition limits the opportunity to earn economic profit. Thus, there is an incentive for a firm to escape competition in any market setting. **Collusion** refers to the act of firms working together (cooperating) to establish the price and level of output in a particular market. By colluding with each other, firms hope to escape or at least lessen the pressures of competition. However, the opportunity to successfully collude is dependent upon the structure of the market in which firms operate.

Perfectly competitive markets are characterized by a large number of small firms. The firms in the market have absolutely no market power and take price

Collusion
The act of firms working together (cooperating) to establish the price and level of output in a particular market.

as given. The fact that each firm produces a homogeneous product eliminates the possibility of escaping competition through product differentiation. In addition, because of the large number of firms, it would be extremely difficult if not impossible to coordinate efforts to restrict market output as a means of forcing up the market price. The only alternative available to competitive firms is to reduce costs, which results in short-run economic profits.

Monopolistic competition affords the individual firm greater opportunities for escaping the pressures of competition. Product differentiation and, in some cases, the effects of regulation lessen the competitive pressures faced by the firm. However, the facts that firms are small relative to the market, that there is usually a large number of firms, and that entry is relatively easy, all serve to maintain a fair degree of competitive pressure. Just as in the case of perfect competition, the likelihood of successful collusion is extremely small.

We have already seen that the costs of competition among oligopolists can be high—loss of market share and economic profit. Hence, there is a strong tendency for firms in this situation to seek out alternatives to competition. Cooperation, and in particular, collusion, is one such alternative. The fact that oligopoly is characterized by a small number of firms enhances the attractiveness of this alternative.

Explicit collusion among firms is illegal in the United States. Specific laws have been passed (which are discussed in Chapter 13) that prohibit firms from working together to set price and the level of output in a particular market. Collusion nonetheless occurs and can take a variety of forms. These include the formation of cartels, price leadership, and secret agreements among firms.

Cartels   A **cartel** consists of a group of firms that have explicitly and openly agreed to work together to set the price that will be charged in a particular market. A cartel also sets production quotas for each participant. The quotas are designed to ensure that price is not driven below the agreed-upon level. The most widely recognized example of a cartel is the Organization of Petroleum Exporting Countries (OPEC). OPEC is legally able to operate because it is an international organization and is not prohibited by any international law. The International Tin Cartel is another example of a cartel that operated successfully for many years.

Cartel
A group of firms that have explicitly and openly agreed to work together to set the price that will be charged in a particular market.

Price Leadership   **Price leadership** refers to a situation in which one firm in an industry establishes the market price and the remaining firms in the industry follow suit. Successful price leadership requires implicit agreement among firms as to who the price leader will be. A number of instances of price leadership have occurred in the United States. U.S. Steel historically took the lead in setting price in the steel industry.[5] R. J. Reynolds assumed a similar role in the tobacco industry. Price leadership is usually the result of dominance in the industry by one firm. However, instances can also arise in which the least-cost producer in the industry emerges as the price leader.

The price leader benefits from its role in two ways. First, it is able to set a price that enables it to earn economic profit without concern about potential price reductions by rival firms. In addition, the price leader can exercise its

Price leadership
A situation in which one firm in an industry establishes the market price and the remaining firms in the industry follow suit.

---

[5]Interestingly, however, the price of steel did not necessarily change every time U.S. Steel changed its price. In some cases, when the new price was announced, the other firms did not follow. The announced price was then rolled back to the original price.

price-setting power in such a way that the other firms in the industry are able to make a small profit as well. The continued presence of the smaller firms shields the dominant firm from charges of monopolization of the market or possession of excessive market power.

Price leadership, although not necessarily intentional, is observed on a regular basis in the automobile industry. Each year, one or another of the three major U.S. producers announces its price changes for the upcoming model year. The remaining firms follow with announcements, usually a week or so later. Generally, the price adjustments are strikingly similar. In this case, the firms in the industry take turns being the price leader. This same general phenomenon is also observed with respect to rebate programs. Once one of three manufacturers announces a set of rebates for selected models, the other manufacturers are usually quick to follow with similar programs.

Secret Agreements Situations have arisen in which firms have worked together, secretly (and illegally) to control the price in a particular industry. In one of the more famous cases, a group of firms, including Westinghouse and General Electric, worked together to fix prices in the heavy-duty electric equipment industry. Once the plan was uncovered, the Justice Department brought suit against the offending companies. The trial that followed resulted in fines for twenty-nine companies and jail terms for many of the individuals involved.

Regardless of the specific form of collusion, the result is that firms in the industry are able to act jointly as a monopolist. By cooperating with each other, they are able to maximize the joint profits in the industry. However, because a number of firms are working together, they must agree on a number of issues including what the price should be and the level of output each firm should produce. Depending upon the nature of the output produced, such agreements can be quite complicated.

At one extreme, firms producing a homogeneous product have a rather simple problem. Once the profit-maximizing price is determined, it is simply a matter of determining what share of the market each firm will control. At the other extreme, if the firms produce a differentiated product, there will almost certainly be a set of prices rather than a single price. Dividing up market shares will consequently be more difficult to agree upon.

SECTION RECAP
Collusion enables firms to escape the pressures of competition and can increase economic profits. There are a number of forms of collusion including cartels, price leadership, and secret agreements.

Successful Collusion

For a collusive agreement to be successful, it is important that all of the firms in the industry implement the terms of the agreement. However, there is a strong incentive for individual firms to cheat on the agreement. Consequently, the industry must continually monitor the behavior of individual firms.

Cheating is a considerable obstacle to successful collusion. This results from the conflict between the individual firm's welfare and the welfare of the group as a whole. Each firm in the agreement recognizes that there are benefits from collusion and benefits from cheating on the agreement once it has been reached. Whether a given firm actually cheats on the agreement will depend on the benefits and costs of doing so.

On the one hand, a collusive agreement benefits each firm by protecting it from the adverse effects of competition from its rivals. Adherence to the agreement by all of the firms involved ensures that the joint profits of the parties to the agreement are maximized. So long as all firms continue to cooperate, and demand and cost conditions are not adversely affected, economic profits will persist over the long run.

On the other hand, cheating offers a single firm the possibility of additional benefits. If the other participating firms all adhere to the terms of the agreement, the remaining firm can cheat on the agreement by lowering price, and increasing output and its share of profits. To the extent that the firm does not cheat, these potential benefits are lost.

Cheating can take a number of forms. For example, a firm might offer secret discounts to buyers and increase its sales as a result. So long as price remains above the average total cost of production for all the additional units sold, the firm will increase its profits. The cheating firm can also increase sales by offering a higher level of quality than its competitors at the going price. The provision of extra benefits such as buyer credit and extended warranties can also increase the firm's sales at the expense of its rivals.

Cheating is obviously a major obstacle to successful collusion among firms in an industry. The success of a cooperative agreement among firms depends upon a number of other factors as well. These factors include: 1) the degree of product differentiation, 2) the extent of cost differences among firms, 3) the number of firms involved, and 4) the availability of substitute products produced by firms outside the industry. Market conditions such as the stability of demand — is it increasing or decreasing or staying the same — also affect the ability to successfully collude.

Product differentiation complicates efforts to agree upon prices and the market share to be controlled by each firm. In addition, differences in product quality among firms make it easier for individual firms to hide discounts (cheat on the agreement). As cost differences among firms become larger, identifying a price or set of prices that benefits all the firms becomes more difficult. Once again, cost differences create an incentive to cheat. Finally, as the number of firms in the market increases, it is more difficult to police the agreement and ensure adherence to the agreement by each of the firms involved. It is this fact that renders collusion unworkable in the case of perfect competition or monopolistic competition.

The stability of market demand and its effect on the ability of firms to successfully collude is best illustrated by reference to the near-collapse of OPEC in the mid-1980s. The oil market experienced a large increase in supply and a simultaneous decrease in the rate of growth of demand. The resulting excess supply put substantial downward pressure on oil prices, and many of the members of OPEC began to undercut the cartel's agreed-upon minimum price to bolster their sagging profits. As a consequence, the pump price of gasoline fell in some places to well below a dollar per gallon. Finally, in late 1988, the cartel reached a new agreement to once again reduce output and raise prices in an effort to regain their control of world prices. However, in 1989, evidence suggested that members were already cheating on the new agreement.

SECTION RECAP
The degree to which collusion is successful depends upon a number of factors, including the degree to which firms cheat, the degree of product differentiation, the extent of cost differences among firms, the number of firms involved, and the availability of substitute products produced by firms outside the industry.

Government Regulation and Cartel-Like Behavior

Government regulation has, on occasion, served to strengthen the cartel-like behavior of firms in an oligopoly. This is especially true when regulation results in the establishment of barriers to entry in the industry. Examples of industries in which this has occurred include the Interstate Commerce Commission's regulation of the trucking and railroad industries and the Civil Aeronautics

Board's regulation of the airline industry. In each of these cases, one of the major results of regulation of the industry was the creation of cartel-like conditions which led to significant profits for firms in each industry.

Regulation in each of these industries focused, in part, on the number of firms that enter and compete in the industry. In each case, it was argued that an excess of competition would result in reduced quality of service to the firms' customers. Therefore, entry into the market was restricted. However, the restrictions on entry also allowed firms to work more closely to establish prices and available levels of service. In addition, regulation had the effect of preventing any firm from cheating, since prices were legally enforced. It is interesting to note that these same industries have been the target of deregulation in recent years. The effects of deregulation are discussed in Chapter 13.

Mergers

Mergers between firms can also provide a means of reducing the degree of competition faced by individual firms. There are several types of mergers. A **horizontal merger** is a merger into a single firm of two or more firms producing the same or similar products. The merger of USAir Group, Inc. and Piedmont Airlines, which was initiated in 1987 and completed in 1989, is an example of a horizontal merger. A **vertical merger** is a merger into a single firm of two or more firms at different levels in the chain of production. A merger between a grain distributor and a breakfast food company would be a vertical merger. When two or more firms whose outputs are unrelated merge, it is referred to as a **conglomerate merger**. A merger between an oil company and a retail chain, such as the merger between Mobil Oil and Montgomery Ward, would be a conglomerate merger.

The effect of a merger, in particular, a horizontal or vertical merger, on competition and economic efficiency depends upon the specific market situation. In the case of a horizontal merger, if the merger results in a significantly higher degree of market concentration, it could open the door to collusive behavior on the part of the dominant firms. This is so if for no other reason than because the *potential* for successful collusion is now greater. On the other hand, a horizontal merger can result in the realization of greater economies of scale. To the extent that prices decline as a result of the decrease in costs, consumers could benefit from the merger.

Vertical mergers also have the potential to create substantial competitive advantages for a firm. For example, if a firm takes control of a supplier of a vital input, the firm may experience lower costs in the short run, enabling it to reduce prices. This would benefit consumers, who would be able to purchase the product at a lower price. However, it may also drive other firms out of the market. Recall our earlier discussion about the different barriers to entry. In the long run, it is likely that the firm could establish what amounts to a monopoly position by controlling all or most of the available supply of an input to the production process. Consumers would then bear the costs of the inefficiencies associated with monopoly.

As the foregoing discussion suggests, the ambiguity of the outcome of a particular merger makes the evaluation, and therefore the regulation, of mergers difficult. This difficulty has led to considerable disagreement over the benefits and costs of mergers within our economy and the appropriate policy to adopt with respect to proposed mergers of various types. Over time, the attitude

---

Horizontal merger
A merger into a single firm of two or more firms producing the same or similar products.

Vertical merger
A merger into a single firm of two or more firms at different levels in the chain of production.

Conglomerate merger
Two or more firms whose outputs are unrelated merge.

SECTION RECAP
Like collusion, government regulation and merger can enable firms to escape or reduce the pressures of competition. However, there may be benefits to both consumers and firms, as when product quality is improved, or production costs and therefore prices are reduced.

toward mergers has shifted, and mergers are now treated much more leniently than they once were. The current policy toward mergers is discussed in detail in Chapter 13.

Oligopoly: Economic Profits and Efficiency

Economic Profits

Recall once again that *oligopoly is, in part, a result of barriers to entry. It is possible for firms to earn economic profits in both the short run and the long run. However, economic profits are not guaranteed.* Indeed, many of the oligopolistic industries in the United States have experienced losses over the last decade. Whether a firm actually earns economic profits in the short run depends upon the demand and cost conditions faced by the firm. In this respect, firms in an oligopoly are faced with essentially the same situation as a monopolist. These similarities can extend into the long run as well.

Both the steel and auto industries have been hard hit by the effects of recession and competition from foreign producers in recent years. The steel industry experienced losses as a result of competition from foreign producers, most notably Japan and West Germany, who enjoyed the benefits of more modern production methods that result in lower average costs. In the late 1970s and early 1980s, and again in 1990 and 1991, the auto industry felt the effects of recession and the shift in consumers' tastes toward smaller, more fuel-efficient cars.

Economic Efficiency

The fact that oligopolistic firms are able to exercise considerable economic power suggests that such firms may take advantage of that power and earn economic profits at the expense of efficiency. However, as we have already noted, it is often the case that oligopolies arise as a result of the existence of significant economies of scale. This implies that oligopoly is economically desirable to the extent that the average costs of production are minimized through the existence of a small, as opposed to a large, number of firms in the industry. However, it may or may not be the case that society actually benefits.

The fact that a particular good is produced at the lowest possible average cost does not ensure that the price paid for the good accurately reflects that cost. Indeed, as we have already seen, there is a strong incentive for firms in an oligopoly setting to collude and behave, in effect, like a monopolist. In this case, the price of the good will exceed the marginal cost of production, resulting in allocative inefficiency.

In addition to the potential benefits associated with economies of scale, some economists have argued that as a result of the larger pool of resources which they are able to draw upon, firms in oligopolistic (and monopolistic) markets have a greater ability to invest in research and development (R&D). R&D can lead to increased economies of scale, improved product quality, and new products, all of which can result in improved social welfare.

As the preceding discussion suggests, the ability of oligopolistic firms to earn economic profits is not guaranteed. In addition, the efficiency effects of oligopoly are unclear. In fact, many economists maintain that in certain situations, the fact that an industry is dominated by a few firms may not have any adverse effects on efficiency.

Does It Make Economic Sense?

With a Monopoly on Natural Gas, Why Advertise?

In recent years the natural gas industry has undertaken a program to increase its sales of natural gas. In support of that program, in 1988, regulators in Texas approved a 100 percent increase in the amount of advertising expenses that gas utilities in the state can pass through to their customers.* However, considering the monopoly position that each natural gas utility enjoys in its market territory—natural gas utilities are natural monopolies, a condition that has prompted policymakers to grant a franchise to a single provider of natural gas in each geographic region—it would seem that advertising would be an unnecessary expenditure and would simply cause the price paid by the utility's customers to increase. Indeed, regulatory commissions allow utilities to pass on to customers any costs that have been approved by the commission. In light of these facts it is worth asking, Does advertising for a generic fuel make economic sense?

To analyze this problem, we need to think in terms of the major sources of energy—nuclear, natural gas, hydro-power, coal and oil. (Note that the generation of electricity requires the input of one of these fuels.) Viewed at this broader level, the market for energy consists of a set of competitors that are each vying for market share. Natural gas, for example, has controlled approximately 23 percent of the fuels market over the past decade. Although there may be only one supplier of natural gas in a particular region, there are substitutes for natural gas. For residential customers, electricity is the obvious substitute, although heating oil can also be substituted for natural gas in specific uses. For industrial users, the set of substitutes is larger. As we have already noted, electricity can be produced using nuclear fuel, coal, oil, natural gas, or hydro-electric generation techniques. As a result of competition in the fuels market, the actual number of customers served by a natural gas utility can vary.

The price paid by each of the customers of a natural gas utility reflects (1) the price paid by the utility for the natural gas, and (2) the average costs (fixed and variable) associated with distributing the gas to the utility's customers. The natural gas industry is characterized by significant economies of scale. This is due to the fact that the majority of the costs associated with the provision of natural gas involve the distribution network of pipes that are used to bring the gas from the producer to the purchaser. A large portion of the total costs incurred in the natural gas industry consist of fixed costs.

The share of the total fixed costs borne by an individual customer depends on the total number of customers served and the amount of gas sold. An increase in the number of customers or the amount of gas sold would allow the fixed costs to be spread over a larger number of units of output. This would in turn translate into a lower per-unit price for natural gas. Consequently, it is possible that existing customers could experience a decrease in the cost per unit of natural gas delivered to their door and a decrease in their total natural gas bill. This could occur even with the increase in advertising expenditures that is passed on to the gas company's customers. So long as the reduction in the average costs of serving customers is greater than the increase in average costs attributable to the additional advertising, existing gas customers would benefit from the increased advertising in the form of lower prices.

Only time will tell whether the decision to increase the allowable amount of advertising by natural gas companies was economically justified. However, it is clear that there is a sound theoretical basis for doing so.

*"Natural-Gas Industry Goes on the Marketing Offensive," *Wall Street Journal,* January 23, 1988.

The Theory of Contestable Markets One theory that has received increasing attention over the last few years maintains that oligopoly may be quite efficient due to the competitive pressures that exist despite the small number of firms in the industry. The **theory of contestable markets** maintains that so long as entry and exit are costless, firms will produce at minimum cost and earn no economic profits.

Briefly, costless entry and exit imply that there are potential competitors who could enter the market and operate at the same level of costs as existing firms. Moreover, the potential competitors could leave the market without the loss of capital. Thus, in contestable markets there are no sunk costs. It is also assumed that consumers in contestable markets are not influenced by such factors as brand loyalty and instead will purchase the lowest-priced product available.

In a contestable market, existing firms are faced with the threat of hit-and-run entry by firms outside the industry. Outside firms are able to enter the market, undercut the price of existing firms, and draw customers away from existing firms before the existing firms are able to respond. As soon as economic profits disappear, the new entrants leave. Because of the threat of hit-and-run entry, existing firms are forced to set their prices at the competitive level on a permanent basis. If they do not, they run the risk of attracting entrants and incurring short-run economic losses.

The following two examples illustrate this situation. The first example involves airline service between two cities.[6] Airline equipment, which consists primarily of airplanes, is highly mobile. In effect, entry and exit into specific markets is costless. Thus, airlines can move into and out of markets at minimal cost. The resulting threat of hit-and-run entry puts downward pressure on prices for air travel. Hotels and motels, on the other hand, involve considerable sunk costs (it is not simply a matter of picking up a hotel and moving it to a new location). Thus, the threat of entry, at least in the short run, is much less. The hotel industry is not contestable.

Under the assumption that entry and exit are costless, the number of firms operating in the market, that is, the degree of market concentration, is largely irrelevant. The mere threat of viable competition creates an incentive sufficient to induce existing firms to produce and price efficiently. Although the theory of contestable markets is not applicable in all cases, it nonetheless suggests that in many instances oligopoly and monopoly may better serve society's interest in efficiency than would perfect competition or monopolistic competition.

Because of the potential for inefficiency, the U.S. government has actively sought to exert a degree of control over oligopolistic markets. As we discussed above, direct regulation has been relied on in some instances to control the behavior of firms in a particular industry. At a more general level, a body of law called *antitrust legislation* has been developed that places specific restrictions on the behavior of firms. This legislation, the purpose of which is to prevent the formation of monopolies and excessive market concentration, is one of the major topics of the next chapter.

Theory of contestable markets
So long as entry and exit are costless, firms will produce at minimum cost and earn no economic profits, regardless of the other characteristics of the market.

SECTION RECAP
Oligopolistic firms may or may not earn economic profits in the short run and long run. In addition, the efficiency effects of oligopoly are unclear. The theory of contestable markets suggests that, in fact, the behavior of oligopolistic firms may be similar to that of perfect competitors.

Summary

This chapter has examined the behavior of markets that are characterized by a small number of firms that control the majority of output in the industry. In the extreme case, a single firm controls the market. This type of market

---

[6]This example is taken from Baumol, Panzar, and Willig, *Contestable Markets and the Theory of Industry Structure* (New York: Harcourt Brace Jovanovich, 1982.)

structure is called **monopoly.** The situation in which the market is dominated by a few large firms is called **oligopoly.**

Monopoly and oligopoly are the result of **barriers to entry,** which result in resource immobility and impede the level of competition that exists in affected markets.

It is possible for a monopolist to earn economic profits in both the short run and the long run. However, economic profits are not guaranteed. Although a monopolist acts as a price searcher, its ability to set price is limited by the market demand curve—the monopolist cannot set a price for a level of output that is higher than consumers are willing to pay. Consequently, depending upon demand and cost conditions, it is also possible for a monopolist to incur an economic loss.

A **natural monopoly** is the result of economies of scale. In this case, efficiency is best served by having a single firm produce for the market. One firm can satisfy market demand at a lower average cost than could two or more firms. However, the considerable market power enjoyed by natural monopolists has led to regulation to limit that power and protect the interests of consumers. Regulation of natural monopolies usually relies on **rate-of-return regulation.** This approach involves establishing a price for the good or service in question that simultaneously is fair to the consumer and allows the producer to earn a fair return on investment.

Oligopoly is similar to monopoly to the extent that it is possible for firms to earn economic profits in both the short run and the long run. It also true that oligopoly generally results in an inefficient level of output.

Firms in an oligopolistic setting have a strong incentive to avoid competing with each other. As a consequence, firms seek alternatives to competition. These alternatives often consist of some form of **collusion,** including the formation of **cartels, price leadership,** and the use of **secret agreements** among firms to fix price and limit output.

Government regulation and mergers can both result in cartel-like behavior by firms and allow firms to reduce or avoid competition. Although the purpose of government regulation is to protect the interests of consumers, regulation that limits entry into certain markets may reduce the level of competition and the incentive for firms to price at marginal cost.

Although oligopoly is often associated with an inefficient level of output, economies of scale can result in lower costs than would exist under competitive conditions. Consequently, it may be desirable to have the government intervene in the market by means of direct regulation or through the enforcement of antitrust legislation.

Questions for Thought

Knowledge Questions

1. List and describe the major characteristics of monopoly and oligopoly. How do these two market structures differ from the other market structures we have considered?

2. How is it possible for monopolists and oligopolistic firms to earn long-run economic profits?
3. What is the principle behind rate-of-return regulation and how does it work? What are the advantages and disadvantages of rate-of-return regulation?
4. What are the principal forms of collusion? How does each one work to control price and the level of output in an oligopoly?

Application Questions

5. Assume that you are the economic advisor to a regulatory commission that is in the process of determining the rates to be paid by three separate classes of customers of a natural gas utility. Assume that the rate base is $5 million; operating expenses are $30,000; the rate of return has been set at 10 percent; and marginal cost equals average revenue equals 5¢ at 10 million units of output. Determine the amount of revenues the utility should be allowed to collect. Will this utility be able to produce the efficient level of output and cover costs by charging the same price to customers in all three classes?
6. Many economists and policymakers argue that when a market is characterized as a natural monopoly, regulation is the appropriate policy response. Do you agree or disagree with this view? Does your response differ depending upon the particular situation? Why or why not?
7. In recent years, OPEC has had difficulty ensuring that the individual members abide by the agreed-upon price and output quotas of the cartel. What factors do you think are most responsible?
8. Construct a graph that depicts a monopolist earning economic profits. Now assume that as a result of a shortage of an essential resource, costs increase and force the monopolist to incur a loss. Graphically illustrate the increase in costs and explain what will happen over the long run.

Synthesis Questions

9. "Because of the huge data requirements and the uncertainty as to what the competitively determined equilibrium would be, an unregulated monopoly is preferred to a regulated monopoly." Do you agree or disagree with this statement? Why?
10. The majority of utilities in the United States are privately owned and operated, but subject to rate-of-return regulation. However, some utilities are publicly owned and operated. These publicly owned utilities usually are not controlled by a regulatory commission. In your opinion, which approach is more beneficial to society and why?
11. Construct a demand curve for a single oligopolistic firm that illustrates the mutual interdependence among firms in an oligopolistic market. (Hint: Your demand curve should not be a straight line.)
12. In the chapter it was noted that economies of scale often force a tradeoff between producing efficiently and producing the efficient level of output. Compare and contrast the benefits of producing efficiently and producing the efficient level of output, respectively. Which do you think is more important from the perspective of society's welfare? Why?

OVERVIEW

Our analysis of the economic behavior of firms operating in different market structures has demonstrated that in a market economy, competition is important for the promotion of economically efficient prices and output levels. The absence of competition results in *market failure,* that is, the failure of the market to produce the efficient level of output.

The Regulation of Business Behavior: Policy in Transition

In this chapter we consider three approaches the government can use to attempt to improve market efficiency in the event of market failure: direct regulation, antitrust legislation, and direct government ownership and operation of specific businesses. We will consider the objectives of each approach, its economic ramifications, and the impact that each approach has had on efficiency in the markets where it has been used.

In this chapter we also examine the trend toward deregulation of previously regulated markets and analyze the impacts of deregulation. In the course of our analysis, we identify effects of regulation that may, in fact, argue for deregulation of specific markets.

Before proceeding, it is worth noting that economists are divided on the question of when competitive pressures are weak or nonexistent and, therefore, when and where intervention in the market is desirable. For example, there is considerable disagreement over issues such as whether the "bigness" of a firm, in and of itself, implies a lack of competition and is

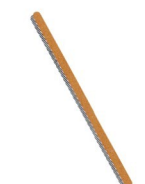

CHAPTER 13

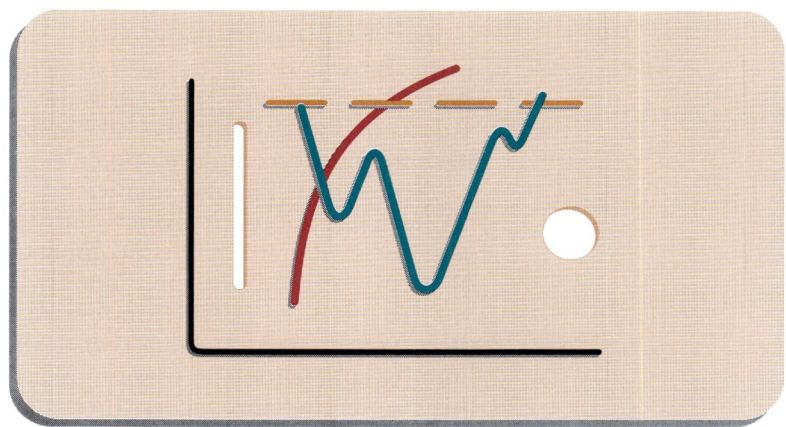

therefore bad from an economic efficiency perspective. Two questions you should ask yourself as you read this chapter are, Does the policy being discussed appear to be warranted on efficiency or equity grounds, and What have the actual results of the policy been?

Learning Objectives

After reading and studying this chapter, you will be able to:

1. Identify market conditions that can lead to market failure and government intervention.
2. Discuss the alternatives available to policymakers when a lack of competition results in inefficient market outcomes.
3. Explain how government ownership addresses the problem of market failure.
4. Describe the evolution of antitrust legislation and its impact on monopolies and oligopolies.
5. Discuss the potential problems associated with the direct regulation and the rationale for deregulation of previously regulated markets.
6. Summarize the potential benefits of deregulation.

Lack of Competition and Market Outcomes

Lack of Competition Causes Inefficiency

A lack of competition can result in long-run economic inefficiency. In Chapters 11 and 12 we saw that in imperfectly competitive markets, the equilibrium output level is generally too low (allocatively inefficient) and the equilibrium price is too high. Long-run economic inefficiency is referred to as **market failure**.[1]

Traditionally, the degree of competition in a particular market has been viewed as being closely related to the number of firms in the market. The monopoly market structure constitutes the polar opposite of perfect competition. The monopolist is the only producer in the industry; it is constrained only by the market demand curve when setting price. As we saw in Chapter 12, an unconstrained monopolist produces an inefficient level of output relative to the perfectly competitive market.

Oligopolistic markets are often characterized by a lack of competition as well. Consequently, the general results associated with monopoly — a level of output that is below the economically efficient level and a price that is too high — have traditionally been associated with oligopoly. However, more recently, economic theories such as the theory of contestable markets have raised serious questions about the validity of this long-held view.[2] The implications of these more recent developments are explored later in the chapter.

The potential market inefficiencies associated with monopoly and oligopoly have been of much greater concern to policymakers than the inefficiencies associated with monopolistic competition. In part, this is due to the importance of monopoly and oligopoly markets relative to the value of all goods and services produced in the economy. Also, as we noted in Chapter 11, much of the policy directed at monopolistically competitive markets has focused on limiting competition in these markets rather than increasing it. The bulk of this chapter therefore focuses on the approaches that policymakers have taken to address the potential lack of competition associated with monopoly and oligopoly.

Can Market Failure Be Corrected?

Can market failure be corrected? The answer is a qualified yes. According to economic theory, appropriately designed policies can result in a more efficient level of output than would occur in the absence of such policies. In effect, policies can be designed that force producers to provide the economically efficient level of output. However, efforts to remedy market failures can also take us farther away from the economically efficient outcome. Indeed, economists and policymakers increasingly have questioned the actual gains associated with intervention in many markets.

When market failure occurs, an opportunity exists for government to take action to improve upon the market outcome. A quick glance at the historical

Market failure
The forces of supply and demand do not yield the economically efficient level of output.

SECTION RECAP
A lack of competition in a market can lead to market failure, that is, an ineffi-
(continued)

---

[1]Other sources of market failure also exist. The most important of these — public goods, externalities, and common property resources — are discussed in Chapter 19. For the remainder of this chapter, market failure is used to refer to the case in which, due to a lack of competition, firms produce an inefficient level of output.

[2]For a review of the theory of contestable markets, see Chapter 12, pp. 324–25.

record shows that government has not been shy about assuming this role. The substantial body of antitrust legislation, the large number of administrative agencies created to regulate specific industries and activities, and the vast body of regulations these agencies have developed are all evidence of government attempts to alter market outcomes. While the specific reasons for regulation vary, *economic efficiency has traditionally been a major objective of government intervention in markets.*

> **SECTION RECAP**
> *(continued)*
> cient level of output. Government has employed a variety of measures to remedy market failure.

Collective Decision-Making Options

The government can use three alternatives to influence economic activity: 1) direct government ownership, 2) the establishment and enforcement of legislation to promote a competitive environment, and 3) direct regulation of firm behavior. In all three cases, the actions involved affect, either directly or indirectly, the exercise of **property rights** by private individuals. Consequently, before we examine these various policy options, it is important that we have a clear understanding of what is meant by the term *property rights*.

> **Property rights**
> The legally sanctioned control that an individual exercises over a collection of goods, resources, and services.

Definition of Property Rights

The concept of property rights refers to the legally sanctioned control that an individual exercises over a collection of goods, resources, and services. For example, in a capitalist economy such as the United States, individuals possess the property right to their labor skills. Similarly, when a person purchases a productive resource such as land, he or she is able to exercise a property right (within legal limits) over that land. The same is true for capital and technological innovations.

Society determines, through its system of laws, how property rights are to be established and exercised. Property rights are continually exercised and exchanged in day-to-day transactions. In the context of production, producers obtain the property rights to labor through the payment of wages and salaries. The goods produced are then sold at the market price. In the cases of monopoly and oligopoly, and to a lesser extent monopolistic competition, that price may exceed the costs of production. In such cases, the corresponding level of output falls short of the efficient level. Society may, therefore, determine that it is in the interest of economic efficiency and social welfare to limit, or otherwise control, the property rights exercised by producers.

Government Ownership of Business

One means of remedying market failure is to substitute government ownership and operation of industry for that of the private sector. This approach is more widespread in other economies than in the United States. In many socialist economies, for example, most productive resources are owned by the government. However, the federal, state, and local governments in the United States have on occasion opted to own and operate specific businesses in lieu of private ownership combined with some form of legislated or regulatory control.

Government-owned businesses, known as **public enterprises**, are usually found in situations perceived to be natural monopolies. State and local governments own and operate utilities such as water and sewage treatment, and

> **Public enterprise**
> A government-owned business.

to a lesser extent, electric and natural gas utilities. The United States Postal Service and the Tennessee Valley Authority are examples of federally owned businesses.

Policy Objectives   A number of objectives are associated with government ownership of business. The most important of these are: (1) to ensure that the good or service is provided at a competitive price, (2) to ensure that the product meets minimum quality standards, and (3) to ensure that the good or service is available to all who need or desire it.

In some instances, production of a particular good or service may require substantial capital outlays that private industry is not willing to undertake. If the government feels that the good or service is socially beneficial, the government may choose to undertake production of the good. Public transportation and municipally owned water companies are all good examples. In other cases, although private business may be willing to undertake production of the good, policymakers may feel that greater control could be exercised, and greater efficiencies achieved, through public ownership. This may occur when it is believed that the costs incurred in monitoring and enforcing restrictions on privately owned firms would be excessive.

Lack of Competitive Pressure   One of the most obvious drawbacks associated with government ownership of business is the lack of competitive pressure. We have already noted that in most instances government ownership involves a monopoly. In addition, there are usually legislated restrictions on entry by private firms into the industry. Consequently, the only pressure to produce efficiently comes from within the organization and, to a lesser extent, from voters.

One example in which competitive pressures have come to bear on a government-owned business is in the overnight shipment of mail. A number of privately owned firms including Federal Express, Emery, UPS, and DHL have entered this market in recent years. The result has been increased competition for a share of the overnight-delivery market and mail service in general. While the United States Postal Service has experienced a decline in business as a result of the creation of this specialized market, consumers have clearly benefited. Indeed, the Postal Service lowered overnight postage rates from $10.75 to $8.75 in 1989, presumably due to competition.[3]

Although economic theorists have shown that under certain circumstances publicly owned firms can generate the same results that would occur in a competitive environment,[4] concerns about the prospects for efficiency resulting from government ownership of business are noteworthy. In particular, the objectives of the firms' managers and problems such as the information needs associated with a government-owned monopoly raise questions about the actual degree of efficiency that can be realized.

Political Issues   It is not clear whether government ownership actually results in an economically efficient outcome. In particular, questions arise concerning the motivations of politicians. Public ownership of business is ultimately the

---

[3]It is interesting to note that, at approximately the same time, the Postal Service raised its rates for first-class postage.
[4]See S. Breyer, *Regulation and Its Reform* (Cambridge, MA: Harvard, 1982), p. 182 and the references cited therein.

result of an act by the governing political body. Public ownership may be pursued for the benefits it will generate for specific segments of society rather than society as a whole. In addition, concerns have been expressed about how staffing decisions for government-owned firms are made. This concern is reflected in Ambrose Bierce's definition of a lighthouse as a "tall building on the seashore in which the government maintains a lamp and the friend of a politician."[5] Finally, the possibility exists that the staff of the government-owned firm may use the firm as a vehicle to further objectives other than economic efficiency.

SECTION RECAP
Government has three alternatives when it wants to influence economic activity: direct ownership, legislation, and regulation. The overall effect of direct ownership on the efficiency of a market is not clear.

Establishment and Enforcement of Rules for a Competitive Environment

A second approach to ensuring economic efficiency in the event of market failure involves the imposition of laws concerning the accumulation and exercise of specific types of property rights. A large body of law, known as **antitrust legislation**, has been developed over time. The purpose of this legislation has been to establish rules that firms must follow in their decisions on production, how large the firm will be, and other relevant factors. Of particular importance are the restrictions on the size a particular firm can assume relative to the industry in which it operates. Laws have been developed that limit the ability of firms to acquire competitors and accumulate additional property rights to productive resources.

Antitrust legislation
A body of law that establishes rules firms must follow in their decisions on production, how large the firm will be, and other relevant factors that influence the efficiency of market outcomes.

Historical Development of Antitrust Legislation   One of the major characteristics of an oligopolistic industry is the high degree of interdependence among firms. We saw in Chapter 12 that interdependence creates an incentive for firms to avoid competing with each other. In the extreme, firms may form cartels or other similar collusive arrangements to avoid competition. Firms involved in these interactions conspire to restrict output and raise price in an effort to maximize profits. In essence, the firms behave collectively as a monopoly supplier of the good or service in question.

One of the earliest forms of such behavior in the United States entailed the formation of **trusts**. A trust consists of a group of firms that agree to work together to restrict the level of total output in their efforts to maximize profits. In effect, the firms in a trust act as a monopolist.

Trust
A group of firms that agree to work together to restrict total output in order to maximize profits.

The *Sherman Antitrust Act,* passed in 1890, was designed to counteract the effects of trusts by prohibiting the formation and operation of trusts. In particular, the Sherman Act states that "every contract, combination in the form of a trust or otherwise, or conspiracy, in restraint of trade or commerce among the several States, or with foreign nations" is illegal. It also states that any person or group of individuals who attempts to monopolize trade between the states or with foreign nations is guilty of a felony.

Several other important pieces of antitrust legislation followed the Sherman Antitrust Act. The *Clayton Act,* passed in 1914, was intended to strengthen the Sherman Act by prohibiting specific monopolistic practices. Outlawed practices include (1) price discrimination[6] that is not justified by cost differences, (2) the use of exclusive, or *tying contracts* (which require the buyer to purchase

---
[5]Breyer, p. 182.
[6]Price discrimination, which was discussed in Chapter 12, refers to the practice of charging different customers different prices for the same good or service in an effort to increase revenues and profits.

other goods or services from the seller of the good in question and not from competitors), (3) the acquisition of stock in competing companies if that acquisition would lessen competition, and (4) the establishment of interlocking directorates (in which the same individual sits on the board of directors of two or more competing firms) if the result would be a lessening of competition.

The *Federal Trade Commission Act*, which was also enacted in 1914, established the Federal Trade Commission (FTC). The FTC is responsible for investigating charges of anticompetitive practices and prosecuting individuals or firms charged with unfair practices.

The *Robinson–Patman Act* of 1936, the *Wheeler–Lea Act* of 1938, and the *Celler–Kefauver* Act of 1950 all amended the Clayton Act in various ways. The Robinson–Patman Act broadened the Clayton Act's restrictions on price discrimination. The Wheeler–Lea Act focused on unfair or deceptive practices and, in particular, false or deceptive advertising. The Celler–Kefauver Act dealt primarily with mergers. Specifically, Celler–Kefauver disallowed vertical and conglomerate mergers that resulted in a substantial lessening of competition. Recall that a vertical merger involves the combining of firms that operate at different stages in the production process. For example, the purchase of a steel company by an auto manufacturer would constitute a vertical merger. A conglomerate merger occurs when firms producing unrelated products combine to form a single company. Horizontal mergers, which involve firms producing the same product, had already been addressed in the Clayton Act.

Impact of Antitrust Legislation   The actual impact of antitrust legislation has varied over time. In large part, this is due to the varied interpretations that courts have applied to these statutes. In particular, over time there has been disagreement as to whether bigness, per se, is a violation of the antitrust statutes or whether the behavior of the firm should be of paramount concern. These shifts in interpretation are best illustrated by reference to a series of landmark court cases.

Bigness versus Behavior.   The first set of cases involved the American Tobacco Company (1911), Standard Oil (1911), and U.S. Steel (1920). In the course of hearing these cases, courts developed the doctrine of the **rule of reason**, which stated that only business practices that were considered unfair (such as pricing below cost to drive competitors out of business) or illegal could be considered unreasonable. Businesses guilty of such practices would be in violation of the Sherman Act. In the cases involving the American Tobacco Company and Standard Oil, the Supreme Court maintained that the behavior of each company was clearly unreasonable because they had engaged in unreasonable restraints on trade. Therefore they were in violation of the Sherman Act. However, in a case brought against U.S. Steel, the court held that although U.S. Steel controlled approximately 60 percent of the market, it did not behave in an unreasonable manner. Therefore, U.S. Steel was not found to be in violation of the Sherman Act.

The rule of reason focused on the behavior of firms rather than solely on their size. However, in 1945, the Supreme Court reversed itself in a case involving ALCOA. Specifically, the Court ruled that the mere size of a firm could and, in the case of ALCOA with 90 percent of the aluminum market, did constitute a violation of the Sherman Act.

Rule of reason
Only business practices that are considered unfair or illegal should be considered unreasonable.

The Court's ruling in the ALCOA case constituted a major departure from previously held views on the distinction between mere size and the behavior of the firm. The ALCOA decision raised questions about the legality of any firm holding a significant share of the total market. Since the ALCOA case, however, views have moderated and behavior has once again become the more crucial issue. Two important cases, involving IBM and AT&T, illustrate this change.

The Justice Department first filed suit against IBM in 1969, alleging that IBM "attempted to monopolize and has monopolized . . . the general purpose computer and peripheral equipment industry." The suit charged that in addition to using anticompetitive techniques, such as pricing schemes designed to discourage the entry and reduce the competitiveness of producers of peripheral equipment for computers (for example, software), IBM controlled over 70 percent of the market for mainframe computers.

During this time, IBM was also involved in a number of civil suits brought by individual firms. In many of these cases, IBM either won the case outright or reached a settlement agreed upon by all the involved parties. Then, in 1982, the Justice Department dropped its case against IBM, concluding that IBM no longer monopolized the computer industry. This decision reflected a changing attitude toward the existence and behavior of large firms and the ability of the government to fashion a result more efficient than that which could be determined by the market.

Another recent major antitrust case involved AT&T's monopolization of the telecommunications industry. A series of suits initiated by the federal government culminated in a suit brought in 1974. In that suit, the Justice Department argued that AT&T should be broken up, charging that the company was using its monopoly over local markets to retain control of the long-distance market by preventing potential competitors from hooking up to local transmission lines.

In what many observers considered a surprising move, AT&T agreed, in 1982, to dissolve its existing structure. Specifically, AT&T agreed to divest itself of parts of Western Electric (its equipment manufacturer) and its local telephone companies. In return, AT&T was allowed to retain its long-distance service operations and most of Western Electric and was granted permission to enter the data communications (information services) market.

While the AT&T breakup can be considered at least a partial victory for competition, it is important to note that the case against AT&T centered primarily on the firm's behavior, rather than on its size. The IBM case focused primarily on IBM's size relative to the industry, and was ultimately found to be without merit. In a case brought against the Du Pont Company in 1947 (and decided in 1956), it was argued that Du Pont held a virtual monopoly in the cellophane market. However, by interpreting the cellophane market to include all substitutes for cellophane, such as wax paper and aluminum foil, the court concluded that Du Pont was innocent of any wrongdoing. Each of these cases points to a clear trend away from the emphasis on the size of a firm relative to the market in which it operates. In the AT&T and IBM cases, the decision ultimately centered on the firm's behavior. In the Du Pont case, the pivotal issue centered on defining the relevant market.

Merger. Efforts by the government to control the market power of firms have also focused on mergers. Recall that the Clayton Act and Celler–Kefauver

Act addressed the practice of horizontal, and vertical and conglomerate mergers, respectively. Horizontal and vertical mergers were discouraged by the government as recently as the early 1970s. Two cases exemplify the government's earlier position. In 1962, the government blocked a merger between Brown Shoe and Kinney Shoe, although they ranked only third and eighth in the industry, respectively. In 1966, the Supreme Court found a merger between Von's Grocery and Shopping Bag, the third- and sixth-largest supermarket chains in Los Angeles, to be illegal, citing concern over a "trend towards concentration," although the firms had a combined share of only 7.5 percent of the market.

For a time, the FTC and the Justice Department also vigorously pursued efforts to block conglomerate mergers when it was felt that domination of a market would result. In these cases, suit was brought on the grounds that the proposed merger had the *potential* to threaten competition in the affected markets. Almost half of the cases brought by the government in the 1960s and early 1970s were successful. However, after 1973, the burden of proof was placed on the government to show that the proposed merger would *actually* reduce or eliminate competition. This change in the burden of proof substantially reduced the ability of the government to block conglomerate mergers.

Since 1973, government actions designed to block potential mergers have dropped significantly. Conglomerate mergers have drawn considerably less attention. Since the early 1980s, many vertical and horizontal mergers have been given approval as well. For example, between 1982 and 1986, the Federal Trade Commission and the Justice Department brought actions against only fifty-six of the more than 7700 mergers that were reported.[7]

Since 1982, the Justice Department has relied upon new sets of guidelines, including the use of the Herfindahl–Hirschman Index (HHI),[8] to gauge the effects on market concentration of potential vertical and horizontal mergers. The five-part process established by the 1982 Guidelines for evaluating horizontal mergers includes 1) identification of the relevant market involved, 2) calculation of the HHI before and after the merger, 3) evaluation of the likelihood of entry into the market by new firms, 4) evaluation of other factors that might affect the likelihood of successful collusion, and 5) evaluation of any efficiency effects resulting from the proposed merger.

The switch to the new guidelines has resulted in a tendency toward a more lenient view of mergers than was the case previously. This approach reflects, in part, the effects of the theory of contestable markets that was discussed in Chapter 12. Recall that a market is contestable if it is possible for firms to enter and leave the market at minimal cost. This threat of hit-and-run entry forces existing firms in the industry to set prices at the competitive level. Mergers between firms in a contestable market should not have an effect on the ability of firms to sustain long-run economic profits or the efficiency of the new equilibrium.

The new approach to mergers is also indicative of a clear shift in views on how the size of the firm affects the potential for competition and the economic

---

[7]S. C. Salop, "Symposium on Mergers and Antitrust," *Journal of Economic Perspectives*, Vol. 1, No. 2, pp. 3–12.

[8]For a review of the mechanics of the HHI, see Chapter 12, pp. 314–15.

efficiency of the resulting market equilibrium. This new attitude is exemplified by the merger between Chrysler and American Motors, which was announced in March 1987 and finalized in the fall of that year. Other examples of significant mergers that have occurred in recent years include the merger of USAir Group, Inc., and Piedmont Airlines, the acquisition of Ozark Airlines by TWA, the merger of Northwest and Republic Airlines, the takeover of Kraft by Phillip Morris, and the merger of R.J. Reynolds and Nabisco. However, it is also worth noting that the Justice Department blocked the proposed acquisitions of Dr. Pepper by Coca-Cola and Seven-Up by PepsiCo.

Many analysts view the new merger guidelines as a more economically defensible approach to merger policy. By focusing on such questions as ease of entry into the market, the potential benefits with respect to cost savings, and the likelihood of successful collusion, attention is focused on the efficiency implications of the proposed merger. Although disagreement still exists over matters such as the level of the HHI that constitutes excessive market concentration, the general conclusion is that the new guidelines have resulted in a more efficient approach to policy on mergers.

SECTION RECAP
Antitrust legislation addresses issues including trusts, competitive practices, size and behavior of firms, and mergers between firms. Over time, there has been considerable variation in the interpretation and enforcement of specific antitrust laws.

Regulation of Firm Behavior

A third approach to addressing market failure is the use of direct regulation. This approach, most often associated with natural monopolies, was analyzed at some length in Chapter 12. In the case of natural monopolies, the objectives of direct regulation are to ensure that the efficient level of the good or service is produced and that it is offered for sale at a so-called fair price, which allows firms to earn a normal profit. The issue of property rights arises in the sense that although the objective of regulators is to achieve an efficient of level of output, they are restricted from forcing businesses to use their property (capital and resources) in such a way that the businesses would incur an economic loss.

As we saw in Chapter 11, direct regulation has also been employed to *limit* the amount of competition in a market, for example, by limiting the number of taxi cabs that are allowed to operate in a market. In effect, restrictions are imposed that limit who may exercise property rights in a particular market. Although someone may possess the property rights to resources (a driver's license and a car) that would enable her to produce and compete in a market (the taxi cab market), entry may be barred.

The ostensible objective of regulation of competitive markets is to maintain product quality and otherwise protect the interests of consumers. The concern is that excessive competition might result in inferior goods or services as firms cut costs in their efforts to compete and earn profits. Interestingly, while we might be tempted to conclude that firms would resist any type of regulatory restrictions, many economists and policymakers have argued that some industries want to be regulated as a way of establishing a legally sanctioned cartel with the attendant benefits (such as a reduction in competitive pressures).

The question of when, or whether, to regulate is a subject of considerable debate among economists. The evidence on the effects of regulation, while not conclusive, does raise questions about the extent to which regulation

Why the **Disagreement?**

Should We Reregulate Cable TV?

In 1984 the Congress passed the *Cable Communications Policy Act*, which reduced the amount of regulation of the cable television industry. In addition, during the 1970s and early 1980s, the Federal Communications Commission passed a number of rulings that greatly reduced programming and other restrictions on cable broadcast companies. As a result of these actions, firms were allowed to set rates for subscribers on the basis of market demand. In effect, because most localities are served by a single provider of cable, cable companies were allowed to act as unregulated monopolists. Subsequent to deregulation, rates for cable TV have increased dramatically in many areas of the country. According to one study, the average monthly basic rate rose approximately 80 percent between 1984 and 1990, with rate increases in excess of 115 percent in some areas of the country.* In addition, a growing percentage of subscribers have expressed dissatisfaction with the service provided by their cable company. In light of these facts, many members of Congress have proposed legislation that would reregulate the cable TV industry. However, a number of individuals, including industry representatives, industry analysts, and cable customers oppose such a move. In light of the broad range of individuals opposed to reregulation, it is worth asking the question, Why the disagreement? The answer to this question requires consideration of a number of factors. Clearly, those in favor of reregulation see such a move as the most direct means of controlling the rates that are charged to cable customers and the level of service that is offered. In most of the proposals, regulation of rates would occur at the local level. As such, agencies charged with the oversight of cable companies would be able to ensure that 1) rates charged for cable service reflect the true cost of providing service to local customers, and 2) customers receive adequate service. Opponents of such a move argue that the regulation of rates at the local level would impede the efficiency of the system and, in particular, its ability to adjust to new developments such as programming alternatives. They point out that to accommodate changes in programming such as the expansion of services, the owners of cable systems, which provide service on a region-by-region basis, would have to renegotiate rates with thousands of independent municipalities. This would create an excessive cost burden for cable

---

actually results in greater economic efficiency. The issues involved include the following:

1. The possibility of regulatory capture: Regulatory capture refers to the fact that many of the individuals who staff regulatory agencies are former employees of the firms being regulated. In addition, many agency employees who return to the private sector go to work for the firms they previously regulated. In either case, questions exist about whose interests — society's or the industry's — are actually served by the regulatory agency.

2. The information problem: Because regulators must often rely on the regulated firm for most of their information, the reliability of such information is often questioned. Recall from our discussion in Chapter 12 that, in most cases, prices are established on the basis of the costs of production.

3. Empirical studies: A study by Stigler and Friedland[9] examined the rates charged by regulated and unregulated electric utilities during the period from 1912 to 1937. The study indicated that there was no statistically significant difference in the rates charged by the two types of firms, suggesting that reg-

---

[9]George Stigler and Claire Friedland, "What Can Regulators Regulate? The Case of Electricity," in Paul MacAvoy, ed., *The Crisis of the Regulatory Commissions* (New York: W.W. Norton, 1970).

companies. Many cable customers oppose direct regulation of rates for fear of the adverse effect that it might have on the variety of programs offered by the cable company. It is also possible that cable companies would withdraw service from localities where the regulated rate was considered too low to allow the company to earn a reasonable profit, thus restricting the television viewer's options.

Another factor in the debate over reregulation concerns the potential for competition within the television industry to hold down rates. The most likely source of new competition is a technology known as direct broadcast satellite, or DBS. With DBS, communications companies can use satellites to broadcast signals directly to homes equipped with receiving dishes. Unlike existing satellite systems, which require large receiver dishes many feet in diameter, a DBS receiver dish is only one foot wide—about the size of a receiver for cable TV. In addition, providers of DBS maintain that their system is capable of broadcasting 108 different channels, compared to thirty-six channels for the average cable company.

To the extent that DBS is a success and it is able to compete on the basis of price with cable companies, it is reasonable to expect that DBS would create incentives for cable companies to hold down their rates to the lowest level possible. However, industry analysts have pointed out that DBS faces a number of technological hurdles that may reduce its advantages relative to cable TV. In addition, many cable companies are considering becoming providers of DBS. This could also blunt the effects of competition to the extent that DBS and cable are packaged in such a way that they become complements, rather than substitutes.

Whether Congress should, in fact, reregulate cable television is clearly a matter for debate. Studies of the effects of regulation such as those cited elsewhere in this chapter suggest that in many cases, direct regulation has no appreciable effect on the rates ultimately charged to customers. In addition, there is a good possibility that competition within the broadcasting industry may provide the pressure needed to maintain rates at a competitive level. On the other hand, experience since 1984 suggests that the customers of cable TV have paid a considerable price as a result of deregulation. The only thing that appears to be certain is that the cable television industry will be experiencing additional changes.

*"Untangling the Debate Over Cable Television," *Wall Street Journal,* March 19, 1990, p. B1.

---

ulation does not significantly alter the market-determined outcome. More recent studies tend to support this finding.[10]

4. **The true degree of monopoly power:** In some cases, economists have questioned the assertion that a monopoly actually exists. To the extent that viable substitutes are available for a good or service, the monopolist might be forced to behave in a much more competitive manner than would otherwise be expected. The Du Pont case referred to earlier is an excellent example of this issue.

5. **Legal cartel theory of regulation:** Some observers have argued that some industries prefer the certainty provided by regulation relative to the uncertainties associated with operating in a competitive environment. Recall from Chapter 11 that many otherwise competitive industries have been regulated in an effort to protect the interests of consumers and the general public. However, this regulation has also resulted in barriers to entry, creating a form of *legal cartel*. As we will see in our discussion of the recent move toward deregulation, certain industries, such as the trucking industry, worked hard to maintain a regulated environment to operate in.

SECTION RECAP
Direct regulation has been used to influence the pricing and output decisions of certain firms and, in other cases, limit the amount of competition in certain markets. The actual effects of direct regulation on the efficiency of markets is subject to considerable debate.

[10]See for example William G. Shepard, "Causes of Increased Competition in the U.S. Economy," *Review of Economics and Statistics,* November 1982, p. 617.

The Deregulation of Business Behavior

Deregulation
The removal of specific regulations that govern the economic activity of the firms in a particular market or industry.

Regulation has traditionally been viewed as a means to increase the level of efficiency in specific markets and otherwise promote the interests of consumers. However, in the last decade we have witnessed a growing trend toward the **deregulation** of previously regulated industries. This trend, which began during the Ford and Carter Administrations, was intensified by the Reagan Administration. Examples of recently deregulated industries include airlines, banking, trucking, railroads, buses, natural gas, and telecommunications.

It is important to note that the term *deregulation* is not meant to imply that all regulations governing the firms in a particular industry are eliminated. Instead, deregulation refers to any situation in which at least part of the regulations governing a particular production activity are removed or relaxed. All of the industries that have been deregulated in the last decade are still subject to some degree of regulation. However, firms in those industries are now more responsive to changes in market forces than they were before deregulation.

A Brief Review of Significant Deregulation Developments

Table 1 summarizes the major pieces of legislation passed since 1978 directed at deregulation of specific markets. As the table indicates, deregulation has not

TABLE 1

Major deregulation legislation since 1978

Date	Act	Major Provisions
1978	Airline Deregulation Act	Allowed increased freedom of entry and exit in markets and price competition. Provided for phase-out of the Civil Aeronautics Board.
1978	Natural Gas Policy Act	Provided for gradual decontrol of wellhead prices of natural gas.
1980	Motor Carrier Act	Provided individual trucking firms more control over rates. Eased restrictions on entry into new markets by new and existing firms and abandonment of unprofitable routes.
1980	Staggers Rail Act	Granted railroads more control over rates charged. Also provided easier methods for abandoning unprofitable routes.
1980	Depository Institutions Deregulation and Monetary Control Act	Equalization of regulations governing all depository institutions. Began phase-out of Regulation Q (interest rate ceilings). Authorization for expansion of specific services offered by depository institutions.
1982	Bus Regulatory Reform Act	Eased conditions to be met by new firms entering the market. Superceded many state regulations that restricted operation of buses between states.
1982	Garn–St. Germain Depository Institutions Act	Allowed depository institutions to offer money market deposit accounts. Accelerated the phase-out of Regulation Q.

been limited to any one sector of the economy. Its effects have been felt in such diverse areas as the transportation, finance, and energy sectors.

One of Congress's first major moves in the direction of deregulation was passage of the *Airline Deregulation Act* in 1978. This law reflected a growing awareness of the potential for workable competition in the airline industry. Its purpose was to facilitate increased competition, which was in turn expected to result in more efficient production, lower fares, improved service options, and, in general, prices that more closely matched the costs of production. The law also provided for the elimination of public subsidies to the airline industry. As is shown below, deregulation of the airline industry appears to have resulted in many of the predicted outcomes. However, it is still too early to assess all the long-run effects, positive and negative, of airline deregulation.

Ground transportation has also been deregulated. The *Motor Carrier Act* of 1980 gave individual trucking firms more control over rates and increased the ability of new and existing firms to enter and compete in new markets and abandon unprofitable routes. The *Staggers Rail Act,* passed in the same year, gave railroads more control over the rates they could charge and established easier methods for abandoning service routes that were unprofitable. In 1982, the Congress passed the *Bus Regulatory Reform Act,* which eased the conditions that must be met by new firms entering the market. This act also removed many state regulations that had restricted the operation of buses between states.

The banking sector has felt the effects of deregulation as well. In 1978, the Federal Reserve began to loosen its control on the interest rates that banks can pay on savings deposits. This move came in response to increased competition for savings through the development by investment firms of money market mutual funds[11] and other interest-bearing assets that were not subject to the same restrictions as depository institution savings accounts.

In 1980, after earlier failed attempts, the Congress passed a sweeping reform bill entitled the *Depository Institutions Deregulation and Monetary Control Act (DIDMCA).* The DIDMCA was designed to improve the competitive position of depository institutions relative to other financial institutions. As a follow-up to the DIDMCA, in 1982 Congress passed the *Garn–St. Germain Depository Institutions Act,* which was directed primarily at ailing savings and loan institutions. A major effect of this law was to allow depository institutions to develop accounts, called money market deposit accounts, that could compete directly with money market mutual funds by offering comparable rates of return and conditions for participation in the fund. In addition, the DIDMCA had already set in motion the process of phasing out the difference in interest rates on savings accounts paid by savings and loan institutions and commercial banks. The Garn–St. Germain Depository Institutions Act also reduced the amount of time over which this phase-out would occur.

Deregulation first came to the natural gas industry with the passage of the *Natural Gas Policy Act (NGPA)* in 1978. The major thrust of the NGPA was to allow a gradual decontrol of the wellhead price of natural gas. (The wellhead price refers to the price of a unit of natural gas as it is extracted from the ground.) This decontrol was to be phased in over a period of time, depending upon the specific source of the gas in question. The purpose of the NGPA was

SECTION RECAP
Over the last fifteen years, a number of industries including airlines, banking, trucking, railroads, buses, natural gas, and telecommunications have been *(continued)*

---

[11]A money market mutual fund pools the contributions of a large number of investors and buys high quality short-term highly liquid assets including commercial paper (the short-term bonds of large corporations) and Treasury bills.

SECTION RECAP
(continued)
deregulated. The purpose of deregulation is to allow firms to respond more directly to market forces that affect pricing and output decisions.

to improve the supply of natural gas by allowing market forces to send the appropriate price signals to producers of natural gas.

As the next section indicates, deregulation can, in fact, result in more efficient levels of output and prices. This is not meant to imply that deregulation is necessarily appropriate for all currently regulated industries. Rather, it suggests that policymakers must keep abreast of ever-changing market conditions to ensure that regulation continues to promote, rather than limit, market competition.

The Case for Deregulation

Regulation Influences the Form of Competition

Regulation of a particular industry is seldom complete. That is, the restrictions placed on firms in a regulated industry are not designed to control all the different aspects of firm behavior. Instead, regulation usually focuses on the price charged by each firm in an effort to ensure that consumers pay a price for the good that reflects the costs of production. This price also enables producers to earn a normal return on their investment. In such cases, the usual response of regulated firms is to find some other way of competing with each other.

Airlines: Nonprice (Service) Competition Prior to 1978, the Civil Aeronautics Board (CAB) exerted considerable influence over the structure and pricing policies of the airline industry. In particular, the CAB controlled the number of major interstate airlines (formerly referred to as *trunk* airlines) that were allowed to operate, the number of airlines operating between any two cities (called *city-pairs*), and the fares that could be charged for specific flights. Consequently, airlines were unable to compete on the basis of these characteristics.

As a result of such restrictions, airlines tended to compete instead on the basis of quality of service. Service includes such characteristics as the number of flights between city-pairs, on-time performance, seating comfort, meals, drinks, and availability of seating. This tendency illustrates the powerful incentive to earn economic profits and the degree to which firms respond to this incentive.

Many analysts argued that the rates airlines were permitted to charge induced them to offer a higher level of service than they would have under competitive conditions. It was argued that competition would result in a reduction not only in fares, but the quality of service offered as well. This is because the regulated fares airlines were allowed to charge (set by the CAB) exceeded the costs of production (including a normal profit). Airlines then used this difference between price and cost to finance an increase in service above the level associated with the competitively determined price. In support of this view, Alfred Kahn, a noted economist and one-time chairman of the CAB, has argued that "essentially unregulated competition among the certificated carriers in scheduling and in the quality of service [airlines] offered generally brought costs into line with CAB-determined fares on all types of routes—upward toward the prescribed fare levels in the markets where those

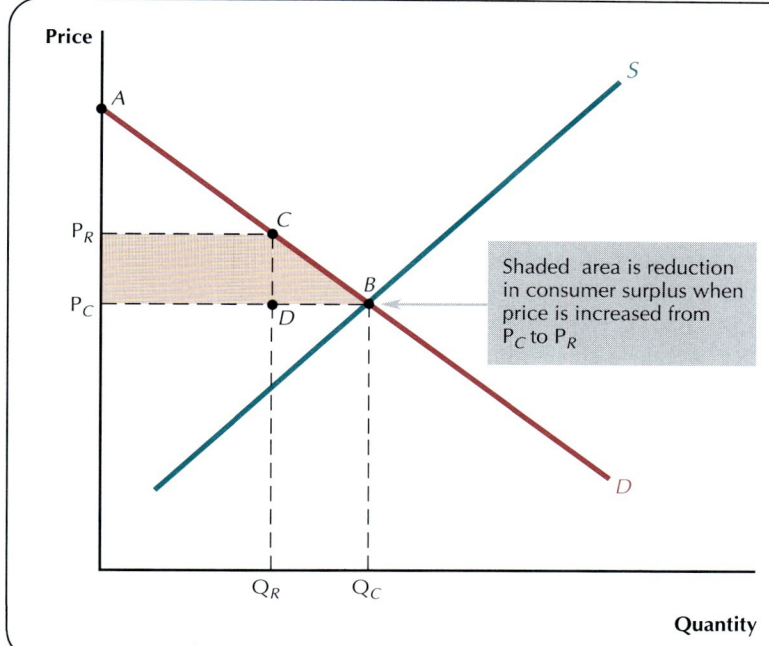

FIGURE 1
Regulated pricing and the redistribution of income. Under competitive conditions, the equilibrium price and output would be P_c and Q_c, respectively. Consumer surplus would be equal to the area $P_c AB$. However, if the price is instead set at P_R, Q_R units will be sold. Consumer surplus is thus reduced by the area $P_c P_R CB$. Of this amount, the area DCB represents a deadweight loss to society. The remaining area, $P_c P_R CD$, is redistributed to producers.

fares were set above standard costs, downward, with skimpy services, where the fares would otherwise have been unremunerative."[12]

Regulation Redistributes Income Deliberately or Arbitrarily

The usual intent of regulation is to ensure that consumers receive the product they want at a price that reflects the costs of production. However, it is often the case that regulation also results, either intentionally or unintentionally, in the redistribution of income.

Separation of Price and Cost   When the price charged for a product exceeds the marginal cost of production, the results are an inefficient level of output and the potential for the creation of economic profits. (Recall that firms earn economic profits when the price of the product sold exceeds the average total cost of production.) In effect, economic profits constitute a redistribution of income from consumers to producers. This is because consumers end up paying a per-unit price that is higher than the price that would be charged under competitive conditions.

This type of redistribution of income is illustrated in Figure 1. The market demand for and supply of the good are illustrated by the curves labeled D and S, respectively. In the case of competition, the equilibrium market price and output would be P_C and Q_C. Consumer surplus is therefore equal to the area

---

[12]Alfred Kahn, "Deregulation and Vested Interests: The Case of Airlines," in R. G. Noll and B. M. Owen, eds., *The Political Economy of Deregulation* (American Enterprise Institute for Public Policy Research, 1983), p. 135.

P_CAB. However, if the price were instead set at P_R, which is greater than P_C, output would fall to Q_R. As a result, consumer surplus is reduced by the shaded region P_CP_RCB. This loss is composed of two parts. The triangle DCB is a deadweight loss.[13] The rectangle P_CP_RCD would now constitute income to the producer. Consequently, income has been redistributed from consumers to producers.

A logical question at this point is, Why would regulators set a price that is above the competitively determined price? One possible answer is that because the industry is regulated, some of the benefits of competition are forgone. In particular, the costs faced by firms may not reflect the costs that would result if firms were forced to compete more actively. (Recall that competition encourages firms to constantly seek out less-costly methods of production in their efforts to maximize profits.)

Another possible answer is that price is purposely set above cost to create profits that can then be used to *subsidize* the purchases consumers make in other markets. This approach is known as cross subsidization.

Cross Subsidies Another means by which regulation can result in a redistribution of income is through the effects of **cross subsidization**. Cross subsidizations occur in a variety of situations. Consider, for example, the situation in which there are two (or more) groups of purchasers of the same product. It is often the case that the costs of producing the product for each group will differ. A good example is the provision of airline service. Per-unit costs of production are lower for heavily traveled routes of a given distance than they are for lightly traveled routes covering the same distance (because fixed costs are spread over more passengers). If each group were charged according to the costs of production, they would pay different prices for the service.

However, as a result of regulation, one of the groups (for example, passengers on heavily traveled routes) often ends up paying a price that is higher than that which would be determined in a competitive market. The other group (for example, passengers on less heavily traveled routes), on the other hand, pays a price that is actually below cost. Consequently, the excess profits earned from one group can be used to pay part of the other group's costs. One group subsidizes the purchases of the other group.

The regulation of air fares prior to 1978 resulted in cross subsidies of the type described above. The CAB set fares on longer, more heavily traveled routes above cost and fares on shorter, less heavily traveled routes below cost. It justified this approach as a means of facilitating the continued development of the air transportation system by encouraging air travel on shorter and less heavily traveled flights. The profits resulting from the regulated fares charged to customers on the major routes were used to cover part of the costs of providing service on shorter and less popular routes.

As a result of this approach, customers on the heavily traveled routes paid a higher price than they would in a competitive situation. Customers on less heavily traveled routes paid less than they would in a competitive situation. From an economic perspective, the result of the regulated air fares and cross subsidization was a redistribution of income from customers on heavily traveled routes to customers on less heavily traveled routes.

Cross subsidization The practice of charging different prices to different groups of customers and using profits from one group to cover the losses generated by another group.

---

[13] This deadweight loss consists of the consumer surplus that is not captured by the monopolist and is instead lost to society.

The effect of this cross subsidization is shown graphically in Figure 2. Figure 2(a) illustrates the demand and cost conditions for flights on usually longer-distance and heavily traveled routes. Figure 2(b) illustrates the demand and cost conditions for flights on shorter-distance and less heavily traveled routes. P_R represents the regulated price in each market. With the price set at P_R (not necessarily the same in each market) it is clear from Figure 2(a) that firms in this market will earn an economic profit. The amount of profit is indicated by the shaded rectangle. With price set at P_R in Figure 2(b), Q_R units of output will be produced. However, this will result in an economic loss equal to the shaded area. As a result of cross subsidization, however, the profits earned in the market illustrated in Figure 2(a) can be used to offset the losses

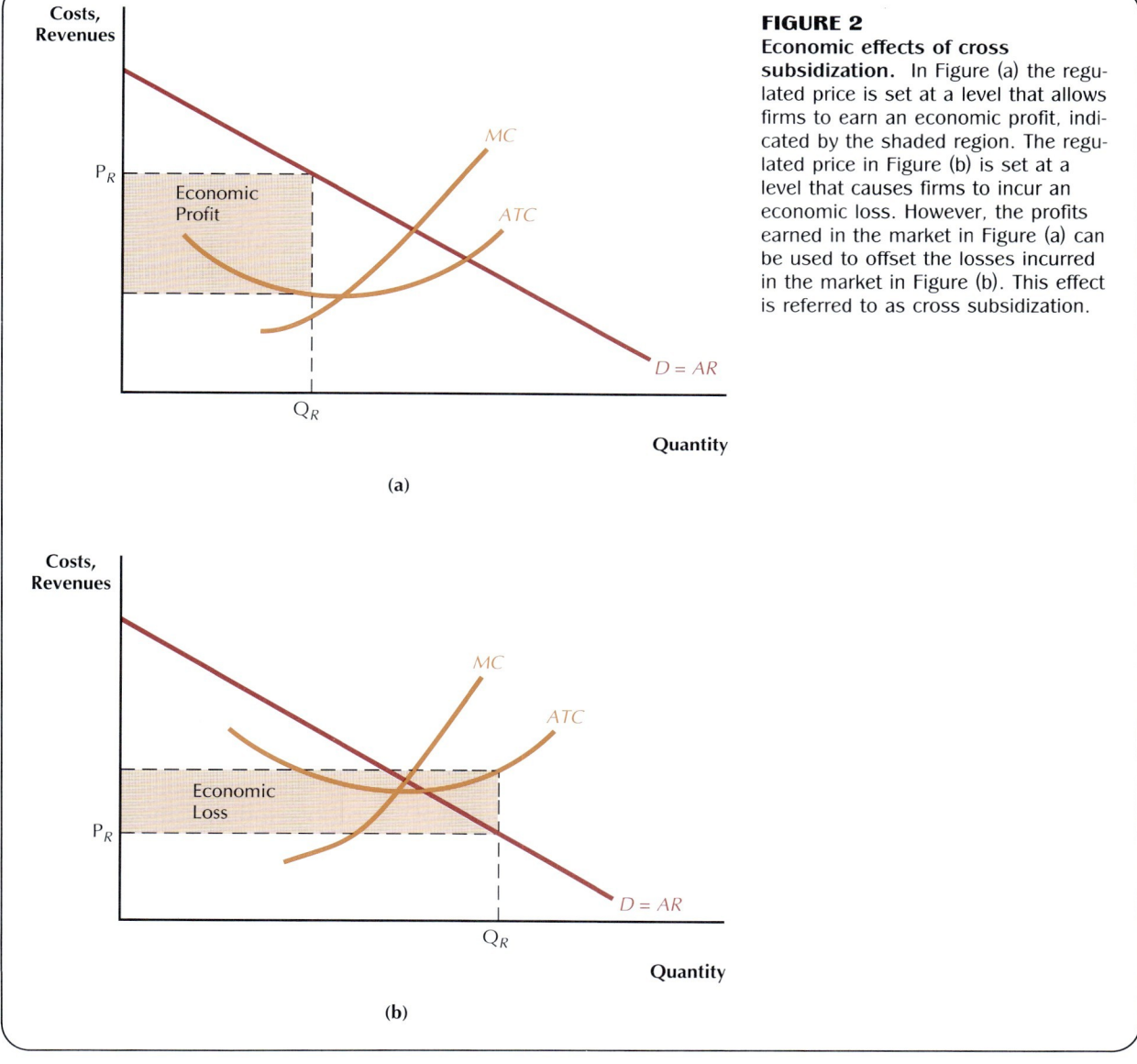

FIGURE 2
Economic effects of cross subsidization. In Figure (a) the regulated price is set at a level that allows firms to earn an economic profit, indicated by the shaded region. The regulated price in Figure (b) is set at a level that causes firms to incur an economic loss. However, the profits earned in the market in Figure (a) can be used to offset the losses incurred in the market in Figure (b). This effect is referred to as cross subsidization.

incurred in the market depicted in Figure 2(b). An additional result is that the optimal, or efficient, quantity of the good is not produced in either market. Instead, the quantity produced is either less than or greater than the efficient level, depending on the market in question.

Regulation Can Reduce Competition and Efficiency: The Establishment of Cartel-Like Conditions

In some instances policymakers have concluded that too much competition is, in fact, undesirable from the consumer's point of view. This conclusion was one of the principal motivations for regulation of the airline industry. However, the effort to limit competition as a means of improving product quality may lead to the creation of cartel-like conditions as entry into the market is restricted. The cartel-like conditions reduce the competitive pressures that firms might otherwise face in their day-to-day operations. A major result is that there is less incentive for firms to reduce costs or pursue research and development intended to provide consumers with a better product or service. As we have already noted, the CAB's pricing and entry policies had essentially this effect on the airline industry.

If restrictions on entry are removed and the firms in the industry are forced to compete, one possible result is a reduction in costs. The potential for economic profits—which will accrue to firms that reduce costs below those of existing firms—creates an incentive for the entry of additional firms into the market. As firms enter, existing firms reduce costs and product prices in response to the increased competition. The result of freedom of entry into the market is that firms now produce a larger amount of output than before and sell it at a lower price.

Studies of the effects of deregulation of the airline industry suggest that airlines have responded to increased competition in the manner just described. In particular, there is strong evidence to suggest that, at least through 1989, fares were lower than they would have been under the pre-1978 regulatory scheme. In addition, the empirical evidence indicates that the average number of carriers that serve a particular route increased by approximately 25 percent during the period from 1978 to 1988.[14]

Before deregulation, cartel-like conditions existed in the trucking industry as well. It is not surprising that among the strongest opponents of deregulation of the trucking industry were the trucking firms themselves. It was clear to existing firms that deregulation would force an increase in the already growing level of competition as new firms entered existing markets. Consequently, when Congress began to consider deregulation of the trucking industry, existing firms vehemently opposed such action. Increased competition was expected to reduce profitability and induce efforts to increase productivity. However, despite the well-organized opposition of the trucking industry, the *Motor Carrier Act* of 1980 was passed and observers have argued that society has benefited considerably.[15]

SECTION RECAP
Proponents of deregulation argue that regulation can have a number of undesirable effects, including an emphasis on costly nonprice competition, redistribution of income, and a reduction in the efficiency of regulated markets.

---

[14]S. A. Morrison and C. Winston, "The Dynamics of Airline Pricing and Competition," *American Economic Review*, 1990, Vol. 80, pp. 389–393.

[15]Marcus Alexis, "The Political Economy of Federal Regulation of Surface Transportation," in R. G. Noll and B. M. Owen, eds., *The Political Economy of Deregulation* (American Enterprise Institute for Public Policy Research, 1983), p. 129.

Airline Deregulation: A Case Study

In the early 1930s, many airlines were experiencing financial difficulties, and the number of airline accidents was increasing. Many observers blamed these conditions on the high degree of competition in the airline industry. It was argued that the increase in accidents was the result of a lack of attention to safety-related measures in an effort to hold down costs. Consequently, Congress passed the *Civil Aeronautics Act* of 1938, which established the Civil Aeronautics Board (CAB) and empowered it to set fares and limit the amount of competition on individual routes. The theory behind this action was that with decreased competition firms would be more financially stable and could therefore devote more attention to factors such as safety and service.

However, the policies of the CAB resulted in what amounted to a cartel in the interstate flights market. Before the passage of the Airline Deregulation Act of 1978, eleven airlines (the trunk airlines) dominated the routes between major cities and controlled almost 90 percent of the total market revenue and traffic. The CAB maintained this oligopolistic market structure by rejecting all of the seventy-nine applications for new major airlines filed between 1938 and 1978. The CAB's reasoning was that reduced competition would encourage airlines to focus more of their attention on safety and service.

During the time that the airlines were regulated, the average level of service offered by airlines did improve. The financial stability of the major airlines licensed to operate in the interstate market also steadily improved, and airline safety increased. However, fares tended to exceed competitively determined levels and consumer choice between airlines on a given route was restricted. Moreover, because fares were set by the CAB and requests for increases or decreases in fares could be matched by competitors, there was little incentive for firms to invest in strategies designed to reduce costs. Consequently, some would argue that the increased service and improved financial stability of the industry would have occurred even in the *absence* of regulation.

An analysis of the effect of deregulation on prices and service indicates that while average real fares have decreased, the average level of service has actually increased. A study by the U.S. General Accounting Office stated that between 1978 and 1984, while nominal fares increased, the real average fare (the nominal fare adjusted for the effects of inflation) per revenue passenger mile (a measure of output for airlines) fell by approximately 6 percent. Also, the study concluded that fares appeared to be more closely related to costs than was the case prior to 1978.[16]

Many analysts had argued that the average level of service would decline after deregulation as competition brought fares and service in line with each other. However, the data indicate that the average level of service, in fact, increased between 1978 and 1984. It has been suggested that this improvement may have been the result of an increase in the number of shorter, less heavily traveled routes offered by the airlines. This, in turn, resulted in a greater total availability of flights and departure times, thus benefiting the air-traveling public.

These results—lower fares and improved service—suggest that, at least through 1984, society benefited from deregulation of the airline industry. This

---

[16]Report of the U.S. General Accounting Office, "Deregulation: Increased Competition Is Making Airlines More Efficient and Responsive to Consumers." GAO/RCED-86-26. November 6, 1985.

TABLE 2

Early results of airline deregulation: 1978–1984

	1978	1984
1. Number of competing airlines	30	37
2. Market share[a] (percent)		
Trunk	87.2	73.3
Local service	8.8	12.2
Intrastate	2.4	3.9
Other[b]	1.6	10.6
3. Markets served by 2 or more airlines[c]	1180	1831
4. Average fares per revenue passenger mile (cents)	5.9	4.8
5. Competition in individual markets		
Total through-plane markets in 1978	5158	—
Change in number of competitors in individual markets during the period 1978–1984		
No change	—	1567
More	—	1185
Fewer	—	291
No longer in service	—	−2115
New service	—	2380
Total through-plane markets in 1984	—	5423

[a] Based on passenger revenue miles.
[b] Includes commuter flights.
[c] Data restricted to markets providing through-plane service.
Source: U.S. General Accounting Office, "Deregulation: Increased Competition Is Making Airlines More Efficient and Responsive to Consumers." GAO/RCED-86-26. November 6, 1985.

does not imply, however, that at least some groups did not lose as a result of deregulation. Table 2 summarizes statistics on the early effects of deregulation. As the table indicates, a large number of markets lost through-plane service (when passengers do not have to change planes on stop-overs) as a result of deregulation. However, the total number of markets receiving through-plane service increased between 1978 and 1984.

    More recent developments in the airline industry have led some observers to question the benefits of deregulation indicated in the GAO study. First, full fares have increased. Thus, certain groups are now paying an increased price for air travel. The increase in full fares, however, has been more than offset by even lower discount fares (fares offered subject to specific restrictions on travel times, length of stay, and other factors).[17] Consequently, average real fares have continued to decline. In addition, consumers now enjoy a wider range of fares then ever before. While the increased number of fares reflects an increase in price discrimination designed to increase profits, it also reflects the effects of increased competition for customers. Customers benefit from

[17] G. W. James, "The Airline Industry." Presented to the Transportation Research Board, Washington, DC, January 11, 1988.

Does It Make **Economic Sense?**

Regulation vs. Deregulation in the Airline Industry

Deregulation of the airline industry has resulted in, among other things, an increase in the number of flights into and out of many of the airports in the United States. Obviously, this has increased the pressure on those individuals responsible for safety in air travel. During the same period, the number of air traffic controllers has decreased substantially. This reduction came as a result of the air traffic controllers' strike in 1981 and the subsequent dismissal of a large number of the controllers employed at the time. One of the recent, most-often-cited problems with the air transportation industry is the need for more airport and traffic controllers to handle the increased volume of traffic.

In response to this problem, many analysts have called for additional deregulation of the airline industry.* They maintain that such a move would reduce many of the problems noted above. To some, this appears to be the complete opposite of what should be done. Rather than further deregulating the industry, many observers have argued that it is time to reregulate the airline industry. From an economic perspective, the question arises whether further deregulation makes economic sense in view of the problems that have arisen.

To analyze this question it is important to realize that only one portion of the air transportation industry was actually deregulated in 1978 — the airlines. Airports and the air traffic control system continue to operate within the applicable regulatory framework that existed prior to 1978. Under those regulations, the prices that airlines and other airport users pay for landing rights fail to reflect the scarcity of landing slots during peak demand periods or the type of aircraft seeking to land. That is, prices are not differentiated according to the characteristics that determine demand for landing slots.

Proposed additional deregulation would allow airports to set prices for landing rights according to their marginal value. Consequently, the pricing of landing slots would reflect the characteristics of the slots. For example, because flights with afternoon arrival times are more popular, landing at 4:00 in the afternoon would cost more than landing the same plane at the same airport at midnight. Such a pricing strategy would presumably reduce congestion at airports during peak times. More importantly, it would allow the market to allocate landing slots to those individuals who value them most.

The change in the cost of landing rights should also appear in the price of airline tickets. To be specific, all else constant, a ticket with an arrival time of 3:00 A.M. should be less expensive than a ticket with an arrival time of 4:00 P.M. Hence, airline customers could be offered an increased variety of fare and service options.

While it appears that this form of deregulation could indeed increase the efficiency of the airline industry, it should not be concluded that this action, in and of itself, would completely solve the problem of airport crowding. As the number of flights into and out of specific areas increases, there will be a growing need for additional space, either by expanding existing airports or by building new ones to accommodate the increase. In addition, reallocation of landing slots does not address the problem of the shortage of the number of available air traffic controllers.

On a different note, because there is often only a single airport in a particular geographic region, allocation of landing slots on the basis of price could create a monopoly position for such airports. Viewed from another perspective, differentiated pricing of landing slots could create an advantage for users who are able to pay higher rates for preferred landing slots. This could create a competitive advantage for some airlines and, in effect, reduce the overall level of competition in the airline industry. Clearly, this issue will require considerable analysis before a consensus on the appropriate approach to eliminating airport crowding can be reached.

*James Gattuso, "Airline Passengers Need Full Deregulation," *Cato Policy Report*, Vol. IX, No. 6, pp. 6–8.

this competition in the form of an increase in the number of fares they can choose from.

Second, there has been a decline in the number of airlines operating in the United States. A number of medium and small carriers have gone out of business in recent years. Between 1984 and 1986, eighty-two certificated carriers and commuter airlines declared bankruptcy or ceased operations.[18] In addition, a number of mergers, such as the purchase of Ozark Airlines by TWA, have reduced the number of competing firms. However, as we noted earlier, the level of competition per route—the usual measure of the competitiveness of the airline industry—increased through 1988.

Third, a number of serious accidents has led to questions about the safety associated with air travel. Some observers have linked this apparent decrease in safety to deregulation. The argument has been made that increased competition has led some airlines to reduce safety-related expenditures to hold down production costs. However, statistics for the period January 1983 to March 1986 indicate that the total number of accidents, as well as fatal accidents, has actually been declining.[19] In addition, the *Economic Report of the President, 1988* stated that for each one billion passenger miles that are flown rather than driven, there are thirty-five fewer deaths.[20] Finally, safety regulations were *not* affected by the Airline Deregulation Act and continue to be enforced by the Federal Aviation Administration.

While the foregoing arguments deserve serious consideration, the available evidence does not appear to support the contention that, overall, deregulation has had an adverse effect on the service or efficiency aspects of air travel. On the contrary, it appears that deregulation has resulted in considerable benefits to air travelers as a group.

In the airline industry, customers have witnessed a dramatic increase in the number of available fare–service options. Depending upon a customer's needs, substantial savings in air travel can be realized. For example, many airlines regularly offer reduced fares on selected flights subject to specific restrictions. These restrictions usually involve days and times when tickets are valid, required length of stay, and refund limitations. While such offerings obviously are not appropriate for everyone (business travelers, for example), they nonetheless constitute an increase in the amount of choice available to consumers. One study has estimated the annual welfare gains from deregulation of the airline industry to be approximately $8 billion (in 1977 dollars) with no substantial losses to any specific group in society.[21]

SECTION RECAP
Recent evidence indicates that as a result of deregulation in the airline industry, full fares have increased, but average real fares have declined. Also, although the number of airlines has declined, competition per route increased through 1988. The level of safety also appears to be increasing.

The Market Mechanism in Action

Deregulation Spurs the Market on

The forgoing discussion suggests that where the potential for competition exists, deregulation can encourage product development and hence expand the set of choices available to consumers. Competition constantly forces firms to

---

[18]James, "The Airline Industry."

[19]Annual Review of Aircraft Accident Data, U.S. Department of Transportation. January 8, 1987.

[20]*Economic Report of the President, 1988*, p. 211.

[21]S. A. Morrison and C. Winston, *The Effects of Airline Deregulation* (Washington, DC: The Brookings Institution, 1986), p. 51.

attempt to minimize costs (to maximize profits) and to upgrade and improve products in the effort to maintain or increase their share of the market. From the consumers' standpoint, where the potential for workable competition exists, deregulation constitutes a preferred policy option.

The experiences of the airline and trucking industries tend to support the argument that deregulation can be beneficial from society's point of view. As we have seen, after deregulation of the airline industry, average fares decreased and the average level of service actually improved. In a similar fashion, rates in the trucking industry tended to decline while the level of productivity increased. However, it is still too early to assess the overall impacts, positive and negative, of deregulation in either of these industries.

Conditions within the economy and particular markets or industries are constantly changing. Consequently, what may have been appropriate policy at one point in time may become inappropriate over time. Moreover, it is quite possible that policies originally designed to improve the efficiency of a particular market may in time lead to increased inefficiencies. When these results arise it is important for policymakers to step back and reevaluate the policies that have been put in place. Just as the economy is constantly changing, so should government policy be ready to change to achieve the greatest amount of social welfare possible.

Summary

Government has several alternatives in the event of market failure that results from a lack of competition. The alternatives include government ownership of business, antitrust legislation, and the direct regulation of business.

Government ownership **(public enterprise)** is used much less extensively in the United States than it is in other countries. The objectives of government ownership are essentially the same as those of direct regulation: to provide an adequate supply of the good or service at a fair price. However, depending upon the objectives of the firm's managers, efficiency in production may not be realized.

Antitrust legislation is designed to control business behavior ranging from pricing policies to mergers to false or deceptive advertising. The enforcement of antitrust policy has varied along the lines of bigness versus behavior.

Direct regulation has been used extensively in the United States. Regulation has been aimed primarily at two different situations: (1) industries that are characterized as natural monopolies, and (2) situations in which it is felt that competition is excessive and that allowing it to persist without regulation would result in a monopoly or some other socially undesirable outcome.

An examination of the broad body of regulation and legislation that has been developed over time suggests that, in many cases, the restrictions imposed on a particular industry have served more to protect existing firms than to benefit consumers. This emerging awareness has resulted in a trend toward **deregulation** in many sectors of the economy.

One of the underlying themes in the deregulation movement has been the emphasis on competition. Arguments for deregulation have centered on the effects of regulation on the competitiveness of the industry in question. In many cases (for example, the airline, trucking, and telecommunications industries) it has been argued that regulation limited competition and led to industry cartels. This resulted in excess costs and, consequently, prices in excess of those that would result in a more competitive environment.

Consumers appear to have generally benefited from the effects of deregulation. These benefits have accrued in the form of lower prices as costs have declined in the face of increased competition. Gains have also been realized in the form of increased consumer choice as firms develop new and different products in an effort to maintain and increase market share.

There have also been losers as a result of deregulation. As is always the case when choices must be made, opportunity costs will be incurred. The decision by airlines to increase the number of flights in some markets has led to declines in the number of flights in other markets. Similarly, deregulation in the trucking industry has resulted in reduced service options on some routes.

Questions for Thought

Knowledge Questions

1. List and discuss the three basic approaches to market failure that are employed in the United States. In your discussion of each alternative be sure to list the basic features of each approach.
2. How has the interpretation and application of antitrust policy evolved over time? What is the *rule of reason*? Cite influential cases in your answer.
3. List the major pieces of deregulation legislation that have been passed since 1978, and discuss the major features of each piece of legislation. In general, what has prompted the move toward deregulation?
4. What is meant by the term *cross subsidization*? What is its purpose in a regulatory setting? Give an example of the use of cross subsidization in regulation and how it worked.

Application Questions

5. Government ownership of business has been employed in a number of instances in the United States as a means of dealing with the problem of market failure. What businesses do you think are best suited to this type of approach? Why? In your opinion, are there any businesses for which this approach is not suitable? List them.
6. It was noted that the airline industry has experienced an increase in the number of mergers and failures in recent years. What factors would you consider in determining whether this is leading to a decrease in competitive pressures in the industry? Why, and how, are the factors you have listed important?
7. Regulation Q, which limited the rate of interest that banks could pay to depositors, was originally intended to protect smaller banks from the effects of competition by larger banks for savings deposits. Do you think that this regulation was justified on the basis of competition? Why or why not?
8. Explain how price discrimination could be used to eliminate the inefficiencies associated with a monopoly. Could price discrimination serve as a substitute for the regulation of monopolies? What problems do you perceive with price discrimination?

Synthesis Questions

9. On the question of bigness versus behavior, the courts have tended to focus on the behavior of a firm in determining whether the firm is in violation of antitrust laws. Do you agree with this approach? Why or why not? (State specific reasons.)
10. Assume that industry X is currently regulated on the basis of the number of firms that can enter into and compete for customers in its market. Many analysts have begun to argue, however, that industry X should be deregulated to promote increased competition and the resulting benefits that competition can bring to consumers. What questions would you consider important in determining whether industry X should, in fact, be deregulated?
11. Many analysts are predicting that the financial sector of the economy is destined for more changes in the near future as competition between depository and nondepository institutions increases. In fact, it is argued that some day such a distinction will not exist. What would be the likely result if the government continued to regulate depository institutions while nondepository institutions were left basically free of regulation? Would this be good for consumers? Explain.

The Theory of Resource Markets

OVERVIEW

We have focused thus far on product markets. The analysis of how prices and levels of output of final goods and services are determined is based upon a few simple yet powerful ideas. The most important principle is that economic decisions are based on marginal costs and benefits. Rational choices by consumers yield downward-sloping demand curves for goods and services. In a similar manner, supply schedules are derived from application of the marginal benefit–marginal cost rule to profit-maximizing firms.

Your investment of time and mental energy in the preceding chapters now pays off in two ways. First, we have gained important insights into how product markets and the price system work to allocate goods and services efficiently. Second, and perhaps more importantly, the same principles can be applied to other types of markets where individuals face choices involving costs and benefits.

In this section we apply the demand and supply model to resource markets. To produce finished goods and services, firms must employ resources such as labor, capital goods, raw materials, and energy. These resources are supplied by other firms or individuals. In the resource markets the roles of firms and households are reversed from product markets—firms comprise the demand side of the market, and individuals are the suppliers.

Just as the interaction of supply and demand determines equilibrium price in product markets, resource prices are set by supply and demand. Under competitive conditions, these prices result in an efficient allocation of resources to firms. Each resource is attracted to the firm where the value of the output produced by the resource is highest.

This chapter provides a general introduction to the

CHAPTER 14

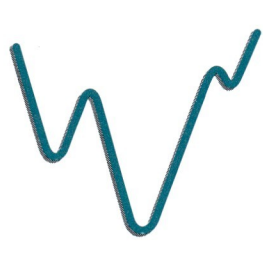

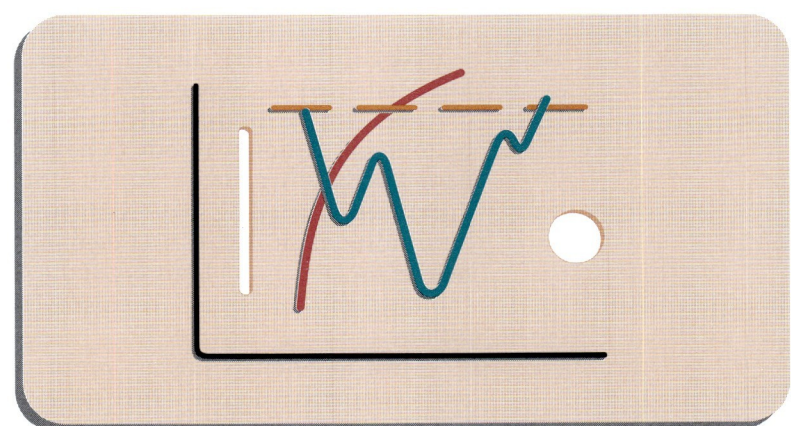

functioning of resource markets and the decision making of firms and resource owners in these markets. Subsequent chapters apply the concepts developed here to the labor and capital markets.

Learning Objectives
After reading and studying this chapter, you will be able to:

1. Explain the concept of *derived demand*.
2. Define and calculate marginal revenue product and marginal resource cost.
3. Derive the firm's resource demand function and identify the three major factors affecting short-run resource demand.
4. Calculate the price elasticity of resource demand and identify the major determinants of resource demand elasticity.
5. Identify the major determinants of supply elasticity.
6. Summarize the efficiency properties of competitive resource market outcomes.

Determinants of Resource Prices

Our focus is still on the decision making of households and firms. However, these economic agents assume roles in the resource markets that are the reverse of their roles in the product markets. In the product markets, households are on the demand side. In the resource markets, households are suppliers. They own the available resources—labor, capital, land, and entrepreneurial skill—and seek to maximize the per-unit price they receive from the sale of their resources. They use the resulting income to purchase goods and services in the product market. In resource markets, firms are on the demand side—they demand resources to produce and supply goods and services that consumers wish to buy in the product markets.

The decisions that households and firms make in the resource markets are just as important to their economic well-being as the decisions they make in the product market. Because household income and costs incurred by firms are determined in resource markets, the product and resource markets are linked. Changing conditions in resource markets affect resource prices. As resource prices change, the cost of supplying output changes and the product market equilibrium is altered. Consequently, *an understanding of resource markets is necessary for a complete understanding of a market economy.*

The income of an individual in a market economy depends upon the quantity of economic resources he or she supplies to the market and the prices paid for these resources. Suppose Smith is a professor of law. His income depends on the going salaries of law school lecturers. This price is determined by conditions of supply and demand in a resource market—in this case, the market for law school lecturers. If the supply of qualified legal scholars doubles (holding all other factors constant), we can predict that Smith's income will decline.

Most individuals possess property rights to significant amounts of only one economic resource—their own labor. Compensation for labor services (wages, salaries, and benefits) has always accounted for most of our national income. During the 1980s, an estimated 75 percent of annual national income was earned by households as employee compensation. The remaining quarter of the national income included payments for land (rent), financial capital (interest), buildings (rent), and entrepreneurship (profit). Labor market outcomes, therefore, have very significant implications for the distribution of income in the United States. Because of their importance in the determination of income distribution, labor markets are the focus of a significant amount of public policymaking. As we shall see in later chapters, a great deal of legislation is aimed at affecting the distribution of income by altering the outcomes of labor markets.

The Firm's Demand for Resources

Resource demand schedule
The quantity of a resource demanded at each price.

The price of a resource affects the amount of the resource that a firm wishes to employ in the production of goods and services. The relationship between price and quantity demanded is captured in the firm's **resource demand schedule.** The first step in analyzing resource demand is to ask, Why do firms employ resources (labor, capital, or land)? A little reflection yields the obvious answer. Firms employ resources to produce a product that the firm expects to sell at a profit. That is, the demand for a resource is a **derived demand**. A firm's resource demands are derived from (depend upon) the demand for its final product. This simple yet crucial idea links the product market with the resource market. If the demand for the firm's product falls to zero, so too will the firm's demands for resources.

The concept of derived demand explains why firms employ resources, but not why they employ particular quantities of resources. Assuming that the firm's goal is to maximize profits, the employment decision boils down to the question, What level of resource utilization generates the greatest profit for the firm? Applying the general rule for profit maximization, profits are maximized when resources are employed such that the marginal revenue attributable to the *last* unit of each resource equals its marginal cost. This marginal revenue is a function of both the additional output produced by the last unit of the input employed and the price at which the additional output is sold.

Expanding employment of a resource increases the firm's output and revenues, but it also increases costs. If the increase in revenues associated with one more unit of a resource exceeds the increase in costs incurred by hiring another unit of the resource, profits will increase. *So long as the increase in revenues resulting from the employment of an additional unit of a resource is greater than the increase in costs, the firm adds to its profits by employing more of the resource.* Expansion stops when employment reaches the level at which marginal revenue product equals marginal resource cost. The marginal revenue–marginal cost rule means that the employer must weigh three pieces of information when making a hiring decision: (1) the productivity of the resource, (2) the marginal revenue of the output, and (3) the cost of the resource.

Marginal Physical Product

The demand for a resource is derived from its value in producing a final product. The greater the productivity of the resource, the more valuable it is as an input to the firm. To make our discussion less abstract we will consider the case of a particular input, labor. However, you should keep in mind that the basic principles developed below apply equally to other resources.

The productivity of labor depends on a number of factors, including the technology used by the firm, the amount of other resources (such as capital goods) that are employed, and the efficiency of management (that is, how skilled management is at combining various resources in the most efficient manner). These variables are all captured in the firm's *production function*, which characterizes the relationship between the quantity of inputs employed and the quantity of output produced.[1] Table 1 presents the production function for a typical firm. It is a short-run production function, showing only how output responds to changes in the amount of labor employed. The other inputs in the production process are assumed to be fixed in amount.

In this example, as additional units of labor are combined with the fixed capital input, output increases.[2] The change in the firm's total physical product (TP) caused by a change in employment (by one worker in this case) is called the **marginal physical product** of labor (MPL). As shown in column 2 of

Derived demand
The demand for a resource is derived from the demand for the product the resource is used to produce.

SECTION RECAP
The demand for a resource is derived from the demand for the product it is used to produce. Additional units of a resource are hired up to the point at which the addition to profit of the marginal unit is zero.

Marginal physical product
The change in total output that results from employing an additional unit of a resource.

---
[1] The production function was introduced and discussed in detail in Chapter 9.
[2] Note, however, that the MP of the ninth worker is negative and therefore total output begins to decline beyond the eighth unit of labor.

TABLE 1

The short-run production function and marginal revenue product schedule for a firm with one variable input

(1) Number of Workers	(2) Total Physical Product (TP) (lbs./hour)	(3) Marginal Physical Product (MP) (lbs./hour)	(4) Marginal Revenue Product (MRP) ($/hour)
1	10	10	$20
2	22	12	24
3	36	14	28
4	48	12	24
5	58	10	20
6	66	8	16
7	70	4	8
8	72	2	4
9	70	−2	−4

(Note: Product price and marginal revenue are assumed to be $2.00)

Table 1, adding the second worker causes total output to increase from ten pounds to twenty-two pounds—thus the marginal physical product of the second worker is twelve pounds (as shown in column 3). The marginal physical product of the third worker is fourteen pounds of output.

The marginal physical product of labor is important information for the firm. Calculating the change in total physical product for each additional worker yields the marginal physical product schedule. The important feature of the marginal physical product schedule is how, beginning with the fourth worker, marginal physical product declines continuously. As more workers are added, the addition to output becomes smaller and smaller. In our example, marginal physical product actually turns negative with the ninth worker. This production function thus conforms to the law of diminishing returns. As more of the variable resource, labor, is combined with the fixed inputs, the marginal physical product of labor ultimately declines. This technological law is responsible for the downward-sloping portion of the marginal physical product schedule shown in Figure 1 (a).

Product Price and Marginal Revenue Product

The marginal physical product of an input is essential information for a firm. However, additional information is required to determine resource demand. The rational firm employs additional units of an input up to the point at which the *revenue* attributable to the marginal unit of the input is equal to its cost. Consequently, marginal physical product must be transformed into its dollar value to the firm. Even if an input, like labor, is very productive, the dollar value of additional workers to the firm will be relatively low if the market price

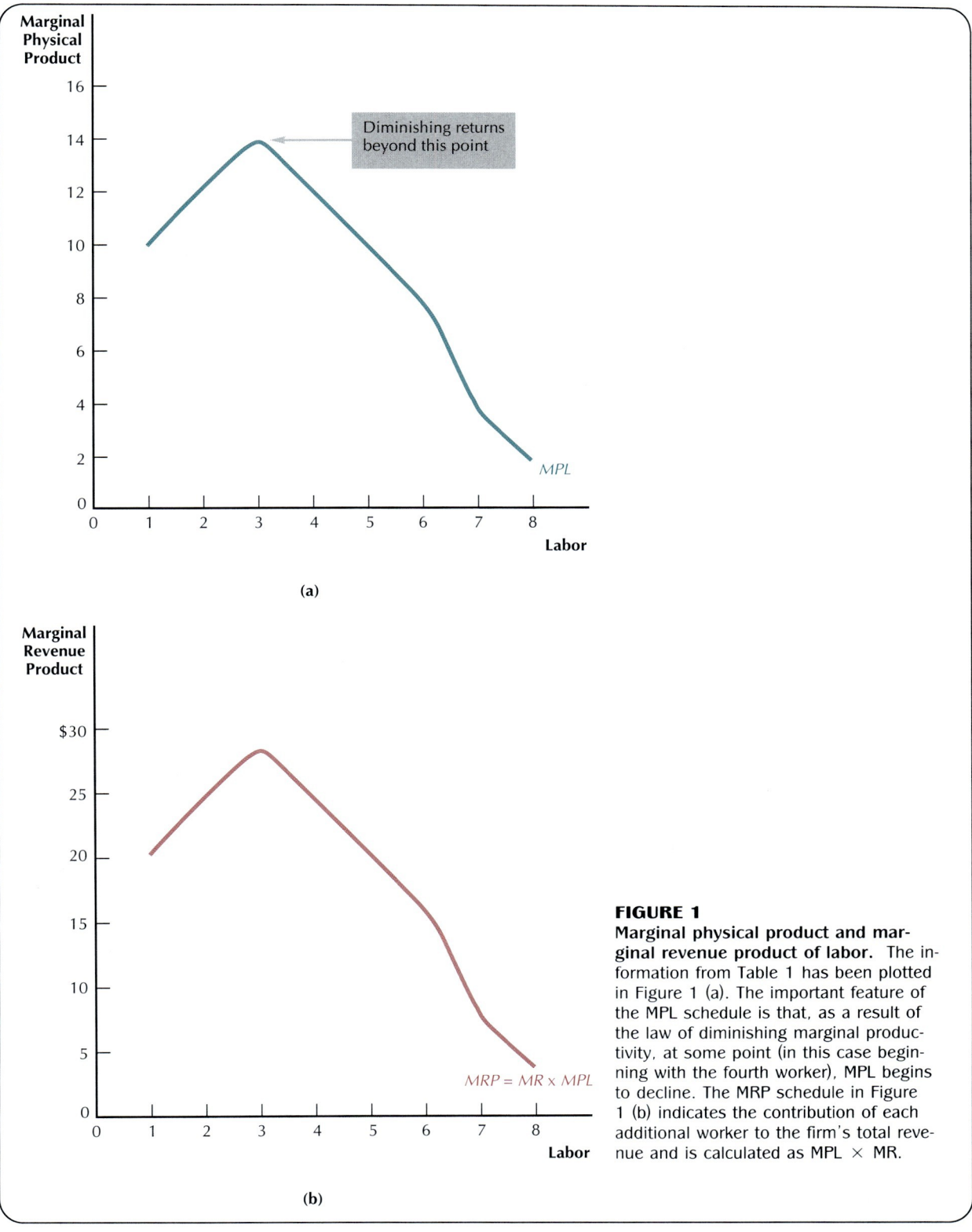

FIGURE 1
Marginal physical product and marginal revenue product of labor. The information from Table 1 has been plotted in Figure 1 (a). The important feature of the MPL schedule is that, as a result of the law of diminishing marginal productivity, at some point (in this case beginning with the fourth worker), MPL begins to decline. The MRP schedule in Figure 1 (b) indicates the contribution of each additional worker to the firm's total revenue and is calculated as MPL × MR.

of the product is low. Again, the demand for a resource is derived from conditions in the product market.

The dollar value to the firm of each additional unit of an input, measured as the change in total revenue, is equal to the marginal physical product of the marginal unit of the input times the marginal revenue (MR) of each unit of output. This measure of marginal productivity is called **marginal revenue product** (MRP). In mathematical notation:

$$MRP = MP \times MR$$

Marginal revenue product
The change in total revenue resulting from the employment of an additional unit of a resource.

Marginal revenue product is the change in total revenue that results from employing an additional unit of an input.

If the firm sells its output in a perfectly competitive product market, the firm is a price taker. For the price-taking firm, marginal revenue is constant and equal to the per-unit price of output (price equals marginal revenue). In our example, a perfectly competitive firm sells the marginal output of the first worker and the eighth worker for the same price. This means that marginal revenue product for the competitive firm is equal to marginal physical product multiplied times the price of the product:

$$MRP = MP \times P$$

for a perfectly competitive firm.

SECTION RECAP
For a perfectly competitive firm, the marginal revenue product (MRP) of a resource is calculated as MP times the market price of output. MRP is the addition to total revenue gained by employing the marginal unit of the resource.

Column 4 of Table 1 is created by multiplying column 3 by $2, the market price of each pound of output. The marginal revenue product of the fourth worker is $24 — this worker brings in $24 to the firm by producing an extra twelve pounds, which can be sold for $2 each. The marginal revenue product of the fifth worker is $20 per hour, and so forth.

The marginal revenue product schedule is shown in Figure 1 (b). It indicates the contribution of each additional worker to the firm's total revenues. Note that it takes the same shape as the marginal physical product schedule. The value of the marginal worker to the firm declines as more units of labor are employed, reflecting diminishing marginal returns.[3]

Marginal Resource Cost and the Demand Schedule for Labor

The marginal productivity of an input and the price of the product combine to determine marginal revenue product, which, in the case of the perfectly competitive firm, is the value of the marginal worker to the firm. The final ingredient in the hiring decision is the **marginal resource cost** (MRC). Marginal resource cost is the change in total resource costs to the firm when it changes the level of employment of a resource by one unit. The profit-maximizing firm compares marginal revenue product with marginal resource cost in determining how much of each resource to employ.

Marginal resource cost
The change in total cost resulting from the employment of an additional unit of a resource.

We already have assumed that our firm sells its output in a perfectly competitive product market. Assume also that the firm hires labor in a perfectly competitive resource market. Perfect competition in a resource market means that each firm is a price taker — it is such a small part of the overall market

---

[3] Up to this point, we have considered the situation for a perfectly competitive firm — a price taker. In the case of the price-searching firm, MR < P at each level of output. In addition, MR declines as output increases and the firm moves down its demand curve. Consequently, the MRP curve for a price-searching firm is steeper than the MRP curve for a competitive firm, *ceteris paribus*.

that its decision about how much to employ cannot affect the market price of the resource. For example, a law firm in New York City does not set the wage it pays its secretaries. Rather, it must pay the going wage that is determined by the interaction of market demand and supply in the New York market for secretarial workers.

For the competitive employer of labor, the marginal resource cost of an extra worker is simply equal to the wage (W) paid to the extra worker (MRC = W). Since the wages of all previously hired workers are unaffected when an additional worker is hired, total labor cost is increased by the wage paid to the marginal worker.

Knowing the marginal revenue product and the marginal resource cost of each worker, the firm has all the information it needs to determine the profit-maximizing number of workers. All workers for which marginal revenue product is greater than marginal resource cost (or equivalently, marginal revenue product is greater than W) will be hired.

Referring to Figure 1 (b) again, suppose the wage for this type of worker is $19 per hour. How many workers will be employed? As indicated in the figure, the marginal revenue product is greater than marginal resource cost for each unit of labor up to and including the fifth worker. The fifth worker adds $20 to revenues but only $19 to costs. Consequently, the firm increases its profits by $1 by hiring the fifth worker. However, the firm will not expand to six employees because marginal revenue product is less than marginal resource cost for the sixth worker, and the firm would lose $3 by hiring the sixth worker at $19 per hour. At a wage of $19 per hour, the profit-maximizing firm hires five workers.

Now suppose the wage drops to $15 per hour. Employment will expand to six workers. At the lower wage the sixth worker adds $1 to profits. By the same reasoning, if the wage were to increase to $21 per hour the firm would cut back to four workers.

The marginal revenue product schedule determines the amount of labor the firm will demand at different wage rates. *The marginal revenue product schedule is the firm's demand schedule for labor.* Given any wage rate, the competitive firm employs labor up to the point where marginal revenue product equals marginal resource cost (which is in turn equal to the market wage). As the wage rises or falls, the firm moves up or down the marginal revenue product schedule, decreasing or increasing the quantity of the resource it employs.

For any given wage rate the level of employment can be read off the marginal revenue product schedule. The marginal revenue product schedule and the firm's resource demand schedule are synonymous.[4] The firm's demand schedule for labor, or any other resource, is downward sloping. This is a consequence of two factors: diminishing marginal productivity of the resource and the profit-maximizing behavior of firms.

SECTION RECAP
The amount of a resource that will be employed is determined by equating its MRC and MRP. As MRC changes, we move along the MRP schedule. Hence, the MRP schedule is the firm's resource demand curve.

Market Demand for Resources

The market price of the resource was taken as a given in deriving the firm's resource demand schedule. The next logical step is to consider how these resource prices are determined. The answer requires an analysis of total market

---

[4]For reasons we need not enter into here, only the downward-sloping portion of the MRP schedule represents the firm's resource demand. We ignore the upward-sloping portion.

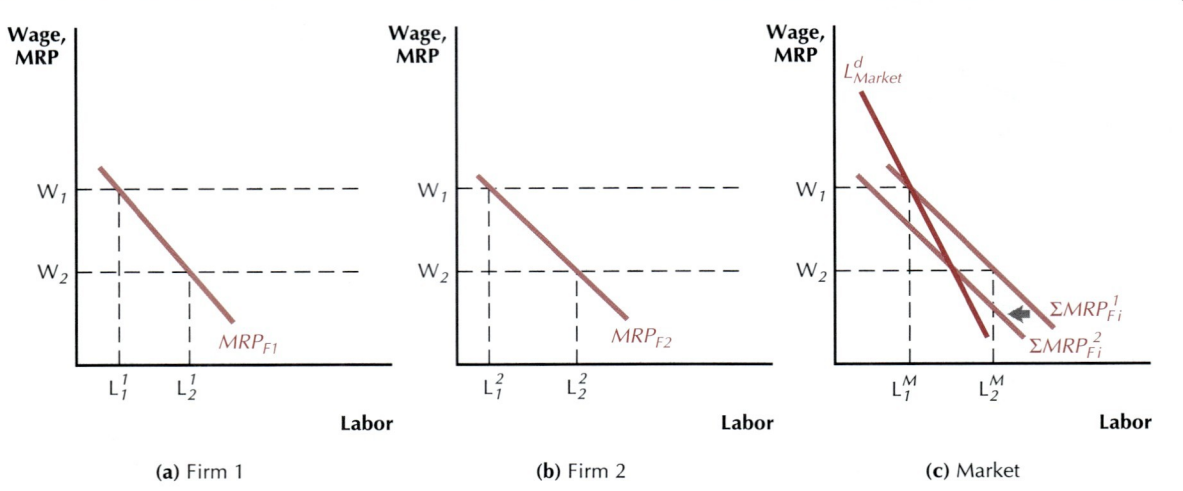

FIGURE 2
Deriving the market demand curve for a resource. *(a) Firm 1 (b) Firm 2 (c) Market.* At each wage rate, total labor demanded is the sum of the quantity demanded by each firm. At W_1 total demand is $L_1^1 + L_1^2 = L_1^M$. Diminishing marginal productivity is one reason for the negative slope of the market demand curve for labor. However, suppose the wage falls to W_2 and all firms expand employment. The resulting increase in total output must drive down the product price as well. When product price falls, each firm's MRP schedule shifts back to the left. The market demand curve for labor, L_{Market}^d, is steeper than the horizontal sum of the individual firms' labor demand curves because of the feedback from the product market.

demand and supply. We begin by deriving the market demand curve for a resource.

Market demand for a resource is obtained in a familiar fashion. Continuing with our labor market example, we begin by horizontally summing the labor demand schedules of the individual firms. This aggregation is illustrated in Figure 2. Suppose there are n firms. (In Figure 2 it is assumed, for simplicity, that n = 2.) At each wage rate, total labor demanded is the sum of the quantity of labor demanded by each firm. At any given wage rate we obtain the quantity of labor demanded from each of the n firms' demand schedules, and then we sum these quantities across all n firms. At W_1 total demand is $L_1^1 + L_1^2 + \ldots + L_1^n = L_1^M$. (Subscripts refer to the wage level, superscripts refer to each firm.) At W_2 each firm demands more, so that $L_2^1 + L_2^2 \ldots + L_2^n = L_2^M > L_1^M$. Since the quantity of labor demanded by each firm increases as the wage falls, the market demand schedule is also downward sloping. One reason is diminishing marginal productivity, which determines the slope of individual firms' demand schedules.

However, there is another factor that explains why the market resource demand curve is downward sloping. In analyzing the individual firm's resource demand curve, product price was assumed constant as the firm expanded output and employment. This assumption must be dropped when deriving the market demand schedule. Suppose the wage falls to W_2 and all firms expand employment. The resulting increase in total output drives down the product price as well. (As supply increases, the product supply curve shifts to the right, causing the equilibrium price to decline.) This, in turn, causes each firm's marginal revenue product schedule (P × MPL) to shift to the left. That is, there is a decrease in demand for the resource. This is shown in the graph for the market by a leftward shift of the curve labeled ΣMRP^1_{Fi} to ΣMRP^2_{Fi}. The net result is that total market employment expands by less than that given by the horizontal sum of the marginal revenue product curves of the individual firms. The fall in product price tempers the incentive for firms to expand employment when the wage falls. Likewise, the fall in employment that is caused by rising wages is offset by rising product prices.

Remember that the product and resource markets are linked. In Figure 2, when product price falls, each firm's marginal revenue product schedule shifts to the left. The market demand curve for labor is steeper than the horizontal sum of the individual firms' labor demand curves because of the feedback from the product market to the resource market through changes in market price.

The shape of the market resource demand curve has extremely important implications for society, and especially for labor. Negatively sloped resource demand curves imply that employment opportunities are negatively related to input prices. Higher input prices imply fewer employment opportunities and vice versa. In the labor market, attempts to raise wage rates through legislation or collective bargaining will result in fewer jobs and consequently lower employment (unless there are offsetting increases in labor productivity).

> **SECTION RECAP**
> The market demand curve for a resource is downward sloping. It is steeper than the firm's demand curve due to the feedback effects of changes in market output and price on MRP.

Price Elasticity of Demand for Resources

Frequently, we need to know not only the relationship between the quantity of a resource demanded and its price, but also by how much quantity demanded changes when the price changes. For example, unions need to know by how much employment will fall if higher wages are negotiated. Congress must estimate how much additional employment will result if wages are subsidized through tax credits. OPEC would like to know how much the quantity of oil demanded will change if OPEC raises the price of oil by a certain percentage. Many decisions depend upon the sensitivity of resource users to changes in resource prices. This sensitivity is called the **price elasticity of resource demand**. It is a measure of how responsive demanders of resources are to changes in resource prices.

Price elasticity of resource demand is based on the same general concept as the price elasticity of product demand introduced in Chapter 7. In that situation, we used the notion of price elasticity to measure the sensitivity of consumers to changes in the prices of consumer goods and services. This concept can also be applied to firms' demands for resources.

The **coefficient of elasticity** is the ratio of the percentage change in quantity demanded to the percentage change in price, or:

$$e_r = \frac{\%\text{ change in quantity of resource demanded}}{\%\text{ change in price}}$$

where e_r is the elasticity coefficient.[5] (The subscript r indicates that the elasticity coefficient is for resource demand.) *The value of the elasticity coefficient allows*

Price elasticity of resource demand
A measure of how responsive the quantity demanded of a resource is to a change in its price.

Coefficient of elasticity
The ratio of the percentage change in quantity demanded to the percentage change in price.

---

[5] As in the case of the price elasticity of a good, the elasticity coefficient has a negative sign as a result of the inverse relationship between price and quantity demanded. However, we once again drop the negative sign for convenience.

us to calculate the amount by which quantity demanded changes in response to a given price change. As in the case of consumer goods, resource price elasticities vary across markets. For example, suppose employment of labor falls by 2 percent when the wage rate rises 1 percent. The elasticity coefficient would be 2.0, indicating a relatively elastic market demand for labor. In another labor market, a 1 percent wage increase may only reduce employment by 0.5 percent. The elasticity coefficient would be equal to 0.5, revealing demand to be relatively inelastic.

The elasticity coefficient of 1.0 is an important benchmark. When the absolute value of the elasticity coefficient is greater than 1.0 (2.0 for example) and resource demand is therefore relatively elastic, a change in the resource price causes total income received by the resource owners to move in the opposite direction. Resource price and income move in the same direction when the absolute value of e_r is less than 1.0, for example 0.5. If the elasticity of resource demand is less than 1.0, a rise in the resource price is not fully offset by the drop in employment. While fewer units of the resource are employed when price rises, the higher price each unit receives leads to an increase in total income paid to the resource. However, if the elasticity coefficient is 2.0, a 1 percent rise in the resource price will be more than offset by a 2 percent decline in employment. While each employed unit of the resource earns more, the large loss in employment means lower total income.[6]

SECTION RECAP
The price elasticity of resource demand measures the sensitivity of quantity demanded to a change in the price of a resource.

Determinants of Resource Price Elasticity

This section considers factors that influence the elasticity of resource demand. As in the case of consumer goods, the availability of substitutes is an important factor affecting resource price elasticity. Elasticity of resource demand is greater in the long run than in the short run. This results from the fact that over a longer period of time firms are able to make more adjustments to price changes. Stated differently, firms have more alternatives available to them over a longer period of time.

Price Elasticity in the Short Run

Four factors influence short-run resource demand elasticity. First, the slower the rate at which marginal productivity declines, the more elastic is resource demand. As the price of a resource—marginal resource cost—declines, the quantity demanded of the resource increases to maintain equality of marginal revenue product and marginal resource cost. If the marginal physical product, and hence marginal revenue product, of additional units of the resource decrease slowly, the firm will expand its employment of the resource by more than it would if marginal physical product fell rapidly. The percentage by which the quantity demanded of a resource responds to a percentage change in price is greater, the slower the decline in the marginal physical product of the resource.

Second, the greater the price elasticity of demand for the industry's product, the more elastic is resource demand. Recall that changes in the employment

---

[6]Note that the relationship between elasticity of resource demand and the impact of a price change on the income of resource owners is the same as the relationship between elasticity of product demand and the income of suppliers. This relationship was discussed at length in Chapter 6.

of a factor of production are dampened by changes in the price of the industry's product. For example, as wage rates rise, firms economize on labor and reduce employment. Layoffs are partially offset by the decline in industry output, which increases product price. The greater the elasticity of demand for the product, however, the less product price rises when output declines. This means that the dampening effect of changes in product price is smaller and employment changes in response to changed resource prices are greater when product demand is elastic.

This particular adjustment process is called *substitution in consumption*. When consumers are relatively insensitive to product price changes (product demand is inelastic), an increase in an input price causes a smaller decrease in employment of the resource (resource demand is more inelastic). A timely example illustrates this point. American automobile manufacturers are more responsive today to changes in auto workers' earnings than in the 1960s. A major reason is that the price elasticity of demand for American cars is higher today, as a result of increased competition from Europe and Japan. Being less able to pass along higher labor costs by raising prices, domestic auto makers are more likely to reduce employment when wages rise.

Third, the greater the share of total costs represented by the resource, the more elastic is resource demand. Suppose wage costs are 80 percent of total production costs in industry X but just 10 percent of total costs in industry Y. An increase in wages of 10 percent for workers in both industries will raise total costs by 8 percent for industry X, but only by 1 percent in industry Y. If product price elasticities are the same for both industries, profit-maximizing output and employment fall by more in industry X.

Fourth, the greater the availability of substitutes for a resource, the more elastic is resource demand. Recall that the elasticity of demand for a good or service increases with the availability of good substitutes. This is because buyers have a larger number of alternatives to choose from in the event of a price increase. The same logic applies to the elasticity of resource demand. As the number of available substitutes for a resource increases, a firm's ability to alter the combination of resources it uses in its production process increases as well. In this case, the quantity demanded of a resource is relatively sensitive to a change in its price. Just the opposite is true in the case where there are few or no good substitutes for a resource.

SECTION RECAP
The short-run price elasticity of resource demand increases 1) the slower the rate of decline of MP, 2) the greater the price elasticity of the firm's output, 3) the greater the share of total costs accounted for by the resource, and 4) the greater the availability of good substitutes for the resource.

Price Elasticity in the Long Run

Resource demand elasticity is greater in the long run. In the short run, a firm may be unable to substitute a cheaper input when the price of a particular resource rises. However, given enough time such substitution possibilities arise. The primary long-run determinant of resource demand elasticity is the relative ease of substitution of other inputs in production. This avenue of adjustment by the firm is called *substitution in production*.

In general, it is technically possible to produce products using different combinations of inputs. A canal can be dug using 500 workers with hand shovels, or one worker with a steam shovel. The choice of inputs depends upon the relative costs of labor and capital. If labor is relatively cheap, the canal will be dug using a labor-intensive technique. When the wage rate rises, the firm will want to substitute relatively cheaper capital for labor, but it is unable to do so in the short run. The decrease in labor employment depends

Does It Make **Economic Sense?**

Management, Unions, and Trade Policy

Organized labor and business management are almost always adversaries, whether in collective bargaining or in lobbying federal or state governments for favorable legislation. On issues of domestic economic policy, the positions of business trade associations and the various labor unions, such as the AFL–CIO, generally are diametrically opposed to one another. However, the two sides have joined forces to lobby the federal government about a particular policy issue. The issue is international trade policy.

Competition from foreign suppliers has been depressing the earnings, sales, and employment of many U.S. businesses. Industries suffering from successful foreign competition include automobiles, steel, computer chip makers, and shoes. Both organized labor and the business community strongly support trade restrictions. They continually encourage Congress to enact legislation that erects barriers to the importation of foreign goods. Does it make sense that both labor and management take this position?

It is clear why U.S. manufacturers want to restrict imports. With less competition, domestic manufacturers are able to exert greater market power. Consequently, they can charge higher prices and enjoy greater profits than they can in the face of foreign competition. But why should organized labor favor a policy that is supposedly probusiness? The answer lies in the elasticity of demand for union labor. Unions are constrained from pushing wages up by the downward-sloping labor demand schedule. The more elastic is labor demand, the greater the employment loss from any given wage increase.

---

solely upon the short-run elasticity determinants discussed above. Over the long run, however, capital can be substituted for labor and the employment of labor will decline further. *This extent to which capital can be substituted for labor depends upon the technology employed, and varies across industries. As the technical feasibility of input substitution increases, so does the long-run demand elasticity of each input.*

Often, we understate the ability of firms to substitute inputs in production, and thereby understate the elasticity of resource demand. For example, consider the airline industry. Most passenger jets flown in the 1970s required three pilots. Throughout this period, pilots' earnings escalated rapidly. In the short run, the airlines were technically unable to respond to these higher wage costs. The 1980s, however, brought the introduction of Boeing 757s and 767s, which require only two pilots. The airlines, given enough time, were eventually able to substitute capital for the more expensive labor. Similarly, most observers were surprised by how much industry in the United States was able to reduce its petroleum usage by substituting other inputs for energy when energy prices rose sharply in the 1970s.

Supply of Resources

In analyzing the relationship between market price and quantities of a resource willingly supplied to the market, we assume that resource owners seek to maximize the income derived from employment of their resources (subject to constraints). The sale of their resources determines the income with which resource owners purchase consumption goods and services. Thus, resource owners supply their resources to those employment opportunities offering the

Unions would prefer the demand schedule to be more inelastic to minimize the number of jobs lost as a result of increased wages.

One of the major determinants of resource demand elasticity is the elasticity of demand for the good or service the resource is used to produce. The potential for substitution in consumption — the act of substituting one consumption good for another — influences the elasticity of demand for resources like labor. By increasing the number of available substitutes, foreign competition makes the demand for products more elastic, thus increasing the elasticity of demand for labor. With import barriers, U.S. firms are more willing to agree to higher wages, as they are better able to raise prices without losing market share. Clearly then, it is in unions' interests to advocate trade barriers, since they reduce the elasticity of demand for American workers by reducing the elasticity of demand for the products they produce.

It is no secret why steel and automobile manufacturers have demanded, and won, major concessions from organized labor in the 1980s. Stiff foreign competition has brought considerable pressure to bear on U.S. manufacturers and forced them to take a stronger position against wage increases. The increase in competition in the product market has also made the labor market more competitive. Essentially, U.S. workers now are competing with Japanese workers through the product market. In short, the increased competition has had adverse effects on both business and labor. Thus we have a rare instance of agreement between the two sides regarding economic policy. Both sides stand to gain from restrictions on free trade.

---

highest price. The owners of capital equipment seek to rent or sell the equipment to the highest bidder. Land owners rent their land to those who offer the highest rent. From the jobs available to workers, they select those jobs offering the highest rate of pay. (Other conditions of employment may be as important as the wage. These will be discussed in the next chapter. For now we assume that only the rate of pay matters to workers.)

The income-seeking behavior of resource owners suggests that resource supply functions are positively sloped — market price and quantities willingly supplied to the market are positively related. Higher resource prices attract more resources. However, the mobility of resources and the time available for response to price changes exert a strong influence on the precise relationship between market price and quantities supplied. **Price elasticity of supply** is the percentage change in the quantity supplied that is caused by a percentage change in market price. This supply elasticity measure is used to consider further the determinants of the shape of the supply curve.

Price elasticity of supply A measure of the responsiveness of quantity supplied to a change in market price.

Resource Supply in the Short Run

When discussing resource supply, care must be taken to identify the use of or the market for the resource. The resource supply curve depends upon how broadly defined that use or market is.[7] The range of alternative uses is determined by our definition of a market. The more broadly the market is defined, the less elastic the resource supply schedule tends to be.

---

[7] Remember that the availability of substitutes or alternatives plays an important role in determining the sensitivity of decision makers to price changes.

Consider the supply of land. For practical purposes, the total supply of land to the entire U.S. economy is fixed in the short run. When the supply of a resource is fixed, the supply curve is perfectly inelastic, as in Figure 3 (a). In the short run, the supply of land is inelastic because owners will not withdraw land from production should land rents fall. Land cannot be used for purposes other than U.S. production. In other words, the opportunity cost of its use in the United States is zero. Similarly, if rents should increase, no additional land can be brought into use. In the short run, there are no alternatives for users of U.S. land.

The economy-wide short-run supply curve of other resources is also very inelastic, although not necessarily perfectly inelastic. The quantities of labor or equipment supplied to the economy in the short run are relatively unresponsive to price changes, but if price movements are sufficiently large, some supply response may occur. These resources are more mobile than land in the short run. The supply of resources to specific uses, or more narrowly defined markets, is positively sloped, as shown in Figure 3 (b).

Resources generally have a variety of uses. Resource owners seeking to maximize their income employ their resources in the most profitable opportunities available and are therefore sensitive to price changes. If the price paid for resources in one market rises, resource owners respond by moving their resources from other employment opportunities to the new, more rewarding use. To hire additional resources firms must bid them away from other employment opportunities.

The elasticity of supply depends on the mobility of resources. **Resource mobility** refers to the ability of resources to move among alternative uses. Resources that move easily and inexpensively between uses are said to be highly mobile. Resources that are difficult and costly to move between uses are said

Resource mobility
The ability of resources to move among alternative uses.

FIGURE 3
The supply of a resource. *(a) Land in United States (b) Land in U.S. Agriculture.* When supply is fixed, the supply curve is perfectly inelastic, as in Figure 3 (a). The supply of resources to specific uses, or more narrowly defined markets, is positively sloped, as shown in Figure 3 (b).

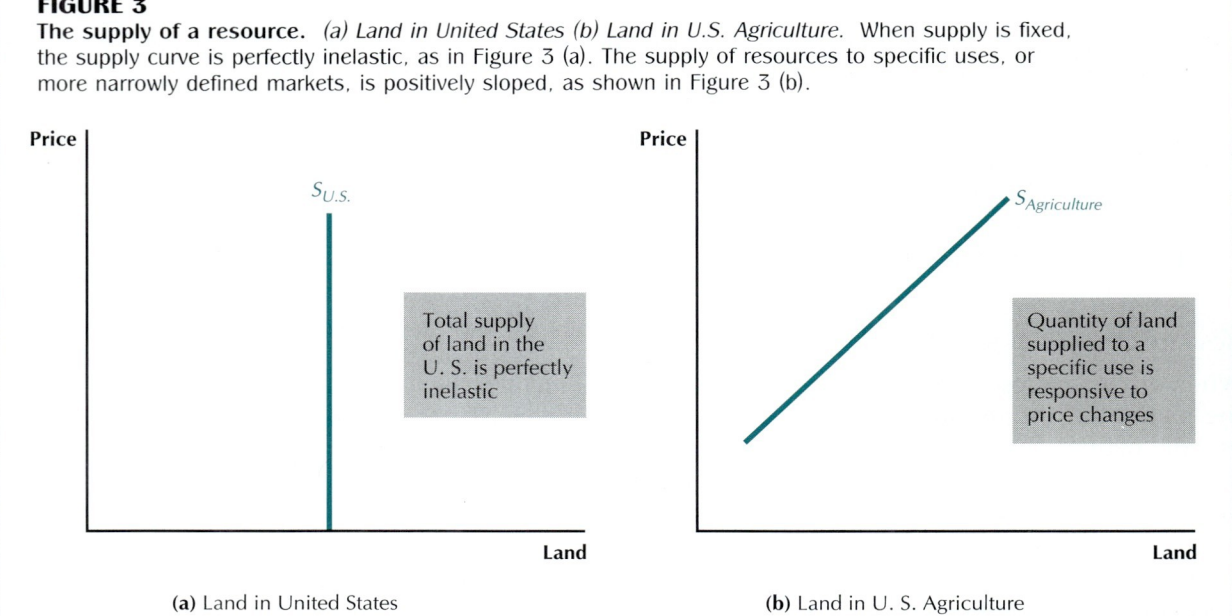

(a) Land in United States

(b) Land in U. S. Agriculture

to be highly immobile. *The more mobile a resource is, the more sensitive its supply is to price changes, and the more elastic is the resource supply function.*

It may sound strange to say that land is mobile, but land is quite mobile between many uses. The supply of land to different industries is positively sloped. Land can be used for growing crops, housing families, or building golf courses. A positively sloped supply curve for agricultural land implies that land rents must rise to draw additional acres into agriculture [Figure 3 (b)]. This follows from the imperfect substitutability of different types of land. At low agricultural prices, land best suited for agriculture is used first. The payments made to its owners do not need to be high, as this land has a low value in alternative production. As agriculture expands, land more suitable for other activities must be brought into production. To expand farming, additional land must be bid away from alternative uses. The rents paid to land more suitable for housing or shopping malls must be higher because the opportunity cost is greater.

The supply of land to a particular agricultural market, say sunflowers, is even more elastic because there are even more land alternatives available. Sunflower production is such a small portion of the agricultural market that it could expand greatly without firms in the sunflower industry having to pay substantially higher rents. On the other hand, if sunflower prices fell, and the returns to land used for this purpose declined even slightly, the land could easily be used to produce a different crop.

Of course, land does not physically move between locations. If land becomes very valuable in the center of downtown Los Angeles, the rising land prices do not attract more land to downtown LA. The supply of land at a particular location is perfectly inelastic. The fixed amount of land at a desirable location simply earns greater rent to reflect its value and inelastic supply.

The mobility and elasticity of labor vary. Geographic moves are costly. Labor of a given quality is highly mobile within a geographic area, such as a city or metropolitan area, but much less mobile when alternative employment opportunities are some distance away. In addition, the skill level of labor affects the elasticity of supply. The supply of higher-skilled workers is less elastic in the short run because of the costly training that is required to develop the skill. In the short run, the supply of machine operators is more elastic than the supply of cardiovascular surgeons.

The supply elasticity of machinery, equipment, and buildings also varies, depending upon the nature of the resource. The more general the purpose of the resource, the more mobile it is and the more elastic is its short-run supply. Fork lifts, desks, lathes, and drills are fairly mobile. Special purpose equipment and buildings are very immobile. It is probably fair to say that most physical capital is relatively immobile. Steel-making machines cannot be used to make computer cabinets. An old downtown warehouse is not suitable for housing an auto assembly plant.

SECTION RECAP
Generally, short-run resource supply curves are positively sloped. The price elasticity of supply depends upon how mobile the resource is.

Resource Supply in the Long Run

The long-run supply curve for all resources is positively sloped. Over time, resources may be depleted or deteriorate, but we can also add to our stock of resources through investment. The amounts of available resources typically grow over time; investment adds resources at a rate that exceeds the rate of depreciation.

Why the **Disagreement?**

The Tin Cartel: Doomed to Fail?

An understanding of markets yields insights into how a supplier can earn substantial economic profits by gaining control of the supply of a product, or resource, that is valuable in consumption, or production, but for which there are no substitutes. This strategy has been pursued on numerous occasions by groups of suppliers who form a *cartel*—a group of individuals, firms, or countries who agree to cooperate in an action to benefit the group.

A cartel of suppliers enlists as many of the industry suppliers as possible and then agrees to cooperate in supplying a good to market. The objective is to increase the profits of the cartel members. Many people believe cartels are successful in making suppliers better off. In particular, it is widely believed that by forming a cartel, participating firms will earn greater profits over the long run. However, our analysis in this chapter (and Chapter 12) suggests such arrangements will be difficult to implement successfully and that long-run profits are by no means guaranteed. What accounts for these two different perspectives; why the disagreement?

The simple answer is that a cartel has a much greater chance of success in the short run than in the long run. Consider the history of one particular cartel, the International Tin Council (ITC), an organization of some twenty tin-producing and -consuming countries. There has been some kind of cartel in the tin industry since the 1920s. The *stated* objective of the cartel is to stabilize prices, but some cartel members argue that its recent collapse occurred because it was attempting to push prices too high. The ITC attempted to stabilize tin prices by buying and selling tin to keep the price within an agreed-upon range.* Cartel members contributed to a fund used to make these purchases. Figure 4 illustrates the way the cartel attempted to stabilize prices. As with many agricultural and mined commodities, the short-run supply of tin is relatively price inelastic. Consequently, demand shifts cause wide price fluctuations. Consider Figure 4 (a) first. Suppose the cartel wants to stabilize the price of tin at P_e, the market equilibrium price when demand is D_e. If demand were less, say D_A, the cartel would enter the market as a buyer, driving demand back to the right and the price of tin back to the desired equilibrium. The cartel purchases $Q_e - Q_A$ units, which it holds until demand is strong enough to push price above the desired equilibrium [see Figure 4 (b)]. When demand exceeds expectations, such as at D'_A, the cartel sells off its holdings, increasing supply to S_{SR+C} and depressing price back to the desired equilibrium. The cartel sells $Q'_A - Q_e$ units of tin.

This system works fairly well so long as the desired market price, P_e, is close to a long-run equilibrium price. However, if cartel members try to use this price-support scheme to push tin prices above the long-run equilibrium, trouble will develop. This is, in fact, what the ITC did. The above-equilibrium price set in motion forces on both the demand and supply side of the market that weakened the organization.

Tin is used in the production of many different products. When the ITC pushed up the price of tin, it made tin a relatively more expensive input. Tin users began to look for substitutes for tin that would keep production costs down. The demand for tin began to fall.

A similar long-run process began on the supply side. The higher tin price made tin mining more profitable. Tin companies began to expand production. Entrepreneurs in non-ITC countries began mining tin. While these investments took time to make, they ultimately resulted in increased supplies of tin available from non-ITC sources. The long-run price elasticity of demand and supply for tin was greater than the short-run elasticity. The higher price caused tin consumers to find alternatives and new producers to enter the tin industry. The result was a worsening of conditions in the tin market for

---

The quantity of resources supplied to the market in the long run depends upon resource prices. Resource prices influence the profitability of investments, and therefore the amount of investment and the rate at which it is undertaken. If the price of oil rises relative to the price of other resources, the relative profitability of investment in the search for and development of new oil supplies increases. These profit opportunities attract investors who finance the

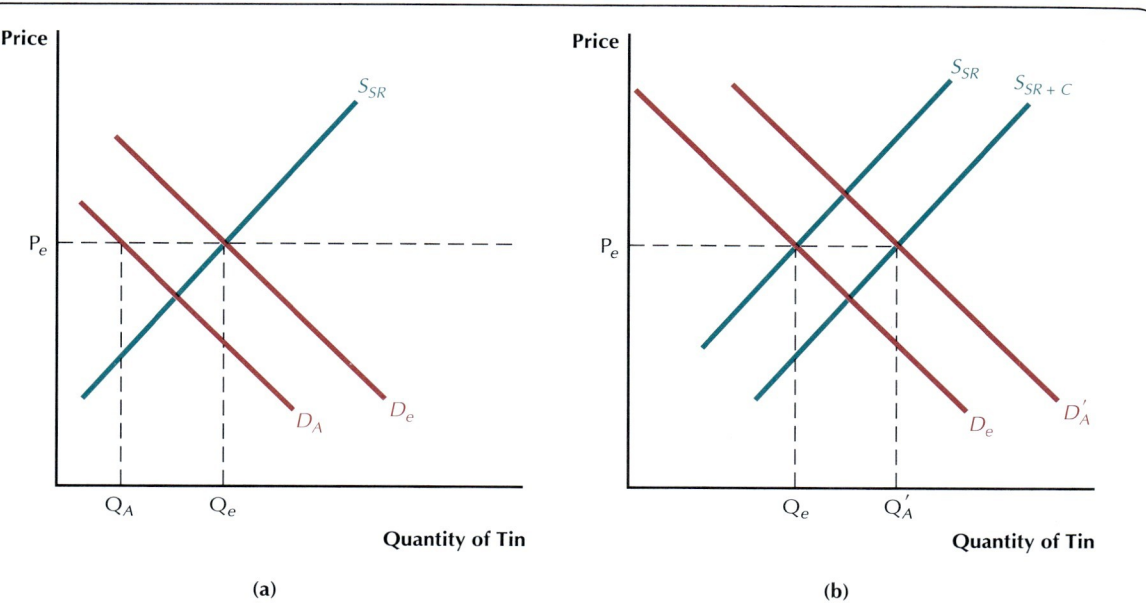

FIGURE 4
The economic effects of the international tin cartel. Referring to Figure 4 (a), suppose the cartel wants to stabilize the tin price at P_e, the equilibrium price when demand is D_e. If demand is less, say D_A, the cartel steps in as a buyer, driving demand back to the right and price back to the desired equilibrium. The cartel purchases $Q_e - Q_A$ units, which it holds until demand is strong enough to push price above the desired equilibrium (see Figure 4 (b)). When demand exceeds expectations, D'_A, the cartel sells off its holdings, increasing supply to S_{SR+C} and depressing price back to the desired equilibrium. The cartel sells $Q'_A - Q_e$ units of tin.

ITC producers. Demand fell and supply increased. The result: an even lower long-run equilibrium price for tin. To maintain the old price would require greater financial commitments to the ITC price-support system. Many member countries were unwilling to make this commitment. In 1985 the ITC ended its price-support system and tin prices were thereafter determined by the unfettered working of the world tin market. In the short run, the ITC succeeded, but its short-run success set in motion the long-run market forces that ultimately defeated it.

*The cartel must include most tin producers. To the extent that some tin producers opt out of the cartel, its control of supply is weakened.

search for new oil. The resources committed to the development of new oil are drawn from other investment opportunities. As a result of these investments, the future supply of oil increases.

Time is a key factor affecting the elasticity of supply. Investments require considerable amounts of time to increase resource supplies. Figure 5 shows three supply curves for oil, S_{SR}, S_{MR}, and S_{LR} (where the subscripts refer to the

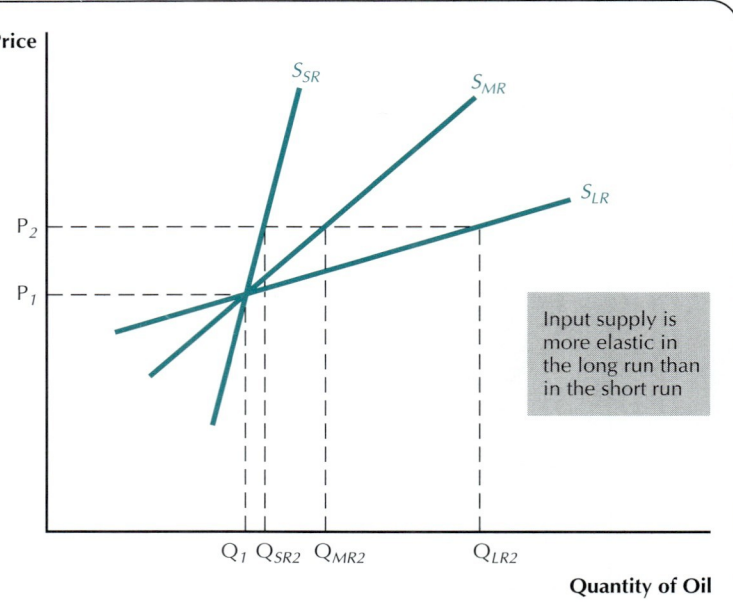

FIGURE 5
The elasticity of resource supply over time: the oil market. In this figure, three supply curves for oil, S_{SR}, S_{MR}, and S_{LR}, have been constructed so that each reflects the supply over a different period of time—one, two, and three years, respectively. The longer the period of time available, the more elastic is the supply curve. Note the effect of a price increase from P_1 to P_2. At P_1, quantity supplied, Q_1, is the same in all three cases. However, when price increases to P_2, the longer the time period being considered, the greater the response of quantity supplied will be, that is, $Q_{SR2} < Q_{MR2} < Q_{LR2}$.

Input supply is more elastic in the long run than in the short run

short run, intermediate run, and long run). Each curve reflects the supply over a different period of time—one, two, and three years. The longer the period of time available, the more elastic is the supply curve. The effect of the varying elasticities is illustrated by observing the effect of a price increase from P_1 to P_2. At the original price, P_1, quantity supplied, Q_1, is the same in all three cases. However, when price increases to P_2, *the response of quantity supplied is greater the longer the time period being considered.* That is, $Q_{SR2} < Q_{MR2} < Q_{LR2}$.

In the long run, even the total supply of land is not fixed. If land prices were to rise high enough, it might become profitable to use other resources to expand the supply of productive land. We could drain lakes, fertilize deserts, or reclaim seashores. These measures may sound outlandish at present land values, but they might be reasonable projects if land prices were much higher than current levels. The higher prices would make these costly investments profitable. Japan is a country with a land problem. It is an island country whose population size is very large relative to its land area. As a consequence, land values are extremely high; the Japanese do take steps to use their land more efficiently than we do in the United States. They have built facilities on land created by filling in the shores around parts of the islands. This additional land was added by long-run investment projects.

Human capital refers to the productivity-determining skills and abilities embodied in labor. We make investments in human capital in much the same way as we do physical capital. We acquire additional education and training to increase our productivity and our earnings. We make such human capital investments on the basis of profitability. We acquire costly training when we believe that the benefits in terms of higher earnings will exceed the training costs. There is considerable evidence that the long-run supply of college- and graduate school-educated workers responds to relative earnings.

Human capital
The productivity-determining skills and abilities embodied in labor.

Growing college enrollments in the late 1960s and early 1970s caused the demand for graduate-educated faculty to rise. The increase in demand bid faculty salaries up, attracting many students into Ph.D. programs and then into college teaching. However, as enrollment growth slowed, and then ended in the 1980s, the demand for university faculty fell sharply, and faculty salaries fell relative to other occupational groups. The poor prospects in higher education reduced the number of people seeking these positions.

Note again the importance of the time dimension. Training takes time. It may take a matter of weeks or months to train people as carpenters, mechanics, machine operators, secretaries, and data entry operators. It takes years to train people for other occupations—attorneys, actuaries, scientists, physicians. The investments necessary for any of these occupations slow the response to higher pay in such jobs. *The short-run supply elasticity is much lower than the long-run elasticity.*

SECTION RECAP
In the long run, the curve for all resources is positively sloped. Also, the price elasticity of supply is greater in the long run than in the short run.

The Labor Supply Schedule: Costs and Benefits . . . Again

The supply of labor to the American economy is a matter of much practical interest. Since World War II, the percentage of the potential labor force that has actually entered the labor market has increased steadily. In 1946 the **labor force participation rate,** the percentage of the noninstitutionalized, nonmilitary population between ages 16 and 70 who were employed or who were without a job but looking for work was 59 percent. In 1989, this percentage was up to 66.5 percent. This overall trend masks very different underlying trends. The participation rate of older males has fallen, while that for married women has nearly doubled, from 32 percent to 57 percent over the same period.

Labor force participation rate
The percentage of the noninstitutionalized, non-military population between ages 16 and 70 who are employed or without a job but looking for work.

What determines the aggregate supply of labor? How responsive is total labor supply to changes in average wage rates? Why has the labor supply of older men and married women moved in opposite directions?

Each individual weighs the costs and benefits of time spent at work. Each person has limited time to devote to either working for pay, working at home (housekeeping or do-it-yourself tasks), or pure leisure. The opportunity cost of an hour spent at leisure or working at home is simply the market wage—what the person gives up by not working at a job. The person who is deciding if and how much to work in the market must weigh the benefits of leisure or work at home against the cost of forgone wages.

When the wage rises, the opportunity cost of not working in the market goes up. Economic theory suggests that as the cost of nonmarket time rises, rational individuals demand less of it. There is a substitution of work time for home time. This adjustment to a wage change is called the *substitution effect*. Perhaps you may have heard very highly paid professionals claim that they "can't afford to take a vacation." What they mean is that the opportunity cost of not working is too high to take time off. For example, available data indicates that surgeons take shorter vacations than general practitioners, reflecting the higher opportunity costs incurred by the relatively higher-priced surgeons. The substitution effect suggests that the individual's supply of labor curve will be positively sloped, as higher wages attract the worker from the home into market work.

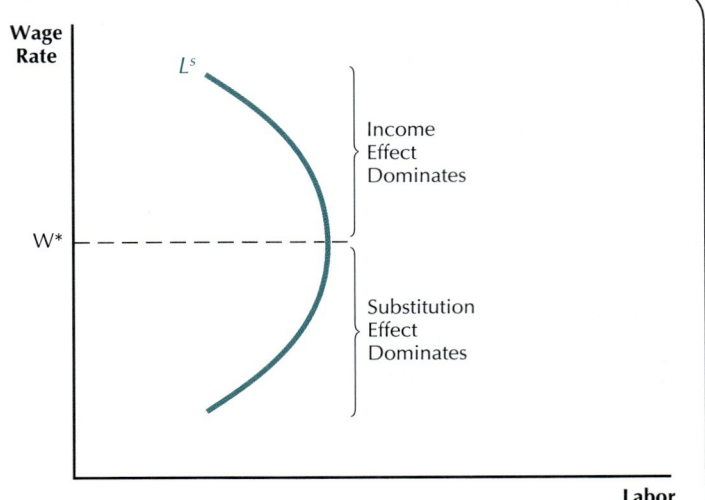

FIGURE 6
A backward-bending labor supply curve. As the wage rate increases, a worker substitutes labor for leisure. Thus, at lower wage rates, the labor supply curve is upward sloping. However, as the wage rate continues to increase, the income effect may dominate, and the worker begins to work less. Thus the labor supply curve bends backward.

At the same time, higher wages raise a worker's income. If leisure time is a normal good, the demand for leisure increases as wages and income rise. The increased consumption of leisure implies less work time. This tendency to consume more leisure is called the *income effect* of a wage change. The income effect tends to offset the substitution effect. What happens to hours of labor supplied to the market as wages rise depends upon which effect is stronger. If the substitution effect outweighs the income effect, the labor supply schedule has the familiar positive slope. However, a negative slope is possible if the income effect becomes stronger with higher wages and dominates the substitution effect. In this case, we see a backward-bending labor supply curve, which is illustrated in Figure 6. At lower wage rates the labor supply curve is upward sloping. However, above the wage rate where the income effect begins to dominate the substitution effect, W^*, the labor supply curve bends backward and successively higher wage rates are associated with successively lower levels of employment.

Statistical studies have indicated that the total supply of labor is rather inelastic, implying income and substitution effects that are offsetting. However, the labor supply schedule of married women is quite elastic. Apparently, rising real wages since World War II have attracted women into the labor force. On the other hand, the decline of labor supply by older men suggests a strong income effect, as wealthier workers now take earlier retirement.

SECTION RECAP
The long-run supply of labor appears to be rather inelastic, suggesting that the income effect and substitution effect offset each other.

Equilibrium in the Resource Market

The competition of firms for resources—the demand for resources—and the competition of resource owners for available employment—the supply of resources—combine to determine market equilibrium in resource markets. The interaction of demand and supply in the resource market is, in general, just like the interaction in product markets. Equilibrium is reached when the price is such that the quantity of the resource demanded by firms equals the quantity resource owners are willing to supply. At the equilibrium price, neither buyer nor seller has an incentive to bid the price up or down. All parties are satisfied, in the sense that they are able to buy or sell as much as they desire at the equilibrium price.

In resource markets, just as in product markets, the equilibrium adjustment process takes time. A change in the demand for a resource causes a short-run change in the market outcome, which then sets in motion a long-run change. Ultimately, a new long-run equilibrium is established. Suppose the demand for coal increases because OPEC nations double the price of oil. Firms look for alternatives to oil, such as coal. Figure 7 illustrates the changes in the coal market.

In the short run, the increase in demand for coal from D_1 to D_2 drives the market price up to P_2 from P_1. This new price is determined by the intersection

FIGURE 7
Long-run supply in the coal market. This figure illustrates the effects in the coal market of an increase in the price of oil. The increase in demand for coal from D_1 to D_2 drives the market price up from P_1 to P_3. Because there are now more profitable opportunities in coal, more resources are attracted into the industry over time, causing the short-run supply curve to shift to S_{SR2}. The market price for coal is driven down and a new long-run equilibrium will be established at a price of P_2 where the new short-run supply curve, S_{SR2}, and the demand curve, D_2, intersect. The long-run supply curve for coal is found by drawing a straight line through the original short-run price–quantity combination and the new short-run equilibrium.

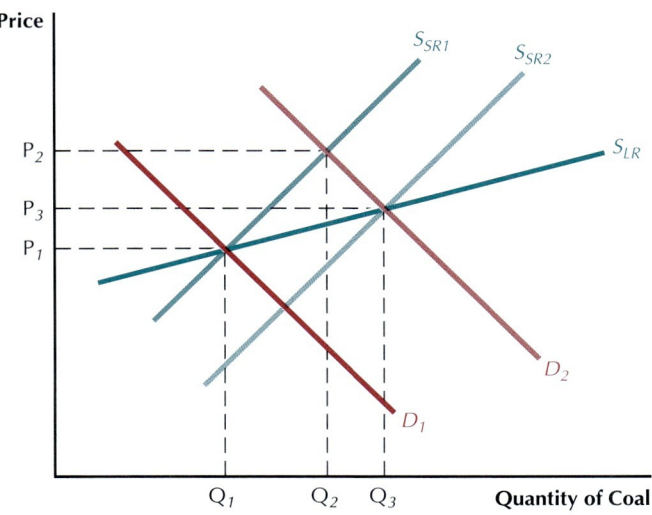

of the short-run supply of coal, S_{SR1}, and D_2. Existing coal producers expand production, responding to the new profit opportunities made available through OPEC's actions. However, the higher coal price attracts more attention. There are now more profitable opportunities in coal. More resources are attracted into the industry over time. Existing firms expand their mines. New firms open new mines. These new investments take time to implement, but after a period of time the supply of coal at the new price rises.

As new supplies come to market, the short-run supply curve shifts to S_{SR2} and the market price for coal is driven down. A new long-run equilibrium is established at a price of P_3. At this new equilibrium the new short-run supply curve, S_{SR2}, and the demand curve, D_2, intersect. The long-run supply curve for coal is found by drawing a straight line through the original short-run price–quantity combination and the new short-run equilibrium, as shown in Figure 7. The long-run equilibrium price is lower than the short-run price, while output has increased even more.

As in the case of product markets, long-run equilibrium in competitive resource markets has several properties that are desirable from an efficiency perspective:

1. There is no surplus or shortage of the resource. Price adjustments guarantee that quantity demanded equals quantity supplied. This takes on special significance in the labor market, where excess supply is another term for unemployment.

2. Resources are allocated to their most valuable use. Industries that experience an increased demand for their final product, or that experience productivity gains, expand. Suppose the demand for an industry's product rises. Its product price rises and so does its demand for resources. Similarly, an increase in resource productivity shifts each firm's marginal revenue product schedule to the right, raising total market demand. Declining industries reduce their resource demands, causing resources to be reallocated to industries that are expanding.

3. The value of the marginal resource in production equals its opportunity cost. In a competitive market, all resources whose marginal revenue product exceeds their price are employed. Remember that, for perfectly competitive firms, marginal revenue product equals product price times marginal physical product. The resource price is a measure of the opportunity cost of the resource, or its value in the next-best alternative use. All resources are employed in the market in which they are most productive. If a resource is more productive in another industry, its marginal revenue product will be less than its opportunity cost. Stated differently, the resource would be paid a higher price in the industry where it is more productive. Thus the market allocation of resources is efficient.

4. All resources are paid a price equal to the value of their marginal product. This is a requirement for an efficient allocation of resources, but it also has important implications for income distribution. In a perfectly competitive market economy, each individual receives an income equal to the contribution of his resources to national output.

SECTION RECAP
Assuming competitive markets, in long-run equilibrium, resources are allocated efficiently, that is, to their most highly valued uses.

Summary

The demand for a resource is a **derived demand.** A firm's resource demands are derived from (depend upon) the demand for its final product. The firm's resource demand curve is its **marginal revenue product** curve. It is downward sloping because of diminishing marginal productivity. The firm maximizes profits by hiring resources until the marginal revenue product is just equal to the **marginal resource cost.** Industry resource demand is less elastic than firm demand because increases in industry output (and employment) reduce market price. Thus, declining marginal physical product and market price cause marginal revenue product to fall.

The short-run **elasticity of resource demand** is greater (a) the slower the decline in marginal physical product, (b) the greater the elasticity of demand for the industry product, (c) the greater the share of total firm costs accounted for by a resource, and (d) the greater the availability of good substitutes for a resource. It is through the second factor that consumer behavior influences resource demand.

In the long run, firms are able to substitute among inputs. The greater the relative ease of substituting one input for another, the greater the long-run elasticity of resource demand. Because there are more substitution possibilities in the long run, the long-run resource elasticity of demand is greater than the short-run elasticity of demand.

The quantity of resources willingly supplied to the market is generally directly related to market price. Resource owners seek to employ their resources in the most profitable employment alternatives to maximize their incomes. The **price elasticity of resource supply** is determined primarily by resource mobility, the relative ease with which resources move between alternatives.

Long-run supply is also positively related to price. Investment adds to our stock of resources, while depreciation reduces the stock of capital. Resource prices influence the relative profitability of investments. Higher relative prices make investment more attractive and thereby expand the long-run supply of the resource.

Resource market equilibrium is achieved by the interaction of supply and demand. An equilibrium price that equates quantity supplied and demanded is established by market forces. The allocation of resources achieved by this equilibrium is efficient. Each resource is employed in the activity for which its marginal revenue product ($P \times MP$) is highest. No other allocation of resources could result in a higher value of output for consumers.

One of the most important applications of this resource market analysis is to the labor market. The shape of the labor supply curve depends upon two opposing forces: the substitution effect (higher wages make leisure more costly) and the income effect (higher wages increase the demand for leisure).

On the demand side of the labor market, the negatively sloped resource demand curve yields an inverse relationship between resource price (the wage) and employment. This tradeoff is a crucial aspect of analysis of the labor market. The next two chapters demonstrate how the demand schedule for labor and its elasticity determine the success of government or trade union policies to raise wage rates.

Questions for Thought

Knowledge Questions

1. The marginal revenue product of a worker is the contribution of that worker to the firm's revenue. Explain how the worker's marginal revenue product is determined.
2. Calculate the price elasticity of the demand for oil if a 10 percent oil price increases causes the quantity of oil demanded to fall by 4 percent. Is demand elastic or inelastic?
3. List four factors that influence the elasticity of demand for a resource.
4. Explain how the income effect and the substitution effect work together to generate a backward-bending labor supply curve.

Application Questions

5. Calculate the marginal physical product of labor from the following short-run production function (assume other inputs fixed):

Units of Labor	Total Daily Output
2	100
3	150
4	195
5	232
6	262
7	285
8	300
9	308
10	308

Graph the marginal physical product function. Assume this firm is a perfectly competitive firm and market price is $2 per unit of output. Calculate and graph the marginal revenue product function. To maximize profits, how much output would the firm produce if the daily wage rate were $30? What would happen to output if the wage rose to $46 a day?

6. Do you think organized labor would support or oppose legislation that restricted immigration into the United States? Explain.
7. Suppose that the oil and coal markets are initially in long-run equilibrium and then the price of oil falls relative to the price of coal. What happens to coal price and output in the short run? Long run?
8. What happens to the demand for labor in question 5 above when the product market price rises to $2.50 per unit? What happens to the profit-maximizing level of employment?

Synthesis Questions

9. Long-run price elasticity is greater than short-run price elasticity on both the demand and supply sides of resource markets. Account for this pattern on both sides of the market using the concept of alternatives.

10. We have used an abstract model of production to derive the firm's short-run demand function for labor. We observe some workers being paid by the hour and others being paid by the piece (the units of output actually produced). What factors would influence the manner in which a worker was paid?
11. Use the resource market equilibrium analysis to explain the impact of an effective price ceiling in the gasoline market on the long-run supply of oil.
12. Assume that the total supply of land in the United States is fixed. What is the price elasticity of supply? What determines the equilibrium price of land? What impact would a land tax have on the price of land?

OVERVIEW

In the preceding chapter we presented a general theory of how the prices and levels of employment are determined. In this chapter we apply that theory to a specific resource — labor. The practical issues that can be analyzed by applying market analysis to labor questions are among the most important in economics. Why do some workers earn more than others? For example, why do physicians make more than janitors?

The Market for Labor

Is an economy where basketball players' salaries are ten times that of teachers rational? Why do some individuals go to college, while others drop out of high school? Are workers in risky jobs exploited? Why do women and blacks earn less than males and whites?

Political scientists, sociologists, and industrial psychologists have written volumes about these and other labor market problems. The economists' approach to the same issues is distinguished by its use of market analysis and its emphasis on the efficiency aspects of these issues. The principles of supply and demand are applied to the determination of wages and employment. In effect, labor is treated as any other product or resource. The application of one set of economic principles to all types of markets sets economists apart from other social scientists. Our understanding of economic principles and market behavior is used to address a number of important economic and social issues.

CHAPTER 15

Learning Objectives

After reading and studying this chapter, you will be able to:

1. Explain why labor is such an important resource in the economy.
2. Identify the determinants of equalizing wage differences and explain the causes of nonequalizing wage differences.
3. Distinguish between equilibrium and disequilibrium wage differences.
4. Identify the factors that influence the profitability of human capital investments.
5. Compare the wage and employment outcomes of a monopsonistic and a competitive labor market.

Significance of Labor in the Economy

Many individuals object to a market analysis of labor on the grounds that it is dehumanizing to speak of labor as a commodity, traded as if it were bushels of corn or bars of gold. However, such an objection misses the fundamental point of market analysis: We apply economic principles to labor issues because we believe that wages and the level of employment are determined by the same economic forces that determine the prices and outputs of other goods and resources. Whether labor is more important than, say, capital is a *normative* question. What happens to wage rates when worker productivity rises is a *positive* question that can be answered by economic theory and scientific inquiry, regardless of subjective feelings about how wages and productivity should be related.

If the labor market operates fundamentally just as any other market does, why single it out for special attention? In fact, the labor market has several unique aspects that set it apart from other markets.

Labor cannot be divorced from its owner. Excuse the expression, but "Labor is us!" Since the abolition of slavery, the owner and the supplier of labor are the same person. The owner must be present when labor is employed. This one seemingly trivial difference between labor and other resources is extremely important because it means that nonwage factors are important in labor markets. Employees may be willing to sacrifice higher wages to have jobs that are safer, less boring, or more prestigious. The owner of capital is concerned only with the price that will be paid for the capital, not the conditions under which it will be used.

The distribution of income is largely determined by the outcomes in the labor market. Over 70 percent of national income is paid out in wages and salaries. The distribution of earnings among labor, capital, and land, called the **functional distribution of income**, reflects the workings of the labor market and other resource markets. The large share of national income that accrues to labor suggests that labor also accounts for a large share of production costs. The share of total costs attributable to labor varies across industries, but in general the labor share is large. (Therefore, economizing on labor can substantially reduce costs.) In addition, labor market outcomes determine how total labor income is distributed among various types of workers — physicians, teachers, grape pickers, miners, and so forth. Income differences by occupation, industry, and so on, largely determine the **personal distribution of income** — how income is distributed among individuals and households in the economy.

The labor market is probably the focus of more government regulation than any other market in the economy. Employment and wages are affected by the Thirteenth Amendment (which outlawed slavery), Social Security, minimum wage laws, affirmative action regulations, occupational licensing, workers' compensation, occupational safety and health regulations, unemployment insurance, and collective bargaining legislation, as well as other regulations. However, this does not mean that the forces of supply and demand do not affect labor market outcomes. The regulator who ignores the economic behavior of workers and firms may be surprised when the impact of regulations turns out to be different than expected or desired.

Labor market disequilibrium has implications for the unemployment rate. If wages are too high for equilibrium, a surplus, or excess supply, results. Excess supply, which is inefficient in any market, is another name for labor market unemployment, with all of its attendant social consequences.

Functional distribution of income
The distribution of earnings among the factors of production.

Personal distribution of income
The distribution of income among individuals and households in the economy.

SECTION RECAP
Labor costs account for over 70 percent of national income. Outcomes in specific labor markets determine how income is distributed among workers.

The Labor Market as an Abstraction

This book is organized around markets. A market is often thought of as a place where trading occurs, such as a livestock auction pen, an open-air farmer's market, or the trading floor of the New York Stock Exchange. However, in the case of labor, it is clear that the market refers to an abstract, rather than a physical, concept. "The San Francisco labor market" refers to general wage and employment conditions in the San Francisco area, not one location in the city where labor is traded.

The **labor market** is the interplay of buyers and sellers of labor services. There are few markets today in which workers and firms come together in a single place to set wages and employment. Undergraduate business majors wonder, for example, what the market for accountants will be like when they graduate, even though there is no one place where accountants' services are auctioned. *Equilibrium wage and employment levels are established by competition among employers for workers and competition among workers for jobs.*

Labor market
The interplay of buyers and sellers of labor services.

A Labor Market for Each Skill

Workers, of course, differ. Some are unskilled while others are highly trained. Similarly, some firms use unskilled labor while others utilize production processes requiring a highly trained work force. These two types of labor obviously are not traded in the same market. In general, there is a different labor market for each skill.

Labor markets may also be regionally segmented. Consequently, it may not be accurate to conclude that an increase in the demand for teachers in Florida will raise teachers' salaries in South Dakota. Imperfect information about employment opportunities elsewhere and the costs of moving may create geographically distinct markets, particularly for less-skilled workers.

One can push the separation of labor markets by skill and space too far, however. If wages for skilled employees rise high enough, unskilled workers will try to obtain the training that will allow them to compete in this market. Similarly, if teachers' wages in Florida are high enough relative to wages paid to teachers in South Dakota, at least some of the teachers in South Dakota will migrate to Florida. In a broad, long-run sense, all labor is traded in the same market.

The Aggregate Labor Market: Wage and Employment Determination

As a starting point, it is useful to think of all labor as being traded in the same market. If we assume that all workers have the same skills, job information is costlessly obtained, and moving has a zero cost, we can aggregate all labor demand and supply schedules into one labor market for the U.S. economy. Figure 1 (a) illustrates equilibrium in the aggregate labor market. L^d represents the aggregation of all industry demand schedules for labor into economy-wide demand. If all industries are competitive, L^d approximates an aggregate marginal revenue product schedule.

The equilibrium wage in the economy is W_e, and the equilibrium level of employment is L_e. Wage flexibility ensures the realization of this equilibrium.

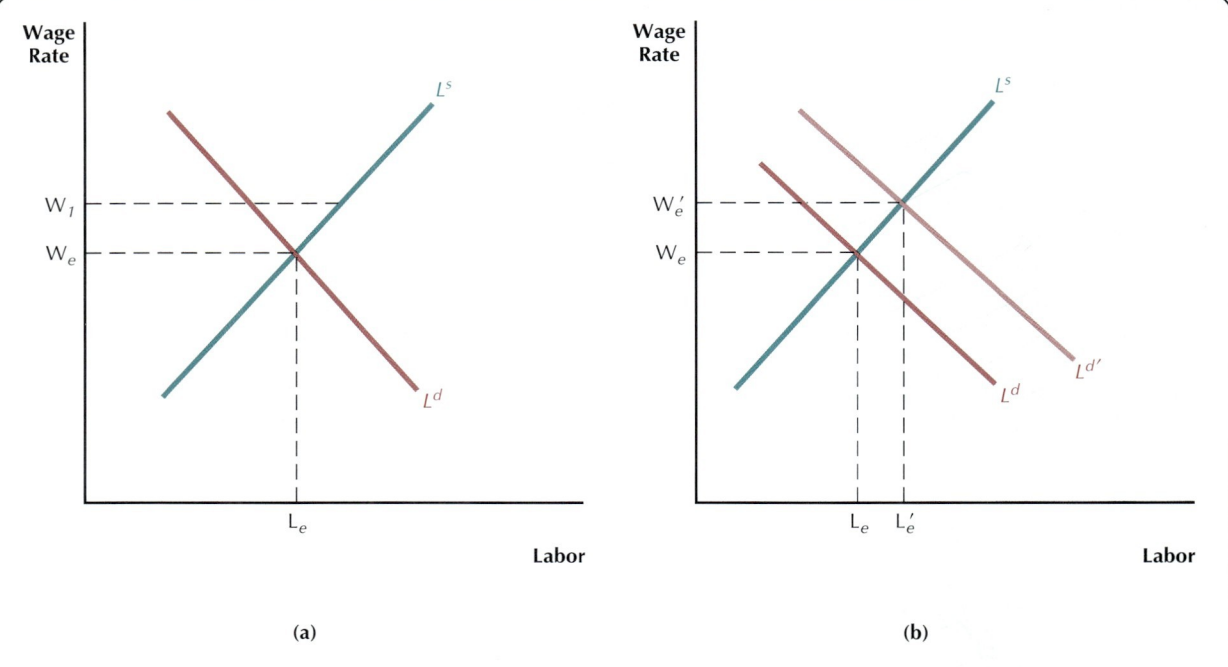

FIGURE 1
Supply and demand for labor and the equilibrium wage. The curve labeled L^d in Figure 1 (a) represents the total industry demand for labor. L^s is the aggregate supply of labor. The equilibrium wage and level of employment are W_e and L_e. At any wage above W_e, such as W_1, there is an excess supply of labor—competition will bid the wage down. In Figure 1 (b), an increase in labor productivity shifts labor demand right to $L^{d'}$, causing the equilibrium nominal wage and level of employment to increase to W'_e and L'_e. Since $W'_e/P_1 > W_e/P_1$, the real wage is now higher.

At any wage above W_e, such as W_1, the number of individuals seeking work is greater than the number of jobs: An excess supply of labor exists. Competition among individuals seeking employment will bid the wage down. As the wage falls to W_e, firms increase hiring and some workers drop out of the labor market. The number of jobs and workers is equal when W_e is reached. The aggregate labor market equilibrium has several desirable properties:

1. There is no unemployment. Wage flexibility guarantees that the number of workers firms wish to hire equals the number of workers who are willing to work at the going wage. Those who are not hired—those on the supply schedule above W_e—are not seeking work because W_e is too low to compensate them for sacrificing nonmarket work activities or leisure time. They are considered to be out of the labor force. They are *not* considered unemployed. To be unemployed, a worker must be actively seeking, but unable to find, work at the current wage.

2. The wage equals the marginal revenue product for the last worker hired. Assuming that all firms and industries are perfectly competitive, marginal revenue product is equal to product price times marginal physical product. As is illustrated in Figure 1 (a), the marginal revenue product of the last worker hired is exactly equal to what she is paid, W_e. (Recall that the demand curve

for labor is the marginal revenue product curve: It shows the value of the last unit of output generated by each additional worker.)

3. The marginal worker's productivity in the labor market equals the opportunity cost of time. Recall from the previous chapter that the resource price is a measure of the opportunity cost of obtaining a unit of a resource. In the case of the aggregate labor market, the alternatives to market work are leisure or work at home. A labor market equilibrium ensures that workers whose market productivity is greater than the value of their time at home are, indeed, working.

The aggregate labor market illustrated in Figure 1 (a) is, of course, an abstraction. However, it is a useful model for evaluating broad labor market issues. Consider the relationship between labor productivity and real wages — the nominal wage divided by the price level. Suppose the United States devotes more of its resources to the education and training of its workforce. Average worker productivity should rise as a result, shifting the aggregate demand schedule for labor to the right. Given the relative inelasticity of aggregate labor supply, and assuming the price level does not change, the result will be higher real wages and a modest increase in employment.

The link between aggregate productivity and the general level of real wages is illustrated in Figure 1 (b). An increase in labor productivity causes labor demand to shift right to $L^{d'}$. This causes the equilibrium nominal wage to increase to W'_e and the equilibrium level of employment increases to L'_e. For a given level of prices, P_1, the real wage is now higher since $W'_e/P_1 > W_e/P_1$.

The simple model of one labor market in the economy also serves as a useful benchmark. We know how such a market would function if it existed. The conditions necessary for an economy to have one aggregate labor market with one equilibrium wage are equivalent to those required for any perfectly competitive product or factor market. In the labor market these conditions take the following form:

1. Workers must be identical. All units of labor must be homogeneous with respect to tastes and productivity characteristics.
2. Jobs must be identical. Since nonwage aspects of employment matter, all jobs must be the same in all dimensions.
3. Labor must be perfectly mobile. Resource mobility allows prices to move to equilibrium levels when market equilibrium is disturbed.

These assumptions imply that labor is truly just a commodity. However, labor services are provided by human beings with diverse skills, preferences, and attitudes. Thus, the first of these three assumptions does not hold. In addition, we know that assumptions 2 and 3 do not hold in the real world — jobs are not all identical and labor is not perfectly mobile. The result is a distribution of wages across a set of labor markets. These three criteria can, however, be used to explain the observed differences in wages.

SECTION RECAP
The fact that workers and jobs are not identical and that labor is not perfectly mobile can be used to explain differences in wages across labor markets.

Explaining Observed Wage Differences

Contrary to the implications of Figure 1, we know from personal experience and observation that not all workers are paid the same wage. In fact, wages vary widely. Table 1 lists the average yearly earnings for males in several different occupations. The disparities are striking. Why does a physician earn

TABLE 1

Annual earnings by selected occupations for males in 1987

Occupation	Mean Income
Cashiers	$13,728
Farm operators and managers	16,918
Construction laborers	18,343
Auto mechanics	19,926
Carpenters	20,360
Motor vehicle operators	23,375
Computer equipment operators	24,375
Primary and secondary school teachers	29,914
Accountants and auditors	40,055
Engineers	41,209
Lawyers and judges	61,477
Health-diagnosing occupations	77,677

Source: U.S. Bureau of the Census, Current Population Reports, Series P-60, No. 162, *Money Income of Households, Families, and Persons in the United States: 1987*. U.S. Government Printing Office, Washington, DC, 1989. Table 39.

more than an engineer? A cashier less than a computer operator? A lawyer more than a school teacher?

The answers to these questions are important. If wage differences are due to luck or discrimination, a strong case can be made for legislation that seeks to alter the distribution of earnings to suit society's notions of efficiency and equity. However, if wages vary according to ability, or the costs of education and training, or other systematic differences in workers or jobs, government policies designed to alter or equalize wages may have adverse consequences in the labor market. In general, wage differences can be classified into two broad categories: equalizing and nonequalizing.

Equalizing Wage Differences

Equalizing wage differences
Differences in wages that are based on nonwage job characteristics, and that tend to equalize the total benefits offered by different jobs.

Equalizing wage differences exist to compensate workers for nonwage job attributes. Jobs differ in many respects, and these differences matter to workers. Certain jobs require extensive education and training, are unpleasant, involve seasonal unemployment, or impose high levels of physical risk on workers. A wage premium must be paid to attract workers into these jobs. Otherwise, all workers would choose pleasant and safe occupations with steady employment. Similarly, workers in jobs that have desirable nonwage attributes—prestige, interesting work, beautiful scenery—earn less, *ceteris paribus*. *Wage differences based on nonwage job characteristics tend to equalize the total benefits offered by different jobs.*

So long as labor markets are competitive, equalizing wage differences will result. Figure 2 makes this result clear. L_A^s is the supply curve for job A, for which nonwage job characteristics are favorable: The work is in an air-conditioned office, with low noise levels, and little risk of injury or death.

Occupation A is assumed to be such a small part of the total labor market that the supply curve is perfectly elastic. Firms can hire all the workers they require at W_A.

However, what about the supply of workers to occupation B, where the boss is subject to periodic fits of rage and machinery produces both loud noise and noxious fumes? If job B paid W_A, no one would want the work. They could earn the same wage under the more pleasant working conditions in job A. To entice workers into job B, a higher wage must be offered. This wage must be high enough to compensate for the unpleasant characteristics of the job. The amount $W_B - W_A$ is such an equalizing wage difference. It is just sufficient to make workers indifferent between jobs A and B. At any wage less than W_B, job A is preferred and the supply of labor to job B is zero.

So long as workers are free to choose whichever job they prefer, equalizing wage differences must be paid. Jobs that are unpleasant will carry a higher wage. By the same reasoning, an occupation that requires a costly training or apprenticeship period must pay a higher wage to compensate for the extra costs of entering that labor market. Physicians must be paid more than unskilled labor, or else few will incur the considerable costs of college and medical school.

This reasoning can be reversed to show that jobs with very favorable job characteristics will pay a lower wage. Workers will crowd into these jobs until the wage has fallen low enough to equalize the total benefits of favorable and unfavorable jobs.

Worker Preferences Affect Relative Wages An equalizing wage difference is a wage premium that must be paid to attract labor to less desirable jobs. Figure 2 illustrated such a premium—a wage premium equal to $W_B - W_A$ had to be paid to workers in job B to attract any workers to job B. Worker perceptions about the value of the differences in job traits determine the size of the wage differential. In Figure 2, it was implicitly assumed that all workers had

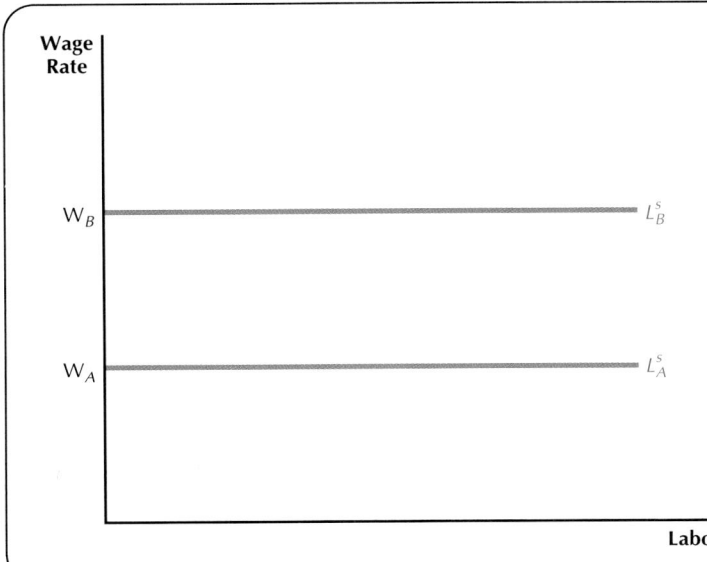

FIGURE 2
Variations in job quality and equalizing differences. In this figure, L_A^s is the supply schedule to job A, for which nonwage job characteristics are favorable. Occupation A is assumed to be such a small part of the total labor market that the supply schedule is perfectly elastic. Firms can hire all the workers they require at W_A. L_B^s is the supply curve for job B, which has a number of undesirable characteristics. If job B paid W_A, no one would want the work. To entice workers into job B, the wage must be high enough to compensate for the unpleasant job characteristics. The amount $W_B - W_A$ is an *equalizing wage difference*. It is sufficient to make workers indifferent between jobs A and B. At any wage less than W_B, job A is preferred and the supply of labor to job B is zero.

the same perceptions. As such, the wage difference was the same for each level of employment.

Since worker preferences vary, however, the premium necessary to attract workers into less preferred jobs also varies. In fact, what one person considers to be an attractive work environment might be the very same environment that someone else finds quite unattractive. Some of the observed differences in wages are attributable to these differences in preferences.

Figure 3 illustrates the impact of worker preferences on observed wage differences. Consider once again jobs A and B, where job B is generally less preferred than job A. Since worker tastes with respect to job attributes vary, the supply of labor to job B is no longer perfectly elastic at the exactly equalizing wage difference in Figure 2. When worker tastes vary, different workers are willing to go to job B at different wage differences and, hence, L_B^s is now upward sloping.

In Figure 3, the wage difference, D, ($D = W_B - W_A$) between job A and B, and not the absolute wage, is measured on the vertical axis. A few workers might actually prefer job B to job A — they would be willing to work in B at a wage lower than the wage in job A. The availability of such people is shown by a supply curve that intersects the vertical axis at a value of D that is less than 0. When $W_B - W_A < 0$, $D < 0$. Employers offering job B hire those workers who dislike job B least because it minimizes labor costs.

The wage difference is determined by supply and demand. When demand is equal to L_1^d, the equalizing wage difference is D_1. However, as demand for job B workers rises, employers must bid away more and more job A workers by offering larger and larger wage premiums. As illustrated in Figure 3, if demand increases to L_2^d, the equilibrium wage difference will increase to D_2. Thus, the observed difference in wages between A and B depends not only on the differences in the two jobs, but also the distribution of worker preferences for the attributes of A and B and the demand for workers in each job.

SECTION RECAP
Equalizing wage differences compensate workers for differences in non-wage job attributes. In general, less attractive jobs command a higher wage premium.

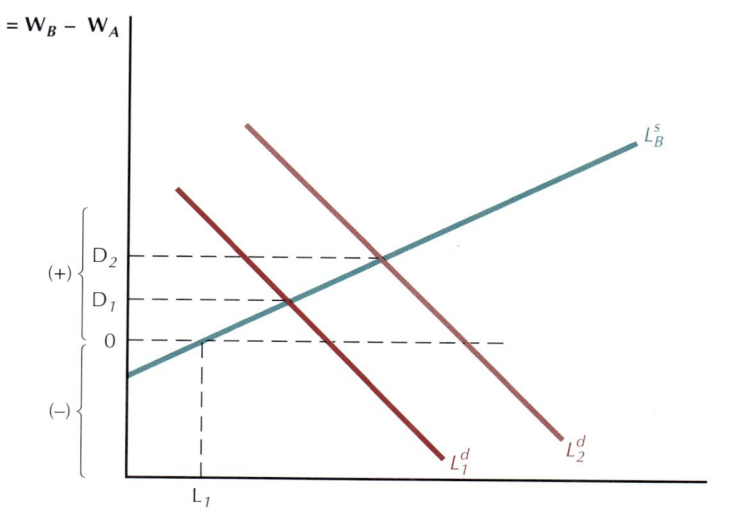

FIGURE 3
Equalizing wage differences and the level of labor demand. When workers' tastes vary, different workers are willing to go to job B at different wage differences. Hence, L_B^s is upward sloping. The wage difference, D, between job A and B is measured on the vertical axis. A few workers, L_1, might in fact prefer job B to job A. The availability of these people is illustrated by a supply curve that intersects the vertical axis at a value of D that is less than 0. When demand is equal to L_1^d, the equalizing wage difference is D_1. However, if demand increases to L_2^d, the equalizing wage difference will increase to d_2.

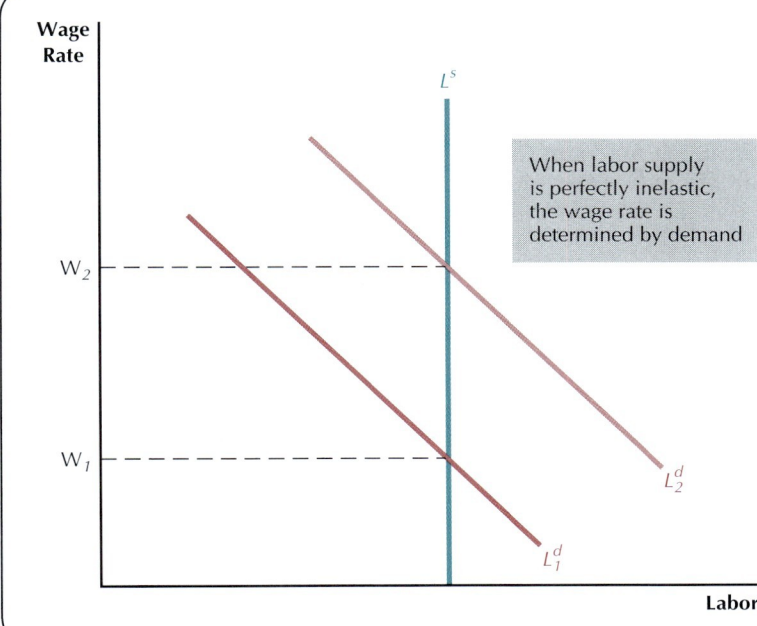

FIGURE 4
Supply of and demand for specialized skills. This figure illustrates the manner in which prices are determined for rare labor skills. There are few, and some would say no, other players who possess the basketball talents that Michael Jordan does. Thus, the supply of those talents is perfectly inelastic—the supply curve, L^s, is vertical. In this situation, the wage paid to Jordan or other such talented players is determined by demand. Jordan receives W_1 if demand is L_1^d. If demand rises to L_2^d, the wage rises to W_2. There is no change in quantity supplied in the short run or the long run. Jordan has a monopoly on those rare, special skills in demand for basketball.

Nonequalizing Wage Differences

As the term implies, **nonequalizing wage differences** are not necessary to attract and retain workers in given occupations. Nonequalizing wage differences cause the total benefits of working in different jobs to vary, with the result that some occupations are, all things considered, preferred to others. We would expect nonequalizing differences to be competed away if workers are free to enter any occupation they wish. Workers would crowd into the preferred jobs until the nonequalizing wage difference is eliminated. *For nonequalizing wage differences to persist, there must be a barrier to the entry of new workers, which limits the degree of competition among workers for the better jobs.* Resource immobility arises for a variety of reasons; we mention three important ones.

Special Skills When a few individuals (maybe only one person) possess a special, unique skill, in effect they have monopoly power conferred upon them. Dr. Robert Kerlan, the famed sports surgeon, earns much more than other orthopedic specialists. His earnings premium is based upon a rare ability. It cannot be competed away because other surgeons, lacking his skill, are not really competitors. Similarly, an individual may be willing to play basketball for the Chicago Bulls for much less than Michael Jordan is paid. The fact that the Bulls don't take the individual up on his offer suggests that he is not competing in the same labor market as Jordan.

Figure 4 illustrates the manner in which prices are determined for such rare skills. This figure represents the market for Michael Jordan's basketball skills. There are few (some would say no) other players who possess the basketball talents that Jordan does. Thus, the supply of those talents is perfectly inelastic—the supply curve is vertical. In this situation, the wage paid to Jordan

Nonequalizing wage differences
Differences in wages that cause the total benefits of working in different jobs to vary.

Does It Make **Economic Sense?**

Market Wages: Professional Sports versus Education

In 1990 many of the top players in professional baseball were able to negotiate multiyear contracts worth millions of dollars per year. José Canseco of the Oakland Athletics became baseball's highest-paid player when he signed a contract worth more than $5 million per year over a five-year period. During the same period, the minimum salary for a draft choice in the National Basketball Association rose to more than $100,000 per year and the median salary exceeded $750,000.

In contrast to the salaries in professional sports, starting salaries for elementary school teachers averaged less than $20,000 per year. In addition, many teachers across the country received raises that fell short of the rate of inflation, resulting in a loss in real buying power. This disparity in outcomes in the sports and teaching labor markets clearly does not make sense to most Americans. For many, this is evidence of the irrationality of American society — that we pay individuals who play catch or jump around in shorts so much more than those who largely shape the abilities and attitudes of our children. Does this make economic sense? Possibly.

To understand how such seemingly illogical differences exist, we must consider the characteristics of supply and demand in each of these two markets. The forces of supply and demand set wages based upon the value of the marginal worker, not the average. The fact that a professional athlete earns more than a teacher cannot be taken as evidence that society values professional sports more than educating its young. Consider Figure 5, which illustrates the supply and demand for teachers and professional baseball players.

The demand for baseball players is less than the demand for teachers because society places a higher total value on education. In addition, demand for professional baseball players is restricted by the number of teams that are allowed to compete and the number of players that a team can have on its roster. However, the supply of teachers is much greater than the supply of professional baseball players. A limited number of baseball players possess the skills required to enable them to compete effectively in the market for baseball players. In relative terms, a much larger number of individuals possess the skills necessary to compete in the market for teachers.

Price elasticity of demand also plays a role in the differences between the two markets. In baseball, a certain number of players are required to compete in a game. In addition, it is important to maintain a number of reserves in the event of injury to a starter. Quantity demanded is relatively fixed, regardless of price. In contrast, it is possible to alter the number of teachers needed to edu-

---

Reservation wage
The minimum amount of money that would attract a worker into a particular line of employment.

Economic rent
The amount of income in excess of a worker's reservation wage.

or other such talented players is determined by demand. Jordan receives W_1 if demand is L_1^d. If demand rises, the wage rises. There is no change in quantity supplied in the short run. Nor is there an increase in supply over the long run. Jordan has a monopoly on those rare, special skills in demand for basketball.

In this situation, Jordan, or whoever has the special skills in demand, earns a wage that is far in excess of the minimum amount that would just make him willing to play basketball. The wage at which he would be attracted into basketball is called the **reservation wage**. The amount he earns above and beyond his reservation wage is called **economic rent**. Most of Jordan's salary, and that of others with special skills, is economic rent.

Trade Union Restrictions   Trade union actions can create nonequalizing wage differences. Labor unions may restrict entry into an occupation or trade, or convince workers not to work for a lower wage. If union efforts are successful, supply may actually fall, pushing up wages. Alternatively, unions may simply bargain for a higher-than-equilibrium wage and then ration entrance into the

cate a fixed number of students by altering the number of classes an instructor must teach, the number of students per instructor (class size) and so forth. These differences imply that the demand for professional baseball players is inelastic relative to the demand for teachers.

As a result of the differences in supply and demand in the two markets, salaries for teachers, W_T, are well below those paid to baseball players, W_{BP}. While the total value to society of teachers is much higher, the marginal value of one more or one less teacher is small. Just the opposite is true with respect to the marginal baseball player.

To demonstrate that society is irrational, one would have to show that teachers would earn less if they were as rare as athletes — a doubtful proposition. Society's valuation of the two occupations is reflected in the demand curve. But it is the interaction of demand and supply that determines wage rates.

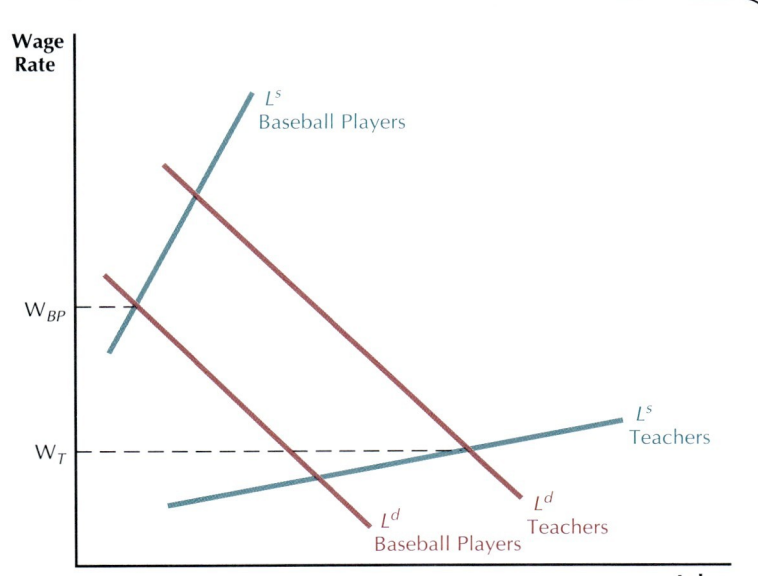

FIGURE 5
Comparing the salaries of teachers and professional baseball players.
The demand for baseball players is less than the demand for teachers because society places a higher total value on education. However, salaries for teachers, W_T, are well below those paid to baseball players, W_{BP}, because the supply of teachers is much greater. Baseball players earn more because so few have the required skill, relative to demand.

occupation. In both cases their actions restrict entry and prevent the higher wage levels from attracting additional workers into the jobs.

Government Restrictions Occupational licensing laws also may prevent free entry and cause wages for licensed workers to be higher than they otherwise would be. Entry into certain occupations, such as medicine, hairstyling, and nursing, is regulated through licensing and training requirements. These regulations are established to ensure a minimum level of competency for all those individuals who practice in one of these occupations. However, these regulations have supply-side effects as well. They are much like union effects to the extent that they restrict entry into the occupation, causing wages to be higher than they would be in the absence of restrictions on entry. The federal government enforces laws that prevent some wages from falling. An example is the *Davis–Bacon Act*, which requires that federal construction projects pay the going wage in the area, prohibiting contractors from hiring construction workers at a lower wage.

SECTION RECAP
Nonequalizing wage differences cause some occupations to be preferred. They reflect resource immobility that can be the result of special skills, and trade union or government restrictions.

Disequilibrium Wage Differences

Whether equalizing or not, wage differences caused by differences in working conditions, special skills, or competitive restrictions are equilibrium wage differences. That is, they will continue to exist over the long run until fundamental demand and supply conditions change.

Ours is a dynamic economy, however. Constantly changing technology and changing demands for products mean that labor markets are always adjusting to a new equilibrium. **Disequilibrium wage differences**, or *transitional wage differences*, are commonly observed. These wage differences are eliminated in the long run.

Consider, for example, the earnings of newly graduated engineers and accountants. In long-run equilibrium, these occupations should have roughly similar starting salaries, since both require a similar level of education. If the demand for accountants dramatically increases, the starting salary of accountants initially rises, and there is a transitory disequilibrium wage difference between accountants and engineers. This wage difference is competed away in the long run, however, as college students switch their majors from engineering to accounting. The increased supply of accountants pushes their starting salaries back down, while the relative scarcity of engineers drives up their starting salaries. Long-run equilibrium is reestablished when engineers and accountants again have the same starting salaries, and the transitory wage difference is eliminated.

You might well ask, How long is the long run? Transitory wage differences might last for a few weeks or years, depending upon how quickly workers can change occupations. In the case of temporary, unskilled jobs in the same geographic area, wage differences are eliminated very quickly. However, an increased demand for brain surgeons produces a disequilibrium wage difference of much longer duration. The supply of brain surgeons cannot increase overnight. It takes years for new individuals to acquire the necessary education and training to enter this market.

Similarly, wage differences for the same skill across different regions may persist for a long time. These transitory wage differences are eliminated by workers moving from low to high demand areas. However, moving is costly, particularly for older workers. It may take the next generation to move to where employment opportunities are more attractive before long-run labor market equilibrium is reached.

Disequilibrium wage differences
Differences in wages that are caused by a short-run disequilibrium in one or more labor markets.

SECTION RECAP
Disequilibrium wage differences are the result of short-run changes in the supply of or demand for a resource. Over the long run, these differences tend to disappear.

Investment in Education: Costs and Benefits . . . Again

The way economists explain education decisions is a good example of how economists view the world differently than other social scientists do. Sociologists emphasize the roles of culture, family background, and social expectations in the decision to attend college. While not dismissing these as unimportant, economists focus on education as an economic choice, with rational individuals once again comparing costs and benefits. Economists consider an investment in education a **human capital** investment. Education choices are similar to firms' decisions to purchase physical capital. Both types of investment require large initial cash outlays, but yield a continuing stream of benefits into the future. For the individual considering college, the costs are both explicit

Human capital
The productivity-determining skills and abilities embodied in labor.

(tuition, books, fees, and so on) and implicit (the loss of full-time earnings for four years). After these costs are incurred, the investment is expected to yield returns in the form of higher earnings throughout the college graduate's working career. The increase in earnings associated with the additional education represents the benefits of the investment.

The benefit–cost comparison is illustrated in Figure 6, where two *age–earnings profiles* are depicted. The curve labeled "high school" measures the annual earnings over a lifetime for those with a high school education. The curve labeled "college" measures the annual earnings for those with a college degree. The profiles have markedly different shapes. The high school graduate goes to work at age 18 and works to age 65. Annual earnings rise gradually over the work life. On the other hand, the person who goes to college forgoes market work for four years, until graduation at age 22. The implicit cost of the education is the market earnings forgone because of the four-year education: the difference between high-school graduate and college graduate earnings until the two become equal. Moreover, the college student incurs explicit education costs such as tuition and fees. Total cost of the education is the sum of implicit and explicit costs, or the area between the high school and college earnings profiles between age 18 and the age at which earnings for the two groups are equal.

The benefit of the investment in college is the anticipated earnings increase associated with college that accrues over a substantial portion of a lifetime. When should a person undertake such a human capital investment? Whenever the expected benefits are greater than the expected costs. Because the costs and benefits of this choice problem occur over a long period of time, however, the decision-making process should take account of the fact that a given amount of benefits received in the future is less valuable than the same amount of benefits received today. To adjust for this difference, we calculate the value today, or the *present value*, of expected costs and benefits over the individual's

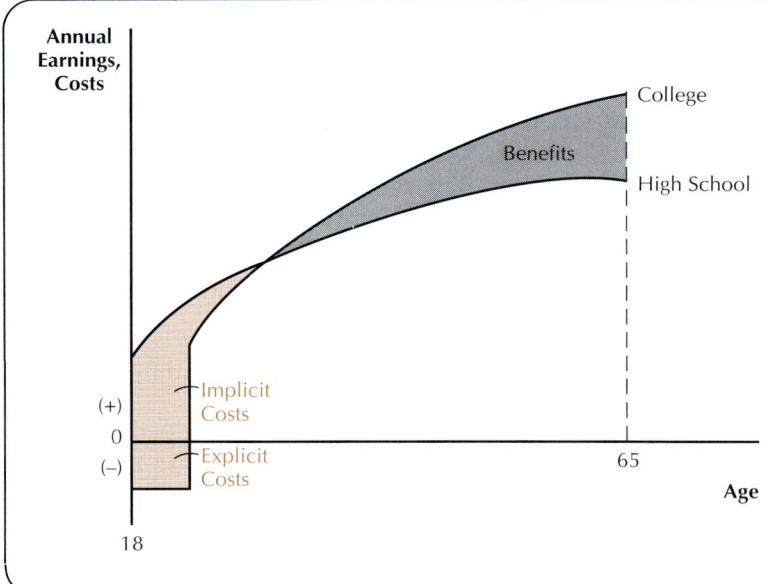

FIGURE 6
Age–earnings profiles for high school versus college graduates. This figure illustrates two *age–earnings profiles.* The curve labeled "high school" measures the annual earnings over a lifetime for those with a high school education. The curve labeled "college" measures the annual earnings for those with a college degree. It is assumed that the high school graduate goes to work at age 18 and works to age 65. For the college student, the implicit cost of education is the market earnings forgone during the four years of school; explicit costs include tuition and fees. Total cost of the education is the sum of implicit and explicit costs, or the area between the high school and college earnings profiles between age 18 and the year that earnings for the two groups are equal.

lifetime.[1] If the present value of the increased earnings exceeds the present value of implicit plus explicit costs, a rational individual will choose to attend college.

This is another illustration of the equalizing wage difference for occupations requiring schooling or other kinds of training. Since a college education is costly, the wage in occupations requiring a college education must exceed the wage in alternative occupations that require no degree by enough to compensate workers for the cost of the training. Otherwise, workers will not be attracted into occupations that require a college education.

This wage differential serves as the mechanism for adjusting relative supplies of college-educated and high-school-educated workers. If the wage of college-educated workers rises, it makes a college education look more profitable. Enrollments increase as people are attracted by the now more-profitable investment. After a few years, this change in the profitability of college will increase the supply of college-educated workers and reduce the supply of high-school-educated workers. These supply shifts decrease wages for college-educated workers and increase wages for high-school-educated workers. These shifts reduce the benefits of a college education, causing the number of individuals seeking college training to fall and relative wages to return toward an equilibrium level.

The analysis of a college education as a human capital investment is not meant to suggest that economists deny noneconomic motives for attending college. College can be viewed as a consumption good as well. However, the investment motive is an important one, and we expect the general predictions of the human capital model to be correct. For example, a reduction in federal subsidies for higher education would reduce enrollments. On the other hand, a widening of the earnings differential between high school and college graduates is predicted to increase college attendance. While not the full story, the theory of human capital has proven enormously valuable in understanding a wide range of labor issues.

SECTION RECAP
From an economic perspective, the decision to invest in education is an investment in human capital. It requires a comparison of the benefits and costs of additional education.

Discrimination in the Labor Market

So far we have considered how wages vary by occupation or educational attainment. Another very important policy issue is how and why wages vary across other groupings of individuals. There is strong evidence that, on average, blacks are paid less than whites, and females earn less than males. Currently, the average full-time level of earnings of blacks is 70 percent that of whites. Females employed full-time earn about 70 percent of what males earn, on average. This evidence suggests, at first glance, that widespread discrimination against blacks and women exists in labor markets. Yet one cannot simply attribute observed earnings differences to a single factor like labor market discrimination. Measuring labor market discrimination is a difficult task. Explaining its origins is even more complex.

Labor market discrimination
Equally productive workers are paid less because of race or sex.

Labor market discrimination is said to exist if equally productive workers are paid less because of race or sex. Obtaining a measure of average discrim-

---

[1]The present value of a future amount, say $100 in the year 2000, is simply the amount that, if invested today, with the effects of compounded interest, would be worth $100 in the year 2000. Chapter 17 contains a more technical discussion of how the present value of a stream of benefits is calculated.

ination requires that the observed earnings differences for blacks and females be adjusted for average differences in their productive abilities.

Blacks have significantly lower average education levels than whites. Various studies have indicated that between 50 and 80 percent of black–white earnings differences is due to measurable differences in productivity characteristics. This implies that if a black worker and a white worker have equal levels of education and training, that is, they are equally productive, the black will earn 85 to 94 percent of what the white worker is paid.[2] The remaining 6 to 15 percent gap may be due to labor market discrimination, or it may be that there is some unmeasured productivity difference between blacks and whites. We simply do not know how much to attribute to discrimination.

On the other hand, many would argue that observed differences in productivity characteristics, like levels of educational attainment, may be due to more complex patterns of discrimination in society. For instance, we would expect a smaller percentage of blacks to acquire a college education if the wages of black college graduates were not as high relative to the wages of high-school-educated blacks as were the relative wages of these two schooling groups for whites. The payoff for a college education may be less for blacks than for whites. Discrimination in access to education may also account for differences in educational attainment.

Estimating the extent of discrimination by sex also requires an accounting for differences in productive characteristics between men and women. The most important of these appear to be job training and experience. For several reasons, women are likely to have less job experience at any given age and to work in occupations where less training is provided. The primary cause of these differences is that women are more likely to work in the home, particularly when small children are present. If a woman expects to be dropping out of the labor market intermittently during child-rearing years, her incentive to choose a job that requires much training and an uninterrupted career to recoup the costs of that training is diluted. At the same time, firms may be reluctant to invest in training women, given their greater likelihood of quitting. It might be less risky to hire men for jobs that involve training costs for the firm.

One result of such differences is occupational segregation, a primary factor in female–male earnings differentials. Women tend to crowd (or be crowded) into lower-paying jobs with less opportunity for advancement, such as clerical and retail sales. Occupational segregation may be due to the reluctance of firms to train females for more responsible, higher-paying positions. However, it is also possible that some females prefer more casual employment. Clerical and retail jobs do not require a high level of training—they can be easily entered and exited. Further, many of these jobs have flexible hours, which is important for women who, for whatever reasons, have the primary responsibility for homemaking.

Approximately half of the male–female earnings gap can be attributed to differences in training and experience. Again, the remainder of the gap is the result of a combination of discrimination and unmeasured productivity differences between men and women.

SECTION RECAP
Labor market discrimination exists when equally productive workers are paid different wage rates. Empirical evidence suggests that minorities and women may be victims of labor market discrimination.

---

[2]This range is calculated as follows: According to the statistics cited, blacks are paid an average of 30 percent less than whites, and 50 to 80 percent of this difference is due to productivity differences. In other words, 15 (.5 × 30) to 24 (.8 × 30) percent of the difference in wages is accounted for by productivity differences. Eliminating productivity differences would increase the salaries of blacks to 85 (70 + 15) to 94 (70 + 24) percent of what whites earn.

Why the **Disagreement?**

Wage Setting by Comparable Worth

For well over thirty years the wages of women who work full time, year round, averaged somewhat less than two thirds of the wages of men working full time, year round. (This figure has risen more recently to approximately 70 percent.) Many people attribute this wage gap (or at least part of it) to labor market discrimination. The apparent lack of success of previous legislative efforts to eliminate this form of discrimination has led to a new proposal to eliminate sex discrimination in the work place and close the male–female wage gap. The proposal is referred to as the *comparable worth doctrine*.

Comparable worth is a criterion for wage setting that supplants the market determination of wages. Employers would establish pay levels for different jobs by evaluating the characteristics of the job and basing wage payments on the skills, responsibilities, and working conditions of the job—regardless of what current market wages for these jobs are. Jobs deemed to be of comparable worth would pay the same wages. While a few state governments have adopted job evaluation and pay determination plans based on this basic principle, the comparable worth proposals have met with strong opposition, much of it from economists. Why the disagreement?

Comparable worth proponents believe that women are discriminated against in the workplace—that they are crowded into so-called women's jobs that pay low wages. Moreover, they believe this discrimination is embodied in labor market institutions. Essentially they believe that "women's work,"—such as secretarial work and retail sales—is low paying because it is viewed as women's work, and that these jobs will remain poorly paid. Comparable worth is a strategy designed to circumvent market forces and establish wage levels that better represent the comparable worth of jobs and establish a fairer distribution of wages.

Opponents of comparable worth believe that the proposal is impractical and they dispute the contention that the antidiscrimination legislation of the past twenty-five years has been ineffective. They conclude that comparable worth policies might worsen the economic welfare of many of the women it is intended to help.

Opponents of the plan argue that it is practically impossible to devise a system for sensibly measuring job characteristics and comparing widely diverse jobs to establish appropriately objective wage rates. A great deal of judgment by someone is required. Which job characteristics will be included in the evaluation? How does one measure the extent of responsibility or skill levels? And even more problematic, what weight is given to dimensions like responsibility and skill so that they

---

Noncompetitive Labor Markets

An important assumption of this chapter is that workers are paid a wage equal to the value of their marginal product, that is, their marginal revenue product, when the labor and product markets are perfectly competitive. It is important to understand the reasoning behind this result. If a worker's marginal revenue product exceeds his wage, another employer has a profit incentive to hire away that worker because he adds more to the employer's revenue than to cost.

However, in some situations the additional cost of hiring the worker is greater than the wage. Such a condition arises in the case of a **monopsony**. Monopsonistic firms may not have an incentive to expand employment until marginal revenue product equals the wage.

A monopsony is said to exist when there is only one employer in a labor market. For example, the school board in an isolated small town may be the only employer of local teachers. The National Football League is said to be a monopsonist since it is the sole employer of professional football players in the United States. *The crucial difference between a monopsonist and a perfectly competitive employer is the monopsonist's incentive to restrict employment to hold*

Monopsony
Only one buyer of a good or resource; for example, only one employer of labor in a particular location.

can be added up? The complexity of these questions suggests that a comparable worth program would produce a very expensive administrative burden that might never yield a system satisfactory to everyone. It is worth noting that the different comparable worth systems developed so far have evaluated similar jobs very differently, an indication of the potential problems with these schemes.

Opponents of the proposal also disagree with the proponents' interpretation of labor market evidence. What explains the fact that women earn two thirds the wages of men when both are employed full time and that this differential has persisted for a long time? Differences in productivity characteristics such as education attainment and job market experience explain a significant fraction of the gap. Even among full-time workers, women work fewer hours annually, thus accumulating less experience.

One reason for the persistence of the gap is the large influx of women, many of them relatively unskilled, into the labor force in the last forty years. Between 1950 and 1990, the labor force increased by more than 60 million people. Women accounted for over 60 percent of the increase. A supply increase of this magnitude tends to depress the average wage for women. Thus, while many women have chosen to pursue professional careers, have acquired more education and experience, and have gone to work in well-paid professional employment, many other less-skilled women have entered the labor force and taken traditional women's jobs. At the aggregate level, the average wage for all full-time women workers would be held down by the large influx of less-skilled women.

Finally, opponents argue that comparable worth legislation might harm many of the women whom it is intended to help. If comparable worth legislation raised the wages paid for traditional women's employment, it would set in motion market forces with adverse consequences. Higher wages for these jobs would reduce employment opportunities (demand is negatively sloped) in both the short run and long run, and the higher wages would encourage additional women to enter the labor force. A few women who kept their jobs in the now-higher wage sector would be better off, but many other women would be without jobs or in less attractive employment.

The elimination of labor market discrimination is an established and worthy normative goal for society. However, in developing policies to achieve this goal it is important that we incorporate incentives that will reinforce the intended objective. So far, comparable worth proposals appear to generate strong counterproductive effects.

---

down wages. Unlike a competitive employer who faces a perfectly elastic supply schedule for labor, a monopsonist confronts the entire market supply schedule.

In Figure 7 (a), the market supply curve is upward sloping. This means that the monopsonist must pay a higher wage to attract more workers. Contrast this situation with the competitive employer in Figure 7 (b). The competitive employer's demand for labor is such a small portion of the total market that it can hire all it requires at the going wage. Supply and marginal resource cost (MRC) are identical for the competitive employer; both equal W_C.

However, marginal resource cost is greater than the wage for a monopsonist. It not only must pay a higher wage to attract new employees, but also must increase the wage of all employees who were previously hired at a lower wage. Suppose a monopsonist can employ ten workers at $5 per hour, but the eleventh worker requires $6 per hour. The marginal cost of the eleventh employee is $16—the wage, $6, plus the additional $1 per hour that must be paid to the other ten employees to bring them up to $6 per hour. The monopsonist's MRC curve lies above the supply curve as shown in Figure 7 (a).

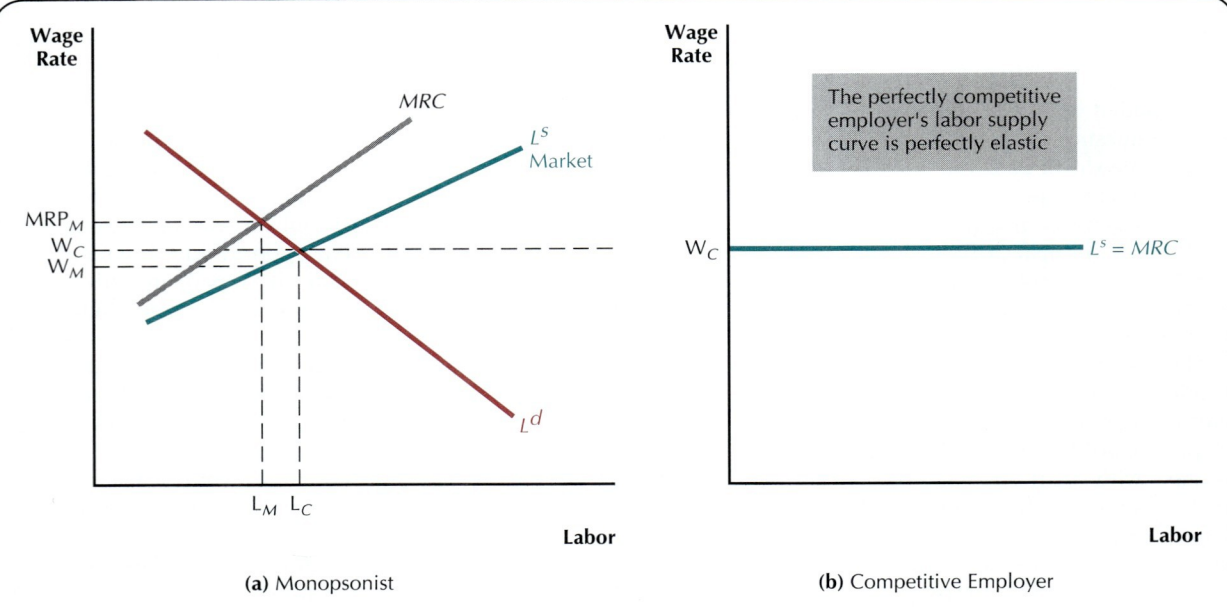

FIGURE 7
Equilibrium in monopsony versus a competitive market. *(a) Monopsonist (b) Competitive Employer.*
Figure 7 (a) illustrates the situation faced by a monopsonist. As Figure 7 (b) illustrates, supply and marginal resource cost (MRC) are identical for the competitive employer—both equal W_c. However, because the market supply schedule is upward sloping, marginal resource cost is greater than the wage for the monopsonist. It not only must pay a higher wage to attract the new employee, but also must increase the wage of all employees who were previously hired at a lower wage. Given its MRP schedule, the monopsonist will hire L_M workers at a wage of W_M. Note that the wage and employment would be W_C and L_C if the labor market in Figure 7 (a) were competitive. Monopsony results in lower wages ($W_M < W_C$) and employment ($L_M < L_C$) because, unlike the competitive employer, a monopsonist can reduce wages by restricting employment.

Fewer workers are employed in a monopsony situation than when the labor market is perfectly competitive. Given its marginal revenue product schedule in Figure 7 (a), the monopsonist hires workers up to the point where marginal revenue product equals marginal resource cost. Thus, L_M workers will be hired. The supply curve in turn tells us that the monopsonist must offer a wage of W_M. Note that the wage and employment would be W_C and L_C if the labor market of Figure 7 (a) were competitive. Each competitive firm, such as the one shown in Figure 7 (b), would continue to hire workers until marginal revenue product equals the wage. *Monopsony results in lower wages ($W_M < W_C$) and employment ($L_M < L_C$) because, unlike the competitive employer, a monopsonist can reduce wages by restricting employment.*

Note also that monopsony breaks the equality of the wage and marginal revenue product. If the monopsonist sells its output in a competitive product market, marginal revenue product is equal to marginal resource cost. However, in Figure 7 (a), the L_Mth worker is paid W_M, which is less than his marginal revenue product. This gap creates an incentive for another employer to hire the L_Mth worker. However, by definition, there is no other employer. Competition is needed to ensure that workers are paid the value of their productivity.

SECTION RECAP
In a monopsony, workers are paid a wage that is less than their MRP. Monopsonies result in lower employment and lower wages than perfectly competitive labor markets.

Long-Term Employment Contracts

An important feature of labor markets in the United States is the long-term nature of much employment. Professor Robert Hall of Stanford University has estimated that 40 percent of men above the age of 30 hold jobs that they will stay in for at least twenty years.[3] The simple competitive labor market model does not reveal why workers and employers should form such strong attachments. Instead, it implies that workers will quit their jobs whenever another firm offers even a temporarily higher wage, or that firms will always lay off workers whenever their marginal revenue product declines below their current wage.

In fact, the labor market appears to be much less responsive to short-term fluctuations in demand and supply than other markets are. Unlike the wheat market, for example, where prices and quantities fluctuate widely, wages and employment are more rigid. Some economists believe that the relative rigidity of labor markets suggests that supply and demand conditions are relatively unimportant in determining wages and employment. However, there are good reasons why, even in very competitive labor markets, workers and firms make long-term employment commitments and ignore temporary fluctuations in market conditions.

There are at least three reasons why workers and firms can benefit from continuous employment:

1. Many jobs require some initial training. The time and cost of training a new employee in the firm's particular production, management, or marketing techniques constitute investments that make workers more productive. The sooner workers quit, the lower the return on this investment. Firms pay trained workers high-than-market wages to establish an incentive for long job tenure. Alternatively, firms may offer employees deferred compensation in the form of bonuses or pensions as a means of retaining trained employees. The result of such incentives is that both the firm and the worker share in the returns. Both will want to continue the employment relationship unless marginal revenue product drops substantially or another firm offers a very large wage increase.

2. Work incentives. The productivity of a worker depends upon her effort. Employees may be able to shirk, or work less productively than expected, if firms are unable to monitor a worker's effort. Without a long-term employment agreement, shirking is riskless: If the worker is caught and fired, she can move to another employer at the same wage. Many firms, however, promise workers a bonus if they remain with the firm for a long duration. The bonus may be in the form of a high wage paid to senior employees, or a pension. Either way, the worker who is dismissed for shirking loses the bonus. The delayed-payment incentive reduces shirking and increases career worker productivity, benefiting both the worker and the firm.

3. Employees prefer stable wages (and incomes). Some economists argue that stable wages reflect workers' dislike for risk. If so, workers and firms may form long-term employment agreements in which firms agree to pay stable wages, even though product demand fluctuations shift the marginal revenue product schedule. Firms in effect insure workers against temporarily adverse demand

---

[3]Robert E. Hall, "The Importance of Lifetime Jobs in the U.S. Economy," *American Economic Review* (September 1982) 72(4), pp. 716–724.

conditions. Workers, for their part, agree not to leave the firm when labor demand is temporarily high and other firms are offering higher wages.

Whenever there are long-term labor commitments, the wage might be different from the worker's marginal revenue product in any given period. For example, the firm may pay a bonus to a worker, pushing the wage above the worker's marginal revenue product late in his career. Normally, we would expect that firms would lay off workers whenever the wage exceeds marginal revenue product, but in this case the firm has promised the bonus as part of the contract. The profit-maximizing condition for hiring workers when long-term contracts are present is that the total marginal revenue product, summed over the worker's career with the firm, equals the total value of wages paid.

SECTION RECAP
Long-term employment contracts benefit both workers and firms by lowering training costs, creating incentives for increased productivity, and providing workers with a stable income.

Summary

We observe a distribution of wages in the labor market. Equilibrium wage differences exist that are equalizing and nonequalizing. There are also disequilibrium wage differences.

Equalizing wage differences exist to compensate workers for differences in nonwage job attributes. When preferred employment opportunities are available, workers must be attracted into less-preferred jobs by wage premiums that equalize the overall attractiveness of different jobs.

Nonequalizing wage differences arise when labor mobility is restricted. Competition on the supply side is reduced and wage levels above competitive long-run equilibrium levels persist. These wage differences arise when special skills become valuable in the market, and when unions or government policies restrict entry into certain occupations or jobs.

Both equalizing and nonequalizing wage differences are equilibrium differences. **Disequilibrium wage differences** occur due to shifts in supply or demand in the market. An increase in demand for one occupation causes wages to rise, but only in the short run. As workers are attracted to the occupation, supply shifts and a new equilibrium is established. These disequilibrium differences are important allocation and rationing functions of the labor market.

The acquisition of education or other skills that improve productivity is a **human capital** investment. An individual undertakes the costs of the investment only if the expected benefits are at least as great as expected costs. The benefits of human capital investments usually accrue in the form of increased earnings. Changes in relative wages of workers with different skills change the profitability of these investments and prompt adjustments in the supply of workers with these skills.

Labor market discrimination exists when groups of equally productive workers are paid different wages. There is substantial evidence of labor market discrimination by race and sex. Blacks and women earn less than whites and men, even after accounting for differences in productivity characteristics such as educational attainment.

When there is only one employer in a labor market a **monopsony** exists. The monopsonist faces a positively sloped labor supply curve and must pay all workers higher wages when each additional worker is hired. The result is that the marginal resource cost of a worker exceeds his wage. The monopsonist has an incentive to reduce employment to save on labor costs. A monopsonist's wage and employment levels are less than those for an employer in a competitive labor market.

Finally, there is considerable employment stability in the United States. Workers tend to remain employed by one firm for relatively long periods of time. These longer-term employment relationships make labor markets less responsive to market changes. Labor market rigidity is beneficial to firms and workers in a number of ways. Long-term relationships make human capital investments more profitable. Longer-term payment schemes may improve worker productivity. Since workers prefer wage stability, employers keep wages constant while product demand fluctuates, and equate worker costs and productivity over a longer period of time.

Questions for Thought

Knowledge Questions

1. What is the difference between a disequilibrium wage difference and a nonequalizing wage difference?
2. Define labor market discrimination.
3. Define human capital investment.
4. What role does resource mobility play in the determination of equilibrium wage rates?

Application Questions

5. Why are nonprice (wage) working conditions important in the labor market but not in other resource markets?
6. Suppose there are only two occupations, X and Y, and that workers are employed in the labor force for only two years. Occupation X is unskilled work, but occupation Y requires a year of training. If the annual salary in X is $10,000, what will the annual salary be for Y? Explain.
7. Use the aggregate labor market model to explore the wage and employment consequences of immigration restrictions that prevent families from migrating to the United States from other countries. What happens to equilibrium wages and employment?
8. In what sense is a wage premium for noisy, dusty work equalizing?

Synthesis Questions

9. According to the definition of unemployment used in the United States, a person is considered unemployed if he or she is currently not working, is available for work, and is actively seeking a job. Can this definition lead to an underestimate of the number of people without jobs who would like to be working at current wage rates? Explain.
10. A biotechnology company expending millions of dollars on research for a new drug is much like a talented high school baseball player training and working to develop into the best baseball player he can be. In what way are these two situations similar? (Hint: Compare economic rent to monopoly profit.)

Trade Unions and Collective Bargaining

OVERVIEW

In the preceding chapter, we stressed the unique characteristic of labor markets: Owners of labor services accompany their delivery to the workplace. Therefore, both monetary and nonmonetary conditions of employment are important to workers. The bulk of most people's incomes is determined in the workplace, and workers spend a large portion of their time in their places of employment. We also showed how monopoly power on the buyer's side — labor market monopsony — can lower wages and employment. Throughout modern economic history, workers have sought to achieve more favorable employment conditions for themselves by generating their own monopoly power on the sellers' side of the labor market. They have tried to develop this market power through the organization of workers into labor unions.

Some of the most important issues in labor economics concern unions. In this chapter we examine a number of these issues. One might imagine that the introduction of such a major noncompetitive element as a labor union would cause us to abandon the supply and demand model of wages and employment. Such is not the case. In fact, we will rely heavily on the analysis of the two preceding chapters in evaluating the impact of unions. The underlying competitive supply and demand conditions in labor markets have a substantial effect on how successfully unions meet their goals. Unions, contrary to popular thinking, cannot set wages independently of market conditions. In this respect, unions are like monopolies. We have seen that monopoly

CHAPTER 16

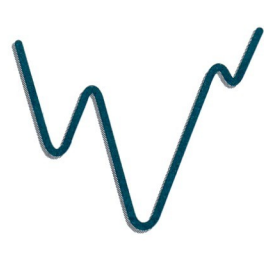

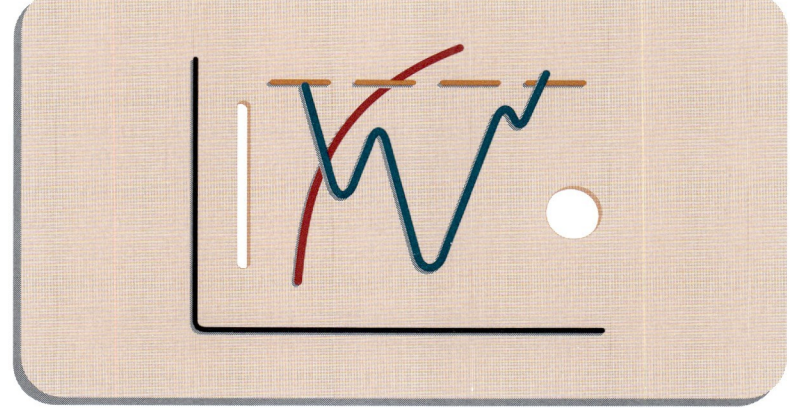

power in the product market does not give a firm unlimited power to raise prices and profits. Like monopolists, unions are constrained by the level and elasticity of market demand.

Learning Objectives

After reading and studying this chapter, you will be able to:

1. Define labor unions and distinguish between craft and industrial unions.
2. Summarize briefly the history and development of organized labor in the United States.
3. Identify factors contributing to the decline of labor unions in recent years.
4. Identify the factors that limit the ability of unions to increase the wages of their members.
5. Describe the objectives and economic impacts of labor unions.

The Purpose of Labor Unions

Labor union
A group of employees who band together to improve their terms of employment.

A **labor union** is an organization whose goal is to improve the terms of employment—both wages and working conditions—for its employee members, primarily by controlling the supply of labor to an industry. Sometimes these organizations are called *trade unions* because the early labor unions were organizations of skilled tradespeople such as carpenters, electricians, and cigar makers. Professional organizations like the National Education Association, the National Football League Players Association, and the Airline Pilots Association are also labor unions in the sense that they devote considerable resources to furthering the economic well-being of their members by using traditional labor union methods.

Unions seek to establish more favorable work rules surrounding the exchange of labor between a firm and its employees. Many aspects of the labor exchange have a public goods rather than private goods character to them. Recall from Chapter 5 that public goods are economic goods consumed jointly; the consumption of the good by one person does not reduce the quantity available for other consumers. In addition, it is difficult, if not impossible, to exclude specific individuals from consuming the public good. Workplace rules governing such things as safety procedures or conditions, established procedures for layoffs or overtime work, expected production per hour, and the responsibility assigned to supervisors have a public goods dimension. Once established, they tend to benefit all employees at no additional cost. Like other public goods, however, they are underproduced if they are generated by individual action. Workers tend to free-ride. Why should I risk my job to complain about workplace hazards if Joe will complain? The problem is that individuals do not have an incentive to convey the true value of workplace rules to their employers. An organization representing the preferences of all workers can improve upon this free rider situation.

Craft union
An organization that represents a particular type of skilled workers such as electricians, pipe fitters, or carpenters.

There are two main types of trade unions. The first employee organizations were **craft unions** (earlier called *guilds*), which sought to organize members of a particular skilled occupation. Today craft unions represent such skilled workers as electricians, pipe fitters, plumbers, boilermakers, and carpenters. *Craft unions attempt to raise wages by restricting entry into the union and occupation, frequently by controlling access to training opportunities for the craft.* Today much craft training occurs through union apprenticeship programs. When craft unions are able to reduce the supply of labor, as shown in Figure 1, wages rise while employment falls. Because the equilibrium wage with the union, W_U, is higher than the equilibrium wage without the union, W_1, those workers who are fortunate enough to be admitted and obtain employment will benefit. However, the higher-than-equilibrium wage creates an excess supply of workers. The union is forced to ration training opportunities as a result.

Industrial union
An organization of workers in an entire industry; membership is not determined on the basis of a particular skill.

Industrial unions seek to organize all workers—regardless of skill—in an entire industry. This type of union developed much later than craft unions. The most commonly recognized examples of this type of union include the United Auto Workers (UAW) and the Teamsters Union. Since industrial unions represent less-skilled workers, they *must* try to organize all potential employees. If industrial unions restricted membership, firms could simply ignore the union and hire from the pool of excluded workers. *Industrial unions attempt to improve wages and working conditions by direct negotiation with employers.* The primary source of an industrial union's bargaining power is its ability to withhold labor

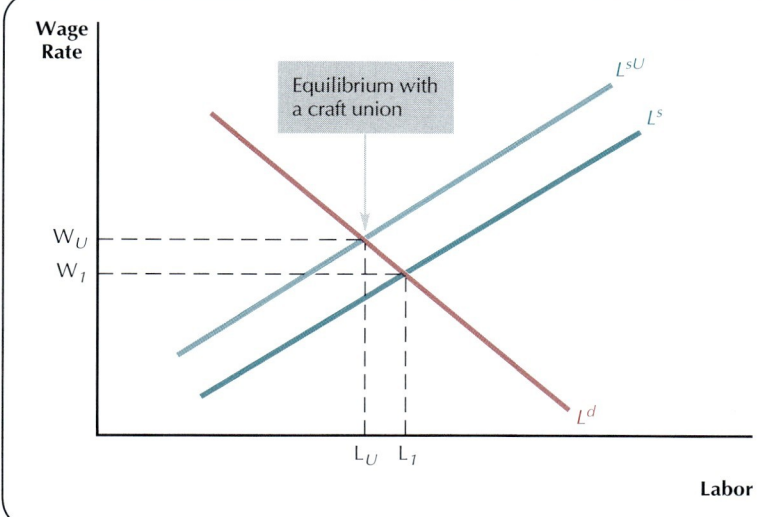

FIGURE 1
Craft unions and the supply of labor. When craft unions are able to reduce the supply of labor, shown by the shift of the labor supply curve from L^s to L^{sU}, the equilibrium wage rises—$W_U > W_1$—and the equilibrium level of employment falls—$L_U < L_1$. Those workers who are fortunate enough to be admitted and obtain employment will benefit. However, the higher-than-equilibrium wage creates an excess supply of workers.

from the industry. If employment terms are unacceptable to the union, it attempts to obtain more favorable conditions by preventing the firm from producing output. The union attempts to persuade all employees to refuse to work and to prevent the firm from hiring replacement workers. The refusal to work is called a **strike**.

In Figure 2, all workers agree not to work for less than W_U, altering the effective labor supply schedule to $W_U a L^s$, as shown by the heavy black line. Even though $L_1 - L_U$ workers are unemployed at this above-equilibrium wage,

Strike
An organized refusal by employees to work that is designed to obtain more favorable working conditions by preventing the firm from producing output.

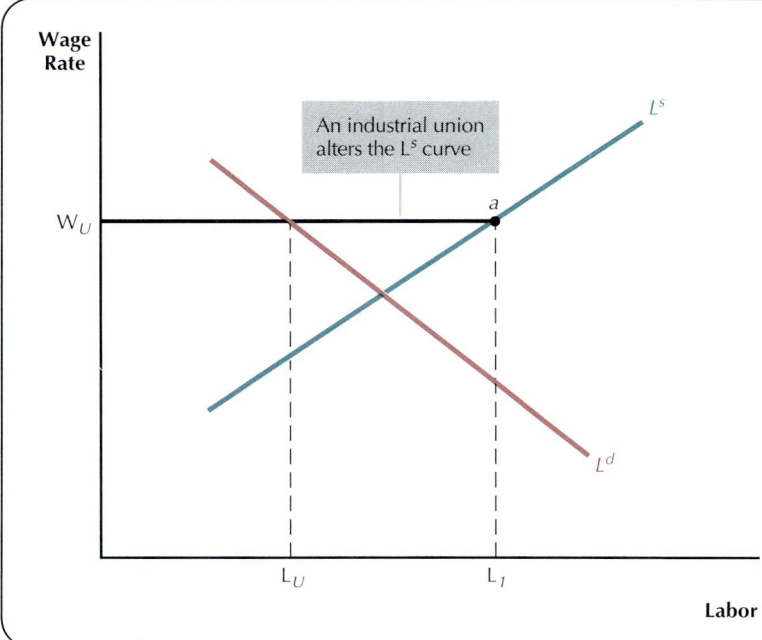

FIGURE 2
Industrial unions and the level of wages. The primary source of an industrial union's bargaining power is its ability to withhold labor from the industry. In this way, the wage can be driven above the competitively determined equilibrium. As illustrated in this figure, if all workers agree not to work for less than W_U, this will alter the effective labor supply schedule to $W_U a L^s$ as shown by the heavy black line. Even though $L_1 - L_U$ workers are unemployed at this above-equilibrium wage, they have agreed not to work for less.

Does It Make **Economic Sense?**

Are Strikes Logical?

Why do strikes occur? Management would prefer that they never did. Firms may find it less costly to raise wages and benefits than to incur the costs of being shut down. For the union, the right to strike is an important source of bargaining power. Unions feel that the strike threat is effective only if the strike weapon is used every so often. Nonetheless, strikes are costly to both sides: Firms lose production and profits and workers forfeit wages. Moreover, any final contract agreement could have been reached without a strike. Do strikes make economic sense?

One theory is that strikes are a result of imperfect information; they occur when one side underestimates the bargaining strength and resolve of the other. The process of collective bargaining begins with both sides making offers that are far apart. In Figure 3, the union's initial demand is W_U, while the firm offers W_C. That the two sides are initially far apart reflects optimal bargaining strategy. The costs of making an offer are low because there is plenty of time before the strike deadline (T_S) to make concessions. At the same time there is always the possibility that the other side will accept, or be so impressed that it revises downward its expectations of what it can get and begin to make concessions faster. In the early stages of bargaining, you should expect to hear union leaders complaining that "management is trying to take away everything we have achieved over the last twenty-five years." Management pleads that unions are out to "bankrupt" the firm.

As the strike deadline approaches, each side begins to make concessions for two reasons: (1) the probability of a strike increases, and (2) each side learns more about the other's bargaining strength. An agreement is reached when the union and firm offer curves intersect, and both sides agree to W^* in Figure 3. As depicted, both sides make concessions near the deadline, and a strike is averted.

Why do the bargainers waste time early with unrealistic bargaining positions, only to have marathon round-the-clock sessions up to the strike deadline? Again, optimal bargaining strategy requires each side to withhold major concessions until the last minute, hoping that the other side will compromise more. The last-minute rush is a feature of any bargaining situation, whether it be arms reduction talks between the United States and the Soviet Union, salary negotiations between a professional athlete and a sports team, or legislative negotiations between the House and Senate.

However, suppose the two sides remain far apart at the strike deadline, as depicted by the dashed offer curves. A strike results when bargainers believe that the benefits of a better contract (resulting from a strike) outweigh the costs of the strike. Each side believes it can do better by refusing the other's last offer and continuing to negotiate during the strike. Negotiations continue and eventually W^* is reached after a strike of $T_1 - T_S$ days. In hindsight, both sides realize that W^* could have been agreed to without a costly strike. A strike has occurred because one side was mistaken about the concessions the other side would make.

Note that strikes do not occur if one party is in a much stronger position than the other. If the industry faces a high demand for its product and low inventories, and if the union has a rich strike fund

---

Collective bargaining
A union represents a group of employees in their negotiations with the employer.

they have agreed not to work for less. *Taking wages out of competition* is an important union goal. There is evidence that unions have been successful in raising the wages of their members relative to nonunion labor.

In the United States, both craft and industrial unions seek to negotiate with the employer a written contract which governs the terms of employment. These contracts are very comprehensive, covering a wide array of workplace issues: wages, hours of work, vacations, pensions, length of work breaks, which job classes do which assignments, how worker grievances are handled, and much more. Because the union represents a group of employees in its negotiations with the employer, this process is called **collective bargaining**. For that segment of the U.S. workforce — approximately 15 percent — that belongs

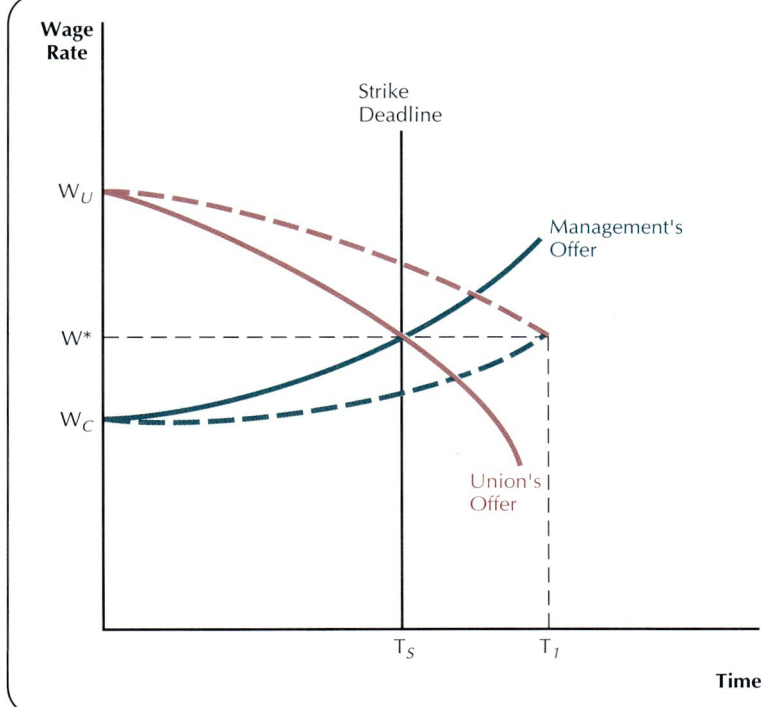

FIGURE 3
Wage bargaining in the face of a strike deadline. One theory of strikes is that they occur when one side underestimates the bargaining strength and resolve of the other. In this figure, the union's initial demand is W_u, while the firm offers W_c. As the strike deadline approaches, each side will begin to make concessions. An agreement is reached when the union offer and firm offer curves intersect, and both sides agree to W^*. However, suppose the two sides remain far apart at the strike deadline, as depicted by the dashed offer curves. A strike results when bargainers believe that the benefits of a better contract (resulting from a strike) will outweigh the costs of the strike. Negotiations continue during the strike and eventually W^* is reached after a strike of $T_1 - T_s$ days.

to pay benefits to its members, management knows that the union is in a strong position. It is better for management to yield quickly to the inevitable higher wage than to suffer a strike and still end up paying more.

The *mistake theory* suggests that strikes do not make economic sense, and thus should be fairly rare. The tremendous media attention that surrounds a strike may give the impression that collective bargaining frequently breaks down without agreement. Such is not the case. U.S. Department of Labor statistics indicate that from 1980 to 1984 less than 5 percent of union members were affected by a strike in any given year, and the United States lost less than one tenth of one percent of work time to strikes in each of those years.

to a trade union, collective bargaining constitutes a significant departure from the perfectly competitive labor market model. Under competition, workers compete against each other for jobs by bidding down the wage rate. The essence of collective bargaining is that workers agree not to compete with one another, even if some workers become unemployed.

In the United States, there are over 200,000 collective bargaining contracts in existence. These contracts, typically two or three years in length, are usually renewed through union and management negotiations as the contract term expires. Most strikes occur during this period of negotiations. Strikes receive considerable attention. Firms shut down and workers go without pay. Strikes may even be accompanied by violence; they always produce frustration and

SECTION RECAP
Labor unions work to improve wages and working conditions by using a variety of methods including restrictions on labor supply and direct negotiation with employers.

anger for both sides. However, it is important to note that most contracts — more than 95 percent on average — are renegotiated without incident.

American Unionism: Structure and Membership

Currently, 15 percent of the American work force belongs to a labor union. Most of these approximately 17 million workers are members of the American Federation of Labor–Congress of Industrial Organizations (AFL–CIO). The AFL–CIO is a federation of approximately 100 independent national unions including such diverse industries and occupations as musicians, college teachers, auto workers, and machinists. The AFL–CIO is an umbrella organization. It does not engage in collective bargaining; rather it supports the entire trade union movement by focusing on the broader issues of organized labor's membership and influence. Perhaps the most important function of the AFL–CIO is to represent organized labor in political affairs. The AFL–CIO formulates positions on public policy issues and seeks to achieve favorable state and federal legislation through lobbying and support for pro-union political candidates.

The true power of organized labor in the United States resides with the national unions and their local union affiliates. There are about 200 national

TABLE 1
Who are union members?

Category	Percent Union*
Industry	
Government	43.6
Transportation and public utilities	34.1
Manufacturing	23.1
Wholesale and retail trade	7.0
Occupation	
Operators, fabricators, and laborers	29.0
Managerial and professional specialty	18.2
Technical, sales, and administrative support	12.1
Sex	
Male	21.8
Female	14.9
Race	
Black	25.4
White	17.7
Hispanic	16.8

*Data is for 1989.
Source: U.S. Department of Labor, *Employment and Earnings*, January 1990.

unions. As we noted above, approximately one half are affiliated with the AFL–CIO, while others are independents. Each national union represents workers in the same industry or occupation, depending upon whether it is an industrial or craft union. Most of the 65,000 local unions are affiliated with a national union. Whether part of the AFL–CIO structure or not, much of the power of organized labor is focused in the national unions' offices. Generally, contract negotiations are conducted by the national unions, with ratification by local unions. The national unions exercise strong control over the locals. For example, frequently only the national union can authorize a strike.

Local unions represent grass-roots unionization. They administer the contract, perform the important function of overseeing the grievance machinery, and communicate the concerns of union members to the national office.

The characteristics of the 17 million union members reveal much about the past growth and future prospects of the trade union movement in the United States. Table 1 shows that union membership is highest in the public sector. Unionism is also strong in the transportation and public utilities sector and manufacturing industries. Blue-collar workers are more likely to be union members than are white-collar employees, and males are more likely than females to belong to unions. Finally, unions organize a greater share of nonwhites than whites.

These patterns should be interpreted with caution. The differences do not necessarily reflect a greater preference for unions among males or nonwhites. They may merely reflect the occupational and industrial patterns of unionization. For example, females are more likely than males to hold white-collar service jobs, which traditionally have had low rates of unionization.

SECTION RECAP
Currently, approximately 15 percent of the workforce is unionized. The majority of union members are public service employees and blue-collar workers in the utility and manufacturing sectors of the economy.

Union Membership in the United States: Growth and Decline

Table 2 reveals that the extent of unionization in the United States has been far from constant. Through 1930, unions represented a very small portion of the work force. However, the Great Depression saw a spurt in union membership that continued through World War II and peaked in the mid-1950s at about 25 percent. Since then, union membership has steadily declined as a percentage of the work force. What explains this pattern of growth and decline?

Labor Unions Prior to the 1930s

Trade unions were formed in the United States shortly after the birth of the Republic. However, as Table 2 shows, they really did not gain a significant foothold until 150 years later. This is explained, in part, by the fact that before 1935, there was no federal legislation that guaranteed the right of workers to organize and bargain collectively. Instead, the courts were left to rule over disputes between a union and a firm's management, and the legal system was generally hostile towards unions.

In these early cases, courts applied the common law doctrine of criminal conspiracy to union organizing. They held that a union was, by definition, an organization that sought to artificially raise the price of labor, and thus was illegal, just as a cartel of businesses that engaged in price fixing would be illegal. Later decisions relaxed the position that unions were per se illegal, but

TABLE 2
Union membership, selected years

Year	Membership (millions)	Percentage of Labor Force	Percentage of Nonagricultural Employment
1880	0.2	n.a.	2.3
1890	0.4	n.a.	2.7
1900	0.8	n.a.	5.2
1910	2.1	n.a.	9.8
1920	5.0	n.a.	18.3
1930	3.4	6.8	11.6
1940	8.7	15.5	26.9
1950	14.3	22.3	31.5
1955	16.8	24.7	33.2
1960	17.0	23.6	31.4
1965	17.3	22.4	28.5
1970	19.4	22.6	27.4
1975	19.6	20.3	25.5
1980	20.0	18.8	22.1
1985*	17.0	14.4	16.3
1989*	17.0	13.7	14.9

*These figures include membership in professional associations.
Source: *Handbook of Labor Statistics*, U.S. Department of Labor, 1980; 1985; *Employment and Earnings*, Bureau of Labor Statistics, U.S. Department of Labor, January, 1987, 1990.

the courts still allowed management an arsenal of powerful union-busting tools. Among these were (1) court injunctions against striking, (2) *yellow dog contracts*, through which a worker agreed not to join the union as a condition of employment, and (3) the right to refuse to bargain if a union were formed.

Organized Labor's Golden Years: 1935 to 1955

The 1930s brought both the Great Depression and the New Deal. The Roosevelt administration actively encouraged the growth of trade unions and delivered two favorable pieces of legislation that kicked off twenty years of union growth. The *Norris–La Guardia Act* of 1932 effectively eliminated two of management's strongest antiunion weapons. It declared the yellow dog contract to be unenforceable in federal courts and severely restricted the ability of employers to gain federal court injunctions.

The *Wagner Act (National Labor Relations Act of 1935)* was even more favorable to unions. Essentially, its provisions sought to enforce the idea that the decision of whether or not to join a union was the worker's alone. The Wagner Act established legal procedures for conducting unionization elections as well as sanctions against employers who attempted to interfere with union organizing efforts. Perhaps more importantly, it established that management had a legal obligation to bargain in good faith once workers established a union. Failure to do so was an unfair labor practice punishable under federal law. The Wagner Act established an independent regulatory authority, the National Labor Relations Board, to implement provisions of the legislation.

By the 1930s the character of America's modern industrial relations system was taking shape. The legislation in this period embodied its most important feature: free collective bargaining. From this period to the present, the government has attempted to establish the rules of the game for labor–management relations, while leaving both parties alone to settle the specific terms of their relationship. Often it is a delicate balancing act. Government control of labor–management relationships is intended to be objective, not giving an advantage to labor or management. The legislation attempts to protect the rights of individual workers to free choice in their relationship with their employers, while it also recognizes the rights of groups—unions—who do succeed in improving the terms of employment for all employees.

Assisted by this legislation, industrial unionism grew rapidly. The Congress of Industrial Organizations (then separate from the American Federation of Labor) quickly organized many major industries, including meat packing, rubber, and steel.

Stagnation and Decline: 1955 to the Present

Since reaching its peak in 1955, the union sector has slowly but steadily declined as a percentage of the total work force. The obvious question is whether this trend will continue, or whether a reversal of union fortunes can be expected in the coming decades. The answer depends upon what caused the decline. While there is much disagreement about the relevant factors, several possible explanations have been offered:

1. Unfavorable legislation: In 1947, a more conservative Congress enacted the *Taft–Hartley Act*. This legislation significantly reduced the power of organized labor and was designed to balance the power of labor and management. The new law altered the union security provision that defines the relationship between the firm's employees and the union. It outlawed the **closed shop** provision, which had required employers to hire only union members, in favor of the **union shop**, which allowed employers to hire anyone they wished, but required the new employees to join the union after they had been hired. The union shop is a compromise between the closed shop and an **open shop**, an arrangement whereby employees do not have to belong to a union if they choose not to.

The Taft–Hartley Act also established more stringent unfair labor practices for unions. The act's most controversial provision allowed individual states to pass *right-to-work* legislation, which allows a worker the option of not joining a union even if the workplace is organized. States can essentially establish the open shop rule by enacting right-to-work legislation. At present, twenty-one states have adopted right-to-work statutes. Organized labor has sought unsuccessfully to repeal or modify Taft–Hartley since its inception.

2. Structural changes in the economy: This hypothesis recognizes that certain sectors of the economy are more conducive to unionization. The data cited earlier suggest that goods-producing industries are more receptive to unioni-

Closed shop
Employers are only able to hire union members.

Union shop
Employers can hire anyone they wish; however, new employees must join the union after they have been hired.

Open shop
Employees are not required to belong to a union if they choose not to.

zation than service industries. Also, blue-collar and male workers seem more likely to join unions than female and white-collar employees. Over the period that the union sector has been in decline, growth in total employment in the United States has favored the nonunion sector. In the post-war period, goods-producing employment has fallen relative to that in the service sector, and white-collar employment has grown faster than blue-collar employment. This period also has seen a dramatic increase in the number of women entering the labor force. Another factor is the expansion of employment in traditionally nonunion southern and southwestern states. These structural changes suggest that union membership would have declined even if basic attitudes toward unionization were unchanged.

3. Substitution of government for unions: Many of the social services now provided by state and federal government had their roots in early union contracts. Programs such as Social Security, workers' compensation, unemployment insurance, and occupational safety and health regulations have roots in collective bargaining. Gradually, government has replaced the trade union as the supplier of these services. One view of union decline is that, with the government so heavily involved in providing benefits and employment security, workers no longer feel it is necessary to belong to a union. In essence, government substitutes for unions.

There are two problems with this theory, however. Expansion of government services does not reduce union bargaining strength. If unions have the power to compel employers to provide costly fringe benefits or improved job safety, why don't they bargain for higher wages or other benefits when the government takes over the former? Second, there is the intriguing question of why the AFL–CIO has strongly supported the expanded role of government if the effect is to diminish its own influence. Currently, organized labor endorses national health care. Are they aware that this would diminish the value of union contracts, which generally provide very generous health care benefits, or are they confident that, with the federal government guaranteeing health care, they could bargain instead for higher wages?

4. Active management opposition: There is evidence that employers are becoming more aggressive in opposing the introduction of unions and in decertifying unions that are already in place. (Just as workers have a legal right to vote to establish a union, they also have the same right to vote to throw out an existing union. The latter process is accomplished through a **decertification election.**) At the national level, conservatives have begun to press their views that federal labor legislation is unbalanced and bestows too much power on organized labor.

In the case of Eastern Airlines in the late 1980s, for example, management was unsuccessful in getting labor to agree to a wage cut that management maintained was necessary for Eastern to remain competitive. Subsequently, Texas Air, which controlled both Eastern and Continental (which was nonunion) began selling part of Eastern's operations to Continental. However, a federal judge ruled that this was a violation of federal labor law and ordered Texas Air to stop. Eastern's mechanics went on strike when management refused to settle on a new contract.

Decertification election Workers vote on whether to remove an existing union from their workplace.

SECTION RECAP
As a percentage of the workforce, membership in unions peaked in the 1950s and has steadily declined since then. Possible explanations for this decline include unfavorable legislation, structural changes in the economy, substitution of government provision of certain services, and active management opposition to unions.

The Goals of Labor Unions

The impact of trade unions cannot be evaluated until we have a theory of what unions try to do. When we assumed single-minded objectives for consumers and producers, namely utility and profit maximization, we were able to derive fairly specific predictions about their behavior in markets. Unfortunately, identifying similarly single-minded labor union goal appears to be impossible. Samuel Gompers, a cigar maker and the first president of the AFL, was once asked just exactly what trade unions wanted from employers. His response was straightforward: "More, more, and more." While Gompers's opinion on union goals may be accurate, it misses an important point. Clearly, unions would prefer to maximize both employment and wage rates. However, the downward-sloping demand curve for labor implies a tradeoff between these goals.

The weakness of always pursuing only a higher-wages objective is apparent from Figure 4. Given downward-sloping labor demand, the wage rate is maximized when only one worker is employed. Of course, no rational union leader would pursue a strategy that causes all members but one to lose their jobs. This patently absurd result suggests that, in general, unions do not always demand more and more, even if they are powerful enough to impose their demands on the industry.

The union must be prepared to trade off higher wages against employment losses. Readers who think this is just a sterile theoretical point—that unions, practically speaking, never are able to push wages high enough to worry about excessive employment losses—should review the collective bargaining expe-

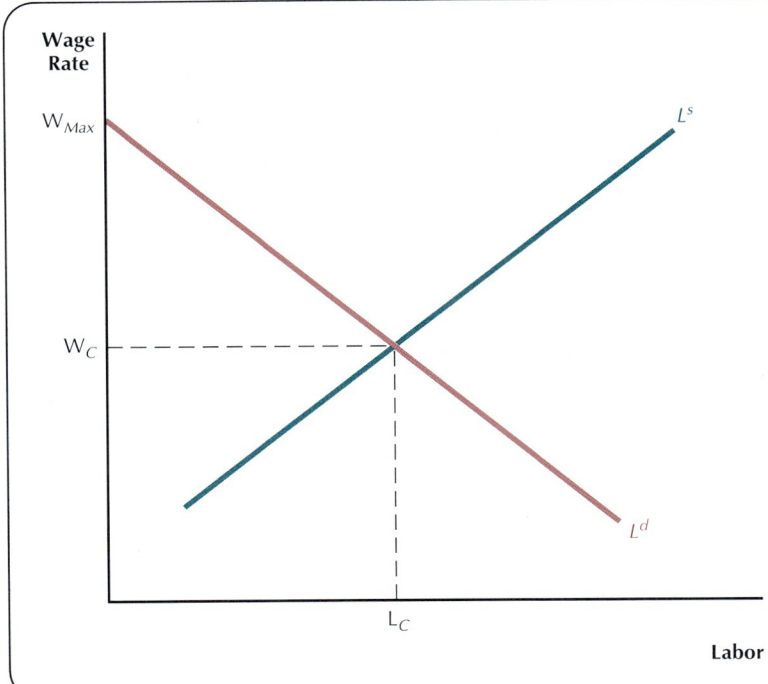

FIGURE 4
Higher wages as a union objective.
This figure illustrates the weakness of always pursuing only a higher-wages objective. Given downward-sloping labor demand, the wage rate is maximized (at W_{Max}) when only one worker is employed. Of course, no rational union leader would pursue a strategy that causes all members but one to lose their jobs. This patently absurd result suggests that, in general, unions will not always demand more and more, even if they are powerful enough to impose their demands on the industry.

riences of the 1980s, when the economy went through the worst recession since World War II. To save jobs, many unions actually agreed to accept reduced compensation. Frequently the alternative to such givebacks was a plant closing.

A Public Choice Model of Union Decision Making

The emphasis thus far has been on unions as organizations whose aim is higher wages. However, for understanding union objectives and behavior, probably the most useful way to view unions is as political organizations. Unions are organizations of workers who represent the collective preferences of their members. The aims of labor unions reflect the aims of their members. Union leaders and members face a situation very similar to that faced by voters and politicians. Union leaders are elected by the membership. Their job is to achieve the goals of the membership. Thus, we can better understand union behavior by applying the simple principles of the economics of public choice that we first introduced in Chapter 5.

The goals of the membership are determined by the preferences of the union members, their heterogeneity, and the economic environment of the firm and the economy. (The price elasticity of demand for labor is an important determinant of union goals and strategy.) The objective of union leaders is to be reelected by delivering those benefits that the membership wants. Failure to do so can cost the leader his job.

Workers are motivated by better pay and working conditions. We expect these to be general union goals. More specific objectives vary by union, industry, and period of time. Within the same company, at a given point in time some workers would rather have higher wages, while others would rather have lower wages but a better pension plan. Others want more paid time off instead of higher wages. Since members essentially vote to determine the union's specific objectives in a given bargaining year, the size and heterogeneity of the union influence the extent of consensus within the union on its objectives. Smaller craft unions have an easier time establishing priorities because the members are very similar. Larger industrial unions have a much more difficult time agreeing on specific objectives. Worker groups with different skills want different benefits, different age groups have different needs. The size and political power of these groups determine their relative influence in the union's decision making. If the union votes by majority rule, there is always a significant number of members at least somewhat dissatisfied with the leadership. This factor explains some of the observed internal dissension in unions.

A union's bargaining goals vary with economic conditions. When employment is strong and growing, workers tend to want to push for better pay, more time off, and so forth. For example, in inflationary periods many unions negotiated automatic wage increases tied to increases in the cost of living, so-called **cost of living adjustment** clauses, or COLAs. During periods of substantial inflation union members wanted this type of inflation protection. At the same time a strong demand for labor eased the employment consequences of wage increases.

However, during recessions the environment is much different, and union objectives change. With slow growth or no growth in output, unemployment becomes a concern. Wage demands are moderated because the employment consequences are more severe. In fact, if unemployment is rising, unions may make job security one of their top demands. Unions seek to negotiate contracts

Cost of living adjustment
A negotiated automatic wage increase that is tied to increases in the cost of living.

that protect union members from layoffs and spread available work to more workers. In recessions there is less concern about inflation among members and they are more willing to give up COLAs in exchange for other benefits.

Only one thing is clear: *No one goal can adequately describe the actions of all labor unions.* Unions are organizations whose purpose is to improve the collective welfare of their membership. While they seek generally better terms of employment, they are constrained by market forces to a greater or lesser degree. Their structure is designed to ensure (ignoring corruption) that their leaders will attempt to achieve whatever gains most members want under prevailing economic conditions.

SECTION RECAP
According to the public choice theory of union behavior, unions' objectives vary with economic conditions. The goal of a union's leadership is to satisfy the majority of the union's members.

A Model of Unions' Impact on Wages and Employment

This section examines the economic impact of successful union efforts to obtain above-equilibrium wages for their members. A reasonable assumption is that a union will strive to negotiate wages that are somewhat higher than the prevailing level in the absence of the union. To simplify the analysis, assume that all labor in the United States is demanded by the two competitive industries shown in Figure 5. Assume also that all workers have the same skills and that

FIGURE 5
The effect of a union on union and nonunion wages. *(a) Industry A (b) Industry B.* This figure illustrates the economic impact of successful union efforts to obtain above-equilibrium wages for their members. Assume that all labor in the United States is demanded by the two competitive industries A and B, that all workers have the same skills, and that jobs in the two industries have identical nonwage characteristics. Initially, all workers receive the same wage, W_C. Now assume that workers in industry A (Figure 5 (a)) are organized into a trade union that immediately negotiates a wage of W_U. The effective supply schedule to industry A becomes $W_U a L^s$. The result is a higher wage but lower employment. Those who have lost jobs may be expected to spill over into nonunion industry B (Figure 5 (b)), raising employment and lowering wages in industry B. As a result, 1) a union–nonunion wage differential of $W_U - W_{NU}$ occurs, and 2) employment declines in the union sector, but increases in the nonunion sector.

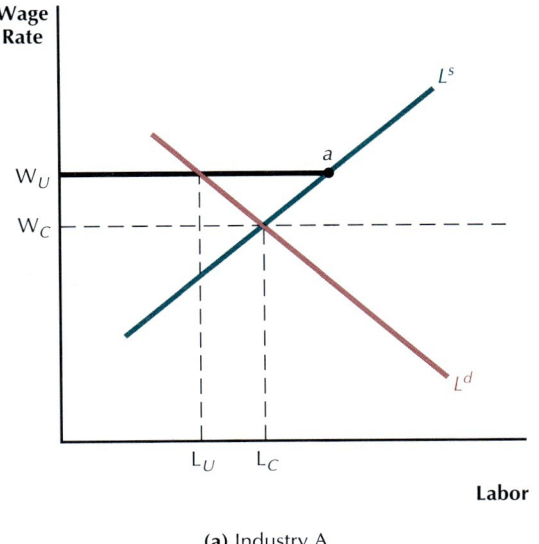

(a) Industry A

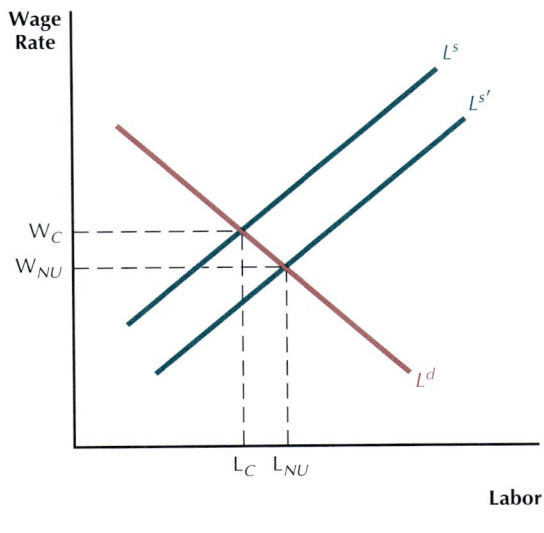

(b) Industry B

jobs in the two industries have identical nonwage characteristics. Under these assumptions workers receive the same wage in either industry, W_C. Now assume that workers in industry A [Figure 5 (a)] are organized into a trade union which immediately negotiates a wage of W_U. The effective supply schedule to industry A becomes $W_U a L_s$, as union workers agree not to undercut the *union scale* of W_U. The result is a higher wage but lower employment; $L_C^A - L_U^A$ workers lose their jobs in industry A.

Unless there is some mechanism to spread the unemployment across all L_C workers evenly (such as *work sharing* in the form of a shorter work week for everyone), those who have lost jobs may be expected to spill over into nonunion industry B [Figure 5 (b)]. The increased supply of labor raises employment and lowers wages in industry B. This spillover effect means that unionizing industry A has had adverse consequences on workers in industry B.

The impact of the union in competitive labor markets can be summarized as follows: (1) a union–nonunion wage differential of $W_U - W_{NU}$ appears, and (2) employment declines in the union sector, but increases in the nonunion sector. The reallocation of labor lowers economic efficiency and welfare. Workers who were more productive in industry A are now employed in industry B, where their marginal revenue product is lower. Not surprisingly, if labor is efficiently allocated by competitive labor markets, anything that disturbs this equilibrium reduces economic welfare.

Threat effect
The possibility that workers in a particular firm or industry will form a union if their wage demands are not met.

Also note that the union causes no involuntary unemployment. All workers who become unemployed by the higher wage in industry A and are willing to work at the lower wage of W_{NU} find work in industry B. However, there is another possibility that could lead to unemployment. Suppose firms in industry B fear that their workers also will organize a union and therefore counter this threat by raising wages above W_C. They hope that workers will be satisfied with a wage close to W_U and will not undergo the expense of an organization drive and union dues. Wages rise in industry B due to a **threat effect**. If wages are higher in both industries, employment must fall and some workers become unemployed.

SECTION RECAP
Although unions can raise the wages of their members, this may lead to lower wages in nonunionized industries. The latter effect depends on how displaced workers in the unionized industry and management in the nonunionized industry react to the increase in wages.

Unemployment also results if workers decide not to spill over into industry B. Workers who lose their jobs in industry A may feel they are better off waiting for a vacancy to open as a result of a quit, layoff, or retirement. (In addition, unemployment compensation may make it easier for workers to resist moving to industry B.) If the chance of a higher union wage is preferred to the certainty of a lower nonunion wage, workers will not spill over and unemployment will occur in industry A. Note, however, that this is voluntary unemployment—workers are willing to remain unemployed in hopes of earning higher wages in industry A.

Policies to Increase Union Power

Unacceptable job losses constrain the union from seeking a wage higher than W_U. For any given wage increase, employment loss is greater the more elastic the labor demand schedule. Thus unions press harder to raise wages when demand elasticity is low. Recalling the determinants of resource demand elasticity, unions are in a stronger position when (1) the available substitutes for union labor are fewer, (2) demand for the product is less elastic, and (3) the ratio of labor costs to total costs is lower.

It should come as no surprise that unions have been unwilling to passively accept restrictions on their ability to raise wages. Instead, organized labor strives to improve the tradeoff between wages and employment. Much of the behavior of unions can be understood as an attempt to shift the labor demand curve outward and reduce its elasticity. Unions also support policies that reduce the likelihood that workers will undercut the union wage.

Policies to Alter the Demand Curve

Union organizations are aware of the consequences of obtaining above-equilibrium wage rates, although individual union members may not be. Union organizations are also aware of the factors that influence these consequences. Wage increases motivate employers to look for substitutes — either cheaper labor or other inputs to substitute for labor, or both. Unions try to offset these forces. They advertise the union label and encourage consumers to buy union-made products in an effort to increase demand for goods that become more costly with union success. (It is not clear that this campaign has much impact.) Unions also negotiate restrictive work rules to limit employers' opportunities to reduce employment. These work rules are known as *featherbedding* practices. When railroads switched from steam to diesel locomotives, they continued to employ the fireman, a third crew member who was really not needed on the new diesels. When technology reduced the need to employ linotypists to set some kinds of print for newspapers, the union negotiated contracts requiring that the type be set by linotypists anyway — and then destroyed.

We already know that unions support trade barriers to increase the demand for union members and reduce its elasticity. Limiting foreign competition means that U.S. industry faces a less elastic product demand. Union efforts to organize the many nonunion workers in the south can also be viewed as a policy to reduce the elasticity of union labor demand. While unions argue that they are organizing the south to bring the benefits of organized labor to these less fortunate workers, we know that organizing southern workers also increases the power of unions to raise the wages of their northern counterparts. If southern labor is unionized, the ability of firms to use a nonunion substitute by relocating in the south is eliminated.

Similar reasoning suggests why unions must organize a significant share of an entire industry. The more nonunion firms and workers, the greater the number of substitutes for union labor and the greater the elasticity of demand for the unionized firm's product. Unionized mines in West Virginia must take a very tough bargaining stance, because they compete with nonunion western coal.

As another example, nonunion supermarket chains have provided an increasing amount of competition for unionized chains in local markets. In many areas of the country, local chains that utilize nonunion labor have been able to gain control of a growing share of the market. This increased market share has come at the expense of unionized national chains such as A&P, Kroger, Safeway, and Eagle supermarkets.

Policies to Prevent Undercutting the Union Wage

An important concern of unions is what happens to the workers who lose their jobs. A large number of unemployed workers is a potential threat to a union. If the unemployed are willing to work for less than the union wage, nonunion firms will hire them and produce at lower cost. This would force the union to

SECTION RECAP
Unions attempt to improve their bargaining position by increasing the demand for labor and reducing the supply of available substitutes.

Why the Disagreement?

Increasing the Minimum Wage

In 1989, the Congress and President George Bush agreed upon legislation which will eventually increase the minimum wage from its previous level of $3.35 an hour to $4.25 an hour. (In addition, the new law contains a provision that allows employers to pay a lower training wage to teen-aged employees.) However, the new legislation was not passed without controversy. An earlier version of the bill that had been approved by the Congress would have raised the minimum wage to $4.65 per hour. President Bush vetoed that bill, arguing that the increase was too large, and that it would have considerable adverse effects on minimum-wage earners and the economy as a whole. The last time Congress voted to increase the minimum wage was in 1977. In total, the minimum wage has been increased sixteen times since it was first established as part of the Fair Labor Standards Act in 1938. (The first minimum wage was 25¢ an hour.) Every time an increase in the minimum wage has been considered, it has been accompanied by considerable controversy. Why the disagreement?

On the one hand, employers — especially employers of low-wage labor — opposed an increase. The U.S. Chamber of Commerce and the National Restaurant Association took a strong stand against the most recent increase. They argued that an increase would cause more unemployment among the least-skilled workers and that a higher minimum wage would deny more young people the opportunity for on-the-job training that is important to get them started on careers of productive employment. On the other hand, supporters of the increase pointed out that full-time work at the prevailing minimum wage yields an annual income that is insufficient for a minimum standard of living. It would be, in fact, below the official poverty line. Organized labor was an especially strong proponent of an increase in the minimum wage. They argued that an increase was needed to ensure that everyone who works earns a decent wage. (However, as we shall see below, they also had self-serving motivations for supporting an increase in the minimum wage.)

Much of the rationale behind the opposing views on this old, established law can be understood through a simple supply and demand analysis. The minimum wage is a price floor, established above the equilibrium wage in the market for relatively unskilled workers. Experienced and educated workers are not directly affected by the law, since they earn wages in excess of those proposed for the new law. Figure 6 illustrates the impact of the law in this less-skilled market, assuming that the market is in equilibrium at the old minimum wage level.

The new minimum wage decreases the quantity of labor demanded by $L_e - L^d$ and increases the quantity of labor supplied by $L^s - L_e$. Some workers previously employed lose their jobs and some individuals previously out of the labor force are now attracted into the market to look for work. Reduced employment occurs because of the negatively sloped demand curve. Labor is now more expensive to employers. In the short run, employers reduce output because of the higher costs. In the long run they attempt to minimize the cost increase by adopting production techniques that rely on less of the now more-expensive labor. This adjustment process is the one noted by the business community.

Organized labor's position is that those who do keep their jobs have a higher income. Notice another impact of the legislation that is generally beneficial to unions. Since unions are always attempting to increase wages and improve working conditions for their members, they must face up to the adverse employment consequences of higher labor costs. Unions attempt to minimize management's opportunities to substitute other inputs for unionized labor. Unskilled minimum-wage labor is one kind of substitute for union labor. When the price of this substitute rises because the minimum wage lower its wage demands to allow organized firms to compete. Union leaders worry that the unemployed will become a nonunion substitute, or more colorfully, will *scab*.

Unions have supported a number of public policies to reduce this threat. Unemployment insurance provides income support to the unemployed, reducing the likelihood that workers, desperate for income, will undercut the

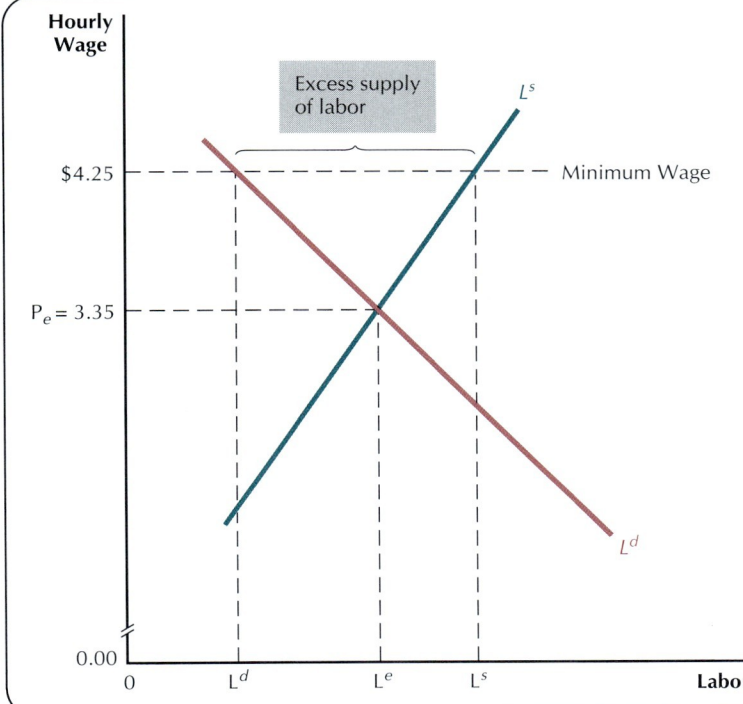

FIGURE 6
The economic effect of an increase in the minimum wage. This figure illustrates the impact of an increase in the minimum wage. Assuming that the market is in equilibrium at the old minimum wage level, $P_e = \$3.35$, the new minimum wage, \$4.28, would decrease the quantity of labor demanded by $L_e - L^d$ and increase the quantity of labor supplied by $L^s - L_e$. Some workers previously employed would lose their jobs and some individuals previously out of the labor force would now be attracted into the market to look for work. Reduced employment occurs because of the negatively sloped demand curve. Labor is now more expensive to employers.

rises, the gains to the employer from using this substitute are reduced. In a relative sense, union labor is less costly. A higher minimum wage makes the demand for union labor less elastic.

This simple analysis has touched on only a few of the many issues associated with the minimum wage law. However, it is clear that both business and labor have strong vested interests in minimum wage legislation. Of course, the important question for society is the net effect of the law. There are gainers and losers in many parts of the economy. However, is the net effect of a higher minimum wage beneficial? If the law causes unemployment, it reduces economic efficiency in society. As a policy to reduce poverty, the law's impact is questionable. It reduces employment opportunities for low-wage workers. Those workers who maintain employment at the higher wage might not be members of low-income families. Many beneficiaries are young people, some of whom are from poor families but many of whom are from middle-income or even upper-income families.

While the net impact of the minimum wage legislation is difficult to ascertain, it is clear that much of the debate about the law is focused on the gains or losses to different groups in society and not on the overall net effect of the law on society and the economy.

union wage. Unions strongly support the concept of work sharing, which spreads the costs of unemployment. Instead of a minority of workers totally unemployed, work sharing means that all workers are prevented from working as many hours as they would like. The requirement that any work above forty hours per week be paid at time-and-one-half encourages firms to employ more workers rather than fewer workers more intensively. Firms find it less costly to add another shift than to use overtime. Union support for the four-day workweek also is consistent with work sharing.

Unions and Wages: The Evidence

Unions are able to raise wages because they control the supply of labor to an industry. If the union can effectively threaten to withhold all labor — to strike — management must weigh the costs of higher wages against the lost sales from being shut down. Thus, unions' bargaining strength varies across industries as the costs of a strike to management are different. How high unions desire to push wages depends upon the elasticity of labor demand, which varies by industry. Not surprisingly, unions have had varying degrees of success at raising wages relative to nonunion members.

Ideally, we would like to measure the size of $W_U - W_C$ in Figure 5, which represents the increase in wages due to unionization. However, we only observe $W_U - W_{NU}$, the difference between equally productive union and nonunion workers. The wage of nonunion workers may be either higher or lower due to the union, depending upon whether the threat effect or spillover effect is greater.

Recent surveys of statistical evidence[1] reveal that union workers earn from zero to 50 percent more than their nonunion counterparts, depending upon occupation and industry. Unions appear to be more effective at raising wages in the construction industry and for blue-collar workers. The average wage gain across all industries and jobs has been estimated to fall in the range of 15 to 25 percent. In addition, there is evidence that the average union–nonunion gap varies countercyclically, rising in a recession (unemployment in the economy is rising) and falling during an expansion (unemployment in the economy is falling).

Other studies point to a spillover effect that is larger than the threat effect. Unions, on average, lower the wages of nonunion workers. Finally, Richard Freeman[2] of Harvard University has shown that earnings dispersion is narrower among union members. Wage differences among union members in similar occupations is less than the variation in the same jobs held by nonunion workers. Thus unions appear to have made progress toward their goal of equalizing, as well as raising, members' wages.

The evidence concerning the success of unions at raising the wages of their members raises another question: Who pays for these union gains? We have already indicated that the wages of nonunion workers can be reduced by union actions. There is strong evidence to support this hypothesis. It was noted in the preceding chapter that a large share (approximately two thirds) of national income accrues to labor. This share has remained virtually constant over the past fifty years, a period when union influence expanded greatly. *If unions have achieved wage gains, they have come from other workers. To the extent that unions raise production costs, consumers also pay for union gains.* Higher production costs tend to raise consumer prices.

---

[1] H. Gregg Lewis, *Union Relative Wage Effects* (Chicago: University of Chicago Press, 1986), and Barry T. Hirsch and John T. Addison, *The Economic Analysis of Unions: New Approaches and Evidence* (Boston: Allen and Unwin, 1986).

[2] Richard B. Freeman, "Union Wage Practices and Wage Dispersion Within Establishments," *Industrial and Labor Relations Review* (1982), Vol. 36, No. 1.

The Effects of Unions: Monopsony

It comes as no surprise that if labor markets are otherwise competitive, unions have a negative effect on economic efficiency. However, what if employers have monopsony power? Figure 7 shows that unions may be able to offset an employer's monopsony power and simultaneously raise wages and employment.

In the absence of a union, the monopsonist employs L_M workers, where MRP = MRC, and pays a wage of W_M. Now suppose a union is organized to counter the firm's monopsony power. It bargains for a wage of W_U. The union wage floor changes the labor supply schedule to $W_U a L^s$, as before. Importantly, the new MRC schedule is equal to W_U up to L_U workers. The monopsonist is forced to pay the same constant wage whether one or L_U workers is hired. As a result it employs L_U workers, where the new MRC equals MRP. The union has increased wages and employment.

The reason the union can do both is that the wage floor removes the monopsonist's incentive to restrict hiring. No longer can the monopsonist reduce the wage by hiring fewer workers. The union counteracts monopsony power. Consequently, the potential for economic efficiency is enhanced. So long as the union does not raise the wage above W', employment and efficiency rise.

Unions and Economic Welfare: A Broader View

The similarity between a trade union and a monopolist in a product market is striking. Unions raise wages and reduce employment. The reallocation of labor reduces total economic welfare. This economic analysis of union effects is a positive one; the normative judgment that is difficult to avoid based on the above analysis is that unions, like other forms of monopoly power, should be discouraged.

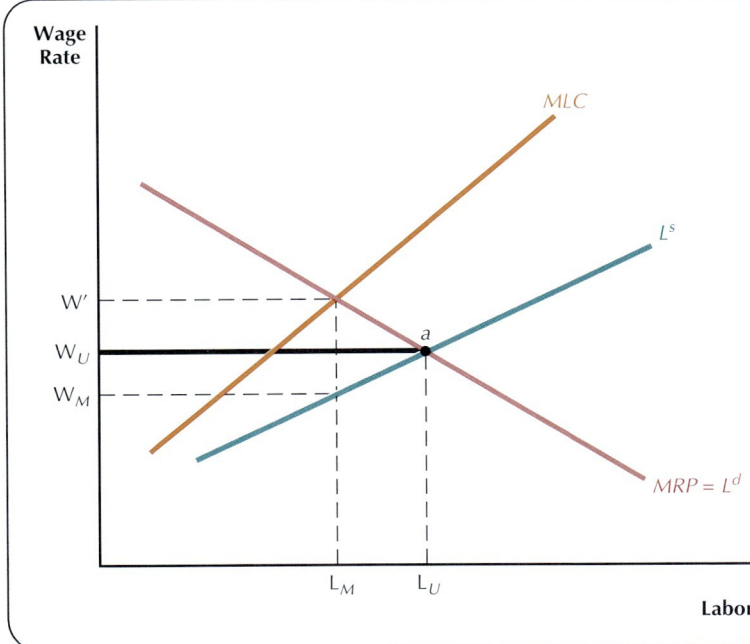

FIGURE 7
The effect of a union in a monopsony situation. Unions may be able to offset an employer's monopsony power and raise wages and employment. In the absence of a union, the monopsonist employs L_M workers, where MRP = MRC, and pays a wage of W_M. Assuming a union is organized, it could bargain for a wage of W_U. The union wage floor changes the labor supply schedule to $W_U a L^s$. Importantly, the new MRC schedule is equal to W_U up to L_U workers. The monopsonist is forced to pay the same constant wage whether one or L_U workers is hired. As a result it employs L_U workers, where the new MRC equals MRP. So long as the union does not raise the wage above W', employment and efficiency rise.

The reader should keep in mind, however, that we have focused on only one function of the union. Professors Richard Freeman and James Medoff[3] of Harvard University have forcefully advocated their view that unions, on net, are good for the economy. They argue that unions play a much broader role than simply bargaining for higher wages, and that the other union functions raise worker morale, job satisfaction, and productivity. Freeman and Medoff cite the grievance machinery, which reduces the likelihood that workers will be fired without cause; the reduction in compensation disparities; the seniority system; administering the pension fund; and many other important union roles.

One major difference between the monopoly view of unions and the broader perspective of Freeman and Medoff is the effect of unions on productivity. The former suggests that unions lower productivity. If their main goal is to raise wages while protecting against job loss, unions will pursue contract provisions that establish minimum staffing requirements and restrict management's ability to adjust the production process. The union goal of wage equalization also may reduce productivity: If more productive employees are not paid more, there is little incentive to work harder.

Freeman and Medoff suggest that a more inclusive evaluation raises the possibility that unions may enhance worker productivity by improving worker morale and job satisfaction. In addition, the union provides a formal mechanism for transmitting production process improvements from the shop floor to the boardroom.

A weakness of the Freeman and Medoff hypothesis is that it conflicts with historic opposition to unions by management. If unions raise productivity, why doesn't management invite them in? There is evidence that, in fact, unions lower profitability and stock prices. Whether unions, on average, raise or lower worker productivity, Freeman and Medoff remind us that the role of unions is not confined to simply monopolizing the supply of labor. Economists increasingly are investigating the broader impacts of unions on productivity, on the allocation of capital through their control of pension funds, and on the political process.

Summary

Labor unions organize workers to improve the terms of employment for the membership. Unions represent a significant departure from the competitive labor markets described in the previous chapter. Yet it is easy to overstate the power of organized labor. Unions represent fewer than one in five American workers. In addition, unions do not have unlimited power to raise wages. Like the monopolist, a union is constrained by a downward-sloping demand schedule. Estimates are that unions raise wages on the average of 15 to 25 percent.

Unions also may have a negative effect on nonunion wages. One measure of the welfare of all workers is the share of national income received by labor. This ratio has remained virtually constant over the past fifty years, a period when union influence has expanded greatly, suggesting that union gains come at the expense of nonunion workers.

Legislation has played an important role in shaping the character and size of the labor movement in the United States. The government has attempted to establish the rules of the game and leave management and labor free to

---

[3]Richard B. Freeman and James L. Medoff, *What Do Unions Do?* (New York: Basic Books, 1982).

determine their own particular economic relationship. This system of **collective bargaining** involves the negotiation of written contracts between labor and management; these contracts cover virtually every facet of the labor exchange. This free industrial relations system is structured through two key pieces of legislation, the National Labor Relations Act of 1935 and the Taft–Hartley Act of 1947.

The negatively sloped demand for labor function is an important constraint on union efforts to improve wages and working conditions. Thus, unions have pursued an array of economic and political strategies to (1) shift the labor demand curve to the right, and (2) decrease the price elasticity of demand for labor. In general, unions attempt to reduce the range of substitutes for union labor available to the firm and/or increase their cost to the firm.

Evaluating a union in its role as an agent of monopoly leads to the conclusion that unionization makes some workers better off, makes others worse off, and lowers net economic welfare. However, a more complete analysis requires recognizing the trade union's broader functions — as the arbiter of workplace disputes, communicator of employee concerns, fiduciary of union pension funds, lobbyist for pro-union legislation, and numerous others. Not all of these are necessarily beneficial for society in general, but they must be addressed before one comes to a judgment as to the net effect of unionization in the workplace and in society.

Questions for Thought

Knowledge Questions

1. In what years was the unionized share of the labor force the largest? How would you describe the pattern in this variable since World War II?
2. What piece of legislation is associated with the first real period of union growth? Why was this legislation a factor in union growth?
3. What is the average wage effect of unions?
4. Do unions increase or decrease the wages of nonunion workers? Explain.

Application Questions

5. Industrial unions pioneered the use of the *sit down strike* in the 1930s. In this situation the striking workers just sit down and refuse to leave the plant. Why would this technique be adopted by industrial unions? Why is it effective?
6. Explain why the incidence of strikes tends to fall during recessions.
7. Management prefers an open shop; labor wants a union shop. Why?

Synthesis Questions

8. Occupations and industries in which women account for a large share of employment have usually had low rates of unionization. In recent years more women have been spending a larger fraction of their adult lifetimes in the labor market. Do you think this increased commitment to labor market participation will alter women's traditional lack of interest in unions? Explain.
9. The chapter discussion of unions makes clear the potential benefits to union membership. What are the costs of being a union member? Explain, considering true opportunity costs and the way a union might alter worker behavior in the work place.
10. In recent years, workers in some new firms have voted against unionization. Can you think of economic arguments for why labor may behave in this fashion?

OVERVIEW

In the preceding two chapters we examined the labor market, labor unions, and labor legislation in some detail. Now we turn our attention to another important resource market: the capital market. In Chapter 1 we defined capital as any man-made aid to production. It refers to any good produced for use in producing other goods or services — assembly lines, drill presses, earth movers, computers, electric generators, and so forth.

A country's real wealth is its ability to produce goods and services, and that depends to a large extent upon the stock of real physical capital. Technological advancement and subsequent growth in the capital stock is the basis for the amazing rise in the standard of living among developed countries in the last one hundred fifty years. The large stock of capital per worker in the United States accounts for much of its high level of productivity and real income.

Note that the concern of this chapter is the creation of *physical* capital. In everyday parlance, the term *capital* is often used to denote financial capital — money assets. However, money only facilitates investment in real capital by providing a convenient way to transfer funds from savers to investors through financial markets.

The capital market is similar to the labor market. Capital

The Capital Market

is a productive input, and the general principles of supply and demand that determine the price and employment of any resource apply to capital as well. The level of capital investment and its allocation among competing uses is determined by the interaction of suppliers of investment funds (savers) with demanders of those funds (investors) in credit markets.

CHAPTER 17

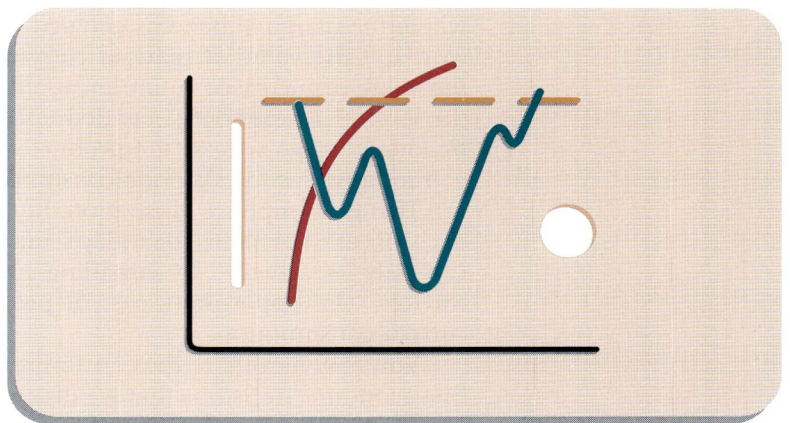

This chapter formally considers the definition of capital, examines the determinants of capital investment, and looks at the relationship between capital investment and savings. The role of financial markets and the rate of interest in the creation of capital are also considered.

Learning Objectives

After reading and studying this chapter, you will be able to:

1. Define the term *capital* and distinguish between a consumption good and an investment good.
2. Define the present value of a future sum and calculate the profitability of an investment using the present value technique.
3. Define rate of return to capital.
4. Define a firm's demand function for capital.
5. Explain the relationship between saving and investment.

Consumption or Investment: Costs and Benefits... Again

One of the first economic choices that confronted human beings was whether to consume or to save and invest. People noticed that, if they were patient, they could increase their ability to produce and consume goods and services in the future by consuming less now and producing capital goods instead. Consider a community of early cave dwellers, which supported itself completely by scavenging for dead beasts. Initially, cave dwellers were scavengers — their bounty was limited to what they could find that had been killed by animals. Then someone realized that they could bring home more meat and hides if they killed their own beasts using spears. The problem was that someone would have to stay home and make the spears, which would mean less manpower available to scavenge for dead beasts and, temporarily, less current consumption of meat and hides. This was the opportunity cost of building spears (investing in capital).

If the cave dwellers were rational, they invested in spears up to the point where the marginal benefits equaled the marginal opportunity costs. In other words, if the value of reduced current consumption of beasts was less than the value of increased future meat and hides, the spears were made. Clearly, the level of investment depended upon two factors: how many beasts would be killed by the spears (the productivity of the capital) and how willing the community was to postpone consumption.

This is a simplistic illustration, but the main ingredients in the investment decision are the same for today's modern economies. Investment in capital can only be achieved by curtailing current consumption of final goods and services. The opportunity cost of producing capital is the value of reduced current consumption.

You may recall that the consumption–investment decision was one of the first economic decisions that we discussed in the book. Figure 1 illustrates the

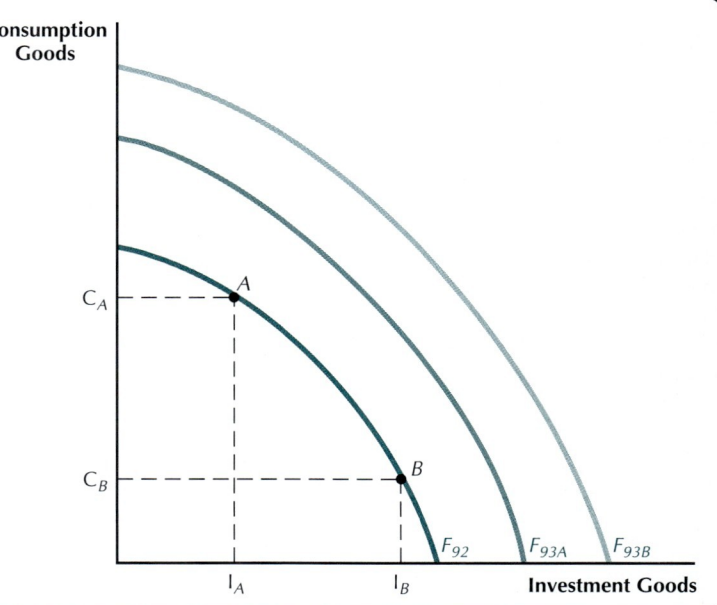

FIGURE 1
Consumption versus investment: shifts in the PPF. Figure 1 illustrates the effects when society chooses between two uses of its resources: consumption (C) or investment (I). Beginning with the production possibility frontier (PPF) labeled F_{92}, society can choose any combination of C and I as long as it is on or within the PPF. If, in 1992, society chose combination B rather than combination A, it would forgo more current consumption for greater investment. The gain is an increased future stock of resources, yielding PPF F_{93B} instead of PPF F_{93A}.

basic decision. Society can choose between two uses of its resources: consumption (C) or investment (I). If its production possibilities frontier (PPF) is F_{92} it can choose any combination of C and I as long as it is on or within its PPF, F_{92}. The investment option adds to the capital stock, generating increased quantities of goods and services in the future. The investment payoff is additional future resources and greater future output. If, in 1992, we choose combination B rather than combination A, we forgo more current consumption for greater investment. Our gain is an increased future stock of resources, yielding PPF F_{93B} instead of PPF F_{93A}.

Investment decisions must balance the cost — forgone consumption — against the benefits — an increased ability to consume in the future. The fundamental determinants of investment are (1) the productivity of capital goods, and (2) the willingness of households to save a portion of their incomes, in other words, to forgo current consumption.

SECTION RECAP
The decision to invest in capital goods involves a tradeoff between current and future consumption. An increase in investment requires a decrease in current consumption.

The Investment Decision

An important characteristic of investment, which you have probably already noticed, is that it takes time. We take resources out of consumption today, use them to produce additions to the capital stock, and then later employ the new capital stock to produce more output. *Investment is a long-run decision.* The costs and benefits accrue over a period of time, and often the benefits accrue over a much longer period of time than do the costs. The long-run nature of investment decisions has two important implications.

First, the costs of the investment must be weighed against its benefits. However, to determine the optimal level of investment and the equilibrium price for investment, we must compare benefits and costs through time. Since a dollar received or spent today has a value different from one received or spent next year, we must develop a way to make these comparisons through time.

Second, an investment decision is based on *anticipated* costs and benefits. We have acted as if the benefits and costs of investment are known with certainty, but they are not. Since costs and benefits are spread out into the future, they can only be anticipated or predicted. Investment decisions, therefore, are made with an element of uncertainty. This uncertainty can make investment activity more volatile than consumption. Investment is very sensitive to expectations and changes in expectations.

Demand for Capital

Like the demand for labor, the demand for capital is a derived demand. Firms invest in capital if it adds more to revenues than to costs. Just as with other productive inputs, *the amount of capital a firm employs depends on the physical productivity of capital, the price of the product, and the cost of capital.* However, there is one major difference between employment of capital and employment of other inputs. Employment of labor can be adjusted with relative ease. If the price of a firm's product declines, the firm can quickly lay off workers whose marginal revenue product has fallen below the wage. However, the firm cannot adjust its capital input so readily. A decision to purchase capital is a long-run commitment. If product demand declines unexpectedly, the firm may be stuck with a capital stock that is too large (unless it is able to sell off part of the

Rate of return
Calculated as the amount of profit attributable to a productive input expressed as a percentage of its cost.

Time value of money
The amount of interest that a sum of money could earn over a fixed period of time.

Present value
The amount of money that would have to be invested today at the market rate of interest to yield a future sum.

Future value
An amount of money held today plus the amount of interest that would accrue over the time period in question.

capital stock). It cannot lay off plant and equipment. The firm must estimate the productivity of capital and product price for the length of the useful life of the capital. Comparing future benefits with current costs requires calculating the **rate of return** to dollars spent on capital.

Consider a manufacturing company that is planning to purchase a computer to improve inventory control. The computer has a cost of $1000 and is expected to lower costs and therefore raise profits by $400 in each of the next three years before becoming obsolete. The computer will be purchased if it adds more to future profits than its initial cost. However, we cannot simply sum up future increases in profits and compare this sum with current costs. A dollar of profit to be received in the future is worth less than a dollar that is spent on the computer today. This is because a dollar spent on the computer could have been earning the market rate of interest. The **time value of money** must be incorporated into our investment decisions. We illustrate how this is done with a simple example before we solve the computer investment problem.

Present Value of a Future Sum

To understand how to compare dollar benefits or costs that accrue over time, we need to begin by discussing the compound interest problem. Suppose that you invest $100 for one year at a 7 percent market rate of interest. The **present value**, or PV, is the $100 you hold at present. The value of the $100 in one year, its **future value** (FV), when invested at 7 percent, is calculated as follows:

$$FV = PV(1+0.07) = \$100(1.07) = \$107$$

The investment problem requires a calculation that is the reverse of the compound interest problem. That problem involves determining the value today, PV, of a sum available in the future, FV. For the example above, the present value of $107 available in one year if the interest rate is 7 percent is calculated as:

$$FV = PV(1+0.07)$$

$$\$107 = PV(1.07)$$

$$\frac{\$107}{1.07} = PV = \$100$$

The present value of $107 to be received in one year is that amount which, invested at 7 percent, yields $107 in one year. Similarly, the present value of $107 to be received in two years is:

$$PV = \frac{\$107}{(1+.07)(1+.07)} = \frac{\$107}{(1.07)^2} = \$93.46$$

The future value of $93.46 invested for two years at 7 percent is $107. In general, the present value of any sum, $X, to be received n years into the future is equal to:

$$PV_x = \frac{\$X}{(1+r)^n}$$

where r is the market rate of interest, and n is the number of time periods.

Discounting
The technique used to calculate the present value of a future sum.

The process by which present value is calculated is called **discounting**, which is an abbreviated expression for *discounting to present value*. Amounts to be received in the future are discounted more (1) the further into the future they are to be received, and (2) the greater the interest rate.

The Computer Investment

Using the formula derived above, and assuming the interest rate is 7 percent, the present value of the benefits from the computer purchase is:

$$PV = \frac{\$400}{(1+.07)} + \frac{\$400}{(1+.07)^2} + \frac{\$400}{(1+.07)^3}$$
$$= \$373.83 + 349.38 + 326.52$$
$$= \$1,049.73$$

Since the $1000 cost of the computer is incurred in the current period, it is not discounted. At a rate of interest of 7 percent, the present value of the benefits of the computer exceeds its cost, and the profit-maximizing firm will make the investment. The interest rate is a measure of the opportunity cost of investing the funds in the piece of capital. The higher the interest rate, the more costly it is to tie funds up in an investment. If the interest rate were 12 percent, the present value of the future profits would be only $960.73. In this case, the gain from the purchase is less than its cost. The computer would not be purchased.

In the computer example, the critical interest rate, denoted r*, is 9.7 percent. At any rate above 9.7 percent the company will not make the investment because the present value of the investment would be less than $1,000. At an interest rate of 9.7 percent:

$$PV = \frac{\$400}{(1.097)} + \frac{\$400}{(1.097)^2} + \frac{\$400}{(1.097)^3} = \$1000$$

The critical rate of interest, 9.7 percent, is the **internal rate of return** earned by the $1000 investment. The internal rate of return of an investment is defined as the interest rate that makes the present value of the stream of profits accruing from this piece of capital exactly equal to the present value of its costs. Of course, the greater the dollar returns from an investment, the greater its internal rate of return. If the computer yielded $500 per period in increased profits, the critical interest rate would be greater than 9.7 percent.

Internal rate of return The interest rate that makes the present value of the stream of profits accruing from a piece of capital exactly equal to the present value of its costs.

SECTION RECAP
Because the decision to invest in capital is a long-run decision, it is necessary to calculate the net present value of the stream of benefits from a capital purchase to determine whether it will be profitable.

Demand Curve for Capital

Ranking all possible capital investment projects by their internal rates of return, from highest to lowest, yields a demand curve for capital. Figure 2 is such a demand curve. It indicates that investment in capital for this firm yields internal rates of return ranging from 20 percent to zero. The declining internal rate of return to successive investments reflects the assumption that capital, like other inputs, is subject to declining marginal productivity.

We already know that a firm will employ any input up to the quantity at which marginal revenue product equals its marginal cost. Because the return to capital is computed as an annual rate, we must compute the annual cost of capital. Whether the firm borrows the funds to purchase the capital or uses its own funds, the annual cost of the investment is equal to the market rate of interest. If funds are borrowed, the cost is explicit. If the firm uses its own funds, buying the capital good imposes an opportunity cost — the interest that could have been earned if the funds had been invested elsewhere.

In a world of certainty, the profit-maximizing firm invests in all capital projects whose rates of return exceed the market rate of interest. If the market

Why the **Disagreement?**

Private versus Social Discount Rates*

Investment in capital stock—regardless of whether it is undertaken by a private firm or the public sector—entails the use of scarce resources. As such, before undertaking a particular investment, it is important to compare the expected benefits and costs to better ensure that resources are used efficiently. However, many investment projects yield a stream of benefits over a number of years. For instance, in the computer example in this chapter (a private investment decision) the firm expected to earn profits over a four-year period. In a similar manner, the decision to use tax dollars to construct a dam on a river to create a reservoir (a public investment decision) would provide benefits to both current and future generations. Because of the time dimension in these situations, it is necessary to discount all benefits and costs to their present value.

Discounting enables decision makers to compare benefits and costs that accrue over time. However, depending on the value of the interest rate that is used, the relationship between benefits and costs can vary widely, and even be reversed. The discount rate used in private investment decisions is determined in the market: It is a private discount rate. However, there is disagreement over what discount rate should be used in public investment decisions. Many individuals maintain that, just as in the case of private investment decisions, the private rate of interest should be used. Other individuals have argued that a social discount rate—which is lower than the private interest rate—should be used. In view of the ramifications of this controversy, it is worth asking, Why the disagreement?

Individuals who support the use of the private interest rate argue that the use of a common interest rate to discount all costs and benefits, regardless of whether they are associated with private or public investment, increases efficiency. Resources are scarce and the use of resources for public investment is not different from the use of resources for private investment in terms of the opportunity cost incurred. The use of a social discount rate for public investment decisions and a (higher) private discount rate for private investment decisions would skew the relative opportunity costs and benefits of the investments being considered.

Individuals who support the use of a social discount rate in public investment decisions argue that decisions regarding private consumption alternatives are myopic. In other words, a disproportionate weight is attached to present consumption alternatives relative to future options. This myopia in turn results in private discount rates that are too high, and therefore the present value of future benefits is understated. As such, the social discount rate should be set lower than the private rate to correct this imbalance and facilitate a more accurate assessment of the present value of benefits and costs.

It is also argued that, in many cases, greed leads individuals to give inadequate consideration to the welfare of future generations in the course of making decisions. Consequently, the level of private investment is too low. Government can help remedy this situation by applying a lower social discount rate to public investment decisions, thereby increasing the overall level of investment. However, critics point out that government is subject to many of the same problems—myopia and greed—as private individuals. Thus, it is unreasonable to expect that the social discount rate will be any more accurate than the private rate.

The use of a higher or lower discount rate could have a major impact on the relative benefits and costs of many public investment projects. In fact, it could be the deciding factor in many cases. Given the range of issues—both positive and normative—involved in this debate, there does not appear to be a solution to this problem that is both efficient and fair and that will be agreed upon by all parties. There also is little doubt that this disagreement will persist into the foreseeable future.

*Much of this discussion is drawn from R.A. Musgrave and P.B. Musgrave, *Public Finance in Theory and Practice* (New York: McGraw–Hill, 1980).

SECTION RECAP
A firm will find it profitable to invest in capital projects so long as the in- *(continued)*

interest rate is 8 percent, a firm increases its profits by investing in all capital that yields an annual return higher than 8 percent. Therefore, the ranking of investment projects in Figure 2 is a demand schedule for capital. Given a market rate of 8 percent, the firm invests in the computer and all other capital whose rate of return is greater than 8 percent. A proposed plant expansion that earns

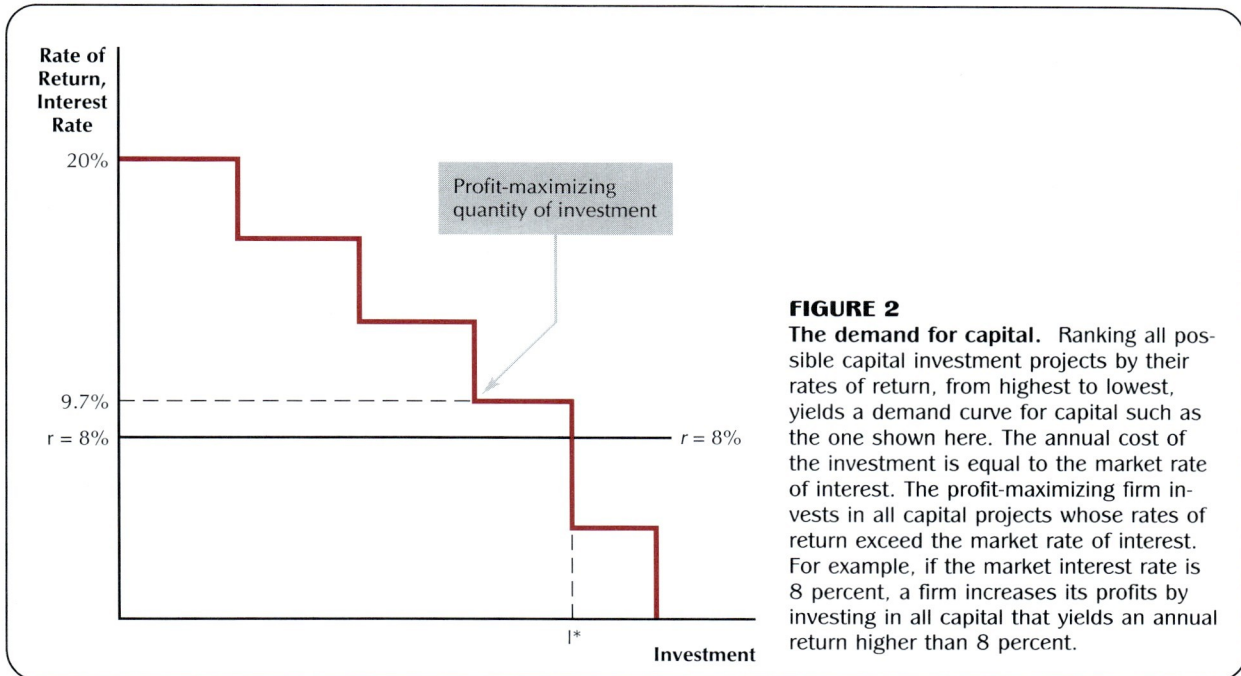

FIGURE 2
The demand for capital. Ranking all possible capital investment projects by their rates of return, from highest to lowest, yields a demand curve for capital such as the one shown here. The annual cost of the investment is equal to the market rate of interest. The profit-maximizing firm invests in all capital projects whose rates of return exceed the market rate of interest. For example, if the market interest rate is 8 percent, a firm increases its profits by investing in all capital that yields an annual return higher than 8 percent.

7 percent will not be undertaken, however, unless the market rate falls to 7 percent or below. According to Figure 2, the desired stock of capital depends upon the productivity of capital, the product price, and the market rate of interest. The first two factors determine the rate of return to capital investments, while the latter is the marginal cost of capital.

SECTION RECAP
(continued)
ternal rate of return exceeds the market rate of interest.

Investment Benefits

The computer example illustrated how to calculate the gain from an investment in a new computer. The gain came in the form of reduced production costs and increased profits. It is also useful to consider the gains from investment activity in a broader framework. The social gains from investment activity include reduced production costs, new goods and services of value to consumers, and increased productivity.

Reduced Costs

Additions to society's capital stock through investment activity can reduce costs in two ways—by taking advantage of economies of scale and technological innovation that results in lower average total costs of production at all output levels. Any time a firm adjusts its capital stock, that is, makes an investment decision, it is making a long-run resource allocation decision. When demand for a product increases, firms respond to the increased profit opportunities by expanding output. This long-run process involves the firm's adoption of a new cost-minimizing production function for the expected higher level of output. In Figure 3, such investment activity is represented by a shift from one short-run cost function, $SRATC_1$, to a new cost function at a higher output level, $SRATC_2$. The investment in new plant and equipment is profitable because it

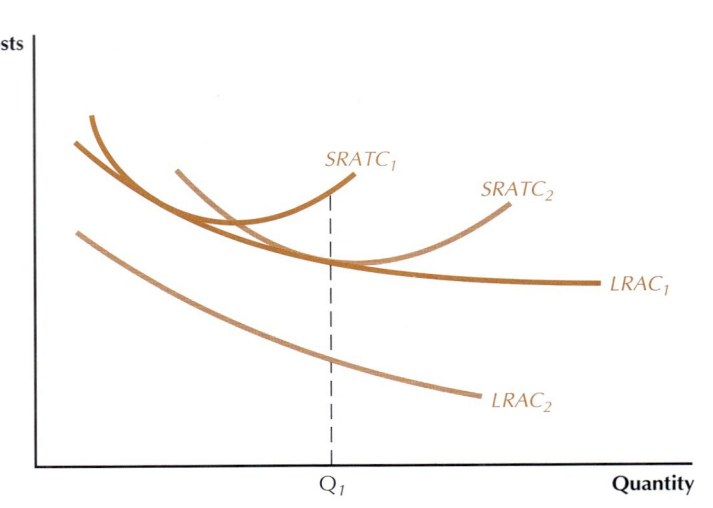

FIGURE 3
Improvements in technology and long-run average total costs. Additions to society's capital stock through investment activity can reduce costs in two ways. First, investment activity represented by a shift from $SRATC_1$ to $SRATC_2$ is profitable because the firm can produce greater output at a lower unit cost. Second, the long-run average cost function, $LRAC_1$, represents the cost frontier for society. Investment in research and development can generate new, even more efficient production techniques, resulting in an overall decrease in production costs as shown by the shift of the long-run minimum cost frontier down, to something like $LRAC_2$.

allows the firm to produce the greater output at a lower unit cost than it would have experienced employing the old production process. Compare, for example, the average cost of producing Q_1 units of output with $SRATC_1$ and with $SRATC_2$.

When economies of scale exist,[1] the average costs of production vary with the expected level of output: The larger the expected level of output, the lower are average costs. When economies of scale exist, the firms' investment for expansion results in even greater cost savings.

The long-run average cost function, $LRAC_1$ in Figure 3, represents the *cost frontier* for society. Given existing technology, costs cannot be reduced below that frontier. However, the devotion of time, effort, and money to research and development (R&D) can generate new, even more efficient production techniques. Note that R&D constitutes a specialized form of investment. The purpose of R&D is to create a more efficient, productive capital stock. Expenditures on R&D can result in increased production—which is generally associated with increased investment.

In the case of R&D, the investment payoff is an overall decrease in production costs. This decrease means that society can have more output with the same quantity of inputs. The investment payoff is the reduced cost. Such technological progress, requiring lengthy investment periods, can shift the long-run minimum cost frontier down, to something like $LRAC_2$ in Figure 3.

Two recent examples of such developments illustrate the concepts just discussed. One advance involves a new process for making paper that may reduce energy costs by 50 percent. Another is the discovery of materials to achieve superconductivity at much higher temperatures than were previously believed possible. Although neither one has yet been adopted for commercial production, these developments hold out the promise for reduced costs of production and even greater computing power in smaller machines, as well as numerous other advances.

[1] Economies of scale were defined and discussed in Chapter 9.

Does It Make Economic Sense?

Labor Opposition to Technological Change

Investment in plant and equipment reduces costs by making workers more productive. The same output can be produced with fewer workers. For instance, new auto manufacturing plants built in the last few years can produce the same annual volume of cars produced by the older plants, but with 25 to 50 percent fewer workers. Organized labor has often vigorously opposed productivity advances through robots and other automated equipment. They claim that new capital equipment and technological change are causing unemployment. Does this opposition make economic sense?

There are two parts to this problem; one is transitory, the other long term. We tackle the latter one first. Additional capital investment is undertaken when it is profitable to do so. The new auto plants are more efficient in a productive sense: Production costs are lower. These lower costs result in short-run profits that are competed away through lower auto prices. Increased profitability ultimately causes output to expand. The increase in supply (a rightward shift in the supply function) causes equilibrium price to fall, increasing the equilibrium quantity of cars produced and sold. Increased sales lead to increases in production and the demand for labor. Thus, some of the workers displaced by the more productive capital stay employed because of increased production.

There are long-term effects that extend beyond the auto market as well. In particular, if cars cost less, consumers have more income to spend on other goods and services. The additional spending elsewhere increases the demand for other goods and services, causing the demand for labor to increase in the affected industries. Hence, although increased productivity in the auto industry may reduce the number of workers employed by auto makers, it can indirectly cause employment to expand in other industries. In short, because production of cars now requires fewer scarce resources, we can spend more on other goods, causing employment to be reallocated from autos to other industries.

However, this long-run economy-wide adjustment to a productivity change in one market does overlook a transitory development caused by costly mobility and information. The auto workers who lose their jobs experience some unemployment, if only because they have to acquire information on other employment opportunities, search these opportunities out, and possibly move to a new location. Furthermore, some of the auto workers who become unemployed may be unemployed for a long time — several years — or they simply may not seek another job. Workers who are in their fifties and who have been employed in the industry for many years may have great difficulty making the transition to new jobs.

In summary, technological change such as the development of productivity-enhancing capital in the auto industry makes society better off — we have more output as a result. However, the temporary unemployment associated with this market reallocation of resources may be especially burdensome to one relatively small group of workers (relative to the total labor force). If these workers are members of a union, it is understandable that the union would protest such developments. Viewed from the perspective of the individual, labor opposition to technological change can in fact make economic sense.

In general, jobs lost to improved capital and technological change are made up elsewhere in the economy because the increased productivity generates savings that can be spent in other parts of the economy. However, it is nonetheless true that technological change can also cause considerable hardships in affected labor markets. As such, for both equity and efficiency considerations, it may be reasonable for society to assist these individuals through subsidies for unemployment, training, or relocation.

TABLE 1

Productivity: annual rates of change in output per hour

Period	Annual Rate of Change
1950–1960	2.6%
1960–1970	2.8
1970–1980	1.4
1980–1985	1.5
1950–1985	2.2

Source: U.S. Department of Labor, Bureau of Labor Statistics, *Handbook of Labor Statistics*, Bulletin 2217, 1985, Table 91.

Productivity
The amount of output produced per unit of input per time period.

TABLE 2

U.S. annual productivity growth

Years	Annual Productivity Growth
1947–1955	2.9%
1955–1968	2.5%
1968–1973	1.5%
1973–1980	0.4%
1980–1986	1.1%

Source: Stanley Fischer, "Symposium on the Slowdown in Productivity Growth," *Journal of Economic Perspectives* (1988), Vol. 2, No. 4, pp. 3–7.

New Products

Investments in research and development also produce new final products, some of which are improvements on old products and some of which are completely new products or ideas. These products make consumers better off in some way. They may reduce work effort around the house, save consumers' time, or simply satisfy consumers' tastes in a better way. Here the payoff for the investment is in the form of profits to the firm whose investment has resulted in new products. Consumer electronics is a good example. New ideas and technologies in electronics, for example the semiconductor and the microchip, have produced a host of new products for use as inputs as well as consumer products.

The investment process is driven by potential profitability. The examples above demonstrate this important force. Firms cannot control market prices. However, they can control costs within limits. Since the difference in revenue and costs is their motivation for being in business, there is a relentless effort to keep costs to a minimum and to develop new products expected to be of value to consumers. Investment in new capital and technology is an important path to lower costs and greater profit for business firms.

Productivity Growth

Investment in improved capital can also result in increased **productivity** and, therefore, increase the overall level of output. When we speak of the economy's rate of productivity or changes in the rate, we usually refer to a measure of output per employee hour. Table 1 contains annual rates of change in output per hour for selected years. Just exactly what kind of productivity measure is this? The best way to explain the concept is to note what it is not. Output per (employee) hour is not a pure measure of the productivity of labor. This is because output per employee hour also reflects spillover effects of improvement in capital and technology which increase labor's ability to produce output.[2]

Technically, output per hour is a ratio of an index of the output of goods and services to an index of hours of labor employed. It tells us output produced per hour of labor employed. If the output per hour index rises by 3 percent in a year, we would read in the local newspaper that productivity increased 3 percent last year. On average we were able to produce 3 percent more output with a given amount of labor.

Noting that productivity has increased leads to the question, To what is the increased productivity attributable? The answer to this question depends on all the factors of production and the extent of their utilization. For example, workers could be more productive, holding constant other inputs. Alternatively, additions to the capital stock—new equipment or improved technologies—could have accounted for the increased output. In addition, it could simply be greater utilization of existing plant and equipment. The increase could have resulted from better management techniques. Finally, it could be a combination of all these factors. This measure of productivity is a general

---

[2] Output per employee hour may be a better measure of the productivity of capital, although it is really not clear exactly what it measures, other than changes in total output relative to total employee hours.

The Economist's Tool Kit

An Unemployment Measure for Capital

When we think of unemployment, we usually think of unemployed labor. However, we do have a rough measure of capital employment, and therefore unemployment, as well. It is called the **capacity utilization rate**, and is defined as the current output of goods and services as a share of total output that could be produced with existing plant and equipment. This measure is calculated for the manufacturing sector of the economy. Rates for the recent past are summarized in Table 3.

The capacity utilization rate is a measure of the share of existing capital equipment being used for current production. It is similar to labor unemployment in two ways. First, it fluctuates over the business cycle, rising as economy-wide output increases and falling during recessions as output is cut back. In the recession of the early 1980s, capacity utilization dropped to as low as 70 percent from a peak value of 85 percent at the end of the long expansion that occurred during the period 1975–1979. Labor unemployment followed a similar pattern but simply moved in the opposite direction.

Second, just as labor unemployment seldom approaches zero percent, the capacity utilization rate seldom approaches 100 percent. In a large, dynamic, and growing market economy, resources constantly are moving around or are being switched from one use to another. These changes keep some of both capital and labor unemployed at all times. Furthermore, as the economy approaches its potential level of output, inflationary pressures build, prompting government measures to slow the growth rate. Output is seldom allowed to reach its potential.

Capacity utilization also affects investment decisions. If existing plant and equipment are underutilized, output can be increased without new investment. The gains from capital investment depend upon the extent to which the capital is employed to produce output. When the capital utilization rate is low, expected profitability of new business investment is probably low also.

TABLE 3
Capacity utilization rates in manufacturing, 1976–1990

Year	Utilization Rate
1976	77%
1977	81
1978	84
1979	85
1980	79
1981	78
1982	70
1983	74
1984	81
1985	80
1986	80
1987	82
1988	84
1989	84
1990 (January)	82

Source: Capacity utilization rates from Board of Governors of the Federal Reserve System, *Capacity Utilization in Manufacturing, Mining, Utilities, and Industrial Materials,* G-3, monthly.

---

one; it tells us only that we have been able to produce more — or less — output per hour worked than in previous periods.

This productivity measure does allow us to compare changes in productivity across industries and countries. For instance, between 1977 and 1982, output per hour declined about 5.5 percent annually in steel foundries, but rose about 1.5 percent annually in railroad transportation. We can see from Table 1 that overall productivity growth slowed in the 1970s and 1980s; we have yet to regain a growth rate in excess of 2 percent.

Table 2 provides further evidence of the recent slowdown in the growth rate of productivity. As the table indicates, the annual growth rate of productivity fell steadily over the period 1947–1980. In particular, the growth rate of productivity fell to only 0.4 percent in the period 1973–1980. As the economy rebounded from the recession of the early 1980s, the growth rate once again began to rise. Changes in the growth rate of productivity have important implications for both the growth rate of output and the level of real income in the economy. In particular, increases in productivity, *ceteris paribus*, increase the economy's capacity to produce. In addition, as productivity increases, so does the level of real income earned by labor.

Capacity utilization rate The current output of goods and services as a share of total output that could be produced with existing plant and equipment.

SECTION RECAP
Investment in capital goods can benefit society in a number of ways, including reductions in production costs through the development of more efficient capital, the development of new or improved products, and increases in labor productivity.

Investment Costs: The Interest Rate

Each individual firm takes the interest rate as given when it chooses its optimal level of capital stock. But what determines the interest rate? The interest rate is the price of investment funds. It is also the *real* rate of interest, to be distinguished from the nominal rate of interest, which may include an expected inflation component. It is the cost of borrowing money and the return to saving. The interaction of the supply of savings and the demand for investment funds real rate of exchange determines the equilibrium interest rate. It is the between current and future goods.

Suppose all borrowers are equally creditworthy and all loans are for the same length of time. Further assume that investment funds are easily transferred to where they earn their highest return and that there is good information about relative interest rates across different credit markets. (Resources are mobile.) If so, all borrowing and lending can be treated as if it occurred in one credit market. Only one interest rate could exist, because any differences would be quickly eliminated by the flow of funds away from low-interest to high-interest markets.

Figure 4 depicts such an aggregate credit market. Demand for investment funds is negatively sloped. A decline in the interest rate increases firms' desired employment of capital, raising the quantity of funds demanded to finance the expansion. This increase is temporary for individual firms. Once the increased capital stock is reached, the firm no longer requires more investment funds. However, new firms are continually being organized, and at the lower interest rate each of these will demand greater investment funds to begin operations with a greater level of capital. Thus, a lower interest rate should lead to a permanently higher level of borrowing.

The rate of interest also is the payment for saving. Therefore, as the interest rate rises, households reduce current consumption because its opportunity cost

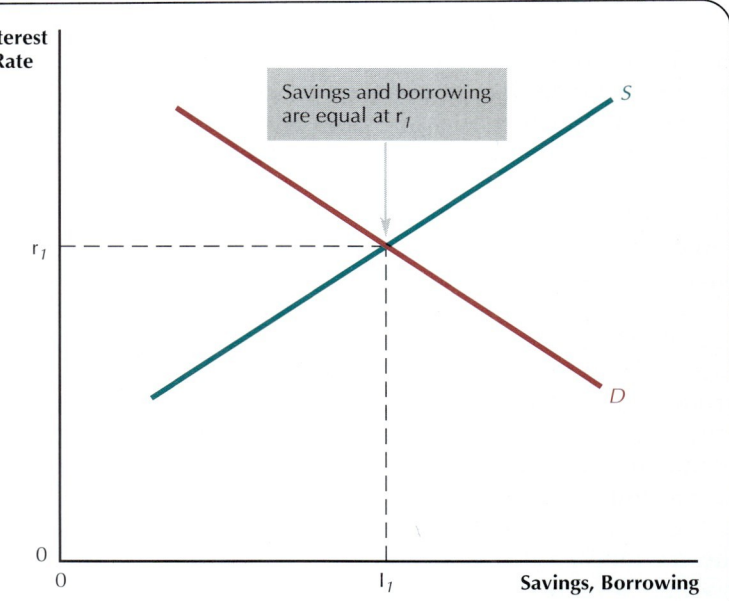

FIGURE 4
Savings, borrowing, and the Interest rate. This figure depicts an aggregate credit market. Demand for investment funds is downward sloping: a decline in the interest rate increases firms' desired employment of capital. The rate of interest also is the payment for saving. Therefore, as the interest rate rises, households reduce current consumption. Thus the supply of saving is upward sloping. At the equilibrium rate of interest, r_1, borrowing and saving equal I_1.

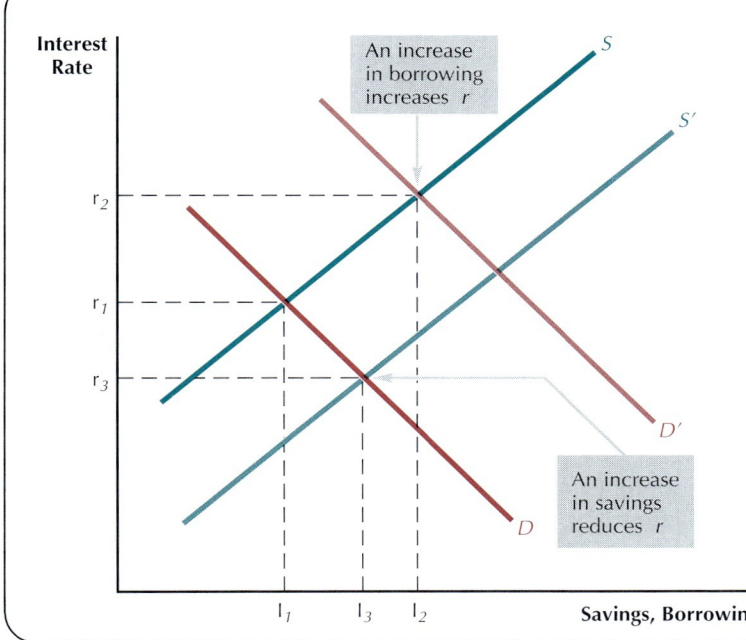

FIGURE 5
Shifting the supply and demand curves for savings. The basic determinants of investment spending are the productivity of capital and the willingness of individuals to save. Starting at an interest rate equal to r_1, if capital becomes more productive, total demand for investment funds will shift from D to D', pushing up equilibrium borrowing, saving, and the interest rate to I_2 and r_2, respectively. Alternatively, an increase in the thriftiness of an economy would raise the level of saving at all interest rates, shifting the supply of savings curve rightward from S to S'. The resulting decline in the equilibrium interest rate to r_3 would induce more spending for investment.

has risen. An increase in the interest rate means that households will be able to earn a larger dollar return on their savings. In comparing the benefits and costs of consumption, formerly marginally profitable consumption expenditures now generate costs, equal to the dollar expenditure plus the interest forgone on savings, that exceed the benefits realized. Assuming that income is fixed, lower consumption means higher saving. Thus the supply of saving is upward sloping.

The equilibrium rate of interest is r_1, with investment and saving equal to I_1. Only at r_1 does the available quantity of investment funds (savings) equal the desired level of investment spending.

In the cave dweller community that was discussed at the beginning of this chapter, the amount of investment depended upon their willingness to save. While investors and savers in a real-world economy are likely to be different people, the basic principle that investment in capital requires reduced current consumption still holds true. The credit market reconciles the willingness of households to save and the desire of businesses to borrow and invest. Flexible interest rates ensure that, when the economy is in equilibrium, the level of saving matches desired investment spending.

We earlier stated that the basic determinants of investment spending in an economy are the productivity of capital and the willingness of individuals to save. Figure 5 shows why. Suppose capital becomes more productive. Each firm's marginal revenue product schedule for capital shifts to the right, causing its desired capital stock to increase. Total demand for investment funds shifts to the right, to D', pushing up equilibrium borrowing, saving, and the interest rate. The interest rate increases from r_1 to r_2 and borrowing and savings increase from I_1 to I_2.

Alternatively, an increase in the thriftiness of an economy raises the level of saving at all interest rates, shifting the supply of savings curve rightward to

S'. The resulting decline in the equilibrium interest rate to r_3 induces more spending for investment—borrowing and saving increase from I_1 to I_3.

For the past decade many respected economists, business leaders, and government officials have been concerned that the level of saving and investment has been too low in the United States. They have argued that greater investment is necessary to increase our rate of economic growth and allow American business to become more competitive in world markets. Congress and the Reagan administration apparently agreed. Since 1981, many changes in the federal tax code have been enacted with the goal of increased savings and investment. Two of the chief measures contained in the *Economic Recovery Tax Act* of 1981—the accelerated depreciation provision and the investment tax credit—were designed to stimulate the demand for capital.[3] (Essentially, accelerated depreciation reduced taxes on profits generated by increased investment in capital, raising its after-tax return.) The predicted result is an increased demand for capital and therefore investment funds from D to D' in Figure 5.

Congress also sought to stimulate investment indirectly, by raising the after-tax returns to saving. The most significant changes reduced the top marginal income tax rate from 70 percent in 1981 to the current 33 percent and established special tax-deferred savings funds, such as Individual Retirement Accounts (IRAs). (IRAs were sharply curtailed in the 1986 tax reform act.) The goal was to shift the supply curve of savings to S'. The combination of increased demand and supply should lead to increased investment spending.

Have these policies worked? As is frequently the case, it is difficult to tell. Since 1982, business fixed investment has risen substantially. This partially reflects the recovery from the 1981–1982 recession. In addition, the federal government has taken an increasing share of private savings to finance its own budget deficit since 1981. Increased federal borrowing may have offset new saving and investment incentives. It remains too early to evaluate the net effects of these policies on capital formation in the 1980s. However, real gross investment was very strong in the 1980s.

The Rate of Interest and the Return to Capital

The rate of interest is both the cost of borrowing and the payment to savers. However, we can also think of interest as the return to capital as a factor of production. Over the long run, the marginal productivity of capital tends to equal the market rate of interest. Each firm maximizes profit by investing in capital until the rate of return to the marginal unit equals the market rate of interest. In equilibrium, the rate of interest must equal the marginal revenue product of capital (expressed as a percentage rate), just as the wage equals the marginal revenue product of labor.

SECTION RECAP
The interest rate equilibrates investment spending and savings (the source of investment funds). Efforts to increase savings and/or investment (that is, to shift each schedule to the right) can result in increased investment and therefore an increase in economic growth.

---

[3]Both of these measures were sharply curtailed in the 1986 tax reform act. This change came about, in part, as a result of arguments that the previous tax breaks had failed to generate productive investment and were therefore too costly in terms of the tax revenues forgone. These arguments were, however, countered by equally compelling arguments that the tax breaks enacted in 1981 helped to spur on the economic recovery that followed the recession in 1981–1982.

Why Do Interest Rates Differ?

In reality, the interest rate of Figures 4 and 5 is a set of rates: the *prime* rate, 90-day Treasury bill rate, AAA corporate bond rates, home mortgage rates, and credit card interest rates, to name a few. Why is the rate on credit card balances higher than the prime rate? Why does the rate on ten-year corporate bonds differ from bonds of shorter maturity? The answer to these and similar questions is that borrowers and loan conditions are different. We arrived at one equilibrium interest rate based upon the assumption of equal risk and loan length. In reality, differences in at least four major loan characteristics result in different interest rates.

1. Differences in risk: The lender assumes a risk that the borrower will default — not repay the principal and interest. Default risk is higher for consumer loans than for business loans, so lending institutions charge higher rates to consumers to compensate for this higher risk. Similarly, the low default risk of U.S. Treasury bonds makes individuals willing to lend to the federal government at rates below those paid by corporate borrowers.

2. Differences in loan length: Generally, lenders prefer not to tie up their savings for long periods. This is called a preference for liquidity. Long-term borrowing generally requires a higher rate of interest to compensate lenders for reduced liquidity. In addition, and possibly more importantly, conventional loans made for a long period of time lock the lender in at a fixed rate of interest. Higher interest rates may therefore be charged on long-term loans as a form of insurance against subsequent increases in the interest rate.

One of the primary causes of rising interest rates is an increase in the inflation rate. During the 1970s, increases in the rate of inflation drove market interest rates to very high levels. Interest rates on certificates of deposit rose to 18 percent and more. As lenders pay higher interest rates for loanable funds (money deposited by savers) the return on existing loans decreases. Thus lenders attempt to set interest rates on loans at a level that accounts for this possibility.

3. Economies of scale in service costs: Large loans have lower costs of administration per dollar loaned. A loan of $5,000 may entail the same amount of clerical, credit investigation, and administrative time as one of $50,000. The fixed administrative costs are spread thinner in the larger loan, making rates on larger loans lower. This is one reason why credit cards, which usually involve loans of relatively small amounts, carry interest charges that are relatively high.

4. Differences in tax treatment: The federal government provides tax incentives to encourage borrowing and lending for certain purposes. To the extent that federal tax treatment differs, favored borrowers are able to pay lower interest rates. For example, interest earned on bonds issued by state and local governments is not subject to federal income tax. Thus savers are willing to hold such bonds at interest rates below those paid on corporate bonds (which pay a taxable yield).

Each of the factors listed above gives rise to a compensating interest rate premium or discount. In equilibrium, the spread of rates must exactly offset the differences in risk, maturity, service cost, and tax treatment.

SECTION RECAP
There is a range of interest rates in the economy. Differences in interest rates reflect differences in the degree of risk, length, cost of providing credit, and tax treatment associated with different loans.

Financial Markets and Intermediaries

The highly simplified credit market of Figure 4 showed that investment decisions must be financed by savings of equal amount. In the United States the transfer of funds from saver to investor is facilitated by a highly developed system of **financial intermediaries**. Commercial banks, savings and loan associations, credit unions, and mutual savings banks accept the deposits of small savers and make these available to firms for capital investment. The financial middlemen play a valuable role. They encourage saving and investment by reducing the risk of saving. Without financial intermediaries, investors would have to borrow directly from savers. If a corporation wanted to build a new plant, it would have to sell bonds directly to individuals. But most savers could only afford to purchase the bonds of a few corporations and would be subject to the considerable risk that one of the corporations would default. The high risk would discourage saving.

A financial intermediary, however, can make large loans with little risk. Because it has pooled the savings of many individuals, it can lend to a diversified group of enterprises, reducing the risk that a default will inflict major losses. In addition, it is able to gather information on borrowers at less cost than would many different lenders who are providing funds to a single borrower. Since the intermediary can lend with little risk, it is able to offer small savers a less risky and more liquid way to save — the passbook savings account, for example. The opportunity to save at low risk allows corporations to tap the savings of people with moderate to low incomes indirectly. By increasing the yields to small savers and decreasing costs to big borrowers, financial intermediaries increase the supply of and demand for borrowed funds, increasing the amount of capital investment.

> **Financial intermediary**
> An institution, such as a bank or savings and loan association, that facilitates the interaction between lenders and borrowers.

Summary

Capital is a productive input. When choosing the optimal quantity of capital, the firm considers the same criteria that apply to any other input: productivity of the input, product price, and marginal resource cost. The major analytical difference between capital and labor is that investment in capital yields productive returns well into future periods.

To properly compare benefits and costs through time we must take account of the time value of money. Income and expenses in the future are valued less than income or expenses today because of the forgone opportunities between now and the future. The market interest is a good measure of forgone opportunities. A dollar received next year is worth less than one today because I can invest the one I have today for a year and earn interest.

The **present value** of a sum available in the future is the amount of money that would yield the future sum if invested until then at the market interest rate. In investment decisions, we compare the present value of costs to the present value of the benefits; an investment is profitable if benefits exceed costs.

The rate of interest that equates the benefits and costs of an investment is called the **internal rate of return** for the investment. The firm's demand for capital is its ranking of investment projects according to their rates of return. The condition for optimal employment of capital is to invest in all projects that yield a rate of return above the market interest rate.

Production of capital goods requires the sacrifice of current consumption, or saving. The mechanism for ensuring that the sum of investment and saving decisions match in a market economy is the interest rate. The interest rate measures both the cost of borrowing and the return to saving. Flexibility of the interest rate ensures that the quantity of investment funds supplied (savings) equals the quantity of funds demanded.

Ultimately, the level of capital investment in an economy depends upon the productivity of capital and willingness of consumers to save.

We have more than one interest rate in the economy because of differences in borrowers, loans, and resource mobility. Capital markets are made more efficient by the presence of financial intermediaries who serve as middlemen for savers and investors.

Questions for Thought

Knowledge Questions

1. Why is investment a long-run decision?
2. Define present value. Explain why an increase in the interest rate reduces present value.
3. Why is there more than one equilibrium market interest rate?
4. What is the difference between financial and physical capital?

Application Questions

5. Suppose households decide to increase their rate of savings. What happens to the market equilibrium rate of interest and quantity of investment? Explain using a graphical analysis.
6. What impact does the tax deductibility of home-mortgage interest payments have on the demand for mortgages (loans for homes)? Explain.
7. Will the following developments increase or decrease the profitability of an investment in a college education? Explain each.
   a. An increase in the interest rate.
   b. An increase in the cost of housing.
   c. A decrease in earnings of college graduates relative to high school graduates.
   d. A decrease in tuition costs.
8. If a building contractor buys a truck for $15,000 with annual operating expenses of $1500 a year, he will save $7500 a year in other expenses. He plans to keep the truck for three years, after which it will have no market value. Should he buy the truck if the rate of interest is 5 percent? Ten percent?

Synthesis Questions

9. Why have electric power companies opted to build nuclear-powered rather than coal-fired electricity generating plans? Are they more profitable? Why have these decisions caused so much controversy?
10. We noted that increases in productivity can have a positive effect on the level of real income earned by labor. Explain how this can occur.
11. Consumers are often faced with a choice between purchasing a big-ticket item such as new car today, and putting the purchase off to the future. What factors should enter the consumer's decision of whether to buy today?
12. Discuss the issues that must be considered by a developing country when it decides how much to invest in its capital stock versus production that would raise the current standard of living.

OVERVIEW

Most of the economic decisions we have analyzed thus far have involved individual choices. Yet one of the most fundamental economic decisions must be made through a collective process. In the process of deciding how, what, and for whom society's goods and services are to be produced, we decide how income should be distributed. Questions of income distribution and redistribution involve both equity and efficiency considerations.

Few among us are in favor of allowing income to be distributed wholly by the marketplace. However, although a consensus exists that some income redistribution by government is appropriate, substantial disagreement exists as to how income should be redistributed, and to what extent. The notion of a fair income distribution is a normative one; no generally accepted definition of what is fair exists. Nor is there any obvious way to determine what individuals are willing to pay for a more equal income distribution.

Although economic analysis alone cannot settle these issues, it can provide important information to enlighten judgment on this crucial social choice. This chapter provides such information. We define ways to measure the distribution of income and then use these measures to describe the current distribution of income and its trend over time. The causes of unequal income distribution are also

Income Inequality and Poverty

CHAPTER 18

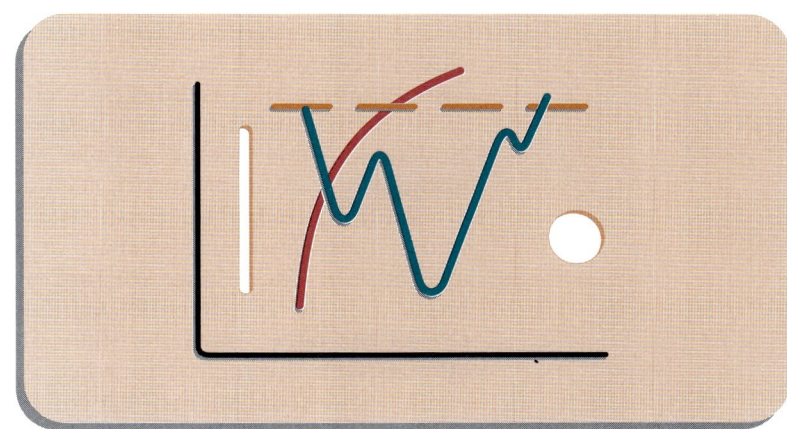

important. Policies adopted to alter the distribution of income, as well as the costs of reduced inequality, depend upon whether income differences are due primarily to differences in ability and productivity or, for example, simply luck.

An important part of our concern about income distribution is our concern for the members of society with low incomes. With respect to the poverty problem in the United States, we explore the difficulties encountered in defining poverty and the extent of so-called official poverty in the United States. Evidence is presented on the characteristics of the poor and the causes of poverty, and federal antipoverty programs are described and evaluated.

Learning Objectives

After reading and studying this chapter, you will be able to:

1. Characterize the degree of income inequality in the United States.
2. Use a Lorenz curve to describe income inequality.
3. Explain the reasons for observed income inequality and assess the shortcomings of annual income as a measure of income inequality.
4. Explain why there is a tradeoff between efficiency and equity in income redistribution policies.
5. Describe the incidence of poverty in the United States and identify the major causes of poverty.
6. Summarize the characteristics of antipoverty programs in the United States.

The Distribution of Income in the United States

Income differences are a fact of life in the United States. From our own personal experiences we are familiar with variations in income even among our own families and friends. We are also accustomed to changes in income. We regularly observe individual and family incomes rising and falling. Before attempting to evaluate society's efforts to redistribute income, we must summarize the pattern of observed income differences in society. We begin with a very aggregated look at the distribution of income in the United States.

The **personal distribution of income** can be described by calculating the share of all personal income received by families at different income levels. Income data are collected by the U.S. Bureau of the Census each year. The Census Bureau's income measure focuses on family income, which represents the total income received from all members of a family. The Census Bureau includes as family members only those members residing in the same house. In addition to income received as wages, salaries, royalties, interest payments, stock dividends, and rent from real property, the income measure includes all money income received as transfer payments from governments. Thus it includes income from such sources as Social Security payments, unemployment compensation, and disability payments. Family income measures gross income received by families from the employment of their resources and assets. Excluded from this income measure are capital gains income and the value of nonmoney transfer payments, such as food stamps or medical care.

Table 1 presents the personal distribution of family income for selected years. The table shows the share of income received by families grouped by income level. For instance, the first row of the table shows the share of income received by the 20 percent of families with the lowest incomes, and the fifth row of the table shows the share of income received by the 20 percent of families with the highest incomes. A perfectly equal distribution of income would yield equal shares of income for the five fifths of families: Each 20 percent of families would receive 20 percent of income.

Personal distribution of income
The share of all personal income received by families at different income levels.

TABLE 1

The distribution of family income in the United States, selected years

Families by Income Quintile	1929	1947	1960	1970	1980	1989	Cumulative Distribution for 1989
Lowest Fifth	3.5%	5.0%	4.8%	5.5%	5.2%	4.6%	4.6%
Second Fifth	9.0	11.9	12.2	12.2	11.5	10.6	15.2
Third Fifth	13.8	17.0	17.8	17.6	17.5	16.5	31.7
Fourth Fifth	19.3	23.1	24.0	23.8	24.3	23.7	55.4
Top Fifth	54.4	43.0	41.3	40.9	41.5	44.6	100.0
Top 5%	30.0	17.5	15.9	15.6	15.3	17.9	

Source: U.S. Bureau of the Census, Current Population Reports, series P-60, No. 168, *Money Income and Poverty Status in the United States: 1989* (Advance Data from the March 1990 Current Population Survey), U.S. Government Printing Office, Washington, DC, 1990, and earlier issues.

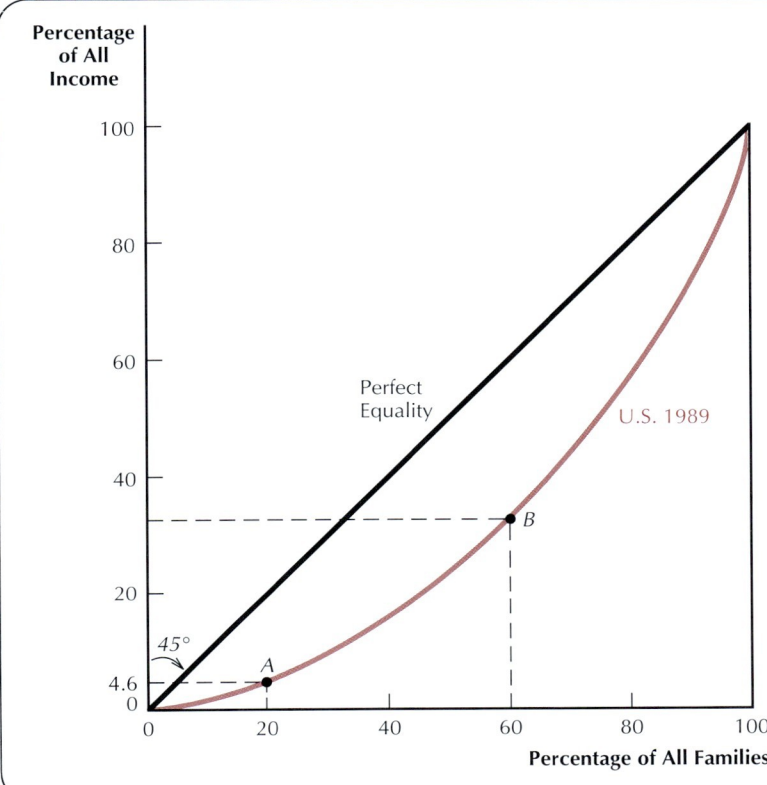

FIGURE 1
Lorenz curve for the United States.
This figure depicts the Lorenz curve for the 1989 income distribution in the United States. The 45-degree line represents perfect income equality. When the Lorenz curve is bowed—as it is in this figure—income is unequally distributed. Point A on the curve shows that the poorest 20 percent of families received less than 5 percent of total income. Point B indicates that the bottom 60 percent of families received 32 percent of total income.

Table 1 reveals substantial income inequality in any year. In 1989, the 20 percent of families with the lowest incomes received just 4.6 percent of total income, while those families in the top quintile (the top 20 percent) received 44.6 percent. The top 5 percent of families accounted for 17.9 percent of income in 1989.

The distribution of income in the United States has been remarkably stable since 1950. Between 1929 and 1950, income inequality was substantially reduced. This change was probably not the result of deliberate government policy, but more likely reflected developments such as the loss of great fortunes during the Depression, and rising real wages and farm incomes during World War II. Since 1950, however, the distribution of income has been essentially unchanged with one exception: It appears that in the 1980s the share of income going to the richest 20 percent of the population has increased.

The personal distribution of income for a given year can be illustrated graphically by plotting the relationship between the percent of families who receive income and the cumulative share of total income received. This functional relationship is called a **Lorenz curve** after M. O. Lorenz, who developed the measure in the early twentieth century. The Lorenz curve for the 1988 income distribution in the United States is plotted in Figure 1. The 45-degree line represents perfect income equality—each quintile receives 20 percent of income. When the Lorenz curve is bowed down and away from the 45-degree

Lorenz curve
A functional relationship that indicates the percentage of the population that receives a given percentage of the total income in the economy.

line, income is unequally distributed. Point A on the curve shows that the poorest 20 percent of families received less than 5 percent of total income. The income of the lowest quintile was just over one tenth of the income of the wealthiest quintile. At point B, we see that the bottom 60 percent of families received 32 percent of total income.

The divergence of the Lorenz curve from the 45-degree line measures the extent of income inequality (the area between the 45-degree line and the Lorenz curve serves as a quantitative indicator of inequality). The less equal is the income distribution, the more bow-shaped the Lorenz curve appears. If one percent of the population received 99 percent of the income, the curve would approximate a backward L. Between 1929 and 1980 the income distribution shifted toward more equality, thus the Lorenz curve shifted toward the 45-degree line.

How does income inequality in the United States compare with that of other economies? Answering this question quantitatively is difficult because of differences in the way countries collect economic data and define economic variables. However, the International Labour Organization has calculated income distributions for a number of countries after adjusting each country's income data to make it comparable with that of other countries. Based on their study, the income distribution in the United States can be considered middle of the road compared to income distributions of other countries.

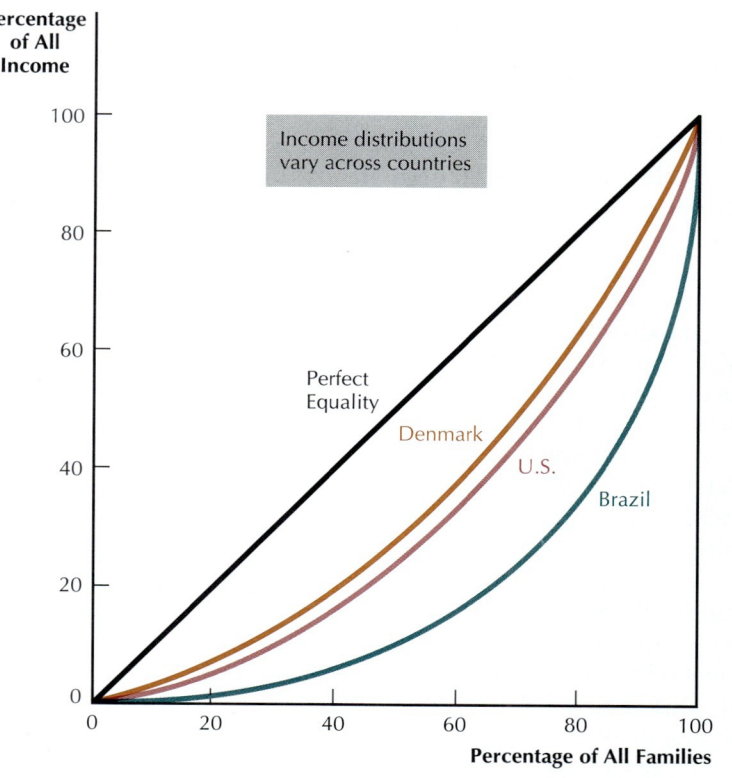

FIGURE 2
Lorenz curves for selected countries.
This figure depicts Lorenz curves for three representative countries. Denmark's Lorenz curve shows that it has an income distribution more equal than that of the United States. This situation is representative of countries that engage in extensive income redistribution through very progressive tax structures and social programs. Developing countries tend to have more unequal income distributions. Brazil's Lorenz curve demonstrates relatively extreme income inequality.

Lorenz curves for three representative countries are provided in Figure 2. Denmark's Lorenz curve shows that it has an income distribution more equal than that of the United States. The income distributions of Sweden and Great Britain are quite similar to Denmark's. These countries engage in extensive income redistribution through very progressive tax structures[1] and social programs that provide generous benefits such as medical services, unemployment compensation, and relocation assistance. The income distribution in France, on the other hand, is very similar to that of the United States.

Developing countries tend to have more unequal income distributions. Brazil's Lorenz curve demonstrates relatively extreme income inequality. For instance, 80 percent of families receive just 35 percent of total income, while the top 20 percent of families receive about 65 percent of income. This kind of income distribution is representative of many developing countries, such as Mexico, Zambia, and Honduras.

The personal distribution of income, as represented by the Lorenz curve, provides a very aggregated picture of the extent of income inequality in an economy. Since our primary interest is (a) whether the observed income distribution is somehow satisfactory to society and, if not, (b) what kind of income redistribution should be undertaken, we must dig deeper. Is the Lorenz curve measure of income inequality an accurate and useful measure of inequality? What causes the kind of inequality we observe by whatever measure? Given our understanding of the extent and causes of inequality, what policies, if any, are appropriate for the redistribution of income?

SECTION RECAP

Over the period 1929–1980, income distribution in the United States has tended to move toward equality. However, there is still a fairly unequal distribution of income. Countries with extensive social programs tend to have a more equal distribution of income while developing countries tend to have a more unequal distribution.

Family Income as a Measure of Well-Being

The data in Table 1 suggest substantial inequality in personal income in the United States. However, these figures probably overstate income inequality for several reasons. First, income is measured before personal taxes are paid. Personal taxes include federal, state, and local income taxes, sales taxes, payroll taxes, and property taxes. If the overall personal tax system is *progressive*—that is, if families with higher incomes pay a higher percentage of income in taxes—the after-tax distribution of income will be more equal.

Table 2 shows that the personal tax system was progressive in 1989. After taxes, low-income groups received a higher share of after-tax income, at the expense of wealthier families.[2] However, the progressivity of the U.S. tax system has been reduced in the 1980s, as marginal income tax rates have been cut and payroll taxes have risen. This trend was partially offset by the reduction of income taxes paid by poor families. Still, it is safe to say that the tax system became less progressive in the 1980s.

Family income data also exclude nonmonetary government transfers. Many government transfer programs provide economic goods to families, either in kind or through subsidies for the purchase of goods and services. Lower- and middle-income families receive subsidized meals, medical care, housing, and

---

[1] In a progressive tax structure, the percentage of income paid out in taxes is an increasing function of the amount of income earned.

[2] It should be noted that the overall progressivity of personal taxes is a function of the federal income tax system. Payroll, sales, and property taxes are regressive—families with lower incomes pay a larger percentage of their income in these types of taxes—and tend to partially offset the redistributive effects of personal taxes.

TABLE 2

The impact of personal taxes on the distribution of income, 1989

Income Quintile	Change in Percentage Income Share after Taxes
Lowest Fifth	+0.7
Second Fifth	+1.1
Third Fifth	+0.6
Fourth Fifth	−0.4
Top Fifth	−2.2

Source: U.S. Bureau of the Census, Current Population Reports, Series P-60, No. 169-RD, *Measuring the Effects of Benefits and Taxes on Income and Poverty: 1989*, U.S. Government Printing Office, Washington, DC, 1990.

education. The benefits of these programs have a cash value to the recipients. Since most of the beneficiaries are low-income families, counting noncash benefits will raise their share of real income.

Edgar Browning of Texas A&M University has attempted to calculate a more accurate distribution of real, spendable income by adding the value of noncash government transfers and subtracting personal taxes.[3] Table 1 implies that the top quintile receives almost ten times the before-tax income of the poorest families. Adjusting for personal taxes by using the figures of Table 2 lowers this ratio to eight–to–one. Browning's adjustments for government transfer payments further lower the ratio of richest to poorest incomes to three–to–one, implying that government transfers also substantially reduce income inequality.

SECTION RECAP
The effects of progressive taxation and government transfer programs tend to reduce the actual inequality of the distribution of income in the economy.

Family income measures also omit the value of services produced and consumed in the household. The work done in the household by both spouses — such as cooking, cleaning, child care, and maintenance of home and autos — is valuable to the family and improves real economic well-being. The value of this economic activity is omitted from family income, although when these same services are purchased in the market by families they are included in income. This omission also may alter the distribution of income.

Distribution of Lifetime Incomes

Another important reason why the personal income distribution overstates inequality is that it gives us a picture of family incomes at one point in time. Thus, it ignores **income mobility**, or what we might call the Horatio Alger effect. Some families and individuals who are in the poorest quintile in one year move into a higher income group in a later year. Consider a common case. Bill Hansen, just married, enrolls in medical school, while his wife Kris enters graduate school. Their low combined money income while in school lands them in the poorest 20 percent of families. After Bill receives his M.D. and Kris her master's degree, their combined incomes move them into the top

Income mobility
The tendency of individuals and families to move among income groups over time.

---

[3]Edgar K. Browning, *Redistribution and the Welfare System* (Washington, DC: American Enterprise Institute, 1975).

20 percent. Later, Kris leaves her job to have children, and they drop back to the fourth quintile. When the kids enter school, it's back to the job for Kris and back to the top quintile for the Hansen family. In retirement, Bill's and Kris's pensions, Social Security, and interest and dividend earnings are only enough to place them in the third quintile, but because the Hansen children are gone and the mortgage is paid, their real standard of living does not decline.

Clearly, it would be wrong to consider the young Hansen couple poor, given their considerable lifetime income. Differences in lifetime incomes across families are a much better measure of inequality. Yet, even if all families had identical lifetime incomes, the Lorenz curve for any one year would show substantial inequality as families' incomes vary from year to year based upon age, child rearing, and just plain luck. For the figures in Table 1 to show perfect equality, not only would lifetime incomes have to be equal for all, but income would have to be identical in every year.

So long as there is mobility across income groups over time, the Lorenz curve will overstate income inequality. Several studies have demonstrated substantial mobility among income classes in the United States. In one study, a large number of families was followed for a number of years, allowing social scientists to monitor changes in their economic status over time. Table 3 contains information on the extent of movement by these families among income quintiles during a seven-year period, 1971–1978. The income changes are striking. About half of families in the highest and lowest income quintiles had moved to other quintiles after seven years. Some families from the highest (lowest) income quintile had actually moved to the lowest (highest) quintile, and about two thirds of all families in the middle quintiles (the second through the fourth) in 1971 changed quintiles within the seven-year period.

TABLE 3

Changes in family income, 1971–1978
(Percentage of individuals in 1971 family income quintile)*

Family Income Quintile, 1971	Family Income Quintile, 1978					
	Highest	Second	Third	Fourth	Lowest	Total
Highest	48.5%	29.5%	14.0%	4.5%	3.5%	100%
Second	22.0	31.5	25.5	15.0	6.0	100
Third	14.0	18.5	30.5	23.5	13.5	100
Fourth	9.0	13.5	21.5	34.5	21.5	100
Lowest	6.0	7.0	9.5	22.0	55.5	100

Source: Mark Lilla, "Why the 'Income Distribution' is So Misleading," *The Public Interest*, No. 77, Fall 1984, p. 70. Adapted from Table 1.1 in Greg J. Duncan, et al., *Years of Poverty, Years of Plenty: The Changing Fortunes of American Workers and Families* (Ann Arbor: Institute for Social Research, University of Michigan, 1984).

*Note: The table is read as follows. Reading across each row indicates, for a given income quintile in 1971, the percentage of families that fell into each income quintile in 1978. For example, of the total number of families in the highest quintile in 1971, in 1978 48.5 percent were still in the highest quintile, 29.5 percent had moved to the second quintile, 14 percent had moved to the third quintile, and so forth.

Income Differences by Family Characteristics

SECTION RECAP
The Lorenz curve overstates income inequality to the extent that there is mobility across income groups. Most families move across income quintiles over time.

Having established that income is unequally distributed in the United States, it is natural to inquire about the causes of income differences. If income inequality results primarily from differences in individuals' abilities and productivity, we are more likely to view the income distribution as fair, especially if individuals have equal opportunities to acquire productivity-enhancing skills. On the other hand, if income differences are based upon discrimination or privilege, or if there is not equal opportunity to climb the economic ladder, society is more likely to choose redistributionist policies.

A review of more specific income patterns by a variety of family characteristics suggests that a mix of factors influences the distribution of income. These differences are summarized in Table 4. For each category in this table,

TABLE 4
Family income by family characteristics, 1987

Characteristic	All Races — Number of Families (1000)	All Races — Mean Income (dollars)	All Races — Per Capita Income (dollars)	Whites — Number of Families (1000)	Whites — Mean Income (dollars)	Whites — Per Capita Income (dollars)	Blacks — Number of Families (1000)	Blacks — Mean Income (dollars)	Blacks — Per Capita Income (dollars)
Age of Householder									
15–24 years	2,926	18,696	6,818	2,348	19,979	7,352	502	12,212	4,266
25–34 years	15,008	31,024	9,280	12,547	33,017	9,935	1,984	19,016	5,484
35–44 years	15,852	41,530	11,101	13,551	43,186	11,604	1,764	27,906	7,273
45–54 years	11,138	47,522	13,929	9,516	49,695	14,806	1,188	30,897	3,360
55–64 years	9,707	40,088	14,650	8,660	41,444	15,592	832	25,171	7,385
65 years and over	10,502	27,107	11,571	9,421	27,895	12,293	906	17,800	5,914
Education of Householder									
less than 8 years	4,263	19,110	5,665	3,259	19,825	6,056	821	16,396	4,534
8 years	3,235	21,960	7,652	2,798	22,550	8,129	382	17,958	5,191
high school, 1–3 yrs	7,475	25,494	8,002	6,036	27,335	8,915	1,306	17,018	4,587
high school, 4 yrs	22,945	33,223	10,442	20,020	34,437	11,029	2,467	23,695	6,582
college, 1–3 yrs	10,519	40,087	12,466	9,184	41,142	12,897	1,006	30,019	8,929
college, 4 yrs or more	13,769	58,100	18,047	12,398	59,211	18,484	692	42,664	13,401
Occupation of Householder									
White collar									
manager/professional	13,773	57,729	17,731	12,562	58,487	18,029	718	43,808	13,350
sales/clerical	11,253	41,724	13,191	9,772	43,159	13,749	1,092	27,400	8,442
Blue collar									
skilled	9,068	36,910	10,697	8,373	37,138	10,846	544	33,078	8,728
semi- & unskilled	8,739	31,472	9,197	7,326	32,068	9,506	1,211	27,834	7,610

mean family income and **per capita income** are reported. The income measure used in this table is the same one used in the Lorenz curves — before-tax income. Mean family income is the average income for families in a particular category. Per capita income is the average income for individuals in a particular category.

Age, Education, and Occupation Income differences within these three categories are clearly defined. Income rises with age until about age 55 to 60 and then declines. Mean income varies positively with level of education. White-collar workers have higher incomes than blue-collar workers, blue-collar workers have higher incomes than service workers, and farm workers have the lowest incomes. Differences in education and training (work experience) account for a large part of these income differences.

Mean family income The average income for families in a particular category.

Per capita income The average income for each individual in a particular category.

TABLE 4
(continued)

	All Races			Whites			Blacks		
Characteristic	Number of Families (1000)	Mean Income (dollars)	Per Capita Income (dollars)	Number of Families (1000)	Mean Income (dollars)	Per Capita Income (dollars)	Number of Families (1000)	Mean Income (dollars)	Per Capita Income (dollars)
Occupation of Householder									
Service workers	4,906	25,776	7,934	3,548	27,749	8,816	1,162	19,967	5,627
Farm, forestry, fishing	1,820	26,220	7,760	1,709	26,452	7,909	79	18,420	4,691
Marital Status of Householder									
Male, total	51,464	39,894	12,423	46,335	40,595	12,796	3,621	30,244	8,580
married, spouse present	48,748	40,472	12,489	44,170	41,060	12,836	3,200	31,435	8,711
divorced	898	31,515	11,919	756	32,695	12,472	112	21,748	7,803
never married	889	26,365	10,290	687	27,783	11,068	150	20,359	7,328
Female, total	16,669	24,043	7,938	9,709	26,784	9,338	3,556	16,132	4,672
married, spouse present	3,061	40,619	12,629	2,474	42,152	13,584	482	31,369	8,364
divorced	3,833	21,423	4,924	3,056	21,947	7,882	680	18,702	5,708
never married	2,250	14,412	7,453	1,089	18,747	7,186	1,104	9,735	2,984
Work Experience of Householder									
Worked last year	49,625	41,318	12,508	43,345	42,625	13,024	4,813	28,657	8,186
full-time job	45,040	42,915	12,836	39,457	44,136	13,309	4,217	30,595	8,694
part-time job	4,586	25,626	8,811	3,888	27,290	9,635	595	14,925	4,427
Did not work last year	14,684	20,928	7,699	12,039	22,729	8,901	2,228	11,530	3,332

Source: U.S. Bureau of the Census, Current Population Reports, Series P-60, 160–163, *Income of Households, Families and Persons in the United States: 1987* (Washington, DC: U.S. Government Printing Office, 1989), Table 14.

The more education and training one has, generally the higher one's earnings will be. The per capita income measure adjusts for differences in family size. The positive relationship between both education and experience and per capita income demonstrates the strong influence that education and experience have on earning capacity. The age–income relationship also reflects some differences in labor supply: Younger people work less because many are acquiring education and training into their late twenties. Older workers reduce their work hours, ultimately retiring to live off their savings, Social Security, and other retirement income. The differences in income by occupational group reflect significant differences in education and training, as well as differences in jobs (wage differences) and labor supply.

Sex and Race   Table 4 also shows significant income differences between different race and sex groups. In every category the income of whites exceeds the income of blacks, and in almost every category male income exceeds female income. Although a portion of these differences can be attributed to differences in education and training, part of the gap between male and female and white and black earnings appears to be attributable to discrimination.

Other Reasons for Income Inequality   In addition to the factors noted above, several other factors generate income inequality:

1. Differences in individual ability and preferences: One of the wonderful characteristics of human beings is their individuality. People have different innate abilities and widely varying preferences. These differences cause differences in earnings, reflecting voluntary differences in behavior, about which policymakers need not worry. Differences in intelligence, physical dexterity, visual acuity, motivation, willingness to work, and thrift can all have an impact on the opportunities available to people and the extent to which people take advantage of those opportunities. Some observed income differences are attributable to these sometimes subtle individual differences. Of course, income differences attributable to physical or mental handicaps are another matter; providing for the handicapped has long been recognized as an appropriate role for the government.

2. Risk taking: We might consider the willingness to take risks as one of the individual differences described in the preceding section. However, since the willingness to take risks can cause large income differences in a market economy, we have separated it out into its own category. The willingness to gamble one's wealth on a single venture or idea can make a person exceedingly rich — or exceedingly poor. Because many business decisions are made in situations of uncertainty, the willingness to assume risks is well rewarded in a market economy. Sam Walton believed that he could develop a discount retailing business that would improve upon the existing approaches, and he became the richest man in America because of Wal-Mart. Steven Jobs and Stephen Wozniak believed they could build a small home computer and sell it at a low enough price that families would buy it; thus, Apple Computer and the microcomputer industry were born.

3. Transfers of wealth: The incomes of some fortunate people are altered by the industriousness, thrift, and generosity of others. Individuals inherit or are

given wealth acquired by others. When we think of inherited wealth, we usually think of the extreme cases in which an exceedingly wealthy family passes on its assets to members of the next generation. However, the process is much more common than that. Many families pass on some wealth to the next generation. Middle-income parents purchase cars, pay for or heavily subsidize college educations, and make the down payments on first homes for their children. Parents use their resources to improve the earnings opportunities of their children and give their children assets that generate income streams.

4. **Luck:** A factor in determining income differences in one year and often over a number of years is plain old luck. Sometimes it is difficult to separate luck from other factors, such as the willingness to take risks or to work hard. However, luck does play a role in altering incomes. One person wins a million-dollar lottery. Another person's father invested in an obscure business machine company years ago (International Business Machines). Yet another's brother becomes president of the United States. Some people marry into wealth. Others choose low-paying occupations and then their incomes rise unexpectedly. It is easy to think of other examples in which luck changes someone's income or income prospects. The outcome of many decisions is affected by chance happenings.

SECTION RECAP
There are a number of factors that influence income inequality including age, education, occupation, sex, race, differences in abilities and preferences, willingness to take risks, transfers of wealth, and luck.

Marginal Productivity Theory and Income Distribution

How does the observed distribution of income fit with the model of resource price determination developed in Chapter 14? A fundamental result of competitive resource market theory is that the payment paid each resource equals its marginal revenue product. Thus, each individual's income is equal to the marginal revenue product of the resources he or she supplies. For most individuals, income is determined by wage payments equal to the marginal revenue product of their labor. Workers who are more productive receive higher wages and incomes. Those who also own capital (shares of stock in corporations) receive additional income based upon the marginal productivity of capital.

One implication of the marginal productivity theory is that income differences reflect different contributions to total output. Those who supply a greater amount of more productive resources are rewarded with higher incomes. Note that this is not a theory of what the income distribution should be; rather it merely seeks to describe how the income distribution would be determined in a competitive market economy. Nevertheless, the theory is the basis for a case against income redistribution. For some, an income distribution based upon each individual's contribution to national output has a ring of fairness to it. Further, if the marginal productivity theory is correct, attempts to redistribute income will reduce the efficiency of the economy.

A fundamental criticism of the marginal productivity theory and the income distribution it implies is that resource markets are not competitive. Under this view, labor markets are characterized by monopsony, trade unions, and discrimination. We have seen how each of these factors can cause wages to vary. As a result, wages are determined not only by relative marginal productivities but also by race and sex, the degree of exploitation by monopsonies, or the ability to gain admittance to a trade union.

While there is evidence in the existing distribution of income that individual ability and effort (productivity) influence income determination, factors such as inherited wealth and luck also matter. In addition, mean income data by race and sex indicate that discrimination may be an important factor in determining income differences. These facts support a policy of redistribution. Few are likely to believe that income determined by discrimination, luck, or accident of birth is fair. Further, if factor payments do not reflect marginal contributions to output, there may be little efficiency loss from redistribution.

Income Redistribution

We have seen that substantial income inequality exists in the United States. We have also noted some of the reasons for the inequality. Our theory of resource price determination does not provide any normative support for the fairness of the observed income distribution, and we know from earlier discussion that economic efficiency is not tied to a particular distribution of income. Our analysis of markets does, however, demonstrate the importance of some inequality in the economy. Opportunities for gain are what cause markets to function as well as they do.

The question, "What distribution of income is consistent with our concerns for economic efficiency and social equity?" is normative. Its answer requires that value judgments be made. We generally recognize the value of some inequality in society. On the other hand, we generally agree that some income redistribution is appropriate. A broad consensus exists on these matters. The controversy centers on how much income redistribution to undertake and by what methods. We can only note some important guidelines in making these important social decisions.

The Equity–Efficiency Tradeoff   Economics teaches us a very important principle of human behavior: Incentives matter. People sell their inputs because they aim to make themselves better off. This desire for individual gain is the driving force in an economy. Income redistribution can weaken this incentive. By taking from those with high incomes and giving to those with low incomes, we run the risk of reducing rewards to those who have been successful as well as those who have been unsuccessful in contributing to society's output. In the extreme, the incentive to work and to produce is removed; each individual gets the same share of output regardless of effort. The result is less output and smaller shares for everyone. Therefore, redistribution policies that preserve individual incentives are preferable to those that destroy incentives.

Equality of Opportunity   Income redistribution policies that provide for equality of opportunity rather than equality of results seem generally consistent with our desire to preserve incentives and to make the notion of redistribution more acceptable to society, at least in the United States. Americans appear to tolerate, even cheer, disparities in income, so long as there appears to be a fighting chance that a poor person, through hard work and sacrifice, can pull himself up by the bootstraps and become prosperous. The opportunity, not just the result, is crucial in American capitalism. Our policies to combat discrimination attempt to provide equal opportunity and thereby alter the differences in income between whites and blacks, men and women. Of course, the controversy that has surrounded these policies is often centered on the question of whether such laws provide more than equal opportunity.

Some of our tax laws dealing with inheritances attempt to provide equality of opportunity across generations. In this society we accept — sometimes grudgingly — the notion that the wealth earned by one generation need not — perhaps should not — be fully passed on to the next generation. Some of it can be taxed away and used to provide benefits to other members of society. Inheritance taxes make it more difficult for families to amass more and more wealth over a number of generations, thus helping to preserve the notion of equality of opportunity and sufficient incentives.

A Minimum Standard of Living In the United States, concern with policies that redistribute income and preserve incentives to contribute is balanced by a desire to establish programs and policies that ensure a minimum standard of living for the least fortunate in society. The objective is to reduce the incidence of poverty. These policies are among the most controversial income redistribution policies in existence. The next section analyzes these policies, defining the notion of poverty, examining the extent of poverty in the United States, and explaining the kinds of programs that have been established to fight poverty.

SECTION RECAP
On efficiency grounds, income redistribution policies that favor equality of opportunity rather than equality of income are preferable because of the incentives they create. In the United States, such policies are balanced by the desire to provide a minimum standard of living for the least fortunate.

Poverty in the United States

Poverty is a close relative of the income distribution issue. Antipoverty policy is one of the most controversial, demanding, and important issues in the United States today. Fundamental disagreement exists over the extent of poverty, what its causes are, and what, if anything, can be done to reduce poverty and dependency.

Consider first the problem of measuring how many people are poor. It is relatively easy to describe income inequality objectively — one can measure income and construct a Lorenz curve as we did in Figure 1. However, defining which families at the lowest relative income levels are poor requires a subjective judgment. Is poverty a low income relative to the rest of the population, regardless of the absolute level of income? If so, we would define those with the lowest *x* percent of incomes as poor. A problem with such a relative definition is that it equates poverty with income inequality. Poverty could never decline unless income inequality diminished, regardless of how much the real incomes of the poor increased. Comparison of the percentage distribution of income in 1947 and 1989 would suggest that no reduction in poverty has occurred, despite the fact that the real incomes of the poorest quintile are substantially higher today.

Another approach is to determine minimum needs of a typical family and count as poor those families who have insufficient income to purchase these necessities. Under such an absolute standard, poverty is unrelated to income distribution and, at least theoretically, poverty could be eradicated. The difficulty of this approach lies in reaching agreement on what constitutes the bare necessities of life. Should we define a poverty level income as that which provides just enough food and shelter to keep the poor alive? Or should provision be made to allow an occasional steak or even a movie? Today ownership of an automobile is considered a necessity, and yet in the United States sixty-five years ago (or in the Soviet Union today), an auto was a luxury. The

Poverty
The result of a level of income that is insufficient to ensure some predetermined minimum standard of living.

TABLE 5
Percent of population in families with poverty incomes, 1959–1988

Family Group	1959	1969	1979	1983	1984	1985	1986	1987	1988
Total persons	22.4%	12.1%	11.7%	15.2%	14.4%	14.0%	13.6%	13.4%	13.1%
Blacks	55.1	32.2	31.0	35.7	33.8	31.3	31.1	32.6	31.6
Age 65 and over	35.2	25.3	15.2	13.8	12.4	12.6	12.4	12.5	12.0
Single female head of household	50.2	38.4	32.0	35.6	34.0	34.0	34.6	31.3	31.2

Source: U.S. Bureau of the Census, Current Population Reports, *Consumer Income,* Series P-60, selected issues.

point is that even an absolute definition of poverty involves a relative comparison of the poor with the standard of living of the nonpoor.[4]

In the United States, the official measurement of poverty is based upon a minimum needs definition. The government's definition of poverty was first developed by the Social Security Administration (in 1965). It is an income measure. A *poverty income* is an income less than the income level defined as sufficient to provide a minimally adequate standard of living. This standard of living is best described as one whose diet is just nutritionally sound. The poverty level of income is adjusted to account for factors such as size of family, number of children in the family, age and sex of household head, and inflation. In 1989, a family of four was considered to be in poverty if its before-tax money income was below $12,676.

Table 5 summarizes the incidence of poverty (that is, poverty rates) for different groups in the United States over the last thirty years. According to the most recent figures, 13.1 percent of individuals live in families with incomes below the official poverty level. It is also evident that poverty rates differ by characteristics and circumstances. The poverty rates for blacks and families headed by females are over twice that of the national average. Surprisingly, in light of much political rhetoric, the poverty rate for the elderly is *below* the average.

The time trend reveals that poverty declined significantly for all groups between 1959 and 1969. The incidence of poverty stabilized somewhat in the 1970s, then rose in the early 1980s. In the last few years it has again fallen. A probable explanation for these trends is that the strength of the economic expansion in the last half of the 1960s reduced unemployment and pulled many of the poor out of poverty. However, economic growth slowed in the early 1970s and unemployment rates increased. The expansion in the last half of the 1970s raised the incomes of many poor. In the early 1980s the Reagan administration reduced funding for many cash-transfer programs serving the poor (funding for in-kind transfers, such as food stamps, increased), and at

---

[4]Studies have indicated that the self-avowed happiness of people depends rather heavily on their perceived *relative* situation. This has important implications for social policy, since raising the absolute standard of living to very high levels might not increase the happiness of those at the bottom of the income distribution. For an interesting discussion of the conditions necessary for happiness and their impact on social policy, see Charles Murray, *In Pursuit: Of Happiness and Good Government* (New York: Simon and Schuster, 1988).

the same time the United States experienced another recession. The recent downturn in the incidence of poverty coincides with yet another economic expansion.

The poverty rate for those 65 years old and older is the exception to these broad trends: It steadily and strongly declined between 1959 and the early 1980s. Since most in this group are retired, the performance of the economy is not a major factor affecting their incomes. The more likely explanation for this trend is the rapid expansion of cash benefits under the Social Security, Medicare, and Supplemental Security Income programs that took place throughout the 1970s. The wealth of the elderly has also increased dramatically relative to earlier decades, and many elderly have substantial incomes from interest and dividend payments.[5]

> SECTION RECAP
> In the United States, poverty is based on a *minimum needs* definition. Approximately 13 percent of the population lives below the poverty level. Poverty fell slightly in the 1970s but rose again in the 1980s.

Is the Incidence of Poverty Overstated?

The statistics in Table 5 indicate that a significant portion of the population remains in poverty. However, these figures may overstate the extent of officially defined poverty. First, only cash income is counted, yet low-income families receive substantial noncash benefits. The in-kind income of the poor includes food stamps, subsidized housing, and federal medical insurance. These benefits have a monetary value—their provision preserves the cash income of the recipient. The Census Bureau has estimated that including these benefits in measured income would reduce the poverty rate by about 2 to 4 percentage points, depending upon how such benefits are valued.

Another shortcoming in the official poverty statistics is that they are *static*. We have previously discussed mobility across income categories over individuals' lifetimes. At any given time families whose total lifetime income is above the poverty level may have, for a variety of reasons, current incomes below the poverty line. For example, a family headed by a middle-income wage earner may fall into poverty one year due to a lengthy strike. Yet the family's prospects for recovering the next year are excellent. For policy purposes we would be less concerned about this family than about another that was perpetually in poverty. Studies suggest that about 45 percent of poverty spells end within one year and 70 percent end within three years. Only 13 percent of poverty spells lasts more than eight years.[6]

Finally, our understanding of the extent of poverty is only as good as our data and definitions of income. Many economists agree that the Consumer Price Index (which is used to measure the rate of change in the prices of consumer goods) is upward biased as a measure of the true change in the cost of living because it overemphasizes the value of housing as a share of the goods and services purchased by consumers. If the poverty level of income is adjusted each year based on changes in the Consumer Price Index, the poverty income level will rise faster than average price increases. One reason for the increase in the share of the population below the poverty line between 1979 and the early 1980s is the rapid increase in prices experienced from 1979 to 1981. Part of the apparent increase in the number of families in poverty was simply due to errors in the measurement of the *actual* rise in the cost of living.

> SECTION RECAP
> Statistics may overstate the actual extent of poverty since they do not take account of in-kind transfers, income mobility, or the actual change in the cost of living for specific individuals.

---

[5]For a discussion of the increasing affluence of the elderly, see Subrata N. Chakravarty with Katherine Weisman, "Consuming Our Children?" *Forbes* (November 14, 1988), pp. 222–232.
[6]Isabel V. Sawhill, "Poverty in the U.S.: Why Is It So Persistent?" *Journal of Economic Literature* 26 (September 1988), p. 1081.

Why the **Disagreement?**

Should Welfare Be Workfare?

The most controversial antipoverty programs are those designed for the working poor. The largest, most visible such program is Aid to Families With Dependent Children (AFDC). This program provides a minimum cash income to single-parent families (and sometimes to families with two parents, at least one of whom is unemployed). Program benefits are reduced dollar for dollar as the recipient earns income. Critics of AFDC argue that recipients can become dependent on it instead of attempting to find employment that pays an income sufficient to allow the recipient to leave the program.

These long-standing criticisms have been translated into actual and proposed changes in the program in the last few years. Most of the changes involve a work requirement. Eligibility for the program would require the recipient's willingness to work, usually for some government agency or office. Experimental programs with work requirements are being, or have been, conducted in California, Illinois, and Massachusetts. A federal law passed in 1988 (the *Family Support Act of 1988*) requires all states to develop and begin to implement workfare programs by 1994. The concept of workfare has a long history. The poor were required to work to obtain state assistance as early as the sixteenth century in England. Yet the opponents of workfare are numerous and vociferous. Why the disagreement over work requirements for welfare recipients?*

Proponents of a work requirement say that it is a good indicator of need. One's willingness to work for aid is a good test of how badly one needs help. In addition, a work requirement contributes to future employability by keeping people in the labor market, where they have a chance to improve their skills or at least prevent them from deteriorating, as can happen during unemployment. Requiring work also reduces welfare costs. The cost of welfare payments is offset by the value of the goods or services produced by welfare recipients. Moreover, if the work requirement is really a good indicator of need, the number of people on welfare may be reduced by the requirement, further reducing program costs. Finally, a work requirement helped satisfy an equity concern. Families who are poor but employed and not in a welfare program have a low income and also work, while families in AFDC have a low income but do not have to work. (They may also be eligible for nonmonetary benefits unavailable to the working poor.) A work requirement would make the economic circumstances of the two groups

Causes of Poverty

Formulating effective antipoverty policies requires an understanding of the causes of poverty. It is convenient to assume that poverty has one or two causes. Some people believe poverty arises from a basic unwillingness to work; we might label this argument the some-people-are-lazy theory. Others argue that poverty arises because people lack skills to be productive or society simply does not generate enough jobs to employ all those who wish to work. Actually, people have low incomes for a variety of reasons.

A more detailed look at who the poor are gives us more clues about the causes of poverty. Table 6 provides information on the number of poor people and the incidence of poverty among various groups. Whites, who comprise about 80 percent of the population, account for two thirds of the poverty population. However, the percentage of blacks living in poverty is much higher than the percentage of whites. Almost a third of the black population lives in families with incomes below the poverty level. (Only 10.5 percent of whites are in poverty.) The number of poor in families headed by women and those headed by men is about equal, but a much larger percentage of the population in families headed by women is in poverty. The incidence of poverty is high among families whose head is young, between the ages of 15 and 24. Ap-

more equitable.

Critics of workfare proposals offer a number of arguments to counter the case made by proponents. An important argument is that workfare stigmatizes welfare recipients even more. Welfare reformers have attempted to develop programs that provide income to poor people, regardless of circumstances. This principle greatly mitigates the stigma associated with seeking assistance through an antipoverty program; workfare proposals are a move in the opposite direction. Critics also believe that dependency is not an issue. Most program recipients are in the program for short periods of time because low incomes are often due to temporary problems such as unemployment or divorce. In a sense, welfare is an insurance scheme rather than a long-term care program.

Workfare opponents also argue that an additional needs test is unnecessary. Eligibility is now limited to those with very low incomes and few assets. Thus, workfare would not reduce welfare caseloads much at all. A final argument concerns the viability of a successful workfare program. For workfare to be successful — as defined by its proponents — it must provide jobs that deliver skill training and produce socially valuable output. In addition, there must be enough jobs for all program participants, and they must be organized to be effective in the context of short employment tenure and high turnover. Finally, if these public sector jobs compete with established job opportunities, public-sector employees will claim that they are being displaced by free labor.

The disagreement over the merits of workfare has both positive and normative elements. Although the results of experimental programs have resolved some questions, many of these programs have yielded inconclusive results thus far. Other arguments involve value judgments about the generosity of benefits, the element of compulsion in the programs, and how to help the poor while allowing them to maintain their dignity and self-respect. Despite the continuing disagreements over the merits of workfare, the Family Support Act of 1988 requires states to implement workfare programs. The benefits and costs of workfare will surely be clearer in the wake of widespread experience with it.

*The arguments for and against workfare discussed here are based on a comprehensive paper by Michael Wiseman about workfare, the experimental welfare programs, and evaluations of these programs that appeared in *Focus*, University of Wisconsin Institute for Research on Poverty, Fall and Winter 1986.

---

proximately 30 percent of families with such young household heads are in poverty, and a striking 56.7 percent of such black families are in poverty.

These patterns provide some hints about the causes of poverty. The incidence of poverty is high among black families, young families, and families headed by women. Low incomes in these groups can be attributed to a lack of skills, education, and experience relative to white males, reduced amounts of labor supplied to the market, and race and sex discrimination in employment. Young people, especially black youths, experience relatively high rates of unemployment. Women who are single parents must balance the need for income against the needs of their children. Even though over half of all women with children — even young children — now work, many work only part time or part of the year. In addition, changes in family structure seem to have a disproportionately adverse effect on women's income. When families break up because of death or divorce, women who have not been in the labor market face limited employment opportunities.

Since family income, especially at low-income levels, is comprised primarily of wage earnings, poverty income can be attributed to low wage earnings. Thus poverty, in an accounting sense, is caused by (1) labor force nonparticipation, (2) unemployment, and (3) employment at low wages. Pov-

TABLE 6

The incidence of poverty by family characteristics, 1987

Characteristic	Numbers			Percent		
	All Races	Whites	Blacks	All Races	Whites	Blacks
Persons (millions)						
All persons	32.6	21.4	9.7	13.5	10.5	33.1
Female householder no husband present	12.1	—	—	38.3	—	—
All other households	12.9	—	—	7.4	—	—
Families	25.0	15.8	8.0	12.1	9.1	31.8
Adults	12.6	7.8	3.7	8.8	6.3	23.7
Children less than 18 years old	12.4	7.6	4.3	20.0	15.0	45.1
Unrelated individual	6.8	5.1	1.5	20.8	18.2	38.3
Families (thousands) by age of householder						
15–24 years old	863	558	285	29.5	23.8	56.7
25–64 years old	5445	3523	1650	10.5	8.0	28.6
65 years and older	751	511	215	7.2	5.4	23.7

Source: U.S. Bureau of the Census, Current Population Reports, Series P-60, No. 160, *Money Income and Poverty Status of Families and Persons in the U.S.: 1987* (Washington, DC: U.S. Government Printing Office, 1987).

---

erty that is associated with nonparticipation — individuals neither working nor seeking work — could be caused by a disability or, in the case of a family headed by the mother, child-care responsibilities. Appropriate policies would include income transfers or provision of child-care subsidies to allow the parent to work. If the major cause is unemployment or low earnings, however, policies should focus on increasing the demand for and skills of low-income workers or promoting high-employment macroeconomic conditions.

Table 7 shows that there were 7,022,000 heads of families in poverty in 1987. About half did no work in 1987 for a variety of reasons. Foremost among these were home duties and illness or disability. There were 414,000 heads of families who were unable to find work.[7] Of the half who did work in 1987, 1,334,000 were employed full time. For this group, about 20 percent of poor family heads, poverty is a result of low wages. The remainder of the working poor did not work full time, due to unemployment or nonparticipation. While we do not know how many of this latter group would have remained in poverty had they been employed full time, lack of full-time employment, rather than low wages, is the immediate cause of most poverty in the United States.

The data in Table 7 also highlight the difference in labor force activity between single female household heads and other household heads. Although about 40 percent of these women worked, only about 8 percent worked full

---

[7]Some economists have labeled these workers *discouraged workers*. They are not counted as unemployed because they did not actively look for work — one of the conditions that must be met to be officially considered unemployed.

TABLE 7

Work experience of heads of poverty families, 1987

Characteristic	Number (1000)	Percent of Total
All poverty householders	7,022	100.0%
Worked	3,311	47.2%
Worked year round	1,334	
Worked 1–49 weeks	1,977	
Did not work	3,711	52.8%
Ill or disabled	870	
Keeping house	1,523	
In school	213	
Unable to find work	414	
Other	691	
Female householder, no husband present	3,637	100.0%
Worked	1,428	39.3%
Worked year round	282	
Worked 1–49 weeks	1,146	
Did not work	2,209	60.7%
Ill or disabled	386	
Keeping house	1,346	
In school	124	
Unable to find work	223	
Other	130	
All other families	3,385	100.0%
Worked	1,883	55.6%
Worked year round	1,425	
Worked 1–49 weeks	458	
Did not work	1,502	44.4%
Ill or disabled	484	
Keeping house	177	
In school	89	
Unable to find work	191	
Other	561	

Source: U.S. Bureau of the Census, Current Population Reports, Series P-60, No. 160, *Money Income and Poverty Status of Families and Persons in the U.S.: 1987* (Washington, DC: U.S. Government Printing Office, 1987).

time. And among those who did not work, over half were involved in home duties or child care. Less than 10 percent of this group would have taken a job if they could have found one. By contrast, over half of other household heads worked, and most of them worked full time. The majority of those who did not work were sick or disabled, in school, or so-called discouraged workers.

This picture of the poor suggests that the causes of poverty are varied but that we can group most of the poor into one of a few categories. We have the *working poor* — those poor who are employed or would like to work but cannot find a job. Some working poor work less than year round or only part time. Improved skills, equal opportunity, and economic growth would help this poverty population. The *nonworking poor* include the sick and disabled, some retirees, and single mothers. We do not expect the sick and disabled and the retired to work. To reduce poverty among this group, the government must provide them with transfer income.

Society's attitudes toward the labor market participation of female household heads with children, especially those who are single (divorced, widowed, or never married), have been quite ambiguous over the past twenty-five years or so. Before World War II, single mothers were not expected to work. However, as the role of women in U.S. society has changed, societal views about the labor market participation of single mothers have changed, too. Many people now believe single mothers should be encouraged to work. The appropriate nature of programs targeted at this population is, as a result of this ambiguity, also unclear.

SECTION RECAP
The incidence of poverty is high among black families, young families, and families headed by women. In an accounting sense, poverty is caused by labor force nonparticipation, unemployment, and employment at low wages.

Income Redistribution and Antipoverty Policy

Economists emphasize the importance of economic efficiency in formulating public policy. On the other hand, government policy decisions generally place more weight on the income distributional consequences of a decision than on efficiency concerns. In such areas as tax reform, health care, deregulation, industrial and trade policy, and Social Security the most decisive arguments concern the impacts on the poor and middle class. While Congress seldom explicitly debates what the optimal distribution of income should be, distribution is implicit in most of its policy debates.

Consider recent proposals to impose and increase insurance deductibles in the Medicare program. Economic efficiency argues for requiring the patient to bear a share of any medical costs. This provides both the doctor and the patient with an incentive to use the most cost-effective treatment consistent with sound medical practice. It is widely recognized that full medical insurance has led to significant health-care cost inflation and misallocation of resources by removing financial incentives to hold down costs. However, the opposition to proposals to increase patient fees, based on income distribution grounds, has been fierce: Raising the costs of medical care would reduce the welfare of the elderly. (An implicit assumption, contrary to fact, in the debate over Medicare and Social Security is that the elderly are more likely than younger people to be poor.)

And so it goes on, issue after issue. Should economic policy promote a high-growth, efficient economy? Or should we be more concerned with equality? This philosophical question is at the heart of the income distribution issue. The cost of increased equality is a decreased reliance upon market forces and reduced individual incentives.

Antipoverty Policies

We have seen that approximately one in seven Americans is in poverty, as it is officially defined. The figure is substantially higher for blacks. This continuing level of poverty, twenty-five years after President Johnson confidently declared a war on poverty, is a major disappointment to policymakers. Antipoverty policy first became a top national priority in the Kennedy and Johnson administrations (1960–1968). President Johnson launched a series of so-called Great Society programs that, it was hoped, would eradicate poverty. Most of the programs initiated during this era still exist today and receive much higher funding levels. Between 1966 and 1985, real federal payments to individuals through an array of social programs increased by 400 percent, from $46.3 billion to $185.5 billion (in constant 1972 dollars). As a share of the rising federal budget, transfers rose from 25.3 percent to 46.7 percent of the budget.

Federal Antipoverty Programs   Federal antipoverty programs have had two main thrusts. One is to strike at the root of poverty — poor employment prospects. The Job Corps and *Comprehensive Employment and Training Act (CETA)* sought to provide training in job skills. CETA also employed workers in public sector jobs. CETA has since been replaced by a much less costly *Jobs Training Partnership Act (JTPA)*, which shifts much of the responsibility for training to private employers. While the JTPA seeks to augment the supply of skills, another program, the Targeted Jobs Tax Credit, seeks to raise the demand for disadvantaged workers. Employers who hire workers from welfare-eligible families may take a portion of their wages as a credit against federal income taxes.

The second thrust is to provide income support to the poor who are unable to work or whose earnings are not sufficient to pull them out of poverty. Some programs, such as Social Security, unemployment insurance, Social Security disability payments, and Medicare are not conditional upon income. While they undoubtedly do have an impact on the poor, they are not targeted for the poor only. The wealthy, along with the poor, may benefit from these programs. A number of other programs are targeted specifically at poor families. To be eligible for benefits, a person's or family's income or assets cannot exceed a predetermined level.

The most widely known example of the latter type of program is Aid to Families with Dependent Children (AFDC). AFDC is a joint federal–state program providing cash payments to needy families in which at least one parent is deceased, disabled, absent from home, or unemployed. Benefits vary from state to state, depending upon the definition of need. As income rises, benefits are reduced, and benefits end when family income rises above 150 percent of the state's definition of need. AFDC families automatically qualify for medical assistance under the Medicaid program.

Food and nutrition assistance to low-income families is provided by a number of federal programs. Food stamps, which reduce the cost of food purchases, are provided based upon income and family size. Child nutrition programs subsidize meals for children in schools and day-care programs. Housing assistance is provided by rent subsidies. The Supplemental Security Income program (SSI) provides cash support for the low-income aged, blind, and disabled poor. SSI recipients also are eligible for Medicaid benefits.

The Welfare Dilemma   Perhaps you have heard someone say, in jest or frustration, "I'm tired of working. I'm going to quit my job and go on welfare." While

Does It Make **Economic Sense?**

Diverging Poverty Rates

The overall fraction of the population with incomes below the poverty line has remained fairly stable since the mid-1960s, averaging between 12 and 15 percent of the population. However, two different age groups have shown markedly divergent trends. The poverty rate for adults over the age of 65 has been reduced by more than half, falling from over 25 percent in the mid-1960s to about 12.4 percent in 1986. On the other hand, the poverty rate for children less than 18 years of age has risen from about 13 percent in the 1960s to over 20 percent in 1986. Do these opposite trends make economic sense?

The income transfer program with the most direct effect on the economic well-being of the elderly is Social Security. Large increases in Social Security benefits explain most of the decrease in the rate of poverty among older citizens. By 1972, the Congress had tied Social Security benefit levels to changes in consumer prices. In fact, the benefit formula contained an error that actually overcompensated beneficiaries for the effects of inflation. The relatively high rates of inflation in the 1970s raised Social Security benefits substantially. Between 1970 and 1985, average monthly benefits increased just over 400 percent, while prices rose by about 275 percent.

Children have not been so fortunate. The welfare program that has the strongest impact on the economic well-being of children in poverty families is Aid to Families with Dependent Children (AFDC). In 1985 some 58 percent of children in poverty were in families receiving AFDC benefits. In 1979, over 70 percent of these children were receiving AFDC support. During the Reagan administration, the Congress restricted eligibility for

---

such threats are rarely carried out, programs such as AFDC, food stamps, and housing assistance do pose a major dilemma for policymakers. Scarcity of government resources requires that benefits be targeted to the truly needy. However, if a dollar of benefits is lost when earned income goes up by a dollar, the incentive for the poor to work at low-wage jobs is weakened. Thus two important goals — targeting benefits to the poor and establishing work incentives — are in conflict.

Why would the AFDC program establish such a work disincentive? If benefits are not reduced, more families with higher incomes will be eligible for benefits, leaving less for the truly needy. Thus the fundamental welfare dilemma: Targeting benefits to those truly in need creates stiff disincentives for work.

How Effective Have Antipoverty Programs Been? The trend of the data in Table 5 reveals that poverty decreased substantially through 1970. Since then, however, there appears to have been little progress. Ironically, the rate of poverty stabilized at about the same time the Great Society poverty programs were fully implemented (that is, before effects attributable to the programs themselves could be felt in the economy). This lack of progress has led some social critics to question the effectiveness of federal antipoverty programs.

The strongest challenge to the Great Society approach comes from Charles Murray in his 1984 book *Losing Ground*.[8] Murray contends that (1) poverty has increased since the inception of the War on Poverty, and (2) rising federal welfare expenditures are the main culprit. Specifically, Murray is critical of the

[8] New York: Basic Books, 1984.

the program and reduced benefit levels. These cuts had an especially serious impact on children, since they are the primary beneficiaries of AFDC funds (two thirds of AFDC recipients are children).

One of the primary factors leading to this difference in treatment of the two age groups has to do with society's attitude about their proper status. In the case of Social Security benefits, retirees are not expected to work. Thus, work incentives have been a relatively minor issue in discussions of income support programs for the elderly.

On the other hand, the AFDC program has been one of the most controversial poverty programs, in large part because of concerns about the work disincentives built into the program. One of the objectives of recent changes to the AFDC program requirements was to increase the incentives for working-age recipients, and the parents of children who receive AFDC benefits, to find work. However, as the empirical evidence indicates, efforts to achieve this objective have come at the expense of child recipients.

Of course, there is a public choice issue here too. The elderly vote and children do not. Consequently, politicians are more sensitive to the possible adverse effects of changes in Social Security benefits than, say, AFDC. Furthermore, the growth in the size of the older age groups has given them more political influence.

As the preceding observations suggest, there is a logical explanation of how the poverty rates for senior citizens and children have diverged over time. Part of the explanation lies in the changes in the amount of benefits going to recipients of government aid programs in each age group. Another part of the explanation lies with the politics of income redistribution.

incentives conveyed by income transfer programs. We have already seen how such targeted programs diminish the incentives of the poor to work. In addition, Murray and others charge that AFDC destabilizes the family and encourages a cycle of poverty by encouraging fathers to leave home and teenagers to become pregnant out of wedlock.

Murray uses the hypothetical Pennsylvania couple, Harold and Phyllis, to press his points. If Phyllis became pregnant in 1960, the couple would have been better off if they had married and Harold had taken a low-wage job. However, by 1970, more generous AFDC benefits and the requirement that Harold be absent would have raised the income of Phyllis and her baby if she remained single.

More generally, Murray criticizes a fundamental change in policy and attitudes toward the poor: a change from assisting the poor to improve their own economic well-being to providing a guaranteed minimum income for them; a change from providing equal opportunity to establishing equal outcomes.

Losing Ground is a very controversial book and was met with vigorous rebuttal. Glen Cain of the University of Wisconsin disputes Murray's claim that poverty programs have led to increased poverty. Cain believes that a sluggish economy was responsible for the failure of poverty rates to decline in the 1970s. Along with the sharp drop in poverty during the high-growth 1960s, this suggests that a strong economy is perhaps the most potent antipoverty weapon.

In her survey of poverty studies, Isabel Sawhill also concludes that high unemployment in the 1970s and early 1980s was the major factor increasing

SECTION RECAP

The government has developed a number of programs to eliminate poverty in the United States. However, many of these programs pose a dilemma because it is difficult to provide both benefits and an incentive to work. In addition, there is considerable debate over the effectiveness of existing antipoverty programs.

poverty rates.[9] Others have noted that Murray's critique is leveled at only a small percentage of welfare recipients. The SSI program, for example, benefits the aged, blind, and disabled poor, and its work disincentives would seem to be irrelevant. Indeed, the poverty rate for the elderly fell continuously through the 1970s. Still others argue that the AFDC program grew because of a greater incidence of divorce in society, not because it encouraged marital instability itself. However, the existence of AFDC does encourage young single mothers to establish independent households, rather than living with relatives. Such female-headed households adds to the poverty rate, as Sawhill notes.

Despite the disagreement over the effectiveness of existing antipoverty programs, there is a consensus emerging among policy experts that new policies and revisions in the existing programs in the 1980s should emphasize work opportunities and strengthened family responsibilities. The *Family Support Act* of 1988 represents a major philosophical change in direction, since it requires many recipients of public aid to work part time in government jobs. In addition, families with unemployed fathers residing in the household will be eligible for program benefits.

Summary

Income distribution and antipoverty policy choices involve a tradeoff between equity and efficiency. Inequality of income in the United States has remained approximately stable since World War II. Countries with more progressive tax structures and more generous social programs have more equal income distributions than the United States does. Incomes in developing countries tend to be much more unequal relative to U.S. income.

Income inequality can be measured in a number of ways. A **Lorenz curve** is used to make comparisons through time and across countries. The use of annual income to measure income inequality has its shortcomings. Income measures omit the value of nonmarket goods and services, and concentration on annual income fails to capture the income mobility that most families experience.

Observed variations in income occur for many reasons, including differences in education, jobs, individual abilities and preferences, and the amount of labor supplied to the market. Discrimination, intergenerational transfers of wealth, and luck also affect the income distribution. Some income differences arise because of differences in productivity and work effort. In a market economy some inequality is necessary to provide incentives for productive activity.

Poverty is measured by counting all families with incomes below the amount necessary to provide a minimally adequate standard of living. In 1989, this poverty income level for a family of four was about $12,700. About 13.1 percent of all U.S. families have incomes below the poverty level. The incidence of poverty is greatest among black families and those households headed by single women.

An array of programs addressing the poverty problem exists. Such programs as Social Security, unemployment compensation, and Medicare raise the incomes of both poor and nonpoor. Programs targeted specifically at the poor include Job Corps, food stamps, Medicare and Medicaid, and Aid to Families with Dependent Children. Spending on these social programs has increased

[9]"Poverty in the U.S.: Why Is It So Persistent?" *Journal of Economic Literature* 26 (September 1988), p. 1081.

dramatically in the past twenty-five years, while the incidence of poverty has changed little, except for the greatly reduced poverty rate among people over the age of 65.

Critics of poverty programs maintain that poverty has not been reduced over time because the programs themselves encourage participants to work less and become more dependent on government assistance. Proponents of the poverty programs argue that recessions are primarily responsible for the continued incidence of poverty and that basic demographic trends have contributed to the poverty problem.

Questions for Thought

Knowledge Questions

1. Explain the equity–efficiency tradeoff associated with income redistribution.
2. Although whites constitute two thirds of the poverty population, the incidence of poverty is greatest among blacks. How can both statements be true?
3. The distribution of income in the United States should be more equal! It should be less equal! Choose one side of this debate and construct a good defense of your position. (You might try it out on a friend.)

Application Questions

4. Suppose that adjustments in family income data for noncash government transfers and the value of household services yield an income distribution as follows:

Quintile	Percent of Income
Lowest fifth	8.0
Second fifth	14.0
Third fifth	18.0
Fourth fifth	22.0
Top fifth	38.0

Construct a Lorenz curve for the 1989 data in Table 1 and for the income distribution above. Which is more equal?

5. In designing income transfer programs to help the poor, why is it important to distinguish between the poor we expect to work and the poor who are not expected to work? In which category do single female household heads belong? Explain.
6. What is the justification for increasing the poverty income level when consumer prices rise? For example, the poverty income level for a family of four was $4275 in 1972, but $12,676 in 1989.

Synthesis Questions

7. What do you consider a minimally acceptable standard of living? Do you think the official poverty income level is sufficient to support this standard of living?
8. Using the factors that the text mentions as affecting family income, explain the differences in family income by marital status of the householder in Table 4. Explain the low per capita incomes of never-married men and women. Explain the difference in per capita incomes between divorced men and women.
9. The minimum wage law is touted as an antipoverty program. In terms of the provision of new jobs and additional training opportunities, how does it compare to a program like the Comprehensive Employment and Training Act? Explain.

OVERVIEW

In previous chapters we identified the conditions necessary for markets to efficiently allocate scarce resources to satisfy competing wants. In many situations, however, the market allocation of resources is not efficient and market failure is said to occur. This chapter considers three specific sources of market failure — externalities, public goods, and common-property resources — and

Externalities, Public Goods, and Common-Property Resources: Problems for the Market Mechanism

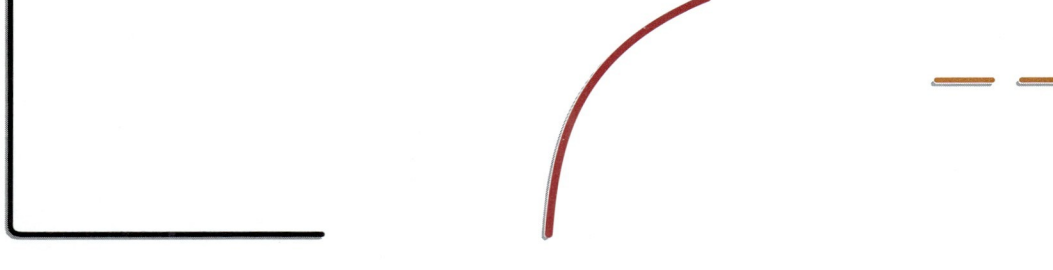

describes policies designed to correct each type of failure.

In addition, this chapter explores the causes and consequences of a classic source of market failure: environmental pollution. We will examine the sources of pollution — where it comes from and where it goes —

and discuss the important role played by property rights in creating or limiting the extent of this externality. A number of pollution control policy options are also identified and analyzed.

In the course of considering the policy prescriptions for each of the different types of

market failure analyzed, we will discuss the difficulties involved in determining the best course of action to take to cope with market failure. We will show that the way in which property rights are assigned will have an important effect on the extent to which market failure occurs.

CHAPTER 19

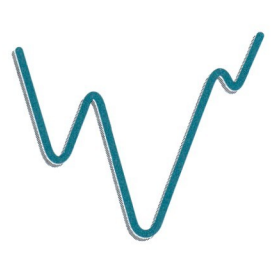
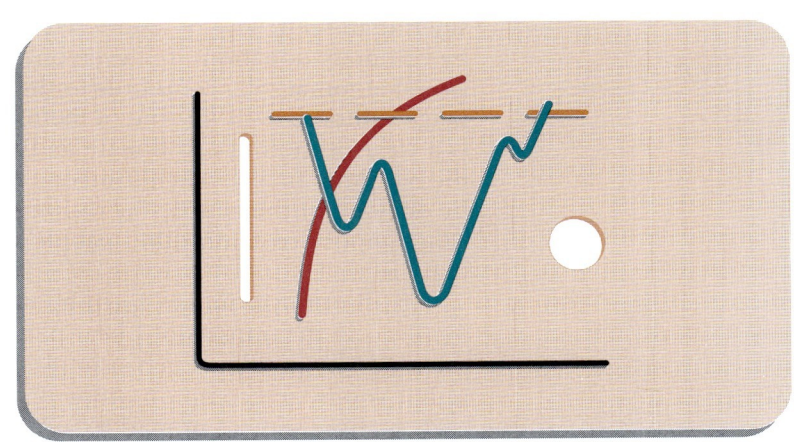

Learning Objectives

After reading and studying this chapter, you will be able to:

1. Explain how poorly defined property rights can be a source of externalities.
2. Explain how external costs and benefits affect the efficiency of equilibrium market price and output.
3. Describe various approaches that can be used to reduce the level of pollution to the socially efficient level.
4. Derive the market demand curve for a public good.
5. Explain the problems associated with common-property resources.
6. Discuss the steps that must be taken in a cost–benefit study.

Conditions That Lead to Inefficient Market Outcomes

According to economic theory, rational choice requires that consumers and producers consider all the marginal benefits and marginal costs of their choices. In each of the situations we have considered thus far, the additional, or marginal, benefits and costs have been *private*, or internal, to the individual. All resources have been assumed to be privately owned, and markets control the allocation of each resource. If the production process requires labor, land, and capital, the producer pays for all the labor, land, and capital used. We have also assumed that when a consumer buys a good, all the benefits of consumption are enjoyed by the consumer.

However, many consumption and production decisions confer benefits or costs on individuals who are not involved in the original market transaction. For example, assume a steel mill uses a river as the dumping ground for its effluent (wastes). If this action forces a nearby municipality to build additional water treatment facilities, the municipality is, in effect, bearing the cost of properly disposing of the effluent. Next, assume that a neighborhood is considering the purchase of land to create a park. The purchase will be financed by voluntary donations, but everyone will be allowed to use the park. This act would automatically contribute to the increased well-being of everyone in the neighborhood, even if some of them do not donate funds. In this case, there is a clear disincentive to donate and instead to rely on the other guy to foot the bill. And, finally, when someone allows his cattle to graze on public land, he does so for the benefits he realizes. However, this action may, at the same time, impose costs on other people who would like to let their cattle graze there as well.

In all of the examples listed above, third parties (individuals not directly involved in the transaction) bear part of the costs or benefits associated with the action in question. Such examples illustrate the problems of external costs, public goods, and common-property resources, respectively. Before examining each of these sources of market failure in detail it is necessary to examine the problems that impede the proper functioning of the market mechanism.

Property Rights Revisited

Property rights
The legally sanctioned control that an individual exercises over a collection of goods, resources, and services.

One of the major characteristics of market economies is the existence of **property rights**. Private market transactions are exchanges of property rights. For example, you may exchange something you have the right to (money income) for something a store owner has a right to (a pound of coffee beans). After the exchange the store owner has the property right to the money and you have the property right to the coffee.

For some goods, however, the question of who actually owns the property right to the good in question is unclear. For example, with whom would you exchange your income (profits) if your company wanted to buy the right to use a river to dispose of its effluents? Using a river as a dumping ground causes market failure because no one has clear property rights to the river. The cost of disposing of the effluent in the river becomes an external one — no exchange of property rights can take place. The river is treated as being costless for the firm to use.

A system of well-defined property rights goes a long way toward alleviating such problems. If clearly established property rights were assigned to the air and water, one would not be able to emit pollution unless the owner of the affected resource was compensated for its use. However, establishing property rights in such cases is not easy. This is especially true given the lack of information on the value different individuals attach to such property rights. The following example illustrates the role of poorly defined property rights as a source of external costs.

Suppose you walk into your dorm room only to find that your new roommate smokes. Because you dislike cigarette smoke, you start considering what you can do about the external cost your roommate is imposing on you. So long as the university does not define who has the property right to the clean air in dorm rooms, the first one to the room has, in effect, the opportunity to seize the property right. If one or the other of you were given clear property rights, the two of you could negotiate an exchange of rights; you might be willing to exchange your rights to clean air for the right to use your roomie's personal computer a certain amount of time. However, without clearly defined property rights, the most likely solution to the external cost problem is arbitration by the dorm staff or some other authority. Furthermore, there is no guarantee that the ruling will distribute the property right optimally. That is, the property right might not go to the individual who values it most.

SECTION RECAP
When property rights are poorly defined, there is an increased potential for external costs that are borne by third parties.

The Coase Theorem

In 1960, Ronald Coase addressed the notion that intervention is always required in the case of market failure.[1] When a small number of people are affected, and when transaction costs are low, he argued, private negotiation can result in an optimum allocation of resources. The only things needed for private negotiation to work are a clear assignment of transferable property rights and the ability to identify and bring together all the affected parties. This argument is known as the **Coase Theorem**. According to the Coase Theorem, if individuals stand to gain from a transaction (that is, if the marginal benefits exceed the marginal costs), they will undertake it.

The Coase Theorem is illustrated in Figure 1, which depicts the situation faced by you and your chain-smoking roommate. The curve labeled MPB indicates the marginal private benefits your roommate receives from each additional unit of smoking. The curve labeled MEC shows the marginal external cost you incur breathing the smoke-filled air. (The cost is external in the sense that your roommate generates it but you bear it.)

In the absence of property rights to clean air (and assuming that you do not throttle her), your roommate will generate Q_{Max} units of smoking. This is because the marginal cost to her of each additional unit of smoking is zero. Thus, for your roommate, marginal private benefits equal marginal private costs at Q_{Max}. (Note that beyond Q_{Max} marginal benefits are negative.) You, on the other hand, are left to endure marginal external costs of ab dollars (and hence total costs of dba dollars). Clearly this is inefficient. The efficient level of smoke is at Q^*, where the additional benefits of smoking to your roommate (MPB) equal the additional cost of the smoke to you (MEC).

Assume the university assigns the property right to you, giving you the exclusive right to clean air in the room. Now you have the right to restrict your

Coase Theorem
So long as all affected parties stand to gain from a transaction (an exchange of property rights), and transactions costs are low, the transaction will take place.

---

[1] Ronald Coase, "The Problem of Social Cost," *Journal of Law and Economics*, Vol. 3, October 1960, pp. 1–44.

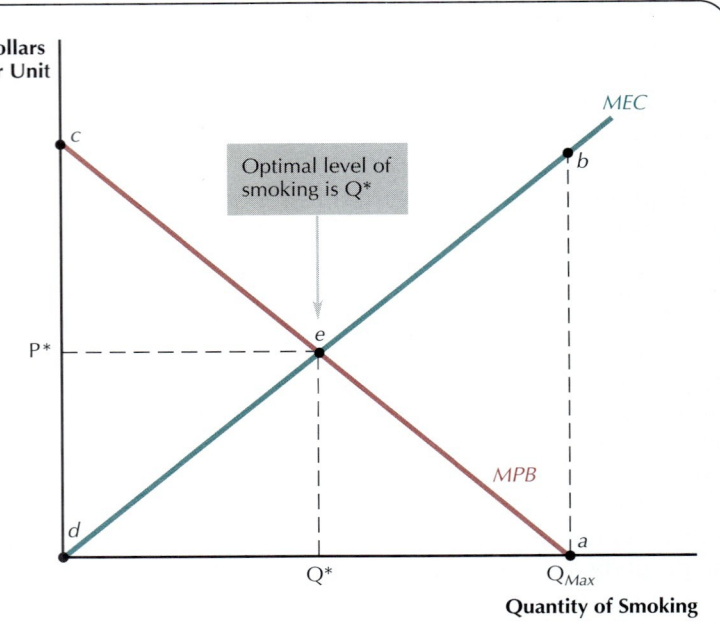

FIGURE 1
The Coase theorem. The curves labeled MPB and MEC show the marginal private benefits and the marginal external cost of smoking. The optimum level of smoking is Q^*. If you have the property right to clean air, you can restrict your roommate's smoking to $Q = 0$. However, so long as she is willing to pay you an amount sufficient to cover the external cost of her smoking, it is in your best interest to accept the payment. The amount of the bribe paid will lie between deQ^* and $dceQ^*$. If, instead, your roommate has the property right, it is in your best interest to bribe her not to smoke as much. In this case the total amount of the bribe will lie between Q^*ea and Q^*eba.

roommate's smoking to $Q = 0$. However, suppose she offers you a bribe to endure some amount of her smoking. So long as she is willing to pay you an amount sufficient to cover the external cost of her smoking, it is in your best interest to accept. MPB shows your roommate's maximum willingness to pay to be allowed to smoke. MEC shows your minimum willingness to accept compensation to endure each unit of smoke. So long as she offers you more than the minimum amount you are willing to accept, you will be better off doing so. The additional benefit of the bribe exceeds the additional cost of the smoke. This implies that when negotiations are finished you would be willing to allow your roommate the pleasure of generating Q^* units of smoke. The amount of the total bribe paid will lie between the amounts deQ^* and $dceQ^*$. DeQ^* is the minimum bribe you would be willing to accept and $dceQ^*$ is the maximum amount your roommate would be willing to pay.

Suppose instead that the university gives the property right to your roommate. In this case, you can bribe her not to smoke as much. So long as the additional benefit you receive from a reduction in smoke exceeds the additional cost to you, it is in your best interest to offer a bribe. When negotiations are complete, you will offer a bribe to your roommate sufficient to induce her to reduce her smoking to Q^* units per day. The total amount of the bribe will lie between Q^*ea, the minimum bribe your roommate would be willing to accept, and Q^*eba, the maximum bribe you would be willing to pay.

When the number of affected parties is small, assigning clear property rights facilitates private negotiation toward the optimal amount of pollution. It does not matter who is initially given the property right. So long as both parties stand to gain from an exchange of property rights, private negotiation will produce a socially efficient outcome.

However, merely assigning property rights is not a panacea. Suppose the number of parties affected by smoking is large, for example, passengers on a flight from Honolulu to St. Louis, and that the property rights to clean air have been given to nonsmokers on all flights. In theory, the smokers could get together and offer a bribe to the nonsmokers to allow them to smoke. However, as a practical matter it would be much more difficult to negotiate an efficient solution now that such a large number of people is involved. Also, there is an incentive for individuals to understate their willingness to pay to smoke. This point is made by Coase — in many cases transactions costs will be so large as to preclude negotiations. Instead, resolution of the dispute will have to be handled by a third party such as the courts.

The preceding discussion serves to illustrate the importance of a lack of clearly defined property rights as a source of market failure. To the extent that property rights are poorly defined and transactions costs are high, it often is likely that in the absence of intervention, the market will not generate a socially efficient level of output. This important point is considered in more detail below.

SECTION RECAP
When transactions costs are low, private negotiation will produce an optimal allocation of property rights. However, in many cases transactions costs are such that property rights disputes must be arbitrated by a third party such as the courts.

Externalities

Economists refer to costs and benefits that spill over into other people's lives as spillovers, neighborhood effects, or more commonly, *externalities*. Externalities that have a negative effect on the well-being of third parties are referred to as **external costs**. Alternatively, externalities can be positive or beneficial, in which case they are referred to as **external benefits**.

In the presence of externalities we need to change our requirement for rational choice. Knowing only the marginal *private* costs and benefits is no longer sufficient to determine the optimal level of output. We must now broaden our perspective to consider the marginal *social* benefits and costs, that is, the costs and benefits borne by society as a whole. The **social benefits** and **social costs** of production and consumption activities are determined by adding the external costs and benefits to the private costs and benefits, respectively.

External cost
A cost resulting from a production or consumption decision that is borne by a third party who is not part of the original transaction.

External benefit
A benefit resulting from a production or consumption decision that is borne by a third party who is not part of the original transaction.

Social costs
The sum of the private and external costs of a production or consumption activity.

Social benefits
The sum of the private and external benefits of a production or consumption activity.

External Costs

As an example of external costs, consider a dentist who sets up her practice on the ground floor of a new building. Over time, word spreads that she is a skilled, caring dentist and she quickly develops a number of loyal patients. Consequently, her practice does very well.

One day a pastry shop opens next door to the dentist's office. Shortly after the opening of the pastry shop the dentist notices that whenever the store runs its giant dough-mixing machines the whole office shakes. While the mixing machines are operating she finds it increasingly difficult to do her work as efficiently as before. The resulting tremors from the mixing machines disrupt the dentist's practice and cause many of her patients to seek a more stable dentist's chair.

In this situation the pastry shop has imposed an external cost on the dentist in the form of decreased profits resulting from the loss of clientele. As this example illustrates, an external cost is a cost of production (or consumption) that is imposed on some third party, for which the generator of the cost is not charged. In our example, the shop owner has imposed the cost of the vibrations on the dentist rather than bearing the costs himself through the purchase of vibration-control equipment. This contrasts with the internal costs of production, which the store owner does pay. The internal costs consist of the fixed and variable costs of production — workers' salaries, rent on shop space, utility bills, the cost of ingredients, plates, and napkins.

From a social point of view the marginal social cost (MSC) of producing pastries is equal to the marginal private (or internal) cost (MC) plus the marginal external cost. Figure 2 depicts the market for pastries. The curve labeled MSB shows the marginal social benefits of additional pastries, assuming no external benefits are generated by their production. The curve labeled MPC shows the marginal private cost of producing pastries.

In the situation where the pastry shop owner does not install vibration-control equipment, profits are maximized by producing Q_P pastries per month, at a price of P_P dollars per pastry. This output–price combination occurs where the marginal social benefit from pastries equals the marginal *private* cost of producing the pastries. However, due to the external costs, output level Q_P is inefficient.

If we add the marginal external cost to the marginal private costs, the marginal social cost curve (MSC) lies above the marginal private cost curve as shown in Figure 2. The efficient level of output is found where marginal social benefit equals marginal social cost. Thus, output falls to Q_s and price rises to P_s. Clearly, *failure to consider the external costs of production results in overproduction of the good (and hence an overallocation of resources to production of the good) and too low a market price.*

The actual efficiency (or welfare) loss associated with producing Q_P units of output is measured as follows. For each unit of output where MSC exceeds MSB, production is inefficient. Producing units beyond Q_s adds more to costs

SECTION RECAP
In the absence of market intervention, external costs will result in an overallocation of resources to the production of goods and services.

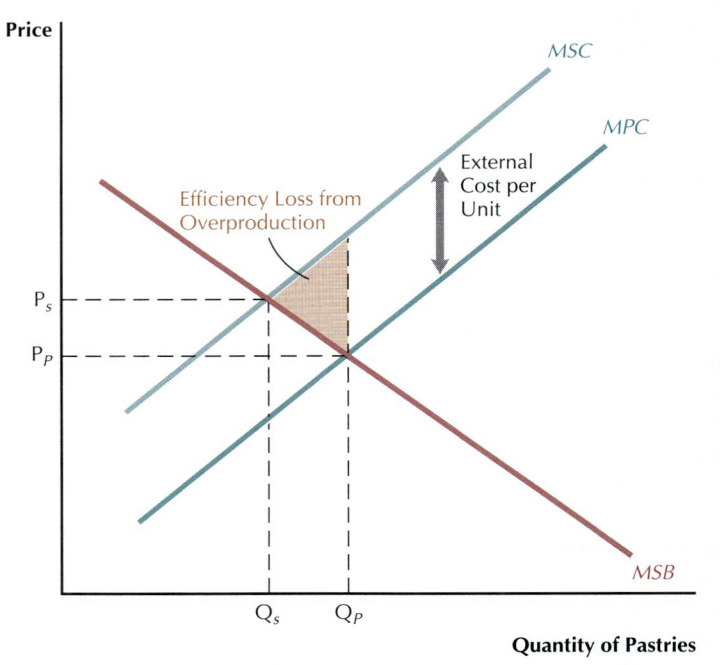

FIGURE 2
Efficiency and the effects of external costs. The curve labeled MSB measures the marginal social benefits of each unit of pastries produced. The curves labeled MPC and MSC measure the marginal private and marginal social costs per unit produced. The vertical difference between MPC and MSC measures the external cost per unit. The market solution would be Q_P units at a price of P_P per unit. However, the inclusion of external costs reduces output to Q_s and price rises to P_s—the efficient equilibrium. The shaded area is the welfare loss associated with the overproduction of pastries when only private costs are considered. A tax equal to the vertical distance between MPC and MSC would induce firms to produce the efficient level of output.

than to benefits. Thus, each level of output from Q_s to Q_P involves an efficiency loss. The shaded triangle in Figure 2 measures the total efficiency loss associated with overproduction of pastries at Q_P.

External Benefits

Not all externalities need impose a cost on others. For example, suppose that after listening to a news broadcast about a possible flu epidemic during the coming winter, you decide to pay the required fee and get the appropriate vaccination. As a result, you incur all the costs of receiving the vaccination. However, not all of the benefits of getting the shot are enjoyed by you alone. Your busy roommate, who cannot find the time to get the (much-feared) shot, your family, and your friends also benefit since you do not expose them to the virus.

In this situation all those getting flu vaccinations confer external benefits on their shot-shy neighbors in the form of reduced chances of contracting the flu virus. As this example illustrates, an external benefit is an unintended benefit of consumption (or production) enjoyed by some third party, for which the generator of the benefit is not compensated. This contrasts with the internal benefits of consumption that are enjoyed solely by the consumer.

From society's point of view the marginal social benefit (MSB) of being vaccinated is equal to the marginal private benefit (MPB) plus the marginal external benefit. Figure 3 depicts the market for flu vaccinations. The curve labeled MSC shows the marginal social cost of flu shots, assuming no external costs are generated. The curve labeled MPB is the marginal private benefit derived from flu shots (reduced chance of illness).

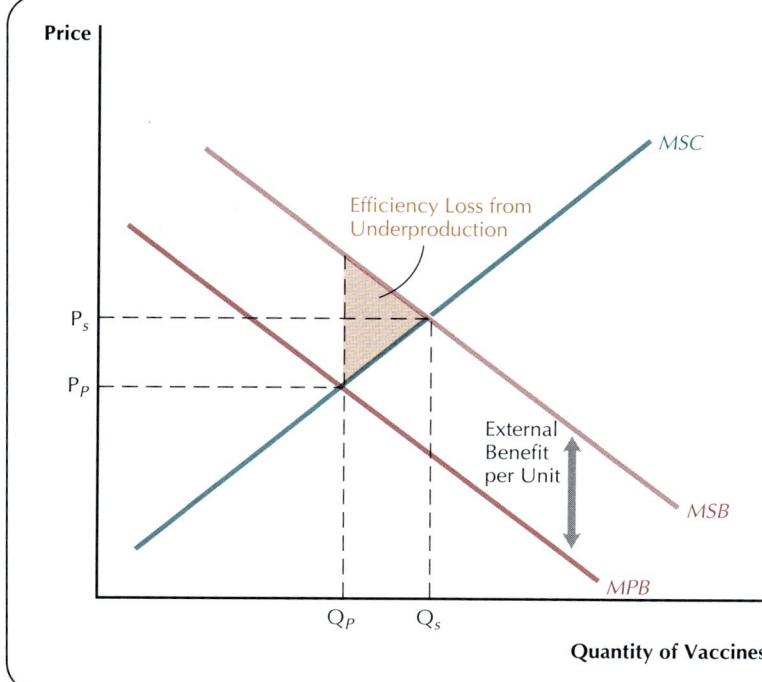

FIGURE 3
Efficiency and the effects of external benefits. The curve labeled MSC measures the marginal social cost of vaccines produced. The curves labeled MPB and MSB measure the marginal private and marginal social benefits per unit of vaccines produced. The vertical difference between MPB and MSB measures the external benefit per unit. The market solution is Q_P units produced at a price of P_P per unit. However, the inclusion of external benefits increases output to Q_s and price falls to P_s—the efficient equilibrium. The shaded area is the welfare loss resulting from the underproduction of flu vaccines when only private benefits are considered. A subsidy to consumers equal to the vertical distance between MPB and MSB would induce the market to produce the efficient level of output.

Ignoring external benefits, the equilibrium level of vaccinations is Q_p shots per month, at a price of P_P dollars per shot. However, this number of shots is too low. When the marginal external benefits are added to the marginal private benefit the MSB curve lies above the MPB curve. The efficient price and number of shots are found where marginal social benefit equals marginal social cost. Thus, the efficient number of shots is Q_s and the efficient price is P_s. *Failure to consider the external benefits of consumption results in the underproduction of the good (and hence an underallocation of resources to production of the good) and too low a market price.*

> **SECTION RECAP**
> In the absence of market intervention, external benefits will result in an underallocation of resources to the production of goods and services.

The MSC curve shows the additional cost to society of producing one more vaccination, and the MSB curve shows the additional social benefit of producing one more vaccination. So long as MSB exceeds MSC, producing that unit is efficient—it adds more to benefits than to costs. Thus, failure to produce each unit of output from Q_P to Q_s involves some efficiency loss. The shaded triangle measures the total efficiency loss resulting from the underproduction of vaccinations at Q_P.

Policy Prescriptions

Because markets fail to account for externalities, they result in an inefficient allocation of resources. However, the market has no choice but to fail. When one does not have to pay to use a productive input, or when one does not have to pay to consume a good, the market will necessarily overproduce (in the case of external costs) or underproduce (in the case of external benefits) the good or service in question. Consequently, this is one area where intervening in the market can increase efficiency.

In the case of external costs, the objective of intervention in the market is to *internalize* the external costs. That is, we attempt to create the conditions necessary to ensure that the individual or firm responsible for the external costs pays for all the costs incurred. There are a number of ways to accomplish this.

One obvious way to control negative externalities is to charge those responsible for the costs imposed on others. For example, if the pastry shop owner were taxed an amount equal to the marginal external cost imposed on the dentist, he would see his costs of production rise. This would in turn alter the shop owner's profit-maximizing level of output. Specifically, the shop owner would have an incentive (higher profits) to reduce output.

The imposition of an excise tax raises the cost of producing each unit of a good and shifts the marginal private cost curve upward by the amount of the tax. In the pastry shop example, if the tax, T, were set exactly equal to the marginal external cost of production, marginal private costs would increase to MSC in Figure 2. As a result of the tax, the shop owner would reduce output to Q_s and the market price would rise to P_s. Production would occur where MSC = MSB and we would have an efficient level of output.

Although straightforward in principle, setting an excise tax at the correct level is difficult in practice because many external costs are difficult to measure accurately. In the case of the dentist and the pastry shop it was relatively simple—external costs could be measured as the reduced profits of the dentist. However, how does one measure the cost of health problems or death caused by toxic pollutants? Incomplete knowledge of external costs can lead to the imposition of a tax that is either too high or too low. A tax that is too high causes the MPC curve to shift to a level higher than MSC, resulting in too low a level of output. A tax that is too low shifts the MPC curve to a level lower than MSC, resulting in an output level that is still too high.

External benefits also require intervention in the market. To internalize an external benefit, we could *subsidize* the consumers of the good. In the flu vaccine example, we saw that those who buy the vaccine pass on an external benefit to others. If a per-unit subsidy were offered to those who buy the vaccination, it would raise the marginal private benefit of getting a vaccination at each quantity of vaccinations. (The buyers now get a shot *and* cash in their pockets.) A subsidy exactly equal to the marginal external benefit would shift the MPB curve up to MSB in Figure 3. The producers of the flu shots would have an incentive to increase the quantity of vaccines supplied (as a result of the higher price), and consumers would pay less than before. Once again, as a result of the subsidy marginal social benefit equals marginal social cost, and an efficient level of output results.

However, just as it is difficult to set a tax exactly equal to marginal external cost, it is also difficult to set a subsidy so that it is exactly equal to the marginal external benefit. In particular, how does one determine the dollar value of the reduction in health risk associated with the flu vaccination? If the subsidy is overestimated, too many vaccinations will be given. If it is underestimated, too few will be given.

SECTION RECAP
In theory, external costs can be internalized by imposing a tax equal to the marginal external cost on the generator of the externality. In a similar manner, positive externalities can be internalized by subsidizing the consumers of the good in question.

External Costs and Environmental Pollution

When one considers the concept of negative externalities, the first example that usually comes to mind is pollution. The tradeoffs involved in using air, water, and land as a waste dump have drawn increased attention in the last twenty-five years. Initially, research and legislation focused on the short-run and long-run health consequences of so-called classical air, water, and land pollutants.[2] More recently, attention has been focused on how to control the disposal of the enormous quantities of toxic wastes that are produced annually by U.S. industries. These latter pollutants include substances that are highly poisonous, such as arsenic, mercury, and polychlorinated biphenyls (PCBs).

When Is Pollution a Social Problem?

It is important to understand that not all air or water pollution is caused by production and consumption activities, and not all pollution endangers public welfare. Natural degradation of organic material in water can lead to foul-smelling streams and ponds. Lightning-induced forest fires and volcanic eruptions have contributed greatly to local and global air pollution. In turn, environmental media (such as the air and waterways) have a natural ability to absorb, or assimilate, some pollutants. In other words, the environment has some **assimilative capacity**. For example, some effluents dumped into a stream can be consumed by stream biota and rendered harmless. In a similar manner,

Assimilative capacity
The environment's natural ability to absorb or assimilate some pollutants.

---

[2]The term *classical air pollutants* is used to refer to the air pollutants initially regulated by the U.S. Environmental Protection Agency. These so-called criteria pollutants include carbon monoxide (CO), sulfur dioxide (SO_2), total suspended particulates (TSP), lead (Pb), nitrogen dioxide (NO_2), volatile organic compounds (VOCs) or hydrocarbons, and lower-atmosphere ozone (O_3).

air pollutants can be diluted as a result of the mixing and dispersion caused by air currents.

However, *when the discharge of a pollutant is so great that it exceeds the assimilative capacity of the environment, the pollutant becomes a social problem.* That is when we notice the impact of a production or consumption activity on social welfare.

Opportunity Cost of Improved Environmental Quality

One of the first lessons students learn in economics is that choices always involve tradeoffs. Yet when the question "What is the optimal amount of pollution?" is raised, the answer most students give is "Zero." We need to bear in mind, however, that the reduction of pollution requires investment in pollution-control capital (such as smokestack scrubbers for coal-fired electric utilities) and the use of additional resources that could have been used to produce other goods and services. *The opportunity cost of improved environmental quality is the amount of other goods forgone.* Again we are faced with choices. We cannot have both an increase in the output of goods and services and an increase in environmental quality without a change in technology or a change in the stock of resources.

Many people object to this seemingly cavalier acceptance of the consequences of pollution. However, so long as we continue to consume goods whose production generates at least some pollution, there *will* be some damage to vegetation, materials, and human health. The relevant question is not whether to eliminate pollution but whether the additional benefits from the goods we consume are greater than the additional cost of the pollution that is generated. A different, but equivalent, question is, Do the additional benefits of pollution control outweigh the additional costs incurred?

Individuals argue, nonetheless, that there is no way one could put a finite value on an increase in the chance of becoming ill, let alone on an increase in the chance of dying. This argument implies that human health and life have an infinite value. However, individuals' daily actions indicate otherwise. If you drive a car without wearing a seat belt, you increase the chance that you will suffer head injuries in the event of a head-on collision. If you eat foods that are not good for you, you increase the chance that you will die of heart disease, obesity, or cancer.

Almost everyone makes choices involving tradeoffs between enjoyment from consumption of goods and an increase in the chance he will become ill or die. This reveals that people do place a value that is considerably less than infinite on human health and life. The trouble is, we often deny that the choices we make convey any risk at all. However, denial does not make it so. Thus, it is important to recognize the implicit tradeoffs we make in our daily actions. Efficient decisions on the optimal level of environmental quality require a recognition of the tradeoffs involved.

Optimal Amount of Environmental Quality: Balancing Benefits and Costs

Figure 4 depicts the market for environment quality (EQ). The quantity (level) of environmental quality is measured on the horizontal axis. The market price per unit of environmental quality is measured on the vertical axis. An indi-

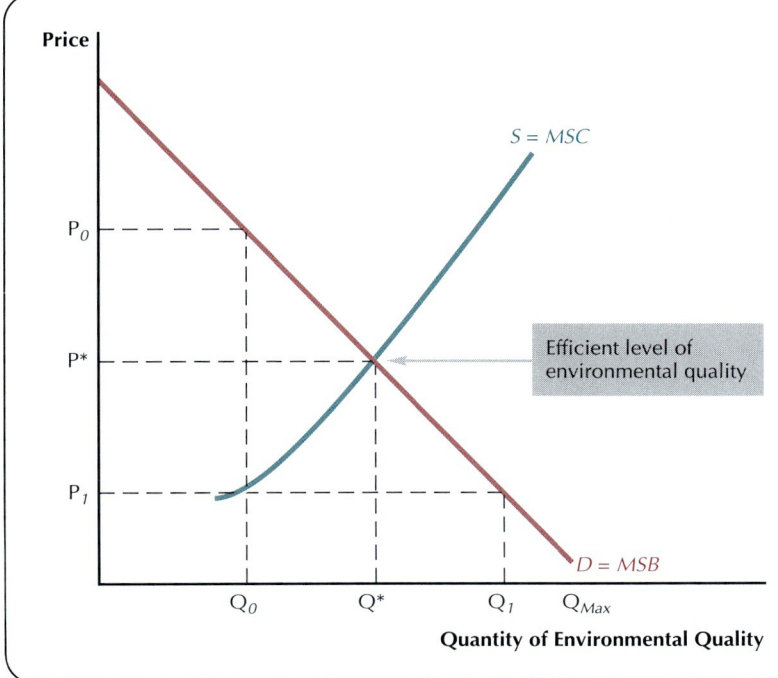

FIGURE 4
The socially efficient level of pollution control. This figure depicts the market for environmental quality (EQ), where EQ is measured as a *decrease* in sulfur dioxide emissions. The demand curve, D, represents society's willingness to pay for additional units of EQ—the marginal social benefits (MSB) of pollution control. The supply curve, S, represents the marginal social costs of pollution control (or increased EQ). The efficient level of pollution control occurs where MSB equals marginal cost, at Q^* units of EQ.

vidual's marginal benefit from environmental quality is measured by his or her willingness to pay for each additional unit. The demand curve, D, is the vertical sum of each individual's marginal benefits and represents the society's willingness to pay for additional units of environmental quality. It is, in fact, the marginal social benefits of pollution control. The horizontal sum of each firm's marginal private costs of producing environmental quality (that is, reducing pollution) is shown by the supply curve S and represents the marginal social costs of pollution control. The question we want to answer is, What is the optimal amount of environmental quality? Put another way, What is the optimal amount of pollution?

The belief that the optimal level of pollution is zero ignores two very important lessons about consumption. First, as you consume more of a good in a given time period, your willingness to pay for additional units of the good declines. In Figure 4, as environmental quality increases (that is, as pollution is reduced) each additional unit of environmental quality is valued less. At low levels of environmental quality, for example, Q_0, consumers are willing to pay P_0 for an additional unit of improvement. However, when the environment is less polluted, for example at Q_1, consumers are only willing to pay P_1 for an additional unit of improvement. Second, there are always tradeoffs. To have more environmental quality, resources must be diverted from the production and consumption of other goods. It is a technical fact that the marginal cost of controlling the emission of additional units of a given source of pollution usually increases. This is reflected in the upward slope of the supply curve of environmental quality.

For levels of environmental quality between 0 and Q^*, the additional benefits of increasing environmental quality exceed the additional costs of

Does It Make **Economic Sense?**

The Benefits and Costs of Reducing Pollution from Wood-Burning Stoves*

There was a time when wood-burning stoves were symbols of the back-to-nature movement. They were synonymous with the desire to turn away from the polluted atmosphere generated by large centralized power-generating stations. If everyone burned wood, there would be no need to heat one's home with the energy generated from coal-fired or nuclear-fired power plants. However, certain states and the federal government have recently begun to regulate the use of wood-burning stoves as an alternative source of heat. Given the commonly expressed desire to reduce the United States' dependence on foreign sources of energy, such as petroleum, as well as the amount of pollution generated by conventional sources of energy, does this make economic sense?

To answer this question it is important to note that, in fact, the solution has now become a problem: in some areas, wood-burning stoves are a major source of particulate pollution. Smoke pollution from wood-burning stoves first became a noticeable problem in the mountainous regions of Oregon, Colorado, Utah, and Vermont. On still, windless days the smoke remains trapped in the forests and valleys, throwing a smoglike pall over many rural areas. The average stove emits about 30 to 40 grams of particulates an hour, which can lead to a substantial amount of air pollution when a number of stoves are burning during a temperature inversion.

To address this problem, the Environmental Protection Agency has imposed regulations, modeled after Colorado and Oregon laws, that limit the average amount of particulates a stove may emit per hour. These regulations, which took effect in July 1988 and apply to stoves manufactured or sold after July 1988 allow only 5.5 grams of particulates an hour to be emitted from the flue of a stove equipped with a catalytic combustor. In July 1990, the allowable amount was dropped to 4.1 grams.

SECTION RECAP
Pollutants are a problem when they are discharged at a rate that exceeds the assimilative capacity of the environment. The economically efficient level of pollution control occurs at the point at which the marginal benefits and marginal costs of pollution control are equal.

doing so. At levels of environmental quality from Q^* to Q_{Max}, the additional costs of increasing environmental quality exceed the additional benefits of doing so. Hence, *the optimal amount of environmental quality is Q^*, where the marginal benefits equal the marginal costs*, which is, in this case, not at zero pollution (Q_{Max}).

Pollution-Control Policies

It is now time to take a look at how policies designed to internalize pollution externalities are formulated. Two different types of control policies are considered. The first approach is to use government regulation directly, through the setting of emission standards. The second approach is to establish the conditions under which the market may work toward the socially optimal equilibrium. This approach also uses government intervention, but indirectly, in the form of emission charges, transferable discharge permits, and specific property rights.

Direct Regulation The most direct way to reduce the incentive firms have to pollute is to forbid it outright through the use of an **emission (or effluent) standard.** An emission standard constitutes a legal limit on the amount of a pollutant an individual source is allowed to emit. Such a standard could, for example, require that a source emit, on average, no more than 235 micrograms per cubic meter of sulfur dioxide into the atmosphere during any one-hour period.

Emission standard
A legal limit on the amount of a pollutant an individual source is allowed to emit.

For stoves not equipped with a catalyst, the standards allowed 8.5 grams per hour until July 1990, when the standard dropped to 7.5 grams per hour.

To meet these standards, manufacturers must either equip all new stoves with a catalytic combustor or find some other way to reduce emissions significantly. The catalytic combustor cleans up the particulates in much the same way a catalytic converter works on automobile pollution. The smoke that would normally leave the stove is captured by the combustor and burned. In addition to burning many of the pollutants that would normally have escaped, this creates heat as well.

The regulation was predicted to add from $120 to $200 to the price of a stove equipped with a catalytic combustor. However, this additional expense not only reduces the external costs of using a wood-burning stove, it also reduces the private (or internal) costs. By burning the smoke, the combustor increases the fuel value of the wood used by 50 percent. This means that two cords of wood will provide the heat previously generated by three cords. The combustor also reduces, by 90 percent, the amount of creosote (sooty tar) that accumulates on the internal wall of the chimney. Because creosote is the major source of chimney fires, use of the combustor reduces the probability of a house fire.**

Clearly, the move to regulate the use of wood-burning stoves will result in benefits and costs. Depending upon the amount of money saved relative to other sources of energy, benefits may still exceed costs. In any event, the regulations described here represent an attempt to avoid simply trading one source of pollution for another.

*Adapted from Peter Tonge, "Clearing the Air," *Christian Science Monitor*, January 20, 1987, p. 29.

**To some people, the additional benefits from increased safety outweigh the additional cost. "Never mind the economics, safety is the most important contribution to come from the catalytic combustor," said one stove manufacturer. Do you find anything wrong with that statement?

Ideally a standard is set such that the resulting market equilibrium is the efficient equilibrium. This case is illustrated in Figure 5, which depicts the market for steel. Assuming that there are no external benefits from the consumption of steel, the demand curve, D, represents marginal social benefits (MSB). The sum of the individual producers' marginal private costs (MPC) is shown by the supply curve, S. However, the production of steel generates a number of air pollutants, most notably sulfur dioxide (SO_2). This results in external costs that cause marginal social costs (MSC) to exceed the marginal private costs of production by the amount C.

In the absence of intervention in the market, the steel industry will produce Q_P units of steel per year, to be sold at a market price of P_P dollars per unit. However, this solution is inefficient, since the production of Q_P units results in a marginal external cost of C dollars from the sulfur dioxide emissions. The efficient level of output and price are found where MSC = MSB, at Q_s units, and at a price of P_s dollars per unit. Once again, the privately determined output is greater than the efficient output, and the privately determined price is lower than the efficient price.

Suppose the government decides to impose an emission standard. The optimal standard should be set such that the industry's output of steel is Q_s units per year. To meet a given standard, each firm in the industry must install pollution-control equipment. Assuming this raises the marginal private cost of production, the market supply curve will shift to the left. If the standard increases marginal costs by the amount C, the industry's private optimum will be identical to the efficient level of output, Q_s, and will be sold at a price of

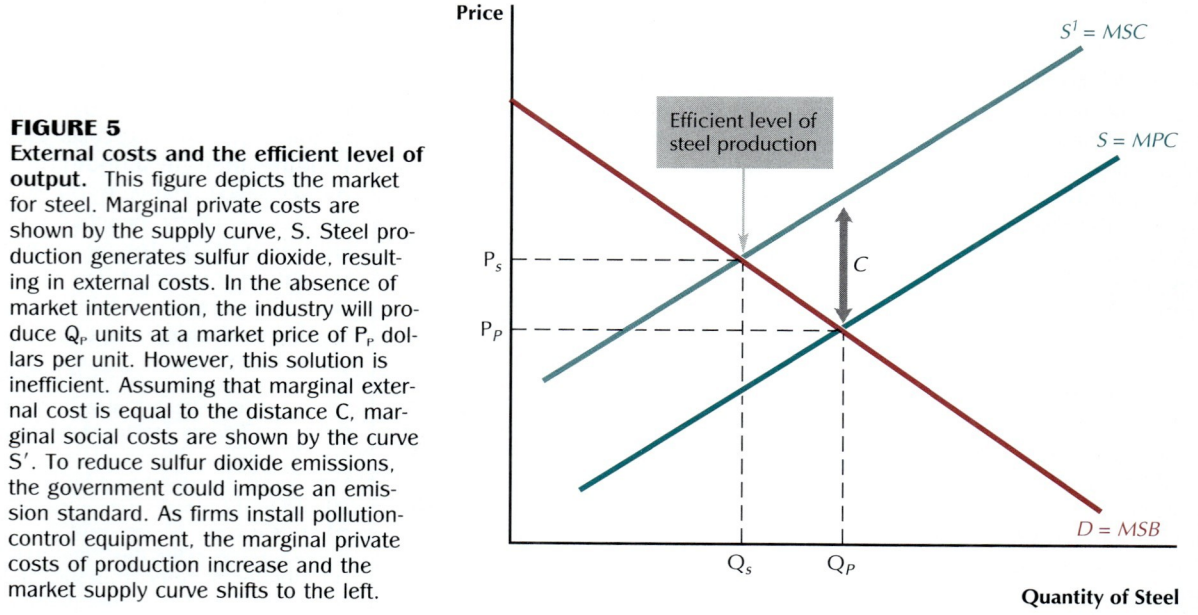

FIGURE 5
External costs and the efficient level of output. This figure depicts the market for steel. Marginal private costs are shown by the supply curve, S. Steel production generates sulfur dioxide, resulting in external costs. In the absence of market intervention, the industry will produce Q_P units at a market price of P_P dollars per unit. However, this solution is inefficient. Assuming that marginal external cost is equal to the distance C, marginal social costs are shown by the curve S'. To reduce sulfur dioxide emissions, the government could impose an emission standard. As firms install pollution-control equipment, the marginal private costs of production increase and the market supply curve shifts to the left.

P_s. Thus the emission standard eliminates the inefficiency associated with the production of steel.

It is easy to see the potential for the standard to be inefficient. If the emissions standard is set too low (is too restrictive) and results in marginal compliance costs greater than C, the supply curve will shift too far to the left, and output will be inefficient (too low). If the standard is set too high (is not restrictive enough), the supply curve will not shift far enough to the left, and output will again be inefficient (too high).

Another source of inefficiency with the standards approach stems from the fact that emission standards are usually uniform across firms. However, individual firms are not likely to face the same pollution control costs, and the external costs of pollution are not likely to be as high in rural areas as they are in urban areas. This implies that the marginal social benefits and the marginal costs of pollution control vary across firms. For efficiency, emission standards should be stricter for firms that can reduce pollution at lower cost or are located in heavily populated areas than for firms with higher control costs or sparse surrounding populations.

However, setting different standards for different size firms and firms in different areas is an administrative nightmare that would greatly increase the already high cost of setting and enforcing emission standards. In response, economists have developed alternative approaches the government can use to promote an efficient level of pollution, approaches which recognize differences in individual firms' cost of control and differences in the social cost of pollution.

Incentives-Based Mechanisms As an alternative to direct regulation, the government can obtain the same result at a lower cost by creating financial disincentives to pollute. It can also create property rights where none existed previously. If these property rights are well specified, the generators of an externality will have an incentive to reduce pollution to the efficient level, again at a lower cost.

When producers are charged an amount equal to the external cost their production imposes on others, they have an incentive to reduce their output to a more efficient level. Thus, the government can use **emission charges** to reduce pollution. Emission charges consist of taxes on the pollution emitted by a firm. The tax can be set as a per-unit tax, in which case each firm's marginal private cost rises by the amount of the tax or the per-unit cost of pollution abatement—whichever is less. Referring to Figure 5, a tax equal to the marginal external cost, C, would raise the marginal private costs of production and cause a leftward shift in the industry supply curve from S to S'. As a result of the tax, the industry would reduce output to Q_s.

One of the problems with emission charges is knowing at exactly which level to set the tax. In practice, the information needed to determine the marginal external cost of production is extremely difficult to obtain. In the absence of knowledge of the exact increase in each firm's marginal private cost that would be necessary to drive output (and, hence, pollution) to the efficient level, the control agency must take a hit-and-miss approach. It must set a tax, monitor the resulting level of pollution, and compare that level with the efficient one. If the new output is still too high, the tax must be increased. If the new output is too low, the tax must be lowered.

As an alternative to emissions charges, the government can establish a program of **transferable discharge permits (TDP)**. A TDP program creates a market for pollution rights. If a firm wants to dump effluent into a stream or emit carbon monoxide into the air, it must now pay for the right to do so. The government essentially has created a property right to a good for which property rights had not been established previously.

A TDP program works as follows: First, the control agency must set a limit on the total amount of the pollutant that can be generated and released into the environment. Second, the control agency must issue permits to affected firms. These permits entitle the bearer to emit a specified amount of pollution per period. For example, each permit might allow the holder to dump one pound of effluent per day into a nearby river. Without a permit, a firm may not discharge any effluent into the river.

Permits can be issued by the pollution-control agency in a number of ways. They can be sold to the highest bidder, given away on a first-come-first-served basis, or divided evenly among existing firms. *With respect to efficiency, it does not matter how the permits are issued. What does matter is that the permit owners must have the right to transfer their ownership of the permit to someone else.* (Note, however, that the way in which the permits are initially distributed will affect the distribution of income.)

Figure 6 illustrates the effect of a TDP program. Assume the control agency sets the pollution limit at Q^* units per year. It will then create only enough permits to allow Q^* units to be emitted. Therefore, the supply of permits is a vertical line at Q^*. The MB curve is the affected firms' demand curve for permits. The market-clearing price for permits is found where the supply of permits (S_P) and the demand for permits (D_P) intersect, at P^* dollars. If a firm's marginal pollution control cost is greater than P^*, it would be cheaper to buy the necessary permits at the market price of P^* dollars each than to pay the additional control costs. If a firm's marginal pollution control cost is less than

Emission charge
A tax imposed on each unit of pollution emitted by a firm.

Transferable discharge permit (TDP)
A property right to discharge a specified quantity of a particular pollutant; it can be traded among affected parties.

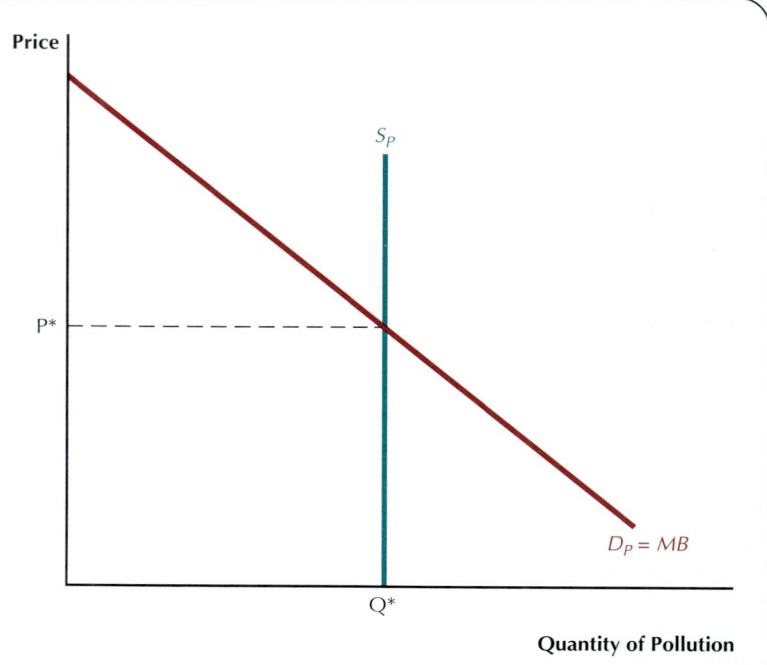

FIGURE 6
The equilibrium price of TDPs. Suppose the control agency sets the pollution limit at Q^* units per year. It will then create only enough permits to allow Q^* units to be emitted. Therefore the supply of permits is a vertical line at Q^*. The MB curve is the affected firms' demand curve for permits. The market-clearing price occurs where the supply of permits (S_P) and the demand for permits (D_P) intersect, at P^* dollars.

Offset program
Allows a new pollution source in a particular geographic region to pay existing sources to reduce their emissions below that required by the existing standard, in lieu of installing control technology at the new plant.

Bubble policy
Treats a group of closely situated pollution sources as if they were encased in a giant bubble; the pollution standard then applies to emissions coming out of the bubble.

Emission banking
A program that grants a firm credit for reducing emissions below the existing standard; the credit can be saved for later use or for sale to another firm.

P^*, it would be cheaper to pay the additional control costs rather than buy the permits at the market price of P^* dollars each.

Emissions charges and TDP programs constitute two alternatives to the standards approach to pollution control. In addition, the U.S. Environmental Protection Agency has recently begun to implement a number of reforms of its air pollution control program. Three innovations currently in operation reflect a move toward greater use of economic incentives — the offset program, the bubble policy, and emission banking.

The **offset program** allows new air pollution sources in a particular geographic region to pay existing sources to reduce their emissions below that required by the standard in lieu of installing control technology at the new plant, so long as the total level of the pollutant does not increase. This program enables new sources to find the least expensive way to reduce pollution in the geographic region. So long as the air quality in the region is better after the new plant moves in, the offset is allowed.

The **bubble policy** attempts to treat a number of closely situated sources, usually within a given production facility, as if they were encased in a giant bubble. The standard then applies to emissions coming out of the bubble. This allows a firm to reduce emissions from those sources within the production facility that are the cheapest to control and to relax controls on the more costly sources. The firm can thus attain the standard at a reduced cost. The only restriction is that tradeoffs may only be made between sources emitting the same pollutant.

The **emission banking** program gives firms credit for reducing emissions below the emissions level allowed by the standard. This credit is then deposited in an emissions bank for later use or for sale to another firm. This approach

Why the **Disagreement?**

Reauthorization of the Clean Air Act*

When the Congress amended the Clean Air Act in 1977, it was intended that this legislation would result in a significant improvement in the level of air quality in the United States. However, as time passed it became clear that additional legislation was needed to generate the degree of reductions in air emissions that had been sought previously. By 1990, the air emissions of only seven toxic chemicals, of which there are hundreds, had been regulated. In addition, acid rain, chlorofluorocarbons, and particulates emissions continue to pose a significant threat to human health and environmental quality.

Most individuals agree that additional steps must be taken to clean up the atmosphere and reduce the amount of air emissions that are generated annually. While the U.S. public expresses a wide range of divergent opinions regarding issues such as national defense and aid to the poor, there is a broad consensus that improvement of environmental quality—including air quality—should be a major priority for policymakers. However, despite this widespread agreement, there has been continuing disagreement over who should be responsible for cleanup and to what extent. This disagreement was most evident in the recent debate over reauthorization of the Clean Air Act. Why the disagreement? Clearly, industry will be required to bear the initial burden of reducing the amount of air pollution that is generated. Analysts have put the cost of the new Clean Air Act legislation that was passed in late 1990 at $25 billion annually by the year 2005. While agreeing that improvements in air quality will be costly, however, specific industries disagree over who should do the most to reduce air emissions. For example, when the new legislation was being debated, the steel industry argued that under most proposals it would be forced to bear a disproportionate share of the burden of cleanup. Industry representatives estimated that proposed legislation would cost the industry in excess of $5 billion by 1995. This, they argue, would hurt their competitiveness by taking money away from efforts at modernization.

The coal industry argued that certain provisions of proposed legislation would result in substantial employment of coal miners. Indeed, it has been estimated that the legislation that was finally passed could result in the loss of as many as 15,000 coal mining jobs by the year 2000. These job losses are a result of the effort to reduce acid rain by limiting the amount of sulfur dioxide that is emitted into the atmosphere by electric utility plants fueled by high-sulfur coal. Along these same lines, many midwest electric utilities, which are the major users of high-sulfur coal, argued that they will bear a disproportionate share of the burden associated with efforts to reduce acid rain.

Automobile manufacturers also disagreed with the types of steps that were proposed to reduce auto emissions. Many proposals contained provisions that would require a certain percentage of new cars to use alternative fuels, such as natural gas, by specified dates. Automobile manufacturers lobbied instead for a program that would rely on reformulated gasoline. Note that this would minimize the amount of work that must be done to modify engines to run on the new fuels. However, oil companies countered that it would be extremely difficult, if not impossible, to reformulate gas and cut emissions significantly in a relatively short period of time. The final legislation requires both development of vehicles that run on alternative fuels and reformulation of gasoline to reduce emissions of hydrocarbons and toxic pollutants.

The disagreement among industry representatives was exacerbated by calls from environmental group lobbyists for stricter measures than those that had been proposed. In many cases, environmentalists argued, the proposed restrictions did not go far enough to provide an adequate margin of safety for the environment and human health. For many individuals, cost should not be an issue. They point out that, in many cases, once a certain level of damage is incurred, no amount of expenditure will be capable of restoring environmental quality to its previous level. This is especially true in cases where pollution results in the extinction of a particular plant or animal species.

It is still too soon to consider here the actual effects that the requirements of the new Clean Air Act will have on the economy, human health, and the environment. However, it is certain that the new law will impose substantial costs on U.S. industry. It is also clear, given the forces of supply and demand, that although some industries will incur greater costs than others, ultimately many of these costs will be borne by U.S. consumers.

*R. Gutfeld and B. Rosewicz, "Sky War," *The Wall Street Journal*, April 4, 1990, p. A1, and B. Rosewicz, "Price Tag Is Producing Groans Already," *The Wall Street Journal*, October 9, 1990, p. A7.

SECTION RECAP
Government can use direct regulation or incentives-based mechanisms, such as taxes or transferable discharge permits, to control pollution. The latter approach achieves the same level of control at lower cost and is more efficient.

Public good
A good whose consumption is nonrival and nonexcludable; markets will not produce the efficient level of public goods.

gives existing firms an incentive to adopt new, cost-saving pollution-control technologies. The resulting emissions reduction can be banked and used on days when the control technology is not functioning properly, used to temporarily expand the plant's operations, or sold to a new firm wishing to locate in the area.

Public Goods

Most of the goods we buy are produced by private firms and are referred to as *private* goods. However, a number of goods we consume are not produced by private firms but instead by public agencies. Examples include national defense, lighthouses, national parks, and police and fire protection. These are examples of **public goods**. A number of other goods have characteristics of both public and private goods and are often referred to as *quasi-public goods*. Public roads, education, and libraries are all examples of quasi-public goods.

Public goods differ from private goods in two important ways. First, public goods are *nonrival*. Rivalry does not exist among consumers of public goods because one person's consumption of the good does not diminish the amount available for anyone else. National defense and police protection are good examples of public goods. The benefits I receive from these services do not reduce the benefits you receive. In fact, we are consuming the same good at the same time.

A second difference between public goods and private goods is that public goods are *nonexcludable*. This means that the benefits from consumption of public goods are available to all regardless of whether they pay for the good. If the government builds a dam to reduce the chance of flooding in a particular area, everyone who lives downstream from the dam is protected. In addition, the level of benefits each individual receives does not depend on the amount he or she contributes to any taxes raised to construct the dam. Nonexcludability is present whenever it is prohibitively expensive (if not impossible) to exclude individuals from using the good once it has been made available for consumption.

Determining the Optimal Quantity of Public Goods

The production of public goods clearly generates external benefits. Consequently, as we have already seen, the market will not provide the optimal amount of the public good. In fact, it is often the case that the market would not provide the public good *at all*. This is the rationale behind government provision of public goods. As with any good that produces external benefits, the optimum quantity is found where the marginal social cost, MSC, of production equals the marginal social benefit, MSB, of consumption. Determining the MSB of public goods, however, requires taking a different approach to aggregating, or adding together, individual demand curves. This difference is illustrated in Figures 7 and 8.

Individual demand curves are summed horizontally to determine the market demand curve for a private good. Figures 7 (a) and 7 (b) show the marginal benefit two individuals each derive from consumption of increasing amounts of a private good. Market demand is simply the horizontal sum of the individuals' demand curves, as shown in Figure 7 (c).

An important distinction between private goods and public goods concerns the effects of one individual's consumption on the consumption of another

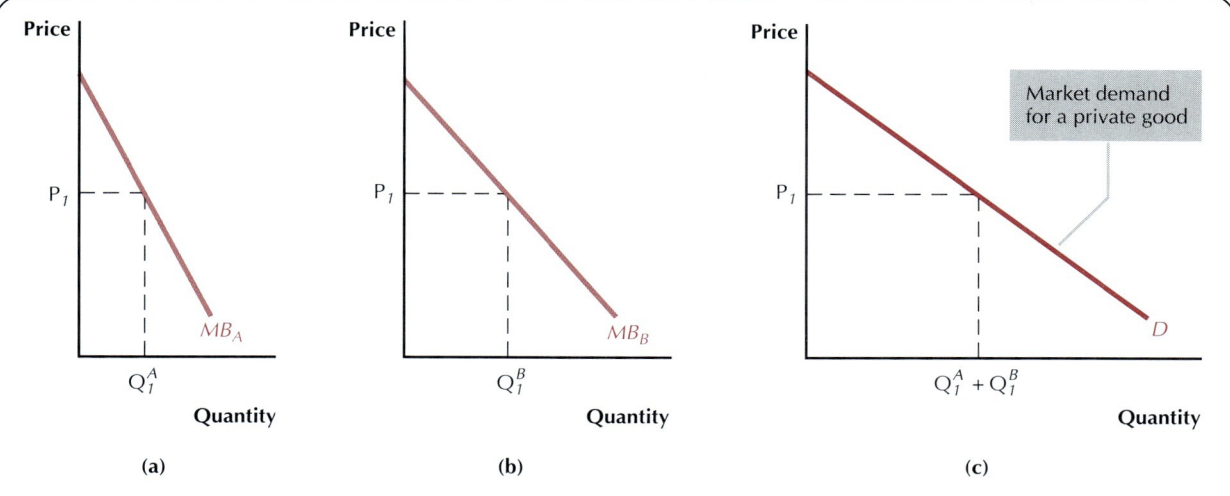

FIGURE 7
Determination of the market demand curve for a private good. Figure 7 (a) and Figure 7 (b) show the additional benefit each of two individuals derives from consumption of increasing amounts of a private good. The curve in each panel is simply the demand curve for each individual. The market demand curve is the horizontal sum of the individuals' demand curves, as shown in Figure 7 (c). For a private good, the market demand curve shows how much of the good will be purchased at a given price.

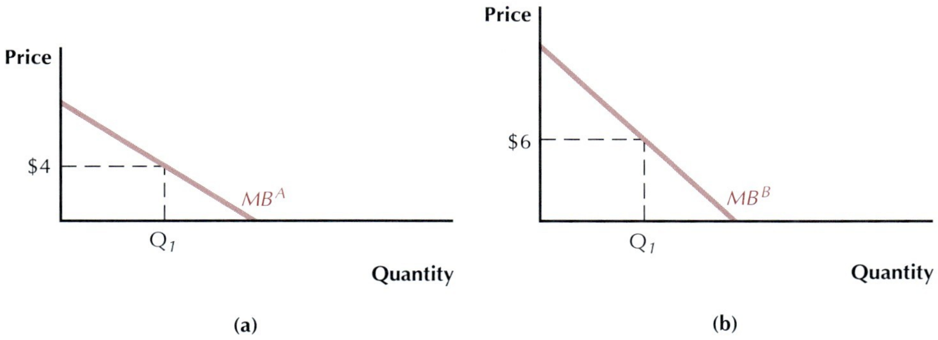

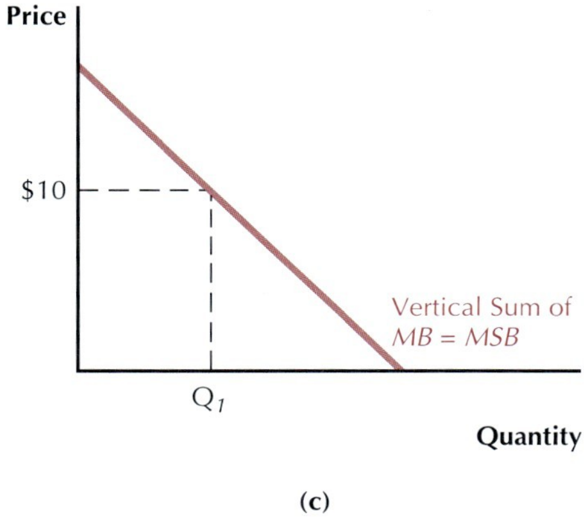

FIGURE 8
Determination of the market demand curve for a public good. Determining the market demand for a public good is illustrated in this figure. Figure 8 (a) and Figure 8 (b) show the marginal private benefits two individuals receive from consuming a public good. The marginal social benefit of any given amount (unit) of the public good is found by adding up the marginal private benefits enjoyed by each of the consumers. Thus, Figure 8 (c) indicates the marginal social benefits for each unit of the public good. This is the amount that society would be willing to pay, as a whole, for that unit of the public good.

individual. A private good can only be consumed by one person. If I buy a shirt, you and I cannot consume it (wear it) at the same time. This is the logic behind horizontal summation. At a given price, the marginal private benefit received by each individual is summed to obtain the marginal social benefit of the good for the market as a whole.

In contrast, a public good can be consumed by more than one individual simultaneously. As we noted above, my consumption of national defense does not reduce the amount available for you to consume. As a result, *the marginal social benefit of a unit of a public good equals the vertical sum of the marginal private benefits of the individual consumers.* That is, it is equal to the total amount that all the individuals involved are willing to pay to consume the *same* unit of the public good.

Figures 8 (a) and 8 (b) show the marginal private benefits two individuals receive from consuming a public good. The marginal social benefit of any given amount of the public good is determined by adding up the marginal private benefits enjoyed by each of the consumers. As shown in Figures 8 (a) and 8 (b), for Q_1 units of the public good, individuals A and B derive marginal benefits of \$4 and \$6, respectively. Thus the marginal social benefit of Q_1 units of the public good is the vertical summation of the individual marginal benefits, or \$10, as shown in Figure 8 (c).

It is important to understand that the marginal social benefit curve for a public good is *not* a demand curve in the usual sense. Individuals 1 and 2 would not be willing to pay \$10 each to consume the first unit of the public good. However, because the sum of their willingness to pay totals \$10, if the good can be provided at a marginal cost of \$10 or less, the combined payments of both individuals would be enough to cover the additional cost of providing it.

> **SECTION RECAP**
> Due to nonrivalry and nonexcludability, the private sector cannot be relied on to produce public goods. Consequently, the government must intervene. The optimal quantity of a public good is determined by equating marginal cost with aggregate marginal willingness to pay.

The Problem of Free Riders

In the old west, when a rancher's livestock was threatened by rustlers the other ranchers would band together and ride the fences to discourage thieves. Everyone contributed to this public good (increased security). However, over time, individual ranchers began to realize that they would get the same protection regardless of the number of hours spent with the posse. As a result, they began spending less time riding, or dropped out of the group altogether. These ranchers became known as **free riders** for their failure to contribute to the safety provided for them by others. The behavior of the free riders led eventually to the dissolution of the group and an increase in the amount of cattle rustling.

Note that each individual rancher who dropped out of the posse was behaving rationally. If one individual failed to contribute to the provision of the good, he would still be able to enjoy the benefits. However, what is rational behavior for the individual turns out to be disastrous if followed by all. As another example of free riders, consider households that watch public television shows regularly (or listen to public radio shows regularly) but never contribute during the station's fund-raising drives.

Free rider
An individual who receives benefits from a public good but does not pay for those benefits.

Policy Prescriptions

Because public goods are nonexcludable, individuals cannot be prevented from consuming them, even if they are free riders. However, if everyone acts as a free rider, the public good will not be produced. (This is the reason public radio and television stations rely so heavily on government support.) Thus, the role of a fully informed government is to recognize the social benefits of public goods and establish policies that set marginal social benefits equal to marginal social costs so that the efficient level of the public good will be provided.

One approach the government can use to encourage the efficient level of output of public goods is to subsidize the producers of the public good (as is the case with public radio and television stations). A subsidy to producers serves to reduce the marginal cost of producing the public good. If an omniscient government offered the correct subsidy, the optimum number of programs would be produced. However, determining the correct subsidy is extremely difficult in actual practice — government is not omniscient. A second approach is for the government to produce the good. Production is financed by tax revenues. Indeed, this is how many of the public goods we consume — national defense, public roads, and national parks to name a few — are produced.

Common-Property Resources

Just as public goods generate positive externalities, another class of goods generates negative externalities when consumed. These goods are referred to as **common-property resources**. Property rights to common-property resources are not clearly specified, or they do not exist at all. Examples include the air, oceans, common grazing land (commons), and fisheries. Because no one has property rights to these resources, they tend to be overexploited.

Garrett Hardin[3] used the example of open grazing areas, or commons, to illustrate the tendency of producers to overexploit common-property resources. The commons was usually an open field near a town where livestock owners were allowed to graze their animals without charge. Each individual had an incentive to consider only the additional benefits and costs to him of feeding another animal on the commons before letting the animal graze there. Because the additional cost to the individual was virtually zero, grazing increased until the commons was denuded of grass and was of no benefit to anyone. Thus, the increased grazing imposed an external cost on other users of the commons.

The "tragedy of the commons," as Hardin labeled it, is that the failure to limit the use of common-property resources will result in their overuse or destruction. Thus, the problem of overgrazing is another example of external costs of production. Because the private cost of using common-property resources is lower than the social cost, the amount of the resource used is too high. Figure 9 shows this result for the market for another common-property resource, lobsters. The horizontal axis measures the number of lobsters caught per year. The vertical axis measures the dollar value of the additional benefits from the costs of harvesting lobsters.

Assuming no external benefits from the harvesting of lobsters, MSB shows the marginal social benefits of harvesting. The marginal private cost of harvesting the lobsters is shown by the curve labeled MPC. Left alone, the market will generate an equilibrium harvest of Q_P. The marginal external cost of

Common-property resource
A resource for which property rights are poorly defined or nonexistent and whose consumption results in a negative externality.

[3]Garrett Hardin, "The Tragedy of the Commons," *Science*, Vol. 162, December 13, 1968, pp. 1243–1248.

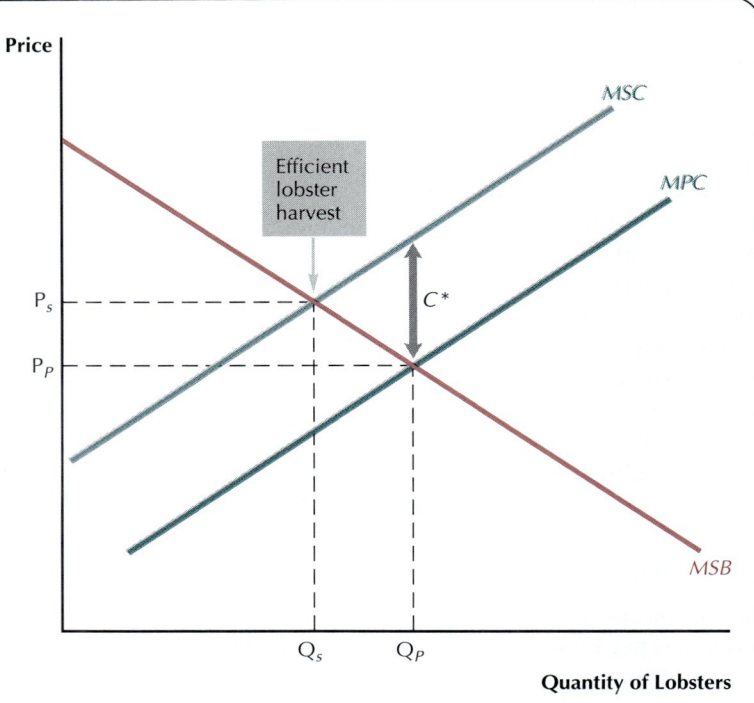

FIGURE 9
MEC in the case of a common-property resource. This figure depicts the market for lobsters. The curve labeled MSB shows the marginal social benefits of harvesting lobsters. The marginal private cost of harvesting the lobsters is shown by MPC. In the absence of intervention into the market, the equilibrium quantity Q_P will be harvested. The marginal external cost of harvesting a lobster today, which is equal to the losses suffered by future fishermen who will have fewer lobsters to harvest, is equal to C^* as indicated in the graph. Hence, the efficient harvest occurs where MSB = MSC, at Q_s lobsters per year.

harvesting a lobster today is equal to the losses suffered by future fishermen who will have fewer lobsters to harvest. (As additional lobsters are harvested today, the number of lobsters that can procreate is reduced. Future populations will therefore be smaller, *ceteris paribus*.) This marginal external cost is equal to C^* as indicated in Figure 9. When this external cost is added to the private costs, the socially efficient harvest occurs where marginal social benefit equals marginal social cost, at Q_s lobsters per year.

SECTION RECAP

Because of the potential for overexploitation of common property resources, it is often necessary for the government to intervene in the market to encourage efficient use of such resources.

Policy Prescription

One approach to generating a market solution is to tax the fisherman an amount equal to C^*, the external cost of harvesting. In this way the producer has an incentive to reduce harvests to the efficient level Q_s. However, the problem that once again arises is trying to determine the correct value of C^*. Without this information it is likely that the tax ultimately imposed will result in a level of harvests that is either greater or less than the efficient level.

Cost of Information

Decisions Made in Ignorance

The primary sources of market failure in each of the examples discussed above are the absence of a clearly defined set of property rights and a lack of information. In those situations in which there are no clearly defined property rights to the air, for example, producers make a decision to compensate no one for any of the air pollution they generate. In other cases, the property right in question may not be assigned initially to the party who values it most. In either of these cases, an inefficient allocation of resources is the likely outcome — especially where the number of affected parties is large.

Likewise, without knowledge of the extent to which individuals derive benefits from consuming specific public goods the market will not, in all likelihood, generate the efficient level of output of such goods. As we have seen, decisions made without this information result in an inefficient output level and price. A lack of information is also the source of some of the major problems with implementing such policy prescriptions as taxes and subsidies.

Each of the policy actions discussed above assumed perfect information on the part of the government. The dollar value of the external costs of a production or consumption activity, the dollar value of the external benefit associated with a public good, and the future social cost associated with overuse of a common property resource all must be known with certainty so that the government can establish the correct tax, subsidy, or restrictions on use.

Efficiency Considerations

Decision makers must search for and evaluate the information referred to above. One common technique is called **cost–benefit analysis**. Efficiency requires considering the costs and benefits of policies aimed at eliminating external costs, increasing the provision of public goods, or avoiding overuse of common-property resources.

Cost–benefit analysis The identification and evaluation of all the costs and benefits associated with a particular public policy alternative.

Cost–benefit analysis is used to provide decision makers with information that will help them make efficient choices regarding the reallocation of resources. It is essentially a sophisticated version of what you do when you decide whether to skip economics to study for your calculus exam. You weigh the costs of skipping — important information missed, ability to get class notes, and so on — against the benefits of spending the additional time studying for the calculus exam. If the estimated benefits outweigh the estimated costs, you skip the class and study calculus.

Cost–benefit analyses start from this point of view and go one step further by attempting to place a dollar value on the costs and benefits of public policies. For example,[4] suppose a local planning board wants to know whether it is worthwhile to build a bridge connecting their small island to the mainland. Travel to and from the island is now completed by ferry. The bridge would be a public good so, to avoid free ridership, a bridge toll or a local tax would have to be imposed to finance the project. To make a rational choice, the planners need to:

1. Identify the effects of the project.
2. Value the costs and benefits.
3. Adjust the costs and benefits for equity considerations.
4. Evaluate alternative projects.

First the board must identify the impacts of the project on the local economy. Who will be affected and in what way? Will the bridge cause additional

---

[4]This example is adapted from William C. Apgar and H. James Brown, *Microeconomics and Public Policy* (Glenview, IL: Scott Foresman, 1987), pp. 344–359.

problems as well as solve the traffic flow problem? The next step is to quantify the costs and benefits to all parties affected by the project. Once the costs and benefits of the proposed project have been determined, the board must compare the gains and losses.

Equity Considerations

One way to make this comparison is to give the benefits and costs equal weight and approve the project if the benefits of building the bridge exceed the costs. However, giving the benefits and costs equal weight may cause problems. Suppose the benefits accrue to a small group of off-island travelers and tourists and the costs are borne by the citizens of the island. What if the costs accrue right away but the benefits will not be enjoyed for several years? If the existence of the bridge puts the ferry operators out of business, what would happen if the bridge should one day fail (due to a violent coastal storm)?

In such cases, the costs and benefits must be adjusted for equity considerations, the fact that costs and benefits accrue at different times, and the increased risks involved in relying on the bridge. This adjustment process is accomplished by weighting each of the factors being considered. It is in the attempt to determine these weights that the greatest disagreement over the results of cost-benefit analysis occurs. Those bearing the costs want the costs to be weighted more heavily. Those enjoying the benefits want the benefits to be weighted more heavily. Those fighting against the project want future benefits to be weighted less heavily.

Policy Prescriptions

It is important to identify and, to the extent possible, quantify all the costs and benefits of a proposed policy so that they can be viewed in a common light. Not surprisingly, however, it is often difficult to put a dollar value on some benefits (and costs), even though they are very important. For example, suppose reducing the amount of toxic material dumped in a local landfill would result in a decrease in the number of birth defects experienced near the landfill. What dollar value do we place on the reduction in the number of birth defects? Where such situations arise, even though quantification of all benefits and costs may not be possible, it is nonetheless useful to recognize the additional sources of costs and benefits. This is because it is often conceivable that, depending upon the potential magnitude of these unknown values, the conclusions of a cost–benefit analysis could be reversed.

The limitations of cost–benefit analysis do not imply that it is useless. Relative to decisions made in ignorance, or on the basis of emotional feelings toward the situation, or for political favor, cost–benefit analysis is an important source of information for policy makers. It is one way to promote rational choice outside the market mechanism.

SECTION RECAP
Government decision making on programs designed to internalize externalities, to increase the provision of public goods, or to reduce the overexploitation of common property resources can be improved by cost–benefit analysis. However, determining the costs and benefits of policy options can be very difficult.

Opportunities for Collective Action

The Challenge of Good Public Policy

Good public policy requires evaluating the additional costs and benefits of policy actions. However, as we have seen, this is not always easy. The task of making good policy decisions is made even more difficult when a decision must be made with less-than-adequate information. The alternative to making a decision based on less-than-adequate information is to do nothing at all while new information is gathered.

An excellent example of this type of dilemma is found in the case of potentially toxic substances. With the ever-increasing production, use, and disposal of hazardous substances, policymakers must face another tradeoff. While additional information is gathered on the potential costs and benefits of controlling the production, consumption, and disposal of toxic substances, more lives may be threatened. The decision maker must then weigh the perceived costs of waiting for more complete information against the perceived benefits of such information.

The Complications of Political Behavior

The formulation of good public policy can also be hampered by the political climate in which it is engendered. The government often finds it necessary to collect taxes to provide a public good, or to give an individual an incentive to internalize an external cost. However, the response of the majority of those taxed is invariably negative.

For example, suppose the government wants to increase the public accessibility of our national forests. If it wishes to imitate the market's provision of this public good it will set a tax such that the total marginal private benefits enjoyed by the consumers of a given level of the public good equal the marginal social cost of providing it. However, this approach will quickly run into trouble. Because access to a national forest is a public good, everyone will receive the same amount of the good for any given tax. However, although consumers receive the same quantity, they do not all enjoy the same marginal private benefit. (Think of the difference in marginal valuation that would be given by an environmentalist and an antienvironmentalist.)

If the government taxed each individual according to his marginal private benefit, enough money would be raised to provide the optimal amount of the public good. However, this approach is bound to run into the problem of free riders, since individuals have an incentive to understate their marginal private benefit. Hence any attempt by the government to set a charge equal to each individual's marginal private benefit will most likely result in failure.

The upshot of the above example is that, although the imposition of a single tax on all users will be inefficient from the individual's perspective, it does help to get around the problem of free riders. In addition, it is obviously much easier, and probably fairer given the free rider problem, to charge everyone the same fee.

Summary

Normal market transactions involve an exchange of **property rights.** If property rights, to clean air for example, are not well defined no such exchange is possible and anyone may use the air as he or she wishes. This is true even if one individual's use of the air reduces another individual's ability to use it as well.

Costs or benefits of a production or consumption activity that affect other people's welfare are called externalities. An **external cost** is an unintended cost imposed on some third party or individual. An **external benefit** is an unintended benefit enjoyed by some third party or individual. In the presence of either of these externalities the result is an inefficient level of output.

Pollution is one example of an external cost that most everyone is familiar with. The optimal level of pollution is not always zero. The optimal level of environmental quality is found by comparing the marginal benefits of controlling pollution to the marginal costs of doing so.

The marginal cost of an increase in environmental quality is measured in terms of opportunity costs, the value of goods that must be forgone to reallocate resources to the production of pollution control. Marginal benefits are measured by society's willingness to pay for the improvement in environmental quality.

Pollution control policies include direct regulation, such as **emission standards** that place a legal limit on the amount of specific pollutants. Policies are also available that promote an optimal level of environmental quality without sacrificing economic efficiency. These policies include **emission charges** — taxes on the output of firms that pollute excessively, **transferable discharge permits,** which create a market for environmental quality and allow the market to determine each firm's level of pollution control responsibility, or some form of **emissions banking, offset,** or **bubble program.**

Public goods are another source of market failure. Unlike private goods, public goods are *nonexcludable* — you cannot be excluded from consuming a public good if you do not pay for it. They are also *nonrival* — one person's consumption of the good does not diminish the amount available for anyone else to consume. Given the nature of public goods and the problem of **free riders,** private firms cannot be relied on to produce the optimum quantity of public goods.

Just as public goods generate external benefits, the consumption of **common-property resources** generates external costs. Common-property resources do not have clearly specified property rights, hence they tend to be overexploited, that is, consumed without concern for the availability of future stocks.

Questions for Thought

Knowledge Questions

1. State in your own words what the term *externalities* means.
2. How do public and private goods differ? Illustrate this difference graphically.
3. According to the Coase Theorem, under what conditions is government regulation of externalities unnecessary?
4. In your own words, describe how a program of transferable discharge permits would operate.

Application Questions

5. Until the nineteenth century, a vast herd of bison roamed the Great Plains. Now what few bison are left are in zoos and private reserves. What factor contributed most to their relative extinction?

6. "The optimal level of air pollution is zero. So long as someone is suffering from the effects of air pollution it must be reduced—regardless of the cost." Do you agree or disagree with this statement? Explain why.
7. A new lead smelter opens at the edge of town. It produces 1000 tons of lead ingots per year, at a cost of $100,000. The smelter also emits lead particles into the air over the town. As a consequence of this air pollution the townspeople find their medical bills rising by $17,000; their wages fall by $6000 from lost work due to being ill; and their house-painting expenses rise by $2000. What are the marginal private, marginal external, and marginal social costs of producing the 1000 tons of lead ingots? (Let one ton = one unit of lead ingots.)
8. Suppose the town imposes a per-unit tax of $25 on the output of the firm in question 7. (Assume one unit is equal to one ton of ingots.) What effect would this have on the firm's output? On the price paid for lead ingots? On the social costs of production of lead?

Synthesis Questions

9. How are the gains and losses from public policy programs designed to internalize external costs shared? (Be careful—this is not as easy as you may think.)
10. Competitive firms earn zero economic profits in the long run. Does this imply that the imposition of an emission charge will result in all of the firms going out of business?
11. In this chapter we have demonstrated that the optimal level of pollution is rarely zero. Do you think this argument also applies to other social ills, such as crime? Could we also argue that the optimal level of risk is also rarely zero? If your answers differ, explain why; if they do not differ, explain why not.

OVERVIEW

In the past few decades, economists have used economic theory to study all sorts of nontraditional issues. One area receiving a growing amount of attention has been the area of political decision making. Following the lead of Anthony Downs, James Buchanan, and Gordon Tullock, a host of economists has investigated the behavior of so-called political markets using both theoretical models and statistical techniques. In this chapter we survey the economic approach to analyzing political decision making, an approach known as public choice analysis.

Economic analysis is built on the premise that individuals maximize something. The next section applies the maximization principle to elected officials and voters.

Public Choice

We examine the conditions necessary for efficient outcomes in the legislative marketplace and discuss features of the political process that prevent effective competition and lead to inefficient outcomes. This discussion revolves around the costs and benefits to voters of being informed about political decisions and the existence of special-interest groups that carry weight beyond the numbers of voters they represent.

We turn next to the theory of bureaucracy and to a survey of the evidence on the relative efficiency of public service providers compared to private companies providing the same types of services. Finally, we examine the burgeoning area known as constitutional economics — the study of the optimal rules with which to constrain governmental behavior.

The purpose of this chapter is to demonstrate that a number of competing forces influence the manner in which government policy is actually carried out.

CHAPTER 20

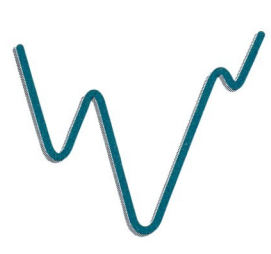

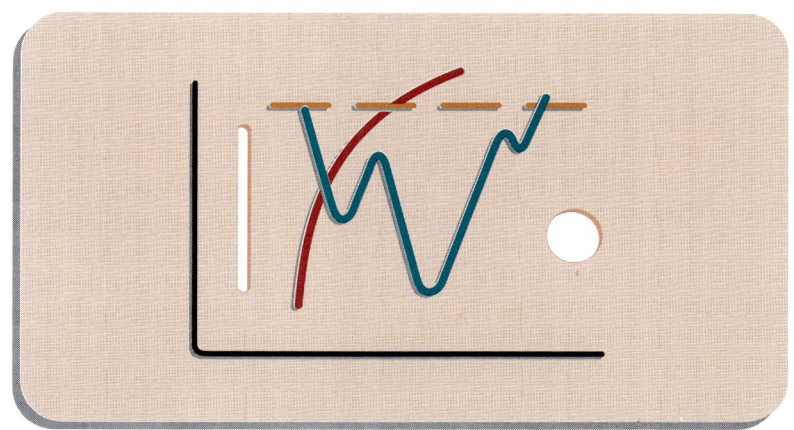

Government intervention does not automatically produce results that are more efficient or more equitable than those produced by private markets. However, the market does not work perfectly in all instances, so governments play a role in the economy even though government policy is often flawed.

Learning Objectives

After reading and studying this chapter, you will be able to:

1. Apply a model of maximizing behavior to government decision makers.
2. Explain why so many voters choose to remain uninformed about the political process.
3. Describe how special-interest groups can muster enough votes to pass the legislation they want.
4. Describe the basic theory of bureaucracy and explain why incentives are so important in understanding bureaucratic behavior.
5. Explain how constitutional constraints on government behavior can improve the functioning of the economy.

Behavior of Elected Legislatures

The concept of utility maximization lies at the heart of economic analysis. Individuals are assumed to use the resources at their disposal in the manner that produces the greatest personal satisfaction. From this proposition the laws of demand and supply are derived. Profit maximization by business managers is a corollary of utility maximization. By maximizing profits, the owners of firms provide themselves with the maximum revenue to spend on the goods and services they desire.

Public choice theory views public officials as utility-maximizing suppliers of public services. Elected officials attempt to maximize their utility subject to constraints placed on them by voters who demand public services.

What Do Elected Officials Maximize?

Elected officials serve at the pleasure of the electorate. If voters become displeased with elected officials, they have the opportunity to express that displeasure by voting them out of office at the next election. Realizing this, we can surmise that *the first priority of most elected officials is to be reelected to office.* The legislative goals of elected officials cannot be realized unless the officials remain in office. To do so they must please enough voters and, given the importance and expense of campaigns, enough contributors to support their reelection.

Following the above logic, we assume that elected officials maximize the probability of reelection.[1] They adopt positions and support legislation that they believe appeal to the majority of voters in their districts. This does not mean that individual officials do not promote legislation that supports their own views of the world. If voters are ignorant of the positions legislators take on most issues, the legislators are relatively free to vote as they please. However, legislative positions are usually modified when elected officials believe that unpopular stands may cost them their jobs.

Maximizing the probability of reelection does not imply that an elected official will vote in the manner preferred by a majority of his constituents on every issue. As we will see later in the chapter, pleasing some minority interests can be more important than pleasing the majority. On issues that elicit intense interest from the general public, however, elected officials usually vote as the majority of their constituents desire.

Voter Behavior

Numerous polls have shown that the typical American voter is not well informed about the major political issues confronting the nation at any point in time. Do U.S. voters act against their own interests when they make little or no effort to become informed about political issues? Or is this rational, self-interested behavior?

Costs and Benefits of Being Informed   Economic analysis indicates that people tend to undertake an activity to the point at which the marginal benefit from the activity equals its marginal cost. The cost–benefit calculus can be applied

---

[1]This is the assumption used in the first major work on public choice theory, *An Economic Theory of Democracy*, by Anthony Downs (New York: Harper and Row, 1957). Most studies of legislative markets make this assumption.

to the voter-information problem. Voters spend resources — money, time, effort — to obtain information only so long as the marginal benefits they expect to receive from the information exceed the marginal costs of obtaining it.

Most voters derive very little direct benefit from becoming informed about most political issues. One reason for this is that the voting population is so large. The opinions of a single voter are not likely to have much impact on a member of Congress or senator, nor is a single vote likely to have any effect on the outcome of an election. Unless a voter is willing to gather wider support for her position, expressing her views to her legislator will probably accomplish little. Since coalition building is expensive — in time and effort, if not in money — voters tend to be informed and politically active only about issues that affect them personally to a significant extent. For most issues and most voters, the marginal costs of becoming an informed participant in the political process exceed the marginal benefits. In short, it is rational to be uninformed about many issues, since the cost of becoming informed exceeds any benefits likely to be gained from understanding the issues.

To some extent the problem of uninformed voters is overcome through labels and endorsements. Virtually all candidates for elected office carry some brand-name label, such as "Democrat" or "Republican." Many candidates go even further, calling themselves "liberals" or "conservatives" or "environmentalists" or "probusiness." Such labels convey information to voters about a candidate's general views on a wide range of issues. Without bothering to research the details of a candidate's platform, voters know the general position the candidate will take on a number of issues.

Any candidate elected as, say, a conservative Republican who then proceeds to vote like a liberal Democrat faces a problem as the next election approaches. Conservative Republican challengers have the incentive to provide information to voters about the incumbent's true voting record. By showing that the incumbent voted the wrong way on a number of crucial issues, conservative Republican challengers may be able to defeat the incumbent in a primary election. Thus, once a candidate adopts a label, he has a strong incentive to vote as the label suggests he will vote, at least on major issues.

Another way in which voter ignorance is overcome is through endorsements. A voter who is in general agreement with the editorial positions taken by a particular newspaper or magazine may simply choose to vote for the candidates it endorses. Voters can free-ride on the knowledge of editors they trust.

Importance of Intensity of Preference The attention a voter pays to an issue depends not only on *how* the voter feels about the issue but also on *how important* the issue is to him. Intensity of preference matters. Although most voters have opinions about a wide range of issues, they are moved to political action on only a few of them. The prospective gains from political action must be high enough to cover the costs of involvement or a rational voter will not become involved.

This important principle goes a long way toward explaining the importance of special-interest groups in the political process. A **special-interest group** is a group of people who have a particular interest in one issue or set of issues. Special-interest groups form when the marginal benefits to be derived from political action outweigh the marginal costs of information, organization, and lobbying.

Special-interest group Group of people with an intense interest in a particular issue or set of related issues.

In the absence of well-informed voters, special-interest groups can have an impact on legislators all out of proportion to the number of voters they represent. Since such groups stand to gain or lose a great deal from legislation pertaining to their issues, they are willing to spend a lot of time and money lobbying for their positions. Often the opponents of special-interest legislation are totally unorganized and do almost no lobbying, instead remaining rationally ignorant of the issues being considered. Since each of the opponents stands to lose relatively little from the special-interest legislation, it is less costly to do nothing and accept the legislation than to work against it. Consequently, special-interest legislation that harms the majority of voters to some slight extent each, while benefiting the special-interest group greatly, can become law. Although the total harm done may be much greater than the total gains realized by the members of the special-interest group, because the harm is spread around so thinly, no organized opposition to the legislation emerges.

Many government programs harm the majority a little while benefiting a minority a great deal. Agricultural programs that increase food prices and quotas and tariffs that limit the importation of foreign goods fit into this category. In both cases a relatively small number of producers gains, while a much larger number of consumers loses.

Outcomes in Political Markets

The major factor determining whether the price–quantity outcomes in economic markets maximize the welfare of both demanders and suppliers is whether effective competition exists. In highly competitive markets, producers are driven to supply goods at the lowest possible prices, and consumers purchase goods to the point where the marginal benefit of consuming the goods equals the market price. It should come as no surprise to find that competition is also the major factor determining how well political markets perform in maximizing voter welfare.[2]

Competition and Efficiency   The conditions producing efficiency in political markets are similar to those producing efficiency in economic markets. For efficient political outcomes, at least two conditions must be met.

1. Voters must be informed about the behavior of their elected representatives. Representatives have an incentive to vote as a majority of their constituents prefer only if their constituents monitor their votes. As noted above, party or ideological labels and the endorsements of newspapers and magazines can substitute for individual information to some extent.

2. There must be free entry into the political process. Barriers to entry, such as extremely high campaign costs, can reduce political competition by keeping potential candidates from running for office. Election laws that make it very difficult for independent candidates to get on the ballot also reduce competition.

These two conditions assure some degree of political competition, thus ensuring that voter preferences are respected.

The Concept of Efficiency in Political Markets. An efficient political outcome differs from an efficient market outcome in important respects. Individual

---

[2]Perhaps the foremost proponent of the view that political markets can be efficient is Donald Wittman, a professor at the University of California, Santa Cruz. For a sample of his arguments, see "Why Democracies Produce Efficient Results," *Journal of Political Economy* 97 (December 1989), pp. 1395–1424.

consumers purchase private goods only if the marginal benefit from consuming such goods equals or exceeds the price they must pay for the goods. Consumers choose to buy or to refrain from buying on a good-by-good basis. Voters must make a different choice. When a voter casts a ballot for a particular candidate, she votes for the entire bundle of public goods the representative will provide. Along with the public goods the voter actually desires, she may obtain a number of public goods she would rather not pay for. In short, public decision making often overrides personal preferences.

Political efficiency differs from economic efficiency in another way. Most issues are decided by a simple majority vote. Thus, even if a representative votes the way a majority of his constituents want on *every* issue, he may continually harm a minority of the voters in his district. Of necessity, public decision making forces some citizens to pay for public goods that they do not want.

Political Power and Legislative Outcomes

Just as market power alters the price–quantity equilibrium reached in an economic market, political power alters the outcomes reached in political markets. In representative democracies, political power is wielded by special-interest groups, whose intense preferences for or against particular types of legislation are signaled to legislators through lobbying and campaign contributions.

It is not difficult to understand why particular legislators might vote for bills favored by only a minority of their constituents. General voter ignorance and the high intensity of preferences of a minority of voters could lead legislators to represent minority views on many issues. This does not explain how bills favored by a minority of all voters become law, however. How do special-interest groups persuade *enough* legislators to vote for their favored bills? The question is important, since many or most legislators may have no members of the special-interest group as constituents. For example, how does the steel industry win protection from foreign competition when very few congressional districts have steel mills? The answer lies in vote trading, or what public choice theorists call **logrolling**.

Logrolling Many of the bills considered by Congress during any session have little direct impact on the constituents of any particular district. A bill to support the price of wheat directly affects only those districts where wheat is grown. The indirect effects are much broader. Members of Congress from districts with farm equipment manufacturing facilities may also favor wheat price supports, and consumers and taxpayers all over the nation are affected by higher food prices, as well as either higher taxes or a higher federal deficit. However, the size of the direct effects on individual wheat farmers and the people who supply them with inputs is much larger than the size of the indirect effects on individual consumers and taxpayers. Each farmer stands to gain a great deal from wheat price supports, while each consumer and taxpayer loses a relatively small amount.

Since wheat price supports are the most important issue to voters in wheat-farming districts, a legislator who can produce on this issue is likely to be reelected even if he votes against his constituents' interests on other, less important, issues. Because the intensity of voter preferences differs from issue to issue, legislators can increase the net benefits they provide to their constituents

Logrolling
Vote trading to acquire sufficient support for issues otherwise supported by a minority of voters.

TABLE 1
Intensity of preferences and the potential for logrolling

	Income Effect on Citizens in	
	District W	District P
Wheat Bill passes	+ $500	− $25
Peanut Bill passes	− $25	+ $500

by trading votes on issues. The following example illustrates how the vote trading, or logrolling, process works.

Table 1 shows the change in disposable income each voter in two particular districts experiences from the passage of two bills. The Wheat Bill supports the price of wheat, while the Peanut Bill supports the price of peanuts. People in district W, where wheat is grown, each gain $500 from the introduction of higher wheat prices. Individuals in district P, where no wheat is grown, must foot part of the bill for the more expensive wheat. Each person in district P loses $25 if the Wheat Bill passes. The situation is reversed for the Peanut Bill. The citizens of district P are big winners, while the people in district W each lose a little.

Citizens in districts that grow neither wheat nor peanuts lose from the passage of either bill. Assume that by themselves legislators from either wheat or peanut districts are in the minority, but that together wheat district and peanut district legislators form a majority in the legislature. Then the wheat and peanut district legislators can produce a net gain of $475 for each of their constituents by agreeing to vote for each other's bills. Citizens in districts that grow neither wheat nor peanuts are each stuck with a $50 net loss from the passage of the two bills.

The logrolling that takes place in Congress and in state legislatures and local councils is often much more complex than our example, but the principle followed is the same. To muster enough votes to support wheat prices, legislators from wheat-farming districts may have to agree to vote for a dozen other pieces of legislation. Voting patterns that would appear inexplicable in the absence of logrolling result. Legislators from tobacco-producing states are among the strongest endorsers of dairy price support legislation, while members of Congress from the breadbasket of the midwest consistently vote to support tobacco farmers. Legislators from auto-producing states support textile quotas in return for support for automobile quotas, and Congress passes a seemingly unending stream of public construction bills, containing projects for dozens of congressional districts. The list of issues subject to logrolling is almost limitless.

Dominance of Producer Groups Not every group of people with a common interest forms a lobbying group.[3] A group of people with similar interests will undertake collective action only if the benefits each person expects to gain from organizing outweigh the costs of organization. This favors producers over consumers in the formation of special interest groups. Producers — either the

---

[3] Mancur Olsen investigates the conditions necessary for political cooperation in *The Logic of Collective Action* (Cambridge, MA: Harvard University Press, 1965).

owners of companies or the workers in those companies — stand to gain a great deal from legislation that promotes their product. Price supports or import quotas can mean thousands or millions of dollars to individual producers of politically favored products. Legislation restricting competition in the labor market can enable unions to bargain for much higher wages than workers would receive otherwise. The benefits of organization outweigh the costs for such groups.

Consumers of products face a totally different situation. Producers gain by extracting a small amount of income from a large number of people. Although consumers may be angered at having to pay $2 per gallon for milk, instead of, say, $1.50, the total annual loss suffered by a household from milk price supports is relatively small. It is not worth a consumer's time and effort to work diligently in opposition to milk price supports if such supports cost the household only $100 per year. The costs to consumers of organizing a Free the Milk! campaign outweigh the expected benefits, although some suppliers, such as retailers, may gain from such an organizing effort.

The number of producers relative to the number of consumers also works in favor of producer groups. Organization costs are much smaller for producer groups because the number of people involved in forming an effective coalition is much smaller. High organization costs hinder the development of consumer-interest groups.

Special-Interest Groups and Long-Run Economic Behavior The harm done by special-interest groups may extend beyond the inequitable redistribution of income. University of Maryland economist Mancur Olsen has argued that the growth of special-interest groups and collusive business and labor organizations actually increases the unemployment rate and slows economic growth.[4] The long-run consequences of special-interest politics may be more harmful than the short-run income redistribution.

Olsen's thesis is that the economy becomes less flexible when special-interest groups and business and labor coalitions use political or market power to raise their incomes. A competitive market system responds quickly to demand or supply shocks. As relative prices change to reflect the new set of demands and supplies, resources are reallocated. The faster firms and workers respond to the new economic conditions, the sooner the economy returns to its natural level of output.

Special-interest groups and economic coalitions respond to shocks much more slowly than competitive firms. It is more difficult and time consuming to forge a new political consensus than it is for a competitive firm to alter its price and output levels. This rigidity places the firms that are part of special-interest groups or coalitions at a disadvantage during turbulent times. Since they cannot react to the new economic conditions quickly, they continue to produce at inefficient levels or with inefficient techniques for some time.

The most rigid economies are those that have been politically stable for the longest periods of time. Professor Olsen notes that Great Britain and the United States, two societies with very long histories of stable government, were harmed more by the macroeconomic shocks of the 1970s than were Japan and West Germany, whose political systems were destroyed by World War II. He maintains that because a smaller number of special-interest groups had

SECTION RECAP
Public choice theory treats elected officials as utility maximizers who vote in the manner that maximizes the probability that they will be reelected. Most voters remain rationally ignorant of the positions taken by elected officials on most issues. Special-interest groups, which have a lot to gain from particular types of legislation, attempt to influence legislation and often succeed through the process of logrolling.

[4]*The Rise and Decline of Nations* (New Haven, CT: Yale University Press, 1982).

had time to arise in those countries, their economies were more flexible and able to respond to shocks than were the more rigid U.S. and British economies.[5]

Bureaucracy

The term *bureaucrat* is used in this book to mean anyone employed by a government agency in the administration of government programs. In particular we are interested in the bureaucrats who occupy the middle- and upper-management positions in bureaus, who have substantial decision-making authority.

What Do Bureaucrats Maximize?

Managers of profit-seeking businesses can increase their utility in two ways. One way is to increase the profitability of the firms they manage. Many managers earn part of their incomes in the form of bonuses that are tied to the amount of profit earned by their firms. Other corporations reward their managers for satisfactory profit performance by increasing their salaries. Either way, managers gain from efficient operations, since minimizing costs for a given level of output is equivalent to maximizing profit.

The second way in which managers increase their utility is by increasing the perquisites of their positions. **Perquisites** (commonly called "perks") are the nonincome benefits of jobs, such as expense accounts, company cars, plush offices, and flexible working hours, all of which are costly to firms. Thus, managers face a tradeoff: Increasing perquisites increases costs and reduces profits. Managers of profit-seeking businesses have the incentive to restrict the number of perquisites they enjoy in order to maximize profits and their own incomes.

Perquisites ("perks")
Nonincome benefits of a job.

Managers of nonprofit organizations, including government agencies, face a different incentive structure. Since their organizations do not seek to maximize profits, such managers are not rewarded for efficiency. They do not gain financially if they hold costs to a minimum. Most managers of government agencies can increase their utility in two ways: by increasing perquisites or by increasing the size of their agencies. In general, the salaries of government managers reflect the size of the organizations they manage. Thus, *bureaucrats tend to be budget maximizers*, rather than profit maximizers, since larger budgets enable them to both hire more employees and enjoy more perquisites.

Nature of Bureaus

Government agencies (bureaus) differ from most profit-seeking businesses in two important ways. First, as just discussed, government agencies do not attempt to maximize profits. Instead, agencies are given budgets and required to perform a certain number of tasks. Within the constraints imposed by their budget, the managers of a government agency have the incentive to maximize their perquisites. They also have the incentive to lobby for a larger budget, sufficient to hire more employees and to acquire more perquisites. The organization itself provides no incentive to operate efficiently.

---

[5]It goes without saying that neither Professor Olsen nor the authors are advocating war or revolution as a way to increase the flexibility of the U.S. economy!

The second major difference between government agencies and most profit-seeking firms is the absence of competition in the public sector. Most government agencies have no competitors in the provision of services. Even in the absence of internal organizational incentives to be efficient, competition from private firms could force government agencies to operate efficiently. Otherwise, they would lose all their business to private competitors. Most government agencies are monopolists, however, so no external incentives to be efficient exist.

The incentive structure of bureaucracy leads economists to predict that government agencies will (1) operate inefficiently, with higher costs of production than profit-seeking firms producing the same services, and (2) expand beyond the profit-maximizing level, particularly by hiring more employees than profit-seeking firms would hire.

Evidence

Many economists have studied the relative efficiency of government agencies.[6] This section draws on a survey of a large number of studies by James T. Bennett and Manuel H. Johnson to provide evidence on the relative efficiency of government agencies.[7]

Trash Collection   Three basic approaches to trash collection are available to cities: direct government provision of the service; trash collection by a single private firm under contract to the city; and collection by a number of private, competing firms. Since all three approaches are widely used, economists have devoted a good deal of attention to the relative costs of the different approaches to trash collection.

When all the factors affecting the cost of trash collection are accounted for, it appears that the costs of public trash collection are much higher than the costs of private trash collection, either under contract or by private competitors. A study of trash collection in the Virginia suburbs of Washington, D.C., concluded that public trash collection was approximately twice as expensive as private trash collection.

Health Care and Hospitals   Studies of the performance of profit-seeking and nonprofit health care organizations reveal that profit-seeking organizations operate at much lower cost. For example, a study of firms processing Medicare claims found that nonprofit firms have processing costs that are 45 percent higher than those of profit-seeking firms. The error rate of nonprofit firms is also 140 percent higher. Studies of hospitals in Los Angeles and San Francisco found that the wages paid by private nonprofit and government hospitals were higher than the wages paid by profit-seeking hospitals in virtually all job categories. Since wages are a major element in hospital costs, we once again find that the costs of profit-seeking organizations are lower.

Ship Repair   Large ships require continual maintenance if they are to remain shipshape. In 1978 the U.S. government's General Accounting Office studied

---

[6]See the studies summarized in Dennis C. Mueller, *Public Choice II* (New York: Cambridge University Press, 1989), Table 14.1, pp. 262–265.

[7]"Tax Reduction Without Sacrifice: Private-Sector Production of Public Services," *Public Finance Quarterly* 8 (October 1980), pp. 363–396.

Does It Make Economic Sense?

Fighting Fires for Profit

As far back as Adam Smith (1776), economists recognized that public goods could not be provided efficiently by competing firms. Recall that a public good has two important characteristics: My consumption of it does not detract from your consumption and neither of us can be excluded from consuming the good if it is provided to the other person. The classic example of a public good is national defense. If the United States defends me against attack by nuclear missiles, it automatically defends you as well.

Many goods provided at the local level also have characteristics of publicness. Road maintenance and street lights are to a large extent public goods. Even firefighting is typically viewed as a public good in urban areas, where buildings are close together and fire spreads easily. Nearly all cities support fire departments because firefighting is viewed as a public good. Nearly all, but not quite all; one U.S. city—Scottsdale, Arizona—does things a bit differently. Scottsdale hires a private firm to fight its fires. If firefighting is a public good, does this make economic sense?

Even goods that are public in *consumption* need not be public in *provision*. A community may provide a service for all its citizens and finance the service with tax revenues without actually producing the service itself. Scottsdale has taken such an approach to fire protection. Rather than maintaining a public fire department, Scottsdale contracts with a private firm for fire protection services. The city carefully specifies the standards it expects the firm to meet, preserving governmental control over the quality of the service. Although Rural-Metro, the company holding the Scottsdale contract, is a profit-seeking firm and has the incentive to minimize costs, it cannot cut the quality of its service without risking the loss of its contract.

How well has the private approach to fire protection worked? According to National Fire Protection Association estimates, the per capita cost of fire protection in Scottsdale is about half the per capita cost in cities of comparable size. Furthermore, a comparison of response times and dollar losses per capita from fires with the neighboring cities of Tempe, Mesa, and Glendale, Arizona, which have public fire departments, showed that the Scottsdale department was the fastest of the four and allowed the least damage.* Quality of service is no problem in Scottsdale, as attested by the fact that its fire insurance rating is no different from that of other comparable cities.

Proponents of *privatization*—the production of public services by private firms—see it as a way to cut the costs of public services dramatically without reducing services. Privatization is not without its detractors, however. Government employees, of course, have a vested interest in maintaining public provision of services. Other critics note that close supervision of private firms would be necessary in many types of production. Such supervision is costly and might eat up any cost savings from private production. Since the idea of privatization is gaining momentum, both in the United States and abroad, more evidence on the efficiency and quality of service of private producers will undoubtedly be available over the next few years.

*Randall Fitzgerald, *When Government Goes Private: Successful Alternatives to Public Services* (New York: Universe Books, 1988), pp. 77–78.

---

the costs of maintenance of Navy support vessels relative to the maintenance costs of similar commercial vessels. They found the costs of repairs of various types by the Navy to be from three to fifty-two times as expensive as similar repairs made by commercial firms. Furthermore, the repair of Navy ships took longer and was done in port, while most commercial ships were repaired while at sea—even though the crews of commercial ships were much smaller than the crews on comparable naval vessels. Once again, government costs exceeded private costs by a wide margin.

Airline Service   Airline services in Australia are provided by two firms, one private and one public. Duke University economist David Davies studied the performance of the two airlines from 1958 to 1974, a period during which the private airline (Ansett) was regulated by the Australian government to prevent it from having any competitive advantages over the public airline (Trans Australian). Despite the extensive regulation of the private airline, which forced it to operate in a manner nearly identical to the public airline, the private airline had lower costs. On average the private airline carried twice as many tons of freight and mail per employee as the public airline. It enjoyed smaller advantages in passengers carried per employee and revenue earned per employee.

Employment Levels in Public and Private Firms   Studies of the relative employment levels of public agencies and private firms appear to confirm the prediction that public firms hire more workers than similar private firms. One study of trash collection concluded that public trash collection requires 97 percent more employees than does private collection, other factors held constant. A study of private and public colleges concluded that public colleges in a state employ about 40 percent more labor than private colleges for the same size capital stock.

Conclusions   Most of the evidence that has been collected on the efficiency and size of government agencies relative to profit-seeking firms confirms the predictions of bureaucracy theory. The lack of managerial incentives and competition from private producers frees bureaucrats from the need to operate efficiently. Consequently, production of services by public agencies is usually accomplished at a higher cost and with more employees than would be required by profit-seeking private firms.

> **SECTION RECAP**
> Bureaucrats lack the incentives to operate efficiently faced by managers of profit-maximizing firms. Thus, bureaus tend to operate at a higher cost and with more employees than profit-maximizing firms engaged in similar activities.

Constitutional Economics

The economic activities of private individuals and firms are conducted within the framework of rules determined and enforced by government. These rules specify what are and are not permissible forms of behavior. The most important set of rules determining behavior in a market economy is the set of **property rights** — the rights of individuals to own and use personal property as they see fit, within broad limits. Property rights allow owners of property to reap the benefits of activities that increase their property and force them to bear the costs of activities that decrease their property.

The existence of firmly established property rights underlies all successful market economies. Property rights substitute individual initiative and accountability for direct control by a centralized agency. In a command economy, a small elite hands down instructions regarding the particular activities individuals are to engage in. In a market economy, no such commands are given. Rather, a general order is created within which individuals compete and cooperate as they pursue their own self-interests. The credit for explaining that a society can operate in a well-behaved fashion without hierarchical control goes to the seventeenth-century English philosopher John Locke. Locke believed in individual freedom to determine for oneself, within broad limits, how one would live. The *natural rights* doctrine that all individuals have the right to life, liberty, and the pursuit of property was developed extensively in the writings of Locke and some of his contemporaries.

Property rights
Rights of individuals to own and use personal property as they see fit, within broad limits.

Why the Disagreement?

The Firemen First Principle

There seems to be no end to the disagreement between people who believe that much government spending on social services is wasteful and those who believe that social service agencies are seriously underfunded. Hardly a day goes by that a major newspaper doesn't carry one or more stories on the plight of people who need more governmentally provided services. Yet many of the same newspapers carry stories describing in great detail the wastefulness of many government programs. This disagreement seems to be one that could be settled empirically: Are social service agencies underfunded, or are they not? If answering this question merely requires looking at the empirical evidence, then the length of this argument is surprising. Why the disagreement? Bureaucratic behavior may explain much of the continuing disagreement. When confronted with a budget reduction, bureaucrats have the incentive to *maximize*, rather than minimize, the pain caused by the budget cut. If a lot of fat exists in an agency's budget, it may totally escape the budget-cutter's knife. Muscle — productive services — may be cut instead. Charles Peters, editor of *The Washington Monthly*, calls this the *Firemen First Principle*.*

The theory of bureaucracy asserts that bureaucrats will attempt to maximize their agencies' budgets. Thus, it is important that an outside agency keep watch over the government bureaucracy if the budget is to be kept under control. The major agency performing this watchdog task at the federal level is the Office of Management and Budget (OMB). When a cabinet-level department, such as the Defense Department or the Department of Health and Human Services, submits its annual budget request, OMB assigns six or seven people to examine the request carefully, looking for waste. While this sounds very thorough, it should be noted that 400 to 500 people may have been involved in creating the budget request. Each of them stands to gain from *hiding* wasteful spending. The odds are stacked against the OMB auditors right from the start.

If the OMB auditors are clever enough to find the waste, and Congress is willing to trim the agency's budget request, the Firemen First Principle comes into play. This principle asserts that "when faced with a budget cut, the bureaucrat translates it into bad news for members of Congress who are powerful enough to restore the amount eliminated. In other words, he chops where it will hurt constituents the most, not the least."**

Why would bureaucrats cut important services rather than eliminate waste? Cutting services generates public anger over the budget cut. Voters write and call their legislators to complain. If voters are unhappy, legislators are unhappy. They seek ways to restore the services so valued by their constituents. The budget cut may be reversed very quickly.

The Firemen First Principle asserts that, if a city faces a budget squeeze, it will not fire office workers; it will fire firemen first. Since firefighting is a service people are not willing to do without, such a cut is very painful. School districts facing reduced funding will fire teachers rather than central office personnel. A classic example of the principle occurred when Congress decided to reduce funding for Amtrak in 1975. Amtrak officials promptly responded by announcing they were going to cut a number of routes. The routes selected went through the home districts of the chairmen of the House Appropriations Transportation Subcommittee, the Senate Appropriations Committee, the Senate Commerce Committee, the Senate Appropriations Transportation Subcommittee, the Senate Commerce Surface Transportation Subcommittee, and the House Commerce Committee. Not surprisingly, the budget cuts were restored.

The paradoxical truth about the disagreement between those who believe bureaucracy is wasteful and those who think that important services are underfunded is that both may be right. There is no doubt that a large amount of wasteful spending is incorporated into the budget of virtually every government agency. But the important services of these agencies may well be underfunded. Agencies have powerful incentives to pad their payrolls with nonproductive employees. Unfortunately, when the budget ax falls, it rarely falls on these unnecessary workers. Instead it pares firemen first.

---

*Charles Peters, *How Washington Really Works* (Reading, MA: Addison–Wesley, 1980), especially Chapter 3.

**Peters, p. 40.

Despite his emphasis on individual freedom, Locke saw an important role for government. Government should enforce the society's laws that prevent some individuals from using force of any kind to deprive other individuals of life, liberty, or property. In effect, government should serve as a referee enforcing the rules within which private individuals operate, including the rules that limit economic activity. This is not the only legitimate role for government in such a liberal society, however. Government should also provide public goods. Public goods would be underprovided if private producers were to supply them, because the demanders of such goods have an incentive to free-ride on the payments of others. Collectively, too little would be spent purchasing such goods. Everyone benefits if government provides public goods, paying for them by taxing the citizens benefiting from the goods.

Once government begins to provide public goods, it becomes an active participant in the economy, while continuing to be the referee of the rules of the game. This creates an obvious problem: What rules will constrain the economic activities of government? In the absence of constraining rules, the people who are governing have the incentive to use government power to obtain things they could not obtain as individuals competing in the market. (Such behavior is what public choice theory analyzes.) The search for optimal rules to constrain governmental behavior is the subject matter of **constitutional economics**.

Constitutional economics Study of the optimal rules with which to constrain government behavior.

Freedom and Leviathan

Since the issue addressed by constitutional economics is constraining government, the first question that must be asked is what government should be prevented from doing. Following Locke and the authors of the U.S. Constitution, whose thinking was dominated by Locke's ideas, constitutional economists assert that the basic value to be protected from governmental abuse is individual freedom. Government must be restrained from trampling individuals underfoot by depriving them of life, liberty, or the pursuit of property.

If government were controlled by people who would never think of using governmental power to unduly limit individual freedom, constitutional limits on government would be unnecessary. Thus, the search for optimal constitutional limits presumes that the people controlling government will, to some degree, attempt to use governmental powers for their own purposes. Since constitutional economists want to prevent such abuses of power, they typically approach the issue by assuming the worst — that the people controlling government will use it to the maximum extent possible to achieve their own personal ends. Although this assumption is probably not realistic, it is appropriate since such governmental behavior is what the economists wish to prevent. The assumption that the people controlling government will use it to further their own ends is called the **Leviathan model**. This name comes from the title of a book by the seventeenth-century English philosopher Thomas Hobbes, who asserted that only two types of social arrangement exist — anarchy or complete control by government (Leviathan).

Leviathan model Model of government that assumes that the people controlling government will use it to further their own ends.

The men who wrote the U.S. Constitution had a Leviathan model in mind when they developed a set of constitutional constraints designed to make it very difficult for people to use government to their personal advantage. Liberty, not democracy, was what the framers of the Constitution sought to preserve, so they placed numerous obstacles in the way of legislation. Turning a bill into law is a cumbersome, time-consuming operation — just as the writers of the Constitution intended. They sought to prevent the abuse of individual rights—even if a majority of the people favor such abuse—by limiting the power of the national government.

Federalism The thorny practical issue confronting constitutional economists is how to limit government while allowing it enough flexibility to carry out its legitimate function: providing public goods. Since different goods have different degrees of "publicness," one solution was to devise a **federal republic**. Several levels of government coexist in the United States. The different levels reflect the fact that the extent of some public goods is very wide, while the extent of other public goods is much narrower. For example, national defense must be the responsibility of the federal government. However, street repair in Durham, North Carolina, while of importance to the citizens of Durham, is of little benefit to people living elsewhere. Thus, it makes sense for local governments to repair streets. Justifying federal responsibility for such local public goods is difficult.

Just as market competition limits the power of individuals, competition among governments limits the exploitation of citizens by government. If local or state governments create an unpleasant environment for their citizens, the citizens can vote with their feet by moving to another political district. When the federal government is the problem, moving away is a much less viable option. Hence, state and local governments are likely to be more responsive to the desires of constituents than is the federal government. This is a strong argument in favor of placing as much responsibility as possible at the state and local levels.

Private Goods and Public Provision A benefit of tightly constraining government's economic activities is that such constraints limit the attractiveness of government as a resource to be exploited by private interests. When the government plays an extensive role in the economy and takes responsibility for achieving particular outcomes (as opposed to maintaining a general structure), special-interest groups have a greater incentive to seek to influence government decisions. Different groups begin competing for government benefits, spending resources in lobbying efforts that produce nothing. Society as a whole gains nothing from such activities—in fact it loses, as energy is diverted from production to politics. Constraining government with rules that prohibit government intervention in the production of private goods and services reduces the incentive to use government as a redistributive device and frees resources for use in socially productive endeavors. Thus, constitutional rules can be viewed as a public good, the provision of which benefits society.

Benefits of Restraint

Without laws no freedom exists. In the absence of a framework that prevents self-interested individuals from imposing their will on others, anarchy reigns. Anarchy implies not freedom but its absence—the rule of power. Just as individuals must be prevented from directly forcing their wills on others, they must be prevented from using government as a tool of personal power. Constitutional economics has become a practical issue during the 1980s, as voters have imposed or attempted to impose constraints on government behavior. California's Proposition 13, which limited property taxes, is an example of a rule constraining government behavior. The balanced budget amendment to

---

Federal republic
A system of representative government with several coexisting levels of government handling different sets of issues.

SECTION RECAP
Constitutional economics studies how to constrain government so as to guarantee personal liberty while still enabling government to provide the services demanded by taxpayers. Federalism is one approach to this problem. By providing local public goods through local governments, goods with a somewhat higher degree of publicness through state governments, and true public goods through the federal government, *(continued)*

the U.S. Constitution, while not yet enacted, represents another attempt by citizens to control the behavior of government. Other constitutional constraints are sure to be proposed in the future, since economists and political scientists are now devoting a great deal of energy to studying how best to constrain governmental power.[8]

SECTION RECAP
(continued)
the responsiveness of government to the wishes of the public is enhanced.

So What's the Bottom Line?

For a variety of reasons economic markets do not always produce outcomes we are willing to accept. The existence of externalities, information deficiencies, market power, and sticky prices and wages has led economists to search for ways in which government can intervene to improve economic performance. In the same manner economists are now investigating the ways in which government institutions perform poorly. Neither the market nor the government is perfect, and the performance of either is to a large extent determined by the laws, regulations, and customs that constrain the actions of individuals.

This chapter is *not* intended to convince you that government is incapable of performing valuable economic functions quite efficiently. It *is* intended to demonstrate that turning a problem over to government is no guarantee that things will get better. You should now have a better appreciation for why that conclusion is valid.

Public finance economists are seeking to determine what organizational structures produce desired outcomes with the fewest negative side effects. They consider such questions as, Should government services be provided at the federal, state, or local level? How can spending programs be designed to run efficiently? Could many public services be provided more efficiently by contracting them out to private firms? What effects on government behavior do constitutional constraints on spending have? The list of questions is almost endless, and we do not have room to discuss the answers here. Suffice it to say that less-than-perfect market performance is not a sufficient argument for replacing private arrangements with government programs. Some evidence must be presented that the performance of government will not be as bad as or worse than the market's performance.

Summary

In recent years the tools of economics have been used to study political processes. **Public choice** theory assumes that government officials are self-interested utility maximizers. This assumption implies that elected officials attempt to maximize the probability of reelection and bureaucrats attempt to maximize their agencies' budgets.

The efficiency of political outcomes depends upon the degree of competition in political markets. Public officials sometimes vote against the interests of the majority of voters because voters typically know very little about the issues being considered. **Rational ignorance** prevails among voters who believe that the marginal benefits of becoming informed and politically active are

---

[8] A good introduction to constitutional economics is Dwight R. Lee and Richard B. McKenzie, *Regulating Government* (Lexington, MA: Lexington Books, 1987).

outweighed by the marginal costs. Only those individuals or groups who stand to gain or lose a great deal from a particular piece of legislation tend to become involved. This helps explain why **special-interest groups** are so important.

Special-interest legislation becomes law because legislators are willing to trade votes on issues. Such vote trading is called **logrolling**. Producer groups tend to dominate this process, since individual producers have more to gain or lose from legislation affecting their product than do consumers.

The theory of **bureaucracy** asserts that bureaucrats are more interested in expanding their bureaus than in holding down costs. Evidence from a number of studies supports this view. Government agencies appear inefficient compared to profit-seeking firms.

Constitutional economics is the study of how to devise optimal rules to constrain government behavior. The basic value economists seek to preserve is individual freedom, the right to life, liberty, and the pursuit of property. By limiting what government is allowed to do, constitutional constraints reduce the incentive for interest groups to attempt to use government to achieve their own ends.

Questions for Thought

Knowledge Questions

1. What are legislators and bureaucrats assumed to maximize in public choice models?
2. What is logrolling? Why is it important?
3. Why do producer groups seem to dominate the political process rather than consumer groups?
4. Why are interest groups less likely to devote resources to affecting governmental behavior if government is constrained by strict rules than if government is free to act with few constraints?

Application Questions

5. If intensity of preference did not matter in determining how voters relate to the political process, how would things change?
6. Government has long regarded education as a public good, because of the external benefits that educated people confer on others. Must the provision of public education be through public agencies? What problems and benefits might arise if public education were funded publicly but provided privately?
7. Suppose the Congress, as part of a deficit-reduction package, said that any bureaucrats introducing cost-cutting measures that do not reduce the level or quality of services may keep a portion of the savings. How would this change the behavior of the bureaucracy?

Synthesis Questions

8. What are the economic incentives that may lead voters to ignore most of the political battles being waged in Congress?
9. Explain why intensity of preferences is an important determinant of political outcomes in a system such as that of the United States.
10. Why do special-interest groups appear to be so successful in obtaining the legislation they want from Congress?

OVERVIEW

Macroeconomics is the study of the total economy. Macroeconomics focuses on such variables as the level and growth of output produced by the economy, the rate at which the economy's average price level changes, and the percentage of people who want to work but are unemployed. Macroeconomics provides an overview of the economy, rather than a close-up picture of the behavior of particular individuals or markets. However, economic activity depends on individual choices and actions. Goods, services, and assets are traded in particular markets, not in some macromarket. Thus, we cannot study the macroeconomy without examining the individual choices and microeconomic market outcomes that determine macroeconomic outcomes.

From Individual Choice to Macroeconomics

The relationship between macroeconomics and individual behavior is rather like the relationship between a forest and the trees within it. One cannot understand what a forest is like by examining individual trees in isolation. A forest is more than just a lot of trees. Nevertheless, it is impossible to understand what a forest is like without understanding the nature of trees. So it is with macroeconomics. We cannot ignore individual behavior and hope to understand macroeconomic behavior, but we must push beyond examining the behavior of individual economic agents to consider how the interactions of large numbers of agents form the forest that is examined by macroeconomics.

We begin this chapter by considering the basic and universal problem of every individual economic unit, be it a household or a business firm: deciding what to buy and how much to save when constrained by limited income. We then turn to the problem of determining how the decisions of individual economic units affect the behavior of the entire economy. To accomplish this we must add up the decisions of individual

CHAPTER 21

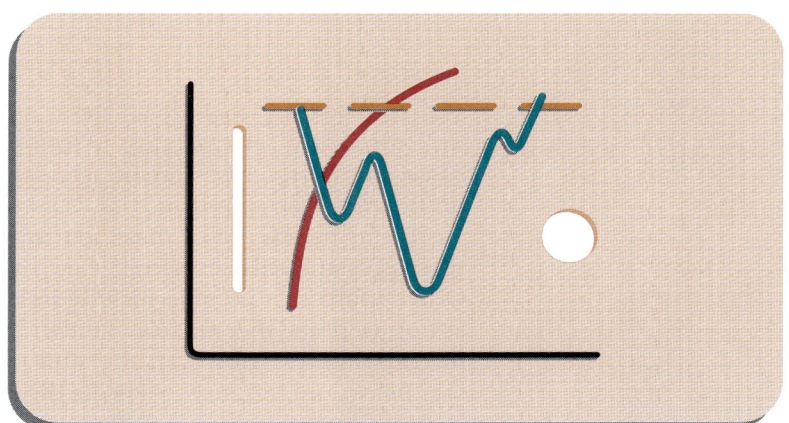

economic units to determine how the macroeconomy behaves. We will see that many of the constraints faced by individuals are also faced by the macroeconomy.

After moving from the individual to the aggregate, or economy-wide, level, we discuss how aggregate prices and output are measured. This discussion carries us into the realm of price indexes and gross national product (GNP) accounting.

Learning Objectives

After reading and studying this chapter, you will be able to:

1. Identify the limits that confront people making spending or saving decisions.
2. Discuss how the rest of the economy is affected when demand or supply changes in a particular market.
3. Show how the aggregate budget constraint is related to individual budget constraints.
4. Define gross national product and differentiate between GNP and real GNP.
5. Derive a price index and describe how aggregate production can be measured.

The Economic Choice Problem

The decisions that determine the level of economic activity in an economy are made by millions of people. Very few individuals have the ability to affect the macroeconomy to any significant extent. However, millions of individuals reacting similarly to emerging events can change the course of the economy. In this chapter we provide the link between individual economic behavior and macroeconomic behavior by building from individual choices to macroeconomic choices.

The basic framework of the individual's choice problem should be familiar to you. The total number of dollars spent during a time period must equal the total number of dollars acquired. In economic terminology, *sources of funds must equal uses of funds during any time period*. The truth of this statement may not be completely obvious, however. Surely someone will think, "There are plenty of months when I spend more than I earn." That is undoubtedly true. Thus, to establish the truth of the statement, the precise meaning of the words *sources* and *uses* must be defined.

Sources of Funds

Sources of funds
All the ways an individual can obtain spendable funds.

Sources of funds include all the ways a person can obtain spendable funds. Individuals can acquire funds in four basic ways: by earning income, by selling assets, by borrowing, and by receiving gifts or transfers of funds for which nothing is given in return.

By far the largest of these four major sources of funds is labor income — the wages and salaries people earn by supplying labor services to employers. Other sources of income include interest income from financial assets, such as bonds, rental income from land or buildings, and dividends from the profits of corporations. However, the sum of individual incomes calculated in this manner would seriously overstate the total income earned by private economic units in the economy because many individuals pay interest as well as receive interest. Only *net* interest payments — interest received minus interest paid — enter into the economy's total income.

Other ways of obtaining spendable funds exist. Individuals can obtain spendable funds by selling assets. Individuals sell some assets through organized markets, such as the New York Stock Exchange. A person wanting to convert one hundred shares of IBM stock into money need only direct a stockbroker to sell the shares. Other people sell assets in more informal markets, as when a family has a garage sale and sells old clothing and furniture to bargain hunters. In either case, the asset seller acquires spendable funds.

Another source of funds for individuals is borrowing. Borrowers obtain funds from lenders in return for a promise to repay the funds, plus interest, at a later date.

A final way that an individual can obtain spendable funds is by receiving a gift or a transfer of funds for which nothing is given in return. Families pass down huge quantities of assets from generation to generation, private agencies transfer funds or goods and services from contributors to the needy, and the government taxes the incomes of taxpayers to make **transfer payments** to recipients of various types.

Transfer payment
Transfer of tax revenue to recipients who give the government nothing in return.

Although sales of assets, borrowing, and gifts and transfer payments are important sources of funds for individuals, they do not add to society's income.

The reason is fairly obvious. Asset sales, borrowing, and transfer receipts represent a shuffling of funds from one person to another. Nothing is produced, and no income is generated. *Production is the only source of income for the economy.*[1] Only production creates things of value, things that can be purchased with the income earned from their production. Sources of funds other than income do not add to the quantity of goods and services people can consume.

Uses of Funds

Uses of funds can be grouped into four basic categories:

1. An individual can use funds to purchase newly produced goods or services. This category includes both goods that are consumed within a very short time and durable goods, such as *new* houses and cars, which last for years. This category is often referred to as **spending**. Spending on durable goods adds to the economy's stock of real assets.

2. An individual can use funds to purchase financial assets or used real assets. This category includes such financial assets as savings deposits at banks, stock in corporations, and U.S. government bonds. It also includes the purchase of *used* cars and houses. Real assets included in this category are traded by one person to another, but nothing new is produced.

3. An individual can use funds to repay debts incurred during some earlier period or to pay interest on debts.

4. An individual can give funds to others as gifts or pay taxes.

Only spending on newly produced goods and services (category 1) contributes to an economy's total income. The other three categories of uses represent the transfer of funds from one person to another. Combining this fact with the similar fact that only income earned by producing goods and services contributes to total income, we can derive an important result: *Total spending on newly produced goods and services in the economy equals total income earned by members of the economy (including governmental income).*

The constrained choice problem confronting an individual economic unit is illustrated in Figure 1. This schematic drawing indicates all the possible sources and uses of funds, without indicating the choices any particular individual will make.

Uses of funds
All the ways an individual can dispose of spendable funds.

Spending
Using funds to purchase newly produced goods and services.

SECTION RECAP
All spending must be financed in some manner. Funds can be raised by earning income, by selling assets, by borrowing, or by receiving gifts or transfer payments. Funds can be spent on newly produced goods and services, financial assets and used real assets, to repay debts, or as gifts or taxes.

Individual Choice and the Budget Constraint

The actual choices a person makes depend upon the individual's preferences, the set of available prices, and the individual's **budget constraint** — the resources available to support spending and asset purchases. The **absolute level of prices** — how high they are in dollar terms — combines with the budget constraint to determine *how much* an individual can buy. **Relative prices** — the prices of products compared to the prices of other products — combine with an individual's preferences to determine *what* the individual will buy.

Budget constraint
Total sources of funds available to purchase goods, services, and assets and make transfers.

Absolute price level
Dollar level of prices.

Relative price
Price of a good compared to the prices of other goods.

---

[1] This statement ignores international transfers between nations but holds true for the world economy.

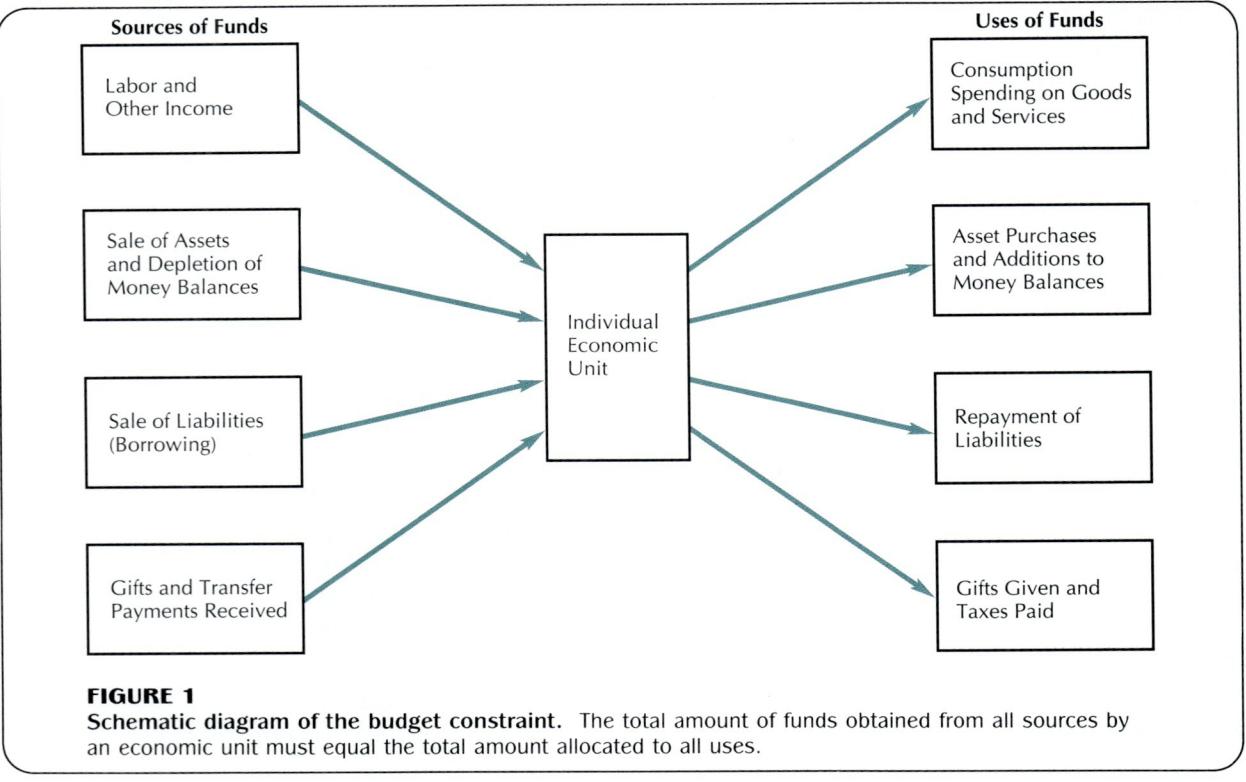

FIGURE 1
Schematic diagram of the budget constraint. The total amount of funds obtained from all sources by an economic unit must equal the total amount allocated to all uses.

An Example

Let's begin with an example. Suppose that Ricardo purchases only three goods and services: food, tickets to entertainment events, and clothing. The only real item he sells is labor services. He owns two financial assets, a savings deposit and money. He does not currently have any debts, though he realizes that he can borrow should he choose to.

The total of Ricardo's spending on food, tickets, and clothing plus any additions to his holdings of financial assets (savings deposits and money) must equal the total of his income plus any funds derived by selling financial assets (depleting his savings deposit or money balances). Thus, Ricardo's budget constraint takes the following form:

Sources of Funds		Uses of Funds
Labor income	=	Spending on food
+		+
Deductions from savings deposit		Spending on tickets
+		+
Deductions from money holdings		Spending on clothing
		+
		Additions to savings deposit
		+
		Additions to money holdings

TABLE 1
The sources and uses of Ricardo's funds

Item	Price	×	Quantity	=	Received	or	Used
Labor	$ 8		40		$320		
Food	2		24				$ 48
Tickets	12		2				24
Clothing	25		8				200
Savings deposit addition	1		40				40
Money addition	1		8				8
Total sources					$320		
Total uses							$320

(We have ignored any interest earned on Ricardo's savings deposit for the sake of simplicity. Interest earnings would add a small amount to the sources side of the budget constraint without significantly changing the results.)

It is important to note that during any time period Ricardo's asset holdings cannot both rise and fall. For example, if during a particular month his savings deposit balance increases, the category "deductions from savings deposit" must be zero. The same holds true for money holdings.

Inserting some numbers into the budget constraint should clarify Ricardo's situation. Suppose Ricardo works forty hours per week at a wage of $8 per hour. His labor income is the wage rate, $W = \$8$, times the number of hours worked, forty, or $320. If Ricardo does not reduce either his savings deposit or money balances, the left-hand side of the budget constraint simplifies to $W \times Q_L$ (where Q_L is the quantity of labor Ricardo supplies, forty hours), or $\$8 \times 40 = \$320$. Ricardo's spendable funds during the week total $320.

On the right-hand side of the equation are the uses of Ricardo's funds. These uses must total $320. Suppose that Ricardo purchases 24 units of food at $2 per unit, 2 units of tickets at $12 per unit, and 8 units of clothing at $25 per unit. His total expenditures on goods and services equal ($2 × 24) + ($12 × 2) + ($25 × 8) = $272. Ricardo chooses to add the remaining $48 to his savings deposit ($40) and his money holdings ($8). Table 1 summarizes this information.

The pattern of sources and uses illustrated in Table 1 is only one among an infinite number of possible patterns. The combination selected by Ricardo reflects his preferences, his income, and the relative prices of the goods and assets. Note that Ricardo's preferences also affect his income. If he chose to do so, he could work more hours and earn more. The only variables Ricardo cannot control are the prices of goods, labor, and assets.[2]

---

[2] Another price relevant to Ricardo's choice of consumption goods, financial assets, and labor supply is the interest rate. Funds deposited in savings deposits earn interest. Although the price of a unit of savings deposit is constant at $1, the interest earned on savings deposits is variable. Changes in the interest rate offered on savings deposits may affect Ricardo's consumption–saving choice.

The General Case

In general, the budget constraint reduces to the following:

Sources		Uses
Total earned from sale of goods and services	=	Total spent on goods and services
+		+
Asset earnings: interest, dividends		Interest payments on liabilities
+		+
Earnings from asset sales		Purchases of assets
+		+
Money supplied to market		Additional money demanded
+		+
Borrowing by issuing debts		Repayment of debts
+		+
Gifts received		Gifts given

SECTION RECAP
The budget constraint, which arises because all spending must be financed, links together an individual's spending and financing decisions. A decision to alter one spending or financing flow necessarily affects at least one other spending or financing flow.

Note that several of the preceding terms are the sums of the quantities of the various items bought or sold times their prices. For example, spending on goods and services equals the price of milk times the quantity of milk purchased per week, plus the price of gasoline times the number of gallons purchased per week, plus the price of books times the number of books purchased per week, plus the prices of all other goods and services times their quantities. In short, the uses and sources of funds are closely linked to demand and supply of goods and assets and market-clearing prices.

Market Demands and Supplies

A budget constraint applies at the market level as well as at the individual level. Chapter 3 showed that market demand and supply are the summation of individual demands and supplies. The total quantity of a good demanded at a particular price equals the sum of the individual quantities demanded at that price. If the quantities demanded of goods and services, assets, and money must equal the quantities supplied for each individual and we add together the budget constraints of all individuals, the *sum of quantities demanded in all markets must equal the sum of quantities supplied in all markets.*

For example, in Ricardo's case, the sum of quantities demanded equaled his labor income (his only source of funds), $320. Suppose a second consumer's budget constraint shows that the total quantity of goods and services, assets, and money she demands is $400, which equals her labor income (also her only source of funds). Adding their budget constraints together yields the following:

$$\begin{array}{ccc} \text{Income (sources)} & & \text{Quantities demanded (uses)} \\ \$320 + 400 & = & \$320 + 400 \end{array}$$

The budget constraint holds not only for individuals separately, but also for all individuals collectively: *Sources of funds must equal uses of funds in the aggregate.*

Interdependence of Markets

Because the aggregate budget constraint applies to the entire economy, market demands and supplies are interdependent, just as individual demands and supplies are interdependent. The preferences of millions of people determine the quantities of goods, services, and assets supplied to and demanded in markets. These preferences also determine the relative prices at which goods, services, and assets are traded. When preferences change, the composition of production and prices also change.

The demand for any particular product depends in general on the demands and supplies for all other goods, services, and assets in the economy. For example, a decrease in the market demand for bicycles implies that at least one other market demand or supply must also change. The market demand for motor scooters might rise by the amount that the demand for bicycles falls. In this case the composition of production changes, although the total level of production might remain constant. Another possibility is that the market supply of labor might decrease by enough to offset the decline in demand. In this case total production falls, as people choose to produce and consume less and enjoy more leisure. The budget constraint does not tell us exactly what happens, but it does tell us that *something* adjusts to maintain equality of total demands and supplies.

Changes in market demands and supplies generate changes in the economy's relative price structure. Figure 2 illustrates this proposition. If the de-

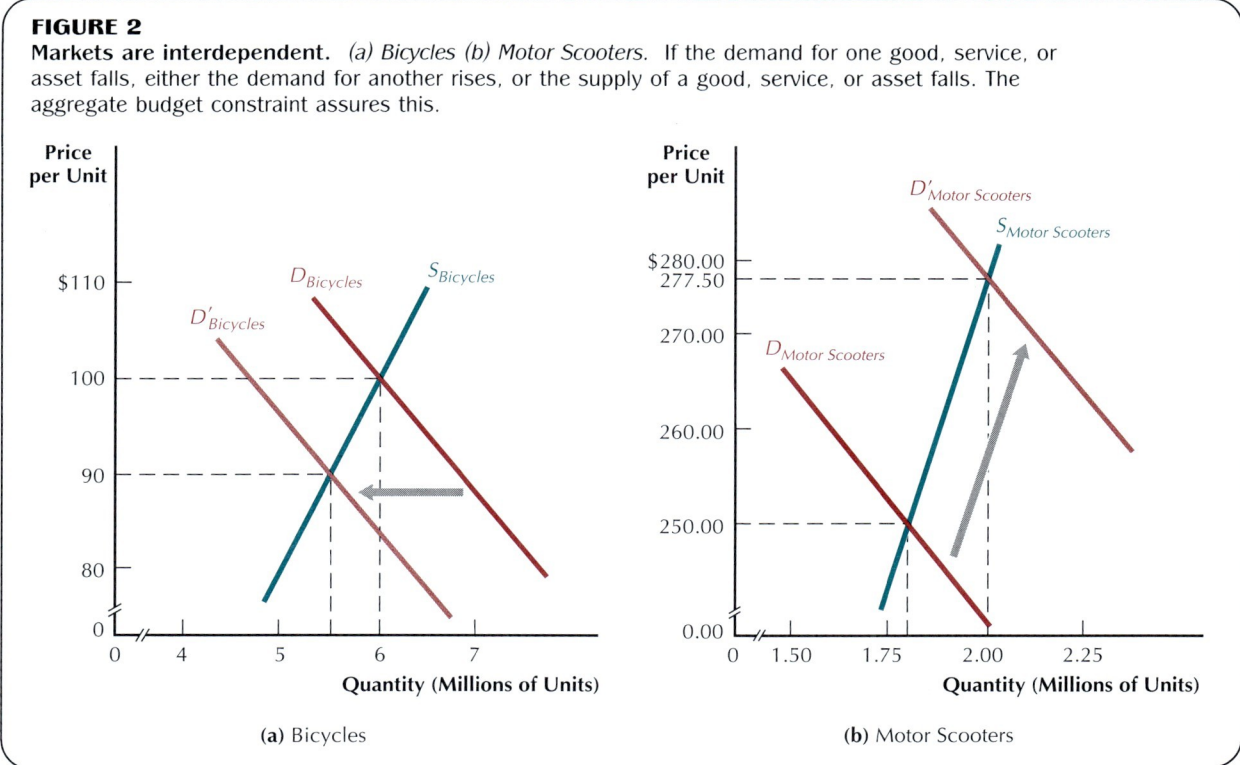

FIGURE 2
Markets are interdependent. *(a) Bicycles (b) Motor Scooters.* If the demand for one good, service, or asset falls, either the demand for another rises, or the supply of a good, service, or asset falls. The aggregate budget constraint assures this.

(a) Bicycles

(b) Motor Scooters

mand for bicycles declines and the decline is offset by an increase in the demand for motor scooters, the price of bicycles declines while the price of motor scooters increases. Note that this rearrangement of market prices need not disturb the total dollar value of the demand for goods and services. Figure 2 (a) shows that total expenditures on bicycles fall from $100 × 6 million = $600 million to $90 × 5.5 million = $495 million, a decline of $105 million. However, expenditures on motor scooters rise from $250 × 1.8 million = $450 million to $277.50 × 2 million = $555 million, an increase of $105 million [Figure 2 (b)]. Total expenditures on goods and services remain the same.

This example illustrates a very important point: *Even if the total value of goods and services bought and sold in the economy during a particular time period remains constant, relative prices and market quantities traded can change significantly.* This fact is important to remember as we study macroeconomics. It means that even in an economy that appears stable, a great deal of price and quantity shifting may be occurring.

One more very important point implied by the aggregate budget constraint must be highlighted. The budget constraint states that the total sources of funds in the economy equal the total uses of funds. Put another way, the total dollar value of the demand for goods and services plus additions to asset and money holdings equals the total dollar value of goods and services supplied plus reductions in asset and money holdings. The budget constraint does *not* state that at any existing set of prices, all markets are in equilibrium. It is quite possible that quantity demanded exceeds quantity supplied in some markets, while quantity supplied exceeds quantity demanded in others *at a particular set of prices*. Such disequilibrium causes relative prices to change, with excess demand driving prices up in some markets and excess supply driving prices down in others.

SECTION RECAP
A change in demand or supply in one market causes offsetting changes in at least one other market.

Aggregation across Markets

Moving from the level of the individual to the level of the market represents an immense simplification. However, to clarify the discussion of changes in the aggregate economy, we must further simplify things. Although there are fewer markets than individual economic agents in an economy, a very large number of markets exists. The markets for bicycles and motor scooters represent only two of thousands of markets that make up the macroeconomy.

It is not possible for us to study the behavior of the aggregate economy by keeping track of what happens in thousands of different markets. In fact, most of what goes on in individual markets is of very little interest to a macroeconomist. Most of the demand and supply changes and the resulting relative price changes have little effect on the aggregate levels of spending, output, and employment. How can we further simplify the model?

A logical way to proceed is to add up the production of all goods and services into one number. To do this we must use a common unit of measurement; we cannot add bushels of wheat and gallons of paint and come up with a meaningful number. However, adding the dollar value of wheat produced and sold to the dollar value of paint produced and sold solves the measurement problem. The dollar value of goods and services produced during a particular time period is a meaningful concept.

Summing the dollar amounts spent in individual markets yields the following:

>Total receipts from the sale of goods and services +
>Total receipts from the sale of assets +
>Money supplied from money balances =
>Total spending on goods and services
>+ Total spending on assets
>+ Money demanded to add to money balances

All the preceding terms are denominated in dollars and can be added together.

Gross National Product

Earlier in the chapter we argued that only production creates goods and services available for consumption and generates income. All other sources and uses of funds are merely exchanges of assets. The aggregate budget constraint illustrates the equality of the value of spending on goods and services and the value of income from producing goods and services:

>Total spending on goods and services =
>Total receipts from the sale of goods and services

The total market value of all goods and services produced for final use during a period of time is called the **gross national product**, or **GNP**. As the budget equation shows, GNP can be measured by adding up either total spending on new goods and services or total income earned from the production of new goods and services. We examine each approach in turn.

Expenditure Approach In calculating GNP, economists include only spending on goods and services produced for final use. Spending on goods and services used to produce other goods and services is omitted. For example, spending on the basic **factor inputs** — labor, raw materials, and energy — used to produce goods and services is not counted as part of GNP, because the value of factor inputs is included in the value of final products. Similarly, spending on **intermediate goods** that go into the production of final goods is excluded for the same reason. For example, the amount spent by General Motors to purchase steel for their automobiles is not included in GNP, because the value of the finished autos includes the value of the steel. Counting the value of both the steel and the autos would be double counting.

GNP is calculated by adding up the dollar value of final goods and services produced in each market in the economy. Table 2 illustrates this process for a simple three-good economy. The table shows that in Year 1 GNP equals $205,000. This represents the current dollar — or *nominal* — value of food, clothing, and shelter produced that year.

When actually calculating GNP, economists group expenditures into four basic categories. The largest category, **consumption expenditures**, includes all spending on goods and services by households. **Investment spending** includes business purchases of plant and equipment and inventory, as well as residential construction. If a family purchases a newly built house, the production of the house is counted in the residential construction category. **Government purchases** of goods and services include both consumption and investment items,

Gross national product (GNP)
Total market value of final goods and services produced during a time period.

Factor inputs
Unprocessed materials and labor services used to produce goods and services.

Intermediate goods
Produced goods that enter into the production of other goods or services.

Consumption expenditures
All spending by households on new goods and services, with the exception of the purchase of new houses.

Investment spending
Purchases of plant, equipment, and inventories by businesses and of new houses by households.

Government purchases
Spending on goods and services; excludes transfer payments.

TABLE 2
GNP in a three-good economy

Year	Food Price	Food Quantity	Clothing Price	Clothing Quantity	Shelter Price	Shelter Quantity	GNP
1	$20	4000	$25	3000	$100	500	$205,000
2	$22	4200	$23	2700	$120	510	$215,700

Note: GNP equals the sum of P × Q for food, clothing, and shelter.

---

though the national income accounts do not show this. That is, some government purchases are used up immediately or in a very short time, while others, such as buildings or road construction, last for years. Government transfer payments represent the redistribution of income from taxpayers to transfer recipients and are not included in GNP.

Finally, **net exports**—exports minus imports—must be added to expenditures. **Exports** are foreign spending on domestically produced goods and services. Such expenditures must be added to obtain a measure of expenditures on domestic production. However, not all domestic spending goes toward the purchase of domestically produced goods and services. A substantial amount of spending is on **imports**—domestic purchases of goods and services produced in foreign economies. Goods imported from other economies do not add to spending on domestic production, although such purchases are included in consumption, investment, and government purchases. To avoid counting them as part of the demand for domestic production, the value of imports must be subtracted from total spending to obtain a correct measure of GNP.

The spending approach to GNP is summarized by the following equation:

$$GNP = C + I + G + NX$$

where C is consumption spending, I is investment spending, G is government purchases, and NX is net exports.

The expenditure approach to GNP calculation contains two complications that deserve comment. First, even in a market economy, not all goods and services produced can be valued at market prices, since not all goods included in GNP are actually traded in markets. Thus, GNP includes estimates of some nontraded goods and services, such as the value of food grown and consumed by farm families. Also included is the estimated value of the housing services consumed by families who own their own homes. This adjustment is included so that the value of rental housing services and that of owner-occupied housing services are treated the same way. Since some two thirds of all housing in the United States is owner-occupied, the housing adjustment is a large one. A number of other imputed values are also included in GNP.

The second complication is that GNP is a measure of the market value of *production*, not of *sales* (as the budget constraint implies). It is possible for the value of goods produced during a period to differ by several billion dollars from the value of sales in that period. The difference is reflected in **inventory changes**—increases or decreases in the value of inventories held by businesses.

Net exports
Exports minus imports.

Exports
Sales of domestically produced goods and services to foreigners.

Imports
Purchases of foreign-produced goods and services by domestic households, businesses, and governmental units.

Inventory changes
Increases or decreases in business holdings of raw materials, unfinished goods, or finished goods ready for sale.

Inventory accumulation or liquidation is counted as positive or negative spending in the GNP accounts. Thus, expenditures equal production by definition. For example, suppose that in a certain year all the business firms in the economy produce $5000 billion worth of goods and services but sell only $4950 billion worth. The other $50 billion worth of goods is added to business inventories (services cannot be stored; only goods can be inventoried). This $50 billion is recorded in the National Income and Product Accounts as business investment. Thus, officially recorded expenditures equal the value of production.

Income (Value Added) Approach All expenditures on goods and services represent income for somebody. The clearest example of this is when someone is hired to provide a service requiring no input other than labor. For example, if you hire Bryan, a young neighbor, to mow your lawn, using your lawnmower and gasoline, the wage you pay to Bryan represents his income. Bryan has no input expenses to subtract.

The principle still applies if Bryan provides his own lawnmower and gasoline. Suppose you pay Bryan $10 for the job. He uses $1 worth of fuel and puts another 50¢ into an account to repair or replace the mower when it wears out. In this case, Bryan's net income is $8.50. However, the dollar spent on gasoline becomes income for someone else. The service station attendant, the service station owner, the petroleum distributor, the refining company, and perhaps an Arab shiek all get a little piece of that dollar. The 50¢ placed in the mower replacement account will also eventually provide income for others. The $10 paid to Bryan becomes income whether Bryan gets to keep all of it or not.

The income earned by producing goods can also be calculated by summing the value added to the product at each stage of production. **Value added** is the difference between the value of a product and the value of the material inputs used in the production of the product. As an example of the value-added approach, consider the steps in the production chain of a simple head of lettuce. The lettuce is grown in California. The grower sells the lettuce to a processing company for 10¢ per head. The processing company grades the lettuce, washes it, and packs it in crates, before selling it for 15¢ a head to a distributor. The distributor ships the lettuce all over the country to wholesalers. The price charged to a wholesaler depends upon the distance the lettuce must be shipped. Let's assume that the price in the midwest is 30¢ per head. The wholesaler sells the lettuce to a retailer for 40¢ per head. The retailer, a supermarket, washes the lettuce again, wraps it in cellophane, and places it in a refrigerated display unit. The retailer charges shoppers 65¢ per head.

Summing up the value added at each stage of the process yields 10 + 5 + 15 + 10 + 25 = 65 cents. This equals the final value of the produce sold to the consumer. This result is perfectly general: *The total value added to a product in its various production stages equals the final market value of the product.*

Concentrating on value added focuses attention on the income earned from production. Adding up all incomes earned in a particular year generates a total called **national income**. This reflects the income earned by all private economic units (households and business firms) from the production of goods and services during the year. National income does not equal gross national product, however. The reason is simple: Not quite all spending gets to private economic units as income. Two major categories must be subtracted from

Value added
Difference between the market value of a good or service and the value of the material inputs used in its production.

National income
Total income earned by private economic units (households and businesses) during a period.

Why the Disagreement?

Social Welfare and Real GNP

Real GNP is a measure of the goods and services produced by an economy during a particular period. These goods and services are available for current consumption or for investment that increases future production and consumption. How the economy's production is distributed is very important, but setting that issue aside, it seems clear that, for a given population, the higher the level of real GNP, the better off the citizens of a nation are. A higher real GNP means that there are more goods and services per person to be enjoyed.

Yet it is easy to find economists who disagree with the assertion that higher real GNP implies higher social welfare. Why the disagreement?

The basic issue is very simple: Real GNP and social welfare are not the same thing. Real GNP measures the production of goods and services. It does not measure a host of other factors that affect national well-being. For example, a sharp increase in robberies and vandalism nationwide might cause real GNP to rise. Households would attempt to protect themselves and their property by purchasing deadbolt locks for their doors, putting bars on first-floor windows, installing burglar alarm systems, and perhaps buying guard dogs or firearms. The production of such theft-prevention goods and the installation services of people selling them would add to measured real GNP. However, it would be difficult to maintain that a nation under siege from within is better off than it was before the crime wave and the increase in real GNP that accompanied it.

Real GNP is not meant to be a measure of social welfare. It ignores some things that make people better off while counting production that yields little or no

---

SECTION RECAP

Gross national product is an aggregate measure of production during a period of time in current prices. Prices and quantities produced in individual markets can rise and fall even if GNP is constant. GNP can be measured either by adding up spending on newly produced final goods and services or by adding up the incomes earned in the production of new final goods and services.

spending to derive national income: capital consumption allowances (depreciation) and indirect business taxes.

When Bryan mowed your lawn using his own lawnmower, he set aside 50¢ to cover the repair and replacement of the mower. The 50¢ went into Bryan's capital consumption allowance account. Someday it will be spent to replace his depreciated mower. For now, it should not be counted as anyone's income. It should not be counted as part of Bryan's income, because Bryan's failure to replace his mower will put him out of business. Just to maintain his present business condition Bryan must replace his depreciated equipment. However, so long as he retains the funds in his capital consumption account, the funds do not represent income to anyone else either.

The second category—indirect business taxes—is even easier to understand. Most states charge sales tax on goods sold at the retail level. Stores collect the sales tax for the state (and possibly for the local) government. This part of spending, which usually ranges from 3 to 8 percent of the purchase price, goes directly to government. It is not counted as part of national income.

When capital consumption allowances and indirect business taxes (plus a few minor items) are added to the incomes earned by private economic units, the total equals gross national product.

Measuring Production When Prices Are Changing

Gross national product is a reasonable measure of an economy's output during a particular time period. However, because GNP measures output in terms of dollar prices, price changes can alter the value of GNP. Furthermore, when

consumer satisfaction. As another example, GNP does not include the value of leisure. The average number of hours worked each week is much lower now than it was in the nineteenth century. Although real GNP is much higher now than it was then, the higher value reflects only the increased production of goods and services. It does not reflect the extra leisure time we enjoy along with more goods and services.

On the other hand, the production of GNP can generate negative effects that reduce social welfare. Increased industrial production pollutes the environment. Large-scale production forces large numbers of people to live in small areas, thus producing traffic congestion and other urban problems. The chemicals used to boost agricultural productivity seep into water systems, and excessive plowing leads to soil erosion. All the goods and services we consume come in packages or containers. When we dispose of them, we create mountains of garbage. None of these factors is accounted for by GNP statistics.

Given all these problems, are GNP figures of any use at all? The answer to that question is an unqualified yes. Economic growth from one year to another, measured by a rise in real GNP, usually signals an increase in economic well-being. If other social or ecological conditions have not changed dramatically, a real GNP increase probably does signal an increase in welfare. Furthermore, knowing how the productive sector of the economy is performing is important to economists and policymakers. Without data, it is difficult to diagnose problems or propose remedies. Thus, we are *not* arguing that GNP statistics are of little value; we *are* arguing that the limits of such statistics should be understood.

---

both prices and quantities are changing, some rising and some falling, it becomes difficult to determine whether total production has increased or decreased.

We can illustrate this problem by returning to the simple three-good economy discussed earlier. Looking back at Table 2, we see that the value of GNP in the three-good economy rose from $205,000 to $215,700 from Year 1 to Year 2. Does this mean that more goods and services were produced in Year 2 than in Year 1? Not necessarily. GNP obviously rose, but production was mixed, rising in the food and shelter markets and falling in the clothing market. Since GNP is the sum of individual quantities *multiplied by individual prices*, it is possible that production fell even though GNP rose. To determine whether production rose or fell, we need a measure of total production that is not affected by price changes.

Constructing such a measure requires a bit of thought, since we cannot just add quantities together; we must measure production using a common unit, such as dollars. Economists solve the measurement problem by measuring production in terms of constant prices. For example, suppose we choose Year 1 as the **base year**—the year to which all other years' prices and outputs are compared. We calculate GNP for Year 1 by multiplying individual prices times quantities and adding the expenditures. However, since we wish to find out if actual production has increased from Year 1 to Year 2, we derive GNP for Year 2 a bit differently. We obtain our measure of GNP for Year 2 by multiplying *Year 1 prices* times *Year 2 quantities*. That is, we hold prices constant at their Year 1 values, but we allow quantities to change to their Year 2 values.

Table 3 replicates Table 2, with one important difference: All prices are held at their Year 1 levels. The GNP figures given in the final column are for Year 1 prices; Year 1 is the base year.

Base year
Year to which other years' price and output levels are compared.

TABLE 3
GNP in a three-good economy in base-year prices

Year	Food Price	Food Quantity	Clothing Price	Clothing Quantity	Shelter Price	Shelter Quantity	GNP
1	$20	4000	$25	3000	$100	500	$205,000
2	$20	4200	$25	2700	$100	510	$202,500

Note: GNP equals the sum of Year 1 prices times Year 1 and Year 2 quantities of food, clothing, and shelter.

When the GNP figure for Year 2 is recalculated using base-year (Year 1) prices, the value falls sharply. According to this calculation, the *real value of production* — the value of production in base-year prices — declined from Year 1 to Year 2. The apparent increase in production, as measured by GNP values, was due to price increases.

When economists measure GNP in base-year prices rather than current-year prices, they call the measure **real GNP (RGNP)**. Real GNP is a measure of aggregate production relative to some base year — the year from which prices are derived. The selection of a base year is essentially arbitrary, although reasons exist for choosing a "normal" year rather than, say, a war year or a year in the depths of a depression. These reasons have to do with the construction of price indexes, the topic to which we now turn.

Real GNP (RGNP)
GNP measured in base-year prices.

Price Indexes

Just how much did prices rise from Year 1 to Year 2 in Table 2? When we ask such a question, we are really asking about the movement in the **general** or **average price level** — the average of all prices of new goods and services in the economy. Different prices obviously rose by different amounts. Food prices rose by 10 percent (from $20 to $22), clothing prices *fell* by 8 percent, and the price of shelter rose by 20 percent. But how much did the average price level rise?

We could simply add together the three percentage price changes and divide by three. This would yield (10 − 8 + 20)/3 = 7.33 percent. However, this simple approach assumes that an equal number of units of food, clothing, and shelter were purchased. It does not account for the fact that a great many units of food may be purchased each month while relatively few units of clothing are bought. A nickel increase in the price of a gallon of milk may have a greater impact on consumers than a $5 increase in the price of designer jeans. Somehow we need to adjust for quantities purchased.

The way economists adjust for uneven buying patterns is by using a weighted average of prices. Each price is weighted by the number of units of that good purchased. The derivation of one such index is straightforward. Divide the GNP value for a given year in current prices by the GNP value for that same year in base-year prices, then multiply by 100 to put the price index in

Average or General price level
Weighted average of prices of a collection of goods and services or assets.

Price Indexes

Let's look at the price index a bit more closely to derive its general form. The price index derived here is called the *implicit price deflator*. As we saw in the example, for any year, PI = (GNP/RGNP) × 100, where GNP is gross national product in current prices and RGNP is gross national product in base-year prices. Dissecting GNP and RGNP, we derive the following equation for PI:

$$PI = \frac{(Pc_1 Qc_1 + Pc_2 Qc_2 + \ldots + Pc_n Qc_n)}{(Pb_1 Qc_1 + Pb_2 Qc_2 + \ldots + Pb_n Qc_n)} \times 100$$

where Pc and Pb stand for current and base-year prices, respectively, Qc stands for current-year quantities, and the subscript numbers index all the goods and services produced in markets 1 through n (all the markets for goods and services).

One can see from the equation that *the implicit price deflator uses current-year quantity weights,* since current-year quantities appear in both the numerator and the denominator.

Such a price index is not the only kind one can estimate. The most publicized aggregate price index is the *consumer price index (CPI)*. It is formed slightly differently. The CPI uses *base-year quantity weights.* That is, it divides the sum of all the (Pc × Qb) terms by the sum of the (Pb × Qb) terms. (By the way, it is because the CPI type of index uses base-year quantity weights that the base year should be "normal." Choosing an abnormal year would lead to abnormal weights.) Unlike the implicit price deflator, the CPI does not include the prices of all final goods and services produced in the economy. The CPI includes only a market basket of commonly consumed goods, as chosen by government statisticians:

$$CPI = \frac{(Pc_1 Qb_1 + Pc_2 Qb_2 + \ldots + Pc_n Qb_n)}{(Pb_1 Qb_1 + Pb_2 Qb_2 + \ldots + Pb_n Qb_n)} \times 100$$

Going back to the GNP example in Tables 2 and 3, we can construct a consumer price index for the three-good economy. The value of the CPI in Year 1 (the base year) is of course 100. To obtain the value in Year 2 we multiply Year 2 prices times Year 1 quantities and divide by Year 1 GNP. Multiplying Year 2 prices by Year 1 quantities, we obtain:

$$(\$22 \times 4000) + (\$23 \times 3000) + (\$120 \times 500) = \$217,000$$

Dividing by Year 1 GNP and multiplying by 100 yields:

$$(\$217,000/\$205,000) \times 100 = 1.059 \times 100 = 105.9$$

a figure that in this example is a bit lower than the implicit price deflator value of 106.5.

Why calculate the CPI in this manner? One reason is that it is simpler. The CPI is published monthly, when good estimates of current quantities are not available. Initial estimates of the CPI are produced only a few weeks after a month ends. The implicit price deflator requires a much larger amount of current data. Hence, it takes longer to calculate and is published only quarterly. A second reason is that the CPI measures the prices of a group of goods actually consumed by U.S. consumers in the base year, rather than the prices of all goods produced. A final reason is that, because the CPI quantity weights do not change from year to year, movements in the CPI reflect pure price changes. Movements in the implicit price deflator reflect movements in both prices and quantities.

The Economist's *Tool Kit*

Does It Make Economic Sense?

Are GNP Comparisons Among Nations Worth Making?

Gross national product is a measure of production during a particular period of time in a particular economy. By converting GNP to real GNP terms, the level of production within an economy at different points in time can be compared. How do we know if these RGNP levels are high or low? What is the measuring stick used to determine whether our economy is performing well or poorly? There is no absolute yardstick for determining whether the production level within an economy is satisfactory. Indeed, the answer is quite subjective, since satisfactory performance may have little correspondence to the level of real GNP. If real GNP is used to measure performance, however, the measuring stick often used is real GNP in other economies. The question asked becomes, How does the U.S. level of real GNP compare with that of other economies? Given vast differences among nations, does it make sense to compare their GNPs?

If this is to be a sensible comparison, some adjustment for absolute size of economies must be made. It hardly makes sense to compare the production level of a country with 248 million inhabitants with the production level of a country of 20 million. Thus, GNP figures are typically put on a per capita basis. Per capita GNP is GNP divided by the population of a country. It attempts to measure the amount of goods and services each individual receives on the average. Table 4 shows per capita GNP figures in terms of U.S. dollars for the year 1988 for several countries. The table indicates that in 1988,

TABLE 4
Per capita GNP for 1988 in U.S. dollars

Country	GNP
Japan	$21,020
United States	19,840
Sweden	19,300
Brazil	2,160
India	340
Nigeria	290
Bangladesh	170

Source: *World Development Report 1990* (Oxford University Press for the World Bank, 1990), Table 1, pp. 178–179.

the average U.S. citizen had a per capita GNP share of $19,840. Although actual individual incomes ranged from much lower to much higher than that figure, the average

percentage form. In compact notation:

$$PI = (GNP/RGNP) \times 100$$

where PI stands for price index.

In our example, the GNP value in Year 1 was $205,000 in both current and base-year prices (since Year 1 *is* the base year). Thus, the Year 1 value of the price index is ($205,000/$205,000) × 100 = 1 × 100 = 100. *The value of the price index in the base year is always 100.* The price index for Year 2 is ($215,700/$202,500) × 100 = 1.065 × 100 = 106.5. This indicates that the general level of prices rose by 6.5 percent from Year 1 to Year 2.

Reversing Directions In the previous example, we derived the implicit price deflator, PI, by dividing nominal GNP by real GNP and multiplying by 100. Data on nominal and real GNP are used to derive PI. It is just as simple to use data on GNP and PI to derive real GNP. Consider again the PI formula:

$$PI = (GNP/RGNP) \times 100$$

Multiplying both sides of the equation by RGNP yields:

$$PI \times RGNP = GNP \times 100$$

Now, divide both sides by PI:

$$RGNP = (GNP/PI) \times 100$$

gives some information on the economic status of the inhabitants of a country.

Note that the per capita GNP share in India in 1988 was only $340, less than 2 percent of the U.S. figure. The figure for Bangladesh was only 50 percent of the Indian figure, or less than 0.9 percent of the U.S. figure. Is it possible for an individual to live on $170 a year? Does it make economic sense?

It is safe to say that an individual could not survive in the United States on $170 — or even $290 (the Nigerian per capita GNP) — per year. Yet a hundred million citizens of Bangladesh do. What does this say about the validity of comparing GNP data across countries? At the very least, it demonstrates the need for extreme caution.

Different items are included in GNP in different countries. In the United States, most of the food produced is sold through markets and recorded as part of GNP. In many countries where agriculture still forms the backbone of the economy, most people grow their own food. The major portion of food production never passes through the market and thus never shows up in GNP. Similarly, U.S. GNP estimates include a large component representing the value of housing. In many nations, this is omitted from GNP. Many other differences exist.

Another factor to be considered is the large difference in the absolute levels of prices in different countries. In underdeveloped nations, where a large portion of the population is not really a part of the world economy, prices of the basic items that the peasants purchase are, by U.S. or European standards, incredibly low.

Comparisons of per capita GNP among nations can have some use. They indicate the relative economic condition of nations in a rough way. It is clear the the average American is much better off economically than the average Indian. However, such statistics should not be used to make precise statements about relative living standards (such as "The average American is fifty times better off than the average Indian"). The statistics were not constructed for such purposes, and using them in that manner is very misleading. The analysis of relative conditions in different countries is too complex to be reduced to one simple number such as per capita GNP.

Given data on nominal GNP and the price index, it is simple to derive real GNP.

Restating the Aggregate Budget Constraint The concept of a price index can be used to restate the aggregate budget constraint in a convenient form. Using the preceding discussion of price indexes and real GNP, we can write the aggregate budget constraint as follows:

$$(PI \times RGNP^d) + (PI^A \times A^d) + M^d =$$
$$(PI \times RGNP^s) + (PI^A \times A^s) + M^s$$

(Total spending on goods and services) is replaced by $(PI \times RGNP^d)$; (total spending on assets) by $(PI^A \times A^d)$; and (money demanded to add to money holdings) by M^d. On the sources side, (total receipts from the sale of goods and services), (total receipts from the sale of assets), and (money supplied to the market) are replaced by $(PI \times RGNP^s)$, $(PI^A \times A^s)$, and M^s, respectively. Price indexes for new goods and services (PI) and for assets (PI^A) replace individual prices, and aggregate quantities of goods and services (RGNP) and assets (A) replace individual quantities. Just as before, markets are interdependent. Aggregate demand for goods and services cannot rise unless some other aggregate demand falls or some aggregate supply rises.

SECTION RECAP
A price index is a weighted average of prices, where the weights reflect the quantities of various goods produced or consumed. Real GNP is GNP adjusted for price changes. It is found by calculating GNP at base-year prices. Real GNP and the price index are measured relative to a base year.

Summary

Having bridged the gap between individual economic behavior and aggregate economic behavior, we are now ready to begin our inquiry into the behavior of the aggregate economy. The **individual's budget constraint,** which ties together individual economic decisions, has an aggregate counterpart. This is no mere coincidence, because the **aggregate budget constraint** is derived by aggregating over individual budget constraints. The individual budget constraints were added up to derive the aggregate constraint.

The aggregate budget constraint demonstrates that **markets are interdependent.** Within both the production and financial sectors of the economy, markets are connected, and the overall condition of the production sector is not independent of the state of supply and demand in the financial sector. The demand for and supply of money are connected to both asset and product markets.

The discussion of the aggregate budget constraint also led to the discovery that the value of aggregate production equals the value of aggregate income, including some income not immediately earned by individuals. Translating this into the terminology of national income accounting, we found that **gross national product** equals **national income** plus **capital consumption allowances** and **indirect business taxes.**

Since GNP is calculated on the basis of current prices, it is of limited value in tracking the behavior of actual production over time. **Real GNP,** measured in **base-year prices,** is a better measure of production. Dividing GNP for a given year by real GNP for that same year, and multiplying by 100, yields a measure of the **average price level** known as the **implicit price deflator.**

A discussion of finer categories of the **national income accounts** appears in the chapter appendix. There we discuss the relationship among such categories as gross national product, net national product, national income, personal income, and disposable income.

Questions for Thought

Knowledge Questions

1. What are the sources from which an individual can derive spendable funds? What are the uses to which the funds can be put?
2. What is the aggregate budget constraint? How is it derived?
3. Define gross national product.
4. What is an aggregate price index?

Application Questions

5. Suppose that the economy is in macroeconomic equilibrium ($RGNP^d = RGNP^s$) and the asset market is also in equilibrium. What is the condition in the money market? If we know the conditions in two aggregated markets, do we need to specify what conditions prevail in the third market? Why or why not?
6. The people of the island nation of Simplicity produced the following goods during 1991:

   Rice — 2000 tons at 200 wan (the wan is the currency unit) per ton

   Bananas — 1000 tons at 700 wan per ton

Chicken — 800 tons at 1600 wan per ton

Cotton — 1500 bales at 250 wan per bale

Shoes — 2000 pairs at 40 wan per pair

Calculate the value of gross national product for the year.

7. Which of the following items belongs in gross national product?
    a. The value of processed leather sold to shoe companies.
    b. The value of raw rice sold in supermarkets.
    c. The value of stocks sold on the New York Stock Exchange during the year.
    d. The income of stockbrokers who deal on the New York Stock Exchange.
    e. The value of used houses traded during a year.
    f. The value of auto parts sold over the counter by auto-supply stores during a year.

8. Given the following data for the United States, calculate real GNP for the years 1984–1988:

Year	GNP	Implicit Price Deflator
1984	3,772.2	107.73
1985	4,014.9	110.95
1986	4,231.6	113.82
1987	4,524.3	117.40
1988	4,880.6	121.28

PI equals 100 in 1982. GNP is in billions of dollars.

9. Given the following U.S. data, calculate the value of the implicit price deflator for the years 1980–1984:

Year	GNP	RGNP
1980	2,732.0	3,187.1
1981	3,052.6	3,248.8
1982	3,166.0	3,166.0
1983	3,405.7	3,279.1
1984	3,772.2	3,501.4

What year is the base year for the price index?

Synthesis Questions

10. Suppose that Mad Max flies over the nation in the dead of night in his jet-powered helicopter dropping money on every household and business. There is method to Max's madness; he drops just enough money on each household and business to exactly double its money holdings. What will all the people who received this gift do with the money? Will this doubling of money balances have any effect on the quantities of goods and services produced? Why or why not?

11. An excess supply of money is related to the conditions prevailing in the product and asset markets. Suppose that an initial position of equilibrium is disturbed by an increase in the money supply. If, in a given year, the money supply rises by $30 billion while money demand is initially constant, what will happen to the extra $30 billion put into the economy? How will this affect the product and asset markets? Do you believe this will tend to restore equilibrium?

12. Suppose you were asked to develop a measure of social welfare. What elements of GNP would you include in the measure? What elements would you exclude? What measurable variables not included in GNP would you want to include in your measure?

Appendix to CHAPTER 21

National Income and Product Accounts

The National Income and Product Accounts (NIPA) are quite detailed. Gross national product is only one statistic that can be derived from these accounts. Many other income categories less inclusive than GNP, such as national income, are also estimated. This section discusses several other income categories.

The broadest measure of income and production is gross national product. GNP is *gross*; it does not adjust for the replacement of capital equipment worn out in the production of new goods and services. If capital consumption allowances are subtracted from GNP, we derive a measure of production adjusted for depreciation, called **net national product (NNP)**. It measures the economy's output after depreciated capital goods have been replaced. NNP is a measure of sustainable production. Figure 3 illustrates the relationship of NNP to GNP and to the other categories derived from NNP.

Subtracting indirect business taxes from net national product leaves national income. As noted in the discussion of the income approach to the determination of GNP, national income is the income of private economic units. Thus, national income is divided between the income of households and the income of corporations. Subtracting undistributed profits (net business saving) and Social Security taxes from national

Net national product (NNP)
GNP adjusted for capital depreciation.

FIGURE 3
National income accounts categories. GNP can be broken down into a number of smaller categories, including net national product (NNP), national income (NI), personal income (PIn), and personal disposable income (DI). This figure shows the relationships among these categories for the United States in 1990.

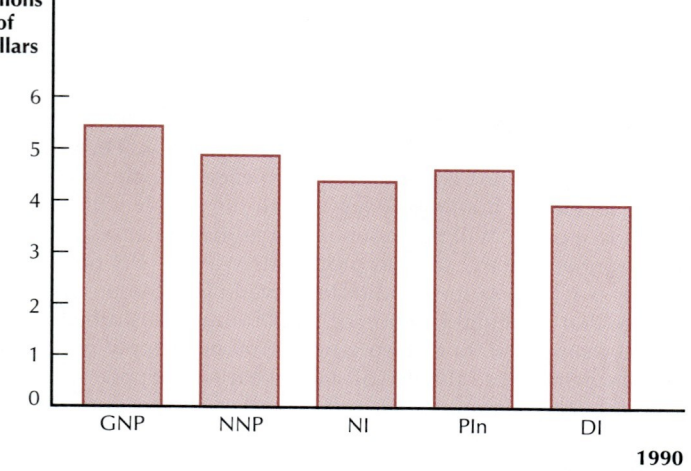

TABLE 5

National income and product accounts

1990 Data in Billions of Dollars

GNP	=	5463.0	
	−	575.7	Capital Consumption Allowances
NNP	=	4887.4	
	−	469.9	Indirect Business Taxes
NI	=	4417.5	
	−	506.9	Social Security Taxes
	−	764.2	Corporate Profits and Net Interest Payments
	+	804.7	Personal Interest and Dividend Income
	+	694.5	Government and Business Transfer Payments
PIn	=	4645.6	
	−	699.8	Personal Taxes
DI	=	3945.8	

Source: *Economic Report of the President, 1991*, Tables B-22, B-23, and B-26.

income, and adding transfer payments and interest payments, yields **personal income** — the income of household units. To obtain an estimate of personal **disposable income** — what households have available to spend or save from personal income — we subtract personal taxes. Households then either spend their disposable income on consumption goods or put it into the financial market through the personal saving stream.

Table 5 displays these NIPA categories in compact form.

Personal income
Total income of households.

Disposable income
Personal income available to spend or save.

OVERVIEW

Overview of Macroeconomics

The study of macroeconomics makes use of a rather sophisticated model. The model must explain the consumption and saving behavior of households, the investment behavior of business firms, and their effects on each other. Since both households and firms are affected by government taxing and spending, the interactions of government and the private sector must also be explained. Furthermore, the U.S. economy is not independent of the world economy; a good macroeconomic model must be able to explain the interaction between the domestic economy and foreign economies.

Pulling together all the pieces of a macroeconomic model takes time. The next eight chapters are devoted to constructing the basic macroeconomic model and using it to show how government policies work. Of necessity, we must construct the model piece by piece. This chapter provides a roadmap to where we are headed. As we noted in the previous chapter, it is easy to lose sight of the forest because of all the trees. By providing you with a brief overview of what is to come, this chapter should help keep the individual pieces of the model (the trees) in perspective.

We begin the chapter with an examination of a circular flow model of the economy. Circular flow models show how the flows of spending and income circulate through the economy. After discussing the circular flow model, we examine the behavior over the past two decades of several key macroeconomic variables. Discussing the behavior of the U.S. economy enables us to introduce some of the issues to be addressed in

CHAPTER 22

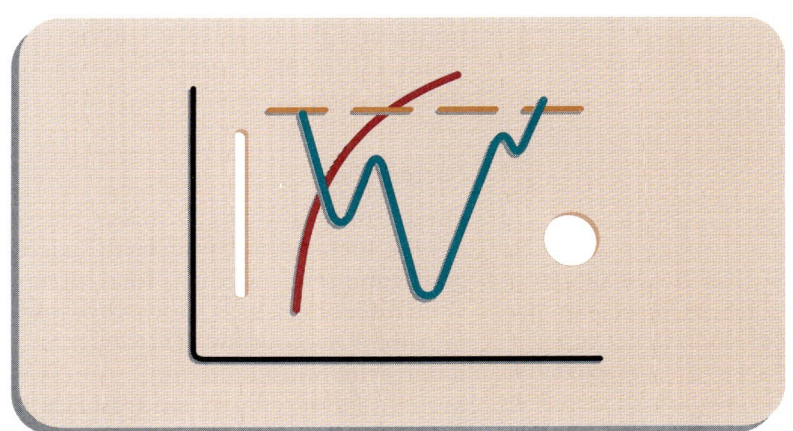

later chapters. We then turn our attention to the four major markets that are the focus of macroeconomic analysis, briefly discussing the markets for labor, goods and services, credit, and money.

Learning Objectives

After reading and studying this chapter, you will be able to:

1. Use a circular flow model to show how the various markets in the macroeconomy are related.
2. Describe in general terms how the U.S. economy is related to other economies.
3. Describe in general terms the behavior of output, prices, employment, and unemployment in the United States over the past two decades.
4. List the important variables determined in each of the four major macroeconomic markets.

The Macroeconomic System

The macroeconomy is made up of thousands of individual markets in which millions of decision makers interact. Microeconomics analyzes the effect of changes in economic variables on equilibrium in individual markets, while typically ignoring the interactions among markets. Such interactions are the essence of macroeconomics. Whereas microeconomics focuses on narrowly defined markets, macroeconomics examines aggregate markets, analyzing how changes in economic variables affect particular aggregate markets and how the effects are transmitted across markets.

A circular flow model serves as a good device to illustrate the scope of macroeconomics. A **circular flow model** shows the flow of spending on goods and services from households to business firms and the flow of income from businesses to households as payment for factors of production. More complicated circular flow models also include the flow of saving from households through financial markets to business firms, the flow of taxes to government and government purchases and transfer payments to businesses and households, and the flows of spending and assets to and from foreign economies. In the following sections we develop both simple and complex circular flow models.

Circular flow model
Illustrates the flows of resources, spending, and income that connect the various sectors of the economy.

Circular Flow

The circular flow model makes use of the fact that one person's spending is another person's income. In the aggregate, total spending on newly produced goods and services equals total income. Figure 1 illustrates this with a **circular flow diagram**, which shows the flows of real resources and money payments in a market economy. This diagram is a highly simplified two-sector model linking the household and business sectors. Figure 1 shows that real resource inputs—labor services, land, and capital—are supplied by households to business firms. In return the households receive income payments. The households use the income earned from supplying resource inputs to purchase the goods

Circular flow diagram
Graphical illustration of the economy's circular flow of spending and income.

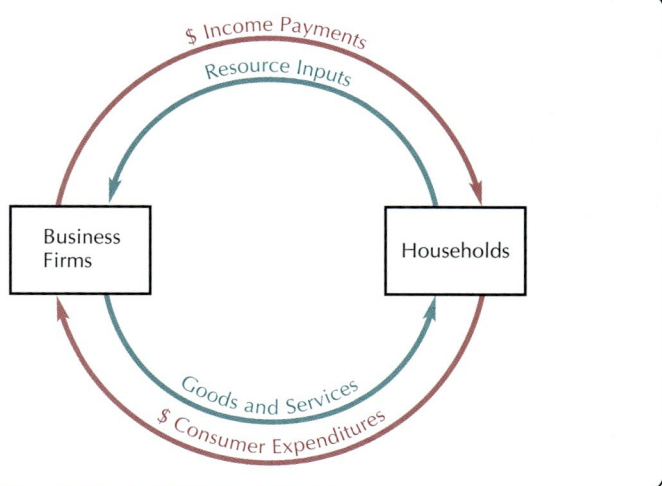

FIGURE 1
Simple circular flow diagram. The inner flow of real goods, services, and inputs moving between households and business firms is financed by the outer monetary flow of consumer expenditures and income payments.

and services produced by businesses. Money payments flow from households to businesses as consumer expenditures, while real goods and services flow from businesses to households in return.

The simple two-sector model ignores the financial sector, the government sector, and the foreign sector. It implicitly assumes that households use all the income they earn to purchase goods and services produced by firms. However, the diagram is useful, because it shows that a complete flow of physical resources and goods and services (the inner circle) is balanced by a complete flow of money incomes and expenditures (the outer circle). The amount of income earned by households depends on the demand for inputs by businesses. At the same time, the business demand for inputs depends on the flow of consumer spending. The level of output and spending are determined jointly.

The fact that the flow of expenditures on goods and services equals the flow of income to households enables us to measure aggregate production (GNP) in two ways: by measuring the expenditures themselves or by measuring the incomes received. This is true for both the two-sector circular flow model, which includes only consumption expenditures, and the expanded circular flow model, which includes flows of spending on investment goods, government purchases, and net exports. As we saw in the previous chapter, these alternative approaches are called the expenditure approach and the income approach to GNP calculation.

Income and Expenditure Categories

Table 1 shows U.S. GNP in 1990 broken into expenditure and income categories. Column 1 presents the breakdown by sources of income. The numbers in parentheses beside each income category represent the percentage of total income included in that category. It is obvious that wages and salaries form

TABLE 1
GNP by income and expenditure categories (1990 percentages)

Income Categories	Expenditure Categories
Wages and salaries (59.4)	Consumer expenditures (67.0)
Capital consumption (10.5)	Government purchases (20.1)
Net interest (8.5)	Gross investment (13.6)
Indirect business taxes (8.1)	Net exports (−0.7)
Corporate profits (5.4)	[Exports (12.3)]
Proprietors' income (7.4)	[Imports (13.0)]
Rental income of persons (0.1)	

GNP = $5,463.0 Billion

Definitions: Capital consumption allowances — business earnings used to replace worn-out plant and equipment. Net interest — excess of interest payments made by the business sector over interest payments received by the business sector. Indirect business taxes — primarily sales and excise taxes. Rental income of persons — includes rent paid and the estimated value of rent in effect paid by homeowners to themselves, net of costs.
Note: Percentages do not add to 100 due to rounding error.
Source: *Economic Report of the President, 1991,* Tables B-1, B-22, and B-24.

the most important category. When it is recognized that proprietors' income includes a large amount of wage and salary income, it becomes clear that about two thirds of GNP is earned in the form of wages and salaries. (Proprietors' income is the income of individuals who work for themselves and thus includes both salaries and profits.) Note that the unusual income categories are defined at the bottom of Table 1.

The second column of the table shows the expenditure categories into which GNP can be broken. This breakdown is very important in macroeconomic modeling. The theory of macroeconomic behavior is based on understanding the behavior of the aggregate expenditure categories. The percentages in parentheses indicate that consumption expenditures account for the bulk of spending on new goods and services in the United States. Net exports can be either positive or negative, but either way it is always the smallest category of expenditures. (This is not to say it is unimportant; $50 billion or more is not peanuts!)

One last feature concerning an expenditure category should be reiterated. The government purchases category includes only government spending on goods and services. It does *not* include the billions of dollars of transfer payments made by federal, state, and local governments each year. Transfer payments represent the redistribution of income. The government receives nothing in return for these payments. Some of the major transfer payments are Social Security payments, Aid to Families with Dependent Children, unemployment insurance benefits, and veterans' benefits. Again, these payments are not included in the government purchases figure in Table 1.

Expanded Circular Flow Model

Since the circular flow diagram in Figure 1 includes only the household and business sectors, it is somewhat misleading. Not all income finds its way back to businesses in the form of consumer expenditures. Some household income is saved. It flows through the financial sector to borrowers of many types — businesses, governmental units, and foreign borrowers. (And of course some households borrow, while others save.) Some income is paid to government in the form of taxes. Government uses tax revenues to purchase goods and services and redistribute income through transfer payments. Even some consumer spending does not flow to domestic businesses. Some flows abroad to pay for imports. Figure 2 presents an expanded circular flow diagram that illustrates how the financial system, the government sector, and the foreign sector affect the aggregate flow of goods and services.

Financial sector
Markets and institutions that transfer funds from savers to borrowers.

The inclusion of the **financial sector** in the circular flow model enables us to discuss the tendency of households and firms to save and borrow. Not all income is immediately consumed by households. A portion is saved in the form of financial assets. Such assets might include savings accounts at banks (which provide funds for bank lending) and stocks and bonds issued by corporations. Whatever the exact form of a financial claim, such a claim represents the transfer of money from income earners through the financial sector to borrowers who wish to spend more than they have earned during the current period. Both households and businesses save and borrow, although the household sector is the only net saving sector (that is, the only sector that saves more than it borrows).

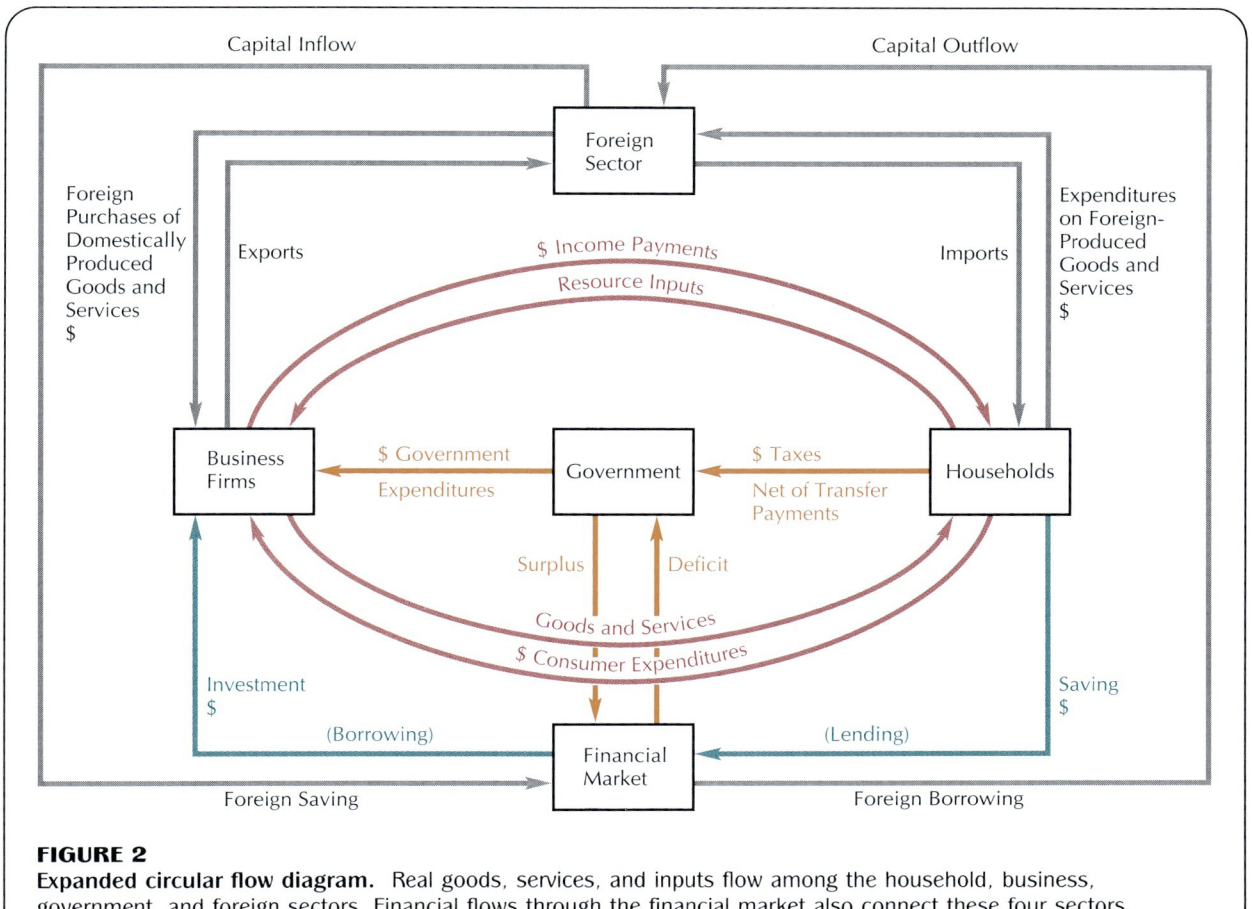

FIGURE 2
Expanded circular flow diagram. Real goods, services, and inputs flow among the household, business, government, and foreign sectors. Financial flows through the financial market also connect these four sectors.

The financial sector is important because it allows households and firms that want to spend less than they earn to channel their savings into productive uses. In particular, the financial sector connects savers with businesses that want to borrow funds to expand their productive capacity. Without a financial market in which they can borrow or sell stock, businesses would not be able to raise investment funds as cheaply or as easily. Investment spending would be lower than it is in the presence of developed financial markets. Since investment spending is a significant portion of aggregate spending, GNP would be lower if investment spending were lower. Thus, the entire circular flow of production and income would be smaller without a financial sector to channel savings back into the spending stream.

The **government sector** is extremely important in modern economies. Governments claim a sizable share of GNP as taxes, draining funds out of the spending flow. However, government purchases and transfer payments add to the flow of spending and income, respectively. Figure 2 shows government expenditures going exclusively to business firms. However, a large share of actual government spending goes toward the purchase of labor services from

Government sector
Spending, revenue, and financial flows to and from governmental units.

Does It Make **Economic Sense?**

Say's Law of Markets

The basic circular flow of production and income, presented in Figure 1, clarifies an important fact of economic life: Income depends on production. Households supply resources to firms, which in turn use the resources to produce goods and services. The income earned by providing resources to firms enables households to buy the goods and services. The income earned from production is the source of demand for the goods produced. This idea was recognized nearly two hundred years ago by the French economist Jean-Baptiste Say. Say's ideas were distilled by others into *Say's Law of Markets:* Supply creates its own demand. Some early nineteenth-century English economists used Say's Law to argue that the economy could never go into a general slump. Certainly, too many goods of one type could be produced and too few of others, but prices would change and resources would move to the markets where they were needed. Since resources do not move immediately from one market to another, a temporary decline in production and income was possible. However, no *general* slump, with unsold goods piling up in all or most markets, was possible, because supply creates its own demand. The act of production itself creates the income necessary to assure sufficient demand for goods and services in the aggregate. Since we know that economies do occasionally experience general slumps, Say's Law seems suspect. Yet, its basic idea is not unreasonable. Does Say's Law make economic sense?

Budget deficit
Excess of government expenditures over tax revenues.

Budget surplus
Excess of government tax revenues over expenditures.

Foreign sector
Export, import, and capital flows to and from foreign economies.

households. The flow from households to government is labeled "Taxes net of Transfer Payments" in recognition of the fact that transfer payments from government to households are like negative taxes. Households receive payments from government in the form of Social Security or welfare benefits rather than sending money to government in the form of taxes.

The government sector is linked to the financial sector by both borrowing and saving. The U.S. government has become famous for spending more than it takes in through taxation, that is, for running **budget deficits**. However, state and local governments often run **budget surpluses** by collecting receipts from taxes and fees that exceed their expenditures. Like private savings, government budget surpluses are used to purchase financial assets or to repay liabilities.

The **foreign sector** must also be included in any complete diagram of the macroeconomy. The reason is twofold. First, some expenditures by households are not received by domestic (that is, U.S.) firms, but rather go to foreign firms. If a consumer purchases a Volvo or a pair of Italian shoes, the money spent goes to the producing companies—overseas. Imports thus drain funds out of the domestic spending flow.

Foreign trading is not a one-way street, however. U.S. companies export a huge variety of goods and services, including agricultural products, computer software, and heavy equipment. Exports bring the U.S. firms dollars spent by foreign households, businesses, and governments. Thus, exports increase the size of the spending (and production) flow. When discussing the foreign sector, we will often subtract imports from exports and speak of net exports.

Referring back to Table 1, you can see that net exports were negative in 1990, as they have been every year since the early 1980s. When Americans purchase more goods and services from foreigners than foreigners buy from U.S. producers, foreigners end up holding dollars. If net exports are positive, Americans end up holding foreign currencies. This brings us to the second

As we noted in beginning this discussion, production is the source of income. Say's Law is built on a true foundation. However, all the income created by production need not be returned to firms in the form of demand for their products. The expanded circular flow diagram of Figure 2 clearly shows this. After earning income, households can choose to spend it on goods and services or save it. If households save by buying financial assets, such as corporate bonds, the income finds its way back to the business sector through the financial market. Firms use borrowed funds to finance investment spending — spending which creates a demand for the products of other firms. Households can hold their savings in other forms, however. If households choose to hold their savings in the form of money, the savings of households may not be available to support business investment. By increasing their money holdings, households drain income out of the circular flow, but they do not inject it back into the flow through the financial market. In this case, total demand for goods and services — by households and firms — falls. Unsold inventories of goods can build up in markets all across the economy, leading producers to eventually curtail production. In other words, the expanded circular flow model shows that a general slump is quite possible.

As with many aphorisms, Say's Law is based on a kernel of truth, but it can be misused to argue that what plainly happens is impossible. When used out of context, it does not make economic sense.

reason the international sector must be included in the circular flow model. Foreign savings flow into the financial market to purchase U.S. assets and domestic savings flow out of the economy to finance foreign investment. These **capital flows** have been quite important to the U.S. economy in recent years. Because net exports have been negative in recent years, more capital has flowed into the U.S. financial sector than out of it. Net inflows exceeded $100 billion per year in the late 1980s, as savers in Japan and Western Europe used part of their earnings from foreign trade to buy U.S. financial assets.

Recent Behavior of the U.S. Economy

The expanded circular flow model indicates some of the macroeconomic variables of interest to observers of the U.S. economy. In this section we briefly examine the major trends in key economic variables over the past two decades. This overview introduces some of the issues confronting macroeconomists and government policymakers.

Output and Prices

Aggregate output is important for two reasons. First, if a country's population is growing, aggregate output must also grow or per capita income — and consumption — will fall. If the nation's standard of living is to increase, output must grow faster than the population. Second, the stability of output growth is important to households. If output grows in spurts, falling periodically, household income and consumption will be erratic. Such an income pattern is less desirable to most people than a smoother income pattern.

Figure 3 illustrates the behavior of output (measured by real GNP) since 1970. As the figure shows, the U.S. economy has grown significantly in the

SECTION RECAP

A circular flow model shows the monetary and real flows among the household, business, government, financial, and foreign sectors. Each flow of real goods, services, or inputs is balanced by a flow of monetary payments.

Capital flow

Flow of money into or out of the economy to purchase financial assets.

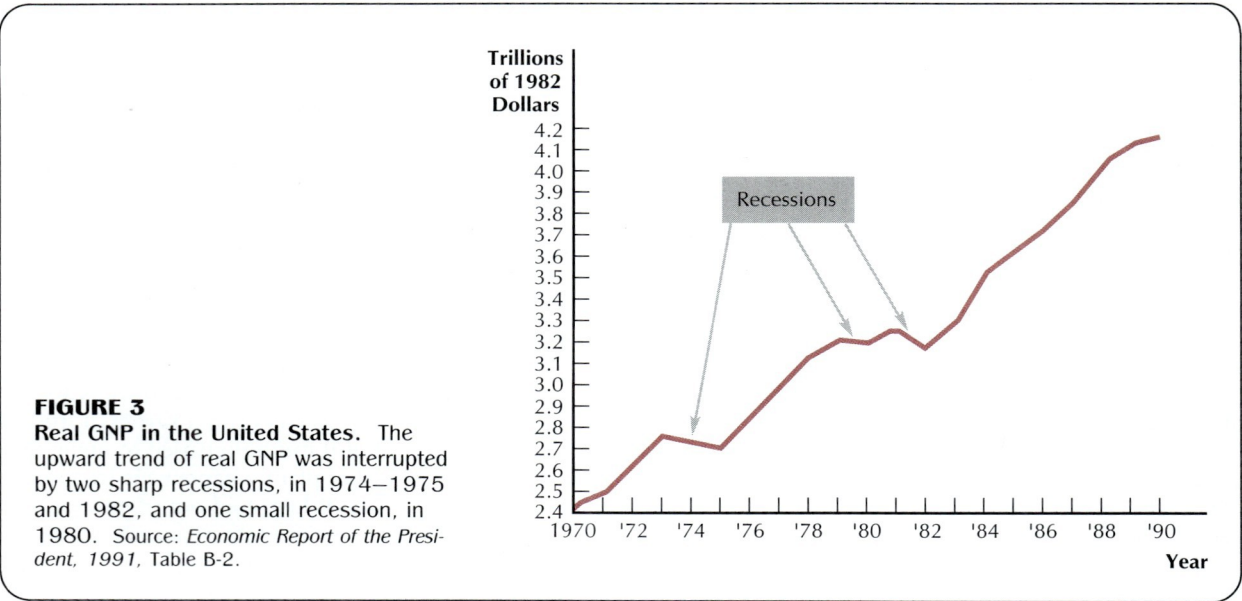

FIGURE 3
Real GNP in the United States. The upward trend of real GNP was interrupted by two sharp recessions, in 1974–1975 and 1982, and one small recession, in 1980. Source: *Economic Report of the President, 1991*, Table B-2.

Expansion
Period when real GNP is rising.

Recession
Period when real GNP is falling.

Business cycle
Includes an expansion and a recession; measured from peak to peak or trough to trough.

Trough
The low point of a recession.

Peak
The high point of an expansion.

past two decades. Real GNP (in 1982 prices) rose from $2,416.2 billion in 1970 to $4,155.8 billion in 1990. However, the increase in real GNP was not smooth. Instead, periods of fairly rapid economic growth—called **expansions**—were interrupted by periods when real GNP actually fell. The periods of declining real GNP are called **recessions**. Figure 3 shows that real GNP fell in 1974, 1975, 1980, and 1982.

When output falls in a recession, the economy moves to the interior of its production possibilities frontier. Resources are wasted, including the most important resource of all, labor services. Many workers lose their jobs during recessions, and income falls, reducing the consumption opportunities of affected households. In addition to the economic costs of recessions, psychologists and sociologists have discovered that the unemployment and reduced income increase the incidence and severity of emotional and family problems.

An expansion and the recession that precedes or follows it are jointly called a **business cycle**. Figure 4 traces out the four phases of a business cycle. The low point in a recession is called the **trough**. The trough represents a turning point; real GNP begins to rise after the trough is reached. The high point of an expansion is called the **peak**. It is also a turning point; real GNP falls after the peak is reached. Business cycles can be measured either from trough to trough or from peak to peak.

One of the major questions of macroeconomics is, What causes business cycles? A secondary question is, Can they be prevented? A number of different views on the major causes of business cycles coexist today. After we have assembled our model of the macroeconomy, we will be in a position to examine some of the answers being given to the business cycle puzzle.

Figure 5 (a) shows that, in addition to output, prices rose throughout the 1970s and 1980s. As was the case with output, the growth of prices was not even. Figure 5 (b) clearly shows the uneven nature of price movements. The

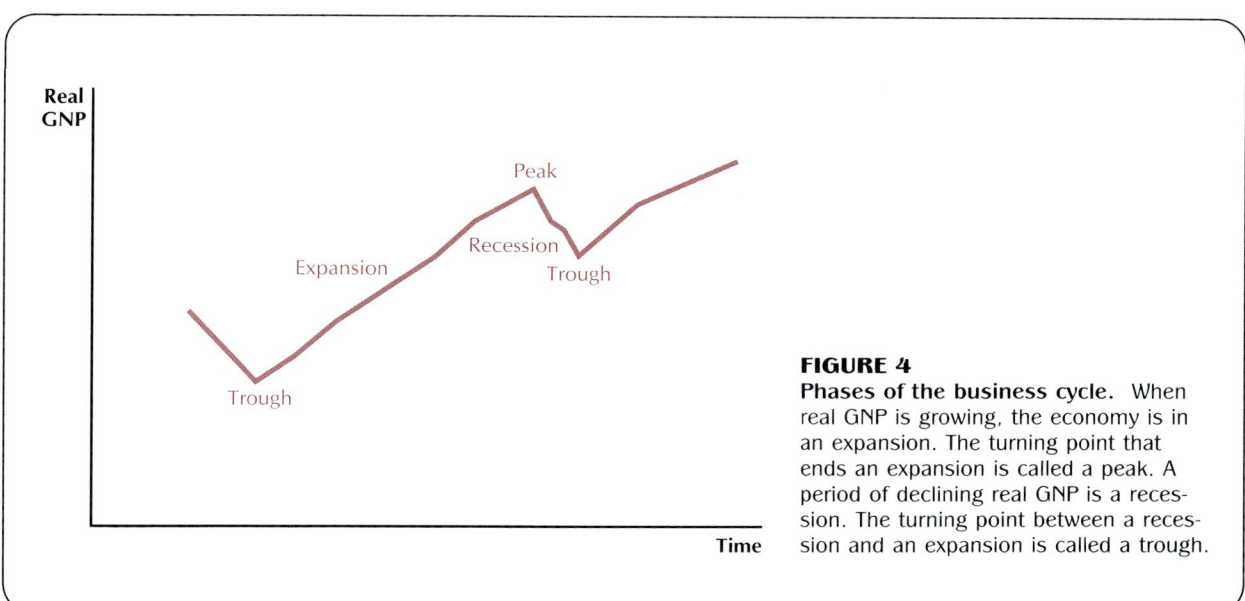

FIGURE 4
Phases of the business cycle. When real GNP is growing, the economy is in an expansion. The turning point that ends an expansion is called a peak. A period of declining real GNP is a recession. The turning point between a recession and an expansion is called a trough.

inflation rate, graphed in Figure 5 (b), shows the percentage change in the aggregate price level from one year to the next. Although prices rose every year from 1970 to 1990, they rose especially fast during the 1974–1981 period.

The magnitude and instability of inflation are major concerns of macroeconomists. Inflation can harm the economy in a number of ways. If the ag-

Inflation rate
Percentage rate of change of the aggregate price level from one period to another.

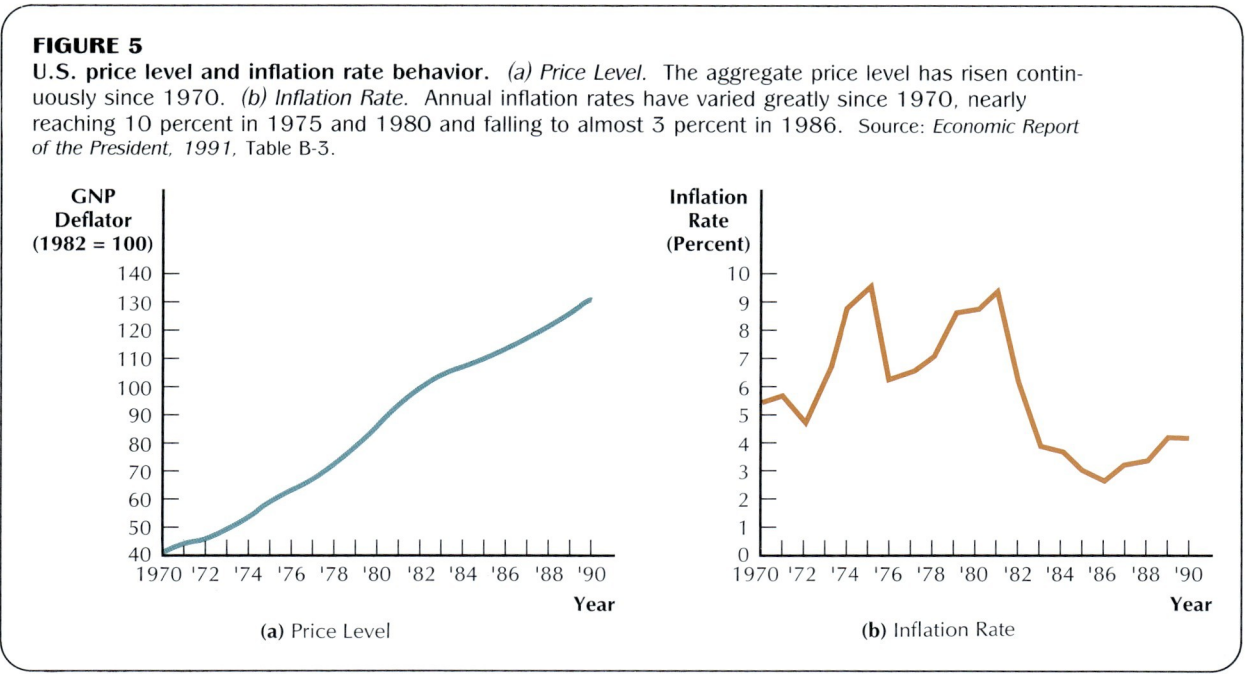

FIGURE 5
U.S. price level and inflation rate behavior. *(a) Price Level.* The aggregate price level has risen continuously since 1970. *(b) Inflation Rate.* Annual inflation rates have varied greatly since 1970, nearly reaching 10 percent in 1975 and 1980 and falling to almost 3 percent in 1986. Source: *Economic Report of the President, 1991,* Table B-3.

(a) Price Level

(b) Inflation Rate

gregate price level is stable, all price movements are relative price changes, reflecting changes in the demand for or supply of particular goods and services. However, if the aggregate price level is as unstable as shown in Figure 5, economic decision makers find it hard to distinguish between relative price movements and movements in the aggregate price level. Thus, it becomes harder to make good business decisions. Productivity can easily suffer, reducing output growth.

Inflation is not related to business cycle movements in any simple way, as can be seen by comparing the behavior of the inflation rate [shown in Figure 5 (b)] to the behavior of real GNP (shown in Figure 3). Inflation shot upward in 1974 and 1975, when the economy was in a recession. After falling sharply in 1976, inflation then began to climb again, this time while real GNP was growing. The inflation rate continued to rise during the recession of 1980, but fell sharply during the recession of 1982. The decline in inflation continued until 1986 when the inflation rate once again headed upward.

In light of the costs of inflation and the complex way in which the inflation rate has moved, it is not surprising that economists ask such questions as "Why has the price level risen so much during the past few decades?" and "Why has inflation varied so much from year to year?" Our macroeconomic model will be quite useful for addressing such questions.

Employment and Unemployment

In the circular flow model the flow of goods and services from firms to households tells only half the story. The other half consists of the flow of real inputs from households to firms. The most important input in the production process is labor services. An increase in the output of goods and services of the magnitude shown in Figure 3 can only occur if the quantity of labor employed also increases. Figure 6 shows that the number of people employed in the U.S.

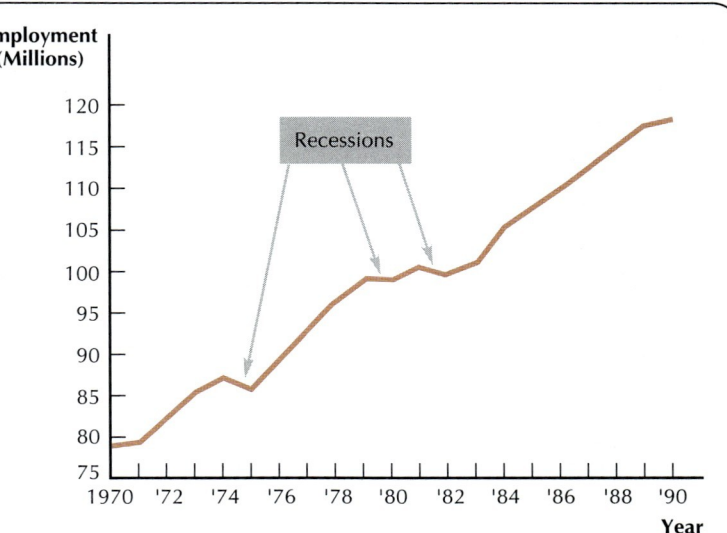

FIGURE 6
Employment in the United States. Employment grew by nearly 50 percent from 1970 to 1990. Source: *Economic Report of the President, 1991*, Table B-33.

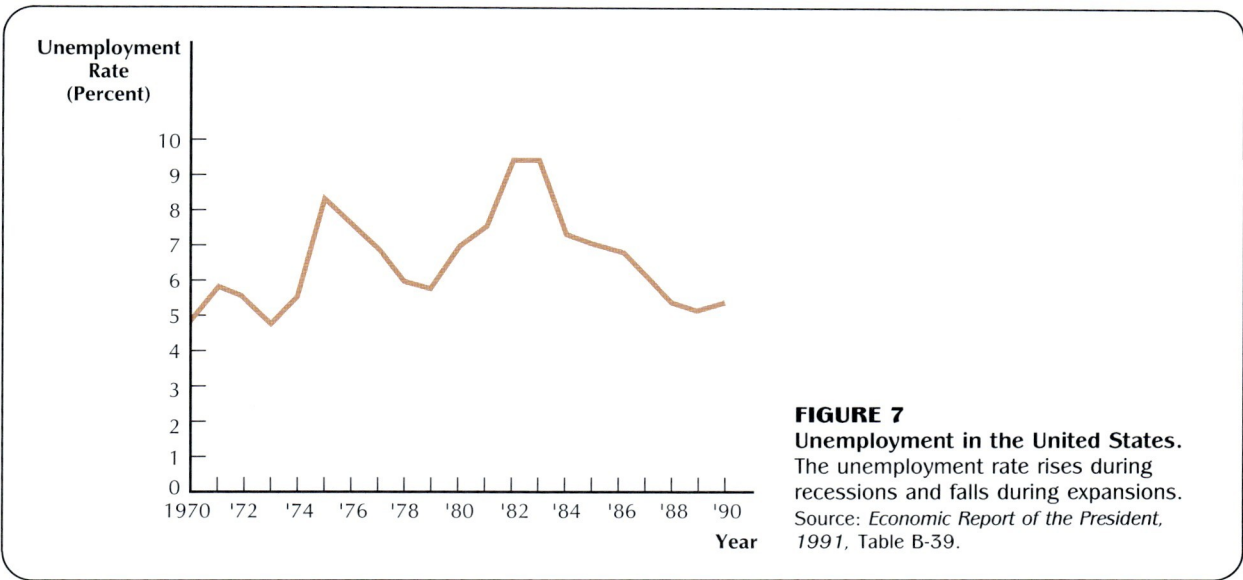

FIGURE 7
Unemployment in the United States.
The unemployment rate rises during recessions and falls during expansions.
Source: *Economic Report of the President, 1991*, Table B-39.

economy increased by nearly 50 percent from 1970 to 1990. Such growth in employment was possible (and necessary) because the working-age population in the United States was also growing rapidly during the 1970s and 1980s.

Even though employment grew dramatically during the past two decades, not everyone who wanted a job at any particular time could find one. During recessions, when employment actually fell, this is not surprising. However, Figure 7 shows that even during expansions the **unemployment rate** is positive. A person is counted as unemployed if he or she is actively searching for employment but is unable to find work. The unemployment rate equals the number of currently unemployed people divided by the total number of people working or searching for jobs.

Why is the unemployment rate always positive? Although we must develop a model of labor market behavior to adequately answer this question, at this point we can list several contributing factors. Some unemployment results when workers are displaced from their jobs by technology or by the transfer of industries to other areas or nations. People who lose their jobs in such a manner often take several months to find a new job. Meanwhile they are unemployed. Other people are unemployed because they are in the process of changing jobs, but do not move immediately from one job to another. Finally, and most important to a macroeconomist, some people are unemployed during recessions because firms lay off or fire workers rather than reducing their wages when the demand for the firms' products declines.

As Figure 7 demonstrates, the unemployment rate has jumped around a great deal over the past two decades. Since the costs of unemployment are so high — in terms of lost output and psychological damage inflicted on the unemployed — economists are very concerned to discover the causes of unemployment. We will pay a great deal of attention to labor market behavior in later chapters.

Unemployment rate
Number of people without jobs who are actively looking for work divided by the number of workers plus the number actively seeking jobs.

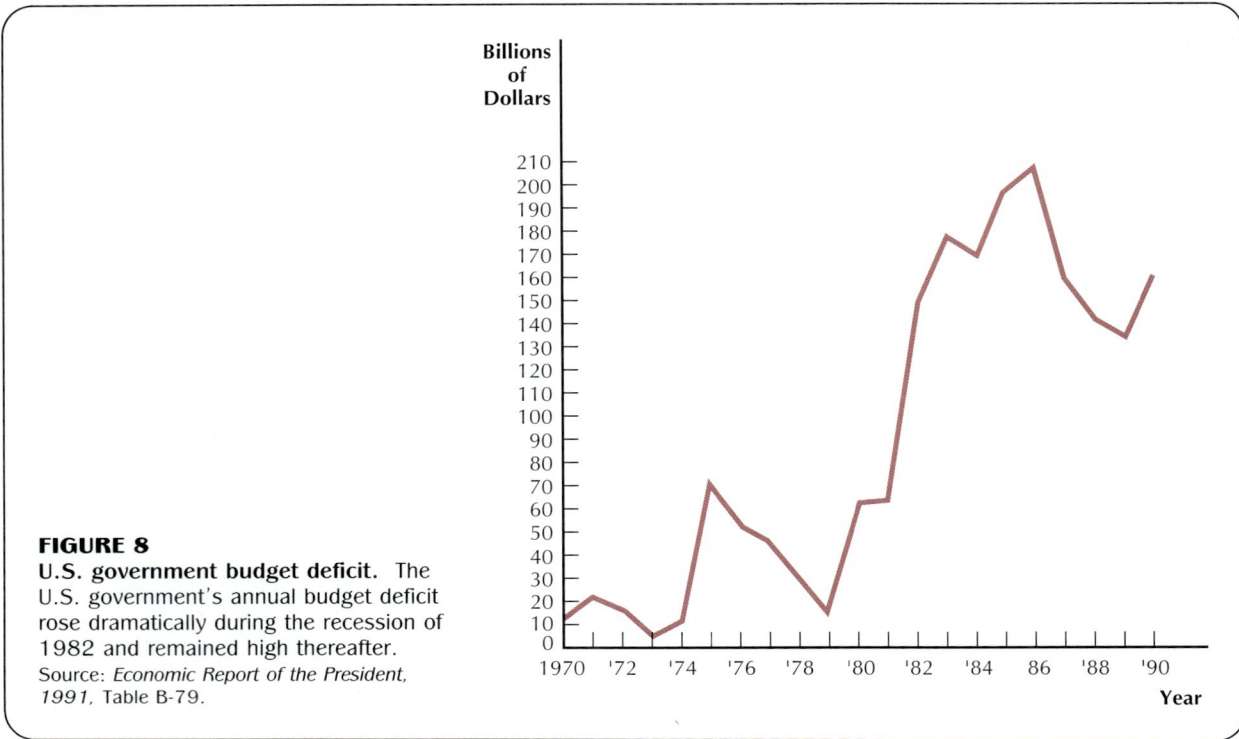

FIGURE 8
U.S. government budget deficit. The U.S. government's annual budget deficit rose dramatically during the recession of 1982 and remained high thereafter.
Source: *Economic Report of the President, 1991*, Table B-79.

The Twin Deficits

During the late 1980s the news media paid a great deal of attention to the U.S. economy's so-called twin deficits. The two deficits referred to are the U.S. government's budget deficit and the U.S. economy's international trade deficit.

As we saw earlier in the chapter, the government's budget deficit is the amount by which government expenditures exceed government revenues. Figure 8 illustrates the federal government's budget deficit. It is clear that the size of the annual deficit rose dramatically in the early 1980s. The deficit has remained high, in current dollar terms, since then. Is the government's budget deficit harmful? Economists disagree among themselves on this question. Some economists argue that the deficit is actually quite harmless; others argue that it creates a number of current and future problems. We examine this issue in detail in the chapter on government finance and fiscal policy.

Some of the critics of government budget deficits argue that the government's overspending has contributed to the development of large international trade deficits. Figure 9 demonstrates that the U.S. **balance of trade** moved sharply in a negative direction during the 1980s. The balance of trade is an accounting term for the difference between the dollar value of exports of goods and services to other countries and the dollar value of imports of foreign goods and services. The trade deficit indicates that during the 1980s the United States bought more goods and services from abroad than American firms sold to foreigners. This left foreigners holding billions of dollars, which they invested in the U.S. financial market.

Balance of trade
Difference between the dollar value of exports and imports.

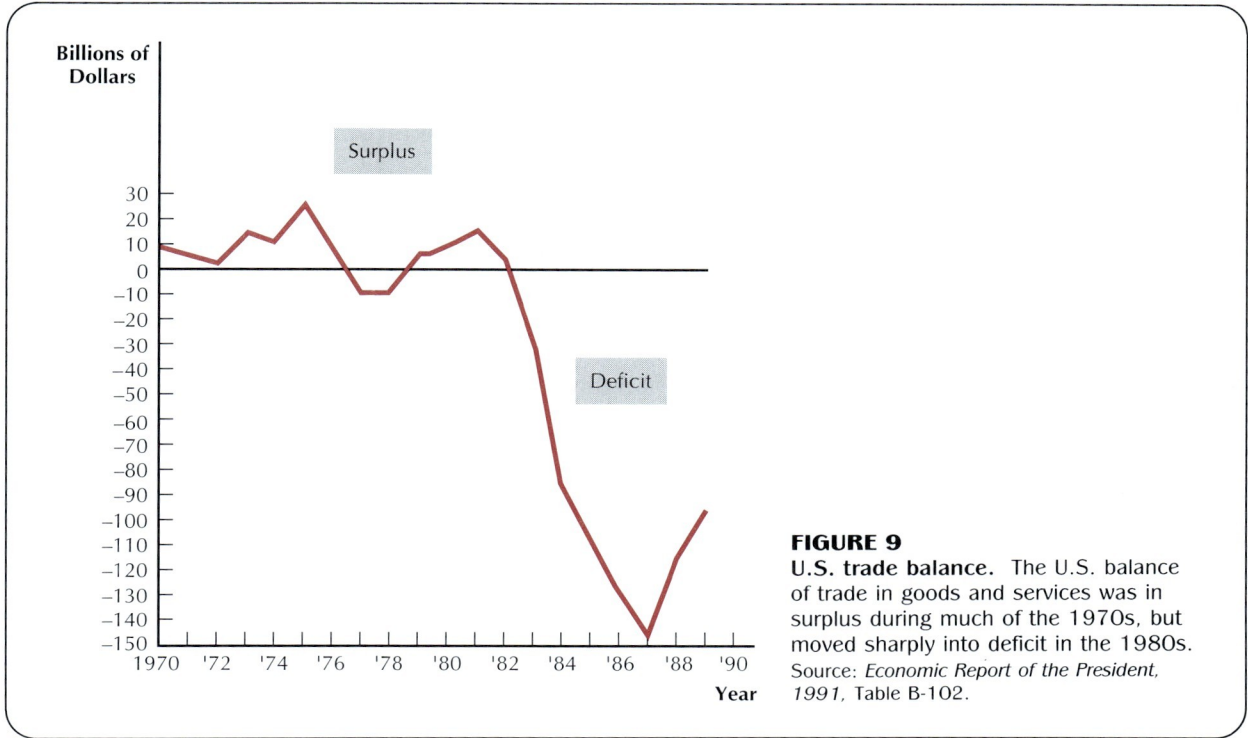

FIGURE 9
U.S. trade balance. The U.S. balance of trade in goods and services was in surplus during much of the 1970s, but moved sharply into deficit in the 1980s.
Source: *Economic Report of the President, 1991,* Table B-102.

The extent to which the trade deficit is a result of the government's budget deficit is hotly debated. The relationship between the budget deficit and the trade deficit is quite complex, involving the connection between both the government and foreign sectors and the financial sector. If we are to address the twin deficits issue without committing serious errors, we must design a model capable of tracing out the relationship between the two deficits. We undertake this task in the chapters on international trade and open-economy macroeconomics.

Macroeconomic Goals

Since World War II the federal government has attempted to influence the course of the macroeconomy. Government policymakers have pursued four goals: rapid output growth, stable output growth, stable prices, and low unemployment. The data presented in Figures 3 through 9 indicate that, on numerous occasions, actual macroeconomic performance has been much poorer than desired. Why has economic growth been so unstable? Why have prices risen so persistently and so erratically? Why has unemployment been so high so much of the time? Are policymakers incompetent, or is the world simply too complex to manage?

As the following chapters demonstrate, the complexity of modern economies makes policymaking a risky business. Often it is not clear what policymakers should do or when they should do it. Furthermore, the four macroeconomic goals are not mutually consistent over short periods of time.

SECTION RECAP
The four goals of macroeconomic policy are strong output growth, stable output growth, price level stability, and low unemployment. U.S. data show that output growth has not been stable since 1970, that prices have risen every year, though at varying rates, and that in-
(continued)

SECTION RECAP
(continued)
flation has surged in two major recessions.

Reducing the inflation rate may also reduce output growth and drive unemployment upward. Promoting rapid long-term growth may require policies that actually reduce output and increase unemployment for a time. In short, tradeoffs make policymaking an often painful exercise.

Complex Issues Require Sophisticated Analysis

Macroeconomics represents an attempt to understand the behavior of the real-world economy. Thus, macroeconomists have developed models that attempt to explain jointly the behavior of aggregate output and price level, employment movements, and the causes and effects of government budget deficits and international trade deficits and surpluses. Without an understanding of why the economy behaves as it does, there is no possibility of designing institutions or policies to improve economic behavior.

The next section outlines the macroeconomic model that we develop in the next few chapters. The complete macroeconomic model includes models of the markets for goods and services, labor, credit, and money. We develop the complete model piece by piece. If you understand each component part as it is developed, you should have little trouble understanding the total macro model.

The Macroeconomic Framework

Macroeconomic analysis focuses on the behavior of a number of important variables, including the levels and rates of growth of prices, output, and employment. The macroeconomic model constructed in this book focuses on four major markets: the labor market, the aggregate market for goods and services, the credit market, and the money market. The outcomes produced in these four markets are interrelated and directly or indirectly affect the price, output, and employment variables of interest to us. The following sections briefly explain why each of these markets is important and describe the approach we will take in modeling the behavior of each market.

Goods and Services Market

Aggregate demand
Total quantity of goods and services demanded by households, business firms, governmental units, and foreigners at various price levels.

Aggregate supply
Total quantity of goods and services supplied by business firms at various price levels.

The quantity of goods and services produced in a period depends on the aggregate demand for and aggregate supply of goods and services. **Aggregate demand** relates the total quantity of output consumers, businesses, governments, and foreigners want to buy to various aggregate price levels. **Aggregate supply** is the maximum quantity of goods and services businesses want to supply at various price levels. The next two chapters are devoted to developing the theory of aggregate demand and the theory of aggregate supply.

Aggregate demand limits the quantity of goods and services all firms can profitably produce and sell. Aggregate demand is broken into the same four spending components as GNP: consumption demand by households, investment demand by businesses, government purchases of goods and services, and net exports (exports minus imports). Changes in any component part of aggregate demand can have important effects on the quantity of output produced.

Aggregate supply depends on several factors, including the availability of resources, the productive capabilities of firms, and the level of product prices relative to costs of production. This last factor—prices relative to costs—changes significantly over time. When product prices rise faster than costs of production, firms have an incentive to increase production. As costs catch up with product prices, firms reduce output. Since the most important cost of production is wages, which are determined in the labor market, it is important that we understand the basic features of labor market behavior.

After developing aggregate demand (AD) and aggregate supply (AS) curves in the next two chapters, we will devote two more chapters to using the aggregate model to determine the equilibrium level of prices and real GNP and to explain changes in the price and output levels.

Labor Market

The **labor market** is the network of institutions and arrangements linking workers and job hunters with employers. The labor market is important to the study of macroeconomics because labor is the most important input in the production of goods and services. Payments to workers account for almost two thirds of GNP. Labor is important for another reason as well: Unlike other inputs to the production process, labor services cannot be separated from the people providing them. If workers are to be productive, they must be satisfied with their working conditions and wages; other inputs make no such demands on their employers.

Labor market
Network of institutions and arrangements linking workers and job hunters with employers.

The demand for labor by firms depends on the productivity of labor—how much workers can produce—and the value of the product being produced. When either the productivity of workers or the relative price of a firm's output increases, workers become more valuable to the firm. Firms hire workers until their marginal value to the firm equals their marginal cost—the wage rate. Thus, changes in the wage rate affect the quantity of labor firms want to hire. The supply of labor also depends on the nominal wage rate received by workers, as well as on the prices workers must pay for goods and services. The higher the level of prices, the higher the wage rate must be to enable a worker to buy a particular quantity of goods and services. The interaction of the demand for and supply of labor determines the equilibrium wage rate and level of employment.

The level of labor employment is one important determinant of the quantity of output (real GNP) produced by the economy. (The amount of plant and equipment and the extent to which it is utilized are also very important.) Over short periods of time, real GNP cannot vary much unless the quantity of labor employed changes. Thus, the behavior of the labor market is an important component of our theory of the aggregate supply of goods and services.

Credit Market

In discussing the expanded circular flow model, we noted the importance of borrowing and lending to the smooth functioning of the economy. Households save for various reasons, reducing the flow of spending. However, firms often want to spend more than they can finance out of current revenues to buy

Credit market
Markets and institutions that link savers to borrowers.

machines or build factories or offices. The credit market enables firms to make use of the savings of households. The **credit market** includes the markets and financial institutions that link savers to borrowers. Household savers lend their savings to business borrowers through the credit market. Of course, some households also borrow, and some firms save, but the principle is the same: transferring funds from those with excess current income to those who want to spend more than current income.

Credit is the rental use of money for a period of time. The price of credit is the **interest rate**. The demand for credit is negatively related to the interest rate, since the interest rate represents the cost of funds to borrowers. Other factors affecting the demand for credit include the level of real GNP and the extent to which businesses are utilizing their plant and equipment. When firms are producing at very high levels—close to capacity—the incentive to invest increases. When investment increases, so does the demand for credit. Another factor affecting the demand for credit is the size of the government budget deficit. When the government runs a deficit, it must finance the deficit by borrowing.

Interest rate
The price of credit, expressed as percent per year.

In the chapter on the credit market we explain how the demand for credit and the supply of credit interact to determine the equilibrium interest rate. This analysis enables us to understand the interaction between real GNP and interest rate movements and the impact of government deficits on the economy. Since the cost of credit limits the willingness of firms and households to borrow and purchase productive equipment or expensive consumer goods, such as cars and furniture, the interest rate affects aggregate demand. Changes in the interest rate thus affect the equilibrium values of the price level and real GNP.

Money Market

Money market
Shorthand term for the demand for and supply of money; money trades in all markets.

The **money market** refers to the demand for and supply of money in the economy. In reality, there is no special market for money. Instead, money is exchanged in all markets, since money serves as the medium of exchange in which transactions are made. A **medium of exchange** is an asset that is generally accepted in exchange and so becomes part of most transactions. When making a purchase or selling a good, people expect to pay with or receive money. In the United States, money primarily consists of coins issued by the U.S. Treasury, paper notes issued by the Federal Reserve System, and checking deposits in banks.

Medium of exchange
Asset generally accepted in exchange and used in most transactions.

Because money is the medium through which the vast majority of market exchanges are made, the ease or difficulty of obtaining money has an important effect on the economy. The interest rate is a measure of the cost of borrowing money or the reward for lending it. As we saw in the previous chapter, the credit market is linked to the money market through the aggregate budget constraint. A change in the demand for or supply of money affects the credit market, the market for goods and services, or both. Because of this budget constraint linkage we can use either the credit market or the money market to determine the equilibrium interest rate. Sometimes it is simpler to use the credit market model to determine the interest rate, while at other times it is simpler to use the money market model. We will make use of both models as we develop our complete macroeconomic model.

SECTION RECAP
The macroeconomic model developed in this book consists of models of four aggregate markets: the market for goods and services, the labor market, the credit market, and the money market. By using *(continued)*

Why the **Disagreement?**

Is Macroeconomics Possible?

Macroeconomics in its modern form was born in the 1930s. Since then many elements of macroeconomic theory have changed, although the basic approach to the analysis of the economy has not changed. Despite being widely practiced for a half century, however, macroeconomic analysis is called simply impossible by some economists. Thousands of macroeconomists disagree. Why the disagreement?

The critics of the concept of macroeconomics lodge a number of arguments, three of which we will note. One problem, according to the critics, has to do with aggregation. Certainly one can calculate GNP, real GNP, and a large number of other aggregate variables. But what do those variables *mean*? Critics note that the meaning of aggregate variables changes with the composition of those variables. For example, the calculated value of GNP could remain constant while the production of steel fell rapidly and the production of hamburgers rose rapidly. The constant value of GNP masks a major change in the economy. Critics lament that paying too much attention to aggregates such as GNP causes economists to lose sight of the real behavior of the economy.

A second problem is related to the problem of aggregation. As the economy grows over time, different sectors grow at different rates. Some sectors adjust to new conditions (move to equilibrium) very quickly, while other sectors adjust very slowly. Even a rapidly growing economy can contain industries or geographical areas that are performing poorly. Concentrating on the macroeconomy glosses over industries and areas moving against the main trend.

A third problem concerns how government policies affect the economy. Macroeconomics is used to study the effects of government policies as though their effects on the economy were even throughout all sectors and regions. In fact, policy effects vary across different industries and different regions. Monetary policy affects interest-sensitive industries more than industries that are not sensitive to interest rate changes. Government purchases directly affect the producers of the goods government buys, while having very little effect on many other producers. Similarly, changes in the tax and transfer payments systems affect different people differently. Macroeconomic theory does not account for such variation.

Although in basic agreement with the critics on all three of these problems, we still believe that macroeconomic theory is useful — provided that its limitations are kept in mind. Macroeconomic theory provides us with a good first approximation of the results of different changes in the economy. When supplemented with microeconomic analysis of particular markets, macroeconomic theory is very useful. The macro section of this text makes use of both the basic macroeconomic model and microeconomic analysis. You should always remember that economic activity takes place in individual markets and affects individual people. Our use of both macroeconomic and microeconomic models to describe economic events represents an attempt to capture the big picture without losing sight of the impact of economics on individuals.

Putting It All Together

Because macroeconomics focuses on the relationships among aggregate markets, answering most macroeconomic questions will require us to analyze three or four markets simultaneously. For example, when the government engages in monetary policy, all four markets are affected in important ways. Thus, to see how the policy affects the economy we must examine how the effects in the money market spill over into the other aggregate markets. One of the keys to understanding macroeconomics is always keeping in mind how changes in one market affect other markets. We will remind you of these connections throughout the remainder of the book.

SECTION RECAP
(continued)

these four models simultaneously to analyze economic changes, we can explain the behavior of the levels of real output, prices, employment, and the interest rate.

Summary

The **macroeconomy** is a complex system of interdependent markets. Changes in demand or supply in one market spill over into other markets. The **circular flow** diagram shows how aggregate markets are interconnected. The flow of spending from households to business firms is augmented by business spending on capital goods, government purchases of goods and services, and foreign purchases of domestically produced goods (exports). Not all household income is spent on domestic production, however. Some is used to purchase foreign-made goods (imports).

The household sector is a net saving sector; households save more than they borrow. The funds saved go through the financial system to finance business **investment** and government **budget deficits**.

Macroeconomics is concerned with explaining the behavior of real-world economies. Thus, the ability to interpret and use macroeconomic data is very important. We will refer to actual data throughout the remainder of the text, both to motivate our development of macroeconomic theory and to apply theory already developed.

This book analyzes the economy with the aid of models of four major markets. The **market for goods and services** determines the aggregate price level and equilibrium real GNP. The **labor market** determines the equilibrium wage rate and employment level. The **credit market** determines the interest rate, although the **money market** model can also be used for that purpose.

In the next chapter we begin the process of constructing the basic macroeconomic model by developing a theory of aggregate demand. This theory is based on theories of consumption demand, investment demand, and the behavior of net exports. The theory of aggregate demand forms half of our model of the market for goods and services.

Questions for Thought

Knowledge Questions

1. Why is the financial sector important to the economy?
2. Why must the foreign sector be included in the economy's circular flow diagram?
3. What is the largest expenditure category of GNP? What is the largest income category?
4. List the components of aggregate demand.

Application Questions

5. Use the circular flow model to determine what happens to the flow of spending if households decide to save more.
6. Why does the government purchases category of expenditures exclude transfer payments?
7. Given the following information, solve for the values of net exports and imports.

   GNP = $4880.6 billion   C = $3235.1 billion
   I = $750.3 billion   G = $968.9 billion
   X = $547.7 billion (X stands for exports)

Synthesis Questions

8. Use the expanded circular flow diagram in Figure 2 to answer this question. Suppose the flow of consumption spending by households remains constant from Year 1 to Year 2. Taxes and saving also remain constant. However, government spending and investment spending both increase. Determine what must happen to net exports. (Hint: Government spending and investment spending must be financed. Where will the financing come from?)
9. Use the expanded circular flow diagram to consider this question. Suppose foreigners want to increase their holdings of U.S. financial assets, such as U.S. government bonds and stock in major U.S. corporations. Such an increase in demand could occur if the world economy were moving toward recession, while the U.S. economy appeared to be strong. What changes in the real and monetary flows would probably occur? (Remember that it is not possible to change only *one* flow; budget constraints force spending to be financed.)
10. Examine the behavior of output in Figure 3 closely. Calculate the average length of recessions during the 1970 to 1990 period. (Note : 1974 and 1975 were part of a single recession.) Next, calculate the average length of expansions. What generalization can you draw about business cycles over the past two decades?

OVERVIEW

Every day almost everyone is involved in some sort of purchase, ranging from buying a doughnut on the way to school to taking in a movie in the evening or paying the electric bill once a month. Less frequently we buy a big-ticket item — a car, a stereo, a refrigerator. Most of our income (sometimes more than our current income) goes into these purchases. Consumption spending accounts for about two thirds of total spending in the economy. In a very real sense, consumption spending drives the economy.

Not all spending is for purposes of immediate gratification, however. A substantial portion of spending goes to purchase items that will themselves be productive in the future.

Aggregate Demand for Goods and Services

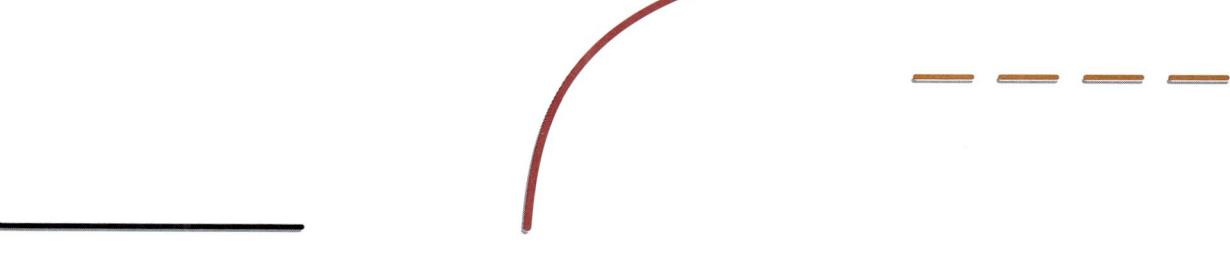

Such investment spending makes up a far smaller portion of total spending than does consumption, but because of its volatile character, we shall pay as much attention to investment as to consumption. Indeed, investment spending is extremely important to the health of an economy. If consumption spending drives the economy right now, investment spending puts in place the capital stock that makes it possible for the economy to produce in the future. Together, consumption and investment spending account for over three fourths of total spending.

Government purchases of goods and services and net exports make up the remainder of aggregate spending. Government purchases (federal plus state and local) exceed 20 percent of GNP. Net exports, though the smallest aggregate demand category, are important because the level of net exports can change significantly from year to year, pushing aggregate demand up or down.

CHAPTER 23

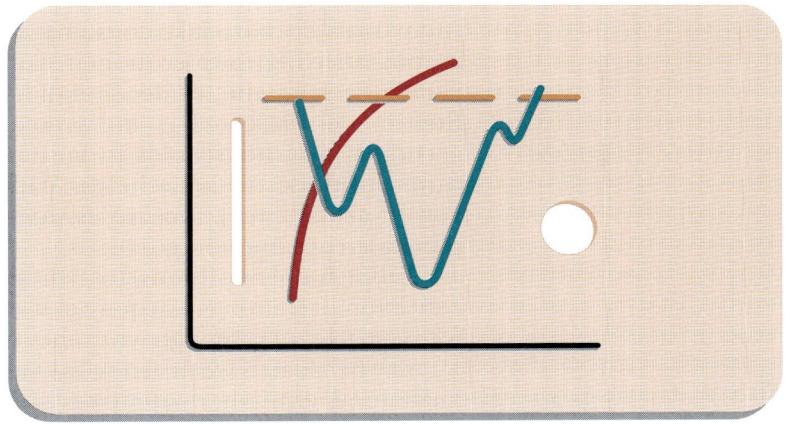

In this chapter we investigate the factors that influence the magnitude of consumption and investment demand, government purchases, and net exports. Adding together these four types of demand, we derive the aggregate demand for goods and services. In turn, aggregate demand serves as one half of our model of the aggregate goods and services market.

Learning Objectives

After reading and studying this chapter, you will be able to:

1. Understand the relationship between income and consumption and why temporary income changes have different effects than permanent income changes have.
2. Explain why different components of consumption demand behave differently over time.
3. Define the term investment as economists use it.
4. List the major factors affecting the level of investment demand, and explain why investment demand is so unstable.
5. List the major factors affecting the level of net exports.
6. Describe how the aggregate demand curve shifts when one of the major determinants of aggregate demand changes.

Consumption Demand

Aggregate demand
Total desired spending on newly produced goods and services; consists of consumption, investment, government purchases, and net exports.

Aggregate demand is total desired spending on newly produced goods and services by households (consumption), businesses (investment), governments, and foreigners (net exports) during a period of time. The largest single component of aggregate demand is consumption expenditures by households. A variety of factors influences household consumption behavior. Rather obviously, the major factor influencing consumption demand is income. But the amount of income a household earns is related to other decisions the household makes. One important decision concerns the amount of labor households want to supply to the labor market. Approximately two thirds of all income is earned as wages or salaries. Another important determinant is the desire of households to save for the future. In the following sections we discuss these topics as we develop a theory of consumption behavior.

Interdependence of Consumption Demand and Labor Supply

Individuals do not make consumption decisions in isolation from other decisions affecting their economic status. The consumption decision is made simultaneously with the decision of how much labor to supply. As the circular flow model presented in the preceding chapter demonstrates, the flow of spending from households to businesses is financed by the flow of income from businesses to households. Without supplying labor to businesses (or governmental units), most of us would have very little income with which to purchase consumption goods.

Labor supply decisions are typically long-term decisions. People invest in education or training to acquire skills that will serve them in the labor market for years to come. Though we cannot see into the future and predict what skills we may need later, we nevertheless make long-term plans. The fact that people make long-term labor supply decisions has important implications for consumption behavior, as we shall see shortly.

Income and Consumption: Keynesian Theory

In *The General Theory of Employment, Interest, and Money*, John Maynard Keynes proposed a "psychological" principle of consumption behavior. Keynes asserted that when income changes, consumption changes in the same direction but by a smaller magnitude. In other words, a positive relationship exists between income and consumption, although consumption does not change dollar-for-dollar with income; saving changes, too. The changes in saving and consumption together equal the change in after-tax income. Thus was born the **consumption function**, which shows the direct relationship between consumption and after-tax income. As after-tax income increases, consumption increases, but by a somewhat smaller amount.

Consumption function
Mathematical relationship between consumption spending and disposable income.

Economists call after-tax income **disposable income** (DI). Disposable income is the income households have left to spend or save after paying taxes and receiving transfer payments. We define disposable income as:

$$DI = GNP - T + Tr$$

Disposable income
Household income net of income and payroll taxes and transfer payments.

where T is the amount of taxes taken out of income (income and payroll taxes,

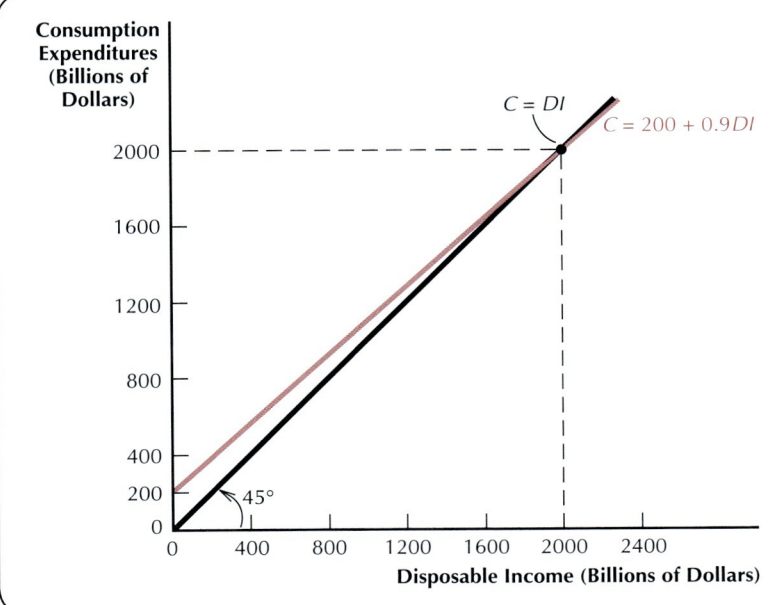

FIGURE 1
Keynesian consumption function. The Keynesian consumption function relates current consumption directly to current disposable income. As disposable income rises, consumption increases, but by a smaller amount. The consumption function illustrated here is C = $200 billion + 0.9(DI). When disposable income equals $2000 billion, C = DI; the consumption function intersects the 45-degree line at this point.

such as the Social Security tax) and Tr is the amount of transfer payments from government to households.[1]

The relationship between consumption and disposable income, as postulated by Keynes, is illustrated graphically in Figure 1. Here, for simplicity, we assume a linear relationship between consumption and disposable income. That is, we assume that the effect on consumption of a dollar change in disposable income is the same regardless of the level of disposable income. The consumption function can be expressed algebraically as:

$$C = a + b(DI)$$

In this equation, a is **autonomous consumption expenditures**, consumption expenditures that do not depend directly on current income. Autonomous expenditures include those financed out of savings or by the sale of assets. Keynes called the fraction of a change in disposable income that is consumed, b, the **marginal propensity to consume** (MPC). Note that the marginal propensity to consume equals the change in consumption divided by the change in disposable income:[2] MPC = $\Delta C/\Delta DI$. The MPC is a fraction: $0 < b < 1$.

The consumption function graphed in Figure 1 shows a specific relationship between consumption and disposable income. The particular consumption function graphed is:

$$C = 200 + 0.9(DI)$$

Autonomous consumption expenditures
Consumption spending not based on current income, but financed out of savings or asset sales.

Marginal propensity to consume
Fraction of an additional dollar of disposable income that is consumed; equals the change in consumption divided by the change in disposable income.

---

[1]Astute observers will note that this definition of disposable income is not correct in terms of National Income Accounts standards. It ignores several items, such as depreciation and indirect business taxes, that must be subtracted from GNP to derive DI. We define DI in this way in the interest of simplicity.

[2]The MPC does *not* equal total consumption divided by total income (a variable called the *average propensity to consume*).

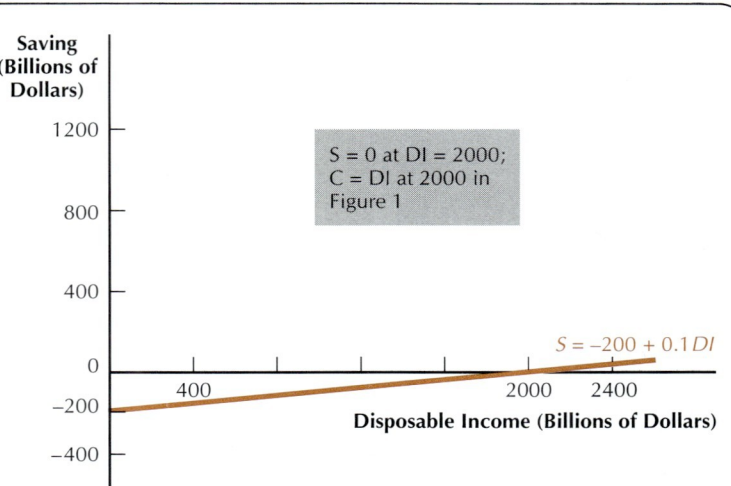

FIGURE 2
Keynesian saving function. The saving function equals DI − C. Thus, S = DI − (a + b(DI)) = −a + (1 − b)DI. This particular saving function corresponds to the consumption function in Figure 1 and takes the form S = −$200 billion + 0.1(DI). At a disposable income level of $2000 billion, S = 0. This is the level of disposable income at which consumption equals disposable income.

The 45-degree line in Figure 1 shows all the points where consumption equals disposable income. Thus, consumption exceeds disposable income when DI is less than $2000 billion (because autonomous consumption equals $200 billion), and consumption falls short of disposable income when DI exceeds $2000 billion (because consumption rises more slowly than disposable income). That is, at disposable income levels greater than $2000 billion, households save part of their disposable income.

A decision to consume is also a decision to save, because disposable income is allocated either to consumption or to saving. In the aggregate, no other choices exist. (Gifts or other income transfers do not violate this principle; the recipients of transfers have only two choices, to consume or to save.) Since consumption plus saving equals disposable income, saving must be the difference between disposable income and consumption. Thus:

$$S = DI - C$$

Substituting for C, we obtain:

$$S = DI - [a + b(DI)]$$

which reduces to:

$$S = -a + (1 - b)DI$$

Marginal propensity to save
Fraction of an additional dollar of disposable income that is saved; equals the change in savings divided by the change in disposable income.

The term $(1 - b)$, which is equivalent to $(1 - MPC)$, is known as the **marginal propensity to save** (MPS). The MPS is the change in savings divided by the change in disposable income. The saving function graphed in Figure 2 corresponds to the consumption function of Figure 1. Its formula is S = −200 + 0.1(DI). Note that, at DI = $2000 billion, S = 0. This must be the case, since C = DI when DI = $2000 billion.

Empirical Evidence on Consumption

Keynes's theory of consumption links *current* consumption to *current* disposable income. Undoubtedly, his insight that consumption depends directly on disposable income is correct. However, there are reasons to doubt that consumption depends on *current* disposable income. Economic theory suggests that people might make their consumption decisions on the same basis that they make their labor supply decisions. That is, they might take a longer view when forming consumption habits. Furthermore, the fact that a consumption decision is also a saving decision also points into the future. Saving amounts to accumulating assets that can be used to support *future* consumption. If people are concerned about future consumption as well as current consumption, logic suggests that they take into consideration the income they expect to earn in the future when formulating current consumption plans.

Empirical evidence also indicates that the relationship between consumption and disposable income differs from the current relationship posited by Keynes. The actual consumption behavior observed in the United States and other developed economies differs from what the Keynesian theory predicts in two ways: (1) in the long run, the ratio of consumption to disposable income has not fallen as Keynesian theory predicts, and (2) in the short run, consumption spending is more stable than Keynesian theory predicts.

Figure 3 illustrates the relationship between consumption and disposable income over time. Real consumption and real disposable income levels (in 1982 dollars) are plotted for each year during the period 1947–1989. The relationship between the two variables is relatively stable and is approximately described by the equation $C = 0.9(DI)$. As disposable income has risen over time, consumption has risen by approximately 0.9 times the increase in disposable income. For every dollar added to disposable income, consumption spending has risen by about 90¢. Note that saving has remained stable at approximately 0.1 times disposable income. No autonomous consumption spending is obvious. The ratio of consumption to disposable income has remained approximately stable. Keynesian theory predicts that this ratio will fall as disposable income rises.

The pattern illustrated in Figure 3 is the long-term relationship between consumption and disposable income. The short-run relationship between consumption and disposable income is quite different. Not every change in income is regarded as permanent by those affected. Many occupations have seasonal or cyclical down times, when income is temporarily depressed. The construction industry provides a good illustration of this principle. Construction workers are accustomed to job interruptions. One project ends, and some time elapses before another begins. The down time is usually anticipated. Income is saved from periods when it is earned, and consumption continues as usual during short periods of inactivity. Only if the layoff period continues longer than anticipated is consumption spending modified.

As this example suggests, temporary increases or decreases in disposable income generate smaller changes in consumption spending than do permanent increases or decreases in income. The major part of a temporary income change is absorbed by a change in saving. Like construction workers, most people meet temporary periods of low income by withdrawing funds from savings and continuing to consume at a nearly normal level. Most of a temporary increase in disposable income finds its way into savings.

If consumption is more stable than disposable income, the marginal propensity to consume over short periods of time will be unstable. The numerator of the MPC (the change in consumption) will remain relatively stable while the denominator (the change in disposable income) moves up and down. As

SECTION RECAP
Keynesian theory says that consumption depends on current disposable income. Empirical evidence indicates that over long periods, consumption is a *(continued)*

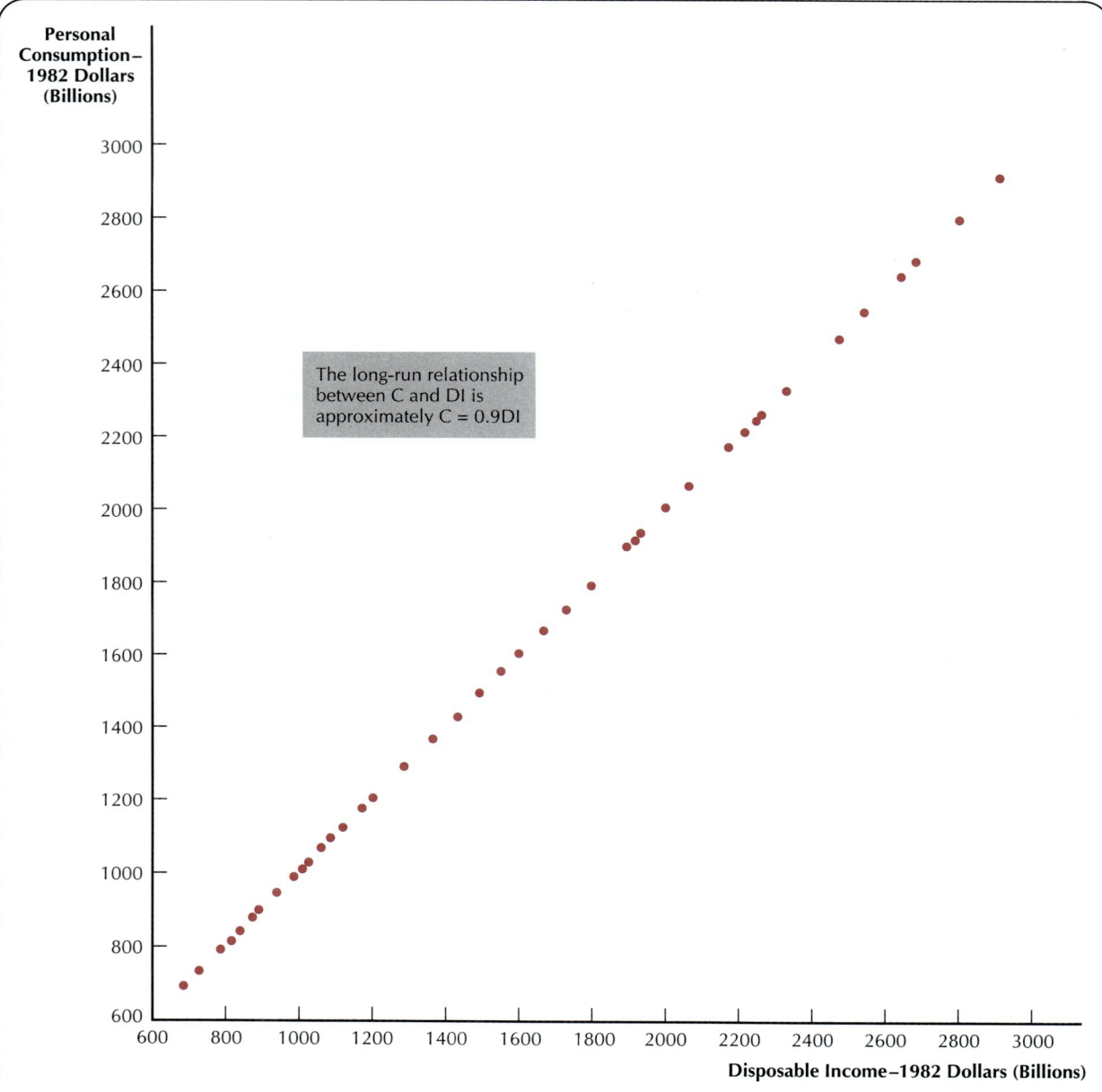

FIGURE 3
Real consumption–disposable income relationship. Real consumption is a fairly stable fraction of real disposable income. This figure shows annual real consumption–real disposable income combinations for the years 1946–1989. Source: *Economic Report of the President, 1990,* Table C-26.

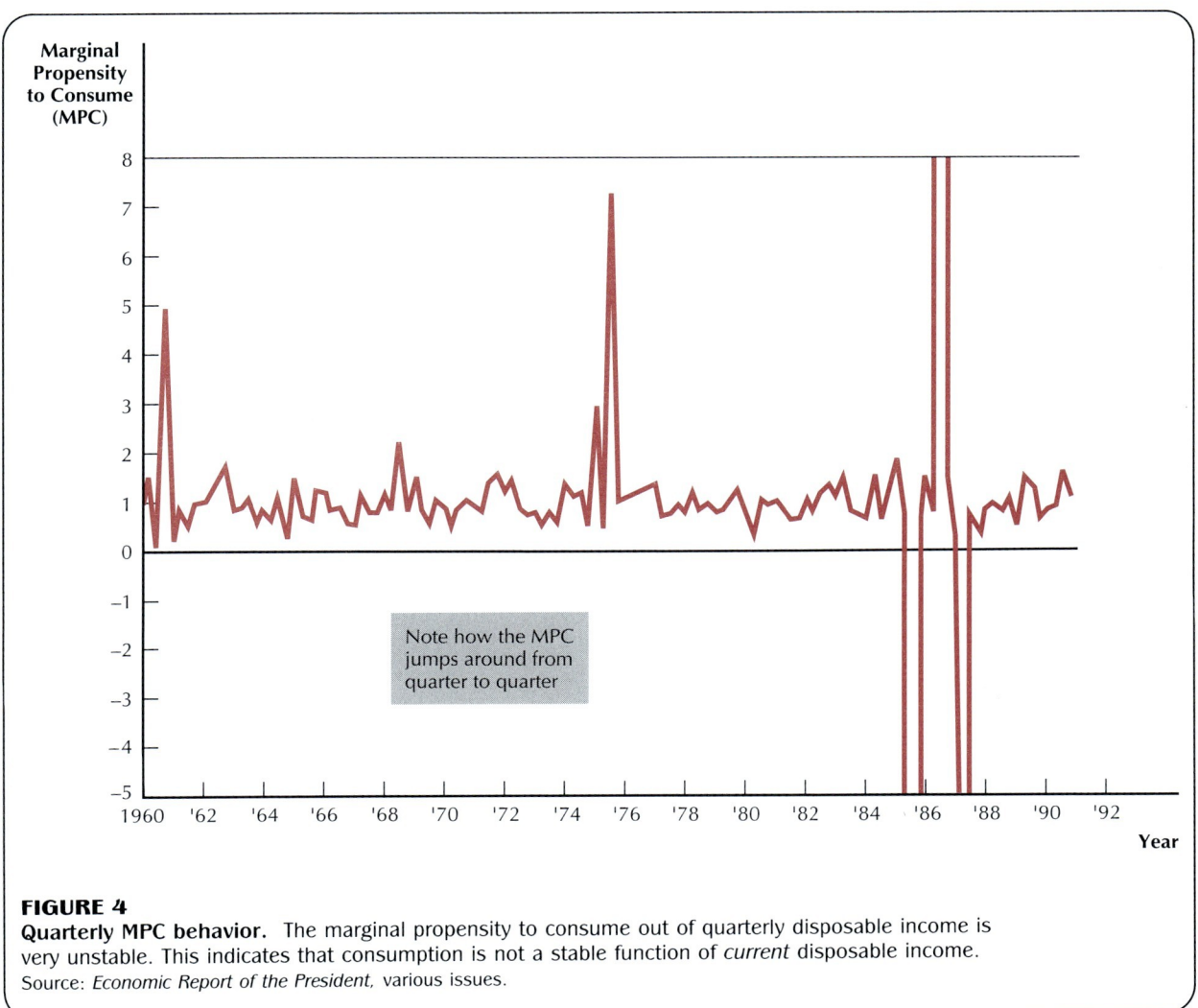

FIGURE 4
Quarterly MPC behavior. The marginal propensity to consume out of quarterly disposable income is very unstable. This indicates that consumption is not a stable function of *current* disposable income.
Source: *Economic Report of the President*, various issues.

Figure 4, which plots data on the quarterly marginal propensity to consume, shows, the quarter-to-quarter behavior of the MPC is very unstable. Such instability indicates that current consumption is not closely related to current disposable income. If it were, the MPC would be stable. However, if consumption is related to people's long-run expected income, we would expect to observe a highly unstable MPC. Thus, the quarterly MPC data indicate that current consumption is not closely related to current disposable income, as Keynes supposed it to be.

Theory of Consumption

The key to understanding consumption behavior is focusing on the long-run behavior of households. In the 1950s, economists Franco Modigliani and Milton Friedman independently developed theories of consumption behavior that explain the data much better than the simple Keynesian theory does. Both Modigliani's

SECTION RECAP
(continued)
stable fraction of disposable income, and that over short periods the MPC is very unstable. Both facts contradict the simple Keynesian theory.

life cycle hypothesis and Friedman's permanent income hypothesis assume that households are concerned with long-term consumption. We present a simplified theory that captures the most important features of the two technical theories.

The modern theory of consumption is based on two assumptions about human behavior: (1) individuals attempt to maximize their welfare over long periods of time, that is, people plan for the future, and (2) a reasonably stable pattern of consumption over time is preferred to an all-or-nothing consumption pattern. The theory is also based on two facts of economic life: (1) people can generate a consumption pattern that differs from their income pattern by borrowing and saving, and (2) most people's income streams vary significantly over the course of their lifetimes.

The assumptions of the theory suggest that disposable income and consumption spending are related to one another only on a long-run average basis. Just as we make long-term labor supply decisions, we make long-term consumption decisions. If we could predict with any accuracy our income streams over our entire lifetimes, we would attempt to match up our average income levels with our average consumption levels. Not being able to see into the future, we nevertheless behave much as though we could. We derive estimates of our long-term incomes by combining our current income levels with future expected earnings. Our consumption is then primarily related to this estimate of our long-term income prospects.

Long-Run Income   Most people have some idea of what their long-term average income will be. This long-term income estimate may be quite different from their current income level. Such is the case for most college students, for example. A typical college student has a modest income, but expects to earn much more upon graduation. For this reason, the consumption level of average college students exceeds the level at which the same individuals would consume if they expected to permanently have their current level of income. Most college students are consuming future income, as they incur debts while in college to finance an acceptable lifestyle until their incomes rise. Students overconsume in this manner because they expect their future incomes to be higher than their current incomes. In effect, they are consuming future income. If they had no expectations of higher incomes, most students would consume at a lower level than they presently do.

If this theory is correct, a change in income will affect consumption demand differently depending upon whether it is perceived to be permanent or temporary. The data on the consumption–disposable income relationship over time suggest that a permanent $1 million change in disposable income alters consumption spending by about $900,000. A temporary $1 million change in income has a much smaller effect on consumption, since a temporary change in income has a much smaller effect on long-term average income.[3]

For example, suppose that Peggy forms her estimate of long-term income by adding up her current annual income and the income she expects to earn over the next nine years and dividing by ten. She assumes that taxes will take

---

[3]Empirical evidence on the magnitude of the effect of temporary income changes on consumption is presented in Alan Blinder and Angus Deaton, "The Time Series Consumption Function Revisited," *Brookings Papers on Economic Activity* 16, No. 2 (1985), pp. 465–521.

10 percent of her gross income. Her current and expected income figures are shown in Table 1. Her estimated annual long-term average disposable income is $28,440.

Assume that Peggy's consumption function takes the form C = 0.9(LDI), where LDI stands for her long-term disposable income. Then her consumption level in the current year is C = 0.9(28,440) = $25,596. This exceeds her current gross income level, but represents a sustainable level of consumption if her income expectations are met. (We are ignoring the fact that Peggy must pay interest on the funds she borrows. This simplifies the problem greatly and does not change the main points.)

How does Peggy react if her current income changes? It depends upon whether she perceives the current income change as a one-time bonus or she believes it represents a permanent increase, one that will be reflected in higher future earnings as well as higher current income. If her current disposable income rises by $1000, and she believes the rise signifies a permanent annual increase of $1000, Peggy revises her estimate of her long-term average income upward by $1000. Her consumption rises by 0.9(1000) = $900. However, if Peggy views the $1000 income increase as a one-time event, she revises her long-term annual income upward by a much smaller amount. In this case, her long-term average income is $28,540 ($285,400/10). Her consumption spending increases to 0.9(28,540) = $25,686 — an increase in consumption spending of only $90.

In summary, the simplest way to think about consumption behavior is to think of consumption as being a *stable percentage of long-run average disposable income*. Permanent changes in income significantly change this long-run average, changing consumption spending significantly. Temporary changes in income alter the long-run average only slightly and thus only minimally affect current consumption. Households whose income is temporarily high increase their saving and consume much of the temporary income in the future, when

TABLE 1
Peggy's long-term income

Year	Gross Income	Disposable Income
1	$18,000	$16,200
2	20,000	18,000
3	22,000	19,800
4	25,000	22,500
5	28,000	25,200
6	32,000	28,800
7	36,000	32,400
8	40,000	36,000
9	45,000	40,500
10	50,000	45,000
	$316,000	$284,400
Long-term average	$31,600	$28,440

Does It Make Economic Sense?

Borrowing to Sustain Consumption

Long-term consumption theory assumes that households consume at relatively stable rates over time. They maintain their stable consumption paths by saving when current disposable income is higher than the desired consumption level and by dissaving or borrowing when disposable income is less than desired consumption. If households are able to save and to borrow as they choose, their consumption is constrained only by their long-term disposable incomes.

The assumption that households can save when current income is relatively high is quite reasonable. But what about the assumption that households can borrow when current income is relatively low? Are the young and unemployed really able to obtain loans to finance consumption? Do banks and other lending institutions really make loans on the basis of long-term disposable income? Does it make economic sense to assume that consumers can borrow as much as they need to maintain desired consumption when their incomes are temporarily low?

Economists have been interested in questions such as these for some time. Since the 1950s, economists have realized that consumption is more stable than current income. However, accumulating evidence indicates that the effect of an income change on consumption is larger than the pure theory of long-term consumption predicts. That is, although consumption spending is much less sensitive to income changes than the Keynesian theory predicts, it is more sensitive to temporary income changes than the long-term consumption theory predicts. One reason for the unexpectedly large consumption movements appears to be the inability of consumers to borrow when their incomes are relatively low.

A consumer who cannot borrow to maintain current consumption is said to be *liquidity constrained*. Although the consumer's long-term income is sufficient to support the desired level of current consumption, she cannot borrow the funds needed to maintain her desired spending level. The consumer's long-term disposable income is not liquid (immediately spendable). Thus, when her current income falls, the consumer has no choice but to reduce consumption spending. In effect, *the consumption function of a liquidity-constrained consumer is the simple Keynesian consumption function,* $C = a + b(DI)$.

Recent research indicates that a they spend what they have saved. Households whose income is temporarily low maintain consumption by using savings they have accumulated in the past and by borrowing.

The theory of consumption we have developed applies to *consumption* rather than to *consumer expenditures*. That is, the theory is based on the idea that people want to consume at a fairly even rate. Thus, the theory really applies only to services and to goods that are consumed rather quickly. It does not apply to goods such as furniture and appliances, which last for many years. The section on *durable* consumer goods shows that purchases of durable goods have many of the same features as saving.

Why Is the Form of the Consumption Function Important? This rather protracted discussion of the relationship between consumption spending and changes in income is not of academic interest only. The behavior of consumption spending is a prime determinant of the stability of the economy over time. If consumption spending depends primarily on long-term average (permanent) income, consumption will vary little when income rises and falls temporarily over the course of business cycles. The stability of consumption spending will, in turn, make the whole economy more stable. A long-run consumption func-

---

SECTION RECAP
Modern consumption theory says that consumption depends on long-run av- *(continued)*

substantial percentage of households may be liquidity constrained at some point in time. A study of individual households conducted by Robert E. Hall and Frederic S. Mishkin estimated that about 20 percent of all households are liquidity constrained.* A more recent study by James A. Wilcox argues that the percentage of liquidity-constrained households varies over time.** Wilcox estimates that the percentage of households that face liquidity constraints has ranged from about 15 percent (in the 1950s, when unemployment and interest rates were low) to over 35 percent (in the recession of 1981–1982).

The existence of liquidity-constrained households means that consumption spending is more sensitive to changes in aggregate disposable income than it would be if consumers could borrow freely on the basis of long-term disposable income. This result has important policy implications. The greater the sensitivity of consumption spending to changes in disposable income, the greater the effect government can have on consumption spending through changes in taxes and transfer payments that affect disposable income. Even temporary government policy actions may have some effect. However, the more unstable consumption spending is, the more need there may be for government policies designed to stabilize aggregate demand. If consumption spending is unstable, the government may choose to use tax and transfer policies to try to limit the size of fluctuations in real GNP.

The evidence indicates that the long-term income theory of consumption fits a majority of households quite well. However, the minority of households that are liquidity constrained can be substantial at times. The resulting aggregate consumption behavior is much more stable than the simple Keynesian model predicts, but less stable than the pure long-term income model predicts.

---

*"The Sensitivity of Consumption to Transitory Income: Estimates from Panel Data on Households," *Econometrica* 50 (March 1982), pp. 461–481.

**"Liquidity Constraints on Consumption: The Real Effects of 'Real' Lending Policies," Federal Reserve Bank of San Francisco *Economic Review* (Fall 1989), pp. 39–52.

---

tion implies a much more stable economy than does a Keynesian consumption function.

If the government chooses to try to increase or decrease consumption spending, its chances for success also depend upon the form of the consumption function. If consumption responds very little to temporary changes in disposable income, the government can only affect consumption significantly by changing disposable income permanently. Thus, the extent to which temporary changes in disposable income affect current consumption spending is an important policy issue. Both the *Does It Make Economic Sense?* section and the section on durable consumer goods contribute to our understanding of this issue.

Durable Consumer Goods

To this point we have discussed consumption demand as though all consumption spending were of the same type. Obviously, this is not the case. Some consumption items — what might be called pure consumption goods — are purchased and immediately consumed. A hamburger, five gallons of gasoline, or a kilowatt hour of electricity all fit into this category. Economists

---

SECTION RECAP
(continued)

erage disposable income. Temporary changes in current income have little effect on long-run average income and thus have little effect on consumption. Permanent changes in income have large effects on consumption.

Nondurable consumption goods Goods that are usually consumed within a short time after their purchase.

Durable consumer goods Goods that are not themselves consumed, but which provide services over a period of time.

classify such items as **nondurable consumption goods**. Such items are purchased as they are needed, and most are used up shortly after purchase. The consumption of services is usually lumped with nondurable consumption spending.

Some consumption items do not fit this category. A refrigerator, a sofa, or an automobile is purchased for the services it will provide over a number of years. Strictly speaking, we do not consume such items; rather, we consume the services they provide. Such goods have many of the characteristics of investment goods purchased by businesses. Consumer goods that provide services over long time periods are called **durable consumer goods**.

Figure 5 illustrates how durable and nondurable consumption and GNP have behaved over time. The relative stability of nondurable consumption spending and the relative instability of durable consumption expenditures are immediately obvious. The data suggest that changes in income have a different impact on durable consumption expenditures than on nondurable spending.

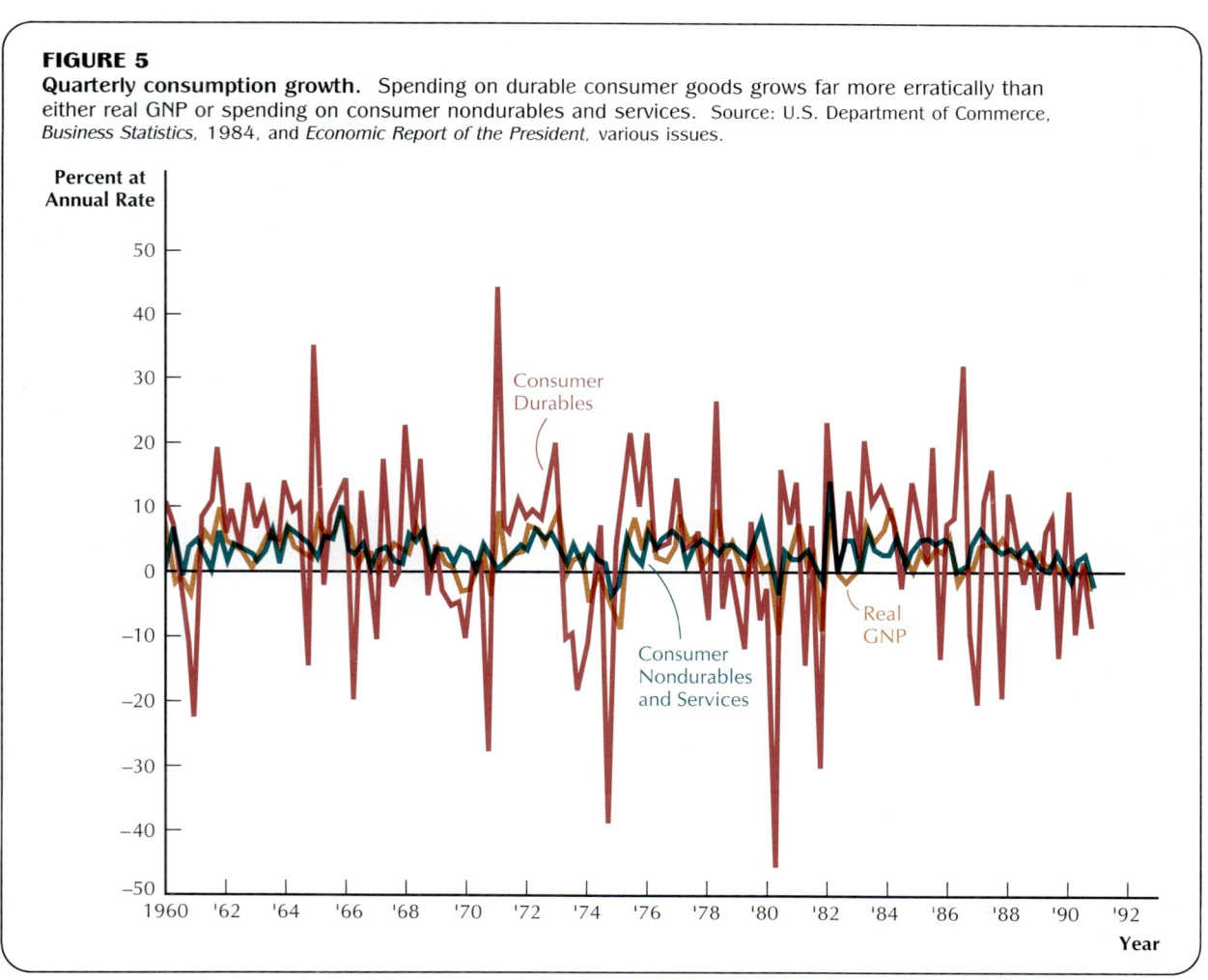

FIGURE 5
Quarterly consumption growth. Spending on durable consumer goods grows far more erratically than either real GNP or spending on consumer nondurables and services. Source: U.S. Department of Commerce, *Business Statistics*, 1984, and *Economic Report of the President*, various issues.

Why does the behavior of durable consumer goods spending violate the theory of long-term consumption? Because the theory applies to actual consumption rather than to consumption spending. When a household purchases a new sofa, it expects to consume the services provided by the sofa over a large number of years. In this respect, buying a sofa has more in common with saving to finance future consumption than it has with buying nondurable goods and services for immediate consumption. Although financial savings provide the saver with more options in the future, the purchase of durable goods provides future consumption just as surely as saved income does.

Since the purchase of durable consumer goods is similar to saving, it is not surprising that spending on durable goods behaves like saving behaves. When disposable income is temporarily high, households save *and* buy durable consumer goods. When disposable income is temporarily low, households postpone both saving and the purchase of durable goods.

What does this imply for the behavior of the economy? Economists have estimated that the marginal propensity to consume from temporary income in the United States is only one third to one half as large as the long-term marginal propensity to consume. However, even an MPC of 0.30 to 0.45 is considerably higher than the MPC predicted by the pure theory of long-term consumption. The main reason the actual MPC out of temporary income is higher than theory would lead us to expect is durable consumption spending. When disposable income temporarily increases, households both save more and purchase more durable consumer goods. When experiencing a temporary decrease in income, households dip into savings to finance current consumption, while also delaying the purchase of new durable goods. Such behavior strengthens the connection between current income and current consumption spending and causes the aggregate demand to be less stable than it would otherwise be.

SECTION RECAP
Spending on durable consumer goods is much less stable than spending on nondurable goods and services. This reflects the fact that durable goods are like savings; they provide a flow of consumption services in the future. Thus, like saving, durable goods spending rises and falls with current income.

Income Taxes, Transfer Payments, and Consumption

Since consumption spending depends on disposable income, the government is able to influence the level of consumption spending. By varying income and payroll tax rates and transfer payments, the government can push disposable income up or down. An increase in the income tax rate or in the Social Security payroll tax rate reduces disposable income and consumption spending. An increase in transfer payments increases disposable income and consumption. All this is straightforward. However, one complication is overlooked. Changes in the level of taxation or transfers can be either permanent or temporary. The effect of a change in disposable income on consumption differs according to the perceived duration of the change. The impact of a change in taxes or transfer payments on the level of consumption spending depends on whether the change is perceived to be temporary or permanent.

The long-term theory of consumption suggests that any changes in taxes or transfer payments perceived to be temporary will have a very limited effect on current nondurable consumption spending. In fact, this is the case. Several well-documented instances of temporary income tax changes in recent U.S. history provide evidence in favor of the notion that temporary tax changes have little immediate impact on nondurable consumption demand. The *Why the Disagreement?* section discusses one such episode.

Why the Disagreement?

Temporary Tax Changes

Economic stability is a goal of government economic policy. Policymakers hope to avoid both excessively large and rapid expansions, which can cause prices to rise, and prolonged or severe recessions, which increase the number of people unemployed. One of the major questions confronting macroeconomists is how to promote economic stability: What policies are likely to be stabilizing?

In the late 1960s, policymakers sought ways to slow the growth of spending to prevent prices from rising. The economy had been growing rapidly since the early 1960s, at least partly because of policies pursued by the Kennedy and Johnson administrations. President Kennedy advocated a permanent tax cut and higher government spending, both of which were accomplished by his successor. Beginning in 1965, government spending on both social programs and the war in Vietnam were greatly expanded. The increased government spending generated tremendous economic growth, as shown in Table 2. Only during 1967 was the growth rate near the long-term average of 3 percent. This rapid growth pushed the unemployment rate below 4 percent in the first quarter of 1966, where it remained until 1970.

Such rapid economic growth and low unemployment led economists to predict a surge in inflation. President Johnson resisted the call for a tax increase, not wishing to end the expansion. Finally, in late 1967, he called for a *temporary tax surcharge* of 10 percent. Individuals would calculate their income taxes in the usual fashion, then add 10 percent. The surcharge was to be in effect for only fifteen months,

TABLE 2

Year	Real GNP Growth	Unemployment Rate
1965	5.5	4.5
1966	4.1	3.8
1967	3.1	3.8
1968	4.3	3.6

Source: *Economic Report of the President, 1986.* All data are in percentage terms. Growth rates are from fourth quarter to fourth quarter.

Investment Demand

Real versus Financial Investment

The second major component of aggregate demand is investment. By **investment** an economist means the purchase of capital goods that are used to produce goods or services in the future. Economic investment must be differentiated from **financial investment** — the use of savings by households or businesses to purchase financial assets. Financial investment is, in economic terms, the allocation of savings to particular assets. Savings, channelled to businesses through financial markets and financial institutions, provide the funds needed to support economic investment.

What is included in economic investment? Investment spending typically is divided into three major categories: fixed business investment, changes in business inventory levels, and residential construction. Note that the purchase of a newly built home by a family is included in investment for official statistical purposes. The purchase of a new house is the only household expenditure counted as investment spending. It is treated as investment because of the length of time a house remains in use.

Investment
Purchase of capital goods used to produce goods or services.

Financial investment
Allocation of savings to the purchase of financial assets.

TABLE 3
Effects of the 1968 income tax surcharge

	First Half	Second Half
Consumption	78.2	78.2
Saving	6.3	4.8
Taxes	13.4	14.9

All data are expressed as a percentage of personal income. Data were drawn from Robert J. Gordon, "Post-War Macroeconomics: The Evolution of Events and Ideas," in M.S. Feldstein, ed., *The American Economy in Transition*, National Bureau of Economic Research, 1982, p. 136.

from April 1, 1968 through June 30, 1969.

Some economists immediately argued that the temporary tax surcharge would not slow the growth of consumption spending. Administration officials argued that by decreasing disposable income, the surcharge would reduce consumer expenditures. Why the disagreement?

In 1967 many economists, including President Johnson's advisers, did not understand the importance of the temporary–permanent income distinction. They thought that a temporary tax increase, which reduces disposable income, would reduce consumption spending, thus reducing the aggregate demand for goods and services. However, the theory of consumption demand asserts that temporary changes in income have relatively small effects on consumer spending. That was the case in 1968.

Table 3 shows the behavior of consumption, saving, and taxes as a percentage of personal before-tax income in 1968. Taxes as a percentage of income rose by 1.5 percentage points from the first half of the year to the second half, but saving as a percentage of income *fell* by an identical 1.5 percentage points. The net result was that consumption spending as a percentage of personal income was unchanged. The temporary income tax surcharge had *no* effect on consumer spending during 1968.

The inflationary pressures expected by economists began to be felt in 1968. Inflation more than doubled from the level of the previous year, rising to 4.9 percent, and went still higher in 1969. This episode greatly weakened policymakers' faith in the effectiveness of temporary policy changes.

Gross and Net Investment

Suppose a business firm purchases a machine to expand its production level. The purchase obviously fits our definition of investment. But what if the machine is purchased to replace an identical machine that has worn out? Is this an investment?

According to our definition, the machine is counted as a business investment whether it adds to productive capacity or merely maintains the previous level of capacity. To the economy, however, a difference exists. Replacement of worn-out capital goods maintains the previous level of capacity but does not allow for growth. Adding to the existing capital stock permits the economy to produce more. Thus, it makes sense to separate the two categories.

Gross investment includes all spending on capital goods, whether to replace worn-out, or **depreciated**, capital goods or to add to the capital stock. Additions to the economy's capital stock are called **net investment**. Net investment enables the economy to produce more over time. Net investment is the difference between gross investment and replacement of depreciated capital. Note that *gross investment is the category that is included in aggregate demand*.

Gross investment
Total spending on capital goods, including replacement of depreciated capital goods and additions to the capital stock.

Depreciation
Wearing out a capital good.

Net investment
Additions to the existing capital stock.

Common Sense of Net Investment

Why do business firms invest in new capital goods? The simple answer is that they expect to increase their profits. That is, they believe that the earnings from the sale of the products produced with the capital goods will cover the cost of the capital goods, plus interest, and will yield an acceptable profit over and above the costs. The major elements in the investment decision, then, are the expected revenues that can be earned, the cost of the investment goods, and the interest rate at which the investment goods must be financed or which the firm could earn if it purchased financial assets instead of capital goods.

The interest rate affects the investment decision regardless of whether the firm must borrow the funds to purchase the new capital goods or uses retained earnings, since the interest rate represents the opportunity cost of investing funds in the business rather than making a financial investment. When making an investment decision, managers must compare the expected return on the investment with the return on the best alternative given up to undertake the investment project. The opportunity cost of investment is the cost of borrowing if the firm must borrow to finance the project. However, if the firm has saved enough from previous income to finance the project, the opportunity cost is the interest that could be earned by purchasing financial assets with the savings.

One way to simplify the investment decision is to compare the rate of return on investment with the interest rate at which the firm could borrow or lend. (For simplicity, assume the borrowing and lending rates are the same.) The **rate of return on investment** is, in effect, the interest rate earned on the funds invested in the new capital. It equals net income produced by the capital good (after operating and maintenance costs are subtracted) divided by the cost of the capital good. If the rate of return on the investment project exceeds the interest rate on loans, the project is profitable. If the rate of return on the investment is less than the market interest rate, the project is unprofitable. (Another approach to the investment decision—more technical but more precise—is described in the appendix to this chapter.)

Investment Demand Curve

Suppose a firm ranks its investment projects in terms of their expected rates of return. The firm lists the project with the highest rate of return first, the next-highest second, and so on down to the project with the lowest rate of return. To compensate for the effects of changes in the price level, the firm adjusts its rates of return for expected inflation. That is, the firm calculates the expected rate of return on investment projects in terms of constant prices. The rate of return in constant prices is called the **real rate of return**. Such an ordering is shown in Figure 6.

Once the firm's investment possibilities are ordered in this manner, all one must do to determine the amount of investment spending to be undertaken is to compare the real rate of return on investment to the expected real (constant-price) cost of borrowing. The expected real cost of borrowing is the **expected real interest rate**, which equals the market (or *nominal*) interest rate adjusted for expected changes in the price level. The expected real interest rate represents the cost of borrowing (and the return to lending) in terms of dollars of constant buying power. In equation form:

$$r^e = i - p^e$$

Rate of return on investment
Net income earned by an investment project as a percentage of its cost.

SECTION RECAP
Business firms invest in capital goods when the expected rate of return earned by the capital goods equals or exceeds the expected cost of financing the capital goods.

Real rate of return
Rate of return calculated in terms of constant prices, that is, adjusted for inflation.

Expected real interest rate
Nominal rate of interest adjusted for the expected inflation rate; $r^e = i - p^e$.

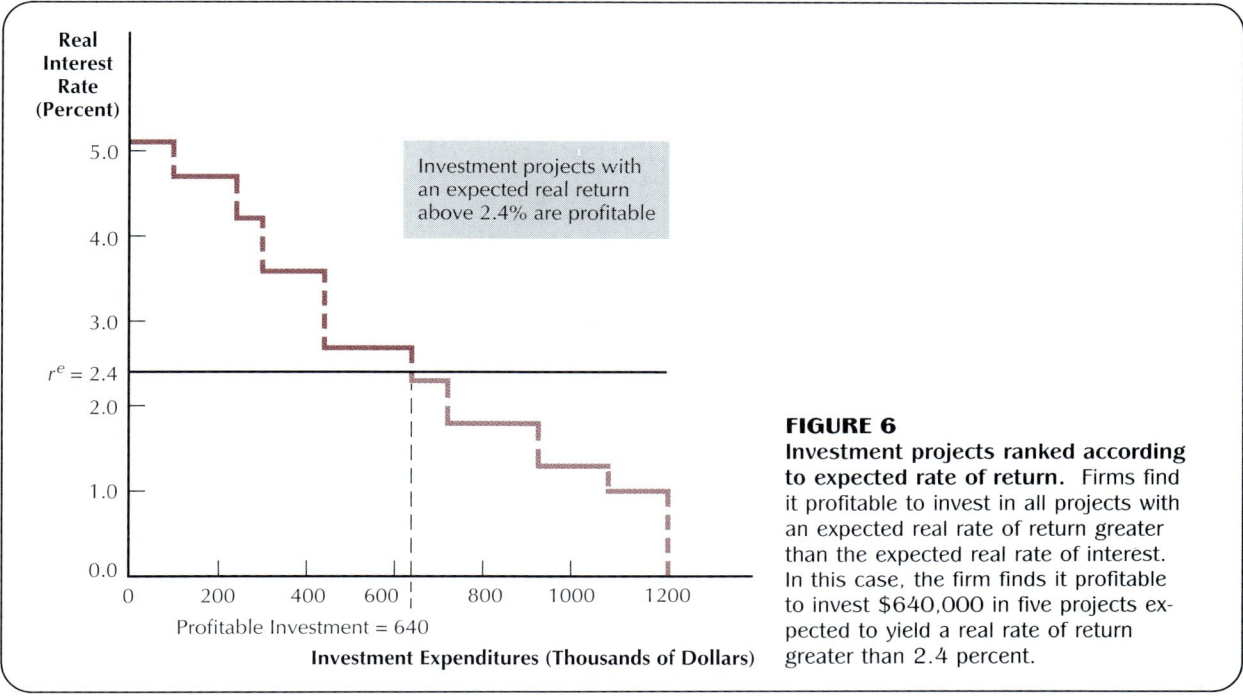

FIGURE 6
Investment projects ranked according to expected rate of return. Firms find it profitable to invest in all projects with an expected real rate of return greater than the expected real rate of interest. In this case, the firm finds it profitable to invest $640,000 in five projects expected to yield a real rate of return greater than 2.4 percent.

where r^e is the expected real interest rate, i is the nominal interest rate, and p^e is the expected rate of inflation for the duration of the loan.

In Figure 6 the expected real interest rate equals 2.4 percent. All investment projects with an expected real rate of return greater than 2.4 percent are expected to be profitable. Projects with expected rates of return below 2.4 percent will not be undertaken.

If this procedure were followed by all the businesses in the economy and the individual investment possibility orderings were added up, the result would be an investment demand curve for the economy. Such a curve is shown in Figure 7. The curve is drawn as a smooth line rather than as a step diagram to reflect the fact that so many investment opportunities exist for the whole economy that even a small change in the expected real interest rate changes the aggregate level of investment a little.

Expectations play a big role in determining how much investment firms undertake. Managers must form estimates of the income they expect investment projects to produce in the future and of the inflation rate they believe will prevail in the future. The expected real rate of return on investment projects depends on these estimates. If changing economic conditions cause entrepreneurs to lower their estimates of future income from capital goods, thereby reducing the expected rate of return on investment projects, the investment demand curve shifts to the left. An increase in the expected rate of return on investment shifts the investment demand curve to the right. Changes in the expected real interest rate cause movements along the investment demand curve.

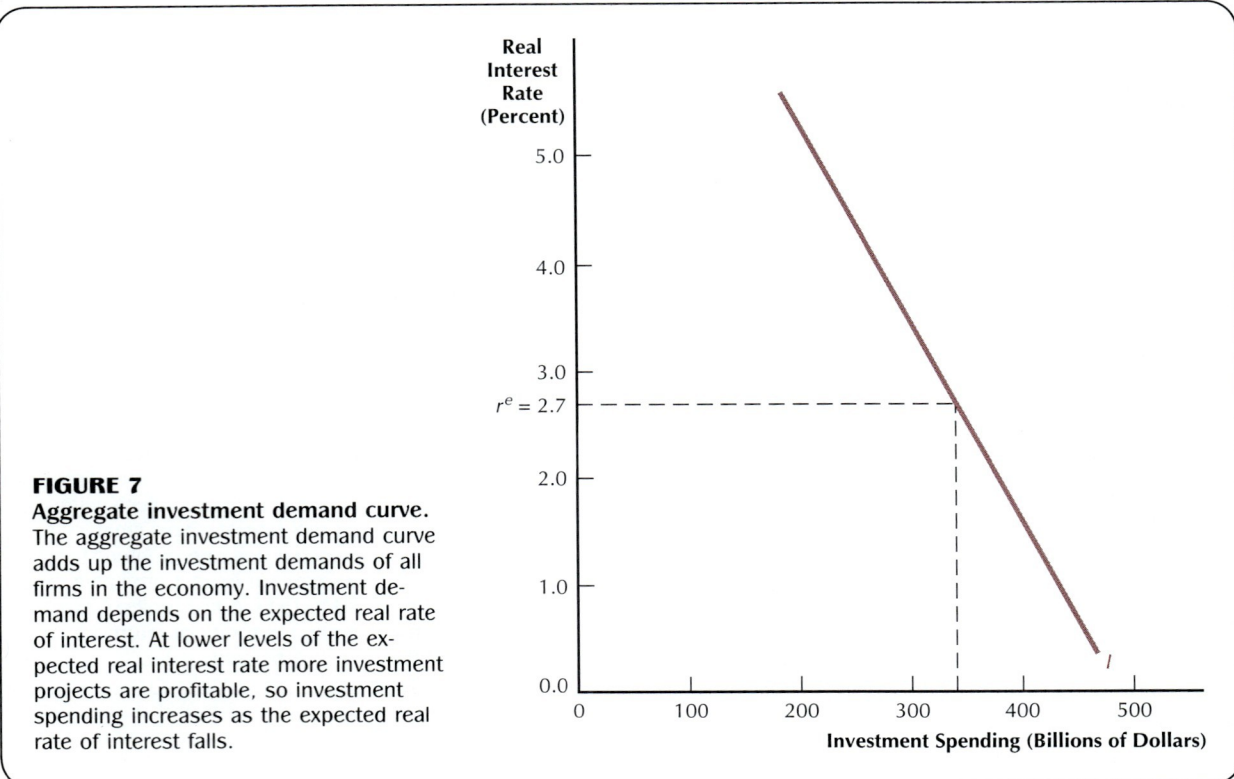

FIGURE 7
Aggregate investment demand curve.
The aggregate investment demand curve adds up the investment demands of all firms in the economy. Investment demand depends on the expected real rate of interest. At lower levels of the expected real interest rate more investment projects are profitable, so investment spending increases as the expected real rate of interest falls.

Factors Affecting Investment Demand

Firms buy new capital goods if they expect to earn a profit by producing goods or services with the capital good. When expectations change, that is, when business decision makers become more optimistic or more pessimistic, investment demand rises or falls. But what factors affect profit expectations? Are any *quantifiable* economic variables useful in predicting the level of investment demand?

A number of quantifiable economic variables are related to the level of investment. However, even the best projections of investment spending are none too good. A large element of uncertainty exists in the investment decision. Since we are dealing with profit *expectations*, we must realize that businesspeople confronted with the same objective data will make different investment decisions depending on whether they interpret the data optimistically or pessimistically. Keynes summarized this uncertainty by saying that investors are moved by "animal spirits" to increase or decrease the level of investment spending.

Income Investment demand is related to income. A large economy with a high level of income invests more than a small economy with a low level of income. When income increases, investment also rises. The number of profitable ventures increases when consumers, businesses, and government agencies spend more. When income declines, investment spending falls; less spending on goods and services reduces the need for firms to expand their production facilities.[4]

Capacity Utilization   Over short periods of time an important factor affecting investment demand is the **capacity utilization rate** of industry—the level of production in an industry as a percent of the industry's maximum production level. Economists have determined that when the capital in an industry is fully employed, the industry has a capacity utilization rate of about 85 percent. This less than 100 percent rate reflects the fact that some capital must always be held in reserve, some is always undergoing maintenance, and some is usually broken down.

When the capacity utilization rate rises above the 85 percent level, net investment usually increases. Below that figure, firms can expand output without investing in new capital. Thus, investment responds much more to increases in income when the capacity utilization rate is high than when it is low.

Tax Policy   Business managers attempt to maximize the after-tax profits earned by their companies. Government tax policies can affect the profitability of investments and hence the amount of investment spending in a number of ways. One direct way is through **investment tax credits**, which allow businesses to deduct a percentage of the cost of investments from the taxes they owe. This directly raises after-tax profits. Investment tax credits lower the cost of investment projects, as government subsidizes the new capital goods. This increases the expected real rate of return on investment projects. Not surprisingly, investment tax credits are an effective way for government to encourage an increase in investment spending.

Another way in which tax policy affects investment is through the corporate profits tax. Martin Feldstein and other economists have argued that taxing corporate profits reduces investment by limiting the amount of internal funds available for investment spending. It is assumed that companies prefer to use internally generated funds (savings) rather than borrowing. If this line of thinking is correct, reducing the corporate profits tax should encourage more investment spending.

Inventory Investment

The word *investment* usually brings to mind purchases of such assets as machines, buildings, or trucks. However, businesses are constantly investing in other assets as well. Nearly every manufacturing, wholesale, or retail business carries substantial **inventories** of raw materials, goods in process, or finished goods—stocks of goods on hand at some stage of the production process. Inventories are part of the capital stock of the firm. (Inventories have traditionally been referred to as circulating capital, because they are used up and replenished frequently.)

When a firm changes the level of its inventory of goods, it is investing (or disinvesting—changes are often negative). Note that *changes* in the level of

Capacity utilization rate
Level of industry production as a percentage of maximum production.

Investment tax credit
Allows firms to deduct a portion of their investment spending from the corporate taxes they owe.

SECTION RECAP
Investment demand depends positively on the level of national income and the capacity utilization rate. Tax policy can favor investment through investment tax credits or can reduce investment by taxing corporate profits.

Inventory
Stock of raw materials or unfinished goods to be used in the production process or of finished goods waiting to be sold.

---

[4]Investment spending is related not only to the level of income but also to the *change* in income. This relationship is quite important. It has been summarized in something called the accelerator model of investment, which is developed in the chapter on business cycles.

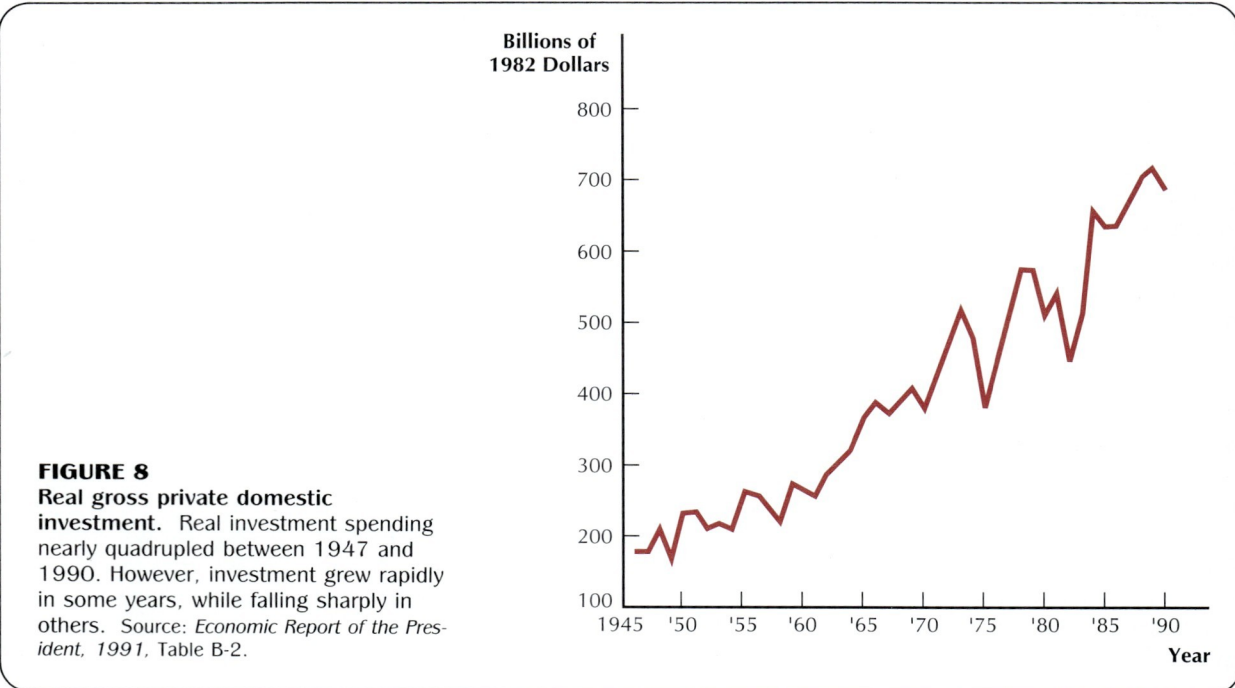

FIGURE 8
Real gross private domestic investment. Real investment spending nearly quadrupled between 1947 and 1990. However, investment grew rapidly in some years, while falling sharply in others. Source: *Economic Report of the President, 1991*, Table B-2.

inventory are investment. This definition is consistent with the definition of net investment in fixed capital. Changes in the level of fixed capital are net investment.

Inventory investment is the most unstable component of gross private domestic investment, because business firms do not have full control over the amount of inventory they carry at all times. If a firm's managers envision increased sales and order more inventory to meet the demand, but the sales do not materialize, the firm is left with an expanded level of inventory. Similarly, unforeseen increases in sales can deplete inventory levels, registering as inventory disinvestment in the official statistics.

Like fixed capital investment, inventory investment is affected by interest rates. Businesses typically borrow short term to finance inventory holdings. When short-term interest rates are high, firms attempt to economize on inventory holdings by purchasing smaller amounts at more frequent intervals.

Instability of Investment Spending

We have already noted that investment spending is quite unstable. Figure 8 shows the actual behavior of investment spending in the post-World War II period. Investment spending is extremely **procyclical**, moving in the same direction as real GNP over the course of business cycles.[5] When real GNP is growing during business cycle expansions, investment spending grows. When output growth is declining or negative during recessions, investment spending also declines. In fact, the investment cycle is much larger, in percentage terms,

Procyclical
Moving in the same direction as real GNP over the course of the business cycle.

---
[5] An economic variable that moves in the opposite direction of the business cycle (that is, that decreases in expansions and increases in recessions) is said to be *countercyclical*.

than is the cycle of total spending. Figure 9 compares the quarter-to-quarter percentage growth rates of real investment spending and total real spending. As you can see, the percentage fluctuations in investment growth are much larger than the percentage fluctuations in the growth of real GNP.

Why is the total spending cycle more stable than the investment cycle? A moment's thought should provide the answer. Consumption demand, especially that portion devoted to nondurable goods and services, tends to be very stable. Since consumption spending is a much larger proportion of total spending than is investment spending, the stability of consumption demand reduces the overall percentage change in total spending.

Investment spending is unstable for a number of reasons:

1. Fixed business investment is very sensitive to changes in real GNP, especially when the economy is operating near full capacity.
2. Fixed business investment is also sensitive to changes in the degree of optimism of business decision makers about the future.

SECTION RECAP
Investment spending is the most unstable component of aggregate demand. Inventory investment is particularly unstable, but fixed business *(continued)*

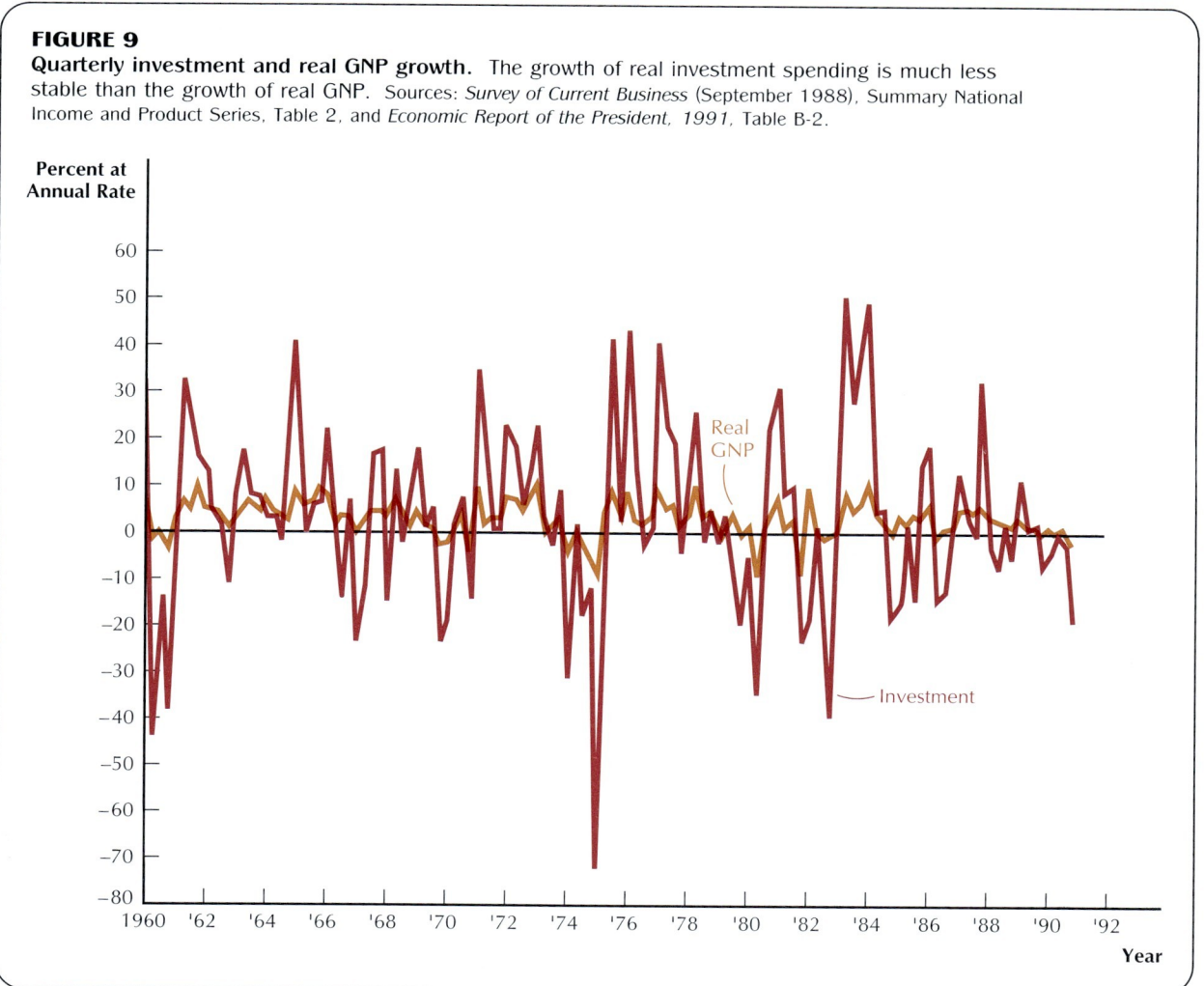

FIGURE 9
Quarterly investment and real GNP growth. The growth of real investment spending is much less stable than the growth of real GNP. Sources: *Survey of Current Business* (September 1988), Summary National Income and Product Series, Table 2, and *Economic Report of the President, 1991*, Table B-2.

SECTION RECAP
(continued)
investment, which is very sensitive to changes in real GNP, and residential construction, which is very sensitive to changes in the mortgage interest rate, are also unstable.

3. Residential construction is very sensitive to changes in the real interest rate.
4. Inventory investment is very sensitive to changes in spending.

Some economists believe that investment instability is a primary cause of business cycles. Keynes made investment instability the central feature in his theory of cyclical instability. Just how investment instability might generate business cycle behavior and what other factors are required in addition to investment instability are discussed after we have assembled a complete model of the economy.

Government Demand for Goods and Services

Federal, state, and local governments are major purchasers of goods and services in the United States. Altogether, government purchases account for slightly over 20 percent of aggregate demand. The factors affecting government demand are mostly political rather than economic. As government provides more and more services (from education to road maintenance to national defense), it demands more and more goods and services, adding to aggregate demand.

In this book we treat government demand as a policy variable. Elected officials determine the level of government spending. They base their decisions on a number of factors, some related to macroeconomic policy, and others unrelated to macroeconomic conditions. At the national level, government spending may be undertaken specifically to increase aggregate demand. At the local level, however, spending has little to do with macroeconomics. For example, when a municipality decides to build a new sewage treatment plant, it does so for reasons that have little to do with macroeconomic conditions. However, the construction of the sewage treatment plant adds to aggregate demand and, to some degree, affects the macroeconomy. When the impact of thousands of such government projects is added together, the effect on aggregate demand is very important.

SECTION RECAP
Government purchases of goods and services are treated as a policy variable; we do not attempt to explain why such purchases rise and fall.

Net Exports

Exports of domestically produced goods and services to foreign consumers, businesses, and governments adds to the aggregate demand for U.S. products. However, imports of foreign-produced goods purchased by U.S. consumers, businesses, and governmental units represent a flow of spending out of the domestic economy. Net exports, the difference between exports and imports, reflect the net effect of international trade on U.S. aggregate demand.

The factors that cause domestic consumers and businesses to buy more consumption and investment goods also cause foreign consumers and businesses to buy more. U.S. exports depend heavily on foreign income levels. As foreign incomes rise, foreign consumers buy more consumption goods, some of which are produced in the United States. Foreign firms buy more capital goods, some U.S. produced. As U.S. income rises, U.S. consumers and businesses buy more goods, some of which are foreign made. Thus, imports are positively related to the level of U.S. income.

When U.S. income rises more rapidly than foreign incomes, imports rise faster than exports, *ceteris paribus*. Thus, relatively rapid U.S. income growth tends to reduce net exports. Net exports are also influenced by the price of U.S. goods relative to the dollar price of foreign-produced goods.

The price of U.S. goods relative to the price of foreign goods depends on two things: the U.S. price level relative to foreign price levels and the rate at which foreign currencies exchange for U.S. dollars. If foreign prices are rising faster than U.S. prices (that is, the foreign inflation rate is higher than the U.S. inflation rate), U.S. goods become relatively cheaper to foreigners. This encourages foreigners to purchase U.S. goods, increasing U.S. exports. Relatively higher foreign prices discourage Americans from purchasing foreign-made goods, and imports fall. Both effects increase net exports, adding to the aggregate demand for U.S. products.

When the **exchange rate** — the number of units of foreign currency that exchange for one dollar — falls, fewer units of foreign currency are required to purchase a dollar. For example, if the exchange rate between the dollar and the German deutschemark falls from 2.00 deutschemarks per dollar to 1.50 deutschemarks per dollar, Germans can obtain more dollars for the same number of deutschemarks. This reduces the deutschemark price of U.S. goods and encourages Germans to buy more U.S. goods. For example, the deutschemark price of a pair of Levi jeans costing $25 falls from 50 deutschemarks (DM2 × 25) to only 37.5 deutschemarks (DM1.50 × 25). Demand for the American-made jeans rises as the price in Germany falls, increasing U.S. exports in the process. In general, as U.S. goods become cheaper to foreigners, foreign demand for U.S. exports tends to rise. Conversely, the decline in the exchange rate makes foreign-produced goods more expensive for Americans, who must give up a larger number of dollars to acquire foreign currencies. Thus, a lower exchange rate discourages imports as it encourages exports; net exports tend to rise when the exchange rate falls.[6]

Exchange rate
Number of units of foreign currency that exchange for one unit of the domestic currency.

SECTION RECAP
Net exports depend on domestic and foreign real income levels, the exchange rate, and the ratio of domestic to foreign prices. Changes in any of these variables alter net exports.

Aggregate Demand for Goods and Services

Aggregate demand equals consumption demand plus investment demand plus government purchases plus net exports. Thus, the theory of aggregate demand draws directly on the theories of consumption, investment, and net exports. Aggregate demand rises and falls with its component parts. The factors affecting aggregate demand are the same factors that affect the individual expenditure categories. In this section we show how changes in consumption, investment, net exports, and government purchases affect aggregate demand. We also derive an aggregate demand curve and examine how it shifts in response to changes in the factors that determine aggregate demand.

Factors Affecting Aggregate Demand

At a particular price level, measured by the price index value PI_0 in Figure 10, the real quantity of goods and services demanded depends on the real demands

---

[6]This discussion of the exchange rate ignores that fact that the exchange rate is a market-determined price. A more complex model of the economy would include a foreign-exchange market. Our treatment has the virtue of being much simpler, while allowing us to discuss the most important points of international macroeconomics.

of consumers, firms, governmental units, and foreign purchasers of domestic products. That is, at price level PI_0:

$$RGNP_0 = C_0 + I_0 + G_0 + NX_0$$

The level of aggregate demand depends on a number of autonomous variables. An **autonomous variable** is a variable whose value does not directly depend on the level of real GNP. An autonomous variable affects the level of real GNP, but is not affected by it in turn. The autonomous variables that determine the quantity of aggregate demand at a particular price level include the following:

Autonomous variable
Variable whose value does not directly depend on the level of real GNP or the price level.

1. Income and payroll tax rates and transfer payments. Consumption depends on long-run disposable income, which is affected by taxes and transfer payments.

2. The level of the expected real interest rate. Investment spending depends on the expected real rate. The expected real interest rate is determined by the nominal interest rate and the expected inflation rate. We will see later that the nominal interest rate is affected by changes in the money supply, which is a policy variable.

3. The level of business taxes and investment tax credits. Investment spending is affected by both.

4. The level of government purchases of goods and services. This policy variable directly affects aggregate demand.

5. The ratio of domestic to foreign prices, the exchange rate, and the foreign real income level. The price ratio and the exchange rate affect the prices of domestically produced goods compared to foreign-produced goods. When either the price ratio or the exchange rate changes, net exports are affected. The foreign real income level affects the foreign demand for U.S. exports.

Changes in any of the autonomous variables on which aggregate demand depends cause the level of real GNP to change at any given price level. For example, an increase in government purchases would increase the RGNP level associated with PI_0 in Figure 10.

Aggregate Demand Curve

The quantity of real GNP demanded is affected by changes in the aggregate price level, as well as by changes in autonomous variables. The graphical relationship between the quantity of real output demanded and the price level (pictured in Figure 10) is the **aggregate demand (AD) curve**. The AD curve is *not* just an ordinary demand curve blown up to account for total demand for goods and services. Although it looks like an ordinary demand curve, since real GNP rises as the price level falls, its slope depends on factors totally different from those that cause ordinary demand curves to slope negatively.

Aggregate demand (AD) curve
Graphical relationship between the total quantity of goods and services demanded in an economy and the economy's aggregate price level.

Suppose that the current aggregate output–price level combination is $RGNP_0$, PI_0, as shown in Figure 10. To derive the aggregate demand curve, we must determine the effect of an increase in the price level, as measured by the price index, on real output demanded. Assume PI rises from PI_0 to PI_1. What happens to RGNP demanded?

To answer this question, we must understand what the *ceteris paribus* clause contains. What other things are being held constant as PI rises? In this instance *the things held constant are the autonomous variables that determine the quantity of real GNP demanded at any price level*: income and payroll tax rates, transfer

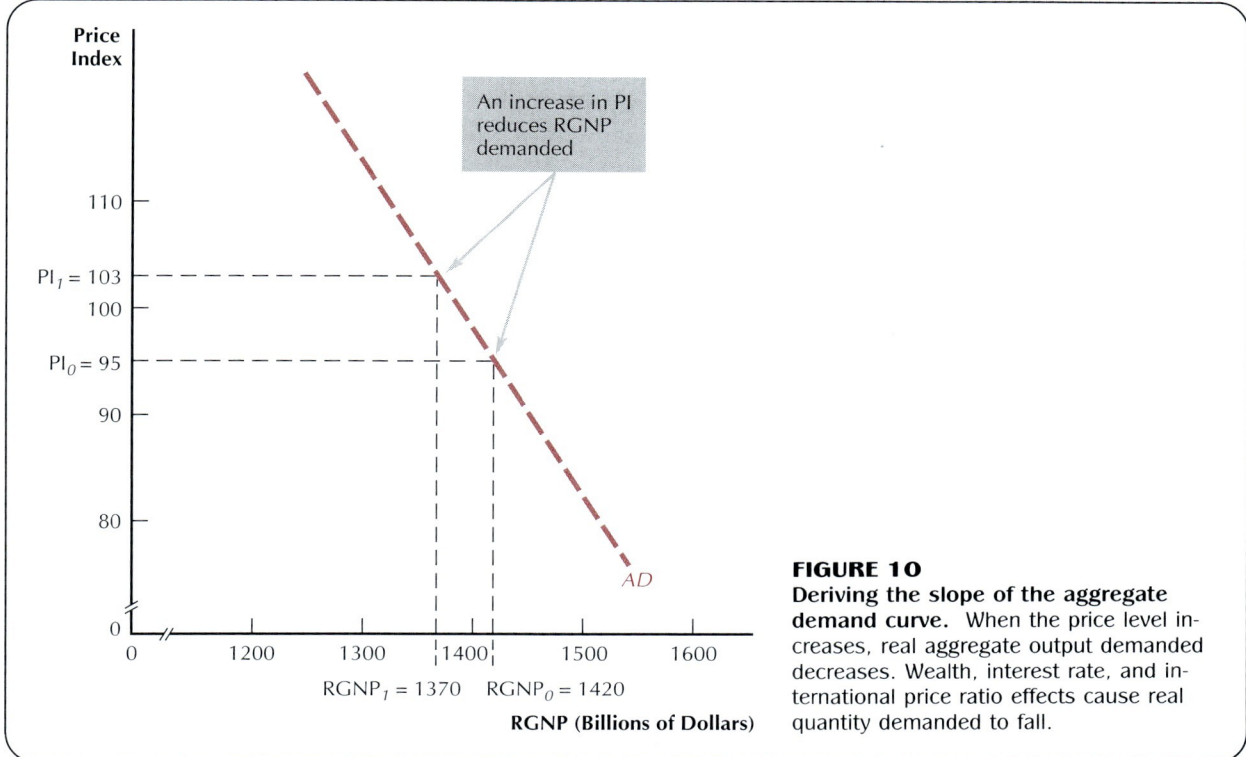

FIGURE 10
Deriving the slope of the aggregate demand curve. When the price level increases, real aggregate output demanded decreases. Wealth, interest rate, and international price ratio effects cause real quantity demanded to fall.

payments, the expected inflation rate, the money supply, business income tax rates and investment tax credits, government purchases, foreign price and real income levels, and the exchange rate. It is perhaps easier to list the variables *not* held constant: PI, the interest rate, and any variables directly affected by them.

An increase in PI affects RGNP demanded through three channels:

1. Direct wealth effect. As PI rises, the buying power of the money and government bonds held by households declines. Both money and bonds are denominated in dollars, and dollars are worth less when prices rise. As household *real* wealth declines, many households reduce their consumption purchases and save more to restore the real value of their savings. The reduction in consumption spending has a negative effect on RGNP demanded.

2. Indirect interest rate effect. At higher prices, businesses require more dollars to purchase the same quantity of investment goods. To finance their investment purchases, firms increase their demand for loans in the credit market. As in any market, an increase in demand *(ceteris paribus)* increases the price of credit, which happens to be the interest rate. If the expected inflation rate remains constant, the expected real interest rate rises. This causes real investment spending to decline, reducing RGNP demanded.

3. International price ratio effect. As PI rises, the ratio of domestic to foreign price levels increases. Domestically produced goods become more expensive relative to foreign-produced goods both at home and abroad. This causes exports to decrease and imports to increase, thus decreasing net exports. A fall in net exports reduces real GNP demanded.

The three effects of PI on RGNP demanded reinforce one another. Thus, as the price level rises from PI_0 to PI_1 in Figure 10, the real quantity of goods and services demanded falls from $RGNP_0$ to $RGNP_1$; the aggregate demand curve slopes negatively.

Shifting the AD Curve

Anything that increases C, I, G, or NX, unless offset by another factor, increases aggregate demand. For example, a decrease in the income tax rate increases disposable income. If consumers perceive the tax cut to be permanent, they react by increasing their consumption spending significantly. The AD curve shifts to the right, as in Figure 11. At a lower income tax rate, the real quantity of goods and services demanded is higher at every level of the price index.

Other factors that could increase aggregate demand include an increase in business optimism that increases investment spending; a decrease in business taxes that encourages investment spending; an increase in government purchases of goods and services; and a decline in the exchange rate that makes dollars cheaper in terms of foreign currencies, thus encouraging exports and discouraging imports. Reversing the direction of any of these factors causes some component of aggregate demand to fall and shifts the AD curve to the left.

In later chapters we will see that changes in aggregate demand are a major determinant of real GNP fluctuations. Most (though not all) recessions in the

SECTION RECAP
The AD curve is negatively sloped because an increase in the price level reduces real income and consumption spending, increases the real interest rate, thus reducing invest- *(continued)*

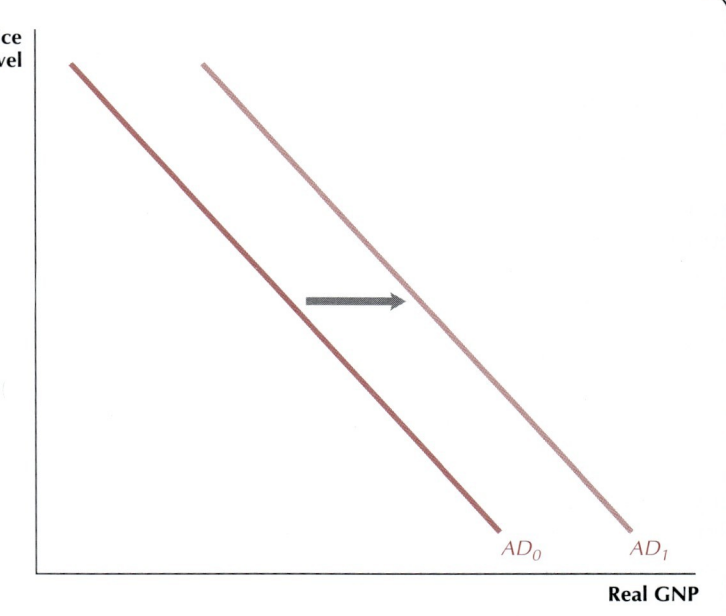

FIGURE 11
Increase in aggregate demand. When any of the autonomous factors affecting the level of C, I, G, or NX changes, causing spending to rise, the AD curve shifts to the right.

United States in this century have been caused by a reduction in aggregate demand. Similarly, most (but not all) periods of rising inflation can be traced to rapidly growing aggregate demand. Stability of real GNP and the aggregate price level cannot be achieved if aggregate demand changes by large amounts from year to year.

We cannot analyze macroeconomic behavior using only an aggregate demand curve. The next chapter develops the theory of aggregate supply. We use the labor market as the starting point for our development of aggregate supply theory. Once we have developed a theory of aggregate supply, we can combine it with aggregate demand theory to explain macroeconomic behavior.

> **SECTION RECAP**
> *(continued)*
> ment spending, and reduces net exports by raising the ratio of domestic to foreign prices. A change in any of the factors (other than the price level) affecting C, I, G, or NX shifts the AD curve.

Summary

Consumption demand theory is based on the idea that households attempt to maximize their welfare over long periods of time and thus form notions of their long-term income levels and consume on the basis of a long-term plan. This implies that the consumption path of a household over time may be smoother than the household's income pattern. Indeed, when a person's entire life is considered, this is almost universally the case. Very few people earn much when they are very young or very old.

Since **long-term income** is the most important determinant of consumption spending—particularly of the consumption of nondurable goods and services—the factors that most affect consumption demand are those that alter long-term income. Thus, the distinction between permanent and temporary changes in income is important. A permanent tax increase or reduction in transfer payments permanently lowers disposable income and is likely to have a significant effect on consumption demand. A temporary tax or transfer payments reduction has little effect on long-term disposable income and thus has little impact on consumption spending.

Durable consumption spending has many of the attributes of saving. It is more unstable than nondurable consumption spending for that reason. Changing interest rates and temporary reductions in disposable income have a greater impact on durable consumption spending than on nondurable consumption.

The **theory of investment demand** is not so precise as consumption theory, primarily because of the large role played by expectations of the future in determining investment expenditures. Nevertheless, several quantifiable factors are related to investment spending in a systematic way, the most important of which is aggregate spending. As total spending rises and businesses run out of productive capacity, **fixed business investment** rises.

The expected real interest rate also affects investment demand, as it represents the opportunity cost of both fixed and inventory investment. Changes in interest rates have an especially great effect on prospective home buyers, who must finance a large mortgage loan for a long period of time. Small changes in the mortgage interest rate can significantly change the size of monthly house payments.

Inventory changes are the least predictable component of investment spending, primarily because businesses do not have complete control of inventory levels. Misestimation of future sales leads to excess accumulation or reduction of inventories.

Government purchases of goods and services are treated as an autonomous policy variable. **Net exports** depend on domestic and foreign income levels, domestic prices relative to foreign prices, and the exchange rate.

Aggregate demand is the summation of consumption demand, investment demand, government purchases, and net exports. The **aggregate demand (AD) curve** relates the real quantity of output demanded to the level of the price index. A negative relationship exists between PI and RGNP because increases in PI (1) reduce the buying power of money and other financial assets, causing consumption spending to decline, (2) increase the demand for loans, forcing up the interest rate and reducing real investment spending, and (3) increase the domestic-to-foreign price ratio, thus causing net exports to decline.

Questions for Thought

Knowledge Questions

1. What are the categories into which consumption spending is typically divided?
2. Why does it make sense for an individual to base his or her consumption on long-term average income rather than on current income?
3. How is the purchase of consumer durable goods similar to saving?
4. Inventory investment is extremely unstable because businesses are not able to control inventory levels completely. Why can't firms control inventory levels precisely?

Application Questions

5. Why should the relationship of consumption to income on a month-to-month basis (that is, the monthly MPC) be less stable than on a year-to-year basis?
6. Compare the consumption patterns over time of nondurable goods and services and durable goods. Why are the patterns different?
7. Why are expectations so important in making investment decisions?
8. Both ordinary commodity demand curves and the aggregate demand curve have negative slopes. Why does a commodity demand curve slope negatively? Why does the AD curve slope negatively?

Synthesis Questions

9. Theories of consumption based on long-term income assume that consumers are able to transfer income over time by saving and borrowing. What effect would the inability to borrow have on a household's short-run consumption behavior? Why?
10. If consumption spending in the United States is over four times as large as investment spending, why do economists who are concerned with business cycles worry so much about investment spending?
11. Investment spending is both unstable and difficult to predict. Is it possible for a variable to be unstable over time but highly predictable? Explain your answer.

12. Suppose the exchange rate between the dollar and the Japanese yen moves proportionally in the opposite direction every time the ratio of U.S. prices to Japanese prices moves. For example, if the price level ratio rises by 5 percent, the exchange rate falls by 5 percent, so that when U.S. prices rise 5 percent relative to Japanese prices, a given quantity of yen buys 5 percent more dollars. Under such conditions, what effect would an increase in the price ratio have on aggregate demand? Explain.

Appendix to CHAPTER 23

The Present Value Approach to Investment Decisions

The decision to invest in a new capital good hinges on the issue of profitability. Will the new capital good increase firm profitability? One way to decide is to calculate the rate of return on the investment and compare it to the interest rate at which the funds to purchase the good must be borrowed. This approach (which was discussed in the chapter) has some technical difficulties, however, the most important being that sometimes the solution of the rate of return problem yields multiple answers. Obviously, this is not good.

The preferred approach to investment decision making is the present discounted value approach, which stresses comparing the present discounted value of the investment project with the present discounted cost of undertaking it.

What is present value? It is easiest to derive the answer by asking a question. Suppose we offered you the choice between receiving a gift of $100 today or receiving the same gift one year from today. Which would you prefer? Unless you are a truly unusual individual, you would choose the $100 today, because having the $100 today gives you options unavailable to you if you must wait a year to receive it. You could spend the $100 on a new ten-speed bike and enjoy the services of it for a year. Or you could save the $100 in an interest-bearing account, in which case you would have more than $100 a year from now. Most people prefer money now to money later; we have *positive time preference*. Thus, $100 to be received one year from now is worth less to us than $100 to be received today.

The present value (or, more precisely, the present discounted value) of $100 to be received in one year is $100 discounted by the interest rate that we could earn on the money if we had it to save today. That is:

$$PV = \$100/(1 + i)$$

Suppose that the appropriate interest rate is 8 percent. Then:

$$PV = \$100/(1.08) = \$92.59$$

If you were given $92.59 today, and you invested it at 8 percent interest for one year, you would receive $100 at the end of that year. Thus, $92.59 today is equal in present value to $100 to be received one year in the future.

Suppose the offer had been between $92.59 now and $100 *two* years in the future. Would the amounts still be equivalent? No, because investing $92.59 at 8 percent interest for two years would yield more than $100. It would yield $92.59(1.08)(1.08) = $108.00. So the present value of $100 to be received two years in the future is less than $92.59. The precise figure is:

$$PV = \$100/(1.08)^2 = \$85.73$$

Present value calculations are important to the investment decision, because the income produced by the investment good is received in the future, while some of the cost is incurred immediately, the rest being spread out over time. By using the present value formula, one can compare the value of income and cost streams.

The *net present value* of an investment project is given by the formula:

$$NPV = -C_0 + \frac{(Y_1 - C_1)}{1 + i} + \frac{(Y_2 - C_2)}{(1 + i)^2} + \ldots + \frac{(Y_n - C_n)}{(1 + i)^n}$$

where Y_1 through Y_n are the income values expected to be produced by the investment good; C_0 through C_n are the costs of operating, maintaining, and paying for the investment good; and 0 through n are the time periods (years) when the income is earned and the costs incurred. If NPV is positive, the investment is profitable.

An example should help to illustrate how the NPV formula is used. Eric manages the Hardy Plants Nursery, which specializes in disease-resistant vegetables. He must decide whether to invest in a new sprayer, with which pesticides can be sprayed on the plants to control insects. The sprayer costs $2500, of which $2000 must be financed with a 12 percent loan from the bank. It has an expected useful life of four years and will have $100 scrap value at the end of that time.

Eric estimates that the annual operating costs of the sprayer, including chemicals and maintenance, will be $1000. He estimates that the added value of produce saved from the bugs will be $2200 annually. He must make an immediate down payment of $500 on the sprayer and will repay the $2000 loan at the end of four years. Interest payments of $240 (12 percent of $2000) must be made annually. Should he buy the sprayer?

The net present value formula will give us an answer. Arranging costs and income in a table makes the calculation simpler.

Year	Income	Cost	Net Income
0 (now)	0	500	−500
1	2200	1240	960
2	2200	1240	960
3	2200	1240	960
4	2300	3240	−940

The annual cost figures are derived from adding operating costs to interest costs. In Year 4, the $2000 loan must be repaid. Income rises in Year 4 due to the scrap value of the sprayer.

Putting the data into the NPV formula with a 12 percent discount rate yields:

$$\begin{aligned} \text{NPV} &= -\$500 + 960/1.12 + 960/(1.12)^2 + 960/(1.12)^3 - 940/(1.12)^4 \\ &= -\$500 + 960.1/12 + 960/1.25 + 960/1.40 - 940/1.57 \\ &= -\$500 + 857.14 + 765.31 + 683.31 - 597.39 \\ &= \$1208.37 \end{aligned}$$

The investment in the sprayer would appear to be a very profitable one.

Note that the profitability of the investment project depends on the interest rate, which appears in the denominator of the net present value formulation. A higher rate reduces NPV. For example, if the bank loan rate had been 14 percent rather than 12 percent, the NPV of the sprayer in the above example would have been reduced to $1055.66. For this very profitable project, a 2 percentage point increase in the rate of interest does not reverse the decision. For projects with smaller NPVs, a rise in the interest rate can drive the NPV below zero, indicating an unprofitable investment. Thus, whether the net present value or the rate of return approach is used, a rise in the real interest rate reduces investment demand.

O V E R V I E W

Production is the lifeblood of an economy. A nation's economic standard of living depends on its ability to produce goods and services. A wide variety of factors affects the quantity of goods and services produced by an economy. In this chapter we examine the factors affecting the aggregate supply of goods and services and construct a theory of aggregate supply.

Aggregate Supply of Goods and Services

The labor market — which really consists of a large number of markets for particular types of labor — is central to the discussion of aggregate supply. Labor is the most important input in the production process. The quantity of labor services supplied to producers when the labor market is in equilibrium is an important determinant of the economy's long-run sustainable output level. We will call this level of output the *natural output level*. Changes in labor demand and labor supply can cause output to vary away from the natural level.

After developing labor market theory, we look at the factors determining the natural output level in some detail. The economy's actual output can deviate significantly from the natural level for short periods of time, but tends toward the natural level over time. The natural output level depends on factors that are subject to control, such as the tax structure, and on factors beyond human control, such as natural resource supplies.

CHAPTER 24

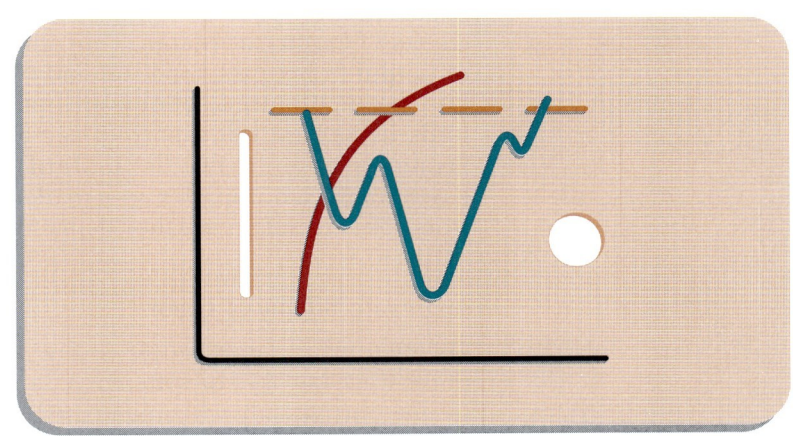

The theory of short-run aggregate supply explains why aggregate output moves away from the natural level. The labor market is central to this discussion; how rapidly wages adjust to changes in the price level determines how aggregate output responds to price level movements.

Learning Objectives

After reading and studying this chapter, you will be able to:

1. List the factors underlying the demand for labor and supply of labor that determine equilibrium wage rate and employment level.
2. Discuss the concept of the natural output level and explain why the economy tends toward the natural output level over time.
3. Use the labor market model to develop the short-run aggregate supply curve.
4. Explain why expectations are important to the short-run behavior of the economy.
5. Explain the importance of contracts and wage rigidity for the theory of the short-run aggregate supply curve.

Labor Market

A substantial number of factors influence the quantity of output produced by the economy. In the long run such factors as the availability of resources, the size of the capital stock, the level of technology, and the way economic activity is organized and regulated are important determinants of output. In this century, technological advances have revolutionized the economy. For example, we have moved from steam locomotives and the telegraph to jumbo jets and cellular telephones in only a few decades.

The quantity and quality of labor available to producers is another important determinant of output. However, labor differs from the other determinants of output in one very important way. The supplies of resources and capital, the level of technology, and the way markets are organized typically change little from year to year. However, the supply of labor often changes significantly from year to year in response to changes in the price level. Such labor supply changes, when combined with large changes in labor demand, can yield significant changes in employment and the average wage rate over relatively short periods of time. These changes are highly related to short-run changes in aggregate output. Thus, changes in the labor market affect the level of output in both the long run and the short run.

The importance of labor as an input in the production of goods and services leads us to base our theory of aggregate supply on labor market behavior. Economists use the familiar tools of demand and supply to analyze the behavior of the labor market. The market wage rate and employment level result from the interaction of labor demand and supply.[1]

Aggregate Supply of Labor

Nominal wage rate
Wage rate in current dollars.

Expected price level
Average price level workers expect to prevail during some future period.

Expected real wage rate
Wage rate in dollars of constant buying power that workers expect to receive.

The quantity of labor people choose to supply depends on the buying power of the wage rate they are offered. A particular wage rate can be judged attractive or unattractive only when compared to the prices of goods workers must buy with their wages. For example, an annual wage of $5000 would place a family of four well below the poverty line today, but would have put them among the wealthy in 1900. (An income of $5000 in 1900 would have been equivalent to an income of about $84,000 in 1989.) Thus, the labor supply decision depends on the **nominal wage rate** (W) — the current dollar wage rate — and the **expected price level** (PI^e) — the average price level the worker *expects* to prevail during the upcoming period when the wage rate is being paid. Dividing the nominal wage rate by the expected price level, we derive the **expected real wage rate** — an estimate of the value of the wage rate in dollars of constant buying power. The quantity of labor services people choose to supply to the labor market depends of the expected real wage rate (W/PI^e).

Holding the expected price level constant, an increase in the nominal wage rate increases the real return to labor (W/PI^e). As the real wage rate rises, the incentive for people to supply more labor increases. However, the positive effect of a higher real wage rate on the quantity of labor supplied is partially offset by the higher income that accompanies a higher wage rate. A higher income enables some people to reduce the quantity of labor they supply to

---

[1] This section presents an aggregate theory of labor market behavior. Students interested in the microeconomic foundations of the labor market should read the appendix to this chapter. The appendix can be read before reading the remainder of the chapter.

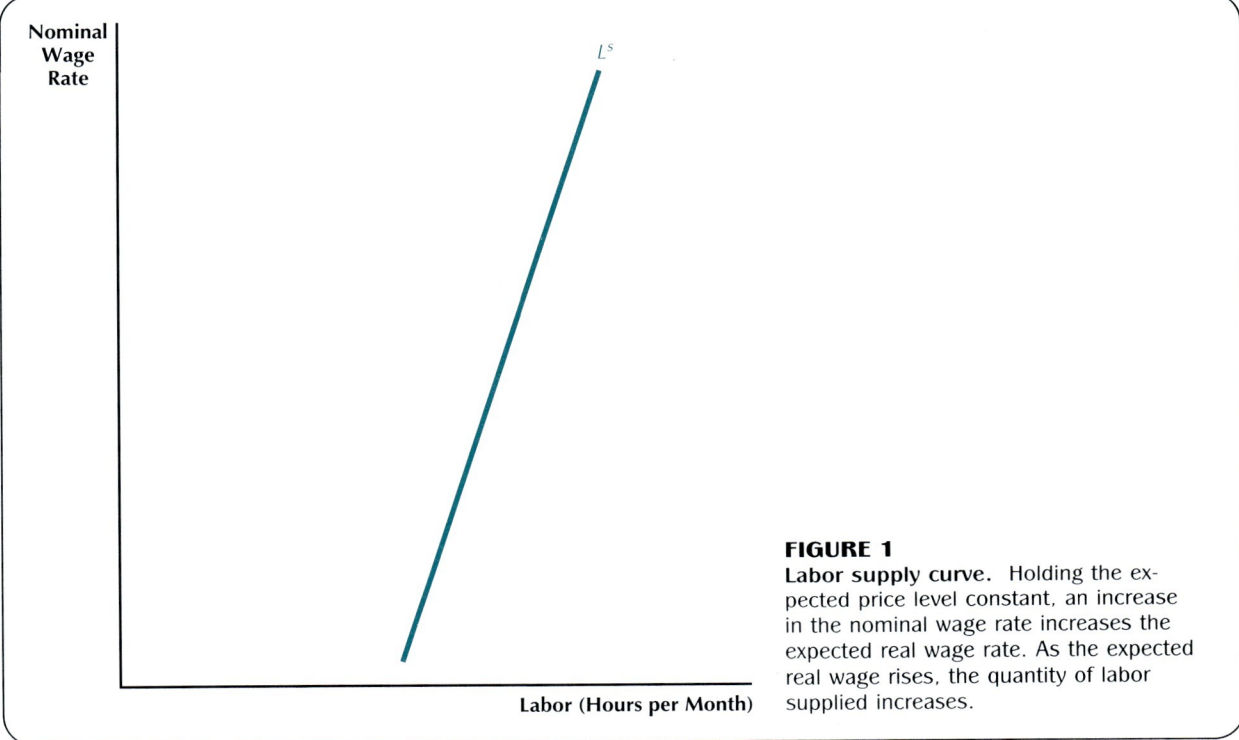

FIGURE 1
Labor supply curve. Holding the expected price level constant, an increase in the nominal wage rate increases the expected real wage rate. As the expected real wage rises, the quantity of labor supplied increases.

the market. For example, a real wage increase in a full-time job might cause some moonlighting workers to drop their part-time jobs.

The net effect of a higher real wage rate on the quantity of labor supplied appears to be fairly small. Holding constant other factors, *including the expected price level* (the *ceteris paribus* assumption), the labor supply curve slopes positively but steeply in Figure 1. For a given expected price level, an increase in the nominal wage rate induces workers to supply more labor to the market. Workers respond to an expected increase in the buying power of their wages. However, such an increase in the expected real wage rate has a rather small effect on the quantity of labor supplied, as reflected in the steep slope of the labor supply curve.

The **aggregate labor supply curve** shows the quantity of labor workers are willing to supply at various expected real wage rates. Each labor supply curve is based on a particular expected price level. When the expected price level changes, the real value of a nominal wage also changes, and the labor supply curve shifts. Suppose the expected price level increases. Then the expected real wage (that is, the expected *buying power* of the wage) falls, and the real return to working declines. The labor supply curve shifts to the left, as in Figure 2. At every level of the nominal wage rate the expected real return from working is now lower and less labor is supplied to the market.

Other factors affecting the position of the aggregate labor supply curve include the size of the working-age population and social factors that determine the attitudes of certain groups toward employment outside the home. An increase in population usually translates into an increase in the labor supply,

Aggregate labor supply curve
Shows the aggregate quantity of labor workers are willing to supply at various real wage rates; the curve is graphed with the nominal wage rate on the vertical axis and the expected price level held constant, so that changes in the nominal wage rate also change the expected real wage rate.

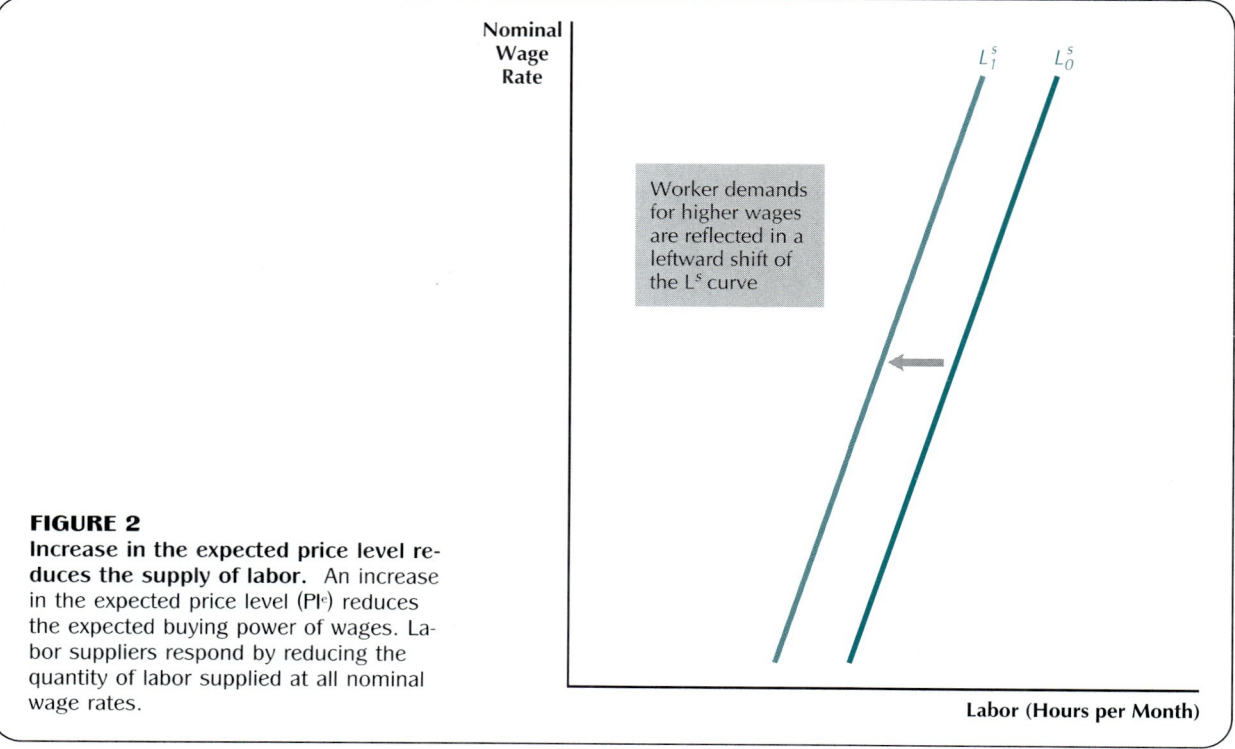

FIGURE 2
Increase in the expected price level reduces the supply of labor. An increase in the expected price level (Pl^e) reduces the expected buying power of wages. Labor suppliers respond by reducing the quantity of labor supplied at all nominal wage rates.

as the United States experienced with the post-World War II baby boom. The children born in the late 1940s and the 1950s began to join the labor force in the mid-1960s. As a result, the labor force grew rapidly, both in absolute size and as a percentage of the adult population. The labor supply curve shifted to the right as the baby boomers entered the labor market.

Changing social attitudes can also have major impacts on the supply of labor. Throughout the 1960s and 1970s, the number of adult women entering the labor force increased rapidly. Working mothers became typical rather than unusual. The **labor force participation rate** of females—the percentage of females 20 years old and over who are working or seeking work—rose from 35 percent in 1954 to 57 percent in 1989. The increase had more to do with social trends than with economics narrowly defined, but the impact on the economy was significant. The number of adult women in the labor force grew by 181 percent from 1954 to 1989, while the number of adult men in the labor force rose by only 49 percent. The effect was to shift the labor supply curve sharply to the right, relative to where it would have been had previous employment trends continued.

Although the impact of demographic and social changes on labor supply is usually small in any one year, the cumulative effect of such factors over a number of years can be sizable.

Aggregate Demand for Labor

Firms demand labor services as an input into the production process. The **aggregate labor demand curve** shows the quantity of labor firms want to hire

Labor force participation rate
Percentage of the working-age population that has a job or is actively looking for work.

SECTION RECAP
The aggregate quantity of labor supplied is positively related to the expected real wage rate. A change in the expected price level, in the labor force participation rate, or in the size of the labor force shifts the labor supply curve.

at various wage rates. The value of a worker to a firm depends on the value of the output the worker can produce. The value of output equals the physical quantity of output a worker can produce times the additional revenue a unit of output generates for the firm. Firms compare the value produced by workers to the wage rate workers must be paid to determine the quantity of labor demanded. Thus, aggregate labor demand depends on the wage rate, the price level, and the productivity of labor. Figure 3 illustrates the labor demand curve.

In the short run, the quantity of capital — machines and factory and office space — available for use by firms is fixed. Although firms can hire more workers and purchase more material inputs, they cannot quickly alter the size of the capital stock. The presence of fixed capital affects the demand for labor by affecting the **marginal productivity of labor** — the addition to total output produced by one more unit of labor.

Suppose a manufacturing firm wants to expand production immediately. The firm can hire more workers and purchase more material inputs, but it cannot add more machines or factory space. Instead, the firm must use its capital stock more intensively. Some machines can be used at only one speed, so bottlenecks in the production process occur. Some workers find themselves waiting for others to catch up. Furthermore, more time is required to move larger inventories around the factory. Thus, in the short run the marginal productivity of labor declines, because the firm is able to increase output, but less than proportionately. The newly hired workers are not able to produce as much output as the original workers; the marginal productivity of the new workers is lower.

Aggregate labor demand curve
Shows the aggregate quantity of labor demanded by firms at various wage rates, holding the aggregate price level and labor productivity constant.

Marginal productivity of labor
Addition to total output produced by one more unit of labor.

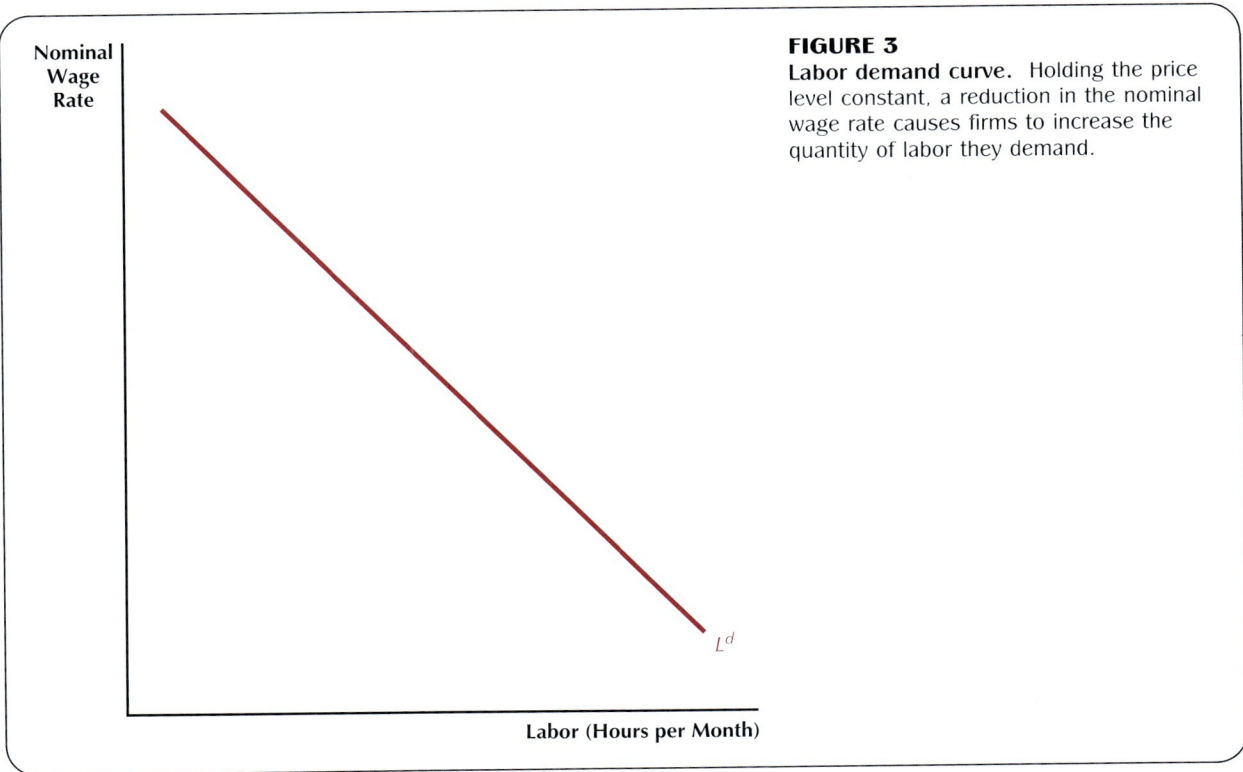

FIGURE 3
Labor demand curve. Holding the price level constant, a reduction in the nominal wage rate causes firms to increase the quantity of labor they demand.

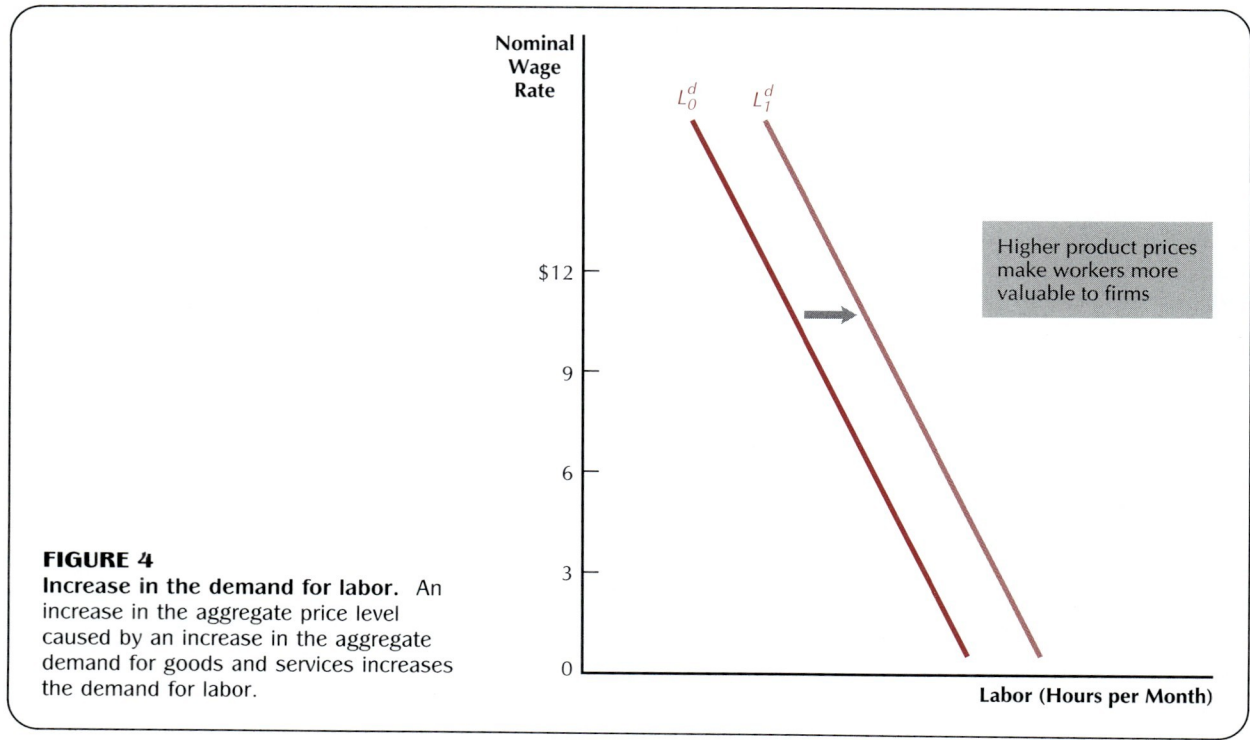

FIGURE 4
Increase in the demand for labor. An increase in the aggregate price level caused by an increase in the aggregate demand for goods and services increases the demand for labor.

Declining marginal productivity of labor means that the marginal benefit to firms of hiring additional workers falls as employment expands. Holding the price level and capital stock constant, firms hire more workers only if the wage rate falls so that the lower revenue generated by additional workers is offset by a lower wage cost. Thus, the labor demand curve is negatively sloped.

The position of the labor demand curve depends on both the price level and the productivity of workers. When the prices firms receive for their products change or when the size or productivity of the capital stock changes, the demand for labor curve shifts. Suppose that, *ceteris paribus*, the prices received by firms for their products rise. The higher product prices make workers more valuable to firms. The labor demand curve shifts to the right, as shown in Figure 4. At every wage rate, firms are willing to hire more labor than before. Technological improvements that increase the quantity of goods workers can produce or increases in the capital stock that enable workers to produce more also shift the labor demand curve to the right.

Labor Market Equilibrium

The **short-run equilibrium** wage rate and employment level are determined by the intersection of the labor demand and labor supply curves, illustrated in Figure 5. Given the level of productivity and the price level underlying the labor demand curve and the expected price level underlying the labor supply curve, the market-clearing nominal wage rate is $8 per hour. At any wage rate

SECTION RECAP
The aggregate quantity of labor demanded is negatively related to the nominal wage rate. Changes in the price level or labor productivity shift the labor demand curve.

Short-run labor market equilibrium
Market-clearing wage rate and employment level, given the currently existing price level and expected price level (which may differ).

other than $8 per hour the quantity of labor supplied to the market does not equal the quantity demanded. Excess demand or excess supply pressure pushes the wage rate toward W_0.

The labor market equilibrium shown in Figure 5 may change rather quickly. A short-run equilibrium simply equates the current quantities of labor being supplied and demanded. Changes in any of the factors underlying the labor demand or supply curves will change the equilibrium wage and employment levels. In particular, if the expected price level on which the labor supply curve is based does not equal the economy's actual price level, workers will soon recognize their mistake. When workers realize that the actual price level is higher or lower than their original expectations, they will revise both their expectations and their wage demands. The labor supply curve shifts in response to a revision in the expected price level, changing both the wage rate and employment level.

When the expected price level on which workers base their labor supply decisions equals the price level that actually prevails in the economy, workers have no reason to change the quantity of labor they are willing to supply. The labor supply curve remains stationary rather than shifting to catch up with unexpected movements of the price level. When workers' expected price level equals the economy's actual price level, and both firms and workers have fully adjusted to the actual price level, the labor market is in **long-run equilibrium**. The employment level generated by long-run labor market equilibrium is called the **natural level of employment**. The natural level of employment is the employment level that exists when the expected price level equals the actual price level.

Long-run labor market equilibrium Market-clearing wage rate and employment level when the economy's actual price level equals workers' expected price level and all wages have adjusted fully to expectations.

Natural level of employment Employment level that prevails in long-run labor market equilibrium.

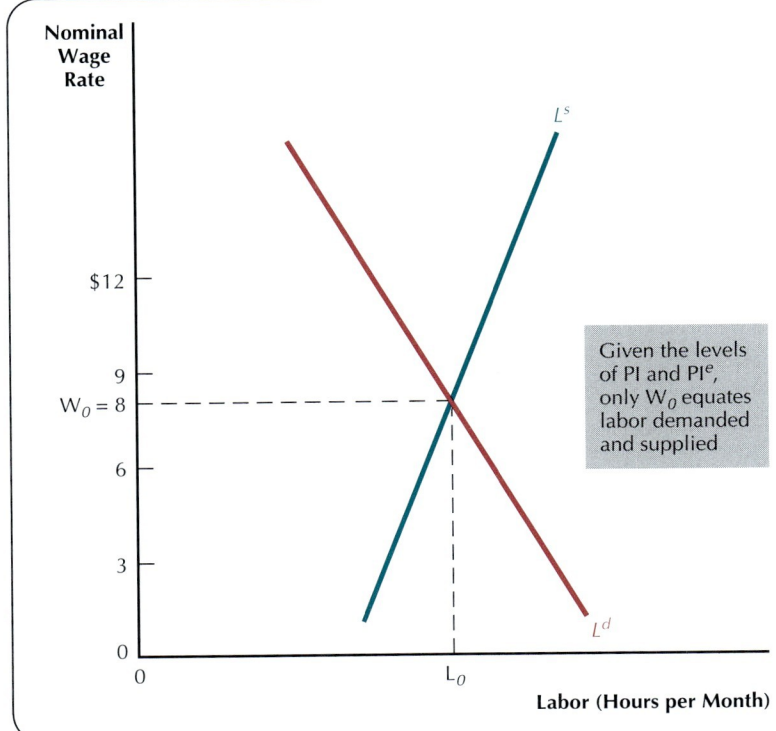

FIGURE 5
Equilibrium wage rate and employment level. The equilibrium wage rate and employment level are determined by the intersection of the labor demand and labor supply curves. The aggregate price level and the expected price level are held constant when drawing the labor demand and supply curves.

Given the levels of PI and PI^e, only W_0 equates labor demanded and supplied

Why the Disagreement?

Immigration: Good or Bad for the United States?

The United States is a nation of immigrants. The ancestors of all but a small fraction of Americans immigrated to the United States within the past 300 years. In recent years, about 600,000 people have immigrated into the United States annually. Such a large number of immigrants has important economic consequences. Most immigrants enter the labor force, thus increasing the supply of labor. Recall that the labor market consists of many markets for different types of labor. Immigration significantly affects some labor markets. Although the number of immigrants is smaller than it once was, it is large enough to concern many people, including some legislators. Of particular concern is the large number of illegal immigrants entering the United States each year. Opposition to illegal immigration stirred politicians to action in the 1980s. In 1986, Congress passed the *Immigration Reform and Control Act*, which sought to limit illegal immigration by imposing penalties on employers who hire illegal immigrants.*

The attempt to limit immigration touched off a heated debate. Proponents of free immigration argue that the economy gains by admitting all who want to immigrate. Those seeking to limit immigration argue that the economic and social costs of immigration are excessively high. Economists and sociologists who have carefully studied the effects of immigration are on both sides of the debate. Why the disagreement?

On an economic level, much of the disagreement is between those who focus on the effects of immigration on the total economy, particularly in the long run, and those who focus on the unequal effects of immigration on different groups, in the short run and long run. A staunch advocate of the free immigration position is University of Maryland economist Julian L. Simon. In a recent book,** Professor Simon argues that people are the ultimate resource. Immigrants are usually in their early working years, ambitious, and self-motivated. They come to work, and they benefit the economy in a number of ways: They supply much-needed labor in many industries, particularly in low-wage industries; they increase the size of the U.S. market, enabling U.S. firms to produce and sell more; they pay Social Security taxes for many years, helping to support retired workers. Ultimately, Professor Simon argues, they boost productivity, investment, and economic growth, benefiting the economy tremendously.

Most economists would not want to argue with the proposition that immigration benefits the economy in a number of ways. However, many argue that the benefits are not without costs and that the costs have been rising faster than the benefits. A recent study by University of California economist

---

Changes in the price level do not affect the natural level of employment. Suppose PI rises, as in Figure 6. Firms respond to the higher price level by demanding more labor; the labor demand curve shifts to the right. If the increase in the price level is unexpected and workers do not immediately demand a higher nominal wage rate, employment temporarily increases. However, when workers have had time to adjust their wage demands to reflect the higher price level, the labor supply curve shifts to the left. A higher nominal wage rate is required to persuade workers to supply as much labor as before. The net result of these two movements is an increase in the nominal wage rate from W_0 to W_1 and *no change in the level of employment*. The wage rate increases proportionately with the price level, leaving the real wage unchanged: $W_0/PI_0 = W_1/PI_1$. A change in the aggregate price level affects neither the natural employment level nor the long-run equilibrium *real* wage rate.

In contrast to changes in the price level, changes in any of the *real* factors determining labor demand or labor supply alter both the natural level of employment and the real wage rate. If increased investment spending or technological advances increase worker productivity, workers become more valuable to firms. The demand for labor increases, pushing up both the wage rate

George J. Borjas found that the labor market quality of immigrants has been deteriorating for a couple of decades.† Newer immigrants are more poorly educated, are less attached to the labor market, and have higher unemployment and poverty rates than earlier immigrants. The cost of providing government social services to such immigrants is high, and U.S. taxpayers must pay for the services. Borjas estimates that the net cost to the economy of recent immigrants is several billion dollars per year. Even that may badly understate the true cost of immigration, since Borjas's study examined only the effects of legal immigration. The costs of illegal immigration can be quite high in the short run and can fall disproportionately on those who can least afford them. Most illegal immigrants to the United States come from Mexico. Although studies have shown that these immigrants are not the least skilled and poorest people in Mexico, they are very low skilled by American standards. They compete for jobs with Americans who also have very few skills. The effect of this increased supply of unskilled labor is a reduction in the wage rate for unskilled labor. This reduces the income of the lowest-paid American workers even further. Rice University economist Donald Huddle has estimated that every hundred illegal immigrants who entered the Houston, Texas, labor market in the early 1980s displaced seventy low-wage American workers.‡

Despite the high costs of illegal immigration, some economists argue that the *economic* benefits of immigration far outweigh the costs.§ However, many of the costs of immigration—both legal and illegal—are not economic and are difficult to quantify. Increasing congestion, strains on the environment, cultural clashes between people with different backgrounds—all are made worse by increased immigration. Considering the strong arguments made by both proponents and opponents of immigration, the argument over immigration does not seem likely to end soon.

---

*The Act also granted amnesty to illegal immigrants who had been in the United States continuously since January 1, 1982. Such immigrants were allowed to apply for resident alien status. Thus, the legislation was designed to stop the flow of illegal immigrants without punishing those who had been in residence in the United States for a long time.

**The Economic Consequences of Immigration* (New York: Basil Blackwell, 1989).

†George J. Borjas, *Friends or Strangers: The Impact of Immigrants on the U.S. Economy* (New York: Basic Books, 1989).

‡Donald Huddle, "Give Us Your Huddled Masses" (review of the books by Simon and Borjas), *Chronicles*, July 1990, pp. 28–30.

§See Barry R. Chiswick, "Illegal Immigration and Immigration Control," *Journal of Economic Perspectives* 2 (Summer 1988), pp. 101–115 for a discussion of illegal immigration.

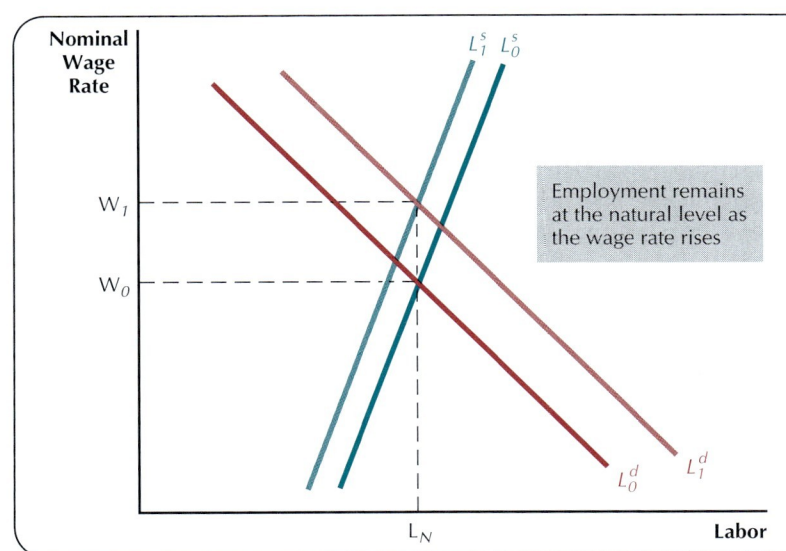

FIGURE 6
Long-run equilibrium in the labor market. The natural level of employment is not affected by a change in the price level. The expected price level rises by the same amount as the actual price level, shifting the labor supply curve by the same amount as the labor demand curve.

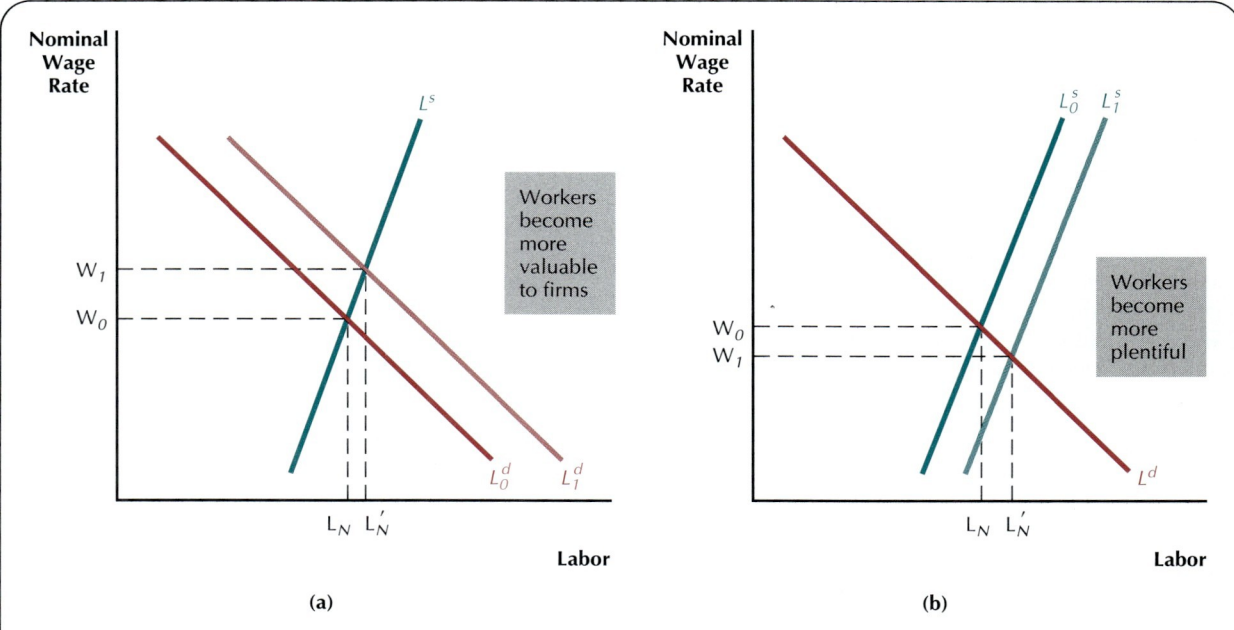

FIGURE 7
Changes in the natural level of employment. An increase in capital per worker or improved technology shifts the labor demand curve to the right, increasing the nominal and real wage rates and the natural level of employment (a). An increase in labor force participation shifts the labor supply curve to the right, decreasing nominal and real wage rates and increasing the natural employment level (b).

Natural output level
Output level determined by the economy's natural employment level, resources, technology, and economic organization.

SECTION RECAP
Short-run labor market equilibrium is determined by the intersection of the labor demand and supply curves. Long-run labor market equilibrium occurs when the price level expectations held by workers are correct, so there is no tendency to revise wage demands.

and employment, as in Figure 7 (a). Since the price level is assumed constant, the real wage rises. The natural level of employment is now L'_N rather than L^2_N.

Changes in the supply of labor also have an impact on the values of the equilibrium real wage and the natural employment level. The large increase in the labor force participation rate of women that took place in the United States between the 1950s and the 1980s and the entry of the baby-boom generation into the labor force shifted the labor supply curve to the right. Figure 7 (b) shows that such an increase in labor supply tends to push the equilibrium wage rate downward. Since labor demand also rose during this period, the average wage rate actually increased (the average manufacturing wage rose from $1.78 per hour in 1954 to $10.47 per hour in 1989). However, both the nominal and the real wage rates would have been even higher if labor supply had not increased so much.

The natural level of employment is a major determinant of the economy's **natural output level**—the output level produced when people have fully adjusted to all changes in the price level. Since labor is not the only input into the production process, we now need to examine the other factors that combine with labor to determine the natural output level.

---

[2]It is true that some capital investment replaces workers. Nevertheless, the net effect of capital investment over the years clearly has been to increase the demand for labor and the wage rate.

Natural Output Level

The natural level of output is the maximum level of output that can be sustained over extended periods without generating inflation. At the natural output level, producers are willing to continue producing at current levels indefinitely, without demanding higher prices or being forced to reduce prices. Input markets are also in equilibrium, in the sense that no pressure to raise or lower input prices exists. When production deviates from the natural level in the short run, prices and wages begin to move in such a manner as to push output back toward its natural level.

Factors Determining the Natural Output Level

A large number of factors combine to determine the natural level of output. Some factors are well known, as they are commented on frequently in the popular media. However, other lesser-known factors appear to be just as important, if not more important, in determining the natural level of production. In addition to labor, the most important factors determining the natural output level are resources, the capital stock, technology, and market organization.

Resources The argument that a certain impoverished country is in that sad economic state because it lacks physical resources is commonplace. The argument appears plausible, because tillable land, water, minerals, and energy are necessary inputs in the production of goods: Physical goods cannot be produced without physical inputs. Little effort is required to list numerous examples of economies that have prospered, at least briefly, by exploiting some physical resource that could be extracted cheaply.

Yet the connection between physical resource supplies and the natural output level in an economy is far from exact. Some countries with very limited physical resources have booming economies, while others with vast mineral and agricultural resources produce at near-subsistence levels. Examples of resource-poor but economically wealthy nations are Japan, Hong Kong, Taiwan, and Singapore. In the nineteenth century Great Britain built itself up in much the same way that Japan has since World War II. Countries with relatively low income levels despite the presence of vast physical resource supplies include Nigeria, Brazil, and the Soviet Union. If resource supplies were of utmost importance in determining an economy's income level, Soviet citizens ought to have a standard of living at least as high as that of U.S. citizens. In reality, the two income levels differ greatly.

How can economies with meager physical resources generate high per capita income levels? The short answer is that they can when they are designed to do so. For example, the Japanese economy is built around importing raw materials and exporting finished products, just as the British economy was in the previous century. In calculating the value of resources, most researchers ignore the most valuable resource of all — the human mind. Most of the mineral resources so highly valued today would be economically worthless had not someone invented a use for them. Oil would be but a sticky nuisance had not the internal combustion engine been invented. The inventiveness of the human mind made oil valuable in the past and is sure to make other resources valuable in the future.[3]

---

[3] A book that stresses the importance of human ingenuity in determining economic performance — and is fun to read besides — is *The Economy in Mind* by Warren T. Brookes (New York: Universe Books, 1982).

Does It Make **Economic Sense?**

Are We Running out of Resources?

From time to time, newspapers and magazines print articles predicting that the world will run out of some important natural resource within the next few years. The resources named vary widely. During the 1970s the most often mentioned resource destined for rapid depletion was oil. Farmland also has been high on the list in recent years. Yet, even after the rise in oil prices caused by the Iraqi invasion of Kuwait in August 1990, the real price of oil (adjusted for inflation) was still lower than it was in the early 1980s, and farm prices fell during much of the 1980s. When faced with the assertions of impending doom and falling resource prices, one is moved to ask, Does this make economic sense?

The notion that the world is running out of valuable resources at a rapid rate is not a new one. The basic idea has been around for centuries. It received its most famous expression in the writings of Thomas Malthus (discussed in the *Why The Disagreement?* section of Chapter 1). Malthus was convinced that the natural physical limitations on the amount of land available to be farmed would eventually result in widespread food shortages as population growth outstripped growth of the food supply. Although it is true that starvation exists in the world today, people are not starving in the heavily populated nations, which Malthusian theory would have predicted, but in sparsely populated countries whose economies have broken down for one reason or another.

In 1865, famed British economist William Stanley Jevons predicted that long-term progress was impossible because the world would soon run out of coal. In 1970, over a century later, it was estimated that enough fossil fuels existed to last 520 years at the 1970 usage rate.* Similar predictions could be cited for any number of other important mineral resources that now have known geological reserves sufficient to last for centuries.** How could so many predictions (and there are literally hundreds, if not thousands, of them) be so wrong?

The main reason that so many predictions have been so far off base is that they concentrate on the technological aspects of resource acquisition and ignore the economic aspects. It is true that the earth contains a finite amount of resources. However, the amount of resources contained in the earth's crust is so great that millions of years of consumption would hardly make a dent in the supplies of most major minerals. If the reserves in the top kilometer of the earth's crust are considered, resource shortages of any major minerals still appear to be over a century away. Furthermore, geo-

---

Capital Stock A nation's capital stock includes both structures (buildings) and productive equipment owned by private businesses and households and by governmental units. Increases in the capital stock contribute directly to production and add to the productivity of the labor force. Just as no direct connection exists between the size of the labor force or the amount of physical resources in an economy and that economy's output level, neither does a direct connection exist between capital stock and output. It is possible to invest millions of dollars in a productive structure that is economically worthless because of world economic conditions. However, when the capital stock is expanded in response to profit opportunities, an increase in capital increases the productive capacity of the economy.

A lack of public capital hinders production in some economies. The road system, water supply system, energy supply system, rail system, or communication system is not developed enough to support a high level of production. The support system of public capital that produces transportation and utility services is called an economy's **infrastructure**. The high costs and wide usage of infrastructure have led government to finance the construction of public capital goods in most countries.

Infrastructure
Public capital used to provide such economic support services as transportation, sewage treatment, and water supply.

logically proven reserves of mineral resources have increased over time.

The economic aspects of resource availability are extremely important. A resource in plentiful supply carries a low price. Little economic incentive exists to spend funds searching for more of the resource or developing substitutes for it. As the demand for a resource rises relative to its supply, the price begins to rise. It becomes profitable to search for more of the resource or to undertake research to develop substitutes for it. This process results in an increase in the proven reserves of the resource or a decline in the demand for it.

A good example of declining demand for a resource because of the development of a good substitute occurred in the latter part of the nineteenth century. Whale oil was used in lamps to light homes in the early-to-mid-1800s. By the later decades of the century, whales were becoming scarce. The supply of whale oil was reduced, and the price rose sharply. This led to the development of the process for refining kerosene from crude petroleum. Within a few years of the whale oil crisis, the price of whale oil had fallen to a small fraction of its previous level. Why? Because the demand for whale oil fell off drastically as nearly everyone shifted to kerosene lamps.

In this century, analysts have repeatedly predicted drastic oil shortages. For example, in 1908 the U.S. Geological Survey predicted that future U.S. production would be a maximum of 22.5 billion barrels. Since then over 35 billion barrels have been produced, and proven reserves now available exceed the 22.5 billion barrel prediction. What happened? Rising oil prices induced oil companies and private individuals to search for more oil deposits. The so-called oil crises of the 1970s had nothing to do with actual resource shortage. They were caused by the decision to reduce production by the nations of the Organization of Petroleum Exporting Countries (OPEC). The higher prices generated by the OPEC production cutback caused non-OPEC production to rise, so that world oil production now is much greater than it was before the production cutback.

Although one cannot say that resource shortages will never hamper economic production, such limits have never been encountered before and are not likely in the foreseeable future.

*William D. Nordhaus, "Resources as a Constraint on Growth," *American Economic Review* 64 (May 1974), p. 24.

**An interesting summary of many of the predictions made over the years—and why they were wrong—is given by David Osterfeld in "Resources, People, and the Neomalthusian Fallacy," *The Cato Journal* 5 (Spring/Summer 1985), pp. 67–102.

A poorly developed infrastructure places strict limits on how much can be produced in an economy. The importance of infrastructure can be seen by considering two economies already mentioned. The so-called Japanese miracle of creating one of the world's largest economies from the ruins of World War II was possible only because the Japanese government devoted vast amounts of resources to the development of an adequate infrastructure. Most of the support given to Japanese manufacturing firms by the government has been in the form of infrastructure development, not production subsidies. On the other hand, resource-wealthy Nigeria is hampered in its development efforts by totally inadequate transportation and communications systems. Vast amounts of physical resources remain unexploited because of the lack of roads to transport resources and agricultural goods from the outlying areas to the cities.

Technology   As new capital stock is put into production, technological advances are introduced. Technological advances may be embodied in the items being produced or in the production process itself. Either way, advances in technology enable firms to produce more output with the same dollar expenditures on capital, labor, and material inputs. Technological advances can lower the per-unit cost of production by (1) reducing the amount of time required to produce a unit, (2) reducing the amount of labor necessary to run the equipment, (3) reducing the amount of capital necessary to produce a unit, or (4) utilizing material inputs more efficiently so that more output can be produced from a given amount of inputs.

Market Organization   One of the most important factors determining the sustainable level of output in an economy is the manner in which the economy is organized. Are individuals given the incentive to produce, or are they hampered by a system that confiscates the fruits of their labor? The answer to that question goes a long way toward determining how productive an economy is.

The economies of northern Europe, the United States, Canada, Australia, and New Zealand developed the highest standards of living in the world before World War II not by accident, but because their economies promoted individual effort. These economies operated basically on free-market principles, which assert that a high percentage of the profits earned on any enterprise should be kept by the people engaging in the production process. In the post–World War II period, several economies adopted this philosophy and expanded rapidly, including Japan, West Germany, South Korea, Hong Kong, and Singapore. Economies that do not allow producers to benefit from their efforts do not grow as rapidly as free-market economies.[4]

The Eastern European nations just beginning to turn from centralized political control of their economies to the market face a massive task. Converting from a highly inefficient, state-controlled economy to an economy able to compete in world markets is incredibly difficult. Workers have made their living producing low-quality goods for sale in state-run stores. Such low-quality goods cannot be exported to market economies and cannot compete domestically with higher-quality imports from market economies. Prices and wages have reflected political decisions, rather than consumer preferences and production costs. Freeing controlled prices and wages to find their market levels will disrupt the incomes of millions of workers.

Over the past few years it has become increasingly clear that the natural output level in centralized economies is much lower than the natural output levels in otherwise comparable market economies. This is one consideration leading to the growing rejection of central planning. The question yet to be resolved in Eastern Europe is how to convert to a market economy with the least pain. At this point, no one is sure what the best course is.

In summary, the aggregate level of output produced in an economy depends on the availability of resources, the size of the capital stock, the level of technology, the way markets are organized, and the quantity of labor employed. Combining the long-run equilibrium (or natural) level of employment with the economy's available resources, capital stock, technology, and institutional organization enables firms to produce the economy's natural level of output.

SECTION RECAP
The natural output level is determined by the economy's natural level of employment, available resources, capital stock, technology, and market organization. The natural output level is the economy's long-run sustainable output level.

---

[4]For example, a recent study of 115 countries concluded that "Politically open societies, which bind themselves to the rule of law, to private property, and to the market allocation of resources, grow at three times . . . the rate [of] . . . those societies in which these freedoms are circumscribed or proscribed." Gerald W. Scully, "The Institutional Framework and Economic Development," *Journal of Political Economy* 96 (June 1988), p. 661.

Aggregate Supply

An economy's **aggregate supply curve** shows the aggregate quantity of goods and services firms choose to produce at various aggregate price levels. The appearance of the aggregate supply curve depends on whether the labor market has fully adjusted to macroeconomic events that alter the price level. In particular, the shape and slope of the aggregate supply curve depends on whether the economy is in short-run or long-run equilibrium.

The *short run* in macroeconomics is the period of time during which markets are still adjusting to a macroeconomic shock.[5] Such a shock can be caused by a natural event, such as a severe and widespread drought, a political event, such as a war, or a policy decision, such as an increase in the money supply. Macroeconomic shocks force economic agents to change the prices they demand or offer. For example, a positive shock to the price level (higher prices) caused by increased aggregate demand causes workers to demand higher wages and forces firms to offer higher wages. However, some amount of time elapses before firms and workers discover the new long-run equilibrium wage level. The time that elapses while the labor market returns to long-run equilibrium is the short run.

The *long run* in macroeconomics is a period of time sufficiently long for all wages and prices to have fully adjusted to any shocks to the price level. In particular, in the long run, the labor market has returned to long-run equilibrium.

Since the behavior of output in the short run is closely related to the quantity of labor employed, we must return to the labor market to construct a theory of short-run output behavior.

> **Aggregate supply curve** Shows the aggregate quantity of goods and services supplied by all firms in the economy at various aggregate price levels.

Sticky Wages, Employment Changes, and Short-Run Aggregate Supply

The labor market is really a complex network of markets. Employers must fill millions of specific jobs with widely varying job requirements. Prospective workers possess a wide range of qualifications and attributes. The evaluation of job applicants is time-consuming and costly, as is the evaluation of employees. The cost of evaluation prevents firms from engaging in frequent evaluations. Instead, most firms evaluate their workers at regular intervals, making wage adjustments only at specific times. Moreover, wage increases are much more frequent than wage reductions, since firms recognize the morale problems that wage cuts can cause. In short, the labor market is not an auction market. The wage rate does not move rapidly to immediately equate demand and supply in the way that the prices of many products move. *Wages are sticky*, moving rather slowly in response to changes in economic conditions.

Consider what happens when an increase in the aggregate demand for goods and services, such as that shown in Figure 8 (b), causes firms to increase production. Initially the labor market is in long-run equilibrium. Workers are receiving the real wages they expected to receive: $W/PI^e = W/PI$. However, an

---

[5] The concept of the macroeconomic short run differs from the concept of microeconomic short run. A firm operates in the short run when at least one input is fixed in quantity. During the short-run adjustment period to a macroeconomic shock, some firms will operate with fixed inputs, while others are able to vary all inputs. Thus, in the macroeconomic short run, some firms operate on their (microeconomic) short-run supply curves, while others operate on their (microeconomic) long-run supply curves.

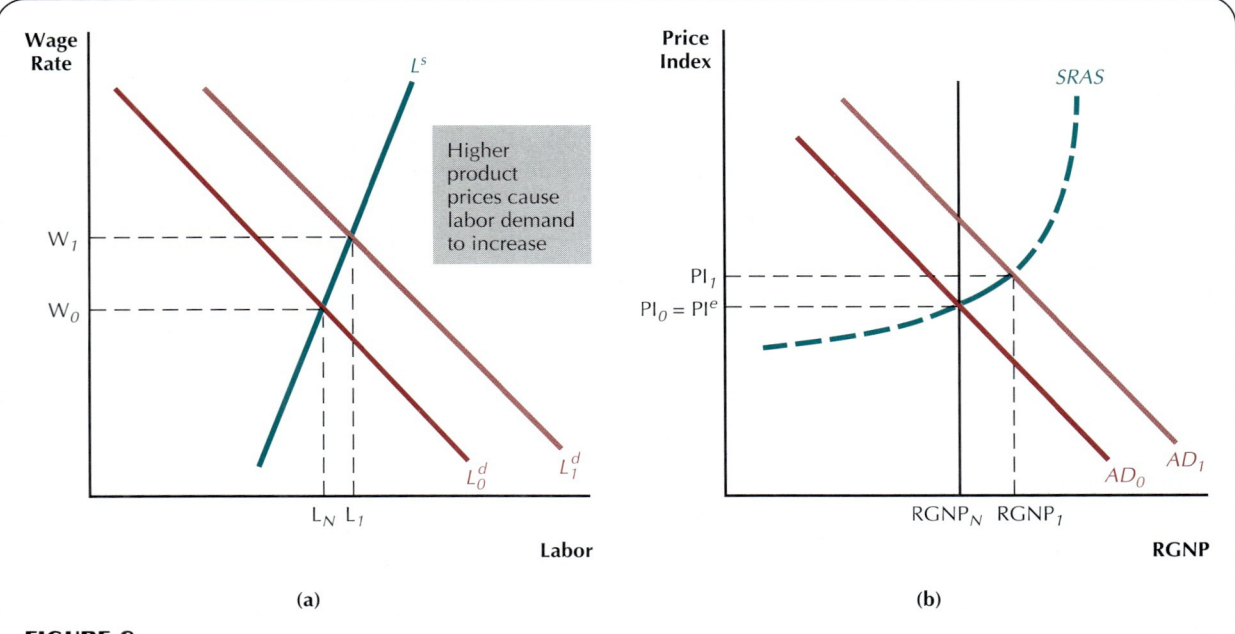

FIGURE 8
Short-run aggregate supply. An increase in aggregate demand puts upward pressure on product prices. Firms demand more labor; the labor demand curve shifts to the right (a). Because wages do not rise proportionately with prices in the short run, labor employed increases to L_1. More output is produced at the higher price level PI_1. The short-run aggregate supply curves slopes positively.

increase in aggregate demand permits firms to charge higher prices for their products. Higher product prices make labor more valuable, shifting the labor demand curve to the right, as shown in Figure 8 (a). To expand production, some firms increase their nominal wage offers and hire more workers. Other firms put their employees on overtime, paying them more for the extra hours worked. The average nominal wage rate in the economy rises from W_0 to W_1, and employment increases from L_N to L_1.

Not all workers receive immediate wage increases, however. Most employees work under explicit or implicit contracts that adjust wages only at specified times. An **explicit contract** is a signed legal agreement setting wages and working conditions. An **implicit contract** is a so-called handshake agreement between a firm and its workers that describes the terms of employment. Most explicit and implicit contracts fix wages for a year or more at a time. When prices rise, wages fixed by such contracts do not immediately adjust to compensate for the higher prices. The result is that, although the average wage rises, prices rise even more, so the real wage (W/PI) falls. This leaves most workers earning a lower real wage than they expected. When the time for wage adjustment arrives (that is, when the current contract expires), workers attempt to restore their lost buying power by demanding higher nominal wages.

The larger quantity of labor employed enables firms to produce more goods and services. As the price level rises above its expected level, output rises above the natural level, as shown in Figure 8 (b). The price level increases because the average wage rate has increased somewhat and because of diminishing

Explicit labor contract
A signed, legal agreement setting wages and working conditions for a specified period.

Implicit labor contract
An informal, often verbal, agreement between employers and workers establishing reasonable expectations about wages and employment conditions.

marginal productivity. As firms use their existing capital stock to produce more goods, the marginal cost of production increases. Thus, the **short-run aggregate supply (SRAS) curve**, which relates the aggregate quantity of output firms wish to produce at a given wage rate to the aggregate price level, slopes positively. At some point, when firms reach the maximum capacity of their capital stock or when acquiring more raw materials or labor becomes impossible, the SRAS curve becomes vertical. Further increases in aggregate demand generate price increases, but no additional output.

When the actual price level equals the expected price level, the economy produces at the natural level of output. Thus, the SRAS curve intersects a vertical line drawn at the natural output level where $PI = PI^e$. When $PI = PI^e$ the labor market is in long-run equilibrium. Employment is at its natural level, L_N. Employing the natural quantity of labor enables firms to produce the economy's natural level of output. On the other hand, when $PI \neq PI^e$, the labor market is *not* in long-run equilibrium. The actual level of employment is greater than or less than L_N. Consequently, the level of output produced does not equal the natural level of output.

The effects of a decrease in the demand for goods and services and a corresponding decrease in the demand for labor are similar, but not identical. A decline in labor demand does not produce an immediate decline in the wage rate. For a number of reasons (discussed thoroughly in the chapter on labor market rigidities and unemployment), firms are reluctant to cut wages when the demand for their products declines. Instead, the wage rate remains more or less constant and employment is reduced by laying off workers, as in Figure 9 (a). The difference between the quantity of labor workers are willing to

> **Short-run aggregate supply (SRAS) curve**
> Relates the aggregate quantity of goods and services supplied at a given level of wages to the aggregate price level.

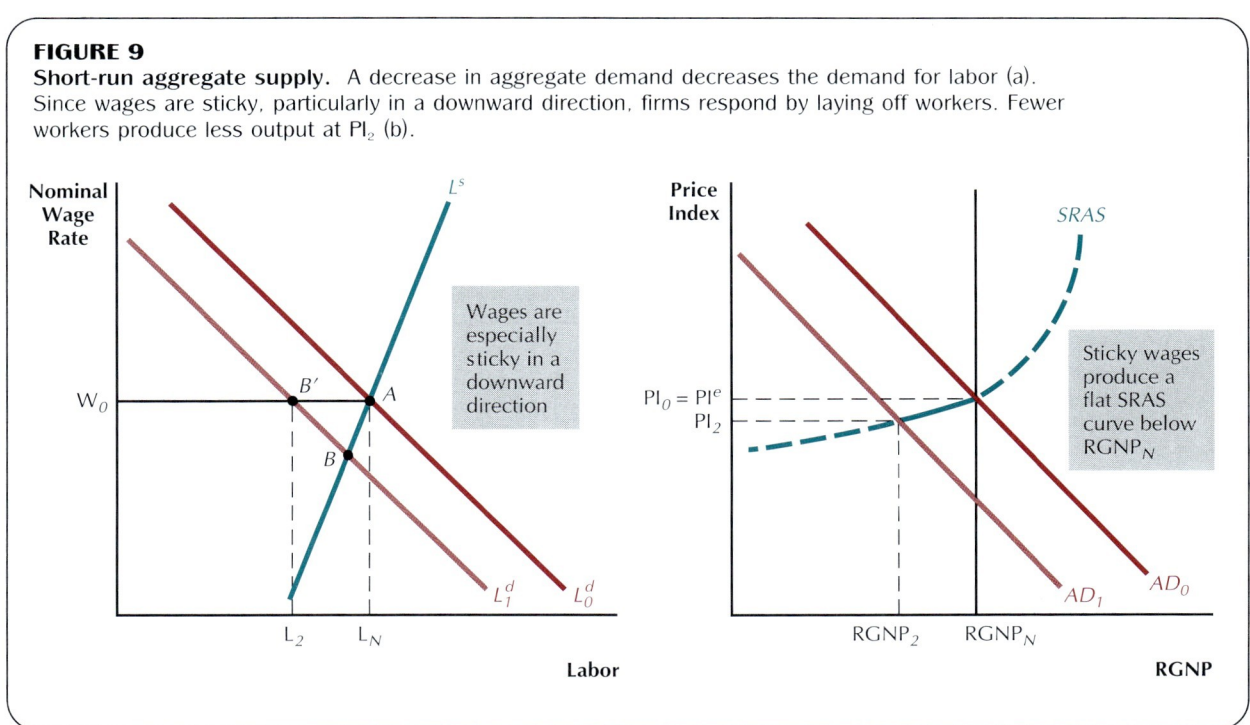

FIGURE 9
Short-run aggregate supply. A decrease in aggregate demand decreases the demand for labor (a). Since wages are sticky, particularly in a downward direction, firms respond by laying off workers. Fewer workers produce less output at PI_2 (b).

Cyclical unemployment
Unemployment caused by a decline in aggregate demand.

supply at W_0 (L_N) and the quantity of labor actually employed (L_2) is **cyclical unemployment** — unemployment caused by a fall in aggregate demand. Such unemployment emerges when the economy enters a recession.

The lower level of employment corresponds to a lower level of production. Output falls below the natural level, as in Figure 9 (b). Since wages are slow to fall, most prices are also slow to fall. When the economy moves into a recession, output usually declines by a larger amount than prices. Consequently, at output levels below the natural output level the SRAS curve is flatter than at output levels above the natural level, where resource constraints come into play.

In real-world economies, not all unemployment is cyclical unemployment. Even when the economy is not in a recession, some unemployment exists. Many factors prevent real-world labor markets from adjusting as rapidly as theoretical markets adjust. The most important factors generating positive unemployment even when the economy is expanding are:

1. The absence of perfect information about jobs and workers.
2. The inability to predict what skills will be needed in the future and to acquire those skills.
3. The unwillingness of workers to relocate.

In the chapter on labor market rigidities and unemployment we discuss the effects of these factors.

SECTION RECAP
Since wages are sticky and do not adjust as fast as many prices, a shift in aggregate demand that alters the price level also changes the real wage rate. The quantity of labor hired by firms and the quantity of output produced both change. Consequently, the short-run aggregate supply curve is positively sloped.

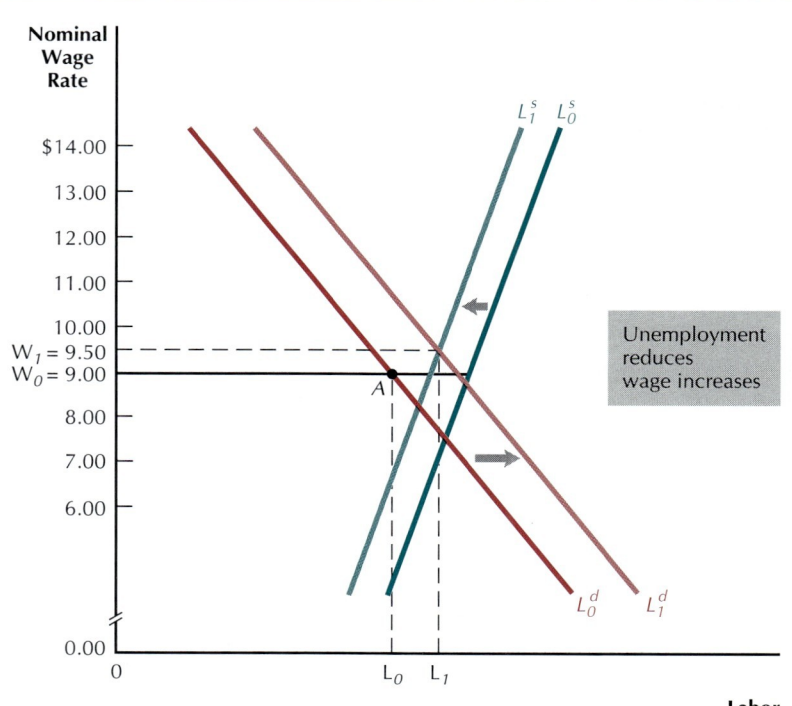

FIGURE 10
Increase in the aggregate price level shifts the labor demand and supply curves. An increase in the aggregate price level caused by an increase in aggregate demand shifts both the labor demand and labor supply curves. The labor demand curve shifts by the proportion by which PI increases. The labor supply curve also shifts, but because the initial position at point A was one of high unemployment, the shift is less than proportional to the change in PI. The result is a small increase in W, a decrease in W/PI, and an increase in labor employed.

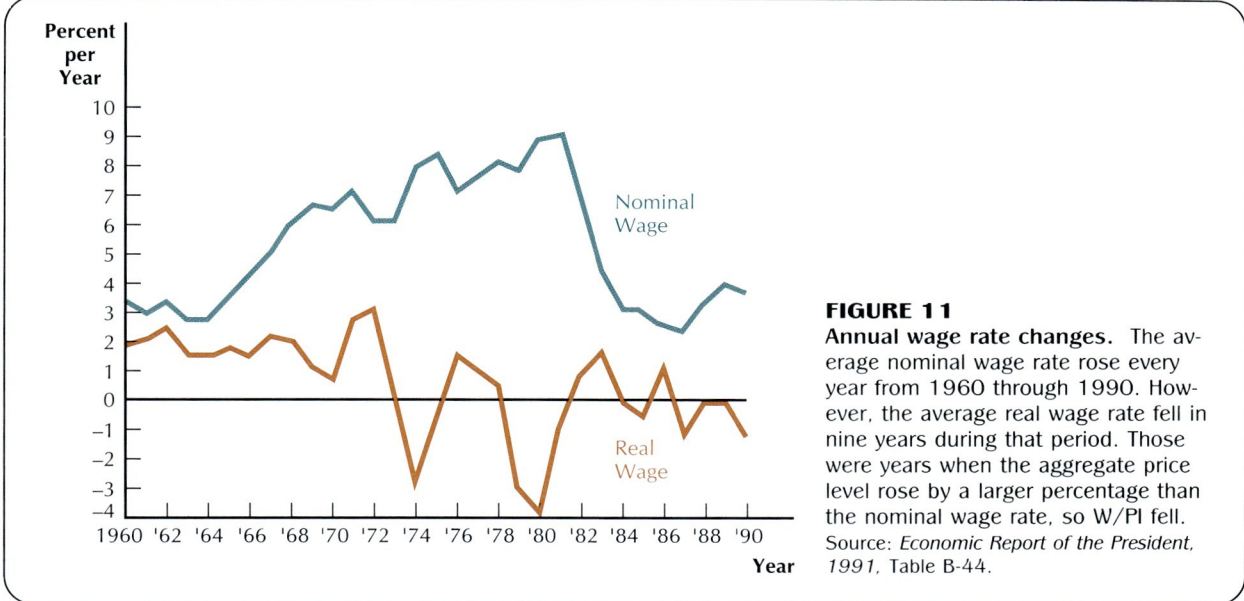

FIGURE 11
Annual wage rate changes. The average nominal wage rate rose every year from 1960 through 1990. However, the average real wage rate fell in nine years during that period. Those were years when the aggregate price level rose by a larger percentage than the nominal wage rate, so W/PI fell.
Source: *Economic Report of the President, 1991,* Table B-44.

Price Level as an Equilibrating Mechanism If nominal wages do not fall in response to a decline in the demand for labor, what restores long-run labor market equilibrium? We can gain insight into this issue by noting that the unemployment at point B' in Figure 9 (a) is accompanied by a *real wage rate* that is too high to maintain labor market equilibrium. Had the nominal wage rate fallen, the labor market would have cleared (at point B). The real wage rate at point B is lower than the real wage rate at point B'.

If labor market rigidities prevent the nominal wage rate from declining, labor market equilibrium can still be restored by an increase in the price level that reduces the *real* wage rate. Recall that changes in the aggregate price level alter the position of both the labor demand and labor supply curves. The labor demand curve shifts to the right when the price level increases. The labor supply curve shifts to the left if workers demand wage increases that reflect the higher cost of living. However, the bargaining position of workers depends crucially on the conditions prevailing in the market when wage rates are negotiated. If the economy is doing well, an increase in the price level will cause workers to demand higher nominal wages. However, if the price level increases when unemployment is relatively high, workers are in no position to demand higher wages. Consequently, although the price level has risen, the labor supply curve may shift very little.

Figure 10 illustrates this process. An increase in the aggregate price level shifts L^d to the right. Because the unemployment level is high when this takes place (at point A), L^s shifts to the left by only a little. The result is a slight increase in nominal wages, but one that is smaller than the increase in the price level. The nominal wage (W) rises, but the real wage (W/PI) falls.

The importance of the price level in restoring labor market equilibrium is illustrated by Figure 11, which shows the annual percentage change in the average nominal and real wage rates. The growth rate of nominal wages — the rate of change of dollar wages — is positive in every year from 1950 to 1990, although the growth rate of real wages — nominal wages adjusted for changes in the price level — falls below zero several times. The declining real wage rate makes labor relatively cheaper to companies and tends to restore labor market equilibrium. Increases in labor productivity also contribute to restoring labor market equilibrium by increasing the demand for labor.

Wage Adjustment, SRAS Shifts, and Long-Run Aggregate Supply

As we have seen, wages do not adjust immediately to changes in the price level. The result is employment variations that correspond to variations in output: The short-run aggregate supply curve is positively sloped. Arguing that wages are sticky is not the same as saying they are fixed, however. Experience confirms what theory predicts: As prices rise, wages also increase. When wages adjust upward or downward, the SRAS curve shifts.

Consider once again the effect of an increase in the aggregate demand for goods and services. The demand for labor shifts to the right [Figure 12 (a)] pushing the average wage rate upward somewhat and increasing employment. Output expands from $RGNP_N$ to $RGNP_1$ [Figure 12 (b)]. The price level rises from PI_0 to PI_1.

Higher prices leave workers with less buying power. They demand higher wages to offset the higher prices, shifting the labor supply curve upward to L_1^s. Since the demand for labor is strong, workers are in a good bargaining

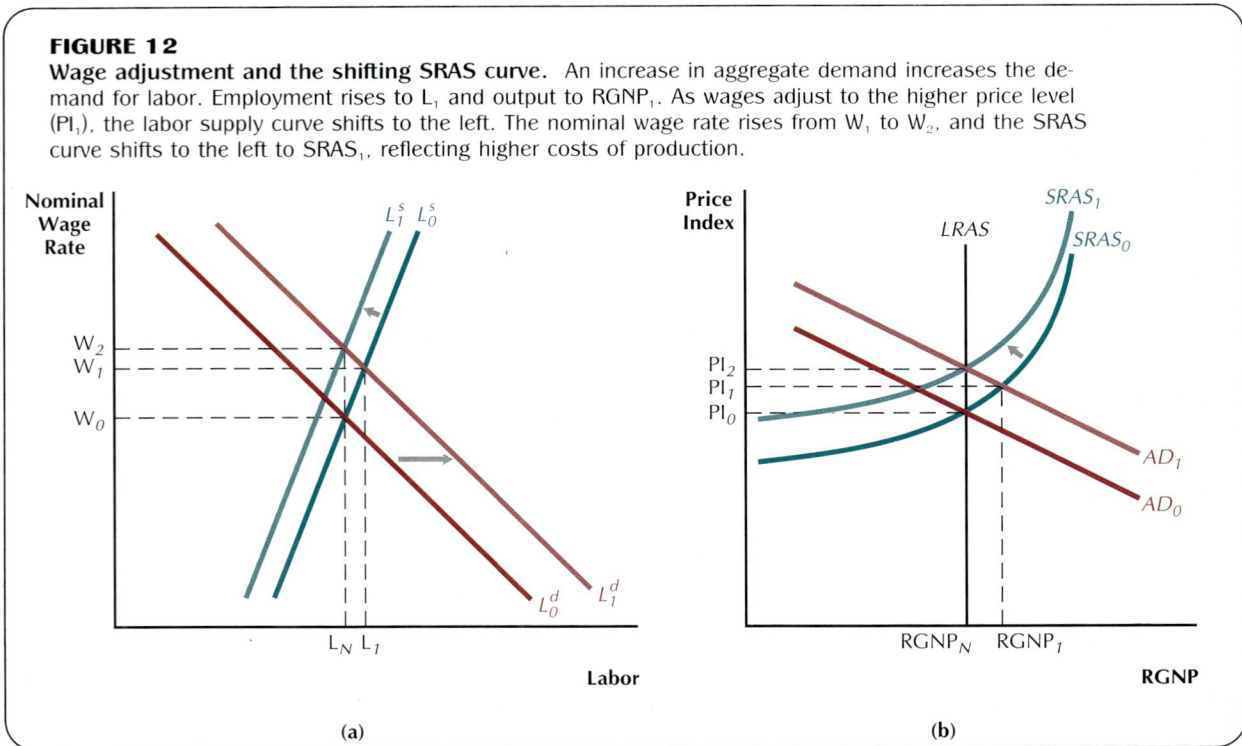

FIGURE 12
Wage adjustment and the shifting SRAS curve. An increase in aggregate demand increases the demand for labor. Employment rises to L_1 and output to $RGNP_1$. As wages adjust to the higher price level (PI_1), the labor supply curve shifts to the left. The nominal wage rate rises from W_1 to W_2, and the SRAS curve shifts to the left to $SRAS_1$, reflecting higher costs of production.

position. High production and profits enable firms to meet the workers' demands for higher wages. The result is an increase in the average wage rate (from W_1 to W_2) and a decrease in employment (from L_1 to L_N).

Higher wages increase the cost of production, shifting the SRAS curve to the left. Only by charging higher prices can firms afford to pay higher wages. Wages and prices continue to rise until wages have fully caught up with prices and employment has returned to its natural level. Output also returns to its natural level ($RGNP_N$). Thus, after the labor market has fully adjusted to an increase in the price level, the natural level of output is associated with a higher price level than before. The economy's **long-run aggregate supply (LRAS) curve**, which illustrates the relationship between output produced and the aggregate price level after all wages and prices have fully adjusted to a change in aggregate demand, is a vertical line at the natural output level. In the long run, output does not depend on the price level. Rather, it depends on the factors that determine the natural output level.

A change in the price of any input that affects the cost of production for a large segment of the economy shifts the SRAS curve. However, not many inputs are important to the whole economy. Besides labor, energy is the most important input on a national level. As a following chapter shows, energy price increases were a major factor contributing to the poor economic performance of the U.S. economy in the 1970s.

Stability of the SRAS Curve

The length of time the SRAS curve remains in one position depends on how rapidly workers' price expectations change. When PI^e changes, wage adjustments soon follow, and the SRAS curve shifts. If price expectations and wages adjust sluggishly, the SRAS curve is fairly stable. In this case, output can deviate from the natural output level for protracted periods of time. If price expectations and wages adjust very rapidly, the SRAS curve shifts rapidly. In this case, the SRAS curve is very unstable. Deviations of output away from the natural level tend to be rather short, since the shifting SRAS curve restores output to its natural level relatively quickly.

The greater the stability of the SRAS curve, the longer the periods when output deviates from the natural level. For example, suppose that expected prices and wages adjust very slowly so that the SRAS curve remains stationary for two or three years at a time. In such a case, a decline in aggregate demand will reduce output below the natural level (and increase unemployment) for two or three years, unless aggregate demand increases in the interim. More rapid adjustment of price expectations and wages would shift the SRAS curve to the right, speeding the return to the natural level of output.

In the next two chapters we combine the theory of aggregate supply with the theory of aggregate demand to develop long-run and short-run models of macroeconomic behavior. We address the long-run behavior of the economy first. There are two reasons for doing this: (1) the long-run model is simpler to use than the short-run model, and (2) the long-run model serves as a benchmark against which short-run behavior can be measured. In the context of the long-run model we talk about the important issues of economic growth and inflation. Our discussion of the behavior of the economy in the long run provides us with a starting point for our discussion of short-run macroeconomic behavior.

Long-run aggregate supply (LRAS) curve Vertical line at the natural output level, showing that output and the price level are unrelated in the long run, when wages have fully adjusted to changes in the price level.

SECTION RECAP
When wages fully adjust to price level changes, the quantity of labor employed does not change. Since wage changes eventually reflect price changes, leaving the real wage rate and the quantity of labor employed unchanged, the long-run aggregate supply curve is vertical.

Summary

Aggregate supply depends on a number of factors, including the quantity of labor employed, the availability of resources, the size of the capital stock, the level of technology, and the manner in which the market is organized. The quantity of labor employed depends on the demand for and supply of labor. The **demand for labor** depends on the marginal productivity of workers, the prices of products, and the wage rate firms must pay. An increase in productivity or product prices increases the demand for labor. An increase in the wage rate reduces the quantity of labor demanded. The **supply of labor** depends on the expected real wage rate. An increase in the expected price level reduces the expected real wage rate and shifts the labor supply curve to the left.

When firms and workers have fully adjusted to price level changes and $PI = PI^e$, the quantity of labor employed is at its natural level. The level of output produced at the natural level of employment is called the **natural output level**. Changes in resource availability, the capital stock, technology, market organization, or labor supply alter the natural output level and shift the **long-run aggregate supply curve**.

The LRAS curve is vertical because wages change proportionally with prices, given sufficient time to adjust. Employment returns to its natural level as wages adjust, and output tends toward its natural level.

The **short-run aggregate supply curve** is derived from labor market behavior. Shifts in labor demand lead to changes in employment in the short run, since wages do not adjust continuously to their long-run equilibrium level. An increase in the demand for goods and services drives up the demand for labor and increases employment. The higher level of employment is used to produce more goods and services. A decline in labor demand reduces employment and output.

The stability of the SRAS curve depends on how quickly wages adjust to price changes. If wages adjust quickly, the SRAS curve is unstable; it shifts upward or downward quickly as higher or lower wages alter production costs. If wages change sluggishly, the SRAS curve is relatively stable. Output can deviate from the natural level for protracted periods.

Questions for Thought

Knowledge Questions

1. What are the major factors determining the position of the long-run aggregate supply curve?
2. Describe the two offsetting effects of an increase in the wage rate on the decision to supply labor.
3. When drawing aggregate labor supply and demand curves, we put the nominal wage rate on the vertical axis and the quantity of labor on the horizontal axis. What are the major *ceteris paribus* assumptions being made when the demand and supply curves are drawn?
4. What major factors shift the labor supply curve? What factors shift the labor demand curve?
5. Define the *value of the marginal product of labor*. What factors affect the VMPL? [Appendix]

Application Questions

6. How would the following changes affect the long-run aggregate supply curve? (Explain which direction LRAS is shifted and the process generating the shift.)
   a. A government project to upgrade the nation's railroad system by improving the roadbed (so that trains can run faster) is completed.
   b. The nation's capital stock diminishes because of several years of little or no investment spending.
   c. New management techniques increase the efficiency of many manufacturing processes.
   d. Continued improvements in computerized robotics lower the cost of producing heavy machinery.
   e. An increase in the price of oil makes a significant portion of the nation's productive capacity uneconomical to operate.
7. What impact would the following changes have on the aggregate supply of labor?
   a. An increase in population.
   b. An increase in the labor force participation rate of women.
   c. A sharp increase in the taxes on labor income.
   d. An increased emphasis on education, combined with government subsidization of advanced schooling.
8. What impact would the following changes have on the aggregate demand for labor?
   a. An increase in technology that increases the productivity of equipment.
   b. An increase in product prices.
   c. An increase in wages relative to product prices.
   d. An increase in the price of energy, making the operation of machines more expensive.
9. What would be the effect of the following on the equilibrium wage rate in the economy?
   a. An increase in the labor force participation rate of women.
   b. An increase in energy prices, making the operation of machines more expensive.
   c. An increase in the aggregate price level, Pl.
10. Analyze the impact of an increase in the number of immigrants permitted to enter the United States each year. What difference would it make if immigration authorities screened potential immigrants for education and skills, admitting only those who were relatively well educated or trained?

Synthesis Questions

11. The long-run aggregate supply curve represents the relationship between the price level and real GNP when wages have fully adjusted to prices. Suppose that private decision makers form their expectations of future prices by using all the information readily available to them, and base their wage offers or wage demands on their price expectations. Furthermore, suppose they systematically use that information, putting it into an economic model, to form the best predictions possible. If contracts are signed on the basis of expectations formed in this manner, what would you expect the aggregate supply curve to look like? What would it look like if price level expectations were wrong?
12. What matters to firms is not nominal wage rates but nominal wages relative to product prices. If this is so, how can the wage rate act to maintain equilibrium in the labor market if nominal wages never fall (as they apparently do not in the United States [refer to Figure 12])?

Appendix to CHAPTER 24

Microfoundations of the Labor Market

Aggregate labor market behavior is built up from the behavior of individual workers and firms. This appendix provides the microeconomic underpinnings for the aggregate labor market model.

Labor Supply Theory

The theory of labor supply begins at the individual level. We will develop a labor supply curve for an individual before aggregating up to the labor supply curve for the entire economy. The theory developed here is highly simplified. We pay no attention to the fact that jobs have different characteristics and workers have different qualifications. The implications of such heterogeneity (jobs and people having different characteristics) are worked out in detail in a later chapter.

Labor–Leisure Tradeoff   The amount of labor services that an individual can supply to the market is constrained by the number of hours in a day. Since everyone requires time to sleep, eat, and relax, the number of hours available for working is significantly less than twenty-four. To simplify things, we will call hours spent in activities other than work *leisure*. According to this definition, there is a direct tradeoff between labor and leisure. If an individual spends one more hour working, then one less hour is available for leisure.

For an individual, the choice of time spent in labor and leisure is not independent of the desired level of consumption and asset accumulation (style of living). Individuals with the same inherent capabilities, but with different desired lifestyles, might make very different labor supply choices. Economists do not attempt to explain such differences. We shall take an individual's preferences as given and concentrate on the rational behavior of a generic individual confronted with changes in the wage rate.

The wage rate is not only the compensation for an hour of labor, it is also the opportunity cost of an hour of leisure. Thus, when we analyze labor market behavior, we may equally well view it as reflecting an individual's preferences with respect to leisure.

Substitution and Income Effects   Figure 13 shows the labor–leisure choices of a young married woman with no children. Jo has chosen a minimum wage beneath which she will not work. Her leisure is more valuable to her than the income she would earn at a wage rate of less than $3 per hour. As the wage rate is raised, the number of hours Jo is willing to work rises, to a maximum of twelve hours per day. Beyond the wage rate of $16 per hour she is unwilling to work any more than twelve hours per day; her labor supply curve becomes vertical. At a wage rate of $22 per hour, the amount of labor time she wishes to supply actually decreases, and her labor supply curve bends backwards. The shape of Jo's labor supply curve can be explained using the concepts of the substitution effect and the income effect.

The substitution effect focuses on relative prices. When the wage rate rises, the relative price of leisure increases. Since leisure is more expensive, Jo substitutes away from it, consequently working more. The additional labor supplied provides Jo with additional income that can be used to purchase goods and services that make the use of her remaining leisure more efficient. For example, Jo might purchase a dishwasher to cut down on the time she and her husband spend washing dishes or a microwave oven to reduce meal preparation time.

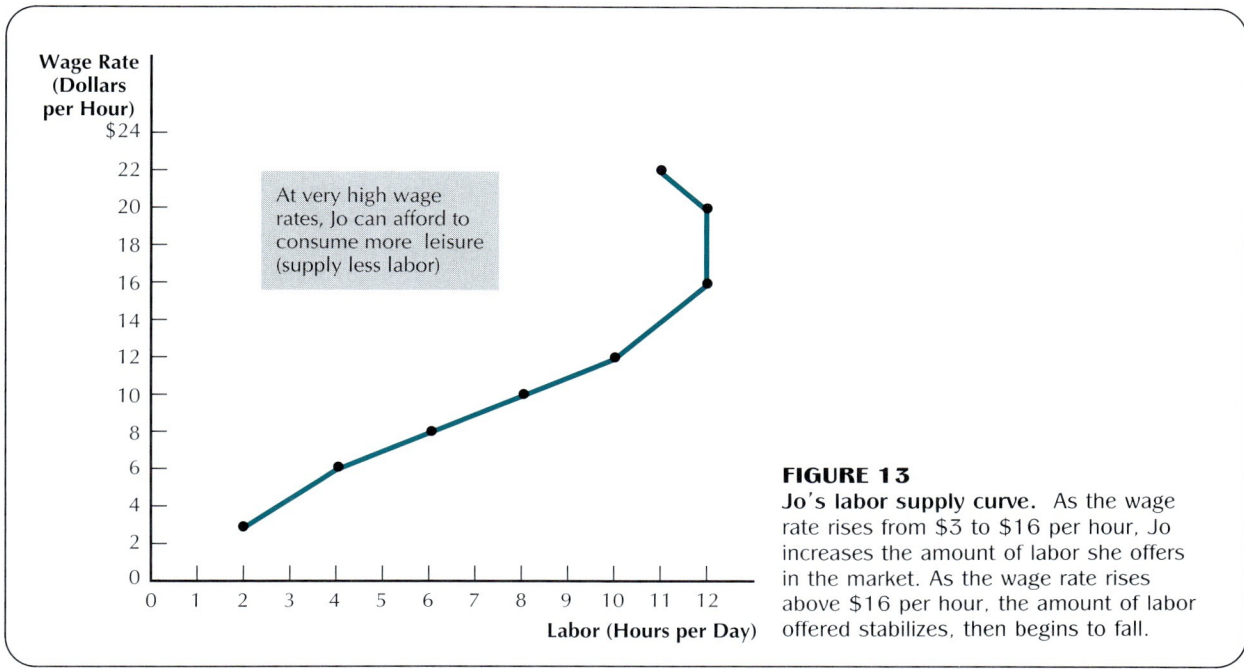

FIGURE 13
Jo's labor supply curve. As the wage rate rises from $3 to $16 per hour, Jo increases the amount of labor she offers in the market. As the wage rate rises above $16 per hour, the amount of labor offered stabilizes, then begins to fall.

The substitution effect always works in the direction of increasing the amount of labor supplied (reducing leisure) as the wage rate rises. It obviously cannot explain the vertical or backward-bending portions of the labor supply curve. The income effect can, however. As Jo's wage rate increases, so does her income. With a larger income Jo can purchase more of any number of goods and services, including more leisure. Leisure is a good, and higher income allows more of it to be purchased and consumed. When the income effect outweighs the substitution effect, the labor supply curve bends backwards.

Household Labor Supply Curve The preceding example, though somewhat contrived, illustrates some important facts about actual labor market behavior of households. Although the way a particular household reacts to changing wage rates cannot be predicted, some well-known behavior patterns provide support for the theory. A couple of examples should suffice to illustrate.

The amount of labor supplied is zero if the wage derived from an hour of labor is less than the opportunity cost of working. Such a situation is not uncommon. A mother with two or more preschool children might find it inefficient to work outside the home, because the income she could derive from working would not pay for child care and still leave enough surplus to make working worthwhile. An increase in the wage rate might raise the income derived from work enough to cause her to join (or rejoin) the labor force. This would translate graphically into a positively sloped labor supply curve.

It is not uncommon for the chief breadwinner in a household to hold down two jobs to make ends meet. If the income derived from the breadwinner's primary job were to increase sufficiently, a reduction in the amount of labor supplied might well take place. The second job would be dropped. If graphed, this would appear as a backward-bending supply curve. Thus, both positively and negatively sloped segments of the labor supply curve are plausible.

Aggregate Labor Supply Curve The aggregate labor supply curve is the horizontal summation of all individual supply curves, as illustrated in Figure 14. It relates the aggregate quantity of labor services, measured in hours per time period, to the wage rate per hour. We assume that the expected aggregate price index (PI^e) is constant when drawing the labor supply curve, so that changes in W translate into changes in expected real wages (W/PI^e). The real wage measures the buying power the worker receives and is thus of utmost importance to the worker. When the price level changes, the labor supply curve shifts.

In the aggregate, we assume that the labor supply curve slopes positively throughout the relevant range (that is, throughout the range of possible wage rates). As the wage rate rises, more people enter the labor force. Many individuals may have backward-bending labor supply curves, but if more people are joining the aggregate labor force as the wage rate rises, the new entrants will offset the reduction in hours of others, leaving a positively sloped supply curve, as shown in Figure 14.

Labor Demand Theory

Labor is demanded by firms, which utilize labor inputs in the production of goods and services. To understand the factors affecting the demand for labor, we must delve into the theory of the firm.

Notion of Derived Demand The demand theory developed in Chapter 3 dealt with what might be called *final demand*. The product in demand was desired by the people demanding it because of the value they attached to it. The value attached to a product by a prospective consumer depends on what the consumer is willing to give up to

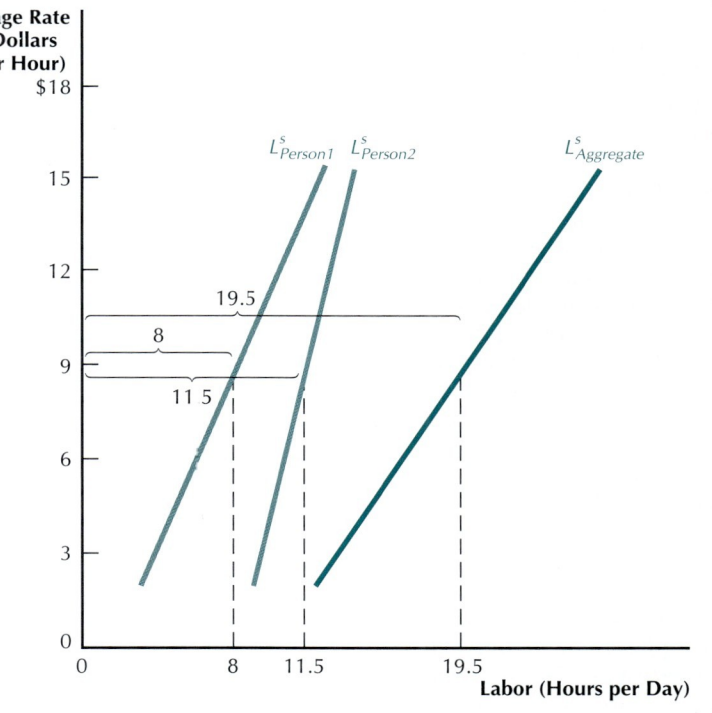

FIGURE 14
Deriving the aggregate labor supply curve. The aggregate labor supply curve is obtained by adding the amounts of labor supplied at each wage rate by all the people supplying labor. For example, at a wage rate of $9 per hour, Person 1 offers 8 hours of labor and Person 2 offers 11.5 hours. The aggregate quantity of labor supplied is 19.5 hours.

obtain the product. The value to the consumer is *subjective*, determined totally by the consumer's preferences. The value of a good may vary widely from consumer to consumer even though the cost of producing the good is constant. Production cost and value are two different things.

The value that a firm attaches to resource inputs, including labor services, is determined differently. A firm purchases labor services to use as inputs in a production process. The value of the labor services is not determined subjectively by the firm, but is determined by the value of the product the firm produces. The demand for labor is derived from the demand of consumers for the products produced by a firm.

Value of a Worker to a Firm The value of a worker to a firm is the marginal benefit the firm gains by employing that worker. The firm measures marginal benefit in dollar terms: *The marginal benefit to the firm of a worker is the dollar value of the additional output produced by the worker.* This depends on two factors: (1) the amount a worker adds to the firm's physical output, and (2) the price consumers are willing to pay for that output. The additional output produced by a unit of labor is called the *marginal product of labor*. The marginal benefit to the firm of employing an additional unit of labor is the *value of the marginal product of labor* (VMPL). It is measured in dollar terms and equals the marginal product of labor (MPL) times the product price (P).* In algebraic form:

$$\text{Marginal benefit} = \text{VMPL} = \text{MPL} \times \text{P}$$

Given a fixed amount of capital to work with, the marginal product of labor diminishes as more and more units are employed. Additional workers add to the firm's output, but each new worker adds less than did previous workers. Workers are restrained by the available capital equipment. They must waste time waiting for machines to become available, or they must transport their work over longer distances inside the factory or office. In short, because the limited amount of capital reduces the efficiency of individual workers, marginal product declines as more workers are employed.

A firm gains from employing additional workers so long as the marginal benefit from adding workers exceeds the *marginal cost*—the cost of hiring more workers. The marginal cost of a worker is the wage rate the worker must be paid. The firm maximizes its total gains from hiring workers and producing goods by following a standard economic guideline: Hire workers until the marginal benefit (of an additional worker) equals the marginal cost. Figure 15 illustrates this. The firm's marginal benefits curve is represented by the value of the marginal product of labor curve. It is negatively sloped because the marginal product of labor declines as more workers are employed. The marginal cost curve is represented by the market wage rate. When the market wage rate equals W_0, the firm gains by hiring labor out to L_0, where the value of the marginal product of labor equals the wage rate.

If the firm employed fewer than L_0 units of labor, it would be giving up some available net gains. At employment levels lower than L_0, the marginal benefits to the firm of additional units of labor exceed the marginal cost. The firm has a net gain from hiring more labor. However, beyond L_0 the marginal cost of labor exceeds its marginal value to the firm.

Firm's Demand for Labor Curve A demand curve tells us the quantity demanded of a good at various prices, other things held constant. The VMPL curve tells us how much labor a firm will demand given its price, the wage rate. Figure 15 showed that the firm

---

*In the microeconomics section of this text, the concept of *marginal revenue product* (MRP) is introduced. Although the MRP of labor is a slightly broader concept than the VMPL (because it does not assume that the firms employing labor are perfectly competitive price takers), the two can be treated as identical for the purposes at hand.

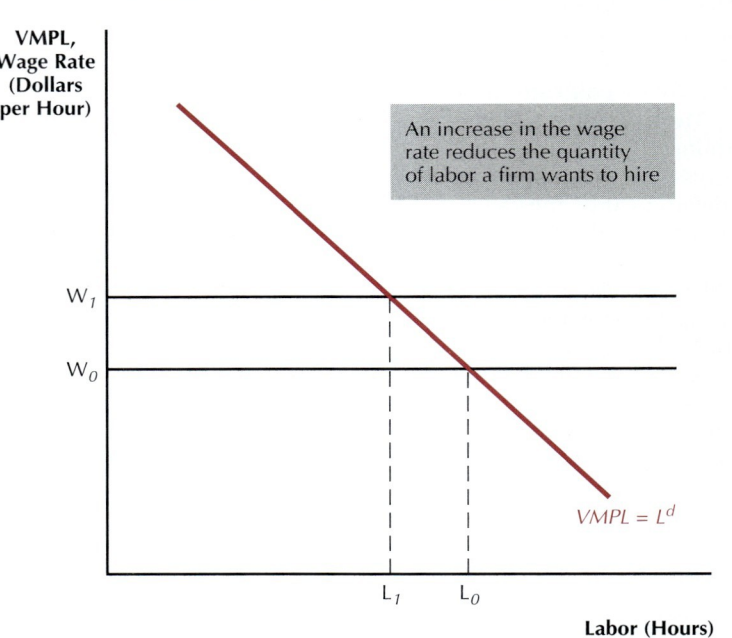

FIGURE 15
Firm's demand for labor curve. The marginal benefit of a unit of labor to a firm is measured by the value of the marginal product of labor (VMPL). The firm maximizes its total net benefits by hiring labor to the point where marginal benefit equals marginal cost. Since the marginal cost of labor is the wage rate, the firm hires labor until VMPL = W. The VMPL curve is the firm's labor demand curve. If the wage rate is W_0, L_0 units of labor are demanded. But if the wage rate rises to W_1, labor demanded drops to L_1.

An increase in the wage rate reduces the quantity of labor a firm wants to hire

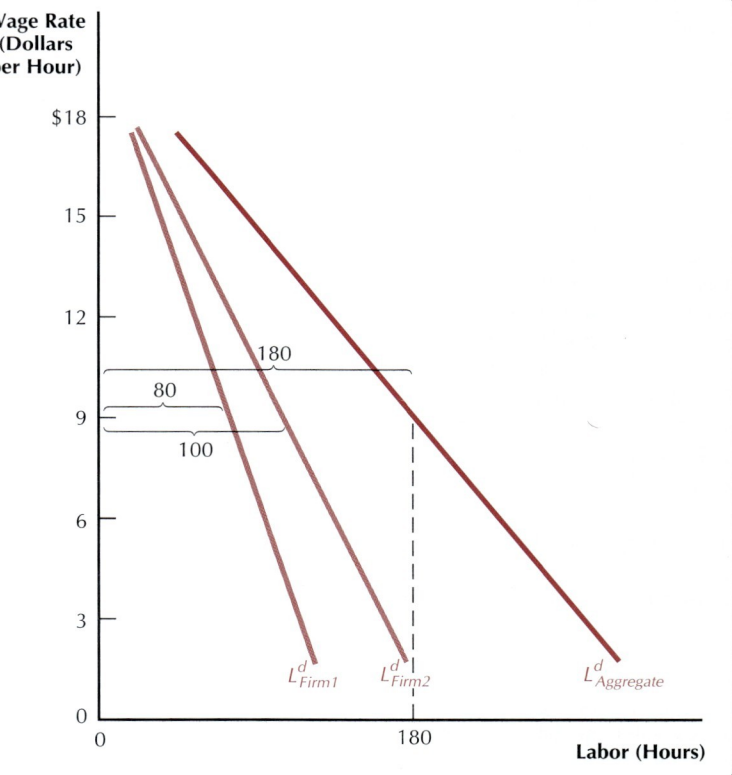

FIGURE 16
Deriving the aggregate labor demand curve. The aggregate labor demand curve is obtained by adding together the quantities of labor demanded at each wage rate by all firms demanding labor. For example, at a wage of $9 per hour, Firm 1 demands 80 hours of labor and Firm 2 demands 100 hours of labor. The aggregate quantity of labor demanded at a wage rate of $9 per hour is 180 hours.

would hire L_0 units of labor at a wage rate of W_0. If the wage rate were to rise to W_1, the firm would equate marginal benefits to marginal cost by hiring L_1 units of labor. Thus, *the VMPL curve is a firm's demand for labor curve.* A firm maximizes its net gain from employing labor by operating at the point on its demand (VMPL) curve where the marginal benefit of a unit of labor equals its marginal cost (the wage rate).

Aggregate Labor Demand Curve   The aggregate labor demand curve is derived by horizontally summing individual firm labor demand curves. (Some strong assumptions must be satisfied for the aggregate demand for labor to be the simple summation of individual firm demands. These technical issues need not affect us here.) Figure 16 shows such a summation for two firms. The aggregate demand for labor curve relates the aggregate quantity of labor demanded to various levels of the wage rate. As before, the quantity of labor is measured in hours per time period.

OVERVIEW

With the basic building blocks now in place, we can assemble the first complete version of our model of the macroeconomy. The model is based on the assumption that prices and wages are free to move to their long-run equilibrium values. Although prices and wages sometimes move flexibly over short periods of time, much of the time they react sluggishly to changes in aggregate demand. Thus, we call the model in this chapter

The Long-Run Model: The Economy with Flexible Prices

the *long-run model* to emphasize the point that prices and wages have had ample time to fully adjust to a change in aggregate demand or aggregate supply.

The long-run model serves two purposes: It provides us with a benchmark for evaluating the behavior of the economy, and it serves as the basis for a discussion of output and price level growth. Since the long-run model shows the natural output level toward which the economy tends over time, the model enables us to determine whether current output is low or high relative to the economy's sustainable output level. The long-run model also focuses our attention on the structural factors that determine the level and growth of natural output. Real-world economies grow almost continuously. The long-run model helps us analyze the factors leading to rapid or slow growth in output — and in prices.

We begin the chapter with an analysis of the long-run model. Because the long-run aggregate supply curve is vertical, the long-run equilibrium (natural) level of output does not depend on aggregate demand. However, prices depend directly on aggregate demand. The policy implications of the long-run model are important.

In the second major section of the chapter we analyze the factors affecting the growth of output in the United States. We also discuss governmental policies that promote or harm growth.

We end the chapter with a discussion of inflation—a sustained increase in the aggregate price level. Since

CHAPTER 25

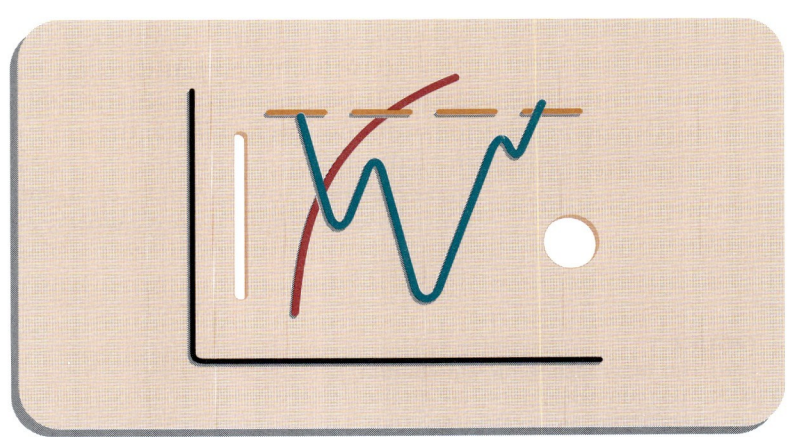

aggregate demand is not limited by physical factors as is aggregate supply, it is possible for aggregate demand to grow more rapidly than aggregate supply. When this occurs, the price level rises. We explore the connection between inflation and money supply growth and use evidence from the United States and other countries to illustrate how money and inflation are related.

Learning Objectives

After reading and studying this chapter, you will be able to:

1. Explain why the natural output level depends only on aggregate supply, while the price level depends on both aggregate supply and aggregate demand.
2. Use the complete aggregate demand–long-run aggregate supply model to analyze the impact of changes in economic variables on the price level and output level.
3. List the major factors affecting economic growth and discuss which factors seem to have been particularly important for the United States.
4. Suggest government policies that could be used to encourage economic growth.
5. Describe the relationship between inflation and money supply growth.

Long-Run Aggregate Equilibrium

In the preceding chapter we saw that the long-run aggregate supply curve is vertical. In the long run, prices and wages have ample time to adjust completely to any macroeconomic shocks. Furthermore, people have time to revise their price level expectations, bringing them into equality with the actual price level. When the expected price level equals the actual price level, the expected real wage rate also equals the actual real wage rate, and the labor market is in long-run equilibrium. The quantity of output produced when the labor market is in long-run equilibrium is the natural level of output. The intersection of the aggregate demand curve with the long-run aggregate supply curve then determines the economy's equilibrium price level. Such a long-run equilibrium is shown in Figure 1.

In long-run equilibrium the output level is completely determined by the level of aggregate supply, while the price level is determined by the intersection of aggregate demand with the long-run aggregate supply curve. This important proposition contrasts sharply with the situation in the short run, when the aggregate supply curve is positively sloped. In the short run, the level of output depends on both aggregate demand and aggregate supply. Changes in aggregate demand shift the AD curve along the SRAS curve and change output. In the long run, however, shifts in the AD curve do not affect output, as you can see in Figure 1. This means that sustained output growth depends on the factors that determine the natural level of output. The economy's productive capacity must grow if output is to grow in the long run.

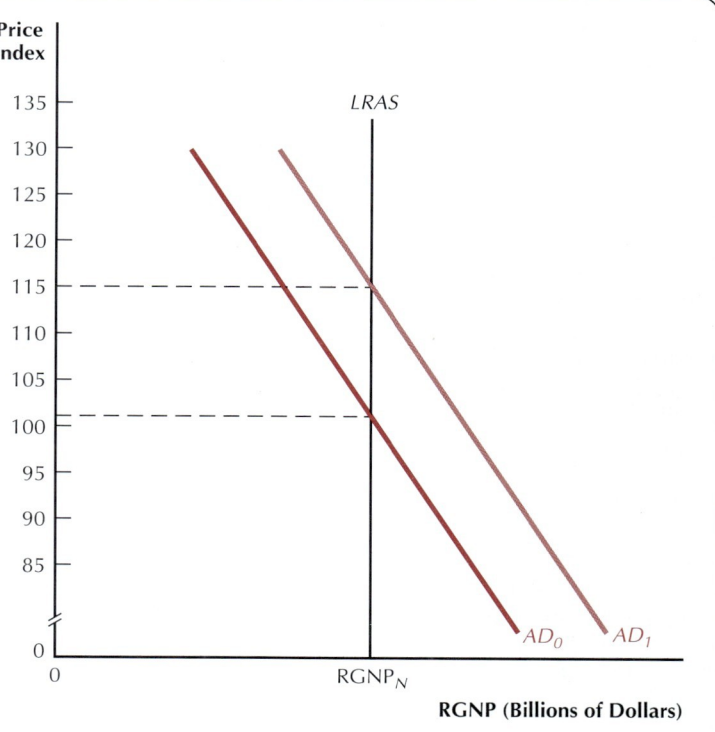

FIGURE 1
Long-run macroeconomic equilibrium.
In the long run, when prices are flexible and expectations are correct, the economy produces at the natural output level.

The Model in Motion: Aggregate Demand Changes

Given a fixed long-run aggregate supply curve, the only effect of a change in aggregate demand is on the equilibrium price level. The effect of an increase in aggregate demand is shown in Figure 2 (a). As AD shifts to the right, both PI and RGNP initially rise along $SRAS_0$. At the new short-run equilibrium (point B), output exceeds the natural level. Output rises because wages initially rise more slowly than prices do.

Figure 2 (b) illustrates the adjustment of the labor market. The increase in aggregate demand drives prices up, causing the demand for labor to increase to L_1^d. Expected prices do not rise immediately, so the labor supply curve remains stationary at L_0^s, and employment rises to L_1. As time passes workers recognize that their real wage has fallen (even though the average nominal wage has risen). Workers demand a higher nominal wage rate, and the labor supply curve shifts to the left. Employment returns to its natural level, and the nominal wage rate rises. The higher nominal wage increases the cost of production for firms, which respond by employing fewer workers and producing less output. The SRAS curve [in Figure 2 (a)] shifts to the left to $SRAS_1$, output returns to its natural level, and the price level rises from PI_1 to PI_2. The economy returns to long-run equilibrium.

Note that the effect of higher aggregate demand ultimately falls only on the price level. The output level is the same before and after the AD shift. *Real* conditions in the labor market are also the same before and after the AD shift. Not only does employment return to its natural level, the real wage rate also returns to its initial level. Although the *nominal* wage rate at point C (W_2) is higher than the *nominal* wage rate at point A (W_0), the *real* wage rate remains the same at both points, because the nominal wage rate rises proportionately with the price level. Since W and PI change by the same proportion, W/PI does not change.

The fact that a shift in aggregate demand leaves the output level unchanged does not imply that the mix of goods and services produced remains the same. Depending on the source of the aggregate demand shift, the demand for particular goods and services may rise more than the demand for other goods and services. Resources, including labor, may be transferred from one particular market to another. However, the aggregate level of output remains constant, even as output rises in some markets and falls in others.

It is worth noting that *nominal* GNP is higher at point C than at point A, because prices are higher while real output is constant. Recall that nominal GNP is the product of the price level times real GNP: GNP = PI × RGNP. Since PI is higher at point C than at point A, while RGNP is the same at both points, GNP rises.

The long-run model indicates that aggregate demand growth has no effect on real output growth. If the model is accurate, over long periods of time we should observe (1) no relationship between aggregate demand growth and output growth, and (2) a strong positive relationship between aggregate demand growth and inflation.

Figure 3 (a) shows the relationship between the average annual growth rates of nominal GNP and real GNP in the United States for each decade of the twentieth century. Nominal GNP growth serves as a measure of growth in aggregate demand, since nominal GNP measures the amount of spending on domestically produced goods and services. As the figure shows, no relationship

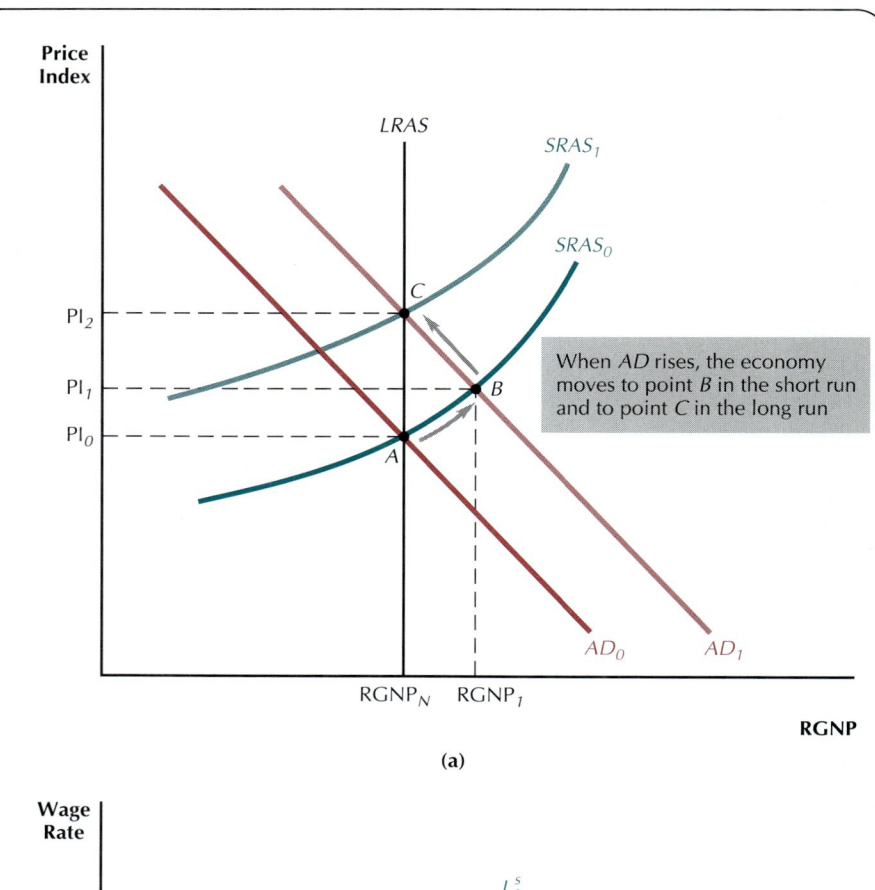

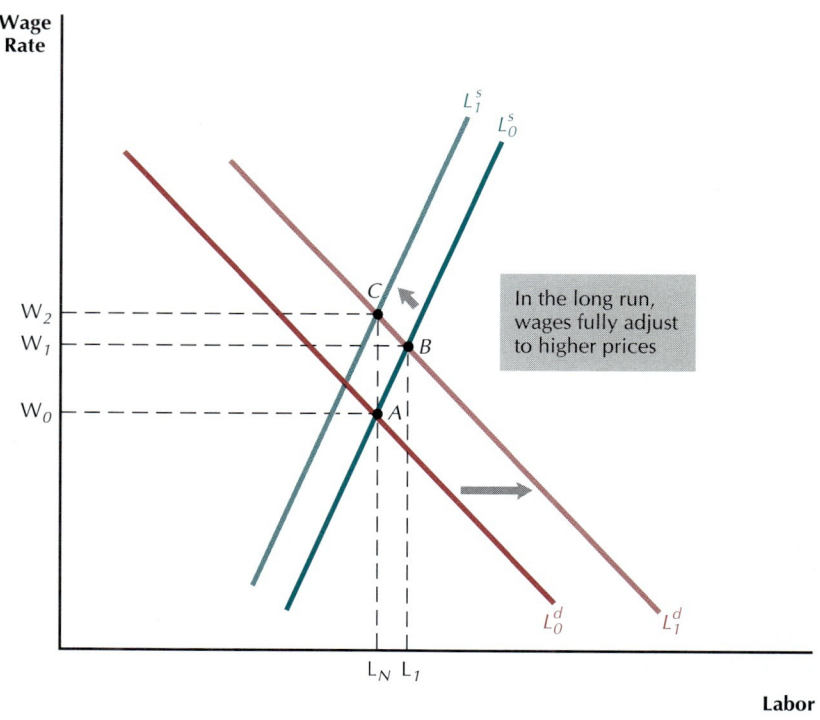

FIGURE 2
Long-run adjustment to an increase in aggregate demand. An increase in aggregate demand increases output in the short run when wages do not fully adjust to higher prices. The economy moves from point A to point B. As wages catch up with higher prices, the labor supply curve shifts to the left, as does the SRAS curve. The economy returns to the natural output level at point C.

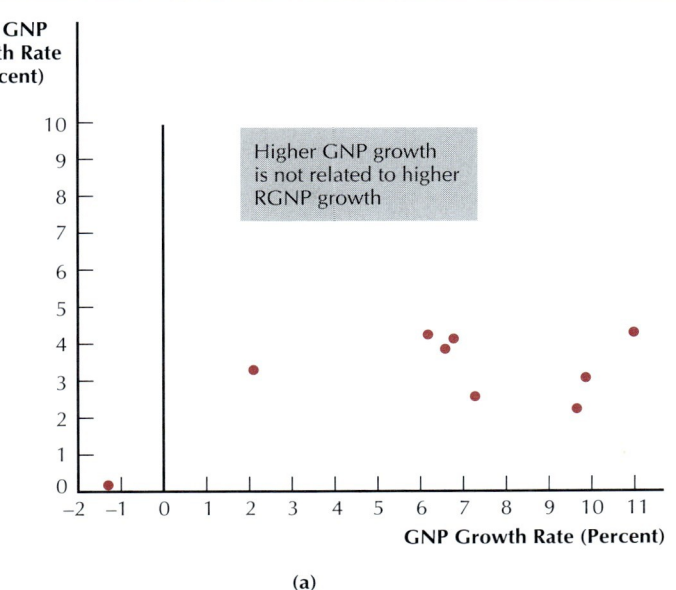

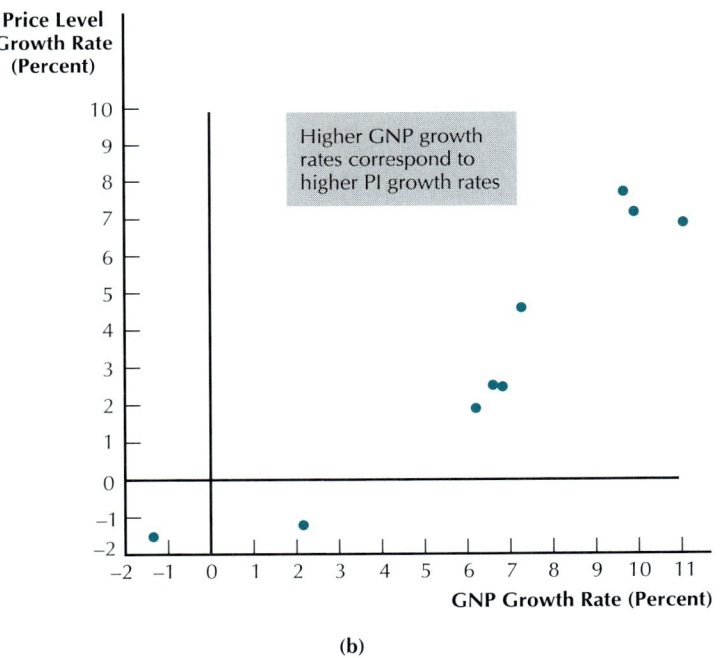

FIGURE 3
GNP growth. *(a) GNP–RGNP Growth Relationship by Decade (b) GNP–PI Growth Relationship by Decade.* GNP growth rates by decade are not related to real GNP growth rates, but are positively related to inflation rates.

between GNP and real GNP growth rates is evident. The real GNP growth rate does not rise systematically as the GNP growth rate rises. The absence of a pattern is consistent with the idea that long-run growth depends solely on aggregate supply. However, Figure 3 (b) shows that GNP growth and price level growth (inflation) are positively related; the higher the GNP growth rate during a decade, the higher the inflation rate is likely to be. Again, this is consistent with the view that aggregate demand growth is the major determinant of the behavior of prices over long periods.

The Model in Motion: Aggregate Supply Changes

Changes in any of the factors that determine the natural output level — natural resources, the labor force, the capital stock, technology, and market organization — shift the long-run aggregate supply curve. Unless aggregate demand changes by an identical amount, such a change also alters the aggregate price level.

As an example, suppose that a technological breakthrough allows petroleum products to be utilized much more efficiently as energy sources. Such a breakthrough shifts LRAS to the right, as shown in Figure 4. With the same amount of resources (oil), more output can now be produced. The per-unit

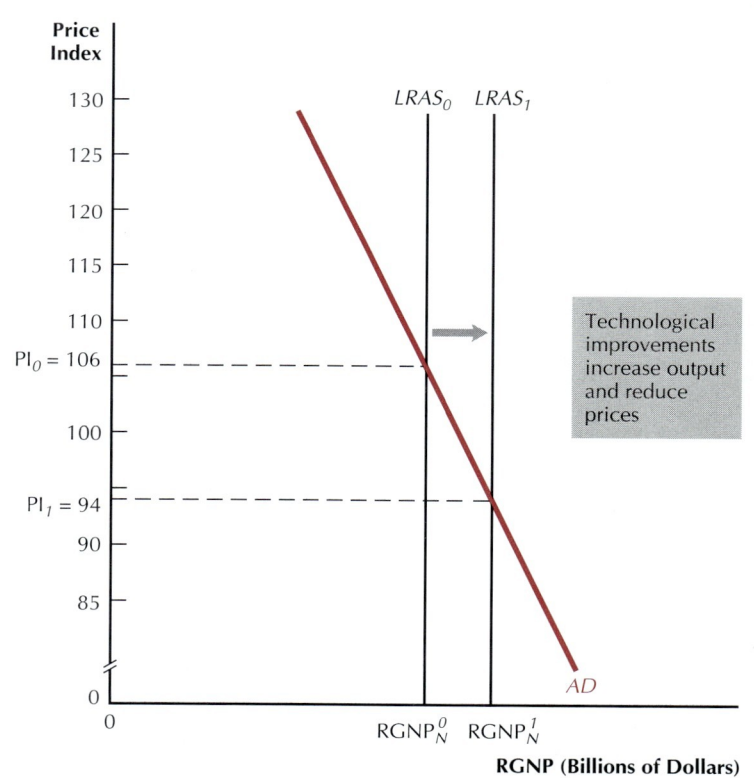

FIGURE 4
Technological improvements increase output and reduce the price level. A technological breakthrough that increases efficiency allows more goods to be produced at a given cost. Lower per-unit costs cause prices to decline if aggregate demand remains constant.

Does It Make **Economic Sense?**

Growing Wealth, Yet Declining Happiness

When one looks across societies, it is by no means obvious that people in the richer nations are more content with their lot than those in the poorer ones. Suicide rates — the percentage of individuals whose levels of satisfaction are so low that life no longer seems worth living — show that higher-income countries usually have relatively more suicides than poorer ones. Nor does the number whose inability to cope with life takes the form of mental illness show any tendency to diminish as incomes increase.*

So says Mancur Olson, who has spent decades studying the process and consequences of economic growth. If Olson is right — and available evidence suggests he is — then one must wonder whether economic growth is a worthwhile goal. Does it make economic sense?

Several issues must be sorted out before the question can be answered. First, does economic growth cause unhappiness or are the two essentially unrelated? Survey research indicates that, within any society, those with higher incomes tend to say they are happier than those with lower incomes. However, as the whole society becomes wealthier (as the United States has over time), people with relatively low incomes do not become happier over time, even though they are becoming wealthier in an absolute sense. It appears that happiness is related at least as much to relative income — where one stands relative to others in society — as to absolute income — the level of wealth. Thus, to some degree, economic growth and happiness are unrelated.

Professor Olson points out that connections between growth and happiness — or unhappiness — do exist, however. The process of growth can have negative effects on how happy people feel. In the process of growth, things change. Relationships that take years to establish are broken up. People are forced to adapt to new jobs and move to new locations. Huge, impersonal organizations dominate the lives of people who no longer have the support of a close circle of family and friends. Even as greater economic wealth makes people better off, the breakdown of relationships makes them worse off. They have higher incomes and more material goods, but feel no happier than they did when they had fewer things but more stable relationships. This phenomenon is by no means restricted to the United States. In Japan, for example, "Those with incomes double the national average complain that they are frustrated with their standard of living — the tiny, ravenously expensive apartments; the long, crushing commutes to work; the tedious days at the gray office." The Japanese call it the " 'paradox of prosperity': rich Japan, poor Japanese."**

Before concluding that economic growth is, on net, bad, we must address another issue. Does growth produce benefits that are not reflected in the dollar value of growing incomes? Professor Olson says it does, supporting his case with the following argument:

Which would you prefer: $25,000 in 1932 dollars, with which you could purchase 1932 goods, or $25,000 today with which you could purchase today's goods? A $25,000 income in 1932 would be equivalent to an income of about $200,000 today. Yet with that 1932 income, you could not purchase a TV set or a personal computer — they did not exist in 1932. If you became ill, your doctor could not prescribe an antibiotic for you for the same reason. So many goods are available today — at very low cost — that did not exist a few decades ago that it is hard to argue that people are not better off today. Certainly, $25,000 would have purchased more food and clothing in 1932 than today, but it would not have purchased the thousands of goods we regularly buy today that did not exist in 1932, goods that make our lives better in untold ways.

So what is the bottom line? Does economic growth make people better off? Professor Olson argues that it does. At the same time, the evidence that economic growth and happiness are only loosely connected warns us that pursuing a policy of growth at any cost does not make sense. As always, trade-offs exist: Economic growth is good, but many noneconomic goods are of higher value than a little bit more material wealth.

*Mancur Olson, "The Social Costs of Economic Growth," *The Wall Street Journal,* December 22, 1988, p. A12.

**"The Dream Out of Reach for Japanese," *Insight,* September 3, 1990, pp. 8–9. This extensive article (which covers pp. 8–17) provides a detailed look at the modern Japanese standard of living.

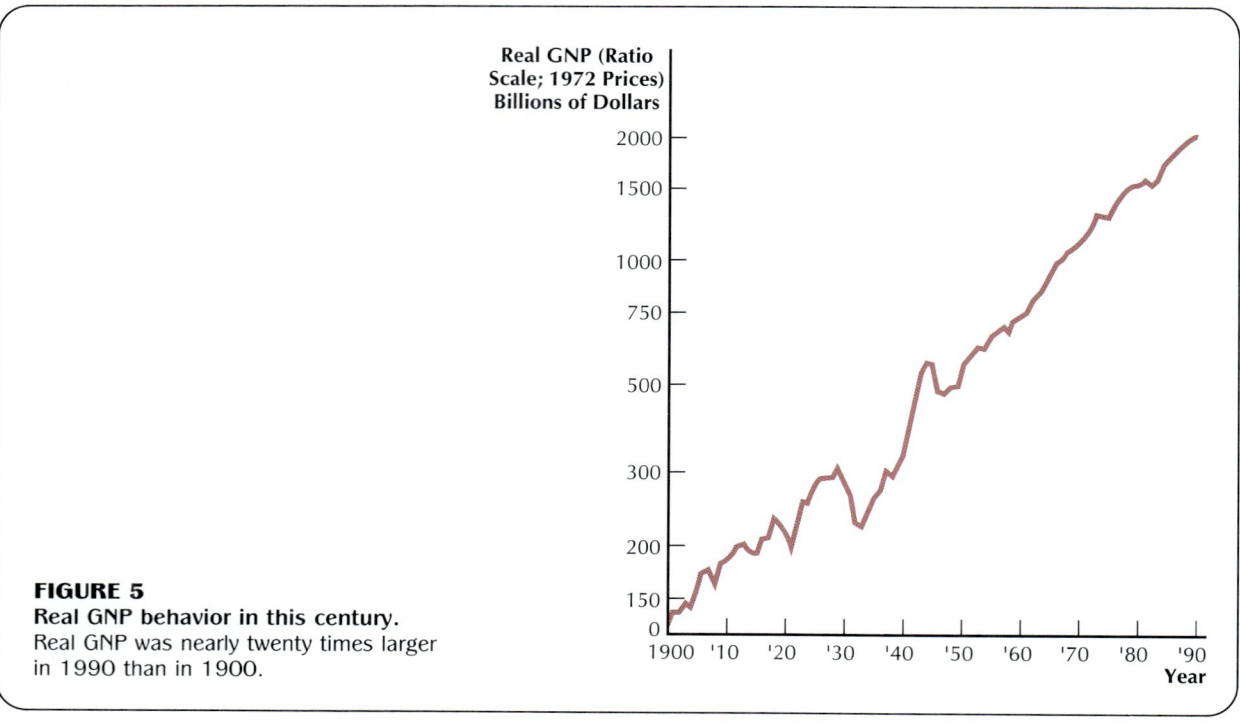

FIGURE 5
Real GNP behavior in this century.
Real GNP was nearly twenty times larger in 1990 than in 1900.

SECTION RECAP
In the long run, the level of output is determined by the factors that affect the natural level of output. Aggregate demand has no effect on output but, in conjunction with long-run aggregate supply, determines the price level.

cost of production falls, resulting in lower prices. Equilibrium output rises, and the equilibrium price level falls.

Increases in the capital stock available for use in production, including improvements in the economy's infrastructure, increases in the size or quality of the labor force, and advances in technology tend to shift the aggregate supply curve to the right. New discoveries of mineral resources or the development of new techniques for extracting such resources also shift LRAS to the right. Increases in government regulation, which prevent businesses from pursuing profit opportunities, or an increase in government planning based on political rather than economic considerations tends to shift the LRAS curve to the left. Even regulation judged to be socially beneficial may imply a tradeoff of lower measureable output for such goods as better air or water quality.

The U.S. long-run aggregate supply curve has shifted to the right almost continuously in the twentieth century. Real GNP in 1900 was only a small fraction of current real output, as Figure 5 illustrates.

The Long-Run Model and Actual Economic Behavior

Both output and prices have risen tremendously in the United States in the twentieth century. In this section we examine the rate of growth of real GNP in the United States during this century and look at some evidence on what generated that growth. Since output growth appears to have slowed over the past twenty years, determining the sources of economic growth is an important issue. We then consider some policy questions pertaining to growth as well as some of the side effects of a growing economy. Finally, we turn to the issue of price level movement and use the AD–LRAS model to discuss the changes in the behavior of the price level during this century.

Output Growth

Real GNP in the United States has been increasing for as long as it has been measured. Although the growth of RGNP has been anything but steady on a year-to-year basis, the pronounced upward trend is strong. Breaking the period 1900–1989 into four long subperiods, and omitting the war years of 1917–1919 and 1941–1946, we see that the average annual growth rate of real GNP was higher during the 1900–1916 and 1947–1973 subperiods than during the interwar period or the period since 1973. The 1920–1940 period included the Great Depression, and the 1973–1989 period included the two major oil price shocks of the 1970s. Dividing the 1973–1989 period into two segments, we see that growth was very slow from 1973 to 1982, but quite rapid from 1982 to 1989.

Period	Average Annual RGNP Growth Rate
1900–1916	3.3%
1920–1940	2.4%
1947–1973	3.7%
1973–1989	2.5%
1973–1982	1.6%
1982–1989	3.9%

Economic analysis of the **factors contributing to growth** typically proceeds by grouping these factors into three categories: (1) growth in the capital stock, (2) growth in the labor supply, and (3) growth in factor productivity. **Factor productivity** is the amount of output produced per unit of factor (capital or labor) input. Changes in technology or government regulations or in the size or quality of the infrastructure affect productivity growth.

Sources of U.S. Growth Table 1 provides estimates of the sources of output growth for the United States for four periods. The estimates were derived by John W. Kendrick, one of the world's foremost experts on economic growth, and are based in part on work by Edward F. Denison, another world-renowned growth expert. The estimates show that economic growth in the 1973–1981 period slowed considerably from the rates of growth over the 1948–1966 and 1966–1973 periods. The major reason for this slump was a sharp decline in factor productivity growth, where this growth is measured by subtracting the growth of total factor inputs from the growth of real GNP. It represents the increase in output per unit of total factor input, where total factor input is a weighted average of labor and capital.

Until the 1973–1981 period, growth of both factor inputs and factor productivity contributed heavily to output growth. During the 1973–1981 period, growth in factor productivity apparently fell off dramatically. Since productivity growth accounted for nearly half of real output growth during the 1966–1973 period and well over half before that, according to Professor Kendrick's estimates, a permanent decline in productivity growth could lead to a permanent reduction in real output growth. Even researchers who believe that productivity

Factors contributing to growth
Typically classified into three categories: growth in the capital stock, growth in the supply of labor, and growth in factor productivity.

Factor productivity
Amount of output produced per unit of factor (labor or capital) input.

TABLE 1

Sources of growth of real GNP
Average annual percentage rates of change

	1929–1948	1948–1966	1966–1973	1973–1981
Real GNP	2.6	3.9	3.5	2.2
Total factor input	0.3	1.1	1.9	2.0
Labor	0.3	0.4	1.4	1.4
Capital	0.3	2.8	3.3	3.2
Total factor productivity	2.3	2.8	1.6	0.1

Note: Total factor input growth is a weighted average of growth of the labor supply and growth of the capital stock.

Sources: John W. Kendrick, "Productivity Trends and the Recent Slowdown: Historical Perspective, Causal Factors, and Policy Options," in William Fellner (ed.), *Contemporary Economic Problems, 1979* (Washington, D.C.: American Enterprise Institute, 1979), Table 4, pp. 33–34; and "Long-Term Economic Projection: Stronger U.S. Growth Ahead," *Southern Economic Journal* 50 (April 1984), Table 1, p. 953.

---

growth was lower before 1966 than Professor Kendrick's estimate agree that the major factor reducing output growth in the 1970s was a decline in productivity growth. Thus, economists have been greatly concerned about declining productivity over the past several years.[1]

Why Has Factor Productivity Growth Declined? Economists have suggested a number of possible explanations for the decline in factor productivity growth. One set of explanations is based on the idea that several things went wrong all at once. Professor Kendrick's analysis of the issue is representative of the findings of most economists studying the problem in the 1970s and 1980s. Professor Kendrick argues that the productivity growth slowdown had multiple sources, some of which will probably reverse themselves naturally. Others may provide cause for changes in government policy.

The decline in total factor productivity growth from the 1966–1973 period to the 1973–1981 period was quite sharp, from 1.6 percent per year to 0.1 percent. (Even the 1966–1973 rate of 1.6 percent was significantly lower than the 1948–1966 rate.) Professor Kendrick finds multiple causes for the decline, the most important being a decline in advances in knowledge and volume

---

[1] Stanford University economist Michael J. Boskin, appointed by President Bush in 1989 to be chairman of the Council of Economic Advisors, puts the importance of a 1 percent decline in the real GNP growth rate in perspective with the following statement:

> The power of compounding even modest increases in the growth rate is enormous. The United Kingdom, growing at only one percentage point per year less than the United States, France and Germany, transformed itself from the wealthiest society on earth to a relatively poor member of the Common Market in less than three generations.

"Tax Policy and Economic Growth: Lessons from the 1980s," *Journal of Economic Perspectives* 2 (Fall 1988), p. 72.

Growth Rates

The major topic of this chapter is economic growth, and the term *growth rate* is used frequently. A **growth rate** measures the percentage change in a variable per unit of time. It is typically calculated on an annual basis. Here we define precisely how to calculate growth rates.

On an annual basis, the growth rate of a variable equals the value of the variable in Year 2 divided by the value of the variable in Year 1, minus one. For example, to calculate the growth rate of GNP from 1975 to 1976, we would do the following: GNP growth rate = $(GNP_{1976}/GNP_{1975}) - 1$. Using actual values (in billions of dollars), we have $(\$1718.0/1549.2) - 1 = 1.109 - 1 = 0.109$, or 10.9 percent.

Calculating annual growth rates over periods not equal to one year is a bit more complicated. Calculating growth rates over longer periods also involves adjusting for compound growth. As the economy grows from year to year, the growth rate not only is based on the value of the variable being measured in Year 1; it also takes account of the growth in subsequent years. Let's use GNP growth from 1975 to illustrate this. We have seen that GNP grew by 10.9 percent from 1975 to 1976. It grew by another 11.6 percent, to $1918 billion, from 1976 to 1977. Now look at the growth from 1975 to 1977. We might calculate this growth as the 1975 GNP value times (1 plus the 1976 growth rate) — which yields 1976 GNP — times (1 plus the 1977 growth rate). That is, 1977 GNP equals $1549.2 × 1.109 × 1.116 = $1917.4. Allowing for rounding error of 0.6, the answer is correct. Now the point of this example: The growth rate was compounded. We multiplied (1 plus the 1976 growth rate) times (1 plus the 1977 growth rate) to derive the correct answer.

To take account of this principle when deriving the growth rate of a variable for periods of more than one year, we must calculate growth rates in the following manner. Call the beginning year of our calculation Year 0. The final year is Year F, where F is the number of years the variable has grown. We can then calculate the annual rate of growth of the variable over the period as $(1 + g) = (X_F/X_0)^{1/F}$. That is, $(1 + g)$ equals the ending value of X divided by the beginning value of X, the quotient raised to the $(1/F)$th power.

An example should clarify this. The GNP level in the United States in 1960 was $506.5 billion. In 1970, ten years later, it was $992.7 billion. Thus, X_0 equals 506.5, X_F is 992.7, and F is 10. Calculating the growth rate:

$$1 + g = (992.7/506.5)^{1/10} = 1.96^{.1} = 1.0696$$

Therefore, g, the growth rate, is $1.0696 - 1 = 0.0696$. The annual rate of growth of GNP from 1960 to 1970 was 6.96 percent.

Suppose we want to calculate the rate of growth of GNP over a period shorter than a year, such as a quarter. (Economists break the year into four three-month quarters. Many data variables are collected quarterly.) From the first quarter of 1981 to the second quarter of the same year, GNP rose from $2853.0 billion to $2885.8 billion. Since the growth of GNP is calculated over a quarter, F = 0.25 (one fourth of a year). The exponent in the growth formula will be $1/F = 1/0.25 = 4$. Using the growth formula, $1 + g = (\$2885.8/2853.0)^4 = 1.047$. Thus, $g = 0.047$ or 4.7 percent. From the first to the second quarter of 1981, GNP grew *at an annual rate* of 4.7 percent.

Growth rate
Percentage change in a variable per unit of time; usually calculated on an annual basis.

The Economist's *Tool Kit*

changes. Professor Kendrick attributes over one quarter of the decline in factor productivity growth to a decline in advances in knowledge. This category includes research and development spending, informal innovation, and the diffusion of the new knowledge produced by such research. (Diffusion is the process of transferring new knowledge from research institutions to the work place.) Knowledge does not affect output until it is taken out of the laboratory and put into the production process. A decline in spending on research and development, informal innovation, and diffusion combined to contribute 0.4 percentage point to the decline in the contribution of knowledge advances to productivity growth.

Volume changes capture the efficiencies resulting from large-scale production. Factories and offices operate more efficiently at high volume than at lower volume. The contribution of volume changes shifted from positive in earlier periods to negative in 1973–1981. The economy operated below its natural level, with unemployed resources, much of the time from 1973 to 1981. Thus, maximum production efficiency was not realized. Operating at less than the natural level of output contributed 0.5 percentage point to the decline in productivity growth. Thus, according to Professor Kendrick's estimates, together a decline in advances in knowledge and operating at a lower production volume accounted for more than half the decline in total factor productivity growth in the 1973–1981 period.

The remaining shortfall in factor productivity growth was accounted for by a number of things, including diminishing productivity in mining industries; smaller productivity gains from reallocating labor from the agricultural sector to nonagricultural jobs; and the effects of tighter government health, safety, and environmental regulations. However, the effects of each of these factors appear to have been minor, leaving a sizeable portion of the reduction in factor productivity growth unexplained.

Even if one accepts Professor Kendrick's estimates of the causes of lower productivity growth in the 1970s, an important question remains: Why did nearly all the factors contributing to productivity growth decline simultaneously? Did something happen to trigger the productivity decline?

Recent research has placed much of the blame for the productivity decline on the large energy price increases experienced in 1973–1975 and 1979–1980. Professor Dale W. Jorgenson of Harvard University argues that higher energy prices affect productivity growth in at least two ways.[2] First, higher energy prices increase the cost of production and reduce the output level. The oil price increases of the 1970s increased production costs and created severe worldwide recessions in 1974–1975 and 1980–1982. Factories and machines sat idle, and workers were unemployed. Excess capacity caused firms to invest less in capital goods, which may have contributed to a decline in innovation. Economist Michael Boskin argues that innovation and investment are linked.[3] In the process of investing in new capital, firms discover new production processes and new products. Thus, the recessions induced by higher energy prices may have negatively affected productivity growth both by causing capital to be utilized at inefficiently low rates and by stifling innovation.

---

[2]"Productivity and Postwar U.S. Economic Growth," *Journal of Economic Perspectives* 2 (Fall 1988), pp. 23–41.

[3]"Tax Policy and Economic Growth: Lessons from the 1980s," *Journal of Economic Perspectives* 2 (Fall 1988), pp. 71–97.

A second way in which higher energy prices reduce productivity growth is by limiting the ability of firms to put new technology and capital in place. Professor Jorgenson found that in most industries, firms must invest in more capital and use more energy to make use of new and improved technology. An increase in energy prices raises production costs and reduces the profitability of technological innovation. Firms invest in less technology, and the productivity gains that would have accompanied the use of improved technology disappear.

Recent work by economists David Aschauer[4] and Alicia Munnell[5] suggests another reason for the decline in productivity growth in the 1970s. The work of Professor Kendrick and other growth experts ignores government investment. However, government capital, especially **core infrastructure** such as highways, airports, mass transit facilities, electric and gas plants, water supply facilities, and sewers, increases the productivity of private capital. Private firms are able to produce more efficiently because of the efficient transportation and utility services provided by government.

The rate of growth of public capital fell from 4.7 percent in 1960–1969 to 2.8 percent in 1969–1973 and to 1.6 percent in 1973–1979. The decline in the growth of public capital coincided with the decline in output growth. Although analysts who ignore public capital blame the decline in output growth on a fall in factor productivity growth, perhaps as much as half of the decline may be due to slower public capital growth. In other words, the research of Aschauer and Munnell suggests that about half of the decline in factor productivity growth is accounted for by the fall in public investment.

Although productivity growth was somewhat higher in the 1980s than in the 1970s, it still was much lower than in the 1948–1973 period. It is not surprising that productivity growth rebounded somewhat in the 1980s, since real energy prices fell in the mid-1980s and the quality of the labor force continued to improve. However, research and development activities continued to lag in the 1980s. The United States spends a far smaller percentage of GNP on nondefense research and development than other industrial nations such as Japan and West Germany — about 1.9 percent of GNP in the United States in 1987, compared to 2.6 percent in West Germany and over 2.7 percent in Japan. Furthermore, the growth in the stock of public capital was even lower in the 1980s than in the 1970s.

A final contributor to the slowdown in factor productivity growth may be the shifting composition of U.S. production. A growing percentage of the labor force is employed in service jobs, rather than in manufacturing jobs. Most economists agree that productivity improvements are harder to come by in many types of service occupations than in manufacturing. Furthermore, the output of many service industries is poorly measured by government statistics. Thus, it is probable that both output growth and factor productivity growth in the service sector are underestimated. If so, the slowdown in factor productivity growth is real, but not quite so bad as the statistics indicate.

Of all the factors contributing to the slowdown in factor productivity growth, the two most significant appear to be the energy-price shocks that lowered

Core infrastructure
Public capital that contributes directly to the productivity of private capital.

SECTION RECAP
U.S. real output growth slowed dramatically in the 1970s. The primary reasons appear to be the decline in factor productivity growth caused by the en-
(continued)

---

[4]"Is Public Expenditure Productive?" *Journal of Monetary Economics* 23 (March 1989), pp. 177–200.

[5]"Why Has Productivity Growth Declined? Productivity and Public Investment," *New England Economic Review* (January/February 1990), pp. 3–22.

SECTION RECAP
(continued)
ergy-related recession of 1974–1975 and the decline in government spending on public capital (infrastructure).

capital utilization and investment in the 1970s and the slowdown in public capital growth that began around 1970.

Output growth depends on growth in the capital stock and the labor force, as well as productivity growth. (Professor Jorgenson rates productivity growth as the least important of the three.) The relatively low rate of investment in the United States concerns many economists as much as slow productivity growth. Both issues are also of increasing concern to politicians.

Role of Government in Promoting Growth

Not long ago the conventional wisdom was that active government participation in the economy could contribute significantly to the growth rate of real GNP. Today most economists are skeptical about such claims, with one important exception—investment in infrastructure. Although government clearly plays an important role in the process of economic growth, that role consists primarily of creating a proper business environment and providing incentives for research and development rather than being an active participant.

The research of Aschauer and Munnell suggests that the greatest direct contribution government can make to economic growth is providing and maintaining the stock of public capital. Reversing the decline in investment in public capital could contribute significantly to output growth. It is well known that a high percentage of the nation's bridges need to be upgraded or replaced. Highway maintenance is also badly needed. Many airports are operating at inefficiently high levels, and other deficiencies in the stock of public capital are becoming more acute. Correcting such deficiencies could directly increase the economy's growth rate.

Although the government can potentially affect economic growth by influencing the growth of the labor supply, the impact of government policies on this variable is generally small. Relaxing restrictions on immigration would have a larger impact on the labor supply that any other government policy. Tax and welfare policies have some impact on labor supply, but the effect is too small to significantly influence economic growth over long periods of time. Eliminating mandatory retirement laws would allow a larger percentage of the older population to hold jobs. Beyond that, government can do little to affect the size of the labor supply.

Policies that seek to increase economic growth by increasing the growth rate of the private capital stock must do one thing—increase the after-tax rate of return on capital. However, the U.S. tax system is antisaving and antiinvestment. The income from investments in productive capital is routinely double taxed. Corporations must pay taxes on their profits, currently at a rate of up to 34 percent. A corporation paying the top corporate tax rate can pay out at most 66 percent of its profits to shareholders in the form of dividends. Individuals must pay income taxes as well, at rates as high as 33 percent. Shareholders paying taxes at the 33 percent rate end up with only 44¢ in after-tax income from every dollar of profit earned by their corporations. Thus, the effective tax rate on income from capital is as high as 56 percent. Such a high tax rate prevents many people from purchasing stock in corporations, making it more difficult for corporations to raise funds for investment purposes. Corporate profit taxes also reduce the amount of retained earnings (business savings) available for investment purposes.

Ultimately, all investment spending must be financed by savings; income that is used for consumption cannot be used to purchase capital goods. Recall that in the aggregate, spending on newly produced goods and services must equal aggregate income. In equation form:

$$C + I + G + NX = C + S + T$$

where the left side of the equation represents spending on domestic production and the right side shows that income can be consumed, saved, or paid to the government as taxes. Note that consumption (C) appears on both sides of the equation. We can cancel it out, leaving:

$$I + G + NX = S + T$$

Rearranging the equation, we can obtain:

$$I = S + (T - G) - NX$$

In words, the amount of investment spending equals domestic savings plus the government's budget surplus minus net exports. Note that $-NX$ represents the amount of foreign savings flowing into the United States to purchase U.S. financial assets.[6] If the government runs a budget deficit, $T - G$ is negative and, other things equal, investment must fall. This happens because the government absorbs savings to finance the deficit. A decline in investment can only be prevented if domestic saving increases (S rises) or if more savings flow into the economy from other countries (NX falls or becomes more negative). Thus, government budget policies are a potentially important factor affecting the growth of the capital stock.

Finally, government may be able to affect the rate of productivity growth through its spending on research and development. Although many people decry the U.S. government's low level of nondefense research and development spending, evidence suggests that government-financed research and development has a smaller impact on productivity than industrial research and development.[7] Thus, policies that encourage firms to invest in research and development, such as permitting competing firms to cooperate on research projects, may be more important than direct government spending. In 1990, the Bush administration began to advocate such industrial cooperation as a way for U.S. firms to compete against foreign companies that do not face the legal restrictions on cooperation restraining U.S. firms.

The federal government's contributions to economic growth during the 1980s were decidedly mixed. Three major tax acts became law. The first two, the *Economic Recovery and Tax Act* of 1981 and the *Tax Equity and Fiscal Responsibility Act* of 1982, apparently encouraged growth by reducing the cost of investment, increasing the after-tax return on investment, and increasing the after-tax return on savings. These acts lowered marginal income tax rates (the rates paid on the last dollar of income), extended investment tax credits, instituted tax credits for research and development, and allowed savers to accumulate savings tax free in Individual Retirement Accounts. The third major

---

[6]When NX is negative, imports exceed exports. Foreigners receive more dollars from Americans than they return in the purchase of goods and services. They use those dollars to buy American financial assets.

[7]Zvi Griliches, "Productivity Puzzles and R&D: Another Nonexplanation," *Journal of Economic Perspectives* 2 (Fall 1988), p. 13.

Why the Disagreement?

Does the United States Have a Savings Crisis?

It is a well-known fact that the U.S. national saving rate has fallen in recent years. The national saving rate measures the saving of households, businesses, and governmental units as a percentage of net national product. Not only has this rate fallen; the U.S. national saving rate is also lower than the corresponding rate in most other developed countries, including Germany, Canada, France, and especially Japan. The Japanese national saving rate, as commonly measured, has been over three times as high as the U.S. rate most of the time for the past twenty-five years.

Many people, including a number of politicians, regard these savings data as ominous. After all, economic growth depends on investment, and investment must be financed by savings. Critics allege that persistent overconsumption and undersaving by Americans has contributed to the decline in U.S. economic growth. They note that since 1960 output growth in Japan has been three times as high as U.S. output growth.

In the face of such statistics, it is surprising to find a growing number of economists arguing that the United States does *not* have a savings crisis. The statistics are there for everyone to see. Why the disagreement?

Most economists who believe that the United States does not have a savings crisis base their arguments to some extent on a criticism of conventional measures of saving. The U.S. National Income Accounts are not directly comparable to other countries' national accounts. One major difference is that the U.S. accounts treat all government purchases as consumption expenditures, while other countries treat government investment as saving. Northwestern University economist Robert Eisner has estimated that simply counting government capital formation as saving would have raised U.S. saving by $53 billion in 1988—an increase of 41 percent.*

Other differences in national income accounting practices exist. For example, Japan measures capital consumption (depreciation) at historical cost, that is, at the original cost of the worn-out capital goods. The United States measures depreciation at replacement cost. During inflationary periods, replacement cost is higher than historical cost. When Professor Fumio Hayashi of the University of Pennsylvania carefully calculated the Japanese saving rate on the same

---

SECTION RECAP

Government can affect growth through its tax policies, which affect the profitability of private in-
(continued)

act, the *Tax Reform Act* of 1986, offset the earlier acts to some extent. Although individual income tax rates were lowered, the tax base was broadened (more income was taxed), and corporations were taxed more heavily. Investment tax credits were eliminated and other tax rules were changed to ensure that corporations pay more taxes. All these changes made investment less attractive.

Throughout the 1980s the federal government ran large budget deficits. To a significant extent, the deficits were financed by inflows of foreign savings. Negative U.S. net exports allowed foreigners to accumulate dollars, which they used both to purchase U.S. government bonds and to buy bonds and equity issued by U.S. corporations. The inflow of foreign savings limited the effect of the U.S. government's budget deficits on investment. Without such inflows, a lack of funding would have reduced investment spending. Nevertheless, many researchers believe that the deficits reduced investment spending by raising the cost of borrowing and by creating uncertainty about the tax laws. Some firms may have postponed investment projects because they expected the federal government to increase taxes to reduce the deficit. Not knowing what form a tax increase will take may cause firms to prefer to wait until after a tax hike to make investment decisions.

As the United States enters the 1990s it finds itself in an increasingly competitive world. Most industrial nations appear to have higher rates of

basis as the U.S. saving rate is calculated, he found that much of the difference between the two nations' saving rates disappears when the same accounting methods are used.** The Japanese saving rate rose steadily from 1957 to 1970, when it was more than double the U.S. rate. From 1970 to 1981 the Japanese rate fell. It was about equal to the U.S. rate from 1978 to 1981. Since 1981 the Japanese rate has again risen, while the U.S. rate has fallen. Consequently, the Japanese rate currently exceeds the U.S. rate, but by a much smaller amount than most people think. Even granting that standardized accounting techniques remove much of the difference between the saving rates of the United States and other countries, it remains true that the U.S. saving rate has fallen significantly since the mid-1970s. Does this decline signal problems for the U.S. economy? Many people, including economists, believe it does. They argue that lower U.S. saving implies one of two things: Either U.S. investment must decline or U.S. firms must borrow from foreign savers. A decline in investment will reduce economic growth. Borrowing from foreigners will lower the U.S. standard of living in the future, as Americans send interest and dividend payments abroad. There is no disagreement about the two possible consequences of low U.S. saving. There is considerable disagreement about how harmful borrowing from foreigners is. Some economists believe that foreign-financed investment increases the nation's wealth to such an extent that U.S. citizens will be better off in the future even after making interest payments to foreign savers. Other economists argue that borrowing from foreigners is simply a passing phase. They note that the United States supplied savings to other nations in the recent past.

The issue of saving and investment is complex enough to support a great deal of controversy. Uncertainty about the ultimate effects of a low national saving rate is sure to feed disagreements into the future.

*Robert Eisner, "Low U.S. Savings Rate: A Myth," *The New York Times* March 1, 1990, p. A19.

**Fumio Hayashi, "Is Japan's Savings Rate High?" Federal Reserve Bank of Minneapolis *Quarterly Review* (Spring 1989), pp. 3–9.

saving, investment, and research and development spending than the United States. The tax rates on investment income paid by U.S. taxpayers are among the highest in the developed world, the U.S. government spends less on nondefense research and development than the governments of most industrialized nations, and government investment in public capital is quite low. The challenge facing U.S. policymakers is to address these problems in the face of large budget deficits that force politicians to talk constantly about tax increases. The economic performance of the United States in the 1990s may depend to a significant degree on how well policymakers address the growth issue.

SECTION RECAP
(continued)
vestment; its budget policies, which affect the national saving rate and the rate of interest; and through the level of public investment in infrastructure.

Theoretical Models and Reality

Economic growth implies change. It is easy to imagine an evenly growing economy, where every industry grows at the same rate, productivity grows evenly across industries, and the growing income is allocated evenly across the growing population. Such an imaginary economy is changing, but only quantitatively. Qualitatively it remains the same. However, when a real economy grows, it changes both quantitatively and qualitatively.

The process of growth can be traumatic. Established industries encounter difficulties and begin to decline, even as new industries are born. Jobs transfer

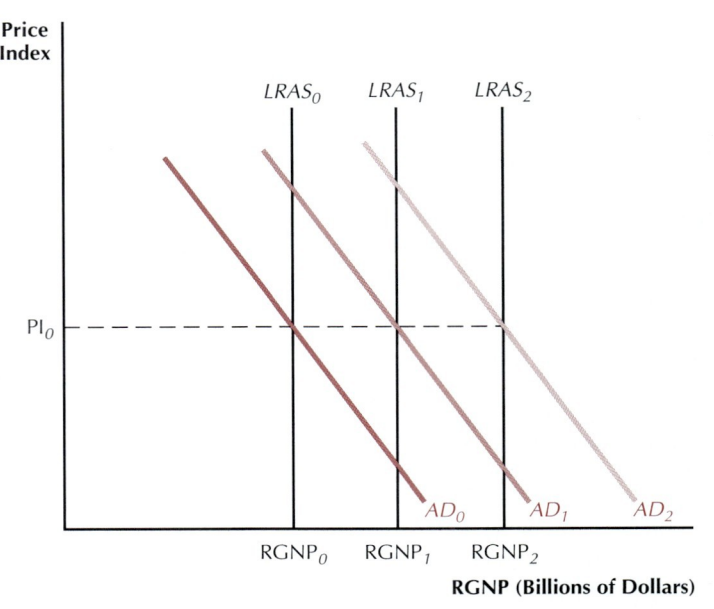

FIGURE 6
Theoretical growth process. Although in theory growth looks orderly, the aggregate model covers up major microeconomic changes across the economy. A real economy changes both quantitatively and qualitatively.

from one area of the country (the Rust Belt) to another (the Sun Belt). Workers who have prospered in the older industries (for example, steelworkers) find their jobs in danger. Yet positions go unfilled in the newer industries (such as computer software) because workers lack the skills to fill them. The actual growth process might not be smooth.

Economic theory often makes the growth process appear much smoother and easier than it is. The long-run aggregate supply curve shifts out over time, and so does the aggregate demand curve. The result, theoretically, is a series of equilibrium points, as shown in Figure 6. So long as aggregate demand and aggregate supply grow at the same rate, not even the price level need change. It all appears so peaceful, so ordered.

Because economic theory makes the process of economic change appear so orderly, theory sometimes becomes the enemy of the market economy whose behavior it seeks to explain. Theory abstracts from most of the details that make up reality. It seeks to explain some important relationships, but ignores many other relationships that are of great importance to some people. Although the growth in real GNP illustrated in Figure 6 may describe the overall position of the actual economy very well, it ignores all the redistributions among industries and individuals that accompany growth.

If people believe that the ordered, smooth growth described by the economic model is how their actual economy *should be* growing, they may become very dissatisfied with the actual growth pattern experienced. The knee-jerk reaction of many dissatisfied people is to demand that government do something to correct the situation. Yet government can do very little to smooth out the process of growth without stifling growth. Policies designed to protect existing industries, jobs, and ways of life invariably reduce economic growth. Although reduced growth can be traded off for less qualitative change, it does not seem possible to maintain a high rate of economic growth and prohibit qualitative change.

Price-Level Growth

Real factors limit the growth of output over time. Output grows more rapidly or more slowly only as the inputs into the production process grow more rapidly or more slowly. Because the growth of the capital stock, the labor force, and the level of technology have real limits, output growth is also limited.

The long-run behavior of the price level is determined by the growth of aggregate demand relative to the growth of real output. Figure 7 illustrates this. Output grows as the long-run aggregate supply curve shifts outward over time. If aggregate demand grows more rapidly than aggregate supply, the price level trends upward [Figure 7 (a)]. Should aggregate demand grow more slowly than aggregate supply, the price level trends downward [Figure 7 (b)].

As Figure 8 shows, the U.S. aggregate price level has trended upward during all but two decades of this century. Every increase in the aggregate price level does not indicate excessive aggregate demand growth; a decrease in aggregate supply can move the economy up along a stationary aggregate demand curve to a higher price level. However, when the price level rises over long periods of time in a growing economy, aggregate demand must have grown faster than aggregate supply.

Money and Excessive AD Growth The theory of aggregate demand recognizes that a number of factors can increase or decrease aggregate demand and thus

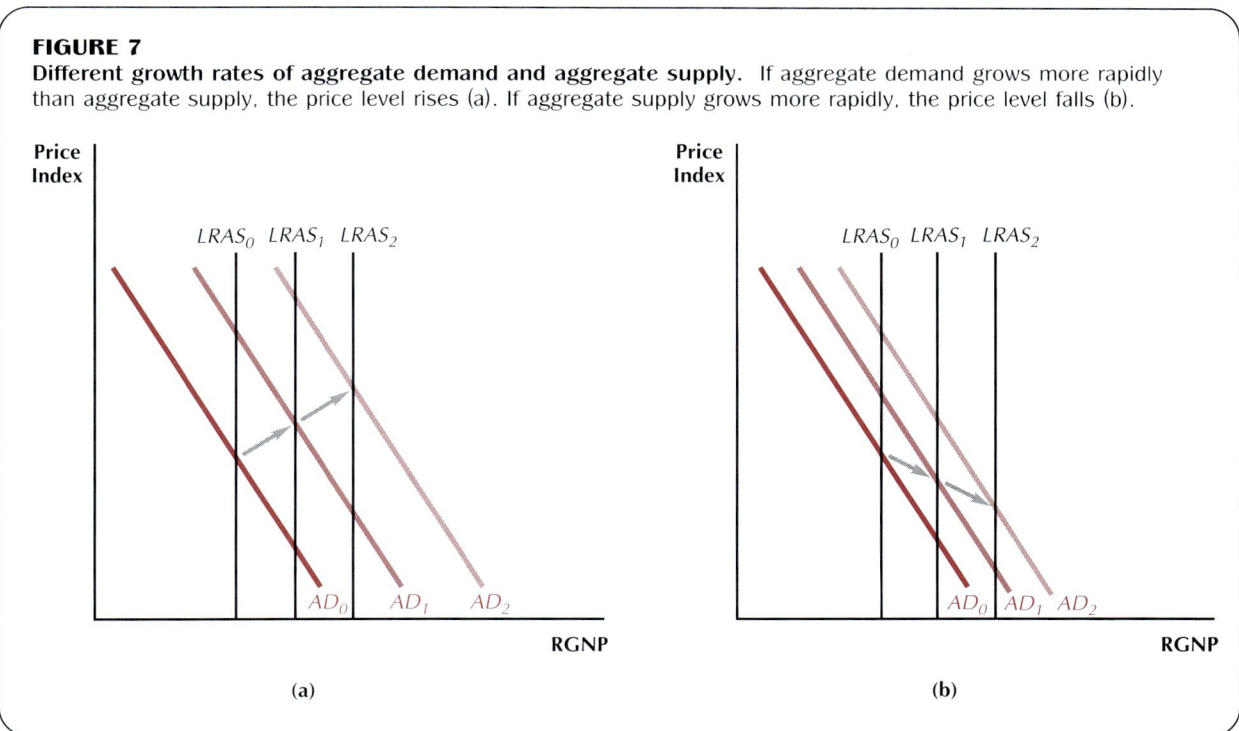

FIGURE 7
Different growth rates of aggregate demand and aggregate supply. If aggregate demand grows more rapidly than aggregate supply, the price level rises (a). If aggregate supply grows more rapidly, the price level falls (b).

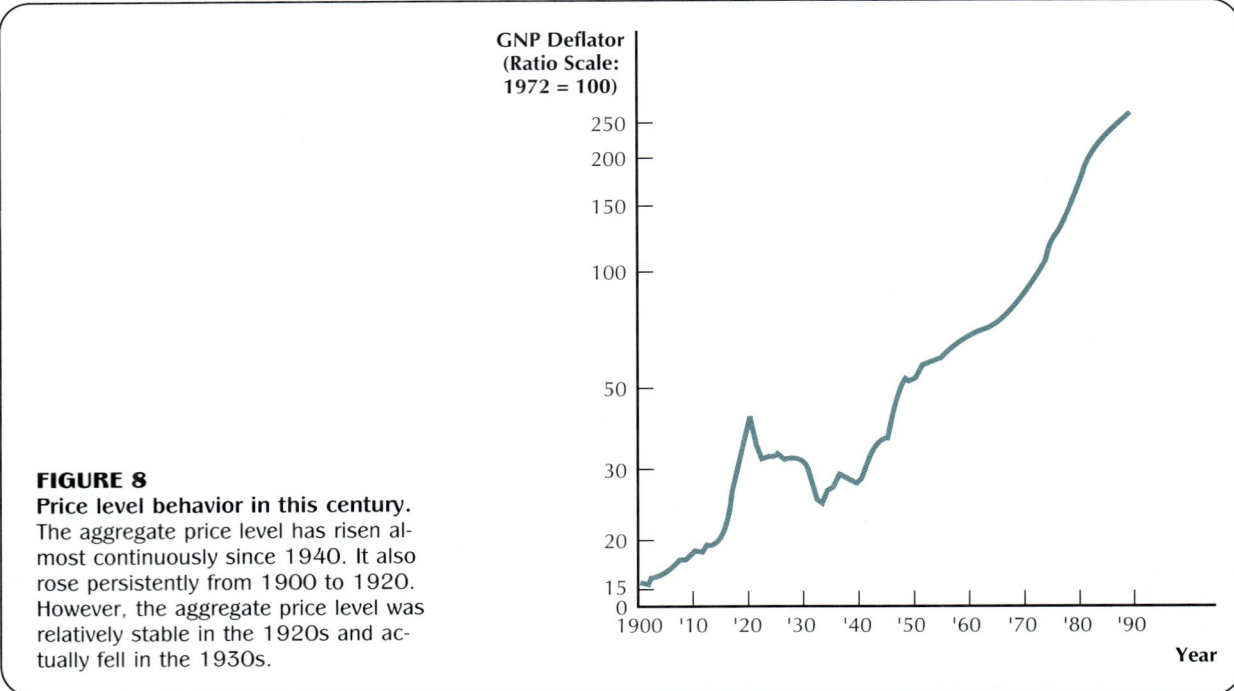

FIGURE 8
Price level behavior in this century.
The aggregate price level has risen almost continuously since 1940. It also rose persistently from 1900 to 1920. However, the aggregate price level was relatively stable in the 1920s and actually fell in the 1930s.

affect the price level. Most of the determinants of aggregate demand cannot themselves grow without limit. However, one determinant of spending may be able to grow without limit. Unless a physical commodity serves as the economy's basic unit of money, no real limit on the growth of the money supply exists. If money consists only of pieces of paper or numbers on the books (or computers) of banks, then the quantity of money can be expanded without any real limit. Excessive money supply growth can generate excessive aggregate demand growth over long periods of time.

A look back at the factors affecting aggregate demand shows why most of them must be rejected as sources of inflation — defined as a *sustained* increase in the aggregate price level. Consumption primarily depends on permanent income. Because saving is positive, consumers spend less than their incomes over protracted periods. Thus, consumption spending grows no faster than income over long periods of time and cannot be the source of increases in the rate of growth of income and spending. Similarly, investment spending depends on income and the real interest rate. Firms invest only to the extent that they believe they will be able to profitably sell the goods they produce. Rapid growth of investment spending for years on end would increase productive capacity to an unprofitable extent. Technological advances make investment projects more profitable and raise investment spending, but they also increase aggregate supply. There is no reason to believe that such innovations should be inflationary.

The rate of growth of government purchases of goods and services is determined more by political than economic factors. But even here spending is limited, since every dollar of government purchases must be financed. Increased government spending requires government to raise taxes, borrow in the credit market, or print money. There is a natural limit to how much tax revenue can be raised (before taxpayers revolt), and borrowing takes funds away from private investors, causing investment spending to fall. However, *under the present monetary system, there is no natural limit to how much money can be created by the government through the central bank.*

Perhaps the oldest economic theory still adhered to by economists is the **quantity theory of money**. In the form accepted by most economists, the quantity theory states that over significant periods of time the inflation rate is closely related to the rate of growth of the money supply. If the money supply grows rapidly for a prolonged period, the inflation rate will increase. If the money supply growth rate falls, so will the inflation rate. *Many factors can cause the aggregate price level to move up or down for a short period of time, but a sustained inflation must be fed by rapid money-supply growth.*

The Empirical Connection Between Money Growth and Inflation Figure 9 plots the growth rates of a broad measure of the money supply (called M2) and the **GNP deflator** for the 1900–1989 period. (M2 includes currency, checking

Quantity theory of money
Asserts that, in the long run, the rate of inflation is closely related to the rate of growth of the money supply, while the growth rate of real GNP is unrelated to the growth rate of money.

GNP (implicit price) deflator
A price index covering all goods and services included in GNP; uses current-year quantity weights.

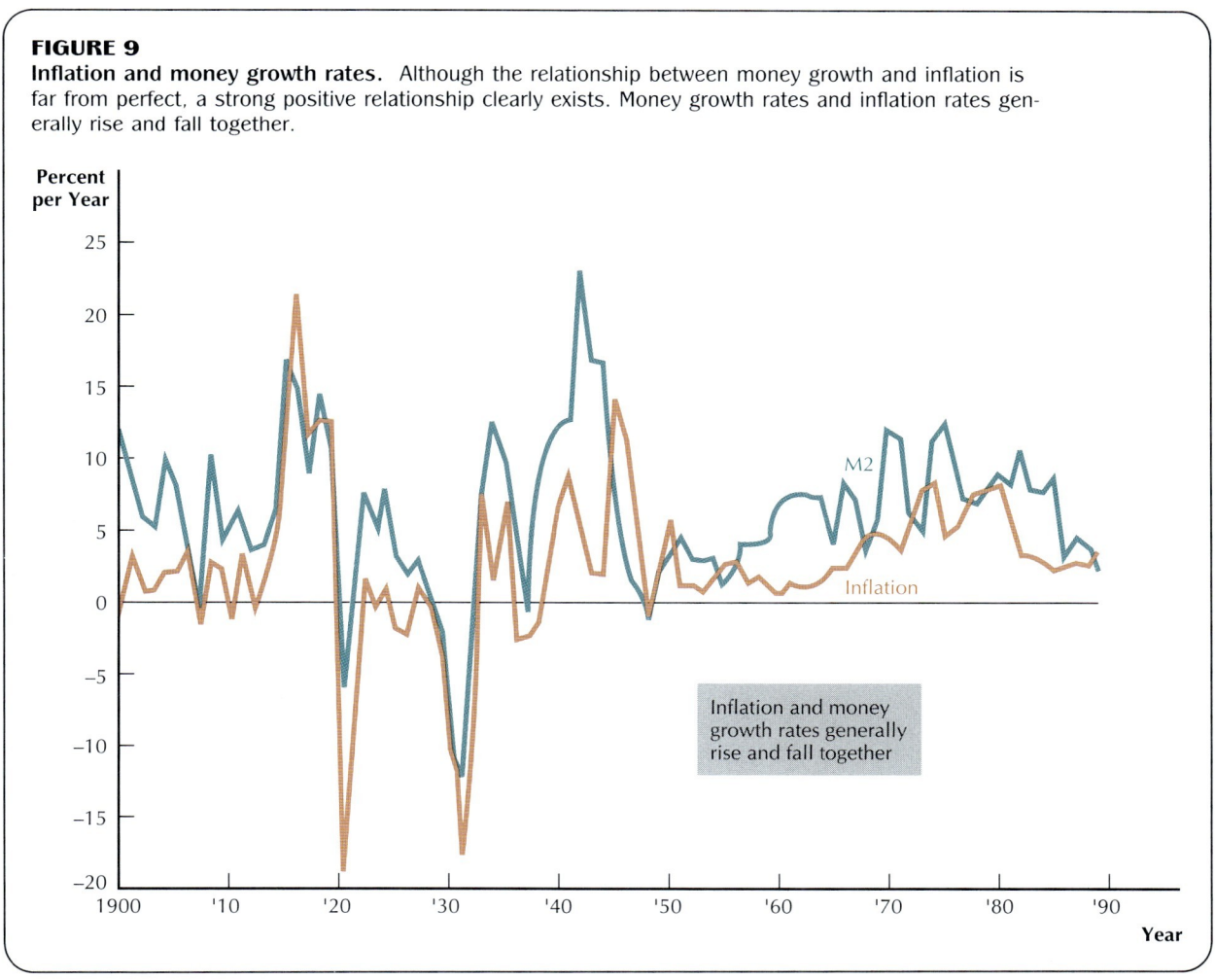

FIGURE 9
Inflation and money growth rates. Although the relationship between money growth and inflation is far from perfect, a strong positive relationship clearly exists. Money growth rates and inflation rates generally rise and fall together.

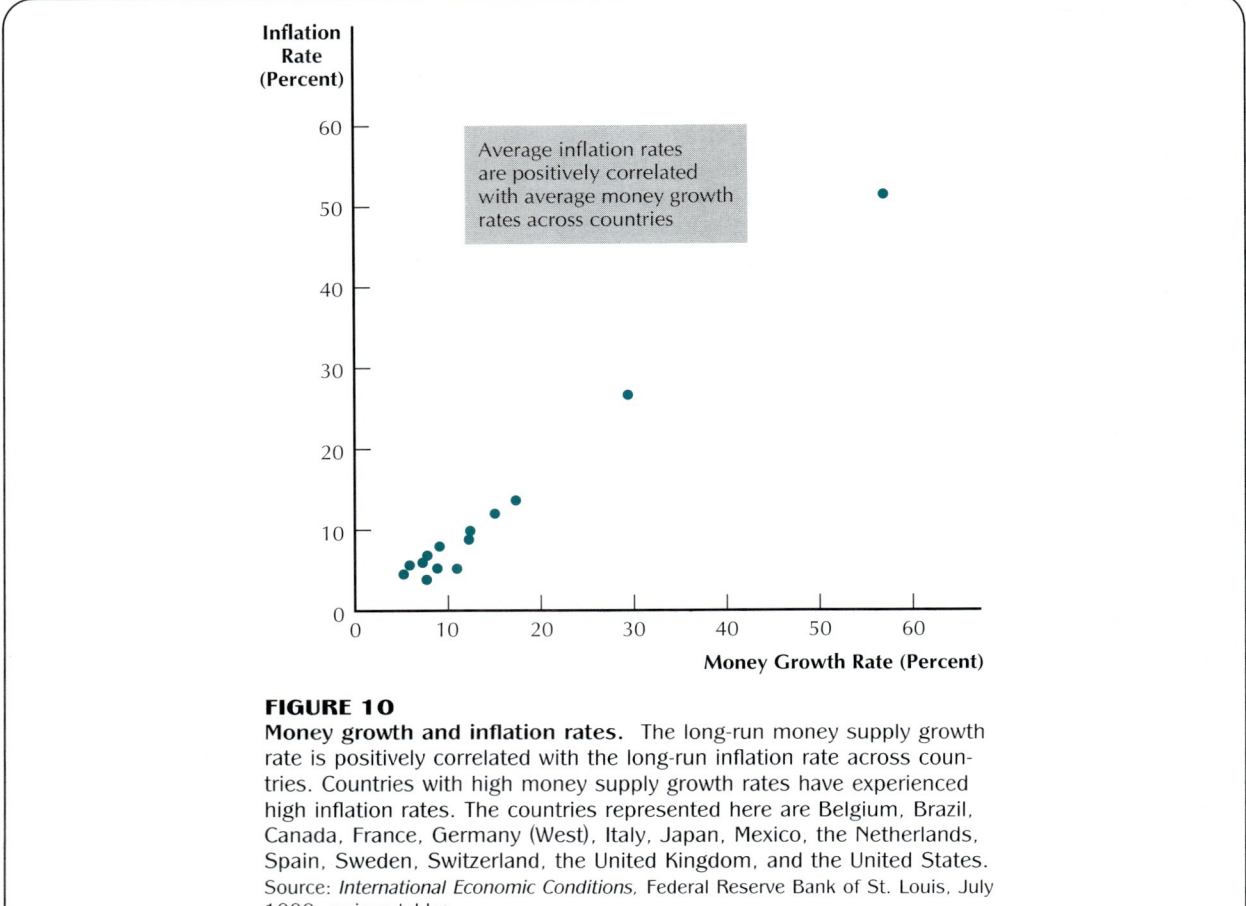

FIGURE 10
Money growth and inflation rates. The long-run money supply growth rate is positively correlated with the long-run inflation rate across countries. Countries with high money supply growth rates have experienced high inflation rates. The countries represented here are Belgium, Brazil, Canada, France, Germany (West), Italy, Japan, Mexico, the Netherlands, Spain, Sweden, Switzerland, the United Kingdom, and the United States.
Source: *International Economic Conditions*, Federal Reserve Bank of St. Louis, July 1990, various tables.

deposits, savings deposits, and small time deposits.) Although the relationship between money supply growth and inflation is certainly not perfect, a relationship clearly exists. High rates of money-supply growth have been accompanied by high inflation rates—and low money growth by low inflation—throughout the twentieth century. Earlier monetary history also corroborates this relationship. Nobel laureate Milton Friedman and his colleague Anna Jacobson Schwartz, in a massive study entitled *A Monetary History of the United States, 1867–1960*, concluded that growth in the money supply was the primary determinant of price-level movements over the entire ninety-four-year period they studied. (We discuss why the money supply might grow so rapidly as to cause inflation in the chapter entitled Monetary Policy: A Further Treatment.)

Figure 10 illustrates the relationship between money growth and inflation over long periods across countries. The figure shows that countries with higher money growth rates also have higher inflation rates. (That is, higher money growth is positively correlated with higher inflation.) A strong positive relationship between a nation's money-supply growth rate and its inflation rate clearly exists.

The relationship between year-to-year price level movements and money-supply growth is not nearly so close. Over periods as short as two or three years, many factors can shift the aggregate demand and aggregate supply curves enough to change the price level significantly. In addition, changes in the money supply often affect aggregate demand with a lag (a delay). Thus, we can say that (1) short-run changes in the money supply and the price level are largely unrelated to one another, and (2) long-run money-supply growth and inflation are highly positively related.[8] The two statements are not inconsistent.

In the following chapter we turn our attention from the long run to the short run. Rather than examining the long-run tendencies of the economy, we examine the immediate movements of output and prices in response to changes in aggregate demand and aggregate supply.

SECTION RECAP
Over long periods the rate of growth of the price level is strongly related to the rate of growth of the money supply. Persistent inflation cannot occur without rapid money growth. However, over short periods, many factors besides the money supply can cause the price level to change.

Summary

The determinants of long-run output and price-level growth differ significantly from the determinants of short-run movements in output and prices. This chapter has used the **long-run model** of the economy to analyze the behavior of output and prices and to suggest the factors that are important for long-run output and price level growth in real economies.

Factors affecting the position of the **LRAS curve** include resource supplies, in particular the labor force (which has both quantity and quality dimensions), the size of the capital stock (including public capital), the state of technology, and the market organization of the economy.

The **long-run price level–RGNP equilibrium** position is determined by the intersection of the AD and LRAS curves. The equilibrium output level is totally determined by the position of the aggregate supply curve in the long run. Changes in the factors affecting LRAS determine the long-run changes in RGNP.

The factors determining real **output growth** include growth in the labor supply, growth in the capital stock, and growth in total factor productivity. During the 1970s **total factor productivity growth** declined sharply. A number of factors apparently combined to produce this decline, but the major factors triggering the slowdown in productivity growth were probably the increase in energy prices and the reduction in government investment in infrastructure. Government policies to enhance productivity growth include providing infrastructure, changing tax law to encourage investment and research and development spending by private businesses and saving by households, directly supporting research and development, increasing government aid for education and training, and removing unnecessary regulations that reduce economic efficiency.

The final topic examined in this chapter was **inflation.** If aggregate demand growth persistently exceeds aggregate supply growth, inflation results. Although many factors can affect the aggregate price level for short periods of time, sustained inflation requires sustained growth of the money supply.

---

[8]This is exactly the conclusion of one recent study. See Gerald P. Dwyer and R.W. Hafer, "Is Money Irrelevant?" St. Louis Federal Reserve Bank *Review* (May/June 1988), pp. 3–17.

Questions for Thought

Knowledge Questions

1. Why is the long-run aggregate supply curve vertical?
2. Why does output depend totally on aggregate supply and not at all on aggregate demand in the long run?
3. Define the term *total factor productivity*. What are the major factors that seem to affect the growth of total factor productivity?
4. Inflation is defined as a sustained increase in the general price level. Explain why inflation cannot be blamed on consumers who spend too much (as at least one U.S. president argued in the 1970s).

Application Questions

5. Suppose the money supply were based on the quantity of gold held by the government. The gold supply expands only as fast as gold can be mined. What effect would this have on the long-run trend of prices? What would be the effect if gold output grew at a slower rate than the output of other goods and services?
6. Economists have discovered that the U.S. real GNP growth rate can be closely approximated by the equation:

$$rgnp = .7l + .3k$$

where *rgnp* is the growth rate of real GNP, l is the growth rate of the labor supply, and k is the growth rate of capital. Suppose that $l = .03$ and $k = .05$ initially, so that $rgnp = .7(.03) + .3(.05) = .036$. If the capital stock equals $6 trillion and net investment equals $300 billion initially, to what level would *investment* spending have to increase to increase *rgnp* by 1 percentage point? Do you think such an increase is feasible?
7. Again using the *rgnp* formula from the previous question, calculate the implied growth rate of the capital stock by decade given the following data on *rgnp* and l.

	rgnp	l
1950–1960	.0330	.0113
1960–1970	.0379	.0174
1970–1980	.0281	.0260
1980–1989	.0296	.0165

Synthesis Questions

8. The process of economic growth is uneven. Some industries grow rapidly, while others grow slowly or shrink. Using the discussion of the factors affecting growth given in this chapter as background, discuss why we should expect growth to be uneven across industries.
9. Changes in economic policy often have different consequences in the long run than they do in the short run. Describe the immediate effects and long-run consequences of the following policy actions:
    a. A reduction in corporate profits taxes causes investment spending on new plant and equipment to increase sharply.
    b. An increase in government benefits for the elderly causes Americans to save less and consume more. (This is a complex one.)
    c. Stricter government regulations force heavy industry to purchase and install costly pollution-control devices.
    d. The government eliminates income taxes on interest earned on savings.

10. During the 1980s, many critics of U.S. government defense spending charged that, by spending more on the defense of Western Europe than European nations spend, the government hurt the international competitiveness of the U.S. economy. Under what conditions would such criticisms be valid?
11. Use the theory of consumption demand, presented in the chapter on aggregate demand, to construct an argument refuting the claim that consumers are the source of sustained inflation.

OVERVIEW

In this chapter we turn our attention to the behavior of the economy over relatively short periods of time. The long-run model of the preceding chapter serves as the benchmark for our evaluation of short-run macroeconomic behavior. Although the economy tends toward the natural output level over time, in the short run—which may last several years—output can deviate from the natural level by large amounts.

The Short-Run Model: The Economy with Wage and Price Rigidities

Short-run economic behavior differs from long-run behavior primarily because of rigidities that prevent prices from moving immediately to their new long-run equilibrium levels. In the short run, wages are usually sticky; they do not move immediately to their new long-run equilibrium value when labor demand rises or falls. Consequently, both the amount of labor employed and output produced change.

We begin the chapter with a discussion of short-run equilibrium. Such equilibrium positions are only temporary, because the labor market is not in long-run equilibrium. As the labor market adjusts to new market conditions, the short-run aggregate supply curve shifts, moving the economy to a new equilibrium position.

How rapidly wages adjust to changes in labor demand depends to a significant extent on how rapidly price level expectations adjust. We examine the effect of changes in autonomous economic variables on macroeconomic equilibrium under two different assumptions about how expectations are formed. We also consider the effects of contracts on labor market and macroeconomic behavior.

The real test of the worth of a macroeconomic model is how well it explains the actual behavior of the economy. We therefore use the short-run model to explain recent U.S. economic history. The model's usefulness is demonstrated by its ability to explain all the major macroeconomic

CHAPTER 26

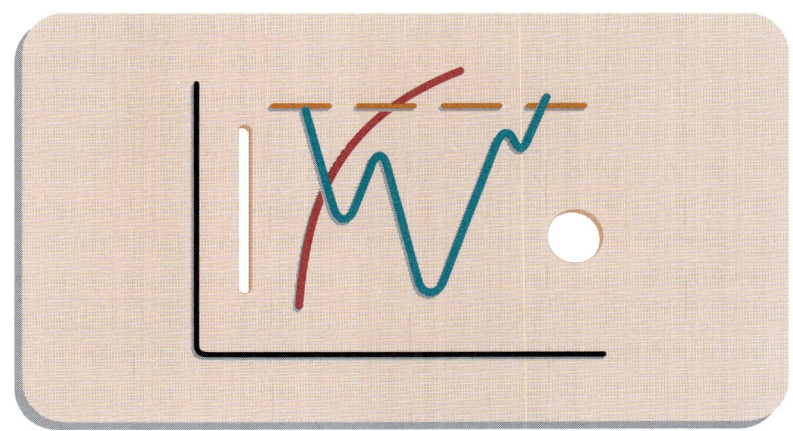

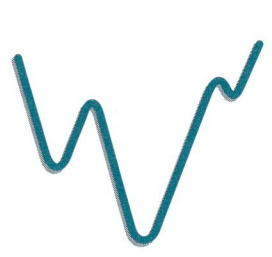

events of the past two decades.

Short-run economic behavior in the United States has often been characterized by instability in output and employment. This instability has led to attempts to stabilize the economy through macroeconomic policy. We conclude the chapter with an introduction to the theory of stabilization policy.

Learning Objectives
After reading and studying this chapter, you will be able to:

1. List the factors that affect the position of the SRAS curve.
2. Define what is meant by *rational expectations* and explain how they affect the economy's short-run behavior.
3. Discuss the effect the form of the consumption function has on the stability of aggregate demand.
4. Determine how long a particular SRAS curve will remain stationary.
5. Use the AD–SRAS model to explain recent U.S. economic history.
6. List the ways government might stabilize real GNP over time.
7. List some of the problems the government is likely to encounter when attempting to stabilize RGNP.

Sticky Wages and Output Movements

We begin our discussion of short-run price level and real GNP movements by assuming that the economy is in long-run equilibrium, with output at its natural level. Since the labor market is in long-run equilibrium, no pressure for wage or price changes exists. Starting from long-run equilibrium at point A in Figure 1, suppose that aggregate demand increases in response to a change in monetary or fiscal policy or to some autonomous change in investment or consumption spending. The effect of this increase on real GNP depends on how wages and prices behave.

If workers do not foresee the increase in aggregate demand, they will be surprised by any price level increase. So long as the expected price level remains constant (PI^e does not change), the labor supply curve does not shift. As the demand for labor rises in Figure 1 (a), employment increases from L_N to L_1. The higher employment level enables firms to produce more goods and services. Thus, output increases as aggregate demand rises. However, higher marginal costs force firms to increase prices. Figure 1 (b) shows that the economy moves from its original equilibrium position at point A, where output equals its natural level, to a new equilibrium at point B, where output exceeds its natural level.

Point B is only a temporary equilibrium, because the labor market is not in long-run equilibrium. Workers expected a price level of PI_0; the actual price

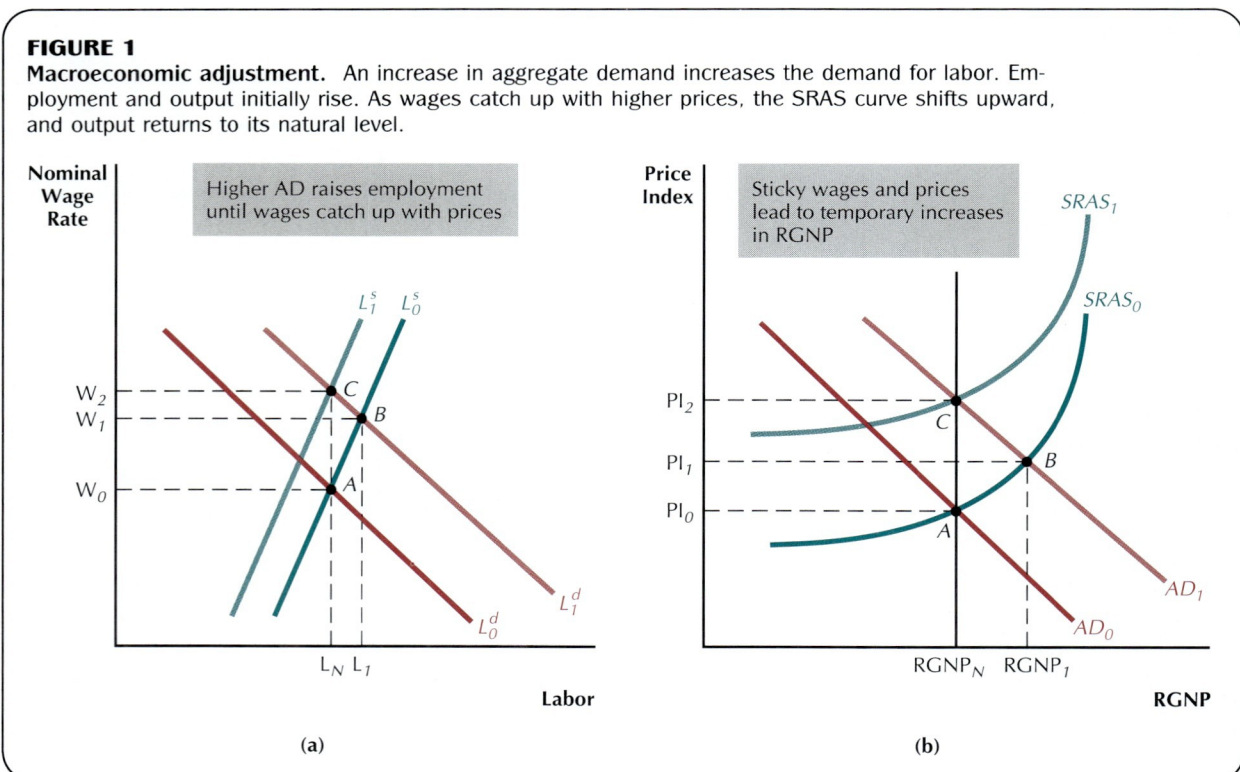

FIGURE 1
Macroeconomic adjustment. An increase in aggregate demand increases the demand for labor. Employment and output initially rise. As wages catch up with higher prices, the SRAS curve shifts upward, and output returns to its natural level.

level is PI_1. When workers realize that prices are higher than expected, they demand higher nominal wages to offset the higher prices. The labor supply curve shifts to the left as a higher expected price level is incorporated into wage demands. The average wage rate rises and employment falls.

Rising wages push up the costs of production. Firms must raise their prices even more to cover the higher costs. The SRAS curve shifts to the left as production costs increase. At the prevailing level of aggregate demand, AD_1 in Figure 1 (b), firms produce fewer goods and services and sell them at higher prices. The price level and the average wage rate continue to rise, and output and employment continue to fall, until a new long-run equilibrium is reached at point C. At that point, the expected price level once again equals the actual price level. Workers have caught up with higher prices, and the actual real wage rate equals the expected real wage rate.

The pattern of price level and real GNP movements traced out in Figure 1 (b) is common in developed economies. Increases in aggregate demand initially drive output above its natural level, but eventually affect only the price level. Actual output movements depend on how rapidly wages adjust to higher prices and on how fully the economy's productive capacity is being used. If the economy is initially operating below the natural output level, output can increase a great deal without generating much pressure on prices. If output is initially at or above its natural level, higher aggregate demand produces a smaller output effect and a larger price level increase.[1] The shape of the SRAS curve depends primarily on the amount that marginal costs rise as production becomes less efficient because of overutilization of capital equipment, higher transportation costs, and overtime wages. The SRAS curve becomes quite steep to the right of the natural output level, as productive capacity is stretched to the limit.

How rapidly SRAS shifts following a change in aggregate demand depends on how quickly wages adjust to higher or lower prices. Wage adjustment, in turn, depends on how expectations are formed and on the existence or absence of labor contracts that prevent wages from adjusting to a new expected price level.

SECTION RECAP
When wages move slowly in response to aggregate demand changes, firms have an incentive to change their levels of production. Thus, aggregate demand changes cause short-term movements in real GNP.

Expectations Formation

The amount of labor supplied depends on the expected real wage rate. Although workers know with certainty the nominal wage they are offered, they do not know how the price level will behave in the upcoming period. Therefore, workers must predict the price level to form an expectation of the real wage being offered. Clearly, some method of estimating the expected price level is needed.

Economists have suggested two different hypotheses about how expectations are formed. The first hypothesis is that expectations are formed adaptively. **Adaptive expectations** use information *from the recent past* to predict the future behavior of variables. Adaptive expectations are backward looking. The hypothesis of adaptive expectations asserts that people form new expectations

Adaptive expectations Expectations of a variable based on the behavior of the variable in the recent past; backward looking.

---
[1]The appendix to this chapter discusses the price adjustment process in detail.

Rational expectations
Expectations of a variable formed on the basis of all available information with an expected marginal value greater than its marginal cost of collection and use; forward looking.

by adapting to past mistakes. The second hypothesis is that expectations are formed rationally. **Rational expectations** are formed by making use of all available information that improves the accuracy of a forecast. Rational expectations are forward looking, since they pay attention to what is happening in the present and what is likely to happen in the future. We examine these two methods of forming expectations in turn.

Adaptive Expectations

Forming expectations adaptively means that future *expected* values of a variable depend on past *actual* values of that variable. For example, if expectations of inflation are being formed adaptively, the past behavior of the inflation rate is used to form predictions of future inflation rates. New data on actual inflation are used to revise expectations.

Because adaptive expectations are backward looking, changes in expectations always trail changes in the actual values of the variable being predicted. For example, when the inflation rate is rising from year to year, the expected rate of inflation (based on lower *past* inflation rates) consistently underestimates actual inflation. When actual inflation begins to fall, the expected inflation rate overshoots the actual rate. So long as the actual rate continues to fall, the backward-looking expected rate exceeds the actual rate. (This is illustrated with a mathematical example in *The Economist's Tool Kit* on adaptive expectations.)

Despite such shortcomings, adaptively formed expectations provide some guide to the future. The problem with adaptive expectations from an economic point of view is not that they miss the mark much of the time. In an uncertain world, *any* method of forming expectations is going to be off target to some extent most of the time. The real problem with adaptive expectations is twofold. First, adaptive expectations make errors in the same direction for long periods of time. For example, whenever inflation is rising, an adaptive equation always underestimates the true inflation rate. Because expected inflation (and thus the expected price level) is too low period after period, an aggregate demand increase or decrease can cause the actual level of real GNP to differ from the natural level for long periods of time.

Figure 2 shows the effects of an aggregate demand increase when expectations are formed adaptively. Output initially rises to $RGNP_1$, while the price level rises to PI_1. Higher prices cause workers to revise their price expectations upward, but by less than the actual price increase. Thus, in period 2 the SRAS curve shifts upward only a little. Output in period 2 remains above the natural level. Over time the actual output level returns to the natural level. However, because expectations lag behind reality, the SRAS curve shifts upward relatively slowly and output remains above the natural level for a long time. *If expectations adjust adaptively, shifts in the aggregate demand curve have long-lasting effects on output.*

The second problem with adaptive expectations is that the adaptive expectations formation process does not apply the principles of economics to expectations formation: The marginal benefits of collecting and processing information to form correct expectations are not equated to the marginal costs. In response to this problem, economist John Muth developed the notion of rational expectations, to which we now turn.

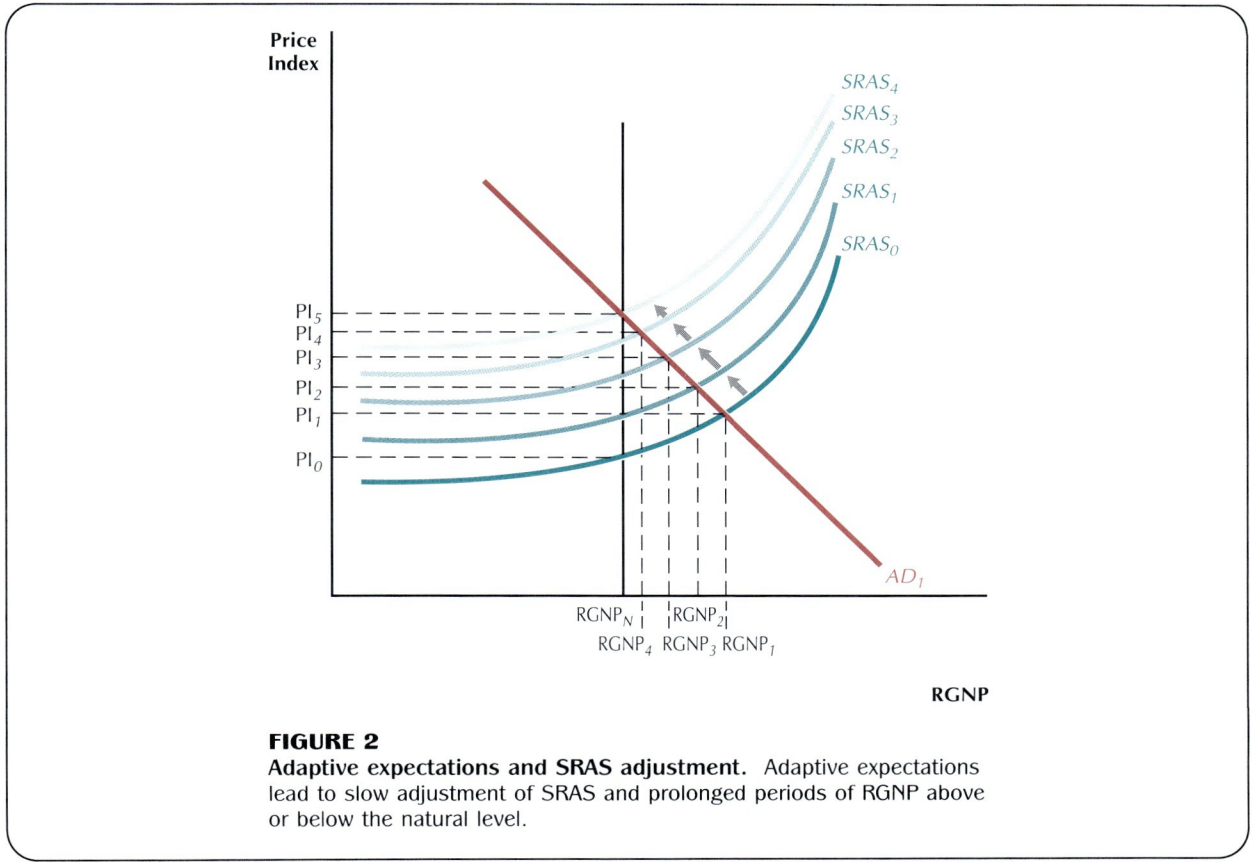

FIGURE 2
Adaptive expectations and SRAS adjustment. Adaptive expectations lead to slow adjustment of SRAS and prolonged periods of RGNP above or below the natural level.

Rational Expectations

Expectations are formed rationally when three criteria are met:

1. Forecasters collect and use information until the marginal benefit equals the marginal cost.
2. Forecasters use a reasonable economic model to process the information.
3. The forecast errors of the model are not systematically positive or negative. That is, forecasts are not too high or too low period after period.

To give a concrete example, suppose that economic decision makers understand the connection between changes in government spending and changes in aggregate demand. They observe that government spending is increasing. Using the available information on government policy and their estimate of the natural level of real GNP, firms and workers (or their bargaining agents) can form an estimate of the probable effect of government policy on the price level.

Suppose forecasters, using the available information on economic capacity, private spending, and government policies, predict that aggregate demand will

TABLE 1
Calculating expected inflation using an adaptive equation

Year	Inflation Rate (Percent)	Expected Inflation Rate (Percent)
1	4	—
2	7	—
3	7	—
4	9	6.7
5	10	8.2
6	11	9.4
7	7	10.5
8	5	8.5
9	3	6.2
10	8	4.0

Note: Expected inflation is calculated according to the formula $p^e = 0.6p_{-1} + 0.3p_{-2} + 0.1p_{-3}$.

The Economist's Tool Kit

Adaptive Expectations

Adaptively formed expectations relate past values of a variable to future expected values. As an example, consider a particular adaptive equation relating expected inflation to past inflation rates:

$$p^e = 0.6p_{-1} + 0.3p_{-2} + 0.1p_{-3}$$

The equation says that the inflation rate expected this year is a weighted average of inflation in the past three years. The most recent annual inflation rate is given the heaviest weight, 0.6. The weights add up to one.

Table 1 presents a series of hypothetical inflation rates for ten years and expected inflation rates for the final seven years. (Three years of data are needed to calculate the first expected inflation rate.) Figure 3 plots the resulting expected rate as well as the actual inflation rate.

---

rise to AD^e in Figure 4. Given their estimate of the natural level of real GNP, $RGNP_N^e$, workers can form an estimate of the level prices will eventually move to, PI^e. Note that forecasters use a reasonable model of the economy to organize the information they collect on the expected levels of aggregate demand and $RGNP_N$. The rationally expected price level is the price level their model of the economy predicts. The expected price level takes into account both the effect of aggregate demand and the effect that higher wage demands will have on prices. *All* relevant information whose marginal benefit is greater than its marginal cost is used to form rational expectations.

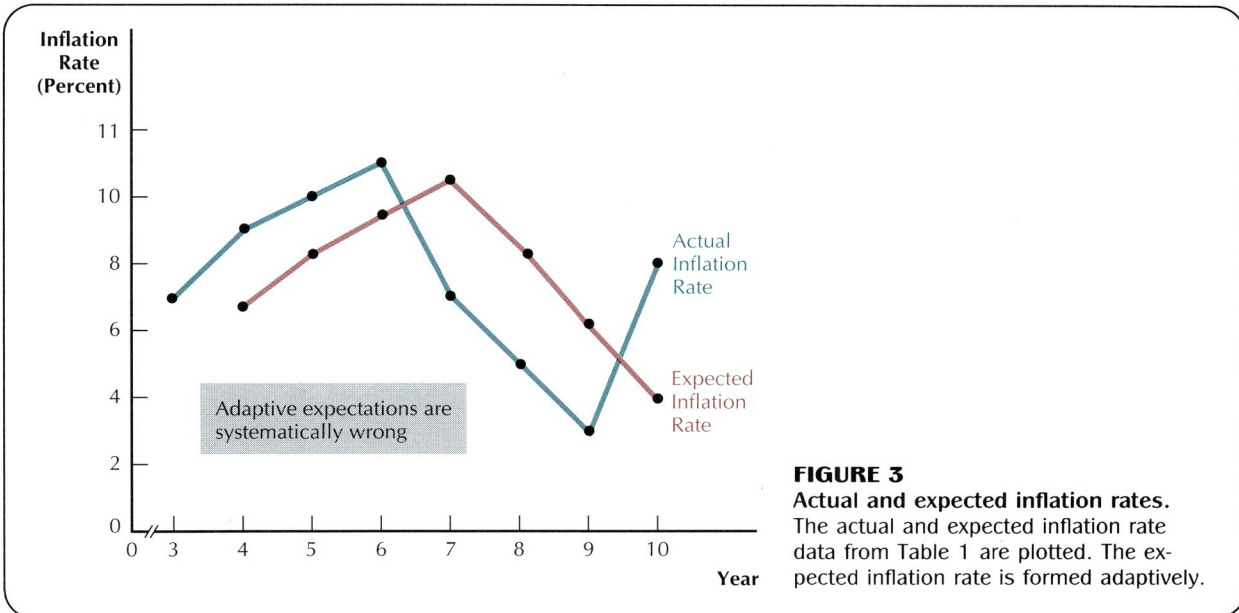

FIGURE 3
Actual and expected inflation rates. The actual and expected inflation rate data from Table 1 are plotted. The expected inflation rate is formed adaptively.

Figure 3 shows that changes in adaptively formed expectations always trail actual changes in the inflation rate. When inflation is rising, the adaptive equation underestimates the true inflation rate. When the inflation rate turns downward, the expected rate overshoots the actual rate. While the actual rate is falling, the equation overestimates inflation. However, the actual pattern of expected inflation rates depends on the values of the weights in the expectations equation. The larger the weight attached to recent values of inflation, the more rapidly expectations adapt to changes in actual inflation. For example, the equation $p^e = 0.9p_{-1} + 0.1p_{-2}$ produces an expected inflation series that catches up to changes in the actual inflation rate more quickly than the equation illustrated in Figure 3.

Are Rational Expectations Reasonable?

Most economists find the idea of rational expectations quite appealing. Economic theory is based on the assumption that people behave rationally, making choices that benefit them the most. The idea of rational expectations is consistent with the basic economic proposition of rationality: People use all the information with an expected marginal benefit greater than its marginal cost of collection and processing to form expectations. In other words, people apply the Fundamental Premise of Economics to expectations formation.

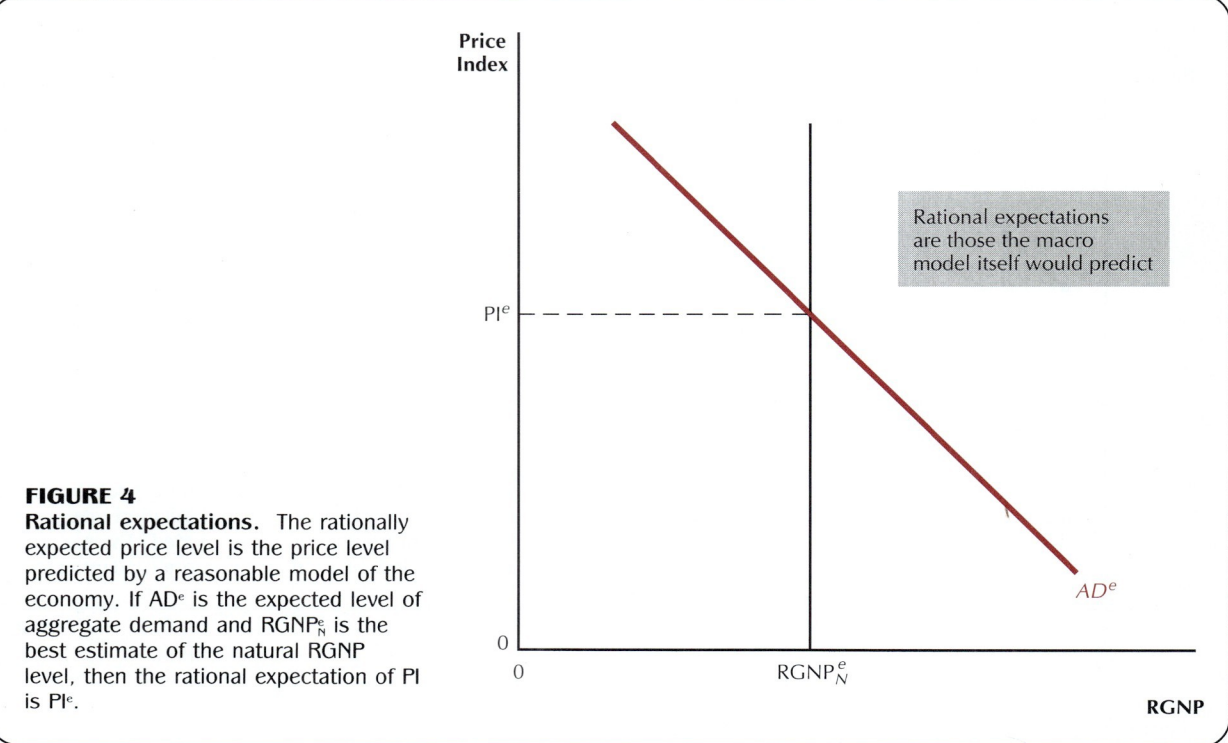

FIGURE 4
Rational expectations. The rationally expected price level is the price level predicted by a reasonable model of the economy. If AD^e is the expected level of aggregate demand and $RGNP_N^e$ is the best estimate of the natural RGNP level, then the rational expectation of PI is PI^e.

Rational expectations are those the macro model itself would predict

When the idea of rational expectations is put into practice, however, many people contend that rational expectations are not reasonable. Most people do not have firm ideas about how the economy works, much less use a formal model to process lots of information. Do people really form expectations by carefully collecting information and using it in a formal economic model?

Even the supporters of rational expectations theory do not contend that everyone understands the economy or that all people make formal calculations of expected future events. After all, not all economists agree on what the best model of the macroeconomy is. Nor do rational expectations theorists deny that most of the information used to predict the future comes from the past — rational expectations are, to some extent, adaptive. However, rational expectations theorists argue that economic decision makers are *forward looking;* they quickly adjust their expectations in response to new information, and they understand enough about the economy to use basic information correctly. The key feature of rational expectations is not that they are always correct — no one contends they are — but that rationally formed expectations adjust to new information more quickly than adaptive expectations.

The speed with which expectations adjust to new information is a key determinant of how long output deviates from the natural level when aggregate demand shifts. The speed of adjustment also determines the gains from an expansive economic policy and the costs of a restrictive policy. For example, at the end of the 1970s the U.S. inflation rate was well above 10 percent. Although most people agreed that inflation should be sharply reduced, economists disagreed about how costly — in terms of lost output and unemployed resources — reducing inflation would be. Proponents of rational expectations

Does It Make **Economic Sense?**

Possibility of a Vertical SRAS Curve

One implication of rational expectations, pointed out in the 1970s by such economists as Robert E. Lucas, Jr., Thomas Sargent, and Neil Wallace, is that only *unanticipated changes in aggregate demand* should affect output. An unanticipated change is one that is not foreseen by economic decision makers. Completely *anticipated AD shifts* — whose direction and size are correctly foreseen — should affect only prices. In response to anticipated AD shifts, the SRAS curve should be vertical. Does this make economic sense?

The possibility of a vertical SRAS curve follows immediately from two assumptions: rational expectations and wage and price flexibility. If workers and business managers, using all available information, correctly anticipate an aggregate demand increase, they are able to form an accurate estimate of what the price level will be in the next period. (This is the proposition illustrated in Figure 4.) To prevent their real wage rate from falling, workers demand higher nominal wages to offset the anticipated price level increase. Thus, the labor supply curve immediately shifts to the left. At the same time, the managers of firms recognize that higher product prices make workers more valuable. Thus, the labor demand curve shifts to the right. The net effect is an increase in the nominal wage rate and no change in the real wage rate, employment, or the level of output.

The *rational expectations hypothesis* says that, when wages and prices are flexible and expectations are formed rationally, only *unanticipated* changes in aggregate demand affect the output level. Fully anticipated aggregate demand changes are incorporated in price expectations, wages adjust immediately, and output does not change. Even if expectations are initially wrong, they should catch up to reality quickly. Thus, movements in real GNP away from the natural level caused by unanticipated AD changes shouldn't last very long. Output should return to its natural level as soon as expectations adjust to new information.

In fact, the output level in the United States has been known to deviate from the natural level for several years at a time. Figure 5 shows the annual level of real GNP as a percentage of natural real GNP for the years 1960 to 1990. As you can see, output has been significantly above or below the natural level for as long as seven consecutive years. Such long-lasting deviations from the natural output level pose a significant problem for the pure rational expectations approach.

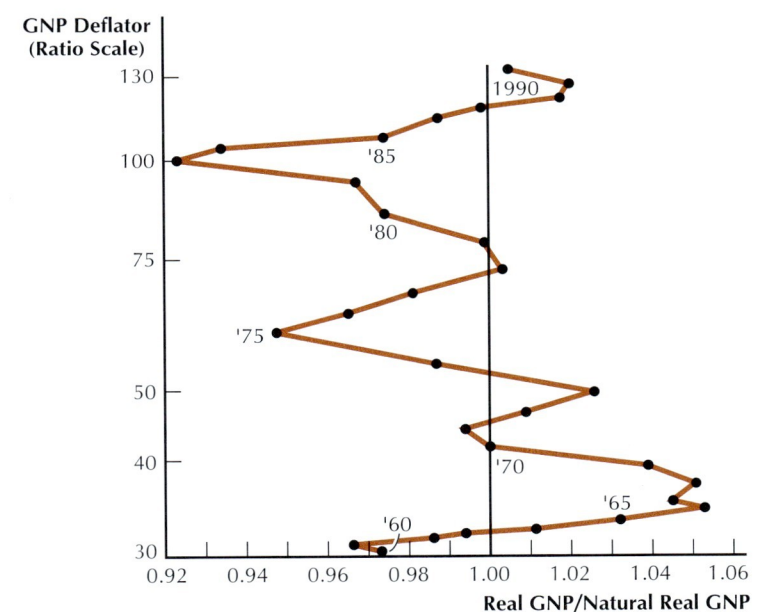

FIGURE 5
Output persistence. In the United States, when output has moved either above or below the natural output level, it has tended to remain relatively high or low for several consecutive years. That is, output movements away from the natural level persist. Such a pattern is contrary to what the rational expectations hypothesis would lead us to expect. Source: *Economic Report of the President, 1991*, Tables B-2 and B-3, and Robert J. Gordon, *Macroeconomics*, 5th ed., (Glenview, IL: Scott, Foresman, 1990).

Restrictive monetary policy
A decrease in the size or growth rate of the money supply, designed to reduce or slow the growth of aggregate demand.

SECTION RECAP
Adaptively formed expectations are backward looking; they fail to take all currently available information into account in forming expectations. Rational expectations are forward looking; they use all available information to forecast future values of economic variables.

Output persistence
Prolonged deviations of output above or below the natural output level.

Real GNP gap
Percentage deviation of actual real GNP from the natural level of real GNP.

argued that once people recognized that the government would no longer tolerate (or promote) inflation, expectations would adjust quickly, the SRAS curve would stop shifting upward, and the output losses from restricting aggregate demand would be minimal. Economists using models based on adaptive expectations disputed such claims. One prominent economic model based on adaptive expectations predicted that output would have to be significantly below the natural level for a decade to reduce inflation to 4 percent.

In 1982 the Federal Reserve's **restrictive monetary policy**, which was designed to slow the growth of aggregate demand, produced the worst recession since World War II. Output fell well below the natural level, and the unemployment rate went above 10 percent. The severity of the recession seemed to indicate that expectations are adaptive. However, the inflation rate fell rapidly, to less than 4 percent in 1983. What the adaptive models predicted would take ten years actually took two years to accomplish. However, although output began to rise again after eleven months of decline, the rate at which output grew was much slower than the pure rational expectations hypothesis predicted. As Figure 5 shows, not until 1987 did output return to its natural level. Thus, the cost of reducing inflation was higher than rational expectationists expected. The mixed evidence — inflation fell faster than adaptive expectations predicted, but output remained low longer than rational expectations predicted — may indicate that some wages and prices react slowly even when price expectations change rapidly.

Problem of Output Persistence

Output persistence refers to prolonged periods of output above or below the natural output level. Output persistence is often measured by the **real GNP gap** — the percentage deviation of actual real GNP from the natural level of real GNP. If a positive or negative RGNP gap persists for several consecutive years, at least one of the assumptions underlying the rational expectations hypothesis must be wrong. Possible sources of output persistence include the following: (1) expectations are not formed rationally, (2) temporary deviations of output from the natural level cause firms to make capital investment mistakes that take time to correct and cause longer-lasting output effects, and (3) prices and wages change only slowly after expectations have adjusted.

Expectations Are Not Formed Rationally   The hypothesis of rational expectations could be wrong. Perhaps people really do form expectations adaptively and ignore information that would be useful in predicting the future course of the economy.

Many economists are very uncomfortable with the thought that expectations are not formed rationally. If expectations are formed adaptively, they can be systematically wrong year after year. Expectations formed adaptively tend to overpredict or underpredict prices for several years running. Such a pattern is irrational in the sense that people can make themselves better off by correcting their *systematic* errors. Why should people harm themselves by choosing to be systematically wrong?

The theory of rational expectations does *not* assert that rationally formed expectations are always correct. It does assert that readily available information on variables that affect the inflation rate will be used efficiently. Using this information improves forecasts, enabling decision makers to make better wage or price decisions by eliminating systematic errors. The attractive features of the rational expectations assumption lead economists to look elsewhere for a solution to the problem of output persistence.

Temporary Output Movements Generate Long-Lasting Effects Output persistence could result from temporary output changes that cause producers to alter the level of productive capacity. For example, an unanticipated increase in aggregate demand might encourage additional investment spending on plant and equipment. Even after expectations adjust to new information, the new capital exists and is used to produce an output level greater than the natural level. Several years of relatively low investment spending are required to return the capital stock to its long-run level.

Several economists have attempted to estimate the effect of temporary overinvestment or underinvestment on output persistence.[2] They have concluded that increases or decreases in the capital stock are a source of output persistence. However, output deviates from the natural level by such large amounts that only a small part of the deviation can be explained by capital stock effects.

Prices and Wages Are Not Perfectly Flexible Price and wage movements might be limited by explicit and implicit contracts. If prices and wages are bound by contracts for two or three years at a time, or if employers and employees determine wages according to an informal but long-accepted pattern, the adjustment of wages and prices to new long-run equilibrium levels could be slow even if expectations are formed rationally and adjust rapidly.

Economists have noted for over two centuries that wages and prices do not always move immediately when demand changes. In particular, wages seem to be inflexible. In 1776, Adam Smith noted that:

> the wages of labour do not in Great Britain fluctuate with the price of provisions. These vary every-where from year to year, frequently from month to month. But in many places the money price of labour remains uniformly the same sometimes for half a century together. (*Wealth of Nations*, I.viii.30)

Most wages today are also relatively inflexible; very few change with every movement in the demand for or supply of labor. The relative inflexibility of wages leads many economists to believe that wage stickiness is the major factor generating output persistence.

Contracts and Persistence

To illustrate the effect labor contracts have on short-run output movements, even when expectations are set rationally, let us consider a simple example. Assume that all workers sign two-year wage contracts at the same time. The wage rate guaranteed by the contracts reflects all the information available to firms and workers at the time the contracts are signed. If aggregate demand behaves as expected over the two years of the contracts, output will equal the natural level and workers will receive the real wage rate they expected when signing the contracts.

---

[2]For example, see Stanley Fischer, "Anticipations and the Nonneutrality of Money," *Journal of Political Economy* 87 (April 1979), pp. 225–252.

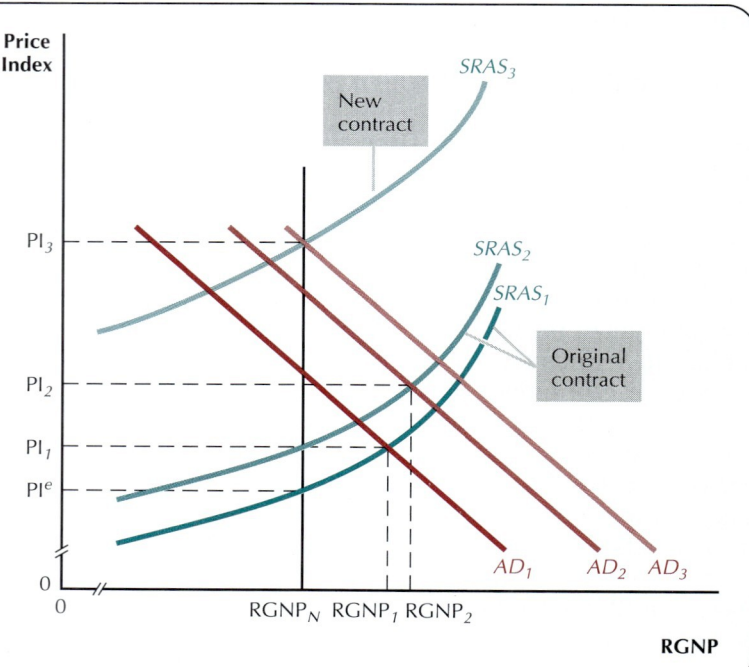

FIGURE 6
Contracts and SRAS adjustment. A two-year wage contract restricts movements in the SRAS curve. The contract sets the position of SRAS in Year 1. When aggregate demand increases more than expected (to AD_1), output rises to $RGNP_1$. In Year 2 wages rise according to the contract. The SRAS curve shifts upward by a relatively small amount. Strong AD growth pushes output higher (to $RGNP_2$). In Year 3 the contract is renegotiated to reflect the higher price level and strong economy. The SRAS curve shifts upward by a large amount, and RGNP returns to its natural level.

SECTION RECAP
The U.S. economy displays output persistence — long periods when real GNP is above or below its natural level. Several factors could cause such persistence. The most important appears to be wage stickiness caused by the existence of explicit and implicit labor contracts.

Now, suppose aggregate demand increases by an unexpectedly large amount after the two-year labor contracts have been signed. Some costs of production rise, but wages remain constant at their contractual level. The AD curve shifts to the right along $SRAS_1$ to AD_1 in Figure 6. In Year 2, wages adjust *according to the contract* rather than according to actual market conditions; the SRAS curve shifts to $SRAS_2$, reflecting the terms of the contract, while aggregate demand rises further to AD_2. Although workers realize they have underestimated the price level, their contract prevents the wage rate from adjusting fully. Only in Year 3, when workers have the chance to sign a new contract, can wages adjust to higher prices. In Year 3 the SRAS curve shifts by a large amount as wages catch up with past price increases. As wages catch up, output moves back toward the natural level.

As the example shows, long-term wage contracts can account for output persistence. In the real world, however, not all contracts are signed at the same time, nor do all contracts last two years. Indeed, most workers do not work under formal contracts. Instead, *implicit* contracts between workers and employers determine when wages will adjust. Some wages move annually or semiannually in response to price level changes. The more rapidly wages adjust to price level changes, the sooner output returns to the natural level.

Working with the Short-Run Model

Changes in either aggregate demand or short-run aggregate supply alter the economy's equilibrium price and output levels. In this section we review the factors that shift the AD curve and we discuss the stability of the AD curve.

We then introduce a factor in addition to wage changes that shifts the SRAS curve. We use the complete short-run model to explain the actual behavior of the U.S. economy during the 1960s, 1970s, and 1980s.

Aggregate Demand Changes

A fairly large number of factors can shift the AD curve. Consumption spending depends on the level of long-run disposable income. Changes in income tax rates or payroll tax rates alter disposable income and change consumption spending in the opposite direction: If tax rates rise, disposable income and consumption fall. Investment spending depends on the level of real income, the expected real interest rate, business taxes and tax credits, and the optimism or pessimism of business decision makers. Government purchases of goods and services affect aggregate demand directly. Finally, net exports depend on relative international price levels, relative international real income levels, and the exchange rate. Table 2 summarizes the factors affecting aggregate demand and shows whether an increase in each factor increases or decreases aggregate demand.

Stability of the AD Curve The amount by which the AD curve shifts when one of the autonomous determinants of aggregate demand changes depends on two factors: (1) the size of the change in the factor triggering the AD shift, and (2) the response of consumers to an initial change in income. (The amount by which real GNP changes of course depends not only on the size of the AD shift but also upon the shape of the SRAS curve.) For example, suppose business expectations of improved profits (increased optimism) cause aggregate demand to rise. Firms purchase new machines and build new factories. Other firms produce machines and factories, and the new investment spending becomes income for such firms. Construction firms and firms that produce capital equipment must hire more workers or ask their current employees to work longer hours to increase production levels. Either way, workers receive more income. If the workers spend all or part of the additional income on con-

TABLE 2

Factors affecting aggregate demand

Autonomous Factor (Increase in)	Affects	Effect on AD
Income, payroll tax rate	C	−
Transfer payments	C	+
Money supply	I (through r^e)	+
Business tax rate	I	−
Investment tax credit	I	+
Business optimism	I	+
Government purchases	G	+
Foreign price level	NX	+
Foreign real income level	NX	+
Exchange rate	NX	−

Multiplier effect
A change in autonomous spending generates changes in consumption spending, causing the ultimate change in aggregate demand to be larger than the initial change in autonomous spending.

sumption goods, aggregate demand rises further. Both investment and consumption spending drive AD to the right, so the total increase in aggregate demand is greater than the increase in investment that triggers the AD shift. Keynes called this the **multiplier effect**.

The multiplier effect works in the following manner. Assume consumption is related to income by a simple Keynesian consumption function of the form $C = a + b(GNP)$. (We ignore income taxes for now.) Further assume a = $400 billion and $b = 0.9$. If investment spending rises by $100 billion, GNP also increases by $100 billion. According to the consumption function, consumption rises by 0.9(100 billion) = $90 billion. The increase in consumption spending further increases income (and nominal output) by $90 billion, since the dollars that you and I spend on consumption goods become the income of the storekeepers and production workers who produce and sell the goods we buy. This further increase in income causes consumption to rise even more. The second-round effect on consumption is an increase of 0.9(90 billion) = $81 billion. This increase in consumption spending further increases income, which then generates a third-round effect on consumption spending, and so on. Table 3 illustrates the process.

The eventual effect on income is some multiple of the initial $100 billion change in spending. Given a marginal propensity to consume of 0.9, consumption increases income by $90 + 81 + 72.90 + \ldots$ billions. The ultimate effect on aggregate demand of the initial $100 billion increase in investment spending is:

$$\$100 \text{ billion} \times \frac{1}{1 - \text{MPC}}$$

In this case, this amounts to:

$$\$100 \text{ billion} \times \frac{1}{1 - 0.9} = 100 \text{ billion} \times \frac{1}{0.1} = 100 \text{ billion} \times 10 = \$1000 \text{ billion}$$

The multiplier is $1/0.1 = 10$. Thus, when the marginal propensity to consume is high, the ultimate effect of a relatively small change in income can be quite large.

TABLE 3

Multiplier process

Round	Change in Income	Change in Consumption
1	100	90
2	90	81
3	81	72.90
4	72.90	65.61
5	65.61	59.05
.	.	.
.	.	.
.	.	.
Final	0	0
Total	1000	900

In contrast to this example, the modern theory of consumption demand suggests that if the initial change in income is perceived by most people to be temporary, the marginal propensity to consume will be quite small. (Recall the example of Peggy in the chapter on aggregate demand.) Suppose the MPC out of temporary income is 0.2. Then the multiplier has a value of $1/(1 - 0.2) = 1/0.8 = 1.25$. The initial increase in income of $100 billion generates an ultimate increase in aggregate demand of only $125 billion, only one eighth as large as the $1000 billion increase of the earlier example.

As these examples demonstrate, the overall stability of aggregate demand depends to a large extent on the degree to which consumption is related to changes in temporary income. *If the marginal propensity to consume from temporary income is small, the multiplier has a low value.* Temporary changes in national income (generated by such factors as changes in investment spending or the money supply) have limited effects on the overall level of spending. If the MPC from temporary income is high, the economy is unstable, because relatively small changes in autonomous spending generate large changes in aggregate spending through consumption spending.

Fortunately, the empirical evidence indicates that the marginal propensity to consume from temporary income is much lower than the MPC from permanent income. While the MPC from permanent disposable income is about 0.90, the MPC from temporary income has been estimated to be from less than one third to one half as large. Temporary spending changes are not likely to have large multiplier effects on the economy. When a change in investment spending, net exports, government purchases, income taxes, or the money supply is perceived to be temporary, consumption spending reinforces the spending change only to a limited extent.

Figure 7 compares the effects on the price and output levels of two increases in aggregate demand, one of which is perceived to be permanent, the other of which is thought to be temporary. When consumers believe that an income increase is permanent, consumption increases by a larger amount. The AD curve shifts farther to the right, putting more pressure on the economy's productive capabilities. Thus, the price and output effects of a permanent change in autonomous spending or in government policy are larger than the price and output effects of a temporary change.

Aggregate Supply Changes

The short-run aggregate supply curve reflects the current costs of production facing firms. When production costs change in most industries, the SRAS curve shifts. The major cost of production affecting the macroeconomy is wages; labor goes into the production of all goods and services. A second input common to some degree in all products is energy. Changes in either the level of wages or energy prices shift the SRAS curve.[3]

The events of 1973–1974 and 1979–1980 demonstrated that energy price increases can significantly affect the SRAS curve. We will examine the actual U.S. data for this period a bit later, but for now we can model the general

SECTION RECAP
The size of an aggregate demand shift depends on the size of the change in the autonomous variable causing the shift and on the size of the expenditures multiplier. If the autonomous change is viewed as permanent, the multiplier is relatively large; if it is viewed as temporary, the multiplier is relatively small.

---

[3]Two other possible sources of SRAS shifts should be mentioned. Changes in technology affect the cost of production and can shift the SRAS curve. However, the effect of technology on SRAS in any particular year is not likely to be large. On the other hand, the SRAS curve sometimes shifts by a significant amount in response to large changes in food production, caused by unusually good or bad weather.

The Expenditure Multiplier

The simple expenditure multiplier tells us how much total spending changes after the economy has fully adjusted to a change in autonomous expenditures (expenditures not directly related to current income). The derivation of this multiplier can be illustrated with a simple example. Suppose total spending in the economy consists of consumption spending plus investment spending. Consumption spending is related to income by the simple Keynesian consumption function, $C = a + b(GNP)$. Assume that investment spending is autonomous; $I = I_0$.

Total spending equals $C + I$, or:

$$\text{Spending} = a + b(GNP) + I_0$$

In equilibrium, spending equals GNP; what is produced is demanded. Thus, in equilibrium:

$$GNP = a + b(GNP) + I_0$$

Solving the equation for GNP yields:

$$GNP - b(GNP) = a + I_0$$

or:

$$(1 - b)GNP = a + I_0$$

The Economist's Tool Kit

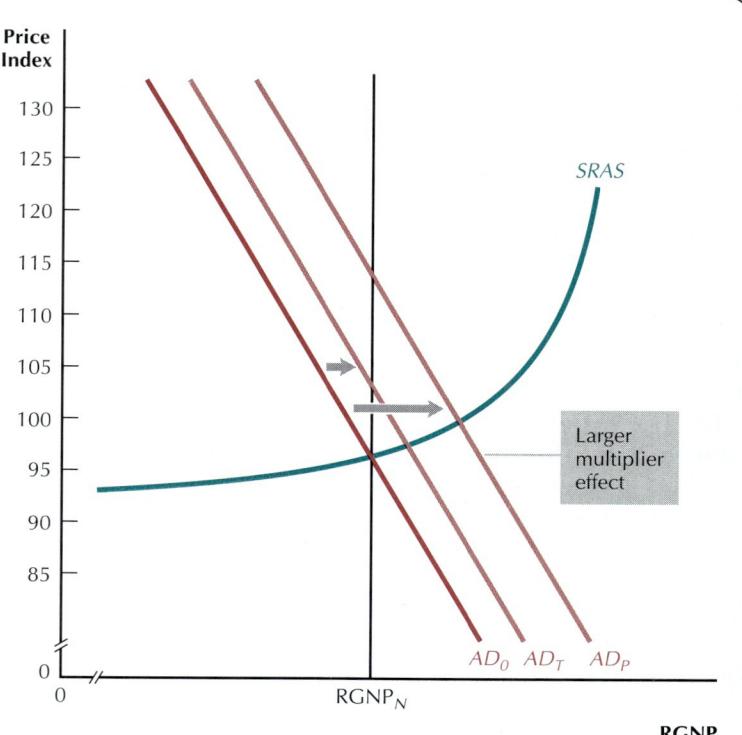

FIGURE 7
Permanent and temporary income changes. A permanent change in income has a larger multiplier effect than a temporary change does.

Thus:

$$\text{GNP} = [1/(1-b)] \times (a + I_0)$$

Any change in autonomous consumption (a) or in investment (I_0) changes GNP by the change in autonomous spending times the multiplier $[1/(1-b)]$.

The multiplier is the solution to the mathematical formula for a convergent geometric series. Refer to Table 3, where the multiplier series is displayed. The increase in autonomous expenditures of 100 increases GNP by 100, causing consumption to rise by 0.9×100 (b equals 0.9). Thus, the second-round effect on GNP is 90, producing another increase in consumption of 81. Note that 81 is $0.9 \times 0.9 \times 100 = (0.9)^2 \times 100$. The changes in income could be rewritten as $100 + (0.9)(100) + (0.9)^2(100) + (0.9)^3(100) + (0.9)^4(100) + \ldots$. Since b lies between zero and one, this is a convergent geometric series (because each term is smaller than the preceding term). The mathematical formula for the value of such a series is:

$$A \times [1/(1-b)]$$

In our example, $A = 100$ and $b = 0.9$.

The simple expenditures multiplier is based on a number of very restrictive assumptions, among them that interest rates remain constant or do not affect spending and that taxes are not related to income. In the text we focus on the logic of the multiplier rather than on its mathematics, because real-world multipliers are much more complex than our simple example.

---

process. If energy prices rise substantially, the costs of production increase in most industries. Higher prices are required to induce firms to produce the quantities of goods they were previously producing; the SRAS curve shifts to the left, as shown in Figure 8. An increase in energy prices, if permanent, also reduces the natural level of output and shifts the LRAS curve to the left. The price level is higher and real GNP is lower than before the supply shock.

The reduced output and higher prices generated by the energy price increases were one factor contributing to the attention given to **supply-side economic policies** by Ronald Reagan in his 1980 presidential campaign. Supply-side policies focus on increasing aggregate supply by altering the incentives to work and produce. The Reagan presidential campaign revolved around the idea that large tax reductions aimed at affecting production incentives could significantly shift both the LRAS and SRAS curves to the right in a short period of time. Although considerable evidence exists that government tax policies have a major impact on the incentive to produce, and thus on the LRAS curve, most economists remain unconvinced that these effects are large enough in the short run to significantly affect SRAS over the period of a year or two.

Supply-side policies Policies designed to shift the aggregate supply curve by changing the incentive to produce goods and services.

The 1960s: Aggregate Demand on the Move

No better time period than the 1960s exists to demonstrate how increases in aggregate demand affect the economy when the short-run aggregate supply curve is stable. As the decade of the 1960s began, output was well below the natural level. Inflation was very low throughout the late 1950s, and the inflation rate was below 2 percent in the early 1960s. Figure 9 illustrates the relationship

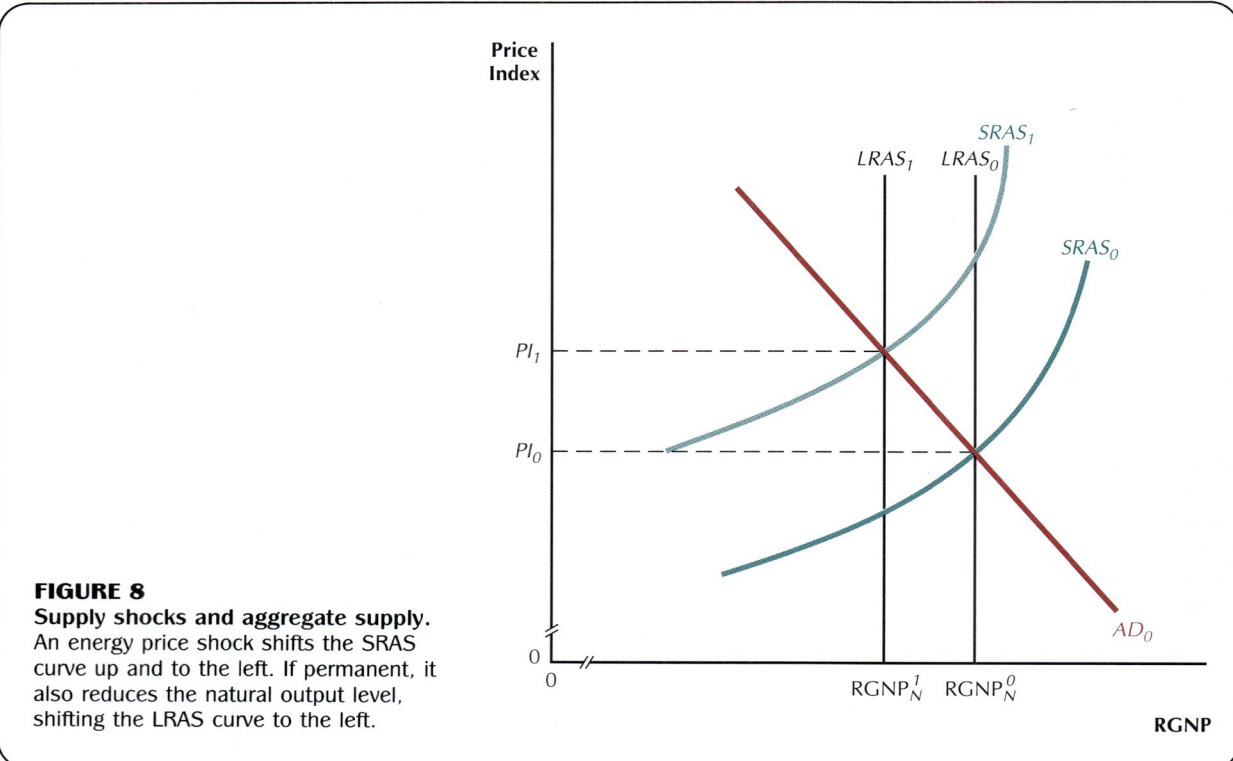

FIGURE 8
Supply shocks and aggregate supply.
An energy price shock shifts the SRAS curve up and to the left. If permanent, it also reduces the natural output level, shifting the LRAS curve to the left.

between the price level and the ratio of real GNP to natural real GNP (RGNP/$RGNP_N$) for the decade. The figure also shows hypothetical SRAS curves. We plot RGNP/$RGNP_N$ along the horizontal axis to take account of the fact that the natural level of RGNP grew during the decade. Thus, Figure 9 shows the level of real GNP relative to its natural level that same year for each year of the 1960s. This enables us to examine short-run movements of RGNP around $RGNP_N$.[4]

Figure 9 shows that from 1961 through 1966 the SRAS curve was apparently stable, while aggregate demand increased continuously. What caused aggregate demand to increase? And why was the SRAS curve stable for so long? The first question is easy to answer. Federal government policy increased aggregate demand throughout the decade. The first half of the decade was characterized by large permanent tax cuts designed to increase consumption and investment demand. Consumption demand increased at an annual rate of 6.6 percent throughout the decade, and investment demand grew even more rapidly, at a 6.7 percent rate. In 1961–1962, defense spending rose significantly as the Kennedy administration sought to overcome the missile gap that was alleged to exist between the United States and the Soviet Union. In 1966, defense expenditures rose sharply as the Vietnam War intensified. The surge in defense spending continued through 1968. In the midst of the Vietnam War buildup,

---

[4]The price index is measured using a ratio scale; the natural logarithm of the price index is measured along the vertical axis. When a ratio scale is used, vertical distances accurately reflect the inflation rate from one year to the next. A simple numerical scale distorts inflation rates.

the Johnson administration pushed its Great Society legislation through Congress. Social spending, particularly in the form of transfer payments, increased dramatically. Not until 1968 was there an attempt to raise taxes to pay for all this additional spending.

In addition to the lower taxes and increased government spending, monetary policy was fairly expansive. The Federal Reserve increased the money supply enough to keep interest rates low, even as income and the demand for money were increasing. Low interest rates increased the profitability of investment projects and made consumer durable spending more affordable, thus encouraging private sector spending.

The result of the rapid growth of government spending and expansive monetary policy was rapid growth of aggregate demand. The economy, which had been stagnant in 1961, operated well above the natural level throughout the second half of the decade.

It is not surprising that the price level did not rise very much in the early 1960s, even though aggregate demand was growing rapidly. Real GNP was below the natural level until 1964. Recall that at output levels below the natural level of real GNP, the SRAS curve tends to be fairly flat. Little pressure is being put on industrial capacity, the labor force, or the transportation system. The implicit price deflator rose at an annual rate of only 1.6 percent over the first half of the decade.

Beginning in 1964, however, actual RGNP exceeded natural RGNP. The economy operated under tighter resource constraints. Not surprisingly, the price level began to rise more rapidly — at a 3.0 percent rate from 1965 through 1967 and a 5.3 percent rate in 1968 and 1969. As capacity constraints forced prices higher and labor markets became tighter, the SRAS curve began to shift upward.

Although the inflation of the early 1960s was not severe, prices did rise year after year. Why did the SRAS curve remain stationary for so long when the price level was rising? A stable SRAS curve presumes stable expectations.

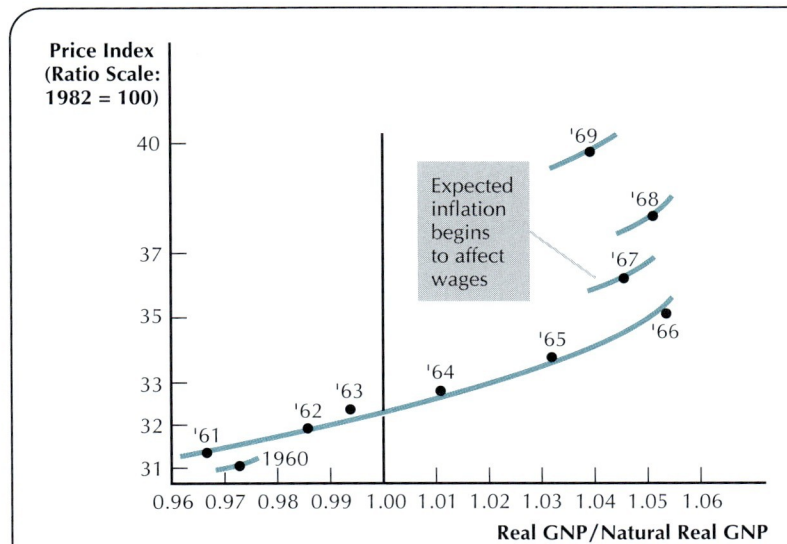

FIGURE 9
The U.S. economy in the 1960s. The short-run aggregate supply curve was relatively stable from 1961 to 1966. In 1967 it began shifting upward as higher expected inflation was incorporated into wages.

Threshold effect
Inflation is incorporated into contracts only when it reaches a level that is too costly to ignore.

SECTION RECAP
The 1960s were characterized by relatively stable short-run aggregate supply and rapidly rising aggregate demand. Inflation increased in the latter half of the decade, and wages began to rise more rapidly to protect real buying power.

If expectations of inflation change, contracts are altered to take the expected higher prices into account. The stability of the SRAS curve during the 1960s indicates that people were paying very little attention to inflation. The aggregate price level had risen very slowly for a long time. From the end of the Korean War through 1966 the annual inflation rate averaged only 2 percent. People simply did not pay much attention to the aggregate price level. It was not that important.

Northwestern University economist Robert J. Gordon has argued that a **threshold effect** exists in incorporating expected inflation into contracts. The threshold is the level at which inflation becomes too costly to ignore. If inflation is very low for a long time, people simply ignore it. However, if it rises above the threshold, causing people to suffer significant losses if they ignore it, inflation affects contracts. The threshold was crossed in the United States around 1967. Wages began to rise, and the SRAS curve began to shift to the left.

The evidence from the 1960s demonstrates that monetary and fiscal policies can have major effects on the level of real GNP, so long as inflation expectations remain constant. However, when expectations begin to change in response to higher inflation, the SRAS curve begins to shift, and output tends back toward its natural level.

The 1970s: The Migration of SRAS

The stability of the SRAS curve until 1967 led some people (including some economists) to believe that the economy could be controlled indefinitely simply by regulating aggregate demand. If the SRAS curve is stable, government fiscal and monetary policies can be used to increase real GNP by increasing aggregate demand or to decrease real GNP by decreasing aggregate demand.

However, not all economists were convinced that SRAS would remain stable. In particular, two economists predicted that it would not. In 1967, before the the SRAS curve began to shift to the left, Milton Friedman and Edmund Phelps argued that it was only a matter of time before expectations would begin to catch up to the new reality and the SRAS curve would begin to shift. They reasoned that workers would be unwilling to accept unexpectedly low real wages for very long. In time, wage demands would rise, shifting the SRAS curve to the left. The late 1960s and early 1970s saw the predictions of Professors Friedman and Phelps fulfilled.

Supply shock
Sudden shift of the SRAS curve caused by a sharp change in the cost of an important factor of production.

Rising wage demands were not the only source of SRAS shifts in the 1970s, however. The 1970s were the decade of **supply shocks**, when world-wide drought and OPEC oil embargoes caused aggregate supply to decrease internationally. A supply shock is a sudden shift in the SRAS curve caused by a sharp change in the cost of an important factor of production. The leftward shifts of SRAS from 1967 to 1971, caused by rising wage demands, were dwarfed in size by the shifts in 1974 and 1975, caused by rising energy and food prices.

Table 4 shows the annual percentage increase in energy prices for the decade of the 1970s. Note that the energy price index includes many commodities in addition to petroleum; oil prices rose much more rapidly in certain years than did the total energy price index. The large increases in energy prices in 1974 and 1979 shifted the SRAS curve far to the left. The 1974 energy price shock was made worse by drought-caused food price increases of over 14 percent in both 1973 and 1974.

TABLE 4
Nominal energy price increases in the 1970s

Annual Percentage Increase

1970	1971	1972	1973	1974	1975	1976	1977	1978	1979
2.7	3.9	2.8	8.0	29.3	10.6	7.2	9.5	6.3	25.2

Source: Bureau of Labor Statistics

Figure 10 shows the instability of short-run aggregate supply in the 1970s. Rising wages throughout the decade combined with supply shocks to shift the SRAS curve frequently. In 1970 the government attempted to reduce inflation by slowing aggregate demand growth. Thereafter aggregate demand grew fairly rapidly for the remainder of the decade. The resulting performance of the economy was the poorest of any decade since the 1930s. Inflation was high during most of the decade, yet the economy operated below the natural level of output much of the time. The 1970s present a vivid portrait of the difficulties inflation-induced wage increases and supply shocks present to policymakers. The 1970s convinced many macroeconomists that attempts to expand output through monetary and fiscal policies are likely to enjoy only temporary success and that even good monetary and fiscal policies cannot insulate the economy from all types of shocks. (The *Why the Disagreement?* section of this chapter deals with policy in the face of supply shocks.)

SECTION RECAP
The 1970s were a decade of macroeconomic instability. Two major oil price shocks and expansive monetary policy generated high inflation. The oil shocks also caused a major recession.

The 1980s: Reversing the Inflationary Spiral

The United States entered the 1980s with inflation at double-digit levels. The supply shocks of 1973–1974 and 1979–1980, coupled with an expansive ag-

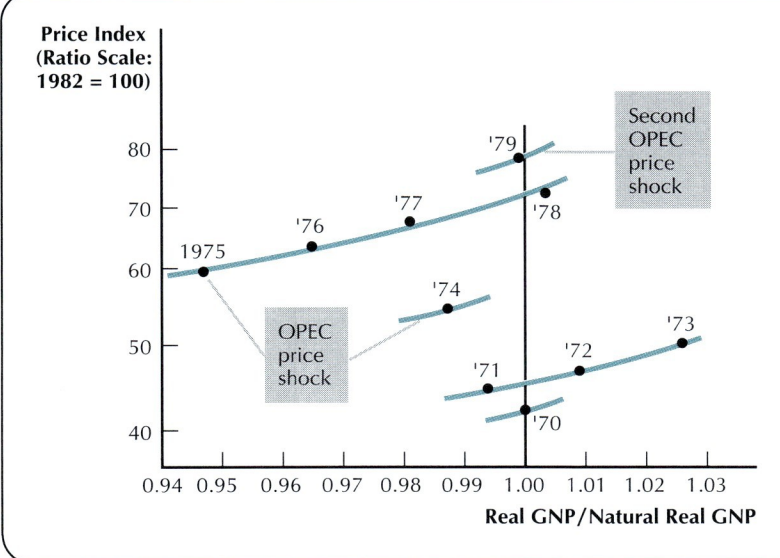

FIGURE 10
The U.S. economy in the 1970s. Wage adjustments and supply shocks caused the SRAS curve to shift upward erratically throughout the 1970s.

gregate demand policy during the Carter presidency (1977–1981), had made inflation public enemy number one. The Federal Reserve began reducing money supply growth in 1979 in an effort to stem inflation. Ronald Reagan's 1980 campaign platform stressed the need to return to price stability. His election meant that the Federal Reserve would receive political support in its anti-inflation efforts.

Figure 11 shows the behavior of the GNP deflator and real GNP from 1979 to 1989. A slowdown in aggregate demand growth in 1980 combined with a 33 percent increase in crude oil prices, which shifted the SRAS curve to the left, led to a mild recession accompanied by 9 percent inflation. Aggregate demand and output grew slowly in 1981, but another increase in energy prices coupled with a large increase in labor costs again shifted the SRAS curve to the left.

In early 1981 the Federal Reserve again tightened monetary policy, this time restricting aggregate demand much more than in 1980. Since the SRAS curve continued to shift upward, primarily because of cost increases already built into the system, such as labor costs (which rose 8.3 percent in 1982), the result was a severe recession. Real GNP fell by 2.5 percent while prices rose by 6.4 percent. Unemployment went above 10 percent as the United States experienced its worst recession since the Great Depression.

The world-wide recession of 1982 set in motion forces contributing to the U.S. economy's strong rebound in the years 1983–1986. Energy prices actually fell 1.3 percent in 1983, mainly because of a world oil glut. The increase in unit labor costs plummeted from 8.3 percent in 1982 to 1.4 percent in 1983, as workers focused on maintaining their jobs rather than on obtaining wage increases. Import prices fell by 2.5 percent. The net result was stability of the SRAS curve for the first time in years. Since aggregate demand grew moderately during 1983, real GNP expanded, while the inflation rate fell.

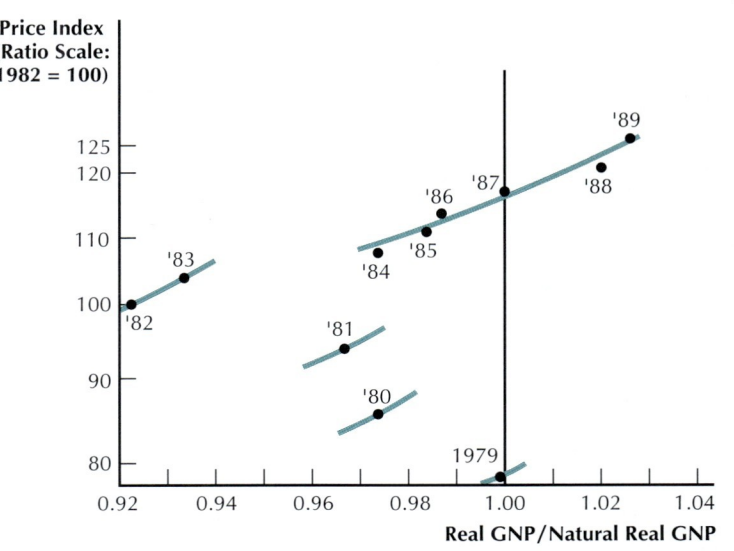

FIGURE 11
The U.S. economy in the 1980s.
High inflation and two recessions marked the early 1980s. However, after the recession of 1981–1982, output grew throughout the remainder of the decade. Inflation was also lower than during the 1970s.

Declining energy prices, declining import prices, and rising labor productivity all contributed to the rightward shift of the SRAS curve in 1984. The increase in aggregate supply largely offset rapid aggregate demand growth, so the price level rose by only 3.7 percent in 1984, while real GNP rose by 6.8 percent. Inflation remained below 3.5 percent per year from 1985 through 1988, while real GNP growth was strong.

The events of the early 1980s demonstrated that the supply-side policies advocated by Ronald Reagan cannot increase aggregate supply quickly enough to prevent a recession when aggregate demand is restricted by monetary policy. However, the large tax cuts that went into effect in 1982 through 1984 did stimulate aggregate demand and may have contributed to the large rightward shift in the SRAS curve that occurred in 1984. Supply-side economics did not cause the 1982 recession — monetary policy deserves the credit (or blame) for that — but neither did it live up to the exaggerated claims made for it by some politicians.

The price level began to rise more rapidly again in 1989. Once again the economy was operating above the natural output level, putting more pressure on input prices. The Federal Reserve acted to restrain aggregate demand by restricting the growth of the money supply and pushing interest rates higher. However, higher inflation continued in 1990. In late 1990 the Iraqi invasion of Kuwait pushed oil prices up sharply. The higher oil prices were an important factor contributing to the recession that ended the longest peacetime expansion on record.

SECTION RECAP
A recession caused by tight monetary policy brought the inflation rate down in the early 1980s, and real GNP grew from 1983 through the end of the decade, the longest peacetime expansion on record.

An Overview of Stabilization Theory

The basic idea underlying stabilization policy is easy to understand. The government attempts to prevent real GNP from deviating by a large amount from its natural level by using fiscal and monetary policy to affect aggregate demand. This section reviews the basic notions about what government stabilization policies might accomplish.

The Stabilization Problem

Stabilization policy is a relevant economic issue only when the economy displays considerable **economic instability** — when real GNP diverges significantly from the natural level of real GNP and the aggregate price level changes significantly over short periods of time. The data presented for the 1960s, 1970s, and 1980s give some indication of the problem. Table 5 shows the levels of actual and natural real GNP and the RGNP gap for selected years. The size of the RGNP gap is a good measure of the degree to which the economy has deviated from the desirable RGNP level.[5]

The table shows that since 1960 the U.S. economy has varied from an RGNP gap (excess aggregate demand) of 5.3 percent in 1966 to a negative RGNP gap (deficient aggregate demand) of −7.7 percent in 1982. This rep-

Economic instability Movements in real GNP away from its natural level and significant changes in the price level over short time periods.

---

[5]This statement assumes that the natural level of real GNP is measured accurately. Measuring the natural level of real GNP is no simple matter, since it is affected by supply shocks. If the natural output level is mismeasured, then of course the RGNP gap is also mismeasured.

TABLE 5
Real GNP, natural RGNP, and the RGNP gap

Year	RGNP	Natural RGNP	RGNP Gap
1960	1665.2	1712.2	−2.7%
1966	2208.4	2096.5	5.3%
1969	2423.3	2332.8	3.9%
1970	2416.2	2416.5	−0.0%
1973	2744.0	2675.0	2.6%
1975	2695.0	2846.5	−5.3%
1978	3115.2	3104.7	0.3%
1982	3166.0	3429.9	−7.7%
1989	4142.6	4038.2	2.6%

Natural RGNP data are taken from Robert J. Gordon, *Macroeconomics*, 5th edition (Glenview, IL: Scott, Foresman, 1990), Appendix A-1. The 1989 value is our estimate. RGNP and Natural RGNP figures are in billions of 1982 dollars. Negative values of the RGNP gap indicate the percentage by which actual RGNP fell short of natural RGNP.

resents considerable instability over a relatively short period of time. It is worth noting, however, that the economy appears to have been more stable in the post–World War II period than it was earlier. (This view has recently been disputed, and we will take up the issue again in the chapter on business cycles.) The RGNP gap varied from a high of 5.5 percent in 1926 to a low of −33.8 percent in 1933. (In 1944, while World War II was still under way, the RGNP gap was an incredible 30.0 percent. The unemployment rate that year was 1.2 percent.)

The basic notion behind stabilization policy is to shift the AD curve whenever RGNP deviates significantly from natural RGNP. Figure 12 illustrates this proposition. AD_0 intersects $SRAS_0$ at $RGNP_0$, which is considerably below the natural output level. If the government can increase AD to AD_1, RGNP will rise to its natural level (and the high unemployment accompanying $RGNP_0$ will be eliminated).

Figure 13 illustrates the case in which AD intersects SRAS at a level of RGNP greater than the natural level. Continued aggregate demand at this level will cause the price level to rise. By shifting AD back to AD_1, policy can lessen the pressure on prices.

Stabilization Policy

The government can alter aggregate demand in three basic ways:

1. By directly changing the aggregate demand for goods and services by purchasing more or fewer goods and services, such as new buildings, new weapons, labor services of bureaucrats, and red tape.
2. By indirectly affecting the level of private spending through changes in taxes or transfer payments.

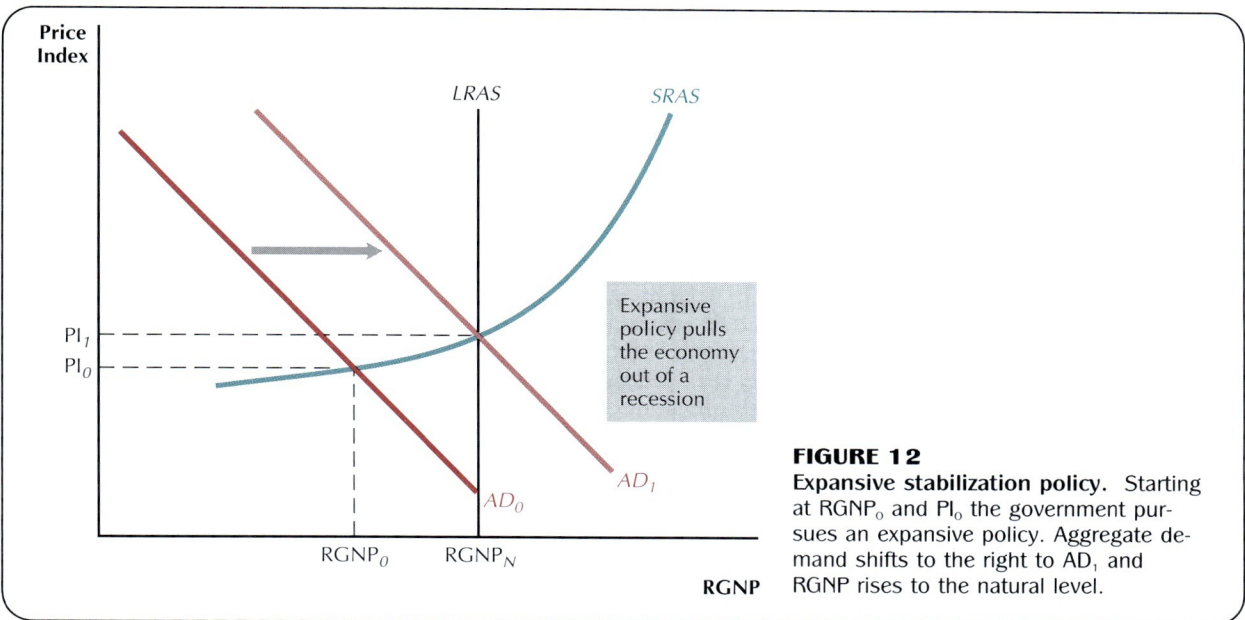

FIGURE 12
Expansive stabilization policy. Starting at $RGNP_0$ and PI_0 the government pursues an expansive policy. Aggregate demand shifts to the right to AD_1 and RGNP rises to the natural level.

3. By using monetary policy to alter the money supply and the level of interest rates.

It is common for the government to combine different types of policies.

When the economy is operating below the natural output level, as in Figure 12, several policy options are available. Without specifying the actual conditions being experienced by the economy, we cannot say which option is best,

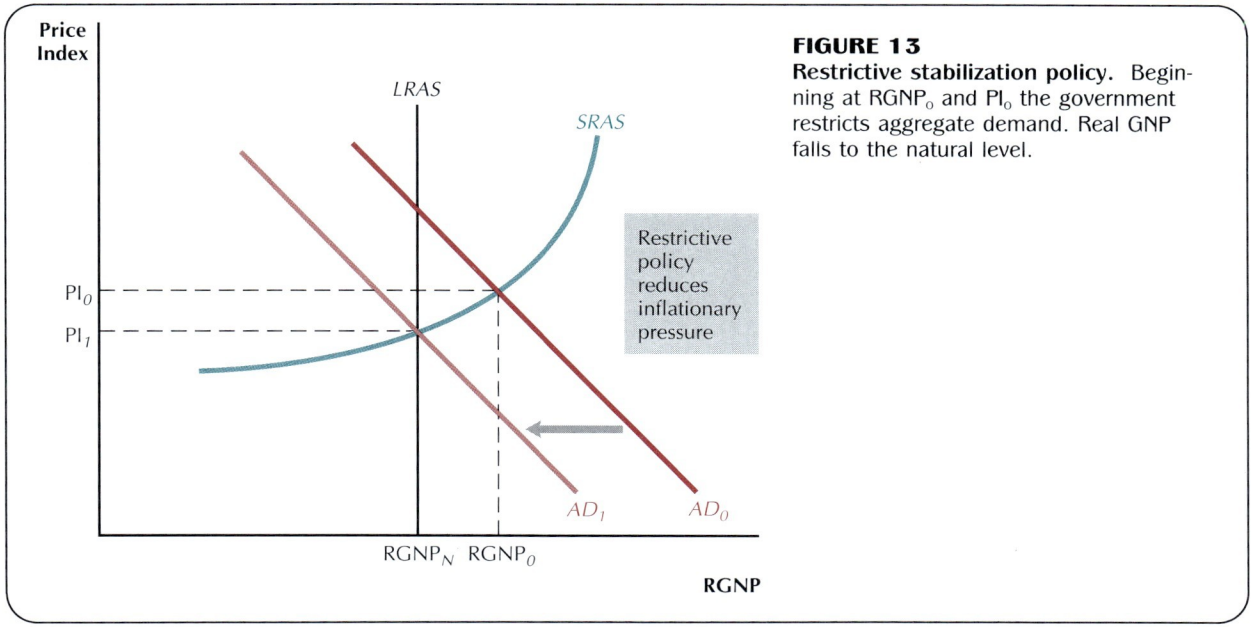

FIGURE 13
Restrictive stabilization policy. Beginning at $RGNP_0$ and PI_0 the government restricts aggregate demand. Real GNP falls to the natural level.

Why the Disagreement?

Responding to Oil Price Shocks

Since 1973, the world has experienced three significant upward jumps in oil prices. In 1973, the Organization of Petroleum Exporting Countries (OPEC) decided to test its market power by embargoing oil sales to the United States and several other countries. In economic terms, the oil embargo was simply a supply restriction. Since petroleum is traded in a world market, the OPEC restriction reduced the world supply of oil and raised oil prices everywhere. OPEC again restricted supply and forced oil prices higher during 1978–1980. The third oil price shock occurred in August 1990, when Iraq invaded Kuwait and the United Nations responded by placing an embargo on oil produced in Iraq and in Iraqi-controlled Kuwait. Large changes in the price of oil have important consequences for the energy-intensive U.S. economy. When real oil prices (oil prices deflated by an aggregate price index) rose by 190 percent from 1973 to 1974, the U.S. economy was hit hard; the real price of an important input in many production processes was nearly three times as expensive in 1974 as in 1973. Rising costs of production shifted the SRAS curve to the left. The natural level of real GNP also fell, because part of the U.S. capital stock could no longer be used profitably at the higher energy prices. The 110 percent increase in the real price of oil from 1978 to 1980 had a similar impact. Figure 14 illustrates the effect of higher energy prices on SRAS and LRAS.

U.S. economic policymakers were confronted with a dilemma when oil prices rose. Should they attempt to moderate the decrease in real GNP by using fiscal and monetary policy to increase aggregate demand? Or should they attempt to minimize the increase in the price level by refusing to pump up aggregate demand? In 1974, in particular, widespread disagreement existed among both economists and government officials. Why the disagreement?

The disagreement reflected differences in opinion about which policy (expansion or restraint) would be most beneficial. The issue really depends on the unknown future behavior of the SRAS curve. Policymakers who favored restraint feared that the oil price shock would initiate a period of high inflation. The oil price shock had already driven the price level upward. If expansive monetary and fiscal policy were used to increase aggregate demand, as in Figure 15, might not wage inflation also set in? If aggregate demand remained at AD_0, output would

FIGURE 14
Impact of higher oil prices on the economy. As oil prices rose the SRAS curve shifted up and to the left. Since higher oil prices also affected the economy's long-run potential, the LRAS curve also shifted to the left.

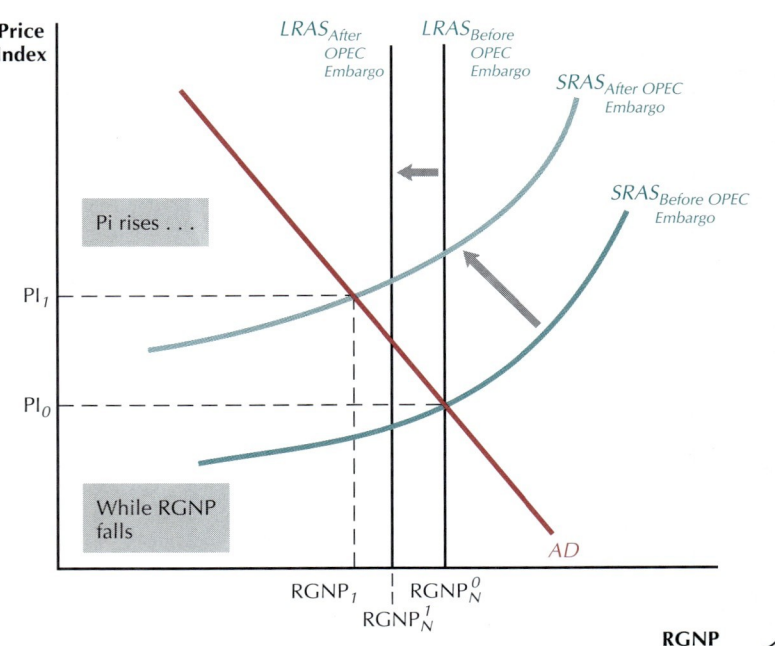

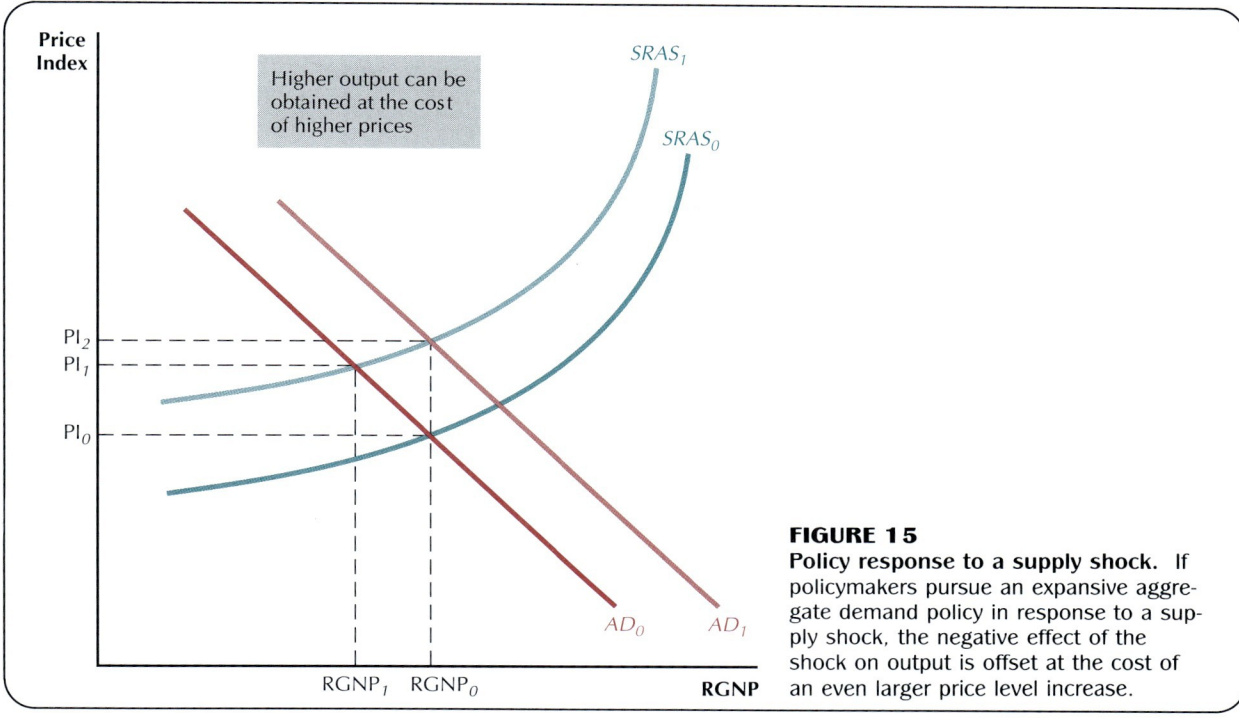

FIGURE 15
Policy response to a supply shock. If policymakers pursue an expansive aggregate demand policy in response to a supply shock, the negative effect of the shock on output is offset at the cost of an even larger price level increase.

fall to $RGNP_1$. At this low output level, unemployment would be high. Workers would be in no position to demand higher wages, which would shift the SRAS curve to the left once again, worsening the inflation problem. Policymakers who feared the effects of inflation and the future costs of bringing it under control argued that accepting a recession in 1974–1975 might work out best in the long run. Inflation would be restrained, and output and employment would eventually return to their natural levels.

Other policymakers argued that the costs of prolonged unemployment were higher than the costs of inflation. Besides, wages were not likely to rise quickly. By the time workers were able to negotiate higher wages, the recession might be over. Then government could restrain aggregate demand and reduce the inflation rate.

Policymakers actually chose to follow the restrained approach. Monetary policy was mildly restrictive in 1974 and 1975, although government transfer payments rose rapidly as many workers lost their jobs. The price level rose sharply anyway, by over 9 percent in 1974 and 1975, and real GNP fell in both years. These results, plus evidence on the wage-adjustment process that indicates considerable short-run rigidity, have led many economists to believe that government policy was too restrictive in 1974 and 1975. A more expansive policy might have increased real GNP without adding much to inflation during those years. However, such a policy might have made the price level even higher eventually.

The experiences of the 1970s helped create a different attitude toward the oil price shock of 1990–1991. As early as the fall of 1990, politicians were urging the Federal Reserve to follow an expansionary monetary policy to prevent a severe recession. Many economists believed that an expansive aggregate demand policy could largely offset the recessionary effects of the relatively small oil price shock (though at the cost of higher prices). It will take time to judge the effectiveness of the expansionary monetary policy that was pursued starting in late 1990. It should be noted that *no* demand-side stabilization policy can offset the long-run effects of a major oil price shock. If energy becomes permanently more expensive (relative to other goods and services), some previously profitable production processes will no longer be economically viable. The natural level of output declines and the long-run aggregate supply curve shifts to the left. Aggregate demand tools are useless against such a shift.

so we will treat the options as equally attractive. The first option is to increase government purchases of goods and services. The government could increase spending on the national highway system or invest in more cancer research or build more missiles. Besides contributing to some social goal, each of these activities adds to GNP, thus addressing the goal of stabilizing the economy. Increased government purchases affect aggregate demand directly and, through their effect on income and consumption spending, they also generate a multiplier effect.

Another option available to policymakers is to reduce taxes. Given the complexity of the U.S. tax system, this is really a large set of options. Reducing income taxes increases disposable income and spurs consumption spending. A tax reduction that people believe is permanent will generate a substantial multiplier effect. Other types of tax cuts are also possible. Cutting corporate income taxes or increasing investment tax credits can be used to encourage more investment spending. Increased investment spending also triggers multiplier effects.

A third policy option would be to use monetary policy to stimulate private spending. An increase in the money supply puts downward pressure on interest rates and makes credit easier to obtain. Lower interest rates reduce the cost of borrowing, making more investment projects profitable. Easier access to credit encourages spending on durable consumption goods. Both add to aggregate demand.

These policy options address the case of deficient aggregate demand. However, the theory of stabilization policy is symmetrical. If aggregate demand is too high, as in Figure 13, the appropriate policies are the opposite of those discussed here: reduce government spending, raise taxes, and contract the money supply. Each of these actions decreases aggregate demand.

A Word of Caution

The basic theory of fiscal and monetary policy seems so simple that you might wonder why the government ever allows output to deviate significantly from its natural level. In fact, the conditions under which fiscal and monetary policies must be carried out are much more complex than the simple theory suggests. The economy is constantly changing, never at rest as the diagrams seem to indicate. The impact of policy actions on private spending is also difficult to predict; it is easy for policymakers to change policy variables by too little or too much. Furthermore, both fiscal and monetary policies take time to work. Time elapses between the implementation of fiscal and monetary policies and the time the policies take effect. Such timing problems complicate matters tremendously. The poor stabilization record of the federal government over the past two decades does not *necessarily* imply policymaker incompetence. Successful policy is very difficult to achieve.

In the next two chapters we investigate the process by which money is created and how it affects the economy. We then examine the credit market, before turning to the governmental expenditure and taxation system. After considering some of the details of how the monetary and fiscal systems work, we will be in a better position to discuss the types of policies that might be most appropriate in our economy.

SECTION RECAP

The government can use its fiscal and monetary policy tools to affect aggregate demand. If the SRAS curve is stable, macro policy can control PI and RGNP. If the SRAS curve is not stable, controlling PI and RGNP is more difficult.

Summary

The basic factor generating deviations of actual RGNP from natural RGNP is **wage rigidity**. If wages were perfectly flexible over even short periods of time, aggregate demand changes would be reflected primarily in price movements. The more rigid wages are, the more a change in the demand for labor affects employment and the quantity of goods and services produced.

As workers begin to incorporate expected price level changes into their wage demands, wages begin to change. The SRAS curve shifts, further raising or lowering the price level, but moving the level of RGNP back toward the natural level.

How rapidly the SRAS curve shifts in response to relatively high aggregate demand depends on how sensitive people are to inflation. If inflation has been very low in the recent past, people may pay little attention to it. Once the **threshold inflation rate** is crossed and people begin to pay attention to inflation, the SRAS curve becomes unstable. Expectations formed **rationally** can adjust very quickly, causing the SRAS curve to shift quickly in response to higher prices.

The **theory of fiscal and monetary policy** suggests that government can minimize the amount of RGNP instability by using government expenditures and taxes and the money supply to offset aggregate demand fluctuations. However, because the real world is very complex, we should not expect too much from policymakers. Certain types of instability, particularly instability resulting from supply shocks, cannot be totally offset by aggregate demand management policies, no matter how well those policies are carried out.

Questions For Thought

Knowledge Questions

1. What determines how long a particular SRAS curve will remain stable?
2. Why does the SRAS curve intersect the LRAS curve where the expected price level equals the actual price level?
3. Define *rational expectations*. How do rational expectations differ from adaptive expectations?
4. What does an economist mean by *economic instability*?

Application Questions

5. "When the aggregate price level rises as the economy moves along a particular SRAS curve, the price rise is not even across all markets." Explain what this statement means. Why must it be so?
6. Explain how an upward revision in price expectations acts to shift the SRAS curve.
7. Why is it that predicted aggregate demand growth of, say, 8 percent is welcomed in some years but viewed as extremely dangerous in others?
8. How does the average rate of inflation over the previous few years affect the economy's performance in the present?

Synthesis Questions

9. It has been noted by Milton Friedman and others that the short-run effect of a change in the money supply on RGNP is not constant over time. That is, sometimes a money supply change has a large impact on RGNP, while other times it does not. Using the AD–SRAS framework, explain this empirical result.
10. If the wage structure in the United States displays a great deal of rigidity—that is, wages change relatively little from year to year—what would seem to be the proper government aggregate demand policy response to a large supply shock? Why?
11. Is it possible for high aggregate demand, which leads to a RGNP level greater than the natural level of RGNP for several years, to be harmful to the economy in the long run (by eventually reducing the natural level of RGNP)? Explain. (*Hint*: Recall the connection between different types of spending and RGNP growth.)

Appendix to CHAPTER 26

Price Adjustment Process

The basic demand–supply model is one of the most useful tools in economics. The effect on prices and quantities of changes in demand and cost conditions can be analyzed efficiently with it. However, although the demand–supply model is extremely useful in describing what ultimately happens in any market when the forces of demand and supply change, it provides an accurate description of the short-run behavior of prices and quantities only for an *auction market* — a market with an auctioneer who calls out prices until prospective buyers and sellers agree on a mutually beneficial price. In auction markets, price moves continually to equate quantity demanded and supplied.

Auction markets confine competition to one dimension — price. The desirability of different sellers' products is equalized by price movements. In contrast to this situation, many sellers in nonauction markets compete in other dimensions as well as with price. For example, banks compete with one another by providing automatic teller machines open twenty-four hours a day or drive-up windows with extended hours. Airlines compete by offering multiple flights between major cities, making it as convenient as possible for travelers to fly on their planes. Convenience stores trade off higher prices for greater customer convenience by staying open around the clock and by locating close to residential areas. Competition can take many forms.

Buyers prefer that sellers carry out some competition in nonprice dimensions. Nearly all shoppers would prefer the supermarket system to an auction market for groceries. Supermarkets allow shoppers to select the most convenient time to shop, offer a wide variety of different products, and are usually located close to major residential areas. The auction alternative would require buyers to assemble at a particular location at a particular time to bid on the products that sellers were selling that particular day. Although buyers would probably obtain better prices if groceries were sold by auction, they would do so at the cost of considerable inconvenience.

Following the lead of Arthur Okun, we will call markets in which nonprice competition takes place *customer markets*. Although such markets may display a great deal of price competition, they are characterized by competition in other dimensions as well, such as time open for business, selection of goods offered, service provided, and location of sales outlets. Because competition in customer markets takes place in multiple dimensions, prices in these markets may not respond immediately to changes in demand or cost conditions.

Auction market
Market with an auctioneer who adjusts prices to bring quantity demanded into equality with quantity supplied.

Customer market
Market with posted prices and competition in nonprice dimensions, such as convenience and service.

Factors Limiting Price Flexibility

Two important reasons for short-run price inflexibility are (1) the existence of long-term customer relationships, and (2) the cost of changing prices. We examine them briefly in turn.

Long-Term Customer Relationships Obtaining price information is costly. A prospective buyer must engage in a search effort, spending time and money acquiring price information. Such a search effort may be very worthwhile for a purchase made infrequently or for a very costly purchase, but most of our purchases are neither infrequent nor relatively costly. Most people spend most of their incomes on relatively low-cost items that are purchased repeatedly. Continuously searching for price information on numerous relatively inexpensive items would be quite costly.

In customer markets, continuity of pricing provides the price information customers desire. Buyers and sellers both benefit from stable pricing patterns. Buyers benefit because the need for more price information is significantly reduced. If stores follow stable pricing policies, shoppers know what prices to expect even before they go shopping. So long as the prices they encounter are reasonably close to those they expect, shoppers are content to make their purchases and return for more shopping.

For customers to adopt this attitude, sellers must convince them that their pricing policies remain consistent. One way to do this is to maintain stable prices in the face of temporary demand fluctuations. By holding inventories of goods, sellers can react to temporary increases or decreases in demand by selling more or less without changing prices. If customers realize that the price of a product rarely changes and they are satisfied with that price, they will not be likely to search for a better price. Their expected marginal benefit of shopping around will not exceed the marginal cost of searching.

Costs of Changing Prices   Another reason for price inflexibility is the costliness of changing prices, often called *menu costs*. For some businesses, this cost can be quite high. Once a catalog is printed, for example, the cost to a mail-order house of changing prices is not trivial. A company such as Sears, Roebuck spends millions of dollars printing its two large semiannual catalogs. Once these catalogs are printed, mail-order prices are fixed for six months (although special sales may be conducted in the interim).

Since most firms do not print catalogs, they do not face the same high costs of changing prices as Sears. Nevertheless, some cost is often attached to changing prices, even if it involves only changing price lists and advising sales personnel of the new price structure. Any cost of price changes encourages less frequent price fluctuations.

Cost-Based Pricing and the Transmission of Inflation

The preceding section was devoted to examining two reasons for inflexible prices. Prices *do* change, however. Price changes occur in some industries every month and in all industries over a period of a few months. What causes these price changes? If firms have an inherent bias against changing prices in order to foster customer relationships, what causes them to change prices as frequently as they do?

Price changes in customer markets are caused by significant long-term movements in demand and, more immediately, in costs. Most sellers will not adjust price unless a demand change is expected to last for quite a while. It is typical for prices to respond quickly and strongly to cost changes but to respond little to changes in demand. In effect, most customer market prices behave as though the market supply curve were relatively flat (elastic), as shown in Figure 16. An increase in demand has only a small effect on price, as in Figure 16 (a). An increase in cost, which shifts the supply curve upward, results in a larger price increase [Figure 16 (b)].

We have good reason to believe that supply curves in many industries are relatively flat over extended quantity ranges. This is certainly true at the retail and wholesale level, where marginal costs rise very little as the quantity sold expands, so long as manufacturers do not raise product prices. Even in many manufacturing industries fairly stable marginal costs are the rule until capacity constraints are reached, at which point marginal costs rise sharply. Only in raw materials markets, which are auction markets, are supply curves not relatively flat over some range. Elastic supply curves generate a particular pattern of price response to aggregate demand changes.

Transmission Process of Demand Increases to Price Increases   Suppose aggregate demand increases, causing product demand to increase in the typical product market. The initial response of retailers is to increase sales at relatively unchanged prices. Retailers run

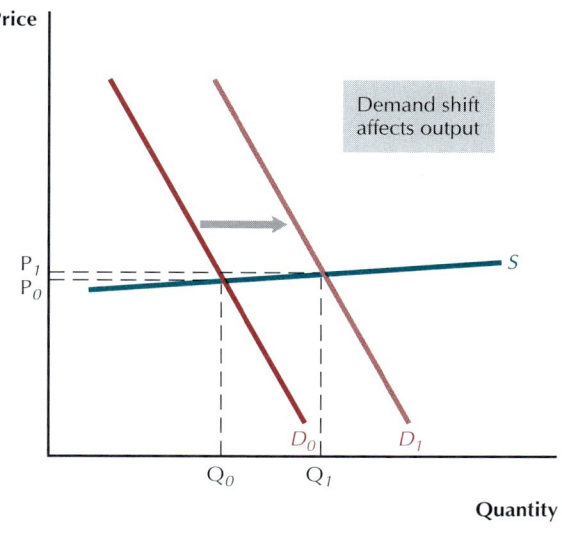

(a)

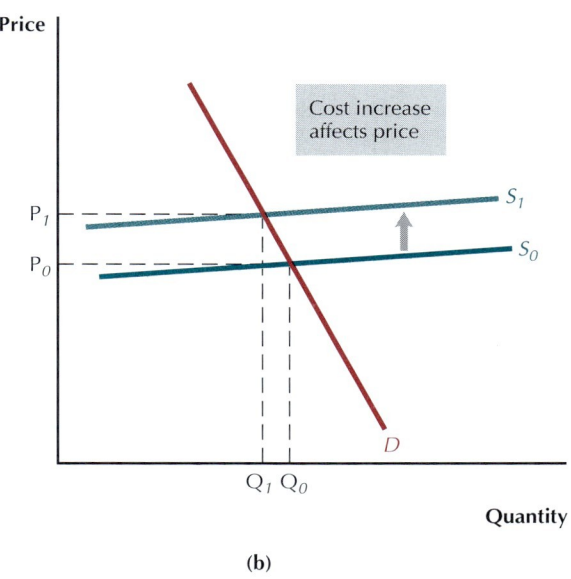

(b)

FIGURE 16
Demand and supply shifts in a customer market. If the supply curve is relatively flat, demand shifts have little effect on price. However, cost increases are passed through to prices.

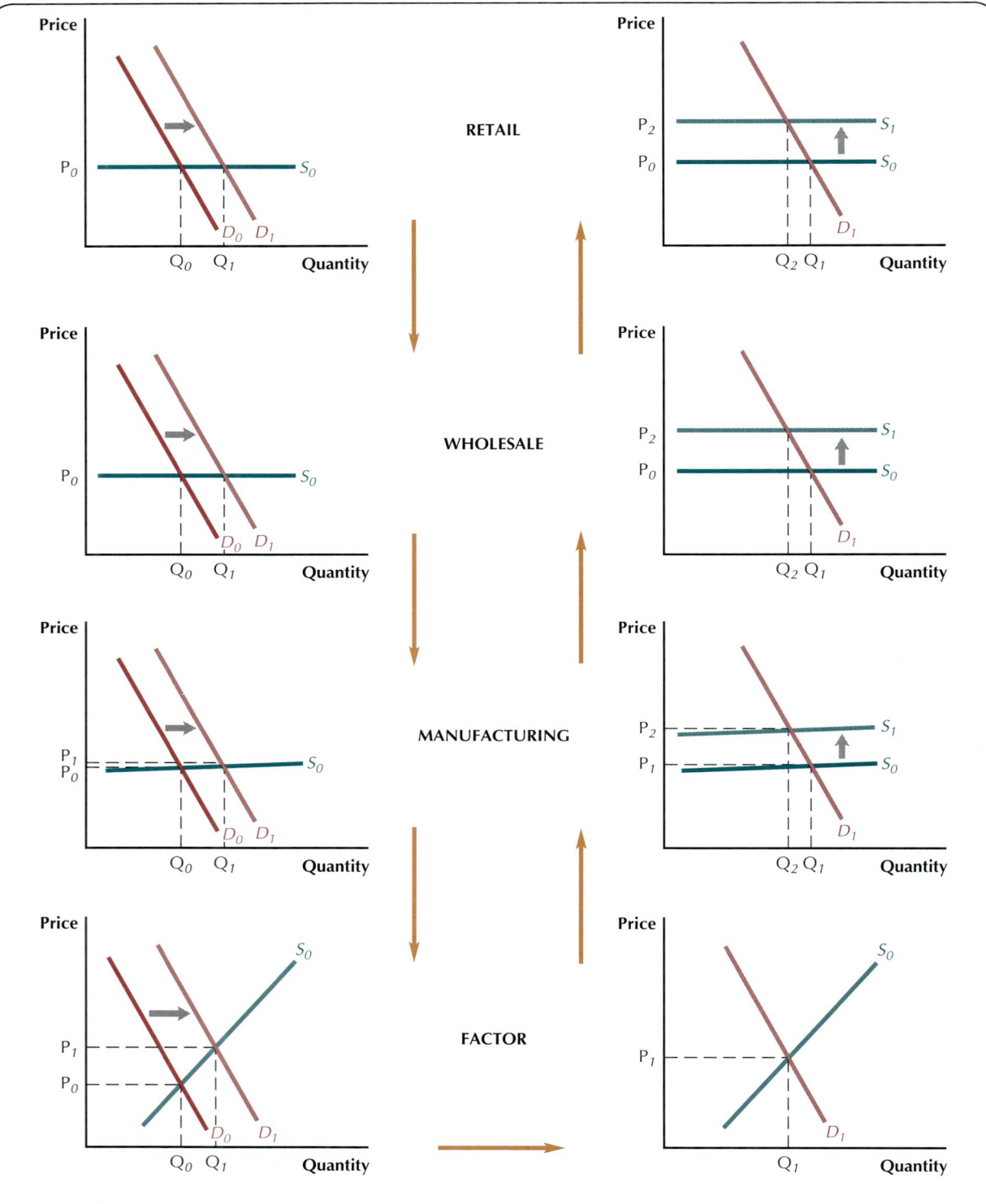

FIGURE 17
Transmission of a demand increase to prices. Demand increases at the retail level. Retailers order more goods from wholesalers, increasing demand at the wholesale level. Wholesalers increase orders from manufacturers, who demand more factor inputs. Factor prices rise, raising manufacturing costs. The higher costs are passed through to wholesalers and retailers.

down their inventories and increase their orders from wholesalers. Wholesalers follow suit by selling from inventories and increasing their orders from manufacturers. Manufacturers increase production levels while holding prices constant so long as their costs do not increase. They demand more labor and more material inputs, shifting the increased demand to the factor markets.

Figure 17 illustrates how the demand increase is passed through from one market level to another. The factor markets are the most basic level in the production process. The demand increase is passed through all the way to this level, at which point increased demand affects quantities supplied—and prices.

Many crude materials prices are set in auction markets. Increased demand for these materials brings forth larger quantities, but materials prices also increase. Higher materials prices raise manufacturing costs.

Increased demand for the most important factor of production—labor—has little immediate impact on the structure of wages because of the existence of implicit and explicit contracts. Employment rises as unemployed workers who wish to work at the prevailing wage structure are hired. If the higher labor demand persists, however, wages begin to rise, causing costs of production at the manufacturing level to increase. As manufacturing costs increase, manufacturers increase their prices. Wholesalers pass the price increase through to retailers, who in turn pass it through to customers. This process is illustrated in Figure 17.

Because an increase in aggregate demand affects prices primarily through costs, a time lag occurs between an increase in aggregate demand and the resulting increase in the price level. An increase in demand must work its way through the system before it has a significant impact on prices. When prices do increase, cost increases seem to be the culprit. Before labeling this an instance of **cost–push inflation**—a process driven by rising costs of production—we should stop to consider what generated the whole process. The causal factor was an increase in aggregate demand.

The moral to this story is that in practice it is very difficult to differentiate between cost–push inflation and **demand–pull inflation**—a process generated by excessive aggregate demand growth. In fact, *any episode of sustained inflation is sure to combine both demand and cost increases.* Both the aggregate demand and short-run aggregate supply curves must be shifting upward continuously, as pictured in Figure 18.

Cost–push inflation
Inflation driven by rising costs of production.

Demand–pull inflation
Inflation driven by increases in aggregate demand.

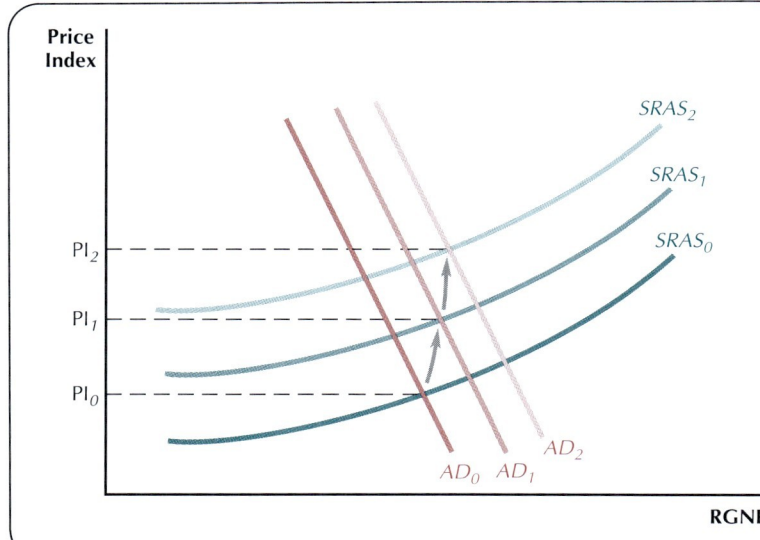

FIGURE 18
Sustained inflation involves both aggregate demand and aggregate supply. Most inflations cannot be characterized as either demand–pull or cost–push, since both demand and costs are rising.

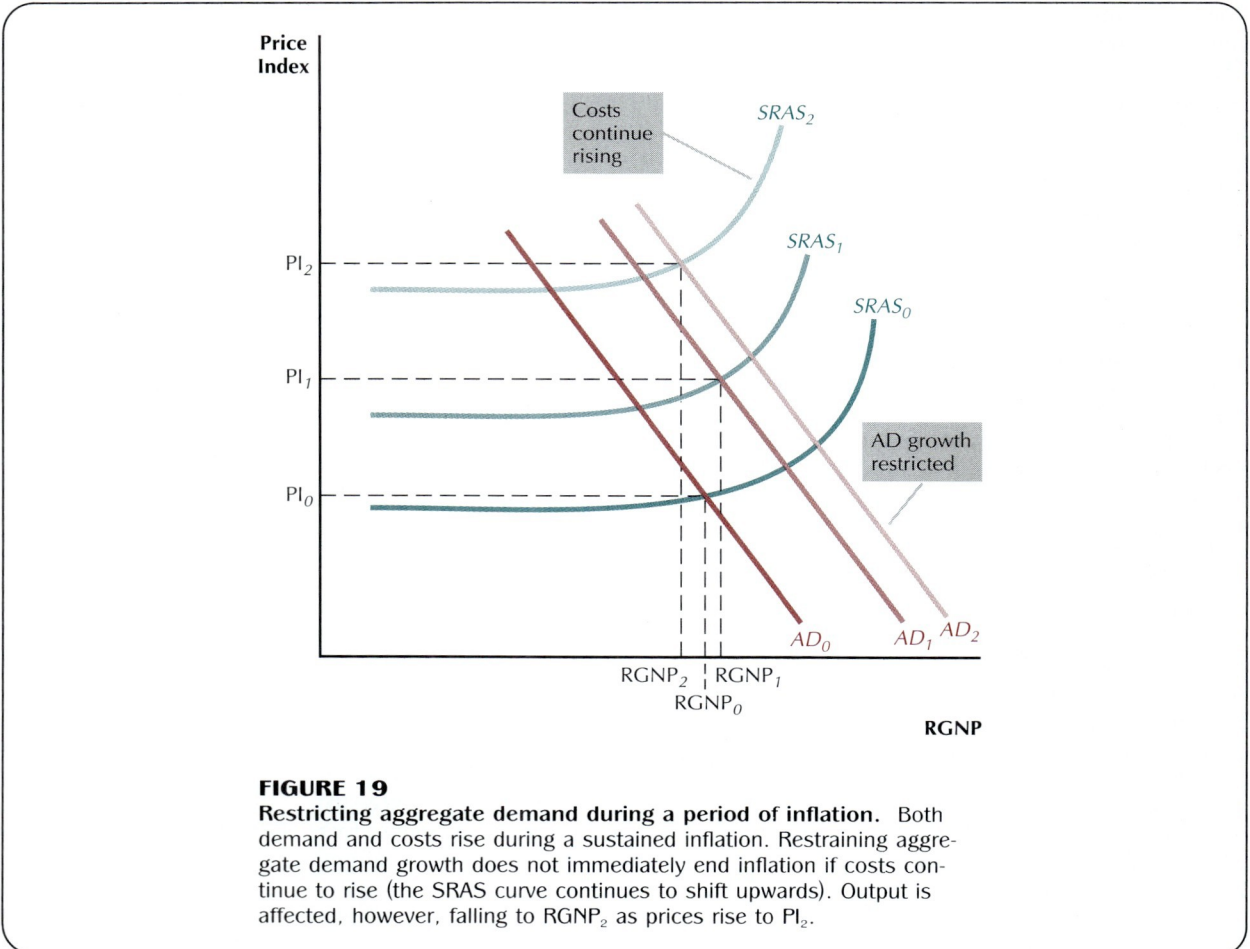

FIGURE 19
Restricting aggregate demand during a period of inflation. Both demand and costs rise during a sustained inflation. Restraining aggregate demand growth does not immediately end inflation if costs continue to rise (the SRAS curve continues to shift upwards). Output is affected, however, falling to $RGNP_2$ as prices rise to PI_2.

The manner in which demand increases are passed through to consumer prices is very important in understanding how restrictive monetary or fiscal policies affect the economy in the short run. Reducing the rate of growth of aggregate demand (or actually decreasing aggregate demand) will not immediately halt price increases. The transmission process of demand changes to price changes and the existence of labor contracts that can increase wages even as labor demand is falling cause the initial impact of declining demand to be primarily on output.

In Figure 19, we see an inflationary process illustrated in the movements of aggregate demand and supply from AD_0 to AD_1 and $SRAS_0$ to $SRAS_1$. (Assume that this process has been going on for some time.) In an effort to reduce the inflation rate, the government institutes a restrictive monetary policy. In Period 2, aggregate demand rises very little. However, the cost increases that were already in effect, coupled with wage increases built into labor contracts, significantly shift the aggregate supply curve upward, to $SRAS_2$. The result is a sharp decrease in aggregate output even as prices continue to climb.

Only when decreased demand pressure has been felt in factor markets will cost increases subside. This means that stopping a well-established inflationary process always entails a temporary reduction in output (and employment). It also points up the importance of maintaining a stable aggregate price level. Once inflation is generated, getting rid of it is a painful exercise.

O V E R V I E W

In this chapter we investigate the nature of money, the factors determining how much money people choose to hold, and how changes in the amount of money people hold affect aggregate spending. We consider such questions as, What makes money valuable? What qualifies one asset as money when other assets do not qualify? What impact does money have on our economy? Could we operate without money? Can

Money: What It Is and Why People Hold It

problems in the monetary system cause problems throughout the economy?

We first examine the nature of money, with the giant question, Why do we use money? driving the discussion. After examining this topic, we turn to the functions of money in a sophisticated modern economy.

We then examine the particular collection of assets qualifying as money in the United States at the present time. This collection includes coins, paper currency, and checking deposits. However, money is not something fixed and unchanging. As society evolves, so does the

monetary system. As the collection of assets actually used as money by the public changes, the relationship between any particular definition of money and aggregate spending also changes. This poses some rather thorny problems for monetary policymakers.

After finishing our discussion of what constitutes the

money supply, we develop the theory of money demand. We examine why people hold the amount of money they do. The particular theory of money demand presented is based on the quantity of transactions people wish to make.

Finally, we examine how changes in the demand for money, relative to the quantity of money supplied to the economy, affect

CHAPTER 27

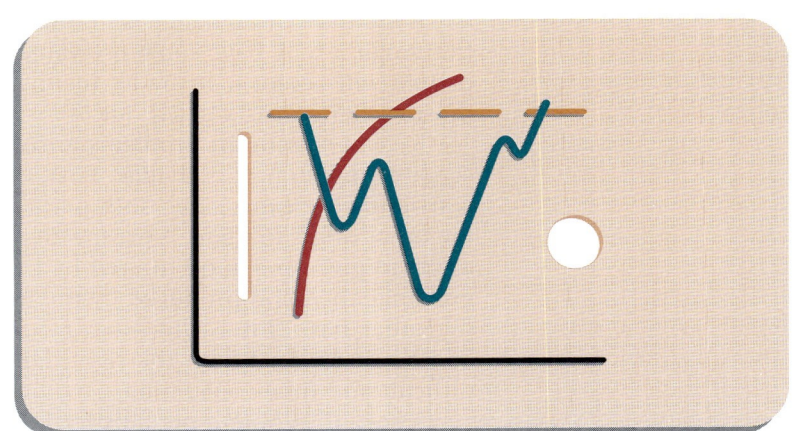

aggregate demand. This enables us to explore the effects of changes in money demand on output and prices and prepares us for an examination of the macroeconomic effects of changes in money supply, a topic pursued in the next chapter.

Learning Objectives

After reading and studying this chapter, you will be able to:

1. State the advantages of a monetary economy over an economy without money (a barter economy).
2. List the functions and characteristics of money.
3. Define the basic U.S. money supply.
4. Discuss the importance of financial innovations for defining money and for monetary control.
5. Use the transactions theory of money demand to predict what effect changes in certain variables will have on the quantity of money demanded.
6. Explain how changes in money demand affect output and prices.

Nature of Money

Perhaps the best way to understand how money benefits the economy is to consider what an economy without money would be like. In such a **barter economy**, people would have to directly exchange the goods and services they produce for goods and services produced by other people.

Barter

In a monetary economy such as ours, some bartering occurs. A person might swap home-grown tomatoes for eggplant grown by a neighbor. An electrician might do some wiring for an accountant in exchange for help with tax preparation. Countless small exchange possibilities exist. However, in a barter economy *all* trades are direct barter trades. No particular good is used specifically to trade for other goods and services. That is, a barter economy has no **medium of exchange** — an asset commonly used to purchase goods and services.

A medium of exchange is not desired primarily for its own intrinsic value (although it may have some use value), but is valued primarily because other people will accept it in trade. In this role, it is the medium through which most exchanges are carried out.

Several significant problems arise in an economy without a generally acceptable medium of exchange. First, the problem of finding a trading partner is magnified greatly, since both parties to a trade must specifically want what the other offers to trade. A prospective trader must locate another person who offers to give up a good desired by the trader *and* who is willing to accept in exchange the good produced by the first trader. Both traders must want what the other has. This is the **double coincidence of wants** problem. Locating another individual with the right demand and supply characteristics can be difficult and time consuming.

A second problem pertains to the production of large, costly goods. Suppose an individual has the equipment and knowledge to produce an automobile. (This is not a small supposition!) Is there any incentive to produce it? Put another way, does anyone have enough items of value to the auto builder to trade for a car? Producing a car is a time-consuming endeavor. The automaker must obtain food, clothing, utilities, and other day-to-day items in return. What prospective buyer has enough of these goods and services to trade for an automobile?

A barter economy would have no large-scale production. It would be difficult to trade large, costly goods in sufficient quantities to make their production profitable. The advantages of capital-intensive, specialized production would be lost. Most people would be forced to engage in the production of goods and services with limited value and for which a large, active market exists. The range of goods and services produced would be much smaller than in modern industrialized economies.

A third problem involves the information needs of traders. People must know the characteristics of any good they acquire in an exchange in order to value it properly. Barter complicates the information problem greatly. Suppose Phil wants to exchange some wood furniture he has built for some bottles of wine. Not only must Phil be able to assess the value of the wine he seeks to acquire, the winemaker must also be able to determine the value of the furniture Phil seeks to trade. A medium of exchange eliminates half of this problem:

Barter economy
An economy without money, in which goods must be traded directly for other goods.

Medium of exchange
An asset that is generally acceptable in exchange and is used to make most purchases.

Double coincidence of wants
Both parties to a trade have what the other wants and want what the other has to trade.

Phil must still be able to assess the value of wine, but the winemaker readily accepts the medium of exchange because its value is evident. *In general, people must spend time and resources obtaining information about any goods they consider accepting in exchange. A medium of exchange with well-known characteristics reduces the information costs of trading.*

Although other problems with a barter economy exist, these three problems show that the information costs and the loss of specialization that would occur in a barter world make barter relatively unattractive.

Efficiency of Indirect Trade

The costs of direct barter exchange would lead traders to look for ways to lower the cost of trading. Somewhat surprisingly, one way to reduce the cost of direct barter trading is to engage in indirect exchanges, involving three or more parties. Although more trading takes place, which may be costly, the problem of the double coincidence of wants is overcome as particular commodities gradually evolve into widely accepted media of exchange.

Consider the role of cashews in Figure 1. Three individuals, Amanda, Becky, and Caroline, each possess a single good, apples, bananas, and cashews, respectively. Amanda wants to trade for bananas, but Becky does not want apples in return. A solution exists, because Caroline is willing to trade cashews for apples and Becky is willing to accept cashews. Thus, Amanda trades some apples to Caroline in exchange for cashews, then exchanges the cashews for some of Becky's bananas. Everyone is better off.

Note how the use of cashews as a medium of exchange reduces the cost of trading. Rather than searching for another trader who has bananas and wants apples, Amanda simply sells her apples for cashews, then uses the cash-

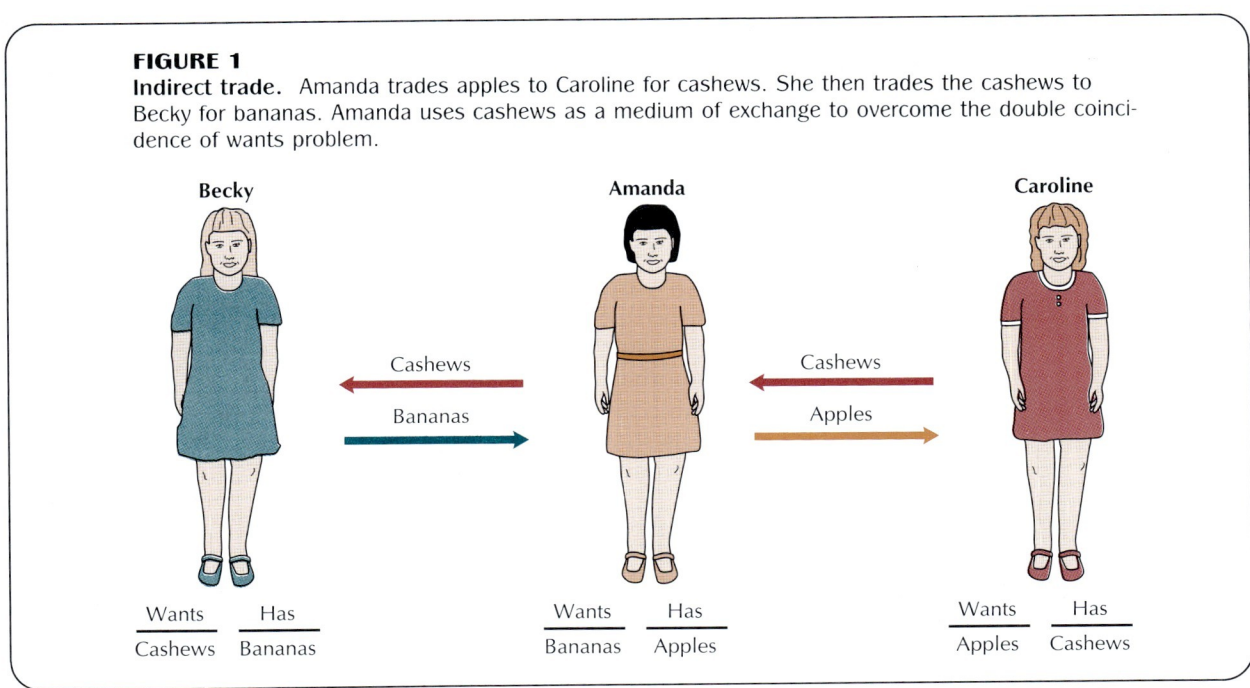

FIGURE 1
Indirect trade. Amanda trades apples to Caroline for cashews. She then trades the cashews to Becky for bananas. Amanda uses cashews as a medium of exchange to overcome the double coincidence of wants problem.

Commodity money
A commodity valued for consumption purposes that also serves as a medium of exchange.

ews to buy the bananas she desires. Cashews serve as more than a commodity (although Becky may eat the cashews she acquires); they serve as a **commodity money** — a good desired both for consumption and for use as a medium of exchange.

Characteristics of a Medium of Exchange

Certain commodities began evolving into media of exchange at an early stage in economic development, before the dawn of recorded history. The commodities that emerged as media of exchange shared one characteristic: They were in widespread demand before they began to be used as media of exchange. Their widespread acceptability led to their use as media of exchange.

An example will clarify this point. Thousands of years ago nomadic cattle cultures were common in Africa, Asia, and Europe. Small groups herded their cattle over large areas. Cattle formed the economic backbone of these societies. Not only were cattle the chief food source, they were also the preferred form of wealth. Because cattle were in widespread demand — they were generally acceptable in trade — they began to be used as a medium of exchange. People began accepting cattle in exchange with the intention of later trading them away for other goods. The use of cattle as a medium of exchange further increased their acceptability in the cattle cultures, reinforcing the tendency to use them as a medium of exchange. As more and more people accepted cattle in exchange for other goods and services, the costs of using cattle as a medium of exchange fell even further.

It is important to note that what led to the widespread use of cattle as a medium of exchange was not a physical characteristic but a social characteristic. Cattle were valued as a source of food and as a store of wealth. Their widespread acceptability led to their use as a medium of exchange, which in turn increased their acceptance in exchange. Had cattle not occupied a central place in the economies of the cattle cultures, cattle would never have evolved into the medium of exchange. The form of society determines what can serve as a medium of exchange. *Only commodities that minimize the costs of trading develop into the medium of exchange.*

Although social acceptability is the most important characteristic of a medium of exchange, several physical characteristics are also important. These include the following:

1. Durability: A medium of exchange should not wear out quickly.
2. Divisibility: Small purchases can be made efficiently only if the medium of exchange can be divided into small units.
3. Portability: The medium of exchange must be easily transported from one market to another.
4. An easily ascertained value.
5. Supply limitations so that supply changes do not radically alter the value over short time periods.

Commodities possessing these characteristics to a greater extent than other commodities make better media of exchange.

Although we cannot trace the history of media of exchange back to barter world beginnings (since such media have existed for thousands of years), we can observe how the items accepted as media of exchange have changed over time. For thousands of years, precious metals have been used in trade. (Note how the desirable physical characteristics listed above fit them.) In the ancient Middle East, copper and bronze were used. Initially the metals were melted and poured into bars or ingots, often called **bullion**. Later they were pounded or minted into coins. Still later, silver became the preferred medium of exchange, largely because it was more valuable per ounce and thus easier to carry. Silver was the dominant medium of exchange in the Middle East until relatively recently.

In Europe, silver served as the dominant medium of exchange until the Spanish began importing tons of gold from the New World. Gold then rivaled and later replaced silver as the dominant medium of exchange. Gold and silver were acceptable in exchange not primarily because they are useful items—in fact their usefulness is rather limited—but because people were confident of their general acceptability. This general acceptability continues to be the primary reason gold and silver are demanded today.

The drive to reduce the information costs of trading led to the replacement of bullion by coins in general trade. Coins replaced bullion because the qualities of coins were easier to judge. The purity of the metal was established by the king, who put his seal (or picture) on the coin. The weight of the coin was guaranteed by milling the edges, so that metal could not be shaved off. (The edges of dimes and quarters are milled to this day.) Such guarantees eliminated the need for traders to spend time or resources establishing the value of the medium of exchange. A simple glance would do.

Bullion
Metal in bulk form, typically melted and poured into bars or ingots.

Functions Served by Money

It should be clear by now that the common term for the medium of exchange is *money*. Money acts as the go-between in the vast majority of exchanges. This function of money is so essential that one common definition of the money supply is "all items that act as media of exchange." However, the medium of exchange function is not the only role played by money. Modern money has two other important functions.

Goods are valued relative to other goods. For example, a gallon of milk may be worth a dozen apples or a pound and a half of hamburger. The use of money as a **standard of value** simplifies the valuation process greatly. A standard of value is a common unit in which values are measured. In the United States the dollar is the standard of value. Quoting all prices in terms of a single standard of value greatly simplifies the pricing process.

The efficiency gains from using a single standard of value are immense. Hundreds of millions of possible exchange ratios between goods are reduced to mere millions of dollar prices. Rather than having to cope with ratios of apples to hamburger, tomatoes to hamburger, running shoes to hamburger, and so on, we simply state the price of hamburger as a dollars-per-pound-of-hamburger ratio. This eliminates the need to quote all the other ratios, drastically reducing the need for information. Yet calculating the relative value of goods is quite simple. The relative value of goods is the ratio of their money prices. For example, if tomatoes cost 75¢ a pound and potatoes cost 25¢ a pound, the price of tomatoes relative to potatoes is 75/25 = 3.

Another important function performed by money is that of **store of value**. A store of value is an item that retains its exchange value over time. Unless an

Standard of value
A unit in terms of which prices are quoted.

Store of value
An asset that retains exchange value over time.

SECTION RECAP
Money arose as a means to reduce transactions costs. The form taken by *(continued)*

SECTION RECAP
(continued)
money depends on the type of society in which the money is used. The most important function of money is that of medium of exchange. Subsidiary functions are standard of value and store of value.

Liquidity
Ability to quickly and easily convert an asset into spendable money at a price near its maximum market value.

item holds its value for at least short periods of time, it will not make a good medium of exchange. No one will be willing to accept it in trade. Inflation reduces the usefulness of money by eroding its usefulness as a store of value.

Money need not be the best store of value available in an economy. Interest-bearing assets are usually better stores of value. Nevertheless, money can be held as an asset and used to transmit value from one time period to another. Savings can be accumulated in the form of money.

Money is important to the economy because it serves as a standard of value, a store of value, and, most importantly, a medium of exchange. Our next task is to examine the collection of assets that perform these functions in the U.S. economy.

The U.S. Money Supply

The money supply in an economy encompasses all the assets that serve the functions of money. However, defining the money supply in a particular economy is not simple, even though the functions performed by money are clear. Uncertainty arises about which assets should be considered money because different assets perform the functions of money to different degrees. In particular, very few assets are media of exchange. However, many assets can be quickly and easily converted into a medium of exchange. Should assets that can be quickly converted into a medium of exchange be counted as money? This is an important question for economic policymakers, who attempt to influence the behavior of the economy by controlling some measure of the money supply.

The **liquidity** of assets — how quickly and easily they can be converted into the medium of exchange at a price near their maximum market values — varies from perfectly liquid to very illiquid. Assets can be ranked along a liquidity spectrum. At the perfectly liquid (immediately spendable) end of the spectrum we would find such assets as currency (coins and paper notes) and checking deposits. Somewhat less liquid, because they cannot be spent without transferring them to currency or to a checking deposit, are passbook savings deposits. Still less liquid are such assets as U.S. Treasury bonds, since converting them into spendable money takes more time and effort than withdrawing funds from a savings deposit. Even less liquid are real assets, such as houses and land. Converting a house into spendable money takes time. People often leave houses on the market for several months in an attempt to obtain the best possible price. Thus, houses violate the quick conversion clause of our liquidity definition.

Where should we draw the line in separating the group of assets known as money from other, less-liquid, assets? This question has no clear answer. Consequently, the Federal Reserve has more than one definition of the U.S. money supply.

Basic Definitions

The Federal Reserve maintains four money supply definitions, rather than designating a particular collection of assets as *the* money supply. The reason for this multiplicity of money supply measures has to do with monetary policy. The main goal of monetary policy is to prevent aggregate demand from growing so rapidly as to cause inflation or so slowly as to cause a recession. Since the Federal Reserve cannot control aggregate demand directly, it attempts to influence demand through its control over the money supply. However, the relationship between aggregate demand and any particular money supply measure is not perfect. No particular measure of money is always superior to others for policy purposes. On the other hand, each of the different money measures provides the Federal Reserve with some useful information on the state of the economy. The Federal Reserve has decided that watching all four money supply measures enables it to do a better job of controlling aggregate demand than it could do by concentrating solely on one particular measure.

The narrowest money supply series calculated by the Federal Reserve is called **M1**. The M1 money supply includes assets that serve as media of exchange: currency in the hands of households and businesses plus checkable deposits at depository institutions held by households and businesses plus traveler's checks. Checkable deposits include zero-interest checking accounts, called **demand deposits**; NOW (negotiable order of withdrawal) and ATS (automatic transfer service) accounts, which pay interest and on which checks may be written; and credit union share draft accounts, all of which may be transferred directly to other people in exchange for goods and services.

The second money supply series calculated by the Federal Reserve is called **M2**. M2 includes all of M1 plus savings deposits and small (less than $100,000) time deposits at depository institutions plus money market deposit accounts at depository institutions plus money market mutual fund accounts plus some other smaller items. **Money market deposit accounts** pay market rates of interest and typically have limited checking privileges. **Money market mutual funds** are organizations that pool the savings of a large number of savers and use them to purchase short-term, liquid, safe assets, such as U.S. Treasury bills. Money market mutual fund accounts are ownership claims against a portion of a fund's assets. Such accounts have limited checking privileges. M2 includes assets that act as media of exchange and other very liquid assets that can be converted into media of exchange very easily at little cost.

The third money supply series calculated by the Federal Reserve, **M3**, includes all of M2 plus large-denomination time deposits ($100,000 or more) and some other minor items.

The fourth, and final, money supply series calculated is not really a money supply series at all. The series is called **L**, which stands for liquid assets. It includes M3 plus household and business holdings of U.S. savings bonds, short-term Treasury securities, commercial paper (short-term corporate bonds) and some minor items. All of these items are liquid and are relatively safe, but they clearly are not money in any typical sense of the word. The L series is calculated to provide an estimate of the amount of assets that the public could quickly convert into money should the need arise.

Table 1 summarizes and defines the components of the various **monetary aggregates** — the collections of assets included in the definitions of money. Figure 2 illustrates the relative size of the components of M1 and M2.

Evolution of the U.S. Money Supply

The money supply definitions presented in Table 1 have been in use only since the early 1980s. Before then a somewhat different set of definitions existed. It is almost a sure bet that some of the definitions in Table 1 will change within

M1
Monetary aggregate that includes only assets that are immediately spendable.

Demand deposits
Zero-interest checking accounts.

M2
Monetary aggregate that includes M1 plus liquid savings instruments.

Money market deposit account
An account at a depository institution that pays a market rate of interest and has limited checking privileges.

Money market mutual fund
An organization that pools the funds of savers and uses them to buy short-term liquid assets.

M3
Monetary aggregate that includes M2 plus some less liquid savings instruments.

L
A broad measure of liquid assets.

Monetary aggregate
A specific collection of financial assets serving as a measure of the money supply.

> **TABLE 1**
>
> **Monetary aggregate definitions**
>
> **M1**
>
> (1) Currency outside the Treasury, Federal Reserve Banks, and vaults of commercial banks; plus
> (2) travelers checks of nonbank issuers; plus
> (3) demand deposits of all commercial banks other than those due to other banks, the U.S. government, and foreign banks and official institutions, less cash items in process of collection and Federal Reserve float (checks which have not cleared); plus
> (4) other checkable deposits consisting of NOW and ATS accounts at depository institutions, credit union draft shares, and demand deposits at thrift institutions.
>
> **M2**
>
> M1 plus overnight (and continuing contract) repurchase agreements issued by all commercial banks and overnight Eurodollars issued to U.S. residents by foreign branches of U.S. banks worldwide, money market deposit accounts, savings and small denomination time deposits, and balances in general purpose and broker/dealer money market mutual funds. Excludes IRA and Keogh balances and all balances held by commercial banks, money market funds, foreign governments, and the U.S. government.
>
> **M3**
>
> M2 plus large-denomination time deposits and term repurchase agreements and Eurodollars.
>
> **L**
>
> M3 plus the nonbank public holdings of U.S. savings bonds, short-term Treasury securities, commercial paper, and bankers acceptances, net of money market mutual fund holdings of these assets.
>
> Source: Federal Reserve *Bulletin*.

the next decade, because money evolves as the economy changes. Just as the form of money in ancient times evolved from cattle to metals in bullion form to coined metal, so the form taken by money changes today. As new technologies alter the costs of various kinds of transactions, the assets used as money change. Money definitions also change when new types of assets are invented, assets which perform some or all of the functions of money.

An excellent example of money supply evolution in the United States occurred in the 1970s. Until then, all checking accounts in the United States were zero-interest demand deposits at commercial banks. Federal Reserve regulations prohibited other depository institutions from issuing checking accounts and prohibited banks from paying interest on their checking accounts. M1 (now called "old M1") consisted of currency plus demand deposits. Then, during the 1970s, mutual savings banks[1] in New England invented the NOW

---

[1] Mutual savings banks are similar to savings and loan associations. Traditionally they collected funds by issuing savings accounts and used the funds to make mortgage loans and to buy corporate bonds. In the 1980s mutual savings banks entered other areas of banking and became more like commercial banks.

(negotiable order of withdrawal) account. Legally, NOW accounts were savings accounts. They paid interest just like passbook savings accounts. The only difference was that the mutual savings banks agreed to honor negotiable orders of withdrawal written on these accounts. Depositors could write negotiable orders of withdrawal on their accounts, using them just like checking accounts.

The Federal Reserve brought legal action against the mutual savings banks, attempting to force them to cease paying interest on what was obviously a checkable deposit. However, the Federal Reserve lost, and the mutual savings banks were permitted to continue issuing NOW accounts. Once it became legal for mutual savings banks to issue NOW accounts, commercial banks and savings and loan associations were put at a competitive disadvantage. Thus, the Federal Reserve was forced to change its regulations, making it legal for commercial banks and savings and loans to issue NOW accounts as well.

The widespread use of NOW accounts forced the Federal Reserve to change its definition of M1. NOW accounts are, of course, checking accounts that can be used just like demand deposit accounts. They should be included in the medium of exchange definition of money, and the definition of M1 was changed to include them.

The development of NOW accounts is one example of **financial innovation** — the development of new financial assets or services by financial institutions. Such innovation is continuous, although the economic conditions prevailing in the 1970s generated an unusually intense outburst of innovation.

Financial innovation Development of new financial assets or services that reduce transactions costs or provide savers with more options.

SECTION RECAP
The Federal Reserve maintains four measures of the U.S. money supply, rang- *(continued)*

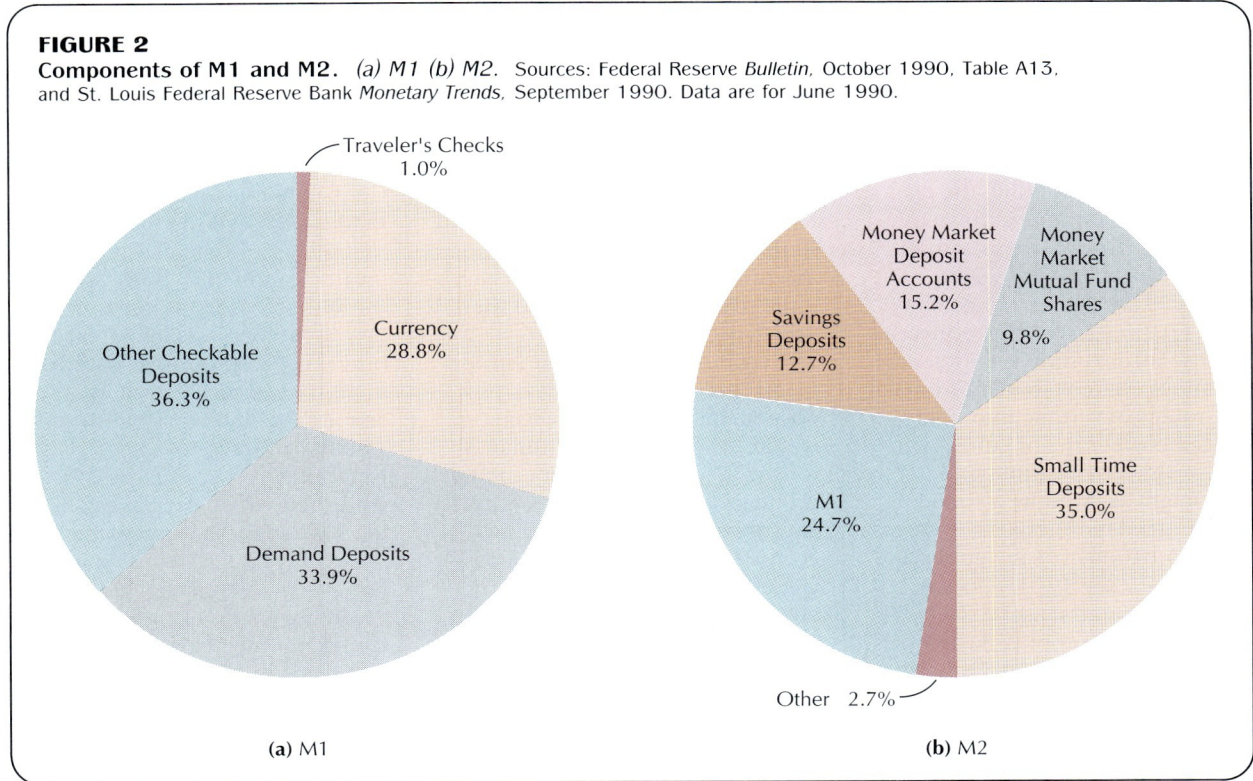

FIGURE 2
Components of M1 and M2. *(a) M1 (b) M2.* Sources: Federal Reserve *Bulletin*, October 1990, Table A13, and St. Louis Federal Reserve Bank *Monetary Trends*, September 1990. Data are for June 1990.

(a) M1

- Traveler's Checks 1.0%
- Currency 28.8%
- Other Checkable Deposits 36.3%
- Demand Deposits 33.9%

(b) M2

- Money Market Deposit Accounts 15.2%
- Money Market Mutual Fund Shares 9.8%
- Savings Deposits 12.7%
- M1 24.7%
- Small Time Deposits 35.0%
- Other 2.7%

Does It Make **Economic Sense?**

Could New Money Rescue the Soviet Economy?

The economic problems faced by the Soviet Union have become well known over the past few years. Even basic food items are often in short supply, and most of the consumer goods Americans and western Europeans take for granted are simply not available. In an attempt to revive the economy, Soviet President Mikhail Gorbachev instituted a number of reforms, the most drastic of which was the confiscation of most 50-ruble and 100-ruble notes.

By outlawing the use of the large ruble notes and by permitting Soviet citizens to convert no more than 1000 rubles into smaller notes, Gorbachev sought to reduce the money supply and thereby reduce prices on the black (unofficial) market. He also indicated his desire to open the Soviet economy to greater international trade with western market economies. Such trade is complicated by many factors, however, including the fact that the Soviet ruble is not a convertible currency. That is, rubles cannot be traded for western money in foreign exchange markets. One suggestion for overcoming the inconvertibility problem is for the Soviet government to make the ruble convertible into gold. Since no other major currency in the world is convertible into gold, this might seem to be a strange recommendation, especially since western nations left the gold standard in the early 1970s. Does it make economic sense?

The monetary problem facing the Soviet Union is simple: Outsiders do not want rubles. The reason no one wants rubles is also simple: The ruble is nearly worthless. At present, the ruble is a paper currency, just like the dollar, the yen, and the deutschemark. None of these currencies is backed by (legally convertible into) anything valuable. Unlike the ruble, however, the dollar, the yen, and the deutschemark *are* valuable. The real key to understanding the ruble problem, then, is understanding why some paper money is valuable, while other paper money is not.

Although U.S. dollars have no *commodity value* (they aren't made out of anything valuable), they have a high *exchange value*. American producers are willing to accept paper dollars from buyers because they in turn can use the dollars to buy things. The incredible productivity of the U.S. economy makes the dollar very valuable. This productivity also explains why the dollar is valued by foreigners. To buy American-made goods, one must have dollars. Foreigners acquire dollars in the foreign exchange market in exchange for foreign currencies, such as the French franc and the British pound sterling. Americans are willing to accept francs and pounds for the same reason the French and the British accept dollars.

The economies of western Europe, Japan, and the United States produce many goods the Soviets would like to buy. Unfortunately for the Soviets, the Soviet economy produces little that is wanted by consumers in developed market economies. This explains the Soviet dilemma: The ruble is worth almost nothing because the Soviet economy produces almost nothing outsiders want. However, there are exceptions to this statement. One exception is gold. The Soviet Union is the world's second-largest producer of gold. Since gold is actively traded in European and American commodity markets, making the ruble convertible into gold would assure its acceptability by foreigners. Once the ruble is acceptable in foreign exchange markets, the problem of opening up trade between the Soviet Union and market economies becomes a bit easier to solve. Gold convertibility would also provide some assurance to Soviet citizens that their hard-earned savings would not be confiscated again.

The eastern European countries that are attempting to convert from command economies to market economies face much the same problem as the Soviet Union. Fortunately for Poland, Hungary, and other eastern European nations, their economies are somewhat more efficient than the Soviet economy, and they are much smaller than the giant Soviet economy. The East German currency problem was solved when West Germany agreed to convert East German ostmarks into deutschemarks as part of the plan to reunite the two Germanies. Of even greater importance, however, was the West German pledge to invest heavily in the East German economy. The West German government understood as well as anyone that money is worth only what it can buy.

Returning to the question of a gold ruble, then, we can say that the idea does make economic sense. By making the ruble internationally acceptable, gold convertibility would bring the Soviet Union one step closer to being a part of the integrated world economy.

High inflation drove interest rates up, making it very costly to hold zero-interest demand deposits, while the increasing use of computers created new possibilities and motivated financial market participants to circumvent federal regulations designed for a different era. By exploiting loopholes in the regulatory system, innovators created a number of attractive new financial assets. After initial attempts to suppress the innovation proved unsuccessful, the Federal Reserve relented and rescinded most of the regulations that led to the innovative activity. The *Depository Institutions Deregulation and Monetary Control Act* of 1980 went even further, greatly simplifying the regulatory system by eliminating a large number of restrictions.

> **SECTION RECAP**
> *(continued)*
> ing from a medium of exchange measure, M1, to a broad measure of liquid assets, L. The assets included in monetary aggregates change over time in response to financial innovations.

Theory of Money Demand

We have seen that people hold money because it lowers the information and transactions costs associated with exchanging goods and services. However, we have not discussed the factors determining how much money people will wish to hold. Because the quantity of money demanded influences the level of aggregate demand, in turn affecting the short-run equilibrium levels of output and prices, the theory of money demand has important policy implications.

The **transactions theory of money demand** is the oldest and most widely accepted money demand theory in economics. It builds on the idea that money is held to reduce the costs associated with exchanging goods, services, and assets — the costs of transactions. The major factor affecting the quantity of money an individual wants to hold is the volume of transactions that individual wants to undertake. Since transactions are closely related to income, the transactions theory of money demand focuses on the effect of real GNP and the price level on money demand. However, the opportunity cost of holding money is also an important consideration, and we will take account of opportunity cost in formulating our complete theory.

> **Transactions theory of money demand**
> Theory based on the idea that money is held primarily to carry out transactions.

Income: The Primary Determinant of Money Demand

What limits the amount of spending by an individual during some period of time? From our earlier analysis of the budget constraint we know that a person can spend no more than he can finance through income, borrowing, or the sale of assets. Assuming that an individual does not continuously increase his borrowing or sell off assets, the ultimate limit on spending is set by income.

Income also provides the source of money holdings for most people. Individuals convert their paychecks into money by cashing them or by depositing them in a checkable deposit account. The funds are then immediately available for exchange. Thus, income provides both the need for money through its close relationship to spending and the source of money for most economic units.

Changes in income are due either to changes in real income or to changes in the price level. The effect on money demand of a change in prices need not be the same as the effect of a change in real income, although they act in the same direction. When real income rises, people typically increase their purchases of goods, services, and assets. They require more money to efficiently carry out a larger number of transactions. Consequently, the demand for money increases when real income (measured by real GNP) rises. Empirical studies indicate that money demand increases less than proportionately when real income rises. For example, a 10 percent increase in real GNP causes people to increase their money holdings by *less than* 10 percent.

Nominal income also rises when prices increase. People need more money to buy the same quantity of goods and services, because the buying power of each dollar they hold has fallen. To maintain a constant level of **real money balances** — money in buying-power terms — people must increase their money holdings proportionately as the price level rises. Real money balances are measured by M/PI, where M is the money stock and PI the aggregate price index. If PI increases by 10 percent, M must also rise by 10 percent to maintain constant real money balances.

An example illustrates the common sense of this. You probably carry several times as much cash with you, on the average, as your grandfather did when he was your age. This is true even if your grandfather was relatively as well off as you are at the same age. Why? Because prices were so much lower in Grandpa's day, he did not need to carry as much cash as you do. The aggregate price level is well over seven times as high now as it was in the 1930s. It takes over $7 today to purchase what $1 would have bought then. Grandpa simply did not need to carry much cash to make the purchases he wanted to make.

We can state the demand for money in equation form as:

$$M^d = f(PI, RGNP, \ldots)$$

which translates to "money demand is a function of (depends on) the price level, real GNP, and other variables (yet to be specified)." Because changes in PI apparently affect money demand by a higher proportion than do changes in RGNP, we separate the two rather than combining them into GNP. However, note that they affect money demand in the same direction.

Role of Opportunity Cost

Income is not the only variable affecting money demand. As with any good, the quantity of money demanded is affected by the opportunity cost of acquiring or holding the good. The opportunity cost of holding money is the income or capital gains forgone by holding money rather than purchasing other assets. A **capital gain** is earned when an asset is sold at a higher price than its purchase price. (A **capital loss** results when an asset is sold for less than its purchase price.)

Either financial or real assets can be held instead of money. The rate of return on financial assets is the interest rate. Many financial assets are safe (relatively free from risk of default) and liquid (easily and cheaply convertible into money), making them excellent alternatives to money. Passbook savings accounts and money market mutual fund shares fill this role for individuals, while Treasury bills are an alternative for large corporations. All these assets pay interest, all are safe, and all can be quickly and cheaply converted into money (the medium of exchange).

As interest rates on nonmoney financial assets rise, the opportunity cost of holding money increases. People respond by conserving on the quantity of money balances they hold. Fewer dollars are left lying idle in checking accounts for weeks on end. More attention is paid to using those dollars to purchase

---

Real money balances
Money holdings of constant buying power.

Capital gain
Income from selling an asset at a price higher than its purchase price.

Capital loss
Loss sustained from selling an asset at a price lower than its purchase price.

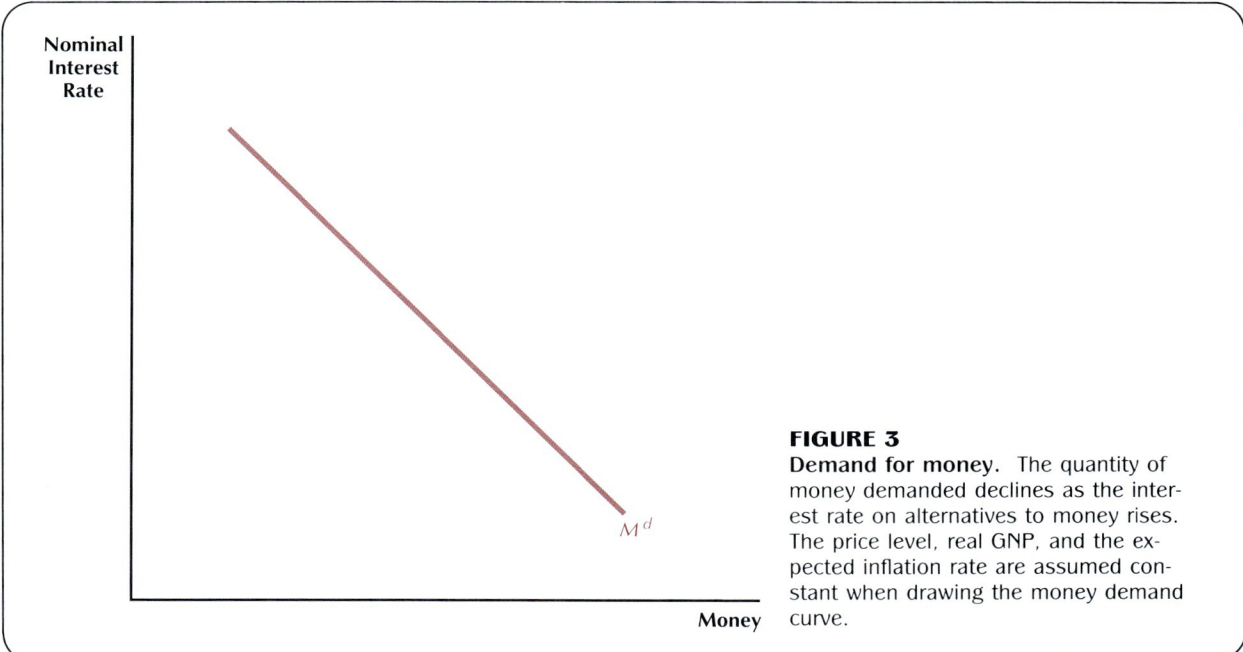

FIGURE 3
Demand for money. The quantity of money demanded declines as the interest rate on alternatives to money rises. The price level, real GNP, and the expected inflation rate are assumed constant when drawing the money demand curve.

financial assets paying a market rate of return. Consequently, the demand for money is negatively related to the nominal interest rate on alternative assets, as shown in Figure 3.

People may also choose to hold real assets rather than money. The rate of return on real assets is represented by the rate of change in the assets' prices. During a period of inflation, individuals can earn a return on real assets by purchasing them before they are needed—and before their prices rise. For example, if you know you will need new tires for your car next year but believe the price of tires will rise by 10 percent between now and then, you can earn a 10 percent rate of return by purchasing the tires now and holding them until they are needed. The expected inflation rate represents both the expected rate of return from holding real assets and the opportunity cost of holding money rather than real assets. If the expected inflation rate, p^e, rises, it becomes more costly to hold money rather than holding real assets whose prices are rising. Consequently, money demand decreases, and the money demand curve shifts to the left, as shown in Figure 4.

The complete equation for money demand can be written as:

$$M^d = f(PI, RGNP, i, p^e)$$

The demand for money is a function of the price level, real GNP, the nominal interest rate on alternative financial assets, and the expected inflation rate. Changes in the price level, real GNP, or the expected inflation rate shift the money demand curve. An increase in real GNP or the price level, which increases the dollar volume of transactions individuals or businesses carry out, or a decline in expected inflation, which reduces the opportunity cost of holding money, shifts the money demand curve to the right. A decrease in real GNP or the price level or an increase in the expected inflation rate shifts the

SECTION RECAP
The transactions theory of money demand says that people hold money primarily to carry out transactions. The major factor determining the amount of money demanded is income. The interest rate on alternative assets and the expected inflation rate are opportunity cost variables affecting the quantity of money demanded.

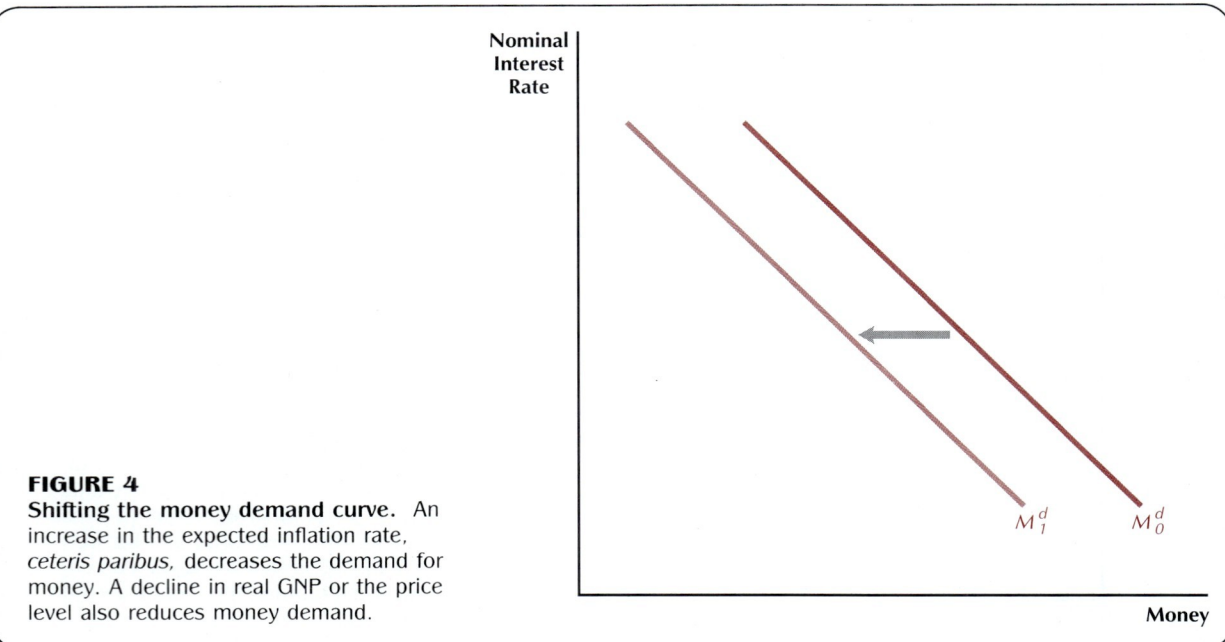

FIGURE 4
Shifting the money demand curve. An increase in the expected inflation rate, *ceteris paribus*, decreases the demand for money. A decline in real GNP or the price level also reduces money demand.

money demand curve to the left, as shown in Figure 4. Changes in the nominal interest rate generate movements *along* the money demand curve.

Credit Cards and Money Demand

The use of credit cards has become extremely widespread in the United States. Many people carry very little cash and write few checks, preferring to use their VISA, Mastercard, or Discover cards to charge most purchases. The increasing use of credit cards has reduced the amount of money people feel they need to keep on hand. Credit cards enable people to make purchases even if their checking accounts are bare. Without credit cards, many people would attempt to hold a significant amount of idle money balances as a precaution against unforeseen events. Credit cards free people from the need to hold precautionary balances. Should an emergency arise—or should a fantastic sale be encountered—the credit card can be used to postpone payment.

Note that *credit cards are not money;* they only postpone the need to transfer money. They enable a card holder to automatically borrow from a bank. The bank must be repaid, however, sometimes with interest. The card holder must transfer money to the bank to pay off the debt incurred. Nevertheless, the use of credit cards has reduced the need to hold idle money balances, shifting the money demand curve to the left over time.

Aggregate Demand and Changes in Money Demand

As we saw in earlier chapters, the level of real GNP produced in the economy depends on aggregate demand and aggregate supply. Aggregate demand is the sum of consumption demand, investment demand, government purchases of goods and services, and net exports. The demand for money is not included in the aggregate demand for goods and services. Nevertheless, the demand for money is an important determinant of aggregate demand. Although the effect on aggregate demand of a change in the demand for money is less direct than a change in consumption demand, it may be just as important. Autonomous changes in money demand can affect aggregate demand through two channels: the budget-constraint channel and the interest-rate channel.

Effects through the Budget Constraint

An economic unit's budget constraint states that sources of funds must equal uses of funds. A household or business cannot spend more than it finances. We can write this budget constraint very simply as follows:

Receipts from the sale of goods and services	=	Spending on goods and services
+		+
Receipts from sales of financial assets		Purchases of financial assets
+		+
Reduction of money holdings		Additions to money holdings

The equality shows that people cannot alter their money holdings without affecting other supply and demand choices. That is, a change in money demand must be financed in some manner. Assuming the supply side (the left-hand side) of the budget constraint is constant, an increase in the demand for money must be accompanied by a reduction in the demand for goods and services or the demand for financial assets. Thus, an increased desire to hold money may lead to a reduction in the demand for goods and services.

The common sense of this is obvious once we drop the budget constraint terminology. Suppose you wish to increase the amount of money held in your checking account. How would you go about it? The obvious way would be to spend less. You might spend less on financial assets (channel less of your income into a savings deposit), or you might spend less on goods and services (eat out less often). Either option would allow you to increase money balances.

The aggregate economy faces a similar budget constraint. The only significant difference is that in the aggregate the money supply can increase or decrease. The aggregate budget constraint can be written as follows:

Supply of goods and services	=	Demand for goods and services
+		+
Supply of more financial assets		Demand for more financial assets
+		+
Supply of more money		Demand for more money

Putting the aggregate budget constraint into equational form, we have the following:

$$(PI \times RGNP^s) + (PI^A \times A^s) + M^s =$$
$$(PI \times RGNP^d) + (PI^A \times A^d) + M^d$$

Just as at the individual level, the demand for more money at the aggregate level is linked to other demands.

Suppose we begin with all three markets (goods and services, assets, and money) in equilibrium. What happens when the demand for money changes?

Obviously, one or more of the other variables must also change to maintain the budget constraint equality. To illustrate this, we will work through a simple example.

Suppose the demand for money increases. That is, at the current levels of PI, RGNP, i, and p^e, the amount of money people want to hold increases. However, assume that the total quantity of money supplied to the economy is constant. This is pictured in Figure 5 (a), where the supply of money is shown as a vertical line. As the demand for money increases from M_0^d to M_1^d, an excess demand for money emerges at the initial interest rate, i_0.

People who want to hold more money attempt to accumulate money by buying fewer goods and services and fewer financial assets. The decreased demand for goods and services reduces the quantity of real GNP demanded at the initial price level, creating an excess supply in the goods and services market [$RGNP_d$ is less than $RGNP_N$ at PI_0 in Figure 5 (b)]. Either real GNP supplied or PI must fall to restore equilibrium. In Figure 5 (b), a new short-run equilibrium emerges as both PI and RGNP supplied fall. The direct negative effect on aggregate demand that results from an autonomous change in money demand is called the **budget-constraint effect**.

The decline in PI and RGNP reduces the demand for money, eliminating some of the excess demand for money that existed after the autonomous increase in money demand. The money demand curve shifts to M_2^d in Figure 5 (a). However, at the initial interest rate, i_0, some excess demand for money remains. The remaining excess demand is eliminated by an increase in the interest rate that results from a change in the demand for financial assets. Of course, a change in the interest rate affects the aggregate demand for goods and services as well as the quantity of money demanded.

Budget-constraint effect (of money demand on aggregate demand) Works through the budget constraint; one way to accumulate more money is to buy fewer goods and services.

SECTION RECAP
A change in the demand for money, *ceteris paribus*, shifts the demand for goods and services in the opposite direction. When money demand increases, the aggregate demand for goods and services falls.

Effects through the Interest Rate

People who want to hold larger money balances reduce both their demand for goods and services and their demand for financial assets. *Ceteris paribus*, a decline in the demand for financial assets reduces the price of such assets. Changing the price of a financial asset also changes the rate of return an asset holder earns. That is, when the price of a financial asset changes, the rate of interest earned on the asset also changes. A change in the rate of interest affects both the quantity of money demanded and the aggregate demand for goods and services.

Consider how the interest rate earned on a one-year discount bond varies as its price changes. A discount bond pays interest by selling at a price less than its face value. For example, a discount bond with a face value of $1000 pays the purchaser $1000 when the bond matures. A buyer earns interest by purchasing the bond at a price below $1000.

Suppose the initial price of one-year discount bonds is $940. A bond purchaser pays $940, holds the bond one year, and then receives $1000. Obviously, the bondholder earns $60 in interest. Dividing the amount of interest by the price of the bond, we obtain the rate of interest earned on the bond: $60/$940 = .0638, or 6.38 percent.

Now, suppose that an increase in the demand for money reduces the demand for one-year discount bonds, reducing the price of such bonds to $930. The amount of interest now earned by bond purchasers is $70, and the

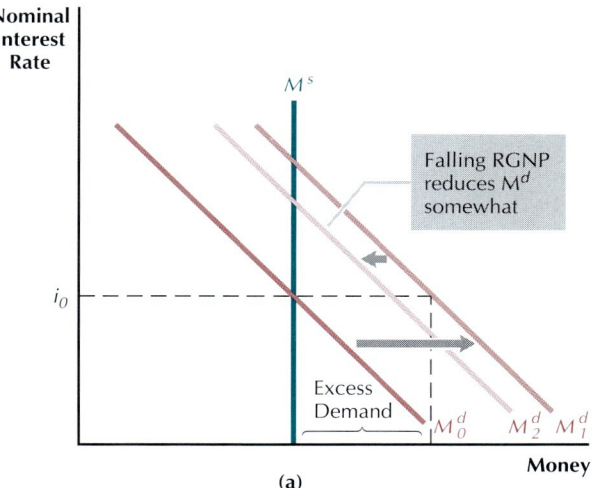

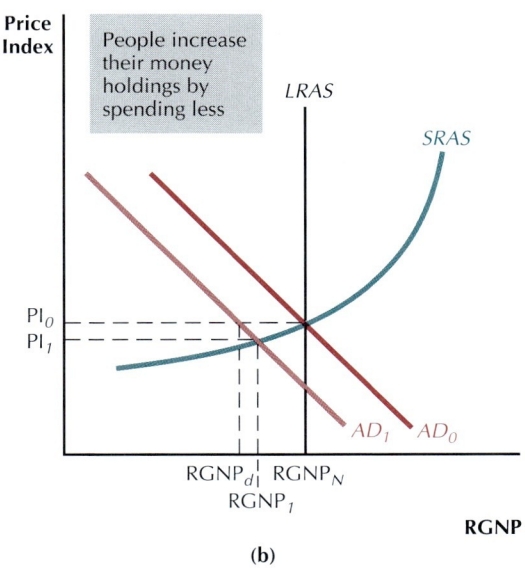

FIGURE 5
Budget-constraint effect of an increase in money demand. An increase in money demand with the money supply constant causes an excess demand for money at i_0. People reduce their demand for goods and services, and the AD curve shifts left to AD_1. The decline in PI and RGNP reduces the demand for money somewhat, shifting the money demand curve to the left to M_2^d and reducing the excess demand for money.

interest rate earned is $70/$930 = .0753, or 7.53 percent. This simple example illustrates a perfectly general result: *When the price of financial assets rises, the interest rate earned on the assets falls, and when the price of financial assets falls, the interest rate rises. Financial asset prices and interest rates are inversely related.*

Now, observe how the increase in the interest rate acts to restore macroeconomic equilibrium. As the interest rate *rises*, the quantity of money demanded *falls* along M_2^d in Figure 6 (a). As the interest rate rises, the excess demand for money diminishes. The higher interest rate also reduces the demand for capital goods by investors, shifting the aggregate demand curve further to the left in Figure 6 (b). This indirect **interest-rate effect** on aggregate demand reinforces the direct budget-constraint effect of an autonomous change in money demand. Note that, as PI and RGNP fall because of lower investment demand, the demand for money also declines, to M_3^d, where money demand once again equals money supply.

Although our example makes it appear as though the budget-constraint and interest-rate effects work sequentially, the two effects really work simultaneously. Given a constant money supply, an increase in money demand immediately affects both the demand for goods and services and the demand for financial assets. The interest rate begins to rise, reducing the quantity of money demanded and the demand for capital goods by investors at the same time that consumers are buying fewer goods and services in order to build up their money holdings.

Sudden changes in the demand for money have the potential to seriously affect the level of economic activity. A large increase in the demand for money can reduce aggregate demand significantly, throwing the economy into a recession. Such an increase could occur as the result of a loss of confidence in financial assets other than money. For example, in October 1987 the stock market nearly collapsed. The price of an average share of stock fell by over 20 percent in two days. Stock prices declined because of massive selling; it seemed that everyone wanted to get rid of stocks and acquire some other asset. Many people bought bonds, but many others demanded money.

The Federal Reserve recognized the potential danger to the economy from a sudden increase in the demand for money. Alan Greenspan, chairman of the Federal Reserve's Board of Governors, pledged to increase the money supply enough to satisfy the increased demand for money. The Federal Reserve's actions held interest rates constant and prevented any decline in aggregate demand. Had the Federal Reserve not responded to the increased demand for money by supplying more money, the economy might well have plunged into a recession.

Money Supply Definitions, Money Demand, and Monetary Policy

As we noted in our discussion of U.S. monetary aggregates, the collection of assets serving as money changes over time. Financial innovation sometimes creates new alternatives to money and sometimes reduces the amount of money required to carry out a particular volume of transactions. In response, the demand for money *as conventionally measured* usually decreases. The new financial innovations enable people to either get by with a smaller amount of money than before or substitute new assets for the old assets counted as part

Interest-rate effect (of money demand on aggregate demand) When money demand changes, the interest rate changes, affecting aggregate demand through borrowing costs and wealth effects.

SECTION RECAP
A change in the demand for money, *ceteris paribus*, shifts the demand for other financial assets in the opposite direction. When money demand increases, the demand for financial assets falls, pushing asset prices down and the interest rate up.

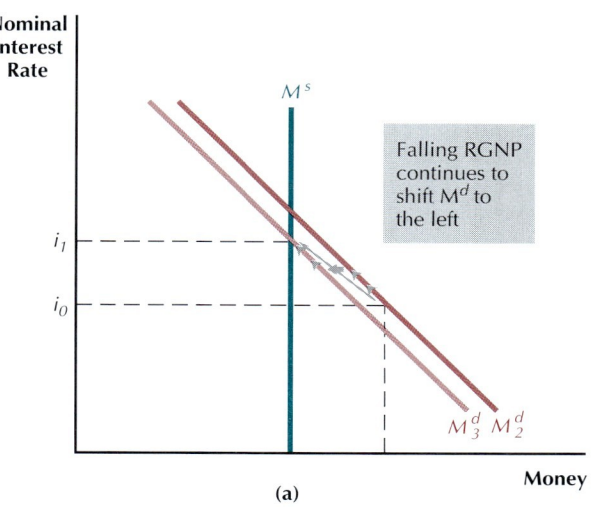

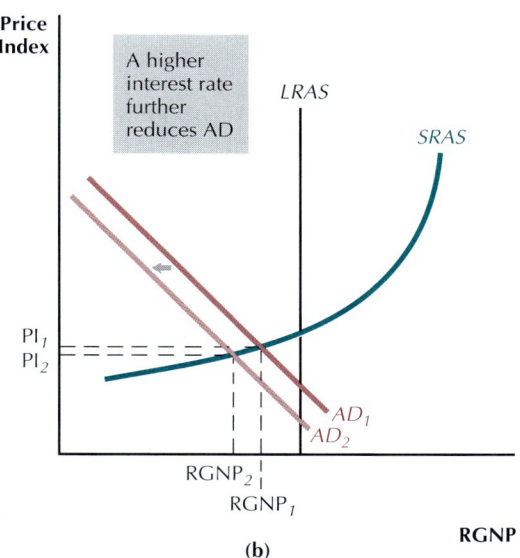

FIGURE 6
Interest-rate effect of an increase in money demand.
An increase in money demand causes the demand for other financial assets to decline. Declining asset demand pushes the interest rate upward. As the interest rate rises, the quantity of money demanded falls along M_2^d. A higher interest rate also reduces investment spending, shifting AD to AD_2 and reducing PI and RGNP. The fall in PI and RGNP reduces the demand for money to M_3^d. The money market returns to equilibrium when the interest rate rises to i_1.

Why the **Disagreement?**

Stable Money Supply Growth

During the early 1970s, an economic doctrine known as *monetarism* came to prominence. Monetarism was the outgrowth of work done by Milton Friedman and later by Karl Brunner, Allan Meltzer, and others. The major policy prescription of monetarism was quite simple: The money supply should grow at a steady rate over time. This would prevent money supply shocks from destabilizing the economy. A smoothly growing money supply would promote smoothly growing aggregate demand, or so said the monetarists. This claim was hotly disputed by a large number of economists. Since this is such an important policy issue, we need to know, Why the disagreement?

Stable money supply growth generates stable aggregate demand growth only if the demand for money is stable. Suppose that the money supply has been growing at a constant rate for some time, so that people are adjusted to that growth rate. If the demand for money is stable, the growth in the money supply causes spending to increase at a stable rate.

Stable money demand means that the money demand curve shifts only when PI, RGNP, or p^e changes. If the demand for money is stable, policymakers can use data on PI, RGNP, and p^e to estimate the position of the money demand curve. If money demand is *unstable*, the money demand curve shifts even when PI, RGNP, and p^e have not changed, and policymakers are uncertain of the position of the money demand curve.

When the Federal Reserve increases the money supply, it creates a situation of monetary disequilibrium, setting off a series of adjustments that reestablish monetary equilibrium ($M^d = M^s$). At the initial levels of i and GNP, the increase in the money supply creates an excess supply of money (Figure 7). Banks have more money to lend and offer lower interest rates on loans. The lower interest rates

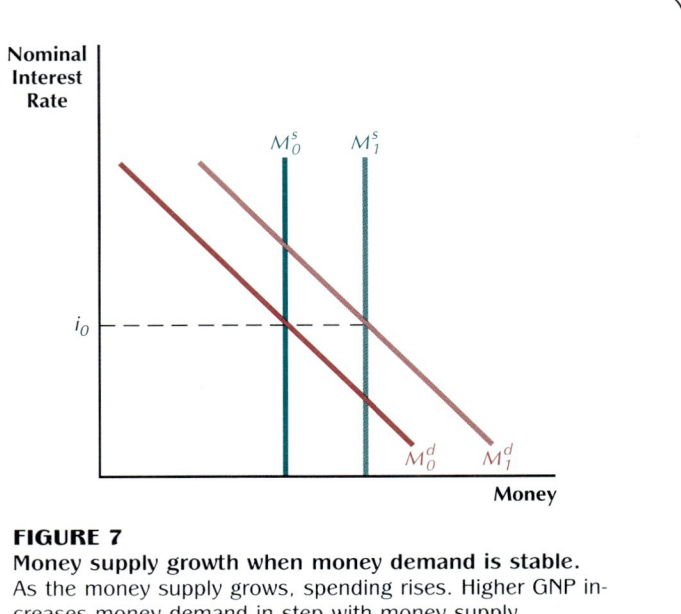

FIGURE 7
Money supply growth when money demand is stable.
As the money supply grows, spending rises. Higher GNP increases money demand in step with money supply.

of the money supply. If monetary policymakers are not aware of what is happening, they can make serious policy errors.[2]

[2]This is not because the Fed is not vigilant. Indeed, the Fed collects an amazing quantity of financial and monetary statistics. It obtains these data directly from banks and other financial institutions. However, the Fed obtains only the data it asks for. If the forms used to acquire data from financial institutions do not ask for data on newly developed financial assets, such data are not collected. And if these data are not collected, the Fed has no way of knowing how important the innovation really is. It is a vicious circle: Unless the innovation is important, no data on it are collected, but unless data are collected, there is no way of knowing how important the innovation is.

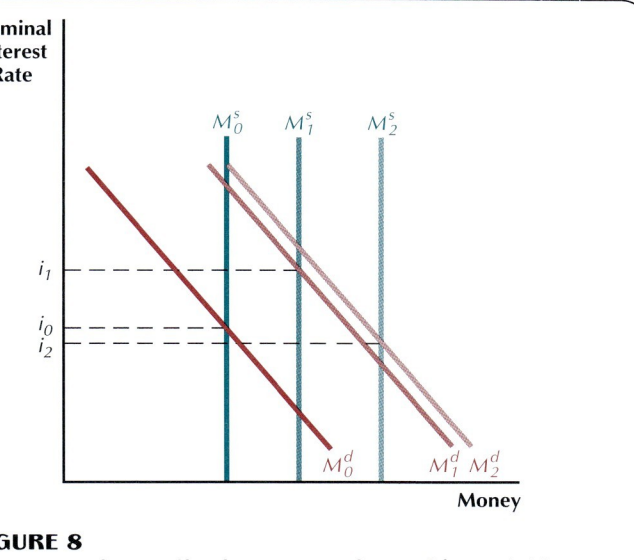

FIGURE 8
Money supply growth when money demand is unstable.
If money demand growth in unstable, stable money supply growth causes the interest rate and GNP to move erratically.

and larger quantity of money encourage spending on new goods and services. As GNP rises, money demand increases (from M_0^d to M_1^d), and a new monetary equilibrium is established. The process of restoring monetary equilibrium can be summarized as:

$$\Delta M^s \rightarrow \Delta i \rightarrow \Delta GNP \rightarrow \Delta M^d$$

A stable money growth policy generates stable aggregate demand growth only if money demand is stable. Many economists doubted (and still doubt) that money demand is stable enough for a constant money growth policy to work well. Consider what happens if a stable money growth policy is followed but money demand is not stable. As the money supply grows steadily from M_0^s to M_1^s to M_2^s in Figure 8, money demand grows erratically. In Period 1, money demand grows much faster than money supply, forcing the interest rate up sharply to i_1. In Period 2, money demand grows more slowly than money supply, pushing the interest rate down to i_2. Stable money supply growth coupled with unstable money demand growth produce erratic fluctuations in the interest rate.

Many economists believe that widely fluctuating interest rates are harmful. Sharp increases in the interest rate disrupt spending, while rapid declines may encourage too much spending. Such beliefs lead many economists to favor a monetary policy approach that pays attention to both the money supply and the interest rate. Except for a three-year period from late 1979 to late 1982, the Federal Reserve has not attempted to control aggregate demand by focusing solely on the growth of monetary aggregates. Under the chairmanship of Alan Greenspan, the Federal Reserve seems firmly committed to watching both money growth and interest rate levels as they attempt to control aggregate demand.

Consider what happens when a financial innovation reduces money demand (as conventionally measured). The money demand curve shifts to the left, creating an excess supply of money at the initial interest rate (Figure 9). People attempt to rid themselves of the excess money balances by purchasing more goods and services and more financial assets. Aggregate demand rises, putting upward pressure on PI and RGNP. The demand for assets rises, pushing asset prices higher and reducing the interest rate. The lower interest rate reinforces the increase in aggregate demand. Higher prices and output and a lower interest rate eventually restore monetary equilibrium ($M^d = M^s$). However, if

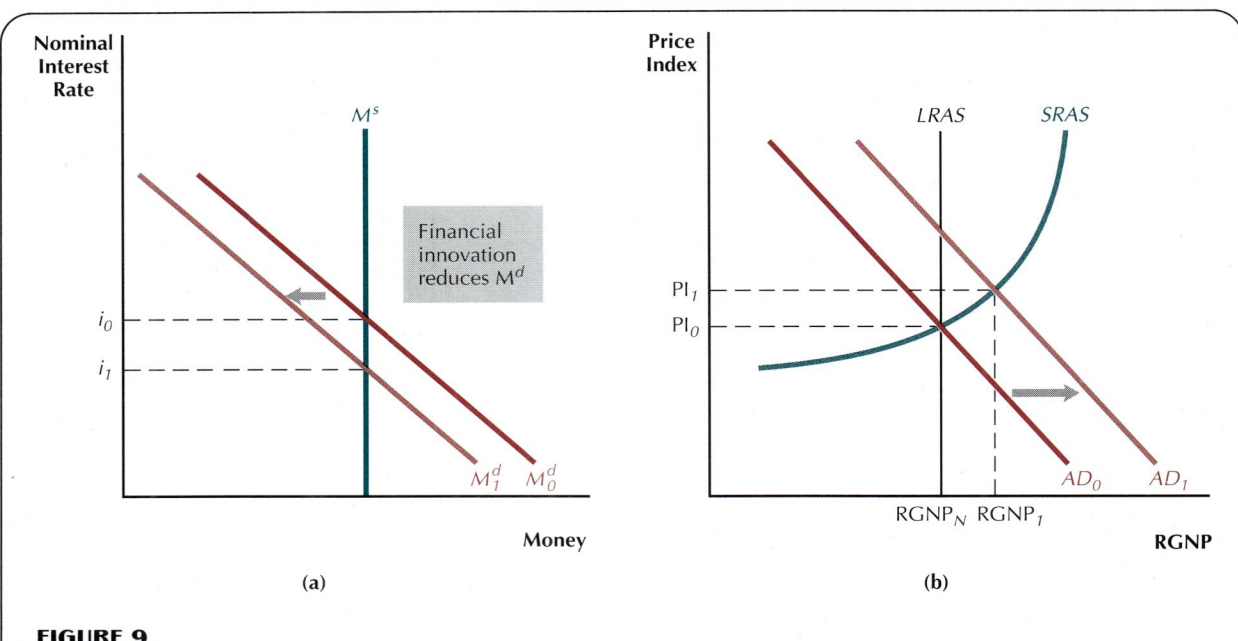

FIGURE 9
Effect of financial innovation. Financial innovation reduces the demand for money as conventionally defined. If monetary policymakers do not reduce the money supply as well, the reduction in money demand increases aggregate demand both through the budget-constraint effect and through the interest-rate effect.

the economy was initially operating near the natural output level, strong inflationary pressures may develop. Some economists believe that this happened in the 1970s.

Throughout the 1950s and 1960s, money demand behaved pretty much as economists thought it should. Using data on the price level, real GNP, and interest rates, economists could predict with great accuracy the amount of money that households and businesses would choose to hold. The money demand function was stable. Then, beginning in 1974, statistical money demand equations began to seriously overpredict money demand. People were not holding as much money as they were supposed to be holding. The money demand curve appeared to shift to the left for no apparent reason. What happened to cause this shift?

A legion of monetary economists began investigating the so-called case of the missing money. Most observers now agree that the main culprit causing the downward shift in money demand was financial innovation. Electronic funds transfer systems and money market mutual funds were two of the primary innovations leading to the decline in money demand.

The increased use of computers contributed to one important innovation in business money-management techniques. Most large businesses have many different deposit accounts. The development in the early 1970s of electronic funds transfer capabilities—the ability to transfer funds by computer or telephone connections among banks—enabled firms to transfer dollars from account to account very rapidly. Firms did not have to hold idle balances in each account to meet unexpected withdrawals. If an account ran low, funds could be transferred quickly from another account. This enabled firms to reduce the total amount of funds held in demand deposit accounts while still making the same level of expenditures. Thus, the same amount of money (as measured by one of the monetary aggregates) supported more spending than before the innovation.

An innovation affecting the household sector was the development of money market mutual funds. A **mutual fund** is an organization that pools the savings of a large number of savers and uses them to purchase financial assets. Mutual funds enable small savers to own a slice of a large financial pie. The value of the slice depends on the market value of the assets owned by the mutual fund. Mutual funds owning stocks and bonds have been around for decades. However, in 1974 a new twist was added when money market mutual funds were created. Money market mutual funds invest only in short-term, liquid, safe assets, including U.S. Treasury bills, commercial paper, and large-denomination certificates of deposit in banks. The major difference between money market mutual funds and other mutual funds is that the price of a share in a money market fund is always equal to one dollar. The interest rate paid on shares goes up and down with market interest rates, but the price of a share never varies.

The combination of safety and a fixed price made money market funds an attractive alternative to savings deposits for many households.[3] During the mid-1970s, market interest rates rose sharply. Money market funds passed the higher interest rates on their assets through to their investors. Banks and other depository institutions were prohibited by law from paying high rates on their savings deposits. As a consequence, depositors removed billions of dollars from banks and savings and loan associations and put their savings into money market mutual funds.

Today money market mutual fund accounts are included in the Federal Reserve's definition of M2. Such was not the case in the mid-1970s. When people pulled funds out of banks and put them into money market funds, the funds were no longer counted as part of M2. Consequently, the Fed underestimated the true value of M2.

Many economists believe that the Federal Reserve misinterpreted what was happening in the 1970s. Monetary policymakers did not understand that the demand for money as conventionally defined had decreased sharply. Instead, they interpreted the decline in money demand as a sign of weakness in the economy. They feared that money demand had fallen because real GNP was lower than it should be. This misinterpretation led the Federal Reserve to conduct an expansive monetary policy throughout much of the 1970s. The result was rapid growth of the true money supply (including financial innovations) and a rising inflation rate.

Mutual fund
Organization that pools the funds of a large number of savers and uses them to buy financial assets, passing the earnings on through to the savers.

SECTION RECAP
Financial innovation reduces the demand for money as conventionally defined. Unless the conventional money supply is also reduced, the money demand shift causes the interest rate to fall and aggregate demand to rise.

---

[3]Another attractive feature of money market funds is the ability of shareholders to write checks on their accounts. Checks must be written for large amounts, however, the minimum amount typically being $500.

Summary

This chapter has taken us from a discussion of the nature of money to a discussion of financial innovations that change our definitions of the money supply. Money is used because it makes trade more efficient. **Barter** is a costly way of exchanging goods and services. The **double coincidence of wants** problem causes the cost of trading to be high, and the absence of a **medium of exchange** eliminates the possibility of extensive specialization. A medium of exchange with well-known properties enables traders to buy and sell at different times with different people, immensely reducing the cost of trading.

The medium of exchange function is not the only function performed by money. Money also acts as the **standard of value,** so that all prices are quoted in terms of a single unit, and serves as a **store of value,** a way to hold wealth over time.

Several money supply definitions are currently reported by the Federal Reserve. The medium of exchange version is called M1. M2, M3, and L are broader definitions of the money supply. Money definitions change as financial innovations create new assets with monetary characteristics.

The **transactions theory of money demand** states that the major determinant of the quantity of money people wish to hold is the level of spending they engage in. In the aggregate, money demand is highly related to GNP. The **interest rate** on nonmoney assets also affects money demand, because it represents the opportunity cost of holding money rather than another financial asset. **Expected inflation** also affects the demand for money, driving it down when expected inflation rises.

Shifts in money demand affect the aggregate demand for goods and services. An increase in money demand reduces aggregate demand. The effect is felt through two channels, the **budget-constraint channel** and the **interest-rate channel.** These effects reinforce one another.

Defining the money supply properly is important for policy purposes. Failing to correctly measure the money supply can lead the Federal Reserve to generate money supply growth that is inappropriately fast or slow. Financial innovation can make it difficult to measure money accurately.

Questions for Thought

Knowledge Questions

1. Define the terms *barter* and *double coincidence of wants.*
2. Why would large-scale specialization and the production of high-value products be impossible in a barter economy?
3. List and define the three primary functions performed by money.
4. What characteristic do all the assets in M1 possess?
5. List the assets included in the M1 definition of money and in the M2 definition.

Application Questions

6. How does a medium of exchange reduce transactions costs?
7. Money demand is systematically related to the price level, real GNP, the interest rate on nonmoney assets, and the expected inflation rate. How would each of

the following changes affect the demand for money?
   a. An increase in the price level.
   b. A decrease in real GNP.
   c. An increase in the interest rate on alternatives to money.
   d. A decrease in the expected inflation rate.
8. Suppose that there is an autonomous increase in the demand for money. (Money demand rises, given the levels of PI, RGNP, and p^e.) What impact would this have on the macroeconomy in the short run? In the long run? Use the full AD–SRAS–LRAS model to explain your answer.

Synthesis Questions

9. Why is it important to have good information about the qualities of any item serving as the medium of exchange? Does your answer explain any of the physical attributes of coins?
10. Explain how financial innovations can disturb a monetary policy that is focused on the growth rate of a particular monetary aggregate.
11. The following table shows the total assets of money market mutual funds for the years 1973 to 1984. What effect do you think this growth pattern had on old M2, which did not include money market funds? Why?

Year	Assets Held by Money Market Funds
1973	—
1974	2.4
1975	3.7
1976	3.7
1977	3.9
1978	10.8
1979	45.2
1980	74.4
1981	181.9
1982	206.9
1983	162.5
1984	209.7

(Assets in billions of dollars.)
Source: Board of Governors of the Federal Reserve System, *Flow of Funds Accounts.*

12. One way to model the effects of financial innovation on the macroeconomy is to recognize that the increasing use of newly created assets reduces the demand for money as traditionally defined. Use the AD–SRAS–LRAS model to illustrate the short-run and long-run effects on the economy of a financial innovation that significantly reduces money demand. Assume that the Federal Reserve holds the money supply (as traditionally defined) constant.

The Banking System, the Federal Reserve, and Monetary Policy

OVERVIEW

Money in a society cannot be separated from the banking and financial system within which it exists. As we saw in the preceding chapter, the assets serving as money change as the financial system changes. In this chapter we examine the U.S. banking system in some detail. Our analysis begins with an examination of the basic business of banking: intermediation. Intermediation involves collecting deposits from savers and making loans to borrowers. The lending process also happens to be the process of money creation. We examine this process carefully, noting the roles played by both banks and the Federal Reserve.

The raw material of the money supply process, called the monetary base, is created by the Federal Reserve System (the nation's central bank). Because the Federal Reserve plays such an important role in the economy, we discuss in detail the Federal Reserve's history, structure, tools, and policies. The rather lengthy discussion is worthwhile, because the Federal Reserve may be the single most important economic institution in the country.

In the final sections of the chapter we merge our new

CHAPTER 28

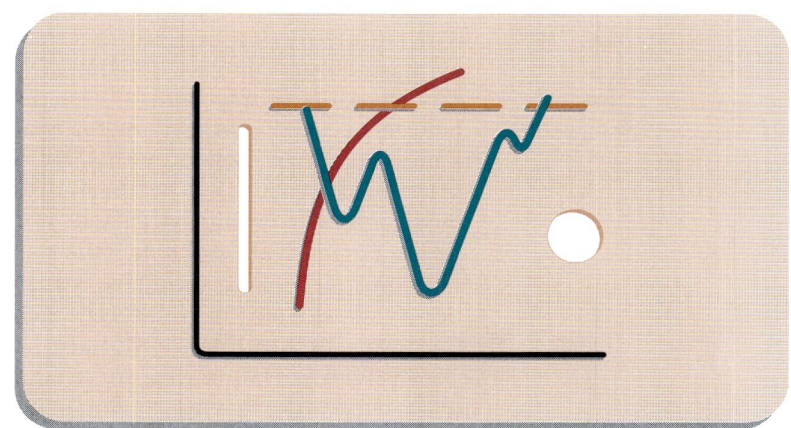

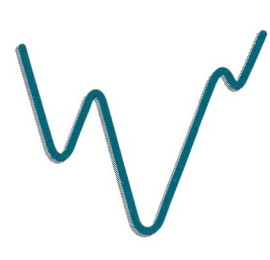

knowledge of the monetary system with the full model of the macroeconomy, enabling us to examine how the economy is affected by changes in Federal Reserve behavior.

Learning Objectives

After reading and studying this chapter, you will be able to:

1. Explain how financial intermediation benefits the economy.
2. Describe the basic structure of the Federal Reserve System.
3. List the Federal Reserve's tools of monetary policy and explain how they work.
4. Explain how the money multiplier process works.
5. Describe how changes in the ratio of reserves to deposits banks hold or changes in the public's desire to hold currency affect the money multiplier.
6. State the major arguments for and against Federal Reserve independence from political control.
7. Use the full macroeconomic model to explain how changes in Federal Reserve behavior affect the economy.

Financial Intermediation

Financial intermediaries
Institutions that collect funds from savers by issuing claims against themselves and use the funds to purchase claims against borrowers.

Firms that collect funds by issuing claims against themselves and use the funds to purchase financial assets or make loans are called **financial intermediaries**. A large number of different financial intermediaries operate in the United States, including insurance companies, pension funds, mutual funds, and depository institutions. The major function of these financial intermediaries is transferring dollars that have been saved by households and businesses that spend less than current income to other households and businesses that spend more than current income. Financial intermediaries bring savers and borrowers together. In doing so, they do more than just shuffle dollars from place to place. Financial intermediaries create claims against themselves (such as savings deposits or insurance policies) that are very different from the financial claims they hold against the borrowers to whom they lend funds (such as mortgages or corporate bonds).

Intermediation
Issuing claims with one set of characteristics to savers and acquiring claims with a different set of characteristics from borrowers.

In the process of **intermediation**—issuing claims to ultimate savers to collect funds with which to purchase claims against ultimate borrowers—financial intermediaries perform several valuable services. First, financial intermediaries issue claims with characteristics that usually differ greatly from the characteristics of the claims they acquire. For example, consider the difference between a NOW account issued by a savings and loan association (S&L) and a mortgage loan owned by the S&L. The NOW account is liquid (it is part of M1) and safe (insured by the Federal Deposit Insurance Corporation). The mortgage loan is illiquid (it will not pay off for years and its market value varies a great deal) and risky (the borrower could default). Savers who would not consider making mortgage loans even if they had the savings to do so are not at all reluctant to hold NOW accounts. Yet, through the S&L, the savers' funds are used to finance mortgage loans.

By issuing claims with the characteristics savers want, financial intermediaries encourage saving. Saving benefits the economy by providing the funds necessary for capital formation, a key element in economic growth.

A second benefit of financial intermediation is the ability to overcome risk that would prevent individual savers from making loans. Financial intermediaries are willing and able to make large, illiquid, risky loans that individual savers could not or would not make. The large amount of funds handled by a typical financial intermediary allows the intermediary to diversify its portfolio (asset holdings), making a large number of different loans to different borrowers. In this way the intermediary can spread the risk of lending. The default of a single loan will not ruin a prudent institution, because such an institution will never make a single loan large enough to break the bank.

A third benefit of intermediation is the reduction in transactions costs that comes through specialization. By specializing in assessing risk, processing loan applications, making loans, and collecting loan payments, financial intermediaries lower the cost of borrowing. Part of the cost savings is shared with savers in the form of higher interest on their savings and with borrowers in the form of lower interest rates on their loans. Both borrowers and savers gain from an efficient system of financial intermediation.

In this chapter we concentrate on the operations of depository institutions, a category that includes commercial banks, savings and loan associations, mutual savings banks, and credit unions. Households and businesses deposit funds in accounts at depository institutions and acquire claims against them in the form of checkable deposits, savings deposits, and time deposits.

A common feature of all claims against depository institutions is their safety. Government agencies, such as the Federal Deposit Insurance Corporation, provide deposit insurance for most deposits (up to $100,000). Since most uninsured deposits can be moved to other institutions rapidly should the need arise, even uninsured deposits are relatively safe. Most deposit claims are also very liquid. They are either money (the medium of exchange) or they can be converted into money very quickly and easily with little or no cost or loss of asset value. Depository institutions use the funds collected through deposits to purchase assets and make loans that are often less liquid and riskier than the deposits they issue.

Before 1980, federal regulations distinguished sharply between commercial banks and other depository institutions. Only commercial banks could issue checkable deposits. Furthermore, commercial banks also differed from other depository institutions in the composition of their asset portfolios. Commercial banks held highly diversified portfolios of consumer loans, commercial loans, mortgage loans, and U.S. government securities. Other depository institutions were more specialized. For example, savings and loan associations specialized in mortgage lending, while credit unions limited their lending to short-term consumer loans.

Increasing competition from other financial intermediaries and changes in the economic environment in the 1970s reduced the profitability of specialized institutions. Congress was forced to change its regulations to permit savings and loan associations, mutual savings banks, and credit unions to diversify both their asset holdings and the types of deposits they offer.[1] Consequently, the nonbank depository institutions became more like banks in the 1980s. Since the process of money creation by a savings and loan association or a credit union is exactly the same as the process of money creation by a bank, we will simply refer to all depository institutions as banks in the remainder of the chapter.

SECTION RECAP
Financial intermediation benefits the economy by encouraging saving, reducing portfolio risk, and lowering the transactions costs of borrowing and lending.

Federal Reserve System

The nation's central bank, the Federal Reserve System, is responsible for controlling the money supply. Since the history of the Federal Reserve explains many of the unusual features of current Federal Reserve structure, we will begin our examination of the Federal Reserve System with a brief historical survey.

A Brief History of the Federal Reserve System

The Federal Reserve System was created by the *Federal Reserve Act* of 1913 and began operations in 1914. Before then the United States did not have a central bank. There was no governmental agency responsible for controlling the size of the money supply. The currency consisted of coins issued by the U.S. Trea-

---
[1]The regulatory changes came too late for many savings and loan associations, which were insolvent (bankrupt) by the time Congress acted. The regulatory changes themselves were badly flawed and contributed to the collapse of the savings and loan industry in the 1980s. An appendix to this chapter discusses the causes of the S&L crisis.

sury and bank notes issued by national banks—banks chartered (licensed) by the U.S. Comptroller of the Currency. Both national banks and state banks—banks chartered by state banking commissions—issued deposits.

During the latter decades of the nineteenth century and the first decade of this century, several major banking crises occurred. Some event would cause depositors to attempt to convert their deposits into currency on a large scale. (Such a widespread demand for conversion of deposits into currency is called a **bank run**.) The problem was that the amount of currency in existence was limited. National banks were required to hold U.S. government bonds as security for any bank notes they issued. Thus, the quantity of notes a bank could issue was limited by the quantity of government bonds it owned. During the late nineteenth century, the U.S. government ran persistent budget surpluses and used them to retire outstanding bonds. Thus, the quantity of bonds held by banks was shrinking, in turn causing the quantity of bank notes to decline.

Then as now, the quantity of bank deposits far exceeded the quantity of currency. As banks ran out of currency during bank runs, they had to close their doors. The limited quantity of government bonds available to back notes prevented banks from satisfying the demand for currency by issuing more bank notes. The supply of currency could not expand and contract to meet changes in the demand for currency.

The primary function of the newly created Federal Reserve System was to protect the banking system from bank runs by providing an **elastic currency** that expanded and contracted as the quantity demanded changed. The Federal Reserve was given the authority to issue paper currency. This currency—Federal Reserve notes—was backed by the gold and silver held by the federal government. During banking crises, the Federal Reserve was supposed to make emergency loans to banks needing currency. By providing extra currency when the public demanded it, the Federal Reserve could allow banks to remain open. When the bank run subsided and confidence in the banking system was restored, people would redeposit the currency in banks, and the banks would repay the Federal Reserve.

Because of political opposition to a powerful central bank in Washington or New York, the Federal Reserve System was given a decentralized form. Rather than creating one central bank, the Federal Reserve Act created twelve district Reserve Banks, each serving a different section of the country. Figure 1 shows the locations of the twelve Federal Reserve Districts and the banks that serve them. The location of the banks reflects the geographical distribution of people and economic activity in 1913.

The Federal Reserve System apparently served its purpose well throughout the 1914 to 1929 period. No major banking crises occurred, and confidence in the banking system was high. During the Great Depression, all this changed. In 1931 and 1932, the Federal Reserve System permitted the banking system and the money supply to collapse. Over 9,000 banks failed from 1930 to 1933. The M2 money supply fell by one third, M1 by one fourth. The Federal Reserve failed to do that for which it had been created.[2]

Bank run
Generalized demand by customers of a bank to convert their deposits into currency.

Elastic currency
Currency whose quantity expands and contracts as the demand for it rises and falls.

---

[2]Why the Federal Reserve failed to protect the banking system is a complicated issue. The major reason appears to be that the Federal Reserve feared losing its gold reserves to foreign countries if it supported the banking system with large-scale loans. For an interesting discussion of the topic, see David Glasner, *Free Banking and Monetary Reform* (New York: Cambridge University Press, 1989), Chapter 6.

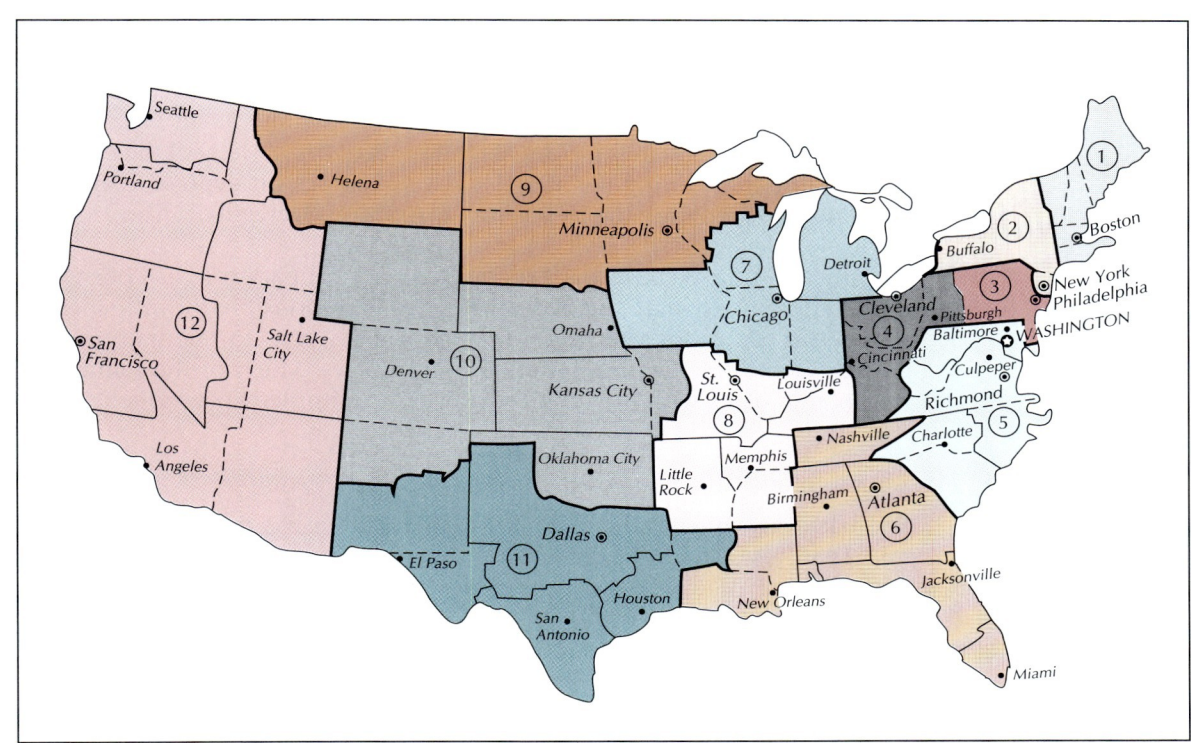

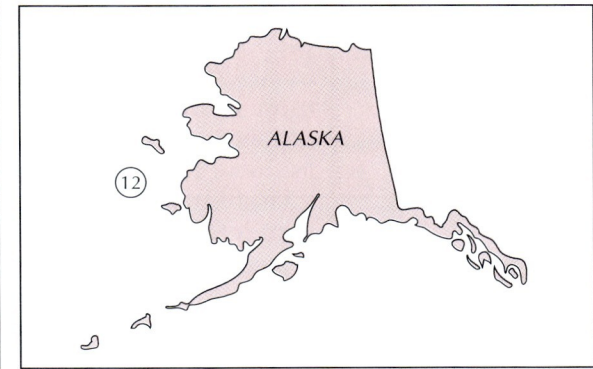

Legend

——— Boundaries of Federal Reserve Districts

——— Boundaries of Federal Reserve Branch Territories

⊙ Board of Governors of the Federal Reserve System

⊙ Federal Reserve Bank Cities

• Federal Reserve Branch Cities

FIGURE 1
Federal reserve bank districts. Source: Federal Reserve *Bulletin*.

In response to the massive banking crisis that accompanied the Great Depression, the Federal Reserve System was reorganized into a more centralized agency of monetary policy. Its regulatory powers were increased greatly. In addition, the Federal Deposit Insurance Corporation was created to insure bank deposits up to a specified amount. The banking system became one of the most highly regulated sectors of the U.S. economy. Many of the regulations placed on banks during the 1930s, such as ceilings on deposit interest rates, were not removed until the Depository Institutions Deregulation and Monetary Control Act of 1980 (DIDMCA) was passed.

Since the early 1950s the Federal Reserve's primary role has been that of monetary policy agent. The Federal Reserve is responsible for influencing the money supply and interest rates in such a manner as to maintain economic growth without generating inflationary pressures. Much of the remainder of the chapter deals with how the Federal Reserve implements monetary policy.

Structure and Functions of the Federal Reserve System

The basic structure of the Federal Reserve System has not changed since the mid-1930s. At the top of the Federal Reserve's organizational chart (Figure 2) is the **Board of Governors**. The Board of Governors is composed of seven individuals appointed by the president of the United States, with the advice and consent of the Senate. Governors are appointed to fourteen-year terms (a new term beginning every two years) and may serve only one full term. (Some governors have served more than fourteen years, because it is possible to finish out the term of a governor who resigns and then be appointed to a full term.)

One of the governors is selected by the president to be the chairman. The chairman serves a four-year term and may be reappointed so long as his term as governor lasts. Although the chairman has no formal powers greater than those of the other governors, other than the power to determine the agenda of meetings, he has a great deal of informal power. The chairman is viewed as the head of the Federal Reserve System. What the chairman says is usually interpreted as the Federal Reserve's official position on an issue. The chairman is universally regarded as the most powerful person in the Federal Reserve System.

Board of Governors Seven-member body that controls the Federal Reserve System.

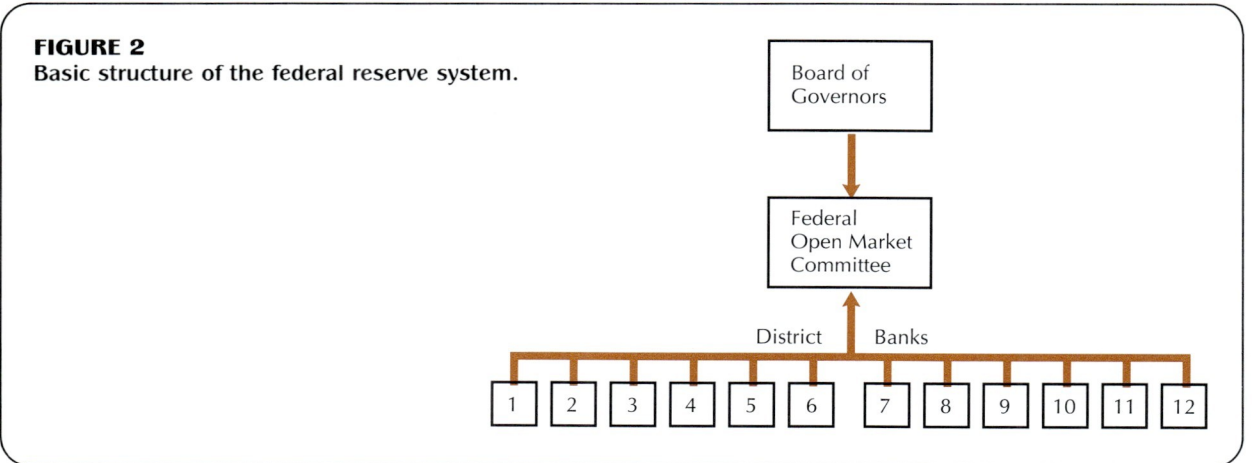

FIGURE 2
Basic structure of the federal reserve system.

The Board of Governors has a large staff of economists and statisticians who collect and analyze economic data. At least twice weekly, staff economists meet with the governors to present the results of their research into the state of the economy and of financial markets. They also present forecasts of what is likely to occur in the near future.

The Federal Reserve uses three policy tools to control the money supply: reserve requirements, the discount rate, and open market operations. The Board of Governors controls two of the three tools. The Board is empowered to set the **reserve requirement ratio**, the minimum legal ratio of reserves to deposits banks must hold. Bank **reserves** include currency held in banks' vaults plus deposits at district Federal Reserve banks. The more reserves banks must hold, the fewer loans they are able to make. Forcing banks to hold more reserves than they would freely choose to hold thus limits the amount of lending—and money creation—banks engage in.

The Board of Governors also determines the **discount rate**—the interest rate the Federal Reserve charges on loans it makes to depository institutions. The discount rate represents the opportunity cost to banks of running short of reserves. By raising the discount rate, the Board increases the cost of excessive lending, inducing banks to make fewer loans. There are also other less important policy tools under the control of the Board of Governors.

Each of the twelve district Reserve Banks has a president. The seven governors join with five district Reserve Bank presidents to form the **Federal Open Market Committee (FOMC)**, the twelve-person committee that determines the course of open market policy. **Open market operations** are the most important tool of policy and the most frequently used means of changing the money supply. The Federal Reserve engages in open market operations when it buys or sells government bonds, trading with government bond dealers in New York and other large cities. As we shall see in the next section, Federal Reserve purchases of bonds increase the quantity of reserves in the banking system, enabling banks to make more loans, while Federal Reserve sales of bonds reduce the quantity of bank reserves and restrict bank lending.

Only five district bank presidents serve on the FOMC at any time in order to allow the seven governors to form a voting majority. The district bank presidents are not appointed by the president or confirmed by the Senate, but are selected by each district Reserve Bank's board of directors and are approved by the Board of Govenors. The FOMC was structured to give presidential appointees the voting majority.

The five district bank presidents serving on the FOMC change annually, with one exception. Eleven presidents rotate into four FOMC positions every second or third year, depending upon which rotation they are in. (There are four rotations, three of them three-bank rotations and the fourth a two-bank rotation.) The fifth position is always filled by the president of the Federal Reserve Bank of New York. All trading in bonds is carried out by the System Open Market Account Manager, who is a vice president of the Federal Reserve Bank of New York.

The twelve district Reserve Banks engage in a host of activities. Checks deposited in banks geographically separated from the banks on which they are written clear (are paid) through the Federal Reserve Banks. The Federal Reserve System also transfers funds electronically. Depository institutions hold reserve deposits in the district Reserve Banks, and the U.S. Treasury keeps its checking accounts in them. The district banks administer the loans made by

---

Reserve requirement ratio
Minimum amount of legal reserves a bank can hold, stated as a percentage of deposits.

Reserves
Vault cash plus bank deposits with district Federal Reserve Banks.

Discount rate
Interest rate set by the Board of Governors on loans of reserves by the Federal Reserve to banks.

Federal Open Market Committee (FOMC)
Twelve-member committee that controls open market operations for the Federal Reserve.

Open market operations
Purchases and sales of U.S. government bonds by the Federal Reserve; such operations affect the quantity of bank reserves.

SECTION RECAP
The Federal Reserve was created to provide the economy with an elastic currency. In the 1930s it was restructured to become an active monetary policy agency. The Board of Governors controls the Federal Reserve System. It sets the discount rate and reserve requirements. The *(continued)*

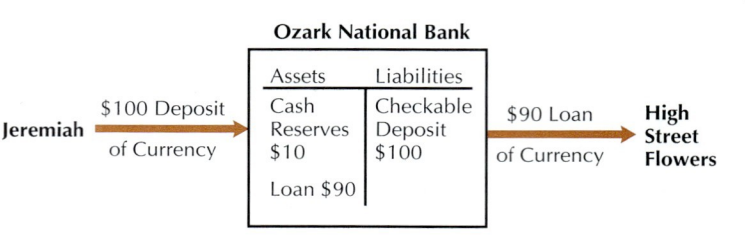

FIGURE 3
Lending and money creation. Ozark National Bank uses most of the $100 in currency deposited by Jeremiah to make a loan. It holds $10 as cash reserves. The money supply increases by $90, because Jeremiah still has his $100 (now in a checkable deposit) and High Street Flowers has an additional $90.

SECTION RECAP
(continued)
Governors, along with five district Reserve Bank presidents, conduct open market operations through the Federal Open Market Committee.

the System to depository institutions. District Reserve Banks also maintain research staffs, who analyze both macroeconomic conditions and business and agricultural conditions within each of the twelve districts.[3]

Although the Federal Reserve System is apparently quite decentralized, all major monetary policy decisions are made by the Board of Governors or by the Federal Open Market Committee, which is dominated by the governors. Thus, it is accurate to say that the United States has a single central bank that acts as the monetary policy agent for the government.

How Money Is Created

The money creation process involves both the Federal Reserve System and the banking system. Since most money is in the form of bank deposits, we will begin our investigation by examining the role banks play in money creation.

In the process of making loans, banks create money. The loan process is a money creation process because of **fractional reserve banking**. Banks do not hold one dollar in cash reserves for every dollar of deposits on their books. Instead, each dollar of deposits is backed by a fraction of a dollar in cash reserves. Thus, when a dollar of currency is deposited in a bank, the bank holds only a few cents (15¢ or less) in reserve and lends out the remainder. The portion that is loaned out adds to the money supply.

Fractional reserve banking
Holding less than one dollar in cash reserves for every dollar in deposits.

Figure 3 illustrates this process. Suppose Jeremiah deposits $100 in Ozark National Bank. At this point the money supply has not changed, either for Jeremiah or for the economy, since both currency and checkable deposits are part of M1. Suppose the bank sets aside $10 as reserves. With the other $90 it makes a loan to the High Street Flower Company. High Street Flowers now has $90 it did not previously have. But Jeremiah has no less money than he began with. The $90 is newly created money, though the banker will say he only loaned out funds that Jeremiah deposited. The key to this paradox is that Jeremiah's $100 deposit is only backed by $10 in reserves. The other $90 backing his deposit is in the form of a loan to High Street Flowers.

Ozark National Bank is able to hold fractional reserves because only a small percentage of its depositors make cash withdrawals on any particular

---

[3]The district Federal Reserve Banks also issue a number of free publications that are useful and informative. Each bank publishes a monthly or quarterly review containing articles about the economy. Several also issue monthly (or even weekly) statistical publications, making it easy to keep up with the movements of important economic variables. Check the library for the addresses of the banks and the names of their publications.

day. Every day as depositors make withdrawals or write checks, drawing down reserves, other depositors make deposits, building up reserves. The net result is that holding reserves equal to 10 percent of deposits is more than adequate to cover normal withdrawals. This is especially the case when a large percentage of deposits are savings or time deposits that are withdrawn infrequently.

Multiplier Process

The loan process does not create money only once. A loan made with dollars newly injected into the banking system sets off a multiple expansion process. The money supply rises by a multiple of the injection of new reserves into the system.

To clarify the basics of the multiplier process, we will make some simplifying assumptions. First, assume that the Federal Reserve requires all banks to hold reserves equal to 10 percent of deposits. That is, the required reserve ratio is 10 percent. Second, assume that banks choose to hold no more than the required amount of reserves. Third, assume that all money is held in the form of bank deposits; no one holds currency. These three assumptions simplify the development of the multiplier. Later we will drop them and deal with a more realistic case.

Suppose the Federal Reserve ("the Fed") makes an open market purchase of a $100 bond from Ozark National Bank. The Fed acquires the bond and the bank receives $100 in return. Ozark National Bank now can make a loan to High Street Flower Company just as before—with one exception. Because Ozark Bank received the new $100 in exchange for a bond—not as a new deposit—it does not need to hold reserves against the $100.

Table 1 illustrates this by showing Ozark Bank's T-account. A T-account shows any changes in Ozark Bank's balance sheet resulting from a transaction. An organization's balance sheet records its assets (on the left side) and liabilities and net worth (on the right side). The two sides of a balance sheet (or a T-account) must balance, because net worth equals assets minus liabilities. A change in one balance sheet item necessitates a corresponding change in another item to maintain the balance, just as a change in one budget constraint item requires another change. Table 1 shows that the sale of bonds to the Federal Reserve does not affect Ozark Bank's deposits. Therefore, its required reserves do not change, and it can lend the entire amount, as shown in Figure 4.

Now suppose Ozark Bank makes a $100 loan to High Street Flower Company by crediting its checking account. The money supply grows by $100, as deposits rise by that amount.

TABLE 1

T-account of Ozark National Bank

Assets		Liabilities & Net Worth
Bonds	− $100	
Reserves	+ $100	

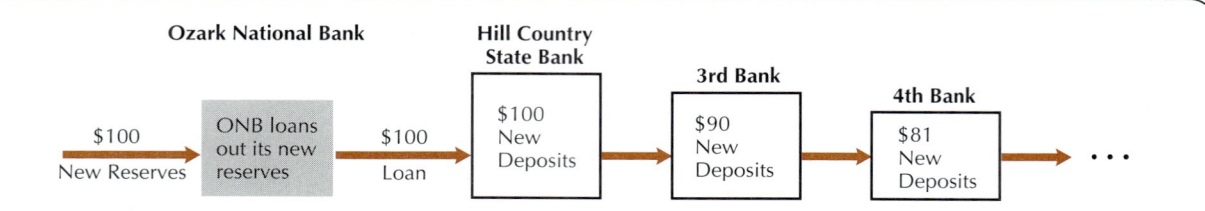

FIGURE 4
Lending and the multiplier process. The acquisition of $100 in reserves from outside the system allows Ozark National Bank to make a $100 loan. When the loan is used to pay a bill, Hill Country State Bank finds its deposits increasing by $100. It holds $10 in reserves and lends $90, which eventually shows up as a deposit at a third bank. The lending process continues until all reserves are held as required reserves.

Most borrowing is done to pay bills. We will assume that High Street Flowers uses the $100 to pay for the main input in its business, cut flowers. A check for $100 is written to Bob's Greenhouse, where the flowers are grown. The funds are transferred from High Street Flower Company's account at Ozark National Bank to Bob's account at Hill Country State Bank. This reduces both the deposits and reserves of Ozark Bank by $100. The deposits and reserves of Hill Country Bank rise by $100.

The stage is set for another round of deposit expansion. Hill Country State Bank needs to hold only $10 in reserves to cover the additional $100 of deposits on its books. It can make loans of $90. Suppose Hill Country Bank lends $90 to Tom, a local farmer. The money supply grows by an additional $90, as deposits rise. This is shown in Table 2, where a T-account for Hill Country State Bank, showing the changes in the bank's balance sheet, is presented. Note that Bob still has the $100 he deposited in his account, and Tom now has $90 he did not have before.

When Tom uses the $90 to pay off a debt, he transfers the money by check to the account of another individual. The deposits of another bank will rise by $90, as will its reserves, since Hill Country State Bank must transfer reserves whenever a check is written on one of its accounts. This third bank may also expand its lending. If its deposits rise by $90, it needs to hold $9 in reserves. It is free to lend $81, thus creating an additional increase in the money supply of $81.

Figure 5 provides a schematic illustration of the money multiplier process. Each bank in the process holds 10 percent of the funds deposited in it and lends out the remaining 90 percent. The dollar amount of loans—and increases in the money supply—gets smaller at each stage of the process. The multiplier

TABLE 2

Hill Country State Bank's T-account

Assets		Liabilities & Net Worth	
Reserves	+ $100	Bob's deposit	+ $100
Loans	+ 90	Tom's deposit	+ 90

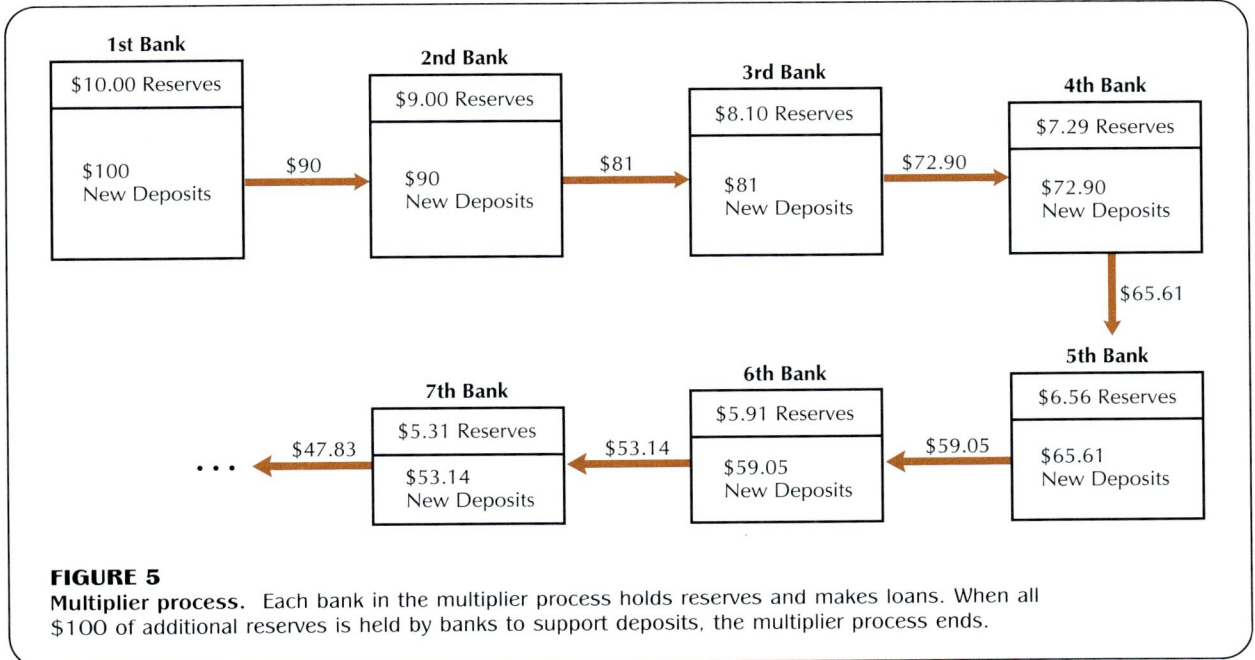

FIGURE 5
Multiplier process. Each bank in the multiplier process holds reserves and makes loans. When all $100 of additional reserves is held by banks to support deposits, the multiplier process ends.

process ends when all the additional reserves injected into the system are being held as required reserves against deposits.

It is easy to calculate the size of the *deposit multiplier*, which tells us how much deposits expand (or contract) for every dollar bank reserves expand (or contract). The multiplier process continues until all the additional reserves are held as required reserves against deposits. Thus, the process ends when:

$$\Delta R = rr \times \Delta D$$

where ΔR equals the change in reserves ($100 was injected in the example above), rr is the reserve requirement ratio (10 percent), and ΔD stands for the change in checkable deposits (the unknown variable). Inserting the numbers from our example into this equation, we have:

$$\$100 = .10 \times \Delta D$$

Dividing by .10 yields:

$$\Delta D = \$100 \times (1/.10) = \$100 \times 10 = \$1000$$

The multiplier is $1/.10 = 10$. In general, the multiplier is $1/rr$, so that, in general:

$$\Delta D = \Delta R \times (1/rr)$$

(Note that this multiplier is based on the assumptions that no one holds any currency, that all deposits are money, and that all banks hold exactly the required amount of reserves. If these assumptions do not hold, the multiplier changes, as we shall see.)

If the required reserve ratio were increased, the multiplier would fall. Suppose rr were raised to 20 percent. The multiplier then falls to $1/.20 = 5$. This happens because every bank in the money expansion process holds a larger quantity of reserves and makes smaller loans. The quantity of money created thus is smaller.

Relaxing Assumptions: The Effect on the Multiplier

We derived the money multiplier under several restrictive assumptions. It is unrealistic to assume that people hold no currency, or that all bank deposits are money (that is, checkable), or even that banks hold exactly the required amount of reserves and no more. What effect would the holding of currency by the nonbank public have on the multiplier? Let's investigate this issue by going through our example again. This time we will assume that every individual wishes to hold currency in addition to deposits.

Ozark National Bank makes a $100 loan to High Street Flowers, as before. The loan is used to pay Bob's Greenhouse for cut flowers. But Bob does not deposit the entire $100 in Hill Country State Bank. Instead, he keeps $20 in currency and deposits only $80. Hill Country Bank can now make loans, but in a smaller amount than in our previous example. The bank must hold .10 × $80 = $8 in reserves against Bob's deposit, so it can make a loan of $72. If Bob had deposited the entire $100, Hill Country Bank could have loaned out $90. Thus, when the nonbank public chooses to hold currency rather than deposit it in a bank, banks have fewer reserves to lend out. *Currency holdings reduce the money multiplier.*[4]

Excess reserves
Reserves in excess of Federal Reserve requirements.

Banks issue deposits other than checkable deposits. Although savings and time deposits are not considered part of the M1 money supply, banks still must hold reserves to support them. Since reserves held to back deposits cannot be loaned out, *the existence of nonmoney deposits against which reserves must be held also reduces the M1 multiplier.*

SECTION RECAP
Deposit money is created through the bank lending process. Since banks hold fractional reserves, deposits are a multiple of reserves. A change in the quantity of reserves leads to a multiple change in the quantity of deposits.

Finally, banks may choose to hold more reserves than required by the Federal Reserve. By definition, such **excess reserves** are not loaned out. They remain in the bank until they are withdrawn or transferred to another bank to clear checks. Since they reduce the flow of loans made by banks, *excess reserves also reduce the size of the money multiplier.*

The existence of currency holdings, nonmoney deposits, and excess reserves causes the M1 multiplier to be much smaller than in the example above. Whereas we constructed a multiplier equal to 10, the real-world M1 multiplier lies between 2.5 and 3.

Monetary Base: The Raw Material for the System

Monetary base
Money created outside the banking system; includes currency held by the public plus bank reserves.

Reserves held by banks are part of the monetary base. The **monetary base** is the ultimate source of money in the United States. It consists of currency held by individuals and business firms plus reserves held by depository institutions (currency in their vaults and deposits at a Federal Reserve Bank). Since banks can convert their deposits at the Federal Reserve into currency at any time, the monetary base is currency plus deposits at the Federal Reserve that are convertible into currency.

---

[4]One complication needs to be mentioned here. Although currency held by the nonbank public reduces the ability of banks to create deposit money, it adds directly to the money supply. Currency is part of the money supply. However, the effect on the money multiplier *is* negative, since a dollar held as currency adds one dollar to money, while a dollar in bank reserves supports several dollars of deposit money.

TABLE 3
Federal Reserve purchase of bonds

Federal Reserve's T-Account

Assets		Liabilities & Net Worth	
Bonds	+ $100,000	Deposit of Ozark Bank	+ $100,000

Ozark National Bank's T-Account

Assets		Liabilities & Net Worth
Bonds	− $100,000	
Reserves	+ 100,000	

The size of the monetary base is determined by the Federal Reserve System. **Federal Reserve notes**—the green paper currency we carry in the United States—and bank deposits at the Federal Reserve form most of the monetary base. The remainder of the base is in the form of Treasury currency, the coins we use for small transactions. Since well over 90 percent of the monetary base is the liability of the Federal Reserve System, it is not inaccurate to say that the Fed controls the base.

The Federal Reserve controls the monetary base primarily by buying and selling financial assets, that is, through open market operations. Whenever the Federal Reserve buys a financial asset, typically a U.S. Treasury bond, it pays for it by creating base money. The New York Federal Reserve Bank (which does all the financial trading for the System) simply writes a check on itself to pay for the bond. When the check is presented for payment, the Federal Reserve Bank credits the deposit account of the bank holding the check.

Table 3 illustrates this process. The Federal Reserve buys a $100,000 government bond from Ozark National Bank and pays for it by check. Ozark National Bank returns the check to the Fed and has its account at the Federal Reserve credited. The quantity of reserves held by Ozark National Bank, and by the banking system, rises by $100,000. Ozark Bank is free to make up to $100,000 in new loans. This sets off the multiplier process, and the money supply rises by a multiple of $100,000.

> **Federal Reserve notes**
> Paper currency issued by the Federal Reserve.

An Empirical Note: Growth of Money and the Monetary Base

The money supply is the product of the monetary base and the money multiplier:

$$M = mm \times B$$

where mm is the money multiplier and B is the base. Changes in either the multiplier or the monetary base change the money supply.

Although changes in the money multiplier can affect the size of the money supply, there are limits on how much the multiplier varies. The value of the multiplier depends on the required reserve ratio and on the amount of currency held by the public, the amount of savings and time deposits against which reserves must be held, and the amount of excess reserves held by banks, relative to the amount of checkable deposits in banks. Although these relative values change to some degree over time, the money multiplier does not rise or fall by large amounts unless economic conditions change drastically.

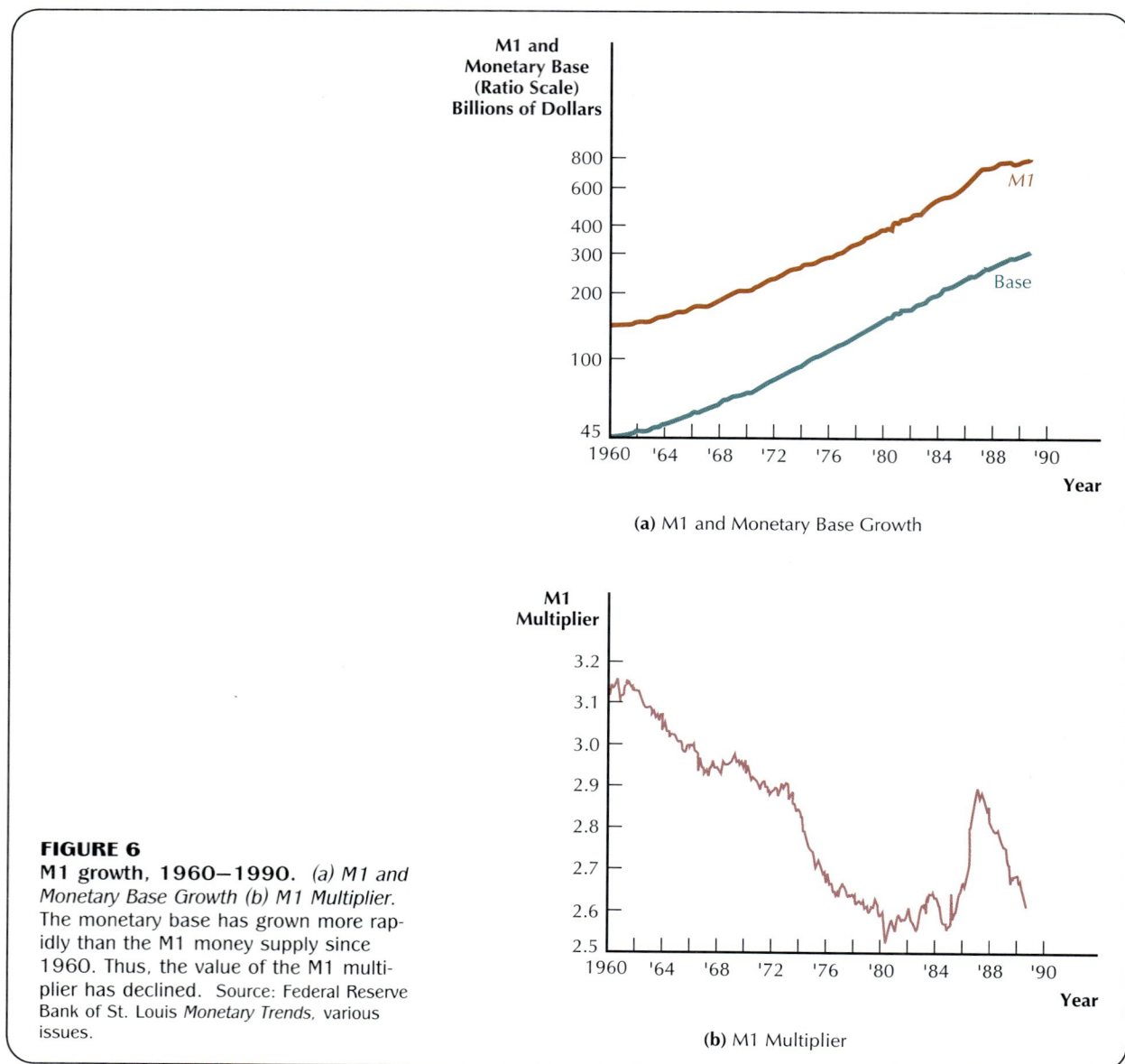

FIGURE 6
M1 growth, 1960–1990. (a) M1 and Monetary Base Growth (b) M1 Multiplier. The monetary base has grown more rapidly than the M1 money supply since 1960. Thus, the value of the M1 multiplier has declined. Source: Federal Reserve Bank of St. Louis *Monetary Trends*, various issues.

SECTION RECAP
By controlling the size of the monetary base, the Federal Reserve exerts control over the money supply. Since most of the monetary base is a liability of the Federal Reserve, the Fed can control the base with great accuracy if it so chooses.

Long-term growth in the money supply is caused by growth in the monetary base. Although the money multiplier fluctuates enough to make the short-run relationship between the money supply and the monetary base less than perfect, the multiplier does not grow and grow without limit. However, there are no natural limits on the growth of the monetary base. So long as the Federal Reserve continues to increase the monetary base, the money supply will grow.

Figure 6 shows the growth of the M1 money supply and the monetary base and the behavior of the money multiplier for the period since 1960. The monetary base has actually grown faster than M1 since 1960; the value of the multiplier has fallen considerably. Therefore, it is clear that growth in the monetary base has been responsible for growth in M1 in recent decades.

Monetary Policy: Tools and Strategy

The Federal Reserve is equipped with several policy tools that can be used to alter the money supply. The three general policy tools — open market operations, the discount rate, and reserve requirement ratio — deserve more in-depth attention than they have been given thus far. As the name *general policy tools* suggests, these instruments of policy affect the monetary system in general and have very broad effects. The Federal Reserve also has a number of specific policy tools that can be used to control particular aspects of financial system behavior.

Mechanics of Open Market Operations

The most frequently used and most important tool of Federal Reserve policy is open market operations. Through the Federal Reserve Bank of New York, the Fed buys and sells U.S. Treasury bonds on the open market. This affects the size of the monetary base and, through the money multiplier process, the size of the money supply.

A concrete example of an open market operation illustrates how this tool works. Suppose that the Federal Open Market Committee has determined that the money supply is growing too slowly. The FOMC directs the System Open Market Account Manager to increase the growth rate of the money supply by a certain amount. The manager must translate this directive into operational terms and decide how many dollars worth of Treasury bonds to purchase to achieve the desired increase in money supply growth.

Suppose the System Open Market Account Manager decides that the Federal Reserve should purchase $500 million of government bonds. The manager directs the bond traders at the trading desk of the New York Federal Reserve Bank to purchase this quantity of bonds. The traders then begin telephoning the bond dealers with whom the Federal Reserve trades, asking for information on prices and quantities of bonds available.

Bond dealers are organizations (such as Salomon Brothers and Merrill Lynch) that buy and sell bonds on their own account. They hold large portfolios of bonds and stand ready to buy or sell bonds at announced bid and asked prices. When the traders at the New York Federal Reserve Bank trading desk have obtained price quotes from all the bond dealers with whom the Fed trades, the manager chooses the offers he thinks are best. A bond purchase as large as $500 million requires the Federal Reserve to buy bonds from a number of dealers.

It should be noted that although the bonds being purchased by the Federal Reserve are U.S. Treasury bonds, the Fed trades with private companies. The bond dealers are private, profit-seeking companies that buy and sell government bonds, creating a *secondary market* (a market for previously issued bonds). The government bonds being traded have been sold to the bond dealers by the individuals or institutions that purchased them from the Treasury. The Federal Reserve is buying U.S. Treasury bonds, but it is buying them from the private sector, which originally purchased them from the Treasury. The Federal Reserve is prohibited by law from purchasing bonds directly from the Treasury.

Suppose the trading desk purchases $40 million of bonds from Acme Bond Company, a dealer in government bonds. Acme Company has a checkable deposit account with a large New York bank. The Federal Reserve carries out

Bond dealers
Privately owned corporations that hold large portfolios of bonds and buy and sell for their own accounts.

the purchase of bonds from Acme Company by depositing $40 million in the reserve deposit account of Acme Company's bank. This account is with the Federal Reserve Bank of New York, so the transaction is easily accomplished. The bank is then notified to credit $40 million to Acme Bond Company's checkable deposit account.

On the books of the Federal Reserve, Acme Company, and Acme Company's bank, the transactions appear as in Table 4. The Federal Reserve's holdings of government bonds rise by $40 million. This is offset by an increase in reserve deposits at the Federal Reserve of $40 million. On the books of Acme Company's bank, reserve deposits at the Fed rise by $40 million and checkable deposits of Acme Bond Company rise by $40 million. On Acme Company's books, $40 million worth of bonds is exchanged for $40 million of checking deposit money.

Acme Bond Company's bank now has $40 million in reserves that it did not previously have. Similar Federal Reserve purchases from other bond dealers increase the reserves in the banking system — and the monetary base — by a total of $500 million. The extra reserves enable the banks holding them to increase their lending. As they make loans, the money supply rises even more. The money multiplier process is under way. The eventual increase in the money supply will be $500 million times the money multiplier.

The bottom line on open market operations is quite simple. *An open market purchase of bonds by the Federal Reserve increases the monetary base and the money supply. An open market sale of bonds by the Federal Reserve decreases the monetary base and the money supply. The size of the increase or decrease in the money supply*

TABLE 4

Open market purchase from Acme Bond Trading Company

Federal Reserve's T-Account

Assets		Liabilities & Net Worth	
Government bonds	+ $40 million	Reserve deposits of Acme Company's bank	+ $40 million

T-Account of Acme Bond Company's Bank

Assets		Liabilities & Net Worth	
Reserve deposit at the Fed	+ $40 million	Checkable deposit of Acme Bond Company	+ $40 million

Acme Bond Company's T-Account

Assets		Liabilities & Net Worth
Government bonds	− $40 million	
Checkable deposits	+ $40 million	

equals the size of the change in the monetary base times the money multiplier. The multiplier works when the monetary base is reduced as well as when it is increased.

Discount Rate

What does a depository institution do when it runs short of reserves? A sudden, unexpected deposit outflow or an unexpected decline in funds flowing into the bank could leave a bank short of reserves. One solution to this problem is to borrow reserves from banks with excess reserves (reserves in excess of what a bank needs to meet its reserve requirement ratio). Such loans of reserves from one bank to another are called **federal funds** trading. The interest rate on these loans is the **federal funds rate**—a market rate determined by the demand for and supply of reserves into the interbank loan market. The name *federal funds* is used because the reserves satisfy the Fed's reserve requirements.

Another option is to borrow reserves from the Federal Reserve. The interest rate charged on borrowing from the Federal Reserve is the discount rate. Unlike the market-determined federal funds rate, the discount rate is an administered rate set by the Board of Governors. By raising or lowering the discount rate, the Federal Reserve can discourage or encourage borrowing by depository institutions.

Bank borrowing from the Federal Reserve affects the size of the monetary base and the money supply. Suppose Piedmont State Bank finds itself $10,000 short of reserves because an expected inflow of reserves did not occur. It chooses to borrow $10,000 from the Federal Reserve. This increases Piedmont Bank's reserves, and the reserves of the banking system, by $10,000. If the required reserve ratio is .10, it enables the banking system to support $100,000 more in deposits than the system could have supported without the extra reserves. Put another way, if the banking system did not acquire an additional $10,000 in reserves, it would have to reduce its loans and deposits by $100,000. Thus, borrowing from the Federal Reserve has an expansionary effect on the money supply.

The Federal Reserve can restrict the money supply by raising the discount rate. This raises the cost of borrowing for depository institutions. To avoid the need for borrowing, banks make fewer loans and hold some excess reserves to make sure they have adequate reserves on hand. If banks make fewer loans, the money supply contracts. Reducing the discount rate makes borrowing from the Federal Reserve more attractive and encourages more aggressive lending by depository institutions.

Not all changes in the discount rate are meant to have large policy effects. Many times the Federal Reserve changes the discount rate to bring it into line with market interest rates. If the rates charged by banks on loans are rising and the Federal Reserve does not increase the discount rate, banks can profit from aggressive lending policies. If they run short of reserves, they can borrow from the Federal Reserve to cover their new deposits. To prevent this sort of behavior, the Federal Reserve attempts to keep the discount rate in line with market interest rates. It also restrains borrowing by reserving the right to refuse loans to any banks it feels are abusing their borrowing privileges. Banks understand that borrowing from the Federal Reserve is a privilege and not a right. The fear that they will not be able to obtain a discount loan when it is desperately needed keeps most banks from borrowing from the Federal Reserve very often.

Federal funds
Loans of reserves by one bank to another bank.

Federal funds rate
Market-determined interest rate on federal funds loans.

Does It Make Economic Sense?

Eliminating Reserve Requirements

As we have seen, the money multiplier depends on the reserve requirement ratio. Even if we take into account other factors ignored by the simple multiplier formula, such as currency held by the public, it remains true that required reserves limit the loan expansion process and the size of the multiplier. The simple multiplier formula seems to indicate that required reserves are necessary to prevent an infinite expansion of the money supply. If $rr = 0$, the multiplier is $mm = 1/0$, which equals infinity. If the simple formula is to be believed, the absence of reserve requirements would allow banks to expand the money supply without limit.

Against this background, a recent proposal for monetary reform appears quite interesting. Jerry Jordan, at one time a member of President Reagan's Council of Economic Advisers, has called for the elimination of reserve requirements.* Since Dr. Jordan is a long-time advocate of slow money growth and stable prices, his proposal appears strange. Does it make economic sense?

To answer whether removing reserve requirements makes sense, we must first determine the purpose of reserve requirements. The reason usually given for reserve requirements is to limit credit and deposit expansion and thereby control the growth of the money supply.** Would credit and deposits expand without limit in the absence of reserve requirements? The answer is clearly no. Even if the required reserve ratio were zero, banks would hold some cash reserves. To remain in business, a bank must stand ready to convert its checkable deposits into currency on demand or to transfer cash reserves to other banks when funds are transferred by check. Any bank unable to immediately convert deposits into currency would rapidly lose its depositors to banks that provide adequate liquidity. Thus, banks would hold cash reserves even if the required ratio were zero.

Although banks would hold reserves in the absence of reserve requirements, it is clear that Federal Reserve regulations require U.S. banks to hold more reserves than the banks need to meet net withdrawals and transfers. Some other

---

SECTION RECAP

The major tool of monetary policy is open market operations. Fed purchases of bonds on the open market increase the monetary base; sales of bonds decrease the base. The Fed affects bank borrowing by *(continued)*

Reserve Requirements

The Board of Governors has the authority to set reserve requirement ratios on bank deposits. Banks would hold reserves even if the Federal Reserve did not require them to do so. However, by setting requirement ratios higher than the ratios banks would choose to hold in the absence of regulation, the Federal Reserve alters the behavior of the banking system.

Our examples have used a single reserve requirement ratio applied to deposits. In reality, different reserve requirement ratios apply to different types of deposits. Checkable deposits are subject to the highest ratios. The reserve requirements against time and savings deposits are much lower. In fact, the Federal Reserve reduced the reserve requirement ratios against time and savings deposits to zero in late 1990.

When the Federal Reserve changes the reserve requirement ratio, it changes the money supply. It does *not* affect the size of the monetary base, however. *Changes in the reserve requirement ratio affect the money supply by changing the value of the money multiplier.* The simple deposit multiplier is $mm = 1/rr$. Since the reserve requirement ratio is in the denominator, an increase in the ratio decreases the multiplier and a decrease in the ratio increases the multiplier.

Even small changes in reserve requirements cause large changes in the money supply unless they are offset by open market operations. In 1990 the monetary base reached $300 billion. A change in the reserve requirement ratio that alters the money multiplier by as much as 0.05 (say, from 2.5 to 2.55)

countries have recognized this fact and have lowered or eliminated reserve requirements. Both Switzerland and Australia eliminated reserve requirements in 1988, the Bank of Canada started the process of eliminating them in 1990, and the reserve requirement ratio in Great Britain is only one half of 1 percent. Even the Federal Reserve has lightened reserve requirements, removing them from all savings and time deposits in 1990. Clearly, the money supply would not expand without limit if reserve requirements were removed. But why bother? What's to be gained from removing reserve requirements? For banks, the big gain lies in the area of income. Reserve requirements act like a tax on bank earnings. When a bank is forced to hold unnecessarily large amounts of cash reserves, it loses the interest it could otherwise have earned on those assets. Earning zero interest on reserves is equivalent to paying a 100 percent tax on the earnings from a portion of the bank's assets. Thus, reserve requirements reduce bank income, making it harder for banks to compete effectively with nonbank financial intermediaries (such as money market mutual funds) and with foreign banks that are not encumbered with high reserve requirement ratios. Placing U.S. banks at a competitive disadvantage reduces the profitability, and ultimately the safety, of the banks. At a time when many banks are experiencing financial problems and many observers fear a repeat of the savings and loan crisis, it seems strange to argue that removing reserve requirements could possibly improve the situation. However, by increasing bank competitiveness and profitability, lower reserve requirements might help stave off some bank failures. From an economic point of view, removing reserve requirements clearly makes sense.

*Dr. Jordan's proposal is recounted in "Let's Kill Bank Reserve Requirements" by Lindley H. Clark, Jr., *Wall Street Journal*, April 3, 1990, p. A24.

**The rationale for reserve requirements has changed over time. See Marvin Goodfriend and Monica Hargraves, "A Historical Assessment of the Rationales and Functions of Reserve Requirements," Federal Reserve Bank of Richmond *Economic Review* 69 (March/April 1983), pp. 3–21.

would change the money supply by $15 billion due to the large size of the monetary base. Thus, in practice, changes in the reserve requirement ratio would have to be very small. Because it is costly for banks to adjust to new reserve requirement ratios, the ratio is seldom changed. Open market operations are a more efficient method of controlling the money supply. The reserve requirement ratio is important because it affects the size of the money multiplier, not because it is used as an active tool of policy.

SECTION RECAP
(continued)
adjusting the discount rate. Changes in reserve requirements change the value of the money multiplier.

Strategy of Monetary Policy

The goals of monetary policy and the policies followed in attempting to attain those goals are referred to as the strategy of monetary policy. In formulating a monetary policy strategy, it is standard to first define the goals and then work backwards to determine the optimal policies to achieve those goals.

Goals of Monetary Policy   The standard goals of macroeconomic policy are high employment, economic growth sufficient to maintain high employment and raise living standards, stability of the price level, and stability of real GNP around trend growth. Other goals could be specified, but they are usually subsidiary to the so-called big four.

The attitudes of policymakers about using monetary policy as an active stabilization tool reflect their views on the stability of the economy. If poli-

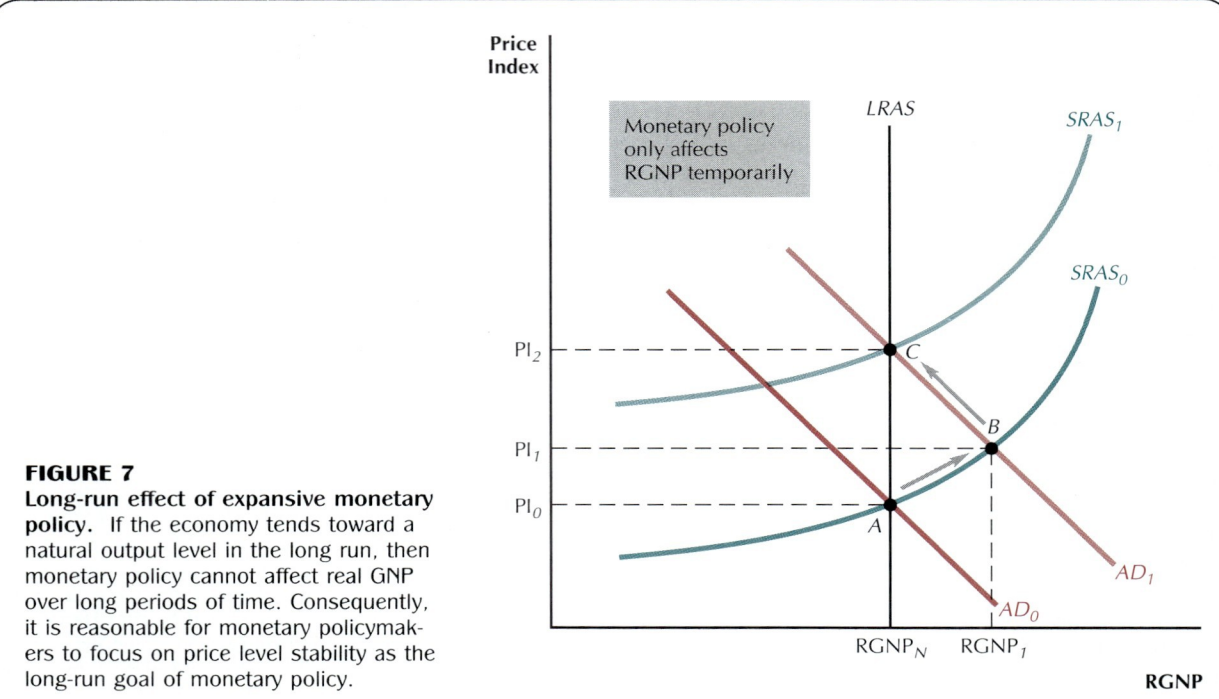

FIGURE 7
Long-run effect of expansive monetary policy. If the economy tends toward a natural output level in the long run, then monetary policy cannot affect real GNP over long periods of time. Consequently, it is reasonable for monetary policymakers to focus on price level stability as the long-run goal of monetary policy.

cymakers believe the economy is basically stable unless subjected to outside shocks (such as money supply shocks), they will not favor using monetary policy to constantly fine tune the level of aggregate demand. Activist policy produces few benefits if aggregate demand is fairly stable. If the monetary authorities believe that aggregate demand is basically unstable, subject to constant shifts due to changes in investment or consumer durable demand, they will be more inclined to intervene frequently. By judiciously expanding or contracting the money supply when aggregate demand falls or rises too rapidly, the Fed may be able to smooth fluctuations in output and employment.

How harmful policymakers believe unemployment to be relative to the harmfulness of inflation also affects policy goals. If policymakers believe that inflation is irritating but not really damaging to the economy, they will be inclined to use monetary policy to fight unemployment. On the other hand, if they believe that inflation seriously harms the economy, perhaps ultimately causing unemployment to rise, they will be less willing to trade off a little more inflation for lower unemployment in the short run.

The macroeconomic model presented in this book suggests that the proper long-run goal for monetary policy is price level stability. If the long-run aggregate supply curve is vertical, as in Figure 7, using monetary policy to increase the growth rate of aggregate demand will lead only to inflation, not to long-term output or employment gains. Expansive monetary policy, which shifts the AD curve to the right and initially increases real GNP, ultimately leads to higher expected inflation. As wages adjust upward to protect the buying power of workers, the SRAS curve shifts to the left. The ultimate result of the expansive monetary policy is a higher price level and the same output level.

Historical experience seems to support this view of the macroeconomy. However, the model does not rule out actively using monetary policy to affect output in the short run. Whether countercyclical policy designed to offset both recessions and excessively large expansions is worthwhile depends on how unstable aggregate demand is. Whether such policy is successful depends on the stability of the short-run aggregate supply curve and the skill of the policymakers. Our theoretical model does not address these issues. Empirical evidence must be used to determine whether the Federal Reserve should focus on more than price level stability in the short run.

Problems in Achieving Monetary Policy Goals   The Federal Reserve cannot directly control prices or output or employment. The levels of prices, output, and employment are determined by the forces of supply and demand interacting in markets. The decisions of millions of individuals act to produce macroeconomic outcomes. Thus, to carry out policy, the Federal Reserve must target some variable that influences the behavior of these individuals. **Monetary policy targets** are variables that the Federal Reserve can affect quickly and with some degree of accuracy and that, through their effect on the behavior of households and businesses, are systematically related to the Fed's policy goals. For example, the target of monetary policy might be the M1 money supply or the M2 money supply, or it might be the level of the interest rate on three-month Treasury bills.

> **Monetary policy targets** Variables that the Federal Reserve can use its policy tools to control with some accuracy.

The complete strategy of monetary policy can be shown in schematic form as:

$$\text{Policy tools} \rightarrow \text{Targets} \rightarrow \text{Policy goals}$$

For example, open market operations (OMO) might be used to increase the money supply in order to drive up spending. This sequence would appear as:

$$\text{OMO} \rightarrow \text{M1} \rightarrow \text{GNP}$$

Alternatively, the Federal Reserve might focus on using open market operations to affect the level of interest rates in the belief that spending is more closely related to interest rates than to the level of the money supply:

$$\text{OMO} \rightarrow i \rightarrow \text{GNP}$$

Federal Reserve officials utilize as targets the variables that seem to have the closest relationship to the goals of policy. Throughout most of the post-World War II period, the Fed has targeted an interest rate (or the general level of interest rates). In the 1970s the Fed began to pay increasing attention to monetary aggregates, in particular to M1. From late 1979 to late 1982 the Fed targeted M1 rather than an interest rate. Since then it has returned to targeting interest rates, while still paying attention to the behavior of monetary aggregates. However, M2 has replaced M1 as the monetary aggregate given the most attention, since the relationship between M2 and GNP has been much closer since 1982 than has the relationship between M1 and GNP.

If the relationship between the targets of monetary policy and the goals of monetary policy is not constant, the exact effects of monetary policy are unpredictable. Historical evidence suggests that the variable best suited to serve as a target of monetary policy changes over time. Thus, the Fed has changed its operating strategy repeatedly. The inability of the Federal Reserve to directly achieve its goals means that an element of uncertainty is always attached to policy actions.

> **SECTION RECAP**
> Monetary policymakers cannot directly control the variables they wish to influence (such as PI and RGNP). They attempt to influence their goal variables by using policy tools to affect targets, such as monetary aggregates or interest rates.

Why the Disagreement?

Should the Federal Reserve System Be Independent?

In a world where much of the government's budget is committed to long-range programs and cannot be changed, and where a major spending or tax bill may take several years to get through Congress, monetary policy is often the only game in town. If the economy is to be encouraged or restrained, the Federal Reserve must shoulder the responsibility. Fiscal policy cannot be implemented quickly enough to do any good.

The Federal Reserve is well-equipped to diagnose and react to changes in the state of the economy. The Board of Governors' staff of economists is respected throughout the world for its high level of technical competence. The people serving as governors and district bank presidents are well educated and well briefed on economic conditions. There may be no better group of policy technicians in the world than at the Federal Reserve. Many economists and businesspeople believe that the Federal Reserve should be left alone to use its immense technical skills in the best way possible.

Other economists and many politicians argue that the Federal Reserve is too independent and that it should be made subject to the directives of elected officials. Why the disagreement?

No one doubts the technical competence of the economists at the Federal Reserve System. However, more than technical competence goes into policymaking. Policymakers must also choose among different and competing goals.

Everyone would like to have a briskly growing economy with low inflation and minimal unemployment, but in the short run these goals may not be compatible. Policymakers may have to sacrifice one or more goals to achieve another.

People who believe that our nation is (or was intended to be) a democracy and that policy goals should be determined democratically are uncomfortable with an independent Federal Reserve System. They do not believe it is appropriate for a group of unelected technicians to determine the economic goals of the nation. They believe that at the very least the Federal Reserve should be directed to pursue policy goals determined by Congress and the president. Some would go so far as to say that the major policy actions taken by the Federal Reserve should be under the direct supervision of elected officials. To this end, Indiana Representative Lee Hamilton introduced legislation in 1989 that would have made the Secretary of the Treasury, an administrative official, a member of the Board of Governors.

Opponents of this democratic view of policymaking argue that monetary policy is too important to be politicized. They might agree that the general goals of policy should be determined by elected officials, but they would allow the technicians considerable latitude in carrying out day-to-day monetary policy. This view of the policy process maintains that the best monetary policy is likely to come from an elite group of technicians who avoid short-run political pressures. Another bill introduced in 1989 by North Carolina Congressman Stephen Neal instructs the Federal Reserve to maintain stable prices, but leaves the details up to Fed officials.

A number of economists and a few legislators hold yet another viewpoint, which stresses the long-run neutrality of the money supply and the need to control inflation. The people holding this view believe that altering the rate of growth of the money supply to increase or reduce real GNP growth is a shortsighted policy. Over extended periods of time, the growth of real GNP is not related to the growth rate of money, but the inflation rate is highly related to money supply growth. (Empirical evidence appears to corroborate this belief.) Monetarists believe that the Federal Reserve should be made to follow a monetary policy rule that prohibits the Fed from changing the growth rate of the money supply every time economic conditions change.

These different views of the proper role of the Federal Reserve System are based as much on political philosophy as on economic evidence. Someone with deeply held democratic views may oppose Federal Reserve independence whatever his views on economics. On the other hand, a person who believes that money supply variability is harmful for the economy might argue for a legislated monetary policy rule even if she believes in political democracy. Attitudes toward the economy are not unimportant in determining how a person feels on the issue of Federal Reserve independence. Nor are they the only thing that matters.

Policy in a Political Environment: The Place of the Federal Reserve in the Governmental System

The theory of monetary policy suggests how monetary policy could best be used. How it is actually used is another matter. Monetary policy is made not in a vacuum but in the political arena. The political position occupied by the Federal Reserve influences monetary policy.

The Federal Reserve System is a unique organization. The Board of Governors is not an administrative agency under the direction of the president, as are the various federal departments. It is a congressional agency. The Federal Reserve System was created by an act of Congress, and it could be altered or eliminated by another act. This means that the Federal Reserve is ultimately responsible to Congress. However, no formal mechanism presently exists for controlling the monetary policy operations of the Federal Reserve. To a large extent, the Federal Reserve System is independent of control by elected officials.

The Federal Reserve System was designed to be free of political pressures. It generates its own operating revenue and is not subject to the congressional appropriations process. Governors are appointed to long terms and cannot be reappointed after serving a full term. This was designed to prevent governors from campaigning for reappointment by serving the political interests of the president. Open market policy is made by twelve people, five of whom (district bank presidents) are neither elected nor appointed by elected officials but are selected by the board of directors of each district Reserve Bank.

The absence of a direct link to the political process does not mean, however, that the Federal Reserve System is unaffected by politics. As noted above, the rules of the game can be altered by a vote of Congress. The governors of the System are always careful not to go against the wishes of the majority of legislators to such a degree that the Federal Reserve Act is revised and their powers diminished. Similarly, the president has considerable informal influence on Federal Reserve decisions. By appointing to the Board of Governors individuals who agree with his basic philosophy, the president can affect monetary policy decisions. By focusing media attention on the Federal Reserve whenever a conflict arises between the Board of Governors and the president, the president can increase the probability that Congress will amend the Federal Reserve Act. In this way, the Federal Reserve can be forced to cooperate with administration wishes much of the time.

To a surprisingly large extent, all governmental agencies take on a life of their own, independent of the desires of elected officials. The Federal Reserve System is probably different in degree, but not in nature, from most other agencies. However, because the activities of the Federal Reserve are of more immediate interest to more people than are the activities of most governmental agencies, attention is focused on the Federal Reserve all the time.

Effect of Changes in the Money Supply on Aggregate Demand

Changes in the money supply affect aggregate demand both through their effects on interest rates and through the direct substitution of money for other assets.

When the Federal Reserve increases the money supply, it puts downward pressure on market interest rates. Lower interest rates encourage additional spending in several ways:

1. Lower interest rates reduce the cost of borrowing to finance investment projects, new houses, or consumer durable goods.

2. Lower interest rates may reduce the incentive to save, since the rate of return on savings is diminished. Present consumption becomes less expensive in terms of future consumption forgone.

3. Lower interest rates make corporate stocks relatively more attractive compared to bonds. As savers turn to stocks, stock prices are driven upward. Corporations find they can raise capital more easily by selling stock than they could before the price increase. This encourages more equity-financed investment spending by corporations.

4. Lower interest rates encourage investment in existing real assets, such as apartment buildings. The rate of return on such assets looks relatively attractive when interest rates fall. As investors purchase used assets, the assets' prices are driven up. As the price of used assets rises, it becomes more attractive to buy new assets. For example, as the price of existing apartment buildings rises, building new apartments becomes more attractive. Such spending on new investment projects increases aggregate demand.

5. Lower interest rates increase the market value of bonds held by households. The market price of a bond rises when the interest rate declines. Households that feel wealthier may spend more on consumption goods.

6. The higher stock prices (point 3) that follow from lower interest rates increase the financial wealth of shareholders who may then increase consumption expenditures.

In addition to the effects that work through interest rate changes, some direct effects may occur from an increase in the money supply.

7. If the increase in the money supply causes households to expect higher prices in the future, such households may increase their purchases of consumer durable goods, adopting a buy-before-the-price-rise mentality.

8. Some of the additional money pumped into the economy may be exchanged directly for goods and services, producing a direct budget-constraint effect on aggregate demand.

Figure 8 summarizes these eight channels.

With so many possible channels through which money supply changes can affect spending, it is no wonder that most economists consider monetary policy very important. Even economists who argue that the proper monetary policy is a constant money supply growth rate that never reacts to changes in economic activity base their argument on the potency of monetary policy. They argue that an activist monetary policy is likely to disrupt the economy. Those economists who argue that the Federal Reserve should be actively involved in managing aggregate demand also believe in the power of monetary policy. They have more faith in the Federal Reserve's abilities and less faith in the inherent stability of the economy.

SECTION RECAP
Money affects aggregate demand through a large number of channels. Changes in the money supply affect AD directly, through expected inflation, and through interest rate changes, which alter the cost of borrowing and the market value of financial assets.

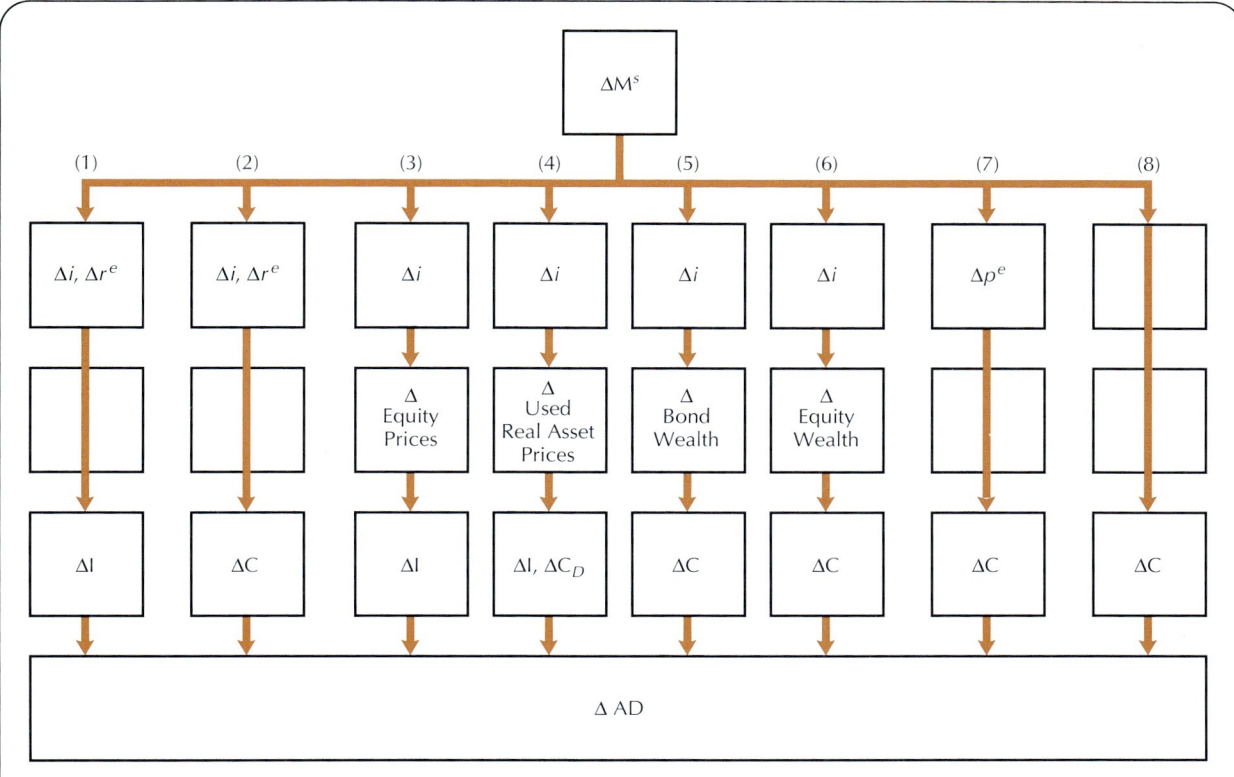

FIGURE 8
Channels through which money affects aggregate demand. Changes in the money supply affect the interest rate, which affects the cost of borrowing and the market value of financial wealth. Money supply changes also affect expected inflation and can affect aggregate demand directly.

Summary

Money is inextricably linked to the financial system that produces it. In the process of **intermediation,** not only do financial intermediaries transform savings into loans, but some of them, the **depository institutions,** create claims against themselves that serve as money. Because the U.S. banking system is a **fractional reserve system,** the loan process generates a **multiplier** effect. An additional dollar of monetary base injected into the banking system supports several dollars of money.

The size of the multiplier process is determined by the amount of reserves banks hold rather than lend and the amount of currency the nonbank public wishes to hold. If the **reserve requirement ratio** is small, banks hold only a few cents in reserves against every dollar of deposits. The remainder of every deposit dollar is loaned and becomes deposits in other banks or currency held by the public. The less currency the public holds (the larger the percentage of money held as bank deposits), the larger the multiplier. Banks have more deposit dollars to lend at each stage of the multiplier process.

The raw material of the money multiplier process is the **monetary base,** which consists of currency in the hands of the public plus the reserves of depository institutions. The monetary base is controlled by the Federal Reserve System, since liabilities of the Federal Reserve form most of the base. **Federal Reserve notes** and **reserve deposits** in **Federal Reserve banks** are both Federal Reserve liabilities and form well over 90 percent of the monetary base.

The **Federal Reserve System** was formed in 1913 to provide an elastic currency. The Federal Reserve was authorized to make loans to banks that needed currency. In the 1930s, the Federal Reserve was reorganized into an agency of monetary policy. The **Board of Governors** was given increased powers. Today monetary policy is the primary function of the Federal Reserve.

The Federal Reserve has several **policy tools** at its disposal. The most important of these is **open market operations,** the buying and selling of government bonds on the open market. The **discount rate** and **reserve requirement ratios** are also controlled by the Federal Reserve.

The goals of monetary policy are to a large extent determined by what policymakers believe about the workings of the economy. If policymakers believe the economy is basically stable when not subjected to outside shocks, they will not attempt to actively manage aggregate demand. If they believe the economy is inherently unstable, they are more likely to take an active role in demand management.

The money supply affects aggregate demand through a number of different channels. Several of these work through changes in interest rates. Wealth effects are also important. Both economists who believe the Federal Reserve should adopt a stable money supply growth rule and economists who favor an activist monetary policy believe in the potency of money supply changes.

Questions for Thought

Knowledge Questions

1. Define *financial intermediation.* Explain why intermediation is important to the efficiency of an economy.
2. Define the terms *monetary base, depository institution,* and *fractional reserve banking.*
3. Within the Federal Reserve System, who controls open market operations? The discount rate? Reserve requirement ratios?
4. What is the difference between the goals of monetary policy and the targets of monetary policy?

Application Questions

5. Suppose the reserve requirement ratio against bank deposits is .12. What is the value of the simple deposit multiplier? If the nonbank public chooses to hold 25 percent of its money in the form of currency, what does this imply about the actual value of the multiplier?
6. Assume the money multiplier has a value of 2.5. If the Federal Reserve wants to increase the money supply by $10 million, what open market operation should it undertake?
7. Suppose the economy is operating at the natural level of real GNP. What would be the effect on PI and RGNP of a large open market purchase of bonds by the Fed in the short run? In the long run?

8. Changes in the money supply can affect aggregate demand through a variety of channels. Explain how an increase in the money supply could affect aggregate demand through the stock market.

Synthesis Questions

9. Explain how the process of bank lending actually creates money.
10. How does the theory of macroeconomic behavior adhered to by policymakers affect the goals they choose for monetary policy? Do theoretical views completely determine policy goals? Explain.
11. What are the major reasons for Federal Reserve independence from the political process? What arguments favor bringing the Federal Reserve under closer political control?
12. Suppose the economy is operating at a real output level below the natural level of output. If the Federal Reserve wishes to use monetary policy to move the economy toward the natural output level, what type of policy should it use? What would be the appropriate open market operation? Change in the discount rate? Change in reserve requirements?

Appendix to CHAPTER 28

The Savings and Loan Crisis

The U.S. financial system experienced the most costly financial collapse in its history in the 1980s, as hundreds of savings and loan associations failed and were taken over by federal regulatory agencies. Estimates of the total losses incurred by the failed S&Ls are usually around $150 billion. The total cost to the U.S. economy of resolving the crisis will probably come to more than $500 billion, a figure that includes the interest that must be paid on bonds sold to finance the closure of insolvent institutions.

What caused such an immense financial catastrophe? Two common responses are fraud and mismanagement on the part of S&L owners and managers, and deregulation of the savings and loan industry by Congress in the early 1980s. While mismanagement and deregulation certainly played a part in the S&L crisis, economists who have studied the situation argue that the biggest factor leading to the widespread failures of S&Ls was regulatory failure. In short, Congress created a regulatory–deposit insurance system that prevented the savings and loan industry from adjusting to an increasingly volatile economy and a more competitive environment. When S&Ls began to fail, Congress changed the regulatory system in a way that encouraged S&L managers to take large risks. Then, as evidence mounted that the industry was in trouble, regulators failed to take prompt action to correct major problems. The result was a costly collapse of the S&L industry, a collapse that need not have occurred.

Background

Although the savings and loan industry has a long history in the United States, savings and loan associations played a minor role in the economy until the 1930s. One part of Franklin Roosevelt's New Deal was the promotion of home ownership. A highly regulated savings and loan industry was to provide financing for home ownership through long-term fixed-interest-rate mortgages. Federal regulations limited competition between S&Ls and other financial institutions, carving out a profitable niche for the specialized mortgage lenders. As a result, the savings and loan business changed very little over the next few decades.

So long as the economic environment remained stable, savings and loan associations prospered. However, a change in the economic environment in the late 1960s, coupled with increased competition from other financial institutions in the 1970s, demonstrated that the specialized structure of savings and loan associations was no longer viable.

Inflation rose sharply from the early 1960s to the mid-1970s. As inflation rose, so did nominal interest rates. Higher interest rates posed two problems for S&Ls. First, because long-term fixed-rate mortgages comprised a large share (around 80 percent) of most S&L asset portfolios, the average rate of return earned by S&Ls on their assets rose very slowly when market interest rates rose. S&Ls could make new mortgage loans at higher rates, but they still held large quantities of older mortgages in their portfolios. These older mortgages yielded relatively low rates of interest, pulling down the average rate of return earned by S&Ls. On the other hand, as short-term interest rates rose, many S&L depositors looked for alternatives to S&L savings deposits. When, in 1973, money market mutual funds were invented, many depositors began pulling their funds out of S&Ls and placing them in money market mutual funds.

If S&Ls had responded to the loss of deposits by increasing the interest rates paid on savings deposits, they would have suffered operating losses. Their cost of funds

TABLE 5

Asset prices and capital

Savings and Loan

Mortgage loans and other assets (at current market prices)	Savings deposits (at fixed dollar value)
	Capital (market value of assets minus fixed value of deposits)

would have risen quickly, while their interest earnings on mortgages rose only slowly. However, federal regulations prevented S&Ls from raising deposit rates. The Federal Reserve's Regulation Q placed a ceiling on the interest rate S&Ls (and banks) could offer. Consequently, S&Ls began losing funds to money market mutual funds and other financial intermediaries offering a higher rate of return.

The second problem caused by rising interest rates was a reduction in the market value of S&L assets. As we saw in the previous chapter, when the market interest rate rises, the price of a discount bond falls. The same is true for a mortgage. The market value of S&L assets fell sharply in the early 1970s. The decline in asset value left many S&Ls with little net worth, also known as capital. Table 5 illustrates this. The amount by which the value of an institution's assets exceeds the value of its liabilities equals its net worth, or capital. During the 1970s the market value of S&L assets fell, while the value of their deposits remained constant. (The price of a deposit is fixed at one dollar.) Consequently, the net worth (capital) of S&Ls evaporated.

When an institution's capital falls below zero, the institution is insolvent (bankrupt). Regulators should take over such an institution and either merge it with a healthy institution or sell off its assets and pay off depositors, using insurance funds to make up any deficiency. However, from 1975 through 1979 regulators resolved only forty-one insolvencies—less than one fourth the number of insolvent S&Ls during that period.[5]

During the 1970s, regulators permitted S&Ls to issue some time deposits bearing market interest rates as a means of attracting funds. However, not until 1980 did Congress act to change the regulations that had generated the problems besetting the savings and loan industry.

Deregulation

In 1980 Congress passed the Depository Institutions Deregulation and Monetary Control Act (DIDMCA). The DIDMCA permitted S&Ls to diversify somewhat by making a limited number of short-term consumer and commercial loans. It also provided for a gradual phasing out of Regulation Q deposit rate ceilings. Almost as an afterthought, the act also increased the amount of deposit insurance provided by the Federal Deposit Insurance Corporation (FDIC) and the Federal Savings and Loan Insurance Corporation (FSLIC) from $40,000 to $100,000 per deposit. This proved to be a serious mistake.

Continued deterioration of the savings and loan industry prompted Congress to remove more regulatory restrictions in 1982. The Garn–St. Germain Act permitted S&Ls wider latitude in lending and investing decisions. A number of states, prominently including Texas, went even further, essentially removing asset restrictions from state-

---

[5]These figures can be found in Edward J. Kane, *The S&L Insurance Mess* (Washington, DC: Urban Institute Press, 1989), p. 26, Table 2-1.

chartered S&Ls. At the same time that Congress and state legislatures were removing regulatory restrictions, the Reagan administration was reducing funds for regulatory supervision of banks and S&Ls. Not only were S&Ls now permitted to engage in more activities, they were able to do so with less supervisory oversight.

Moral Hazard

The combination of reduced asset restrictions and high deposit insurance limits proved lethal. It generated an incentive structure that encouraged the managers of insolvent S&Ls to take large risks in the hope of huge payoffs. Consider the position of the manager of an insolvent S&L: Unless the S&L is returned to solvency (positive net worth), regulators will eventually close the institution, eliminating the manager's job and forcing the institution's stockholders to take losses.[6] The removal of asset restrictions permits the manager to engage in very risky — but potentially very rewarding — investment activities. Deposit insurance provides the manager with a way to attract funds. Since deposits are insured by an agency of the federal government, depositors don't really care about the financial health of the S&L. If the manager offers attractive interest rates on deposits, funds will flow in. Thus, it is a simple matter to attract funds, make risky investments, and hope for the best.

An incentive structure that induces private individuals to make decisions that are privately beneficial but socially harmful is said to create **moral hazard**. The situation created by overly generous deposit insurance limits in the S&L industry is similar to the situation that would exist if a fire insurance company insured homes for far more than their market value. A homeowner would then have an incentive to be careless with fire, since his home is insured for more than it is worth.

As risky lending by S&Ls increased, losses mounted. Institutions that had small negative net worths made risky loans, took losses on the loans, and saw their (negative) capital positions deteriorate further. Regulators permitted losses to mount by practicing **regulatory forbearance** — refraining from closing insolvent S&Ls as was permitted by law. S&L regulators practiced regulatory forbearance because the FSLIC did not have enough reserves to close all the insolvent institutions. In other words, the liabilities of the FSLIC exceeded its assets — the insurance fund was bankrupt. Regulatory forbearance allowed the total losses of insolvent S&Ls to grow dramatically during the 1980s.

Legislative Action

Although the extent of the S&L industry collapse was widely recognized by 1988, Congress did not act to stem the losses until 1989. (Since 1988 was an election year, neither party wanted to deal with the S&L situation. The failure to act promptly added tens of billions of dollars to the ultimate cost of resolving the crisis.) In 1989 Congress passed the *Financial Institutions Reform, Recovery, and Enforcement Act* (FIRREA). This act placed stronger lending restrictions on S&Ls, closed the bankrupt FSLIC and transferred authority for S&L deposit insurance to the FDIC, appropriated funds to begin closing insolvent S&Ls, and authorized a newly created Resolution Trust Corporation to sell bonds to raise more funds to clear up insolvencies. In 1989 and 1990 the FDIC seized hundreds of insolvent S&Ls, merging most with healthy institutions, which took over the insolvent S&Ls' deposits and good assets. The healthy institutions received payment from the FDIC for the amount by which the value of deposits acquired exceeded the value of assets acquired.

FIRREA was a step in the right direction, because it closed many insolvent S&Ls that would have gone deeper into bankruptcy had they been allowed to continue operations. However, FIRREA did nothing to address the root problems besetting the S&L industry. Two fundamental problems must be overcome before the industry can

Moral hazard
A situation in which an individual has the incentive to do something that is socially costly.

Regulatory forbearance
When regulators permit insolvent financial institutions to continue operating, rather than closing them.

---

[6]Many S&Ls are mutual associations, which do not have stockholders. Technically, mutual S&Ls are owned by their depositors. Their capital is in the form of retained earnings.

return to economic health. First, S&Ls must learn to — and must be permitted to — compete with other financial intermediaries in an increasingly competitive financial environment. This means that S&Ls must not be forced to make only one type of loan; they must be permitted to diversify their portfolios, to engage in activities that enable them to spread the risk of lending over a wide variety of assets. They must have the flexibility to react quickly to changing economic conditions. S&Ls cannot be singled out for especially restrictive regulation. Tight regulation ultimately will kill the industry.

The second fundamental problem is the current structure of the deposit insurance system. The current system promotes risk taking by charging all S&Ls the same insurance rate, regardless of how safe or how risky they are, and by removing all depositor discipline from S&Ls. We would think that private insurers were crazy if they charged safe drivers the same auto insurance rates as they charge drivers who have had multiple accidents or who have been repeatedly convicted of driving under the influence of alcohol. Yet the deposit insurance system does just that. Safe S&Ls pay higher insurance rates than they should; risky S&Ls pay less than they should. The effect of the flat payment system is to encourage risk taking.

The $100,000 deposit limit has the same effect. If only, say, 90 percent of deposits were insured by the FDIC, depositors would be concerned about the safety of their funds. They would investigate the safety of an institution before depositing funds in it. Does the institution have a large amount of capital? Capital protects depositors (and the insurance fund) from losses, so depositors would have an interest in capital adequacy. How risky is the institution's asset portfolio? If the institution has a high rate of loan losses, the probability of failure is higher. Depositors would investigate asset quality.

Such concern by depositors would force S&Ls (and other financial institutions) to take fewer risks. Fewer risks mean lower loan losses, fewer failed institutions, and lower liabilities for the deposit insurance fund. Until the deposit insurance problem is resolved, the potential for widespread failure of S&Ls (or of banks) remains.

OVERVIEW

It seems safe to say that interest rates attract more attention than virtually any other prices. Economists are constantly asked their opinions about the future course of interest rates, network television news programs report interest rate movements, and politicians regularly charge that interest rates are too high for the good of the economy (they never seem to be too low).

In the preceding chapters we frequently mentioned

The Credit Market

interest rates, stressing their importance as a factor affecting both consumption and investment spending. Changes in interest rates cause people to alter their spending patterns. For example, temporarily higher interest rates may cause a household to postpone the purchase of a new automobile, even if the household has the funds available to buy the car outright. The fact that higher interest rates do not eliminate the purchase of the new car, but merely postpone it, does not mean that interest rate changes are unimportant. If many consumers simultaneously postpone large expenditures, the path of spending in the economy over time will be very uneven. The economy will be subject to business cycle movements that result, at least partly, from interest rate changes.

In this chapter we consider the basic theory of interest rate determination. First, however, we must clarify what an interest rate is. Understanding the nature of interest rates requires an appreciation of the difference between money and credit. After making this distinction, we discuss the determination of the market level of the interest rate with the same basic tools used to examine any market price: demand and supply.

Because different markets are linked by the aggregate budget constraint, it is possible to analyze interest rate determination either directly through the credit market or indirectly through the monetary sector. In an earlier chapter we made use of the indirect approach,

CHAPTER 29

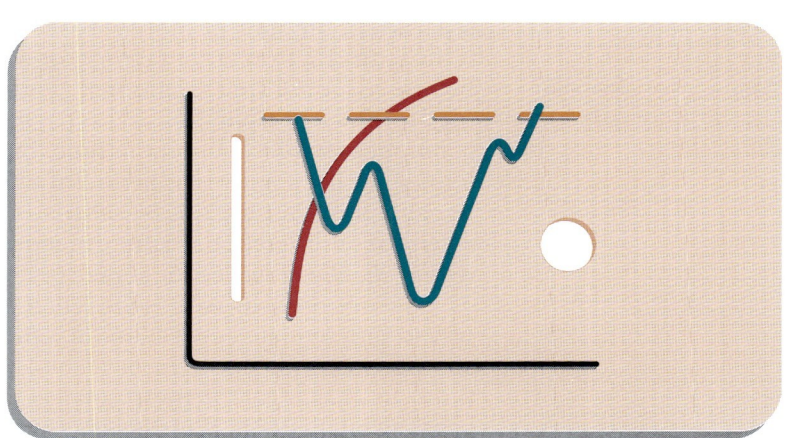

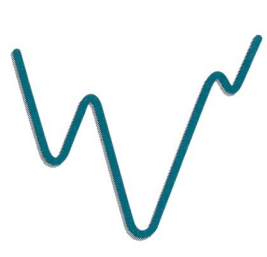

showing how a change in money demand (relative to the money supply) alters the equilibrium interest rate. However, for many purposes it is preferable to address the issue of interest rate determination directly. Thus, in this chapter we develop the credit market model and use it to show how various factors affect the interest rate.

Learning Objectives

After reading and studying this chapter, you will be able to:

1. State the difference between money and credit, and define the term *interest rate*.
2. Relate market interest rates and bond prices.
3. List the factors that affect the demand for credit.
4. List the factors that affect the supply of credit.
5. State the difference between nominal and real interest rates.
6. Discuss the extent to which the Federal Reserve can control the level of interest rates.

The Interest Rate Is the Price of—What?

A longstanding confusion exists among noneconomists concerning what the interest rate is the price of. The answer is clear: *The interest rate is the price of credit.* It is *not* the price of money. The price of money is the *inverse* of the aggregate price level. As PI rises, each dollar buys less; that is, the price of money falls, and money becomes less valuable in terms of goods and services.

Money and Credit: What's the Difference?

Stock
Economic variable that exists at a point in time.

The difference between money and credit can be explained in several different ways. Technically, money is a **stock**, something that exists at a point in time. The money stock consists of the currency issued by government agencies—Federal Reserve notes and U.S. Treasury coins—plus checkable deposits at banks and thrift institutions. It is conceptually possible to count the number of dollars of money existing at a particular point in time, since at any moment, a particular amount of money exists.

Flow
Economic variable that must be measured over a period of time.

Credit is a **flow** over a period of time. It represents the lending of money by one economic unit to another. Lenders exchange their current money holdings for interest payments and repayment of the money in the future. Credit is not measurable at a point in time, but is calculated as the amount of money loaned during a particular period of time. (The dollar value of loans outstanding at a point in time can be calculated, although that figure represents credit extended at different dates for different periods of time.) Credit is, in essence, *renting the use of money* for some specific period of time.

The notion that credit is the rental use of money provides us with a second way to differentiate between money and credit. If Lindsey leases an apartment, she purchases the services of (rents) the apartment for a specific period of time. In exchange for these services, Lindsey pays rent to the owner. The relationship between a borrower and a lender is analogous. When the borrower obtains a loan from the lender, the borrower must repay the loan at some point; that is, the borrower must return the money to the owner. While the borrower has possession of the money, he pays interest to the lender. The interest pays for the services provided by the loan during the period that the loan is outstanding.

It is worth noting that the demand for credit by a borrower is *not* equivalent to a demand for money, since the borrower may immediately use the borrowed funds to make a purchase. The demand for money refers to the desire to *hold* money balances; the demand for credit refers to the desire to obtain funds to finance a purchase.

An Empirical Note on Money Supply and Credit Data The amount of money in existence and the amount of credit extended are related even though they are different. If the money supply is expanding rapidly, it is easier for financial institutions to expand their lending. (As the preceding chapter noted, most of the money supply is created through bank lending.) Nevertheless, the relationship between money and credit is not rigid. It is possible for the amount of credit issued to move sharply upward or downward during a period in which the money supply is relatively constant, since the same units of money can be repeatedly loaned and spent. For example, the average value of the M1 money supply (currency outside the banking system and checkable deposits)

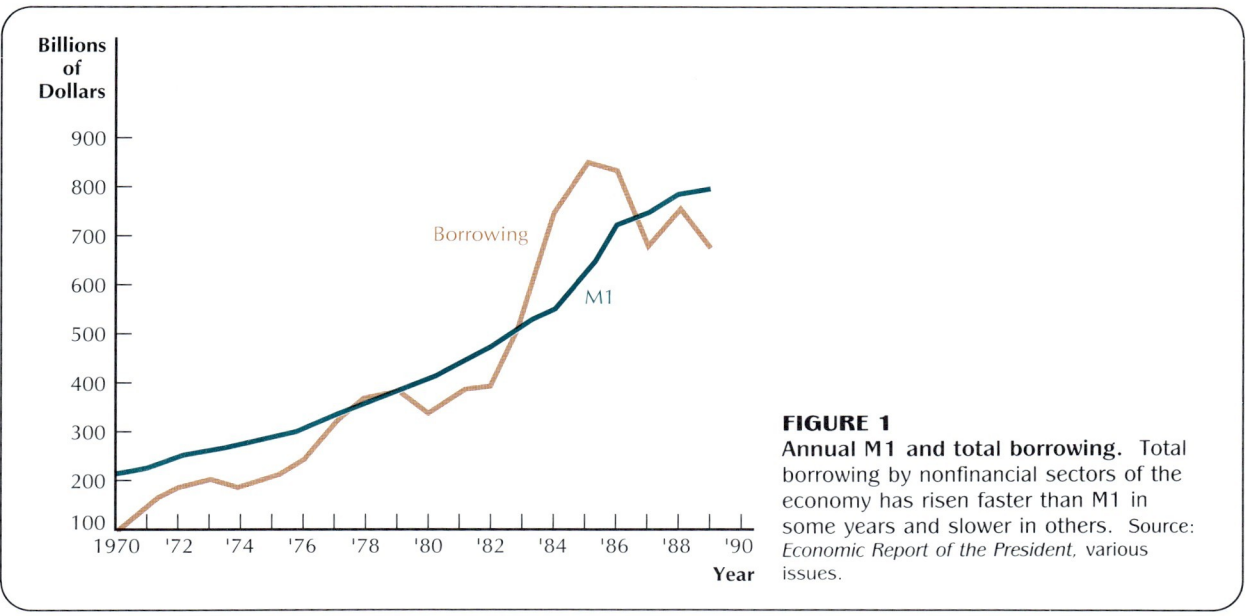

FIGURE 1
Annual M1 and total borrowing. Total borrowing by nonfinancial sectors of the economy has risen faster than M1 in some years and slower in others. Source: *Economic Report of the President*, various issues.

during 1985 was $620.5 billion. The amount of funds raised in U.S. credit markets during 1985 (total net borrowing) was $846.3 billion. Figure 1 illustrates the relationship over time of the M1 money supply and total net borrowing in U.S. credit markets.

Loans and Bonds

When a bank makes an automobile loan or a savings and loan association makes a mortgage loan, credit is extended. When an individual purchases a U.S. savings bond, credit is also extended. The purchaser of the bond loans money to the seller of the bond, the U.S. government. A bond is simply a specific type of loan contract.

Bonds are issued by organizations that borrow repeatedly. By selling bonds directly to the public, corporations and government units can raise more funds than they would be able to acquire by taking out a loan from a single bank. However, only organizations with well-known credit ratings are able to issue bonds. Information on the **default risk** of a bond issue—the probability that the borrower will not repay principal or meet interest payments—must be generally available for bond purchasers to be able to calculate the probable value of the bonds. (Moody's and Standard and Poor's bond-rating services provide such information to bond purchasers.) These two criteria—repeat borrowing and well-known risk status—limit the bond market to moderate-to-large organizations. Smaller and less frequent loans are typically handled by banks or other financial institutions.

Most bonds other than those with very short terms to maturity (a year or less) are **coupon bonds.** Coupon bonds pay a specified amount of interest (the coupon payment) on specified dates (usually semiannually) until they mature, at which point the **face value** is repaid. The face value of a bond is the principal that is paid to the bondholder whenever the bond matures. The

Default risk
Risk that a borrower will fail to meet principal or interest payments on schedule.

Coupon bonds
Bonds that make explicit interest payments on specified dates.

Face value
The principal that is repaid when a bond matures.

Secondary market
Market in which previously issued securities are traded.

face value of a bond is fixed when the bond is issued; neither the face value nor the coupon payment ever changes. Most bonds are issued with face values that are multiples of $1000.

Most widely traded bonds have **secondary markets** in which previously issued bonds can be traded. Secondary markets enable bond purchasers to sell the bonds before the bonds mature, thus greatly increasing their liquidity (the ease and efficiency with which an asset can be converted into money). The company or government unit issuing the bonds is not affected by secondary market transactions. Savers merely trade assets, the original bondholder giving the bond to another saver in return for money. The price at which bonds trade in the secondary market is determined by the demand for and supply of bonds on the market. The existence of secondary markets makes bonds much more attractive to savers by providing a convenient way to convert bonds into money should the need arise.

Bond Prices and Interest Rates

Since the face value and the value of coupon interest payments are fixed when a bond is issued, the rate of return a bondholder receives *when the bond is held to maturity* is also fixed. Consider a $1000 face value bond with an annual coupon payment of $80 and a term to maturity of five years. An individual purchasing this bond at a price of $1000 and holding it to maturity will receive five annual interest payments of $80 each plus a repayment of the $1000 principal at the end of five years. The rate of return on the bond, called the **coupon rate**, is 8 percent. It is derived by dividing the annual coupon interest payment by the face value of the bond: $80/$1000 = .08.

Coupon rate
Coupon payment divided by the bond's face value.

If the bondholder needs money before the bond matures, he or she can sell the bond in the secondary market. Suppose, however, that the market interest rate has risen from 8 percent to 10 percent. Who would want to buy an 8 percent bond when other bonds paying 10 percent interest are available? The bondholder will be able to sell the bond only if it pays a competitive rate of return. The bond holder can offer a competitive rate by selling the bond for less than its face value. Doing so increases the rate of return earned by the buyer.

Suppose a bond with a face value of $1000 and a coupon of $80 has one year remaining to maturity when it is sold. Whoever buys the bond will receive an $80 interest payment and a $1000 principal payment at the end of the year, for a total dollar return of $1080. For the bond to pay a 10 percent return, its price must satisfy the equation:

$$P_B \times (1.10) = \$1080$$

SECTION RECAP
Credit is the rental use of money for a period of time. Credit is extended in the form of loans. Bonds are a standardized form of loans. The market price of a bond or a loan *(continued)*

Solving the equation yields:

$$P_B = (1/1.10) \times \$1080 = \$981.82$$

In other words, a person who pays $981.82 for a bond paying $1080 at the end of one year earns a 10 percent rate of return on the bond.

Note what happened when the market interest rate rose from 8 to 10 percent. The price of the bond fell from $1000 to $981.82. *The price of a bond and the market interest rate are inversely related.* Given fixed coupon interest payments and fixed face value, the only way the rate of return on a bond traded in the secondary bond market can be altered is by changing the bond's market price. *When a bond's price falls, the yield, or rate of return, rises; when the price rises, the yield falls.* (The Appendix to this chapter provides an in-depth discussion of interest rates and bond prices.)

> **SECTION RECAP**
> *(continued)*
> is inversely related to the market interest rate.

Which One Is *the* Interest Rate?

Economics textbooks often speak of *the* interest rate, as though there were only one interest rate in the credit market. (This book is no exception.) Yet it is obvious that literally thousands of different interest rates exist in the sophisticated financial system that is the U.S. credit market. All one has to do to confirm this is thumb through any issue of the *Wall Street Journal*. Page after page of small print provide information on the market yields offered by different types of bonds and loans. How is it that economists think they can refer to *the* interest rate when so many rates exist?

The answer to this question goes back to the definition of interest rates. An interest rate is the rental price of money for a period of time. The thousands of different bonds, loans, and other securities differ in many important ways, so their interest rates also differ. However, they all have one thing in common: They all represent the renting of money. Since the use of money is the common factor, economists view *the* interest rate as the *pure rental price of money*. The interest rate on a particular loan is composed of this **pure interest rate** plus some additional premiums that reflect risk and other factors.

> **Pure interest rate**
> Pure rental price of money, common to all interest rates.

An example should clarify this. Suppose we compare two loans, one of which is regarded as completely safe, the other of which is viewed as risky. The second loan is risky because there is a chance that the borrower will default by failing to pay interest or repay the loan principal on schedule. If the two loans are identical in all characteristics other than default risk (including length of the loan), which loan will carry the higher interest rate? The answer should be obvious: The risky loan will carry a higher interest rate. If the only difference between the two loans is default risk, the difference in interest rates must be a **risk premium**—an addition to interest required to persuade lenders to make the risky loan.

> **Risk premium**
> An addition to the pure interest rate, required to induce lenders to make risky loans.

The common component of the two interest rates is *the* interest rate, the pure rental price of money. This is the interest rate determined by the economy's demand for and supply of credit. The riskier loan carries a rate equal to the pure interest rate plus a risk premium. If the factors determining the pure rate of interest change while the default risk remains constant, both interest rates should change by the same amount. Thus, it is possible to speak of *the* interest rate without doing too much damage to reality, because the macroeconomic factors causing one interest rate to rise or fall are likely to cause nearly all other interest rates to rise or fall as well.

Changes in the expected rate of inflation provide an exception to this rule. Loans of differing lengths or **terms to maturity** often carry different expected inflation premiums. For example, suppose credit market participants expect inflation to be relatively low over the next year, say 3 percent, but they expect the inflation rate to rise to 6 percent the following year. The inflation premium, p^e, added to a one-year bond would be 3 percent, while the inflation premium added to a two-year bond would be approximately 4.5 percent (the average of 3 percent and 6 percent). Changes in the expected rate of inflation can alter

> **Term to maturity**
> Length of time until a bond matures and pays off its face value.

Term structure
Pattern of interest rates on bonds of different maturity lengths.

Time preference
Desire to have something now rather than in the future.

SECTION RECAP
The interest rate on a particular security consists of a pure interest rate common to all loans plus one or more premiums reflecting risk, term to maturity, or other specific features of the security.

the **term structure** of interest rates—the pattern of interest rates on loans of different maturity lengths. If inflation is expected to rise in the future, the inflation premium on long-term loans will be higher than the premium on short-term loans, and long-term interest rates will exceed short-term rates. If the inflation rate is expected to fall in the future, short-term interest rates will carry a larger expected inflation premium and may rise above long-term rates.

The pure interest rate is positive because of **time preference**. People would rather enjoy consumption now than later. If they are to be persuaded to give up control of some of their wealth by lending it to a borrower, they must be compensated. Even if individuals wish to save, they can choose to maintain control over their savings by simply holding money. A positive interest rate provides the incentive to allow another person to use their savings.

For practical purposes, economists often regard a short-term U.S. government bond rate as the pure rate of interest. Short-term Treasury bills (or *T-bills*, as such bonds are often called) have no default risk (since the government has the right to levy taxes or print money to pay its debts), standard tax features, and none of the other peculiarities that sometimes characterize private loans. Additionally, Treasury bills are bought and sold in large quantities by a large number of traders, so no single trader (other than the U.S. Government itself) can affect the interest rate of T-bills to any great extent.

Credit Market Model

In this section we develop a model of interest rate determination that focuses directly on the demand for and supply of credit. Since, in an earlier chapter, we demonstrated that it is possible to use a money demand–money supply model to analyze interest rate behavior, the need for a credit market model must be justified. The credit market model of interest rate determination is useful because

1. it focuses on the factors that directly affect the interest rate, rather than focusing on factors that have indirect effects
2. it is much better suited to the analysis of dynamic processes, such as inflation (a *sustained* increase in the general price level), than the money demand–money supply model
3. it handles changes in economic flows better than the money demand–money supply model, which is a stock model.

The money demand–money supply model enables us to see that a change in money demand or money supply creates either an excess demand for money or an excess supply of money. People react to such a monetary disequilibrium by attempting to adjust their money holdings. This leads them to change the amount of financial assets they hold; that is, people adjust their money holdings by altering the amount of funds they supply to the credit market. We can gain additional insight into the workings of the economy by examining the credit market, where the interest rate is actually determined.

Demand for Credit

The general level of interest rates is determined by the forces of demand and supply. The credit market is undoubtedly the most efficient market in existence.

Changes in demand and supply cause almost immediate changes in interest rates. This section discusses the demand for credit, while the following section covers the supply of credit.

Let us begin our examination of credit demand by separating that demand into demand by different sectors of the economy, just as we did earlier when formulating the theory of aggregate demand. The four sectors examined are the household, business, government, and foreign sectors. Each of these sectors demands credit for different reasons.

Consumer Durables and Housing The major reason for household borrowing is the purchase of consumer durable goods and housing. Many consumer durable items are quite expensive but are nonetheless desirable, because they provide a flow of services for years into the future. This is true of cars, furniture, televisions, kitchen appliances, washers and dryers, and, of course, houses. The services produced by these items are consumed over long periods of time. (The durable goods themselves are not consumed. Rather, they depreciate, or wear out, over the course of their productive lives.) The cost of one of these items, when spread over several years, can appear quite reasonable. (For example, a $600 refrigerator that lasts for ten years costs only $60 per year.[1]) Paying for a durable item out of current income or savings may prove difficult. Hence, the major reason for household borrowing is to purchase consumer durable goods and housing.

What factors influence the desired level of consumer durable purchases? One factor is the interest rate. When the interest rate rises, borrowing becomes more expensive. This has a negative effect on the purchase of consumer durables, as shown by the negative slope of the household credit demand curve in Figure 2.

Two factors influencing the amount of credit households demand at various levels of the interest rate are the level of national income and the amount of borrowing households have already undertaken. When national income rises, households have more income that can be used to purchase consumer goods or to repay debt. As we saw when discussing the theory of consumer demand, purchases of consumer durables are quite cyclical. When the economy is expanding briskly, spending on consumer durables is high; in a recession, it is low. The ability to repay borrowings is the key. Thus, when national income rises, the household demand for credit curve shifts to the right. When income falls, CR^d shifts to the left.

A factor negatively affecting the amount of new borrowing that a household will undertake is the amount of debt the household has already incurred. Given its budget constraint, a household can make a limited amount of loan payments. If households have already borrowed a great deal, an increase in national income or a decrease in interest rates may have a relatively small effect in persuading them to borrow any more. Thus, if households have relatively little debt outstanding, an increase in income shifts CR^d by more than if households already have incurred a relatively large amount of debt.

Investment Business firms borrow to finance long-term projects and short-term inventory needs. Business borrowing is negatively related to the expected

---

[1] This simple calculation ignores the fact that future values must be discounted to find their present value. See the appendix to the chapter on aggregate demand for details.

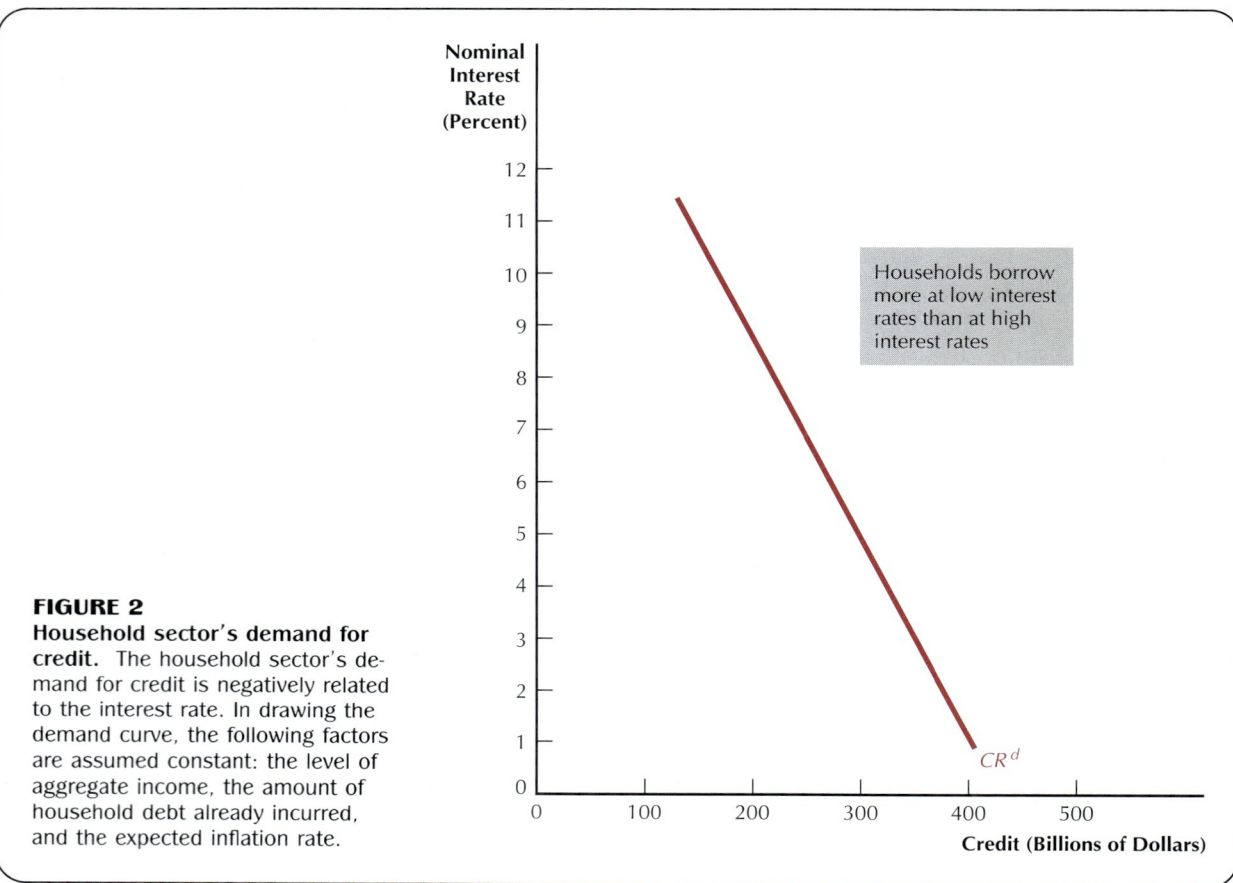

FIGURE 2
Household sector's demand for credit. The household sector's demand for credit is negatively related to the interest rate. In drawing the demand curve, the following factors are assumed constant: the level of aggregate income, the amount of household debt already incurred, and the expected inflation rate.

real interest rate, and the amount of credit demanded by businesses changes with changes in national income, capacity utilization, and tax policy.

Recall that the expected real interest rate is given by the formula:

$$r^e = i - p^e$$

where p^e is the expected inflation rate. When expected inflation rises, other things constant, the expected real rate declines. This increases the desire of business managers to borrow, because they believe that the real cost of borrowing has declined. Thus, the demand for credit curve shifts to the right.

An increase in aggregate income generates increased demand for the products produced by businesses. The need to expand to meet greater customer demand causes business firms to invest when income rises. The income increase causes the business sector's demand for credit curve to shift to the right. An increase in income has a larger effect on investment and the demand for credit when capacity utilization is high and few machines and factories are underemployed.

Tax policy is a very important determinant of investment demand and businesses' demand for credit. A change in the tax laws that makes investment more profitable increases the demand for credit. A tax law revision that reduces the profitability of investment reduces the demand for credit by business firms.

Government Deficits Just like every other economic unit, government units face budget constraints. All expenditures must be financed somehow. If a government unit runs a deficit, spending more than it receives in tax revenues, it must cover the difference by borrowing. (The federal government has another option — creating money.) Government borrowing influences the total demand for credit in the same way private borrowing does. An increase in the total government budget deficit increases the demand for credit, shifting the credit demand curve to the right.

Foreign Demand for Credit The credit market is an international market. Credit moves rapidly around the world as funds are transferred electronically from banks in one country to banks in other countries. Since the U.S. dollar occupies a special place in world finance, serving as an **international reserve currency** — a currency widely used in international transactions — the demand for dollars can lead foreigners to enter the U.S. credit market as borrowers. Foreigners compare the cost of obtaining dollars in the U.S. credit market relative to the cost of obtaining them in international markets. When the expected real interest rate in foreign countries rises relative to the U.S. expected real interest rate, the demand for credit in the U.S. market rises. Foreigners borrow more in the United States, shifting the credit demand curve to the right. A decline in foreign real interest rates reduces the foreign demand for credit in the U.S. market.

International reserve currency
Currency widely used in international transactions.

Factors Affecting Credit Demand: A Summary The aggregate credit demand curve is the horizontal summation of the credit demand curves of the household, business, government, and foreign sectors. Figure 3 shows the summation of these credit demand curves into the aggregate credit demand curve. The gov-

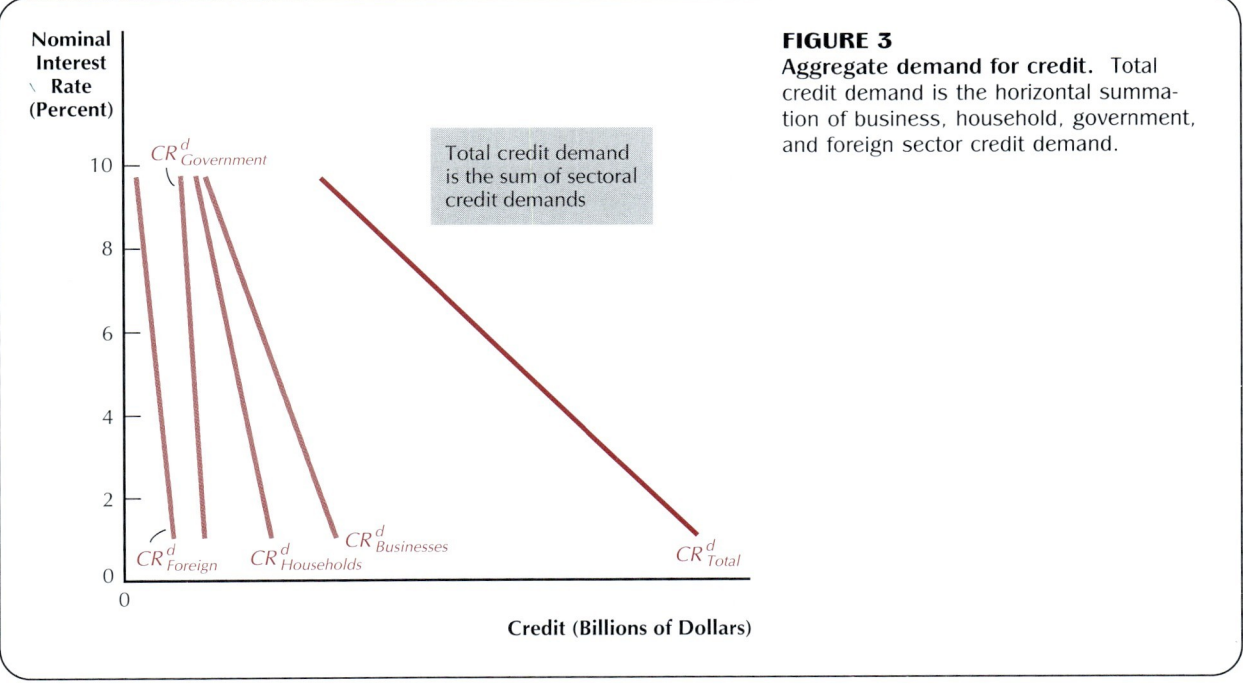

FIGURE 3
Aggregate demand for credit. Total credit demand is the horizontal summation of business, household, government, and foreign sector credit demand.

ernment's demand for credit curve is drawn with a very steep slope, reflecting the fact that the demand for credit by governments is very insensitive to the interest rate. Although local governments pay some attention to interest rates (a school district may delay selling bonds if interest rates are too high, for example), state and federal governments pay very little attention to interest rates. Their spending and taxation decisions are not affected by the level of market rates. Consequently, the total government demand for credit is quite insensitive to changes in the interest rate. However, *because the credit demands of the household and business sectors are interest sensitive, total credit demand is also interest sensitive.*

The following major factors affect the position of CR^d:

1. The level of income: An increase in income generates higher consumer and business borrowing, shifting the credit demand curve to the right; a decrease in income shifts CR^d to the left.

2. The level of consumer debt outstanding: The greater the indebtedness of households, the less additional borrowing they engage in when income increases.

3. The level of capacity utilization of industry: High utilization is conducive to more investment and hence more borrowing.

4. The size of the total government deficit: When government spending exceeds tax revenues, the deficit must be financed by borrowing (although the federal government has the option of creating money). An increase in the deficit increases the demand for credit.

5. An increase in foreign expected real interest rates: Foreign borrowers may look to the U.S. credit market for cheaper credit, increasing CR^d in the U.S. market.

Supply of Credit

The source of credit in any economy is saving. All three domestic sectors of the economy — household, business, and government — are potential savers, and savings can flow into the domestic credit market from foreign savers as well. The household sector is the only *net* saving sector, saving more than it borrows. The business sector saves the most, but since business borrowing to finance new investment projects exceeds business saving, the business sector is a net borrower. The government sector is also a large net borrower. Table 1 provides data on saving for the years 1970, 1975, 1980, 1985, and 1990.

The factors affecting household saving include the real interest rate, income, and the expected rate of inflation. If the real interest rate rises, households earn more on their savings. The higher return to saving caused by an increase in the real rate of interest encourages households to increase their saving. However, when the real interest rate rises, households also earn more interest income on their previously accumulated wealth. Without saving more, their interest earnings rise. If they are satisfied with their previous interest earnings, they might even save less. Thus, a rise in the real interest rate might have a negative effect on saving; people might choose to consume more and save less.

Although empirical evidence on this issue is mixed, we will assume that the quantity of credit supplied increases slightly as the real interest rate rises, indicating that the incentive to save more when the real interest rate rises

TABLE 1
Saving by sector in selected years

Billions of Current Dollars

Sector	1970	1975	1980	1985	1990
Household	57.7	104.6	136.9	125.4	179.1
Business	106.7	198.9	341.5	539.9	604.8
Government	−10.6	−64.9	−34.5	−131.8	−126.0

Source: *Economic Report of the President, 1991*, Table B-28.

slightly outweighs the incentive to save less. The important thing to remember is that saving is not very sensitive to changes in the real rate of interest. Thus, the household saving curve in Figure 4 appears very steep; an increase in the interest rate, holding income and expected inflation constant, generates only a very small increase in saving.

We saw in an earlier chapter that, although consumption spending depends on income, not all income changes affect spending equally. A temporary in-

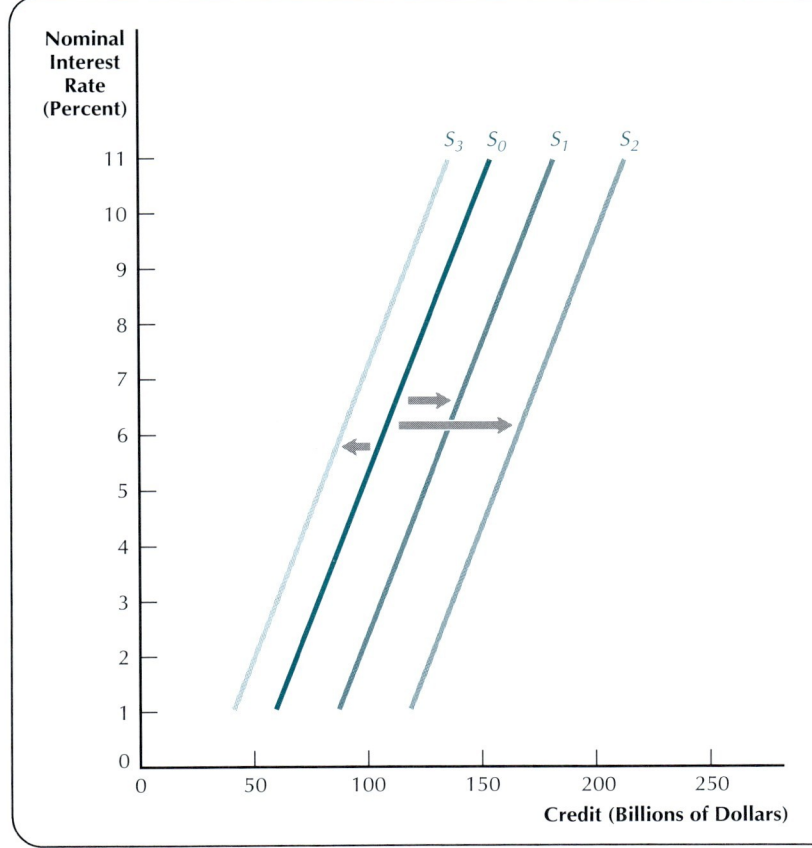

FIGURE 4
Household sector saving (supply of credit). Saving by the household sector supplies credit to borrowers. A temporary increase in income increases saving by more (to S_2) than does a permanent income increase (to S_1). An increase in expected inflation shifts saving to the left (to S_3).

come change generates a relatively small current change in consumption spending. Most households save a large portion of a temporary increase in income. However, liquidity-constrained households, which cannot borrow to sustain consumption during periods of low income, consume most of an income increase as they seek to return to their desired consumption level. Empirical evidence indicates a minority of households are liquidity constrained. Most households are able to borrow and lend to smooth out consumption. Such households increase their saving significantly when income rises temporarily. Thus, most of a temporary increase in income is saved, and most of a temporary shortfall in income is offset by less saving. *Saving is very sensitive to temporary changes in income.*

Permanent changes in income also affect saving, but by a smaller amount. If long-run average income rises by $100 per year, an individual might save an additional $10 per year. A temporary increase in income of $100 might prompt saving of $60 or more. Although the precise amount saved from temporary income is uncertain, it is clear that saving from temporary income is several times greater than saving from long-run average income.

Since it is the real interest rate that is important to households, changes in the expected inflation rate affect the position of the credit supply curve. For a given nominal interest rate, the higher the expected inflation rate, the lower the expected real interest rate and the lower the incentive for households to save. As the expected inflation rate rises, households have the incentive to buy now to avoid future higher prices.

Figure 4 illustrates how the household saving curve shifts when income or expected inflation changes. An increase in permanent (long-run average) income shifts the saving curve to S_1; a temporary increase in income of the same size shifts the saving curve to S_2. An increase in inflationary expectations causes households to decrease their saving at every level of the nominal interest rate. Rather than saving, households might buy furniture or a new car. Thus, the saving curve shifts leftward to S_3 if the expected inflation rate rises.

Businesses save in the form of profits that are not distributed to shareholders — **retained earnings** — and capital consumption allowances. Retained earnings are closely tied to the overall level of profits earned by businesses. They tend to be very cyclical, rising when national income rises during an expansion and falling (even becoming negative) when income falls during a recession. Capital consumption allowances — funds accumulated to replace worn-out plant and equipment — tend to increase as the size of the capital stock increases.

Since income changes affect business saving in the same way that they affect household saving, the relationship between income changes and the saving curve illustrated in Figure 4 continues to hold. An increase in income shifts the saving curve to the right. A temporary increase has a greater impact than a permanent increase. Adding retained earnings and capital consumption allowances to household saving yields total domestic saving in the economy.

One other source of savings has been very important in recent years. Foreign savers have supplied large amounts of credit to U.S. borrowers. If the U.S. real interest rate is higher than foreign real interest rates, foreigners may use their savings to purchase financial assets in the United States, making foreign savings available to support U.S. domestic spending. Over $100 billion of foreign savings flowed into the United States each year from 1985 through 1989. Disagreement exists as to how reliable foreign savings are as a source

---

Retained earnings
Business profits that are not paid out to shareholders as dividends; business savings.

SECTION RECAP
The demand for credit depends negatively on the interest rate. When income, expected inflation, or the government budget deficit rises, the demand *(continued)*

of credit. A decline in the U.S. real interest rate relative to foreign real interest rates could cause the foreign credit supply to the U.S. market to dry up rapidly. (The *Why the Disagreement?* section takes up this issue.)

Factors Affecting Credit Supply: A Summary The supply of credit comes from saving by the household and business sectors of the economy and from foreign savers who want to purchase U.S. financial assets. An increase in saving shifts the credit supply curve to the right. *The supply of credit increases when income rises or when inflationary expectations or foreign real interest rates fall. A decrease in saving shifts CR^s to the left when income falls or inflationary expectations or foreign real interest rates rise.*

> **SECTION RECAP**
> *(continued)*
> for credit increases. The supply of credit comes from saving. It depends positively on the interest rate. When income rises, the supply of credit increases. When expected inflation rises, the supply of credit decreases.

Using the Credit Market Model

Having discussed both the demand for and supply of credit, all that remains is to put together the two sides of the market to determine the equilibrium interest rate. We then use the model to investigate the effect of changes in the factors that affect credit demand and supply on the equilibrium level of the interest rate.

Interest Rate Determination

The interest rate is determined by the intersection of the credit demand and credit supply curves. *The interest rate is the price that brings the quantity of credit demanded into equality with the quantity of credit supplied.* Figure 5 illustrates the determination of the equilibrium level of the interest rate. In the figure, i_0 (equal to 8 percent) is the only interest rate that does not generate either an excess demand for or an excess supply of credit.

Suppose the market interest rate were 10 percent. At this rate, the amount of credit that savers are willing to supply to borrowers exceeds the quantity demanded. Thus, not all savers attempting to make loans at an interest rate of 10 percent are able to do so. Competition among savers drives the interest rate downward, toward i_0. As the interest rate falls, the quantity of credit demanded increases (along CR^d). Simultaneously, the quantity of credit supplied decreases (along CR^s). The process ends when the market interest rate reaches 8 percent, where quantity demanded equals quantity supplied.

Since many real-world credit markets are auction markets, where suppliers and demanders interact with one another face to face, the process of moving from one equilibrium interest rate to a new equilibrium rate is very rapid. Not all interest rates change so rapidly, of course, but even the more stable interest rates (such as those charged by banks) are affected rather quickly by interest rate movements in the auction portion of the market.

Working with the Model

Table 2 lists the major factors affecting the demand for and supply of credit and the equilibrium value of the interest rate. Several factors affect both demand and supply.

An increase in income has a theoretically ambiguous effect on the equilibrium value of the interest rate. An increase in income increases the demand

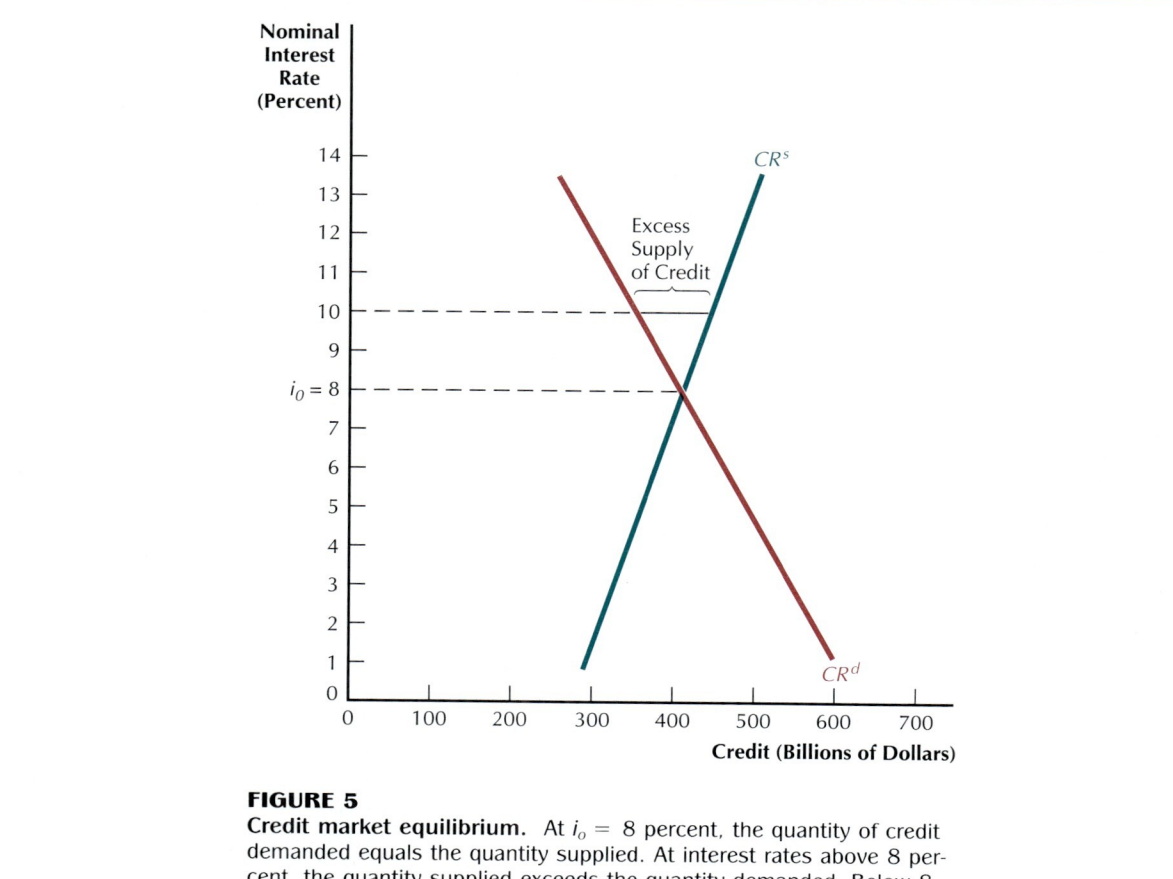

FIGURE 5
Credit market equilibrium. At $i_o = 8$ percent, the quantity of credit demanded equals the quantity supplied. At interest rates above 8 percent, the quantity supplied exceeds the quantity demanded. Below 8 percent, the quantity demanded exceeds the quantity supplied.

TABLE 2

Factors affecting credit demand and supply

Credit Demand	Credit Supply
Position of Curves	
Income	Income (temporary, permanent)
Government deficit	
Inflationary expectations	Inflationary expectations
Foreign real interest rates	Foreign real interest rates
Slope of Curves	
Interest rate	Interest rate

Why the **Disagreement?**

Those Dangerous Foreign Savers

During the 1980s, when the U.S. government was running large budget deficits and soaking up billions of dollars of U.S. savings to finance the deficits, billions of dollars of foreign savings flowed into the U.S. credit market. Foreigners bought government bonds, corporate stock—even Rockefeller Center! The U.S. borrowers who understood the situation were grateful for the foreign credit, since it helped to keep the interest rate much lower than it would otherwise have been. However, the inflow of foreign savings bothered many observers, who argued that foreign lending in the United States will reduce the U.S. standard of living in the future when the loans must be repaid. Other analysts believed the inflow of foreign savings to be quite harmless, indeed necessary given existing international financial arrangements. Why the disagreement?

Foreigners obtain the dollars to purchase U.S. financial assets by selling goods to Americans. The skeptics who fear that the United States will be forced to pay dearly in the future for its borrowings from foreigners point out that an inflow of foreign savings is accompanied by a U.S. trade deficit (negative net exports). Foreigners can accumulate enough dollars to buy financial assets only by selling more goods to Americans than they purchase from U.S. firms. Although some critics believe that trade deficits are themselves harmful, most are simply concerned that relying on foreign savers to finance U.S. spending is setting the United States up for a fall. They fear that foreign savers might decide to pull their savings out of the U.S. market suddenly. Such an outflow could be caused by a number of factors: Foreign real interest rates might rise relative to the U.S. real interest rate in response to investment opportunities in Germany and Eastern Europe; doubts about the safety of U.S. assets might increase because of recession (such as the one that began in the fourth quarter of 1990); or increased consumption in Japan might reduce the outflow of funds. A large outflow of foreign funds would force the U.S. interest rate dramatically higher, possibly triggering severe slowdowns in consumption and investment spending.

In the longer run, skeptics believe that U.S. citizens will be forced to reduce their standard of living to repay the debts they owe to foreigners. In the 1980s, U.S. spending exceeded U.S. production; skeptics say the United States was living beyond its means. Such overconsumption can be paid for only by consuming less than is produced in the future, that is, by running trade surpluses (positive net exports) to earn the foreign currency needed to repay foreign savers.

Not all observers agree that the future is so gloomy. Some argue that the persistent U.S. trade deficit is nothing more than a reflection of the world demand for dollars. Since World War II the U.S. dollar has been widely used in international trade, serving as an international reserve currency. Because international trade is expanding over time, the world demand for dollars is also expanding. Foreign nations can acquire dollars only by running trade surpluses against the United States—which implies that the United States must run trade deficits. So long as the dollar is the major international currency, U.S. trade deficits are inevitable and relatively harmless.

John Mueller, who subscribes to the second viewpoint, notes that the total net foreign debt of the United States—the amount by which foreign holdings of U.S. financial assets exceed U.S. holdings of foreign financial assets—is approximately equal to the dollar holdings of foreign governments.* He argues that U.S. trade deficits are linked rather closely to the demand for dollars by foreign governments, which want dollars because they are the closest thing to a universally accepted money in the world today. Private holdings of U.S. assets by foreigners are approximately equal to private holdings of foreign assets by Americans. The demand of foreign governments for dollars is the major cause of U.S. trade deficits.

Which view is correct? At this point, we cannot say. The disagreement revolves around *why* foreigners choose to hold dollars. Only time will tell whether foreigners will pull their savings out of the U.S. market in the future, forcing U.S. consumers to accept a lower standard of living to repay their debts, or whether foreign governments want dollars so badly that foreign savings will be a constant source of credit for the U.S. market.

---

*John Mueller, "CPI at 7%? Bet Your Reserve Dollar," *Wall Street Journal*, February 24, 1989, p. A10.

for credit, as both households and businesses increase their demand for durable goods. CR^d shifts outward, as in Figure 6. However, an increase in income also increases the supply of credit, and this effect is particularly significant if the income increase is temporary. Thus, CR^s also shifts outward. Whether the interest rate rises or falls depends upon the relative size of the shifts. If CR^s shifts only to CR_1^s, i rises. However, if CR^s shifts to CR_2^s, i falls. Economic theory cannot say which will occur.

Although economic theory cannot say whether an increase in income will cause the interest rate to rise or fall, observation of the behavior of interest rates suggests an answer. Over the course of the business cycle, when income rises and falls, we observe that *interest rates are procyclical*. Other things constant, interest rates tend to rise when income rises and fall when income falls. This suggests that the typical response to an income increase is for credit demand to increase by more than credit supply. Thus, in Figure 6, the typical movement of the interest rate in response to an income increase would be an increase from i_0 to i_1.

An increase in the government deficit increases government's demand for credit. CR^d shifts to the right, increasing the interest rate. It is possible that government borrowing prompts taxpayers to save more in anticipation of the higher *future* taxes needed to pay interest on the government debt or repay the debt. Such a reaction would shift the credit supply curve outward, reducing or offsetting the effect of government borrowing on the interest rate. Although

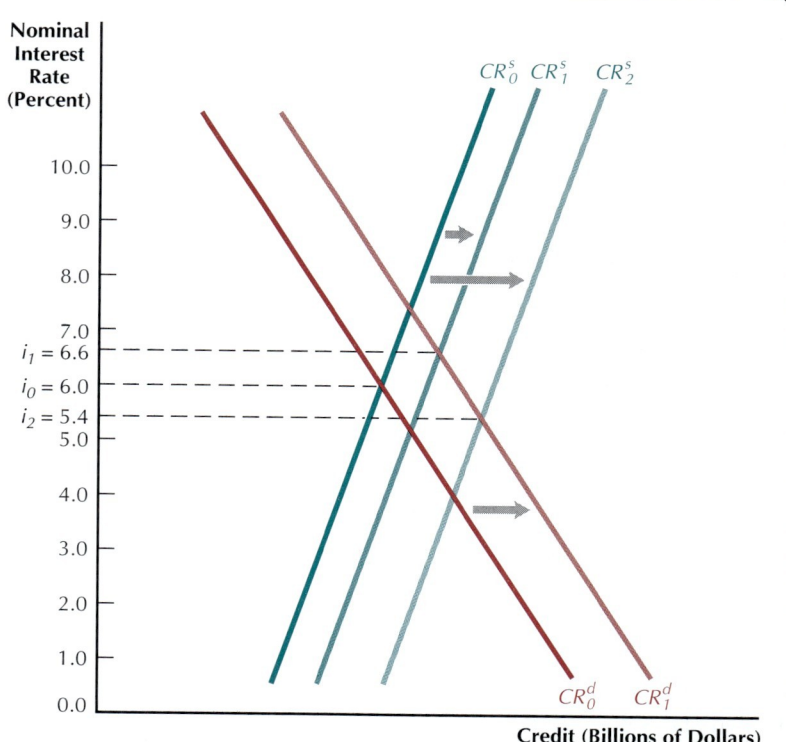

FIGURE 6
Effect of an increase in aggregate income on the interest rate. An increase in aggregate income shifts both the credit demand and credit supply curves to the right. The equilibrium interest rate may rise or fall, depending on whether the credit demand or credit supply shift is larger. Given the shift in credit demand from CR_0^d to CR_1^d, if credit supply shifts to CR_1^s, the interest rate rises; if credit supply shifts to CR_2^s, the interest rate falls.

most statistical evidence suggests that government deficits increase the interest rate, some studies find no relationship between deficits and the interest rate. (This issue is considered further in the next chapter.)

An increase in inflationary expectations has a predictable effect on the interest rate, even though both the demand for and the supply of credit are affected, because it shifts the demand and supply curves in opposite directions. Consider Figure 7. An increase in inflationary expectations shifts CR^d to the right as borrowers realize that the real cost of borrowing at any level of nominal interest has been reduced.

The effect on savers is also predictable. Savers realize that for a given level of the nominal interest rate, they will be able to buy less with their interest earnings in the future. For example, suppose a saver purchases a financial asset costing $100. It matures in one year and bears an interest rate of 10 percent. At the end of the year, the saver receives $110. If prices rise by 10 percent over the next year, $110 received one year from now will buy no more than $100 will buy today. The real rate of return on the asset is zero. Thus, as inflationary expectations rise, the incentive to save diminishes. The supply of credit curve shifts to the left. The net result of the demand and supply shifts is an increase in the nominal rate of interest.

An increase in foreign real interest rates tends to increase foreign borrowing in the U.S. credit market and decrease the flow of foreign savings into the U.S. market. CR^d shifts to the right and CR^s shifts to the left. The result is an increase

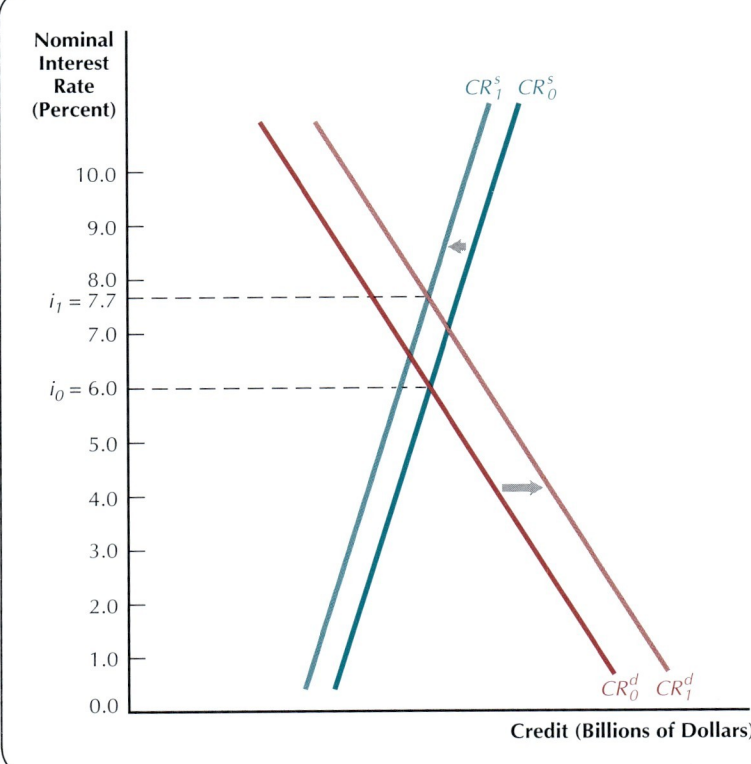

FIGURE 7
Inflationary expectations and the interest rate. An increase in the expected inflation rate causes the credit demand curve to shift to the right and the credit supply curve to shift to the left. The nominal interest rate rises.

in the interest rate—toward the foreign level. *In an international credit market, economic forces tend to push interest rates in all countries toward equality,* although risk, inflation, and other factors prevent exact equality from ever being achieved.

Nominal and Real Interest Rates

The idea of the real rate of interest has already been discussed repeatedly. Here we will illustrate it graphically. Suppose we begin with the situation of zero expected inflation. Both borrowers and lenders expect the price level to remain constant. Credit demand and supply conditions are summarized in Figure 8 by the curves CR_0^d and CR_0^s. The noninflationary interest rate is i_0. Note that in this case the nominal interest rate equals the expected real interest rate: $i_0 = r^e + p^e = r^e + 0$.

Suppose that something changes that causes savers and borrowers to expect a positive rate of inflation. In particular, suppose that inflationary expectations rise to $p^e = 5$ percent. Borrowers (credit demanders) now perceive that the expected real cost of borrowing, $r^e = i - p^e$, has fallen by 5 percent. Hence, the amount that they previously would have borrowed at 3 percent interest

SECTION RECAP
An increase in expected inflation, the government deficit, or foreign real interest rates pushes the U.S. interest rate upward. An increase in aggregate income increases both credit demand and credit *(continued)*

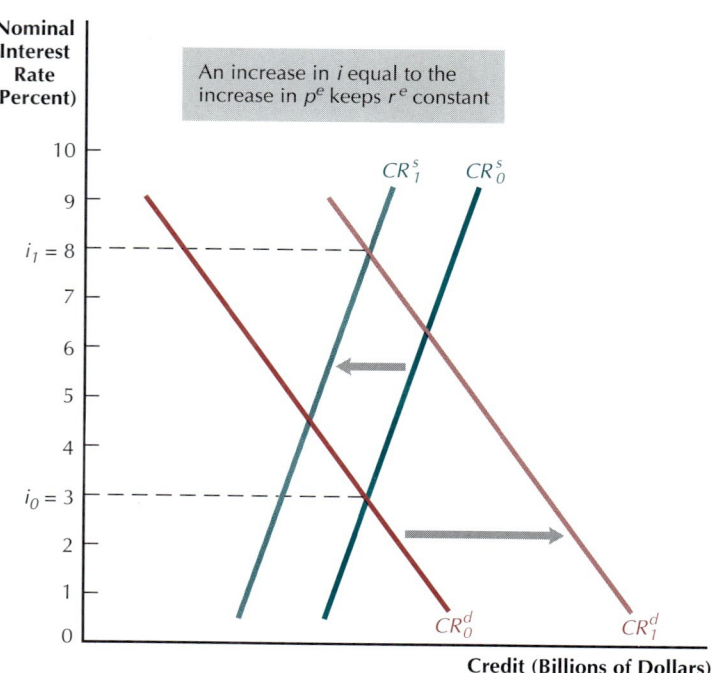

FIGURE 8
Increase in the expected inflation rate. At an expected inflation rate of $p^e = 0$ percent, the expected real rate equals the nominal interest rate: $r^e = i = 3$ percent. When p^e rises to 5 percent, the nominal rate rises to $i = 3$ percent + 5 percent = 8 percent, while the expected real rate remains constant at 3 percent.

rate they are now willing to borrow at 8 percent. The credit demand curve shifts to the right.

Savers realize that the real return on their savings has fallen by 5 percent. Therefore, the amount that they previously saved at $i = 3$ percent will now be saved only if i rises to 8 percent. Thus, the credit supply curve shifts to the left. CR^d and CR^s now intersect at a nominal interest rate of 8 percent. However, the expected real rate of interest remains unchanged at $r^e = 3$ percent. The nominal rate has risen to protect the expected real rate.

SECTION RECAP
(continued)
supply, leaving the change in the interest rate indeterminate. Empirical evidence indicates that the interest rate rises when income increases.

Linking the Two Interest Rate Models

In developing the credit market model we have simplified the model to such an extent that the connection between the credit market model of interest rate determination and the money demand–money supply model of interest rate behavior is not obvious. In this section we explicitly show the connection between the two markets and provide a set of guidelines for applying the two models in the most convenient manner.

Although the dominant source of credit to the economy is saving, another source of credit exists. When money demand or money supply changes, creating an excess demand for or an excess supply of money at the prevailing interest rate, money holders react by changing the quantity of credit they are supplying to the market. As an illustration of this, consider what happens when the demand for money increases. As Figure 9 (a) shows, an increase in money demand creates an excess demand for money at the prevailing interest rate, i_0. People who want to obtain more money react by purchasing fewer goods and services and by purchasing fewer financial assets. However, *buying fewer financial assets, such as bonds, is the same thing as supplying less credit*, since a bond purchaser is making a loan to the bond seller. Thus, an *increase* in the demand for money, *ceteris paribus*, is linked to a *decrease* in the supply of credit, as shown in Figure 9 (b). The reduced supply of credit drives the market interest rate up, restoring equilibrium between money demanded and money supplied.

A change in the supply of money has a similar effect. Figure 10 shows the results of an increase in the money supply by the Federal Reserve, other things constant. At the original interest rate, i_0, an excess supply of money is created. As the Fed increases the monetary base, banks have more funds with which to make loans. They expand the supply of credit, pushing the interest rate downward and restoring equality between money demanded and money supplied.

Neither Figure 9 nor Figure 10 takes account of the effects that changes in money demand and supply have on income, and the resulting second-round effects on money demand and on credit demand and supply. However, the figures demonstrate the budget-constraint connection that exists between the credit and money markets and show that either model can be used to address the issue of interest-rate behavior.

Why bother with two interest rate models? Our answer is pragmatic: It is easier to use one model to address some questions, while the other model works better for other questions. When discussing the effect of a change in the money supply, the money demand–money supply model is quite convenient. When examining the results of a larger government budget deficit, the

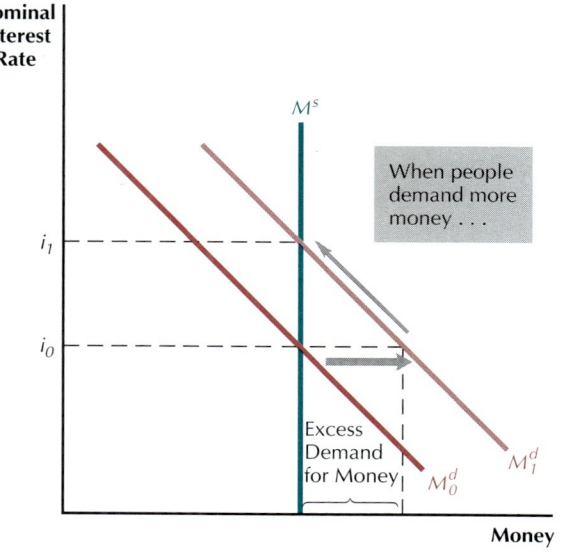

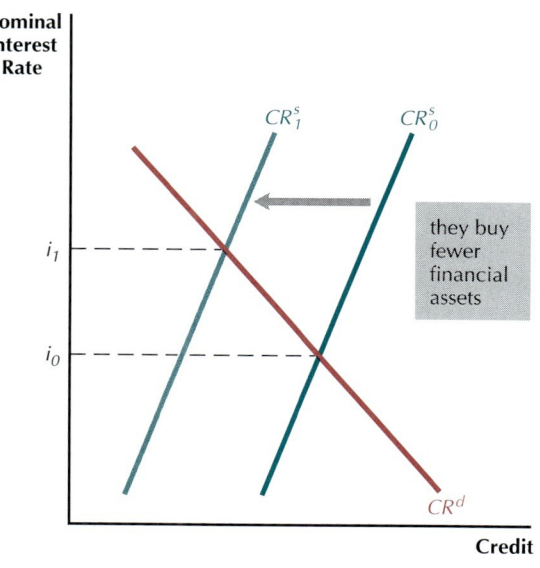

FIGURE 9
Effect on the interest rate of an increase in money demand. An increase in money demand creates an excess demand for money at the prevailing interest rate, i_0 (a). People react by buying fewer financial assets, thus reducing the supply of credit (b). As the supply of credit decreases, the interest rate rises, restoring monetary equilibrium.

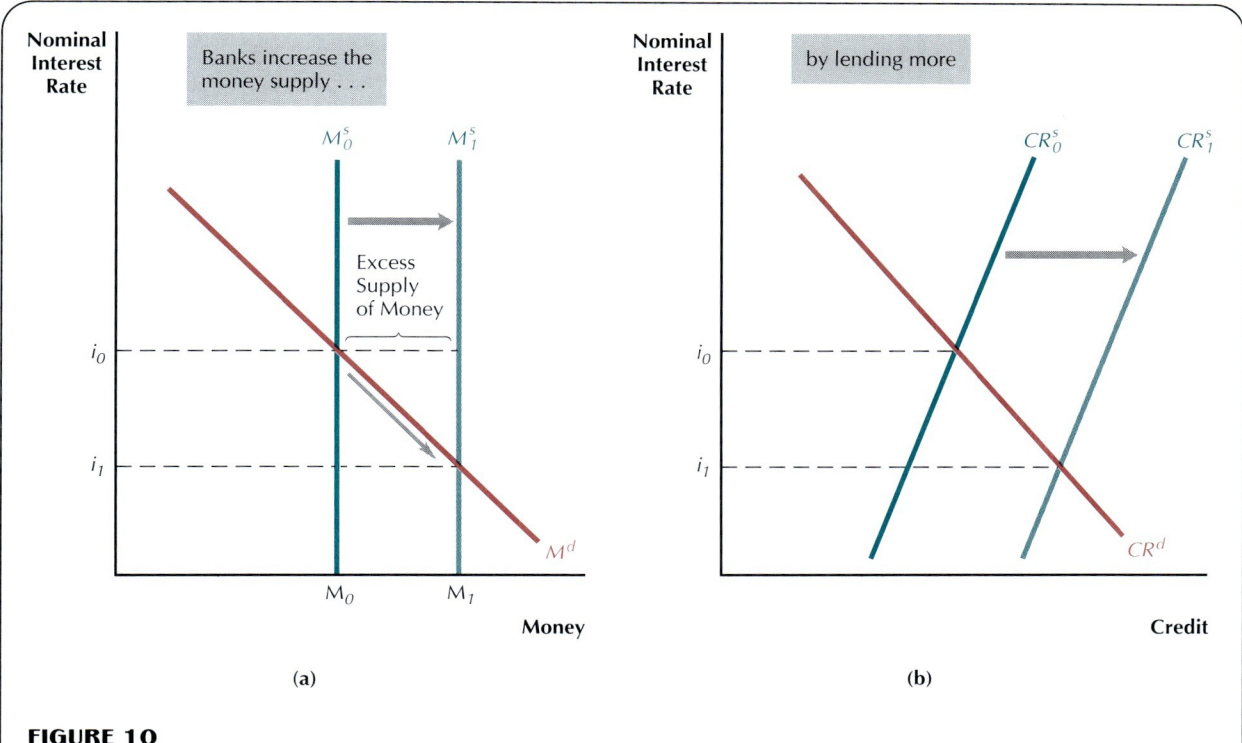

FIGURE 10
Effect on the interest rate of an increase in money supply. An increase in the supply of money creates an excess supply of money at the prevailing interest rate, i_o (a). Banks make more loans and people buy more financial assets, increasing the supply of credit (b). The increased supply of credit pushes the interest rate downward, restoring monetary equilibrium.

credit market model works better. Sometimes it is useful to combine the two models to analyze the complete effect on the interest rate (as in the *Does It Make Economic Sense?* section of this chapter). Table 3 provides a handy reference to the use of each model.

TABLE 3
Guide to using interest rate models

Factor Affecting i	Model to Use
Income	Either model (but money demand–money supply preferred)
Inflationary expectations	Credit market
Government deficit	Credit market
Money supply	Money demand–money supply
Factors affecting investment (capacity utilization, expectations, and so on)	Credit market
Foreign real interest rate	Credit market

Does It Make **Economic Sense?**

Can the Federal Reserve Control Interest Rates?

A large number of factors combine to determine the level of interest rates, as the credit market model illustrates. Most of these factors are not directly controllable by any government agency. For example, consumer expenditures, investment demand, and saving are all determined by millions of private decision makers, acting in their own best interests. Yet it is common to hear complaints that "the Federal Reserve should lower interest rates." Does such a statement make economic sense?

The statement that the Federal Reserve should reduce the level of interest rates presumes that the Fed has the power to push the level of interest rates up or down, if not control it directly. Can the Fed do this?

Consider the money demand–money supply model. The Federal Reserve has no control over the demand for money, but it can control the supply. By increasing the money supply, the Federal Reserve can drive the interest rate downward, at least temporarily. However, the long-term consequences of such a policy are less certain. Suppose the Fed drives the interest rate down by increasing the money supply, as shown in Figure 11. This decline in the interest rate (point B) is only the initial effect of Fed policy. It is called the *liquidity effect,* because people use the newly created liquidity (money) to buy financial assets, driving asset prices up and interest rates down.

The lower interest rate encourages more investment and consumer durable spending, driving real income and prices upward. Money demand is positively related to these variables, so the money demand curve shifts to the right. The *income effect* reverses the down-

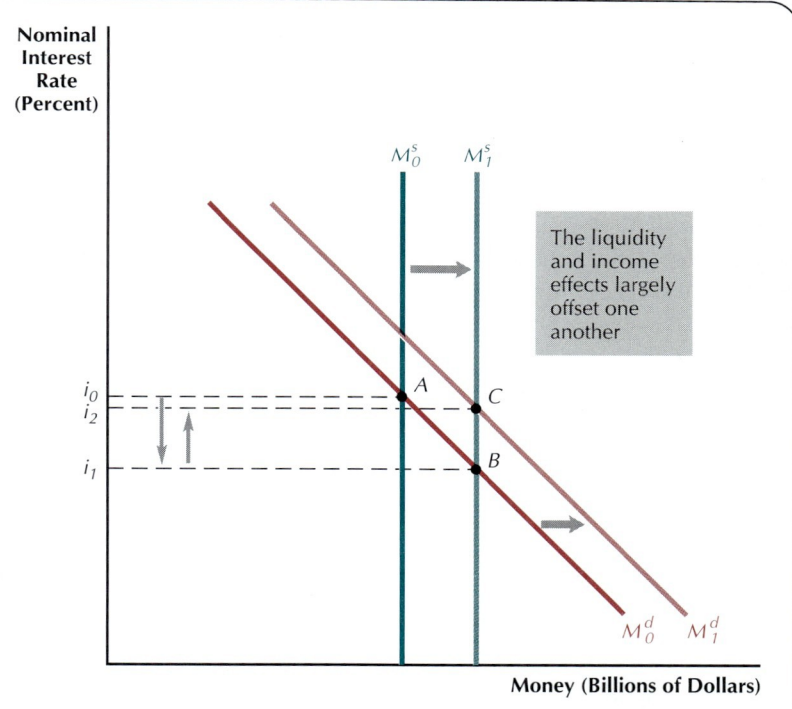

FIGURE 11
Liquidity and income effects. An increase in the money supply initially pushes the interest rate down; this is the liquidity effect. As income rises, money demand increases, pushing the interest rate back upward. This is the income effect.

The liquidity and income effects largely offset one another

ward trend of the interest rate, pushing it back toward its original level, toward point C in Figure 11. If the Federal Reserve persists in its attempt to maintain a lower interest rate, it must continue to increase the money supply. However, historical evidence indicates that money supply growth and inflation are positively related. If market participants react to the increasing money supply by raising their inflation expectations, the interest rate will move even higher. Figure 12 illustrates the relationship between the *inflation expectations effect* and the interest rate in the context of the credit market model. The demand for credit increases, while the supply decreases. The result is that an inflation premium is added to the interest rate. The eventual result of a Federal Reserve attempt to reduce the interest rate might well be an increase in the interest rate. Any initial success might be offset rather quickly by economic factors beyond the Fed's control, as any liquidity effect produced by an increased money supply is offset by the effect of increased spending and higher expected inflation. It is ironic but true that the best monetary policy to maintain low interest rates over long periods of time is a policy of slow money supply growth. To hold interest rates low in the long run, inflation must be held in check. Of course, restraining the money supply can produce high interest rates for a short time. The cost of returning to relatively low interest rates in the long run is accepting relatively high interest rates in the short run.

LEARNING OBJECTIVE 6:
Discuss the extent to which the Federal Reserve can control the level of interest rates.

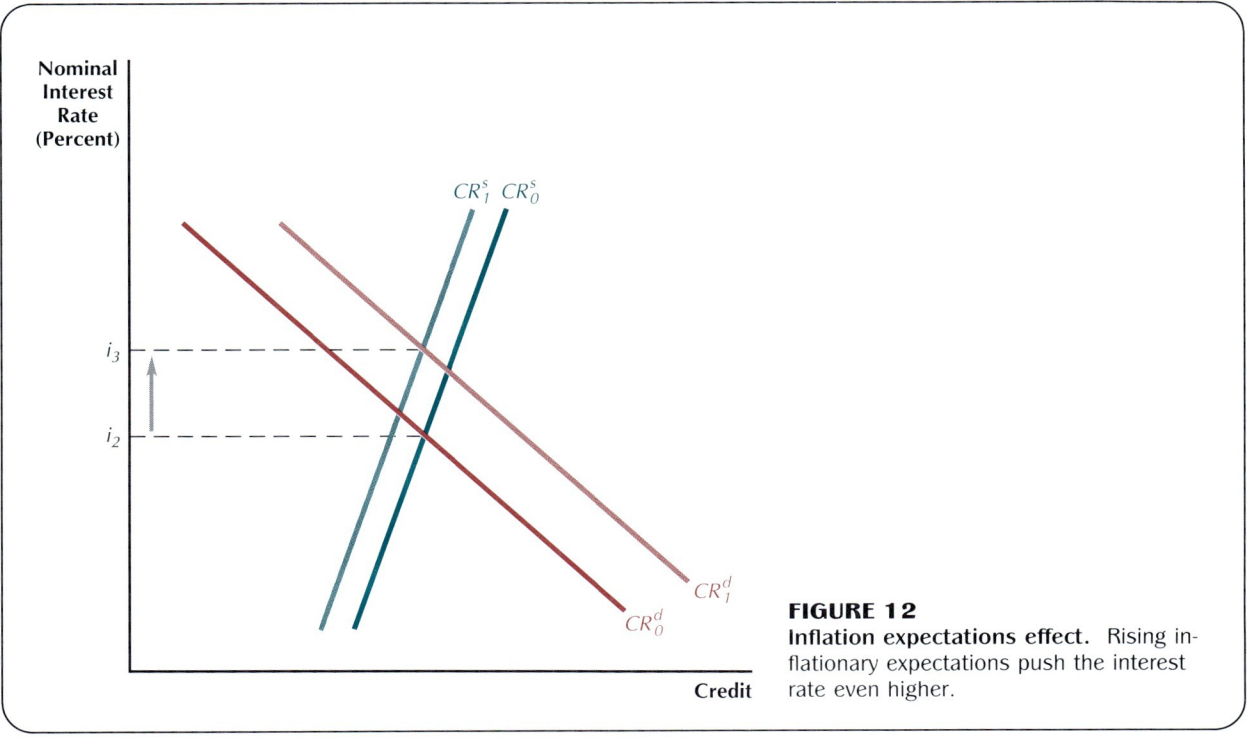

FIGURE 12
Inflation expectations effect. Rising inflationary expectations push the interest rate even higher.

Summary

Interest rates are the prices of credit. **Credit** is the rental use of money for a period of time. Thus, an interest rate is the price of the rental use of money for a period of time.

Since all interest rates are affected by a common set of factors, they tend to move up and down together (though the relationship among rates changes constantly). Thus, it is convenient to speak of *the* interest rate, meaning the component of interest rates that is common to all particular interest rates.

The interest rate is determined by the interaction of the demand for credit with the supply of credit. The **demand for credit** is affected by the factors that influence the demand for consumer durable goods and housing, for capital goods (investment demand) by businesses, of governments for funds to finance budget deficits, and of foreign borrowers. The factors affecting these demands include the level of income, the amount of consumer borrowing already undertaken, the degree of capacity utilization of existing capital equipment and plant, the state of inflationary expectations, and the level of foreign real interest rates. An increase in income, capacity utilization, or inflationary expectations tends to increase the demand for credit. The larger the amount of consumer credit already outstanding, the more reluctant households are to borrow more.

The **supply of credit** is provided by saving. Factors affecting saving include income (permanent or temporary) and inflationary expectations. An increase in income increases saving, and the impact is greater if the income change is thought to be temporary rather than permanent. An increase in inflationary expectations causes households to curtail saving, because at any level of the nominal interest rate, the real interest rate earned on savings declines.

The credit market model is a **flow model.** It is useful for showing the effect on the interest rate of changes in economic flows. It is more convenient to use the **money demand–money supply model** to show the effect on *i* of changes in **stocks,** since the money model is a stock model. It is very useful for showing the effect on *i* of a change in the money supply. The two models give equivalent results when the economy is in equilibrium, because they are linked by the aggregate budget constraint.

Questions for Thought

Knowledge Questions

1. What is an interest rate?
2. What is the difference between money and credit?
3. What are the major sources of demand for credit? Of supply of credit?
4. What is meant by the term *nominal interest rate*? What is meant by *real interest rate*?
5. Why is it legitimate to talk of *the* interest rate, when we know that thousands of different interest rates exist?

Application Questions

6. Explain why it is the expected real rate of interest that is relevant to investment and saving decisions.

7. Other things constant, how would each of the following changes affect the interest rate, in the short run and in the long run, according to the theory of the credit market developed in this chapter?
   a. A decrease in the Federal Reserve's demand for bonds.
   b. An increase in the level of income during a business cycle expansion.
   c. A reduction in the size of the government's budget deficit.
8. Obtain monthly data on the three-month Treasury bill rate and Moody's Aaa bond rate from the *Federal Reserve Bulletin* for the years 1971 through 1975. Plot these data so that you can see how the two series behaved over the course of the business cycle. Do short-term (the T-bill) or long-term (the bond) rates fluctuate more over the course of a cycle?

Synthesis Questions

9. In the chapter on aggregate demand we discussed the income tax surcharge of 1968. This surcharge reduced disposable income, although everyone knew that the reduction was only temporary. What does our theory of the credit market imply for the behavior of interest rates during the period of the income tax surcharge? (Remember to take the theory of consumption spending into account. Also note that your answer will depend upon what you assume about the behavior of consumer durable expenditures.)
10. Obtain data on the annual average value of the three-month Treasury bill rate and the inflation rate (rate of change of the implicit price deflator) from the *Economic Report of the President*. Calculate the real rate of return on three-month Treasury bills year by year for the decade of the 1970s. How might your seemingly strange results be explained? (Note that what you calculated is the *actual* real rate of interest, not the *expected* real rate.)

Appendix to CHAPTER 29

Interest Rates and Bond Prices

A bond represents a promise to make money payments on particular dates in the future. It is a legal claim against future payments. Since these payments are spread out over time, the value of a bond cannot be derived simply by adding up the future payments. The farther into the future a payment is, the lower its value is to a prospective bond purchaser at the present. For example, $100 in hand is worth more than $100 to be received a year from now, because the $100 in hand could be used to purchase a real asset producing services for the next year or a financial asset yielding interest. If the interest rate is 10 percent, $100 now is worth $110 one year from now, because that is the value it would grow to if used to buy a financial asset.

The price of a bond with one year to maturity equals the amount received at the end of the year (principal plus interest) *discounted* by one plus the market interest rate:

$$P_B = \frac{1}{(1 + i)} \times (\text{amount received})$$

Discounting converts future payments into *present value* terms. It tells us what a sum of money to be received in the future is worth today.

The bond price formula is nothing more than the present discounted value formula for a stream of future payments. It is exactly the same formula used in determining the profitability of an investment project in the appendix to the aggregate demand chapter.

We can generalize the bond price formula quite easily. The price of a bond with annual coupon interest payments (CPN) and two years to maturity, when the face value of the bond (FV) is repaid, is:

$$P_B = \frac{CPN}{(1 + i)} + \frac{(CPN + FV)}{(1 + i)^2}$$

The discount factor of the second term is squared because the coupon and face value payments are received after two years. A bondholder earns interest on his investment for a period of two years. If the bondholder invests $100 at 10 percent for two years, he ends the first year with $100 \times (1.10) = $110. This amount earns interest for a second year, leaving the bondholder with $100 \times (1.10) \times (1.10) = $100 \times (1.10)^2 = $121 at the end of two years. Working backwards, the amount received at the end of two years must be discounted by $(1.10)^2$ to take account of compounded interest (interest paid on both the principal invested and on previously earned interest).

In general, the price of a multi-year bond is:

$$P_B = \frac{CPN}{(1 + i)} + \frac{CPN}{(1 + i)^2} + \frac{CPN}{(1 + i)^3} + \ldots + \frac{CPN}{(1 + i)^n} + \frac{FV}{(1 + i)^n}$$

where n is the number of years to maturity. Note that the relationship between the bond price and the interest rate is inverse, just as it was for a one-year bond. The interest rate appears in the denominator of the formula. When the interest rate rises, the bond price falls.

Some short-term bonds do not carry coupons. These *discount bonds* simply pay a fixed amount on maturity. The purchaser earns interest by paying less than the face amount for the bond. For example, a $1000 face value one-year bond, yielding 10 percent interest, would sell for $P_D = \$1000/1.10 = \$909.09$. Here we note that it is a discount bond by labeling its price P_D. The general formula for a one-year discount bond is:

$$P_D = \frac{FV}{(1 + i)}$$

If the discount bond has a maturity of less than one year, the discount factor $[(1 + i)]$ will have a fractional exponential. For example, a bond maturing in six months (one-half year) and paying a 10 percent annual yield would carry a price of $P_D = \$1000/1.10^{.5} = \$953.46$. (Note that 1.10 to the .5 power is the square root of 1.10, or 1.049.)

The discount bond formula can be seen as a simplified form of the coupon bond formula, with CPN = 0. The important property that the market interest rate is inversely related to the bond price is just as true for discount bonds as for coupon bonds.

OVERVIEW

In 1990, federal, state, and local governments spent a combined total of one trillion 907.1 billion dollars. Needless to say, government is a major actor in the U.S. economy. Over sixteen million people are employed by governments, directly earning their incomes by providing labor services. Other millions work in businesses that sell goods and services to government agencies. Still others receive transfer payments. And of

Government Finance and Fiscal Policy

course, the vast majority pay taxes. Few people evade the economic reach of government.

In this chapter we examine the role of government in the economy. We spend significant time covering the basics of fiscal policy — the use of government spending and taxes as policy instruments. We examine the various types of government spending, how government spending is financed, and how financing policies affect private economic behavior.

We begin with a look at the recent trends in government expenditures and revenues. We then use the basic macroeconomic model to analyze the effects on the economy of government spending and taxation. However, not all government expenditure is financed by taxes. In particular, the federal government has resorted to deficit financing in recent years. Whenever

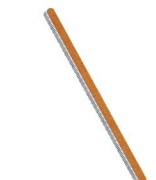

CHAPTER 30

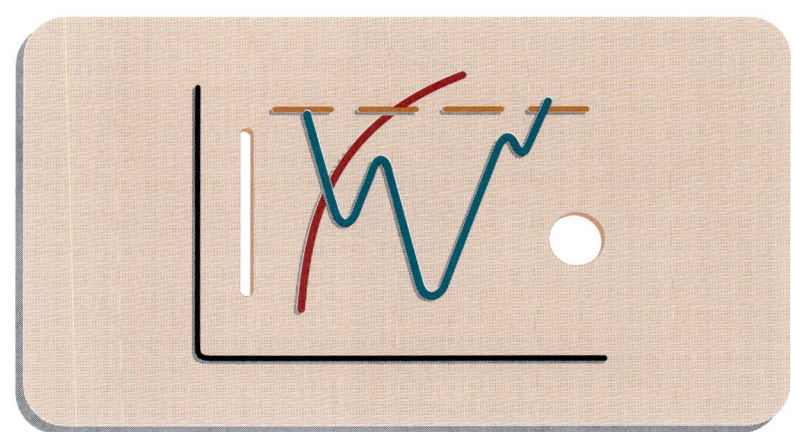

government expenditures exceed tax revenues, the difference, called the deficit, must be financed by borrowing. We examine the effects of deficit financing and the accumulating national debt in the final sections of the chapter.

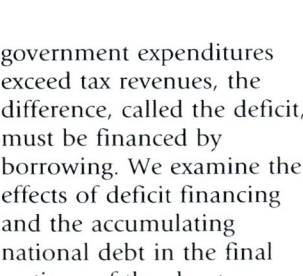

Learning Objectives

After reading and studying this chapter, you will be able to:

1. Discuss the recent trends in government spending.
2. Discuss the recent trends in government revenues.
3. Explain how changes in government purchases of goods and services and transfer payments affect aggregate demand.
4. Explain how changes in taxes affect aggregate demand and aggregate supply.
5. Explain the difference between deficits and high employment deficits.
6. Discuss the difference between nominal and real public debt and explain why the difference is important.

Recent Trends in Government Finance

Government expenditures as a percentage of GNP have risen sharply over the past four decades, from under 22 percent in 1950 to almost 35 percent in 1990. Figure 1 shows the behavior of total government spending as a percentage of GNP.

Not all expenditure categories have behaved similarly in recent years. Figure 2 illustrates the behavior of real government spending (in 1982 dollars) since 1960.

The growth of federal spending, which so concerned Americans in the 1980s, was due primarily to increases in transfer payments. Figure 2 shows that real federal purchases of goods and services have grown only moderately since the mid-1970s and were not much higher in 1990 than in 1968. Federal purchases were high during the late 1960s because of spending on the Vietnam War. When the conflict ended, defense spending was cut, and increased purchases of nondefense goods and services grew more slowly than the price level. Thus, *real* federal purchases fell.

In contrast, state and local purchases of goods and services, a spending category larger than either federal purchases or federal transfer payments, have grown steadily over the past few decades. Americans seem less concerned about the growth of state and local purchases, possibly because they provide services such as police and fire protection, schooling, and street and highway maintenance directly to consumers. Such services are obvious and highly valued. The benefits of federal purchases or transfer payments are not so obvious. It is easier to appreciate services provided locally than those that provide only indirect benefits or that benefit other areas of the country.

Federal, state, and local governments raise revenue in a variety of ways. Although taxes of various sorts account for most revenue, government funding also comes from the earnings of government enterprises, license fees, user charges (such as entrance fees to national or state parks), and interest on

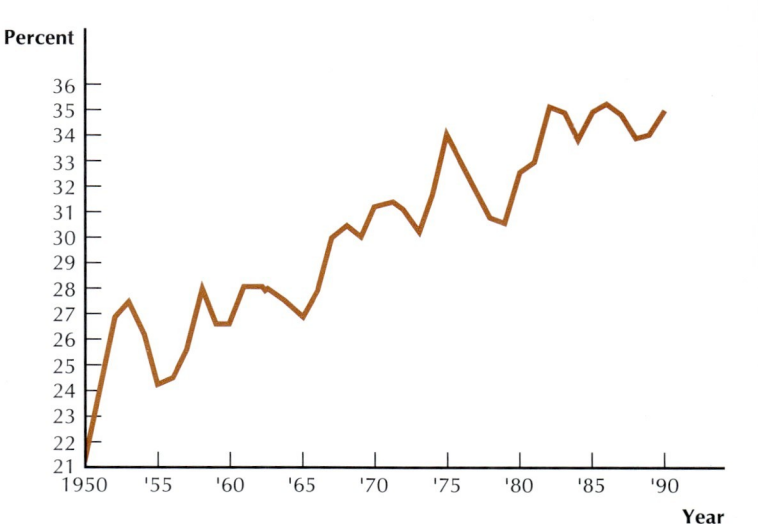

FIGURE 1
Government expenditures as a percentage of GNP. Total government expenditures as a percentage of GNP rose from less than 22 percent in 1950 to 35 percent in 1990. Source: *Economic Report of the President, 1991*, Tables B-1 and B-79.

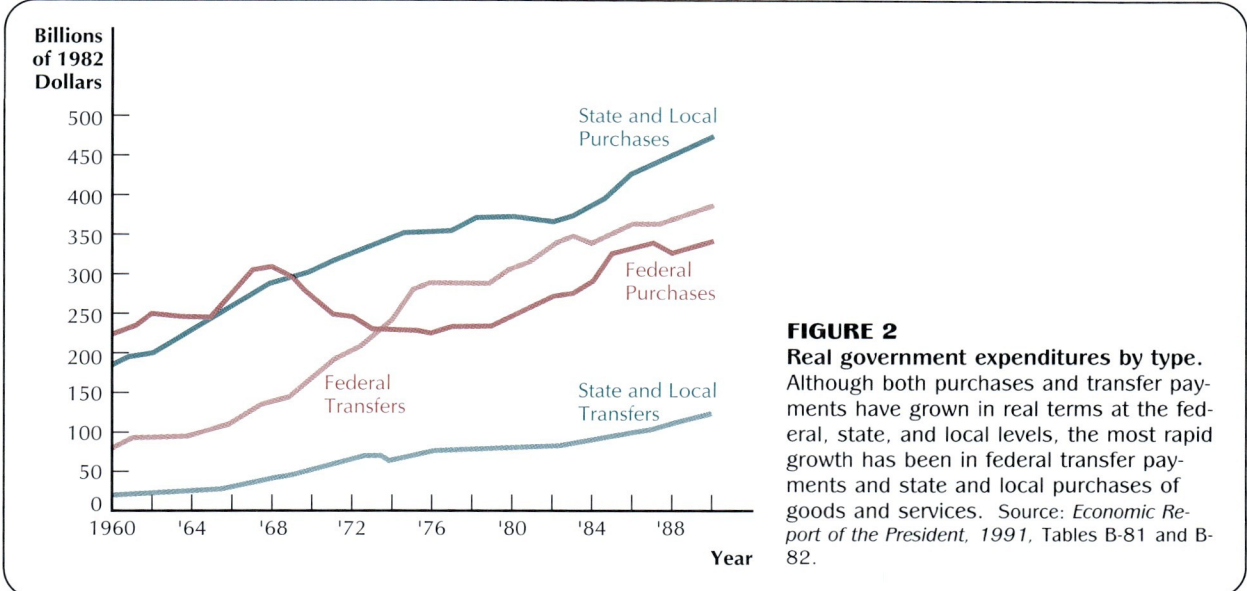

FIGURE 2
Real government expenditures by type. Although both purchases and transfer payments have grown in real terms at the federal, state, and local levels, the most rapid growth has been in federal transfer payments and state and local purchases of goods and services. Source: *Economic Report of the President, 1991*, Tables B-81 and B-82.

government-owned bonds. Governments also borrow through the credit market, both to cover budget deficits and to finance capital investment projects such as new schools and water-treatment facilities. A **government budget deficit** occurs when spending exceeds revenue from taxes and fees.

The trend in real tax revenues for federal and for state and local governments since 1960 is shown in Figure 3. Real tax revenues have risen at both the federal and the state and local levels. However, spending has grown faster

Government budget deficit
Excess of government expenditures over tax receipts.

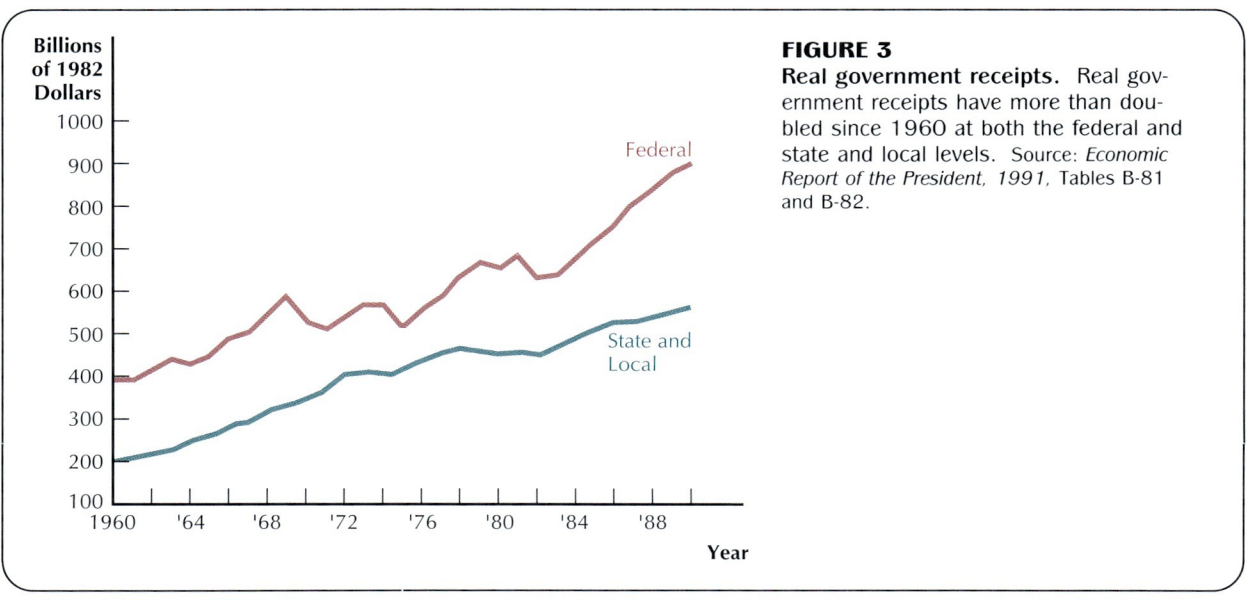

FIGURE 3
Real government receipts. Real government receipts have more than doubled since 1960 at both the federal and state and local levels. Source: *Economic Report of the President, 1991*, Tables B-81 and B-82.

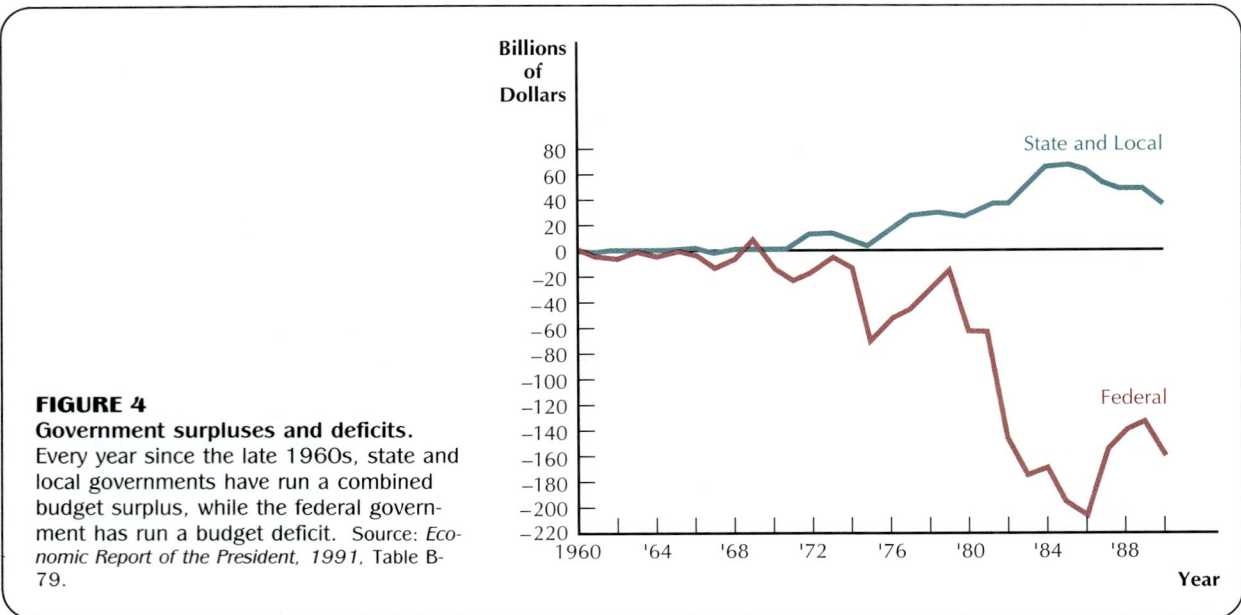

FIGURE 4
Government surpluses and deficits.
Every year since the late 1960s, state and local governments have run a combined budget surplus, while the federal government has run a budget deficit. Source: *Economic Report of the President, 1991*, Table B-79.

than tax revenues at the federal level. The federal budget has been in deficit in most years since 1960. Figure 4 shows the federal and state and local budget deficits or surpluses in current dollars. The federal government has been accumulating deficits for some years while state and local governments have been accumulating surpluses.

Fiscal Policy

Fiscal policy
The use of government expenditures and taxes to affect aggregate demand or aggregate supply.

Fiscal policy is the use of government spending and financing powers to affect aggregate demand or aggregate supply. Although most active fiscal policy — designed specifically to affect the macroeconomy — is carried out at the federal level, expenditure and tax programs at all levels of government affect private spending. Because federal spending and taxing decisions have a greater effect on the economy than do the decisions of any state or local government, we focus our discussion of fiscal policy on the federal government's spending, taxation, and deficit finance policies.

Government Spending and Aggregate Demand

Government spending falls into two broad categories: purchases of goods and services, and transfer payments. Purchases of goods and services include such disparate items as the resurfacing of an interstate highway, wage payments to Department of Agriculture food inspectors, and purchases of stealth bombers. In each case the government acquires goods and services while generating income for the providers of the goods and services.

Other government expenditures represent the transfer of income rather than the acquisition of goods. The government receives nothing in return for such expenditures. Veterans of the armed services receive retirement benefits. Low-income families receive Aid to Families with Dependent Children. The elderly receive Social Security payments and Medicare benefits. Such transfer payments redistribute income from taxpayers to recipients, but do not contribute directly to GNP (though they may contribute indirectly through their effect on consumption expenditures).

Government Purchases and Transfer Payments Work Differently Government purchases of goods and services directly affect the aggregate demand for goods and services. An increase in spending on urban transit systems or on state universities (one of our personal favorites) adds to the demand for goods and services produced by the economy. The aggregate demand curve shifts to the right, as in Figure 5.

Reducing government purchases of goods and services shifts the aggregate demand curve to the left. Major reductions in government purchases have been rare in recent U.S. economic history, with one exception. Whenever a war ends, defense spending falls sharply. This happened following World War II, the Korean War, and the Vietnam War.

Increases or decreases in transfer payments affect aggregate demand indirectly through their effect on consumption spending. We have seen that most households base their consumption on long-run disposable income. Temporary changes in current income have little effect on their consumption, because the households are able to draw on savings or borrow to maintain consumption even if their income is temporarily low. However, low-income households may find it difficult, if not impossible, to save, and they may be

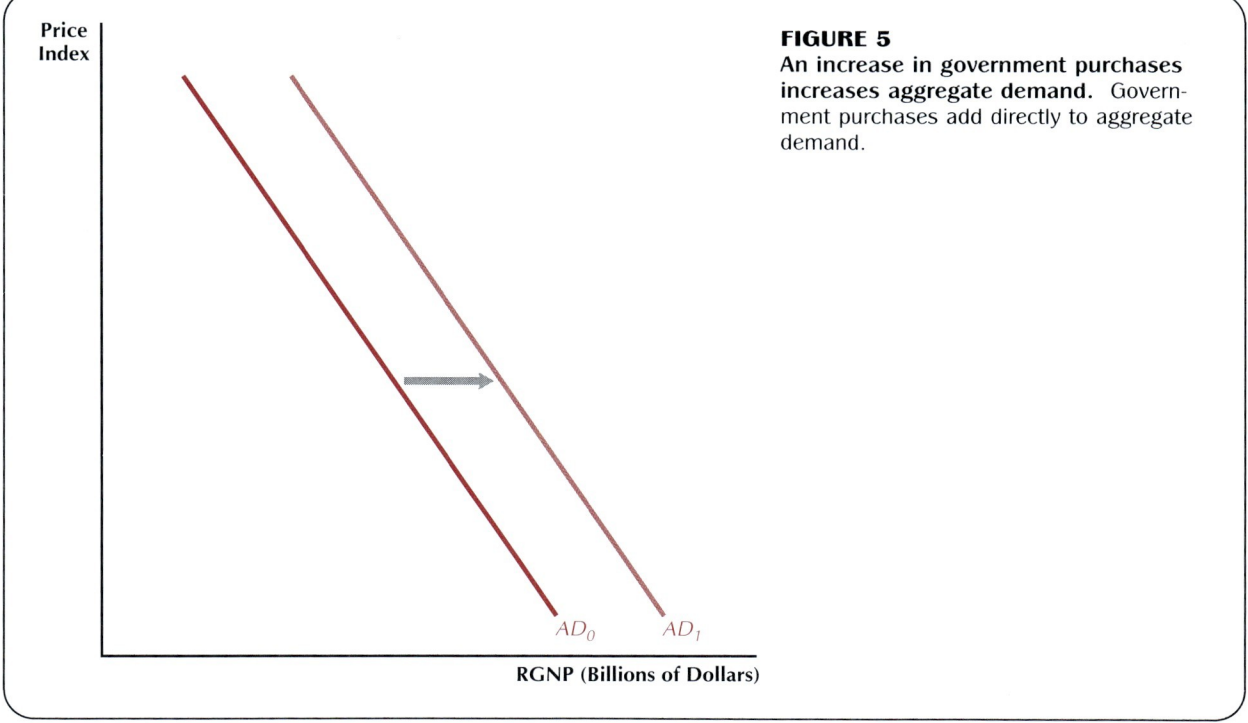

FIGURE 5
An increase in government purchases increases aggregate demand. Government purchases add directly to aggregate demand.

unable to borrow when their income falls. Thus, when the current income of a low-income household falls, the household may be forced to reduce consumption as well. In such a case, consumption is liquidity constrained and depends on the household's current income.

Transfer payments, such as unemployment insurance benefits and food stamps, enable liquidity-constrained households to maintain higher levels of consumption spending than they would be able to maintain without public assistance. Without income maintenance benefits, consumption spending would be lower than it actually is.

Multiplier Effect Changes in government purchases and in transfer payments may cause even larger changes in aggregate demand. A decrease in defense purchases of armored personnel carriers sets off a chain reaction. The private companies producing the personnel carriers experience a reduction in income. They demand fewer engines, less metal plating, fewer transmissions — in short, less of all the intermediate goods that go into the production of personnel carriers. Unless demand for other products increases, the firms will also be forced to lay off workers.

The companies providing the component parts of the personnel carriers lose income. They reduce their demands for raw materials and labor. The workers who are laid off make fewer purchases of consumer durable goods and may even have to cut back on consumption of nondurable goods and services. The final result could be a reduction in GNP substantially larger than the reduction in defense spending.

The size of the multiplier is limited by several factors. Since the consumption of most households depends on permanent rather than current income, consumption is not likely to decline much when government spending declines, at least not for a while. The presence of transfer payments provides income to liquidity-constrained households, allowing them to sustain consumption spending. As income declines, tax payments also decline, cushioning spending; in effect, government absorbs part of the income reduction.

The reduction in government purchases may also push the interest rate down slightly, as the need to borrow to finance deficit spending declines. A lower interest rate encourages spending on investment goods and consumer durables. The existence of all these effects limits the size of the multiplier.

Changes in transfer payments may also generate multiplier effects. However, the transfer payments multiplier is even smaller than the purchases multiplier, because transfer payments do not *directly* affect aggregate demand; they affect aggregate demand only through their effect on consumption spending. The direct effect of government purchases is missing. Thus, the multiplier effect of transfer payments works entirely through the effect of transfer payments on consumption spending.

SECTION RECAP
Government expenditures are part of the aggregate demand for goods and services. Changes in G affect AD in the same direction. Changes in transfer payments also shift AD in the same direction. However, the effect of transfers works through consumption spending. The multiplier effect of government expenditures is larger than the transfer payments multiplier.

Government Spending and Aggregate Supply

Over extended periods of time, government spending patterns may affect aggregate supply. The size of the capital stock available for use in producing goods and services can be affected in two ways: by the composition of government spending and by the effect of transfer payments on saving, which affects the interest rate.

Composition of Government Spending Government spending can be divided into consumption expenditures and investment expenditures. Consumption expenditures are on goods and services that provide direct benefits, but do not increase future production. Spending on recreation, the salaries of most government employees, some defense spending, and most transfer payments would fall into this category.

Government investment expenditures increase the nation's capital stock, leading to higher future production. Building roads, constructing sewage treatment plants, educating students, and vaccinating children for measles all qualify as investments. They upgrade either the economy's infrastructure or the quality of the future labor force. Spending on such items *immediately* adds to aggregate demand, and it *eventually* increases the nation's ability to produce, increasing the natural level of output.

SECTION RECAP
Government spending affects aggregate supply through its effects on public and private investment.

Transfer Payments and Private Saving Government provision of Social Security and Medicare benefits may affect aggregate supply through the effect of such benefits on household saving. Some economists fear that people save less because they believe that Social Security benefits reduce the need for retirement savings. Medicare benefits similarly reduce the incentive to save to pay medical bills after retirement.

If saving is diminished by Social Security benefits, the supply of credit declines. The reduction in credit supply increases the interest rate, as in Figure 6. Higher interest rates discourage capital investment. Lower investment spending leads to a smaller capital stock and lower aggregate supply in the long run.

The actual effects of Social Security benefits on saving are highly uncertain. Although some economists believe that Social Security benefits reduce saving

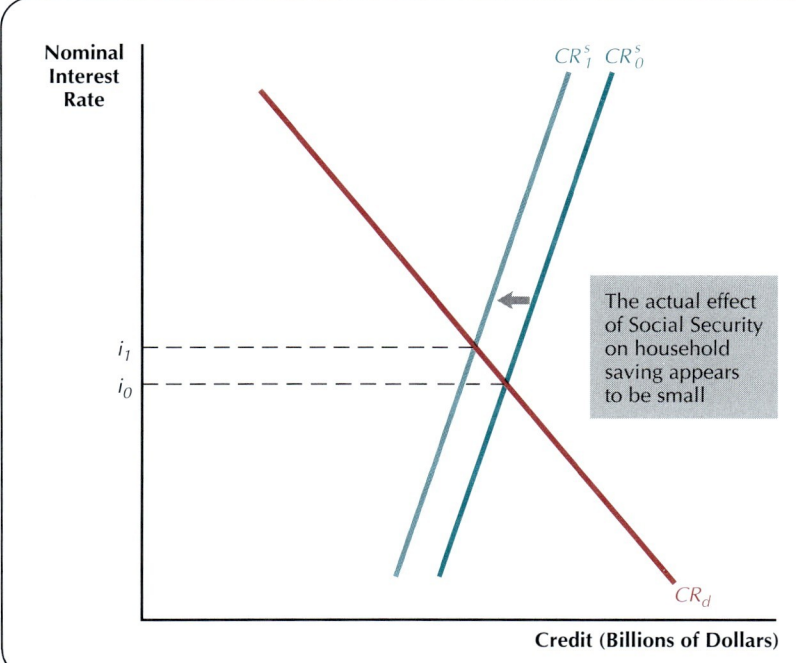

FIGURE 6
Social Security and saving. If the presence of Social Security causes households to save less, the supply of credit is reduced. Given a stable credit demand curve, this increases the interest rate.

(with the results shown in Figure 6), others believe that Social Security has little impact on saving or the interest rate. These economists note that while Social Security reduces the incentive to save for one's own retirement, it also reduces the amount of spending by children on their retired parents. Since adult children spend less on their retired parents, they have more discretionary income out of which to save. This may counterbalance any negative effect of Social Security benefits on saving.

The empirical evidence on this issue is mixed. Most studies appear to indicate that Social Security either reduces saving or has no effect on saving; few indicate that saving increases. Thus, the effects of Social Security on long-run capital formation, if any, are probably negative.

Taxation and Aggregate Demand

Taxes affect aggregate demand through their effect on disposable income. The larger the share of household income claimed as taxes, the smaller the share of income available to spend and save.

The federal government obtains the vast majority of its tax receipts from two sources: individual income taxes and social insurance taxes and contributions. Social insurance taxes, often called **payroll taxes** because they are subtracted directly from paychecks, cover Social Security and Medicare payments and are not used as an active tool of fiscal policy. However, the income tax has been frequently used as a policy tool. Although a much smaller source of revenue than the personal income tax, the corporate profits tax is also important for fiscal policy purposes.

Payroll tax
Tax on income used to support the Social Security system.

Individual Income Tax   The largest source of revenue at the federal level is the individual income tax. The U.S. individual income tax is a **graduated-rate**, or **progressive**, tax. This means that the tax rate rises as individuals move into higher income brackets. The current law, which combines features of laws passed in 1986 and 1990, reduced the number of tax brackets from fifteen to three, and low-income households pay no income tax at all. Under the current, simpler system, individuals pay 15 percent of their taxable income to the federal government if they are in the lowest tax bracket. If they are in the middle income bracket, they pay 28 percent on all income above the lower bracket amount and 15 percent on the lower bracket amount. The high income bracket applies a tax rate of 33 percent to all income above the middle bracket amount.

Graduated-rate (progressive) income tax
Tax rate on the last dollar of income rises as the taxpayer's income increases.

An example will clarify how the system works. Suppose a single individual earned $30,000 in actual income in 1990 and had $24,000 in taxable income after deductions and the personal exemption. (**Deductions** are expenditures that can be subtracted from income before taxes are calculated. Examples include state and local income tax payments, mortgage interest payments, and charitable contributions. The **personal exemption** is the amount that can be subtracted from income simply because the individual exists.) This individual paid 15 percent tax on the first $19,450 in taxable income and 28 percent on the remainder. This amounts to:

Tax deduction
Expenditures that can be subtracted from income before calculating the amount of income tax due.

Personal exemption
Amount every taxpayer is entitled to subtract from income before calculating the amount of income tax due.

$$.15 \times 19{,}450 = \$2917.50 \text{ plus}$$
$$.28 \times 4{,}550 = \$1274$$

Marginal tax rate
Rate paid on the final dollar of income.

or a total of $4191.50 in taxes. The **marginal tax rate** paid by the individual — the rate paid on the final dollar of income earned by the taxpayer — is 28 percent. The **average tax rate** equals the amount of tax paid divided by the taxpayer's income, or $4191.50/$30,000 = 14 percent.

The existence of personal exemptions ($2050 per person in 1990) and itemized deductions or the **standard deduction** that may be taken instead of itemizing deductions, means that low-income households pay no federal income tax at all. For example, a family of four with income of $13,650 or less in 1990 paid no tax, because the personal exemptions for four people equaled $8200 and the standard deduction for a married couple filing jointly was $5450. Taxable income thus was zero.

Corporate Profits Tax The corporate profits tax is levied against the profits remaining after corporations have subtracted costs of production from sales revenue.

A popular theme in recent years has been the notion that corporations do not pay their so-called fair share of taxes. Many politicians and private citizens have called for lower individual income taxes and higher corporate profits taxes. While such a change might appear to be beneficial to individuals, it is doubtful that individual taxpayers would gain much from it. The reason is simple: Corporations don't pay taxes; people do. Corporations are legal fictions. Shareholders, employees, and customers — people — pay the corporate income tax. To the extent that corporations react to higher taxes by raising prices, customers bear the burden of the tax. If corporations pay lower wages because of higher taxes, employees suffer. If after-tax profits are reduced by higher taxes, shareholders suffer as the value of their stock declines. Exactly how the burden of the corporate income tax is distributed is unknown, a fact that causes many economists to oppose this form of taxation.

Income Taxes and Aggregate Demand Taxes affect aggregate demand through their effects on consumption and investment spending. The size of the effect of a change in taxes depends on the precise nature of the change and whether it is expected to be temporary or permanent.

The theory of consumption demand stresses the dependence of consumption on long-run income. Temporary changes in the income tax do not affect households' permanent disposable income very much and consequently have only minor impacts on consumption spending. We have seen that the temporary income tax surcharge imposed in 1968 had little effect on consumption spending. People simply reduced their saving temporarily to support their accustomed level of consumption. (A temporary transfer payment increase in 1974 also had a minimal effect on aggregate demand.) Temporary income tax reductions or increases do not shift the aggregate demand curve significantly.

Permanent changes in income taxes are a different matter. If the federal government increases income tax rates, and this increase is expected to be permanent, household permanent disposable income falls, causing households to reduce their consumption spending. The result is a shift to the left in the aggregate demand curve, as shown in Figure 7. A permanent reduction in income tax rates shifts the aggregate demand curve outward.

Corporate Profits Taxes and Investment Spending The corporate profits tax affects the amount of investment spending undertaken by corporations. Business firms often find it less costly to finance investment projects with their own savings (retained earnings) than with borrowed funds. The corporate profits

Average tax rate
Amount of tax paid divided by the taxpayer's income.

Standard deduction
Deduction that may be taken instead of itemizing specific deductions.

SECTION RECAP
Income taxes affect consumption through their effect on disposable income. An increase in the income tax rate reduces disposable income and consumption spending.
(continued)

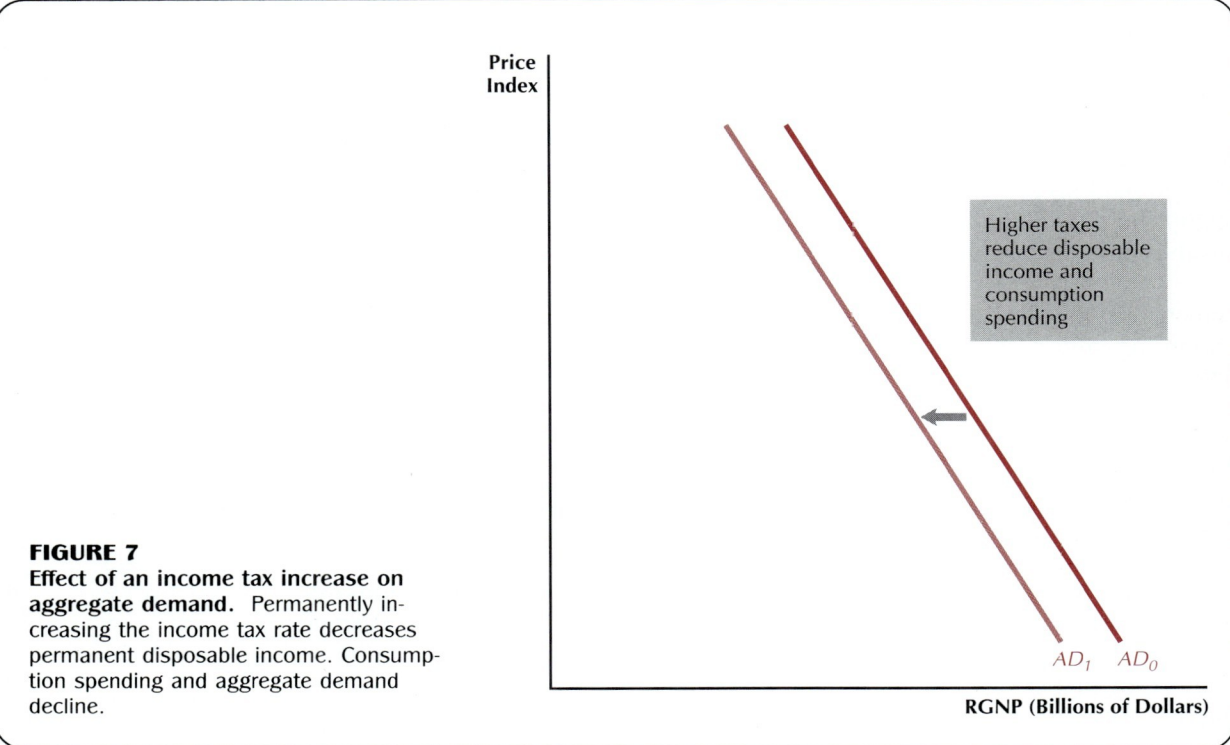

FIGURE 7
Effect of an income tax increase on aggregate demand. Permanently increasing the income tax rate decreases permanent disposable income. Consumption spending and aggregate demand decline.

SECTION RECAP
(continued)
Corporate profits taxes and investment tax credits affect investment spending. Higher profits taxes reduce investment, while higher tax credits encourage investment.

Investment tax credit
Permits businesses to deduct a percentage of their investment expenditures from their corporate profits tax payments.

tax reduces the amount of after-tax business savings available to support investment. An increase in the corporate tax rate may cause fixed investment spending to decline, shifting the aggregate demand curve to the left. A reduction in the corporate tax rate increases after-tax business savings, encouraging investment.

Tax policy affects investment spending in another, even more important way. The government often passes legislation granting investment tax credits to corporations that invest in fixed plant and equipment. An **investment tax credit** allows the corporation to deduct some percentage of the purchase price of investment goods from its tax bill. For example, a 10 percent tax credit on a $10,000 machine would allow a firm to deduct $1000 from its tax bill, in effect lowering the price of the machine to $9000. Lower effective prices for investment goods increase the demand for investment goods by raising the rate of return on the investment project. For a given level of the expected real interest rate, investment spending rises. This shifts the aggregate demand curve to the right in the short run and increases aggregate supply in the long run.

Taxes and Aggregate Supply

The Short Step from Aggregate Demand (Investment) to Aggregate Supply (Capital) Tax policy that influences investment spending in the current period affects the size of the economy's capital stock and the natural output level in future periods. Lower corporate income tax rates and higher investment tax credits encourage firms to invest in more plant and equipment. Over time, such investment shifts the long-run aggregate supply curve to the right as the capital stock grows.

In practice, tax policy cannot be expected to significantly affect the size of the capital stock and the position of the long-run aggregate supply curve over the course of a year or two. The additions to the capital stock in any one year are very small compared to the existing capital stock. However, high levels of investment spending that persist for several years can significantly affect the productive capacity of the economy. The cumulative effects of high investment spending are much larger than the effects in any single year.

Importance of Marginal Tax Rates   Income tax policy can affect aggregate supply in other ways. Most people earn most of their incomes by supplying labor services. The income tax reduces the after-tax earnings from working. An increase in the income tax rate (or in the payroll tax rate used to support the Social Security system) may discourage work by reducing after-tax earnings. Workers previously earning just enough to keep them in the labor market may choose to quit their jobs, reducing the total supply of labor. However, a tax increase has a second, offsetting effect. At a higher tax rate some people may have to work more just to make ends meet. Lower after-tax income forces some people to supply more labor to maintain their standard of living. Thus, the net effect of an income or payroll tax rate increase on a person's labor supply decision is unclear. More or less labor might be supplied.

The aggregate effect of a change in the tax rate is even more complicated, because the effect on aggregate labor supply depends not only on the change in the tax rate, but also on what happens to government spending after tax revenues change. Depending on what happens to government spending, household income may rise, fall, or remain unchanged in the wake of a change in the income tax rate. Since the aggregate labor supply decision depends on both the return to working (the after-tax wage rate) and the total income received, including the value of services provided by the government, the effect on aggregate labor supply of a change in the income tax rate must be determined on a case-by-case basis.[1]

Another way marginal tax rates can affect aggregate supply is through their effect on saving behavior. Interest and dividend income from stocks and bonds purchased with savings is subject to the income tax. Increasing income tax rates reduces the after-tax rate of return on these assets. This discourages saving, shifting the supply of credit curve to the left, as in Figure 8 (a). A higher interest rate results.

Permitting taxpayers to deduct interest payments from income when calculating their taxable income puts even more upward pressure on the interest rate. If interest payments are tax deductible, the after-tax cost of borrowing is reduced. This increases the demand for credit, as shown in Figure 8 (b). The net effect of taxing interest income and making interest payments tax deductible is to increase the interest rate.

SECTION RECAP
Taxes can affect aggregate supply through their effects on the supply of la-
(continued)

---

[1]This issue has been discussed at length in a series of comments and replies resulting from a paper by James D. Gwartney and Richard Stroup. See their paper "Labor Supply and Tax Rates: A Correction of the Record," *American Economic Review* June 1983, pp. 446–451, as well as their replies to comments in the December 1984 (pp. 1108–1109) and March 1986 (pp. 284–285) issues of the same journal. See also the comments by James A. Wilde (December 1984, pp. 1103–1107), Cecil E. Bohanon and T. Norman Van Cott (March 1986, pp. 277–279), and Firouz Gahvari (March 1986, pp. 280–283).

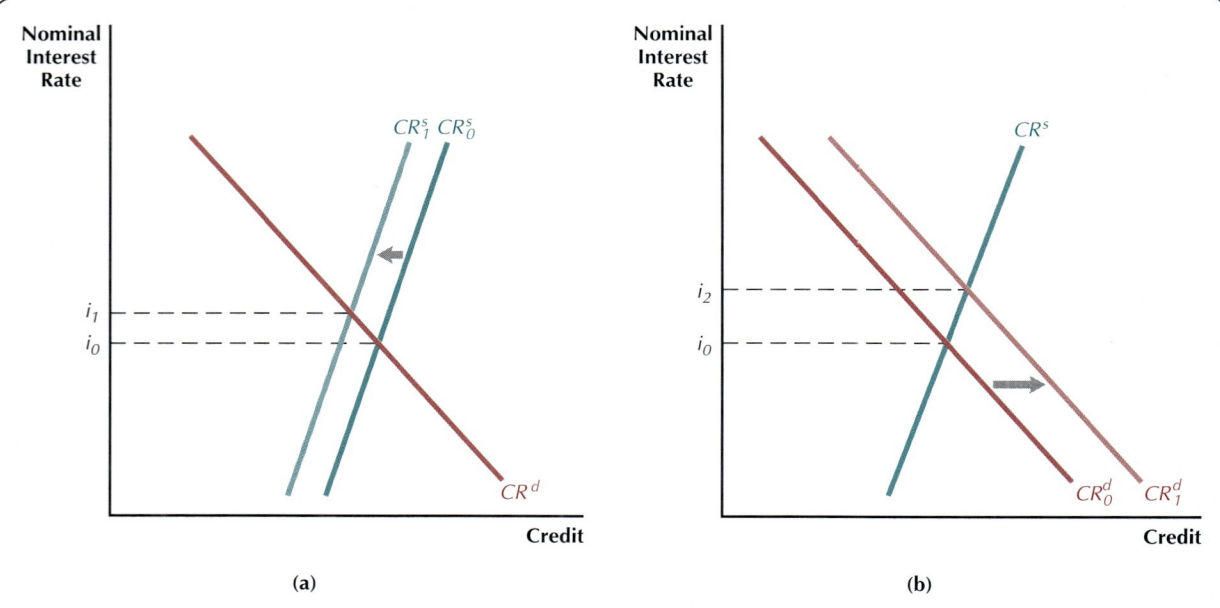

FIGURE 8
Tax effects on the interest rate. A higher tax rate reduces the rate of return on savings. This reduces the incentive to save. The supply of credit declines, and, assuming constant credit demand, the interest rate rises (a). If interest payments are tax deductible, the cost of borrowing is reduced. This shifts the credit demand curve to the right. Given a stable supply of credit, the interest rate rises (b).

SECTION RECAP
(continued)
bor and on the interest rate. The labor supply effect, if any, is unknown. Taxing interest earnings and allowing borrowers to deduct interest payments from their taxable income tends to increase the interest rate.

If the government wanted to increase the growth rate of real GNP by encouraging as much productive investment as possible, it could do so by not taxing the interest earnings on financial assets and by allowing generous investment tax credits. These two policies would increase the supply of credit and the demand for credit for investment purposes. The long-run effects on the capital stock might be quite large. Figure 9 illustrates the potential effects on the natural level of real GNP over time of policies that encourage more saving and investment. An increase in the growth rate of natural real GNP (caused by greater investment) from 3.0 percent per year to 3.3 percent per year results in a real GNP level that is 6 percent higher after only twenty years and 15.7 percent higher after fifty years.[2]

Budget Deficits and Borrowing

All government spending must be financed. Governments face budget constraints, just as households and businesses do. However, governments have some financing options not available to households and businesses. One op-

---

[2] Part of the reason saving and investment in Japan are higher than in the United States may be because the Japanese tax system encourages saving and investment to a much greater extent than does the U.S. tax system.

tion is to levy taxes against the citizens of the nation, state, county, or city. Another option, available only to the federal government, is to finance spending by expanding the monetary base. Newly created base money can be used to pay bills.

The federal government's formal budget constraint is:

$$\begin{array}{cc}\text{(Sources)} & \text{(Uses)} \\ T + \Delta B + \text{Bor} = & G + \text{Tr} + \text{Int}\end{array}$$

where T is tax revenue, ΔB is the change in the monetary base, Bor is borrowing, G is government purchases of goods and services, Tr is transfer payments, and Int is interest payments on outstanding debt, and all variables are measured in current dollars. (If the government runs a surplus, borrowing is replaced by lending.)

By subtracting T from both sides of the budget constraint, we can see that whenever spending (G + Tr + Int) exceeds tax revenues (T), the deficit must be financed by creating more base money or by borrowing in the credit market:

$$G + \text{Tr} + \text{Int} - T = \Delta B + \text{Bor}$$

The federal deficit is largely financed by borrowing in the credit market. The Treasury sells bonds to raise funds. The Federal Reserve may purchase some of those bonds through open market operations, thus increasing the monetary base and substituting money for Treasury bonds in the hands of the public. However, the portion of the deficit *monetized* — converted into money —

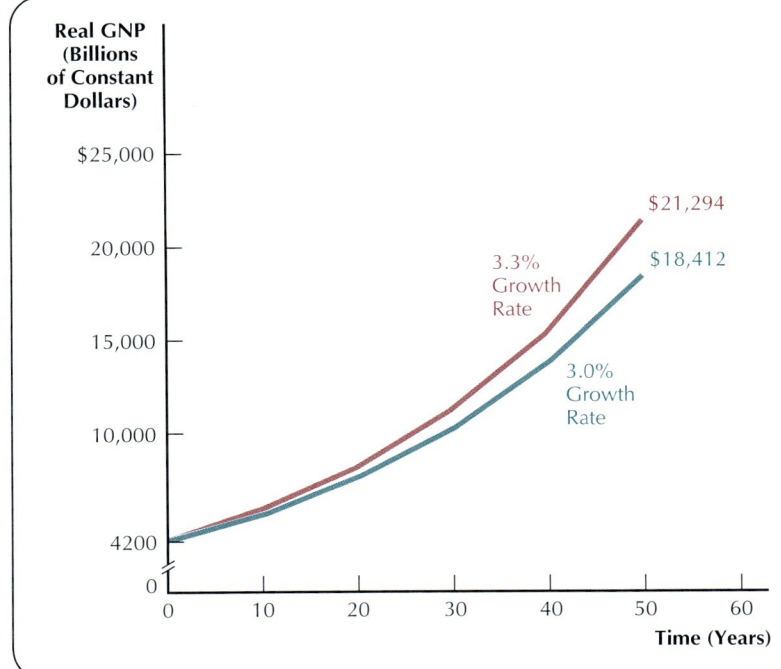

FIGURE 9
Saving, investment, and growth in natural output. Policies that reduce the cost of borrowing to investors and encourage saving by households may have a significant effect on the economy's long-term output level. This example shows the effect of policies that raise the growth rate of natural real GNP from 3.0 percent to 3.3 percent, starting from a real GNP level of $4200 billion (which approximately equaled U.S. real GNP in 1990).

Why the **Disagreement?**

Paying for Social Security

The Social Security system is the U.S. government's largest transfer program. Only the personal income tax brings the federal government more revenue than the Social Security payroll tax. During the early 1980s, when income tax rates were reduced, the Social Security tax rate was increased. This resulted in large surpluses for the Social Security system, as payroll tax receipts far exceeded current payouts to Social Security recipients. At the same time, the federal budget was sharply in deficit. Congress intended to generate large Social Security surpluses when it increased the Social Security tax rate. The system faces a major problem funding the benefits of the baby-boom generation that will begin to retire around 2015. At that time the number of retirees relative to the number of active workers will begin to rise. At the current Social Security tax rate the Social Security system will run surpluses until about 2015, at which time the total Social Security surplus will be in the neighborhood of $5 trillion. The idea behind the tax rate increase was to use the surplus to fund the benefits of the large pool of retirees without having to raise taxes on the smaller pool of workers paying into the system.

It is against this backdrop that, in January 1990, Senator Daniel Patrick Moynihan of New York proposed cutting the Social Security tax rate to eliminate the system's surplus.* Senator Moynihan proposed to put Social Security on a pay-as-you-go basis, with current taxes paying for current benefits. The Moynihan proposal immediately met with vigorous opposition from President Bush, as well as from many members of Congress. However, Moynihan's proposal received widespread support from many other politicians. Why the disagreement?

The issue is really far more than just an argument between those who want to cut taxes and those who do not. Everyone who has studied the Social Security system understands the problem facing the system. Senator Moynihan's proposal followed from his belief that the current Social Security surpluses do nothing to address the funding problem.

Unless the productivity of U.S. workers increases significantly over the next twenty-five years, the economy will not be able to produce enough goods and services to sustain the standard of living reached while the baby boomers were working. However, the Social Security surpluses currently being accumulated do not add to the economy's productivity. Social Security surpluses are invested in U.S. Treasury securities, as the law requires. Thus, in effect the Social Security system lends its surpluses to the federal government, which in turn uses them to support its current spending. Rather than being used to finance new capital and technological improvements, the Social Security surplus is largely spent on public consumption.

---

by Federal Reserve open market purchases typically is small. Borrowing from the public is the federal government's major deficit financing method.

A Historical Look at Deficits

Before the 1970s, the federal government attempted to keep its budget close to balanced. Although it did not maintain a balanced budget every year, it attempted to offset deficits in some years with surpluses in others. Even during the 1960s, when the federal government was becoming more actively involved in managing the economy, the federal budget was in surplus or in deficit by less than $5 billion in six years. The cumulative deficit for the whole decade of the 1960s was only 56.5 billion (in current prices) — and during that time the government financed the Vietnam War and some major social programs in addition to its normal activities.

As Figure 10 shows, federal expenditures chronically began to exceed receipts during the 1970s. Following the large tax reductions that went into effect in 1982, the deficit reached record highs.

Senator Moynihan recognized that Social Security surpluses only mask the true size of the federal deficit, which, excluding Social Security surpluses, exceeded $200 billion per year during most of the late 1980s. Thus, the Moynihan plan has the virtue of showing the true size of the federal government's operating deficit. Furthermore, a payroll tax cut could strengthen the economy. Payroll taxes represent a significant cost to businesses. Workers and firms together must pay 15.3 percent of wages in Social Security taxes. Reducing the tax rate would lower the cost of employing workers, thereby encouraging firms to hire more workers and increase production. Long-run aggregate supply would rise. Aggregate demand would also rise, as workers spend part of their higher disposable income on consumption goods.

On the negative side, the Moynihan plan would require significantly higher payroll taxes in the future to pay for the benefits of a larger pool of retirees. Furthermore, by increasing the size of the federal government's deficit, a Social Security tax cut would require the government to borrow more, pushing up the interest rate and possibly retarding economic growth.

The negative features of the Moynihan plan have led other politicians and social analysts to propose alternatives. Representative John Porter of Illinois proposed that, rather than cutting the payroll tax, the surplus Social Security funds be used to fund Individual Social Security Retirement Accounts for all workers.** These tax-free savings accounts would accumulate throughout the worker's lifetime. At retirement, workers would draw smaller Social Security benefits, using the proceeds of the Retirement Accounts to make up the difference. The funds saved in the Retirement Accounts would be used to support productive investment, thereby increasing the size of the capital stock and providing for a larger real GNP in the future.

Still another proposal has been to tie a current payroll tax reduction to a reduction in future benefits. Former Treasury official Stephen J. Entin notes that the current benefits schedule will provide future retirees with much higher *real* benefits than current retirees receive.† By reducing future benefits somewhat — but still leaving them higher than current benefits — the system could be put on a pay-as-you-go basis without having to raise the payroll tax rate in the future.

As you can see, the issue of how to fund Social Security is quite complex. The disagreement about funding is over how to reform the system. Virtually everyone agrees it needs reform.

*Senator Moynihan's plan is discussed in many places, including "Social Security's 'Dirty Little Secret,'" *Business Week,* January 29, 1990, pp. 66–67.

**John Porter, "Let Workers Own Their Retirement Funds," *The Wall Street Journal,* February 1, 1990, p. A14.

†Stephen J. Entin, "Moynihan is Right — Now, Cut Benefits," *The Wall Street Journal,* January 29, 1990, p. A18.

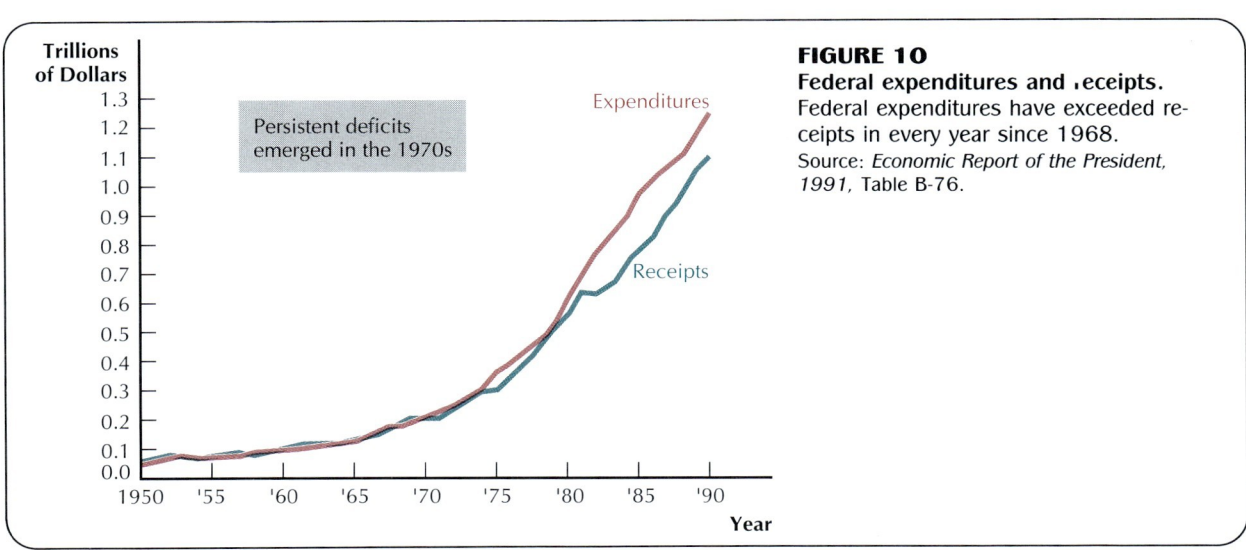

FIGURE 10
Federal expenditures and receipts.
Federal expenditures have exceeded receipts in every year since 1968.
Source: *Economic Report of the President, 1991,* Table B-76.

Actual and High Employment Deficits

The size of the federal deficit is not completely under government control. Since both tax revenues and transfer payments depend to a large extent on national income, changes in national income affect the government budget. For example, a government budget that is balanced (spending equals taxes) when the economy is operating at the natural output level automatically moves into deficit if the economy goes into a recession. As national income falls, tax revenue decreases and transfer payments rise. Thus, spending exceeds tax revenue, and the government budget is in deficit.

The automatic reduction in income and payroll taxes and increase in such transfer payments as unemployment insurance benefits, food stamps, and Aid to Families with Dependent Children acts as an **automatic stabilizer** — a mechanism that reduces the effect of a change in GNP on disposable income and consumption. Automatic stabilizers moderate the effects of aggregate demand shifts, thus stabilizing aggregate income.

Although the government budget naturally moves into deficit in a recession, the deficit does not indicate that fiscal policy has become more expansionary. If the economy were operating at its natural level, the budget would be in balance. Fiscal policy would be neutral, not expansionary.

Because it is affected by cyclical movements in GNP, the actual budget deficit is a poor measure of how expansionary or contractionary fiscal policy is. Figure 11 compares movements in the ratio of the actual budget surplus as a percentage of trend GNP to movements in the unemployment rate. (A negative budget surplus is a deficit.) The cyclical behavior of the surplus-to-GNP ratio shows up clearly, as the ratio falls when the unemployment rate rises in a recession and rises when the unemployment rate falls in an expansion.

To use the deficit as a measure of how expansive or restrictive fiscal policy actually is, we must adjust for cyclical behavior. When this is done we have

Automatic stabilizer
Automatic change in tax receipts or transfer payments in the opposite direction of a change in real GNP thus partially offsetting the real GNP change.

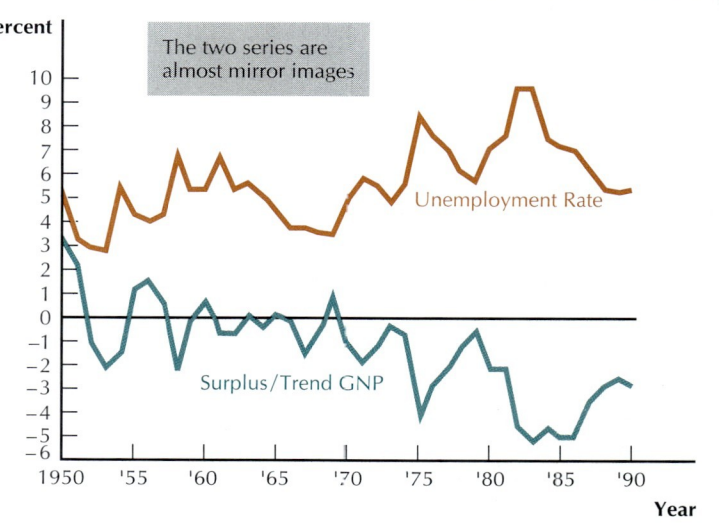

FIGURE 11
Cyclical behavior of deficits. The surplus-to-trend GNP ratio falls whenever the unemployment rate rises. Whenever the unemployment rate declines during an expansion, the budget ratio rises back toward surplus. The unemployment rate and surplus-to-trend GNP ratio series are almost mirror images of each other. Source: *Economic Report of the President, 1991*, Tables B-1, B-39, and B-76.

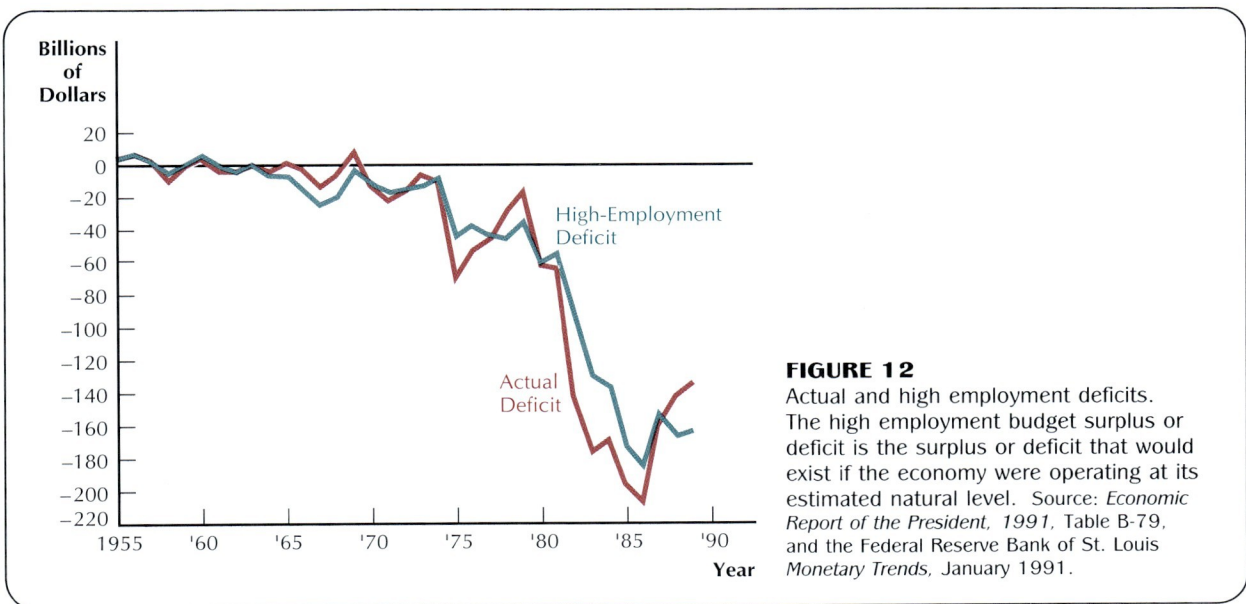

FIGURE 12
Actual and high employment deficits. The high employment budget surplus or deficit is the surplus or deficit that would exist if the economy were operating at its estimated natural level. Source: *Economic Report of the President, 1991,* Table B-79, and the Federal Reserve Bank of St. Louis *Monetary Trends,* January 1991.

the **high employment budget deficit**—the budget deficit that *would* occur *if* the economy were operating at its natural level. In other words, given the current legislation governing taxes and expenditures, the high employment deficit tells us what the difference between expenditures and receipts *would be* if real GNP were at the level estimated to be its natural level. The high employment budget deficit (or surplus) is a measure of the government-determined behavior of the budget, after reactions to the state of the economy have been removed.

The behavior of the high employment budget deficit (sometimes called the **structural deficit**) is shown in Figure 12. The actual federal deficit is also shown for comparison. Even after eliminating cyclical effects, recent deficits are large by historical standards.

High employment budget deficit
What the budget deficit would be, given existing expenditure and tax rates, if the economy were operating at the natural output level.

Structural deficit
Another name for the high employment budget deficit.

Effect of Deficits on the Credit Market

Government budget deficits affect the economy in a number of ways. Since deficits force the government to borrow, some of the effects work through the credit market. When the government sells bonds, it increases the demand for credit. Other things equal, an increase in credit demand increases the interest rate, as shown in Figure 13. However, other things are often not equal. During recessions, private borrowing declines, putting downward pressure on the interest rate. Government borrowing adds to the demand for credit and keeps the interest rate at a higher level than it would otherwise fall to.

If the government runs budget deficits during the expansion phase of business cycles, it pushes the interest rate higher than it would otherwise go. During expansions, private credit demand increases. Adding government demand for credit pushes the credit demand curve further to the right, causing the interest rate to rise more than it otherwise would.

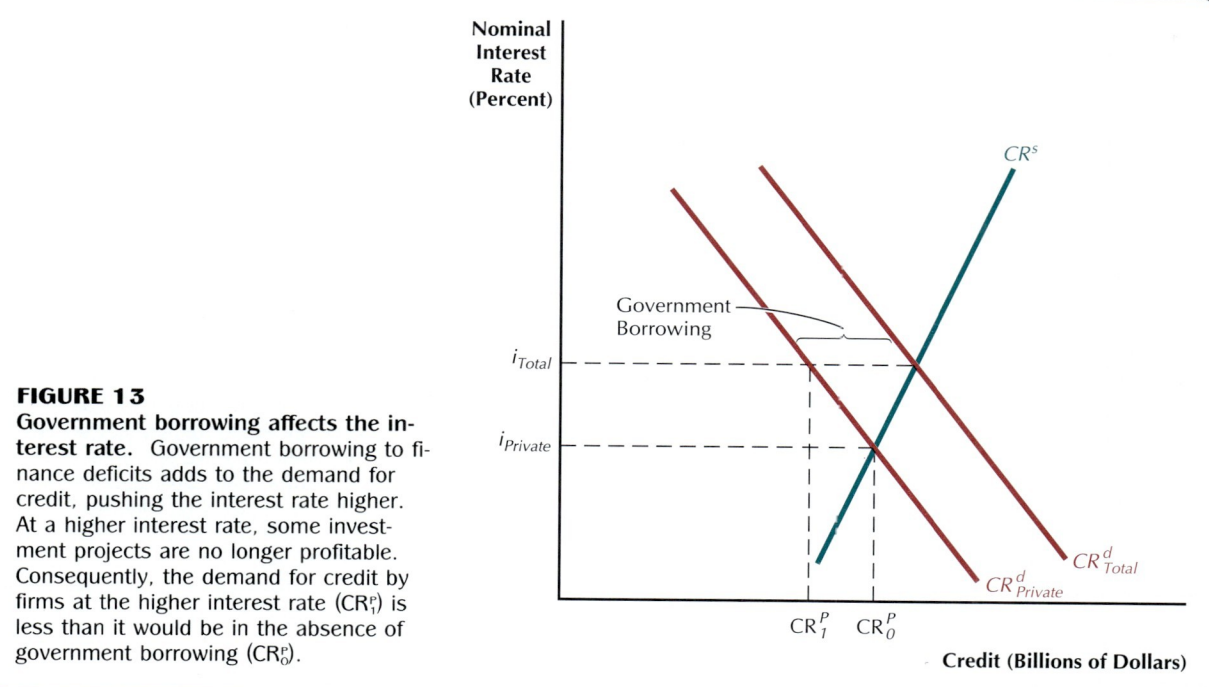

FIGURE 13
Government borrowing affects the interest rate. Government borrowing to finance deficits adds to the demand for credit, pushing the interest rate higher. At a higher interest rate, some investment projects are no longer profitable. Consequently, the demand for credit by firms at the higher interest rate (CR_1^P) is less than it would be in the absence of government borrowing (CR_0^P).

Effect of Deficits on Aggregate Demand

To the extent that government borrowing increases the interest rate, private spending may be reduced, as the government bids funds away from private borrowers. Consider Figure 13, which shows the private demand for credit and the total demand for credit, including government demand. Government borrowing shifts the credit demand curve to the right, forcing the interest rate upward. The quantity of credit demanded by private borrowers declines from CR_0^P to CR_1^P as the interest rate rises and previously profitable investment projects become unprofitable at the higher interest rate.

Private investors are **crowded out** of the market by government borrowing, as shown in Figure 14 (a). Such crowding out is not complete (that is, not exactly equal to government borrowing), because at the higher interest rate people are willing to reduce their money holdings, giving up some money in exchange for government bonds. By purchasing bonds instead of holding money, people add to the supply of credit and moderate the increase in the interest rate. Thus, the negative effect of crowding out on aggregate demand is smaller than the positive effect of increased government deficit spending, as Figure 14 (b) shows.

The extent of crowding out depends on the sensitivity of firms and households to changes in the interest rate. The more sensitive that investment demand, residential construction, and consumer durables demand are to changes in the interest rate, the greater the crowding out effect is. Figure 15 illustrates the case of interest-sensitive credit demand (relative to the credit demand curves shown in Figure 13). By comparing Figures 13 and 15, you can see that an

Crowding out
When government borrowing increases the interest rate, causing businesses to decrease investment spending.

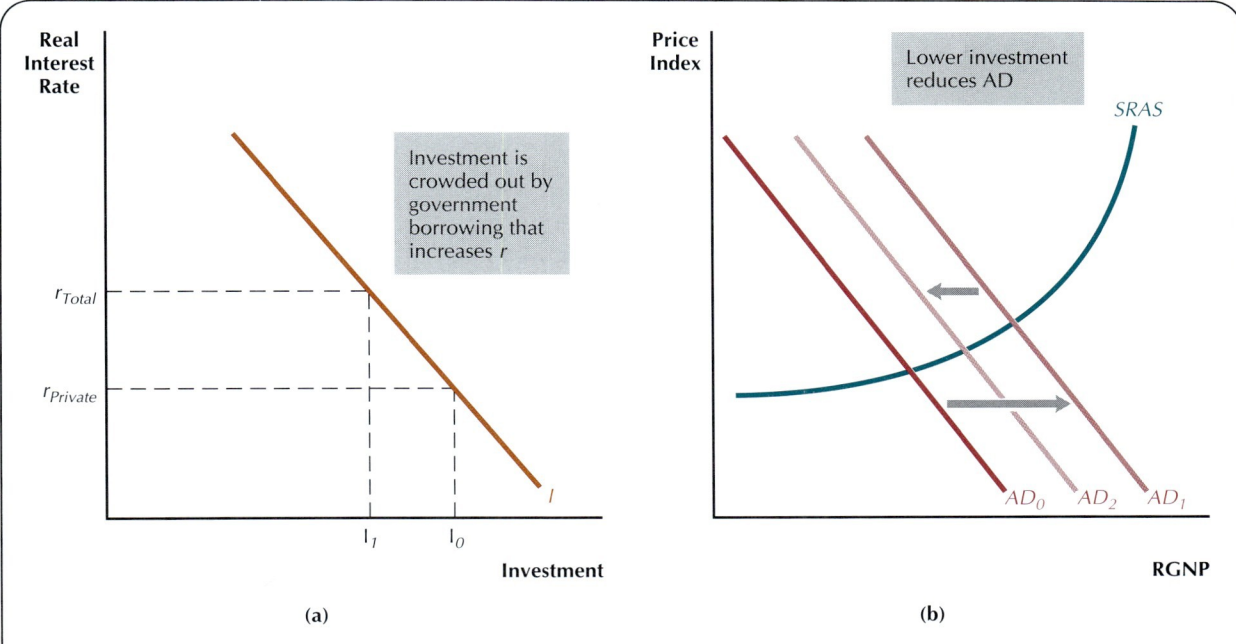

FIGURE 14
Crowding out. As the real interest rate is forced up by government borrowing, investment spending is crowded out of the market. Investment falls from I_0 to I_1 (a). The decline in investment spending offsets the expansionary effect of government deficit spending to some degree (b). The expansionary fiscal policy alone would shift the aggregate demand curve to AD_1; crowding out reduces the expansionary effect, leaving aggregate demand at AD_2.

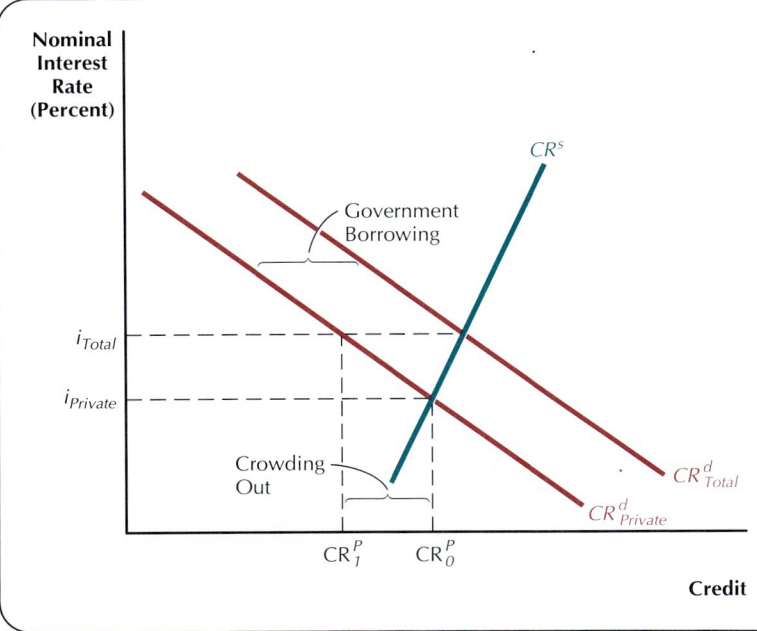

FIGURE 15
Interest sensitivity of credit demand and crowding out. The more sensitive private credit demand is to changes in the interest rate, the greater the crowding out effect of government borrowing is. Crowding out in the interest-sensitive case (shown here) is greater than crowding out in Figure 13, where credit demand is not so interest sensitive.

Does It Make **Economic Sense?**

Ricardian Equivalence Principle

Economic theory has traditionally treated the deficit financing of government expenditures as more expansionary than tax financing, because borrowing does not reduce disposable income as does tax financing. Unless government borrowing crowds out a large amount of private investment, deficit-financed government expenditures should increase aggregate demand by a larger amount than tax-financed expenditures.

However, deficit financing is more expansionary than tax financing only if taxpayers do not recognize that government debt increases future tax liabilities. The more government borrows in the present, the higher taxes must be in the future to pay off that debt. Even if the debt is never paid off, future taxes must rise to pay the interest on the debt. If taxpayers are completely rational, they will save more to meet the future tax increases whenever government borrowing rises. Such an increase in saving reduces consumption spending just as higher taxes would, making deficit-financed spending no more expansionary than tax-financed spending. Are taxes equivalent to debt? Does it make economic sense?

The idea that rational taxpayers will save more whenever government borrowing rises can be traced to the early nineteenth-century English economist David Ricardo. The hypothesis that tax financing and debt financing have equivalent effects on aggregate demand is called the *Ricardian Equivalence Principle*. This principle can be clarified with a simple example. Suppose the government can support an increase in expenditures by collecting one dollar in taxes or by borrowing one dollar from every household in the economy. If it finances the program by borrowing, it must repay the debt, plus interest, next year. That means that next year each household will have to pay $\$(1 + i)$ in taxes — $\$1$ to cover the principal borrowed and $\$i$ to cover interest payments.

Rational households understand that, if the government borrows to finance the program, their taxes will rise by $\$(1 + i)$ next year. They will compensate by increasing their saving by one dollar. Over the course of a year, each household will earn interest on the additional savings. In the second year, when taxes increase by $\$(1 + i)$, savings will have grown by $\$(1 + i)$. The interest earned on the additional savings will be sufficient to pay the interest on the government debt.

The Ricardian Equivalence Principle requires extreme rationality on the part of households. Furthermore, one generation must care about the next. If the present generation adopts a you're-on-your- own attitude toward future generations, it will not save to help future generations pay off the debt.

Do people really behave the way the Ricardian Equivalence Principle assumes? Even David Ricardo had doubts that people are so rational and so concerned about future generations. In the past few years, numerous economists have used advanced statistical techniques to study the question. Their results are mixed. Some studies suggest that Ricardo was at least partially correct. Although households may not increase their savings by one dollar for every dollar the government borrows, they appear to increase savings somewhat. Many studies indicate that 50 percent or more of an increase in government borrowing is offset by increased savings; some studies find Ricardian equivalence to be complete. However, during the 1980s, when the federal government's budget deficit rose to unprecedented levels, the household saving rate (saving as a percentage of disposable income) went down. The conflicting evidence leaves most economists skeptical of the relevance of the Ricardian Equivalence Principle.*

---

*An overview of different views on this topic appears in "Symposium on the Budget Deficit," *Journal of Economic Perspectives* 3 (Spring 1989), pp. 17–93.

Crowding in
When government deficit spending increases real GNP and businesses react by increasing investment spending.

equal increase in government borrowing crowds out a larger amount of private borrowing — and spending — when private credit demand is very interest sensitive. The decline in private borrowing from CR_0^P to CR_1^P in Figure 15 is larger than the decline from CR_0^P to CR_1^P in Figure 13.

The crowding-out effect is not the only way in which government deficit spending affects aggregate demand. To the extent that government deficits increase the level of aggregate income, they may actually have a **crowding-in** effect on investment spending. Crowding in occurs if investment spending depends on real GNP. During a recession, a government deficit limits the size of the decline in real GNP. By maintaining a higher level of real GNP, the deficit may encourage more investment spending than would otherwise occur.

Figure 16 shows the crowding-in effect. During a recession, real GNP falls, pulling investment demand down. However, the government deficit limits the decline in real GNP, so the investment demand curve shifts to the left by a smaller amount than it would in the absence of a government deficit.

Effect of Deficits on Aggregate Supply

How aggregate supply is affected by deficit spending depends on (1) whether deficits crowd in or crowd out private investment spending, and (2) whether the government spending being financed is consumption spending or investment spending.

If deficits crowd out private investment spending, the capital stock will grow more slowly over time, reducing the growth rate of real GNP. The long-run aggregate supply curve will not shift to the right as rapidly as it otherwise

SECTION RECAP
Higher budget deficits increase the demand for credit and, *ceteris paribus*, increase the interest rate. This can crowd out private investment spending. However, if investment depends on the level of real GNP, deficit-financed government spending may also crowd in investment spending.

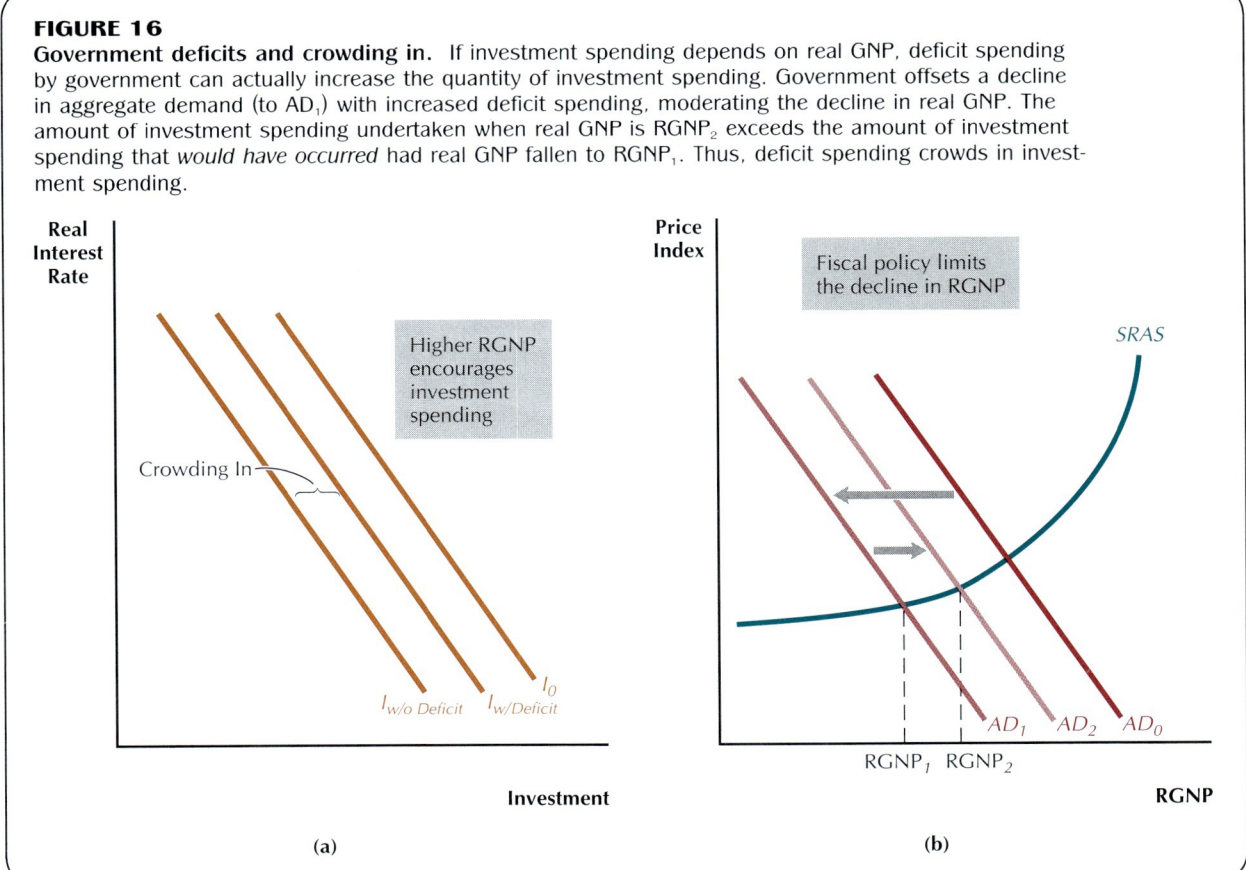

FIGURE 16
Government deficits and crowding in. If investment spending depends on real GNP, deficit spending by government can actually increase the quantity of investment spending. Government offsets a decline in aggregate demand (to AD_1) with increased deficit spending, moderating the decline in real GNP. The amount of investment spending undertaken when real GNP is $RGNP_2$ exceeds the amount of investment spending that *would have occurred* had real GNP fallen to $RGNP_1$. Thus, deficit spending crowds in investment spending.

would. However, if deficits crowd in private investment spending, the effect is just the opposite. The capital stock grows more rapidly than it would without deficits, and the growth rate of real GNP rises. Unfortunately, economists are not sure which effect prevails.

The composition of government spending has clearer effects on aggregate supply. Government can borrow to finance transfer payments or defense spending, or it can borrow to finance the construction of roads and bridges. Transfer payments and defense spending do not add to the future productive capabilities of the economy, but roads and bridges do. They amount to public investment projects.

The U.S. government's accounting system does not separate *current* expenditures on consumption from *capital* expenditures on goods that increase the future productive capacity of the economy. The practice of not separating current from capital expenditures flies in the face of standard accounting practices and makes it very difficult to determine what portion of the deficit encourages consumption, to the detriment of future production, and what portion enhances future production by building up the nation's capital stock.

Although it is difficult to separate government consumption from investment expenditures, it is not impossible. In recent work, David Aschauer has done just that. Aschauer seeks to compare the effects on the economy of government consumption and investment expenditures. Aschauer's findings indicate that the composition of government spending is very important. Not only does public investment in such capital goods as highways, airports, and water supply and sewage facilities add directly to aggregate supply, it also encourages more private investment spending. Aschauer has found that public investment increases the rate of return on private investment, encouraging private firms to add to their productive capacity. Thus, public investment spending adds to aggregate supply both directly and indirectly.[3]

Countercyclical Fiscal Policy versus Balanced Budgets

Federal debt
Total amount of U.S. government bonds outstanding.

Countercyclical fiscal policy
Tax and expenditure policy designed to offset the business cycle.

Before Keynesian theory became widely accepted in the 1960s, the standard view of government finance maintained that the only good budget was a balanced budget. Because of occasional wars and the dependence of tax revenues on income, some budget deficits were inevitable, but such deficits were always offset in subsequent years. Before 1930, the **federal debt** — the total amount of U.S. government bonds outstanding — typically rose during wars and fell during peacetime periods.

The idea that the federal budget could be used as an active stabilization device was presented by John Maynard Keynes in 1936 in *The General Theory*. Abba Lerner and other followers of Keynes promoted the idea that the government budget should be in deficit whenever the economy is below its natural (or what Keynesians called its "full employment") level and in surplus whenever real GNP exceeds the natural level of output. Using the government budget to manage the macroeconomy is called **countercyclical fiscal policy**. Countercyclical fiscal policy, conducted properly, requires the government to in-

[3] David Alan Aschauer, "Does Public Capital Crowd Out Private Capital?" *Journal of Monetary Economics* 24 (March 1989), pp. 171–188.

crease spending and reduce tax rates during recessions and cut spending and raise tax rates during expansions.

A very cautious form of countercyclical policy may have been practiced in the 1950s, during which budget deficits occurred in seven years and budget surpluses in three years. For the whole decade there was a deficit of $17.5 billion. Countercyclical policy was introduced without reservation in the 1960s by the Kennedy and Johnson administrations. That decade saw an accumulated deficit of $56.5 billion, although much of the deficit was due to the Vietnam War.

During the 1970s, the federal government ran a budget deficit every year. The deficits increased during recession years and decreased during expansion years, but there was never a surplus. The cumulative deficit over the course of the decade was $365.2 billion. That figure was dwarfed by the deficit incurred in the 1980–1989 period. In just ten years the government was forced to borrow $1,564 billion. This explosion in the nominal government deficit, combined with increasing dissatisfaction with government programs, led many people to wonder what had gone wrong. This clearly was not what the proponents of countercyclical fiscal policy had in mind.

Do Governments Always Grow?

Although countercyclical fiscal policy sounds reasonable, putting it into practice is not easy. Spending programs, once introduced, are difficult to eliminate. Both the people benefiting from these programs and the government employees administering them lobby against spending cuts. Tax increases are also very unpopular. Politically, it is much easier to increase spending or cut taxes than it is to reduce spending or raise taxes.

Political realities coupled with growing government expenditures and deficits led many people to wonder if the natural course of events is for government to grow without limit. Can government restrain itself, or does the political process make it impossible for legislators to practice fiscal restraint without being voted out of office? Some economists and political observers believe that voluntary restraint on the part of government should not be expected. Some politicians agree. This has led to an intellectual and political backlash against the notion of countercyclical fiscal policy, not because it is faulty in theory, but because it has been used as an excuse to abandon the balanced budgets that once restrained government spending.

The Idea of a Balanced Budget Amendment

The tremendous growth of government deficits during the 1970s and into the 1980s generated support in the early 1980s for a balanced budget amendment to the Constitution. The idea behind such an amendment is simple: If our elected officials cannot or will not voluntarily restrain their deficit spending, we will alter the Constitution to force them to do so. Despite the support of President Reagan and a number of other prominent politicians, no balanced budget amendment came close to passage. However, an ordinary act of Congress with much the same intent — the *Gramm–Rudman–Hollings Act* — was passed into law in 1985. Gramm–Rudman–Hollings sets annual deficit targets for the government. If the budget deficit in one year exceeds the target, the government must either pass a plan to reduce the deficit or impose across-the-board spending cuts on most government programs.

Although drafting a workable balanced budget amendment appears simple, a number of complex issues are actually involved. The primary issue is how to define the budget deficit. Not all government spending or revenue shows up in the official budget. A substantial portion of federal government spending — almost $225 billion in 1990 — does not appear in the official budget. Similarly, a large portion of receipts is also omitted — nearly $282 billion in 1990. Such **off-budget items** include expenditures and receipts that are generated by the numerous federal agencies that operate under governmental authority, but with their own budgets.

Off-budget items Expenditures and receipts not included in the official U.S. government budget.

Another important issue is how capital expenditures are to be treated. Private corporations and state and local governments do not treat capital investment expenditures as current expenses. Instead, the cost of capital goods is spread out over time in the form of depreciation expenses. The federal government, on the other hand, lumps capital investment expenditures with current expenditures, treating investment spending as a current cost. This increases the size of *measured* federal deficits relative to state and local deficits. Indeed, the surpluses enjoyed by state and local governments in recent years (refer to Figure 4) would turn into deficits if state and local governments used the federal government's accounting system. Conversely, if the federal government treated capital spending as an investment in the future, rather than a current expense, the size of the federal deficit would be substantially smaller.

Another problem with a balanced budget amendment is that it gives the federal government the incentive to shift spending programs to state and local governments. By passing laws mandating state spending on particular programs, the federal government could expand total government spending without affecting the official federal budget. States would then be left with the problem of how to finance the newly mandated expenditures. For example, the federal government might pass legislation requiring states to make health insurance available to all people regardless of their ability to pay for it. States would then be left with the problem of funding the program.

How the federal government would cope with cyclical budget deficits under a balanced budget amendment is also unclear. A budget thought to be in balance or even in surplus can quickly go into deficit if the economy moves into an unexpected recession. Would legislators be fined or imprisoned for such cyclical deficits? Or would cyclical deficits be permitted, so long as they are offset by surpluses in expansion years? Perhaps the budget should be balanced over every four-year period instead of every year. Perhaps it should be balanced over the course of every business cycle. A number of possibilities exists.

SECTION RECAP
Rapid growth in government spending and the size of deficits has led many to call for a balanced budget amendment to the Constitution. A number of important problems arise when trying to construct such an amendment, including how the deficit is to be defined and over what *(continued)*

As you can see, implementing a practical balanced budget amendment would not be so simple as might first be supposed. Many technical choices would have to be made. As with any regulation, the amendment would provide the incentive to invent ways to circumvent the spirit of the law while staying within the letter of the law. Furthermore, focusing on balanced budgets rather than on the level of government spending and taxation relative to GNP ignores what many people consider to be the most important issue of government finance — how large should the government sector be? By financing higher expenditures with higher taxes, government could continue to grow even if its budget were balanced. Thus, many economists favor focusing on the ratio of government spending to GNP. By placing a limit on that ratio, Congress could constrain the percentage of the economy's resources controlled by government. If resource consumption, rather than financing, is of ultimate importance, this strategy is superior to a balanced budget approach.

What is the bottom line on a balanced budget amendment? Such an amendment would undoubtedly have a major impact on federal budget practices. Since tax increases are not popular, the growth of government would probably be restrained, but at the cost of reduced fiscal flexibility and diversion of federal programs to the states.

> **SECTION RECAP**
> *(continued)*
> period it should be balanced. Such an amendment would give the federal government the incentive to shift programs to the state governments.

Government Debt

The government debt is the total amount of government bonds outstanding. It represents the accumulation of all the deficits and surpluses generated by the federal government over the years. Deficits add to the national debt, surpluses subtract from it.

The huge additions to the nominal (current dollar) debt in recent years have led to increasing concern over the size of the debt. The belief that the debt is harmful to the economy appears to be widespread. Many people fear that future generations will be saddled with huge debts incurred by their parents and grandparents.

Are such fears reasonable? Is the national debt detrimental to the economic health of the nation? Or is the debt really harmless? We begin our search for answers to these questions by examining the size of the national debt. How big is the national debt, *really*? After examining this issue, we look at the future-generations question and then discuss two other issues related to the effect of the national debt on the economy.

How Large Is the National Debt?

The perception that the nominal value of the national debt has sharply increased is correct. Figure 17 illustrates this convincingly. After rising very little in the first two postwar decades, the debt began to grow more rapidly in the late 1960s. Then, in the early 1980s, the debt skyrocketed.

As with all nominal variables, however, inflation can distort our perception of the behavior of the national debt. If we measure the value of the debt in constant 1982 dollars, the picture is quite different. Figure 18 shows that the real value of the national debt fell from 1945 to 1970 almost without interruption. It rose sharply in the mid-1970s before leveling off and then shot upward again in the 1980s.

The real value of the debt is a better measure of the economic significance of the debt than the nominal value, because it accounts for price increases that have affected nearly all goods and services — and incomes. The increase in the real debt measures the amount by which nominal debt growth exceeds price level growth.

Another way to gauge the significance of the national debt is to compare it to gross national product. The ratio of debt to GNP tells us the percentage of a single year's GNP that would be required to pay off the entire national

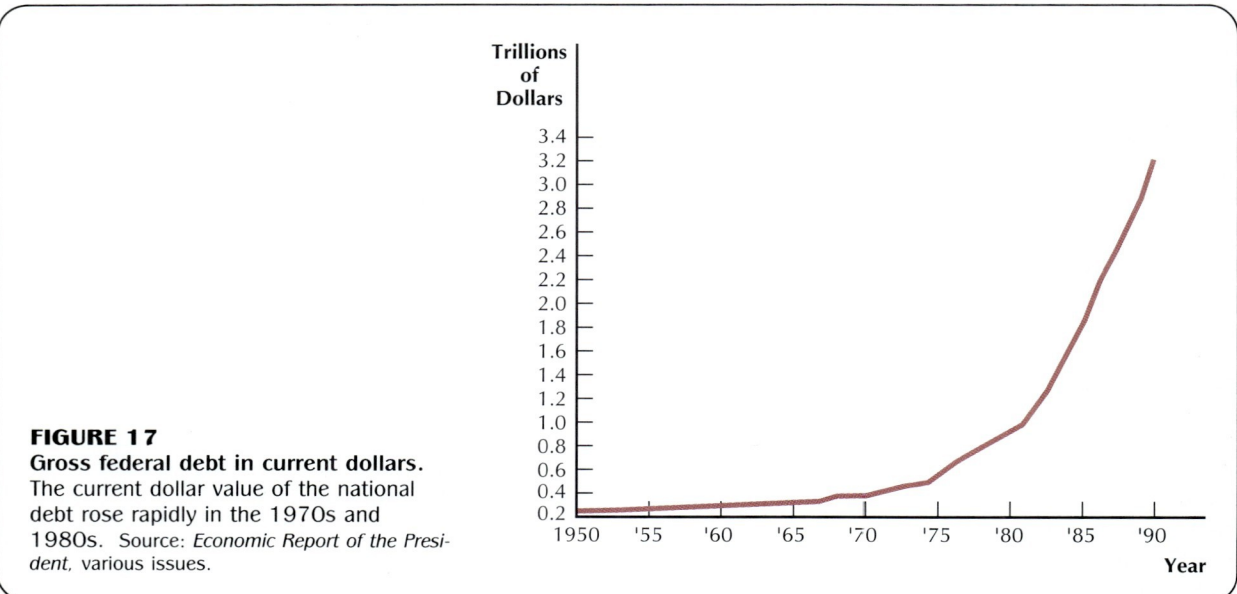

FIGURE 17
Gross federal debt in current dollars.
The current dollar value of the national debt rose rapidly in the 1970s and 1980s. Source: *Economic Report of the President*, various issues.

debt. Figure 19 shows that the debt–GNP ratio has fallen sharply since the end of World War II. Although the ratio rose in the 1980s, it still stands at a level lower than that reached during the 1950s and about equal to the level of the early 1960s.

By measuring the national debt in a number of different ways, we are able to assess its significance much better than by focusing only on the nominal value of the debt. All the debt measures surveyed indicate that the debt rose

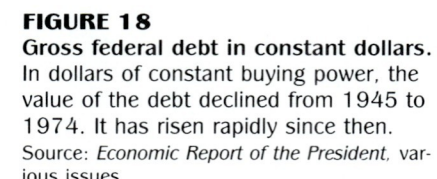

FIGURE 18
Gross federal debt in constant dollars.
In dollars of constant buying power, the value of the debt declined from 1945 to 1974. It has risen rapidly since then.
Source: *Economic Report of the President*, various issues.

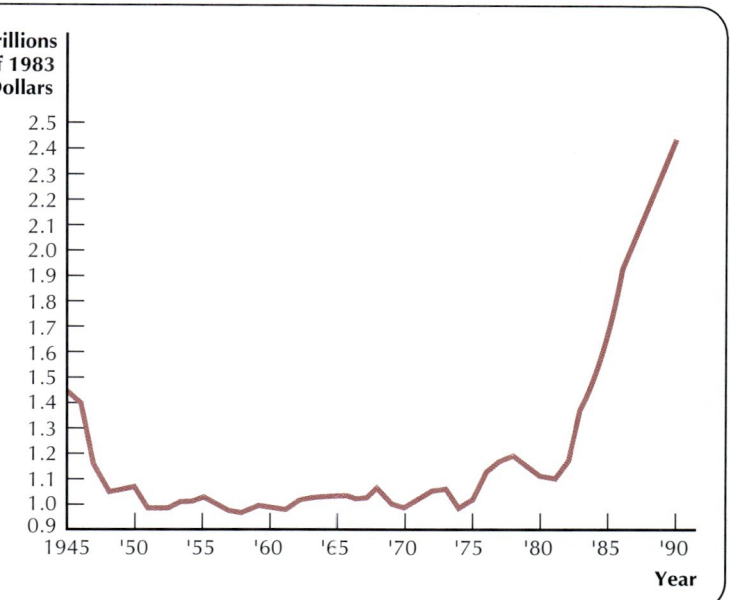

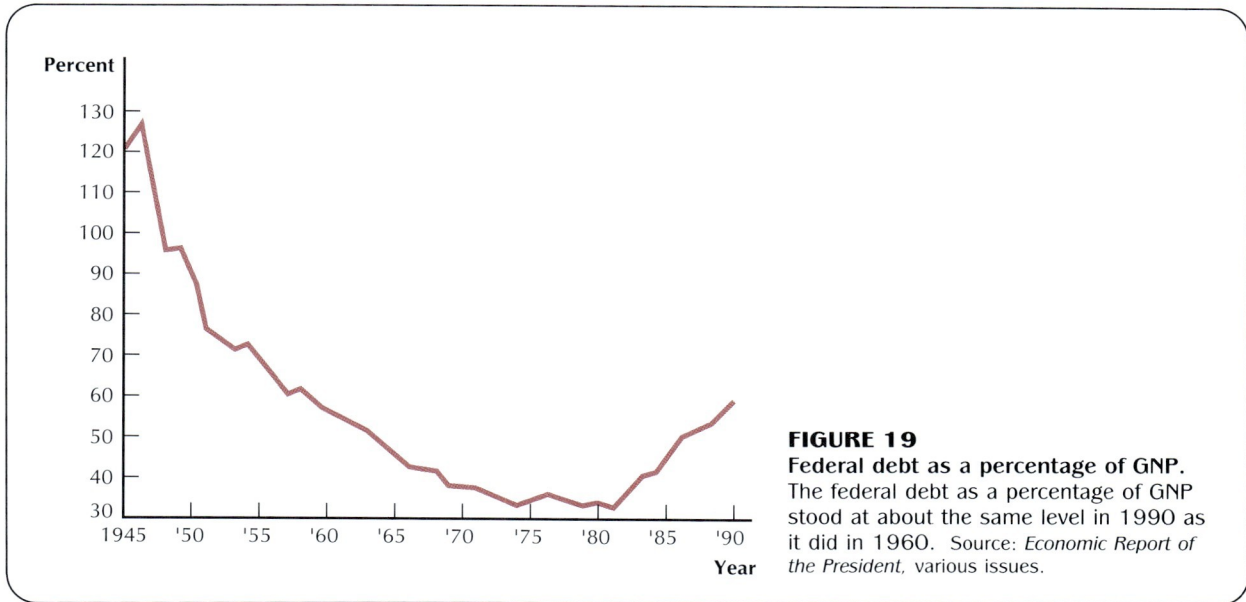

FIGURE 19
Federal debt as a percentage of GNP.
The federal debt as a percentage of GNP stood at about the same level in 1990 as it did in 1960. Source: *Economic Report of the President,* various issues.

in the 1980s. However, the debt–GNP ratio indicates that the current levels of national debt are not unprecedented. Although they may or may not be harmful to the economy, such levels have been experienced before.

Is the Debt a Burden on Future Generations?

One of the most widely expressed fears concerning the size of the national debt is that our generation is imposing a huge debt on future generations, forcing our children and grandchildren to sacrifice to pay for our excesses.

There are two responses to such a fear. The first response is to note that the nation's capacity to repay the debt — should it ever choose to do so — is higher than it was during most of the postwar period. The ratio of debt to GNP is no higher now than it was during the early 1960s.

The second response focuses on who owns the debt. It is estimated that in March 1990 U.S. citizens owned 56.2 percent of the national debt. Another 31.4 percent was held by government agencies or the Federal Reserve System. Only 12.5 percent was held by foreigners. In other words, almost 90 percent of the debt was owed to ourselves. However, the portion of the debt owned by foreigners grew throughout the 1980s (before falling slightly in 1990).

Because most of the debt is owed to Americans, it is not only a national liability but also a national asset. Millions of Americans hold much of their financial wealth — either directly or through financial intermediaries — in the form of U.S. government bonds. If the bonds were paid off, these Americans would receive the payments. Since taxes would have to be increased greatly, Americans owning bonds would also have to pay more. The net effect for individuals could be positive or negative. Some individuals would pay more in taxes than they would receive in debt repayments; others would pay less. Most of the repayments, however, would stay within the U.S. economy.

The portion of the national debt owned by foreigners is a liability for future taxpayers. If that portion of the debt must be repaid, tax dollars will flow out of American accounts and into foreign-owned accounts. Foreigners will be able to claim U.S. goods and services. The national debt owed to foreigners in March 1990 amounted to about 7.2 percent of GNP. Although not an insignificant figure, it does not appear to be a matter for major concern.

Other Possible Negative Effects of the Debt

Though the national debt may not be a heavy burden on future generations, it still may be costly. The major costs appear to be distributional; that is, they affect the way income is distributed across households. As the debt grows, the government must allocate more and more tax dollars to the payment of interest on the debt. Interest payments accounted for 14.6 percent of all federal expenditures in 1990, up from only 7.7 percent in 1978. In eleven years, the federal government lost control of another 6.9 percent of its expenditures, since interest payments are not optional. The government cannot simply choose to reduce them in order to increase spending on other programs. If the government's revenue is constrained, it must cut back on other programs to meet its interest payments.

Another potential cost of the debt concerns long-run economic growth. If households accumulate government debt issued to finance transfer payments and other government consumption programs rather than the debt of private corporations, the economy's capital stock may grow more slowly. This is the long-run component of the crowding-out problem. The future level of natural real GNP may be lower because of the large government debt.

Monetizing the Debt: Inflation and the Budget

When we examined the federal government's budget constraint, we noted that expenditures can be financed in three ways: taxes, borrowing, or increases in the monetary base. When the Federal Reserve finances government expenditures by purchasing government bonds, it creates additional base money. The increase in the monetary base sets off the money multiplier process, causing the money supply to increase by a multiple of the increase in the base. When the Federal Reserve substitutes new money for government bonds, we say it is monetizing the debt.

If using the normal methods of government finance—taxes and borrowing—becomes more difficult for political or economic reasons, monetization of the debt becomes more attractive. For example, suppose that the political climate is hostile to the notion of a tax increase. Further suppose that large-scale government borrowing has significantly increased credit demand, pushing the interest rate relatively high. If a tax increase is political poison and further borrowing would harm the economy by pushing interest rates even higher, the Federal Reserve may be tempted to intervene in an attempt to hold interest rates down. It may offset increased government borrowing by increasing the monetary base.

The short-term effects of debt monetization may be quite favorable. Taxes do not increase and the interest rate is held in check. However, the longer-run effects are not so positive. If a large amount of debt is monetized, the growth rate of the money supply will increase sharply, boosting aggregate demand. If the economy is operating near the natural level of output, where the aggregate

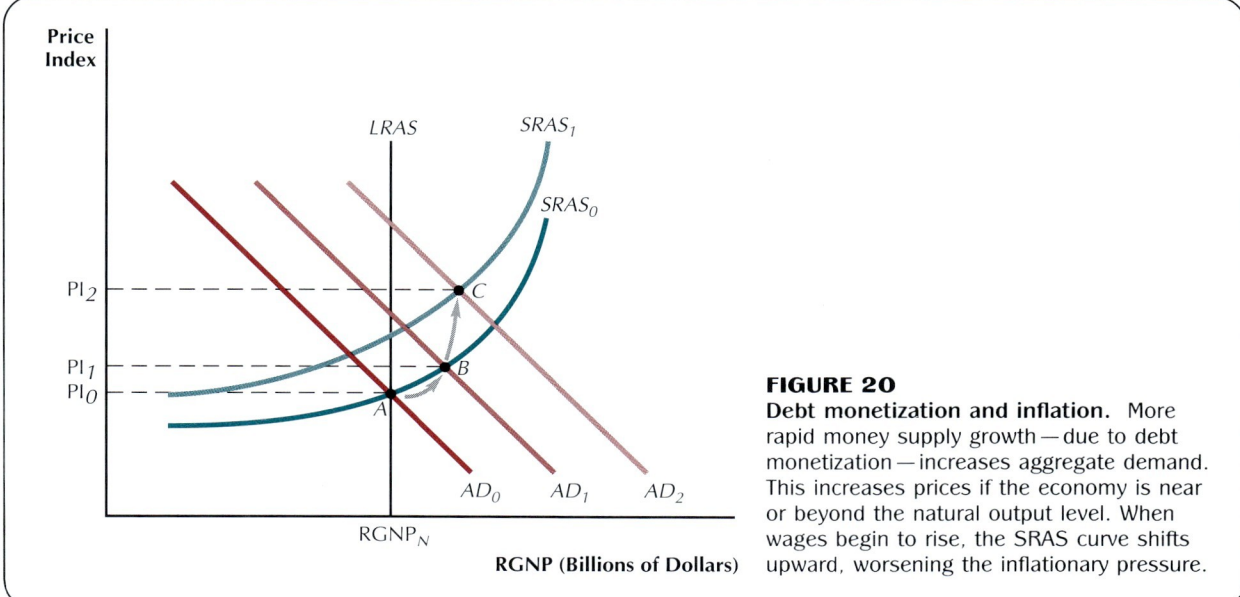

FIGURE 20
Debt monetization and inflation. More rapid money supply growth—due to debt monetization—increases aggregate demand. This increases prices if the economy is near or beyond the natural output level. When wages begin to rise, the SRAS curve shifts upward, worsening the inflationary pressure.

supply curve begins to be steep, increased aggregate demand generates strong inflationary pressures. So long as debt monetization continues, so will rapid money supply growth. The aggregate demand curve will be pushed up along the aggregate supply curve, as in Figure 20. When wages begin to catch up with rising prices, the short-run aggregate supply curve will also shift upward. Since nominal interest rates will rise because of inflation, the Federal Reserve's actions ultimately will fail to prevent the real interest rate from rising.

Little evidence exists that debt monetization in the United States has been an important source of inflation in the past except during major wars. However, the fear that the government could turn to debt monetization in the future causes some people to oppose large-scale deficit financing. Other nations, including Germany, Austria, and Hungary following World War I, have resorted to massive monetization to pay off large government debts. The result in each case was **hyperinflation**—inflation of thousands of percent per *month*. Although such hyperinflation is not likely in the United States, inflation at uncomfortably high levels could easily result from debt monetization. In view of the size of U.S. budget deficits and the resistance of Americans to tax increases or spending reductions, debt monetization and higher inflation remain a possibility.

Hyperinflation
Runaway inflation, sometimes of thousands of percent per month.

SECTION RECAP
Although the national debt has grown rapidly for the last decade, its size relative to GNP is not unprecedented. Most of the debt is owed to U.S. citizens or to government agencies. The biggest effects of the debt appear to be distributional.

Summary

Government is a major actor in the modern economic drama. **Total government spending** is over one third as large as gross national product. The largest single spending category is the purchase of goods and services by state and local governments. Federal government transfer payments rank second in size. Most government revenue comes from taxes. The federal government raises over 80 percent of its revenues through the individual income tax and payroll taxes.

Government purchases of goods and services affect aggregate demand directly and through the multiplier. The initial purchase of a good or service increases the demand for it while increasing the income of the supplier. Increased income promotes additional consumption spending. **Transfer payments** indirectly affect aggregate demand through their effect on household disposable income and enable **liquidity-constrained** households to consume at levels that would not otherwise be possible. The multiplier effect of transfer payments is smaller than the purchases multiplier because of the absence of any direct effect.

Government purchases of goods and services may add to future productive capacity, thus qualifying as investment spending, or they may finance current consumption. Government investment spending increases aggregate supply in the future both directly and through its positive effect on private investment spending.

A permanent increase in income taxes reduces aggregate demand by reducing consumption spending. Taxes also affect investment spending by affecting after-tax profits. The **investment tax credit** promotes investment spending by allowing businesses to reduce their tax payments by some percentage of the purchase price of fixed capital goods, effectively lowering the price of investment goods.

The federal government's **budget deficit** has reached unprecedented peacetime levels during the 1980s. The size of the **national debt** has risen dramatically. The debt–GNP ratio is smaller now than it was during the 1945–1960 period, however. This fact undercuts much of the fear that the debt places a heavy **burden on future generations.** The fact that over 85 percent of the debt is owed by U.S. citizens to themselves further reduces the fear that the debt is extremely harmful. Nevertheless, an increasing debt increases the percentage of government spending that must go to meet interest payments and supports government consumption expenditures at the expense of capital accumulation. It also raises the fear that the Federal Reserve might decide to **monetize the debt,** thus generating substantial inflation.

Questions for Thought

Knowledge Questions

1. Classify spending on each of the following items as either government purchases of goods and services or transfer payments:
   a. Aid to Families with Dependent Children payment.
   b. Salary of a caseworker in the Aid to Families with Dependent Children program.
   c. Salary of a U.S. Senator.
   d. A new municipal sewer system.
   e. A federal scholarship grant to a college student.
2. Define *high employment budget deficit*. Why is it a useful concept?
3. What is *countercyclical fiscal policy*? Has the notion worked well in practice? Explain.
4. What does it mean to *monetize the debt*? What harmful effects might come from such monetization?

Application Questions

5. Why is the multiplier effect generated by a change in government purchases larger than the multiplier effect following from a change in transfer payments?
6. What is the effect on aggregate demand and aggregate supply — in the present or the future — of the following?
   a. Increased spending on resurfacing the interstate highway system.
   b. Increased Social Security payments financed by higher Social Security taxes.
   c. The elimination of investment tax credits.
   d. The erection of a new government office building.
7. How does a 10 percent investment tax credit affect the demand for fixed capital goods? Explain not only the direction of the effect but also the reason it occurs.
8. What effect would eliminating the taxation of interest earnings have on saving and investment? What would be the effect on aggregate demand and supply?

Synthesis Questions

9. Explain the theoretical connection between government deficits and the growth of aggregate supply. Does theory imply that there *must* be a particular connection?
10. Is government spending harmful to the economy? (Consider your answer carefully. On what does government spend? How is it financed? Not all economists agree on the answer to this question.)
11. Explain how government deficits may *crowd out* private spending. When is crowding out likely to be a significant problem?
12. The Ricardian Equivalence Principle maintains that tax and deficit financing have equivalent effects. What conditions must hold for the principle to be true?
13. Have the large federal deficits in recent years placed a large burden on future generations of Americans? Explain.

OVERVIEW

In most markets, prices move relatively quickly to equate the quantity demanded with the quantity supplied. Sometimes stores are forced to run sales to rid themselves of excessively large inventories of goods, but a sale is nothing more than a price reduction in the attempt to clear the market. However, the labor market contrasts sharply with other markets. In the labor market, quantity demanded never seems to equal quantity supplied; unemployment is a constant fact of economic life.

Several million Americans are always counted as unemployed. In this chapter we seek to develop an understanding of what unemployment is, why it exists, and what can be done about it. We begin by briefly recalling how the simple labor market model handles (or fails to handle) unemployment. We then investigate what unemployment is, using the procedures developed by modern labor economists to describe unemployment. We also relate unemployment to the macroeconomic model developed in earlier chapters.

After coming to grips with what unemployment is, we provide an explanation for it. We do this in two stages, first by examining the shortcomings of the simple

Labor Market Rigidities and Unemployment

CHAPTER 31

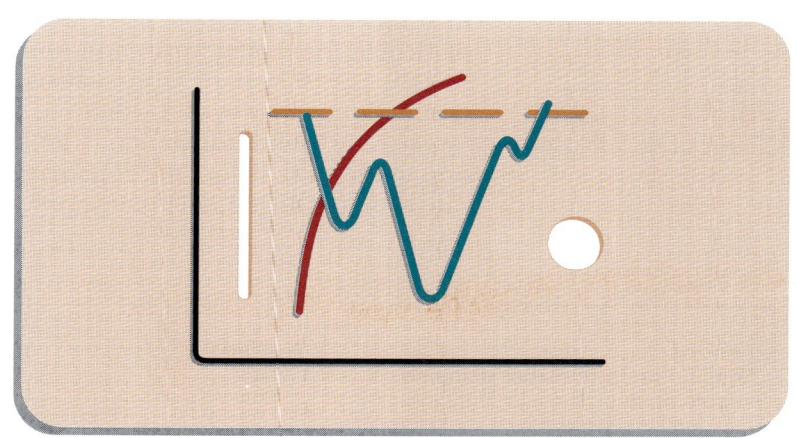

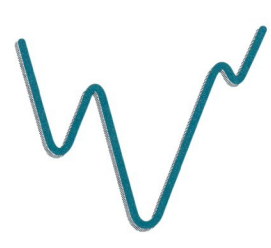

labor demand–labor supply model, then by developing two complementary theories that attempt to explain the existence of unemployment and changes in the level of unemployment. Finally, after developing an understanding of unemployment, we end with a discussion of some possible policy options.

Learning Objectives

After reading and studying this chapter, you will be able to:

1. Define the term *unemployment* as used by economists and list the three categories unemployment can be broken into.
2. State the reasons the simple labor demand–labor supply model fails to adequately explain the existence of unemployment.
3. Explain how the search model improves on the simple labor market model's explanation of labor market behavior.
4. Discuss the benefits derived by employers and employees from entering into implicit or explicit labor contracts.
5. State the types of policy actions that should be successful in reducing unemployment, as well as the types that should have only temporary or negligible effects.

Labor Demand, Labor Supply, and Unemployment

In developing the theory of aggregate supply we made use of a simple demand–supply model of the labor market. We argued that labor demand depends on the marginal productivity of workers, the prices of the goods workers produce, and the wage rate the workers earn. Since the marginal productivity of labor declines in the short run, when the quantity of capital is fixed, the labor demand curve slopes negatively, as shown in Figure 1. Labor supply depends on demographic variables, such as the working-age population, social attitudes toward work, the expected price level, and the wage rate. Because the quantity of labor supplied increases as the expected real wage rate rises, the labor supply curve slopes positively for any given expected price level.

The equilibrium wage rate and level of employment are determined by the intersection of labor demand and labor supply. Changes in productivity, the price level, or the expected price level shift the labor demand or supply curve, altering the equilibrium wage and employment levels. The model's predicted effects correspond to our observations of the real world in most cases. However, in some ways the simple labor demand–supply model is sorely lacking. In particular, the model leaves no room for unemployment.

The U.S. Bureau of Labor Statistics uses a monthly survey to calculate the number of unemployed. It counts as **unemployed** anyone without a job who has actively looked for work or who has been on temporary layoff from a job during the week before the employment survey is taken. The **unemployment rate** is simply the number of unemployed divided by the number of employed

Unemployed
Anyone without a job who has actively looked for work or who has been on temporary layoff during the week before the employment survey is taken.

Unemployment rate
Number of unemployed as a percentage of the labor force.

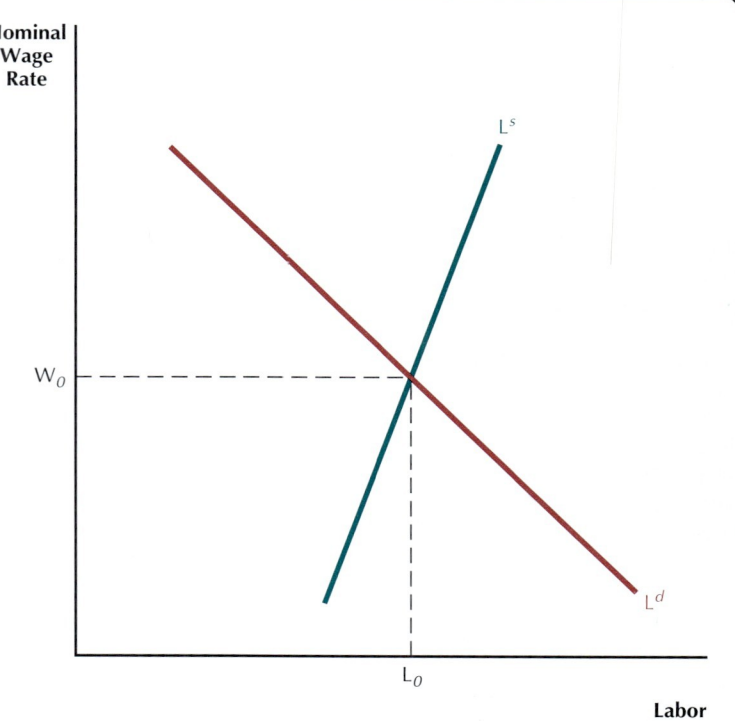

FIGURE 1
Equilibrium in the labor demand–supply model. The equilibrium wage rate and employment level are determined by the intersection of the labor demand and supply curves. At equilibrium, there is no unemployment in this model.

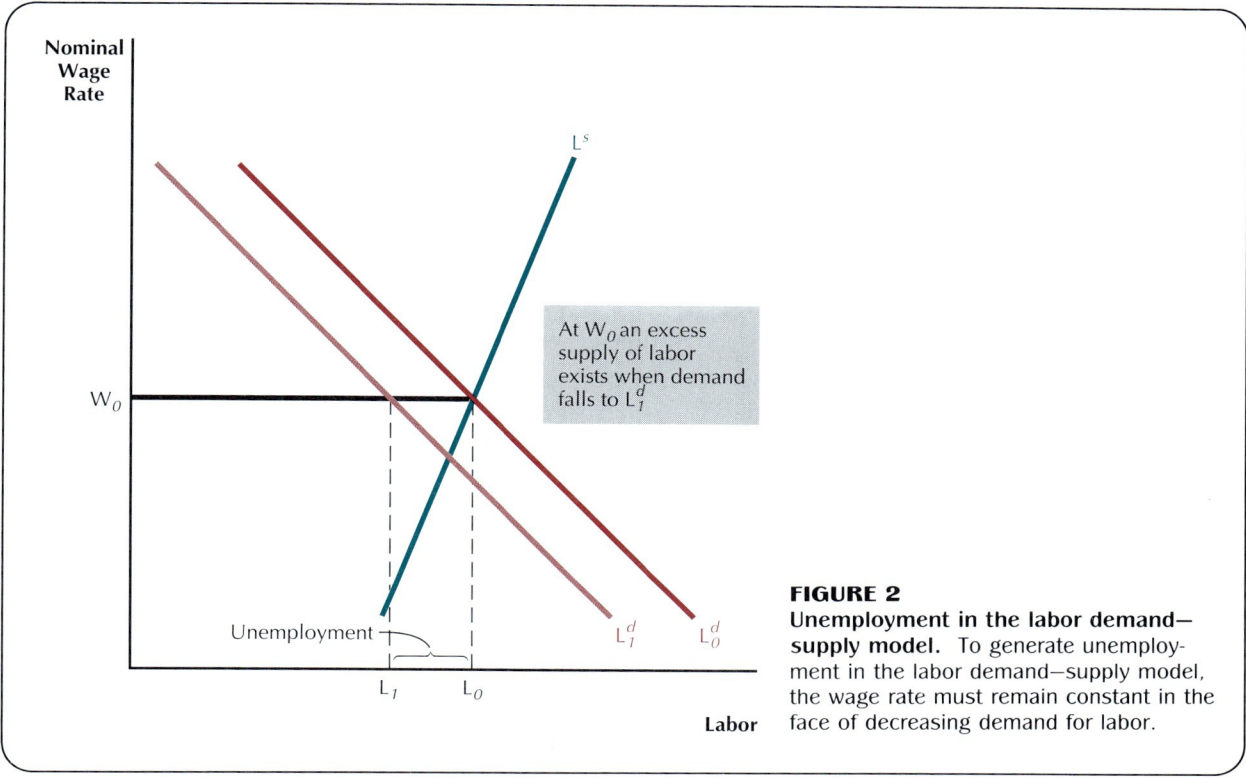

FIGURE 2
Unemployment in the labor demand–supply model. To generate unemployment in the labor demand–supply model, the wage rate must remain constant in the face of decreasing demand for labor.

plus the number of unemployed, a total called the **labor force**. That is:

$$u = \frac{\text{(number of unemployed)}}{\text{(labor force)}}$$

We can generate unemployment in the labor demand–supply model by assuming that the wage rate remains constant when labor demand decreases. Figure 2 shows this possibility. If the wage rate remains constant at W_0 in the face of declining labor demand, firms respond by employing fewer workers. The workers laid off or fired by firms, $L_0 - L_1$ in Figure 2, would be counted as unemployed.

Two problems arise from using the demand–supply model in this way to explain unemployment. The first problem is explaining why the wage rate is rigid in the face of falling labor demand. Why doesn't the wage rate adjust to clear the market? The second problem with using the demand–supply model in this way is that unemployment exists *all the time,* even when the economy is booming. The combination of wage rigidity and falling labor demand explains only the portion of unemployment that arises during recessions.

It is obvious that the simple labor demand–supply model is not adequate to the task of explaining the existence of unemployment. We need to discover why it is inadequate to be able to develop a model that overcomes the simple model's shortcomings. However, before we turn to the task of explaining why unemployment exists, we need to know a bit more about the forms unemployment takes.

Labor force
Number of employed plus the number of unemployed.

Aggregate Unemployment

The labor market is a study in change. People are constantly moving into and out of jobs, and even into and out of the labor force altogether, thus leaving one labor market category to move into another. In this section we develop a model of unemployment that helps organize our thinking about unemployment. We call this model the **flow model of unemployment**, because it stresses the flow of people into and out of the employment and unemployment categories.

Flow model of unemployment Model based on the flow of people into and out of employment and unemployment categories.

Flow Model of Unemployment

The modern theory of unemployment focuses on the flows of people into and out of three pools into which the working-age population is grouped. All noninstitutionalized people age 16 and over are classified as (1) employed, (2) unemployed, or (3) not in the labor force. People in the third category are people who do not have a job outside the home and are not looking for one. Examples of such people include homemakers, full-time students, and retirees. Figure 3 illustrates the three labor market categories and the flows we will analyze.

The flow labeled number 1 is the flow of new entrants and reentrants to the labor force who find jobs with no period of unemployment. These people move directly from a condition of not wanting employment to having a job without spending any time unemployed and searching for work. Included in this flow would be women who return to previously held jobs after taking time off to have a child.

Flow number 2 includes those people who leave jobs in order to withdraw from the labor force. Retirees fit into this category, as do individuals who decide to return to school full time.

The third flow is from the unemployed pool to the employed. This flow includes job finders (successful searchers) and people recalled from layoff.

Flow number 4 measures the number of people who want to work, but who are fired or laid off or who choose to quit their current jobs. These people

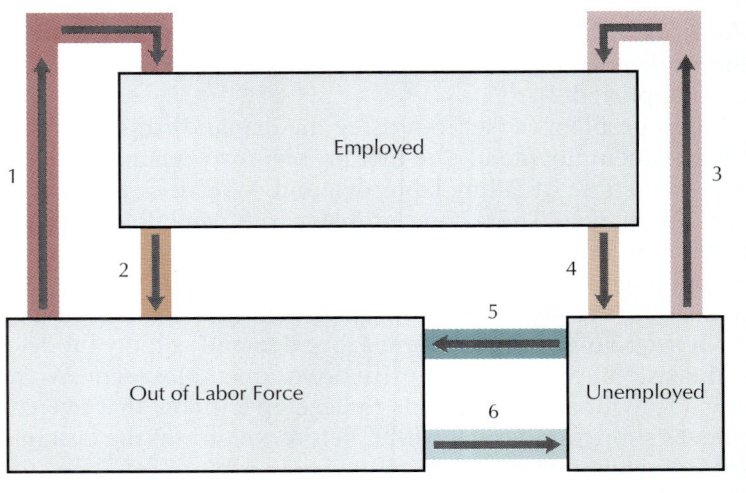

FIGURE 3
Labor market flows. People are constantly moving from one labor market category to another through one of six channels.

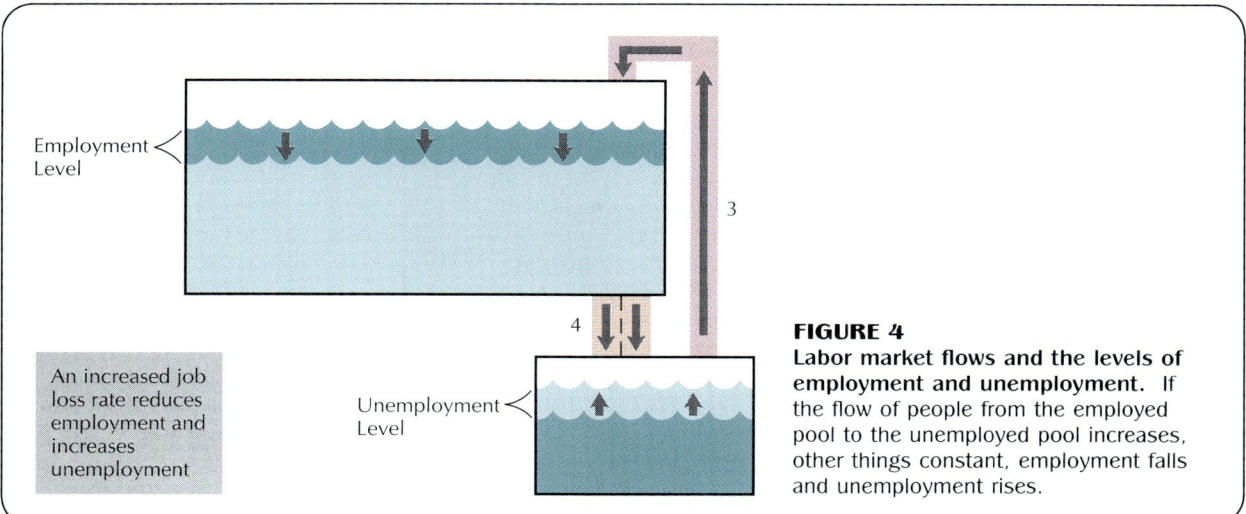

FIGURE 4
Labor market flows and the levels of employment and unemployment. If the flow of people from the employed pool to the unemployed pool increases, other things constant, employment falls and unemployment rises.

remain in the labor force by searching for new jobs or standing ready to return to their previous jobs.

Many of the individuals included in flow 5 are *discouraged workers* — people whose job search efforts have been unsuccessful for a long period of time. After a while, they become convinced that search is useless, and they drop out of the labor force altogether.

Many of the individuals in flow 5 return to the labor force via flow number 6 after a relatively short period outside the labor force. Others included in flow 6 are new entrants and reentrants to the labor force who require some search time to obtain employment.

The unemployment rate depends upon the volume of people flowing into and out of the employment and unemployment pools via these six channels. If U stands for the number of people in the unemployment pool and L is the number of people employed, then the unemployment rate is:

$$u = U/(L + U)$$

Note that $L + U$ is the size of the labor force, those people with jobs plus those searching for jobs.

The unemployment rate rises if the number of people flowing into the unemployed pool exceeds the number flowing out. Consider the simplified flow diagram presented in Figure 4, which focuses on flows 3 and 4. Assume that the unemployment rate initially is constant. What would happen if the rate at which workers were flowing from the employed pool into the unemployed pool (number 4) increased? The effect would be the same as opening a larger hole in the bottom of a bathtub while allowing water to flow into the tub at a constant rate. The water level in the tub would fall. Here the employment level falls while the unemployment level rises. Since U gets larger while $L + U$ remains the same size, the unemployment rate rises.

Economists focus on two statistics that determine the rates of flow into and out of the unemployment pool: frequency of unemployment and duration of unemployment. **Frequency of unemployment** is a measure of the number of unemployment spells that begin in a period of time. The greater the fre-

Frequency of unemployment
A measure of the number of unemployment spells that begin in a time period.

Does It Make Economic Sense?

Average Unemployment Duration and the Long-Term Unemployed

Most unemployment spells are of rather short duration. Except during severe recessions, the percentage of unemployment spells lasting fourteen weeks or less exceeds 70 percent. In the face of this evidence, it is interesting to note that a recent study of unemployment concluded, "Most unemployment, even in tight labor markets [expansion periods], is characterized by relatively few persons who are out of work a large part of the time."* The economists conducting this study are fully aware of the unemployment duration data cited in this chapter. Does this make economic sense? How is it possible for most unemployment spells to be of short duration if most unemployment is due to individuals who are out of work much of the time? These two facts seem to be contradictory. In fact, they are not contradictory, and understanding the truth of both statements provides us with important insights into the policy problems posed by unemployment.

Consider the unemployment situation illustrated in Figure 5. This diagram shows the unemployment experience of ten individuals, labeled A through J. Each line segment represents a period of unemployment. The length of the line segment corresponds to the duration of the unemployment spell.

Fifteen unemployment spells are shown in Figure 5. The total number of people-weeks of unemployment experienced by the ten individuals is 119. Thus, the average duration of an unemployment spell is 119/15 = 7.93 weeks. Furthermore, thirteen of the fifteen spells are fourteen weeks or shorter in length. Thus, we could characterize 86.7 percent of the unemployment spells shown as short term. The story told by these numbers seems to roughly correspond to the actual evidence for the United States.

How much of the unemployment in the diagram is due to lengthy unemployment spells? You might be tempted to say 13.3 percent (100 − 86.7 = 13.3), but that number understates the significance of long-term unemployment. Of the 119 people-weeks of unemployment shown, fifty are due to two unemployment spells. Individual C had a twenty-week spell, and individual I suffered a thirty-week spell. Together, these two long-term spells accounted for 50/119 = 42 percent of total unemployment.

If we look at individuals who were unemployed for more than fifteen weeks during this period, we find that individual C was unemployed a total of twenty-seven weeks, individual I a total of thirty weeks, and individual J a total of seventeen weeks. These three individuals accounted for 74/119 = 62 percent of total unemployment. Thus, it is possible for most unemployment spells to be of short duration, while most unemployment is experienced by a relatively few individuals.

Another factor that may distort the unemployment picture is the number of workers who interrupt their unemployment spells by dropping out of the labor force for short periods of time. The flow of people from the unemployed pool to the out-of-the-labor-force pool and back (flows 5 and 6 in Figure 3) are large relative to the flows from the employed to unemployed pools and back (flows 3 and 4). Many unemployed workers seem to stop searching for work for short periods of time, thus technically dropping out of the unemployed category. The distinction between being unemployed and being out of the labor force is fuzzy.

Breaking up a period of unemployment by temporarily dropping out of the labor force reduces the estimated average duration of an unemployment spell. Suppose that worker C in Figure 5 remained jobless for the four weeks between his two unemployment spells. For whatever reason, he simply stopped looking for work for a month. If we count the entire period he is out of work as a single *nonemployment* spell, the period is thirty-one weeks long. Calculating the average duration of nonemployment for our example — assuming that C is the only temporary labor force dropout — increases our estimate significantly. Now total weeks of nonemployment equals 123, spread over four-

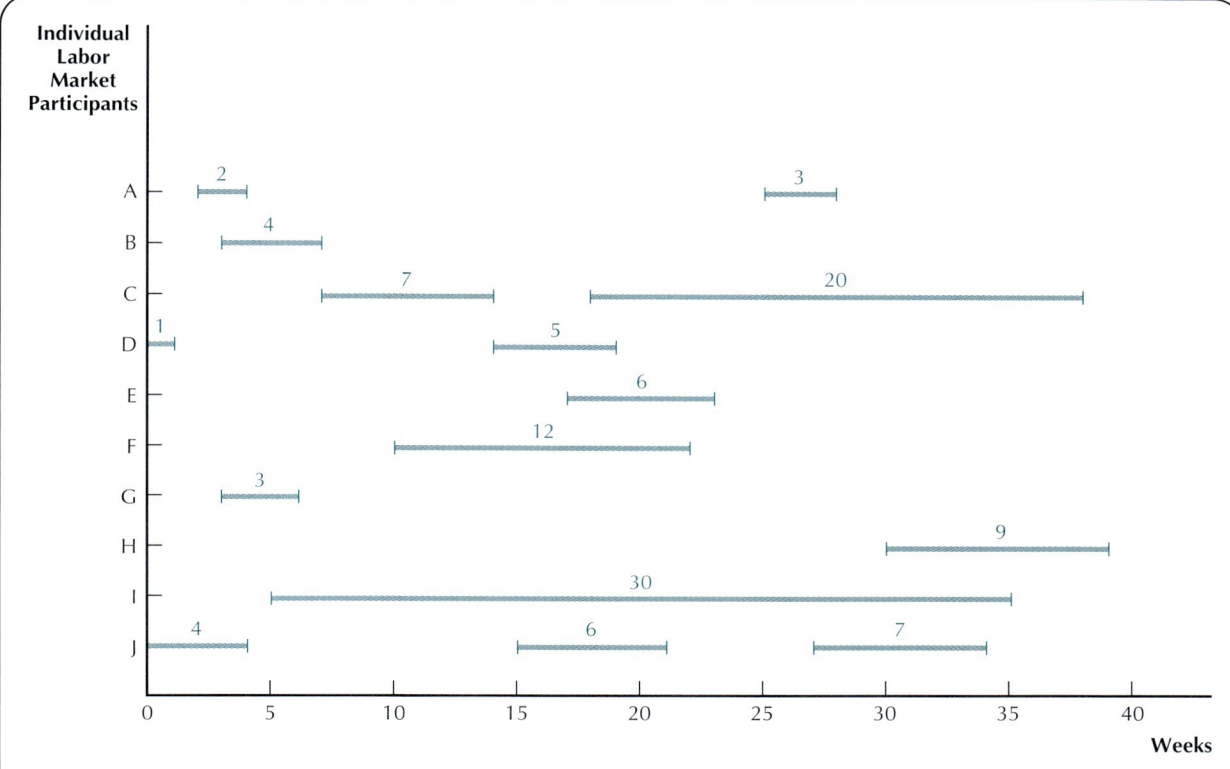

FIGURE 5
Individual unemployment spells and the duration of unemployment. Even though most unemployment spells are short, as is the average duration of an unemployment spell, most of the time spent unemployed may be suffered by relatively few people. In this example, individuals C and I suffer a disproportionate share of total unemployment.

teen spells. The average duration of nonemployment is 123/14 = 8.79 weeks, an increase of 10.7 percent over the estimated average duration of unemployment. The implications of this analysis for policy are important. Unemployment should not be viewed as harmless simply because most unemployment spells are short. Most unemployment is experienced by a relatively small number of people who may be significantly harmed by it.

*Kim B. Clark and Lawrence H. Summers, "Labor Market Dynamics and Unemployment: A Reconsideration," *Brookings Papers on Economic Activity,* 1979:1, p. 14.

TABLE 1
Unemployment duration

Year	Percent of Unemployed Out of Work for			
	Less than 5 Weeks	5–14 Weeks	15–26 Weeks	More than 26 Weeks
1967 (expansion)	55	30	9	6
1971 (recession)	45	32	13	10
1975 (recession)	37	31	17	15
1979 (expansion)	48	32	11	9
1982 (recession)	36	31	16	17
1989 (expansion)	49	30	11	10

Source: *Economic Report of the President, 1990*, Table C-41.

Duration of unemployment
Length of time spent unemployed.

SECTION RECAP
The flow model of unemployment shows the flows of people into and out of three pools: employed, unemployed, and out of the labor force. The number of people unemployed depends on the frequency and the duration of unemployment spells.

Frictional unemployment
Short-term unemployment arising because moving from one job to another takes time.

---

quency, the larger the size of flow 4 from the employed pool to the unemployed pool. All other things constant, an increase in the frequency of unemployment raises the unemployment rate.

The **duration of unemployment** is the amount of time spent unemployed by each of the individuals flowing into the unemployed pool. An increase in the average duration of unemployment means that the unemployed remain on the average in the unemployed pool for a longer period of time. Other things equal, this decreases the flow out of the unemployed pool (number 3) and increases the unemployment rate.

Most unemployment spells are of rather short duration; even during recessions most unemployment spells last less than fifteen weeks. Table 1 provides data on the percentage of unemployed workers out of work for various lengths of time for several recent years. Note that during recession years, the percentage of workers with unemployment spells longer than five weeks increases substantially.

The extremely long periods of unemployment endured by a minority of the unemployed suggests that perhaps they have problems that differ from those encountered by the majority of the unemployed, who return to employment in less than fifteen weeks. This line of thinking has led economists to separate unemployment into three categories, each describing a different problem and requiring a different solution.

Categories of Unemployment

Economists divide unemployment into three categories: frictional (or turnover) unemployment, structural unemployment, and cyclical unemployment.

Frictional (Turnover) Unemployment   **Frictional unemployment** includes people unemployed for a relatively short period of time while searching for employment. Frictional unemployment arises because neither labor market information nor mobility is perfect. Some time is required for searchers to acquire information about available jobs and for firms to obtain information about job candidates or potential job candidates. In addition to the absence of perfect information, new job openings may be in different locations than the unemployed are. Some time may pass before searchers pull up their roots and move to a new location.

Some amount of frictional unemployment always exists in a dynamic economy. If people are allowed to change jobs, some people inevitably will spend some time unemployed. Not all frictional unemployment is desirable, however. If information about employment possibilities and searcher characteristics could be more widely disseminated, the frictional rate might be lowered. The whole economy would benefit from such a reduction in unemployment if the cost of providing the information were relatively low.

Structural Unemployment   A small but significant minority of people unemployed at any point in time are in the midst of periods of long-term unemployment. The problem faced by the chronically unemployed is not informational and often has little to do with immobility. Economists define **structural unemployment** as unemployment resulting from a lack of worker skills or a mismatch between worker skills and job requirements. The long-term unemployed may be out of work for extended periods for one of several reasons, including (1) changes in demand conditions or technology that have eliminated certain types of jobs, (2) changes in world trade patterns that have transferred certain types of production to other countries, and (3) a lack of attractive skills and a good work record.

Structural unemployment Long-term unemployment arising from the mismatch of job requirements and worker characteristics.

Structural unemployment is usually considered to be much more serious than frictional unemployment. Since frictional unemployment measures the turnover between jobs, most individuals who are frictionally unemployed can be expected to return to work within a fairly short period of time. Not so for the structurally unemployed, many of whom have no job prospects other than low-paying, unskilled positions. Some accept such jobs, but others remain unemployed while looking for jobs that match their skill levels or customary wages.

Who are the structurally unemployed? Some concrete examples include steelworkers whose jobs were terminated when many of the steel mills in western Pennsylvania shut down. Because of worldwide excess capacity in steel production, many of these mills will never reopen. Thus, many skilled steelworkers will never return to their former occupations. Skilled and highly paid in steelworking, they find themselves unskilled with respect to other occupations.

Another example of the structurally unemployed are people raised in some of the blighted inner-city neighborhoods of many large, old cities. Manufacturing firms long ago moved out of most inner-city areas, and more recently small businesses have followed. Growing up in conditions of chronic unemployment with no unskilled jobs available in which to acquire experience, many inner-city residents find themselves virtually unemployable by the time they are 25 or 30 years old.

Cyclical Unemployment   The third category of unemployment arises from a macroeconomic problem. **Cyclical unemployment** arises when aggregate demand declines and wages do not fall to clear the labor market.[1] Firms quit hiring,

Cyclical unemployment Unemployment arising from a decline in aggregate demand.

---

[1] Cyclical unemployment is the one type of unemployment the labor demand–supply model is able to explain.

Why the **Disagreement?**

Path to a Career or Just a Dead-End Job?

More American teenagers get their start in the labor market working for McDonald's than for any other corporation. McDonald's currently employs some 240,000 teenagers in over eight thousand restaurants. Other fast food chains also employ large numbers of young people. For many, perhaps most, of these teenagers, frying hamburgers or waiting on customers is their first real job.

A job in a fast food restaurant is especially important to many inner-city youths, who have virtually no other employment options. For many teenagers from poor households, a job at McDonald's means more than just spending money; it may mean adequate meals for the family. Yet earning a living working in a fast food restaurant is no picnic. The pace is often hectic, and the pay is low. Such negative characteristics have led critics of McDonald's and other large fast food chains to charge that the corporations are exploiting America's youth by offering dead-end jobs to those who have no alternatives. However, this viewpoint has not gone unchallenged. Some defenders of the fast food chains have argued that they provide benefits to their employees that go beyond mere wages. Why the disagreement?

Critics of the large fast food chains say that the companies benefit at the expense of people with few options. To earn a profit in the competitive fast food business, a company must hold down its costs. It does this in two ways: by stressing efficiency and by holding down wages. Fast food workers are expected to serve customers promptly, and their speed is timed and recorded by managers. This puts pressure on the young workers to perform. Since the work performed in fast food restaurants is unskilled, wages are low. Turnover is high—McDonald's loses over 70 percent of its work force each year—but replacements can be trained quickly.

---

and new entrants into the labor force cannot find jobs. Cyclical unemployment is caused by insufficient aggregate demand. When the economy moves into an expansion period and output reaches the natural output level, cyclical unemployment disappears. In this respect, it is quite different from structural unemployment, which is relatively unaffected by cyclical conditions.

Natural Rate of Unemployment

Natural rate of unemployment Unemployment rate that exists when the labor market is in long-run equilibrium and toward which the actual unemployment rate tends over time.

The macroeconomic model in this book focuses on the natural level of output toward which the actual output level tends over time. Such a model implies the existence of a **natural rate of unemployment**—an unemployment rate toward which the actual unemployment rate tends. When the labor market has fully adjusted to a change in the price level, and employment has returned to its long-run equilibrium level, some unemployment still exists. Dividing this equilibrium level of unemployment by the labor force yields the natural rate of unemployment. Cyclical swings in the economy cause the actual unemployment rate to deviate from the natural rate much of the time, but the actual rate always tends to return to the natural rate.

The natural rate of unemployment is composed of frictional and structural unemployment. When cyclical unemployment is zero (and the economy is operating at the natural output level), the actual unemployment rate equals the natural rate. Since the actual unemployment rate can be lower than the natural rate, cyclical unemployment can be negative at times. Cyclical unemployment is negative whenever the economy is in an expansion period and is growing at a rate that cannot be sustained for very long. The late 1960s provide an excellent example of such a period.

Where does hard work and determination get a person in the fast food business? Critics argue that it gets them nowhere. If they remain with the company, they are likely to continue in low-paying unskilled jobs indefinitely. If they leave the company, they have obtained no salable skills from their employment. Either way they lose. The conclusion that fast food employees gain nothing of lasting value from their employment has recently been challenged. Defenders of fast food employment, such as Ben Wildasky of the Heritage Foundation, argue that working for McDonald's may give inner-city youths exactly the job skills they need the most: discipline, punctuality, responsibility, courtesy, and the ability to follow directions. Wildasky argues that "McDonald's functions as a de facto job-training program by teaching the basics of *how* to work."*

Many inner-city youths grow up in a culture that differs radically from the dominant American culture in terms of work habits and expectations. Lacking role models, inner-city teens often know little about the basic work habits required to hold a job. Lacking such work habits, they have little chance of ever landing a job with prospects for advancement. However, working at McDonald's teaches the basic skills that such teenagers need. It also gives young people a sense of teamwork and pride of accomplishment, thus adding to their self-esteem.

Dead-end job or a start on a career? Undoubtedly, the value of a job at McDonald's varies from person to person. Highly motivated young people may use a job flipping hamburgers as a springboard to a skilled job with higher pay. Unmotivated workers may earn enough to survive and never move on to anything better. The variety of possible results is sure to keep the disagreement about the value of such jobs alive for some time.

*Quoted in Marcus Mabry, "Inside the Golden Arches," *Newsweek*, December 18, 1989, p. 46.

The behavior of the actual unemployment rate in relation to the natural rate is illustrated in Figure 6. The actual unemployment rate has, of course, been much more erratic than the natural rate. Given time, however, the actual rate has tended to move toward the natural rate. The natural rate itself has changed over time, increasing in the 1970s and leveling off in the 1980s.

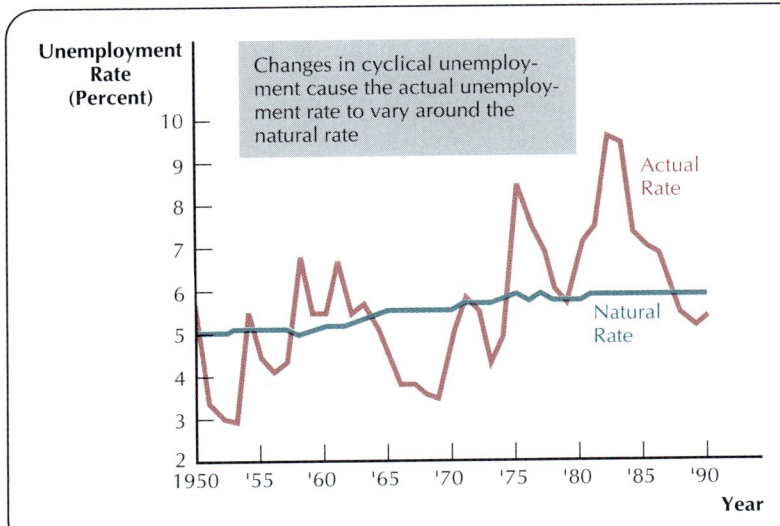

FIGURE 6
Actual and natural unemployment rates. The actual unemployment rate fluctuates around the natural rate of unemployment. Sources: *Economic Report of the President, 1991*, Table B-40, and Robert J. Gordon, *Macroeconomics*, 5th edition (Boston: Scott Foresman, Little, Brown, 1990), Data Appendix.

Factors Affecting the Natural Rate of Unemployment The natural rate of unemployment is the rate the economy naturally tends to produce given the technological, institutional, governmental, and demographic factors existing in the economy. The natural rate is not necessarily the desirable or best unemployment rate, nor is it fixed and unchanging. Changes in both market conditions and government social and tax policies can significantly affect the natural rate.

In general, anything *other than price level changes* that affects the incentive of firms to hire workers or of workers to supply labor alters the natural rate of unemployment. The following is an incomplete list of factors that affect the natural rate of unemployment:

1. Demographic factors: The age–sex composition of the labor force is an important determinant of the natural rate of unemployment. Much of the increase in the natural rate from the 1950s to the 1970s was due to the increased labor force participation of adult women and the entry into the labor force of a relatively large number of young workers (the baby-boom generation). In the 1980s, both of these factors abated, and the natural rate stabilized.

2. Technology, resource availability, and the capital stock: The productivity of labor, and hence the demand for labor, is affected greatly by the factors that are combined with labor services in the production process. More rapid growth in the capital stock can increase the demand for labor, reducing the natural rate of unemployment.

3. Government income maintenance programs: The federal government, as well as most state governments, supports a host of income maintenance programs. These programs range from unemployment insurance benefits to food stamps. By providing individuals with income while they are unemployed, income maintenance programs reduce the incentive to obtain a job quickly. Longer search efforts are now feasible. Hence, income maintenance programs, by lowering the cost of being unemployed, increase the average duration of unemployment and thereby increase the unemployment rate. The effect of popular income maintenance programs on the unemployment rate destroys the argument that the unemployment rate should be as low as possible. One way to reduce the unemployment rate would be to curtail such income maintenance programs as unemployment insurance benefits and food stamps. However, it is not at all clear that society would benefit from a lower unemployment rate obtained in such a manner. Thus, it is important to realize that a positive unemployment rate is not automatically bad, but may be one of the side effects of policies considered humane and appropriate for a wealthy society.

4. Government tax and regulatory policies: The optimal production level of a firm may be affected in a variety of ways by taxes or regulations. Tax policies that increase the cost of investing in new capital or that raise the cost of production may have serious negative effects on the optimal output level and the unemployment rate.

SECTION RECAP
Frictional unemployment is short-term unemployment created by people changing jobs. Structural unemployment reflects long-term mismatches between worker and job characteristics. Cyclical unemployment arises during recessions when aggregate demand falls. The natural rate of unemployment is the rate to which the economy tends over time; it consists of frictional and structural unemployment.

Explaining the Existence of Unemployment

Now that we know something about the forms unemployment takes, we can begin to look for an economic explanation of why unemployment exists. We proceed by first examining the labor demand–supply model to see why it fails to explain unemployment of any but the cyclical variety. After determining the shortcomings of the simple demand–supply model, we use our insights to develop two models which together do a much better job of explaining labor market behavior.

Shortcomings of the Simple Labor Demand–Supply Model

The simple labor market model is useful for various purposes, including showing how employment adjusts to changes in the price level, technology, and demographics. However, the simple model does not handle the existence of unemployment well. Taken literally, the simple labor market model implies that unemployment is zero at equilibrium.

At least four conditions would have to be met for the unemployment rate to be zero when the economy is operating at or above the natural level: (1) all workers must be able to perform all jobs (homogeneity), (2) workers must be willing to move to new jobs *immediately* (mobility), (3) workers and firms must have perfect information about prospective job openings and prospective employees, and (4) neither workers nor firms can have market power. These conditions are not met in actual labor markets.

Worker Heterogeneity   If workers are not all alike, they are not equally desirable to employers. Firms must search for workers with appropriate characteristics, and prospective workers must search for jobs they can handle. Wage rates will differ for different types of workers.

The actual labor market is characterized by workers and job seekers with a wide variety of skills and abilities. Some skill differences are due to training, others to natural factors. For example, many people who are not machine operators or typists could be taught the skills for those jobs. Given the proper wage incentive to train for such positions, there should be workers ready to occupy job openings. On the other hand, the number of people who would be competent brain surgeons, given the proper training, is much smaller. The natural abilities required to be a brain surgeon exclude most of us from pursuing such an occupation, if for no other reason than that we would be unable to absorb the training required for the position.

Just as workers have widely varying characteristics, so also jobs have differing requirements. Some jobs require almost no training. To a great extent, employers hiring workers to fill such unskilled positions regard all workers as alike. The fact that some employees may have capabilities that would enable them to perform well in the skilled jobs is of no consequence to the employer. If the job requires minimal skills, employers have little incentive to try to hire skilled workers or workers with great potential for training. Not surprisingly, the market for unskilled labor appears to operate more like the simple labor market model than does the market for skilled labor.

Since different jobs require workers with different skills, the actual labor market is far more fragmented than the simple labor market model indicates. Teenagers looking for summer jobs and skilled mechanics do not operate in the same market. *The* labor market is really a network of interrelated markets. Workers can move from one specific market to another by acquiring education or training. Employers may be able to substitute one type of labor for another by altering the production process somewhat. Thus, although individual labor markets are interrelated, they also are separated from one another by worker skills and job requirements.

The process of acquiring education or training to move from one segment of the market into another is often costly and time consuming. Furthermore, it is common for workers to resist changing occupations until they are convinced that no opportunities exist in their fields. Thus, in a dynamic economy it is possible for shortages of workers with one type of skill to coexist with surpluses of workers with other skills at prevailing wage scales. Changes in the wages paid for different jobs eventually correct such a problem, but the solution can take a long time.

Labor Immobility If unemployment is to be held close to zero, workers must be ready and willing to go where the job openings are. Although some labor market participants are willing to move on short notice, most people resist locational changes. This is true even in the United States, where labor mobility is probably the highest in the world. Family, friends, school systems, neighborhoods, and locational or weather preferences all act to keep many households in one location for extended periods of time. A lengthy period of unemployment is often required before a person will consider relocating.[2]

Labor immobility contributes to the segmentation of the labor market and to the existence of different unemployment rates in different areas of the country (and world). Because of labor immobility, it is possible for a shortage of skilled labor of a particular sort to drive wages up in one area of the country while a surplus of that type of labor (unemployment) exists in other regions. Changing wage patterns are sufficient to eliminate such shortages and surpluses, but not without a considerable delay.

Imperfect Information An unemployment rate of zero would also require perfect information. Prospective employees would have to know exactly where job openings are and what the requirements for the jobs are. Furthermore, they would need to know the nonwage, nontechnical characteristics of the job. Most people place as much importance on working conditions and relationships with management and coworkers as on wage rates. In the absence of perfect information about the characteristics of jobs, some jobs go unfilled while prospective employees collect the desired information.

Employers need information, too. In the absence of perfect information about such worker characteristics as technical skills, personality, and work habits, employers must spend resources acquiring such information. Job candidates must fill out forms providing basic information. They must be interviewed by trained personnel managers. Often they must take tests of one sort or another to demonstrate their technical competence. It is costly and time consuming for firms to go through such procedures before filling a position, but the process is worthwhile if the firms obtain high-quality workers as a result.

The absence of perfect information causes job seekers to engage in a process of **search**. A good deal of unemployment can be explained by the search process. One of the two major theories of unemployment developed in this

Search
Process whereby job seekers acquire information about the availability and characteristics of jobs.

---

[2]For recent confirmation of the existence of labor immobility, see Hilary Stout, "Jobless Aren't Migrating to Boom Areas," *The Wall Street Journal*, February 21, 1989, p. B1.

chapter is **search theory**—the theory that much unemployment is due to the time required to obtain information about job characteristics and alternatives.

Market Power The simple labor market model is a perfectly competitive model. Neither demanders nor suppliers of labor services are assumed to have any market power. In other words, firms must pay the going wage as determined by the market. Attempting to pay a lower wage would cause them to lose all their employees and paying a higher wage would unnecessarily reduce profits. Workers are wage takers. They may accept or reject the market wage offer, but they are unable to force the wage offer any higher than the market level. As labor demand and supply change, the market wage changes to equate the quantity of labor demanded with the quantity supplied.

The presence of market power affects the equilibrium wage–employment combination. Firms with labor market power offer lower wage rates and hire fewer workers than perfectly competitive firms, *ceteris paribus*. If hiring by a firm drives up the wage the firm must pay to *all* its workers, the firm has an incentive to hold down its wage bill by hiring fewer workers than it otherwise would.

When workers have market power the equilibrium wage–employment combination is also affected, but in the opposite direction. Labor unions seek to increase the wages earned by their members by restricting the supply of labor in particular markets. By negotiating contracts that commit firms to employ only workers who are members of a particular union and by controlling the number of members, the union can force the wage rate up. The union in effect reduces the supply of labor to a particular market, shifting the labor supply curve to the left and increasing the wage rate.

The presence of market power on either the demand or supply side of the labor market explains why the wage–employment combinations in real-world labor markets might differ from the perfectly competitive equilibrium position. Market power does not explain why wages should be downwardly rigid, however. The issue of downwardly rigid wages is the subject of **contract theory**, which focuses on the formal and informal employment relationships between employers and workers. Contract theory is the second major theory of unemployment developed in this chapter.

Two Complementary Theories of Unemployment

The basic notions behind modern theories of unemployment are the absence of perfect information and the existence of contracts that cause wages to be inflexible. Translating these basic ideas into a reasonable theory of unemployment is the task of search and contract theories.

Search Theory The simple labor market model is in reality an auction model. It presumes that labor suppliers and demanders are constantly reacting to the state of demand and supply, employing more or fewer people as the market-determined wage rate rises and falls. Search theory rejects this view of the labor market. The core of search theory includes the following:

1. Prospective employees do not have perfect information about the wages being offered by employers. Instead, they acquire information by sampling job offers. This process of information acquisition takes time.

Search theory
The theory that much unemployment is due to the time required to obtain information about job availability and characteristics.

Contract theory
The theory that explains wage rigidity as the natural outcome of contracts between employers and workers.

SECTION RECAP
The simple labor demand–supply model assumes away the factors that are responsible for unemployment. If all workers are alike, workers are perfectly mobile, information is perfect, and neither firms nor workers have market power, there is no explanation for unemployment, other than cyclical unemployment caused by downward wage rigidity in the face of falling labor demand.

Reservation wage
Minimum wage rate that will induce a searcher to accept a job or a worker to remain in a job.

Hiring rate
Percentage of applicants who choose to accept a firm's employment offer in a time period.

Retention rate
Percentage of a firm's employees who choose to remain in their jobs during a period of time.

Quit rate
Percentage of a firm's employees who choose to quit their jobs in a time period.

2. In sampling the job market, a prospective employee forms an idea of the state of the market. She uses this idea to form a **reservation wage** — a minimum acceptable wage rate. If the searcher receives a wage offer higher than the reservation wage, she accepts the offer and begins working. If the offer is less than the reservation wage, the searcher rejects the offer and continues searching.

3. If a worker already employed by a firm revises his reservation wage upward so that it now exceeds the actual wage, he resigns and looks for another acceptable offer. If the firm cuts the worker's wage to a figure below the reservation wage, the worker quits and searches for another job.

4. Firms set the wage rates they offer so as to maintain the desired flow of workers into and out of the firms. By raising the wage rate, a firm induces more searchers to accept its offer. The **hiring rate** increases. The wage increase also reduces the number of workers who choose to quit their jobs and search for better wages. Thus, the **retention rate** increases, or equivalently, the **quit rate** declines.

Figure 7 illustrates the effect of changing the wage offer on a firm's hiring and quit rates. Figure 7 (a) shows the hiring rate curve facing the firm. The hiring rate curve relates the percentage of searchers accepting the firm's wage offer to the wage rate offered. The higher the wage offer, the higher the percentage of searchers accepting the offer. Figure 7 (b) illustrates the quit rate curve. This curve relates the percentage of current employees who choose to

FIGURE 7
An individual firm's hiring and quit rate curves. A firm can increase its hiring rate and reduce its quit rate by increasing its wage offer. The hiring rate is the percentage of job offers that are accepted each period. The quit rate is the percentage of workers quitting their jobs each period. Reservation wages are assumed constant when drawing these curves.

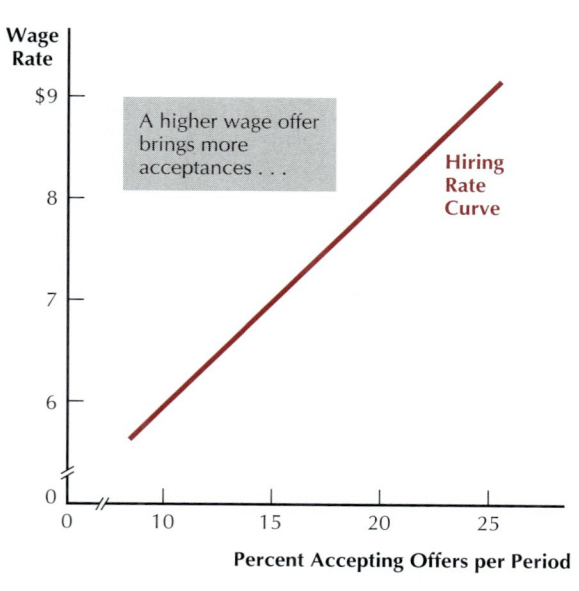
(a)

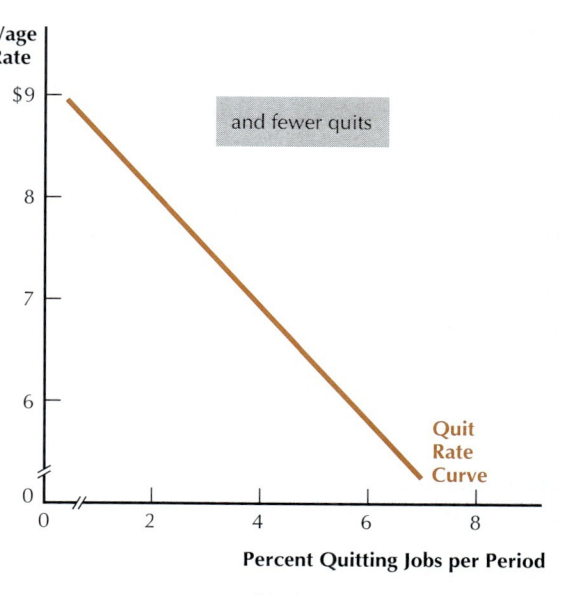
(b)

quit their jobs and enter a search for a better job to the firm's wage offer. As the wage offer rises, the quit rate declines.

It is important to note that *the hiring rate and quit rate curves are drawn under the assumption that searcher and worker reservation wages are constant.* If searchers revise their reservation wages upward, any particular offer made by the firm looks less attractive. Thus, an increase in reservation wages shifts the hiring rate curve to the left and the quit rate curve to the right.

The firm chooses its desired wage rate by determining its desired labor force. For example, consider a firm that currently employs 1000 workers. Suppose it wishes to maintain its work force at that level. The number of workers hired must equal the number quitting. Assume that the firm's quit rate per month is 6 percent if the wage rate is $6 per hour, 4 percent if the wage rate is $7 per hour, and 2 percent if the wage rate is $8 per hour. Also assume that the current wage rate is $7 per hour. The firm expects 4 percent of its labor force to quit each month. This means that $.04 \times 1000 = 40$ workers will leave the firm to search for other employment.

Whether the work force remains stable in size, grows, or diminishes when the wage rate is $7 per hour depends upon the hiring rate and the number of searchers sampling the firm's wage offer. Suppose that 100 workers per month interview with the firm. Also suppose that when the wage rate is $6 per hour, the hiring rate is 10 percent, when it is $7 per hour, the hiring rate is 15 percent, and when it is $8 per hour, the hiring rate is 20 percent. At a wage rate of $7 per hour, the number of new hires per month equals $.15 \times 100 = 15$.

If the number of quits per month is 40 and the number of hires is 15, simple subtraction tells us that the firm's work force shrinks by 25 workers during the month. But we assumed that the firm wanted to maintain a constant work force of 1000 workers. How can the firm offset this unwanted shrinking? By raising its wage rate. If the firm were to increase its wage offer to $8 per hour, the number of quits would decline to $.02 \times 1000 = 20$. The number of hires would increase to $.20 \times 100 = 20$. Thus, a wage offer of $8 per hour would stabilize the size of the firm's work force.

Changing Business Conditions and Employment Behavior. The search model explains cyclical variation in employment and unemployment by referring to the behavior of quit rates and hiring rates over the course of the business cycle. Suppose that a firm experiences an increase in the demand for its product. To meet the increased demand, the firm wishes to expand the size of its work force. It can do so by increasing its wage offer. An increased wage offer increases the hiring rate, thus increasing the number of searchers who accept the firm's offer. It also reduces the quit rate, enabling the firm to retain more of its current workers.

A general increase in demand drives up wage offers throughout the economy. Searchers accept jobs more quickly than they would at lower wage rates, and the aggregate quit rate falls. Since fewer searchers are in the market, *the unemployment rate falls.* Thus, an increase in aggregate demand should bring with it an increase in employment, a decrease in unemployment, and a decline in the quit rate. The unemployment rate declines for two reasons: (1) the quit rate falls, so fewer people become unemployed, and (2) workers accept offers more quickly, so the duration of unemployment declines.

The pattern in a recession is the reverse of the expansion pattern. Firms experience a decline in the demand for their products. In response, they want to reduce their employment levels. (Alternatively, they wish to reduce their costs of production by reducing their wage costs, but reducing wage costs causes employment to fall.) Wage offers are cut. Given the current set of reservation wages, hiring rates decline and quit rates rise. More workers enter the ranks of the unemployed to search for better wages, and the duration of unemployment of searchers lengthens.

Crucial to the story of the business cycle told by the search theory is the *assumption* that *workers revise their reservation wages slowly* in response to aggregate demand changes. When aggregate demand falls and wage offers are cut, quit rates rise only if reservation wages do not fall. If workers sense that a recession is coming and reduce their reservation wages, the decline in actual wage offers will not necessarily cause a fall in employment. Reservation wages must change rather slowly.

Another interesting feature of the search model is the type of unemployment that results. *Searchers are unemployed because they choose to be* so that they can search for a better offer. All unemployment in this model is voluntary frictional unemployment linked to the search process and not due to any structural defects in the economy.

Economic Trends and Revisions in Reservation Wages. The search theory of cyclical behavior assumes that workers are slow in revising their reservation wages when the general level of wage offers rises or falls. But what happens if a lower level of aggregate demand persists for months or years? According to search theory, searchers discover that their reservation wages are too high. After sampling a large number of jobs and finding that all wage offers are lower than the reservation wage, a searcher revises his reservation wage downward. The searcher realizes that the previous reservation wage was unrealistically high. As other searchers recognize the same fact, the whole set of reservation wages held by searchers decreases. This causes the hiring rate curve to shift to the right and, as word spreads, the quit rate curve to shift to the left. Lower wage offers by firms are now associated with higher hiring rates and lower quit rates. Employment rises, the unemployment rate falls, and the average duration of unemployment declines.

The process works in the other direction for rising wages. Suppose that aggregate demand grows by an unexpectedly large amount. Firms increase their wage offers, initially increasing the hiring rate and decreasing the quit rate. Employment rises, unemployment falls. If the higher level of wage offers persists, however, searchers realize that virtually every offer they obtain is satisfactory (above their reservation wage rates). This leads them to revise their estimates of the wage structure upward. They decide that they have been underestimating the true structure of wages. Reservation wages rise, the hiring rate curve shifts to the left, and the quit rate curve shifts to the right. The current level of wage offers is now associated with lower hiring and higher quit rates. The employment level falls and the unemployment rate rises to its natural level.

This point is important enough to be repeated. *According to search theory, an increase or decrease in the general level of wage offers alters the unemployment rate only temporarily.* When labor force participants discover what the new distribution of wages is, they revise their reservation wages. The unemployment rate returns to the level that prevails when workers correctly perceive the distribution of wages.

TABLE 2
Cyclical movements in the labor market

	Search Theory	Evidence
Expansions		
Employment	Increases	Increases
Unemployment	Decreases	Decreases
Quit rate	Decreases	Increases
Average duration of unemployment	Decreases	Decreases
Recessions		
Employment	Decreases	Decreases
Unemployment	Increases	Increases
Quit rate	Increases	Decreases
Average duration of unemployment	Increases	Increases

This view of the labor market implies that some unemployment is beneficial. Searchers should not always accept the first wage offer they receive, because such an offer might not be well suited to their preferences and abilities. When workers are fooled into thinking that the distribution of wage offers is different than it really is, some searchers accept jobs that are not the best for them (or reject offers that are the best). Whenever workers perceive the true state of wage offers, they remain unemployed and search (on average) for the optimal amount of time.

Search Model Predictions and the Evidence. The search model presents us with a well-developed explanation of cyclical movements in employment, unemployment, quit rates, and average duration of unemployment. This explanation may or may not coincide with the empirical evidence, however. In fact, the search model does quite well, with one major exception. Table 2 summarizes the typical business cycle movements actually observed in the labor market as well as the predictions of the search model.

As the table shows, the search model's predictions coincide with the evidence for three variables, but are contradictory to the evidence on the quit rate, which actually falls slightly during recessions, rather than rising as the theory predicts. The quit rate rises a little during expansions, when the theory says it should be falling. Why the discrepancy?

The reason for the incorrect prediction of quit rate behavior is twofold. First, the search model has no room for layoffs. In the search theory, all job separations are due to workers quitting their jobs. In the real economy, however, most job separations are due to layoffs or firings. The search model does not explain layoffs, because it assumes that firms raise or lower their wage offers to induce workers to sign on or quit in greater numbers. Layoffs are a substitute for wage cuts. Instead of lowering wages and inducing quits, firms simply lay off unneeded workers while maintaining stable wages. The second reason is that the quit rate curve shifts in response to information about the

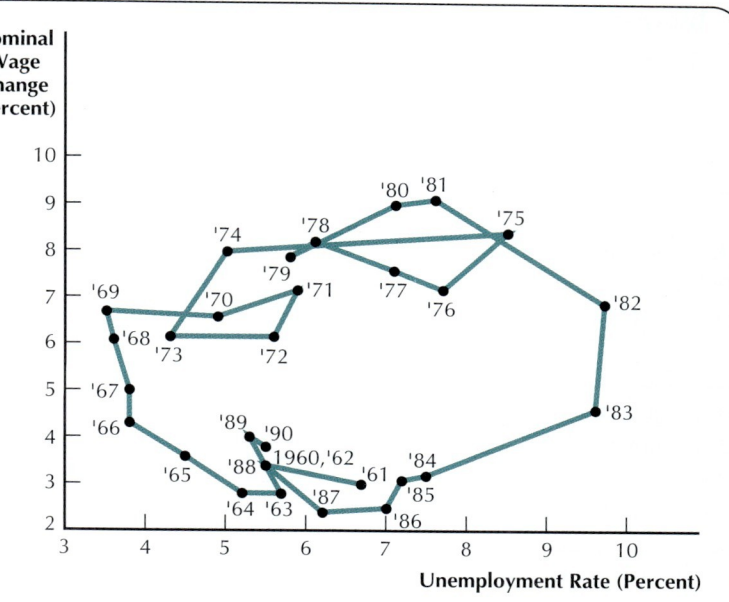

FIGURE 8
Wage growth and the unemployment rate. When nominal wages rose during the 1960s, the unemployment rate fell. When workers adjusted to the higher level of wage growth, the unemployment rate returned to a higher level. During the mid-1980s, both the rate of wage growth and the unemployment rate declined. The behavior of the unemployment rate suggests the existence of a natural rate of unemployment, around which the actual rate varies. Source: *Economic Report of the President, 1991*, Tables B-40 and B-44.

business cycle. When workers realize the economy is in a recession, they are less likely to quit their jobs, knowing that obtaining other jobs will be difficult.

The search model prediction that a permanent increase in the overall level of wage offers only temporarily affects unemployment is borne out by the evidence. Figure 8 shows the relationship between wage rate increases and the unemployment rate for the 1960–1990 period. When wages first began to rise rapidly during the 1960s, unemployment fell. Even though the high rates of wage increase continued into the 1970s, the unemployment rate returned to higher levels. Both wage increases and unemployment fell in the mid-1980s.[3]

Summary of Search Theory. Search theory is superior to the simple auction market model of the labor market. It explains the existence of one type of unemployment (frictional), as well as the cyclical pattern of employment, unemployment, and unemployment duration. It also explains the tendency for increased wage offers to affect the unemployment rate only temporarily. It only partially explains observed wage rigidity (through reservation wage rates), however, and does not account for layoffs. We must seek answers to the question of why wages are rigid in another type of model—the contract model.

Contract Theory In developing the search theory of unemployment, we focused on imperfect information. The lack of perfect information explains the need for search. Contract theory is also concerned with imperfect information, but it also addresses the fact that workers and jobs are not all alike.

Several different types of contract theory have been developed in the past few years. The version presented here, developed by the late Arthur Okun,

SECTION RECAP
Search theory is based on the assumption that workers must search to obtain information about wage offers and job characteristics. Search takes time, creating some frictional unemployment. The amount of unemployment depends on the perceived attractiveness of wage offers.

---

[3]This is exactly the pattern we would expect to find if there is a natural rate of unemployment toward which the actual unemployment rate tends over time.

focuses on the difference between experienced and inexperienced workers and the cost of training new workers.[4] The basic assumptions on which the model rests are as follows:

1. When a firm hires a new worker, it incurs a substantial cost. This cost involves both the cost of **screening** — interviewing and testing job candidates — and the cost of training the worker.

2. Experienced workers are valuable to a firm because the firm does not have to incur screening and training costs. The total cost of an experienced worker is the wage rate. The cost of a new worker is the wage rate plus screening and training costs.

3. Since firms want to minimize screening and training costs, they must develop a wage plan that induces workers to remain with the firm. Since workers do not know the future, they must be persuaded that remaining with a particular firm for a long period of time is in their best interests.

4. Although the reason for wage reductions is not always clear to workers, the reason for layoffs usually is.

Screening
Ascertaining a prospective employee's qualifications through interviews or testing.

Because new workers involve costs that experienced workers do not, firms attempt to shift the costs of screening and training from themselves to the new workers. From the firm's point of view, it would be optimal to pay a new worker an amount equal to the value of the worker's marginal product of labor (VMPL) less screening and training costs. (As explained in the appendix to the chapter on the labor market and aggregate supply, the wage rate equals the VMPL of the last worker, in this case the newly added worker.) However, to hire a new worker, the firm must offer a wage equal to or higher than the prospective employee's reservation wage. Thus, the wage paid to a new worker must lie somewhere between the worker's reservation wage and the value of the worker's marginal product, and the firm may have to absorb some or all of the training cost.

Since the firm wants to retain the worker after training ends, it must offer a long-run wage package that is attractive to the worker. One way for the firm to recoup its training costs while still offering an attractive wage package to new workers is to offer wage increases tied to seniority. For example, new workers are offered a wage (W_N) that is lower than the wage rate of experienced workers (W_X). Thus, new workers accepting job offers realize that it is to their benefit to remain with the firm in order to earn the future higher wage rate of experienced workers.

If a firm is to make this kind of offer, it must either do so in the form of an explicit legal contract or have established a reputation for dealing fairly with workers so that its offer is believable. Many firms, particularly those using union labor, operate with explicit wage contracts. Such contracts make a firm's offer credible by making it legally binding. However, explicit contracts have many costs that firms like to avoid. Some of these costs are direct, such as the legal costs of negotiating a wage agreement. However, the most important costs come in the form of reduced flexibility. Once a firm has committed to an explicit contract, it has very little flexibility in reacting to unforeseen circumstances. For this reason, most firms prefer to operate with implicit contracts.

---

[4]The model is presented in Arthur M. Okun, *Prices and Quantities: A Macroeconomic Analysis* (Washington, D.C.: Brookings Institution, 1981).

Implicit contract
An informal agreement between employer and employees that limits the choices the employer can make by generating expectations on the part of workers.

Implicit Contracts. One of the developers of contract theory defined an **implicit contract** as one "causing a firm to restrict its activities as though a contract exists, even when there is no legal contract."[5] The purpose of restricting its activities is to convince employees that the firm is honest and that its offers are good.

How might a firm go about convincing workers that its offers are credible? One way is to meet the expectations created by the firm's offers. The simplest example of this would be meeting new workers' expectations of a wage increase whenever the probation period ends. If the workers accepted a relatively low starting wage with the expectation that six months or a year later they would receive a substantial wage increase, the firm must meet that expectation. If the firm does not do so, it will destroy its reputation for dealing honestly with new employees. This will harm its ability to hire new workers.

Another simple way of establishing a reputation for honesty is to give workers regular wage increases of some standard size as the workers acquire more seniority. Once such a pattern is established, it becomes dangerous for the firm to deviate from it. Attempting to cut wages, or even to skip the expected wage increase, may cause workers to feel that the firm has reneged on its commitment to them. Such disappointment leads to an increased quit rate. Thus, *in preserving its reputation for dealing fairly with workers, a firm may introduce a significant amount of wage rigidity into its behavior pattern.*

Suppose that the firm is faced with a decrease in the demand for its product. How should it react? Search theory says that the firm should cut its wage offer to induce more workers to quit and fewer searchers to accept its offer. Cutting the wage rate, however, will be viewed by current employees as breaking the implicit contract. Since experienced workers are preferred to new workers (because of training costs), such a wage cut could be quite costly to the firm in the long run.

The firm may believe that the appropriate strategy is to maintain the wage structure but (1) stop hiring new workers completely, and (2) lay off some experienced workers. Since laying off experienced workers increases the quit rate among those workers, it is not costless. However, layoffs may be preferable to reducing the wage rate because of the information conveyed to workers by the two methods of cost reduction.

Layoffs versus Wage Cuts. When a firm lays off workers, the workers know that they are not being exploited. Because layoffs are almost universally accompanied by no-help-wanted signs, the laid-off workers know that they are not being replaced by cheaper labor. Furthermore, the company is deriving no cheap benefits from the workers, as it might have had the wage rate been cut. When firms ask workers to take pay cuts, the workers are unsure whether the pay cuts are necessary or whether the company is attempting to take advantage of them. If workers suspect that the company is attempting to use the wage cut to increase profits, they may feel that the implicit contract has been violated.

Understanding that the real reason for a wage cut may not be clear to workers, firms would rather stop hiring and lay off selected workers than cut wages. Many firms even make the order of layoffs part of the implicit contract.

---

[5]Donald F. Gordon, "A Neo-Classical Theory of Keynesian Unemployment," *Economic Inquiry* (December 1974), p. 443.

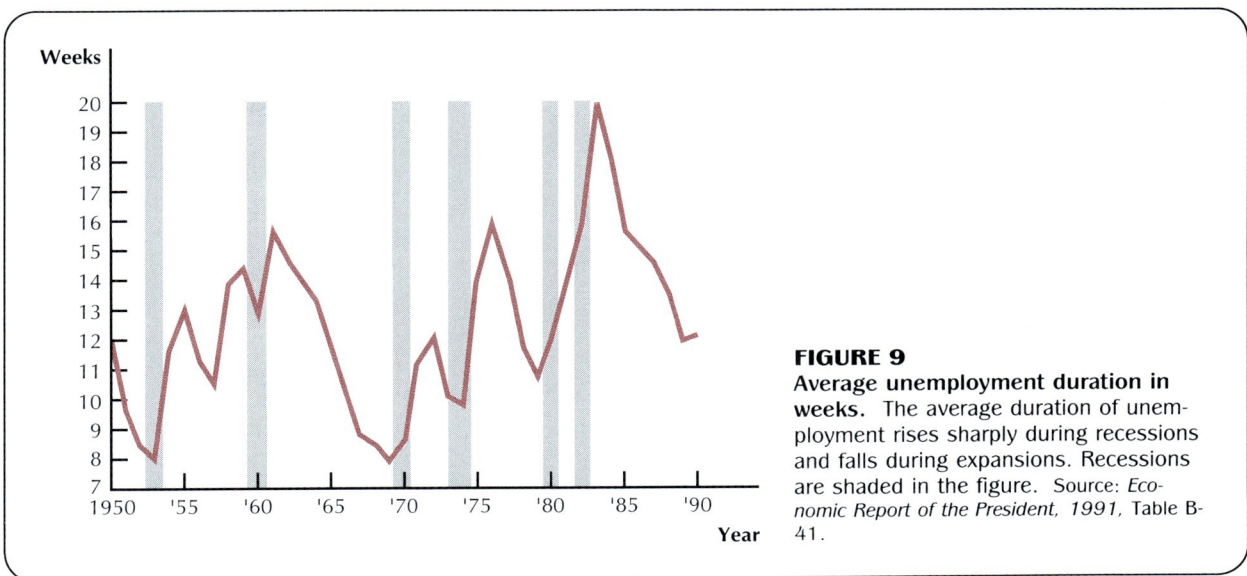

FIGURE 9
Average unemployment duration in weeks. The average duration of unemployment rises sharply during recessions and falls during expansions. Recessions are shaded in the figure. Source: *Economic Report of the President, 1991*, Table B-41.

Junior workers in a particular job category are laid off before senior workers. This provides further incentive for worker loyalty, since senior workers are paid more and are less likely to be laid off.

Cyclical Movements in a World of Contracts. When aggregate demand declines, firms initially respond to the reduced demand for their products by increasing inventories. If the reduction in demand appears to be more than a very brief event, firms cease hiring new workers. Since this makes it more difficult for searchers to locate acceptable job offers, the average duration of search — and of unemployment — rises. Figure 9 shows that the average duration of unemployment rises during recessions and falls during expansions, just as we would expect if search becomes more difficult in a recession.

If the demand reduction persists, firms begin to lay off workers. The unemployment rate rises and employment begins to fall. This is consistent with the predictions of the search model and with real-world behavior. However, the contract model does not explain rising unemployment by saying that quit rates rise. Instead, most workers who become unemployed are assumed to be released by firms. Layoffs, not quits, rise. The contract model does not assume that workers have no information on the general state of the economy. In fact, Americans are engulfed with information on such variables as real economic growth and the aggregate unemployment rate. Knowing the general state of the economy, workers are hesitant to quit their jobs during a recession. Hence, the quit rate actually remains stable or falls during recessions.

Figure 10 shows the behavior of the job loss (layoff plus firing) rate and the quit rate for the period 1967–1990. The job loss rate fluctuates far more over the course of the cycle than does the quit rate.

In terms of the labor demand–labor supply model, *we now have an explanation of downward wage rigidity.* Firms refuse to cut wages in response to temporary reductions in the demand for their products. If labor demand falls, firms respond by holding wages constant and laying off workers. Since the

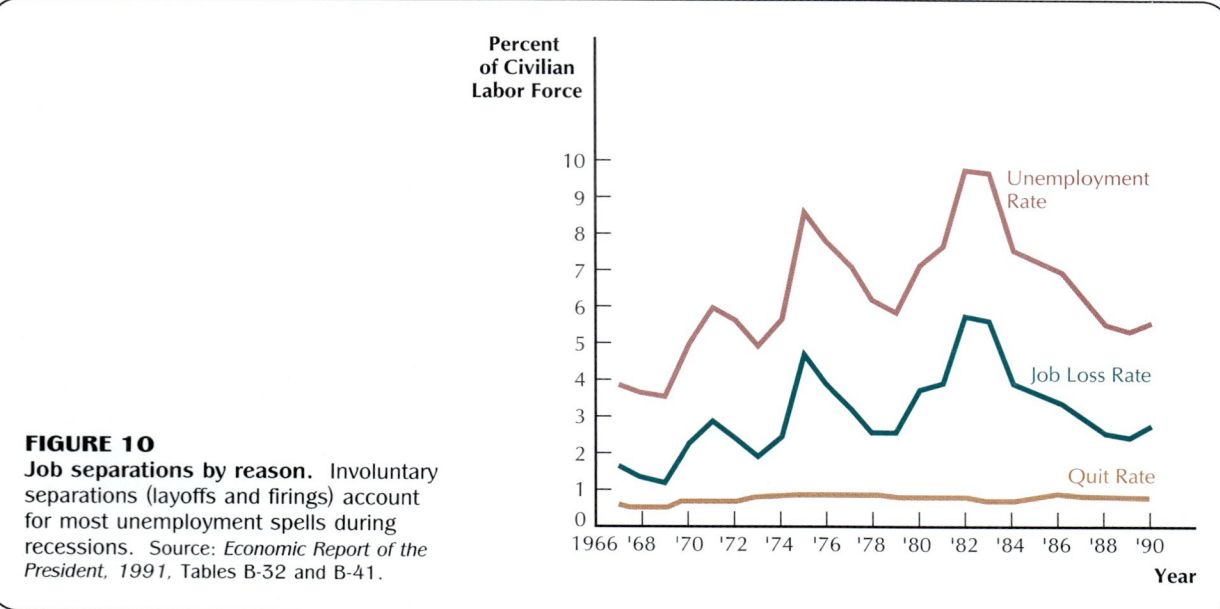

FIGURE 10
Job separations by reason. Involuntary separations (layoffs and firings) account for most unemployment spells during recessions. Source: *Economic Report of the President, 1991,* Tables B-32 and B-41.

laid-off workers would like to be working at current wage rates, they are classified as unemployed.

Contract theory adds one additional twist to this story. Since firms have implicit long-term contracts with their workers and these contracts typically cause workers to expect regular wage increases, firms may grant pay hikes to their remaining employees even while other workers are laid off. Doing so further establishes the firms' reputation for honesty by meeting worker expectations.

Economic Trends and Worker Expectations. Search theory predicts that an increase in demand that drives up wages will only temporarily raise employment. Contract theory agrees with this prediction. If aggregate demand and prices begin rising more rapidly, firms initially raise wages by the amount expected during the period of lower inflation. If higher inflation rates persist, however, workers begin to feel the squeeze when real wages decline. To maintain a fair wage structure, firms must offset the decline in real wages by granting larger wage increases. If a firm does not react in this manner, its reputation for fairness will be tarnished. Thus, faster aggregate demand growth and higher inflation rates increase employment initially, as the labor demand curve shifts to the right faster than the labor supply curve shifts to the left. As inflation persists, workers begin to expect and firms begin to grant larger wage increases. This process is illustrated in Figure 11, where the path of wages and employment is from A to B to C.

One other implication of contract theory is worth mentioning. Wage rigidity is due primarily to the desire of firms to avoid disappointing worker expectations. But what of those firms whose very existence is threatened unless costs are reduced? The theory suggests that if a firm convinces its workers that bankruptcy is imminent unless wages are reduced, workers will be willing to

SECTION RECAP
Contract theory explains wage rigidities by explaining why both firms and *(continued)*

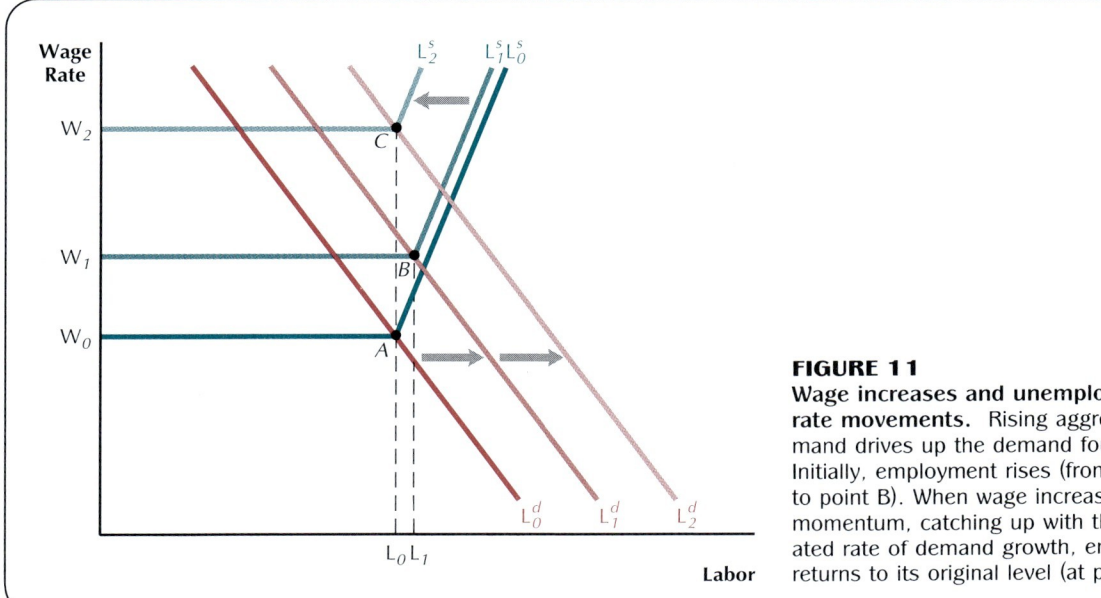

FIGURE 11
Wage increases and unemployment rate movements. Rising aggregate demand drives up the demand for labor. Initially, employment rises (from point A to point B). When wage increases gain momentum, catching up with the accelerated rate of demand growth, employment returns to its original level (at point C).

accept pay cuts. Such a situation is not a violation of the implicit contract. The 1981–1982 recession—the most severe recession of the post-World War II period—saw a considerable amount of wage cutting in certain industries. Contract theory does not say that wages *never* fall but that they fall only under obviously very serious conditions.

By providing an explanation of why wages are downwardly rigid most of the time, contract theory enables us to explain cyclical unemployment. It thus complements search theory, which provides an explanation of frictional unemployment.

SECTION RECAP
(continued)
workers prefer stable wage patterns to perfectly flexible wages. The preference for stable wages leads firms to lay off workers during recessions, rather than reducing wages.

Unemployment Policy

Since 1946, high employment has been an explicit goal of the federal government. Such a goal means that the federal government must formulate policies that limit the number of people who are unemployed at any point in time. In this section we briefly discuss some of the policy options available to the government.

Unemployment Is Really a Variety of Problems

The preceding discussion of the different categories of unemployment implies that no single policy cure for unemployment exists. Just as unemployment has many causes, so any effective policy must include a variety of approaches. Policies designed to reduce the level of frictional unemployment will have almost no impact on the long-term structurally unemployed. Expansive aggregate demand policies intended to pump up the economy may be able to reduce cyclical unemployment to zero and even temporarily drive frictional unemployment down. But such aggregate demand policies do not affect the long-run equilibrium levels of frictional and structural unemployment.

It is helpful to use the aggregate demand–long-run aggregate supply framework to think about unemployment policy. One type of unemployment, cyclical unemployment, can be addressed by controlling the level of aggregate demand. The other two types of unemployment, frictional and structural, determine the natural unemployment rate and contribute to the determination of the natural output level. Policies that affect the aggregate supply characteristics of the economy are necessary to address these types of unemployment.

Cyclical Unemployment: Aggregate Demand Policy

Cyclical unemployment arises when aggregate demand falls and wages do not fall immediately to clear the labor market. Contract theory demonstrates that good reasons exist for wages to be downwardly rigid. Both firms and workers prefer some wage rigidity to perfect wage flexibility. Thus, it is neither realistic nor desirable to attempt to force wages to move freely to clear the market. (It is hard to imagine how the government could enforce wage flexibility even if it wanted to.) This implies that the way to avoid cyclical unemployment is to avoid sharp declines in aggregate demand. Furthermore, should a recession develop, the government can limit the duration of cyclical unemployment by pursuing policies that increase aggregate demand and restore output to its natural level.

As we shall see in the next chapter, avoiding all recessions is easier said than done. Pressures build up over time that can erode the strength of an economic expansion and topple an economy into recession. Attempts to use monetary or fiscal policy to prevent recession may be effective, but they run the risk of generating inflation. Thus, while the cure for cyclical unemployment is obvious, putting it into practice is not simple.

Frictional and Structural Unemployment: Aggregate Supply Policy

Frictional unemployment emerges when people changing jobs spend time searching for information or relocating to new areas. Structural unemployment arises from the mismatch of job requirements and worker characteristics. Neither type of unemployment responds more than temporarily to changes in the level of aggregate demand. Rather, the real incentives for firms to hire workers and for prospective workers to seek and find jobs must change.

Reducing frictional unemployment requires shortening the search process somehow. This may be done in a number of ways. One option is to increase the amount of information available to both employers and prospective employees. The U.S. Job Service does this very thing. Improved information enables searchers to locate desirable job opportunities more quickly, thus reducing search time, the duration of unemployment, and the unemployment rate.

Information deficiencies are not the sole reason for a high level of frictional unemployment, however. Income maintenance programs that reduce the net benefits from working also add to frictional unemployment. Generous unemployment benefits or welfare benefits, especially when combined with high tax rates on labor income, can reduce the incentive for unemployed workers to actively search for new jobs. If, in return for accepting a relatively small reduction in after-tax income, unemployed workers can, in effect, take a vacation for a few weeks, they may not choose to aggressively pursue new jobs. Most Americans believe that income maintenance programs serve a useful purpose, that they benefit society by providing a so-called safety net for those who are unfortunate enough to have no job. However, we now see that such programs also have a social cost, beyond the cost of financing them. An optimal income maintenance program must balance the benefits from providing for the unfortunate against the costs of inducing people to remain unemployed for inordinately long periods of time.

Most economists believe that structural unemployment is the toughest part of the unemployment problem. This is so for two reasons. First, the structurally unemployed tend to remain jobless for much longer than the frictionally or cyclically unemployed. The harm inflicted on particular individuals and their families is greater. Second, no good solutions to the problem of structural unemployment have emerged. Retraining programs and relocation assistance may be the best option for those workers whose jobs have been eliminated by technological advances or changing demand patterns. Yet for older workers with deep roots in their communities, such an option may be none too good.

The inner-city unemployed present an equally difficult problem. In many central-city areas, job opportunities are few and far between. Lacking a good education and means of transportation to areas where employment is available, and often possessing poor work skills, many inner-city unemployed have little hope of finding and holding a good job. Upgrading the skills of inner-city residents through education and training programs can improve their employability. However, until the problem of locational separation of jobs and potential workers is overcome, education and training do little to reduce unemployment. Relocation of the trainees or of jobs (to the center city) also appears necessary.

In some cities, companies have reduced unemployment somewhat by simply providing transportation from the inner city to suburban jobs. However, for the inexperienced, unskilled unemployed of the inner city, the best hope may be bringing productive jobs back into the city. Government-sponsored enterprise zones, which encourage businesses to relocate into depressed areas by offering tax breaks and special subsidies, offer a partial answer to the chronic unemployment problems of many large cities. If induced to locate in depressed areas, firms should be able to provide better training than an outside program could.

Other possible solutions abound. The common thread in all these solutions is that they seek to use microeconomic tools to address what are essentially microeconomic problems. Effective policies must take account of the incentives they provide for prospective workers and for prospective employers. Lower unemployment cannot be legislated. Only by providing the proper production and work incentives can government policy reduce the natural unemployment rate.

SECTION RECAP
Since unemployment is really a variety of problems, no single policy can address all types of unemployment. Cyclical unemployment can be reduced through policies that increase aggregate demand. Frictional and structural unemployment must be addressed with microeconomic policies that affect the conditions of labor demand and supply in particular markets.

Summary

Economists use a flow model to analyze unemployment. The aggregate unemployment rate depends on the **frequency** and **duration** of unemployment. Not all unemployment is alike. **Frictional unemployment** presents a totally different problem than does **structural unemployment,** which is long term.

Cyclical unemployment arises when aggregate demand falls. The **natural rate of unemployment** is the unemployment rate toward which the actual unemployment rate moves, the unemployment rate that corresponds to the natural level of output. Cyclical unemployment is zero at the natural rate.

The labor demand–supply model rests on several restrictive assumptions, including worker homogeneity, perfect labor mobility, perfect information, and perfect competition. In the real world, all of these attributes are absent. Since it is these factors that explain the existence of unemployment, it is no surprise that the simple labor market model has no room for unemployed workers.

Once the assumption of perfect information is discarded, attention must be focused on how prospective employees obtain information about wages and job characteristics and on how firms learn about workers. **Search theory** addresses these issues. Searchers are assumed to obtain information by sampling job offers. The sampling process takes time, thereby generating frictional unemployment. Searchers accept job offers and move from the unemployed pool to the employed pool whenever they receive a wage offer that exceeds their **reservation wage.**

Search theory correctly predicts that unemployment will rise during recessions and fall during expansions, but the process by which this occurs is variation in the quit rate. Search theory predicts that firms will lower wages during recessions, causing more workers to quit. However, quit rates actually decline during recessions, as workers realize that there are fewer alternatives to their present jobs. Unemployment rises during recessions because of layoffs.

To explain the existence of layoffs, we developed **contract theory.** A great deal of **wage rigidity** exists, and contract theory provides a logical explanation of this rigidity. Firms do not regard job applicants as perfect substitutes for experienced workers. Screening and training costs must be added onto the wage rate to determine the total cost of hiring a new worker. Thus, firms attempt to maintain long-term employment relationships with workers. They do so by offering **contracts** that commit the firm to a particular wage structure into the future. Sometimes these contracts are **explicit contracts** — negotiated legal documents — but more often they are **implicit contracts** — informal commitments to treat workers in a particular manner.

Addressing the unemployment problem is quite difficult, because many separate problems really exist. Cyclical unemployment can be addressed with aggregate demand policy, but frictional and structural unemployment are really microeconomic problems. Lowering them affects the natural rate of unemployment and the economy's long-run aggregate supply curve.

Questions for Thought

Knowledge Questions

1. Define the following unemployment terms: *natural rate of unemployment, frictional unemployment, structural unemployment,* and *cyclical unemployment.*
2. What is an implicit contract?
3. What conditions would have to hold in the actual labor market for the simple labor market model to provide a good description of labor market behavior?
4. What is the major weakness of the search model of unemployment?

Application Questions

5. Explain how imperfect information (about workers and about jobs) can generate frictional unemployment.
6. How is it possible for the average duration of unemployment spells to be relatively short while most unemployment is suffered by a relatively few people who are unemployed much of the time?
7. Suppose that the economy is characterized by both rational expectations and long-term contracts. Will government policy changes that are predictable two or three years in advance have any impact on employment and output? What about policy changes that are predictable six months in advance? Is there a significant difference between your answers to these two questions? If so, why?
8. In terms of the flow model of unemployment, explain how an increase in the average duration of unemployment can increase the unemployment rate, even if the frequency of unemployment is unchanged.

Synthesis Questions

9. The market for unskilled labor operates more like an auction market than does the market for skilled labor. Wages are less rigid, relationships of shorter duration. Why is this not surprising?
10. What effect would an increase in welfare or unemployment insurance benefits have on the optimal amount of time spent searching for employment? What are the implications of this for unemployment policy?
11. What is the reservation wage? What part does a sticky reservation wage play in the search theory explanation of business cycle movements? What happens to employment and unemployment when the reservation wage adjusts to new macroeconomic conditions (such as widespread unemployment during a recession or persistently higher inflation)?
12. Explain how rigid wages, no-help-wanted signs, and layoffs all contribute to the cyclical pattern of the average duration of unemployment spells.
13. Is the lowest possible unemployment rate the best unemployment rate for society? Explain.

OVERVIEW

Business cycles are a recurring feature of highly developed market economies. They have existed for over two centuries, surviving dramatic changes in technology, information and transportation services, monetary systems, and government behavior. There have been times when some economists were optimistic enough to talk about the demise of the business cycle (notably during the 1920s and the 1960s) and other times (the 1930s) when pessimism was so widespread that economists discussed little besides the depressed state of the economy. Through all the optimism and pessimism, the business cycle has continued. There is little reason to believe it will soon disappear.

Business cycles are irregular, broad-based movements in a large number of economic variables. Although cycles are primarily discussed in terms of movements in real output or employment and unemployment, many other variables display cyclical patterns. Prices in most industries, short-term interest rates, and business inventories and profits move cyclically. Although every cycle differs in important ways from other cycles, enough similarity in movement exists from cycle to cycle to cause economists to investigate the sources of the patterns that emerge.

What causes cyclical movements? That is the major question addressed in this chapter. After looking briefly at some data describing the business cycle, we investigate several theories of business cycle behavior and attempt to pull together some conclusions. Be forewarned that no

Cyclical Behavior: Theory and Evidence

single answer exists. Most economists reject the notion that a single dominant cause of cyclical fluctuations exists.

After reviewing several theories of the business cycle, we confront the theories with some of the empirical evidence from actual cycles. The test of a good theory is the theory's ability to stand up to the evidence. This exercise helps us form an intelligent opinion about the nature

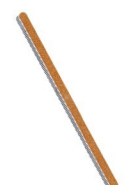

CHAPTER 32

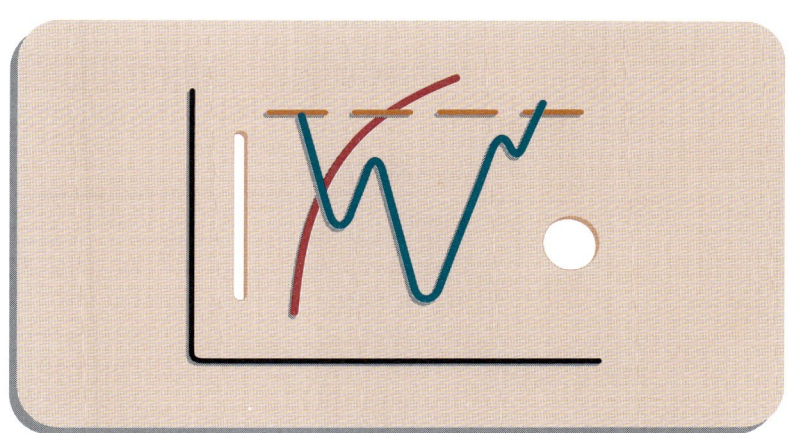

and causes of cyclical fluctuations. We top off our discussion of ordinary cycles by closely examining this century's most extraordinary cycle — the Great Depression.

We end the chapter with a discussion of the types of government policies that might be effective in stabilizing the economy.

Learning Objectives

After reading and studying this chapter, you will be able to:

1. Describe in considerable detail the Keynesian theory of cyclical fluctuations and critique it by showing the ways in which it is contradicted by the empirical evidence.
2. Explain in considerable detail the monetarist theory of cyclical fluctuations and critique it by showing how it is at variance with the empirical evidence.
3. Explain the New Classical and New Keynesian theories of cyclical behavior and critique their performance.
4. List the major factors that turned the recession of 1929–1930 into the Great Depression.
5. Discuss the need for stabilization policy and the specific types of policies that might prove successful.

Charting the Business Cycle

Table 1 lists the dates of all the business cycle peaks and troughs (typically called **turning points**) occurring in this century, along with the duration of expansions and contractions. The data show that the length of business cycles is highly variable. Figures 1 and 2 show that the severity of cycles is also variable. Figure 1 illustrates the behavior of the unemployment rate for the periods 1900–1940 and 1950–1990. Figure 2 shows the movements of real GNP for the same periods. Both figures illustrate the cyclical behavior of the economy. They show that the unemployment rate has been subject to large changes from year to year and that real GNP growth has been anything but stable.

Figures 1 and 2 indicate that since World War II the **amplitude** of cycles — how large the upward and downward swings are — has been smaller than before the war. Though still subject to cycles, the economy appears to have become considerably more stable in the post-World War II period. We say "appears" because recent work by Christina Romer challenges what most economists

Turning points
Cyclical peaks and troughs, where the direction of real GNP growth changes.

Amplitude
The size of the upward and downward movements of real GNP over the course of a business cycle.

TABLE 1

U.S. business cycle expansions and contractions, 1900–1989

Reference Dates		Duration in Months	
Trough	Peak	Contraction	Expansion
December 1900	September 1902	. . .	21
August 1904	May 1907	23	33
June 1908	January 1910	13	19
January 1912	January 1913	24	12
December 1914	August 1918	23	44
March 1919	January 1920	7	10
July 1921	May 1923	18	22
July 1924	October 1926	14	27
November 1927	August 1929	13	21
March 1933	May 1937	43	50
June 1938	February 1945	13	80
October 1945	November 1948	8	37
October 1949	July 1953	11	45
May 1954	August 1957	10	39
April 1958	April 1960	8	24
February 1961	December 1969	10	106
November 1970	November 1973	11	36
March 1975	January 1980	16	58
July 1980	July 1981	6	12
November 1982	June 1990	16	91
Average, 1900–1945		18.1	30.8
Average, 1945–1990		11.0	99.8

Source: National Bureau of Economic Research.

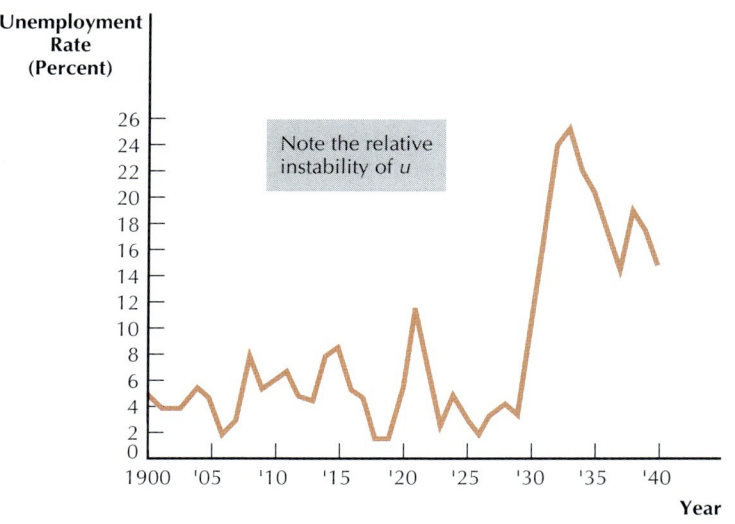

(a) 1900–1940

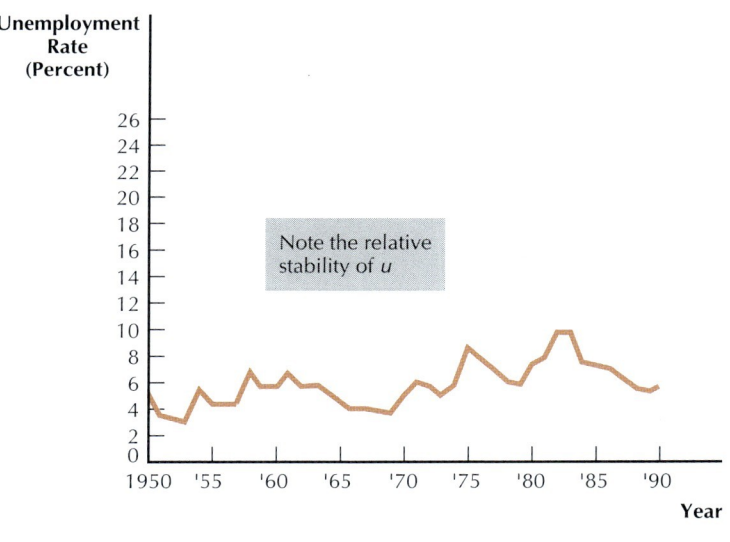

(b) 1950–1990

FIGURE 1
Unemployment rate. (a) 1900–1940 (b) 1950–1990. Sources: *Long-Term Economic Growth, 1860–1970,* Series B1, and *Economic Report of the President, 1991,* Table B-39.

834 CHAPTER 32 CYCLICAL BEHAVIOR: THEORY AND EVIDENCE

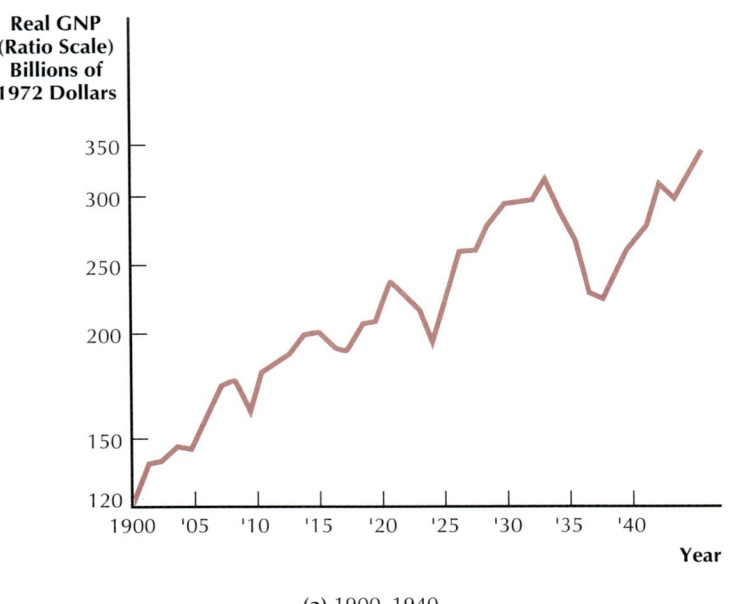

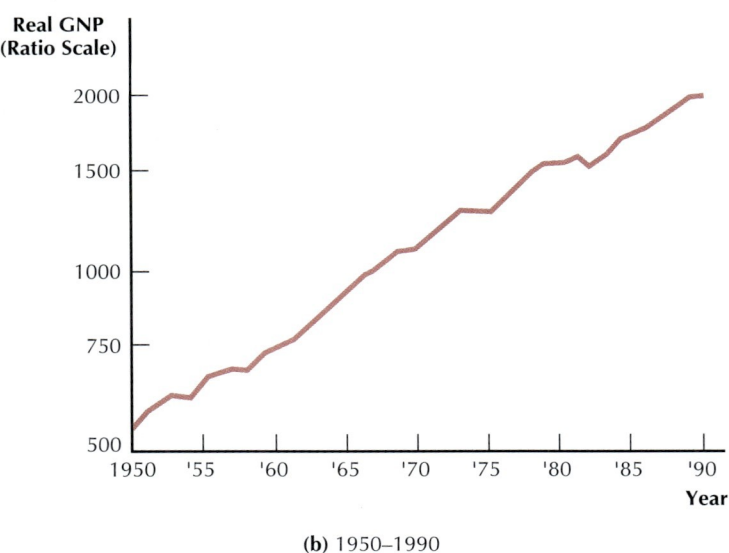

FIGURE 2
Real GNP behavior. *(a) 1900–1940 (b) 1950–1990.* Sources: *National Income and Product Accounts, 1929–1976,* Table 1.2; *Long-Term Economic Growth, 1860–1970,* Series A2; and *Economic Report of the President, 1991,* Table B-2.

have long regarded as fact. Her research indicates that the true size of pre-war cycles may be no larger than postwar cycles. Professor Romer's findings are the subject of this chapter's *Why the Disagreement?* section.

What Causes Business Cycles?

Theories of the business cycle can be grouped into two categories: endogenous and exogenous. **Endogenous theories** stress the internal characteristics of the economy that cause cyclical fluctuations as part of the natural course of events. **Exogenous theories** focus on the impact of outside shocks—such as severe droughts or autonomous changes in the money supply—on a presumably stable economy. The two categories of theories are not mutually exclusive; they can be combined into a hybrid theory of the cycle.

John Maynard Keynes centered his theory of cyclical fluctuations on the instability of investment spending and the tendency of money demand shifts to prevent interest rate movements that would reduce the size of output fluctuations. Keynes's theory was an exogenous theory, since it did not explain why investment spending is unstable, beyond arguing that the expectations held by business managers swing from optimism to pessimism. Keynes's followers developed an endogenous theory by linking investment fluctuations to the growth of real GNP. In this **Keynesian model** of cyclical behavior, investment both responds to and causes fluctuations in real GNP.

The dominant current example of an exogenous theory is the **monetarist model**. Developed by Milton Friedman and some of his colleagues, this approach views money supply instability as the primary cause of cyclical instability. Money supply movements are thought to be determined by the central bank. Hence, they are **exogenous**—determined outside the economic system—and not an inherent feature of the economy. Recent contributions by some nonmonetarist economists have added to, and in some cases drastically altered, the basic monetarist model.

Endogenous cycle theories
Theories that link business cycles to processes naturally occurring within the economy.

Exogenous cycle theories
Theories that link business cycles to factors outside the normal workings of the economy.

Keynesian cycle model
An endogenous theory based on the instability of investment spending.

Monetarist cycle model
An exogenous theory based on the effects of monetary shocks on aggregate demand.

Exogenous
Determined outside the economic system.

Keynesian View: Investment Instability

As noted, Keynes centered his theory of cyclical fluctuations on the behavior of investment spending. In his view, businesses undertake investment projects to the point where the rate of return on investment equals the interest rate. Investment spending is negatively related to the interest rate. The position of the investment demand curve depends crucially on the expectations held by investors.

As Keynes saw it, investment spending is unstable and subject to major changes whenever businesspeople's expectations of future profits change. A sudden collapse in the *expected* rate of return on new capital might cause a sharp downturn in investment spending, shifting the investment demand curve suddenly to the left. Only a large decrease in the (real) interest rate would prevent investment spending from declining significantly. In the Keynesian system, however, the interest rate is determined by the demand for and supply of money. The decline in investment would not automatically decrease the demand for money or the interest rate. Thus, the shift in the investment demand curve would result in a decline in actual investment spending.

Why the **Disagreement?**

Has the Economy Really Become More Stable?

Economists have long accepted the idea that the economy has been a great deal more stable in the post-World War II period than it was before the war. This belief stems from evidence such as that presented in Figures 1 and 2. The data show conclusively—or so it seems—that cyclical fluctuations have been much smaller since World War II than before. However, the conventional view has recently been challenged by a Princeton University professor. Christina Romer argues that appearances are deceiving: The postwar economy has been no more stable than the prewar economy. Why the disagreement?

Professor Romer's attack on the conventional wisdom stems from her examination of how data series were constructed. She has argued that the apparent changes in behavior over time of some important macroeconomic variables are figments of the data.* In particular, the apparent instability of the economy before 1930 compared with its relative stability following World War II may be due to how the macroeconomic data series were constructed. Professor Romer argues that the economy was about as stable before 1930 as it has been in the postwar period. Today the federal government collects an almost unbelievable variety of economic data. Although most of the data series are estimates, the estimates are based on sound statistical techniques. Before World War II, the quantity and quality of data collected were not nearly so high as today. In the absence of good data, economists later constructed data series based on what seemed to be reasonable assumptions about how the estimated series behaved. For example, Romer notes, "The modern unemployment series is based on the Current Population Survey, which began in 1940. The pre-1940 data, on the other hand, are pieced together from census data, industry records, and various state reports." Using accurate census data—collected every ten years—to determine unemployment values in census years, the data collected from these various sources were then used to construct an annual unemployment series for the non-census years.

Evaluating the techniques used to construct the pre-1940 unemployment series, Professor Romer concluded that the estimated series, such as the one shown in Figure 1 (a), greatly overstated the variability of the true unemployment rate. When Professor Romer corrected for sources of systematic error in the pre-1940 estimates, she found that the corrected series was about as stable as the post-World War II series. In other words, Professor Romer argued that if correctly measured, unemployment was no more variable over the 1900–1930 period than it has been since World War II.

Figure 3 compares the standard unemployment rate measure with Professor Romer's measure of unemployment for the 1900–1930 period. The relative stability of her measure is obvious. Professor Romer obtained similar results for such variables as manufacturing output and real GNP.

Romer's findings have not gone unchallenged. Nathan S. Balke and Robert J. Gordon generated a revised real GNP series for the pre-World War I period using new information on output in the transportation, communications, and construction sectors.** Their revised real GNP series fluctuates as severely as the older estimates criticized by Romer. The Balke–Gordon findings led many economists to reject Romer's argument.

Figure 4 (b) shows the sharp decline in the desire to invest caused by the decline in the expected rate of return on capital. Figure 4 (a) shows the money demand and money supply curves. The interest rate is determined by the intersection of money demand and money supply. (Assume that the expected inflation rate is zero, so that the expected real interest rate equals the nominal rate: $r^e = i - p^e = i - 0 = i$.) When the investment curve shifts, the interest rate does not change. Hence, investment spending falls from I_0 to I_1.

The decline in investment spending would surely prove detrimental to the economy. However, investment spending, including residential construction, accounts for no more than 15 percent of gross national product. Even if investment spending fell by 20 percent (a very large decline), such a decrease

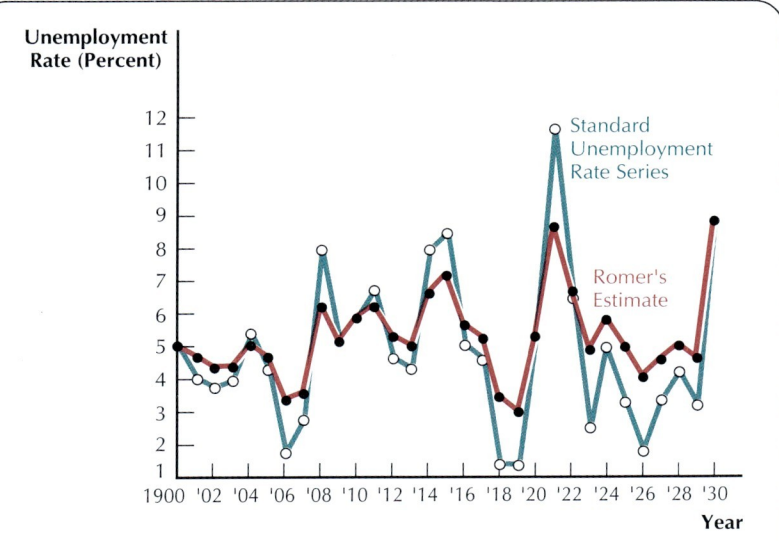

FIGURE 3
Comparison of unemployment series. After correcting the standard unemployment rate calculations for systematic errors, Christina Romer found the corrected series to be far more stable. Source: Christina Romer, "Spurious Volatility in Historical Unemployment Data," *Journal of Political Economy*, February 1986, Table 9.

more stable, the effectiveness of stabilization policies is called into question.

Professor Romer's results also provide a nice object lesson on using economic data. The data are only as good as the techniques used to collect them. Many data series, particularly for the pre-World War II period, are only rough estimates of actual behavior. By calling into question the construction of standard data series, Professor Romer has triggered research into the quality of data. Both economists and policymakers can only gain from such research.

The debate over the stability of the economy more than sixty years ago has important consequences today. If Professor Romer's results are accepted, little or no evidence exists that the business cycle has been smaller in the post-World War II period than it was before 1930. This is an important result, because a generation of economists has argued that the stability of the postwar economy was due to government stabilization policies. If the economy has not been

*Professor Romer's results are presented in "Spurious Volatility in Historical Unemployment Data," *Journal of Political Economy*, February 1986, pp. 1–37; "Is the Stabilization of the Postwar Economy a Figment of the Data?" *American Economic Review*, June 1986, pp. 314–334; and "The Prewar Business Cycle Reconsidered: New Estimates of Gross National Product, 1869–1908," *Journal of Political Economy* 97 (February 1989), pp. 1–37.

**Nathan S. Balke and Robert J. Gordon, "The Estimation of Prewar Gross National Product: Methodology and New Evidence," *Journal of Political Economy* 97 (February 1989), pp. 38–92.

would drive total spending downward by only about 3 percent. Assuming a stable price level, real GNP would fall by 3 percent as well. A decline of this size is more than sufficient to account for the output decline in mild recessions, but is far too small to account for the decline experienced in the early 1930s. During the Great Depression, real GNP declined by 32.6 percent. Since Keynes was attempting to explain the Great Depression, there must be more to his theory than just investment instability.

The additional element that made Keynes's investment theory potent was the autonomous expenditures multiplier. Recall that the Keynesian consumption function makes consumption spending a function of *current* income. A decline in investment spending causes a decline in current income, which

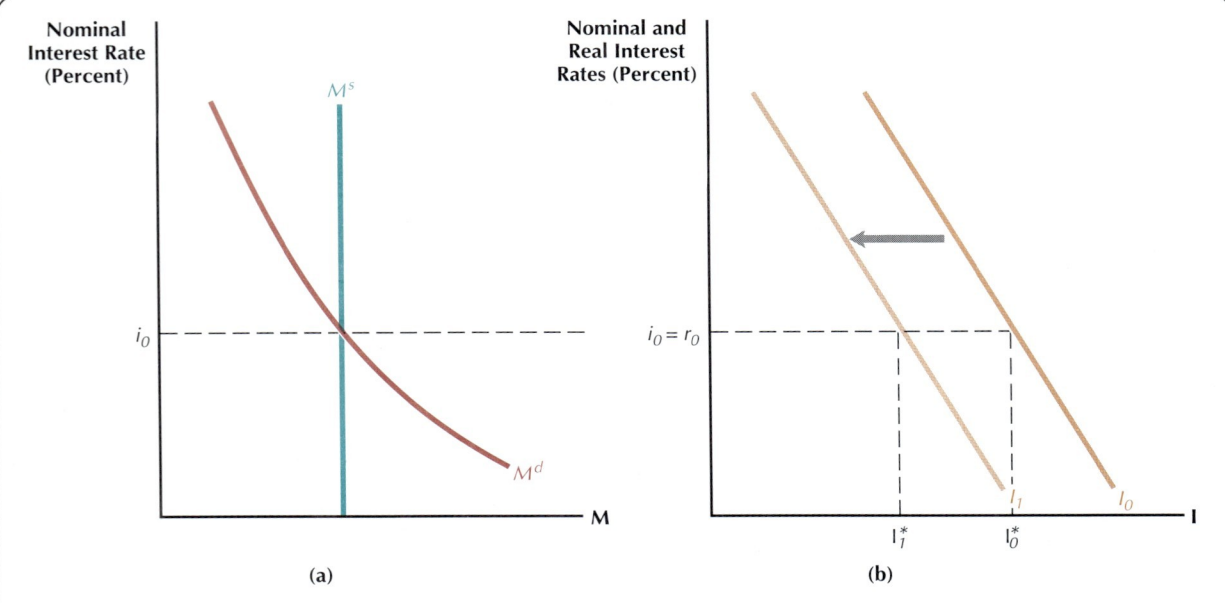

FIGURE 4
A decrease in the expected rate of return on capital reduces investment spending. Investment demand falls from I_0 to I_1 when the expected rate of return on capital declines. Since the interest rate is determined by the intersection of money demand and money supply curves (in the Keynesian model), it does not decline. Consequently, investment spending falls from I_0^* to I_1^*.

reduces consumption spending by the amount of the investment decline times the marginal propensity to consume. The decline in consumption spending further reduces income, which causes second-round consumption decreases, and so on.

In a simple model with no income tax, the multiplier equals $1/(1 - b)$, where b is the marginal propensity to consume. Suppose $b = 0.8$. Then the multiplier equals $1/(1 - 0.8) = 1/0.2 = 5$. Total spending falls by \$5 for every \$1 decline in investment spending. In this way a fall in investment equal to 3 percent of GNP is translated into a spending decline five times as large — 15 percent of GNP.

Unstable investment is the source of aggregate instability, and the multiplier process magnifies the investment spending shifts enough to account for the size. What accounts for the duration of cyclical downturns, in particular, the Great Depression (a decline that lasted forty-three months)? Keynes again turned to the state of expectations to explain the persistence of the depression.[1] He maintained that once a depression is under way, investment spending will not rebound until business confidence rebounds. The economy could get stuck in a depression and remain there indefinitely.

Keynes's theory assumed that the price level would not move to offset the decline in investment spending. Although he did not assume that prices would

---

[1] A depression is an unusually long and severe recession. However, the terms are not defined precisely; no standards exist for determining when a recession becomes a depression.

remain constant as real output falls far below the natural level (what Keynesians call the "full employment level"), Keynes did assume that aggregate demand would fall faster than the price level. Thus, even if wages and prices decline, output does not rise. This is illustrated in Figure 5. The aggregate supply curve shifts downward as output falls below the natural level, but the stickiness of wages and prices prevents SRAS from declining as rapidly as aggregate demand.

What brings the economy out of such a depression? If investment falls very low, the capital stock begins to wear out. Replacement investment can be delayed only so long. As some machines wear out and others are written off as obsolete and abandoned, the size of the capital stock declines. At some point, businesses must undertake new investment to produce even the reduced depression level of output. Confident that producing at this level is profitable, businesses increase investment. The increase in investment spending, through the multiplier effect on consumption spending, propels the economy out of its depressed state. Just as reduced investment spending took the economy into the depression, increased investment spending brings it out.

Of course, this natural recovery process could take a very long time. The major purpose of Keynes's *General Theory* was to argue that government should not wait for the natural recovery. Keynes advocated the use of fiscal policy to pull the economy out of its slump. Increased government purchases of goods and services generate the same multiplier effects as investment spending without having to wait for investor confidence to rise.

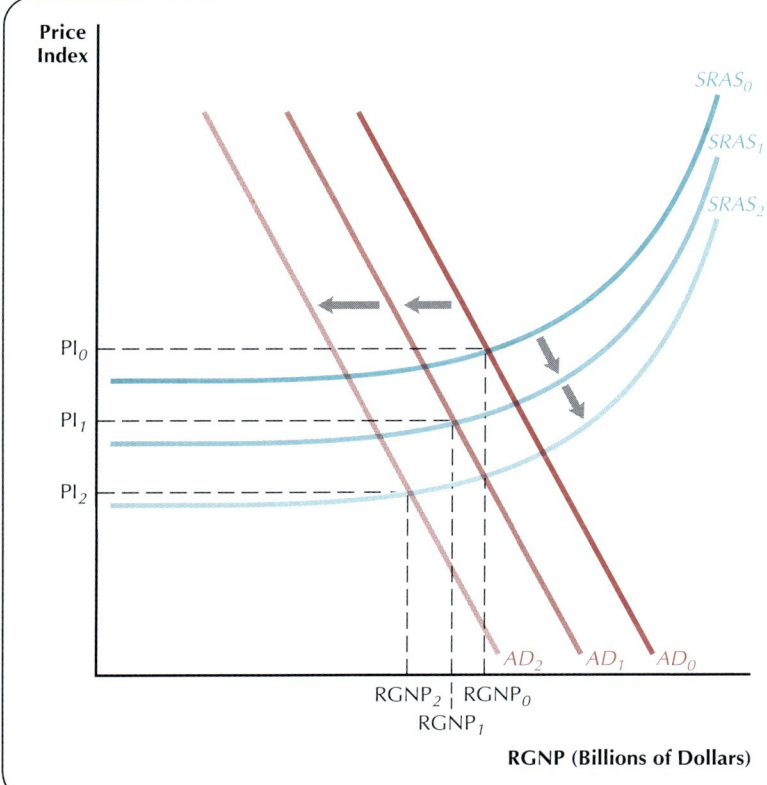

FIGURE 5
Aggregate demand fell faster than wages during the Great Depression. Keynes did not assume that wages and prices are totally rigid; he assumed that wage and price stickiness would prevent the SRAS curve from shifting downward as rapidly as aggregate demand. If this occurs, output falls.

Modifications of Keynes's Original Theory   Although a generation of economists drew their inspiration from Keynes's work, many were bothered by some perceived shortcomings. The major shortcoming of Keynes's theory was the lack of an explanation for the behavior of investment spending. Keynes focused his attention on business expectations. Whenever expectations change, investment spending changes. But Keynes provided no systematic theory of what might cause expectations to change. In Keynes's model, changes in expectations are exogenous (unexplained). Thus, changes in investment spending are also exogenous.

The major development in Keynesian business cycle theory after Keynes was the introduction of the **accelerator principle**, which links investment spending with *changes* in the level of output. The idea behind the accelerator is simple. If output is growing, net investment (which adds to the size of the capital stock) will be positive, because a larger capital stock is needed to produce more output. If output growth levels off, net investment spending falls. Through the multiplier, this causes output to decline, plunging the economy into a recession.

Accelerator principle
Net investment spending depends on the growth of real GNP.

The accelerator–multiplier theory of business cycles is an endogenous theory. Cyclical fluctuations are naturally produced by a model in which the accelerator principle and the multiplier process are at work. To see why this is so, let us talk our way through an ordinary cycle.

We begin with an expanding economy. Assume that the expansion has been under way for some time. Output is growing, and the accelerator effect causes net investment to be high. The investment spending works through the multiplier to generate further increases in output. So long as output continues to grow, investment spending remains strong. However, output cannot grow rapidly forever. Once the natural output level has been reached, further increases in spending generate more upward pressure on prices than on output. The growth of output inevitably must slow.

As output growth slows because of capacity constraints in the economy, net investment spending declines. The accelerator model links net investment to output growth:

$$I_N = j(\Delta RGNP)$$

In this equation, j, the accelerator coefficient, is a positive number (such as 2 or 4). If the *growth* in RGNP declines, the *level* of net investment spending falls. The decline in net investment causes income to fall. The multiplier process multiplies the decline in income, which results in a *decline in the level of RGNP*. The cyclical peak has been reached.

As real output falls, net investment spending may turn negative. (The accelerator equation says that it *will* turn negative, but the economy does not always cooperate.) However, the amount that net investment can decline in a period is limited by the amount of depreciation of capital per period. Net investment equals gross investment (total investment spending) minus depreciation:

$$I_N = I - Dep$$

If gross investment is zero, net investment equals the negative of depreciation.

The lower limit on net investment spending sets a floor on how far output can fall. When investment spending stabilizes, the level of output also tends to stabilize. But when real GNP stops falling, net investment spending rises (to zero — remember, it was negative). This increase in investment spending increases income. Through the multiplier effect, income rises by a multiple of the increase in investment spending. The economy has *passed the trough* of the recession. A new expansion is under way. We are back to the point where we started.

The accelerator–multiplier model describes an economy perpetually fluctuating through an endless series of business cycles. Output growth and investment spending interact to drive output upward in the expansion phase and downward in the contraction phase. Capacity constraints set a ceiling beyond which the economy cannot rise. The minimum amount of investment spending sets a floor below which the economy cannot fall. Output fluctuates between the ceiling and floor limits (which are rising in a growing economy).

The accelerator–multiplier model can be modified to take account of the effect of interest rates on spending. Net investment can be made a function of the real interest rate as well as the change in output. Doing this tends to stabilize the model, making the cyclical fluctuations smaller, if the real interest rate is procyclical. An increase in the real interest rate during expansions tends to reduce the impact of rising output on investment spending. A decline in the real rate during recessions limits the negative effect of declining output on investment. The total effect is to moderate the size of both expansions and contractions.

One criticism of the accelerator–multiplier model is that it completely ignores the financial side of the economy, which many students of business cycles believe is important in explaining cycles. It is possible to append a theory of financial behavior to the accelerator–multiplier model. Nobel laureate James Tobin added financial behavior to the model by arguing that the money supply reacts endogenously to changes in spending. When spending rises, the money supply automatically increases. This increase occurs when banks extend their lending (and money creation) to the limit, using their cash reserves as efficiently as possible. The tendency of the Federal Reserve to offset rising interest rates during expansions by increasing the monetary base adds to the ability of banks to make loans. An increase in the money supply during expansions provides the means of financing investment and consumer durable purchases. Such money supply behavior increases the amplitude of cycles.

In summary, the accelerator–multiplier model, modified to take account of real interest rate movements and endogenous money supply behavior, appears to describe the general pattern of business cycle movements. How well it performs when confronted with more detailed data on cycles is discussed after we present the monetarist view of cycles.

Monetarist View: Money Supply Instability

The monetarist theory of cyclical fluctuations is an exogenous theory. Monetarists tend to view the economy as being quite stable; cycles are primarily the result of shocks to the system. These shocks affect output, but the inherent stabilizing tendencies of the market system cause output to eventually return to its natural level.

The starting point for monetarist theory is the **equation of exchange**. This identity states that the money supply multiplied by the average number of

SECTION RECAP
The Keynesian theory of business cycles focuses on the instability of investment spending. Because of changes in profit expectations or changes in the growth of real GNP, investment changes. Through the multiplier, this causes further changes in real GNP.

Equation of exchange
A mathematical identity equating the quantity of money in existence times the average number of times it is spent during a period to total spending: $M \times V = PI \times RGNP$.

Velocity
The average number of times a unit of money is spent during a time period.

Quantity theory of money
A theory linking money supply changes to changes in real GNP in the short run and to changes in the price level in both the short run and the long run.

times a dollar is spent in a period—**velocity**—equals the total value of spending during that period. In equation form:[2]

$$M \times V = PI \times RGNP$$

Since velocity is defined as the average turnover rate of a dollar, the equation of exchange is true by definition. That is, $V = (PI \times RGNP)/M$, so $M \times V = PI \times RGNP$. However, monetarists have turned the equation into a theory of economic behavior by making some assumptions about the behavior of specific variables in the equation. (They were not the first to do so. The **quantity theory of money**, of which monetarism is the modern version, is over 300 years old.)

The first assumption made by monetarists is that real GNP is determined, in the long run, by real factors. That is, the long-run aggregate supply curve is vertical, and its position depends on the labor supply, resources, capital stock, state of technology, and tax and regulatory structure existing in the economy at a particular point in time. In the short run, however, real output may be affected by aggregate demand.

The second monetarist assumption is that velocity is stable, or at least predictable, and that the value of velocity is not affected by changes in the money supply. This amounts to assuming that velocity does not move systematically to offset changes in M. For example, when M rises, V does not fall, offsetting the effect of M on RGNP and PI.

If both velocity and real output are independent of the money supply in the long run, changes in the money supply must eventually affect the price level. The equation of exchange demonstrates this. Suppose velocity is fixed at a particular value (V_0) and real output is fixed at $RGNP_N$. Then:

$$M \times V_0 = PI \times RGNP_N$$

An increase in M must cause PI to rise proportionately to maintain the equality. Thus, the long-run effect of increasing the money supply is a higher price level.

In the short run, prices are less than totally flexible. If wages are determined on the basis of adaptive expectations, which are backward looking, an increase in spending leads to an increase in output. In his 1967 presidential address to the American Economic Association,[3] Milton Friedman argued that unanticipated aggregate demand increases (due to money supply increases) drive product prices up more rapidly than wages. This means that real wages (W/PI) fall. It becomes profitable for businesses to employ more workers and expand production at the lower real wage rate. Until wages adjust, output rises along a positively sloped short-run aggregate supply curve.

Given slow adjustment of wages and stable velocity, an increase in the money supply shifts the aggregate demand curve outward, causing output to increase, as shown in Figure 6. A decrease in the money supply has the opposite effect.

If that were all there is to monetarist business cycle theory, it would not be too impressive. However, monetarism is founded as much on empirical evidence as on theoretical principle. In a series of papers analyzing the effects of monetary changes on the U.S. economy, Milton Friedman and several col-

---

[2] We should note that the usual form in which you will see this equation is $MV = PQ$, where $P = PI$ and $Q = RGNP$.
[3] "The Role of Monetary Policy," *American Economic Review*, March 1968, pp. 1–17.

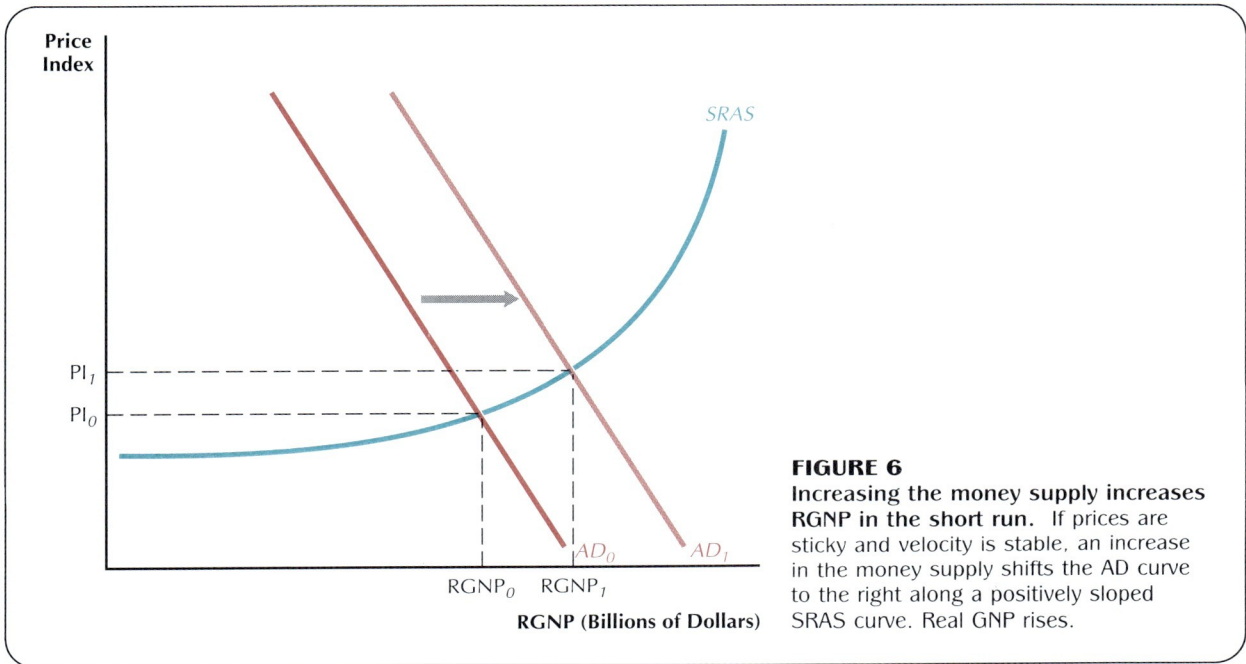

FIGURE 6
Increasing the money supply increases RGNP in the short run. If prices are sticky and velocity is stable, an increase in the money supply shifts the AD curve to the right along a positively sloped SRAS curve. Real GNP rises.

leagues showed that the *timing* of aggregate demand shifts caused by changes in the money supply is very uncertain. The **lags in the effect of money supply changes** are long and variable. The lag in the effect of money supply changes on spending is the time between a change in the money supply and the resulting change in spending.

Because lags are of uncertain length, the effect of a change in the money supply on the economy is uncertain. Suppose the economy is currently in a recession. The Federal Reserve, wishing to pull output back to the natural level, increases the money supply. The increase in the money supply does not immediately affect spending. Its initial effects are on interest rates and wealth. The excess supply of money is used to purchase financial assets, driving their prices up and interest rates down. Eventually the lower interest rates and greater financial wealth cause investment and consumption spending to rise.

Unfortunately, we do not know when "eventually" is. It could be a year or more after the increase in the money supply. By that time the trough of the recession might be several months in the past. If so, the money supply injection will cause the expansion already in progress to be larger, possibly causing the economy to overheat as output rises above the natural level. Such excessive aggregate demand pressure could lead the Federal Reserve to reduce the money supply (or the growth rate of the money supply), which would eventually shift aggregate demand to the left. The timing of this shift is also unknown and could come when the spending growth is slowing down on its own. If so, the money supply reduction could throw the economy into a recession.

Most monetarists believe that money supply changes have been destabilizing in the past. They argue that such changes have magnified the natural tendency of the economy to fluctuate around the natural output level and that the natural fluctuations in output, caused by imperfect information, weather

Lag in the effect of money supply changes Time between a change in the money supply and the consequent change in aggregate demand.

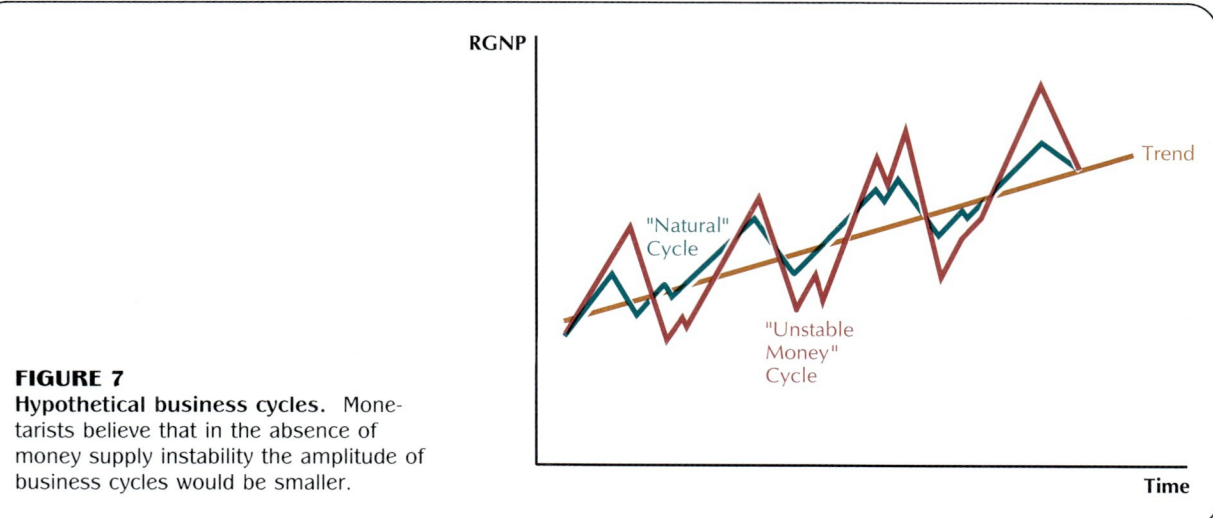

FIGURE 7
Hypothetical business cycles. Monetarists believe that in the absence of money supply instability the amplitude of business cycles would be smaller.

SECTION RECAP
Monetarists argue that money supply instability is the source of most business cycle movements. Exogenous changes in the money supply alter the level of aggregate demand. Since wages and prices are sticky in the short run, real GNP changes.

shocks, or international factors, would be small if they were not reinforced by money supply fluctuations. In effect, monetarists claim that the natural cycle would appear as shown in Figure 7 were it not for a constant string of monetary shocks that causes the cyclical fluctuations to be much larger than they would otherwise be.

Why do monetary policymakers persist in policies that harm the economy? Monetarists do not claim that the monetary authorities are evil or deranged or that they possess wrong motives. Rather, monetarists assert that the Federal Reserve consistently has tried to do more than it is able to do. Monetary policy intended to offset the cycle (*countercyclical* policy) actually magnifies the cycle (*procyclical* policy). The major source of cyclical fluctuations is the government, not the private market economy.

New Classical Modifications of Monetarist Theory

Monetarist theory as developed by Friedman, Karl Brunner, Allan Meltzer, and others was based on the idea that expectations are formed adaptively. If expectations are backward looking, a change in the money supply that increases spending always fools people and generates real output effects in the short run.

The new classical economics revolves around the assumption of rational expectations: People use all available information that is economically efficient in forming their expectations of future price level movements. Surely the information used would include past and future expected levels of the money supply. If people include the expected future money supply in forming their expectations, *and* if prices are flexible and are set on the basis of those expectations, *anticipated changes in the money supply will have no effect on output.* Wages rise in anticipation of higher prices, and the short-run aggregate supply curve shifts upward by the same amount as the aggregate demand curve. Only *unanticipated* changes in the money supply affect output, since wages do not rise immediately and the SRAS curve is temporarily stationary.

The rational expectations hypothesis focuses on the predictability of money supply behavior. If the monetary authorities follow a systematic monetary policy rule, most movements of the money supply (or money supply growth rate) will be predicted. If prices are perfectly flexible, such monetary changes will have no output effects. Prices will move immediately to their new long-run equilibrium levels, and output will not change. If prices are not perfectly flexible, some output effects may result, but they will be offset whenever price changes do occur. Significant and long-lasting output effects must be caused by unanticipated monetary shocks (surprise movements in the money supply) coupled with prices that are rigid for significant periods of time. The contribution of the New Keynesian economics has been to explain why, even in a world of rational expectations, price and wage rigidity is widespread.

New Keynesian Economics

The aggregate supply model in this book is based on the notion that significant wage and price rigidities exist in the real world. Explicit and implicit contracts limit the response of wages to short-run demand shifts. Wage rigidities give rise to a positively sloped short-run aggregate supply curve. **New Keynesian Economics** is concerned with developing the microeconomic foundations of wage and price rigidity and the accompanying unemployment of labor and inventory fluctuations. Whereas Keynesian theory simply assumed that wages and prices were fixed until "full employment" was reached, New Keynesian theory attempts to explain *why* wages and prices are sticky (not fixed — all wages and prices change, though some change very infrequently). Thus, although New Keynesian Economics does not really provide a theory of the business cycle, applying the insights of New Keynesian Economics to Keynesian and monetarist theory helps us to better understand cyclical behavior.

New Keynesian Economics
A branch of theory devoted to developing the microeconomic foundations of wage and price rigidities.

Although New Keynesian theory focuses on the sources of rigidities, it does not ignore expectations, one of the crucial elements of New Classical theory. Expectations are not unimportant in a world with sticky prices. Although anticipated aggregate demand changes are predicted to have output effects in models with wage rigidities, the output effects of anticipated aggregate demand shifts may be smaller than the effects of unanticipated demand shifts.

Consider the following example. Suppose the Federal Reserve reacts systematically to economic conditions. When people observe changes in economic variables, they understand how the Federal Reserve will react. They are able to predict the future course of the money supply based on past Federal Reserve behavior. Now, suppose that events cause people to expect a money supply increase that shifts the aggregate demand curve from AD_0 to AD_1 in Figure 8. If prices were perfectly flexible, the economy would move from its initial position at point A to point D. Output would be unaffected, and prices would rise to their long-run equilibrium level. This is the New Classical result: An anticipated money supply increase (or decrease) does not affect output.

However, if wages and prices are not perfectly flexible, even anticipated demand shifts cause output to change. If wages did not adjust at all to the demand increase, the economy would move to point B. In both New Classical and New Keynesian theory, point B would be the short-run equilibrium position if the money supply increase and aggregate demand shift were *unanticipated*. We assumed, however, that the demand shift was anticipated. It is at this point that the New Keynesian theory differs from its New Classical coun-

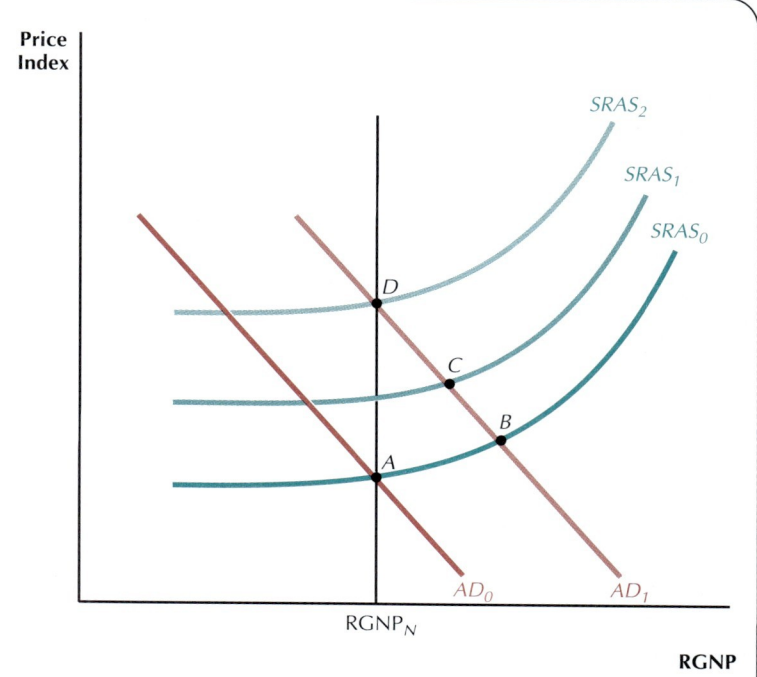

FIGURE 8
Possible outcomes of an aggregate demand increase. If wages are flexible and expectations are rational, an anticipated aggregate demand increase affects only prices; the economy moves from point A to point D. This is the New Classical result. If expectations are rational but some wages are fixed by contracts, the economy moves to point C. This is the New Keynesian result. If expectations are not rational or all wages are fixed in the short run, the economy moves to point B.

SECTION RECAP

New Classical economists appended rational expectations and perfect price flexibility to the monetarist model, yielding a model in which only unanticipated aggregate demand shifts affect real GNP. New Keynesians accept the assumption of rational expectations, but argue that wages are sticky in the short run. In their model, unanticipated aggregate demand shifts affect real GNP more than anticipated AD shifts do.

terpart. Although some wages remain unchanged for one to two years into the future because of preexisting contracts, other wages change immediately as expiring contracts are renegotiated to reflect the new conditions. Thus, an anticipated increase in aggregate demand is accompanied by some wage increases and an upward shift in the aggregate supply curve from $SRAS_0$ to $SRAS_1$. The economy moves to point C, the New Keynesian short-run equilibrium.

Using Figure 8, we can summarize the major results of the New Classical and New Keynesian theories as well as note how they differ. According to New Classical theory, an anticipated increase in aggregate demand affects only prices. The economy moves from point A to point D. An unanticipated increase in aggregate demand increases both prices and output; the economy moves to point B. This is identical to the effect of an unanticipated increase in AD in New Keynesian theory. However, an anticipated increase in aggregate demand increases both PI and RGNP, moving the economy to point C, according to New Keynesian theory. The price effect is larger and the output effect smaller for anticipated aggregate demand shifts than for unanticipated shifts. Thus, only unanticipated aggregate demand changes can cause cyclical fluctuations in New Classical theory, while any aggregate demand change can cause output to fluctuate in New Keynesian theory.

A Look at the Empirical Evidence

Sorting out the factors causing or contributing to cyclical fluctuations in output and employment is not easy. We summarize the major features of the cycle theories discussed above in Table 2.

Confronting the Theories with the Evidence   How well do these theories stand up to the evidence? We will examine the Keynesian theory first. Our analysis revolves around Table 3, which presents expenditure data from eight post-World War II recessions. (The recession that began in late 1990 is not included.)

Reading the Table. The first two columns of Table 3 provide the dates of the recession being analyzed. The third column shows the percentage decline in real GNP from the business cycle peak to the following trough. The remainder of the table provides information on the contribution to the real GNP decline made by seven expenditure categories. This contribution is in percentage terms. For example, consider the number under net exports in the first line of the table. Net exports contributed 26.9 percent of the 1948–1949 decline. In other words, the decline in net exports was equal to 26.9 percent of the total decline in real GNP.

TABLE 2
Summary of major features of cyclical theories

Keynesian   Investment changes, possibly caused by an accelerator relationship $[I = j(\Delta RGNP)]$ have a multiplier effect on AD. Nominal wages are rigid below the natural output level, so RGNP fluctuates with changes in AD.

   Important Prediction:
   Consumption changes are larger than investment changes.

Monetarist   Destabilizing money supply movements cause AD to fluctuate. Money affects spending with a lag of uncertain length. Money supply changes are exogenous. Wages are sticky because expectations are formed adaptively.

   Important Prediction:
   Money supply movements precede changes in GNP.

New Classical   Exogenous money supply shocks destabilize AD. Expectations are formed rationally, so monetary policy is taken into account in forming expectations. Prices and wages are flexible.

   Important Prediction:
   Only unanticipated money supply changes affect RGNP; anticipated changes affect only PI.

New Keynesian   Expectations are formed rationally, but wages are sticky due to explicit and implicit contracts. Both anticipated and unanticipated AD changes affect RGNP.

   Important Prediction:
   Anticipated AD changes affect PI by more and RGNP by less than unanticipated AD changes.

TABLE 3

Economic contractions since World War II

Contraction		% Decline	% of RGNP Decline Accounted for by						
Peak	Trough	RGNP	C_{Non+S}	C_{Dur}	I_{Res}	I_{Nonres}	Inv	Net X	G
1948.4	1949.4	1.35	−31.3	−71.6	−43.3	123.9	194.0	26.9	−98.5
1953.2	1954.3	3.29	−9.7	1.0	−4.4	4.9	44.7	−13.6	76.7
1957.3	1958.1	3.24	5.4	13.1	2.7	26.6	47.3	21.2	−16.2
1960.1	1960.4	1.88	−62.5	8.0	54.5	17.0	197.7	−44.3	−70.5
1969.3	1970.4	1.11	−152.5	59.2	−4.2	76.7	84.2	−7.5	45.0
1973.4	1975.1	6.56	−1.1	14.8	22.8	22.1	56.3	−8.8	−6.3
1980.1	1980.2	2.57	12.7	49.7	28.8	23.1	−5.7	−4.1	−4.7
1981.3	1982.4	3.08	−25.7	−3.0	4.9	33.0	86.6	33.4	−29.4
AVERAGE		2.80	−33.1	8.9	7.7	40.9	88.1	0.4	−13.0

Notation: C_{Non+S} = consumption expenditures on nondurable goods plus services; C_{Dur} = consumption expenditures on durable goods; I_{Res} = investment in residential construction; I_{Nonres} = nonresidential fixed investment; Inv = change in inventory investment; Net X = net exports; G = government purchases of goods and services. Decimals in years refer to quarters.

Data Sources: For the first five cycles, the data are taken from Robert J. Gordon, "Postwar Macroeconomics: The Evolution of Events and Ideas," in Martin Feldstein, ed., *The American Economy in Transition* (Chicago: University of Chicago Press, 1980), pp. 101–182. The data on the last two contractions come from *Economic Indicators*, December 1983.

Negative numbers appear frequently under several expenditure categories. A negative contribution to the decline in real GNP means that the expenditure being considered continued to grow during the recession. For example, in row one we see that nondurable goods and services consumption spending made a negative contribution of 31.3 percent to the 1948–1949 recession. While real GNP was falling, consumption of nondurable goods and services *rose* by an amount equal to 31.3 percent of the real GNP decline. Negative contributions indicate stabilizing factors; they tend to offset the cyclical decline.

Keynesian Theory: The Multiplier. Does consumption spending change in the same direction as autonomous spending changes, producing a multiplier effect on total spending? If by consumption spending we mean purchases of *nondurable goods and services*, the answer is clearly no. Such consumption spending is much better described by theories that stress long-run income than by the Keynesian current income theory. Consumption spending on nondurables and services actually continued to grow during six of eight post–World War II recessions, offsetting rather than reinforcing changes in autonomous spending.

Consumer durable spending has been much less stable. However, since spending on consumer durable goods is only one fifth as great as spending on nondurable goods and services, the multiplier effect produced by changes in consumer durable spending is small. Although consumer durable purchases contributed to the decline in real GNP in six of eight recessions, the average contribution to the RGNP decline was less than 9 percent, as shown in the last line of Table 3. The average contributions of the seven expenditure categories to the eight postwar contractions are shown graphically in Figure 9.

As Table 3 and Figure 9 illustrate, the major contributors to postwar recessions have been declines in inventory investment and nonresidential fixed investment. Inventory investment is the most unstable expenditure category. During the latter stages of an expansion, business inventories grow as consumer spending slows. During the peak quarters of the eight postwar cycles, inventory investment averaged 23 billion 1982 dollars. This inventory buildup left businesses with excess stocks of goods when consumer durable and nonresidential investment spending declined following the business cycle peak. Businesses cut back production (and laid off workers) until inventories fell to acceptable levels. During the trough quarters inventory investment averaged −17.8 billion 1982 dollars. The average swing in inventory investment from peak to trough was 40.8 billion 1982 dollars.

Inventory investment is endogenous. The sharp downturn in inventory investment during most contractions is merely a response to excessive inventory levels, rather than a reflection of business pessimism. When excessive inventories have been reduced, production for inventory resumes. Thus, we can conclude that one important part of investment instability over the cycle is endogenous.

The second largest contributor to cyclical contractions was nonresidential fixed investment. This is what Keynes had in mind when he formulated his theory of the business cycle. During the eight recessions considered here, nonresidential fixed investment fell on average by 19.1 billion 1982 dollars.

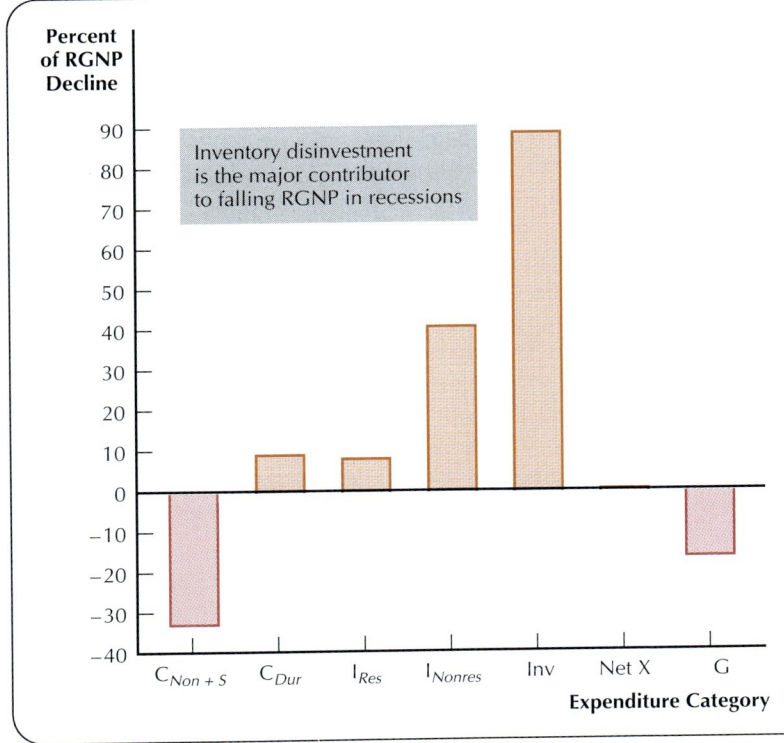

FIGURE 9
Average contribution to contractions. This chart shows the average change in seven expenditure categories during eight postwar recessions as a percentage of the change in real GNP. A negative number indicates that variable typically increased during recessions. Notation: C_{Non+S} = nondurable goods and services consumption, C_{Dur} = durable goods consumption, I_{Res} = residential construction investment, I_{Nonres} = nonresidential fixed (business) investment, Inv = inventory investment, Net X = net exports, G = total government purchases of goods and services.

Although Keynes may have been correct in focusing on business investment spending as the major source of recessions, he does not appear to have been correct with respect to the size of the effects of investment downturns. The largest contributor to recessions — declines in inventory investment — is an endogenous variable that may cause a recession of moderate size, but cannot cause a depression. Although somewhat unstable, nonresidential fixed investment has not been unstable enough to generate a recession of more than moderate size. Because consumption spending has been quite stable, the multiplier effect of investment spending declines is small, as the long-run income theory of consumption predicts. Indeed, the multiplier may well be a fraction.[4]

We can summarize our analysis of the Keynesian theory of the business cycle as follows:

1. Keynesians are correct in focusing on investment spending as the most unstable component of aggregate demand. However, inventory investment, not fixed business (nonresidential) investment, is the most unstable component of aggregate demand.

2. Most investment fluctuations appear to be endogenous responses to changes in spending. This is surely true of inventory investment and to a large degree may be true of fixed business investment.

3. The accelerator model, taken to include inventory investment, may provide a reasonably good model of the cycle.

4. Consumption spending is far more stable than the simple Keynesian consumption function predicts. Because consumption spending is stable, the multiplier effect of investment changes is very small.

5. The economy appears to be reasonably stable, though subject to recurrent cyclical fluctuations of relatively modest size. There appears to be little likelihood of a major depression unless some large outside shock hits the economy. It is noteworthy that the largest postwar recession (in terms of lost output), which occurred from the fourth quarter of 1973 to the first quarter of 1975, was due primarily to an exogenous shock. That was the period when OPEC quadrupled the price of crude oil, forcing production costs up sharply in all industrialized countries.

Monetarist Theory: Money Supply Instability. From our discussion of expenditure patterns we can conclude that one assumption of monetarist theory appears to be correct. The economy seems to be relatively stable. We should note that part of the reason for that stability may be government spending and taxation patterns. As Figure 9 shows, government purchases of goods and services were, on the average, slightly stabilizing in the postwar period (though in a couple of instances they contributed greatly to the recession). Countercyclical transfer payments, financed by borrowing, may have contributed to the stability of consumption spending. Nevertheless, the economy appears to

---

[4]Statistical simulations with a large econometric model of the economy indicate that the multiplier effect of a change in government purchases of goods and services is about 1.3 one year after government spending changes. The size of the multiplier then declines to 1.0 after two years, 0.2 after three years, and −0.9 after four years. See Flint Brayton and Eileen Mauskopf, "Structure and Uses of the MPS Quarterly Econometric Model of the United States," *Federal Reserve Bulletin,* February 1987.

be much more stable than many Keynesians believed it to be as late as the 1960s.

Monetarism asserts that (1) money supply movements are correlated with movements in nominal GNP, (2) money supply movements are the exogenous variable causing GNP movements, not vice versa, (3) since prices are sticky, exogenous money supply movements cause short-term movements in real GNP (cyclical movements), and (4) although the long-run growth rate of real GNP is independent of the growth rate of the money supply, the inflation rate is highly correlated with it. By and large, propositions 1, 3, and 4 are confirmed by the evidence. The status of proposition 2 — that money supply movements are the cause and GNP movements the effect — is somewhat less certain.

Figures 10 and 11 illustrate the relationship between the growth of the M1 money supply and nominal GNP. The relationship has been tighter over some periods than over others. During the 1950s, the connection between the two-quarter growth rate of M1 and the two-quarter growth rate of GNP was very loose. The major cyclical movements over the course of the two complete cycles shown in Figure 10 (a) appear to have been caused by expenditure shifts. Diminished money supply growth may have contributed to the 1957–1958 recession. However, the 1953–1954 recession was primarily the result of a reduction in government purchases of goods and services following the end of the Korean War.

The correlation between money growth and GNP growth was much tighter in the 1960s. The growth rates tend to move up and down together over the course of the longest cycle of this century, shown in Figure 10 (b). As monetarists would expect, changes in the money supply growth rate tend to lead (precede) changes in the GNP growth rate.

The effect of money growth on GNP growth appears even clearer in the 1969 third-quarter to 1980 first-quarter period, shown in Figure 11 (a). M1 growth definitely leads GNP growth throughout this two-cycle period.

The relationship between money growth and GNP growth is not so clear in the 1980s. Declining velocity after 1981 led to a divergence in the growth rates of money and GNP. The money supply grew very rapidly during the 1982–1986 period, but GNP growth did not keep up. People were content to increase the amount of money they held rather than spending all the newly created money.

Although the correlation between money growth and GNP growth is much less than perfect over the course of the postwar period — which implies that velocity has not been completely stable — monetarist proposition 1 seems to be confirmed to a reasonable extent by the data.

The third proposition — that money growth and real GNP are correlated over the course of business cycles — also seems to be valid. If prices are less than perfectly flexible, such correlation is the natural result of correlation between money growth and nominal GNP growth. Figures 12 and 13 illustrate the relationship between money growth and real GNP growth for the same periods as shown in Figures 10 and 11.

The fourth proposition — that long-run real GNP growth is not related to long-run money supply growth and that long-run inflation is highly related to money growth — is supported by the empirical evidence in Table 4, which gives the growth rates of money, real GNP, and the price level for all the nonwartime periods in this century. The periods begin and end with cyclical

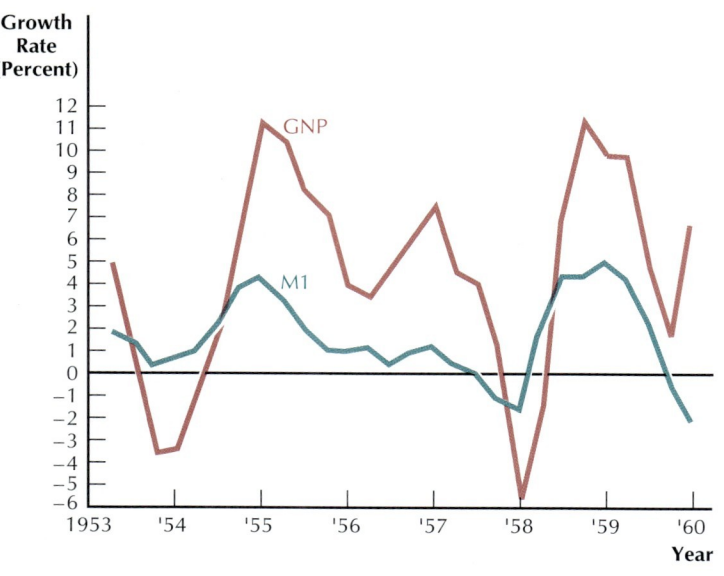

(a) 1953.2–1960.1

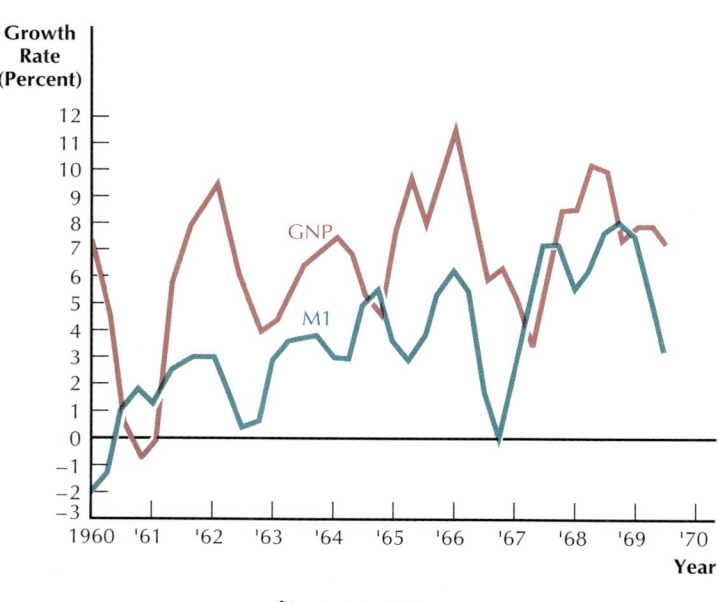

(b) 1960.1–1969.3

FIGURE 10
GNP and M1 growth. *(a) 1953.2–1960.1 (b) 1960.1–1969.3.*
Sources: *Survey of Current Business* and Federal Reserve *Bulletin*, various issues.

WHAT CAUSES BUSINESS CYCLES? ■ 853

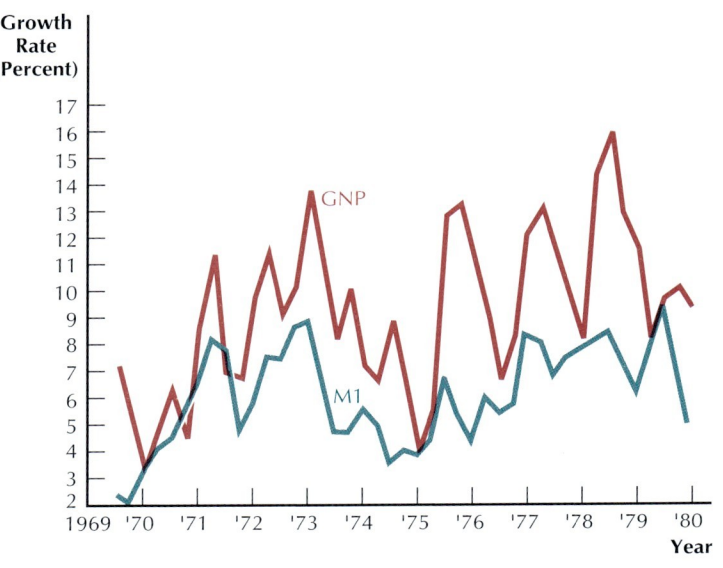

(a) 1969.3–1980.1

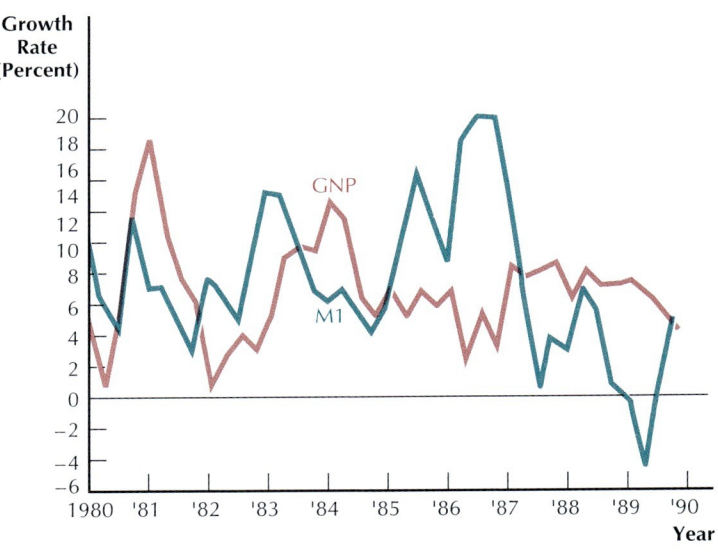

(b) 1980.1–1989.4

FIGURE 11
GNP and M1 growth. (a) 1969.3–1980.1 (b) 1980.1–1989.4.
Sources: *Survey of Current Business* and Federal Reserve *Bulletin*, various issues.

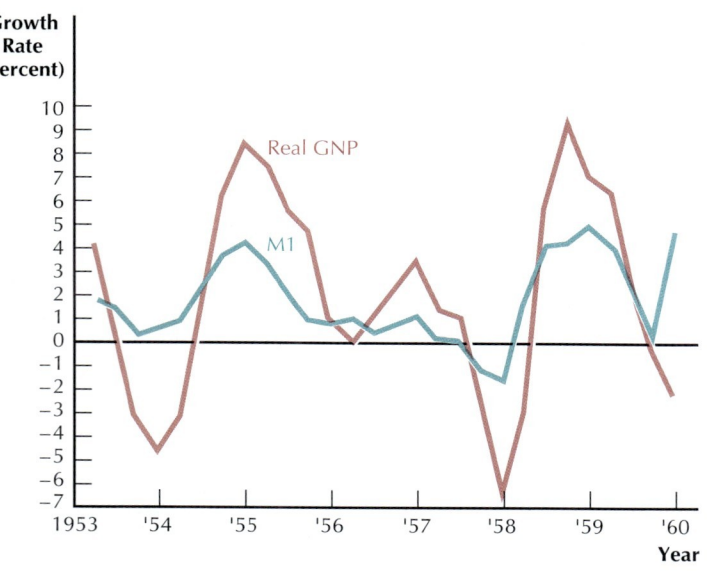

(a) 1953.2–1960.1

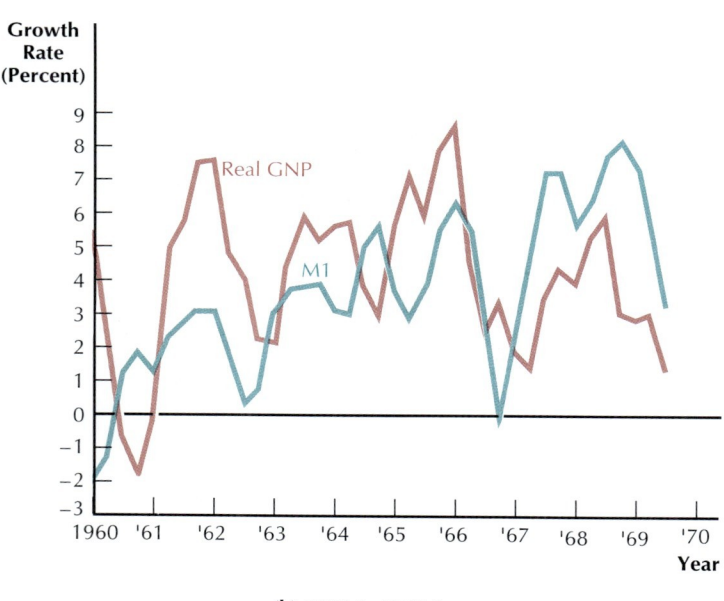

(b) 1960.1–1969.3

FIGURE 12
Real GNP and M1 growth. (a) 1953.2–1960.1 (b) 1960.1–1969.3. Sources: *Survey of Current Business* and Federal Reserve *Bulletin*, various issues.

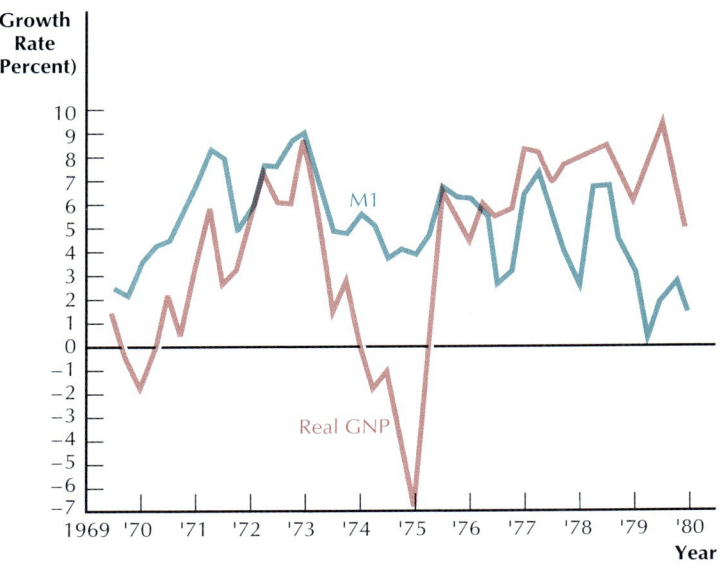

(a) 1969.3–1980.1

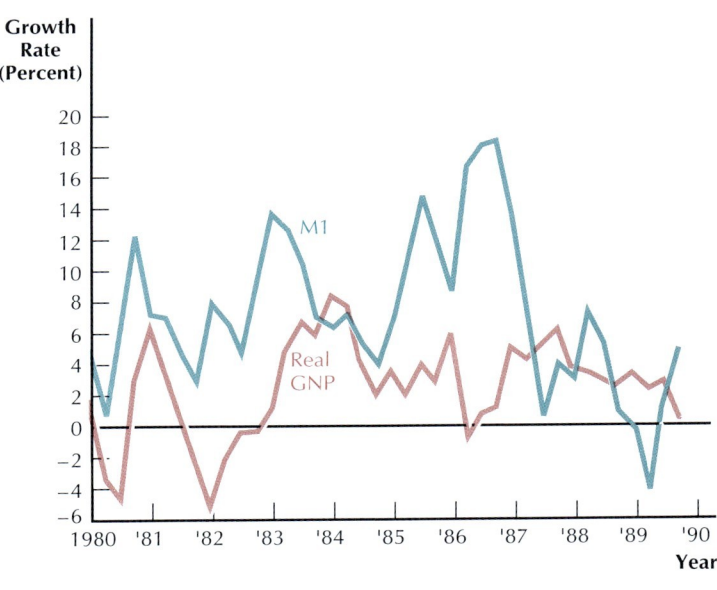

(b) 1980.1–1989.4

FIGURE 13
Real GNP and M1 growth. *(a) 1969.3–1980.1 (b) 1980.1–1989.4.*
Sources: *Survey of Current Business* and Federal Reserve *Bulletin,* various issues.

TABLE 4
Peacetime real GNP, price level, and money growth in the twentieth century

Period	Real GNP Growth	GNP Deflator Growth	M2 Growth
1900.1–1912.4	3.79%	1.71%	6.21%
1920.1–1929.3	3.82	−2.15	3.27
1929.3–1940.2	0.30	−1.18	1.36
1948.4–1960.1	3.59	2.23	3.45
1960.1–1973.4	3.98	3.42	7.96
1973.4–1989.4	2.60	4.93	8.59

Note: Growth rates are on an annual basis. Periods are from cycle peak to cycle peak, except for the last period, which ends with the most recent data available. Decimals in years refer to quarters.
Sources: Data appendix to Robet J. Gordon, "Price Inertia and Policy Ineffectiveness in the United States, 1890–1980," *Journal of Political Economy* 90 (December 1982), pp. 1087–1117; Milton Friedman and Anna J. Schwartz, *A Monetary History of the United States, 1867–1960* (Princeton, NJ: Princeton University Press, 1963); and *Economic Report of the President, 1990*.

peaks to correct for any cyclical effects. Money growth appears to make no difference for real GNP growth over the course of a decade or more. The growth rate of real GNP has been amazingly stable over time, falling outside the 3.5 to 4 percent range only during the Great Depression and during the 1973–1989 periods. Although the relationship between the inflation rate and the money growth rate is far less than perfect, there is some correlation between the two.

The relationship between money growth and the growth in GNP, real GNP, and the price level conforms to the monetarist view of the world. But is money growth the *cause* of the observed patterns in spending, output, and prices? This is an important and a difficult question. It is possible that changes in spending trigger endogenous changes in the money supply. If the Federal Reserve wants to hold interest rates constant, an increase in investment demand, which increases the demand for money, would cause the Fed to increase the money supply to prevent interest rates from rising. Figure 14 illustrates this. The demand for money rises as income increases following the increase in investment spending. Since the Fed wants to hold the interest rate constant at i_0, it increases the money supply. The money supply curve shifts outward, leaving the interest rate unchanged (at least until inflationary expectations rise). In such a case the increase in the money supply is caused by an increase in spending.

Economists have known for a long time that the money supply typically grows more rapidly during the expansion phase of a business cycle than during the contraction phase. This is exactly opposite of what countercyclical policy calls for. Either the Federal Reserve has mismanaged monetary policy, or the money supply has changed endogenously in response to changes in income, or both. Since changes in the form in which people hold money can affect the money multiplier and the size of the money supply, it is quite possible that a large percentage of cyclical money supply movements is endogenous. For ex-

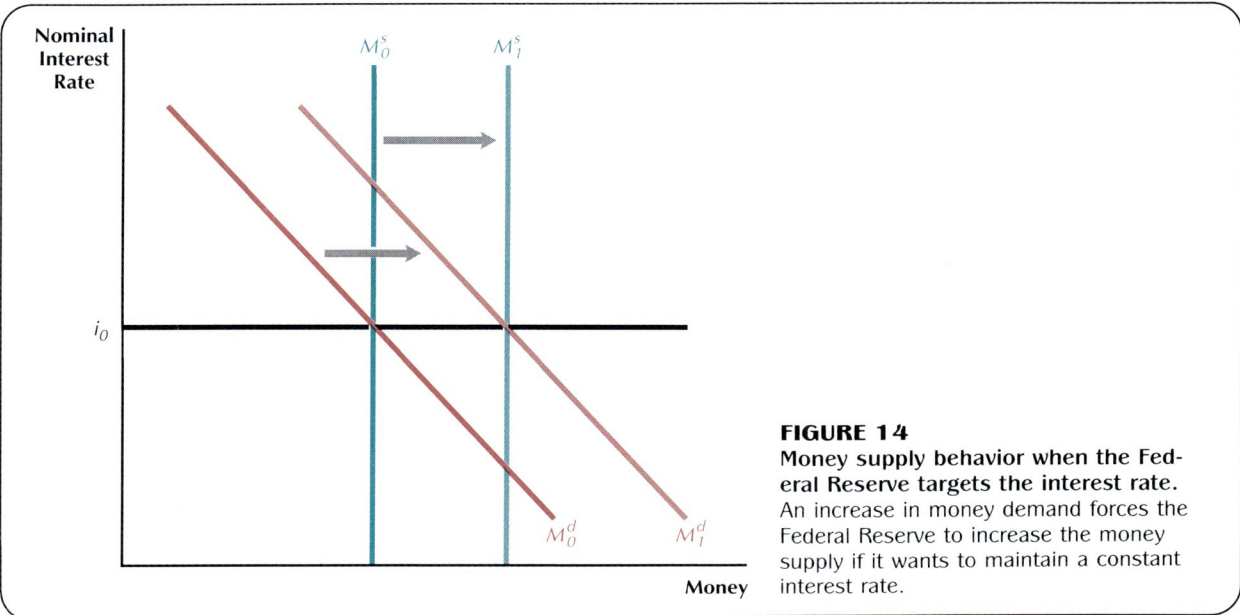

FIGURE 14
Money supply behavior when the Federal Reserve targets the interest rate. An increase in money demand forces the Federal Reserve to increase the money supply if it wants to maintain a constant interest rate.

ample, the reduced rate of money supply growth during recessions may be due in part to the tendency of the public to hold more currency relative to deposits during recessions. Such behavior reduces the money multiplier which, in the absence of faster growth of the monetary base, reduces money supply growth.

It should be noted that the behavior of the money supply during severe depressions is different from its behavior during normal recessions. Severe depressions have always been accompanied by monetary contractions of one type or another, contractions that have caused spending to decline precipitously. We must agree with Professor Friedman's claim that collapses in the money supply and the banking system have caused deep depressions. Money supply collapses do not appear to have been the result of depressions caused by other factors.

New Classical and New Keynesian Theory: Unanticipated Money Supply Shocks. Money supply movements affect both prices and output. Is output affected only by unanticipated money supply movements? The initial evidence presented by researchers such as Robert Barro suggested that was the case: Anticipated money supply growth affects only prices. However, more recent research decisively rejects this conclusion. Anticipated money supply movements — or more generally, anticipated aggregate demand shifts — do generate output effects. This is consistent with the New Keynesian theory, but contradicts the New Classical economics.[5]

---

[5]The evidence presented by Barro in support of the New Classical position appeared in "Unanticipated Money Growth and Unemployment in the United States," *American Economic Review*, March 1977, pp. 101–115. Since then a huge body of research has led to the conclusion that anticipated demand shifts do cause output changes. A good example of this research is Robert J. Gordon, "Price Inertia and Policy Ineffectiveness in the United States, 1890–1980," *Journal of Political Economy*, December 1982, pp. 1087–1117.

The question of whether anticipated demand shifts have larger price and smaller output effects than unanticipated demand shifts is more difficult to resolve. No clear-cut answer has emerged, but there is reason to doubt that unanticipated aggregate demand shifts have larger output effects than anticipated shifts.[6] If no difference between anticipated and unanticipated aggregate demand shifts exists, it must be because the short-run aggregate supply curve is fairly stable. For at least a year or two, aggregate demand shifts have output effects. This result does not mean, however, that government policy can push output to whatever level is desired. It is clear that over time the short-run aggregate supply curve does shift and that it shifts faster during high inflation periods than during low inflation periods.

Summing Up the Evidence on Cycles. Both the Keynesian and monetarist theories of the business cycle have something to contribute to our understanding of cyclical behavior. The monetarist assumption that the economy is basically stable seems correct. The Keynesian idea that fluctuations in investment spending cause aggregate output fluctuations also appears to have merit. The investment fluctuations may be fairly well explained by an accelerator model. Since the multiplier effect is quite small, possibly even a fraction, the fluctuations in investment spending generate real GNP fluctuations of relatively modest size. The average decline of real GNP from peak to trough during the eight recessions since World War II was only 2.8 percent.

Monetary fluctuations contribute to the cyclical behavior of output. During most normal cycles, much of the variation in the money supply growth rate appears to be simply a reaction to the state of the economy. Nevertheless, monetary fluctuations can be quite powerful. The sharp recession of 1981–1982 was primarily a monetary recession. The Federal Reserve acted strongly to reduce inflation from double-digit levels. The sharp reduction in the money supply growth rate caused output to fall by 3.08 percent from the third quarter of 1981 to the fourth quarter of 1982.

As mentioned, deep depression cycles apparently differ from normal cycles largely because the money supply collapses during deep depression cycles. To see how a monetary collapse can turn a normal recession into an economic disaster, we examine the worst contraction of this century, the Great Depression of 1929–1934.

SECTION RECAP
Empirical evidence suggests that the economy is relatively stable, but that endogenous investment fluctuations do contribute to business cycles. Monetary shocks have caused some cycles and appear to be a major factor in severe recessions.

What Causes Some Recessions to Turn into Depressions?

The most common view of the Great Depression is that it was caused by the stock market crash of 1929. Massive bank failures and general market breakdown then followed. The government stepped in and forcefully used fiscal policy to prevent a complete economic collapse. The market system was in such bad shape, however, that the economy remained stagnant in the face of government efforts to spur production. Finally, World War II led to a rebound in aggregate output.

Although this story has a plausible ring to it, it is *not* what happened. It is true that the stock market crash contributed to the recession of 1929–1930,

---

[6]For example, Frederic Mishkin maintains that the effects of anticipated monetary policy are as large as, if not larger than, unanticipated policy. See "Does Anticipated Monetary Policy Matter? An Econometric Investigation," *Journal of Political Economy*, February 1982, pp. 22–51.

TABLE 5

Real GNP and money supply behavior during the Great Depression

Date	Real GNP Index	% Change in RGNP	M2 Index	% Change in M2
1929.3	100.0		100.0	
		−14.5		−3.7
1930.4	85.5		96.3	
		5.9		−3.6
1931.2	88.4		92.8	
		−29.8		−25.0
1933.1	62.1		69.6	
		60.9		40.1
1937.1	99.9		97.5	
		−6.9		−0.5
1938.3	93.0		97.0	
		15.5		11.4
1939.4	107.4		110.3	

Note: Decimals in years refer to quarters.
Source: Data appendix to Robert J. Gordon, "Price Inertia and Policy Ineffectiveness in the United States, 1890–1980," *Journal of Political Economy* 90 (December 1982), pp. 1087–1117.

but the effect ended there. It is true that the government became more involved in economic affairs during the Depression than it had ever been before, but many of the actions taken by the monetary and fiscal authorities made the situation worse, not better. It is true that the market system broke down, but the breakdown was the result of the collapse of the financial system. Markets rebounded when the financial system regained its stability. Bad government policy must take much of the blame for the severity of the Great Depression.

The Great Depression can be broken down into stages. Table 5 presents data on these stages, and Figure 15 illustrates them. The first stage ran from the third quarter of 1929 to the fourth quarter of 1930. This stage appeared

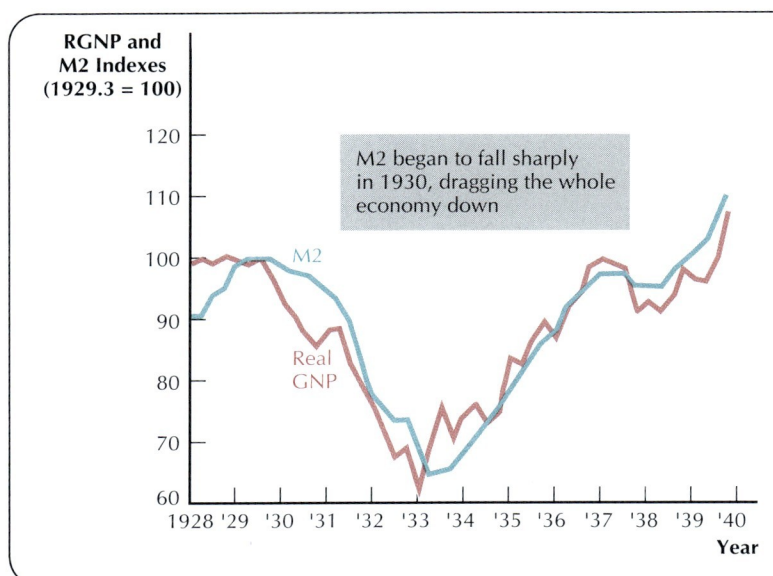

FIGURE 15
Great Depression: real GNP and M2.
The initial stage of the Depression appeared to be a normal, though severe, recession. The collapse of the banking system and the money supply in 1931 and 1932 plunged the economy into a deep depression. Source: Data appendix to Robert J. Gordon, "Price Inertia and Policy Ineffectiveness in the United States, 1890–1980," *Journal of Political Economy* 90 (December 1982), pp. 1087–1117.

to be a normal, though rather sharp, recession. Output fell by 14.5 percent. The recession appeared to be ending in the fourth quarter of 1930, however. Output rose during the first half of 1931; a normal expansion seemed to be under way.

The second stage of the Depression began in the third quarter of 1931. Output fell from the peak in the second quarter of 1931 to the trough of the Depression in the first quarter of 1933. Real GNP declined by 29.8 percent during this period. This was the period during which the monetary system collapsed. The M2 money supply fell by 25 percent during this period, and a massive number of banks failed.

From the trough of the first quarter of 1933, the economy rebounded. Output grew by 60.8 percent (from its low 1933 level) by the first quarter of 1937. However, a tight monetary policy caused another sharp recession in 1937. Finally, in the fourth quarter of 1938, growth resumed and the economy climbed out of its depressed state.

What caused such a massive economic downturn? Several factors contributed. In the middle of 1928 the Federal Reserve began restricting the money supply. The immediate reason for this was to check speculation in the stock market. The tight monetary policy cooled off the economy during 1929. When economic growth subsided, the stock market euphoria evaporated. Stock prices began to fall in September 1929, but trended upward during early October. The decline resumed in mid-October and turned into a panic on October 23. Standard and Poor's index of common stocks fell from 245 on October 10 to 162 on October 29 — a decline of 34 percent.

The stock market crash had almost no effect on the monetary system. The Federal Reserve Bank of New York provided loans to banks during the crisis, and the money supply actually grew slightly. Stock prices continued to decline until February 1930, when they began to rise again. They rose until the middle of the year. The entire episode left stock prices in mid-1930 at almost exactly the same level as in 1928. The speculative bubble of 1929, when prices rose above realistic levels, was removed, but the financial system was still in good condition.

During 1930, the government made a crucial policy mistake. On June 17, President Herbert Hoover signed the *Smoot–Hawley Tariff Act* into law. The act, which was pushed primarily by agricultural interests, placed heavy tariff duties on a wide range of imports. The sponsors' idea was to promote American agriculture and manufacturing by raising the price of foreign goods. The results of the act were tragic.

Other nations retaliated against the United States by increasing tariffs and instituting quotas against U.S. goods. International trade was reduced dramatically. Annual U.S. exports during the 1931–1935 period were 46 percent lower than during the 1926–1929 period. Imports fell by 44 percent. U.S. businesses that produced goods for export were badly harmed. Ironically, so was U.S. agriculture. By 1933, farm exports were less than one third what they had been in 1929.

The decline in foreign sales contributed to the stagnation of the economy in 1931. However, it was monetary forces that led to the drastic decline in production from mid-1931 through the end of 1933. Figure 15 shows that the money supply fell very rapidly over the entire period from mid-1931 through 1933. The decline in the money supply was due to a lack of faith in the financial

Does It Make **Economic Sense?**

Is the Business Cycle Disappearing?

The relative stability of the U.S. economy since World War II and the long expansion from November 1982 to late 1990 led some people to wonder if the business cycle is disappearing. Can the economy simply continue to grow year after year, without falling into a recession? Does a permanently growing economy make economic sense?

Economic data clearly indicate that business cycles have become less severe over time. Before World War II, recessions were more frequent and longer than since World War II. Furthermore, the average size of recessions has apparently declined in the post-War period. Kansas City Federal Reserve Bank economists C. Alan Garner and Richard E. Wurtz conclude that "an examination of the best available statistics and the complete historical record suggests the U.S. business cycle has moderated in the postwar years."* Thus, the behavior of the economy lends some credence to the view that the cycle is slowly disappearing.

A number of theoretical explanations for the smaller size of postwar recessions exist. Garner and Wurtz include among the factors moderating the size of cycles the following:

1. The larger size of government: Government spending is very insensitive to changes in real GNP. Stable government spending helps to stabilize the entire economy. As government spending has grown as a percentage of GNP, aggregate demand has become more stable.

2. The existence of automatic stabilizers: Transfer payments rise and taxes fall naturally during recessions, cushioning the effect on disposable income and stabilizing consumption spending.

3. More active monetary policy: The Federal Reserve has attempted to offset recessions in the postwar period, something it did not do earlier.

4. Growth of the service sector: Employment—and hence the income earned by workers—is more stable in the service sector than in manufacturing. As the percentage of workers employed in service occupations has grown, so has the stability of income and consumption spending.

5. The growth of international trade: In a recession, imports fall, forcing foreign producers to absorb part of the decline in spending. This stabilizes domestic demand.

6. Greater financial sector stability: Deposit insurance and tighter regulation of financial institutions in the postwar period have prevented any major banking crises.

7. New financial instruments: These have made it easier for firms and consumers to obtain credit to support spending. For example, most consumers have at least one credit card, which can be used to support consumption during temporary income shortfalls.

All these factors (and several more) have acted to moderate cyclical fluctuations. But will the cycle disappear? Garner and Wurtz think not. They argue that, while the economy has become more stable, it is still subject to exogenous shocks. A severe drought in agricultural regions, a foreign supply shock, or a poorly timed change in the money supply might topple the economy into a recession if it were already growing slowly. Since such exogenous events are difficult to predict and often impossible to prevent, it is unlikely that the economy can avoid all such shocks in the future. However, since endogenous business cycles are apparently becoming less likely, recessions may well be even less frequent in the future than in the past.

*C. Alan Garner and Richard E. Wurtz, "Is the Business Cycle Disappearing?" Federal Reserve Bank of Kansas City *Economic Review* (May/June 1990), p. 29.

---

system. People withdrew their deposits from banks in large numbers, triggering **bank runs** that drained reserves out of the banking system.

The Federal Reserve was created to prevent the sort of banking crisis that took place in 1931. The Fed was supposed to make loans to banks that needed emergency cash so that those banks could meet the withdrawals of depositors without having to sell their assets at relatively low prices. (Remember, banks keep only a fraction of their assets in the form of cash.) For a number of

Bank run
Large-scale withdrawal of deposits from one or more banks; depletes bank reserves.

reasons, the Fed failed to make such loans. The result was a spreading banking crisis that saw 2,293 banks fail in 1931, another 1,453 fail in 1932, and an astounding 4000 fail in 1933.

The failure of over 9000 banks in the 1930–1933 period contributed mightily to the 30 percent decline in the M2 money supply. Deposits fell sharply at banks that did not fail, as people preferred the safety of holding cash to the risk of holding deposits. Consequently, banks had fewer dollars to lend. The supply of credit largely dried up. It became quite difficult to obtain business loans. Since a modern market economy runs on credit, this was disastrous for economic activity. The result was the worst depression in U.S. history.

The reasons for the Federal Reserve's failure to put a halt to the banking crisis and decline in the money supply are too complex to discuss here in any detail. International considerations had much to do with the Fed's behavior. The United States was on the gold standard at the time, and Federal Reserve officials feared that gold would flow abroad if the money supply were expanded. The theory of monetary policy the Fed was following at that time, which stressed providing only the amount of funds demanded by businesses, also played a part. Whatever the reason for the Fed's policy breakdown, it seems clear that the severity of the Great Depression is directly traceable to the collapse of the monetary system. This must be viewed as largely a policy failure.

Fiscal policy actions in the United States during the Depression were rather small and ineffective. The Roosevelt administration promoted a number of policies that encouraged higher prices and wages—policies that appear to be the opposite of what was needed. Overall it is difficult to see how policymakers can be given a passing grade for their efforts during the fateful decade of the 1930s, though in their defense, they did not have available to them much of the data that economists use today in analyzing their behavior. It is difficult to make good decisions if you do not have good information about the problem.

SECTION RECAP
The Great Depression probably would have been an ordinary recession had the Federal Reserve not permitted the monetary system to collapse. A 25 percent reduction in M2 contributed greatly to the decline in real GNP in 1931 and 1932. Poor fiscal policy and international trade protectionism added to the economy's problems.

What Type of Stabilization Policy Might Be Successful?

A successful stabilization policy is likely to be one that creates a more stable environment for the private economy to operate in. Examples of such policies would be a monetary policy aimed at promoting price level stability over long periods of time and transfer payments that increase and decrease automatically as income falls or rises.

Many economists believe that the attempt to use monetary policy actively to counteract the business cycle contributed greatly to the rising inflation of the 1960s and 1970s. The Federal Reserve attempted to increase the monetary growth rate to offset recessions and decrease it to moderate expansions. Unfortunately, monetary policy does not affect spending immediately; the lag between the time the money supply growth rate changes and the time the growth rate of aggregate demand changes can lead to policy errors.

To carry out a successful countercyclical monetary policy, the Federal Reserve must (1) forecast when the peak or trough of a cycle will occur, (2) alter the money supply growth rate in the appropriate direction *before the cyclical turning point is reached*, and (3) hope that the lag in the effect of the money growth change is the length it expects it to be. Unfortunately, forecasting cyclical turning points is very difficult. Many times the economy has passed a cyclical peak or trough before the authorities realize it. Consequently, an activist monetary policy can easily end up increasing the money supply growth rate during expansions and decreasing it during recessions. This makes cyclical fluctuations worse.

To avoid making recessions more severe, the Federal Reserve has tended in the past to err on the side of expansion. This had the unfortunate side effect of pushing the inflation rate higher throughout the latter half of the 1960s and all of the 1970s. (Oil price shocks complicated things greatly in the 1970s.) Faced with double-digit inflation at the end of the 1970s, the Fed was forced to adopt a restrictive policy. The result was the severe contraction of 1981–1982.

A monetary policy geared toward maintaining price level stability sacrifices short-term output and employment gains in favor of long-term economic stability. Such a policy tends to be naturally somewhat restrictive when aggregate demand is growing rapidly and somewhat expansive when it is growing slowly. This sounds like a countercyclical policy, but the motto of a Federal Reserve committed to long-term price level stability would be "All things in moderation." Sharp policy changes would be carefully avoided. Under the leadership of Alan Greenspan, the Federal Reserve appears to have followed such a policy since 1987.

Transfer payments that change automatically as income rises and falls promote stability by evening out the flow of consumption spending. One of the best things about such automatic stabilizers is that they do not require legislative action. Congress is notoriously slow. By the time a bill designed to offset a recession is passed and implemented, the recession is usually over. Automatic stabilizers avoid the legislative lag.

The income tax system also acts as an automatic stabilizer. When income falls, tax payments decline. In effect, government absorbs part of the decline in income, leaving more dollars to be spent on consumption goods. More people also go on welfare rolls during recessions. Lacking income, they meet the eligibility requirements and automatically qualify for benefits.

The next two chapters analyze monetary and fiscal policy in greater depth. Here we wish only to note that the ideal of a smoothly growing economy, with no business cycles at all, is not something government can provide. The information required to carry out the systematic policy intervention necessary to offset all cyclical fluctuations simply does not exist. If it did exist, other unforeseen consequences might pop up. Too much policy activism can be destabilizing, making cycles larger than they would be if government adopted a more passive stance.

Summary

Business cycles are a recurrent feature of modern monetary economies. Cycles are irregular in their timing, but they have enough common features over time to cause economists to look for a single theory of cyclical behavior.

Four theories of cyclical behavior were discussed. The **Keynesian theory,** in its original form, stressed the extreme volatility of investment spending. Autonomous changes in investment spending due to changes in business expectations affect income. When income changes, so does consumption spending, thus generating a **multiplier effect.** Thus, relatively small changes in investment spending cause large changes in consumption spending and even larger changes in income.

Later versions of Keynesian theory stressed the **accelerator model** of investment spending. This model explains why investment spending might be unstable over the course of the cycle. The multiplier effect is an integral part of these models.

The major problem with the Keynesian theory of business cycles is the lack of a strong multiplier effect. Because consumption depends primarily on long-run income, changes in investment spending do not generate sizable changes in consumption spending. Thus, the multiplier is quite small. Investment is the most unstable component of aggregate demand, but the multiplier is small enough that these investment swings cause only moderately strong fluctuations.

The **monetarist theory** of cyclical fluctuations focuses on the behavior of the money supply over the course of cycles. Changes in the money supply growth rate cause aggregate demand growth to change. Since prices are not perfectly flexible, this generates changes in the growth rate of real output. Such output growth fluctuations last only until prices adjust, however.

The primary difficulty encountered by monetarist theory is demonstrating that changes in money supply growth cause cyclical fluctuations and not the other way around. It seems clear, however, that money supply collapses have been the major cause of deep depressions. The **Great Depression** appeared to be an ordinary recession until the banking system, and with it the money supply, collapsed.

New Classical economic theory is based on the hypothesis that expectations are formed rationally and that price and wages are flexible. Its major short-run conclusion is that only unanticipated monetary policy actions will have output effects. **New Keynesian** theory accepts the rational expectations hypothesis but argues that some wage and price rigidity is also rational. In New Keynesian models, both anticipated and unanticipated policy changes have output effects. The evidence indicates that both types of policy do indeed affect output.

The existence of business cycles does not justify activist countercyclical policy by the government. Such policy could be the source of cyclical fluctuations or could be ineffective in offsetting fluctuations originating in the private sector. Whether countercyclical policy is useful depends upon how costly cyclical fluctuations are thought to be (that is, how long and deep recessions are) and how effective government policy is in controlling aggregate demand.

Questions for Thought

Knowledge Questions

1. What was the primary factor causing cyclical fluctuations in Keynes's original theory of cyclical fluctuations? How did changes in this one variable affect the whole economy?
2. Describe the basic monetarist theory of the business cycle.
3. What are the major differences between the predictions of New Classical theory and standard monetarist theory? What is the source of these differences?

4. In what important ways was the Great Depression different from normal recessions?
5. What categories of spending contribute most heavily to cyclical fluctuations? What categories act as stabilizers, offsetting cyclical movements?

Application Questions

6. "Correlation does not imply causality." What does this statement mean? Give an example of variables that are correlated but are not the cause of one another.
7. Assume expectations are formed rationally and all wages are set for three years by explicit contracts. Every year, one third of the labor contracts expire and are renegotiated. Before wage setting in Year 1, the Federal Reserve announces a one-time increase in the money supply. Trace out the behavior of the economy over Years 1 through 3, explaining why it moves as it does.
8. What has government contributed to the increased stability of the economy since World War II?
9. Why is there reason for skepticism that activist fiscal policy can dampen the size of cycles any more than they have already been dampened?

Synthesis Questions

10. Critique the original Keynesian theory of the business cycle. In what ways does it fail to explain actual behavior?
11. How does the accelerator theory improve the original Keynesian theory of the cycle?
12. Does New Keynesian theory have anything to contribute to the monetarist explanation of cyclical fluctuations? Explain.

OVERVIEW

In recent years, several opinion polls have asked business leaders the question, Who is the most powerful person in the United States? Invariably the president ranks number one. Usually the person ranked second is the chairman of the Board of Governors of the Federal Reserve System. This high ranking reflects the importance attached to monetary policy. For good or for bad, monetary policy is powerful. If conducted properly, it can contribute to the smooth operation of the economy. If conducted poorly, it can generate high inflation, high unemployment, or both.

The basic principles of monetary policy have been described in previous chapters. This chapter investigates some of the more complex issues confronting policymakers.

Monetary Policy: A Further Treatment

Since economists disagree considerably over what constitutes good monetary policy, we will not be able to say one particular type of policy is clearly the best. Nevertheless, after reading this chapter you should understand the important issues involved in making monetary policy decisions. This will enable you to form intelligent opinions about the course of monetary policy in the years ahead.

The chapter begins with a review of the monetary transmission mechanism, the channels by which a change in the money supply affects aggregate demand.

Economists generally agree that the transmission mechanism is quite broad, as we noted in the earlier chapter on monetary policy, although they differ in their appraisals of the relative importance of different channels. We follow this discussion with an examination of the Keynesian and monetarist views of monetary policy. The major difference in policy prescriptions between these two groups has to do

CHAPTER 33

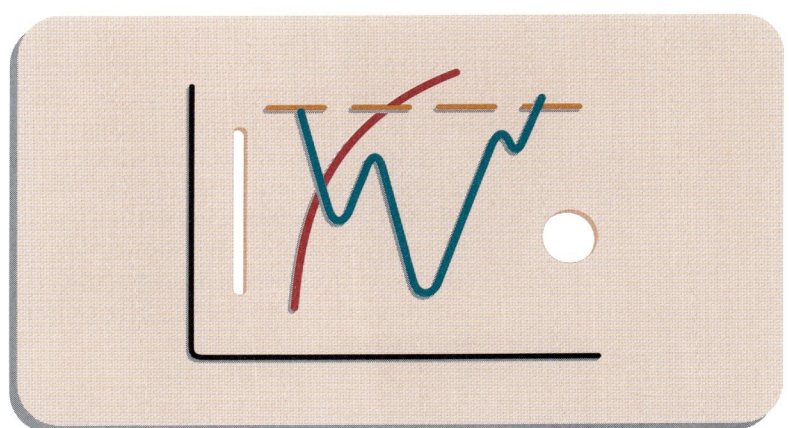

with whether the Federal Reserve should pursue a discretionary countercyclical policy or follow a stable money growth rule. We critique both viewpoints, pointing out the strengths and weaknesses of each. Included in the critique is an assessment of the historical record and a discussion of some technical issues relating to monetary control.

Learning Objectives

After reading and studying this chapter, you will be able to:

1. Explain the Keynesian view of monetary policy and discuss why Keynesians prefer discretionary policy.
2. Define the term *lag in the effect of monetary policy* and explain how lags affect policymaking.
3. Explain the monetarist theory of economic instability and how it relates to monetarist policy prescriptions.
4. Explain how the assumption of rational expectations alters what is considered good monetary policy.
5. Discuss the factors that appear to have caused the relatively poor performance of monetary policy over the past two decades.
6. Assess the ability of economists to forecast well enough to carry out a discretionary monetary policy.
7. State the issues involved in the rules-versus-discretion debate about monetary policy.

Monetary Transmission Mechanism

The modern view of the monetary transmission mechanism is very broad. Money is thought to affect spending in a number of ways. Figure 9 in the chapter entitled "The Banking System, the Federal Reserve, and Monetary Policy" diagrams eight separate channels through which a change in the money supply can affect aggregate demand. The eight effects can be summarized as follows: Starting in equilibrium ($M^d = M^s$), an increase in the money supply creates an excess supply of money at the prevailing interest rate. The excess money is exchanged for financial or real assets. When the demand for bonds and equities (financial assets) rises, the prices of such assets are pushed upward. Since bond prices are inversely related to interest rates, interest rates fall (assuming inflationary expectations do not rise). Higher stock prices and lower real interest rates encourage more investment and consumption spending both because financing current spending is now cheaper (in terms of interest expense) and because the rise in asset prices increases the financial wealth of the public.

An exchange of money for real assets can also take place. Purchases of new real assets drive aggregate demand up directly. Purchases of used real assets push up used asset prices, making new assets more attractive. As people switch to new real assets, aggregate demand is pushed up further.

This view of the way in which money affects economic activity is essentially a monetarist view. The transmission mechanism as developed by Keynes and adopted by his followers in the 1950s and 1960s was much narrower. It stressed the exchange of excess money for bonds, omitting the equity and real asset effects. It thus focused on the effect of money on the interest rate and of the interest rate on spending. The original Keynesian view could be schematized in this way:

$$\uparrow M^s \rightarrow \downarrow i \rightarrow \downarrow r^e \rightarrow \uparrow I \rightarrow \uparrow AD \rightarrow \uparrow RGNP, \uparrow PI$$

In the standard Keynesian view, if changes in the expected real interest rate have little effect on investment spending, the impact of money supply changes on aggregate demand is weak. Figure 1 shows the case of interest-insensitive investment spending. If changes in the expected real interest rate have little effect on the amount of investment spending, the effect on aggregate spending is minimal even if a change in the money supply significantly affects the expected real interest rate.

Monetarists stress not only the effects that work through the interest rate, but also wealth and direct substitution effects. The schematic of the monetarist transmission mechanism is more complicated:

$$\uparrow M^s \rightarrow \downarrow i \rightarrow \downarrow r^e \rightarrow \uparrow I, C_D \rightarrow \uparrow AD \rightarrow \uparrow RGNP, PI$$
(with Direct and Wealth channels)

The monetarist transmission mechanism includes the Keynesian channel (through interest rates), but also stresses the fact that money can be substituted directly for real goods and services and that changes in the money supply can generate wealth effects that also affect spending.

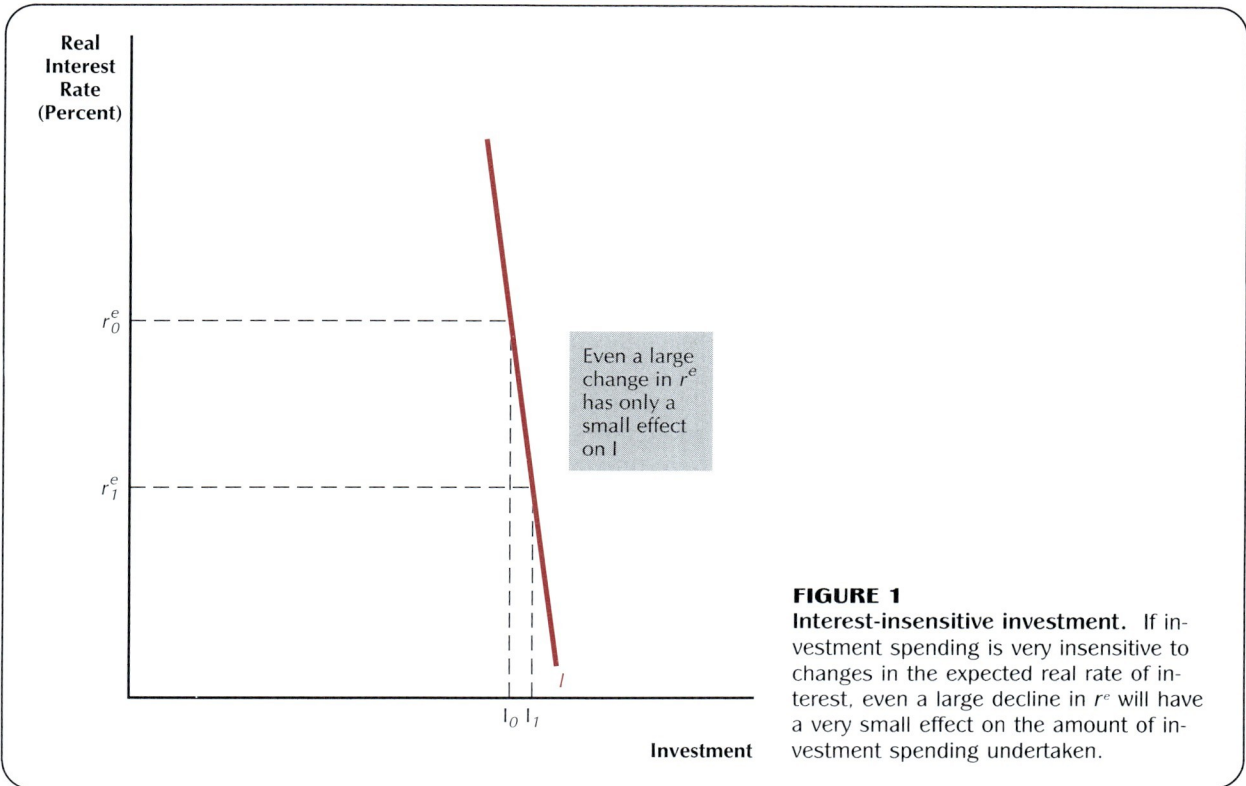

FIGURE 1
Interest-insensitive investment. If investment spending is very insensitive to changes in the expected real rate of interest, even a large decline in r^e will have a very small effect on the amount of investment spending undertaken.

In the monetarist view, even if the effect of money on spending *through the interest rate* is small, monetary policy may still be powerful. Since empirical studies have indicated that some noninterest-rate channels are in fact important, most Keynesians today accept the monetarist view of the transmission mechanism as valid. However, Keynesians still focus on the financial market effects — through interest rates, equity prices, and wealth — and downplay the significance of the direct exchange of money for real assets. Nevertheless, the acceptance of the broad transmission mechanism by Keynesians and monetarists alike means that most economists agree that changes in the money supply have powerful effects on aggregate demand.

SECTION RECAP
Changes in the money supply have powerful effects on aggregate demand, working directly through interest rates and wealth.

Theory of Monetary Policy

What type of monetary policy is best for the economy? An economist would answer that question depending upon his or her view of how the economy functions. Is the private sector of the economy stable or unstable? Are fluctuations in output and employment caused by erratic shifts in private spending or by other factors (government or supply shocks)? Are prices and wages fairly flexible, or are they rigid for long periods of time? Are expectations forward looking (rational) or backward looking (adaptive)? How one answers these questions goes a long way toward determining one's preferred monetary policy. Let us briefly recount the Keynesian and monetarist views of the world.

Keynesian View of the Economy

Keynesian business cycle theory focuses on endogenous changes in investment spending as the main cause of cyclical fluctuations. The accelerator model summarizes the Keynesian view that investment instability lies at the heart of macroeconomic instability. Given a relatively large multiplier, investment fluctuations can generate relatively large aggregate fluctuations.

The Keynesian view of the supply side stresses the rigidities that prevent wages and prices from moving rapidly to clear markets. Wage and price rigidities give rise to a short-run aggregate supply curve that is fairly flat over much of its range and that does not shift rapidly when output differs from its natural level. Keynesians especially stress downward wage and price rigidity; the SRAS curve shifts downward (to the right) only after a protracted period of high unemployment and low output. A decline in investment spending that reduces aggregate demand could reduce output below the natural level for several years in the absence of government policy actions to increase aggregate demand.

Most Keynesians do not deny that the natural corrective powers of the economy will eventually return the economy to the natural output level. However, they believe the time required for such a natural healing process to occur is unacceptably long. The lost output and pain of unemployment suffered while waiting for the economy to right itself are excessive and unnecessary. Thus, the Keynesian view that the Federal Reserve should pursue an activist monetary policy is based on the belief that (1) cyclical fluctuations primarily originate in the private sector, and (2) wage and price rigidities prevent the economy from adjusting quickly to relatively low output levels.

Keynesian Theory of Countercyclical Policy

Countercyclical monetary policy
Policy designed to offset business cycle fluctuations by increasing the money supply as a recession approaches and decreasing the money supply when an expansion overheats.

Given the Keynesian view of the world, a **countercyclical monetary policy** — a policy designed to offset cyclical fluctuations — is appropriate. To offset cyclical downturns the Federal Reserve must increase the money supply at the appropriate time. The increased money supply should encourage more spending at the same time that private spending would be weakening in the absence of an expansive monetary policy. To prevent aggregate demand from becoming excessive and causing inflation, the Federal Reserve must decrease the growth rate of the money supply at the appropriate time.

The basic notion of countercyclical policy is simple: When private demand weakens, increase the money supply to strengthen it, and when private demand is too strong, reduce the money supply to offset inflationary pressures. Unfortunately, monetary policy does not immediately affect aggregate demand. There is a **lag in the effect of monetary policy** on aggregate demand; some time passes before a change in the money supply generates a change in aggregate demand. The presence of lags makes monetary policy much more difficult than it would be if no lags existed.

Lag in the effect of monetary policy
Time that elapses between a change in the money supply and the consequent change in aggregate demand.

Since a change in the money supply affects aggregate demand with a lag, any policy action designed to prevent cyclical fluctuations must be taken *before the turning point in the cycle is reached*. Suppose that the lag in the effect of monetary policy is six months. Then, as shown in Figure 2, to offset the recession that begins at time *t*, the Federal Reserve must increase the money supply at time *t* minus six months. If it waits until time *t*, the recession will be under way before aggregate demand responds to the increased money supply.

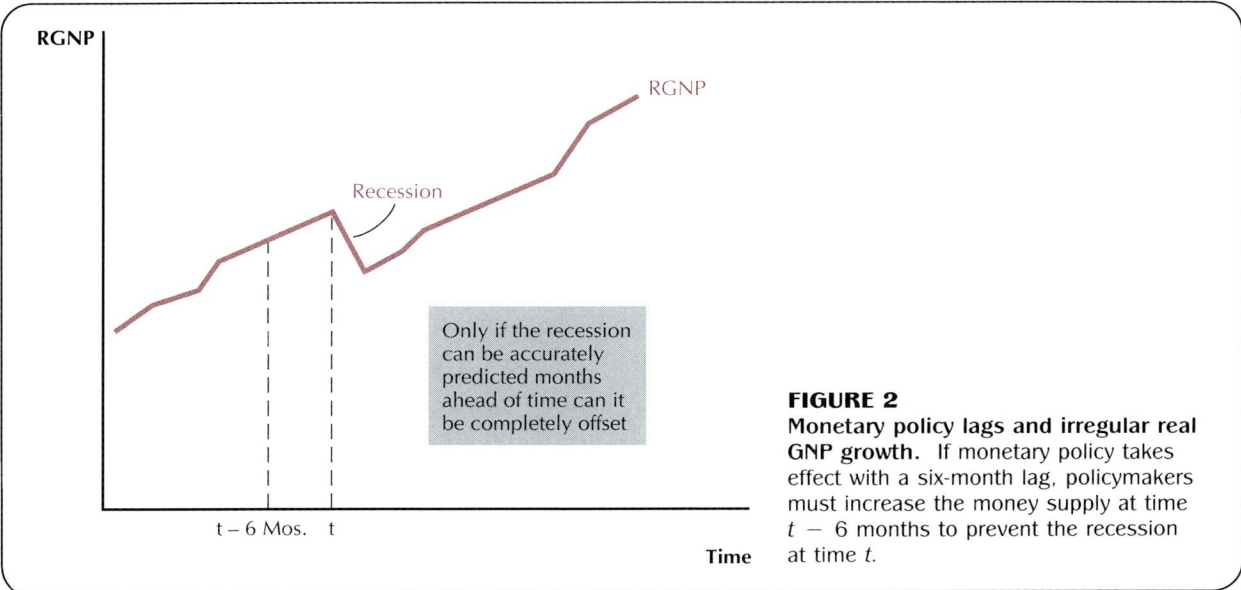

FIGURE 2
Monetary policy lags and irregular real GNP growth. If monetary policy takes effect with a six-month lag, policymakers must increase the money supply at time $t - 6$ months to prevent the recession at time t.

Lags in the effect of monetary policy create problems of two types. First, the Federal Reserve must be able to estimate the length of the lag. If lag length is stable, this is no problem, but if it is unstable, policy becomes very difficult. Second, the Federal Reserve must be able to forecast the course of the business cycle reasonably well. To prevent a cyclical downturn or excessively rapid expansion, the Fed must know the change is imminent.

Even if the Federal Reserve cannot accurately predict cyclical turning points and hence prevent economic fluctuations, countercyclical policy may be useful in reducing the size and duration of recessions. If the economy is characterized by wage and price rigidities, a policy change that is a bit late might still have beneficial effects.

SECTION RECAP
The Keynesian view of monetary policy stresses the need to use policy actively to offset fluctuations in aggregate demand.

Monetarist View of the Economy

Monetarists believe that the private sector of the economy is stable. Taking a quantity theory approach (introduced in the preceding chapter), monetarists maintain that velocity is relatively stable. Although not constant over time, movements in velocity typically are neither large nor erratic. The equation of exchange states that:

$$M \times V = PI \times RGNP$$

The term on the left side of the equation ($M \times V$) represents aggregate demand. If velocity is stable, a policy of holding the money supply stable (or causing it to grow at a stable rate) will produce aggregate demand stability.

The view that velocity is relatively stable implies that aggregate demand instability — if it exists — must be due to money supply instability. In this view, the major cause of cyclical fluctuations is not shifts in private sector spending but stop-and-go monetary policy. Therefore, the proper monetary policy is not a discretionary countercyclical policy, but a policy of allowing the money supply to grow at a stable rate over time. By pursuing stable money growth, the Federal Reserve eliminates monetary shocks as a source of business cycle fluctuations.

The monetarist view of the supply side of the economy also differs from the Keynesian view. Monetarists realize that wages and prices are not perfectly flexible, but they believe that they adjust fairly rapidly to excess demands or supplies. Even when most wages and many prices are sticky in the short run (due to implicit and explicit contracts), they will adjust to new economic conditions without long delays. A stable monetary policy enables people to form expectations with reasonable confidence that the expectations will not be significantly wrong. As contracts adjust, the economy returns to its natural level.

In summary, the monetarist view of the economy is based on the belief that (1) most aggregate demand fluctuations are monetary in origin, and (2) wages and prices adjust quickly enough that lengthy periods of output above or below the natural level are unlikely.

Monetarist Theory of Monetary Policy

If erratic monetary policy is the major source of aggregate demand instability, a stable monetary policy seems appropriate. Over the past twenty years, monetarists and New Classical economists have addressed the question of how monetary stability stabilizes the entire economy. Their answer revolves around the necessity of planning for the future and the harmfulness of uncertainty.

The Need to Plan and the Importance of Uncertainty All successful economic agents plan: Households plan for future expenditures by saving in the present, and businesses plan new facilities to meet anticipated demand growth.

The more stable the economy, the easier it is to make good economic plans. If the economy is stable, tomorrow will be much like today. Business strategies that are successful now will probably work well in the future. Instability makes planning much more difficult. If the economy is subject to extreme instability, business and household planners are more uncertain of future economic conditions. The probability of making planning errors increases.

Neither businesses nor households are willing to risk as much when the future is highly uncertain as when they have some confidence in the future course of events. Economic instability — variability of real GNP growth and inflation — reduces the productivity of an economy. Businesses curtail many long-term projects for fear that they will fail. As a result, the capital stock grows more slowly than it otherwise would, reducing the growth rate of the economy and ultimately harming everyone.

Uncertainty about the future makes households more conservative, too. They are less likely to buy expensive consumer durable goods or invest in new homes if they are unsure about the future. The firms supplying durables or building homes thus suffer.

Monetarists argue that the best monetary policy is to establish a **policy rule** — an announced pattern that is always followed — and stick to it. The rule could be as simple as "Cause the money supply to grow 3 to 5 percent per year," or "Hold the price of gold at $X per ounce." Rules that do not alter the growth rate of the money supply in response to economic events are called **passive rules**. On the other hand, the rule could be an **active rule**, relating

Policy rule
Formal guidelines followed by policymakers.

Passive rule
Policy rule that does not alter the money supply in response to changes in economic activity.

Active rule
Policy rule that adjusts the money supply in response to changes in economic activity.

monetary growth to the unemployment rate, the inflation rate, the GNP growth rate, or to movements in velocity. The fact that a well-known rule exists is more important than the rule itself. Proponents of monetary policy rules argue that a known, stable monetary policy benefits the economy by reducing uncertainty about the future. This stability, rules proponents argue, increases economic growth.

The Incentive for Policymakers to Cheat Even if the Federal Reserve were persuaded to adopt a policy rule, political pressures might lead the monetary authorities to cheat by changing policy unexpectedly. The temptation to violate a policy rule to obtain short-term gains is called the **time-inconsistency problem**. This incentive can be illustrated as follows: Suppose the Federal Reserve has been following a policy rule for some time. Economic agents form their expectations about the effect of money on aggregate demand by using the rule to predict the future. In particular, the monetary rule is valuable in forming expected inflation rates, which in turn affect price and wage contracts.

The policy rule determines the amount by which the money supply is expected to react. Expected prices and wages determine the position of the short-run aggregate supply curve, as in Figure 3. However, the Federal Reserve shocks the economy by increasing the money supply more than is called for by the rule. Aggregate demand shifts to $AD_{Surprise}$ rather than $AD_{Expected}$. Output and prices are unexpectedly high.

The monetary policymakers could plausibly argue that the economy is better off after having been fooled. Real GNP is significantly higher than it would have been, and the inflation cost of this RGNP gain is not great. Unfortunately, if the Federal Reserve frequently breaks the rule, before long no one will believe the rule will be followed. The problem of uncertainty returns. *What is best for the economy in a single instance may not be the best policy over a*

Time-inconsistency problem
Optimal long-run policy differs from the optimal short-run policy, giving policymakers the incentive to cheat on long-run policy rules.

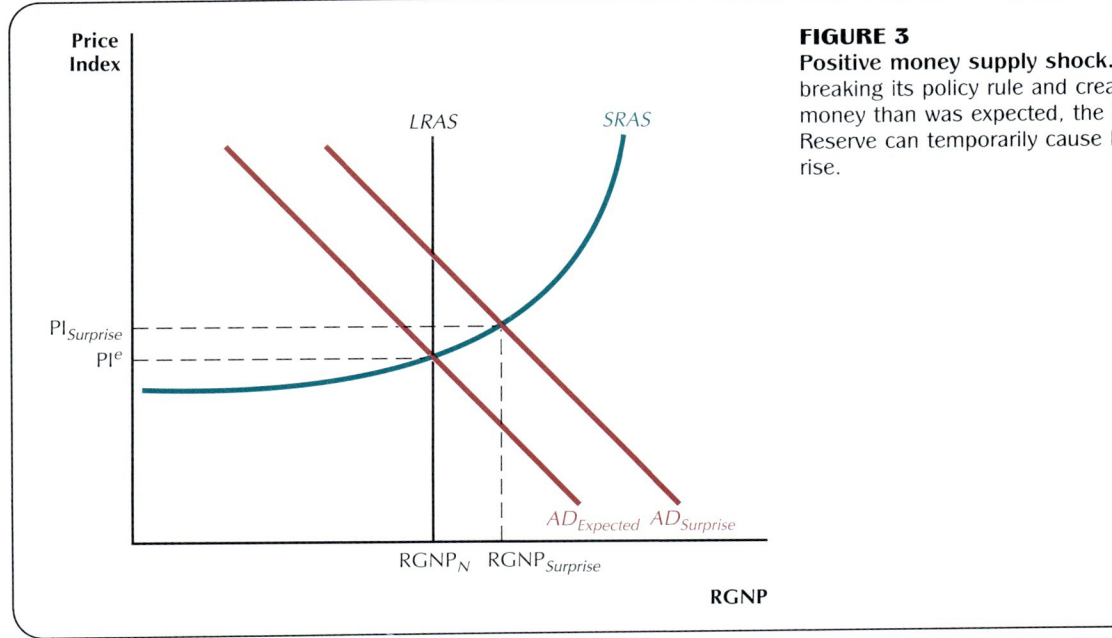

FIGURE 3
Positive money supply shock. By breaking its policy rule and creating more money than was expected, the Federal Reserve can temporarily cause RGNP to rise.

period of time. Short-term gains are inconsistent with optimal long-term policy. Using policy to occasionally increase output may decrease the rate of growth of real output over an extended period of time.

Credibility Thesis If the Federal Reserve wishes to affect the level of real GNP, an unexpected change in money supply growth will accomplish that goal. If, however, the monetary authorities wish to reduce inflation while affecting real GNP as little as possible, a surprise policy is very costly.

Figure 4 shows why this is so. The position of the short-run aggregate supply curve depends, in part, on the expected price level. The SRAS curve cuts the long-run aggregate supply curve where the expected price level equals the actual price level. Now suppose the Federal Reserve wants to reduce the price level from PI_0 to PI_1. (In reality, the inflation rate would be the target, but the principle is the same.) It does so by reducing aggregate demand from AD_0 to AD_1.

If the restrictive policy is unannounced or if private decision makers do not believe the announcement, the SRAS curve will remain stationary. When aggregate demand shifts, real GNP will fall to $RGNP_1$. The effect on the price level will be minimal. If the Federal Reserve's announcement of its intentions were credible, however, the expected price level would decline. The SRAS curve would shift downward to $SRAS_1$, and the negative effect on output would be much smaller. (There would be some output effect because of the existence of long-term contracts still in effect.)

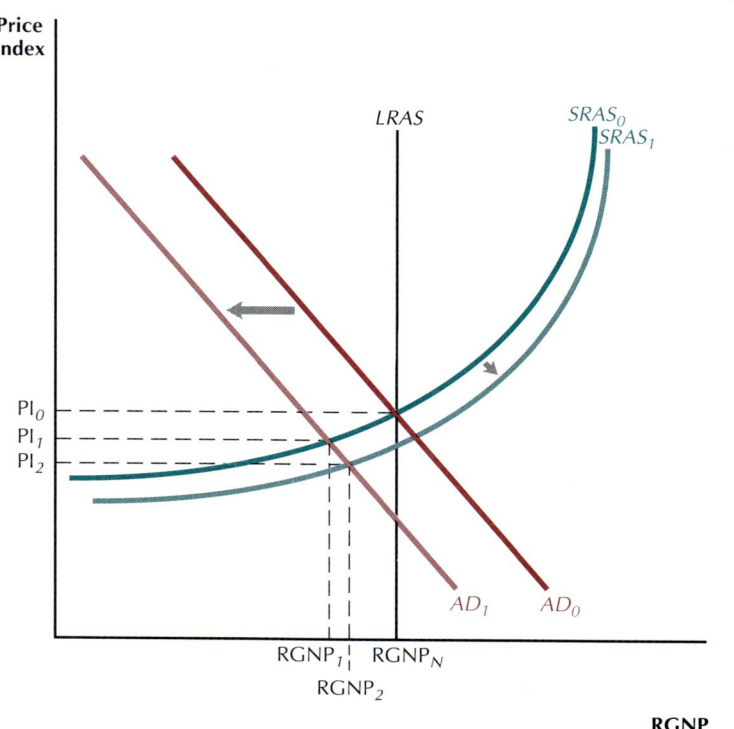

FIGURE 4
Credible monetary policy. If the Federal Reserve unexpectedly reduces the money supply or if its announced intentions are not believed, the short-run aggregate supply curve remains stationary at $SRAS_0$. The result is a small decline in PI and a large decline in RGNP, to PI_1 and $RGNP_1$. If the Fed's policy announcement is credible, the expected price level declines. SRAS shifts down to $SRAS_1$. The resulting fall in PI is larger, while the decline in RGNP is smaller.

The **credibility thesis** simply states that if monetary policymakers do what they say they are going to do, the output effects of anti-inflation policy will be much smaller than if policy is not credible. A credible policy does not guarantee that inflation can be ended without any negative effect on output and employment. However, theory predicts that the output and employment effects of credible policy will be smaller than the effects generated by noncredible policy.

Proponents of monetary policy rules argue that rules promote credible policy. If the Federal Reserve faithfully adheres to a policy rule, its actions become predictable. Thus, any anti-inflation policy is fully expected, and expectations are held with confidence. Prices and wages respond more rapidly than they would otherwise, thus minimizing the recessionary costs of lowering inflation.

The credibility thesis makes sense only if expectations are important. If prices and wages are set in a backward-looking manner, without taking account of expected Federal Reserve behavior, a credible policy is no different from an unpredictable policy. However, if economic agents do base their prices and wages on the expected behavior of monetary policy, credibility is important.

Credibility thesis
Output effects of a credible policy are smaller than the output effects of a noncredible policy.

SECTION RECAP
Monetarists believe the economy is inherently stable and want monetary policy to be stable too. They prefer rules to discretionary policymaking.

Critique of the Theories of Monetary Policy

Although both the Keynesian and monetarist theories of monetary policy are theoretically plausible, each has weaknesses. Furthermore, since they are based on different notions of what causes cyclical instability, they cannot both be correct. Either most fluctuations are caused by monetary instability or they are not. Thus, the first issue to be examined is the most crucial: Has monetary policy been a stabilizing force in the U.S. economy, or has it been the source of most macroeconomic instability? After assessing this issue, we will examine several criticisms that have been leveled against the two theories of policy.

Has Monetary Policy Been Stabilizing?

Judging whether monetary policy has been stabilizing in the post-World War II era is not easy. In the preceding chapter we saw that even the apparent increased stability of real GNP and the unemployment rate in the post-World War II period may be a figment of the data. This apparent stability had been one of the major arguments of those who believe that monetary policy has been stabilizing. Now that the very fact of increased stability has been questioned, the stabilizing properties of monetary policy are even more in doubt. A thorough examination of postwar monetary policy is called for.

Economists generally agree that during some postwar time periods monetary policy was a stabilizing factor and during other times it was destabilizing. An examination of the period from the 1950s to the 1980s — breaking it down by presidential administration — shows that monetary policy was beneficial in certain circumstances and harmful in others.

The Eisenhower Years: Cautious Restraint During World War II and continuing until 1952, the Federal Reserve did not carry out an independent monetary policy. Instead it helped finance the war effort by keeping interest rates low. The Federal Reserve would supply whatever amount of money was required to hold the interest rate to the low target level.

In 1951, the Federal Reserve and the Treasury reached an accord, freeing the Federal Reserve from the low interest rate policy. Federal Reserve economists, concerned that rapid money supply growth and low interest rates would lead to inflationary pressures, wanted to carry out a more cautious policy.

Dwight D. Eisenhower, who became president in 1953, supported the Federal Reserve's cautious anti-inflation approach. Throughout the remainder of the 1950s the Federal Reserve followed a policy of leaning against the wind. In practice, this meant pursuing a mildly stimulative monetary policy whenever the economy was sluggish and a mildly restrictive policy whenever it appeared to be growing too rapidly. Considerable emphasis should be placed on the word *mildly*. Caution was the order of the day, especially in the early years of the Eisenhower administration.

The result of the cautious leaning against the wind was relatively stable money supply growth until 1959. The growth rate of M2 over twelve-month periods neither rose above 5 percent nor fell below 2 percent during Eisenhower's years in office. Monetary policy seems to have been a stabilizing factor during this period. Not until 1959 did the Federal Reserve overdo it, cutting back on money growth sharply enough to cause a recession.

The Kennedy–Johnson Years: Accommodation of Government Spending   Monetary policy became more expansionary in the 1960s. As government spending on both the Vietnam War and social programs expanded, the Federal Reserve increased the money supply growth rate to hold down interest rates. Since inflation had not been a problem for a long time, the expected inflation rate rose very slowly. People were not used to inflation and did not incorporate inflationary expectations into their price, wage, or credit contracts. Consequently, real interest rates were fairly low during most of the 1960s.

As inflationary pressures began to build during the second half of the 1960s, the Federal Reserve became increasingly concerned. In 1967, the growth rate of the money supply was sharply curtailed and interest rates jumped (a negative liquidity effect). The policy was short lived, however, because of concern over the effects of high interest rates and intense pressure from President Johnson to accommodate federal government spending. Reverting to an easy money policy, the Federal Reserve contributed to the inflation that was becoming a problem in 1968.

The Nixon–Ford Years: A Policy Disaster   Both monetary and fiscal policy contributed to the rising inflation of the late 1960s. Immediately after his election, President Nixon urged the Federal Reserve to take steps to control inflation. The Federal Reserve responded by sharply restricting the money supply growth rate, plunging the economy into recession.

Most economists, at that time and now, agree that a restrictive monetary policy was necessary. However, had monetary policy not been so expansionary in 1968, it would not have had to be so restrictive in 1969. Excessive money supply growth led to excessive restraint — exactly what monetarists feared.

Despite the recession of 1969, inflation continued to be a problem. In late 1971, with an election only a year away, President Nixon imposed wage and price controls on the economy. Directly controlling prices was supposed to temporarily relieve the inflationary pressure so that other policies could eliminate the excessive aggregate demand growth causing the inflation. An appropriate monetary policy for the period of wage and price controls would have restricted the growth of the money supply. Instead, at the urging of the administration, the Federal Reserve increased the money supply growth rate.

The short-term effects of combining price controls with an expansionary monetary policy appeared good. The rapid money supply growth increased demand, while the price controls prevented suppliers from raising prices. The excess demand for goods and services was met out of inventories for a while. Consequently, consumers were able to purchase more goods and services at the same time that inflation subsided.

Producers cannot run down inventories for long, however. Over any period of time longer than a few weeks, sales will equal production. Consequently, producers could not meet the excess demand for very long. Soon they began to ration their products by nonprice means. People waited in line to buy gasoline. They bribed suppliers by paying more than the legal price. Suppliers made minor changes in products and charged higher prices for the so-called new items.

The result of this episode was a good deal of inefficiency, caused by distorted prices, reduced output growth, and no reduction in inflation. Studies have concluded that prices rebounded so much after the price controls were removed that the controls did not ultimately reduce inflation at all. Monetary policy deserves a failing mark for the years 1971–1973.

The OPEC oil embargo of 1973–1974 created another real problem for policymakers. Should they accommodate the higher prices caused by the oil embargo, or should they attempt to squeeze the inflation out of the economy? The Federal Reserve adopted the latter approach. Consequently, the 1974–1975 recession was unusually severe. In defense of the monetary authorities, a supply shock of the magnitude of the oil embargo had never been encountered before. It is easy to criticize their performance using hindsight. Surely they do not deserve as much criticism for the years 1974–1975 as for the years 1971–1973, when politics completely dominated economics.

The Carter Years: Pumping Up the Economy When Jimmy Carter took office as president in 1977, the economy was rebounding from the OPEC recession. The unemployment rate was over 7.5 percent, but real GNP grew at a 4.4 percent rate during 1976. Inflation was under 5 percent. The Carter administration made it clear that bringing down the rate of unemployment was its chief concern. Inflation was regarded as strictly a secondary problem.

President Carter appointed a close political ally, G. William Miller, as the new chairman of the Board of Governors in 1977. Mr. Miller agreed with the president that an expansive monetary policy was needed. The growth rate of M1 was increased substantially. Spurred on by rapid money supply growth and increased government spending, aggregate demand growth increased. By the fourth quarter of 1978, the unemployment rate was under 6 percent.

Unfortunately, the expansionary monetary policy purchased lower unemployment at a price. Inflation, as measured by the GNP deflator, increased from 4.7 percent in 1976 to 6.2 percent in 1977, 8.4 percent in 1978, and ultimately to 10.2 percent in 1980. Another OPEC oil price hike contributed to the inflationary environment in 1979.

Unlike the 1960s, when inflationary expectations adjusted to higher inflation rates very sluggishly, inflationary expectations rose rapidly in the late

Foreign exchange market Market in which different currencies trade for one another.

1970s. Higher expected inflation pushed nominal interest rates to double-digit levels in 1979. The rate on short-term Treasury bills topped 10 percent, and the prime rate charged by banks was over 13 percent by year's end.

Foreigners began to lose faith in the dollar. In **foreign exchange markets**, where national currencies are traded for one another, the demand for dollars was growing more slowly than the supply of dollars. The price of the dollar — the exchange rate — fell sharply, reducing the international value of dollar holdings.

In 1979, when the problems experienced by the monetary sector were coming to a head, President Carter appointed a new chairman of the Federal Reserve Board of Governors. G. William Miller resigned to accept the post of Secretary of the Treasury, and Paul Volcker, an experienced veteran of the Federal Reserve System, became chairman of the Board of Governors. In October 1979, following a meeting with European finance ministers, Mr. Volcker initiated a dramatic change in Federal Reserve policies. The discount rate was raised and much more emphasis was placed on controlling the growth rate of M1. The battle against inflation began on October 6, 1979.

When President Carter left office in January 1981, the unemployment rate was 7.4 percent — almost what it had been when he took office. Inflation during the last year of the Carter presidency, 1980, was over twice as high as it had been during the final year of the Ford presidency. Although the expansive monetary policy temporarily pushed the unemployment rate below 6 percent, where it remained throughout 1979, the cost of lowering unemployment by monetary means was unacceptably high. The United States learned a harsh lesson about the limits of monetary policy during the Carter years.

The Reagan Years: The Power of Money   If rapid money supply growth can pump up aggregate demand, slow growth surely can restrict it. Ronald Reagan was elected president on the pledge to reduce inflation to a reasonable level. (He pledged to do this without creating a recession, thus showing more optimism than the situation warranted.)

The main weapon in the fight against inflation was to be monetary policy. Although he occasionally wavered in his support for tight money, President Reagan backed Chairman Volcker's restrictive monetary policy throughout 1981. The policy was quite effective. Aggregate demand growth fell dramatically. Unfortunately, so did real GNP. The economy operated exactly as theory predicted. Wage and cost increases already built into the system continued to push the short-run aggregate supply curve upward, while aggregate demand rose slowly, as pictured in Figure 5. The effect of this combination was the most severe recession (in terms of unemployment) of the postwar period.

The Reagan administration had hoped that so-called supply-side tax cuts would shift the SRAS curve outward while monetary policy restrained aggregate demand growth. Unfortunately, supply-side economics works slowly and cumulatively. Tax policies that affect saving, investment, and labor decisions can affect aggregate supply significantly, but considerable time is needed for the effects to be felt. Monetary policy works on aggregate demand much more quickly.

From 1982 until late 1987, the Federal Reserve pursued a policy of encouraging aggregate demand growth. Some monetarists, among them Milton Friedman, warned that money was growing too rapidly from 1983 to 1987. They feared a return to high inflation rates. Falling oil prices (a negative oil

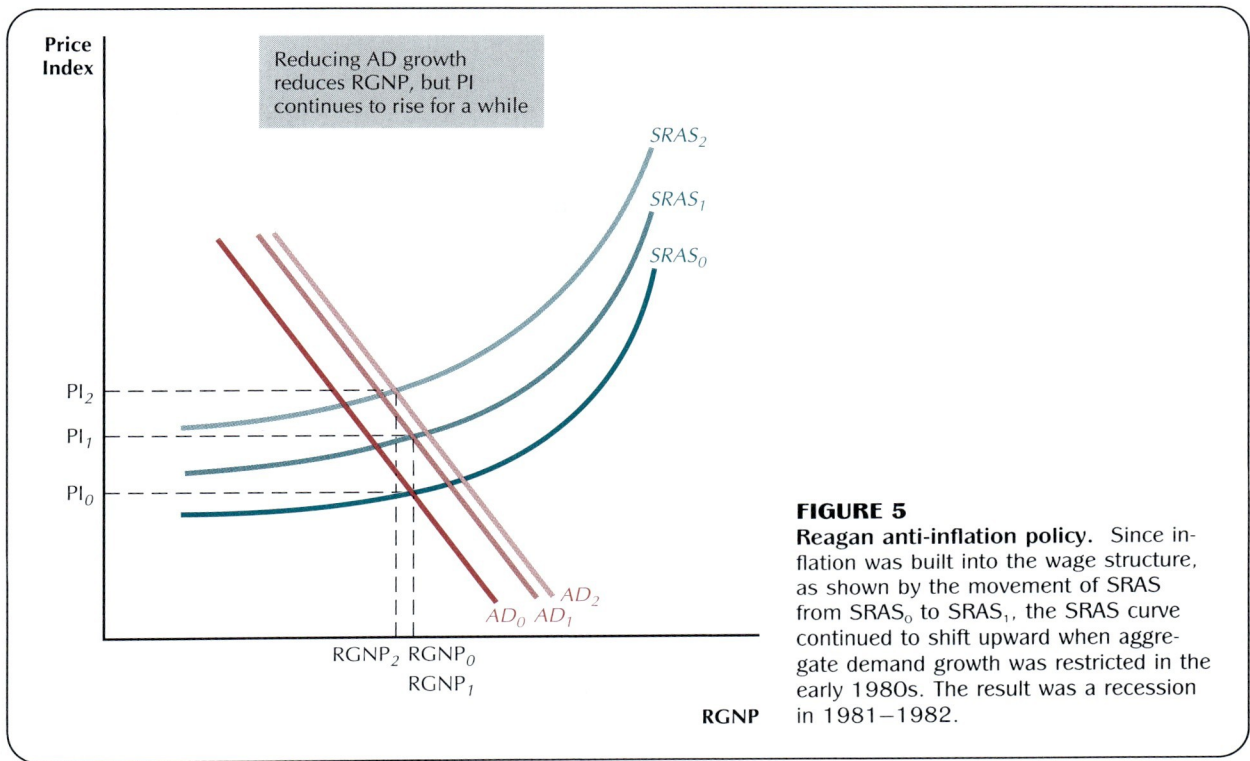

FIGURE 5
Reagan anti-inflation policy. Since inflation was built into the wage structure, as shown by the movement of SRAS from $SRAS_0$ to $SRAS_1$, the SRAS curve continued to shift upward when aggregate demand growth was restricted in the early 1980s. The result was a recession in 1981–1982.

price shock) contributed to the lowest inflation rates in over two decades during 1985 and 1986. Although inflation began climbing again in 1989, the burst of inflation predicted by monetarists did not materialize. The mildly restrictive policy pursued since 1987 by the Federal Reserve under the leadership of Alan Greenspan may have contributed to the rather modest increase in the inflation rate. Declining velocity during the 1980s also contributed, leading many economists to doubt that the relatively rapid money growth of the 1980s was very inflationary. The behavior of recent money supply and velocity growth rates is discussed later in the chapter.

The Verdict: Stabilizing or Destabilizing? Our survey of postwar monetary policy leads us to the conclusion that monetary policy has been destabilizing in several instances. The U.S. economy experienced seven recessions from 1950 to 1989. Four of them were primarily due to restrictive monetary policy. Another was caused by a decline in government spending (at the end of the Korean War), and yet another by the OPEC oil price shock in 1973–1974. Only one recession, lasting from August 1957 to April 1958, appears to fit the Keynesian theory of recession caused by a slump in private investment. Although it may be argued that more investment-led recessions *would have occurred* in the postwar era in the absence of discretionary countercyclical policy, we believe the evidence indicates that most fluctuations during the 1952–1989 period not caused by supply shocks were monetary in origin, perhaps reflecting the time-inconsistency problem. The Federal Reserve overproduced money much of the time, causing inflation and forcing it to adopt contractionary policies on occasion.

SECTION RECAP
Monetary policymaking changed greatly from the 1950s to the 1980s. Policy in the 1950s was very cautious. Monetary policy was used aggressively in the 1960s and 1970s, the decades when inflation rose sharply. A return to monetary restraint and caution marked the 1980s.

Why Hasn't Countercyclical Policy Worked Better?

Given the technical competence of the officials and economists responsible for formulating monetary policy, it may seem odd that money supply shifts have so often been destabilizing. Why hasn't the Federal Reserve been more successful in stabilizing the economy? One reason is suggested by the preceding historical discussion: If the private economy is basically stable, the Federal Reserve may have created problems by trying to do too much. In particular, the Federal Reserve may have set goals that were unattainable, generating instability as a byproduct. We will consider this and three other possible reasons why policy intended to be countercyclical often turned out to be procyclical.

Unrealistic Goals The long-term performance of the economy depends upon a host of factors, including labor force characteristics, the size and growth of the capital stock, the development of new technology, and government tax and regulatory policies. These factors determine the natural level of output and its labor market complement, the natural rate of unemployment.

The Federal Reserve is concerned with both the output level and the unemployment rate. While monetary policy can affect output and unemployment in the short run, it cannot drive them away from their natural levels for very long without generating strong price effects. But what *is* the natural level of output or unemployment? Although we speak of these natural rates as though their values are well known, it is often difficult to determine what the natural rate is until historical experience demonstrates its value.

Suppose the Federal Reserve believes the natural output level is $RGNP_E$ while the actual natural output level is $RGNP_N$ in Figure 6. If actual output is $RGNP_N$, the monetary authorities believe that the actual output level is below

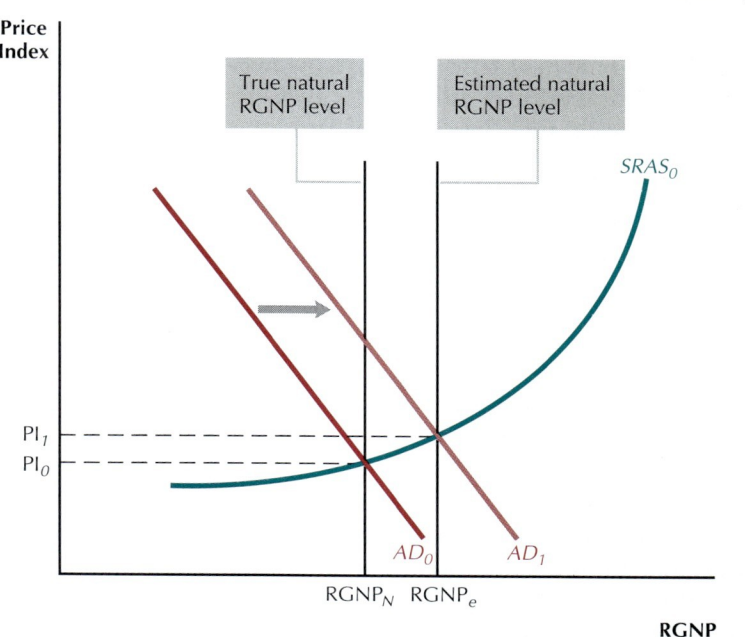

FIGURE 6
Misestimating the natural output level.
Overestimating the natural level of output may have led the Federal Reserve to be more expansionary than it should have been in the 1960s and 1970s. Rather than being content with output of $RGNP_N$, the authorities increased the money supply in an attempt to push output to RGNPE.

its natural level. This could lead them to increase the money supply, shifting aggregate demand outward from AD_0 to AD_1 in an attempt to push output to its "natural" level. If the short-run aggregate supply curve is relatively flat in the neighborhood of the true natural output level, they will be successful in driving output up without affecting the price level very much. This happy state of events is only temporary, however. Excess demand pressure in materials and labor markets will put upward pressure on input prices and wages and the SRAS curve will begin to shift upward. Federal Reserve attempts to maintain output at the $RGNP_E$ level by increasing the money supply further will intensify the inflationary pressures. Eventually prices will begin to rise rapidly, and the Federal Reserve will be faced with the prospect of accepting high and rising inflation or of allowing output to fall to its true natural level.

There is considerable evidence that this is what actually happened in the late 1960s. The unemployment rate was driven as low as 3.4 percent in late 1968 and early 1969. Economists realized that this was below the natural unemployment rate, and that output was above the natural output level, but they did not realize how far below the natural rate unemployment had been pushed. Estimates at the time put the natural unemployment rate at about 4 percent in the late 1960s. More recent research estimates the natural rate to have been around 5.5 percent. Thus, monetary policy (and fiscal policy in this instance) was much too expansionary. The inflation of the early 1970s may be traced directly to poor government policy.

Political Pressure   Politicians are very interested in the state of the economy. This is as it should be, but their interest extends beyond the national welfare to their own jobs. To put it bluntly, a stagnant economy is very bad for incumbents. Thus, during election years the Federal Reserve may come under considerable pressure to pump up the economy.

Since we will discuss the political business cycle in the next chapter, we will not go into the research in this area here. However, recall that our historical discussion of monetary policy mentioned several episodes during which political pressure was an important cause of overly expansive monetary policy. During the Johnson years, intense pressure was applied to the Federal Reserve to accommodate Vietnam War and Great Society spending. It is generally agreed that political pressure by the Nixon administration accounts for the excessive monetary growth in 1971 and 1972. President Carter vowed to use both monetary and fiscal policy to boost the economy in the late 1970s. By placing a close political ally in the position of chairman of the Board of Governors, Carter came as close to controlling the Federal Reserve as a president can come. Finally, the severity of the 1981–1982 recession may have been due to pressure by the Reagan administration to eliminate inflation. Political pressure appears to have played a major role in promoting overly expansive or overly restrictive monetary policy in recent years.

Lags and Forecasting Errors   Changes in the money supply do not generate immediate changes in spending. Monetary policy affects aggregate demand with a lag, forcing policymakers to take countercyclical policy actions before cyclical problems appear. The monetary authorities must accurately forecast the course of the economy if they hope to carry out a successful countercyclical policy.

Thousands of economists make their living forecasting future economic behavior. Some variables are forecast quite accurately, others not. For monetary policy, it is most important to accurately forecast (1) the timing of business cycle turning points, (2) the growth of real GNP, and (3) the growth of the price level.

Forecasting the date of business cycle turning points means forecasting when cyclical peaks and troughs will occur. Sad to say, economists have not done very well in this endeavor. A quote from a 1969 study of economic forecasting by Geoffrey Moore, one of the nation's foremost experts on business cycles, remains appropriate: "The data as a whole suggest that forecasters have yet to establish their ability to detect turning points in aggregate economic activity well in advance of the event. What they do demonstrate is an ability to recognize turns at about the time or shortly after they occur."[1]

Recognizing a cyclical turning point just as it occurs is not to be sneered at. Preliminary economic data are often very confusing. One must be a pretty good economist just to interpret what is currently happening, much less predict the future. Nevertheless, recognizing the current course of events is not good enough if one wants to carry out an activist countercyclical monetary policy. To completely offset cyclical fluctuations, cyclical turning points must be forecast accurately. It is doubtful that such accurate forecasting will ever be possible.

Economists have done somewhat better at forecasting the growth of real GNP and the price level. At that, the record is far from perfect. Economist Stephen McNees of the Federal Reserve Bank of Boston calculated the average forecasting errors of five prominent forecasters for the upcoming year over the 1971–1983 period.[2] He found that the average forecast of real GNP growth for the upcoming year was off by 1.6 percentage points — about 50 percent of average real GNP growth — and the average price level growth forecast was off by 1.4 percentage points.

Even if cyclical turning points could be forecasted accurately, a problem would remain. The lag in the effect of monetary policy is not stable. Research in the 1960s by Milton Friedman and some of his colleagues indicated that the lag in the effect of monetary policy was "long and variable." Professor Friedman and Anna Schwartz calculated the average lag before a business cycle peak to be seven months. The average lag prior to a cyclical trough was calculated to be four months. Unfortunately, actual lags tend to vary widely in length. Although the average lag before peaks is seven months, one third of the time the lag is likely to lie outside the range of zero to fifteen months. In other words, there is a significant probability that the lag will be very long or very short at any particular time.

Data lag
Time required to assemble data on the economy.

Recognition lag
Time required to interpret data correctly.

More recent evidence indicates that the lag may not be quite so variable as calculated for earlier periods. Still, it appears that it is as likely to be ten months as it is to be five. The effectiveness lag, when combined with the **data lag**, the time required for preliminary macroeconomic data to be assembled, and the **recognition lag**, the time required to interpret the data correctly, easily

---

[1]Geoffrey H. Moore, *Business Cycles, Inflation, and Forecasting*, 2nd ed. (Cambridge, MA: Ballinger for NBER, 1983), p. 407.

[2]Stephen K. McNees and John Ries, "The Track Record of Macroeconomic Forecasts," *New England Economic Review* (November/December 1983), pp. 5–18. Also by McNees are papers on forecasting in the May/June and September/October 1981 and March/April 1987 issues of the *New England Economic Review*.

can cause countercyclical policy actions to be delayed a year or more beyond the time they should be taken. These lags can cause policy to be procyclical.

Interest Rate Targeting   This book has focused on the money supply as the variable the Federal Reserve **targets,** or seeks to control. So long as the money supply (1) is controllable by the Federal Reserve, and (2) is linked fairly stably to aggregate demand, it makes a reasonable target for monetary policy. However, the money supply is not the only possible target variable. In fact, it has come into prominence only fairly recently. Before the 1970s, almost no attention was paid to the money supply. Instead, the Federal Reserve targeted an interest rate.

Monetary policy target Economic variable the Federal Reserve seeks to control as a means of influencing other variables.

The major argument in favor of controlling an interest rate is the belief that money affects aggregate demand primarily through interest rates. The most important channel in the monetary transmission mechanism is the interest rate channel. In this view, the expansiveness of monetary policy is measured not by the growth rate of the money supply but by the level of the interest rate. Since it is the expected real interest rate that affects spending, the Federal Reserve must control r^e if an interest rate policy is successful.

Interest rate targeting presents policymakers with several difficulties. First, the interest rates most closely connected to spending are not directly controllable by the Federal Reserve. Long-term corporate bond rates, the prime rate charged by banks, and short-term commercial paper rates are only indirectly affected by monetary policy. The interest rate actually targeted by the Federal Reserve in the past is the **federal funds rate,** the interest rate on loans of reserves by one bank to another.

Federal funds rate Market-determined interest rate on loans of reserves by one bank to another.

The federal funds rate is a very short-term rate. Most federal funds loans are overnight loans. The funds rate is very sensitive to the level of reserves in the banking system. If the Federal Reserve desires to push the federal funds rate downward, it purchases bonds on the open market. When it pays for the bonds, more reserves are pumped into the banking system. Some banks have more reserves to make loans with. In order to earn interest on these reserves, banks immediately offer some of them to other banks. This increases the supply of federal funds and pushes the interest rate downward, as shown in Figure 7.

The level of the federal funds rate may be taken as a measure of the availability of reserves. If banks are anxious to obtain reserves (reserves are relatively scarce), they bid up the funds rate. If reserves are relatively plentiful, the funds rate falls.

A falling funds rate puts downward pressure on other interest rates. With more reserves to lend, banks are more likely to lower the interest rates they charge on loans. Lower bank loan rates put downward pressure on market rates. Companies that had been borrowing in the market, perhaps by selling commercial paper (short-term corporate bonds), switch to bank loans. This reduces the demand for loans in the commercial paper market, forcing the commercial paper rate downward. Falling interest rates spread across the entire financial market.

If inflationary expectations do not rise, falling nominal interest rates translate into falling real interest rates. Lower real rates encourage more spending on investment and consumer durable goods. The entire process might be summarized thusly:

$$\uparrow \text{Reserves} \rightarrow \downarrow i_{ff} \rightarrow \downarrow i \rightarrow \downarrow r^e \rightarrow \uparrow I, C_D \rightarrow \uparrow AD$$

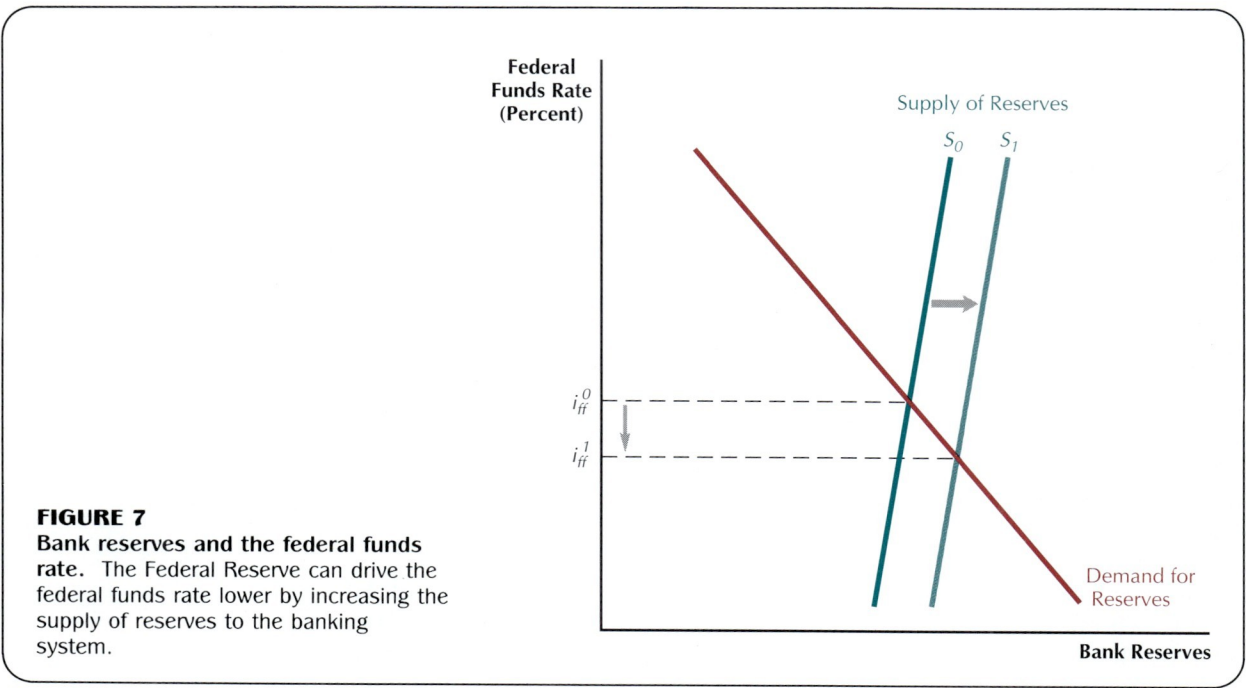

FIGURE 7
Bank reserves and the federal funds rate. The Federal Reserve can drive the federal funds rate lower by increasing the supply of reserves to the banking system.

A change in bank reserves (due to open market operations) changes the federal funds rate, which affects other market rates. If inflationary expectations do not change much, then the expected real interest rate changes. This affects spending on investment and consumer durable goods, thus affecting aggregate demand.

The Ultimate Effect of Money Growth on Interest Rates. The Keynesian transmission mechanism, on which interest rate targeting is founded, presumes that an increase in the money supply growth rate reduces the interest rate. The newly created money is used to purchase bonds, driving bond prices up and interest rates down. Economists call this the **liquidity effect**. The liquidity effect is but the first of three effects money growth ultimately has on the interest rate. Reduced interest rates promote more spending, leading to an **income effect**. As income rises, money demand rises, putting upward pressure on the interest rate, as shown in Figure 8. The income effect counteracts the liquidity effect.

If the increased money growth causes an increase in inflationary expectations, the interest rate rises even higher. Savers demand a higher nominal return on their savings to protect their real rate of return. The credit supply curve shifts to the left, as shown in Figure 9. Borrowers realize that at the current nominal rate the real rate of interest they are paying has fallen, and they increase their demand for credit, shifting the credit demand curve to the right. The actions of borrowers and savers push the nominal interest rate above its initial level. This is the **inflationary expectations**, or **Fisher, effect** (named after the economist who discovered it, Irving Fisher).

An increase in the money supply growth rate ultimately causes interest rates to *increase* rather than decrease if inflationary expectations rise. The entire

Liquidity effect
Effect on the interest rate of an injection of liquidity (money) into the system by the Federal Reserve.

Income effect
Effect on the interest rate of a shift in the demand for money caused by a change in aggregate income.

Inflationary expectations (Fisher) effect
Effect on the interest rate of a change in the expected inflation rate.

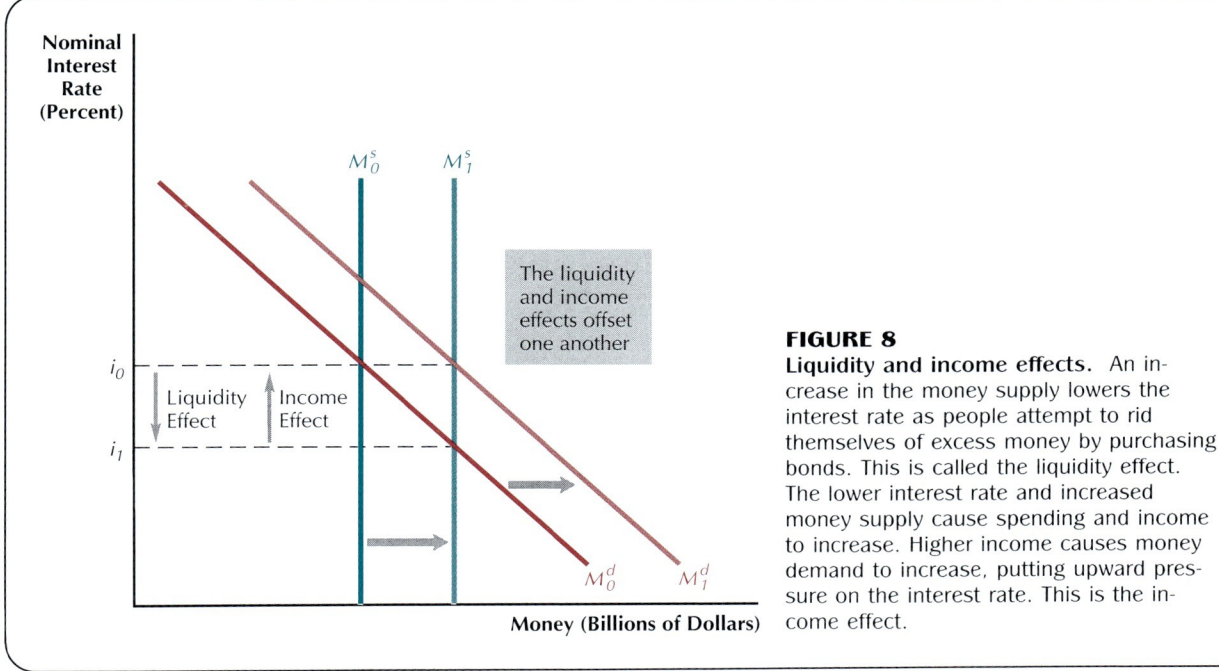

FIGURE 8
Liquidity and income effects. An increase in the money supply lowers the interest rate as people attempt to rid themselves of excess money by purchasing bonds. This is called the liquidity effect. The lower interest rate and increased money supply cause spending and income to increase. Higher income causes money demand to increase, putting upward pressure on the interest rate. This is the income effect.

path of the interest rate over time, in response to an increase in the money supply growth rate at time t, is shown in Figure 10. The path is presented in a way that shows each effect separately. When the money growth rate is increased at time t, the interest rate initially declines (the liquidity effect). When income begins to rise, the interest rate is pushed back up (the income effect).

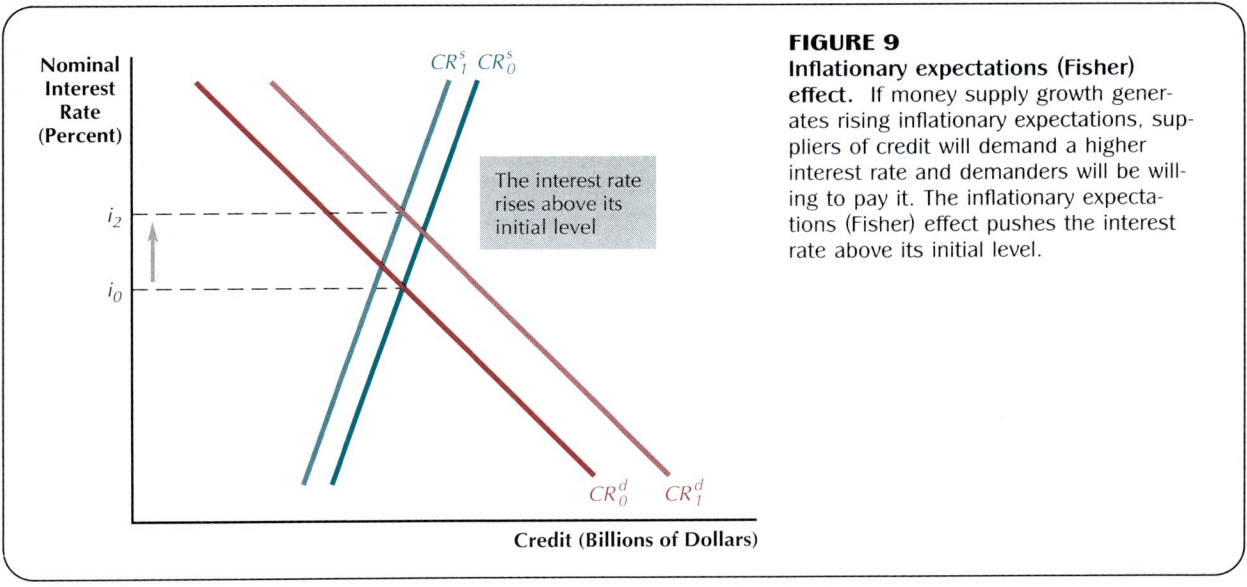

FIGURE 9
Inflationary expectations (Fisher) effect. If money supply growth generates rising inflationary expectations, suppliers of credit will demand a higher interest rate and demanders will be willing to pay it. The inflationary expectations (Fisher) effect pushes the interest rate above its initial level.

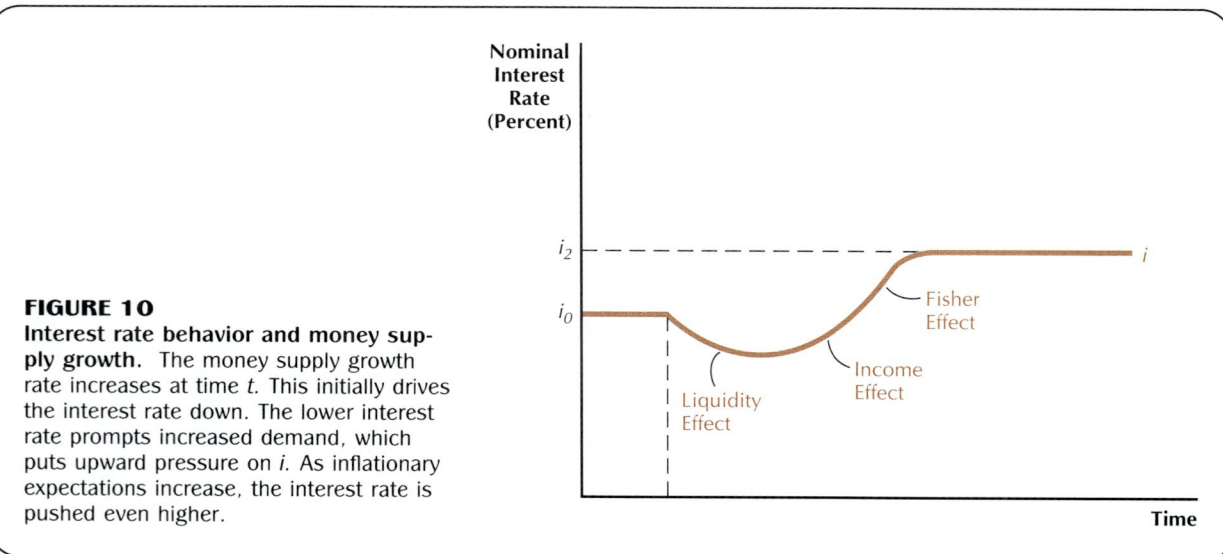

FIGURE 10
Interest rate behavior and money supply growth. The money supply growth rate increases at time *t*. This initially drives the interest rate down. The lower interest rate prompts increased demand, which puts upward pressure on *i*. As inflationary expectations increase, the interest rate is pushed even higher.

Finally, when inflationary expectations rise, the increase in inflation is added to the interest rate (the Fisher effect). So long as the money supply grows at the higher rate, the interest rate will remain at the higher level (other things equal).

The process works in reverse for a reduction in the money supply growth rate. When money growth slows, interest rates initially rise. Thereafter declines in income and expected inflation put downward pressure on the interest rate.

The Impossibility of Controlling Real Interest Rates. The existence of the Fisher effect complicates monetary policy immensely. If expected inflation is positively related to money supply growth (rising when the money supply grows faster), any attempt to permanently drive the real interest rate lower by increasing money supply growth is doomed to failure.

Consider the following simple example. Suppose that the expected inflation rate, p^e, equals the money supply growth rate (m). Further, suppose that the expected real interest rate determined by the credit market is 3 percent. Begin with a money growth rate of 4 percent. If p^e equals m, then $p^e = 4$ percent. Thus, the nominal interest rate is:

$$i = r^e + p^e = 3\% + 4\% = 7\%$$

Suppose the Federal Reserve increases the money supply growth rate to 8 percent. If inflationary expectations adjust immediately to the new money growth rate, the nominal interest rate will rise immediately by four percentage points. The new nominal interest rate will be:

$$i = r^e + p^e = 3\% + 8\% = 11\%$$

The expected real interest rate is unchanged.

It is reasonable to ask whether the expected inflation rate will rise immediately when the money growth rate increases.[3] If it does not, the liquidity effect will push the real interest rate downward. However, as soon as the expected inflation rate increases, the reduction in the real interest rate will be reversed. The real rate will return to the level determined by credit demand and supply.

In fact, the problem faced by the Federal Reserve is even more complicated than described thus far. In our example we treated the expected inflation rate as a known variable. But the Federal Reserve has no way of knowing what *the* expected inflation rate is. It can, and does, estimate the rate of inflation expected by economic agents, but it has no way of knowing exactly what market participants expect. And if the Federal Reserve does not know exactly what the expected inflation rate is, it does not know what the expected real interest rate is either. Since $r^e = i - p^e$, if p^e is unknown, so is r^e.

Misestimates of the Expected Real Rate and Excessive Expansion of the Money Supply. If the Federal Reserve underestimates the public's expected inflation rate, it will overestimate the expected real rate of interest. Suppose the nominal interest rate is 8 percent, the public's actual expected inflation rate is 6 percent, and the Federal Reserve's estimate of the public's expected inflation rate is 4 percent. Then in reality:

$$r^e = i - p^e = 8\% - 6\% = 2\%$$

But the Federal Reserve's perception is that r^e equals 4 percent. If Federal Reserve officials believe 4 percent is too high, they will increase the money supply growth rate.

The Federal Reserve apparently made this mistake frequently in the 1970s. By overestimating the expected real interest rate, the monetary authorities attempted to push it lower than it should have been. By underestimating the effect money has on aggregate demand through noninterest-rate channels, the Fed underestimated the expansiveness of monetary policy. Targeting the interest rate may have contributed significantly to the Federal Reserve's overly expansive policy during the 1970s.

Discretionary Countercyclical Policy: A Verdict   A rather large number of factors may have contributed to the relatively poor performance of countercyclical monetary policy. It is clear that today we have a much better understanding of the technical problems involved in monetary policy than the Federal Reserve had in the 1960s and 1970s. Understanding the limits constraining policy-making is a necessary step on the road to good monetary policy. What is not clear is whether the Federal Reserve will be able to adjust to the new and unforeseen problems of the 1990s any better than it did to the shocks of the 1960s and 1970s.

SECTION RECAP
Unrealistic goals, political pressure, lags in the effect of policy, forecasting errors, and interest-rate targeting all may have contributed to the relatively poor performance of countercyclical monetary policy in the 1960s and 1970s.

---

[3]In fact, recent research indicates that the inflationary expectations effect occurs very quickly when the money supply growth rate changes. The inflationary expectations effect overrides the liquidity effect almost immediately, so an increase in money supply growth causes an immediate increase in the interest rate. The Federal Reserve cannot push the interest rate down even temporarily. See William Reichenstein, "The Impact of Money on Short-Term Interest Rates," *Economic Inquiry,* January 1987, pp. 67–82.

Does It Make Economic Sense?

A Return to the Gold Standard?

For two decades the U.S. monetary system has been entirely free of any connection to gold. One must go back to the early 1930s to find a time when the United States was on a strict gold standard. Most people probably join John Maynard Keynes in viewing gold as a "barbarous relic," once useful as the base for sound monetary systems, but now old fashioned and unnecessary. Yet in the 1980s a number of respected economists and businesspeople began paying a lot of attention to the idea of returning to a gold standard. Would such a relic of bygone times be of any use today? Does it make economic sense?

Before attempting to assess the idea of a return to the gold standard, let us examine what such a standard entails. During the gold standard era of the late nineteenth and early twentieth centuries, governments participated in the gold standard system by standing ready to buy or sell gold at a stated price. Gold served as the international money of the system. Businesses with foreign debts could purchase gold from their government and transport it abroad to satisfy the debts. Most people handled very little gold, instead using paper currency and checkable deposits as we do today. However, the paper currency was convertible into gold on demand, so the value of paper money could not differ from the value of gold within a particular country.

The gold standard promoted price level stability within countries and internationally. Any government that permitted prices to rise relative to prices in other nations would lose gold. As we saw in earlier chapters, one of the factors determining net exports is relative price levels. If, for example, the Federal Reserve created so much paper money that the U.S. price level began to rise, net exports would tend to fall *(ceteris paribus)*. Foreign-made goods would become relatively cheaper than U.S.-made goods; Americans would buy more imported goods, and foreigners would buy fewer U.S.-produced goods.

A trade deficit (negative net exports) must be financed. Unless foreigners want to buy more U.S. financial assets, the trade deficit would be financed by sending gold—the international money—abroad. If the United States is to remain on the gold standard, the government must not allow the U.S. gold stock to dwindle too much. Thus, the Federal Reserve would be forced to take steps to reduce the price level, bringing it back to its international-equilibrium level.

Modern proponents cite the tendency of the gold standard to promote price level stability as its most attractive feature. Opponents note that the gold standard stabilizes prices only at the cost of giving up effective governmental control of the money supply. The gold standard forces all governments to pursue similar policies. Domestic policy goals may have to wait while the government concentrates on protecting its gold stock. Many proponents of the gold standard see this as a benefit rather than a cost of a gold system.

The gold standard is not without other problems. Of particular concern is the way the system behaves when the private (nongovernmental) demand for gold rises sharply. The government cannot simply print more gold and satisfy the demand; it must supply the gold out of its stock. To protect its gold stock, the government may find it necessary to tighten monetary policy, driving interest rates sharply upward. Such a policy protects the gold stock by persuading people to purchase high-yielding bonds rather than holding gold. However, such a policy can plunge the economy into a recession. The government may find itself forced to generate recessions if it is to remain on the gold standard.

So, does a gold standard—or some other *commodity standard* based on a real asset—make sense in our modern world? Yes, such a system makes sense, but it may not be preferable to the *paper standard* system now in place. Each system has advantages and disadvantages. Unless the prevailing system suffers some severe shocks that disrupt the system, a return to gold in the near future is not likely.

Would a Policy Rule Improve Monetary Policy?

The difficulties with countercyclical policy that we have surveyed, plus the expected benefits of stable policy, have led many economists to call for a policy rule. Despite widespread support for strict money supply targeting, widespread opposition also exists. We will discuss three reasons why money supply targeting is opposed by many economists.

Strict Money Supply Targeting Throws Away Valuable Information Advocates of a money supply growth rule argue that the sole target of monetary policy should be some measure of the money supply. The Federal Reserve should not concern itself with short-run movements in interest rates, prices, or output. It should pay attention to money supply growth, period.

Opponents of strict adherence to a money growth rule, such as Benjamin Friedman of Harvard University, argue that this amounts to throwing away a great deal of information about the economy. By focusing only on money supply growth, the Federal Reserve ignores what it can learn about the state of the economy by observing other economic variables. Used intelligently, such information could enable the Federal Reserve to adjust money supply growth upward or downward in a stabilizing fashion. Thus, opponents of a money growth rule do not argue that the money supply should not be the target of policy (or at least *a* target of policy), but that more flexible control of the money supply will produce better performance than following a strict growth rate rule would.

Proponents of a money supply rule counter with two arguments: (1) most cyclical fluctuations are monetary in origin, so a rule will be stabilizing, and (2) while optimal flexible policy looks attractive, actual flexible policy is mistake prone. Professor Thomas Mayer put the monetarist argument succinctly when he said, "The case for a monetary rule is not that it is the best monetary policy conceivable by the mind of man, but that given our lack of knowledge and the Federal Reserve's inadequacies, it is the best we can do. It is a monetary policy for a world of limits—not limits to our resources, but limits to our capacities. These limits are of two kinds: limits to our knowledge of the economy and limits to our administrative ability."[4] As is so often the case, beliefs about the inherent stability of the economy and about the abilities of policymakers determine how one stands on this issue.

Velocity Is Too Unstable for a Money Growth Rule to Work Controlling the money supply makes sense if velocity is stable. Velocity need not be constant, but its growth must be stable and predictable if money supply changes are to have predictable effects on spending.

The equation of exchange states that:

$$M \times V = PI \times RGNP$$

In practice, some particular monetary aggregate must be inserted in place of M. For example, we could write:

$$M1 \times V1 = PI \times RGNP$$

---

[4]"Replacing the FOMC by a PC," *Contemporary Policy Issues*, April 1987, p. 31.

where M1 is a particular definition of the money supply and V1 is the velocity measure corresponding to it.

The Federal Reserve calculates several monetary aggregates: the monetary base (B), M1, M2, M3, and L. Which one should be targeted? Recall that a good target must be controllable and must be linked stably to the variable the Federal Reserve desires to control. Suppose controlling GNP is the Federal Reserve's goal and that it can control any of the monetary aggregates accurately. Then the best target for monetary policy would be the aggregate with the most stable velocity.

Throughout the postwar period, until about 1980, M1 velocity was relatively stable. It trended upward throughout this period, but movements around the trend were relatively small. A policy of stable M1 growth probably would have generated stable aggregate demand growth. But in 1981 the bottom fell out of M1 velocity. Figure 11 shows the behavior of M1 velocity relative to its 1970–1980 trend. After years of growing rather steadily, M1 velocity fell sharply in the 1980s.

A constant M1 growth rate in the 1980s would have resulted in a sharp decline in aggregate demand. Since the collapse in velocity came after years of relative stability, it raises an important question: If the Federal Reserve chooses to follow a growth rate rule because velocity has been stable in the past, is there any guarantee velocity will remain stable in the future? Put another way, was it merely an accident that velocity was so stable in the past? Can we be sure it will not be unstable in the future?

Although there are no guarantees that M1 velocity will be stable in the future, supporters of policy rules note that the early 1980s was an unusually unstable period for the financial system. In 1980, the Depository Institutions Deregulation and Monetary Control Act was passed. This act, and the Garn–St. Germain Act of 1982, allowed banks and other depository institutions to offer a wide range of new deposits. Some of these interest-bearing deposits are checkable and thus are included in M1. However, many people began holding NOW accounts and other interest-bearing checking accounts as savings ac-

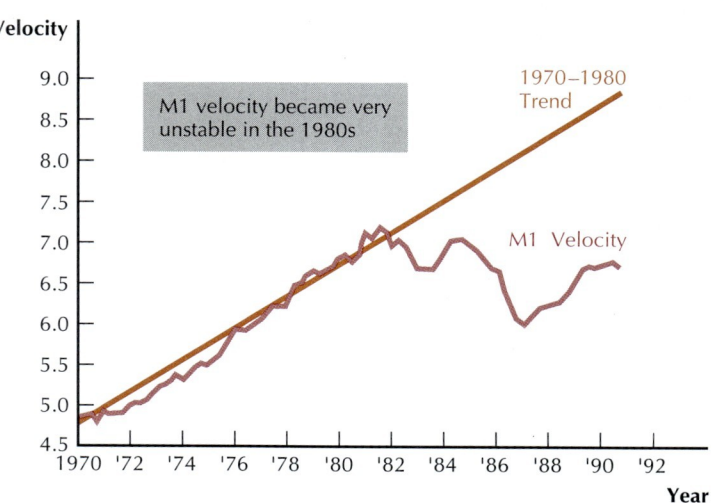

FIGURE 11
M1 velocity. M1 velocity fell far short of its trend in the 1980s. Sources: Federal Reserve *Bulletin* and *Survey of Current Business*, various issues.

counts. This meant that the demand for M1 money rose sharply. Since money demand and velocity are inversely related, M1 velocity fell. One could reasonably argue that what we are experiencing is a downward shift in velocity to a new natural level, after which stability will return. Because part of M1 is now used for savings purposes, M1 money demand will be permanently higher and M1 velocity permanently lower than before the financial innovations of the early 1980s.

Even if M1 velocity does stabilize in the future, the events of the early 1980s are cause for concern. They indicate that financial innovation could play havoc with a money growth rate rule. It would especially be a reason for concern if the velocity of all monetary aggregates had dropped as much as M1 velocity. However, other velocity measures were not as affected by the financial innovations as was M1 velocity. Figure 12 shows that the decline in M2 velocity in the 1980s was relatively minor. A policy of targeting M2 would have been affected to a much smaller degree by the velocity decline.

The events of the 1980s have shaken the faith of some economists in a constant money supply growth rate rule. The unstable velocity experienced recently has led some monetarists to support a more flexible policy rule than the constant growth rule typically advocated by them. Thomas Mayer has proposed adopting a so-called semirule, which adjusts for velocity changes. For example, the Federal Reserve might follow the rule:

$$\text{M1 growth rate} = 4\% - \text{lagged velocity growth rate}$$

If velocity were constant from one year to the next, M1 would grow by 4 percent. If velocity rose by, say, 2 percent, M1 growth would be reduced to 2 percent. If velocity fell by 2 percent, M1 growth would rise to 6 percent. In this manner the effects of velocity fluctuations would be limited to a single year. The next year money growth would offset them.

The concern about velocity instability is a valid one, but it does not destroy the monetarist argument that rules are preferred to discretion. Even a flexible semirule could be well known and understood by the public, thus encouraging

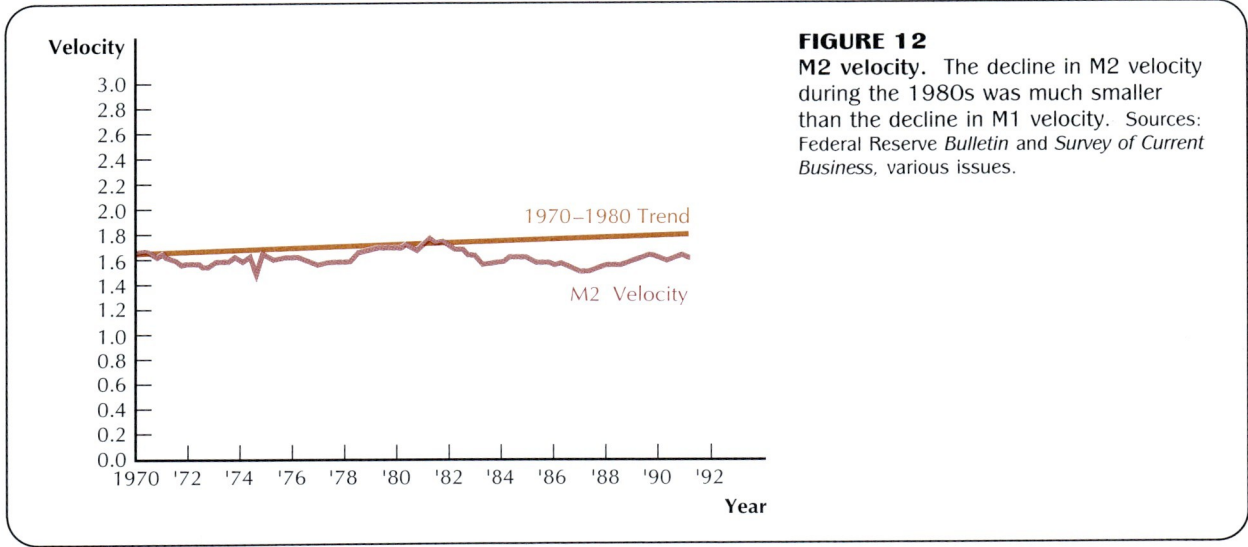

FIGURE 12
M2 velocity. The decline in M2 velocity during the 1980s was much smaller than the decline in M1 velocity. Sources: Federal Reserve *Bulletin* and *Survey of Current Business*, various issues.

Why the Disagreement?

Would a Constant Money Supply Growth Rate Have Caused a Depression in the Early 1980s?

The dramatic change in the growth pattern of M1 velocity is evident in Figure 11. The annual growth economists had come to expect disappeared, as velocity fell in five of the seven years from 1982 through 1988. If M1 had been growing at a historically appropriate constant rate during these years, it seems clear that GNP growth would have been negative. Rather than recovering from the 1981–1982 recession, the economy would have plunged deeper into depression.

The equation of exchange in growth rate form suggests what might have happened. Converting to growth rates, the equation reads:

$$m + v = p + rgnp$$

where the lower case letters represent growth rates. (Growth rates are added rather than multiplied.) If M1 had been growing at a rate of, say, 4 percent per year, GNP growth (which equals $p + rgnp$) would have been close to zero in some years and sharply negative in 1986. For example, velocity fell by 3.3 percent in 1983. Had M1 grown by 4 percent, GNP growth would have been $4 - 3.3 = 0.7$ percent. In 1986, velocity fell 7.4 percent. Four percent money growth would have generated a *decline* in GNP of 3.4 percent.

Such figures indicate that a constant money supply growth rate would have been very contractionary. The conclusion must be that a constant growth rate rule would have caused a depression in the 1980s. Or would it have? Milton Friedman has argued that such a rule would *not* have been contractionary. In the face of the evidence we have cited, this seems to be an unusual position. Why the disagreement?

Professor Friedman* does not deny the validity of the equation of exchange. What he denies is that, if M1 had been growing at a stable rate for a number of years, the behavior of velocity would have been what it was in the 1980s. As we noted above, the sharp decline in M1 velocity was associated with an equally sharp increase in the demand for money. The increase in money demand, in turn, was related to the massive in-

---

long-range planning by stabilizing expectations. As noted earlier, monetarists believe having a well-known rule is more important than the precise nature of the rule. A flexible rule is better than no rule at all.

Supply Shocks and the Need for Flexibility   We saw earlier in the book that the effects of a supply shock cannot be completely offset. Policy can be used to counter the price level effects, but doing so magnifies the output effects. If a supply shock reduces aggregate supply and the Federal Reserve responds by increasing the money supply, prices will rise even higher than they would have in the absence of policy, but the output effects will be smaller.

Supply shocks present a dilemma for proponents of money growth rules. Even if a rule could stabilize aggregate demand, supply shocks can generate severe recessions and significant, though temporary, movements in the price level. Only if the best policy response to a supply shock is no response will a money growth rate rule produce the optimal policy response to a supply shock.

As in the case of financial innovation and large velocity shocks, the Federal Reserve must stand ready to modify its policy rule if a large supply shock hits the economy. However, modifications of the policy rule in force could be part of the Federal Reserve's overall policy strategy. The Federal Reserve has good

novations in the banking system that took place in the late 1970s and early 1980s. It is generally agreed that the innovations were a response to the high inflation–high interest rate environment of the late 1970s. Had inflation not been so high, most of the innovations would not have been developed, and money demand would not have surged.

The gist of Professor Friedman's argument should now be clear. *If* M1 had grown at a low, stable rate (4 or 5 percent per year) from the early 1970s onward, then the inflation rate would not have soared in the late 1970s. Lower inflation would have meant lower interest rates. Lower interest rates would have eliminated the incentive to develop most of the significant financial innovations of that period. Without the innovations, money demand would have remained stable, and velocity growth would not have plunged as it did. The stable behavior of velocity growth would have enabled a constant M1 growth rate to stabilize aggregate demand growth in the 1980s without causing a depression.

Although Professor Friedman's argument is cogent, and many economists find it persuasive, other economists are less confident that a constant growth rate rule would have worked well. There is no simple way to settle this disagreement, because the Friedman argument is counterfactual: It says that *if M1 had grown* at a constant rate since the early 1970s, then velocity *would have been* stable in the 1980s. But of course, M1 did not grow slowly and steadily during the 1970s. Apparently the only way to really test Professor Friedman's hypothesis is to adopt a constant money growth rate rule and follow it for a number of years. Both policymakers and many economists regard this as a dangerous way to test a theory. Unfortunately, we may never know how well a constant growth rate rule might work until we try it.

*Professor Friedman presented his views in a panel discussion at the 1986 Western Economic Association meetings. See Michael R. Darby, *et al.*, "Recent Behavior of the Velocity of Money," *Contemporary Policy Issues* 5, January 1987, pp. 1–33.

information about supply shocks as they occur. For example, when OPEC raised oil prices in 1973–1974 and again in 1979 the Federal Reserve knew it. Although the precise effects of the oil price shocks were unknown before the fact, the Federal Reserve could form reasonable estimates about the size and nature of the effects. Indeed, one could argue that the effects of a supply shock are more predictable than the effects of financial innovation. It would be possible for the Federal Reserve to modify its policy rule in a standard manner any time the economy is hit by a supply shock.

Setting policy according to rules and giving up all flexibility are not the same thing. Monetarists and others who advocate policy rules believe that the elimination of monetary disturbances would more than offset the problems created for policymakers confronted with supply shocks or financial innovation.

SECTION RECAP
Monetary policy rules are not without problems. Strict rules throw away valuable information on the state of the economy, velocity may be too unstable for money growth rules to work well, and no rule handles supply shocks well.

Summary

A number of technical issues have been discussed in this chapter. We began by reviewing the generally accepted version of the **monetary transmission mechanism.** After recalling how money affects spending, we turned to the

Keynesian view of the economy and the **Keynesian theory of countercyclical policy.** Keynesian theory stresses the inherent instability of the private economy and the importance of the interest rate as the connection between monetary policy and aggregate demand.

The **monetarist view** is that most aggregate demand instability is due to monetary instability. This leads monetarists to advocate a stable money supply growth rate rule as the best feasible approach to policy.

Recent monetary history suggests that policy has been destabilizing as often as it has been stabilizing. Four reasons were suggested for this poor record. The Federal Reserve may have pursued **unrealistic goals** during some periods. **Political pressure** is constantly applied to the Federal Reserve, and this pressure appears to have an expansionary bias. This may help to explain why monetary policy was so inflationary in the 1970s. **Lags in the effect of monetary policy** and **forecasting errors** may have caused policy to be procyclical, and **interest rate targeting** may have led the Federal Reserve into errors.

While the performance of countercyclical policy has not been very good, there are a number of objections to following a **policy rule.** Strict adherence to a rule throws away information that might be valuable in adjusting money growth. **Unstable velocity** combined with stable money growth produces aggregate demand instability, and **supply shocks** need to be addressed with flexible policy. All these objections have merit, but it is not clear that they outweigh the arguments in favor of a policy rule.

Questions for Thought

Knowledge Questions

1. Outline the Keynesian transmission mechanism of monetary policy, and describe how it works.
2. Define and explain the liquidity, income, and Fisher effects of changes in money supply growth on the interest rate.
3. Describe the monetarist view of the economy. How does this view relate to the monetarist preference for monetary policy rules?
4. What is the credibility thesis? Explain why credibility might be very important.

Application Questions

5. In the Keynesian system, is monetary policy more powerful when investment spending is sensitive or insensitive to changes in the interest rate? Explain your answer.
6. Monetarists often advocate a constant money supply growth rate rule as a good approach to monetary policy. Using our model of the macroeconomy, explain how a policy of holding the money supply constant could help stabilize real GNP if money demand is stable. (How does the economy react to changes in variables other than money demand?)
7. As in question 6, use the complete macroeconomic model to show the effects of holding the money supply constant, this time in the face of unstable money demand.
8. The Federal Reserve can choose to target the interest rate or the money supply. If money demand is stable, which variable — i or M — is the better target? If money demand is unstable, which variable is better? Explain your answer.

Synthesis Questions

9. The Fisher effect complicates monetary policy by pushing the interest rate in the same direction as the money supply growth rate. Explain the difference it makes for monetary policymakers whether the Fisher effect occurs immediately or with a significant lag when the growth rate of the money supply is changed.
10. What problems are raised for monetary policymakers by the existence of "long and variable" lags and the need to forecast cyclical turning points accurately?
11. Explain how an activist monetary policy could be destabilizing.
12. Why can't the Federal Reserve control real interest rates? Why does the fact that it is the *expected* real interest rate that is important complicate matters even further?

OVERVIEW

Fiscal Policy: A Further Treatment

In the period immediately following World War II, most economists believed that fiscal policy was a more powerful tool than monetary policy for affecting the level of real GNP. Throughout the 1950s and 1960s, faith in the beneficial effects of an intelligently enacted fiscal policy continued to grow. However, the poor economic performance of the 1970s caused many economists and policymakers to wonder whether the advocates of fiscal policy had promised too much. Furthermore, some new theoretical developments cast doubts on the power of fiscal policy. These doubts have led many economists to reexamine the theory of fiscal policy and the empirical evidence on its effectiveness.

In this chapter we examine both the theory and the practice of fiscal policy, particularly focusing on fiscal policy used as a tool to stabilize the business cycle. Our examination of the practice of countercyclical fiscal policy includes an analysis of why fiscal policy actions might be poorly timed. We follow our theoretical discussion with a short history of fiscal policy from the 1950s to 1990. This historical overview serves the same purpose as the overview of monetary policy in the preceding chapter: It enables us to form an opinion on the actual effectiveness of fiscal policy as a countercyclical tool.

Following our discussion of the theory and practice of fiscal policy we attempt to answer the question, How effective is fiscal policy? To answer this question we reexamine the issues of crowding out (and crowding in) and the importance of the composition of government spending. We also discuss the question of how to properly measure the magnitude of deficit-financed government spending.

We end the chapter with a discussion of an alternative to traditional fiscal policy. Proponents of a national industrial policy argue that more direct government control of the economy is necessary if the U.S. economy is to remain competitive in the world economy. Opponents argue that a national industrial policy is a recipe for inefficiency and stagnation.

CHAPTER 34

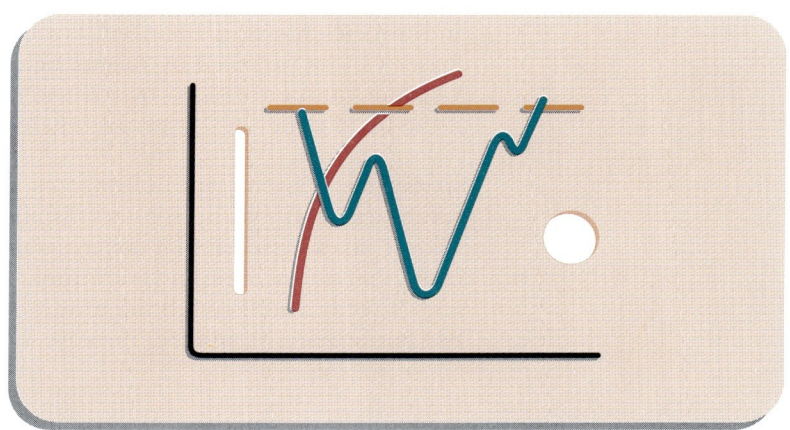

Learning Objectives
After reading and studying this chapter, you will be able to:

1. Use the AD–SRAS model to show how countercyclical fiscal policy is supposed to work.
2. Explain why enactment and implementation lags weaken the case for discretionary fiscal policy and strengthen the case for automatic stabilizers.
3. State the conditions under which crowding out and crowding in are likely to occur.
4. Explain why the composition of government purchases might matter in determining the aggregate output level even in the short run.
5. Discuss the shortcomings of the standard definition of the government budget deficit as a measure of the expansiveness of fiscal policy.
6. List the major arguments for and against a national industrial policy.

Countercyclical Fiscal Policy in Theory and Practice

The basic theory of fiscal policy was discussed in the chapter on government finance and fiscal policy. Here we concentrate on the theory of countercyclical policy.

Theory

Figure 1 illustrates the basic idea behind countercyclical fiscal policy. If real GNP falls below its natural level, as occurs when aggregate demand is at AD_1, government should increase aggregate demand by increasing government purchases of goods and services, increasing transfer payments, or decreasing taxes. If real GNP rises above its natural level and the price level begins to rise, as occurs when aggregate demand is at AD_2, government should decrease aggregate demand by decreasing government purchases or transfer payments or increasing taxes.

The magnitude of the effect of any change in spending or taxes depends on how the change is financed. For example, an increase in government purchases can be financed by raising taxes or by borrowing in the credit market. A tax cut can be financed by reducing spending or by borrowing. The impact of the fiscal policy action on aggregate demand depends on how it is financed.

Tax-Financed Government Expenditures Suppose the government increases its purchases of goods and services, financing the increase by increasing personal income taxes. Assume that taxpayers regard the tax increase as permanent. We know that an increase in government purchases increases aggregate demand, both directly and through the multiplier effect on consumption spending. We also know that a permanent increase in income taxes reduces aggregate demand

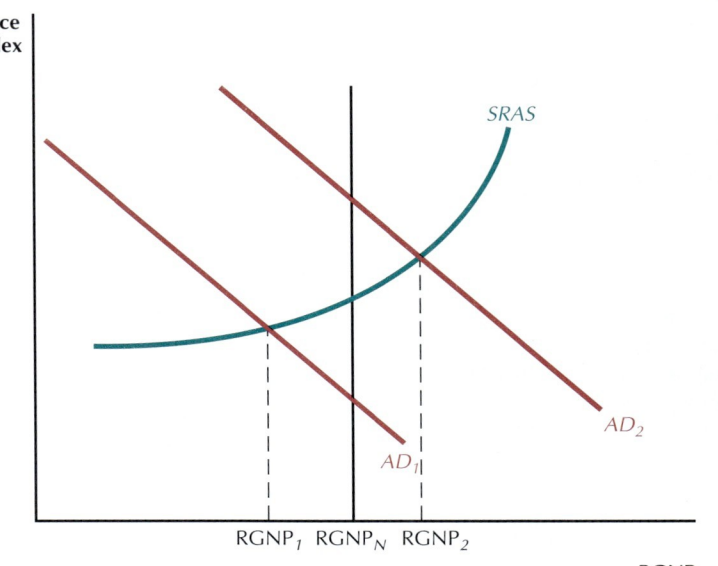

FIGURE 1
Countercyclical policy problem. Countercyclical policy seeks to offset fluctuations in real GNP away from its natural level. If aggregate demand is at AD_1, real GNP is below $RGNP_N$; an expansive fiscal policy is called for. If aggregate demand is at AD_2, real GNP is above $RGNP_N$; a restrictive fiscal policy is appropriate.

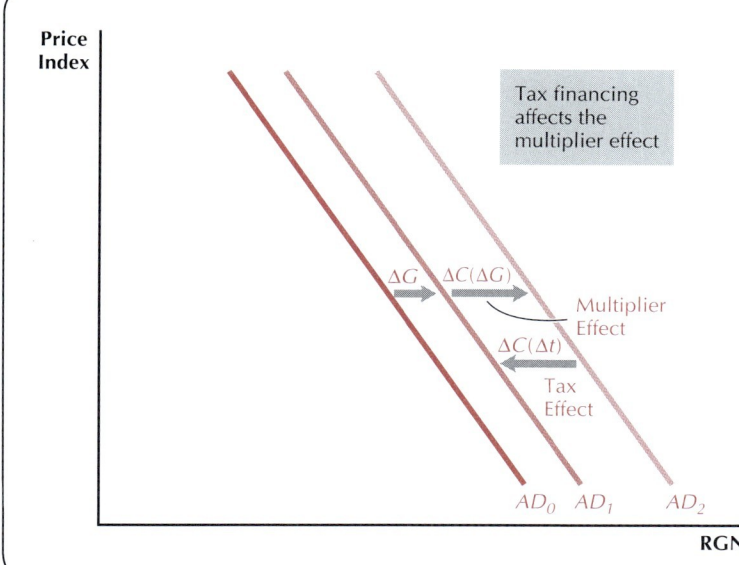

FIGURE 2
Tax-financed increase in government purchases. An increase in government purchases of goods and services, which shifts the AD curve from AD_0 to AD_1, increases disposable income. This generates a further increase in consumption spending, which, *ceteris paribus*, would shift the AD curve to AD_2. However, if taxes rise to finance the expenditure increase, the negative effect of the tax increase on disposable income will reduce consumption spending, offsetting the shift to AD_2. The total effect on consumption will be very small. Thus, aggregate demand increases by about the same amount as government purchases increase, from AD_0 to AD_1.

through its effect on long-run disposable income. Since the increases in purchases and income taxes have offsetting effects on aggregate demand, their combined effect is not immediately obvious. However, further examination provides a clear theoretical prediction for the combined effect.

Additional government purchases increase aggregate demand in two ways. Government purchases add directly to aggregate demand, and they increase disposable income, which has a positive effect on consumption spending. This is shown in Figure 2 as a shift from AD_0 to AD_1 to AD_2. However, the higher income taxes required to finance increased government purchases reduce disposable income. The resulting negative effect on consumption, shown in Figure 2 as a shift back from AD_2 to AD_1, approximately offsets the positive effect on consumption of higher government spending. The total effect of a tax-financed increase in spending is, therefore, positive, because the direct effect of government purchases on aggregate demand is large enough to ensure that the combined effect of purchases and taxes is positive. Though positive, the effect of tax-financed government purchases may be quite small.

The effect on aggregate demand of a tax-financed increase in transfer payments is even smaller. The reason is simple: Transfer payments do not directly affect aggregate demand. Instead, they affect disposable income, which in turn affects consumption spending and aggregate demand. Graphically, the direct effect of government purchases on aggregate demand, shown as the shift from AD_0 to AD_1 in Figure 2, is missing. Transfer payments can be thought of as negative taxes. When they are financed by positive taxes, the total effect on aggregate demand is minimal.

If an increase in tax-financed transfer payments has any positive effect on aggregate demand, it is because the combined tax–transfer policy redistributes income from savers to spenders. The recipients of transfers usually have very high marginal propensities to consume. For example, welfare recipients are unlikely to save any of an increase in transfer payments; such liquidity-constrained consumers spend all of the additional income they receive. On the other hand, most taxpayers do not consume all of their income. They respond to an increase in taxes by both consuming less and saving less. Thus, some tax dollars come from saving, but all transfer receipts are spent on consumption. The net effect on aggregate demand is positive, though quite small.

Spending-Financed Changes in Taxes Tax changes are often used as a primary tool of fiscal policy, as well as to finance changes in spending. Any time the government chooses to reduce taxes, it must finance the tax cut by reducing spending or by borrowing. Consider the effect on aggregate demand of a reduction in income taxes financed by decreased government purchases. Lower income taxes increase disposable income and consumption spending. However, reduced government purchases of goods and services affect aggregate demand negatively, both directly and through the effect of lower disposable income on consumption. The net effect of an income tax cut financed by a reduction in government purchases is negative, as shown in Figure 3. Thus, a countercyclical change in income tax rates cannot be financed by changing government purchases. Financing countercyclical tax changes by altering transfer payments is also ineffective.

Deficit-Financed Government Expenditures Most economists argue that a deficit-financed increase in government expenditures is more expansionary than a tax-financed increase in spending. Tax financing reduces disposable income, thus reducing consumption. However, deficit financing does not reduce dis-

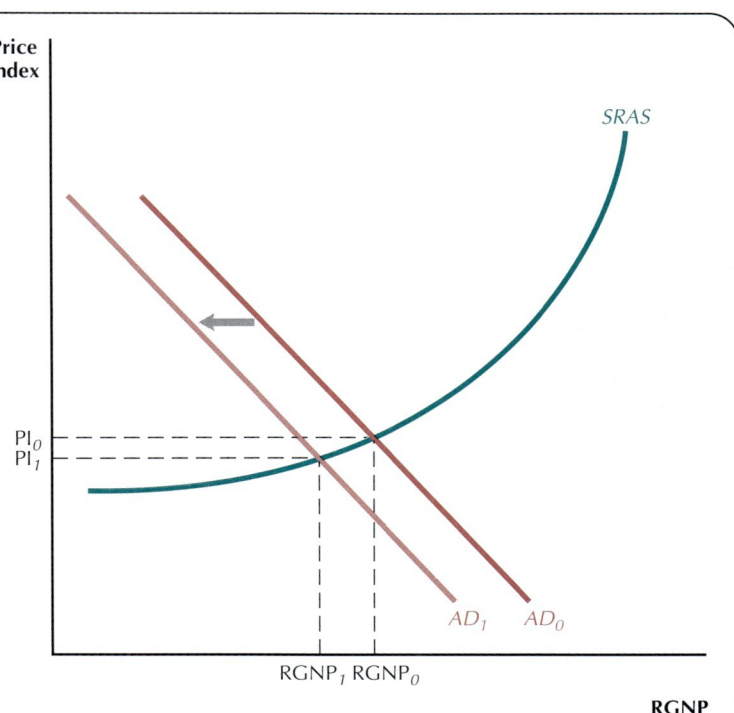

FIGURE 3
Income tax reduction financed by a reduction in government purchases.
The negative effect on aggregate demand of a reduction in government spending outweighs the positive effect of an income tax cut.

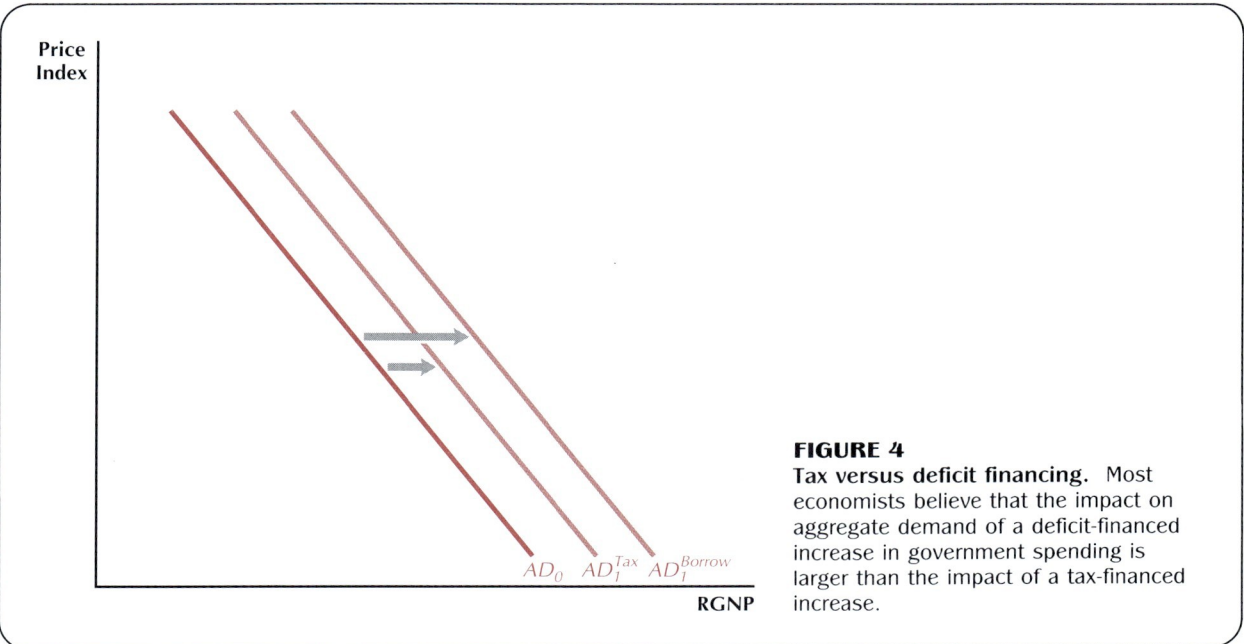

FIGURE 4
Tax versus deficit financing. Most economists believe that the impact on aggregate demand of a deficit-financed increase in government spending is larger than the impact of a tax-financed increase.

posable income. Instead, bonds are sold to savers who wish to purchase them. The purchasers exchange one form of financial wealth — money — for another — government bonds. Such a transaction should have no negative effect on consumption spending. Thus, the total effect on aggregate demand of a deficit-financed increase in government purchases should be larger than the net effect of a tax-financed increase. The same reasoning applies to deficit-financed and tax-financed increases in transfer payments. Figure 4 illustrates this.

Deficit-Financed Tax Changes If changes in income tax rates are to be used as a countercyclical policy tool, they must be deficit financed. A tax reduction financed by cutting government purchases reduces aggregate demand, rather than increasing it as desired. Financing a tax cut by reducing transfer payments has only a minimal effect on aggregate demand. However, a tax reduction financed by borrowing increases aggregate demand through its positive effect on disposable income. Of course, a permanent tax reduction has a larger effect on permanent disposable income and on consumption than does a temporary tax reduction.

Theory of Countercyclical Fiscal Policy: A Summary Our brief discussion of the financing of fiscal policy leads us to conclude that the most powerful countercyclical policy actions are deficit-financed changes in government purchases. Government purchases affect aggregate demand both directly and through their effect on disposable income. Deficit financing eliminates the offsetting effect on disposable income that occurs when purchases are financed through changes in income taxes. The second most powerful fiscal policy tool appears to be deficit-financed changes in income taxes.

SECTION RECAP
The standard theory of fiscal policy leads to the conclusion that deficit-financed government purchases are the most powerful tool of fiscal policy. Deficit-financed tax changes and tax-financed changes in pur-
(continued)

Why the Disagreement?

Pro-Growth or Just Pro-Rich? The Debate over Cutting the Capital-Gains Tax Rate

Capital gains are earned when people sell assets whose value has increased over time. Savers who purchase shares in corporations, hold them for several years, and sell them at a higher price earn capital gains. So do the owners of small businesses who sell at a profit. Both are taxed on the difference between their cost and the selling price.

From 1921 until 1986, capital gains were almost always taxed at a lower rate than ordinary income. However, the Tax Reform Act of 1986 simplified the federal tax code and treated capital gains as ordinary income. This raised the tax rate on capital gains. In his campaign for the presidency in 1988, George Bush argued that the capital-gains tax rate should be reduced and that capital gains should be indexed for inflation, so that only *real* capital gains would be taxed. He continued to support such a reduction after he was elected. Many economists and politicians sided with the president on the issue. However, opposition to his proposal was widespread and vocal. Why the disagreement?

Proponents of a capital-gains tax cut argue that a tax cut would encourage saving and investment, thereby promoting economic growth. A lower capital-gains tax rate would increase the after-tax return to the owners of assets. Savers would respond by making more savings available to entrepreneurs, who in turn would start more new businesses or expand existing businesses. The new investment would increase the economy's productive capacity and create new jobs.

Advocates of a tax reduction note that the cost of capital is lower in many other countries because those countries either tax investment earnings at a lower rate than the United States does, or do not tax investment earnings at all. For example, Japan does not tax capital gains. The Japanese argue that capital gains are not income; rather, they reflect expected earnings flows. That is, asset prices rise because companies are expected to earn more in the future. If those earnings materialize, they are taxed as ordinary income.

Taxing capital gains is especially damaging to venture capitalists who raise capital to start new businesses. Many new firms hire talented executives away from larger firms by offering them shares of stock in the new company. If the company succeeds, the shares rise in value, and the executives can sell them at a large profit. Offering stock rather than high salaries enables entrepreneurs to start new

---

SECTION RECAP
(continued)
chases have smaller effects. Tax-financed changes in transfer payments have very small effects.

This brief overview of the theory of fiscal policy should enable you to understand why, during the 1950s and 1960s, some economists were so optimistic about the prospects for using countercyclical fiscal policy to smooth the business cycle. The theory implies that a proper fiscal policy should be able to offset any major upward or downward shifts in aggregate demand, thus smoothing the growth path of real GNP. As usual, however, putting the theory into practice is not as easy as it first appears.

Practice

Policymakers run into three problems when attempting to use fiscal policy to smooth business cycles:

1. Good information on the *current* state of the economy is scarce. Most macroeconomic data series are reported with a lag of one to three months.
2. Enacting and implementing fiscal policy takes time. As with monetary policy, there are lags in the effect of fiscal policy.
3. Political pressures often make it difficult to enact and implement the policies that would be optimal for macroeconomic purposes.

firms with a smaller amount of capital. Taxing capital gains forces entrepreneurs to offer higher salaries to attract executives, raising the cost of starting new businesses and reducing the number of new businesses actually started.

Proponents of reducing the capital-gains tax also argue that taxing nominal capital gains is simply unfair. If the price of assets merely rises at the same rate as inflation, the real value of the assets does not change. However, owners must pay taxes anyway, thus actually suffering a real loss on the sale.

Opponents of a capital-gains tax cut attack the proposal on three fronts. First, they argue that the beneficiaries of such a tax cut would, for the most part, be the wealthiest Americans. Most capital-gains taxes are paid by the wealthy, so they would receive most of the benefits. Furthermore, the benefits would largely go to people who invested their funds long ago. Reducing their taxes would have no effect on current investment. Since a large share of venture capital comes from pension and retirement funds, whose earnings are not subject to the capital-gains tax, the effect of a tax reduction on investment would be minimal.

A second argument lodged by opponents concerns the effect of a tax reduction on the federal budget. Reducing the capital-gains tax rate might increase tax revenues for one or two years, but thereafter, they argue, tax receipts would fall, worsening the federal budget deficit. The amount of growth promoted by a tax cut would be insufficient to produce enough income tax revenue to replace the lost capital-gains tax revenue.

Opponents also argue that reducing the capital-gains tax rate increases the probability that a host of special-interest tax loopholes will be reintroduced into the tax system. The major benefit of the 1986 tax law was the elimination of many loopholes in return for lower income tax rates. The broader tax base offset the effect of lower tax rates. If the capital-gains tax rate is reduced, other loopholes are sure to follow.

Nearly all economists on both sides of the issue agree that indexing capital gains for inflation would improve both the fairness and the efficiency of the tax. However, since proponents and opponents of a capital-gains tax reduction disagree on the points discussed above and have other arguments in their arsenal, the debate over all other aspects of the issue is likely to continue—even if a reduction becomes law.

Since the data problem has been discussed in the two preceding chapters, we will not review it here. We will, however, discuss how lags can reduce the effectiveness of fiscal policy as a countercyclical tool and how political pressures on economic policymaking might generate business cycles.

Enactment Lags: Democracy Works Slowly   The United States is the oldest constitutional republic in the world. (Great Britain has a much longer history of parliamentary government but has no written constitution.) The U.S. political system owes its basic form to men whose views were shaped by the events of the eighteenth century. Much has changed since then, and the way government operates is very different than its founders would have imagined. Yet today the legislative process is much the same as it was nearly two hundred years ago.

When the United States was born, no one imagined that government would attempt to do the things it does today. Legislators viewed their positions as senators or representatives as part-time jobs. Compared to the flood of legislation working its way through Congress today, the legislation passed in the early years of U.S. history amounted to a mere trickle.

Because the framers of the Constitution and the organizers of Congress did not foresee a need for haste, they created a legislative system that works

Enactment lag
Time required to pass and sign a bill into law.

slowly. The legislative process is filled with checks and balances, designed to ensure that any bill is thoroughly discussed before it becomes law. Only a bill commanding nearly universal support can become law quickly.

The delays experienced by ordinary legislation also affect fiscal policy bills. The time-consuming process by which a bill becomes law creates a long **enactment lag** for most fiscal policy actions. A bill introduced in, say, the House of Representatives must pass through a subcommittee and a full committee before reaching the floor of the House. The bill can be rejected at any level. If it is accepted by the full House, it must go through the same process in the Senate. Often the Senate approves a different version of a bill than the House, necessitating work by a joint conference committee to iron out the differences. Once finally approved, the bill is sent to the president, who may sign or veto it.

The process of enacting a complicated bill can easily take from one to two years or more. Meanwhile, the economy moves on. Legislation designed to offset an impending recession may not be enacted until the next expansion has already begun, since the average recession in the United States lasts less than a year.

Implementation Lags: Writing the Regulations   After a bill has become law, it must be implemented (put into practice). This can be a lengthy process. The time between the passage of a bill and the actual spending of appropriated funds is called the **implementation lag**.

Implementation lag
Time required to put a policy decision into effect.

Any bill that appropriates funds, either to purchase goods and services or to expand transfer payments, is accompanied by regulations specifying how the funds are to be spent. These regulations are written by government bureaucrats in the department overseeing the spending. A fairly simple bill, only a few pages in length, is often augmented by hundreds of pages of bureaucratic regulations. Since the regulations are written after the bill has become law, the process of writing regulations slows the implementation of fiscal policy substantially. Because spending bills are affected to a much greater extent by the regulation process than are tax bills, many economists favor the use of tax changes as the primary tool of discretionary fiscal policy. However, tax bills are just as subject to enactment lags as spending bills. Competition among legislators to obtain the most favorable treatment possible for their constituents often delays the enactment of tax legislation.

Automatic Stabilizers: Avoiding the Problem of Lags   Enactment and implementation lags complicate the practice of discretionary fiscal policy. However, not all fiscal policy actions are subject to such lags. Some fiscal policy tools react automatically to the state of the economy. Such **automatic stabilizers** do not require legislative action to go into effect. Instead, they are triggered by changes in income. Examples of automatic stabilizers include unemployment insurance benefits, welfare payments, and income taxes based on a graduated income tax schedule.

Automatic stabilizer
Fiscal policy tool that varies in response to changes in aggregate income, moderating movements in disposable income.

Whenever the economy moves toward a recession, firms begin laying off workers. Most workers are covered by unemployment insurance, entitling them to receive a fraction of their incomes from state governments in unemployment insurance payments when they are laid off. Without any discretionary action by legislators, unemployed workers begin receiving transfer payments. These transfer payments enable many of the unemployed to continue consuming at a higher level than they would be able to in the absence of unemployment insurance benefits. Increased welfare payments work in a similar fashion.

In the presence of a graduated-rate tax schedule, a decline in income reduces income tax payments more than proportionately. As a laid-off worker's income falls, the worker moves into a lower marginal tax bracket. The worker's income tax liability falls by a larger percentage than his before-tax income. Thus, the worker's after-tax income is protected to some extent by the decline in his income-tax liability.

By their very nature, automatic stabilizers tend to offset business cycle movements. Because they are not subject to lags, automatic stabilizers may be the most useful component of countercyclical fiscal policy.

Political Pressure and Macroeconomic Policy Common sense indicates, and research confirms, that the state of the economy has a powerful influence on political elections. Incumbents are helped and challengers hampered by good economic conditions during election years. Other things equal, the lower the inflation and unemployment rates and the higher the real GNP growth rate, the better an incumbent's chances of reelection are.

Since presidents and members of Congress have the tools of fiscal and (through political pressure on the Federal Reserve) monetary policy at their disposal, an interesting question is whether elected officials attempt to influence the economy in order to increase their reelection chances. Does the government create political business cycles or election cycles in an attempt to protect the jobs of incumbents? Is it possible to manipulate the economy for political purposes? We examine the conditions necessary for political manipulation of the economy to be possible, before turning to the evidence on the political business cycle.

Voter Myopia, Time Horizons, and Election Cycles. Several political and economic conditions must be met if political business cycles are to be possible. First, voters must respond positively to good economic conditions during election years. The evidence indicates that they do, so we will assume this condition is met. Second, voters must place heavy emphasis on the present. They must be myopic (shortsighted), or they must have short time horizons. In other words, either they must not foresee the ultimate consequences of political manipulation of the economy or they must not care about them. Furthermore, they must have short memories or regard the past as irrelevant. Voters who take a long-term perspective on the economy will not approve of policies that attempt to pump up the economy in election years and restrain it in the following years.

The economic conditions that must be met have to do with the power of fiscal and monetary policy. The government must be able to use policy tools to increase aggregate demand, and the increase in aggregate demand must generate an increase in real output. This means that the short-run aggregate supply curve must be relatively flat and stable, as shown in Figure 5 (a), rather than unstable, as in Figure 5 (b), or very steep, as in Figure 5 (c). If the SRAS curve is very steep, or if it shifts upward rapidly in response to aggregate demand pressure, any attempt to pump up the economy will result in higher prices rather than more output.

The ideal economic conditions for the creation of a political business cycle would be a relatively flat short-run aggregate supply curve that shifts upward

SECTION RECAP
Enactment and implementation lags delay the effect of discretionary fiscal policy, reducing its effectiveness as a countercyclical tool. Automatic stabilizers react to changes in the level of national income, thus avoiding the timing problems of discretionary policy.

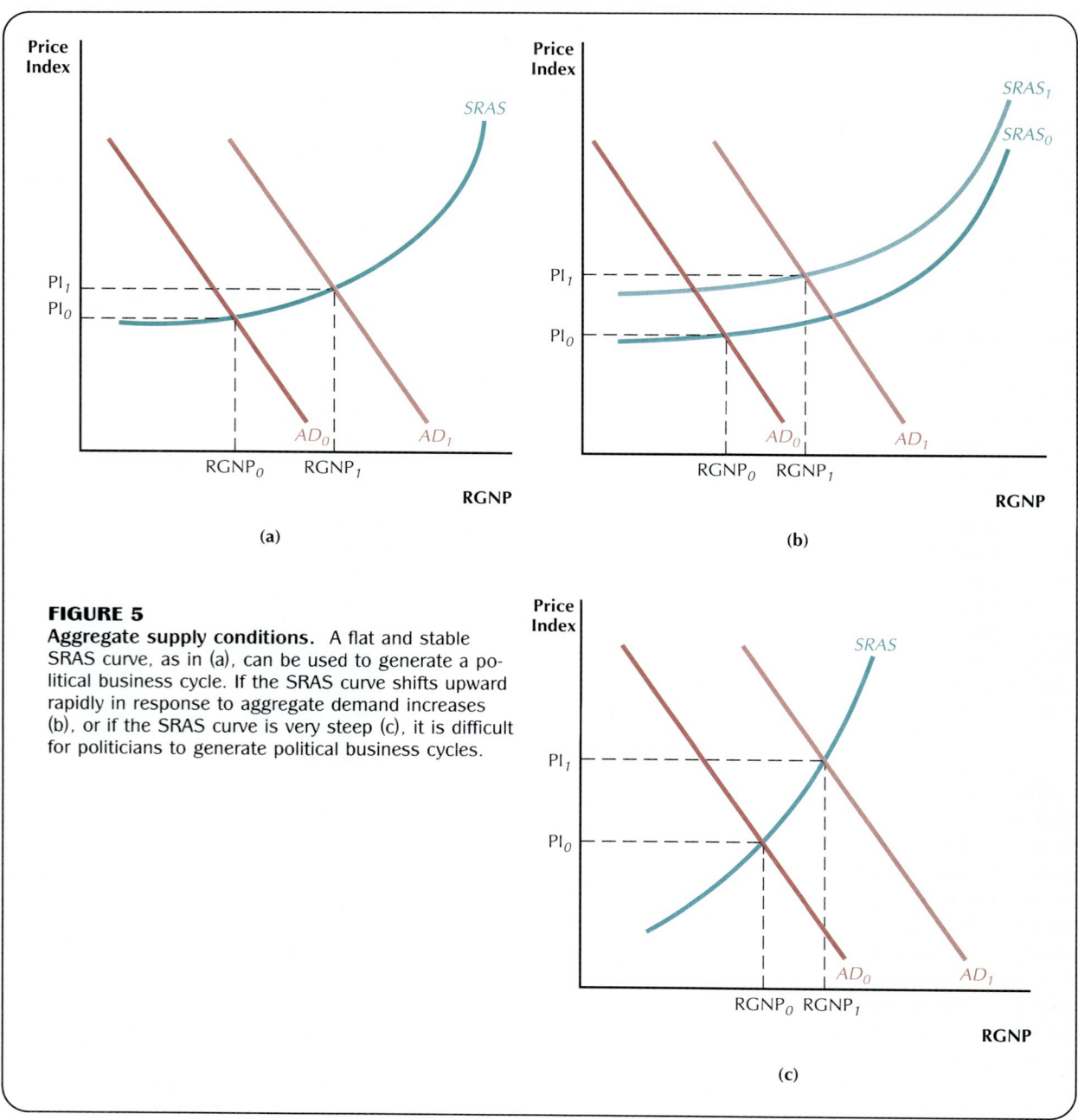

FIGURE 5
Aggregate supply conditions. A flat and stable SRAS curve, as in (a), can be used to generate a political business cycle. If the SRAS curve shifts upward rapidly in response to aggregate demand increases (b), or if the SRAS curve is very steep (c), it is difficult for politicians to generate political business cycles.

with a lag when aggregate demand rises, and an aggregate demand curve that is very responsive to government policy. Under such conditions, the government could generate the following election cycle pattern. Fiscal or monetary policy is used to expand aggregate demand during an election year. This moves the economy from point E_0 to point E_1 in Figure 6, where the economy is operating at election time. In the year following the election the aggregate demand pressure affects costs, and the SRAS curve shifts upward. The economy

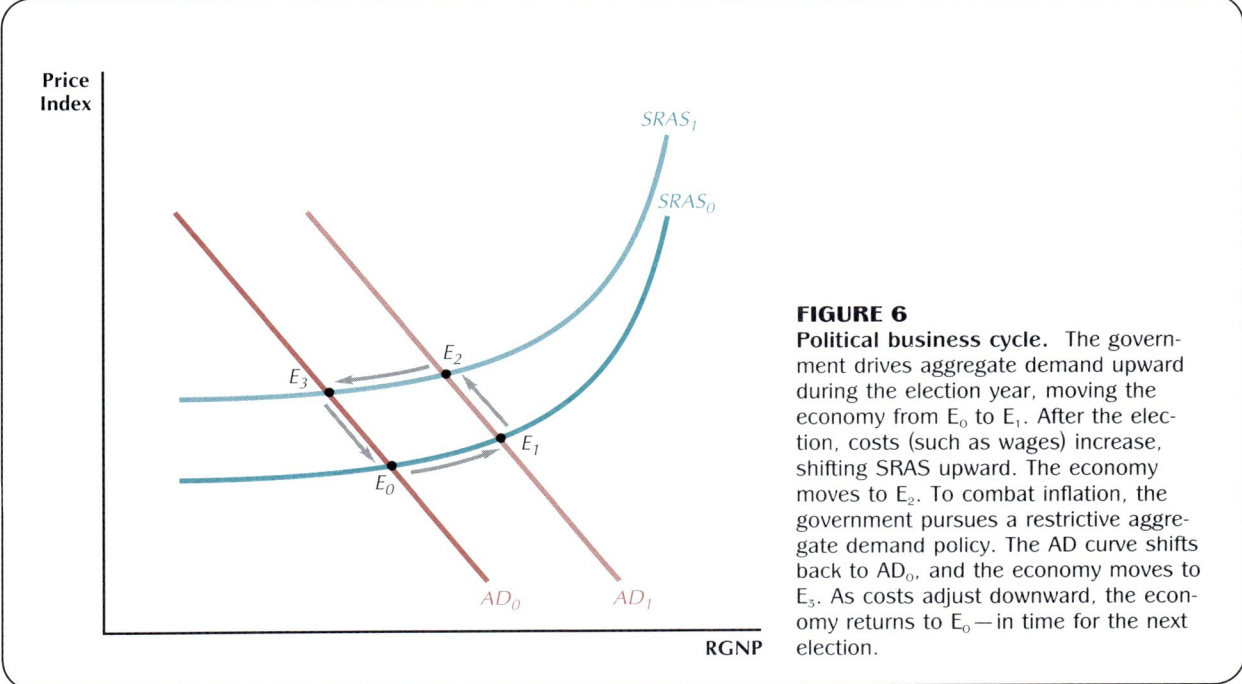

FIGURE 6
Political business cycle. The government drives aggregate demand upward during the election year, moving the economy from E_0 to E_1. After the election, costs (such as wages) increase, shifting SRAS upward. The economy moves to E_2. To combat inflation, the government pursues a restrictive aggregate demand policy. The AD curve shifts back to AD_0, and the economy moves to E_3. As costs adjust downward, the economy returns to E_0—in time for the next election.

moves to E_2. To restrain inflationary pressures, policymakers enact restrictive fiscal or monetary policies, moving the economy to E_3. Costs adjust with a lag, and the economy returns to E_0 where it began. The next election cycle can now begin.

Given the information deficiencies and variable lags built into the real economy, an election cycle so perfect as that shown in Figure 6 is an impossibility. Nevertheless, government could use, or attempt to use, economic policy to increase income and reduce unemployment in election years. Whether policy actually has been used in such a manner is an empirical question.

A Look at the Evidence on Election Cycles. A considerable body of research examining the hypothesis of a political business cycle has accumulated. Although the results are mixed, a significant amount of circumstantial evidence suggests that politicians have tried to influence the economy for political purposes. Some recent highly sophisticated statistical studies indicate that they have consistently succeeded.

In a book entitled *Political Control of the Economy*,[1] political scientist Edward R. Tufte presents evidence in support of the election cycle hypothesis. He shows, for example, that the pattern of transfer payments in election years differs significantly from the pattern in nonelection years. During election years, especially large transfer payments — particularly to Social Security recipients and veterans — are made just before election day. The smooth pattern of nonelection years is absent.

---

[1] Princeton, NJ: Princeton University Press, 1978.

Tufte's study shows that the growth rate of real disposable income is higher in presidential election years than in nonpresidential election years. It is higher in midterm election years than in years when no election is held. Such a pattern is consistent with the hypothesis that incumbents attempt to pep up the economy for elections. Also consistent is the pattern of growth of the monetary base. The growth rate of the base increases in most presidential election years and falls the year following the election.

Although Tufte's arguments in support of the political business cycle hypothesis seem persuasive, Tufte backs them with very little statistical analysis. Indeed, for many years researchers were unable to find any statistical connection between macroeconomic and election behavior. However, recent research by two University of Oregon economists shows that such a connection exists.[2] Using sophisticated statistical techniques, Stephen Haynes and Joe Stone discovered two types of politically generated macroeconomic cycles. They found that inflation and real GNP growth are higher and unemployment is lower during Democratic presidential administrations than during Republican administrations. In other words, a Democratic president encourages more rapid aggregate demand growth, on average, than a Republican president. Haynes and Stone call this effect a **partisan cycle** — different political parties lead to different macroeconomic behavior.

The second type of political business cycle occurs only in Republican administrations. Republican presidents attempt to generate the type of **electoral cycle** discussed earlier. That is, they attempt to create high real GNP growth and low unemployment during election years, and follow with restrictive policies to control inflation in subsequent years. No such pattern emerges for Democratic administrations. Haynes and Stone speculate that the reason Republicans generate electoral cycles and Democrats do not is that, as the minority party, Republicans must attract all the votes possible to be elected. As the majority party, Democrats feel freer to pursue partisan policies.

Fiscal Policy Since World War II

A survey of fiscal policy since the late 1940s shows that policymakers have frequently failed to use fiscal policy as an effective stabilization tool. We will survey fiscal policy by presidential administrations, as we surveyed monetary policy in the preceding chapter.

The Truman Years: From One War to Another   A huge decline in defense expenditures (from $73.7 billion in 1945 to $16.4 billion in 1946) reduced government spending sharply following World War II. The sharp reduction in defense spending immediately pulled real GNP down from its abnormally high wartime level and ultimately led to a mild recession in 1949. In 1950 the Korean War began, and defense spending once again soared. Congress responded to the outbreak of war with an immediate increase in both income and excise taxes. The tax increase helped to offset the expansiveness of war expenditures. Thus, although spending on the Korean War was itself highly destabilizing, the government took steps to minimize the overall impact of defense spending. Con-

---

SECTION RECAP
An incumbent's reelection chances depend partly on the state of the economy. This gives legislators and presidents an incentive to attempt to produce a booming economy at election time. Evidence indicates that economic conditions under Democratic administrations differ significantly from those under Republican administrations and that Republican presidents have produced election cycles.

Partisan cycle
Different political parties consistently produce different macroeconomic behavior.

Electoral cycle
A political business cycle; government policy increases aggregate demand during election years to generate high real GNP growth and low unemployment, then slows aggregate demand growth in subsequent years to reduce inflation.

---

[2]See, in particular, Stephen E. Haynes and Joe A. Stone, "Political Models of the Business Cycle Should Be Revived," *Economic Inquiry* 28 (July 1990), pp. 442–465.

gress and President Truman deserve high marks for fiscal policy during this period.

The Eisenhower Years: Peacetime Prosperity The Korean War was still going on when Dwight D. Eisenhower was elected president in November 1952. At the end of the war, Congress and President Eisenhower reduced income and excise taxes, reversing the tax increases of 1950. The tax reductions were an appropriate response to the decline in defense spending, representing an effective use of fiscal policy as a stabilization tool.

The remainder of the Eisenhower period was marked by a strong economy, punctuated only by a recession in 1958. The government pursued a countercyclical fiscal policy in 1958 by increasing both government purchases and transfer payments. However, just as monetary policy was cautious under Eisenhower, so was fiscal policy. The expansion of government spending, although moderating the recession, was not sufficient to completely offset it.

Overall, fiscal policy during the Eisenhower administration was successful, if somewhat cautious. It should be noted, however, that policymakers were not confronted with any major problems during that period.

The Kennedy–Johnson Years: Fiscal Policy to the Fore The U.S. economy was operating below its natural level when John F. Kennedy was elected president in 1960. Kennedy named several prominent Keynesian economists to his Council of Economic Advisers, economists who believed that fiscal policy should be used aggressively to raise real GNP to its natural level and keep it there. Kennedy's advisers noted that the government was running a high-employment budget surplus, which had a contractionary effect on aggregate demand. They advocated income tax reductions and investment tax credits as a way to reduce the high-employment surplus and drive real GNP toward its natural level.

A package of investment tax incentives was put in place in 1962. In 1964, Congress enacted legislation reducing the income tax and excise taxes, both of which were further reduced in 1965. The tax cuts had the desired effect, turning the high-employment budget surplus of 1963 into a substantial high-employment deficit by 1965. The tax reductions spurred both investment and consumption spending, driving real GNP to its natural level in 1964.

President Johnson continued the expansive fiscal policy by increasing the growth of transfer payments and defense spending without raising taxes. Federal transfer payments grew at an annual rate of about 7 percent from 1961 through 1964; they grew at a rate of almost 14 percent per year from 1965 through 1968. When combined with an increase in defense expenditures of over 50 percent between 1964 and 1968, the result was an overly expansive fiscal policy. Rapid aggregate demand growth generated increasing inflation. The temporary income tax surcharge enacted in 1968 did nothing to check spending growth.

There was no countercyclical fiscal policy as such during the Kennedy–Johnson years, since no recessions occurred. The use of fiscal policy to stimulate the economy was overdone, paving the way for the inflation problems that plagued the U.S. economy throughout the 1970s.

The Nixon–Ford Years: Missed Opportunities Two recessions occurred during the 1969–1976 period, a mild recession in 1970 and a severe recession in 1974–

1975. Reductions in defense spending contributed to the 1970 recession, although tight monetary policy designed to subdue inflation was the major cause of the 1970 downturn. Automatic stabilizers worked well during 1970; disposable income was actually higher at the trough of the recession than it had been at the previous cycle peak. No discretionary fiscal policy actions were taken.

In August 1971 President Nixon imposed a wage–price freeze on the economy in an attempt to check inflation. The three-month freeze was followed by a number of phases of wage and price controls. As we noted in the preceding chapter, rather than accompanying the wage–price controls with a restrictive monetary policy, the Federal Reserve generated rapid monetary growth in 1971 and 1972. The price controls lowered inflation in 1972, but the rebound of prices after the lifting of controls offset any long-term effects of the controls on the price level.

The 1974–1975 recession was caused by the OPEC oil price increases of 1973 and 1974. As we saw in earlier chapters, even a perfect aggregate demand policy cannot offset all the negative effects of supply shocks. Policymakers must choose whether to attempt to minimize the price level effects or the output effects of a supply shock. Monetary policymakers largely concentrated on minimizing the increase in the price level. However, in 1975 Congress did approve both a temporary income tax rebate and a permanent income tax reduction. Thus, the only discretionary fiscal policy action taken during the Nixon–Ford years was countercyclical.

The Carter Years: Self-Inflicted Wounds Inflation rose throughout the Carter years, driven both by rapid aggregate demand growth and, in 1979, by higher oil prices. The Carter administration did not undertake any anti-inflation policy until late in 1979, when the Federal Reserve tightened monetary policy. The most important fiscal policy development of the Carter years was a major increase in payroll taxes. Although payroll taxes reduce disposable income, and hence had some contractionary effect on aggregate demand growth, they also affect prices by affecting the cost of production. Payroll taxes (such as the Social Security tax) are largely shifted by producers to consumers in the form of higher prices. To the extent that the higher payroll taxes imposed during the Carter years drove prices up, they worsened the inflation problem of the late 1970s.

The Reagan Revolution: Tax Cuts and Big Deficits Fiscal policy was central to Ronald Reagan's economic program. Reagan came to office pledging to reduce the size of government. He believed that reducing taxes and cutting government spending would spur the private economy and reinvigorate economic growth in the United States. In 1981 the Reagan administration pushed a major tax reduction bill through Congress. As the federal budget deficit rose in 1982, Congress passed a second act that took back some of the business tax cuts granted by the 1981 act. Finally, another major tax bill became law in 1986. The 1986 act lowered the marginal tax rate on corporate income, but also eliminated the investment tax credit and altered other tax rules in such a way that business tax liabilities rose.

The initial plan of the Reagan administration was to reduce taxes, increase defense spending, and reduce nondefense spending. Reagan's economic advisers believed that sharp reductions in income tax *rates* would generate enough economic growth that tax *revenues* would fall very little. Thus, they argued that the entire fiscal policy package would largely finance itself through economic growth. They were wrong.

The federal government's budget deficit grew from a little more than $70 billion in 1980 (the last year of the Carter administration) to over $200 billion in 1983. Part of the reason for the sharp increase in the deficit was the recession of 1981–1982, which reduced national income and thus lowered tax revenue. However, even after the economy recovered, deficits remained large. In 1988, the last year of the Reagan presidency, the budget deficit was still $155 billion, despite the fact that the ratio of total federal tax receipts to GNP was nearly as high when Reagan left office as when he entered it. (The income tax rate reductions of the early Reagan years were offset by increases in payroll tax rates.)

On the spending side, the Reagan administration managed to accomplish only one of its two goals: defense spending rose both in real terms and as a share of federal expenditures until 1987; however, nondefense spending did not decline. In fact, nominal transfer payments rose at an annual rate of 7 percent during the Reagan years, and real transfer payments rose at a rate of 2.2 percent per year. Furthermore, interest payments on the government debt nearly tripled between 1980 and 1988. The net result was an 82 percent increase in federal government spending from 1980 to 1988. Even a 75.6 percent increase in tax revenues could not prevent the emergence of large budget deficits.

The expansive fiscal policies of the Reagan years helped promote rapid growth from 1983 through 1988. Coming out of the 1982 recession, real GNP grew at an annual rate of 4 percent for the remainder of the Reagan years. When Reagan left office, the economy was operating a bit above its natural output level. However, Reagan bequeathed persistent budget deficits and a huge national debt to his successor.

The Early Bush Years: Focusing on the Deficit The size of the federal government's budget deficit dominated discussions of fiscal policy in 1989 and 1990. Scrambling to avoid across-the-board spending cuts mandated by the Gramm–Rudman–Hollings Act, in the fall of 1990 Congress and President Bush agreed on a package of tax increases and spending cuts to reduce the budget deficit. Ironically, this contractionary fiscal policy legislation was passed just as the economy moved into a recession. Not surprisingly, most economists viewed the legislation unfavorably, arguing that it would worsen the emerging recession.

Summary: What History Tells Us The record of postwar fiscal policy in the United States is decidedly mixed. With only two or three exceptions, fiscal policy has not been used as an effective countercyclical policy tool. As often as not, fiscal policy actions have destabilized the economy. As is the case with monetary policy, countercyclical fiscal policy does not appear to work as well in practice as in theory. Thus, most economists have moved away from the view that activist fiscal policy is practicable. However, fiscal policy can affect the basic position of the macroeconomy greatly, as the Reagan years demonstrated.

SECTION RECAP
With only two or three exceptions, discretionary fiscal policy has not been used effectively as a countercyclical policy tool in the postwar period.

Does It Make Economic Sense?

Is the Economy Depression Proof?

Skepticism about the ability of policymakers to use discretionary policy to offset the business cycle is widespread. A lack of information and the existence of lags make monetary policy an unsure anticyclical device, and the political process dampens enthusiasm for fiscal policy. Yet few economists seem to fear the possibility of another major depression. If the major policy tools used to combat business cycles are so imperfect, does such an attitude make economic sense?

The rather complacent attitude displayed by economists toward the possibility of another major depression stems primarily from two sources. The first source is the belief that the Great Depression required a sequence of events that is unlikely to occur again. In this view, poor government policy was responsible for turning an ordinary recession into a major depression (as explained in the business cycles chapter). In 1929 the Federal Reserve instituted a tight monetary policy in an attempt to squelch stock market speculation. The tight policy was continued even after it became evident that the economy was slipping into a recession. (The economy obviously was slowing before the stock market crashed.) The tight monetary policy started the economy on its downward path.

During the early stages of the recession, some major banks began having liquidity problems. They did not have enough liquid assets to meet the demands for cash facing them. The Federal Reserve failed to provide cash to banks, and the banking system collapsed. Over 9000 banks failed in three years, and the M2 money supply fell by one third. Government further added to this debacle by passing the Smoot–Hawley Tariff Act, which led to dramatic reductions in foreign trade. Hence, many economists believe that the Great Depression was the result of a nearly incredible sequence of bad policy decisions. Such a sequence is unlikely to occur again.

The second source of confidence in the stability of the economy is much less negative toward government. This source stresses the important role government plays in the economy as a major factor preventing another large depression. First, the Federal Reserve System and the Federal Deposit Insurance Corporation are genuinely committed to the safety and solvency of the banking system. These agencies will not allow the banking system to collapse again. Deposit insurance has increased public confidence in the banking system, so the probability of large-scale bank runs is extremely low. It is worth noting that neither the October 1987 stock market crash nor the collapse of the savings and loan industry triggered even a recession, much less a depression.

A number of fiscal policies also contribute to the stability of the economy. The unemployment insurance system supports disposable income and consumption spending during recessions, thus limiting the multiplier effect during a downturn. The welfare system performs a similar role. Furthermore, the large number of people working for government (16.3 percent of the nonagricultural workforce in 1989) is largely recession proof. The size of government acts to prevent another major depression.

One additional factor should be mentioned. A major depression doesn't develop overnight. In a prolonged recession, expansive monetary and fiscal policy could be brought to bear on the economy, offsetting further decline. While discretionary policy may not work well against ordinary cyclical movements, it is still a powerful antidepression tool.

These arguments are persuasive to most economists. Still, there is some concern that the economy might not be 100 percent depression proof. The concern centers mostly on the state of the world financial system. Electronic banking goes on worldwide, and no single central bank can control it. (However, about 40 percent of the world money supply is in three countries—the United States, West Germany, and Japan—so the coordinated action of only three central banks would be very powerful.) A major banking collapse in another part of the world could cause major U.S. banks to fail. Would the Federal Reserve act to save them? If it did, what would be the consequences? Saving major banks from failure might force the Federal Reserve to increase the money supply drastically, possibly generating a great deal of inflation. Policymakers would then be faced with choosing the lesser of two evils, inflation or depression. Thus, as stable as the economy may appear, there is no guarantee that a major depression or inflation will never occur again.

How Powerful Is Fiscal Policy?

The simple theory of fiscal policy indicates that government spending and taxing should have powerful impacts on the economy, especially if such fiscal policy actions are perceived as permanent. However, in recent decades a number of economists have questioned the power of fiscal policy, arguing on both theoretical and empirical grounds that fiscal policy actions often have little lasting impact on the macroeconomy. In this section we discuss three facets of this ongoing debate: crowding out (or crowding in) in the short run and the long run, the importance of the composition of government spending, and the issue of how to measure the degree of expansiveness of deficit-financed fiscal policies.

Crowding out (or in) in the Short Run and the Long

If deficit-financed increases in government spending or reductions in taxes trigger offsetting movements in private spending, the overall effect of the fiscal policy actions may be small. One mechanism that might trigger a reduction in private spending in the face of expansionary fiscal policies is a rise in the interest rate.

The Short Run Government borrowing to finance increased spending or reduced taxation increases the demand for credit. Other things constant, an increase in the demand for credit pushes interest rates upward. As the government bids up the interest rate on its bonds to attract buyers, businesses and households are forced to pay higher interest rates to obtain credit. If investment spending is sensitive to interest rates, the higher rates caused by increased government borrowing reduce investment spending. Government borrowing crowds investors out of the market.

If increased government borrowing occurs when the economy is in a recession, short-run crowding out may be minimal. Suppose the economy is operating at point R in Figure 7. At such a relatively low output level, business investment spending may depend more on income and capacity utilization than on interest rates. Companies that are experiencing low sales and have a large amount of idle capital are probably not very sensitive to moderate changes in their cost of borrowing. Investment projects already under way will be completed, so long as the companies can afford to do so. However, new projects will be postponed until sales improve.

In such circumstances, a deficit-financed increase in government purchases can have a positive effect on investment spending by increasing aggregate demand, and through the multiplier effect, increasing consumer demand for the products of businesses. As output rises to $RGNP_1$, some firms may decide to increase investment spending, further increasing aggregate demand and real GNP. In such a case, deficit-financed government spending *crowds in* private investment spending.

Deficit-financed government spending is more likely to crowd out investment spending when the economy is operating at or above the natural output level. At relatively high output levels, most firms are fully utilizing their plant and equipment. Investment spending is already high, as firms seek to expand

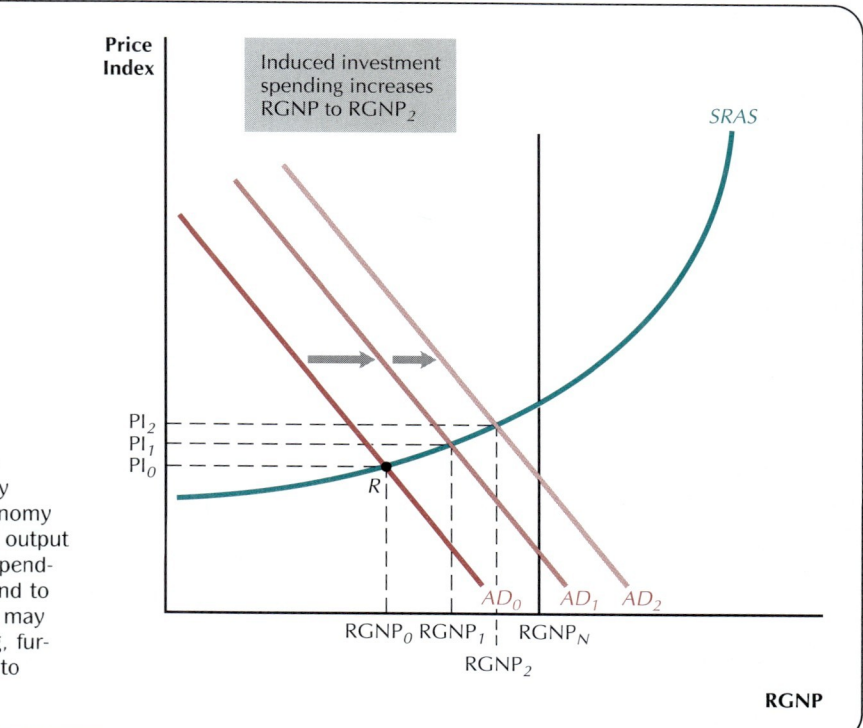

FIGURE 7
Crowding in investment. Deficit-financed government spending may crowd in investment when the economy is operating well below the natural output level. An increase in government spending that increases aggregate demand to AD_1 and raises real GNP to $RGNP_1$ may induce higher investment spending, further increasing aggregate demand to AD_2.

their productive capacity. Government borrowing at such a time can significantly depress investment spending. By pushing the interest rate upward, government borrowing reduces the profitability of investment projects, causing some firms to delay or cancel investment projects. Perhaps even more important is the effect of higher interest rates on home buyers. Monthly house payments are extremely sensitive to changes in mortgage rates because of the length of mortgage loans. Government borrowing when real GNP is at or above the natural level can play havoc with the mortgage market by crowding many prospective home buyers out of the market.

The Long Run Even if the short-run consequences of deficit-financed government spending are beneficial, the long-run consequences may not be. The reason is straightforward: The economy tends toward a natural level of output over time. Assuming the government's actions do not affect the natural output level (perhaps an unrealistic assumption), increased government spending ultimately claims a larger share of output, leaving less to be purchased by investors and consumers.

Figure 8 illustrates this result. Suppose private spending declines and AD shifts to the left, reducing output from $RGNP_N$ to $RGNP_1$. The government responds by increasing its purchases of goods and services. Through the multiplier effect, government spending drives output back to the natural level, $RGNP_N$. Although fiscal policy has returned output to its natural level, the *composition* of aggregate demand differs from its original composition. Government now claims a larger share of real GNP; the private sector receives a

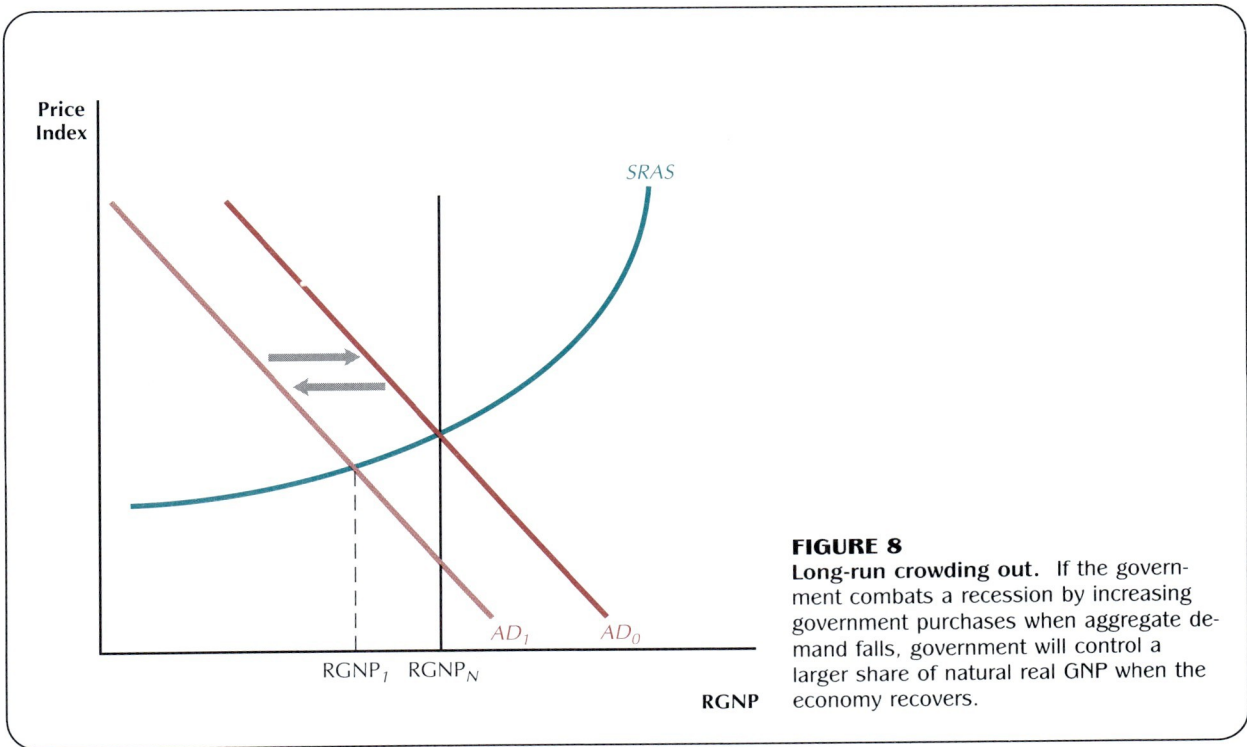

FIGURE 8
Long-run crowding out. If the government combats a recession by increasing government purchases when aggregate demand falls, government will control a larger share of natural real GNP when the economy recovers.

smaller share. Further increases in private sector spending will only result in an increase in the price level, since output cannot exceed $RGNP_N$ for very long.

Government spending on consumption goods that crowds out investment spending harms the long-term health of the economy. The growth of the capital stock slows, reducing the growth of output over time. In graphical terms, the LRAS curve does not shift outward as rapidly as it would if government purchases were lower. Only if government invests in infrastructure development that encourages businesses to produce more — such as road construction, bridge repair, and sewage treatment facilities — does the additional government spending have beneficial long-run effects on output. That is, the *composition* of government spending appears to be important. Recent research indicates that the composition of government spending may matter in the short run as well as in the long run.

Composition of Government Spending

The standard treatment of the effects of government spending found in textbooks (this book included) implicitly assumes that consumers do not value governmentally provided goods and services as income. That is, consumers do not alter their consumption spending in response to changes in government provision of goods and services. The importance of this assumption can be seen by comparing the behavior of consumers who do not count government goods and services as income with the behavior of consumers who *fully* count government goods and services as income. The latter group treats governmen-

SECTION RECAP
In the short run, deficit spending may either crowd out or crowd in private spending. In the long run, however, greater government spending crowds out private spending unless government spending increases economic productivity and the natural output level.

tally provided goods and services as direct substitutes for private consumption goods.[3]

The standard consumption function, in its simple Keynesian form, is:

$$C = a + b(DI)$$

Consumption depends only on autonomous factors (such as accumulated wealth) and on disposable income. Unless government policy affects disposable income, consumption spending does not change.

Consumers who count governmentally provided goods and services as equivalent to privately purchased consumption goods have a consumption function of the following form:

$$C + G_C = a + b(DI)$$

where G_C stands for government consumption goods. Rearranging this equation we obtain:

$$C = a - G_C + b(DI)$$

Now, assume that all consumers count governmentally provided consumption goods as perfect substitutes for private consumption goods; that is, the economy's consumption function is $C = a - G_C + b(DI)$. In this case an *increase* in government consumption expenditures generates an identical *decrease* in private consumption expenditures. Thus, *the increase in government consumption spending has no direct effect on aggregate demand*, being fully offset by the decrease in private consumption spending. Consequently, only government investment purchases affect aggregate demand if consumers fully substitute government consumption goods for private consumption goods.

Perhaps more plausible than either of the two assumptions explored thus far is the assumption that consumers *partially* substitute government consumption for private consumption expenditures. In this case, a change in government consumption spending would be partially offset by a change in private consumption spending. The effect of changes in government consumption spending on aggregate demand would not be zero, but they would be smaller than the traditional approach indicates.

The extent to which government consumption spending actually affects aggregate demand, and through aggregate demand real GNP, is an empirical issue. A number of economists have investigated this question in recent years. Our discussion draws on the work of David Aschauer.[4]

Professor Aschauer began his investigation of the impact of government spending on real GNP by dividing government purchases of goods and services into three categories: consumption spending, military investment spending, and nonmilitary investment spending. He then used statistical techniques to estimate the effect of each type of government purchases on real GNP. His results were eye opening. Professor Aschauer found that government consumption purchases had *no statistically significant effect* on real GNP — even in the short run. The same was true for military investment spending. However, he estimated the impact of nonmilitary investment spending on real GNP to

---

SECTION RECAP

If consumers regard government consumption expenditures as a substitute for private consumption expenditures, government *(continued)*

---

[3]The ideas presented in this section were first developed by Martin J. Bailey in *National Income and the Price Level* (New York: McGraw–Hill, 1962), pp. 71–80.

[4]Professor Aschauer has written a number of theoretical and empirical papers on this topic. Here we draw on "Is Government Spending Stimulative?" *Contemporary Policy Issues* 8 (October 1990), pp. 30–46.

be quite large. Professor Aschauer's work indicates that the multiplier effect of nonmilitary investment spending is around four; a $1 increase in government nonmilitary investment spending generates about a $4 increase in real GNP.

Why is the effect of nonmilitary investment so large? In earlier chapters we discussed the effect of public investment on the productivity of private capital goods. When government provides better infrastructure—roads, bridges, water and sewer systems, and so forth—private capital becomes more productive. Greater productivity encourages private firms to invest more. Thus, public nonmilitary investment spending encourages private investment spending. The effects on real GNP are positive in both the short run and the long run.

The implications of Professor Aschauer's findings are important for short-run fiscal policy. If only nonmilitary investment spending affects aggregate demand to any significant degree, then discretionary fiscal policies that alter the level of government consumption purchases or military purchases are (approximately) useless as countercyclical policy measures. Government is constrained in its choice of projects for countercyclical purposes.[5]

> **SECTION RECAP**
> *(continued)*
> spending may largely replace private spending. Recent statistical work indicates that the effect of government consumption spending on real GNP is very small (with a multiplier of less than 0.5). However, government nonmilitary investment spending has a large impact on the economy, since it encourages more private investment spending.

Measuring the Effect of Fiscal Policy

Another factor complicating the use of fiscal policy is determining whether a particular combination of spending, taxes, and borrowing is expansionary, neutral, or contractionary. At first glance, this would not seem to be a problem. If the government is running a high employment deficit, fiscal policy is expansionary; if the high employment deficit is zero, fiscal policy is neutral; if the government is running a high employment surplus, fiscal policy is contractionary. The issue is not quite so simple, however, as Northwestern University economist Robert Eisner has demonstrated.[6]

Deficit spending is more expansive than tax-financed spending only if the public views the bonds sold by government as part of their wealth.[7] Let us consider what that means. What reason would the American public have to *not* consider their holdings of U.S. government bonds part of their wealth? One possible reason would be if the public viewed the sale of government bonds in the present as an indication that taxes will be higher in the future. If the public believes that current deficits will be paid off in the future, then it makes sense for people to view their bond holdings as savings needed to meet future tax liabilities. In this case, the bonds are not regarded as true wealth.

Now, suppose the American public does treat U.S. government bonds as part of wealth. In this case, the *real* value of government bond wealth at the beginning of a year equals the nominal value of bonds outstanding divided by the price index. Over the course of the year the real value of government

---

[5]This statement applies only to government purchases, not to transfer payments. Note that automatic stabilizers affect the level of transfer payments or taxes.

[6]Professor Eisner argues his case in *How Real Is the Federal Deficit?* (New York: The Free Press, 1986).

[7]Not all economists believe that deficit-financed spending is more expansive than tax-financed spending. Economists who believe that the Ricardian Equivalence Principle (introduced in the earlier fiscal policy chapter) is valid believe the two types of financing are equivalent. Other economists, including David Aschauer, find that when the composition of government spending is accounted for, the size of the deficit makes no difference.

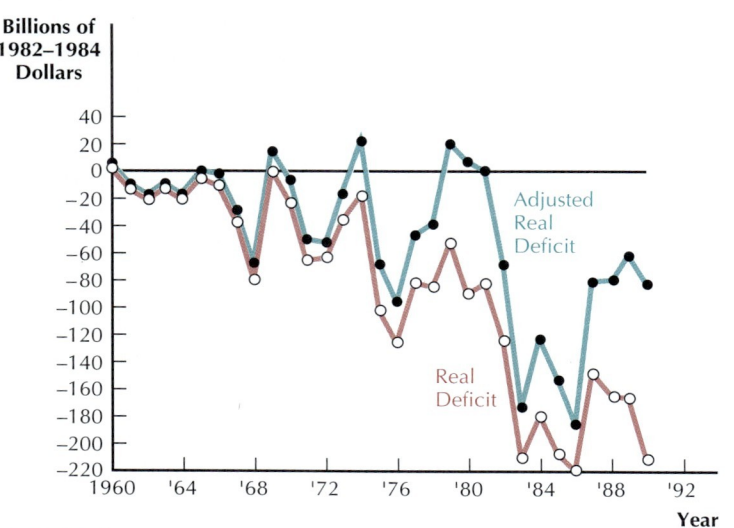

FIGURE 9
Adjusting the real deficit for the effect of inflation on outstanding debt. Rising prices affect not only the real size of current budget deficits; rising prices also affect the buying power of outstanding debt held by households. Inflation reduces the buying power of outstanding debt, thereby reducing the expansive effect of current deficits. When the real deficit is adjusted for decreases in the real value of outstanding debt held by households, the combined effect is a significantly smaller adjusted deficit. In some years the adjusted measure records a surplus.
Source: *Economic Report of the President, 1991*, Tables B-60 and B-76.

bond wealth can change for two different reasons: The government can run a deficit (or a surplus), thus adding to (or subtracting from) the nominal value of the government debt, or the price level can change, thus altering the real buying power of the nominal debt. That is, the change in the real government debt outstanding during a year equals the real deficit run by the government during the year plus the change in the real value of the debt held by the public at the beginning of the year.

The change in the real deficit during a year simply equals the value of the deficit divided by the price index for the year. The change in the real value of the previously issued debt equals the inflation rate for the year times the nominal value of the debt at the beginning of the year. (The inflation rate measures the decline in the purchasing power of money during the year, so multiplying it by the beginning value of the debt tells us how much the real value of the debt declines.)

Robert Eisner has argued that, when account is taken of the effect of inflation on the real value of government debt held by the public, fiscal policy is seen to have been far less expansionary in the 1970s that it was thought to have been. Figure 9 illustrates the conventional measure of the real government deficit and the real deficit adjusted for the change in the real value of government debt held by the public. The conventional measure of the real deficit is larger than the adjusted measure throughout the 1960 to 1990 period, since the inflation rate was positive throughout this period. Professor Eisner argues that one of the reasons for the poor performance of the U.S. economy in 1979 and 1980 was a contractionary fiscal policy, produced by policymakers who failed to take the effect of inflation on the outstanding debt into account in calculating the impact of fiscal policy on the economy. Note that, adjusted for the change in the real value of outstanding debt, the real deficit became a real surplus of $20 billion in 1979 and $7.52 billion in 1980.[8]

The problem of measuring the deficit correctly goes well beyond adjusting for the effects of inflation on outstanding debt. As we mentioned in the earlier fiscal policy chapter, the accounting system used by the U.S. government is peculiar. Unlike corporate and state and local government accounting systems, the federal government does not divide its accounts into a current account and a capital account. All federal investment spending is counted as a current expense, rather than being depreciated over time. Thus, the federal deficit is overstated according to generally accepted accounting practices. Furthermore, a large amount of government spending and revenue never shows up in the official budget. Such off-budget spending and income sometimes add to and sometimes reduce the size of the official deficit.

The various measurement problems, combined with the composition of spending issues raised by Martin J. Bailey and recently revived by David Aschauer, and the issue of Ricardian Equivalence, leave the theory of fiscal policy in something of a flux. No longer is fiscal policy viewed as a simple, direct policy tool. Its effects are complex and difficult to measure.

SECTION RECAP
The size of the real budget deficit may be a poor measure of the impact of fiscal policy on the economy. Deflating the nominal budget deficit only partially corrects for the effect of rising prices. Inflation also reduces the buying power of the outstanding debt held by households. Adjusting the value of outstanding debt for declines in its real value reduces the size of the adjusted budget deficit substantially.

National Industrial Policy

To this point we have discussed fiscal policy as though it consisted solely of the government's spending, taxing, and borrowing policies. However, in many countries the government has followed a more direct approach, by actually intervening in the decision making of private corporations. Although little direct intervention has taken place in the United States, such a policy is not without its advocates. During the early 1980s, some politicians, government officials, and economists who believed that the United States was deindustrializing began calling for such a fiscal policy — a **national industrial policy**. These people believed that high-productivity manufacturing jobs were being lost in large numbers to foreign competitors while the U.S. economy was rapidly converting to a service-based system. They feared that the U.S. labor force would be divided into two groups: a small group of highly paid technicians and a large group of poorly paid unskilled workers. What is needed, they claimed, is a national industrial policy to revitalize the manufacturing sector and restore the United States to its competitive world position.[9]

National industrial policy
Policy designed to affect the long-term growth and industrial composition of the economy.

---

[8]In his book, Professor Eisner also accounts for changes in the market value of debt caused by changes in the interest rate. We have seen that the price of a bond moves inversely with interest rates. Rising interest rates in the late 1970s depressed bond prices, further tightening fiscal policy, in Professor Eisner's view.

[9]Those calling for an industrial policy in the early 1980s included 1984 presidential candidate Walter Mondale; Senator Gary Hart; economists Barry Bluestone, Bennett Harrison, and Lester Thurow; New York investment banker Felix Rohatyn; and the Democratic Caucus Committee on Party Effectiveness. In 1988, presidential candidate Michael Dukakis supported the idea. A variety of industrial policy proposals is summarized in Chapter 1 of Richard B. McKenzie's *Competing Visions: The Political Conflict Over America's Economic Future* (Washington, D.C.: Cato Institute, 1985).

What is a national industrial policy? In truth, the concept means different things to different people. To some a national industrial policy means large-scale planning by a centralized agency, probably a tripartite commission of representatives of government, business, and organized labor. To others a national industrial policy means government subsidization of ailing industries or (the opposite extreme) government subsidization of new industries that show growth potential for the future. Yet others believe that the best policy would be increased government involvement in the process of financing investment. Finally, some would call the system of taxation and regulation a national industrial policy and seek only to reform it. There are approximately as many different ideas about national industrial policy as there are writers on the subject.

Whatever proposals the advocates of a national industrial policy have in mind, they all share two common beliefs: (1) the U.S. economy is on a downward path, a trend that causes the future to appear bleak, and (2) only concerted action by the government will prevent the decline from continuing and worsening.

The national industrial policy position, simplified greatly, might be said to revolve around three specific arguments:

1. The U.S. manufacturing sector is declining, output is falling, and jobs are being lost. Such a trend is dangerous to the health of the economy.

2. Foreign competition is winning the sales battle both in the United States and abroad. Much of the success of foreign companies is due to government support (through industrial policies).

3. Government can do a better job of allocating investment funds than the market. Government should have the right to pick winners and losers and treat them accordingly.

The opponents of a national industrial policy dispute all three arguments. First, they contend the argument that the United States is deindustrializing is a hoax. The share of manufacturing output in real GNP was 21.8 percent in 1988, as high as it had been for three decades. (It was 21.4 percent in 1950, 20.3 percent in 1960, 21.0 percent in 1970, and 20.9 percent in 1980.) Actual manufacturing production rose by 50 percent from 1967 to 1981. Manufacturing output declined in 1981 and 1982, but the worst recession of the post-World War II era occurred during those years. Manufacturing output always declines during recessions.

Although manufacturing output continued to rise during the 1970s, manufacturing employment remained approximately stable over the 1965–1980 period (and throughout the 1980s), at around 20 million workers. How could manufacturing output rise more than 50 percent if employment was stable? Productivity increased. In large part, the failure of manufacturing employment to grow was due to the success of manufacturing industries in enhancing labor productivity.

The evidence on manufacturing output and employment has led most economists to reject the argument that the United States is deindustrializing. As Brookings Institution economist Robert W. Crandall has noted, "The United

States has outperformed every major industrial economy in the world except Japan since 1975."[10]

The second argument — that the competitiveness of U.S. firms in world markets has fallen drastically — also needs close examination. How international competitiveness should be measured is not completely clear. Some simple measures can be misleading. For example, if we use the share of U.S. manufacturing exports in total world manufacturing exports (manufactured goods sold outside the country in which they are produced) as a measure of competitiveness, we find that the U.S. share dropped from 14.8 percent in 1962 to 12.3 percent in 1982. However, the decline in export share came during the very prosperous decade of the 1960s, when no one thought that the U.S. economy was in decline. The U.S. export share fell from 14.8 percent in 1962 to 12.1 percent in 1972, before rising to 12.3 percent in 1982. According to this measure, the decade of the 1970s showed no deterioration of U.S. competitiveness.

Another possible measure of international competitiveness is the nation's **merchandise balance of trade** — the value of a nation's exports of tangible goods minus its imports of tangible goods. The merchandise trade balance was positive for the United States throughout the 1946–1970 period. Since 1970, however, it has been negative most of the time: U.S. imports of merchandise have exceeded U.S. exports.

A close examination of the factors contributing to the decline in the merchandise trade balance shows that the decline does not necessarily imply declining U.S. manufacturing competitiveness. If petroleum exports and imports are subtracted from merchandise exports and imports, the resulting nonpetroleum merchandise balance of trade remained positive throughout the 1970s. Figure 10 shows both the merchandise balance of trade and the nonpetroleum merchandise balance of trade. Not until 1983, at a time when conditions in the U.S. manufacturing sector were improving, did the latter turn negative.

International competition has caused structural shifts in U.S. manufacturing. Some industries have been unable to meet foreign competition and are declining. Other industries have expanded their market share. Older industries with simpler technologies, such as shoe and textile manufacturing, are losing business, but newer, more technologically advanced industries, such as electronics and biogenetics, are on the rise. No evidence exists that U.S. manufacturing industries as a whole are becoming less competitive in the world economy.

The final argument in favor of a national industrial policy is that government should be involved in allocating scarce investment funds. Industries favored by the governmental commission in charge of allocating credit would have access to credit on better terms than industries not favored. Critics make three major arguments against this idea. First, it is extremely difficult to pick winners in the Great Economic Race. Forecasting the needs of different industries is necessary if government planning is to add to economic growth. Growth experts such as John Kendrick doubt that such forecasting is possible with any degree of accuracy.

Merchandise balance of trade
Difference between the value of tangible goods exported and the value of such goods imported.

---

[10]Robert W. Crandall, "Can Industrial Policy Work?" *Washington Post,* Book World section, May 22, 1983, p. 8.

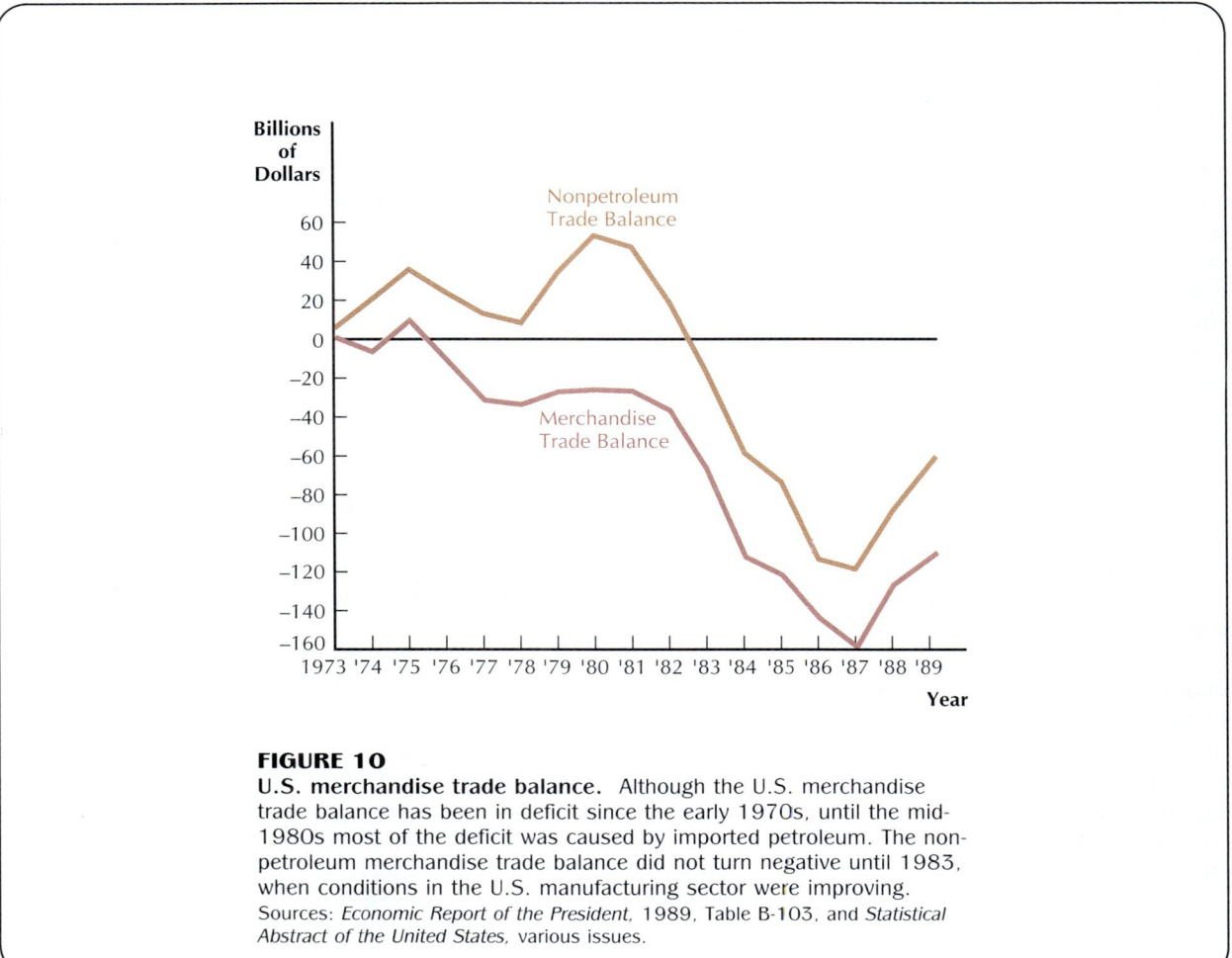

FIGURE 10
U.S. merchandise trade balance. Although the U.S. merchandise trade balance has been in deficit since the early 1970s, until the mid-1980s most of the deficit was caused by imported petroleum. The nonpetroleum merchandise trade balance did not turn negative until 1983, when conditions in the U.S. manufacturing sector were improving.
Sources: *Economic Report of the President*, 1989, Table B-103, and *Statistical Abstract of the United States*, various issues.

Second, central planning commissions encounter a problem that some economists call "the information problem." Having a government agency make investment or production decisions wastes most of the information people have about the economy, since the information relevant to making economic decisions is widely dispersed. Millions of people understand their particular businesses very well and contribute to making economic decisions. Market prices coordinate these decisions. If government decision makers override the market, they eliminate the contributions made by millions of people. The total amount of knowledge applied to economic problems falls drastically. In short, a few government officials cannot possibly know more than a small fraction of the relevant information understood by the millions of decision makers who participate in private market decisions.

The third argument against government financing of chosen industries is political. Advocates of government aid suppose that the aid will go where it will do the most economic good. Critics say it will go where the greatest political power is. Special-interest groups are very good at obtaining public funds, often

SECTION RECAP
A national industrial policy would increase government involvement in *(continued)*

diverting them from very productive uses to less productive uses. Critics maintain that this is exactly what would happen if the government were to become involved in allocating credit among industries. Newer, smaller industries with tremendous growth potential would be robbed of funds by older, larger, stagnant industries, because the older industries would have the political lobbying power to divert funds to themselves.

In summary, the arguments in favor of a national industrial policy are matched by some very strong arguments against such a policy. The basic issues seem to be whether government decision makers can respond to the desires of consumers better than private businesspeople and whether decisions made by a government commission would be free of undue political influence. Experience in other countries has not been kind to those advocating greater government involvement. It is clear that the advocates of a national industrial policy have not proven their case.

> **SECTION RECAP**
> *(continued)*
> investment decisions. Government would favor certain industries in an attempt to improve the performance of the economy. Opponents argue that such a policy would reduce economic efficiency and would enable groups with political power to gain at the expense of less-powerful groups.

Summary

The simple **theory of countercyclical fiscal policy** says that government should offset recessions by increasing government purchases or transfer payments or by reducing taxes. Decreasing spending or increasing taxes is the appropriate response to an excessively large expansion. However, a number of factors complicate fiscal policy in practice. **Lags** in the collection of data and in the **enactment** and **implementation** of discretionary fiscal policy changes often upset the timing of countercyclical fiscal policy. Thus, **automatic stabilizers** typically work better as a stabilization tool than discretionary fiscal policies.

Since voters' views of incumbents are influenced by the state of the economy at election time, elected officials have an incentive to create **political business cycles.** By driving real GNP growth up and unemployment down during election years, incumbents might be able to increase their reelection chances. Recent evidence suggests that they have succeeded in creating such a cycle in the United States.

The effect of fiscal policy on real GNP depends on a number of factors. If the economy is operating near its natural output level, an expansive fiscal policy may simply **crowd out** private spending, having little effect on real GNP. If, however, an expansive fiscal policy is undertaken during a recession, the policy may **crowd in** investment spending by raising real GNP and inducing private corporations to increase their investment spending. In the long run, government spending simply crowds out private spending, unless the government spending contributes to the growth of natural output.

Theory suggests that the **composition of government purchases** may be important in the short run, as well as the long run. If government-provided consumption goods are good substitutes for private consumption goods, an increase in government consumption purchases may be offset, at least partially, by a decline in private consumption spending. Recent empirical work suggests that the effect of government nonmilitary investment spending on real GNP is much larger than the effect of government consumption purchases.

Measuring the expansiveness of fiscal policy is not a simple issue. The size of the real deficit may overstate the expansiveness of fiscal policy in an inflationary environment, since inflation erodes the real value of government debt already held by the public. Furthermore, the U.S. government's accounting system does not separate spending on consumption goods from spending on capital goods, thus biasing the standard measure upward relative to the deficits run by state and local governments.

Some economists and politicians believe that the government should be involved more directly in investment and financing decisions. Supporters of a **national industrial policy** argue that only greater government involvement will maintain U.S. competitiveness in the world economy. Opponents argue that a national industrial policy would simply substitute political decisions for economic decisions, reducing the efficiency of the economy and the standard of living of Americans.

Questions for Thought

Knowledge Questions

1. Define the terms *enactment lag* and *implementation lag*.
2. Define the term *automatic stabilizer*. Give some examples of automatic stabilizers.
3. How (by what process) does a change in government purchases affect aggregate demand? A change in transfer payments? A change in income taxes?
4. Why is discretionary fiscal policy so often ineffective as a countercyclical stabilization tool?

Application Questions

5. Suppose four fiscal policy options are available to government policymakers who want to increase aggregate demand: Increase government investment purchases and finance with taxes, increase transfer payments and finance with taxes, increase investment purchases and deficit finance, and increase transfers and deficit finance. Rank the four options from largest to smallest impact, providing the reasoning for your ranking.
6. Suppose private investment demand and consumer durable demand are very sensitive to changes in the expected real rate of interest. What does this imply for the power of fiscal policy actions, such as increases or decreases in the level of government purchases?
7. Illustrate with the complete AD–SRAS–LRAS model the effects of an expansion in government purchases of consumption goods. Carry your analysis out into the long run.
8. The nominal value of government debt held by the public at the beginning of the year is $2200 billion. During the year the government runs a nominal deficit of $160 billion. The average value of the price index for the year is 180, and the inflation rate for the year is 6 percent. Calculate the change in the real value of the government debt during the year.

Synthesis Questions

9. Compare the effect on PI and real GNP in both the short run and the long run of an increase in government purchases composed mainly of consumption spending with an increase in government purchases composed mainly of investment spending. Explain why the effects differ.
10. Using both the AD–SRAS model and the credit market model, show the different effects of an increase in government purchases financed by borrowing and

an increase in government purchases financed by the creation of base money by the central bank. (You must make clear your assumptions about what happens to inflationary expectations in each case.)

11. Suppose voters take a long view of economic policy. They are more interested in the performance of the economy over a number of years than in any particular year. What incentives would this provide for politicians and policymakers? What type of economic policy do you think would be enacted?

12. Suppose the government decides to support the U.S. semiconductor industry. (Semiconductors are the basic component part of computers.) They refuse to allow foreign-made semiconductors into the United States, and they prop up the price of domestically manufactured semiconductors by purchasing and storing a significant number each year. What effect do you think this policy will have on the semiconductor industry? On industries that use semiconductors as inputs? On the domestic production of semiconductors relative to domestic demand? (In fact, in 1986 the Reagan administration placed a tariff on Japanese semiconductors. What was the result of this action?)

OVERVIEW

International trade is becoming increasingly important to the U.S. economy. Over 12 percent of the goods and services produced by U.S. companies are sold abroad. About 13 percent of the things Americans buy are foreign made. In Chapter 2 we argued that international trade benefits an economy. This chapter reviews and extends the theory of international trade, showing explicitly how trade affects prices and how tampering with free trade reduces the total benefits consumers and producers enjoy.

Trading — either domestically or internationally — does not benefit every member of society, although society as a whole benefits from trade. We discuss both the short-run and long-run gains from trade and the costs of trading. Following that, we examine the effects of devices that artificially restrict trade. In particular we are interested in determining the effects of tariffs and quotas on consumers and producers.

After developing the theory of international trade and trade barriers, we examine the importance of international trade to the U.S. economy. Both exports and imports are huge. In the 1980s, U.S. imports exceeded exports, producing large trade deficits. We discuss the sources of the trade deficits, although no final conclusion can be reached without discussing the international financial system.

International Trade

CHAPTER 35

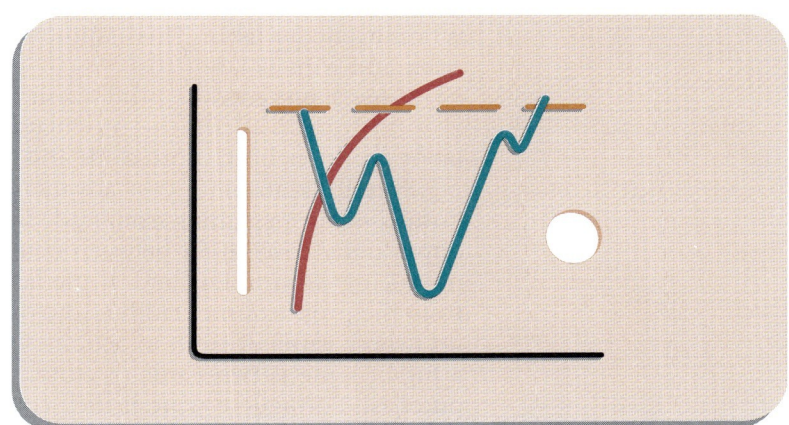

Learning Objectives

After reading and studying this chapter, you will be able to:

1. Explain why international trade is beneficial to society even if some individuals are harmed by it.
2. State the major gains from trade experienced by an economy in the short run and over longer periods of time.
3. Describe the effects of tariffs and quotas on trade patterns, and explain who gains and who loses from such trade barriers.
4. Describe the major trends in world trading and the types of goods and services traded by the United States.

Theory of Trade

The modern theory of international trade originated with the British economist David Ricardo in the 1820s. International trade was a much-discussed topic long before then, but the concept of comparative advantage was not understood until Ricardo and some of his peers developed it. The **principle of comparative advantage** (discussed in Chapter 2) states that two countries (or individuals, for that matter) can benefit by each producing the good for which it has the lowest relative opportunity cost and trading for the good which has a higher relative opportunity cost. The gains from trade that come from comparative advantage are illustrated in the following Ricardian example of trade between England and Portugal.

Principle of comparative advantage
Two countries can maximize the joint production of two goods by each producing the good for which it is the relatively low-opportunity-cost producer and trading for the other good.

Comparative Advantage: An Example

England and Portugal are two countries that each produce wine and cloth. In the interest of simplicity, assume that the only input in the production process is homogeneous labor. This assumption means that the total cost of producing cloth and wine is labor cost.[1]

Table 1 presents the production data for both countries. Portugal has an **absolute advantage** in the production of both goods. The same amount of labor produces both more cloth and more wine in Portugal than in England.

Absolute advantage
The ability to produce a good with fewer resources than another economy can.

Portugal's absolute cost advantage in both goods does not prevent the Portuguese from gaining from trade with the English, because the comparative opportunity costs differ between countries. Consider the opportunity cost of producing cloth in England. If the labor of one worker for one day is shifted from the production of cloth to the production of wine, the English must give up twenty yards of cloth to acquire ten jugs of wine. The opportunity cost of a jug of wine is two yards of cloth. English consumers would be willing to purchase Portuguese wine if they could give up less than two yards of cloth per jug of wine to acquire it. The opportunity cost of a yard of cloth in England is the inverse of the opportunity cost of a jug of wine. English consumers must give up one-half jug of wine to obtain a yard of cloth.

The opportunity cost of a yard of cloth in Portugal is one jug of wine. When labor is shifted from the production of wine to the production of cloth, one jug of wine is given up for each yard of cloth acquired. The Portuguese would be willing to trade with the English if they could acquire more than one yard of cloth for a jug of wine.

Consider the situation facing the two nations. The English are willing to trade if they can give up less than two yards of cloth for a jug of wine. The Portuguese are willing to trade if they can acquire more than one yard of cloth for a jug of wine. Any ratio between one yard of cloth for a jug of wine and two yards of cloth for a jug of wine is acceptable to both nations. That is, any ratio lying between the two nations' opportunity cost ratios presents an opportunity for mutually beneficial trade.

Suppose that England has enough labor to produce either 2000 yards of cloth per year or 1000 jugs of wine, or any linear combination of the two. We will assume that prior to trading with Portugal, the English choose to produce 1250 yards of cloth and 375 jugs of wine. This combination appears as point

---

[1] This approach is closely related to David Ricardo's original treatment of comparative advantage. See his *Principles of Political Economy and Taxation*, Chapter 7.

TABLE 1
Cloth and wine production in England and Portugal

	Output per Person-Day of Labor	
	Cloth (Yards)	Wine (Jugs)
England	20	10
Portugal	30	30

C on England's production possibilities frontier in Figure 1 (a). Portugal, a smaller nation, can produce either 1000 yards of cloth or 1000 jugs of wine, or any linear combination thereof. Before trade begins, the Portuguese choose to produce and consume 500 yards of cloth and 500 jugs of wine, point C' on the Portuguese PPF in Figure 1 (b).

Assume that the two countries trade at a ratio of 1.5 yards of cloth per jug of wine. Because this ratio lies between the two nations' opportunity cost ratios it is acceptable to both countries. Their gains from trade now can be calculated. Instead of producing both cloth and wine, suppose England specializes in the production of cloth. It produces 2000 yards of cloth and trades 750 of them to the Portuguese for $750/1.5 = 500$ jugs of wine. The Portuguese specialize in wine production and trade 500 jugs of wine to the English for $500 \times 1.5 = 750$ yards of cloth. Table 2 and Figure 1 show that the trade benefits both

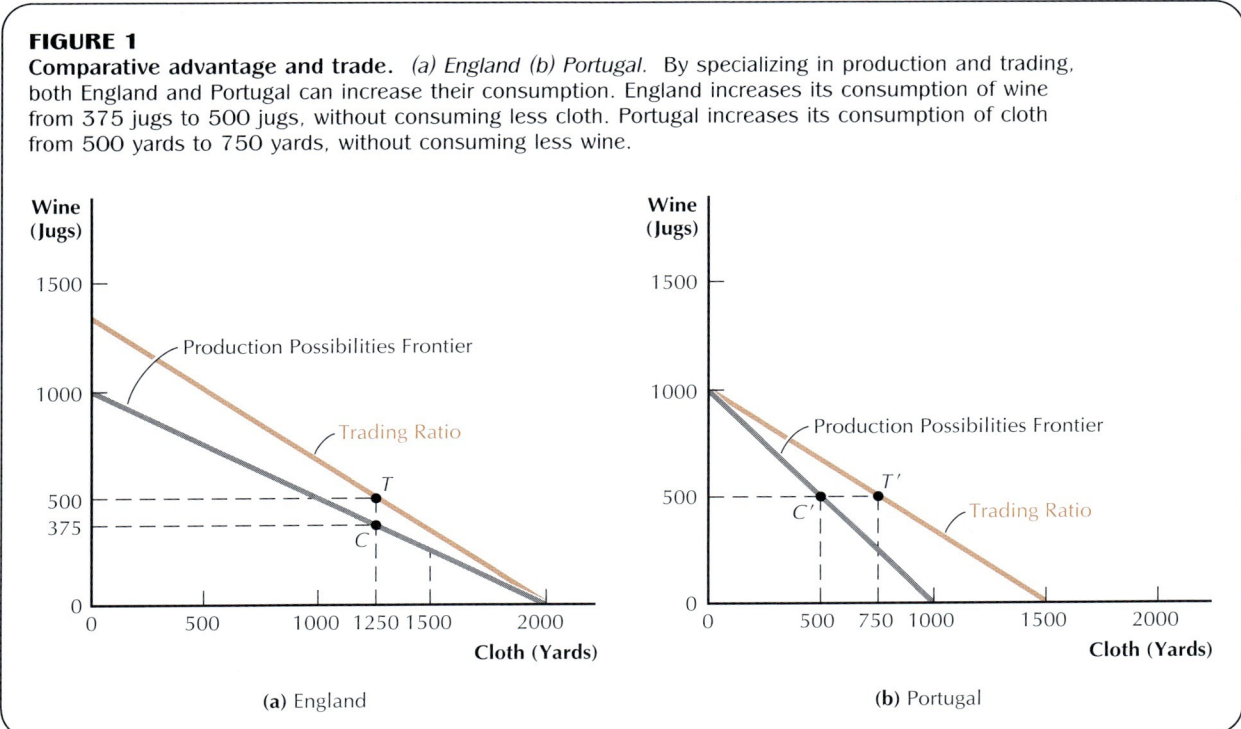

FIGURE 1
Comparative advantage and trade. *(a) England (b) Portugal.* By specializing in production and trading, both England and Portugal can increase their consumption. England increases its consumption of wine from 375 jugs to 500 jugs, without consuming less cloth. Portugal increases its consumption of cloth from 500 yards to 750 yards, without consuming less wine.

nations. English consumption of wine rises by one third with no reduction in cloth consumption [a movement from C to T in Figure 1 (a)], while Portuguese consumption of cloth rises by one half with no reduction in wine consumption [from C' to T' in Figure 1 (b)]. The trading ratio lies outside each country's production possibilities frontier.

By specializing in the production of the low-opportunity-cost good and trading for the other good, both England and Portugal were able to expand their consumption beyond the limits permitted by domestic production possibilities. Specialization and trade make both nations better off.

Terms of Trade

In the preceding example both England and Portugal gained by trading cloth for wine at a 1.5-to-1 ratio. This ratio was used because it lies between 2-to-1 (the English opportunity cost ratio) and 1-to-1 (the Portuguese opportunity cost ratio). In fact, *at any ratio between the two opportunity cost ratios both countries would gain from trading.* The 1.5-to-1 ratio was chosen arbitrarily.

How the gains from trade are split between trading countries depends upon the actual trading ratio chosen. In our example both countries gained substantially. English wine consumption rose by 33 percent, while Portuguese cloth consumption increased by 50 percent. At a different trading ratio the relative gains would differ. Suppose, for example, that the two countries traded at a ratio of 1.25 yards of cloth per jug of wine, rather than 1.5-to-1. Then England could have acquired 500 jugs of Portuguese wine for only 500 × 1.25 = 625 yards of cloth. The English could have consumed 1375 yards of cloth and 500 jugs of wine, increasing their consumption of both goods compared to the no-trade case. However, the Portuguese would not have fared so well at a 1.25-to-1 ratio. They would have 625 yards of cloth and 500 jugs of wine. This is better than they could have done without trading, but inferior to their position at a 1.5-to-1 trading ratio.

In general, a country gains the most from trading when the trading ratio is close to the other country's opportunity cost ratio. This makes sense. If the trading ratio is very close to, say, Portugal's opportunity cost ratio, then the Portuguese will not do much better by trading than by producing their own goods. If the trading ratio is far removed from the opportunity cost ratio, a considerable gain results.

What determines the trading ratio and the relative gains from trade? Within the limits of the two opportunity cost ratios, the strength of demand in each

SECTION RECAP
A nation can gain by specializing in the production of goods in which it is the relatively low-opportunity-cost producer and trading with other nations that are similarly specializing. Any terms of trade lying between the *(continued)*

TABLE 2
Gains from trade

	Consumption			
	Before Trade		After Trade	
	Cloth	Wine	Cloth	Wine
England	1250	375	1250	500
Portugal	500	500	750	500

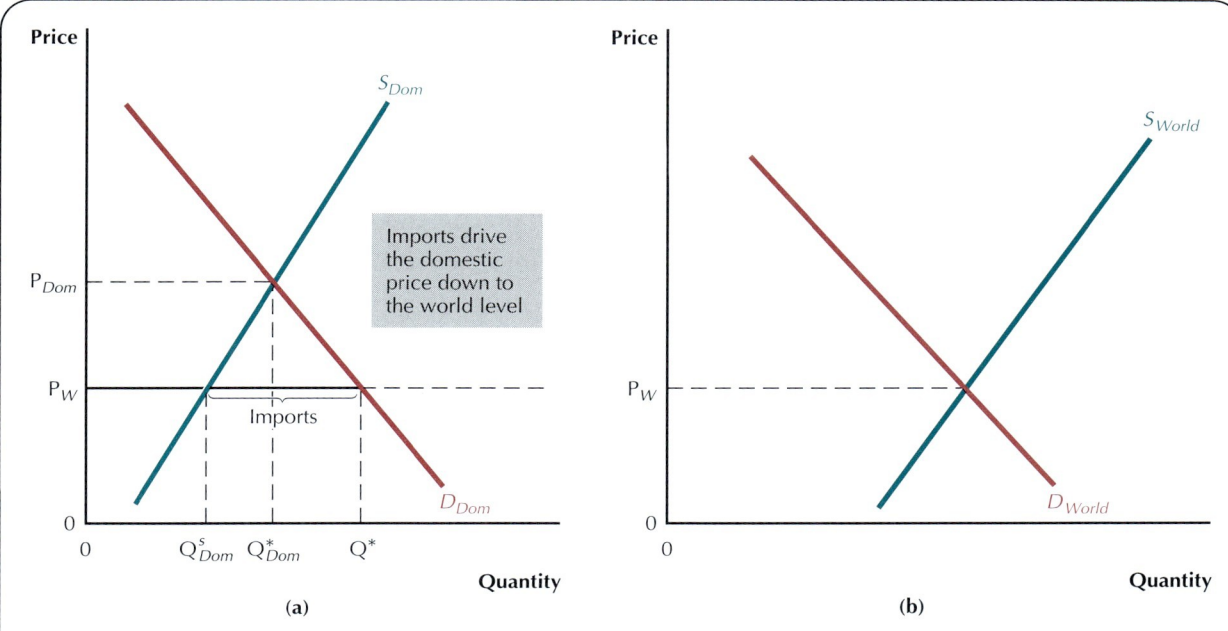

FIGURE 2
Imports and the domestic market. Opening a domestic market to lower-priced imports forces the domestic price down to the world level. Without imports, the domestic price would be P_{Dom} and the quantity traded Q^*_{Dom} (a). Permitting imports drives the price down to P_W, the world price for the good (b). Domestic production falls from Q^*_{Dom} to Q^s_{Dom}, while domestic quantity demanded rises to Q^*.

country determines the trading ratio. The more willing England is to give up cloth to obtain wine (the stronger the English demand for wine), the higher the cloth–wine trading ratio becomes. High demand drives up the price of wine (in terms of cloth). Thus, the terms of trade favor the nation with the relatively weaker demand for the other country's product.[2]

Price Equalization and Gains from Trade

To this point we have analyzed trade in terms of trade ratios between two goods. In reality the ratio that matters to both consumers and producers is the ratio of units of money per unit of product—the product's money price. International trade affects the money prices of traded goods (and the prices of nontraded substitutes and complements as well). Consumers will not purchase an imported product, identical in its characteristics to a domestically produced good, unless the price of the imported good is as low as the domestic price. Similarly, producers will not export goods unless they can receive a higher price abroad than in the home market.

The price effects of international trade are illustrated in Figures 2 and 3. Figure 2 examines the case of imports. The demand and supply curves depicted in Figure 2 (a) are for the domestic market only. If there were no imports the market price would be P_{Dom} (domestic price) and the quantity traded would

SECTION RECAP
(continued)
internal opportunity cost ratios of the trading nations benefit both nations.

---
[2] David Ricardo never figured out what determined the exact terms of trade. That honor belongs to another English economist, John Stuart Mill.

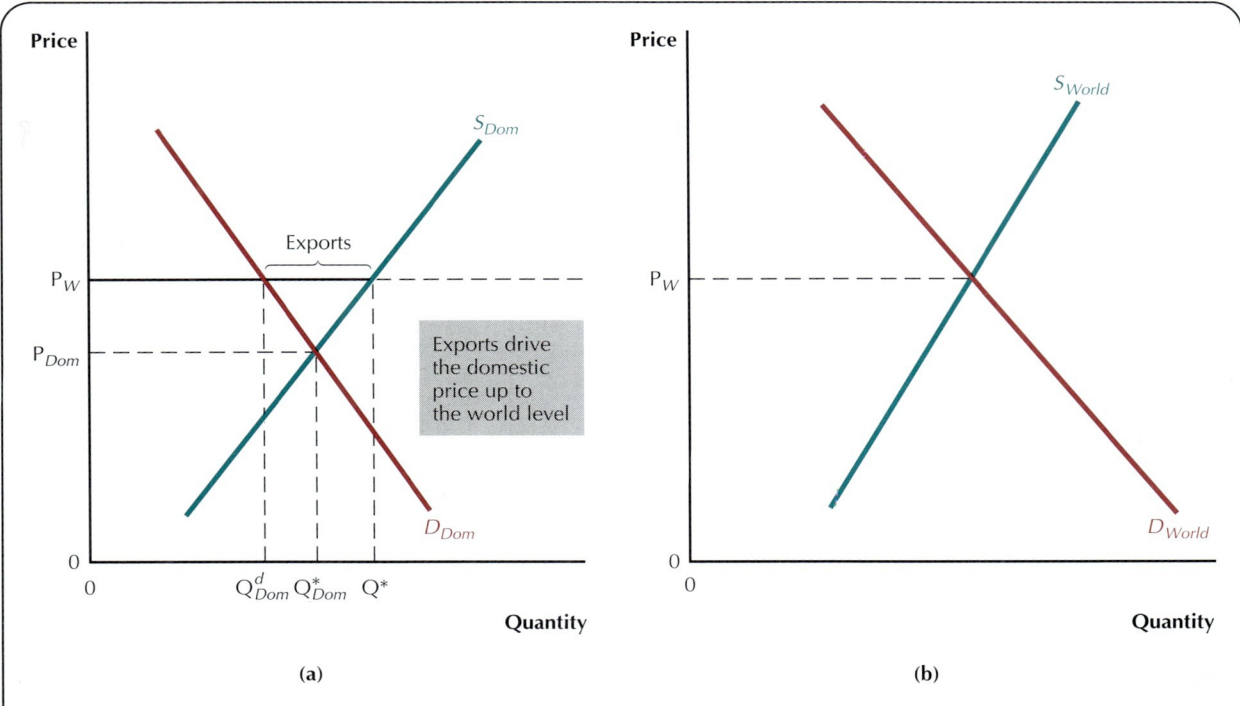

FIGURE 3
Exports and the domestic market. Selling goods on the world market pushes the domestic price up to the world level. Firms prefer to export their products, so long as the world price exceeds the domestic price. When the domestic price rises to P_W, domestic quantity demanded falls from Q^s_{Dom} to Q^d_{Dom}. Domestic producers produce Q^* units of the good, exporting the difference between Q^* and Q^d_{Dom}.

be Q^*_{Dom}. However, the product is produced more cheaply in other countries; as Figure 2 (b) shows, its world market price is below P_{Dom} at P_W. The presence of imports in the domestic market increases the total supply of the good and drives the actual market price down to the world level.

At P_W domestic producers will supply only Q^s_{Dom} units of the good. The difference between Q^* and Q^s_{Dom} is imported. The importation of lower-priced goods enables consumers to pay lower prices for all units of the good, whether produced in foreign countries or domestically. It also causes resources to be reallocated from **import-competing industries**—domestic industries producing goods that can be imported—to other industries.

Some resources will flow into industries that have a comparative advantage in production and can export goods to the rest of the world. In Figure 3 we once again see the domestic demand and supply curves for a product. In this case, however, the domestic price lies below the world price. Domestic producers have a comparative advantage in the production of this good. By selling on the world market, producers can increase their sales and earnings. However, domestic consumers are forced to pay the higher world price for the good, as producers otherwise would ship their entire production abroad at prices higher than the domestic price.

Import-competing industries
Domestic industries that produce goods that can be imported or are close substitutes for imported goods.

The result of this process — imports driving down prices while exports drive them up in the domestic market — tends to equalize prices across countries. Of course, different nations have different currencies, so the price in one country is quoted in different terms than in another country (U.S. dollars versus Japanese yen, for example), but the relative prices of traded goods within different countries should be driven into equality. Differences in domestic and world market prices induce either imports or exports, and the flow of international trading acts to equalize prices.

SECTION RECAP
Specialization and trade tend to drive the domestic prices for traded goods into equality with the world prices of such goods.

Gains from Trade: A Technical Analysis

The gains to society from international trade can be illustrated with the concepts of consumer and producer surplus developed in Chapter 4. Consider Figure 4, which reproduces Figure 2 (a) with some additional notation. In the absence of international trade the market price would be P_{Dom} and the quantity exchanged Q^*_{Dom}. Consumer surplus, the difference between what consumers would be willing to pay and what they actually pay, is the triangle $P_{Dom}bc$. Producer surplus, the difference between what producers would be willing to accept for quantity Q^*_{Dom} and what they actually receive, is the triangle $aP_{Dom}c$. Now, compare this situation to the situation with international trade. The price falls to P_W, while the quantity traded rises to Q^*. Consumer surplus now equals the triangle P_Wbd. Domestic producer surplus is now the triangle aP_We.

Obviously consumers have gained and domestic producers have lost. But have the gains of consumers exceeded the losses of producers? The answer is

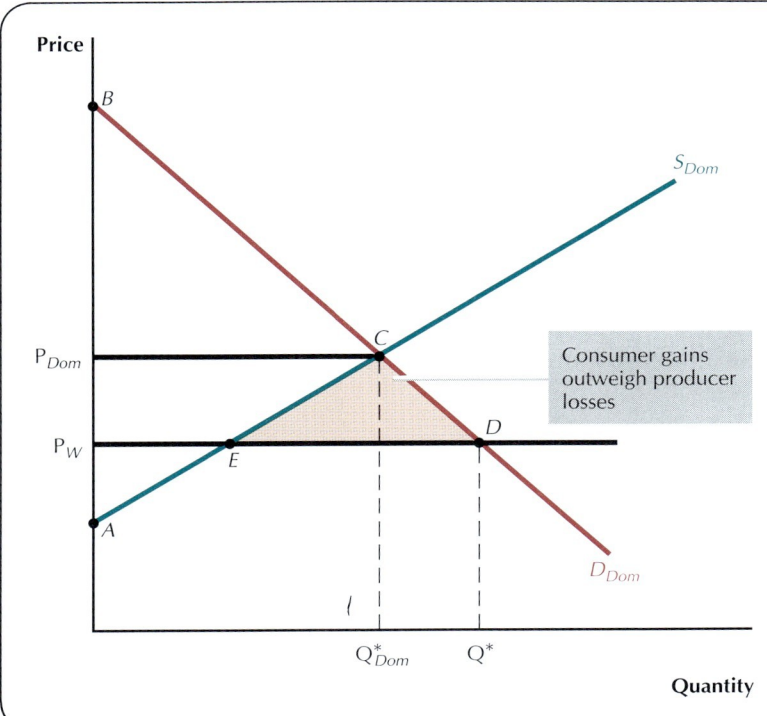

FIGURE 4
Gains from imports. When imports are admitted into an economy, the gains of consumers ($P_WP_{Dom}cd$) exceed the losses of producers ($P_WP_{Dom}ce$) by the amount of the shaded triangle (ecd).

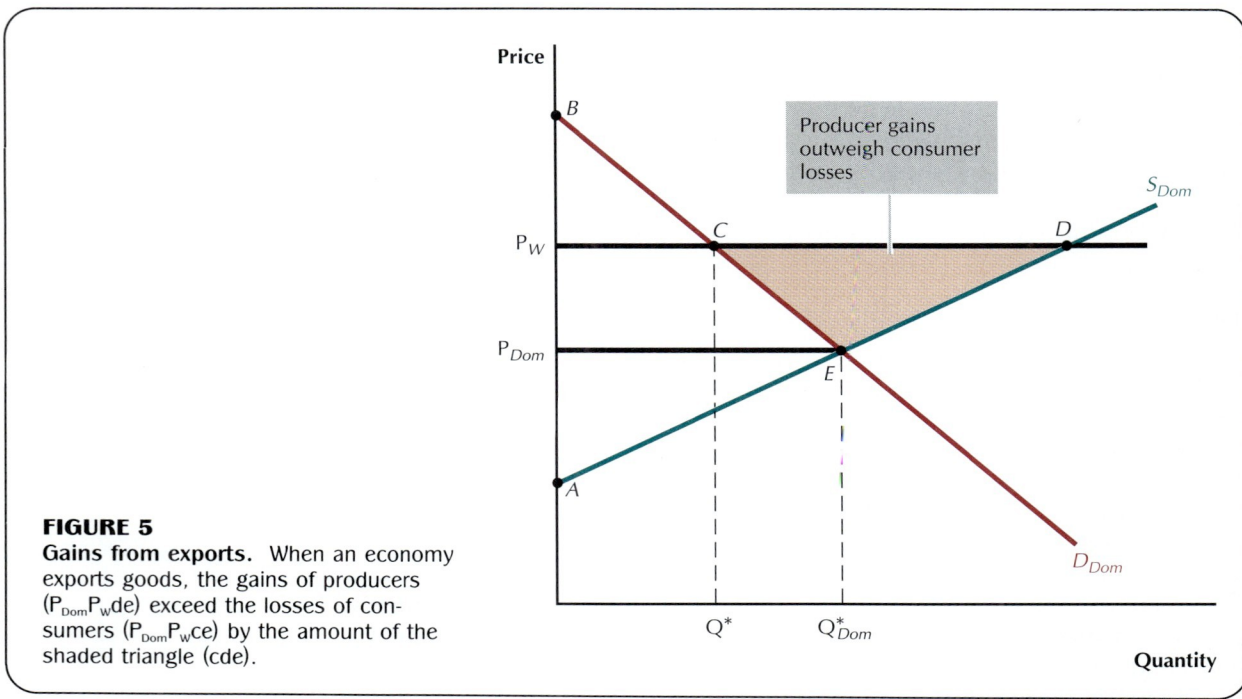

FIGURE 5
Gains from exports. When an economy exports goods, the gains of producers ($P_{Dom}P_wde$) exceed the losses of consumers ($P_{Dom}P_wce$) by the amount of the shaded triangle (cde).

yes. Consumers gain the area $P_wP_{Dom}cd$, while producers lose the area $P_wP_{Dom}ce$. The *net gain* from trading equals the shaded triangle ecd. The gains to consumers exceed the losses of producers by that amount.

Analysis of the case of exports reveals a similar situation. Figure 5 reproduces Figure 3 (a) with some additional notation. When domestic producers begin to export goods in which they have a comparative advantage, the market price is driven upward from P_{Dom} to P_W. The quantity demanded and consumed by domestic consumers falls from Q^*_{Dom} to Q^*. Before trading, consumer surplus equaled the triangle $P_{Dom}be$. After trading, consumer surplus declines to the triangle P_wbc, a loss of the area $P_{Dom}P_wce$. Before trading, producer surplus amounted to the triangle $aP_{Dom}e$. After trading, producer surplus increases to the larger triangle aP_wd. The *net gain* to the economy is the shaded triangle cde. This area represents the amount by which the gains of producers exceed the losses of consumers. Exports, like imports, benefit the economy.

Costs of Adjusting to International Trade

Free trade benefits the world economy. A nation's consumers gain from importing low-priced goods from countries that have a comparative advantage in their production. Exporters gain by selling on the world market those goods for which they have a comparative advantage. The total world output level rises. However, changing trade patterns usually produce problems for companies that lose their comparative advantage. A firm, or a number of firms in an industry, may fall victim to so-called cheap foreign imports. Workers are laid off and capital goes unused. It can take several years for the workers to find other jobs equivalent in pay and status to their old jobs. Some never locate jobs so good as the ones they lost.

It is important to note that this phenomenon is a feature of the market economy. Shifting trading patterns and changing cost conditions affect firms and workers within a country as well as among countries. In the United States in the 1970s, a large transfer of jobs from the Rust Belt of the northeast and upper midwest to the Sun Belt took place. Many firms found costs of production much lower in the south than in the north and transferred their operations. Northern workers were laid off, southern workers hired. Many of the northern workers had difficulty obtaining new jobs with the same characteristics as their old jobs. A large number of northerners simply moved south in search of work. The adjustment problems caused by shifting demand and cost conditions clearly are not limited to international trade.

A recent study of the international competitiveness of U.S. industry concluded that most industries experiencing job loss during the turbulent 1970s did so because of domestic demand shifts. In thirty-eight of the fifty-two industries studied, international trade contributed to employment growth during the 1973–1980 period. In short, domestic demand shifts caused more problems than did international trade shifts.[3]

Having said this, it is clear that the perception that jobs are being lost because of imports generates more public and political concern than jobs being transferred from one area of the country to another. Thus, policies to reduce the adjustment costs incurred by workers and firms hurt by import competition are often proposed and sometimes enacted by Congress. The United States has had laws since the early 1960s authorizing payments to workers displaced by foreign competition. While paying workers special adjustment benefits may seem a humane thing to do, it is not necessarily in the best interests of the economy. The incentives created by such payments may not be desirable.

If workers displaced by foreign competition can receive relatively large government payments for an extended period of time (a year or more), they have less incentive to look for other jobs either before or after they are laid off. Workers can usually predict large-scale layoffs before they occur, and they have the incentive to seek more stable employment before they are fired. Generous adjustment benefits reduce this incentive greatly. Such benefits also subsidize unemployment, causing displaced workers to remain unemployed longer than they might otherwise.

If the cost of adjusting to increased trade is to be shared by society (through government payments), a better approach would be to provide wage subsidies for displaced workers who find employment in other industries.[4] Such a subsidy program would encourage firms to hire displaced workers at higher wages than they might otherwise be willing to pay. The program would allow firms to deduct from their income taxes some percentage of their wage payments to newly hired workers. This would reduce the wage cost of hiring these workers. For example, with a subsidy rate of 20 percent, a worker paid $25,000 would cost the firm only $20,000. The firm would be able to save $5000 on its tax bill (20 percent of $25,000) by hiring the displaced worker.

---

[3] Robert Z. Lawrence, *Can America Compete?* (Washington, D.C.: The Brookings Institution, 1984), Chapter 4.

[4] Such a program is proposed by George R. Neumann in "Adjustment Assistance for Trade-Displaced Workers," in David B. H. Denoon, ed., *The New International Economic Order* (New York: New York University Press, 1979).

SECTION RECAP
Adjusting to any shift in demand or cost conditions causes pain for some people. The effects of international demand shifts do not appear to be any worse than the effects of domestic demand shifts.

Although some program to ease the cost of adjusting to increased trade may be desirable, constructing a program that does not have negative impacts on the economy is not always easy. Policymakers must realize that the gains generated by a market economy depend upon the principle of comparative advantage being allowed to work, both within an economy and among economies. Policies that prevent the reallocation of resources from less-valued to more-valued uses ultimately reduce the efficiency of the economy and reduce the gains to both consumers and producers that come from an efficiently operating market system.

Changing the Terms of Trade

Various government policies can affect the terms at which goods are traded among countries. Such policies also affect the gains from trade experienced by consumers and producers. The two most frequently used trade policies are tariffs and quotas.

Tariffs and Quotas

Tariff
A tax on imported goods.

Quota
A limit on the quantity of a good that may be imported.

A **tariff** is a tax on imported goods. It adds to the price of imports, thus making imported goods less attractive to consumers. A **quota** is a limit on the quantity of a good that may be imported. Limiting the supply of a good also affects its price, as we shall see.

The effect of placing a tariff on an imported good is examined in Figure 6. As in Figures 2 and 4, the world market price lies below what the domestic

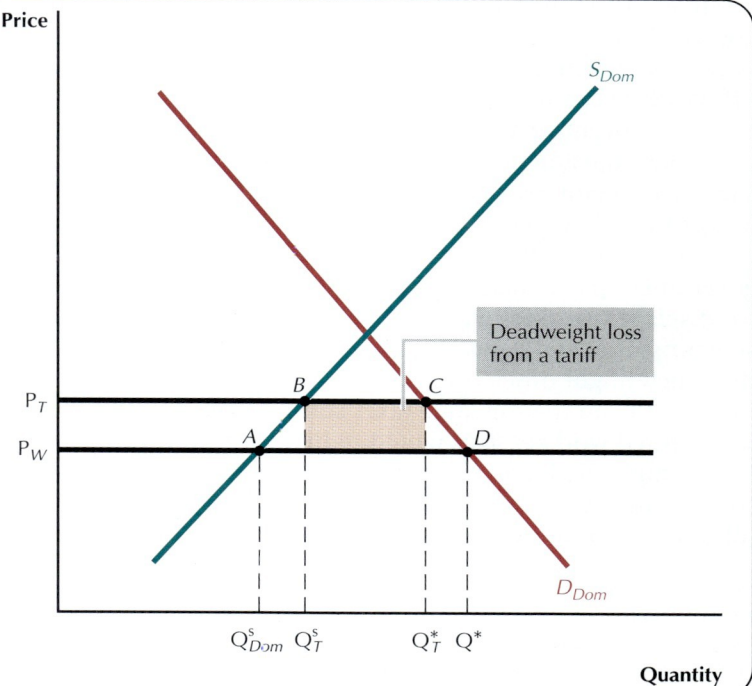

FIGURE 6
Effects of a tariff. Consumers lose more from a tariff ($P_W P_T cd$) than producers gain ($P_W P_T ba$), even if the government distributes tariff revenue (represented by the shaded rectangle) to consumers.

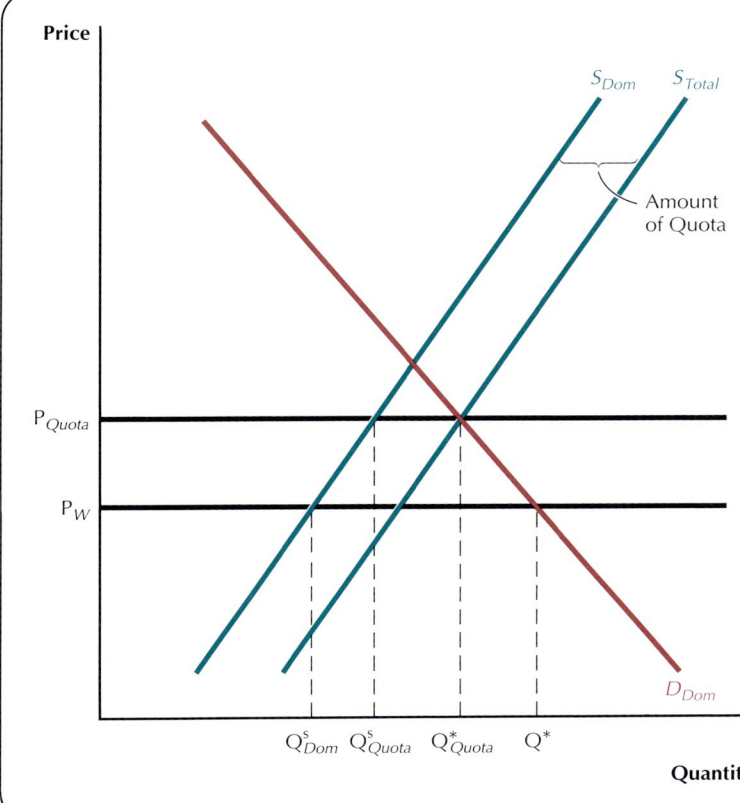

FIGURE 7
Effects of a quota. Domestic producers gain less from a quota than domestic consumers lose, and the government obtains no revenues. A quota pushes the domestic price to P_{Quota}, which is higher than the world price (P_W). Domestic production rises from Q^S_{Dom} to Q^S_{Quota}, while consumption falls from Q^* to Q^*_{Quota}.

price of the good would be if there were no international trade. A tariff adds to the price of imported goods, increasing the price that consumers must pay for imported goods from P_W to P_T. The equilibrium quantity demanded declines from Q^* to Q^*_T. The quantity of domestically produced goods rises from Q^S_{Dom} to Q^S_T. The quantity of imports declines from the amount between Q^S_{Dom} and Q^* to the amount between Q^S_T and Q^*_T. The government collects tariff revenue equal to the area of the shaded rectangle (which represents the amount of the per-unit tariff times the number of units imported).

It is clear that domestic producers gain from the imposition of the tariff. Domestic production expands from Q^S_{Dom} to Q^S_T. However, the gains of the domestic producers come at the expense of domestic consumers. Consumer losses exceed producer gains even if tariff revenues are distributed to consumers by the government. Consumers purchase less of the good and pay a higher price.[5]

Imposing a quota on imports has much the same effect, except that the government does not obtain any tariff revenue. Instead, those foreign producers able to continue selling their goods gain from the higher price. Figure 7 illustrates the effect of a quota. The quantity of imports permitted by the

---

[5] Producer surplus rises by the area $P_W P_T ba$. Consumer surplus declines by $P_W P_T cd$. The net loss to consumers is abcd, which cannot be replaced even if government distributes the tariff revenues to consumers.

quota is added to the domestic supply curve to obtain the total supply to the domestic market. The domestic market price rises to P_{Quota} to clear the market. Domestic production rises from Q^s_{Dom} to Q^s_{Quota}. The higher prices paid by consumers go entirely to domestic and foreign producers; the government obtains no revenue from a quota.

The same output and price results can be obtained from either a tariff or a quota. A quota of the appropriate size has the same effect as some particular tariff. However, if it is decided that a restrictive trade policy is to be pursued, tariffs are preferred to quotas for at least two reasons. First, quotas allocate import rights to foreign companies on the basis of some arbitrary rule. Usually future import limits are tied to past import levels. The allocation rule may allow inefficient foreign firms to sell goods, while preventing efficient firms from doing so. Or foreign companies producing relatively inferior goods may have marketing rights, while firms producing relatively superior products are excluded from the market.

The second reason that tariffs are preferable to quotas is that the entire price increase due to a quota goes to producers. While this may be the desired effect with regard to domestic producers, it merely increases the profits of foreign producers for no good reason. It transfers wealth from domestic consumers to foreign producers. A good example of this was the so-called voluntary import restrictions placed on Japanese automobiles in the early 1980s. U.S. car buyers transferred millions of dollars to Japanese auto companies, whose profits rose considerably after the imposition of the informal quota. This example is discussed in more detail later in the chapter.

A way to overcome the disadvantages of quotas relative to tariffs has been proposed recently: auctioning quota allotments to foreign producers. The foreign companies willing to pay the largest amount to obtain an import quota would be allowed to import goods into the domestic market. Such a policy would allow the government of the importing country to reclaim a share of the excess earnings of the foreign companies generated by the quota. It would also permit efficient foreign firms to outbid inefficient firms, thus serving domestic customers better.

> **SECTION RECAP**
>
> The terms of trade can be altered by imposing tariffs or quotas. Either trade barrier reduces the gains from trade. Tariffs are preferred to quotas, however, because tariffs allow efficient foreign firms to undersell inefficient firms, and because they allow the nation imposing the tariff to capture some of the benefits of higher product prices.

Arguments in Favor of Tariffs

If tariffs reduce the welfare of an economy, why do they seem to be so widely used? In reality, the theory of public choice goes a long way toward explaining why tariffs and quotas are enacted. However, narrow private interest is not often the argument used to defend tariffs. It is hardly an attractive political argument to say, "Everyone should have to pay more so I can increase my profits (or wages)." We will examine several of the more frequently used arguments in favor of tariffs.

Infant-Industry Argument When new firms begin producing a product, they are often relatively inefficient. They have not yet developed the managerial, production or marketing expertise of an experienced firm. Often they begin production at relatively low output levels, when larger output levels can be produced more efficiently using larger factories and more automation. Given time these infant firms become more efficient. Their costs of production decline, and they become competitive in the world market.

The infant-industry argument asserts that firms entering a new market should be protected by tariffs until they develop enough to become efficient. It is often used by less-developed countries, which argue that protection of industry is a necessary part of their development process. Although this argument has a plausible ring to it, it suffers from several problems. First, if private investors believe a product will be profitable to produce eventually, then they will be willing to absorb losses for some time while the firm establishes itself in the world market. Tariff protection forces consumers to share the risks with the owners of the firm, who stand to benefit anyway once the firm becomes profitable.

Another problem is picking winners. The government cannot protect every new industry that develops. Which of the new industries will prove to be profitable and which will not? There is little evidence that the government can pick winners and losers effectively.

Finally there is the problem of getting rid of a tariff. Once a tariff is levied on an imported good, it is very difficult to remove. Domestic producers and their workers argue that removal of the tariff will mean real hardship for them. Since the gains to consumers from removing a tariff are spread out over millions of people, while the costs to producers are concentrated on a much smaller number of individuals, politicians are likely to hear much more protariff than antitariff sentiment. A tariff, once established, often takes on a life of its own.

A slightly different variant of the infant-industry argument also deserves mention. It might be called the **senile-industry argument**: Industries that employ large numbers of workers, but that can no longer compete in the world market, should be afforded protection in order to save jobs. Anyone who understands the notion of comparative advantage can see immediately that this argument simply calls for abandoning international trade whenever a domestic industry is at a comparative disadvantage. The harmfulness of such a policy should be obvious.

Senile-industry argument Industries that are no longer internationally competitive should be protected to save domestic jobs.

Preventing Job Loss to Cheap Foreign Labor A frequently heard argument for tariff protection is that foreign imports are produced cheaply because foreign workers are paid so little. These workers are exploited, being paid a wage barely sufficient to keep them fed and clothed (so the argument often goes). If such cheap goods are allowed to replace domestically produced goods, domestic workers will eventually be driven into poverty too.

It is true that, other things equal, firms using relatively cheap labor have an advantage over firms using relatively expensive labor. However, other things are often not equal. Productivity differs greatly from country to country. Productivity depends to a large extent on the amount of capital provided to workers and the technological sophistication of that capital. One worker in an industrial country using sophisticated machinery often can produce as much as several workers in a less-developed country using only rudimentary tools. The high-productivity worker can be paid much more than a low-productivity worker, while still producing a lower-cost product.

The firms that are being driven out of business in relatively high-wage countries such as the United States by firms in low-wage countries are typically low-capital, low-technology firms. For example, among the U.S. industries suffering most from foreign competition are shoe and textile manufacturing. Both of these industries use rather simple, low-cost machinery. Entrepreneurs

Does It Make **Economic Sense?**

Protectionism and Domestic Employment

The proponents of protectionism usually justify their support of tariffs and quotas on the grounds that such barriers to trade increase the number of jobs in the economy. The logic behind this argument is straightforward. Tariffs and quotas make foreign firms less competitive with import-competing firms in the domestic economy. As domestic firms win a larger share of the domestic market, they expand production. Increased production requires more workers. Thus, trade barriers actually increase employment. Since, in a nation as wealthy as the United States, national income is less of a concern to most people than having enough jobs to go around, this benefits society. Although we know that trade barriers reduce the total consumption level of society, might not trade barriers increase employment? The argument has a certain plausibility. However, two of the nation's foremost experts on the international economy have recently argued in their textbook on international economics that trade barriers actually *decrease* the number of jobs provided by the U.S. economy. Does this make economic sense?

In their textbook, Peter Lindert and Charles Kindleberger argue that protective tariffs quickly cost the U.S. economy more jobs than they protect.* Net job losses result from the facts that (1) exports decline approximately dollar-for-dollar with imports, and (2) more jobs are tied to a billion dollars of exports than to a billion dollars of production of import-competing industries. We will examine these arguments in turn.

Exports decline when imports are restricted for several reasons. First, many exporters use imported inputs in their production. When imports are restricted, the price of their inputs rises, forcing domestic firms to raise their product prices and making them less competitive in world markets. Export sales decline as a result. Second, when foreigners cannot sell goods to us, they cannot afford to buy products from us. Foreigners must have dol-

---

in Third World nations can afford such machinery, and the equipment is simple enough that even uneducated people can run it efficiently. Hence these firms can undersell U.S. firms paying wages eight or ten times higher.

In industries where expensive, sophisticated equipment is used, however, firms in poor, relatively undereducated nations cannot compete with U.S. firms. The productivity of U.S. workers is so much higher that U.S. costs of production are lower even though U.S. workers are much better paid. Protecting workers from cheap foreign labor really amounts to forgoing the benefits of comparative advantage in those industries that are at a relative disadvantage.

National Defense The tariffs-for-national-defense argument stresses the need to maintain production in key industries in case of armed conflict. In a war, imports of vital products might be cut off. Thus, to ensure the ability of the nation to defend itself, industries vital to the defense effort should be protected.

The problems with this argument are twofold. First, how do we define what is vital to national defense? A large number of industries might claim to be important. Where is the line to be drawn? For example, in the mid-1980s the U.S. shoe industry argued for tariff protection because army boots are vital to the nation's defense program. (The argument failed to win them a tariff.) If the shoe industry can argue that it is vital to national defense, what other industries can do so too? (Our argument does not imply that *no* industries are vital to defense, only that the defense argument tends to be overused.)

The second problem with the argument is that only a major war could disrupt supplies of most important imports. (Oil is a major exception. A local

lars to buy American products. They earn those dollars by selling goods in the United States. When imports are curtailed, foreigners earn fewer dollars and thus can afford fewer U.S. products. U.S. export sales decline. Third, when one nation imposes import restrictions, other nations usually retaliate. Increased trade barriers reduce trade worldwide, including U.S. exports. The total effect on exports of these three factors (and some others we have ignored) is to decrease exports by approximately the same amount as the trade restrictions decrease imports. The effect on net exports should be close to zero. If exports and imports fall by about the same amount, shouldn't the net effect on jobs be zero? Not necessarily. The amount of labor used in the production of exports may differ significantly from the amount used by import-competing industries, since different products are being produced by the two groups of industries. Professors Lindert and Kindleberger cite four different studies conducted in the post-World War II period of the number of jobs tied to $1 billion of exports and $1 billion of import-replacing production. All four studies concluded that *more jobs are tied to a billion dollars of exports than are tied to a billion dollars of import-replacing production.* Reducing both exports and imports by $1 billion costs the U.S. economy jobs, since more workers are required to produce $1 billion of goods for export than are required to produce $1 billion of import-replacing goods.

This result adds to the case for international free trade. Trade restrictions reduce both the consumption level and the number of jobs in an economy. Trade restrictions cannot be used as a kind of back door government employment policy, because their effect on employment is negative.

*International Economics, 7th ed. (Homewood, IL: Richard D. Irwin, 1982), pp. 73–77.

war in the Mideast could disrupt the world oil market. However, in the nuclear age the probability of a worldwide conventional war is quite small. The next world war, if it ever occurs, probably will be nuclear and very short. Imports will be the least of our worries in such a case.

Tariffs as a Bargaining Chip   Though many nations pay lip service to free trade, pressure for protectionism is always great. A country that totally disavows tariffs may be put at a competitive disadvantage when dealing with other less-restrained nations. Even though most major trading nations are members of the General Agreement on Tariffs and Trade (GATT) and have pledged themselves to promote free trade, many trade barriers exist, and new ones are popping up all the time.

The best way to promote free trade may be to threaten massive retaliation against any countries that impose tariffs or quotas on an economy's exports. Adam Smith recognized this over two centuries ago, listing it as one of the arguments in favor of tariffs in *The Wealth of Nations*. Threatening retaliation in many cases may be sufficient to persuade trading partners to forgo protectionism. President Reagan used this tactic in late 1986 to gain tariff concessions for U.S. products from the European Economic Community.

As a long-term strategy, using the threat of tariff retaliation works only if a nation is, in fact, willing to retaliate. Sooner or later it will be called upon to back its threats with action. Then what? Adam Smith's suggestion was to back down. While foreign tariffs on our exports are bad, placing tariffs on imported goods just makes things worse. Consumers as well as producers

SECTION RECAP
A number or arguments are made in favor of tariffs. Of these, only the argument that the threat of tariffs serves as an important bargaining chip in the effort to obtain free trade holds up under scrutiny.

suffer. But a consistent policy of backing away from threats will destroy their usefulness. It is sad but true that the best way to preserve mostly free trade in the long run may be to play tit-for-tat in the short run. Tariff retaliation may have its place in the maintenance of mostly free world trade.

Summing Up the Arguments With the possible exception of the retaliation argument, none of the arguments in favor of tariffs holds up under close scrutiny. The bottom line is simple and familiar: Tariffs restrict trade and reduce the gains from trade experienced by an economy. The majority (consumers) loses, while a protected minority (producers) gains. The losses of consumers outweigh the gains of producers (including workers).

Using Trade Theory to Estimate the Cost of the Voluntary Import Agreement on Japanese Automobiles

The recent so-called voluntary export restraints on Japanese automobiles present an excellent opportunity to apply the theory of trade restrictions to a real-world problem. Imported automobiles have been growing in popularity among U.S. car buyers for a long time. In 1960, 6.6 million new cars were sold in the United States. Over 92 percent of them were domestically produced. By 1970, foreign imports accounted for 14.7 percent of the 8.4 million cars sold in the United States. By 1980, following the second major OPEC oil price increase, imported cars accounted for 28.2 percent of the market. This share drifted upward for two more years, reaching 29.3 percent in 1982.[6]

Why did imported automobiles grow so much in popularity? There seem to have been three major reasons. First, imported cars were cheaper than comparable domestic autos. In particular, Japanese auto makers seemed to be able to produce low-priced autos that suited American tastes. Second, the quality of U.S. cars fell relative to the quality of Japanese cars during the 1970s. This was particularly noticeable in small cars, which, of course, most Japanese imports were. Third, the increased price of gasoline, following the OPEC oil price hikes of 1973–1974 and 1979, greatly increased the demand for small cars. Domestic producers were far behind their Japanese competitors in small-car technology.

The demand for domestic cars did not grow much after the late 1960s. Almost all the growth in the domestic car market went to imports. In the wake of the second oil price shock, demand for U.S. cars plummeted. In 1981 U.S. auto makers lost about $4 billion, their worse performance ever. Their pleas for protection received special attention because of their large losses and the high unemployment levels of automobile workers. President Reagan announced that a voluntary export restraint agreement had been reached with Japan. The agreement limited the importation of Japanese cars to 1.68 million per year for the years 1981–1983. It was renewed in 1983 for the period 1984–1985 with a slightly higher limit of 1.85 million units per year. The agreement still exists, the limit being tied to a fixed percentage of domestic production.

The rationale for the quota was to give U.S. auto makers time to adjust to the new conditions of a world of high gasoline prices. The combination of

---

[6]The data and estimates presented in this section are taken from "Import Quotas and the Automobile Industry: The Costs of Protectionism," by Robert W. Crandall, *The Brookings Review* 2 (Summer 1984), pp. 8–16.

increased federal safety and fuel-efficiency regulations and the need to downsize their cars had left U.S. manufacturers in a precarious position. The Japanese, who did not have to worry about downsizing their already small autos, seemed to be at a distinct advantage. By limiting the importation of Japanese cars, it was hoped that U.S. auto companies would have time to retool for small-car production, invest in new facilities using more automated production techniques, improve their inventory management techniques, and negotiate lower-cost wage and benefits packages with their workers. Such a reorganization of the industry would then allow U.S. auto makers to compete successfully with foreign competitors without further quota or tariff protection, it was hoped.

Of course, there is no guarantee that producers will make the adjustments government hopes for when quotas are enacted. Companies instead may choose to increase product prices, earn higher profits, and pay higher wages to their workers. It appears that this is largely what happened in the U.S. auto industry. Investment in new plant and equipment, which had been at all-time highs just before the imposition of the quota, fell dramatically in 1982 and 1983. Industry profits edged into the positive in 1982 and soared in 1983. Auto companies paid out large bonuses to management personnel, and the total hourly compensation paid to workers continued to rise. In 1983 the average American auto worker earned almost 55 percent more than the average U.S. manufacturing worker. (By contrast, Japanese auto workers earned only 27 percent more than the average Japanese manufacturing worker.)

Trade theory says that a quota will increase the prices of both foreign and domestic goods. In this instance the theory was confirmed with a vengeance. The average price of a Japanese car rose by $920 to $960 in 1981–1982 alone. These higher prices transferred more than $2 billion per year from American car buyers to Japanese auto companies. (It is not difficult to understand why the Japanese auto companies chose to go along with the program without protesting.) By 1986, Americans were paying a $2500 premium for Japanese automobiles.[7] Robert Crandall of the Brookings Institution estimates that the average price of domestic cars rose by $370 to $430 during the 1981–1983 period. This increased U.S. auto makers' revenues by between $6.6 billion and $7.7 billion over this period. By 1986 an additional $1000 or more was being added to the price of American cars by the quota.

The most important reason for the quota was to save jobs in the U.S. auto industry. While some jobs were saved, the quota was hardly a success on this score. Crandall estimates that a maximum of 26,200 jobs were saved. (He suspects the true number was considerably smaller.) The cost per job saved was, therefore, about $160,000 per year. This figure is roughly four times the annual income of the average auto worker. In other words, for every $40,000 auto worker job saved, U.S. consumers paid $160,000. The quota did cause Japanese auto makers to transfer some production to the United States, however, generating some jobs for U.S. workers over the course of the decade.

Not all instances of protection turn out so badly. A similar tariff on large motorcycles designed to enable the Harley–Davidson Company to regain its competitiveness worked well. In early 1987, the company was healthy enough that it requested that the tariff on foreign motorcycles be removed a year early.

---

[7]Robert W. Crandall, "Detroit Rode Quotas to Prosperity," *The Wall Street Journal,* January 29, 1986, p. 28.

Sometimes companies do use tariff protection to improve their productive efficiency. (Despite the automobile quota, U.S. automakers improved the quality of their cars significantly during the 1980s.) The problem with tariff protection is that it provides companies with a blank check. More often than not they use the protection afforded by tariffs to increase profits and wages, rather than preparing for a return to international competitiveness.

Exports, Imports, and the Balance of Trade

Trade theory predicts that in the absence of artificial restrictions, nations will export goods for which they have a comparative advantage and will import goods for which they have a comparative disadvantage. This prediction appears to be borne out by the evidence. If nations are grouped into three classifications—those with abundant capital, those with abundant unskilled labor, and those with abundant skilled labor—the trading patterns that emerge are consistent with the theory of comparative advantage. Less-developed countries with little capital and abundant unskilled labor tend to export raw materials and agricultural products, while importing manufactured goods. Developing nations, such as South Korea or Taiwan, that have large unskilled workforces but also have an abundance of basic capital tend to export basic manufactured items, such as textiles and shoes. Developed nations, such as the United States and Japan, have an abundance of skilled labor and tend to export more sophisticated products, such as capital goods and computers.

A nation's **trade balance** is the difference between its exports and its imports. A **trade surplus** indicates a positive trade balance; exports exceed imports. A **trade deficit** indicates that imports exceed exports. There is no reason for a nation's trade balance to be zero in any particular year. When a nation's trade balance is not zero, it must finance the difference by acquiring or issuing financial claims. A country that runs a trade surplus produces more than it consumes and acquires financial claims against other nations (that is, it acquires financial assets in foreign countries). A country that runs a trade deficit consumes more than it produces and issues financial claims against itself (that is, it borrows from foreigners to finance its consumption).

Trade balance
Difference between the money value of a country's exports and the money value of its imports.

Trade surplus
Positive trade balance; exports exceed imports.

Trade deficit
Negative trade balance; exports are less than imports.

Trends in International Trade

In the years immediately following the end of World War II, the United States dominated the world economy. Most of the world's developed economies had been destroyed. Thus, the United States was the source of manufactured goods of all types. U.S. producers had an artificial comparative advantage in many products, such as textiles, because the manufacturing facilities in much of the rest of the world had been destroyed. As late as 1953, U.S. exports of manufactured goods accounted for nearly 30 percent of the world total of manufacturing exports. This was a much higher percentage than before the war and was not a figure that could be sustained as other nations rebuilt their economies.

The trends in international trade that have occurred in the four decades since the war reflect changes in comparative advantage. Less-developed countries (LDCs) have increased their share of world manufacturing exports only slightly overall but have made significant progress in goods that are relatively simple to manufacture. Such countries as South Korea, Hong Kong, Taiwan, and Singapore have greatly expanded their share of world production of textiles and clothing, shoes, small appliances, and electronic components for stereos, TVs, and computers. These manufactured goods require relatively simple capital that can be operated by unskilled labor.

In the manufacture of goods requiring more sophisticated capital and highly skilled labor, the United States, Japan, and West Germany have prospered. For example, in 1953 these three countries accounted for 39.2 percent of world exports of chemicals. In 1976, this figure stood at 36.9 percent. Much the same story appears if exports of machinery and transportation equipment are examined. In 1953, the three nations accounted for 53.8 percent of exports and that figure fell only to 48.6 percent in 1976.[8] What did occur, however, was a major redistribution of market shares among the three industrial giants. Germany, and especially Japan, have gained market share at the expense of the United States over the past three decades.

The most important trends in world trade in recent years were the sharp increase in the value of petroleum exports and imports in the 1970s and the collapse of those values in the 1980s. The quadrupling of oil prices in 1973–1974 and a further doubling of prices in 1979 increased the dollar value of petroleum exports and imports immensely. OPEC nations acquired billions of dollars from oil exports, as did non-OPEC oil-exporting nations such as Great Britain. The oil revenues allowed oil-producing countries to finance all sorts of projects that were previously unaffordable. When oil revenues collapsed along with oil prices in the 1980s, these nations found it very difficult to finance the levels of imports they had been acquiring. The import levels of many oil-producing nations fell dramatically in 1983 and 1984. This affected the export levels of industrial nations, because what one nation imports, another must have exported. If world imports fall, so do world exports.

What Does the United States Trade?

The United States is a major participant in world trade. In 1990, U.S. exports totaled $670.4 billion, equal to 12.3 percent of GNP. Imports were even higher, $708.4 billion, or 13 percent of GNP. In other words, over one ninth of U.S. production was sold to foreigners, and over one eighth of U.S. purchases of new goods and services were from foreigners.

What does the United States export and import? The single most important category of merchandise exports is capital goods other than automotive products. U.S. companies produce and export all kinds of capital equipment, from earth movers to computers. In 1989 the value of such exports was $138 billion, comprising over one fifth of U.S. exports. The second most important merchandise export category is industrial supplies and materials. Included in this category are such things as chemicals and intermediate goods that go into the production of other goods. It may come as a surprise that U.S. exports of services exceed even capital goods exports in value. How is it possible to export services? Insurance and financial and transportation services can be provided to foreigners quite easily, and U.S. producers have a comparative advantage in these skill-intensive areas. Investment income from U.S. investments in foreign countries is also included in the service export category.

[8]These and other figures in this section are drawn from William H. Branson, "Trends in United States International Trade and Investment since World War II," in M. S. Feldstein, ed., *The American Economy in Transition* (Chicago: University of Chicago Press, 1980), pp. 183–273.

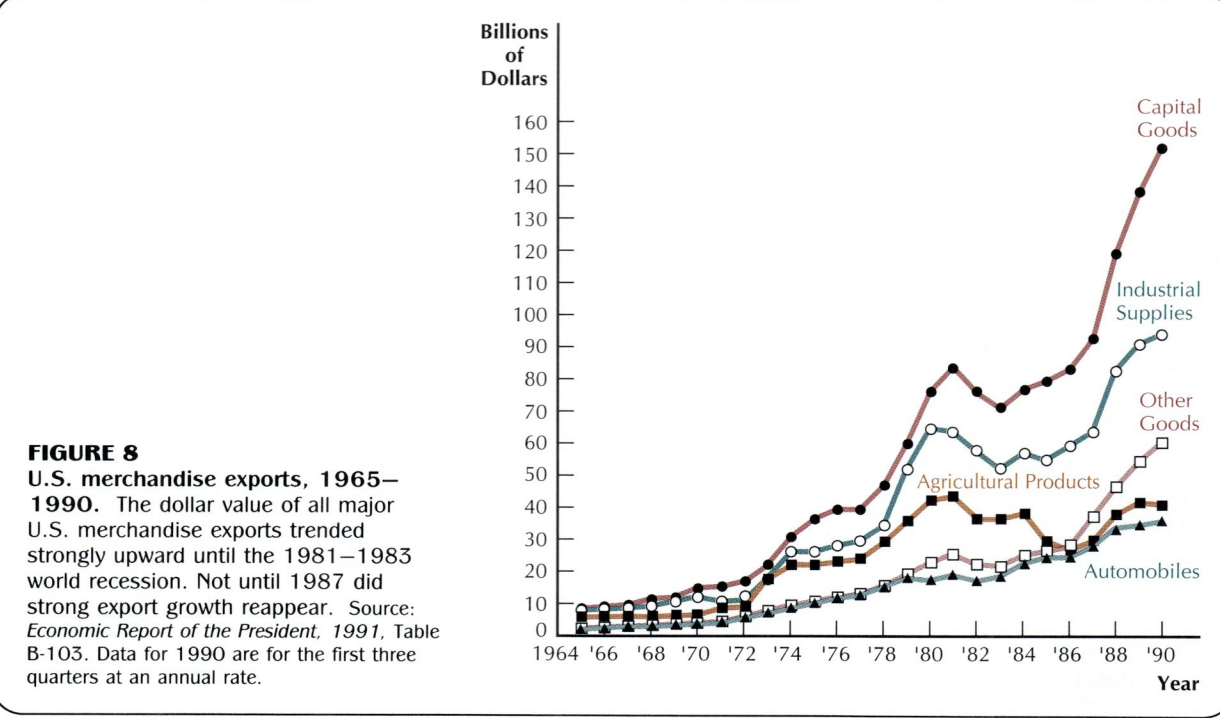

FIGURE 8
U.S. merchandise exports, 1965–1990. The dollar value of all major U.S. merchandise exports trended strongly upward until the 1981–1983 world recession. Not until 1987 did strong export growth reappear. Source: *Economic Report of the President, 1991,* Table B-103. Data for 1990 are for the first three quarters at an annual rate.

Figure 8 shows the behavior of major merchandise export categories over the past two decades. All categories trended upward in current dollar terms, although the growth was not even across categories or over time. Especially evident is the sharp decline in exports in 1982 and 1983 and the small rebound in 1984. The recession experienced in the United States in 1981 and 1982 was worldwide. Demand for all products, including those made in the United States, fell off significantly. This decline in exports had serious implications for the U.S. balance of trade.

The pattern of U.S. merchandise imports is shown in Figure 9, which shows that major growth took place in imports of petroleum in the 1970s and in imports of other goods, primarily consumer goods, in both the 1970s and 1980s. Rapid growth also took place in the importation of automotive products and capital goods.

The United States is a major *net* exporter (exports minus imports) of agricultural products and capital goods (other than automobiles) and a major *net* importer of petroleum products, consumer goods (such as textiles and shoes), and automobiles. These trade patterns reflect a comparative advantage in goods produced by skilled labor working with sophisticated capital and a comparative disadvantage in goods produced with simple capital and unskilled labor. The exception to this is automobiles, where Japanese technology is more advanced than U.S. technology and Japanese auto workers earn less than U.S. auto workers, giving Japan a comparative advantage in automobile production, even though it is a sophisticated industry.

Figure 10 shows the U.S. balance of merchandise trade (excluding services) with several countries or groups of countries. A major feature stands out. The

SECTION RECAP
The United States tends to export goods that require sophisticated capital and skilled labor to produce. U.S. imports primarily in- *(continued)*

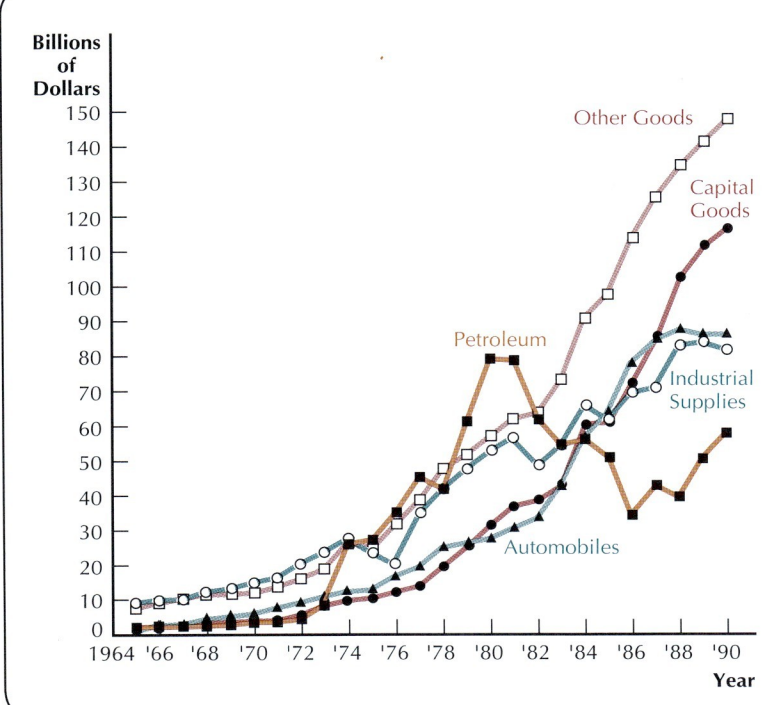

FIGURE 9
U.S. merchandise imports, 1965–1990. The dollar value of petroleum imports leaped upward in 1974–1977 and again in 1979–1980, before dropping off after 1980. The fastest-growing import categories in the 1980s were "other goods" (a category including consumer goods), capital goods, and automobiles. Source: *Economic Report of the President, 1991*, Table B-103. Data for 1990 are for the first three quarters at an annual rate.

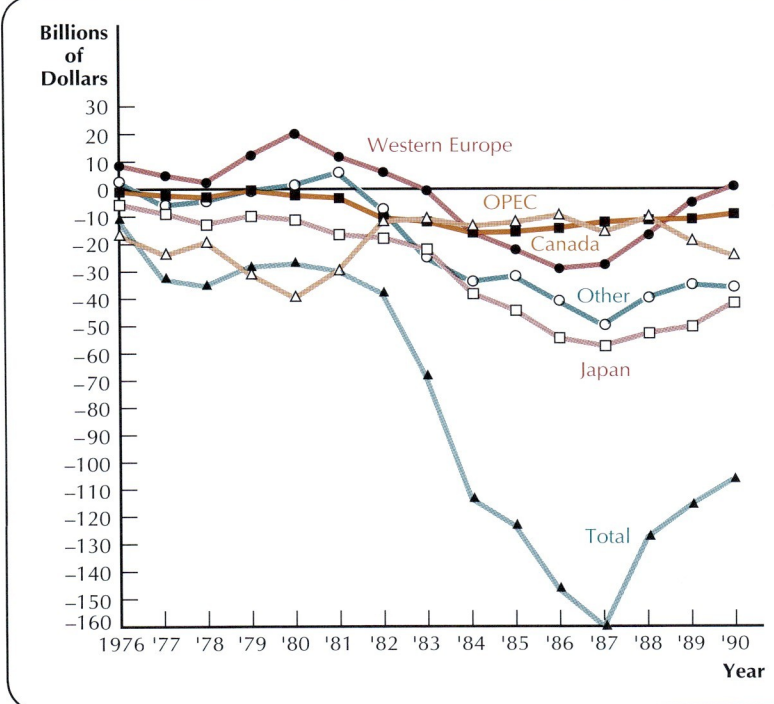

FIGURE 10
U.S. trade balances with selected regions. The U.S. merchandise trade balance plunged sharply into deficit from 1983 to 1987. The U.S. deficit with most major trading nations and regions grew until 1987, when it began to recover. Source: *Economic Report of the President, 1991*, Table B-104. Data for 1990 are for the first three quarters at an annual rate.

Why the **Disagreement?**

Is Japan a Boon or a Threat to the U.S. Economy?

Over 25 percent of the cars bought by Americans in 1989 were built by Japanese companies. Names such as Sony, Canon, and Panasonic are found in almost every American home. In addition, well over 10 percent of U.S. merchandise exports went to Japan in 1989, and the Japanese purchase more U.S. agricultural products than any other nation, indeed, more than all the western European nations combined.

In the face of such facts, it is somewhat surprising to see opinion polls showing that Americans believe that Japanese economic prowess is a greater threat to the United States than Soviet military might. Anti-Japanese attitudes are not confined to blue-collar workers who fear losing their jobs, either. A number of journalists, academics, and politicians have become well known for their anti-Japan sentiments. The view that Japan is a threat to the economic well-being of the United States has become so prevalent that *Fortune* magazine — which does *not* share such hostile views toward the Japanese — felt compelled to run a story entitled "Fear and Loathing of Japan."* Yet most economists take the view that trade with Japan benefits the United States. Why the disagreement?

The argument that Japan poses a threat to the United States stems from four sources: (1) Japan annually runs a large trade surplus against the United States, (2) Japanese companies are very aggressive exporters, (3) trade barriers make entry into Japanese markets much more difficult than entry into U.S. markets, and (4) rapid technological development has made Japanese companies more technologically advanced than their American counterparts in several industries. The "fear and loathing" felt by many Americans seems to reflect a feeling of inferiority combined with the beliefs that the Japanese don't play fair and that they seek to dominate the world economy.

The more articulate opponents of Japan argue that the Japanese are different than westerners, and that they will never have a free market like those in western nations. The conclusion usually drawn from such arguments is that the United States cannot practice free trade with Japan. Instead, the U.S. government must manage trade with the Japanese. That is, the government must protect U.S. industries with tariffs and quotas, while actively coordinating the economic activities of U.S. companies.

There is no question that Japanese growth depends heavily on exports. Such a strategy made sense early in the postwar period, when Japan was attempting to recover from the devastation of the war. However, the aggressive export policy was carried on until huge

---

SECTION RECAP
(continued)
clude goods that can be produced with simple capital and unskilled labor. The worldwide recession of the early 1980s, from which the United States recovered more quickly than other nations, plunged the U.S. balance of trade into deficit. The U.S. trade deficit did not begin to shrink until 1988.

U.S. trade balance turned sharply downward against all countries and groups of countries in the 1980s. Why did this occur? One reason has already been mentioned. The worldwide recession of the early 1980s caused many countries to cut back on their imports. The U.S. economy came out of the recession more quickly than did most other economies. When the U.S. economy began expanding, U.S. consumers began buying more goods — some of which were foreign made. Consequently, imports rebounded but exports did not. As other economies began to grow more rapidly, U.S. exports have increased.

The second reason for the large U.S. trade deficits of the 1980s has to do with the exchange rate, the price of U.S. currency in terms of foreign currencies. The exchange rate rose sharply from 1980 to early 1985. This raised the cost of U.S. products to foreigners and made foreign-produced goods cheaper to Americans. The result was an expansion of imports and a contraction of exports. The exchange rate declined from 1986 to 1990, eventually contributing to the decline in the U.S. trade deficit that began in 1988.

trade surpluses arose. There is also little question that U.S. markets are easier to penetrate than tradition-bound Japanese markets. Furthermore, Japan *has* taken the technological lead in a number of industries. The question is, Do these facts make Japan a threat to the United States? Further, is Japan's success a coordinated effort to dominate the world economy? In a book on why nations succeed or fail in international trade, Harvard Business School professor Michael Porter argues that a government-coordinated plan to dominate the world economy is *not* the source of Japanese success.** Porter credits Japanese companies and sophisticated, demanding consumers. Porter's study of ten countries convinced him that tough competition and high consumer standards are crucial to success in the international market. For example, the international success of Japanese automobile companies stems largely from the cutthroat domestic competition among nine companies. In contrast, the much-larger U.S. economy has only three auto companies. Less competition means that U.S. auto companies do not have to work so hard to remain profitable.

Porter argues that the standard view that government coordination of exports accounts for the success of Japanese companies is simply wrong. Japanese companies do not produce with only the export market in mind. Instead, when a Japanese company develops a new product, it markets it heavily within Japan. When the company's competitors produce similar products and reduce the company's domestic sales, the company turns to foreign markets. The success of Japanese companies has little to do with government direction, but much to do with competition.

So, back to the original question: Is Japan a threat or a boon to the United States? Both countries stand to gain tremendously from free trade. Japan is a threat to the United States only if U.S. companies lose the competitive drive that once made them the world's best. The interests of Americans will be best served if the U.S. government continues to press for open markets in Japan, while promoting active competition within the United States.

*Lee Smith, "Fear and Loathing of Japan," *Fortune*, February 26, 1990.
**Michael Porter, *The Competitive Advantage of Nations* (New York: Free Press, 1990).

Summary

The principle of **comparative advantage** states that producing low-opportunity-cost goods and trading them for high-opportunity-cost goods increases the amount of goods and services a society can consume. Two nations can benefit from trade by specializing and trading one good for another if the opportunity costs of the goods differ between the countries. The **terms of trade** must lie between the two countries' opportunity cost ratios if both nations are to benefit from trade.

As nations trade, resources flow from high-opportunity-cost industries, which become unprofitable, to low-opportunity-cost industries, which become more profitable. The price of traded goods tends to equalize across different economies, as consumers buy from the cheapest producers and producers sell in the markets with the highest prices. Such trading drives prices toward equality across economies.

Restricting international trade is profitable to producers who do not have a comparative advantage in their product. **Tariffs**—import taxes—and **quotas**—import quantity restrictions—are both used to drive up the price of imports and protect domestic producers. Although such policies help the producers of protected goods (owners of companies and workers), the losses suffered by consumers exceed the gains to producers. The recent quotas on Japanese automobiles illustrate this point. For every $40,000 auto-worker job saved by the quotas, American consumers paid $160,000 to U.S. and Japanese car companies.

Tariffs are defended with a number of arguments, including the **infant-industry argument,** the **cheap foreign labor argument,** the **defense argument,** and the **bargaining chip argument.** With the possible exception of the last one, none of these arguments holds up under careful scrutiny. If trade barriers are to be erected, tariffs are preferred to quotas, because tariffs allow consumers to choose the product they wish to purchase and raise revenue for the government, while quotas restrict choice and raise no revenue.

Nations tend to export goods in which they have a comparative advantage in production. Less-developed countries export raw materials and minerals, developing countries export simple manufactured goods, and highly developed economies export sophisticated manufactured goods. The United States is a major net exporter of capital goods and agricultural products and a major net importer of consumer goods, petroleum, and automobiles.

Questions for Thought

Knowledge Questions

1. Define what is meant by the terms *tariff* and *quota*.
2. Explain why, if the domestic market is to be protected, tariffs are preferred to quotas.
3. What is the infant-industry argument? What are its shortcomings?
4. What kinds of goods does the United States export? Why?
5. How does international trade affect domestic aggregate supply?

Application Questions

6. Use a demand–supply diagram to explain what happens when a tariff is applied to an imported product.
7. Using the theory of consumer and producer surplus, show how a tariff applied to an imported good affects consumers and producers.
8. Explain why adjustment benefits for workers displaced by foreign competition might not be good for the economy.
9. The production possibilities frontiers for two countries are provided. Determine the following:
    a. If the countries could benefit from trade.
    b. Which country should specialize in which good.
    c. The limits between which any acceptable trading ratio must lie.

Gondor		Rohan	
Steel (tons)	Wheat (tons)	Steel (tons)	Wheat (tons)
0	100	0	60
20	80	5	48
40	60	10	36
60	40	15	24
80	20	20	12
100	0	25	0

Synthesis Questions

10. Explain why and how the prices of freely traded goods are driven toward equality across nations.
11. It is well known that international trade affects jobs. When a domestic industry loses business to foreign competitors, workers are displaced and incur adjustment costs. Is this problem a uniquely international problem? Explain.
12. Why do you think there is more concern over a job lost to foreign competition than over a job lost to domestic competition?
13. A friend argues that the United States ought to increase tariffs sharply to keep out goods from developing countries. He believes that it is only a matter of time until all U.S. manufacturing jobs are lost and the standard of living in the U.S. is dragged down to a Third World level. How do you counter his argument?

O V E R V I E W

International Finance and the Open-Economy Model

Most international trade is carried on by means of monetary exchanges. In an earlier chapter we explored the advantages of using money as a medium of exchange. When trade is across national borders, however, the process of monetary exchange becomes more complex. The reason is obvious: Different nations use different monies. If you were to walk into the Kaufhaus, a large department store in Munich, Germany, you would be required to use deutsche marks to purchase anything. The clerk serving you would not be interested in your nationality—or in your dollars. Only marks would be accepted.

The principle is exactly the same for a U.S. firm importing Swiss cheese. Although the cheese will ultimately be sold in the United States in exchange for dollars, Swiss producers want to be paid in Swiss francs. They want the currency they must use in their own transactions. Somehow, then, one currency must be exchanged for another. That is the basic fact motivating this chapter.

We begin the chapter with another application of the budget constraint principle. In this case, we apply it to international transactions. Every nation has a balance of payments with other nations as goods, services, financial assets, and money flow from country to country. We then discuss the determination of a country's exchange rate, a process that is closely linked to the nation's balance of payments.

Exchange rates can be market determined or they can be controlled to a greater or lesser degree by governments. It is important for the macroeconomy whether the exchange rate is flexible, changing as market forces change, or fixed by government policy. How the economy adjusts to international trade depends upon the existing exchange rate system. We use an open-economy macro model to examine the behavior of the economy in response to various kinds of demand and supply changes under both exchange rate systems.

CHAPTER 36

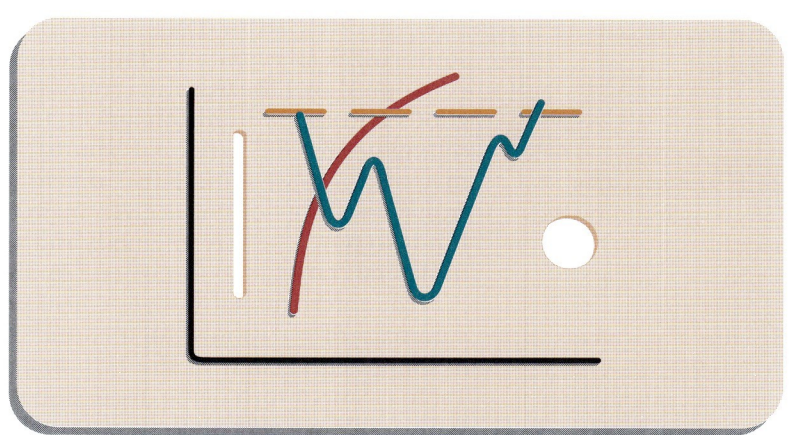

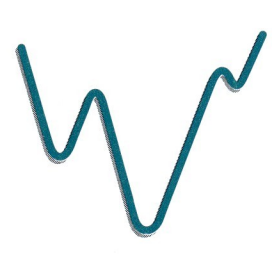

Learning Objectives

After reading and studying this chapter, you will be able to:

1. Define the terms *balance on goods and services* and *balance on current account* and explain what they mean.
2. Describe the types of capital flows that might correspond to current account balances or surpluses.
3. Use the model of exchange rate determination to explain movements in a country's exchange rate.
4. Outline the basic features of flexible and fixed exchange rate systems and their effects on trade flows.
5. List the factors that limit a government's ability to control its exchange rate and describe the sorts of limitations they impose.
6. Explain how an open-economy model differs from a closed-economy model of the macroeconomy.

Balance of Payments

All economic units face budget constraints. The basic idea behind a budget constraint is that an individual, or a family, or a firm, or a government cannot purchase something without financing it in some way. Sources of funds must equal uses of funds. This principle applies as much to nations as to any other economic unit. A nation cannot acquire goods and services from other nations without giving up something in return, unless the acquisition is an outright gift.

Since a nation's budget constraint reflects its transactions with other nations, it looks a bit different from the macroeconomic budget constraint used in earlier chapters. The equation:

$$\begin{array}{c} \text{Exports of goods and services} \\ + \\ \text{Gifts received} \\ + \\ \Delta \text{ Foreign assets in U.S.} \end{array} = \begin{array}{c} \text{Imports of goods and services} \\ + \\ \text{Gifts given} \\ + \\ \Delta \text{ U.S. assets abroad} \end{array}$$

Unilateral transfers Gifts or grants for which nothing is received in return.

Balance of payments Accounting summary of a nation's international transactions, built up from the nation's budget constraint, so that the balance always equals zero.

summarizes an economy's international budget constraint. The left side of the equation shows the ways an economy can obtain the funds needed to purchase goods and assets from foreigners. Domestic citizens obtain foreign funds by selling goods and services (exports) and financial assets to foreigners. They may also receive some gifts from foreigners. Such gifts are called **unilateral transfers**, since nothing is given up in return. Domestic citizens can use foreign funds to purchase foreign goods and services (imports) and assets, or to make unilateral transfers to foreigners. As always, sources of funds must equal uses.

The international budget constraint lies behind the standard accounting summary of a nation's international transactions—its **balance of payments**. A simplified version of the U.S. balance of payments for 1989 is shown in Table 1. Since much of the discussion that follows uses the balance of payments framework, we will carefully work through the table.

We can get from the budget constraint equation to the balance of payments table in the following manner. Subtract the right side terms (uses) from both sides of the equation. Rearranging slightly, we obtain:

$$(\text{Exports} - \text{Imports}) + (\text{Gifts received} - \text{Gifts given}) - (\Delta \text{ in U.S. assets abroad}) + (\Delta \text{ in Foreign assets in U.S.}) = 0$$

Now, rename the gifts term *unilateral transfers, net*. Then the international budget constraint is:

$$(\text{Exports} - \text{Imports}) + \text{Unilateral transfers, net} - (\Delta \text{ in U.S. assets abroad}) + (\Delta \text{ in Foreign assets in U.S.}) = 0$$

From the budget constraint we see that if U.S. net exports are positive and not offset by unilateral transfers, U.S. asset holdings abroad will increase or foreign asset holdings in the United States will decrease. Why? A net export surplus indicates that Americans earn more funds by selling goods and services to foreigners than they spend on foreign-produced goods and services. With the excess funds they either acquire assets from foreigners or repay debts to foreigners (or buy U.S. assets back from foreigners who owned them). The opposite occurs if the United States runs a net export deficit. Americans must sell assets to finance the deficit. U.S. holdings of foreign assets decline, or

TABLE 1
U.S. balance of payments, 1989

(Billions of Dollars)

1. Exports of goods and services	+ $603.2	
2. Imports of goods and services	− 698.5	
Balance on goods and services	− 95.3	
3. Unilateral transfers (net)	− 14.7	
Balance on current account	− 110.0	
4. U.S. assets abroad, net (increase)	− 127.1	
a. U.S. official reserve assets		− 25.3
b. U.S. nonreserve assets		− 101.8
5. Foreign assets in U.S., net (increase)	+ 214.7	
a. Foreign official reserve assets		+ 8.8
b. Foreign nonreserve assets		+ 205.8
6. Statistical discrepancy	+ 22.4	
Balance of Payments	0	

Note: Inflows (sources) of funds are recorded as positive items, outflows (uses) of funds as negative items.
Source: *Survey of Current Business,* December 1990, Table 1.

---

foreign holdings of U.S. assets rise (or both). By construction, the balance of payments always equals zero.

Consider Table 1. In line 1 we see that in 1989 the United States exported goods and services worth $603.2 billion. Since these exports brought funds into the United States, they are recorded as a positive item in the balance of payments. In 1989, Americans purchased $698.5 billion worth of foreign-produced goods and services (line 2). This represented an outflow of funds from the United States, so it is recorded as a negative item in the balance of payments. Adding lines 1 and 2 we derive the **balance on goods and services**. This is the trade balance for 1989.[1]

Unilateral transfers (line 3) include U.S. government grants to foreign nations and private transfers to foreign nationals. An example of the former would be foreign aid grants; an example of the latter would be savings sent back to family in the old country by people who have immigrated to the United States. Of course, transfers may come from foreign governments or citizens to the United States, but in 1989 (as in all recent years) more funds left the United States as gifts to foreigners than came into the United States as gifts to Americans. Thus net unilateral transfers is negative. Adding net unilateral transfers

Balance on goods and services
Dollar value of exports of goods and services minus imports of goods and services.

---

[1] A narrower measure of the trade balance, not included in Table 1, is the *balance on merchandise trade.* It often receives more attention than the balance on goods and services. The merchandise trade balance, which ignores the value of services traded internationally, was −$114.9 billion in 1989. Thus, the United States ran a surplus on services trade of almost $20 billion, which reduced the balance on goods and services deficit. Trade in services includes such things as medical treatment of foreigners and provision of insurance services. Interest and dividends earned on foreign investments are also included as service exports. Since there is no good reason to ignore trade in services, we focus on the broader balance in our discussion.

Current account balance
Sum of balance of goods and services and net unilateral transfers.

Capital flow
Flow of money into or out of a country in exchange for financial assets.

to the balance on goods and services yields the **current account balance**. This is the amount that must be financed by **capital flows**—funds flowing into or out of the domestic economy to purchase financial assets. In 1989, the United States ran a current account deficit of $110.0 billion. This represented a net outflow of funds and had to be offset by a capital inflow of the same size.

Capital flows are of two basic types: changes in official reserve asset holdings and changes in asset holdings other than official reserves. Table 1 shows that in 1989 U.S. asset holdings abroad (line 4) increased by $127.1 billion. This represented a capital outflow—funds that left the United States to purchase foreign assets. The capital outflow was composed of a net increase in U.S. official reserve assets of $25.3 billion (line 4a) and a net increase of nonreserve assets abroad of $101.8 billion (line 4b).

U.S. official reserve assets are U.S. government holdings of gold, convertible (tradable) foreign currencies, reserve position in the International Monetary Fund (IMF), and special drawing rights in the IMF. All these items are acceptable in international trade. Gold was for centuries an international currency, though it is little used for trading purposes now. Foreign currencies are useful when buying products or assets from the countries that issued them. A nation's reserve position in the IMF is an *official checking account* that can be used for transferring funds between governments. Special drawing rights are similar. Both are held in the International Monetary Fund, an agency created following World War II to be a bank for official international transactions. During 1989 the U.S. government acquired $25.3 billion worth of reserve assets from foreign governments.

U.S. holdings of (nonreserve) assets abroad rose by almost $102 billion. This category includes direct private investment by U.S. companies in foreign countries (for example, building factories or transportation facilities), purchases of foreign stocks and bonds by U.S. citizens, increases in American-owned foreign bank deposits, and U.S. government loans to foreign governments or businesses.

Line 5 shows the inflow of funds from increased foreign holdings of U.S. assets. Foreign governments increased their reserve holdings of dollars and dollar-denominated U.S. Treasury bonds by $8.8 billion (line 5a). Nonreserve foreign asset holdings in the United States rose by $205.8 billion, as foreigners invested in facilities in the United States, bought stocks and bonds issued by U.S. companies and the U.S. Treasury, and increased their deposits in U.S. banks. This massive capital inflow financed the current account deficit. Without such an inflow, it would not have been possible to purchase the volume of imports that flowed into the United States in 1989.

The last item in the balance of payments is a statistical discrepancy term (line 6). From the international budget constraint, we know that the current account balance must be offset by a capital flow of the same size. However, data collection is not perfect. The U.S. government collects data both on the value of goods traded and on the financing of those goods. For example, it collects data from exporters on the value of shipments and data on international transactions from banks. Due to deficiencies in the collection process, these values are never exactly equal. The statistical discrepancy term is a measure of the error in data collection.

The balance of payments always balances because it is derived from a budget constraint. *How* it balances is of interest to economists. The behavior of the exchange rate is a crucial determinant of how the balance of payments is achieved.

SECTION RECAP
An economy has an international budget constraint: All purchases from foreigners must be financed. The international budget constraint is reflected in a nation's balance of payments accounts. A surplus or deficit in the trade of goods and services must be financed by a flow of capital into or out of the country. The balance of payments always balances; *how* it balances is of interest to economists.

Determining the Exchange Rate

The **exchange rate** — the number of units of one currency that exchange for one unit of another currency — depends on the demand for a nation's currency by foreigners relative to the supply of the currency to foreigners. The exchange rate is a market price that fluctuates with demand and supply.

Exchange rate
Number of units of one currency that exchange for one unit of another currency.

Demand for a Currency

There are two major reasons why someone in another country might want to obtain U.S. dollars. One is to purchase U.S. products. If a Japanese company desires to buy IBM computers or Lotus software, it must obtain dollars to do so. A second reason foreigners demand dollars is to purchase dollar-denominated financial assets or engage in direct investment in the United States. Corporate stock or U.S. government bonds must be purchased with dollars, and investment goods must be paid for with dollars.

The quantity of dollars demanded varies with the price of the dollar. Figure 1 illustrates the demand for dollars by Germans. The price of the dollar — the exchange rate — is the number of German marks required to purchase one dollar. If the exchange rate is high, Germans must pay a larger quantity of deutsche marks to obtain one dollar. For example, if the exchange rate is 3.00 (DM3/$1), a German must give up three marks to obtain one dollar. If the exchange rate is 2.00, then a German can obtain a dollar for only two marks.

Suppose a German company wants to purchase some electric turbines from a U.S. producer. The turbines cost $100,000 each. They are priced in dollars, because the U.S. company must purchase its material inputs with dollars, pay its workers with dollars, and pay out dividends to its stockholders in dollars.

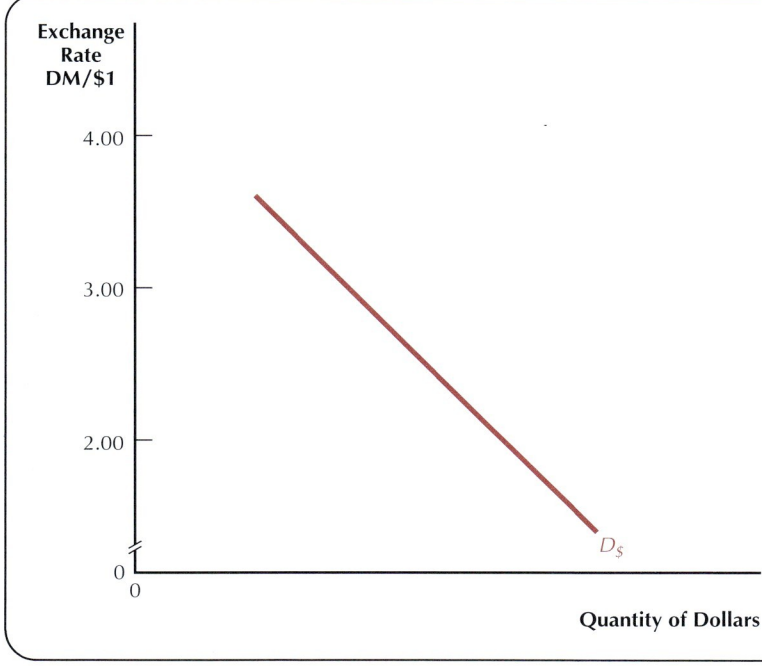

FIGURE 1
Demand for dollars. The demand for dollars is negatively related to the deutsche mark–dollar exchange rate. In drawing the demand curve we assume that the German real income level, the ratio of the U.S. price level to the German price level, and the ratio of the U.S. real interest rate to the German real interest rate are constant.

If the exchange rate is 3.00, then a single turbine costs the German company DM300,000. If the exchange rate is 2.00, the cost is only DM200,000. The cost of a turbine *to the German company* falls by one third when the exchange rate falls by one third. Needless to say, the Germans are likely to purchase more turbines if they cost DM200,000 each than if they cost DM300,000. Hence, the quantity of dollars demanded by Germans rises as the deutsche mark–dollar exchange rate falls. U.S. goods become cheaper to Germans, and Germans demand more dollars in order to purchase more U.S. goods.

As the exchange rate falls, dollar-denominated financial assets also become cheaper to Germans. However, this does not necessarily affect the quantity of dollars demanded. When a German bank buys a U.S. government bond, it is interested in earning the highest real interest rate possible. When the bond matures, the bank must convert the dollars it receives back into deutsche marks. If it buys dollars at DM2/$1 and reconverts into deutsche marks at the same low exchange rate, the bank gains nothing from the low rate. Thus, the value of the exchange rate does not affect the quantity of dollars demanded for financial purposes *unless the exchange rate is expected to rise or fall.* Financial investors can gain from movements in the exchange rate, but they neither gain nor lose if it remains constant.

Three major factors shift the Germans' demand-for-dollars curve:

1. If the real income level rises in Germany, consumption spending increases. German consumers purchase more goods, some of which are American made. Thus, an increase in the German real income level increases the demand for dollars.

2. If the price level in Germany rises more rapidly than the price level in the United States, the German demand for dollars rises. U.S. products become relatively cheaper in such a situation, and German consumers begin to substitute U.S. products for German goods.

3. If the ratio of the real interest rate in the United States to the real interest rate in Germany rises, the demand for dollars increases. If the U.S. real rate is higher than the German real rate, U.S. financial assets are relatively more attractive than German financial assets. German financial investors demand dollars with which to buy dollar-denominated assets.

Any of these three factors will shift the demand curve for dollars to the right. If these factors are reversed, the demand curve shifts to the left.

Supply of a Currency

A currency is supplied to the foreign exchange market when foreign products or financial assets are desired. Returning to our United States–Germany example, the supply of dollars into the foreign exchange market depends upon U.S. demand for German-made goods and for deutsche mark-denominated assets; Americans supply dollars to obtain deutsche marks. The supply curve of dollars is illustrated in Figure 2. It slopes upward because German goods become cheaper to Americans as the exchange rate rises. An Audi with a DM50,000 price tag costs an American $25,000 if the exchange rate is DM2/$1, but costs only $16,667 if the exchange rate is DM3/$1. As the exchange rate rises, the quantity demanded of German-made goods increases, because the dollar price falls.

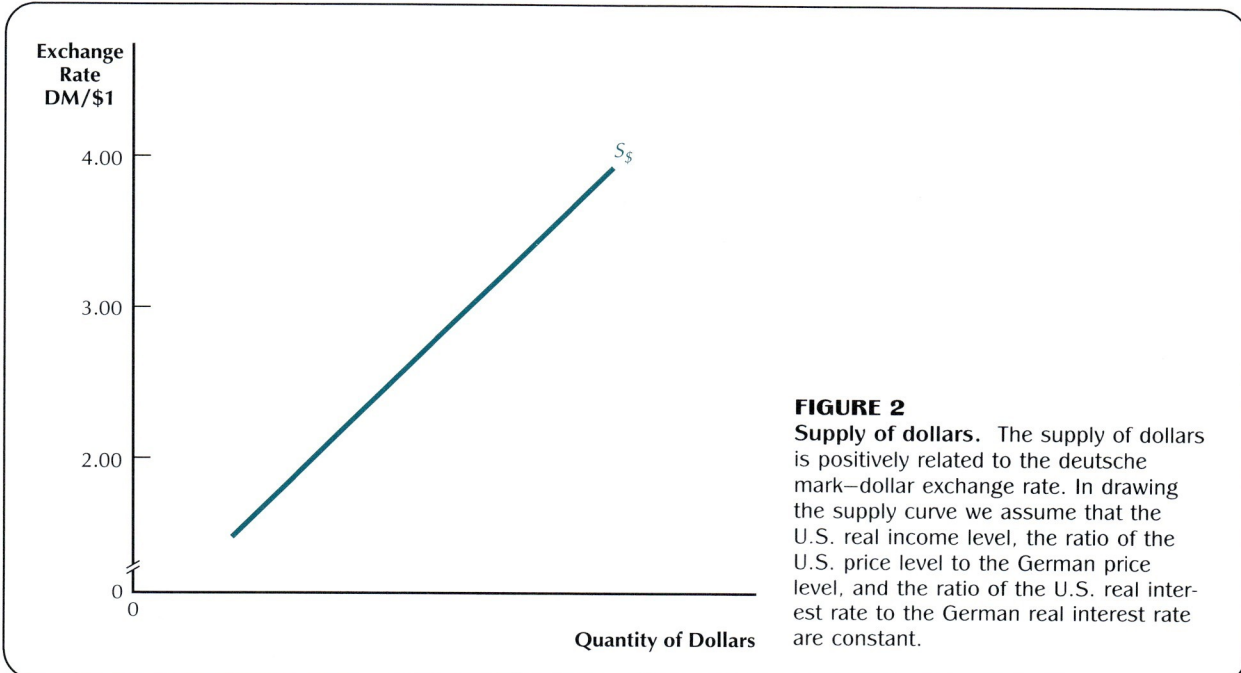

FIGURE 2
Supply of dollars. The supply of dollars is positively related to the deutsche mark–dollar exchange rate. In drawing the supply curve we assume that the U.S. real income level, the ratio of the U.S. price level to the German price level, and the ratio of the U.S. real interest rate to the German real interest rate are constant.

The factors shifting the supply-of-dollars curve are similar to those shifting the demand-for-dollars curve.

1. An increase in the real income level in the United States increases consumption spending. U.S. consumers buy more products of all kinds, including German-made imports. As U.S. purchases of German goods increase, the supply of dollars to Germans increases.

2. If the U.S. price level rises more rapidly than the German price level, German goods become relatively cheaper to Americans. U.S. consumers buy more German-made goods, increasing the supply of dollars to Germans.

3. If the U.S. real interest rate *falls* relative to the German real rate, deutsche mark-denominated assets become more attractive to U.S. savers. As U.S. savers buy German assets, they supply more dollars to Germans.

Each of these factors shifts the supply-of-dollars curve to the right. If these factors are reversed, the supply curve shifts to the left.

It may have become obvious in the preceding discussion that the supply of dollars *is* the demand for deutsche marks by Americans. Similarly, the demand for dollars by Germans *is* their supply of deutsche marks. We could turn the analysis around and examine the dollar–deutsche mark exchange rate just as easily as we have examined its inverse, the deutsche mark–dollar rate. The results would be exactly the same in either case.

Exchange Rate

The interaction of the demand for a currency and its supply determines the exchange rate. Figure 3 shows the determination of the deutsche mark–dollar

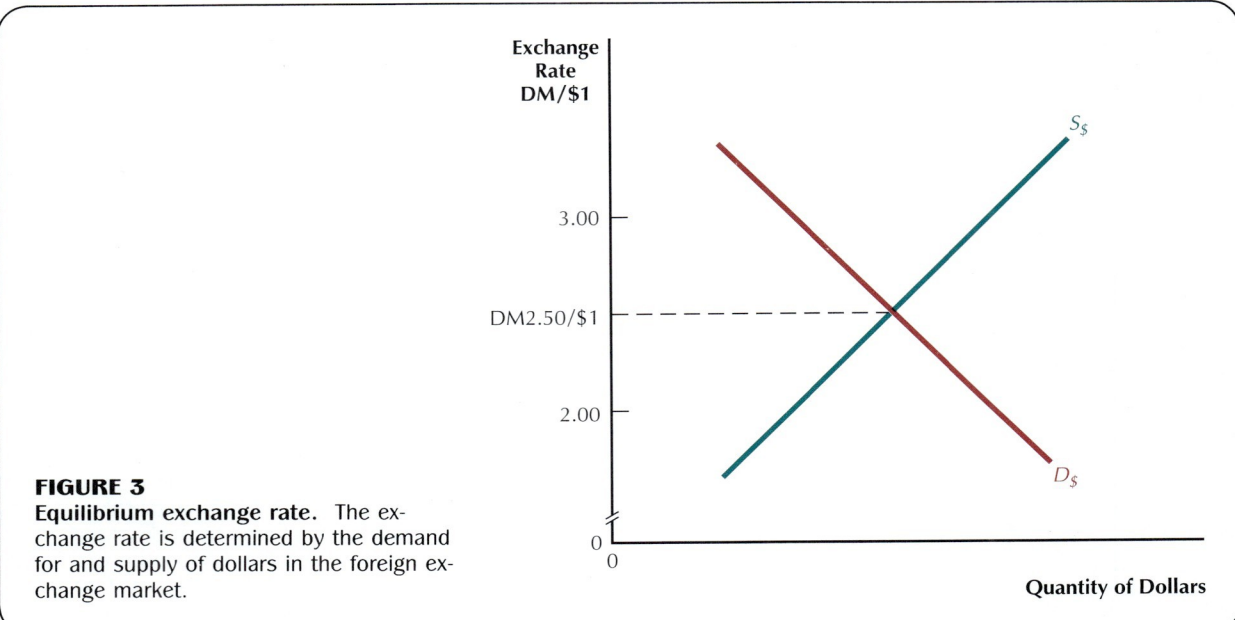

FIGURE 3
Equilibrium exchange rate. The exchange rate is determined by the demand for and supply of dollars in the foreign exchange market.

SECTION RECAP
The exchange rate is determined by the demand for and supply of a currency in the foreign exchange market. The demand for a currency depends on the demand by foreigners for a nation's goods, services, and assets. The supply of a currency depends on the nation's demand for foreign goods, services, and assets.

Appreciation
An increase in the value of a currency relative to other currencies.

Depreciation
A decrease in the value of a currency relative to other currencies.

exchange rate. In this example, the market is in equilibrium at an exchange rate of DM2.50/$1.

Changes in the Exchange Rate Suppose the real interest rate in the United States rises relative to the real rate in Germany. This increases the attractiveness of dollar-denominated assets. As Figure 4 illustrates, the demand for dollars rises, while the supply of dollars falls. The simultaneous increase in demand and decrease in supply causes the exchange rate to rise. In fact, during the first half of the 1980s, the U.S. real interest rate did rise relative to the real rate in Germany, and the exchange rate did increase. Relatively high U.S. real interest rates appear to have played a major part in the extremely high U.S. exchange rates of the early 1980s.

An increase in the exchange rate represents an **appreciation** of the dollar and a **depreciation** of the deutsche mark. As the dollar buys more deutsche marks, the deutsche mark buys fewer fewer dollars. For every currency that appreciates, another depreciates.

Fixed and Flexible Exchange Rates

In the absence of government intervention in the foreign exchange market, the exchange rate moves continuously to equate the quantity demanded of a currency with the quantity supplied. Such exchange rate movements have macroeconomic effects, as we will see shortly. Most of the time, adjustments in the exchange rate are rather small. For example, the deutsche mark–dollar exchange rate does not bounce around from 2.25 to 2.85 to 2.40 from day to day. Instead, the changes tend to be small, from 2.25 to 2.27, for example. In

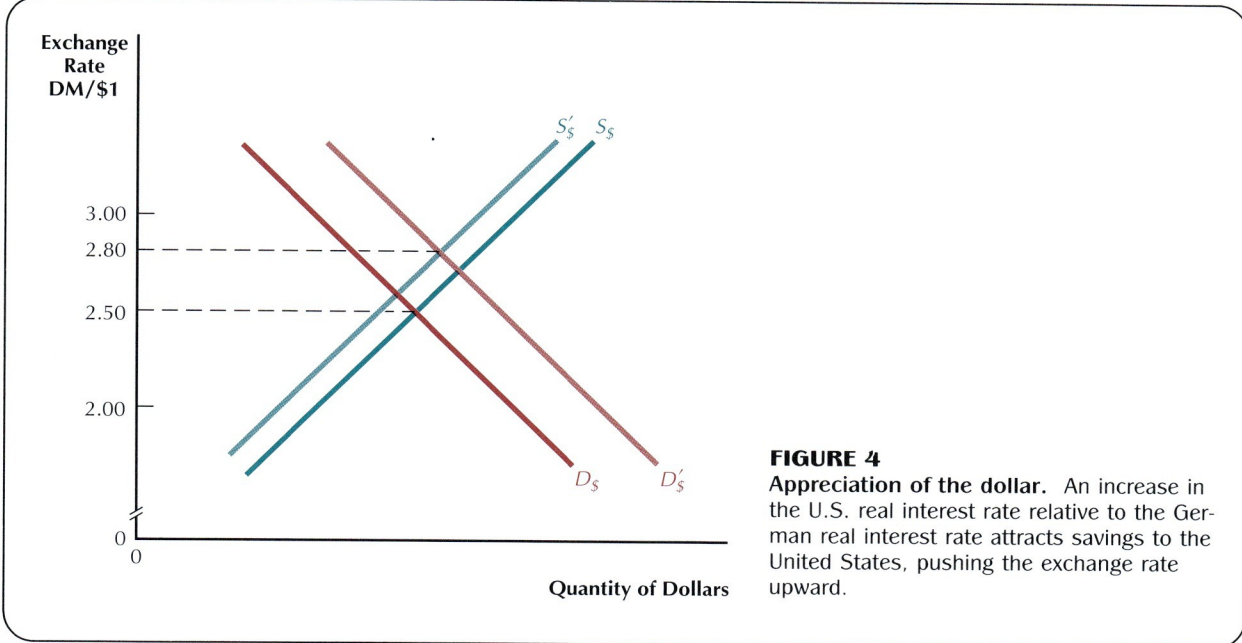

FIGURE 4
Appreciation of the dollar. An increase in the U.S. real interest rate relative to the German real interest rate attracts savings to the United States, pushing the exchange rate upward.

most instances, large changes in the exchange rate accumulate over lengthy periods of time.

The positions of the demand and supply of currency curves are not arbitrary. They depend on the real income levels in both trading nations, the price levels in those nations, and the ratio of real interest rates in the two countries. If these factors are relatively stable, the exchange rate should be relatively stable too, although changes in price level or interest rate expectations cause the exchange rate to vary somewhat from day to day. There is some normal value of the exchange rate determined by economic conditions in trading countries toward which the exchange rate tends.

Purchasing Power Parity

The theory of **purchasing power parity** focuses on relative price levels as a major determinant of the value of the exchange rate. The theory is based on the notion that a certain amount of a currency should purchase the same amount of tradable goods in all countries (ignoring transportation costs and taxes). For example, if a pair of running shoes costs $35 in the United States, then a person should be able to buy the same pair of shoes in West Germany after converting the $35 into deutsche marks. If the deutsche mark price of the shoes is DM70, then the exchange rate should be 2.00 for purchasing power parity to exist.

Of course, purchasing power parity is not determined on the basis of single prices. Ideally, a price index of all tradable goods should be used to determine the parity exchange rate. Only tradable goods should be included, because international competition does not directly affect the prices of nontradable goods. One can hardly fly to Germany for a haircut if he feels the price of the

Purchasing power parity Theory that a specific amount of currency should purchase the same quantity of tradable goods in all countries.

American variety is too high, but a German car can be substituted for an American car quite easily if the price makes it attractive.

What is the logic behind purchasing power parity? Suppose American importers find that at the current exchange rate they can purchase goods in Germany and resell them in the United States more cheaply than the goods can be made in the United States. For example, suppose the exchange rate is 3.00 deutsche marks per dollar and that running shoes that cost $35 in the United States can be bought for only DM70 in Germany. U.S. importers could buy the shoes in Germany for only $23.33 per pair (DM70/3.00) and resell them in the United States. Imports from Germany would increase dramatically, and so would the supply of dollars into the foreign exchange market. A larger supply of dollars into the foreign exchange market would push the exchange rate down, and the *dollar price* of importing shoes from Germany would rise. For example, at an exchange rate of 2.50, the dollar price of imported shoes would rise to $28. This process would continue until purchasing power parity was established on average for all tradable goods. Thus, *the purchasing power parity exchange rate can be viewed as the long-run equilibrium rate toward which the exchange rate tends.*

According to the purchasing power parity theory, the major factor determining the exchange rate is the relative level of prices between countries. In equilibrium (when purchasing power parity holds), the price level of tradable goods in Germany should be equal to the exchange rate (ER) times the price level of tradable goods (PT) in the United States:

$$PT_G = ER \times PT_{US}$$

[Back to the running shoes: DM70 = (DM2.00/$1) × $35.] Dividing through by the U.S. tradable goods price level:

$$ER = PT_G/PT_{US}$$

When the German price level rises relative to the U.S. price level, the exchange rate should rise (the deutsche mark should depreciate). When the German price level falls relative to the U.S. price level, the exchange rate should decline.

Purchasing power parity rarely holds exactly because other factors, such as real income levels and real interest rate levels, also affect the demand for and supply of a currency. Nevertheless, exchange rate *movements* are strongly related to changes in relative inflation rates between countries, a fact that is consistent with the purchasing power parity theory.

Policies to Hold an Exchange Rate Fixed

Governments do not always wish to allow exchange rates to move freely to market-determined levels. Since exchange rates are determined by the forces of supply and demand, however, a nation whose currency is tradable cannot fix its exchange rate at a desired level simply by passing a law. If it wants to hold its exchange rate at a particular level, it must **intervene** in the foreign exchange market by using its official reserve holdings to either demand or supply currency. (Not all nations have tradable, or **convertible**, currencies. Most communist nations and many less-developed countries have inconvertible currencies. Although these nations set official exchange rates by law, the official exchange rates usually differ from the rates that supply and demand

Intervention
Government purchases or sales of currency in the foreign exchange market designed to affect the value of the exchange rate.

Convertible currency
Currency that can be traded in the foreign exchange market for other currencies.

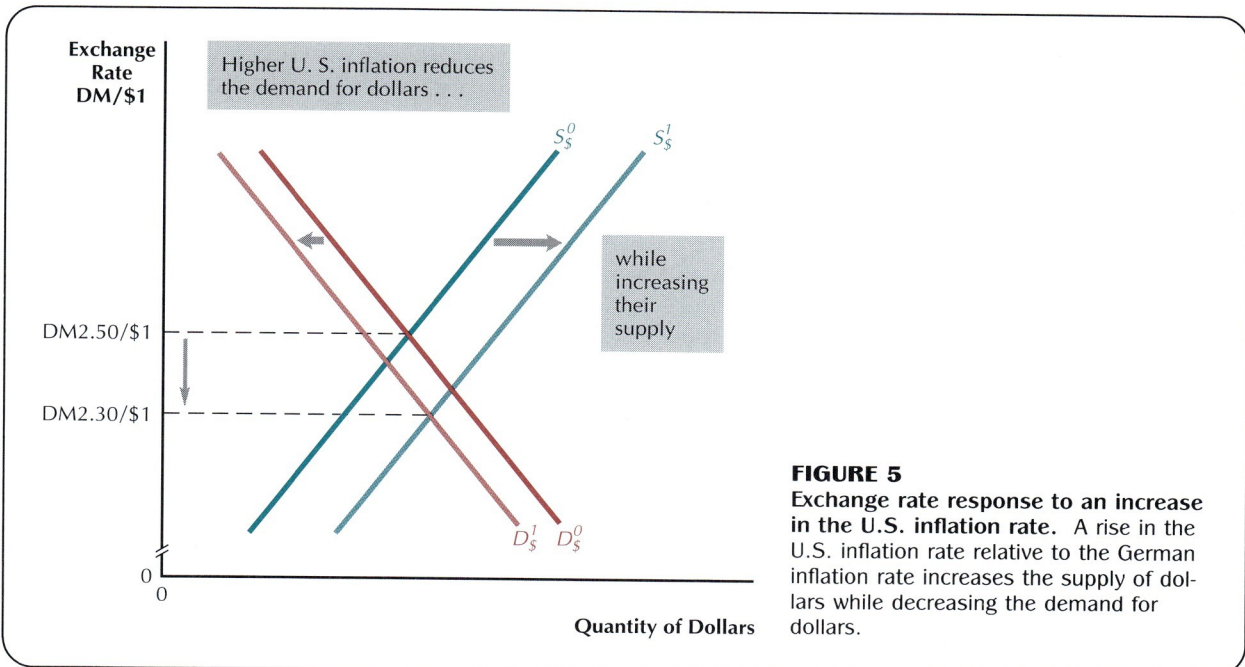

FIGURE 5
Exchange rate response to an increase in the U.S. inflation rate. A rise in the U.S. inflation rate relative to the German inflation rate increases the supply of dollars while decreasing the demand for dollars.

in the market would set. This hinders trade and forces these nations to bend the rules quite frequently.)

Suppose the U.S. government wants to hold the mark–dollar exchange rate at DM2.50/$1.[2] How would it go about fixing the rate at this level? To keep things simple, assume that the market level of the exchange rate initially is 2.50. Now, suppose that the U.S. inflation rate exceeds the German inflation rate. This means that U.S. products become more expensive relative to German products. U.S. consumers respond by demanding more German products and supplying more dollars to obtain them. Germans demand fewer American-made products and thus need fewer dollars. In the absence of intervention, the market level of the exchange rate falls, as shown in Figure 5.

If the U.S. government is to hold the exchange rate constant at 2.50, it must either (1) increase the demand for dollars, or (2) decrease the supply of dollars. To increase the demand for dollars, the U.S. government must use its official reserve holdings to purchase them. That is, the government must use foreign currency or its reserve position holdings at the IMF to increase the demand for dollars. This means that the government must have accumulated official reserve assets at some earlier time or must be able to borrow foreign currency from other governments. If the Federal Reserve, which handles foreign exchange for the U.S. government, has accumulated deutsche marks in the past, or if it can borrow marks from the German Bundesbank (the German equivalent of the Federal Reserve), it can use them to increase the demand for dollars, thus maintaining the exchange rate at the desired level.

---

[2]More realistically, the government would attempt to hold the exchange rate in a narrow band around 2.50, say from 2.48 to 2.52.

However, using foreign exchange reserves to prop up the demand for dollars is only a temporary expedient. The Federal Reserve does not have an unlimited supply of deutsche marks, nor can it borrow them indefinitely. It cannot create deutsche marks as it creates dollars. When its reserve of marks is depleted, the exchange rate will fall to its market level unless something else is done to shift the demand-and-supply-of-dollars curves.

How might the supply of dollars be altered? Americans supply dollars when they want to purchase German products or financial assets. If this desire could be checked, the supply of dollars would decrease, and the market exchange rate would rise back toward the targeted rate of 2.50. The U.S. government could limit the supply of dollars by using monetary and/or fiscal policy to restrict aggregate demand.

Suppose the Federal Reserve decreases the money supply through open market operations. This immediately puts upward pressure on interest rates. If inflation does not fall immediately — and the existence of contracts makes continued inflation likely — real interest rates rise. The ratio of the U.S. real interest rate to the German real interest rate rises. U.S. financial assets become relatively more attractive, leading to an increase in the German demand for dollars and a decline in the U.S. supply of dollars. The market exchange rate moves upward toward the targeted 2.50 level.

The restrictive monetary policy also has a negative impact on real income in the short run and prices in the long run. As real GNP declines, consumption spending drops off a little. The demand for imports, including German imports, falls. This further reduces the supply of dollars in the foreign exchange market, putting more upward pressure on the exchange rate. Eventually the tight monetary policy reduces the inflation rate, which was the original cause of the decline in the exchange rate. As the U.S. inflation rate declines relative to the German inflation rate, the downward pressure on the exchange rate evaporates. Thus, by using monetary policy to affect the real interest rate and real GNP (in the short run) and inflation (in the long run), U.S. policymakers can push the exchange rate toward its desired level.

The process of protecting a fixed exchange rate is much easier if there is international cooperation. If the Germans want to maintain an exchange rate of DM2.50/$1, they also can intervene to prop up the rate. The German Bundesbank could increase the demand for dollars by buying them up with newly created deutsche marks. If they did this — and they could do it indefinitely if they so desired — the United States would not have to adopt a restrictive monetary policy to protect the exchange rate. Note the effect this would have on the German economy, however. By creating more marks the Bundesbank would increase the growth rate of the German money supply. This would increase aggregate demand in Germany, ultimately increasing the German inflation rate. Thus, *maintaining an exchange rate at a targeted level inevitably affects the price level, real GNP, or both in at least one of the two countries involved.*

Gold Standard   Much of the time during the eighteenth, nineteenth, and early twentieth centuries, the developed economies of Europe and the Americas were on the gold standard. Gold served as the international medium of exchange, and a nation's gold stock limited its ability to purchase foreign products. Under the gold standard, domestic currencies were convertible into gold at specified prices. Governments stood ready to buy or sell gold at the official price. Fixing the price of gold in terms of a country's currency also fixed the exchange rate between countries. A simple example illustrates how this works.

Suppose the value of gold in the United States is set at $20 per ounce, while the official value of gold in England is set at £5 sterling per ounce. The ratio of gold prices sets the exchange rate between the dollar and the pound. In this case, ER = \$20/£5 = 4.00. If the exchange rate were to vary from its equilibrium value, the actions of private **arbitragers** — currency traders who buy and sell currencies when their values move away from their equilibrium levels — would quickly force it back to 4.00. Suppose the exchange rate rose to 4.10. With £5 an arbitrager could purchase $20.50 (which equals 4.10 × £5). The arbitrager could then purchase gold at $20 per ounce and sell the gold for £5. At the end of this transaction, the arbitrager would have his original £5 plus a fifty-cent profit. The actions of arbitragers seeking to earn risk-free profits increase the supply of pounds sterling and the demand for dollars in the foreign exchange market. The international value of the pound falls toward its equilibrium value of 4.00. (The costs of transporting gold across the Atlantic might prevent the exchange rate from returning exactly to 4.00, but it would come very close.)

Under the gold standard, gold automatically flowed out of a country when it ran a trade deficit and into a country when it ran a trade surplus. Such automatic gold flows constrained the ability of central banks to create paper money. If a central bank issued so much money that prices were driven up (relative to prices in other countries), a trade deficit would emerge. More gold would flow out of the country than into it. To protect its gold supply, the central bank would be forced to reduce the quantity of paper money, thereby reducing aggregate demand and the price level and restoring a balance of trade equilibrium. This aspect of the gold standard caused price levels to be relatively stable over many decades. Prolonged periods of high inflation were impossible under the gold standard, because the quantity of money in existence was based on a physical commodity.

Arbitragers Traders who buy and sell currencies for profit when exchange rates move away from their equilibrium values.

Fixed Exchange Rates and Macroeconomic Policy Coordination   It is impossible for nations to fix their exchange rates at constant values over long periods of time unless they are willing to coordinate economic policies. The purchasing power parity theory makes this clear. If one nation pursues a high-money-growth, high-inflation policy, while another pursues a low-money-growth, low-inflation policy, the currency of the high-inflation country will depreciate. A nation can prevent exchange-rate movements in the short run by intervening in the foreign exchange market, but to hold the exchange rate constant in the long run, it must limit its inflation rate to the rate prevailing in the other country.

A major reason for the collapse of most fixed exchange rate systems in the past has been the unwillingness of governments to coordinate their monetary and fiscal policies. Different nations have different goals and different fears that keep them from agreeing on optimal policies. Different policies lead to different real GNP and price level growth rates, as well as different real interest rates, and these factors ultimately force the exchange rate to its market level.

A Middle Course: The Dirty Float

Even when countries choose to follow a flexible exchange rate policy, they may not completely forsake intervention in the foreign exchange market. Un-

Does It Make Economic Sense?

Bolshoi Mac, or Why Does McDonald's Want Rubles Anyway?

January 31, 1990 was a big day for 30,000 residents of Moscow. They got to experience a truly American phenomenon—a meal at McDonald's. And not just any McDonald's; they ate lunch or dinner at the world's largest McDonald's. Since its opening, hundreds of thousands of Muscovites have waited in line for hours to pay 3.90 rubles for a Bolshoi Mac (*bolshoi* means *big* in Russian) and fries. By all accounts the restaurant has been a huge success.

Making the first Soviet McDonald's a success was not easy. After George Cohon, president of McDonald's of Canada, Ltd., finally obtained permission to open a restaurant in Moscow, he had to face the difficult task of acquiring high-quality inputs in the necessary quantities. McDonald's personnel soon discovered that the only way to obtain high quality inputs was to participate in their production. Two Canadian agricultural experts spent nine months teaching Russian farmers how to grow russet Burbank potatoes for french fries. McDonald's had to set up its own milk-processing plant to acquire enough pasteurized milk for milkshakes and ice cream. However, after months of preparation, McDonald's pieced together a supply network that enables the restaurant to produce meals that meet McDonald's quality standards.

After the technical difficulties were overcome, one large economic problem remained. All sales at the Moscow McDonald's are in rubles, the Soviet currency. The problem is that the ruble is inconvertible; it does not trade in the foreign exchange market. Furthermore, Soviet law prohibits taking rubles out of the Soviet Union. Therefore, profits earned by the Moscow McDonald's must be spent in the USSR. Unfortunately, the anemic Soviet economy produces very little that westerners would want to buy. This problem casts doubt on the wisdom of selling goods in the Soviet Union. Does it make economic sense?

If the Soviets had permitted McDonald's of Canada to build only one restaurant in Moscow, in which all sales were in rubles, the deal would not have made economic sense. However, the agreement between McDonald's and the Moscow city council permits McDonald's to build more restaurants in the future. McDonald's plans to eventually have twenty restaurants in Moscow. How will more restaurants help? Profits from the first Moscow McDonald's will be used to run the second McDonald's restaurant, scheduled to open in 1991. The second McDonald's will sell only in U.S. dollars. Tourists will comprise the majority of customers. The dollars earned by the second McDonald's restaurant will be the profits for the entire Moscow operation.

Until the Soviet economy begins producing products of a quality acceptable to westerners, deals such as the one worked out by McDonald's will be the only way corporations can profitably sell in the Soviet Union. Although an inconvertible currency is a major obstacle to international trade, making the ruble convertible at this time would help little because of the poor condition of the Soviet economy. Innovative financial deals can overcome inconvertibility, but extensive trade between the Soviet Union and the West requires a strong Soviet economy.

Managed (dirty) float Government intervenes to offset temporary fluctuations in the exchange rate, but allows the rate to move over time in response to long-run changes in demand and supply.

derstanding that a lack of international coordination of monetary and fiscal policies makes a fixed exchange rate system impossible, governments still may choose to use their official reserve holdings to influence the exchange rate temporarily. For example, the government may choose to offset small upward or downward movements in the exchange rate by buying or selling foreign currency, until it is sure that the upward or downward pressure represents a strong trend. Such behavior does not prevent the exchange rate from moving to its market level, but it does smooth the path of such movements. Temporary fluctuations are offset. A policy of offsetting temporary exchange rate fluctuations, while allowing the exchange rate to trend upward or downward to its market level, is called a **managed** or **dirty float**.

One major problem confronts governments attempting to follow a dirty float policy: How do you tell the difference between a temporary exchange rate fluctuation, which would soon be offset by market forces, and an exchange rate trend, which will not be offset? There is no clear answer to this question. In practice, central banks, which carry out foreign exchange transactions for their governments, use information on real income growth rates, inflation rates, and real interest rates to estimate the equilibrium value of the exchange rate. Such estimates are not precise, however, leaving a major role to be played by judgment.

If upward or downward pressure continues in the face of official intervention, the central bank eventually must realize it is fighting a market trend. When this fact becomes obvious, it must withdraw from the market and allow the exchange rate to find its new level.

Open-Economy Macroeconomics

The increasing importance of international trade to the U.S. economy is forcing Americans to come to terms with what citizens of many other nations have known for decades—what happens in the world economy affects the domestic economy. **Open-economy macroeconomics** takes explicit account of how the domestic economy is affected by international factors. Open-economy macroeconomic models take account of how changes in demands and supplies—both at home and abroad—affect net exports and capital flows. Changes in net exports and capital flows in turn affect the exchange rate, setting off further changes. The eventual effects on the price level and real GNP can be quite different from the effects predicted by a model that ignores international trade.

In the following sections we examine the effects on aggregate demand, the price level, and real GNP of four different kinds of demand and supply changes. In particular, we look at the effects of changes in money demand and supply, changes in real domestic demand (such as investment or government purchases), changes in export demand, and changes in the supply of a major import (a supply shock). We examine the effects of these demand and supply changes first in the context of a flexible exchange rate model, then for a fixed exchange rate system.

Flexible Exchange Rate System

Shifts in Money Demand and Supply To a first approximation the effects of an *increase* in money demand are equivalent to the effects of a *decrease* in the money supply. Thus, we can consider the effects of money demand and money supply shifts simultaneously. Suppose the demand for money increases. Such an increase initially drives up the interest rate. In the absence of an immediate fall in the expected inflation rate, the expected real interest rate also rises, since $r^e = i - p^e$. A higher expected real interest rate reduces aggregate demand by increasing the cost of financing capital goods and durable consumer goods. The increased demand for money also reduces consumption spending through the direct budget constraint effect: The surest way to increase money balances is to spend less on consumption goods. If prices are sticky in the short run, the decline in aggregate demand is primarily felt as a decrease in real GNP.

SECTION RECAP
In the absence of government intervention the exchange rate moves to equate the quantity of a currency demanded with the quantity supplied. Governments can maintain fixed exchange rates only by intervening to affect the demand for or supply of their currencies. Maintaining a fixed exchange rate may require a government to accept a lower real income level or a higher real interest rate than otherwise preferred.

Open-economy macroeconomics Takes account of both domestic and international transactions and linkages.

Turning to the international side of the economy, the increase in money demand puts upward pressure on the exchange rate through two channels:

1. The higher expected real interest rate makes domestic financial assets relatively more attractive. Foreigners demand more dollars with which to buy U.S. assets, while Americans supply fewer dollars to foreigners, as the demand for foreign assets declines.

2. The lower level of real GNP leads to reduced consumption spending; imports fall, reducing the supply of dollars into the foreign exchange market. A greater demand for dollars, coupled with a smaller supply of dollars, drives the exchange rate upward.

The rising exchange rate reinforces the effect of the increase in money demand. A higher exchange rate makes imported goods cheaper to Americans and U.S. goods more expensive to foreigners. Foreign goods are substituted for U.S. goods both at home and abroad, and net exports decline. This puts further downward pressure on aggregate demand and real GNP. Thus, in a flexible exchange rate system, an increase in money demand has a larger negative effect on aggregate demand than such an increase has in a closed system with no international trade.

The power of monetary policy is enhanced in a flexible exchange rate system. An increase in the money supply increases aggregate demand through the same channels as in a closed economy. As aggregate demand rises, imports increase, and the supply of dollars into the foreign exchange market rises. This drives the exchange rate downward, as pictured in Figure 6. The falling exchange rate makes imports more expensive (because, for example, a dollar buys fewer deutsche marks), while making domestically produced goods relatively more attractive to foreigners. Domestic consumers substitute domestically produced

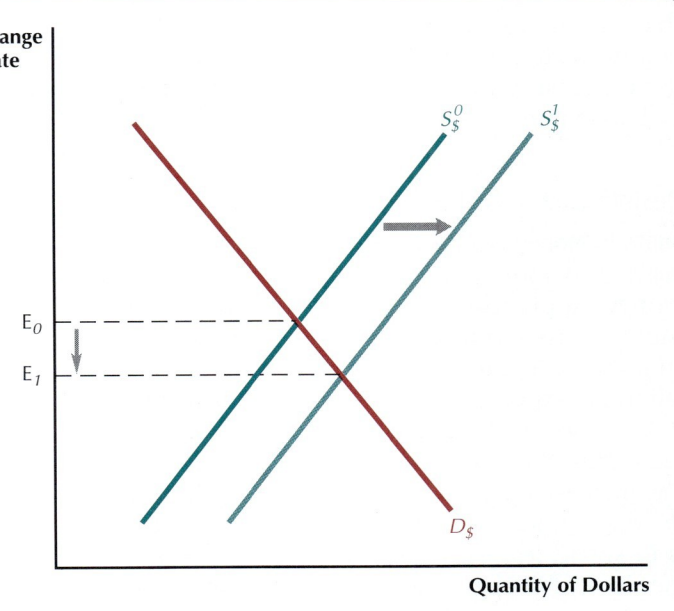

FIGURE 6
Trade deficits and exchange rate movements. A trade deficit tends to drive the exchange rate downward.

goods for imported goods, raising domestic demand, and the demand by foreigners for exports also rises. The net result is a larger increase in aggregate demand in response to a money supply increase under flexible exchange rates than in a closed economy. Monetary policy increases net exports as well as consumption and investment spending.

Shifts in Real Spending   The second case we will examine is the case of a shift in real spending, such as a change in investment spending or government purchases of goods and services. Suppose domestic investment demand falls sharply, reducing aggregate demand. Falling real income reduces the demand for imported goods. Declining imports reduce the supply of domestic currency into the foreign exchange market, putting upward pressure on the exchange rate. However, as investment demand declines, the demand for credit also declines. This pushes the expected real interest rate lower (assuming the expected inflation rate remains constant). As the expected real interest rate falls relative to foreign real interest rates, U.S. assets become relatively less attractive. The demand for dollars by foreigners falls, and the supply of dollars by Americans buying foreign assets increases, putting downward pressure on the exchange rate. Thus, the ultimate effect on the exchange rate depends on whether the effect of decreased imports dominates the effect of a falling real interest rate.

In a world of high **capital mobility**, where savings flow very quickly to the country offering the highest real rate of interest, it is plausible to assume that the real interest rate effect dominates. In this case, a decline in investment spending leads to a fall in the exchange rate. The lower exchange rate, in turn, encourages exports and discourages imports. The resulting increase in net exports partially offsets the initial decline in investment spending. Thus, in a flexible exchange rate system, changes in net exports help stabilize the economy by offsetting real domestic spending changes. Of course, if the real spending change in question is a change in government purchases, the offsetting effect of net exports makes the fiscal policy action *less powerful* than it would be in a closed economy.

Capital mobility
Ease with which capital flows from one country to another in response to changes in real interest rates.

Shifts in Export Demand   The demand for a nation's exports depends on the level of income in other countries and on the exchange rate. Suppose a recession occurs in some area of the world that normally demands a large quantity of exports from the United States. As export demand falls, net exports decline, shifting the U.S. aggregate demand curve to the left and decreasing the demand for dollars, putting downward pressure on the exchange rate. This decreases the price of U.S. exports in terms of foreign currency, making them more attractive to foreigners, and raises the price of imported goods, making them less attractive to Americans. The initial decline in exports, due to lower foreign incomes, is partially offset by the lower exchange rate. Imports of foreign goods also fall. Thus, the decline in the exchange rate helps to stabilize aggregate demand by moderating the fall in net exports.

Import Supply Shocks   The fourth and final situation we will examine is that of an import supply shock. Assume that the good in question is a crucial import, such as oil. When the supply of the import is reduced, its price rises sharply. The money value of imports rises, causing net exports to fall. Aggregate demand shifts to the left. When higher import prices affect production costs, the domestic short-run aggregate supply curve also shifts to the left, raising the price level and reducing real income further.

The increased supply of dollars into the foreign exchange market that accompanies the higher dollar volume of imports drives the exchange rate down. This favors exports and reduces other (nonoil) imports, partially offsetting the decline in aggregate demand. Thus, flexible exchange rates have a modest cushioning effect when an economy is hit by a major import supply shock.

Fixed Exchange Rate System

The effects of demand and supply changes in a fixed exchange rate system can be very different than the effects of the same demand and supply changes in a flexible rate system. The reason is simple: In a fixed exchange rate system, the exchange rate cannot move to reestablish the balance of payments. Instead, the government must make policy adjustments to maintain international equilibrium. We examine the same four demand and supply changes for the fixed exchange rate system that we examined for the flexible rate system.

Shifts in Money Demand and Supply   Once again suppose that the demand for money increases. Aggregate demand declines, both because of the budget constraint effect and because the real interest rate rises. The higher real interest rate attracts capital from other countries and puts upward pressure on the exchange rate. To maintain a fixed exchange rate, the Federal Reserve must offset the upward pressure on the exchange rate. It does so by increasing the supply of dollars into the foreign exchange market. This has two effects:

1. Because the exchange rate does not rise, consumers do not have the incentive to substitute imported goods for domestically produced goods; the negative effect of a higher exchange rate on net exports disappears.
2. As some of the money pumped into the foreign exchange market finds its way into the U.S. economy, the domestic money supply increases. This partially satisfies the increased demand for money, so that the negative effect on aggregate demand of increased money demand is smaller.

Thus, *relative to the flexible exchange rate case, aggregate demand is less affected by a change in the demand for money when the central bank maintains a fixed exchange rate.*

This relative stability in response to money demand shifts carries over to the effect of changes in the money supply. The Federal Reserve loses its monetary policy flexibility under a fixed exchange rate standard. If the exchange rate is hovering around the official rate, called the **par value**, the Federal Reserve cannot undertake policies that would drive the rate up or down significantly, even if policymakers are not satisfied with the behavior of the economy.

For example, suppose the exchange rate is at its par value, but the economy is stagnant. Such a situation is shown in Figure 7 (a). If the Federal Reserve increases the money supply to encourage more spending and push real GNP back to the natural level, it will also affect the equilibrium exchange rate. An increase in the money supply reduces the real interest rate (assuming expected inflation remains constant), encouraging capital to flow abroad. Foreigners pull funds out of the U.S. market, and U.S. savers purchase foreign financial assets. This puts downward pressure on the exchange rate. Furthermore, as

Par value
Official exchange rate in a fixed exchange rate system.

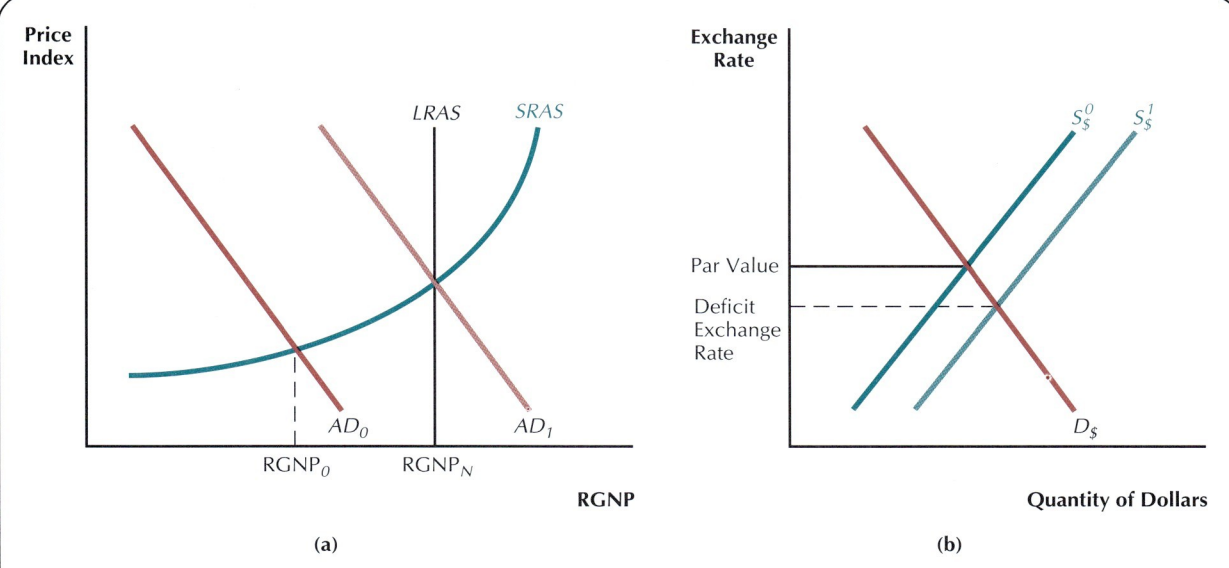

FIGURE 7
Monetary policy in a fixed exchange rate system. If the central bank increases the money supply, driving aggregate demand up to AD₁ and real GNP up to RGNP_N, the trade balance will move into deficit. The supply of dollars will increase, putting downward pressure on the exchange rate. This may prevent policymakers from pursuing the expansive policy.

aggregate demand increases and real GNP rises, the demand for imports also increases. The supply of dollars into the foreign exchange market increases as imports rise [Figure 7 (b)]. Thus, in this case an expansive monetary policy is inconsistent with maintaining the exchange rate at its par value.

Shifts in Real Spending We saw that a flexible exchange rate moderates the effect on aggregate demand of a decline in investment spending. Not surprisingly, maintaining a fixed exchange rate increases the amount by which aggregate demand falls when investment spending declines.

When investment spending declines, so does the demand for credit. The real interest rate falls, reducing the demand for U.S. assets. Consequently, the demand for dollars falls and the supply of dollars increases, putting downward pressure on the exchange rate. To maintain a fixed exchange rate the Federal Reserve must increase the demand for dollars or reduce their supply. It does this by using its official reserves to purchase dollars in the foreign exchange market.

When the Federal Reserve buys dollars, the dollars disappear from the world economy. The effect is equivalent to an open market sale of bonds by the Federal Reserve. The U.S. money supply begins to shrink, putting upward pressure on the real interest rate and ending the downward pressure on the exchange rate. Thus, maintaining a fixed exchange rate in the face of a decline in investment spending ultimately requires the Federal Reserve to contract the money supply. Aggregate demand thus falls by a larger amount than it would if the exchange rate were flexible.

Fiscal policy is very powerful in a fixed exchange rate system, since any changes in government spending or taxes must be accompanied by complementary changes in the money supply. It should be noted, however, that the long-run output effects of fiscal policy are still constrained by the economy's natural output level, just as they are in a closed-economy model.

Shifts in Export Demand A decline in the demand for U.S. exports reduces the demand for dollars, putting downward pressure on the exchange rate. To maintain the official exchange rate, the Federal Reserve must use its official reserve asset holdings to increase the demand for dollars. Such an action ultimately reduces the U.S. money supply, thus reinforcing the negative effect on aggregate demand of the decline in exports. Just as in the case of an investment spending decline, maintaining a fixed exchange rate in the face of declining export demand requires policymakers to reinforce the effect of the original demand shift.

Import Supply Shocks Under any exchange rate system, an increase in the price of a vital import, such as oil, increases both the dollar value of imports and the supply of dollars to the foreign exchange market. Downward pressure on the exchange rate results. To maintain the official exchange rate the Federal Reserve must purchase dollars in the foreign exchange market. As we have seen, this ultimately reduces the domestic money supply, increasing the real interest rate and putting downward pressure on aggregate demand. This magnifies the effects of the supply shock. *Maintaining a fixed exchange rate in the face of an import supply shock reinforces the effect of the shock on domestic real GNP.*

Comparing Flexible and Fixed Exchange Rate Systems

Table 2 summarizes the results of the two preceding sections. As the table shows, a flexible exchange rate system stabilizes domestic real GNP better than a fixed exchange rate system for all types of *real* demand and supply changes: domestic spending, export demand, and import supply. However, a fixed exchange rate system offsets the effects on real GNP of money demand and

> **SECTION RECAP**
> The international sector can magnify or reduce the size of a shock to the economy, depending on the source of the shock and on the exchange rate regime in place. A flexible exchange rate tends to magnify the effects of monetary shocks, but modifies the effects of real shocks. A fixed exchange rate modifies the effects of monetary shocks, but magnifies the effects of spending and supply shocks.

TABLE 2

Comparison of flexible and fixed exchange rate systems

Short-Run Effect on Real GNP of a Change In	Flexible ER	Fixed ER
Money demand or supply	Large	Small
Real domestic spending	Small	Large
Export demand	Small	Large
Import supply	Small	Large

Note: The table records relative effects. For example, the effect of a change in money demand on real GNP in a flexible exchange rate system is large *relative to* the effect of an identical change in a fixed rate system.

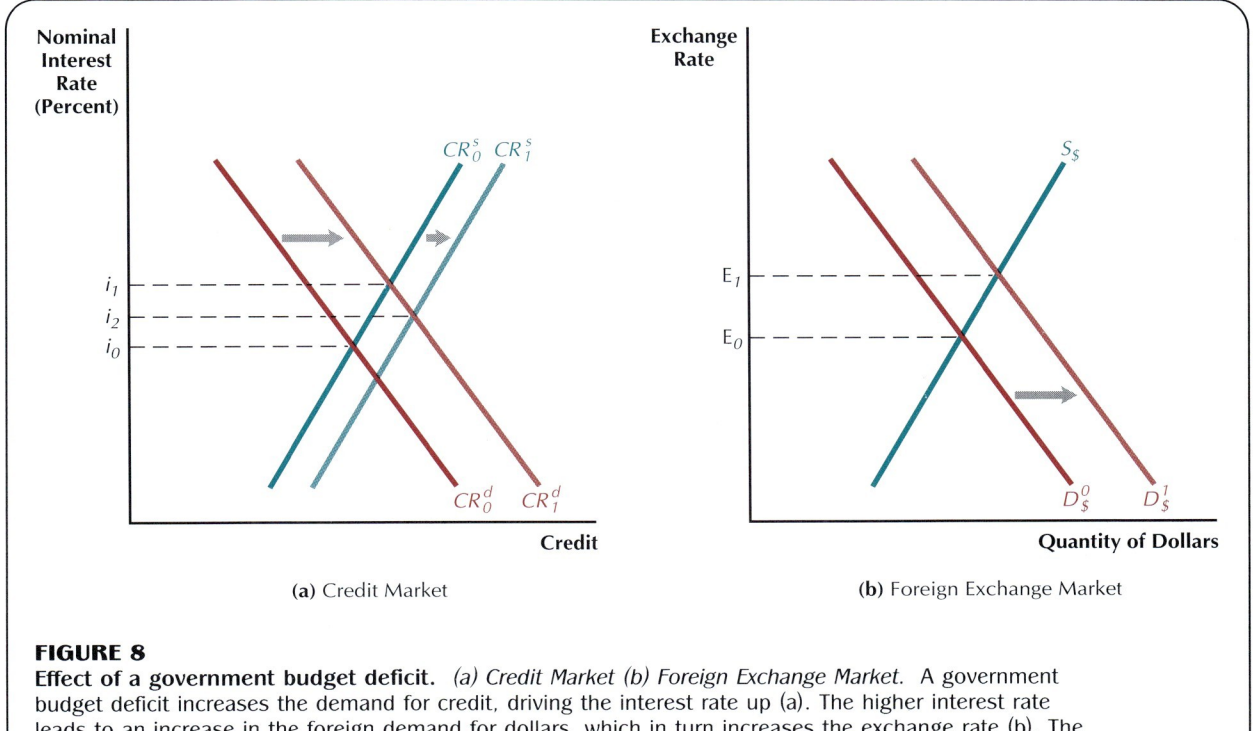

FIGURE 8
Effect of a government budget deficit. *(a) Credit Market (b) Foreign Exchange Market.* A government budget deficit increases the demand for credit, driving the interest rate up (a). The higher interest rate leads to an increase in the foreign demand for dollars, which in turn increases the exchange rate (b). The inflow of dollars increases the supply of credit (to CR_1^s in (a)), moderating the increase in the interest rate.

money supply changes better than a flexible rate system does. Thus, one system is not more stable than the other in all circumstances.

Government Budget Deficits in a Flexible Exchange Rate System

In the preceding sections we examined the economy's response to both monetary and real spending changes. Another type of change that can have major effects on the economy is a capital-flow shock. A **capital-flow shock** is a sudden flow of money into or out of an economy. Capital-flow shocks can have major real effects, positively or negatively affecting the level of real GNP and employment. In the 1980s, the U.S. economy experienced a major inflow of funds. The inflow appeared to be an important factor contributing to the slow aggregate demand growth prevailing from 1985 through 1987. Most economists believe that the capital inflow is linked to the size of U.S. government budget deficits. If so, this provides an example of the limits the international economy places on fiscal policy even under a flexible exchange rate system.

The connection between the government budget deficit and the state of the economy runs through the real interest rate. Large budget deficits in the 1980s forced the government to borrow more in the credit market, pushing up the demand for credit and the real interest rate, as shown in Figure 8 (a). Since the inflation rate fell for several years, the increase in the nominal interest rate also increased the real rate. Foreign financial investors responded to the

Capital-flow shock
Sudden flow of money into or out of the economy to purchase financial assets.

Why the Disagreement?

Selling America

During the 1980s the United States ran the largest trade deficits in its history. The deficits were financed by foreigners who acquired hundreds of billions of dollars worth of U.S. assets. The inflow of foreign savings enabled business investment to grow at the same time that government budget deficits rose to record levels. Had foreign savings not been available, either government borrowing would have crowded out billions of dollars of investment spending or the government would have been forced to cut expenditures or raise taxes to bring its budget closer to balance. In this light, many people see the inflow of foreign funds as a very positive thing. In essence, foreigners financed the U.S. economic expansion of the 1980s.

However, not everyone is happy about the inflow of foreign funds. Such critics as New York investment banker Felix Rohatyn and Missouri Congressman Richard Gephardt have argued that the capital inflows of the 1980s are creating a bleak future for Americans, who will find themselves increasingly under the economic control of foreigners. Both supporters and critics of foreign capital inflows are aware of what has been happening. Why the disagreement?

The increasing criticism of U.S. trade deficits and foreign capital inflows reflects the fear that crucial U.S. industries will fall under the control of foreigners. In the late 1980s, foreign investment in the United States turned away from U.S. government bonds, the preferred asset for many years, to U.S. business assets. Foreign acquisitions of U.S. businesses averaged $10.5 billion per year from 1980 through 1985, then jumped to $24.5 billion in 1986 and $40.4 billion in 1987. The sudden preference for business assets reflects, to some degree, an attempt by foreign investors to protect themselves against U.S. inflation. The real value of bonds is much more likely to be reduced by inflation than is the real value of businesses.

Fueling the fears of foreign takeover is the "fact" that the United States has become a net debtor nation: Foreigners own more U.S. assets than Americans own foreign assets. In 1982, U.S. assets abroad exceeded foreign assets in the United States by about $137 billion; by the end of 1987, foreign holdings of U.S. assets exceeded American holdings of assets abroad by $420 billion. However, these figures do not reflect the true value of holdings, since earnings on foreign assets owned by Americans still exceeded earnings on foreign assets in the United States by $4.78 billion in 1988. American holdings abroad are worth much more than the officially reported figure. Nevertheless, the trend is clear—American companies are being sold to foreigners at an increasing rate.

Critics of the selling-America trend argue that transferring the management decisions of large U.S. companies to foreigners leaves the United States in a precarious position. Foreign managers, making decisions in the best interests of their multinational corporations, could throw American workers out of jobs or otherwise adversely affect the U.S. economy. (It is ironic that foreigners have made the same arguments about U.S. ownership of foreign firms in the past.) The critics are urging Congress to pass laws limiting the share of foreign ownership of firms in important industries.

Many observers believe the recent criticism of foreign purchases of U.S. firms is simply misplaced. When a U.S. corporation purchases a foreign firm, it does so for one reason: profit. U.S. corporations buy foreign firms when they believe a foreign subsidiary will enable them to produce and sell in a foreign market at a lower price. Similarly, foreign corporations purchase U.S. firms as a way to lower the costs of producing and selling in the United States. Attributing anything more than simple economic motives to such purchases is naive: *Japan* didn't buy Rockefeller Center; *Mitsubishi* did.

History shows that the U.S. economy was largely built with foreign capital. The United States was a net debtor nation throughout the nineteenth century—exactly the period when the United States was becoming an economic giant. When foreigners buy U.S. companies, they have a stake in the U.S. economy. A healthy economy benefits not only Americans, but also the foreigners who own businesses in the United States. It is hard to see how such an arrangement harms Americans.

relatively high U.S. real interest rate by purchasing more U.S. financial assets. To acquire U.S. assets, however, they first had to acquire dollars. Thus, the demand for dollars rose, pushing the exchange rate upward as in Figure 8 (b).

The inflow of capital into the United States had several effects. First, it increased the supply of credit [as shown in Figure 8 (a)], maintaining the U.S. interest rate at a lower level than it would have been without foreign savings. The moderation of the interest rate increase helped to reduce the crowding out of domestic investment spending. However, this beneficial effect was offset by the effect of the higher exchange rate on net exports. The higher exchange rate reduced the dollar price of imported goods significantly. U.S. imports rose, while U.S. exports, now higher priced in terms of foreign currency, fell. Net exports plunged sharply into deficit. The trade deficit restrained aggregate demand growth, slowing the recovery from the 1981–1982 recession.

Earlier in this chapter we emphasized the fact that any trade flow is accompanied by a financial flow in the opposite direction. In that discussion we focused on financing the trade of goods. In the 1980s, however, it is probably more accurate to say that *the flow of goods financed the flow of capital.* If foreign investors want dollars in order to purchase dollar-denominated financial assets, how do they obtain them? The natural way is to sell their goods to Americans, obtaining dollars in exchange. This seems to be what happened in the 1980s. The demand for dollars was so strong that it drove the exchange rate up to extremely high levels. This encouraged Americans to import huge quantities of foreign goods, supplying dollars in the process. It also discouraged the foreign consumption of American-made products, leaving foreigners with dollars for financial investment. The result was a sharp decline in U.S. net exports and stagnant aggregate demand.

If this is an accurate description of the situation faced by the U.S. economy in the 1980s, the strongest case against large government budget deficits may be the international case. As noted in our earlier discussion of government budget deficits, evidence that the budget deficit has been harmful to the domestic economy is scarce. However, the absence of large-scale crowding out of domestic investment and consumer durable spending may be due to large capital inflows, which held the interest rate down somewhat. These same capital inflows increased the exchange rate and reduced net exports. Thus, in effect, the budget deficit crowded out exports and domestic goods that compete with imports rather than crowding out investment spending.

SECTION RECAP
The large budget deficits run by the U.S. government in the 1980s may have contributed to the increase in the U.S. trade deficit in the early and mid-1980s. By driving up the U.S. real interest rate, the budget deficit may have induced a capital inflow, which drove up the exchange rate. The high exchange rate made imports cheaper and U.S. exports more expensive.

Summary

International trade is not carried out through barter arrangements. Money flows offset the flow of goods and services. Since different nations use different currencies, a **foreign exchange market** arose in which one currency may be traded for another.

A nation's **balance of payments** reflects its international budget constraint. Inflows of funds must equal outflows of funds. A current account surplus or deficit is accompanied by a capital outflow or inflow, respectively.

The way the balance of payments balances both affects and is affected by the **exchange rate.** The demand for a currency depends on other nations' real income levels, foreign price levels relative to the domestic price level, and foreign real interest rates relative to the domestic real interest rate. The supply of a currency in the foreign exchange market depends upon domestic real income and relative price and real interest rate levels. An increase in foreign real income or price levels, or a relative increase in the domestic real interest rate tends to push a nation's exchange rate upward. An increase in the domestic real income or price levels or a decline in the ratio of domestic to foreign real estate rates tends to push the exchange rate downward.

Exchange rates will **float** to clear the foreign exchange market unless governments **intervene** by altering demand or supply conditions. Governments can maintain **fixed exchange rates** by using their official reserve holdings to affect currency demand or supply in the short run and by using monetary and fiscal policy to manipulate aggregate demand in the long run. They must be willing to accept changes in real GNP, prices, and real interest rates to protect a fixed exchange rate.

The macroeconomy reacts differently to demand and supply changes depending upon whether the exchange rate is fixed or flexible. Internal money demand and supply changes have a larger impact on aggregate demand if the exchange rate is flexible. Changes in real domestic spending, export demand, and import supply all have a smaller effect on real GNP and the price level when the exchange rate is flexible than when it is fixed.

In the 1980s, the U.S. government budget deficit might have been the major factor generating a large trade deficit. By driving up the real interest rate, the deficit made U.S. financial assets very attractive to foreigners. They demanded dollars with which to purchase these assets. This drove the exchange rate very high, which encouraged imports and discouraged exports.

Questions for Thought

Knowledge Questions

1. Define the following terms: *exchange rate, fixed exchange rate system, and intervention.*
2. How would the following factors affect the demand for or supply of dollars in the foreign exchange market? (Indicate whether demand or supply is increased or decreased.)
   a. An increased U.S. demand for Volvos.
   b. An increase in the British real rate of interest.
   c. A sharp reduction in the price of OPEC oil.
   d. A decision by the Italian government to buy IBM computers.
3. What is a *dirty float*?
4. What is a capital inflow? Give an example of a specific form it might take.

Application Questions

5. Suppose the real interest rate in the United States falls relative to the real rate in France, while the real income level in the United States rises relative to the French RGNP level. What will happen to the franc–dollar exchange rate? Why?

6. The U.S. government wants to maintain a fixed exchange rate with the Japanese yen of 175 yen per dollar. Suppose the United States runs a trade deficit with Japan. What could the U.S. government do to protect the exchange rate in the face of the trade deficit? Will the policy actions have any effect on the future size of the trade deficit?
7. Suppose the United States and Germany want to maintain a fixed deutsche mark–dollar exchange rate of DM2.25 = $1. In the United States the inflation rate has been running at about 6 percent; in Germany it has been running at a rate of 3 percent. What impact will this have on the exchange rate? What will it force the governments of the United States and/or Germany to do?
8. Describe the process whereby an economy adjusts to an increase in the internal demand for money under flexible and fixed exchange rates (two cases). In which case is the economy more stable? Why?
9. You are the economic czar of Placidity, a peaceful land that experiences almost no internal economic shocks. However, your economy is buffeted frequently by external shocks to export demand and import supply. What exchange rate system would be best for your domain? Why?

Synthesis Questions

10. Germany and Italy are both members of the European Economic Community (EEC). EEC members attempt to maintain fixed exchange rates relative to each other. The hyperinflation of the 1920s left the Germans with an abiding fear of inflation. They refuse to allow their money supply to grow rapidly enough to be inflationary. The Italians, on the other hand, are more concerned with chronic unemployment. They are known for high money supply growth rates. What problems do you think these tendencies create for the two EEC members?
11. The large U.S. government budget deficits of the 1980s may have been related to the large trade deficits experienced by the United States. What is the alleged connection between the two? Some economists argue that the budget deficit is not what caused the trade deficit. They contend that political and economic instability in many less-developed countries (LDCs), particularly Latin American countries, led to the U.S. trade deficit. The debt problems of LDCs also contributed. How do you think these two factors could have caused the U.S. trade deficit? (Note: You must be resourceful to answer this question. The issue is not mentioned in the chapter.)

OVERVIEW

Comparative Economic Systems: Theory and Evidence

This text has focused on markets as the means of organizing economic behavior and allocating scarce resources. We have assumed that individuals respond to market incentives in predictable ways, and we have shown how the market transmits information and coordinates the decisions made by millions of individuals. Though concentrating on market behavior, we have noted how government can influence market outcomes with its supply and demand capabilities, or how it can override the market altogether. The U.S. economy is a mixed economy, leaving most decisions to the market, but reserving some decisions for government policymakers.

In this chapter our attention turns to alternative systems for organizing economic behavior. Since we need a reference point for our discussion, we begin by briefly restating the major problems any economy must solve. We then examine how market and socialist economies solve these problems. In a pure socialist economy, the government owns the means of production and makes all major economic decisions. Not surprisingly, the resulting solutions to the major economic problems differ greatly from those produced by a market economy. We end our comparison of market and

socialist economies by assessing the relative strengths and weaknesses of the two types of economic systems.

Few real-world economies fit into neat analytical boxes. Different nations have combined elements of pure market and pure socialist economies in very different ways, with results that have varied from success to complete failure. We examine several different economies in an effort to understand the combinations of market and government decision making that seem to work well or not so well. We also examine the difficulties faced by countries seeking to turn from socialism to the market.

CHAPTER 37

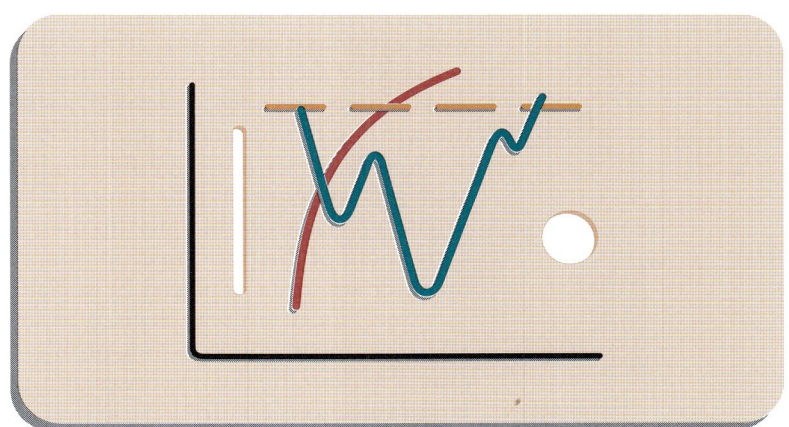

Learning Objectives
After reading and studying this chapter, you will be able to:

1. State the major questions that any economy must answer.
2. Explain how a market economy answers the major economic questions.
3. Explain how a socialist economy answers the major economic questions.
4. Compare how well market and socialist economies perform in answering the major economic questions.
5. List the different combinations of market and socialist elements that exist in actual economies today.
6. Discuss the major strengths and weaknesses of mixed economies and assess why they succeed or fail.

Major Problems Facing Any Economy

Most of the problems that must be addressed by any economy fall into three major categories. We call the following three questions the *major problems of economics*.

1. What should be produced, and in what quantity?
2. How should these goods be produced?
3. How should the product (or income from production) be distributed? (Who reaps the benefits of production?)

Market and Socialist Responses to the Major Economic Problems

Markets evolved over time as people were freed from the constraints of feudalism to pursue their own interests. The rise of the market economy enabled talented entrepreneurs to become very wealthy at a time when most people were extremely poor. The great disparities in wealth between capitalists and workers led social critics two centuries ago to call for redistribution of property and income. The *utopian socialists,* as they are now called, attempted to persuade the wealthy to voluntarily share their wealth with the less fortunate.

Karl Marx set the stage for modern socialism in a number of books that analyzed and criticized the capitalist system. He harbored no illusions that the privileged classes would give up their comfortable existence voluntarily for the betterment of the poor. Instead, Marx argued that capitalism would inevitably break down, to be replaced by socialism and eventually communism.

Since socialism was devised as an alternative to the market economy, it addresses the major economic problems differently than does the market economy. We examine the responses of market and socialist economies to the three major questions in turn.

What, and How Much, to Produce

Consumer sovereignty
Idea that consumers ultimately determine what is produced and in what quantity by buying what they like and refusing to buy what they don't like.

Markets are institutions that bring together consumers and producers. Markets function properly when they provide producers with incentives to respond to the desires of consumers. In a pure market economy, consumers ultimately determine what is produced. **Consumer sovereignty** is a phrase that implies that only those producers who satisfy the desires of consumers will be successful. Provided alternatives, consumers will purchase those goods and services that best satisfy their desires. Ultimately, consumers determine what is produced in a market economy.

The type and quantity of goods actually produced depend on the amount consumers are willing to pay to obtain the goods and the opportunity cost of producing the goods. Market demand and supply curves carry this information. A good is produced to the point where its marginal benefit equals its marginal opportunity cost. At this point the maximum price consumers are willing to pay for an additional unit of the good equals the minimum price producers are willing to accept. The market price both rations the good to the consumers who value it most highly and provides information to producers on how highly consumers value the good.

Pure socialism requires state ownership of the means of production and state determination of what and how much to produce. Marx argued that capitalist production is wasteful and destructive. Producers base their production on estimates of demand, which are often wrong. Resources are wasted on products no one wants, at least at a price equal to their cost of production. Furthermore, workers are controlled by the production process, becoming slaves to capital. Replacing private choice with social choice rationalizes the production process. So the first major difference between pure market and pure socialist societies is who determines what is produced. The consumer is not sovereign in a socialist state, and the individual is viewed as secondary to society.

Having decided what to produce, the government of a socialist state usually issues a **production plan**, which may run for several years. The plan sets production goals for each sector of the economy, detailing how each sector's production is to be allocated across particular factories or farms.

Production plan Government plan setting production goals for a command economy.

When the idea of production plans was first introduced, the difficulty of large-scale planning was not appreciated. This difficulty arises from two sources:

1. Coordinating production: Many firms use the outputs of other firms as inputs in their own production processes. What matches the outputs of some firms with the input needs of other firms?
2. Providing incentives: How can the cooperation of managers and workers be ensured?

The first issue was brought to the fore by Austrian economist Ludwig von Mises. In 1922, Mises contended that without money, markets, and a price system, a socialist government would have no way of coordinating an economic system of any substantial size. The individuals making production decisions would lack the information necessary to make rational calculations. Producers might be able to produce goods without wasting resources in the production process, but they would inevitably produce the wrong quantities, ultimately wasting huge amounts of resources.

The socialist solution to the problem, developed by Oskar Lange and Abba Lerner, was to propose that the government set prices, to which individual managers would respond. The dictated prices would reflect the government's economic and social priorities. Managers would use these prices in determining how goods should be produced and in what quantities.

Though *market socialism* seems to get around the economic coordination problem, Mises and his student Friedrich Hayek argued that the solution was illusory. Market prices carry information about the true opportunity costs society attaches to goods and services. Opportunity costs change continuously in response to changes in resource availability and demand conditions. For government planners to set prices that accurately reflect true opportunity costs is, in a practical sense, impossible. No small group of planners could ever discover all the information required to plan a large (or even a relatively small) economy, much less process the information correctly if they had it.

Doubts may also be raised about the incentive structure of a socialist state. What incentives do workers or managers have to be efficient if their incomes are not affected by their performance? Socialist states have attempted to overcome the incentive problem by equating work effort with patriotism or socialist fervor and by threatening the use of, or actually using, force. Neither solution has worked well. Incentives remain a problem in socialist economies, which have never discovered any good alternatives to market incentives.

How to Produce the Desired Goods

The drive to maximize profits determines how goods are produced in a market economy. Profits — the difference between revenue and costs — are income to the owners of firms. Firms maximize the profits earned at a particular output level by minimizing the costs of production. It is in the best interests of the owners of firms to produce efficiently, using the production techniques and the combination of inputs that minimize costs.

In a competitive market economy, input prices reflect the social opportunity costs of the inputs. By minimizing their own production costs, firms also minimize the social costs of production (assuming no external costs or benefits exist). Since firms must buy inputs in markets, resources are used where they are valued most highly. Resource owners reap the greatest rewards from selling their resources to those who value them the most. Thus, market economies, unhindered by social goals, tend to be efficient.

The managers of socialist firms lack the profit incentive. They do not benefit from minimizing production costs. However, the problem of determining how to produce goods in a socialist economy goes beyond incentives. Unless the managers of firms have correct information on the social opportunity costs of inputs, they cannot minimize the social cost of production, even if they are motivated to do so. To minimize social costs, managers must be provided with price information that reflects the true opportunity costs of the resources used in production. If the prices provided by planners do not reflect true opportunity costs — and the Mises critique suggests they will not — managers cannot determine the most efficient techniques and input combinations.

How Output Is Distributed

Willingness to pay the market price determines who receives the goods and services produced in a market economy. In a perfectly competitive market, only willingness and ability to pay matter. Similarly, the distribution of income from production depends on the productivity of factors of production. In perfectly competitive markets, with so many producers and consumers that no single market participant has any effect on the market price, income from production is distributed according to marginal productivity. For example, the wage rate equals the marginal product of labor, what the final unit of labor contributes to the production process, times the price of the product being produced. The return to capital, what a machine or a building earns for its owner, equals the marginal product of capital. All income is paid out in proportion to its contribution to the value of production.

Though distortions caused by market power (the ability to affect the market price) exist, the bottom line in a market economy still is that most individuals share in the production of the economy *approximately* according to their contribution. Thus, wide variation in incomes may exist, especially since some people may be unable to contribute to the production process due to physical or mental disabilities or age. Large variations in income or significant numbers of people with little or no income may be viewed by society as morally wrong. In such a case, society may act to *redistribute* income through private organizations (such as charities and churches) or through government. The market economy itself does not provide for the unproductive; society must arrange for their support through private or public institutions.

Some income disparities serve a useful economic function. Such disparities provide the incentive to obtain training or education to enter high-wage occupations or to relocate to areas where labor is relatively scarce. They provide the incentive to invest in high-profit industries. Such incentives help to balance and coordinate the economy over time, pulling resources into relatively highly valued uses and out of less-valued uses. This explains why a tradeoff between equality and efficiency often exists. *Removing disparities removes the incentives that promote efficiency.*

Socialism arose in response to the apparent inhumanity and inequities of capitalism. Socialist thinkers contend that capitalism distributes goods inequitably. Socialist economies replace the impersonal forces of the market with planned distribution of output or of the income earned from production. Equality — of outcome rather than opportunity — is stressed.

Pure socialist economies achieve the desired distribution of income by directly setting wages and prices. This, to a significant degree, determines the incomes of workers, since there is little income from capital in socialist economies. Another way to shape the income distribution is through the powers of taxation and spending. Many socialist nations tax workers heavily, while providing a wide range of social services "free" to all citizens.

> **SECTION RECAP**
> In market economies, consumers determine what will be produced through their purchases, managers decide how to produce by comparing the costs of alternatives, and the market determines the distribution of income according to the value of inputs. In socialist economies, planners decide what will be produced and how it will be produced, and the government distributes income either directly or through taxes and subsidies.

Comparing Market and Socialist Economies

The discussion of how market and socialist economies answer the three major economic questions has laid the groundwork for comparing the two types of economies. Once again, we will proceed question by question.

What, and How Much, to Produce

If economic efficiency is the criterion by which we judge an economic system, the market economy wins hands down. Efficiency is the driving force of the market economy. Socialism arose largely as a method of promoting other social goals. Large-scale planning is carried out in such countries as the Soviet Union, China, and some Eastern European countries, but these economies are notoriously inefficient. The absence of a price system prevents the attainment of economic efficiency, while poor incentive structures lead to poor performance by managers and workers.

Many socialist thinkers want to broaden the definition of efficiency, however. They perceive market economies to be wasteful and inefficient in a large social sense. They believe that Madison Avenue advertising creates needs and drives consumers to demand goods that do not really make them better off. Capitalism promotes materialism and drives people to work harder and longer to acquire more and more.

Traditional economic theory (market variety) has ignored such concerns, although some of the criticisms may contain more truth than many economists want to admit. More goods and services and an empty, decaying culture are not necessarily inconsistent. However, economists concerned with individual freedom are quick to ask another question: If individuals, through the market, are not allowed to make their own decisions about what to consume and where and how much to work, who will make these choices for them? Government? Do government officials really know what is best for me better than I know?

At this broader, cultural level, questions of individual freedom versus social responsibility become paramount. A market economy allows individuals to choose the careers they wish to pursue, the lifestyles they like, and where they want to live. Few restrictions are placed on choices, so long as they do not deprive other people of the right to make similar choices. *Socialism must restrict individual freedom to promote equality.* The importance one attaches to individual freedom goes a long way toward determining one's attitude toward the market.

How to Produce the Desired Goods

Again, on a strict economic efficiency criterion, the market economy is far superior to a socialist system. The price system allows producers to choose the production process with the lowest opportunity cost. However, socialists criticize the narrow concept of efficiency at this point too. Many socialist thinkers are more concerned about providing adequate jobs than about the quantity of output actually produced, above some acceptable minimum. They argue that managers ought to take more than opportunity costs into account in choosing production techniques. For example, a relatively more costly labor-intensive production process might be preferred to a more efficient capital-intensive process if unemployment were a major problem.

Supporters of the market counter this argument by noting that profits are the driving force of **entrepreneurship**, the creative management of production. Entrepreneurs spur economic growth and development by seeking to meet demands, or sometimes by producing goods they believe *will* be demanded if provided. Forcing them to consider social goals in their production plans deprives them of the incentive that drives the economy. According to many economists, dampening the entrepreneurial spirit creates unemployment by reducing the willingness of companies to take risks and expand production.[1]

Entrepreneurship Creative management of production.

How Output Is Distributed

Socialist thinking has scored its greatest victory in the area of income distribution.[2] Nearly every developed economy in the world has chosen to use the powers of government to create a more equal distribution of income than the market would generate if unhindered. To be sure, the arguments in favor of income redistribution in market economies are usually not couched in socialist terminology, but the effect is much the same. Government overrides the market to some extent in determining how income is distributed.

Whether government redistribution is good or bad depends upon one's views on equality, the availability of economic opportunities for all, wealth, and poverty. It is clear that the consensus in the United States, Western Europe,

---

[1] This is one the themes of George Gilder's *The Spirit of Enterprise* (New York: Simon and Schuster, 1984).

[2] Assuming that most goods are sold, rather than directly rationed by government, leads directly to the conclusion that the distribution of output will closely resemble the distribution of the income earned by producing the output.

and the British Commonwealth nations is that everyone is entitled to a minimum living standard, the level of which varies from country to country.

Differences in the degree of income redistribution across countries allow us to assess the effects of welfare systems on the economy. The amount of income redistribution that can take place without a perverse incentive structure developing is clearly limited. If the average welfare recipient is as well off as the average manual laborer, where is the incentive to take a relatively low-paying job? And how is a welfare state to be financed? Welfare programs are very costly, requiring high tax rates. High taxes reduce the incentive to work or invest, because most of the fruits of labor or risk taking go to government, not to the individual. Thus, welfare states may be plagued with high absenteeism and low productivity among workers.

The ironic thing about welfare programs is that, when taken beyond some acceptable point, they may help create the very problems they were intended to remedy. High welfare benefits may generate unemployment. Free medical care may cause individuals to become careless about protecting their own health. Free housing may cause the occupants to allow their houses or apartments to deteriorate. In short, divorcing individual income and benefits from individual behavior creates a host of problems. We may not like to admit it, but most people pursue their own personal interests, even to the extent of taking advantage of the system set up for their benefit. The trick for a humane government is to design a welfare system that takes care of the needy without creating the incentive to become needy.

SECTION RECAP
Market economies are much more efficient than socialist economies both in the sense of producing what consumers want and in the sense of producing with little waste. The distribution of income in market economies, unless altered by government, tends to be very unequal. Socialist governments may attempt to equalize incomes through various policies.

A Continuum of Market Types

Between the polar extremes of pure capitalism and pure socialism lies a continuum of possible market types. A nation need not commit itself to an all-or-nothing approach to either capitalism or socialism, though the results of mixing the two systems may not always be desirable. To illustrate the many possible economic arrangements that can arise in the real world, we will place seven different economies on three different capitalist–socialist scales. These three scales represent (1) the degree of state ownership of the means of production (the traditional definition of socialism), (2) the degree of state planning of the economy, and (3) the degree of income distribution carried out by government.

State Ownership of the Means of Production

State ownership of the resources and capital used in the production of goods and services ranges from near zero in our prototype capitalist economy, Hong Kong, to well over 90 percent in the communist nations of China and the Soviet Union. Figure 1 presents the ownership continuum for seven representative economies.

The developing country (colony) of Hong Kong has been one of the success stories of the past three decades. Hong Kong's phenomenal economic growth has been spurred by private entrepreneurship, since the government has taken a very **laissez faire** attitude, providing an environment with low taxes and minimal government involvement in the economy. The government owns almost none of the means of production in Hong Kong. At the other end of

Laissez faire
Literally, "let them do it"; an environment with minimal government intervention.

```
Hong Kong        Sweden          Yugoslavia     Poland
|————————————————————————————————————————————————————|
Private    United States    France              USSR      State
```

FIGURE 1
Ownership of the means of production. The Soviet state owns nearly all the means of production in the Soviet Union. Farms are largely privately owned in Poland and Yugoslavia. The French government owns a number of large companies. Most property is privately owned in Sweden, the United States, and Hong Kong.

the spectrum lies the USSR, where the government owns almost all productive property. Peasants own most of the farmland in both Poland and Yugoslavia, and private ownership of all types of businesses is growing rapidly in Poland.

The French government participates heavily in the economy through its ownership of several large corporations and banking enterprises. Over 90 percent of productive property is privately owned in Sweden, and an even larger percentage is privately owned in the United States.

State Planning of the Economy

The degree of state ownership of productive resources and capital does not necessarily indicate the degree of government involvement in the direction of production. Property may be state owned but privately managed, or the government may, through price controls, tax policies, or direct intervention, heavily influence the uses to which privately owned resources are put. Figure 2 illustrates the planning continuum for our seven representative economies.

The state planning continuum resembles the state ownership continuum, but a little shuffling has taken place. The Soviet economy is now far more thoroughly planned than the Polish economy, which is undergoing a rapid transition to a market economy.[3] The French and Yugoslav economies have switched places. In France the government participates in **indicative planning**, setting production goals for major sectors of the economy. How those goals are met is left up to the management of producing companies. In Yugoslavia, most enterprises are **worker managed**. The workers, who own the firms, make production and marketing decisions. The central government is less involved in this process than the French government is in France's economy.

Indicative planning Government sets goals, provides incentives for private firms to meet those goals, but allows firms to determine *how* they will meet the goals.

Worker-managed firm A firm owned by its workers, who hire and fire managers.

Income Distribution and Welfare

Our final continuum seeks to rank the seven representative economies according to the extent of government involvement in the income distribution process and the provision of welfare services for citizens of these nations. Settling on a definite ranking is not easy, because government involvement in the income distribution process is not the same thing as the level of welfare provided to citizens. For example, since the government sets wages and prices for most jobs and goods, the income distribution in the Soviet Union is almost

[3]As this book is written, the Soviet Union is also undergoing massive economic changes. It is not clear at this point how much authority Soviet central planners will have in 1992 or later.

```
    Hong Kong          Sweden           France       USSR
|-------|---------------|----------------|------------|
Minimal    United States      Poland       Yugoslavia    Total
```

FIGURE 2
State planning of the economy. The Soviet economy is still largely directed by state planners. France engages in indicative planning. Yugoslavia has its own version of indicative planning. Poland is rapidly moving from central planning to markets. Central planning is slight in Sweden, the United States, and Hong Kong.

totally state determined. Yet it is clear that the average Swedish citizen is much better cared for by the Swedish welfare state than the average Soviet citizen by the Soviet socialist state. The main reason is that the absolute standard of living in Sweden is much higher than the standard of living in the Soviet Union. There is also growing evidence that the state-determined distribution of consumer goods and welfare services is very unequal, not only compared to the Swedish welfare state, but also when compared to the U.S. economy.[4]

Our subjectively determined income distribution–welfare continuum appears as Figure 3. It differs considerably from the other rankings, particularly in the placement of the Swedish economy.

SECTION RECAP
The state can intervene in the economy in a number of ways. Different governments intervene in different ways, giving rise to a variety of different economic types.

Mix and Match: Multiple Dimensions of Modern Economies

The different economies we have examined move around in the rankings (with the exception of Hong Kong and the United States, which are always at the free-market end of the continuum). This suggests that nations are able to choose over a fairly wide range of institutional arrangements for their economies. In fact, there are more differences from economy to economy than most people realize. In the next section we examine six of these economies more closely in order to develop a better understanding of the variety of economic types that exists and some of their strengths and weaknesses. We omit further discussion of the U.S. economy, since it has been discussed at length throughout the book.

---

[4]This is the argument of Soviet economist Andrei Kuteinikov in "Soviet Society — Much More Unequal Than U.S.," *The Wall Street Journal,* January 26, 1990, p. A12.

FIGURE 3
State involvement in the distribution of income and welfare. The Soviet and Swedish governments are involved in determining the income distribution of their citizens to a larger extent than the governments of the other five countries represented here.

```
          Hong Kong            Yugoslavia           Poland          USSR
|------------|------------------|--------------------|---------------|
Individual    United States        France             Sweden         State
Responsibility                                                       Provision
```

A Quick Look at Some Representative Economies

A Command Economy: The USSR

For decades the Soviet Union has had the prototypical command economy. Although the government of Mikhail Gorbachev is attempting to expand the use of markets, the Soviet economy remains largely centrally planned, the government plans dictating in minute detail what is expected from each enterprise in the economy. Soviet economic planning goes back to the 1920s, when Josef Stalin instituted the first five-year plan. Although five-year plans are still utilized to set long-range goals for sectoral production, they are less important than the **one-year plans**. One-year plans are highly detailed descriptions of the production goals of state enterprises and the resource movements to meet those production goals. They reflect the priorities of government planners, stating what proportion of resources will be devoted to such areas as military production, capital formation, housing, and consumer goods.

The Soviet planning process is quite complex. The political leadership sends its broad goals for the year to **Gosplan**, the State Planning Commission. Using mountains of data from the ministries in charge of the various industries on the production capacities and resource needs of those industries, Gosplan formulates a detailed preliminary production plan. This plan is reviewed by the industrial ministries, as well as by regional planning officials and plant managers. The planners want to make sure the plan is feasible. After a series of negotiations among all the planners, a final production plan is approved.

The basic philosophy behind the Soviet planning exercise is something called **materials balancing**. In short, the planners attempt to match up the available supplies of resources, including intermediate manufactured goods (which go into other manufactured goods), with the demands for those resources. They take a balance sheet approach, trying to exactly balance the demands for resources with their supplies. To say that this is a difficult task is an understatement. Although the problem is theoretically solvable (through a mathematical technique known as input–output analysis), the number of demands and supplies with which the planners must deal makes a perfect solution of the problem impossible. There is no computer in the world today large enough to handle all the data a solution would require — if such data could be collected. In fact, data collection is always incomplete, so the actual production process involves a great deal of trial-and-error learning.

The production plan gives specific production quotas to the more than 200,000 different Soviet enterprises (firms). Since the plan is not technically perfect, and the planners know this, they attach priorities to different parts of the plan. For example, in case of materials shortages, military production and the production of capital goods may take priority over the production of consumer goods. In this way the damage from breakdowns in the plan is minimized (from the government's point of view; consumers may feel differently).

The state sets the prices enterprises are to pay for their inputs and to receive for their outputs. These prices are *not* market prices; they are *accounting* prices. Product prices are set so that an enterprise of average efficiency, paying official prices for its inputs and receiving the official price for its output, should make neither a profit nor a loss. An enterprise making a profit is more efficient than average; it exceeds the state plan. An enterprise making a loss fails to meet its quota. Profit-and-loss accounting is kept in money terms. **Gosbank**, the state

---

One-year plan
Detailed production goals for all sectors of the economy and all enterprises within sectors.

Gosplan
Soviet state planning commission.

Materials balancing
A balance-sheet approach to matching available supplies of resources to demands for those resources.

Gosbank
The Soviet state bank.

bank, provides each enterprise with just enough money to purchase the inputs needed to meet its production quota. If the enterprise overspends or underspends, it has violated the plan in some manner.

Consumer prices are often much higher than the prices received by producing enterprises. The difference between the prices paid by consumers (in state stores) and the prices received by enterprises is called the *turnover tax*. This is one of the primary ways in which the Soviet government finances investment and military projects. In theory, the authorities can match aggregate demand to the planned aggregate supply of consumer goods by varying the turnover tax. In practice, excess demand or excess supply usually exists.

Markets in the Soviet Union   Although the state owns virtually all productive resources in the Soviet Union, the level of market activity is increasing. Without free market activity in agriculture, the Soviet Union could not come close to feeding its people. As it is, the USSR imports millions of tons of wheat each year—this in a country with some of the world's best wheat-growing land.

Soviet agricultural problems go back to the time of the revolution. During the Russian Revolution in 1917, and for some time thereafter, the new communist regime mistreated the Russian peasantry terribly. Land was confiscated, many of the small landowners were executed, and forced collectivization was attempted. The result was massive famine in the early 1920s. In an attempt to shore up his weak government, Soviet leader Vladimir Lenin instituted the New Economic Policy (NEP), which permitted private ownership of land and wide operation of markets for agricultural goods. The policy was a great success, and Soviet food production grew tremendously.

Lenin died in 1924 and was replaced by Josef Stalin. The new leader was determined to socialize the economy at any cost. He forcibly collectivized agriculture in the late 1920s. The cost was high, in both economic and human terms. Agricultural production fell to famine levels once again, and the communist government punished the peasantry for its lack of socialist fervor by confiscating whatever food could be found. It has been estimated that ten million people died in Stalin's forced collectivization effort in the years 1929–1936.[5]

Against this background it is not surprising that collectivized agriculture has performed poorly in the USSR. A recent estimate of the contribution of private production on small peasant plots illustrates how inefficient the state farms are. Swedish economist Sven Rydenfelt cites Soviet and Swedish sources which indicate that peasants using only 3 percent of the cropland produce 27 percent of total Soviet agricultural output.[6]

Why is collectivized agriculture so inefficient in the Soviet Union? Beyond the resentment of the peasantry for the communist government, the three factors that seem to hamper Soviet agriculture are (1) the inefficiently large size of state farms, (2) the shortage of modern equipment and spare parts, and (3) the lack of incentives for farm workers to be productive. The 21,000 state farms in the Soviet Union have an average size of over 45,000 acres. By comparison, a very large farm in the United States would be in the 1000 to 3000 acre range. The mere size of the state farms prevents effective manage-

---

[5] See Paul Johnson, *Modern Times: The World from the Twenties to the Eighties* (New York: Harper & Row, 1983), p. 272.

[6] *A Pattern for Failure: Socialist Economies in Crisis* (New York: Harcourt Brace Jovanovich, 1984), p. 38.

ment. Furthermore, farm managers are shackled by rules that force them to obtain permission from government bureaucrats before they make even small purchases or sales.[7]

The inability of Soviet farmers to acquire the modern equipment needed to harvest crops and transport them to markets results in tremendous waste in the Soviet agricultural system. Equipment shortages reflect the problems of the Soviet manufacturing and distribution systems. President Gorbachev himself estimates that 20 percent of Soviet farm production spoils before reaching market; other experts think the figure is much higher.

The lack of worker incentives may be an even greater problem, though. Soviet agricultural workers are poorly paid in comparison to industrial workers, and they receive lower welfare benefits when they retire. Since increasing their productivity on the state farms does not increase their income, they tend to devote as little time and effort to their official jobs as possible. They save their energies for tending their private plots, from which they benefit directly.

Outside agriculture, most Soviet market activity consists of the legal (and heavily taxed) moonlighting of service providers, such as doctors, carpenters, and plumbers; recently legalized *cooperatives*; and illegal trading of manufactured goods. Illegal market activity in Soviet manufacturing comes in two forms. Managers of enterprises illegally trade materials with one another to obtain the resources necessary to meet production goals. Such trading is necessary to make the production plan work. The second type of trading takes place in the **underground market**. Private entrepreneurs illegally manufacture goods (sometimes using state factories after hours) and sell them, or illegally transport legally produced goods to areas of the country where they are in short supply and sell them at market prices. Soviet law prescribes heavy penalties for such economic crimes; several people were executed for them in the 1980s.

As part of Gorbachev's attempted restructuring of the Soviet economy, workers are permitted to form cooperatives that produce and sell goods at market prices. Most cooperatives appear to be private firms, run by an entrepreneur or small group of entrepreneurs. By 1990, some 200,000 cooperatives were operating in the Soviet Union, producing around 5 percent of Soviet GNP. The managers of cooperative firms face many difficulties, such as problems acquiring materials from state enterprises, arbitrary seizures of property by government officials, and the hostility of many Soviet citizens toward anyone who appears to be doing better economically than they are.[8]

One other area in which the market plays an important role in the Soviet economy is in the allocation of labor. There is a considerable amount of freedom to change jobs in the Soviet Union, and by paying higher wages in favored industries, the government ensures that high-priority goods are produced. Studies have concluded that the wage differentials among blue collar workers in the Soviet Union are about the same as the wage differentials among such workers in the United States.

Underground market
Market for illegally produced or transported goods.

---

[7] A recent news story reports that one manager of a state farm employing 450 workers cannot spend more than twenty-five rubles — the equivalent of about $4 — on goods for the farm without obtaining permission from bureaucrats in Moscow. See Elisabeth Rubinfien, "Soviet Farm System Hungers for Reform," *The Wall Street Journal*, September 5, 1990, p. A10.

[8] A comment in a magazine article makes the point well: "[S]cratch the average comrade in the streets and you quickly discover that the fury he feels over the party bosses' privileges is rivaled only by his envy of Russia's new private rich." Richard I. Kirkland, Jr., "Can Capitalism Save Perestroika?" *Fortune*, July 30, 1990, pp. 138–144.

Income Distribution The one place where one might expect the Soviet economy to excel is in the provision of an equal distribution of income. In fact, the Soviet income distribution may not be too different from that of the United States and appears to be almost identical to the Swedish income distribution.[9] Furthermore, the fact that so many goods and services are reserved for the political elite has led Soviet economists to argue that Soviet society is actually more unequal than U.S. society. Soviet statistics indicate that a small number of political insiders live very well, a very small middle class lives acceptably, and the mass of Soviet citizens are, by western standards, simply poor.[10]

Perestroika and the Future of the Soviet Economy The Soviet government has fought a continuing battle against inefficiency for decades. Until recently, this battle was fought within the confines of the planned economy. Reforms were designed to improve planning and streamline the command system. However, under the leadership of Mikhail Gorbachev the reform movement has taken on a new look. Under the banner of *perestroika* — economic restructuring — the Soviet government has instituted a number of changes designed to increase the efficiency of the Soviet economy and provide Soviet consumers with more goods.

The initial effects of *perestroika* have not been good. The attempt to combine market incentives with direct commands in the state enterprise sector has led to even greater inefficiency. The bureaucrats who run the Soviet economic system — some 18 million of them — have a vested interest in retaining the centralized command system. Partially freed from government control, but still unconstrained by market forces, the managers of state enterprises have not responded as Gorbachev hoped they would. Consequently, the state distribution system has degenerated dramatically. Real GNP in the Soviet Union has been falling for years, putting immense political pressure on the Soviet leadership to reverse the decline in the standard of living.

How much economic freedom will result from *perestroika* remains to be seen. The Soviet government is in a delicate position. More than one hundred nationalities have been held together as a nation for seven decades, primarily by force. The economic freedom and political openness *(glasnost)* being promoted by Gorbachev have already brought nationalist sentiments to the surface in several Soviet republics, as witnessed by the attempted secession of the Baltic states. Should the political situation appear to be getting out of hand, the move toward economic liberalization could end abruptly.

SECTION RECAP
Until the late 1980s, the Soviet economy was almost totally centrally planned. As the inefficiencies of central planning became more obvious, the Soviet government began to turn toward the market. The abortive coup in August, 1991, and subsequent political changes in the Soviet Union resulted in a rapid weakening of central control of the Soviet economy, accelerating the movement toward a market economy.

Poland: Shock Therapy for a Command Economy

In many ways the pre-1990 Polish economy resembled a smaller version of the Soviet economy. Government bureaucrats made most production decisions, 71 percent of all Polish workers were employed by state-run enterprises, and 88 percent of measured net industrial output was produced by socialized firms. The major difference between the Polish and Soviet economies seemed

---

[9]See Lowell Galloway, "The Folklore of Unemployment and Poverty," in S. Pejovich, *Government Controls and the Free Market* (College Station, TX: Texas A&M University Press, 1976), pp. 41–72.

[10]Andrei Kuteinikov, "Soviet Society — Much More Unequal Than U.S.," *The Wall Street Journal*, January 26, 1990, p. A12.

Why the **Disagreement?**

Slicing the Socialist Pie

Eastern bloc nations face a multitude of problems in converting their economies from socialist command systems to market enterprise systems. One of the major problems is how to privatize existing state enterprises. It is now recognized by virtually all observers that a successful market economy requires private ownership of most firms. Given the entrenched political power of socialist bureaucracies, private firms simply cannot compete effectively in an economy dominated by state-owned firms. However, the agreement over the need for privatization turns into disagreement when the issue of *how* to privatize the socialist economies is raised. Given the extent of agreement over the need to privatize, why the disagreement over how to do it?

The disagreement over the path to a market economy arises largely from the fact that no perfect options exist, as an examination of three potential privatization schemes demonstrates.

One way to privatize state firms is to auction them off to the highest bidder. Auctioning off state enterprises is attractive for a number of reasons. Holding an auction is a quick and relatively simple way to transfer ownership of capital. An auction also has the important benefit of producing the maximum revenue for the governments selling the firms. Given the sad state of the transportation, communication, and public utility systems in such countries as Poland, Czechoslovakia, and Hungary, and the increasing need for funds to support unemployed workers, obtaining the maximum revenue from the sale of state enterprises becomes a major benefit.

On the down side, auctioning off state enterprises is sure to place ownership of the most attractive and economically viable firms in the hands of foreigners. Capitalists from western Europe, North America, and Japan have the resources to outbid entrepreneurs from the socialist nations for the strongest firms. It is asking a lot of the long-suffering citizens of eastern Europe to accept foreign ownership of their largest, most successful firms. Furthermore, an auction approach might find no buyers for a number of currently unprofitable, but potentially salvageable firms. Without buyers, the usable capital owned by the firms would go to waste.

A second option is to privatize firms by giving existing managers and workers ownership of their own firms. Like the auction approach, such spontaneous privatization (as it is called) has the benefit of being relatively quick and simple. It also keeps the own-

to be that Polish farming was largely carried out by peasant farmers working their own land, while Soviet farming is dominated by large collectivized farms.

Politically, Poland was very different from the Soviet Union, however. In the early 1980s the Solidarity movement, under the leadership of Lech Walesa, mounted a campaign of opposition to the policies of the communist government. From its beginnings as a trade union movement, Solidarity slowly grew into a full-fledged political party. As the Polish economy deteriorated in the 1980s, the position of the Polish communist party became more and more tenuous. Finally, in 1989, the communists agreed to free elections. Solidarity candidates displaced communists in large numbers, and Poland became the first country in the world with a centralized command economy and a noncommunist government.

This situation did not last for long. In late 1989 the Solidarity government began planning for a rapid transition from a command economy to a market economy. Following the advice of western economists such as Jeffrey Sachs of Harvard University, Solidarity decided to try shock therapy on the moribund Polish economy: Poland would make a "great leap to the market," beginning January 1, 1990.

ership of firms within the emerging market economies, and it turns ownership over to people who have a vested interest in the success of the firms they own.

Unfortunately, spontaneous privatization also has some drawbacks. First, who wins and who loses from this allocation process would be arbitrary. People who happen to work in stronger firms would gain; workers in weak firms would lose everything if their firms were forced to close. Second, upper-level managers at most state firms hold their positions for political reasons. Why should holdovers from the old regime benefit from the privatization process? Finally, turning firms over to their employees would open them up to the same problems faced by Yugoslav firms (discussed later in this chapter). Worker-managed firms tend to invest too little in new capital, preferring to pay higher wages to their worker owners. The long-term result is slow growth and antiquated facilities.

A third privatization option is to distribute shares in all state firms to all citizens. The benefit of such an approach is the rapid achievement of broad-based ownership. Everyone in the country has a stake in the success of the newly privatized companies. Furthermore, wealth is spread around so that no one benefits from political connections with the old socialist regimes. After shares were distributed to the entire population, a stock market could be organized, through which people could buy and sell their shares. Companies would then be owned by the people who valued them most highly.

This option also has a number of negatives. Compared to the first two options, spreading the wealth is logistically complex. Furthermore, with shares in firms spread so widely, it is not clear that shareholders would have any real control over the management of their firms. Management, technically accountable to everyone, might be practically accountable to no one. Finally, unless prohibited by law from purchasing shares on the stock market, foreigners would surely purchase the shares in the most desirable companies by bidding up their share prices until the natives would sell. It would be simple to prohibit foreign ownership of shares, but that would impose controls on trading that do not exist in most market economies.

Of the three options discussed here, most analysts probably favor the third. However, the problems accompanying even this option make it easy to understand the great disagreement over the path to privatization.

Pre-1990 Economic Conditions Like all economies in Eastern Europe, the Polish economy suffered from chronic excess demand. That is, most prices were set below their market-clearing values, generating shortages at the prevailing set of official prices. Both consumer goods and material inputs were rationed by the state firms producing or selling the goods. Consumers competed for products by standing in line to purchase what they could before supplies ran out. Firms made arrangements with suppliers as best they could. Prices were essentially meaningless, since they reflected neither the value attached to goods by consumers nor the opportunity cost of producing the goods.

Government subsidies enabled Polish firms to sell at below-market prices. The Polish government financed the subsidies through heavy taxation and through rapid money creation. The subsidized firms were very inefficient, employing far too many workers (there was no unemployment in pre-1990 Poland) and using antiquated machinery and production techniques. The policy of subsidizing inefficient production by printing money was possible only because foreign trade was tightly controlled and the Polish currency (the zloty) was inconvertible. At the official exchange rate, the zloty was grossly overvalued in terms of western currencies.

By 1989, Polish economic conditions had reached the crisis stage. Poland was unable to make its debt payments on loans from western governments and banks. Attempts by the communist government to impose some discipline on the economy by reducing subsidies to state firms and decontrolling some prices had resulted in an inflationary spiral of prices and wages. From August through September 1989, the *monthly* inflation rate ranged from 17.7 percent to 54.8 percent.

Economic Reform in 1990   Beginning in January 1990 the Polish government took a number of bold steps to begin the transition from a centralized command economy to a market economy. The major steps included the following:

1. The zloty was radically devalued, and most currency controls were removed. At its new, lower value, the zloty was made convertible into western currencies.

2. Money supply growth was slowed dramatically. Firms that had previously borrowed from the state bank at low interest rates now faced very high interest rates. Most could no longer afford to borrow. As loan creation slowed, so did the growth of the money supply.

3. Most prices were decontrolled. With the exception of the prices of such monopolistically produced goods as electricity, prices were freed to find their market levels. Simultaneously, firms were allowed to sell their products however they wished.

4. Government subsidies to state firms were removed, and the firms were, for the first time, forced to consider the true costs of production. The government announced that unprofitable firms would be allowed to go bankrupt.

5. Most restrictions on foreign trade were removed, with the exception of tariffs on imported consumer goods. The Polish government felt that the quickest way to promote competition was to enter the world economy. By opening the Polish economy to trade, the government encouraged Polish firms to seek new outlets for their products and new suppliers for needed materials.

Results of the 1990 Reforms   The first effect of the 1990 reforms was an intensification of the inflation that had emerged in 1989. Consumer prices rose by 78.6 percent in January 1990. At the same time, the Solidarity government maintained controls over wage increases in an attempt to end the price–wage spiral. Because prices rose rapidly, while wages rose much more slowly, the *real* wage rate of Polish workers fell dramatically — by over 43 percent in one month.

The outburst of inflation did not last long. By March the monthly inflation rate was down to 4.7 percent. Most importantly, higher prices eliminated the shortages that had characterized the Polish economy for decades. Stores were filled with goods, street vendors were sprouting up everywhere, and rationing by price had replaced rationing by queue (waiting in line). Although the real wage of Polish workers had declined drastically, their actual standard of living fell by a much smaller amount. Before the reforms, shortages limited what Poles could buy, reducing the true economic value of their incomes. After the reforms, prices were higher, but goods were actually available.[11]

---

[11]A wealth of information on the Polish economy, as well as a detailed description of the Polish economic reforms, appears in David Lipton and Jeffrey Sachs, "Creating a Market Economy in Eastern Europe: The Case of Poland," *Brookings Papers on Economic Activity*, 1, 1990, pp. 75–147.

Polish workers also felt the harsh effects of reform in a second way—through the emergence and growth of unemployment. Without access to state subsidies or cheap credit, most firms found that they could not produce profitably. Firms began laying off workers, and unemployment emerged and grew. Rather than denying that unemployment would rise sharply, Polish officials boldly argued that unemployment serves a useful purpose. In a dynamic economy, the demand for workers rises and falls at different rates in different industries. Labor is reallocated from low-value uses to higher-value uses. In the process, some unemployment always exists. Furthermore, the complete absence of unemployment that characterized the Polish economy before 1990 led to inefficiency and carelessness on the part of workers, who were essentially guaranteed jobs.[12]

Workers in state firms were not the only ones to feel the effects of reform. Polish farmers were hit hard. Although the prices of farm products rose to ten times their prereform levels, the prices of many inputs rose even more. Since the vast majority of Polish farms are small (twelve to fifteen acres) and inefficient operations, many farmers found themselves unable to earn a profit in the new environment. This led to political opposition to the reforms as early as the summer of 1990.[13] It is clear that, for the Polish economic reforms to succeed, farming must be done by fewer farmers using more equipment on larger farms. The transition from small peasant farming to efficient commercial farming will be difficult and painful.

The entire character of the Polish economy changed after the 1990 reforms. Firms began looking for new markets, seeking foreign trading partners, selling goods directly to consumers, and running down their bloated inventories. Managers were forced to think about product quality and about marketing for the first time. The need to produce efficiently forced managers to begin scrapping antiquated equipment and seeking ways to finance the purchase of modern machinery. Some Polish firms experienced unexpected immediate success in selling to the west,[14] but no one knows how much time will pass before the majority of Polish firms are able to participate effectively in a competitive world marketplace.

Future Reforms As important as the 1990 reforms were, the Polish economy cannot be fully competitive with market economies unless some additional reforms are instituted. Most important is the privatization of state firms and the institution of strong property rights laws. Efficiently operating markets are driven by the profit motive. Decontrolling prices and forcing state-owned firms to pay for their inputs imposes some discipline on the firms' managers, but does not assure that they will attempt to maximize profits. The state's grip on the Polish economy will be loosened only when private individuals are in control of most firms.

Other areas awaiting reform are taxes and regulations. High taxes are a major impediment to the formation of firms, and government regulations still

SECTION RECAP
A democratically elected government turned Poland sharply toward the market in 1990. Central planning was dismantled, subsidies to industries were discontinued, and prices were freed. The shock therapy threw many Poles out of work and forced many inefficient firms to close. However, many other firms quickly adapted to competition.

---

[12]See Barry Newman, "Poland's New Realities Include Joblessness; Solidarity Is Unmoved," *The Wall Street Journal*, June 15, 1990, pp. A1, A19.

[13]See "Farmers Seek the Fruits of Change," *Insight*, August 20, 1990, pp. 34–35.

[14]Quite unexpectedly, Poland ran a trade surplus in 1990, as a number of Polish firms quickly adapted to competition. See Barry Newman, "Poles Flex Unaccustomed Export Muscle," *The Wall Street Journal*, September 12, 1990, p. A19.

make it difficult to start a business. Removing all the vestiges of the communist command economy may take longer than the Solidarity reformers ever imagined.

Market Socialism: Yugoslavia

The southeastern European nation of Yugoslavia was formed out of several smaller states. At the end of World War II it fell under Soviet domination and began to construct an economy following the rigid centralized Soviet model. However, Yugoslavia broke away from the Soviet sphere of influence in 1948. Since then the Yugoslavs have pursued a determinedly independent path, developing their socialist economy to fit their particular situation.

The outstanding feature of the Yugoslav economy is worker management of firms. Unlike command economies, the central government does not develop detailed economic plans that state enterprises must fulfill. Although the state owns the factories and machines, the production decisions of the state-owned enterprises are made by the workers. Each enterprise is free to contract with other enterprises for material inputs, to set its own production goals, and to market its products. The revenues earned from the sale of products are used to pay for materials, energy, and transportation. Whatever remains after these costs have been met is divided among the workers, who act as both the employees and owners of the firms.

State planning does exist in Yugoslavia. However, the type of planning carried out is not centralized—the central government is surprisingly weak—but *indicative*, much as in France (to be discussed next). Enterprises cooperate with one another in forming their production plans, in order to increase the information about market conditions available to the firms. This planning partially supplants the price system as an information provider.[15]

The performance of the Yugoslav economy over the past three decades has deteriorated. Until the 1980s its economic growth rate exceeded the growth rates of both eastern and western European nations but was about equal to the growth rates of so-called middle-income LDCs. However, the Yugoslav economy actually shrank in the 1980s. Real income fell by about one fourth, unemployment rose, and prices exploded into a hyperinflation of some 1500 percent by 1989. High unemployment is particularly troublesome to a socialist government, and Yugoslavia has experienced it despite allowing thousands of workers to cross into western European countries to find work.

Worker management, the distinguishing feature of the Yugoslav economy, appears to be largely responsible for the economy's recent poor performance. The lack of management direction of large firms hampers their ability to compete in the world market. Workers have so much authority that they often override the decisions of the managers (who are hired by the workers) and slow down the large firms' reactions to changes in market conditions. Furthermore, workers have shown a tendency to vote themselves pay raises rather than plowing profits back into their businesses. Since large worker-run firms control many banks, credit has been available even to poorly run, unprofitable firms. Thus, while the Yugoslav model gives workers genuine control over their

---

[15] Good discussions of the Yugoslav system are contained in Stephen R. Sacks, "The Yugoslav Firm," Chapter 14 in Morris Bornstein, ed., *Comparative Economic Systems*, 5th ed. (Homewood, IL: Irwin, 1985), and in Paul R. Gregory and Robert C. Stuart, *Comparative Economic Systems*, 2nd ed. (Boston: Houghton Mufflin, 1985), Chapter 8.

activities, something workers in the Soviet Union do not have, it has weaknesses that neither the Soviet nor the standard market model have.[16]

Yugoslavia's economic problems are further complicated by increasing ethnic strife. The westernmost states of Slovenia and Croatia are openly hostile to the largest state, Serbia. While most Serbs remain committed to communism, most Slovenians and many Croatians would prefer a move to political democracy and market capitalism. The tension reached such a point in 1990 that Slovenia and Serbia were boycotting each other's products. It is quite possible that Slovenia, and perhaps even Croatia, will attempt to secede from Yugoslavia in the near future.

> **SECTION RECAP**
> The Yugoslav economy is in trouble, both because of the inefficiency of worker-managed firms and because of ethnic problems that threaten to tear the country apart.

Government Planning in a Market Economy: France

The French economy, though based on markets, is dominated by the government to a much greater extent than is the U.S. economy. Government influence is felt not only in the usual ways — through government taxation and spending programs and public provision of services — but also through direct ownership of industrial and financial companies and through indicative planning. We will examine the last feature.

The French planning system bears little resemblance to the Soviet system. Although a broad sectoral production plan is formulated in both cases, the command element of the Soviet system is absent in France, where representatives of government, business, and labor form consensus plans for five-year periods. Data are assembled from throughout the economy, and forecasts of attainable economic behavior under different plans are compared. A particular plan is then chosen and publicized.

The French plan is not imposed upon firms; a firm can choose to ignore the plan entirely. This being the case, what is the relevance of planning? If the government cannot force firms to go along with the plan, why should firms cooperate?

The French government obtains cooperation with the plan in three ways:

1. The French government owns a number of large industrial corporations which it can direct to act according to the plan.
2. The government also owns major portions of the financial sector. By controlling the lending practices of much of the banking sector, it can influence the activities of private firms.
3. Through its powers of taxation and spending, the government can influence the direction of private companies.

If a large enough share of the French economy cooperates with the plan, private companies may find it in their interests to cooperate as well. Surveys of business executives have shown that they regard the plans as important, although the degree to which the plans affect their decisions is unclear.

How has indicative planning worked in France? Does it provide a model for overcoming the major problems of market economies, while still providing a free market environment? Observers disagree on the success of the French

---

[16]For interesting accounts of the problems encountered in self-management, see Barry Newman, "Yugoslavia's Workers Find Self-Management Doesn't Make Paradise," *The Wall Street Journal*, March 25, 1987, pp. 1, 16; and "Independence Breeds Dependence," *Insight*, July 4, 1988, pp. 28–29.

model.[17] Most believe it worked fairly well in the 1950s, as France was reconstructing after World War II, but that it has not made much difference since the late 1960s. The French economy performed about equally as well as other western European economies in the 1970s and more poorly than most in the 1980s.

As the European Economic Community moves toward complete economic integration in 1992, indicative planning appears to be less and less important. The French government will not be able to affect the Common Market to the extent it affected the French economy. Thus, the French economy may become more like the U.S. economy in the 1990s, although the French are attempting to persuade the European Community to adopt many of the features of French market socialism.

SECTION RECAP
French indicative planning will probably matter very little when the French economy is fully integrated into a single European Community in 1992.

A Welfare State: Sweden

In the 1960s and early 1970s, many Americans and western European liberals regarded Sweden as the great example of what a welfare state could be. Though nearly all property was privately owned, the Swedish government pursued policies designed to promote full employment (an unemployment rate of 2 percent or less), income equality, economic growth, and price stability. The Swedish economy boomed, and the government instituted a comprehensive social welfare system: generous social insurance and pension benefits, essentially free health care, and free education at all levels. To finance these programs, taxes were raised to relatively high levels, but the consensus among Swedes was that the standard of living was improved greatly by the welfare policies.

Then in 1973–1974, oil prices quadrupled. The Swedish government chose to protect the employment level against the effects of this supply shock by expanding public sector spending. Total public sector expenditures (purchases plus transfer payments) rose to over two thirds of GNP. The expenditures were financed by increased taxes. Swedish payroll taxes (roughly equivalent to U.S. Social Security taxes) rose to over one third of the total payroll, while the average industrial worker faced a marginal income tax rate of 40 percent and middle-income earners faced a rate of 60 percent. Even these rates were not enough; the Swedish government's budget deficit topped 12 percent of GNP in the early 1980s, in relative terms twice as large as the U.S. government's budget deficit.

The Swedish economy did not rebound well from the mid-1970s recession. Productivity fell off sharply, and inflation rose well above the levels experienced by most western European economies. The high wage increases granted to Swedish workers during the inflationary mid-1970s helped price Swedish goods out of the international market.

The recent poor performance of the Swedish economy appears to be linked to the massive welfare state.[18] The generous provision of benefits to workers

---

[17]See Gregory and Stuart, pp. 311–321.

[18]See Erik Lundberg, "The Rise and Fall of the Swedish Economic Model," Chapter 5 in Bornstein, *Comparative Economic Systems*; "The Model Cradle Begins to Creak," *Insight*, March 5, 1990, pp. 30–31; and "Sweden Faces Chill as Economy Stagnates," *The Wall Street Journal*, April 5, 1990, p. A18. It is worth noting that the Swedish economy performed about as well as most western European economies in the 1980s—which is to say not very well in comparison to the U.S. and Japanese economies.

has greatly reduced the incentive to work.[19] The large public sector employs one of three Swedish workers, keeping employment high but producing very little. Funds needed for industrial investment are siphoned off to finance government. Policies that would promote efficiency are resisted because they would also promote income inequality.

The Swedish standard of living, though essentially unchanged for the past two decades, remains among the highest in the world. However, to maintain the welfare state and its emphasis on equality, Swedes may be forced to accept a lower real income level. They have passed the point where income equalization has little effect on economic performance. Wage solidarity has leveled incomes to the point where there is almost no return to training; skilled workers earn about the same wages as unskilled workers. Sweden's eroding position in the world economy led the government to lower marginal income tax rates, the top rate falling to 50 percent in 1991. In 1990, Swedish politicians began talking about joining the European Economic Community, largely to impose some needed competition on the stagnant Swedish economy. The government also introduced restrictive monetary and fiscal policies in an attempt to reduce the inflation rate (which was running at 11 percent).[20] Swedish economists foresee more adjustments to taxes and welfare programs in the future, a process that will be politically painful to Swedes accustomed to cradle-to-grave governmental care.

SECTION RECAP
The Swedish welfare-state economy has stagnated in recent years, forcing the Swedish government to reduce tax rates, lower welfare benefits, and consider joining the European Community.

The Free Market at Work: Hong Kong

One of the great success stories of the past twenty-five years has been the small British colony of Hong Kong. Squeezed into an area of some 400 square miles of rugged terrain, almost devoid of natural resources, Hong Kong has experienced rapid economic growth despite the influx of hundreds of thousands of immigrants. Hong Kong is almost entirely dependent on foreign trade for its economic success, but its industrious people have proven that the free market can increase living standards rapidly if given the opportunity.

The government's attitude toward the economy is quite simple: Interfere as little as possible. Trade is largely unrestricted. The only tariffs on imported goods are low and strictly for revenue purposes. There is little regulation of business, and labor regulations are primarily limited to such basics as restricting the minimum age at which young people may be employed and the number of hours per week workers may be asked to work. Nothing remotely resembling government planning exists.

The results of this approach are startling. From 1961 to 1980 the real income level rose at a rate of about 10 percent per year. This is an astounding figure; many economies *never* grow at a 10 percent rate, even for one year, much less for two decades. The rapid growth enabled per capita real income to rise by three and one half times during this period, despite a population explosion from 3.2 million to 5.2 million people.[21]

---

[19]Abuse of the sick-leave system costs Sweden billions of kroner in sick pay annually. "Some Swedes Not Honoring Sick Pay System," *The Pantagraph* (Bloomington–Normal, IL), March 5, 1989, E3.

[20]"Push and Pull," *The Economist*, November 3, 1990, p. 62.

[21]For a readable discussion of the Hong Kong economy, see A. J. Youngson, *Hong Kong: Economic Growth and Policy* (Oxford: Oxford University Press, 1982).

Does It Make **Economic Sense?**

Is the U.S. Social-Welfare Effort Superior to the Swedish?

Mention "welfare state" and most people automatically think of Sweden. By conventional measures of welfare effort, Sweden surpasses virtually all other countries in the world. For example, according to one standard measure of welfare effort — the percentage of a nation's gross domestic product* spent on social programs — Sweden ranked second only to the Netherlands in the early 1980s. By the same measure the United States ranked eighth, behind such countries as France and Canada and ahead of Australia and Japan. Sweden spent 32.5 percent of its gross domestic product on social programs, while the United States spent only 20.7 percent.

The conventional ranking has been challenged by a University of California at Berkeley professor who argues that Sweden's welfare effort is actually not so good as advertised. In fact, Neil Gilbert argues that the Swedish government's welfare effort is inferior to that of the U.S. government.**

Does this make economic sense? Professor Gilbert's argument is based on a critical assessment of the standard measure of welfare effort — the percentage of GDP spent on social programs. One problem is that the percent-of-GDP measure ignores the fact that different countries have different needs for welfare programs. For example, a country with a relatively large elderly population has a greater need for social security spending than does a country with a relatively small elderly population. The percent-of-GDP approach does not take needs into account.

A second problem with the percent-of-GDP measure is that taxes don't count in assessing welfare effort. It is reasonable to argue that the welfare effort of a high-tax country is lower than that of a low-tax country that spends the

---

SECTION RECAP

Laissez faire economic policies have worked well in generating rapid economic growth in Hong Kong.

Along with such other market-oriented nations as the Republic of (South) Korea, Taiwan, and Singapore, Hong Kong has been one of the economic stars of the past couple of decades. However, it is interesting to note that, even in this bastion of capitalism, the government plays an important role. About 40 percent of the Hong Kong population lives in government-subsidized apartments. Low-income people are provided what amounts to free health care, and education is largely government provided. Such welfare programs do not seem to harm economic incentives at all, since they are financed primarily by tariff revenue and have little direct impact on incomes, and they undoubtedly improve the quality of life for millions of people.

Despite its rapid progress, Hong Kong is still a developing economy. Living standards are much lower than in the United States or Sweden. There is no thought of trading off less-rapid income growth for more equality, because income levels are still relatively low. But even income levels low by U.S. standards represent a vast improvement in the lives of millions of people who were in abject poverty only a few years earlier.

What Are We to Conclude?

Drawing conclusions about comparative economic systems based on the scanty evidence presented in this chapter is dangerous. Nevertheless, several things do seem obvious. First, the theoretical proposition that government-planned economies are inefficient is true. Command economies are designed for control, not efficiency. Second, although various combinations of market and socialist elements are possible, poor performance soon follows when the wel-

same proportion of GDP on social programs. The low-tax country provides the same benefits without taxing away so much of its citizens' incomes.

To avoid these problems, Professor Gilbert created the Need, Expenditure, Tax (NET) index of welfare effort. The NET index takes into account social expenditures as a percent of GDP, tax burdens, and social needs. The measure of needs is based on the number of people likely to need assistance, such as children, the elderly, single-parent families, and the unemployed. Adjusting for needs and tax burdens, Professor Gilbert finds that the welfare-effort ranking changes considerably. Although the Netherlands remains at the top of the list, Japan moves from tenth on the conventional index to second on the NET index. Japan moves up because its tax rates are low, and because families provide many social services in Japan, lessening the need for government programs.

The United States also moves up on the NET index, from eighth to sixth. Most surprisingly, Sweden's ranking plunges from second to tenth. Sweden's extremely high tax burden is primarily responsible for its lower ranking.

Professor Gilbert's exercise reminds us once again not to accept at face value the conventional wisdom. Although no social-welfare index is flawless, the NET index included, many apparently obvious measures of economic welfare are misleading. An intelligent appraisal of welfare effort requires taking more than just social spending into account.

---

*Gross domestic product (GDP) is closely related to gross national product. GDP omits earnings from investments in foreign countries, whereas GNP includes such earnings as part of exports.

**Neil Gilbert, "How to Rate a Social-Welfare System," *The Wall Street Journal*, January 13, 1987, p. 32.

---

fare aspects of socialism begin to destroy the incentive structure of the market economy. Third, both socialist and capitalist economies are subject to the problems of inflation and unemployment, though these may be expressed in different ways. Finally, there seems to be a strong connection between markets and freedom. In a command economy, for the economic plan to be realized all resources—including labor—must be subject to the direction of the planners. The only alternative is to allow wage differentials to exist to attract workers to high-priority industries. Such a policy is *using* the labor market, not supplanting it. The power of the market is evident even in planned economies.

Summary

The **three major problems** any economy must address are (1) what, and how much, to produce, (2) how to produce it, and (3) who should benefit from the production. **Market economies** answer the first question by proclaiming **consumer sovereignty;** producers react to, or attempt to anticipate, consumer demands. The **price system** transfers information to producers on consumer desires and provides incentives for producers to meet those demands. Producers attempt to maximize profits by minimizing costs of production. Income is distributed approximately according to the marginal productivity of factors of production.

Socialist economies override the market. In a pure socialist economy the government owns the means of production. Production decisions are planned. This necessitates overcoming the **coordination problem.** Command economies attempt to do this through **materials balancing,** but the information requirements of such an approach are immense. Choosing production techniques in an economy without a price system is quite difficult; economic inefficiency often results. However, the distribution of income can be socially determined to a much greater degree in a socialist economy than in a market economy.

Economies can be classified as "socialist" or "capitalist" in several dimensions. An economy will not necessarily rank the same when measured with different standards. Some economies in which state ownership of property is pervasive, such as Yugoslavia, permit the market to operate to a significant degree. In other market economies, such as Sweden, **welfare states** have arisen, and the government largely determines the distribution of income, though most property is privately owned.

The Soviet economy is the world's largest **command economy.** The Polish economy is in the transition process from a command system to a market system. Most Yugoslav enterprises are **worker managed,** and state planning is minimal. In France, **indicative planning** has been used since World War II, though its importance may have waned in recent years. The Swedish welfare state has grown to such an extent that the market incentive system has suffered, and Hong Kong has used the free market to develop rapidly over the past three decades.

Questions for Thought

Knowledge Questions

1. What does *consumer sovereignty* mean?
2. What is the basis for the Mises–Hayek argument that government-determined prices cannot replace market prices?
3. How does the broad socialist definition of efficiency differ from the definition of economic efficiency used in this book?
4. Explain the basic principle behind Soviet economic planning.

Application Questions

5. Do income disparities play any useful role in the economy? Explain.
6. Who determines what is produced in a command economy? How is the coordination problem (what and how much to produce) solved?
7. What problems has Sweden encountered in combining an extensive welfare state with a market economy?
8. What is the distinctive feature of Yugoslavian socialism? Do you think this is a true socialist system? Explain.

Synthesis Questions

9. Explain how the price system provides information and incentives for producers to meet consumer demands.

10. By what principle is income distributed in a market economy? How does the presence of market power affect the situation?
11. Why is it difficult to coordinate an economy without a market price system?
12. Is an economy that is *socialist* in one dimension *socialist* in all dimensions? Explain.

GLOSSARY

Absolute advantage Ability to produce a good at a lower resource cost than other producers.

Absolute price level Dollar level of prices.

Accelerator principle Net investment spending depends on the growth of real GNP.

Accounting profit The difference between total revenue and explicit, or accounting, costs.

Active rule Policy that adjusts the money supply in response to changes in economic activity.

Adaptive expectations Expectations of a variable based on the behavior of the variable in the recent past; backward looking.

Aggregate demand Total desired spending on newly produced goods and services; consists of consumption, investment, government purchases, and net exports.

Aggregate demand (AD) curve Graphical relationship between the total quantity of goods and services demanded in an economy and the economy's aggregate price level.

Aggregate labor demand curve Shows the aggregate quantity of labor demanded by firms at various wage rates, holding the aggregate price level and labor productivity constant.

Aggregate labor supply curve Shows the aggregate quantity of labor workers are willing to supply at various real wage rates; the curve is graphed with the nominal wage rate on the vertical axis and the expected price level held constant, so that changes in the nominal wage rate also change the expected real wage rate.

Aggregate supply Total quantity of goods and services supplied by business firms at various price levels.

Aggregate supply curve Shows the aggregate quantity of goods and services supplied by all firms in the economy at various aggregate price levels.

Allocative efficiency Using resources to produce goods with the highest possible value.

Allocatively efficient firms Produce the level of output for which P = MC, where the value of the variable inputs is equal to the value of the output.

Amplitude The size of the upward and downward movements of real GNP over the course of a business cycle.

Anticipated change in aggregate demand Change whose direction and size are correctly forecast.

Antitrust legislation A body of law that establishes rules firms must follow in their decisions on production, how large the firm will be, and other relevant factors that influence the efficiency of market outcomes.

Appreciation An increase in the value of a currency relative to other currencies.

Arbitragers Traders who buy and sell currencies for profit when exchange rates move away from their equilibrium values.

Arc elasticity The price elasticity of demand between any two points on a demand curve.

Assimilative capacity The environment's natural ability to absorb or assimilate some pollutants.

Auction market Market with an auctioneer who adjusts prices to bring quantity demanded into equality with quantity supplied.

Automatic stabilizer Automatic change in tax receipts or transfer payments in the opposite direction of a change in real GNP, thus partially offsetting the real GNP change.

Autonomous consumption expenditures Consumption spending not based on current income, but financed out of savings or asset sales.

Autonomous variable Variable whose value does not directly depend on the level of real GNP or the price level.

Average fixed cost Total fixed cost per unit of output.

Average price level Weighted average of prices of a collection of goods and services or assets.

Average product of a variable input The amount of output per unit of the variable input employed.

Average revenue The amount of revenue per unit of output sold.

Average tax rate Amount of tax paid divided by the taxpayer's income.

Average total cost Total cost per unit of output.

Average variable cost Total variable cost per unit of output.

Balance of payments Accounting summary of a nation's international transactions, built up from the nation's budget constraint, so that the balance always equals zero.

Balance of trade Difference between the dollar value of export and imports.

Balance on goods and services Dollar value of exports of goods and services minus imports of goods and services.

Bank run Large-scale withdrawal of deposits from one or more banks; depletes bank reserves.

Barrier to entry Anything that restricts the free flow of resources between profitable employment alternatives.

Barter economy An economy without money, in which goods must be traded directly for other goods.

Base year Year to which other years' price and output levels are compared.

Block pricing A pricing technique in which a regulated firm is allowed to sell blocks of output at different prices in order to simultaneously earn a normal profit and produce the efficient level of output.

Board of Governors Seven-member body that controls the Federal Reserve System.

Bond A note that promises to pay its holder a specified amount of interest plus the face amount of the bond at a specified point in the future.

Bond dealers Privately owned corporations that hold large portfolios of bonds and buy and sell for their own accounts.

Breakeven point The level of output at which price equals average total cost and economic profit is therefore zero.

Bubble policy Treats a group of closely situated pollution sources as if they were encased in a giant bubble; the pollution standard then applies to emissions coming out of the bubble.

Budget constraint Total sources of funds available to purchase goods, services, and assets and make transfers.

Budget-constraint effect (of money demand on aggregate demand) Works through the budget constraint; one way to accumulate more money is to buy fewer goods and services.

Budget deficit Excess of government expenditures over tax revenues.

Budget surplus Excess of government tax revenues over expenditures.

Bullion Metal in bulk form, typically melted and poured into bars or ingots.

Business cycle Includes an expansion and a recession; measured from peak to peak or trough to trough.

Capacity utilization rate The current output of goods and services as a share of total output that could be produced with existing plant and equipment.

Capital flow Flow of money into or out of a country in exchange for financial assets.

Capital-flow shock Sudden flow of money into or out of the economy to purchase financial assets.

Capital formation Investment in productive capital stock.

Capital gain Income from selling an asset at a price higher than its purchase price.

Capital-intensive production techniques Use more capital relative to labor and other inputs.

Capital loss Loss sustained from selling an asset at a price lower than its purchase price.

Capital mobility Ease with which capital flows from one country to another in response to changes in real interest rates.

Capital stock The factories, machines, and other goods used to produce more goods and services.

Cartel A group of firms that have explicitly and openly agreed to work together to set the price that will be charged in a particular market.

Central bank Governmental agency that controls a nation's money supply.

Ceteris paribus A Latin phrase meaning "other things being equal."

Circular flow diagram Graphical illustration of the economy's circular flow of spending and income.

Circular flow model Illustrates the flows of resources, spending, and income that connect the various sectors of the economy.

Closed shop Employers are only able to hire union members.

Coase Theorem So long as all affected parties stand to gain from a transaction (an exchange of property rights), and transactions costs are low, the transaction will take place.

Coefficient of elasticity The ratio of the percentage change in quantity demanded to the percentage change in price.

Collective bargaining A union represents a group of employees in their negotiations with the employer.

Collude Agree to sell output only at an above-equilibrium price.

Collusion The act of firms working together (cooperating) to establish the price and level of output in a particular market.

Command economy An economy in which decision making is centralized in the hands of a few planners.

Commodity money A commodity valued for consumption purposes that also serves as a medium of exchange.

Commodity standard Basic monetary unit is a specific quantity of a real commodity with a limited supply, such as gold.

Common-property resource A resource for which property rights are poorly defined or nonexistent and whose consumption results in a negative externality.

Comparative advantage Ability to produce a good at a lower opportunity cost than other producers.

Competition A situation in which no individual buyer or seller is able to influence the market price.

Complementary goods Goods that produce more consumer satisfaction when consumed together than when consumed separately.

Concentration ratio A measure of market concentration, that is, the extent to which one or more firms control the level of production in an industry.

Conglomerate merger Two or more firms whose outputs are unrelated merge.

Constant-cost industry Per-unit production costs are constant, causing the long-run supply curve for the market to be horizontal.

Constant economies of scale An increase in the capacity of the firm has no effect on the average total cost of production.

Constitutional economics Study of the optimal rules with which to constrain government behavior.

Consumer decision-maximizing rule To maximize utility, consumers purchase a combination of goods such that the ratio of marginal utility to price is equal across all the goods consumed.

Consumer equilibrium Achieved when the total utility from consuming a combination of goods and services is maximized.

Consumer sovereignty The ability of consumers' preferences to influence the level of output in competitive markets.

Consumers' surplus The difference between the value of a good to consumers and the amount consumers paid to acquire the good.

Consumption expenditures All spending by households on new goods and services, with the exception of the purchase of new houses.

Consumption function Mathematical relationship between consumption spending and disposable income.

Contract theory The theory that explains wage rigidity as the natural outcome of contracts between employers and workers.

Convertible currency Currency that can be traded in the foreign exchange market for other currencies.

Core infrastructure Public capital that contributes directly to the productivity of private capital.

Corporation A legal business entity that is owned by a group of individuals. The corporation can sue and be sued, but the liability of each owner is limited to the amount of money he or she has invested in the firm.

Cost–benefit analysis The identification and evaluation of all the costs and benefits associated with a particular public policy alternative.

Cost of living adjustment A negotiated automatic wage increase that is tied to increases in the cost of living.

Cost–push inflation Inflation driven by rising costs of production.

Costs of production The full opportunity costs of all resources used in the production of the firm's output.

Countercyclical fiscal policy Tax and expenditure policy designed to offset the business cycle.

Countercyclical monetary policy Policy designed to offset business cycle fluctuations by increasing the money supply as a recession approaches and decreasing the money supply when an expansion overheats.

Coupon bonds Bonds that make explicit interest payments on specified dates.

Coupon rate Coupon payments divided by the bond's face value.

Craft union An organization that represents a particular type of skilled workers such as electricians, pipe fitters, or carpenters.

Credibility thesis Output effects of a credible policy are smaller than the output effects of a noncredible policy.

Credit market Markets and institutions that link savers to borrowers.

Cross price elasticity A measure of the responsiveness of the quantity demanded of one good to a percentage change in the price of another good.

Cross subsidization The practice of charging different prices to different groups of customers and using profits from one group to cover the losses generated by another group.

Crowding in When government deficit spending increases real GNP and businesses react by increasing investment spending.

Crowding out When government borrowing increases the interest rate, causing businesses to decrease investment spending.

Current account balance Sum of balance of goods and services and net unilateral transfers.

Customer market Market with posted prices and competition in nonprice dimensions, such as convenience and service.

Cyclical unemployment Unemployment caused by a decline in aggregate demand.

Data lag Time required to assemble data on the economy.

Decertification election Workers vote on whether to remove an existing union from their workplace.

Decision-making costs The time, effort, and risk involved in making a consumption decision.

Default risk Risk that a borrower will fail to meet principal or interest payments on schedule.

Demand deposits Zero-interest checking accounts.

Demand–pull inflation Inflation driven by increases in aggregate demand.

Depreciation A decrease in the value of a currency relative to other currencies.

Depreciation The loss in the value of a piece of capital due to its use in production.

Deregulation The removal of specific regulations that govern the economic activity of the firms in a particular market or industry.

Derived demand The demand for a resource is derived from the demand for the product the resource is used to produce.

Discount rate Interest rate set by the Board of Governors on loans of reserves by the Federal Reserve to banks.

Discounting The technique used to calculate the present value of a future sum.

Diseconomies of scale An increase in the capacity of the firm results in an increase in the average total cost of production.

Disequilibrium Any price–output combination at which market forces are acting to change price or quantity.

Disequilibrium wage differences Differences in wages that are caused by a short-run disequilibrium in one or more labor markets.

Disposable income Household income net of income and payroll taxes and transfer payments.

Dividends The amount of profit per share of stock outstanding that is paid to the firm's stockholders.

Double coincidence of wants Both parties to a trade have what the other wants and want what the other has to trade.

Durable consumer goods Goods that are not themselves consumed, but which provide services over a period of time.

Duration of unemployment Length of time spent unemployed.

Economic efficiency Obtaining the maximum net gain from an action.

Economic instability Movements in real GNP away from its natural level and significant changes in the price level over short time periods.

Economic profit The difference between total revenue and the total opportunity costs of production.

Economic rent The amount of income in excess of a worker's reservation wage.

Economics The study of how people decide to use scarce resources to produce goods and services and distribute them for consumption.

Economics of public choice Application of economic principles to the study of political behavior.

Economies of scale An increase in the capacity of the firm results in a decrease in the average total cost of production.

Elastic currency Currency whose quantity expands and contracts as the demand for it rises and falls.

Elastic demand Quantity demanded is relatively responsive to a change in price; the coefficient of elasticity is greater than one.

Electoral cycle A political business cycle; government policy increases aggregate demand during election years to generate high real GNP growth and low unemployment, then slows aggregate demand in subsequent years to reduce inflation.

Emission banking A program that grants a firm credit for reducing emissions below the existing standard; the credit can be saved for later use or for sale to another firm.

Emission charge A tax imposed on each unit of pollution emitted by a firm.

Emission standard A legal limit on the amount of a pollutant an individual source is allowed to emit.

Enactment lag Time required to pass and sign a bill into law.

Endogenous cycle theories Theories that link business cycles to processes naturally occuring within the economy.

Entrepreneur A person who organizes, manages, and assumes the risks of a business enterprise.

Entrepreneurship Creative management of production.

Equalizing wage differences Differences in wages that are based on nonwage job characteristics, and that tend to equalize the total benefits offered by different jobs.

Equation of exchange A mathematical identity equating the quantity of money in existence times the average number of times it is spent during a period to total spending: $M \times V = Pl \times RGNP$.

Equilibrium A price–output combination at which there is no pressure for either price or output to change.

Excess reserves Reserves in excess of Federal Reserve requirements.

Exchange rate Number of units of one currency that exchange for one unit of another currency.

Exogenous Determined outside the economic system.

Exogenous cycle theories Theories that link business cycles to factors outside the normal workings of the economy.

Expansion Period when real GNP is rising.

Expected price level Average price level workers expect to prevail during some future period.

Expected real interest rate Nominal rate of interest adjusted for the expected inflation rate; $r^e = i - p^e$.

Expected real wage rate Wage rate in dollars of constant buying power that workers expect to receive.

Explicit costs The out-of-pocket expenses incurred by a firm; they involve the expenditure of money to buy resources, raise financial capital, and so on.

Explicit labor contract A signed, legal agreement setting wages and working conditions for a specified period.

Exports Sales of domestically produced goods and services to foreigners.

External benefit A benefit resulting from a production or consumption decision that is borne by a third party who is not part of the original transaction.

External cost A cost resulting from a production or consumption decision that is borne by a third party who is not part of the original transaction.

Externalities (spillover effects) Market exchanges that generate costs or benefits for people not directly involved in the exchanges.

Face value The principal that is repaid when a bond matures.

Factor inputs Unprocessed materials and labor services used to produce goods and services.

Factor of production (input) A resource used in production.

Factor productivity Amount of output produced per unit of factor (labor or capital) input.

Factors contributing to growth Typically classified into three categories: growth in the capital stock, growth in the supply of labor, and growth in factor productivity.

Federal debt Total amount of U.S. government bonds outstanding.

Federal funds Loans of reserves by one bank to another bank.

Federal funds rate Market-determined interest rate on loans of reserves by one bank to another.

Federal Open Market Committee (FOMC) Twelve-member committee that controls open market operations for the Federal Reserve.

Federal republic A system of representative government with several coexisting levels of government handling different sets of issues.

Federal Reserve notes Paper currency issued by the Federal Reserve.

Financial capital The money firms acquire from lending institutions and individuals to finance production activities, including current production, expansion, product development, and so forth.

Financial innovation Development of new financial assets or services that reduce transactions costs or provide savers with more options.

Financial intermediary An institution, such as a bank or savings and loan association, that facilitates the interaction between lenders and borrowers.

Financial investment Allocation of savings to the purchase of financial assets.

Financial sector Markets and institutions that transfer funds from savers to borrowers.

Fiscal policy The use of government expenditures and taxes to affect aggregate demand or aggregate supply.

Fixed cost Any cost that does not vary with output. In the short run, fixed costs are sunk.

Flow Economic variable that must be measured over a period of time.

Flow model of unemployment Model based on the flow of people into and out of employment and unemployment categories.

Foreign exchange market Market in which different currencies trade for one another.

Foreign sector Export, import, and capital flows to and from foreign economies.

Fractional reserve banking Holding less than one dollar in cash reserves for every dollar in deposits.

Free ride To consume without paying an appropriate price.

Free rider An individual who receives benefits from a public good but does not pay for those benefits.

Free rider problem Incentive for consumers of public goods to understate the true value of the good to them in order to reduce the amount they must pay to consume it.

Frequency of unemployment A measure of the number of unemployment spells that begin in a time period.

Frictional unemployment Short-term unemployment arising because moving from one job to another takes time.

Functional distribution of income The distribution of earnings among the factors of production.

Future value An amount of money held today plus the amount of interest that would accrue over the time period in question.

General equilibrium analysis Is concerned with the relationships across markets and the conditions necessary for equilibrium in all markets simultaneously.

GNP (implicit price) deflator A price index covering all goods and services included in GNP; uses current-year quantity rates.

Gosbank The Soviet state bank.

Gosplan Soviet state planning commission.

Government budget deficit Excess of government expenditures over tax receipts.

Government purchases Spending on goods and services; excludes transfer payments.

Government sector Spending, revenue, and financial flows to and from governmental units.

Graduated-rate (progressive) income tax Tax rate on the last dollar of income rises as the taxpayer's income increases.

Gross investment Total spending on capital goods, including replacement of depreciated capital goods and additions to the capital stock.

Gross national product (GNP) Total market value of final goods and services produced during a time period.

Growth rate Percentage change in a variable per unit of time; usually calculated on an annual basis.

High employment budget deficit What the budget deficit would be, given existing expenditure and tax rates, if the economy were operating at the natural output level.

Hiring rate Percentage of applicants who choose to accept a firm's employment offer in a time period.

Horizontal merger A merger into a single firm of two or more firms producing the same or similar products.

Human capital The productivity-determining skills and abilities embodied in labor.

Hyperinflation Runaway inflation, sometimes thousands of percent per month.

Hypothesis An implication of a theory that can (in principle) be shown to be true or false.

Imagined product differentiation The result of efforts such as advertising or packaging that create the impression that two or more products are different when, in fact, they are composed of exactly the same inputs.

Implementation lag Time required to put a policy decision into effect.

Implicit contract An informal agreement between employer and employees that limits the choices an employer can make by generating expectations on the part of workers.

Implicit costs The opportunity costs of using resources that are already owned by the firm.

Implicit labor agreement An informal, often verbal, agreement between employers and workers establishing reasonable expectations about wages and employment conditions.

Import-competing industries Domestic industries that produce goods that can be imported or are close substitutes for imported goods.

Imports Purchases of foreign-produced goods and services by domestic households, businesses, and governmental units.

Income effect Effect on the interest rate of a shift in the demand for money caused by a change in aggregate income.

Income effect The increase in real purchasing power that results from a decrease in the price of a consumption good, *ceteris paribus*.

Income elasticity of demand A measure of the responsiveness of quantity demanded to a change in income.

Income mobility The tendency of individuals and families to move among income groups over time.

Increasing-cost industry Per-unit production costs are an increasing function of the level of output, causing the long-run supply curve for the market to be upward sloping.

Indicative planning Government sets goals, provides incentives for private firms to meet those goals, but allows firms to determine *how* they will meet the goals.

Indifference curve All combinations of two goods, X and Y, that yield the same level of total utility.

Indifference curve map A set of indifference curves, each of which is associated with a different level of total utility; moving up to the right (away from the origin) moves the consumer to higher levels of utility.

Industrial union An organization of workers in an entire industry; membership is not determined on the basis of a particular skill.

Industry A grouping of firms that produce a similar product.

Inelastic demand Quantity demanded is relatively unresponsive to a change in price; the coefficient of elasticity is greater than zero but less than one.

Inflation expectations effect Effect on the interest rate of a change in the expected inflation rate; works through credit demand and supply.

Inflation rate Percentage rate of change of the aggregate price level from one period to another.

Inflationary expectations (Fisher) effect Effect on the interest rate of a change in the expected inflation rate.

Information costs The costs incurred in gathering information to be used in making a consumption decision.

Infrastructure Public capital used to provide such economic support services as transportation, sewage treatment, and water supply.

Interest rate The price of credit, expressed as percent per year.

Interest-rate effect (of money demand on aggregate demand) When money demand changes, the interest rate changes, affecting aggregate demand through borrowing costs and wealth effects.

Intermediate goods Produced goods that enter into the production of other goods and services.

Intermediation Issuing claims with one set of characteristics to savers and acquiring claims with a different set of characteristics from borrowers.

Internal rate of return The interest rate that makes the present value of the stream of profits accruing from a piece of capital exactly equal to the present value of its costs.

International reserve currency Currency widely used in international transactions.

Intervention Government purchases or sales of currency in the foreign exchange market designed to affect the value of the exchange rate.

Inventory Stock of raw materials or unfinished goods to be used in the production process or of finished goods waiting to be sold.

Inventory changes Increases or decreases in business holdings of raw materials, unfinished goods, or finished goods ready for sale.

Investment Purchase of capital goods used to produce goods or services.

Investment spending Purchases of plant, equipment, and inventories by businesses and of new houses by households.

Investment tax credit Allows firms to deduct a portion of their investment spending from the corporate taxes they owe.

Isocost line All the combinations of two inputs that result in the same total cost.

Isoquant All the combinations of a set of inputs that yield the same level of total output.

Isoquant map All the output levels that can be produced with a set of inputs; moving up to the right (away from the origin) moves the firm to higher levels of total output.

Keynesian cycle model An endogenous theory based on the instability of investment spending.

L A broad measure of liquid assets.

Labor force Number of employed plus the number of unemployed.

Labor force participation rate The percentage of the noninstitutionalized, nonmilitary population between ages 16 and 70 who are employed or without a job but looking for work.

Labor-intensive production techniques Use more labor relative to capital and other inputs.

Labor market The interplay of buyers and sellers of labor services.

Labor-market discrimination Equally productive workers are paid less because of race or sex.

Labor union A group of employees who band together to improve their terms of employment.

Lag in the effect of monetary policy Time that elapses between a change in the money supply and the consequent change in aggregate demand.

Lag in the effect of money supply changes Time between a change in the money supply and the consequent change in aggregate demand.

Laissez faire Literally, "let them do it"; an environment with minimal government intervention.

Law of demand The quantity demanded of a good is negatively related to its price, holding constant other factors that affect demand.

Law of diminishing marginal returns At some point, the marginal physical product of an input begins to decline.

Law of diminishing marginal utility As an individual consumes more of a good, the marginal utility of additional units eventually decreases.

Law of supply The quantity supplied of a good is positively related to its price, holding constant other factors that affect supply.

Leviathan model Model of government that assumes that the people controlling government willl use it to further their own ends.

Liquidity Ability to quickly and easily convert an asset into spendable money at a price near its maximum market value.

Liquidity-constrained consumption Current consumption limited not only by long-run disposable income, but also by the inability to borrow during periods when income is temporarily low.

Liquidity effect Effect on the interest rate of an injection of liquidity (money) into the system by the Federal Reserve.

Logrolling Vote trading to acquire sufficient support for issues otherwise supported by a minority of voters.

Long run A period of time sufficient for a firm to vary the quantities of all factors of production.

Long-run aggregate supply (LRAS) curve Vertical line at the natural output level, showing that output and the price level are unrelated in the long run, when wages have fully adjusted to changes in the price level.

Long-run average cost curve The cost of producing different levels of output when all inputs are allowed to vary; it shows the effect on average total cost when the capacity of the firm is varied.

Long-run decision A planning decision. In the long run, all inputs are variable, including the amount of capital stock employed by the firm.

Long-run labor market equilibrium Market-clearing wage rate and employment level when the economy's actual price level equals workers' expected price level and all wages have adjusted fully to expectations.

Lorenz curve A functional relationship that indicates the percentage of the population that receives a given percentage of the total income in the economy.

M1 Monetary aggregate that includes only assets that are immediately spendable.

M2 Monetary aggregate that includes M1 plus liquid savings instruments.

M3 Monetary aggregate that includes M2 plus some less liquid savings instruments.

Macroeconomics Study of the behavior of the whole economy.

Managed (dirty) float Government intervenes to offset temporary fluctuations in the exchange rate, but allows the rate to move over time in response to long-run changes in demand and supply.

Marginal benefit The satisfaction derived from consuming an additional unit of a good.

Marginal cost The addition to total cost associated with the production of an additional unit of output.

Marginal physical product The change in total output that results from employing an additional unit of a resource.

Marginal productivity of labor Addition to total output produced by one more unit of labor.

Marginal propensity to consume Fraction of an additional dollar of disposable income that is consumed; equals the change in consumption divided by the change in disposable income.

Marginal propensity to save Fraction of an additional dollar of disposable income that is saved; equals the change in savings divided by the change in disposable income.

Marginal rate of substitution The ratio of the marginal utilities of two goods, holding total utility constant; the slope of the indifference curve.

Marginal rate of technical substitution MRTS between two inputs, for example, labor (L) and capital (K), is equal to the negative of the ratio of their marginal products, or $-MP_L/MP_K$.

Marginal resource cost The change in total cost resulting from the employment of an additional unit of a resource.

Marginal revenue The change in total revenue associated with a change in output.

Marginal revenue product The change in total revenue resulting from the employment of an additional unit of a resource.

Marginal tax rate Rate paid on the final dollar of income.

Marginal utility The additional benefit the consumer receives from consuming one more unit of a good or service.

Marginal utility per dollar A ratio that measures the additional utility per additional dollar spent on a good or service.

Market economy An economy in which individuals own most property and make most decisions about its use; decisions are coordinated through markets.

Market failure The forces of supply and demand do not yield the economically efficient level of output.

Market price Price established by the interaction of consumers demanding a good and producers supplying the good.

Market structure The characteristics of output markets including the number of firms in the market, the size of the firms, and the variety of products produced by firms, that influence the behavior of firms.

Markets Institutions and arrangements that coordinate the activities of buyers and sellers.

Materials balancing A balance-sheet approach to matching available supplies of resources to demands for those resources.

Maturity The length of time for which a bond is issued.

Mean family income The average income for families in a particular category.

Medium of exchange Asset generally accepted in exchange and used in most transactions.

Merchandise balance of trade Difference between the value of tangible goods exported and the value of such goods imported.

Microeconomics Study of consumer and firm behavior in individual markets.

Mixed economy An economy in which economic decision making is shared by individuals and government.

Mobility costs The expense, time, and effort spent traveling to a particular location to complete a transaction for a consumption good.

Model A simplified representation of reality that focuses attention on the issues the scientist wishes to examine.

Monetarist cycle model An exogenous theory based on the effects of monetary shocks on aggregate demand.

Monetary aggregate A specific collection of financial assets serving as a measure of the money supply.

Monetary base Money created outside the banking system; includes currency held by the public plus bank reserves.

Monetary policy Government control of the money supply as a means of influencing the level of economic activity.

Monetary policy target Economic variable the Federal Reserve seeks to control as a means of influencing other variables.

Money market Shorthand term for the demand for and supply of money; money trades in all markets.

Money market deposit account An account at a depository institution that pays a market rate of interest and has limited checking privileges.

Money market mutual fund An organization that pools the funds of savers and uses them to buy short-term liquid assets.

Monopolistically competitive market A market characterized by a large number of relatively small price-searching firms, resource mobility, and product differentiation.

Monopoly A single firm that produces all the output in a particular market.

Monopsony Only one buyer of a good or resource; for example, only one employer of labor in a particular location.

Moral hazard A situation in which an individual has the incentive to do something that is socially costly.

Multiplier effect A change in autonomous spending generates changes in consumption spending, causing the ultimate change in aggregate demand to be larger than the initial change in autonomous spending.

Mutual fund Organization that pools the funds of a large number of savers and uses them to buy financial assets, passing the earnings on through to the savers.

Mutual interdependence One firm's actions influence the actions of other firms in a market.

National income The total annual income paid to all owners of resources. It is the sum of all wages, rent, interest, and profit.

National industrial policy Policy designed to affect the long-term growth and industrial composition of the economy.

Natural level of employment Employment level that prevails in long-run labor market equilibrium.

Natural monopoly The long-run average costs of production are decreasing over the relevant range of output.

Natural output level Output level determined by the economy's natural employment level, resources, technology, and economic organization.

Natural rate of unemployment Unemployment rate that exists when the labor market is in long-run equilibrium and toward which the actual unemployment rate tends over time.

Net exports Exports minus imports.

Net gain Difference between benefits received and costs incurred.

Net investment Additions to the existing capital stock.

Net national product GNP adjusted for capital depreciation.

New Keynesian Economics A branch of theory devoted to developing the microeconomic foundations of price and wage rigidities.

Nominal wage rate Wage in current dollars.

Nondurable consumption goods Goods that are usually consumed within a short time after their purchase.

Nonequalizing wage differences Differences in wages that cause the total benefits of working in different jobs to vary.

Nonprice competition Activities such as product differentiation and advertising, which are designed to increase the demand for a firm's output.

Normal profit An implicit cost incurred by the firm; the amount of payment that is just sufficient to keep the entrepreneurs/owners in business.

Normative position Based on a set of values; expresses what should be (rather than what is).

Off-budget items Expenditures and receipts not included in the official U.S. government budget.

Offset program Allows a new pollution source in a particular geographic region to pay existing sources to reduce their emissions below that required by the existing standard, in lieu of installing control technology at the new plant.

Oligopoly A small number of firms dominate the market; the economic well-being and behavior of the firms is mutually interdependent.

One-year plan Detailed production goals for all sectors of the economy and all enterprises within sectors.

Open-economy macroeconomics Takes account of both domestic and international transactions and linkages.

Open market operations Purchases and sales of U.S. government bonds by the Federal Reserve; such operations affect the quantity of bank reserves.

Open shop Employees are not required to belong to a union if they choose not to.

Opportunity cost The value of the most desirable alternative given up when choosing an option.

Output persistence Prolonged deviations of output above or below the natural output level.

Paper standard Basic monetary unit has no intrinsic value and can be produced in unlimited quantities.

Par value Official exchange rate in a fixed exchange rate system.

Partial equilibrium analysis Focuses on the conditions necessary for equilibrium in a particular market, independent of other markets in the economy.

Partisan cycle Different political parties consistently produce different macroeconomic behavior.

Partnership A business that is owned by two or more people. Each partner is personally liable for all of the firm's obligations.

Passive rule Policy rule that does not alter the money supply in response to changes in economic activity.

Patent Issued by the government, it entitles its owner to exclusive rights to a production process for a period of seventeen years.

Payroll tax Tax on income used to support the Social Security system.

Peak The high point of an expansion.

Per capita GNP GNP divided by population.

Per capita income The average income for each individual in a particular category.

Perfectly competitive market A large number of relatively small price-taking firms that produce a homogeneous product and for whom entry and exit are relatively costless.

Perfectly elastic demand The percentage change in quantity demanded is infinite for a price decrease, regardless of the value of the percentage change in price; the coefficient of elasticity equals infinity.

Perfectly inelastic demand The percentage change in quantity demanded is zero, regardless of the value of the percentage change in price; the coefficient of elasticity equals zero.

Perquisites ("perks") Nonincome benefits of a job.

Personal distribution of income The share of all personal income received by families at different income levels.

Personal exemption Amount every taxpayer is entitled to subtract from income before calculating the amount of income tax due.

Personal income Total income of households.

Point elasticity of demand Price elasticity at a single point on a demand curve.

Policy rule Formal guidelines followed by policymakers.

Positive science The study of how the world works; an examination of what is (rather than what should be).

Poverty The result of a level of income that is insufficient to ensure some predetermined minimum standard of living.

Present value The amount of money that would have to be invested today at the market rate of interest to yield a future sum.

Price ceiling A law or regulation holding the market price below its equilibrium level.

Price discrimination The practice of charging different prices to different consumers of the same good or service.

Price elasticity of demand The relationship between a change in quantity demanded of a good or service and a change in price.

Price elasticity of resource demand A measure of how responsive the quantity demanded of a resource is to a change in its price.

Price elasticity of supply A measure of the responsiveness of the quantity supplied to a percentage change in market price.

Price floor A law or regulation holding the market price above its equilibrium level.

Price leadership A situation in which one firm in an industry establishes the market price and the remaining firms in the industry follow suit.

Price-searching firm Has some degree of market power; the output decisions of a price searcher affect market price.

Price-taking firm Takes the market price as given; the output decisions of the individual firm have no effect on market price.

Principle of comparative advantage Two countries can maximize the joint production of two goods by each producing the good for which it is the relatively low-opportunity-cost producer and trading for the other good.

Private good A good whose use by one person reduces its availability for use by other people.

Privatization Production of public goods by private firms.

Procyclical Moving in the same direction as real GNP over the course of the business cycle.

Producers' surplus The difference between the revenue received by producers for a good and the opportunity cost of producing the good.

Product differentiation Variations in one or more characteristics of a good that are designed to distinguish the good from its competitors.

Production function Determines the maximum output that can be produced from a given quantity of inputs (and a given level of technology).

Production plan Government plan setting production goals for a command economy.

Production possibilities frontier All the maximum possible combinations of two goods that can be produced with available resouces.

Productive efficiency Operating on the production possibilities frontier; producing without wasting resources.

Productivity The amount of output produced per unit of input per time period.

Profit The difference between total revenue and total cost.

Property rights The legally sanctioned control that an individual exercises over a collection of goods, resources, and services.

Public enterprise A government-owned business.

Public good A good whose consumption is nonrival and nonexcludable; markets will not produce the efficient level of public goods.

Purchasing power parity Theory that a specific amount of currency should purchase the same quantity of tradable goods in all countries.

Pure interest rate Pure rental price of money, common to all interest rates.

Quantity theory of money A theory linking money supply changes to changes in real GNP in the short run and to changes in the price level in both the short run and the long run.

Quit rate Percentage of a firm's employees who choose to quit their jobs in a time period.

Quota A limit on the quantity of a good that may be imported.

Rate of return Calculated as the amount of profit attributable to a productive input expressed as a percentage of its cost.

Rate of return on investment Net income earned by an investment project as a percentage of its cost.

Rate-of-return regulation Prices are set at a level that will cover the costs of production and provide the firm's investors with a competitive rate of return on their investment.

Rational decision maker Someone capable of setting goals and acting purposefully towards achieving those goals.

Rational expectations Expectations of a variable formed on the basis of all available information with an expected marginal value greater than its marginal cost of collection and use; forward looking.

Rational expectations hypothesis Proposition that only unanticipated changes in aggregate demand affect real output.

Real GNP GNP measured in base-year prices.

Real GNP gap Percentage deviation of actual real GNP from the natural level of real GNP.

Real money balances Money holdings of constant buying power.

Real product differentiation Similar products differ as a result of actual characteristics such as quality of inputs or location of the firm.

Real rate of return Rate of return calculated in terms of constant prices, that is, adjusted for inflation.

Recession Period when real GNP is falling.

Recognition lag Time required to interpret data correctly.

Regulatory forbearance When regulators permit insolvent financial institutions to continue operating, rather than closing them.

Relative price Price of a good compared to the prices of other goods.

Reservation wage Minimum wage rate that will induce a searcher to accept a job or a worker to remain in a job.

Reserve requirement ratio Minimum amount of legal reserves a bank can hold, stated as a percentage of deposits.

Reserves Vault cash plus bank deposits with district Federal Reserve Banks.

Resource A raw material or produced good available for use in the production of other goods and services.

Resource constraint Maximum quantity of resources available for use in production or consumption.

Resource demand schedule The quantity demanded of a resource at each price.

Resource endowment The stock of resources available to a person or nation.

Resource mobility The ability of resources to move among alternative uses.

Restrictive monetary policy A decrease in the size or growth rate of the money supply, designed to reduce or slow the growth of aggregate demand.

Retained earnings Business profits that are not paid out to shareholders as dividends; business savings.

Retention rate Percentage of a firm's employees who choose to remain in their jobs during a period of time.

Revenue requirement The amount of money a regulated firm such as a utility must earn to be able to cover its production costs and earn a normal profit.

Risk premium An addition to the pure interest rate, required to induce lenders to make risky loans.

Rule of reason Only business practices that are considered unfair or illegal should be considered unreasonable.

Science The systematic study of how the world works.

Screening Ascertaining a prospective employee's qualifications through interviews or testing.

Search Process whereby job seekers acquire information about the availability and characteristics of jobs.

Search theory The theory that much unemployment is due to the time required to obtain information about job availability and characteristics.

Secondary market Market in which previously issued securities are traded.

Securities markets Secondary markets in which existing shares of stock or bonds are bought and sold.

Security The physical evidence of ownership of debt, such as a stock certificate or promissory note.

Senile-industry argument Industries that are no longer internationally competitive should be protected to save domestic jobs.

Shares of stock Certificates of ownership in a company. **Stockholders** are the owners of the firm.

Short run The period of time during which at least one factor of production is fixed in quantity.

Short-run aggregate supply (SRAS) curve Relates the aggregate quantity of goods and services supplied at a given level of wages to the aggregate price level.

Short-run capacity The level of output at which the average total cost of production is minimized.

Short-run decision A constrained decision. In the short run, the amount of at least one of the inputs employed by the firm is fixed.

Short-run labor market equilibrium Market-clearing wage rate and employment level when the economy's actual price level equals workers' expected price level and all wages have adjusted fully to expectations.

Shortage (excess demand) Quantity demanded exceeds quantity supplied at a particular price.

Shutdown point The price level at which average variable cost is at a minimum. If price falls to this level, the firm minimizes losses by shutting down.

Social benefits The sum of the private and external benefits of a production or consumption activity.

Social costs The sum of the private and external costs of a production or consumption activity.

Sole proprietorship A business that is owned by a single person.

Sources of funds All the ways an individual can obtain spendable funds.

Special-interest group Cohesive group of individuals with a common interest in some economic or social issue.

Spending Using funds to purchase newly produced goods and services.

Standard deduction Deduction that may be taken instead of itemizing specific deductions.

Standard of value A unit in terms of which prices are quoted.

Stock Economic variable that exists at a point in time.

Store of value An asset that retains exchange value over time.

Strike An organized refusal by employees to work that is designed to obtain more favorable working conditions by preventing the firm from producing output.

Structural deficit Another name for the high employment budget deficit.

Structural unemployment Long-term unemployment arising from the mismatch of job requirements and worker characterisitcs.

Substitutes Goods that are alternatives to one another in consumption.

Substitution effect Consumers purchase more of a good whose price has fallen relative to the prices of its substitutes.

Sunk cost A cost that has been incurred in the past that can no longer be recovered. Sunk costs are irrelevant for current decisions.

Supply shock Sudden shift of the SRAS curve caused by a sharp change in the cost of an important factor of production.

Supply-side policies Policies designed to shift the aggregate supply curve by changing the incentive to produce goods and services.

Surplus (excess supply) Quantity supplied exceeds quantity demanded at a particular price.

Tariff A tax on imported goods.

Tax deduction Expenditures that can be subtracted from income before calculating the amount of income tax due.

Technology The application of knowledge about the world to the production of goods and services.

Term structure Pattern of interest rates on bonds of different maturity rates.

Term to maturity Length of time until a bond matures and pays off its face value.

Terms of trade The ratio at which two goods are traded for one another.

Theory A set of generalizations purporting to explain observed regularities.

Theory of contestable markets So long as entry and exit are costless, firms will produce at minimum cost and earn no economic profits, regardless of the other characteristics of the market.

Threat effect The possibility that workers in a particular firm or industry will form a union if their wage demands are not met.

Threshold effect Inflation is incorporated into contracts only when it reaches a level that is too costly to ignore.

Time-inconsistency problem Optimal long-run policy differs from the optimal short-run policy, giving policymakers the incentive to cheat on long-run policy rules.

Time preference Desire to have something now rather than in the future.

Time value of money The amount of interest that a sum of money could earn over a fixed period of time.

Total cost of production The sum of the costs of each input (fixed and variable) used in production.

Total revenue The product of a good's market price and the quantity of the good purchased.

Trade balance Difference between the money value of a country's exports and the money value of its imports.

Trade deficit Negative trade balance; exports are less than imports.

Trade surplus Positive trade balance; exports exceed imports.

Transactions costs Any of the opportunity costs from consumption that are not incorporated in the market price of a good or service.

Transactions theory of money demand Theory based on the idea that money is held primarily to carry out transactions.

Transfer payment Transfer of tax revenue to recipients who give the government nothing in return.

Transferable discharge permit A property right to discharge a specified quantity of a particular pollutant; it can be traded among affected parties.

Trough The low point of a recession.

Trust A group of firms that agree to work together to restrict total output in order to maximize profits.

Turning points Cyclical peaks and troughs, where the direction of real GNP growth changes.

Unanticipated change in aggregate demand Change whose direction or size is unexpected.

Underground market Market for illegally produced or transported goods.

Unemployed Anyone without a job who has actively looked for work or who has been on temporary layoff during the week before the employment survey is taken.

Unemployment rate Number of people without jobs who are actively looking for work divided by the number of workers plus the number actively seeking jobs.

Unilateral transfers Gifts or grants for which nothing is received in return.

Union shop Employers can hire anyone they wish; however, new employees must join the union after they have been hired.

Unitary elastic demand The percentage change in quantity demanded is exactly equal to the percentage change in price; the coefficient of elasticity equals one.

Uses of funds All the ways an individual can dispose of spendable funds.

Utility Economic term for consumer satisfaction.

Value added Difference between the market value of a good or service and the value of the material inputs used in its production.

Value of money Quantity of goods and services a unit of money will buy.

Variable cost Any cost that varies directly with the quantity of output produced.

Velocity The average number of times a unit of money is spent during a time period.

Vertical merger A merger into a single firm of two or more firms at different levels in the chain of production.

Worker-managed firm A firm owned by its workers, who hire and fire managers.

INDEX

Accelerator principle, 840
Accelerator-multiplier model, 840–841
Accounting profit, 203–205
Action, collective, 135
Advantage, absolute, 38, 928
  comparative, 39–45
  principle of comparative, 928
AFL-CIO, 408–409, 411–412
Aggregate demand, 550, 558, 579–583, 621, 657, 696, 732–733, 772, 826, 898–901, 916
  stability of, 659
Aggregate demand curve, 580–582
Aggregate labor demand curve, 592
Aggregate labor supply curve, 591
Aggregate supply, 550, 659, 826
  long-run, 608–09, 620
  short-run, 605
Aggregate supply curve, 603
Aggregation, 553
Agriculture, collectivized, 989
Aid to Families With Dependent Children, , 463–466
Airline Deregulation Act, 340–341
Akerlof, George, 47
Alexis, Marcus, 346
Allocation, 9, 56
Allocative efficiency, 265–266, 289–90, 306, 323
Alternatives, 6
Analysis, economic, 5
  graphical, 7
Antitrust legislation, 331, 333–337
Apgar, William C., 491
Appreciation, exchange rate, 968

Arbitragers, 965
Aschauer, David, 631, 790, 916, 919
Assets, financial, 516, 540
  real, 695
Assimilative capacity, 477–478
Automatic stabilizer, 784
Automobiles , Japanese, 942–943
Autonomous variable, 580
Average fixed cost, 221–223
Average product, 218–219, 223
  relationship to marginal product, 218–219
Average product function, 218–219
Average revenue, 234–236, 251–252
Average revenue function, 234–236
Average total cost, 221–227, 251–53, 285–90, 304–5
Average variable cost, 221–225, 253–54

Backward-bending labor supply curve, 374
Bailey, Martin J., 916, 919
Balance of payments, 954–956
Balance of trade, merchandise, 921
Balance on current account, 956
Balance on goods and services, 955
Balanced budget amendment, 792 791
Balke, Nathan S., 836-837
Bank run, 712, 861
Banking, fractional reserve, 716
Bank(s), central, 134
  commercial, 711
  national, 712
Bar chart, 24

Barriers to entry, 300–306, 314
  in labor markets, 389–392
Barro, Robert, 857
Barter, 684
Base year, 527
Baumol, William, 325
Benefits, external, *see* External benefits
  marginal external, 475–477
  marginal private, 475–477
  marginal social, 475–477
Benefit(s), 3
  external, 126–130
  marginal, 59, 94, 96–97, 615
  net, 50
  of consumption, 75
  private, 127, 130
  social, 94, 127, 130
  total, 96–97
Bierce, Ambrose, 333
Block Pricing, 311
Bluestone, Barry, 919
Bond dealers, 723
Bonds, 200–201, 743–44
  coupon, 743
Borjas, George J., 597
Branson, William H., 945
Brayton, Flint, 850
Breakeven point, 253
Breyer, S., 332-3
Brookes, Warren T., 599
Brown, H. James, 491
Browning, Edgar K. , 448
Bubble policy, 484
Budget constraint, 186–188
Budget-constraint effect, 700 698

1017

Bullion, 687
Bus Regulatory Reform Act, 340–341
Business cycle(s), 544, 832
   empirical evidence on, 846–858
   endogenous theories of, 835
   exogenous theories of, 835
   Keynesian model of, 835–841, 848–850
   monetarist model of, 841–844, 850–857
   political, 905

Cable Communications Policy Act, 338
Capacity, short-run, 224–227, 231–233
Capacity utilization rate, 435, 575
Capital, 2, 216–219, 226, 229–233, 426–428, 431, 434–435, 631
   financial, 68, 198–201
   human, 2, 13, 372–73
   investment in human, 392–94
   social, 15
   public, 631
Capital consumption allowance, 526, 752
Capital flow(s), 543, 956
Capital formation, 13
Capital gain, 694
Capital investment, *see* Investment
Capital loss, 694
Capital mobility, 969
Capital stock, 626 632 600
Capital-flow shock, 973
Capital-intensive production, 210
Cartel, 319
Carter, Jimmy, 666, 877, 881
Celler-Kefauver Act, 334
Chakravarty, Subrata N., 457
Chiswick, Barry R., 597
Choice, individual, 8
Choice, social, 7, 10, 12–13
Circular flow model, 271
Civil Aeronautics Act, 347
Civil Aeronautics Board, 342, 344, 347
Clark, Lindley H., 727
Clark, Kim B., 807
Clayton Act, 333
Clean Air Act, 485
Closed shop, 411
Coase, Ronald, 471
Coase theorem, 471–473
Cohon, George, 966
Collective bargaining, 406–408
Collusion, 125, 318–322
Collyns, Charles, 49, 139
Commodity standard, 888
Common property resource, 470, 489–490
   policy prescriptions, 490
Competition, 57, 101
   foreign, 40, 920, 935
   lack of, 125–126
   unfair, 4
Competitive industry, 201
Competitiveness, international, 935
Complementary goods, 63
Comprehensive Employment and Training Act, 463
Concentration ratio, 314–315

Constant cost industry, 262–263
Constant economies of scale, 232–233
Constraint, budget, 517, 520, 697, 781, 954
Constraint, international budget, 956
   resource, 5, 8, 11
Consumer decision-making rule, 176
Consumer equilibrium, 176
Consumer price index, 529
   and the poverty level, 457
Consumer sovereignty, 264–265
Consumer surplus, 98, 100, 306–307, 343–44, 933–34
Consumer sovereignty, 980
Consumption, 523, 558, 564
   autonomous, 661
   current, 2, 15
   empirical evidence on, 561
   future, 2, 561
   government, 916
   liquidity-constrained, 566
   versus savings and investment, 426–427
Consumption function, 558–559, 566, 837–838
Contract theory, 820–825 815
Contracts, long term, in labor markets, 399–400
Contract(s), Explicit, 604
   Implicit, 604, 656, 822
   Labor, 655
Copernicus, Nicolaus, 17
Cooperatives, 990
Coordination, 20
Corporation, 198–201
Cost, 3
   Law of increasing opportunity, 11
   minimization, 36
Cost curve(s), average total, 221–227
   Average variable, 221–227
   average fixed, 221–223
   long-run average, 231–233, 307–11
   Marginal, 221–227
Cost frontier, *see* Long-Run Average Cost Curve
Cost of living adjustment, 414–415
Costs of production, 202–205
Cost(s), Average total, 251
   average fixed, 221–223
   average total, 221–227, 251–53, 285–90, 304–5
   average variable, 221–225, 253–54
   Explicit, 393
   external, 126–127
   fixed, 219–221, 253–55
   implicit, 393
   information, 137–138, 687
   long run average, 229–234, 307–11
   marginal external, 473–474
   marginal private, 473–474
   marginal social, 473–474
   marginal, 65–67, 94–97, 221–227, 223–224, 238–239, 615
   menu, 676
   opportunity, *see* Opportunity cost
   of production, 67, 75
   private, 127
   social, 94, 127

   total, 96–97, 221–227, 251–253
   transaction, 46, 710, 180–183, 471–473
   unit, *see* Average total cost
   variable, 219–221, 253–54
Cost-benefit analysis, 491–192
Coupon rate, 744
Craft union, *see* Union(s)
Crandall, Robert W, 49, 920-921, 942-943
Credibility thesis, 874 875
Credit, 724
   demand for, 746
   supply of, 750–753
Credit cards, 696
Credit market, 436–438, 785
Credit market model, 753–759
Cross subsidization, 312, 344–346
Crowding in, 788 789
Crowding out, 786, 913
Currency, convertible, 962
   demand for, 957–958
   elastic, 712
Cycle, electoral, 908
Cycle(s), election, 905

Darby, Michael R., 893
Davis-Bacon Act, 391
Deadweight loss, 307, 344
Debt, federal, 790
   government, 793
   monetization of, 797
   national, 793–794
Decertification election, 412
Decision makers, rational, 3
Decision making, 3–5, 123–124
   political, 140–141
   Decision making costs, 181–182
Deficit, federal budget, 910
   government budget, 542, 548, 633, 771, 900, 973
   high employment budget, 785
   Trade, 755
   trade, 548
   twin, 548
Deflator, implicit price, 529–530
Demand, 60
   aggregate labor, 592
   change in, 76, 79–83
   excess, 73, 76, 993
   for labor, 383–385, 388–390
   labor, 802–803
   law of, 59
   final, 614
Demand curve, and the income effect, 178–179, 190–191
   and the substitution effect, 178–179, 190–191
   for Capital, 429–431
   for environmental quality, 479
   market, 63
Demand schedule, 59, 63, 73
   market, 63
Demand theory, labor, 614–617
Denison, Edward F., 627
Deposit insurance, 739 738 739

Depository Institutions Deregulation and Monetary, Control Act, 340–341, 693, 714, 890
Depository institutions, 710 711
Deposits, checkable, 689
  demand, 689
Depreciation, 203, 526
  accounting, 203
  economic, 210
  exchange rate, 960
  real, 571
Depression, 912
Deregulation, 294–295, 340–51
Derived demand, 356–357, 614
  for capital, 427
Diagram, circular flow, 538
  scatter, 24–25
Direct regulation, 337–339
Dirty float, 966
Discount rate, 430, 725
Discounting, 428–430
Discrimination, labor market, 394–395
Diseconomies of scale, 232
Disequilibrium, 73, 522
  market, 102–105
Disequilibrium wage differences, see Wage Differences
Distribution, 13
  income, 982
Distribution of income, 356
Dividends, 200, 516
Doctrine of comparable worth, 396–397
Double coincidence of wants problem, 684
Dukakis, Michael, 919
Dunaway, Steven, 49, 139

Economic rent, 390
Economic efficiency, 36–37, 92, 266, 289–90, 306, 308–311, 323–325, 330
  and labor unions, 421
  and natural monopoly, 308–311
Economic loss, 286–287
  calculating, 251–254
Economic profit, 203–205, 251–252, 284–84, 287–88
  calculating, 251–254
Economic Recovery Act of 1981, 438, 633
Economics, definition of, 2
  New classical, 844–846 857–858
  New keynesian, 857 845–846
  supply-side, 667
Economies of scale, 232, 301, 323
  and investment, 432
  in lending, 439
Economy, barter, 684
  command, 56
  free-market, 602
  market, 56
  mixed, 56
Efficiency, 983
  allocative, 36, 265–266, 289–90, 306, 323
  economic, 36–7, 92, 266, 289–90, 306, 308–11, 323–25, 330

  productive, 36, 68, 216
Eisenhower, Dwight D., 876 909
Eisner, Robert, 917 918
Elasticity, arc, 154
  coefficient of, 149–155
  elastic demand, 152–154
  inelastic demand, 152–154
  point, 154–155
  unitary elastic demand, 153
Elasticity of Demand, 148–164, 287, 293
  and consumer durables, 163–164
  and price discrimination, 158–160
  and slope, 154–155
  and substitutes, 160–164
  and total revenue, 155–158
  cross price, 164–165
  determinants of, 160–164
  long run, 162–164
  short run, 162–164
Elasticity of labor demand, and unions' goals, 416–417
Elasticity of supply, 165
Electronic funds transfer system, 704
Embargo, OPEC oil, 877
Emission banking, 484–485
Emission charge, 483
Emission standard, 480–482
Employment, full, 13
  natural level of, 595
Entin, Stephen J., 783
Entrepreneur, 194
Entrepreneurial ability, 2, 203
Entrepreneurs, 65
Entrepreneurship, 984
Equal output curve, see Isoquant
Equality, 983
Equalizing wage differences, see Wage differences
Equation of exchange, 841
Equilibrium, 71, 73
  long-run aggregate, 620–641
  long-run labor market, 595
  short-run labor market, 594
Equity capital, see stock
European economic community, 998 999 941
Exchange, market, 57
Exchange rate, 579, 878, 957–968
  fixed, 962–963
  flexible, 960–962
Expansion(s), 544
Expectations, 63, 573
  adaptive, 647–648
  inflationary, 884 886 877
  price, 609
  rational, 648
Expenditures, autonomous consumption, 559
Explicit costs, 202–205
Exports, 524, 921, 954
  net, 524, 578, 633
External benefits, 475–477
External costs, 470–478
Externalities, 126–130, 470–77
  and allocation of resources, 474, 476
  internalization of, 476–477
  negative, see External costs
  positive, see External benefits

Factor productivity, 627
Family Support Act, 458–459, 466
Farm Credit System, 256–257
Featherbedding, 417
Federal Deposit Insurance Corporation, 710 711
Federal funds, 725
Federal funds rate, 725, 883
Federal Open Market Committee, 715 723
Federal Reserve, 663, 693, 705, 762, 862–863, 873–874, 876, 878–882
  history of, 711
Federal Reserve Board of Governors, 714 715
Federal Reserve notes, 721
Federal Trade Commission Act, 334
Feldstein, Martin, 575
Financial Institutions Reform, Recovery, and Enforcement Act, 738
Financial intermediaries, 440, 710–11
Firm(s), 65
  worker-managed, 986
Fixed Cost, 219–221, 253–55
  and short-run losses, 254–255, 253–55
Flow, 742
Food Security Act of 1985, 110
Forecasting, 882
Foreign competition, 272
France, 997–998
Franchise, 301
Free lunch, no such thing as, 137
Free rider problem, 131, 488–89
Freeman, Richard B., 420, 422
Friedland, Claire, 338
Friedman, Benjamin, 889
Friedman, Milton, 563, 640, 835, 842
Friedman, Milton, 878, 882, 892-893
Functional distribution of income, 382
Fundamental premise of economics, 3–4, 35, 178, 205, 258, 651
Funds, sources of, 516, 520, 954
  uses of, 517, 520, 954
Future value, 428

Galloway, Lowell, 991
Garn-St.Germain Act, 340–41, 890
Garner, C. Alan, 861
Gattuso, James, 349
General Agreement on Tariffs and Trade(GATT), 941
General Equilibrium Analysis, 271–272
George, P. S., 161
Gephardt, Richard, 974
Germany, 44–45, 692
Gilbert, Neil, 1000-1001
Gilder, George, 984
Goals, 5
  macroeconomic, 549
  social, 19, 110–113
Gold, 692, 888
Gold standard, 964 888
Goods, durable consumer, 566, 568–569
  intermediate, 523
  nondurable consumption, 568
Gompers, Samuel, 413

Goodfriend, Marvin, 727
Gorbachev, Mikhail, 692, 988, 990-991
Gordon, Donald F., 822
Gordon, Robert J., 664, 836, 856, 867
Gosbank, 988
Gosplan, 988
Government expenditures, 770, 772, 774–775
Government ownership, *see* Public enterprise
Government purchases, 523, 578, 773, 898
Gramm-Rudman-Hollings Act, 791
Graphs, time series, 25–26
Great Depression, 627, 838, 858–862
Great Society Program, 463, 663, 881
Greenspan, Alan, 700, 863, 879
Gregory, Paul R., 996
Gross national product (GNP), 523, 553
   expenditure approach, 523
   income approach, 525
   per capita, 530
   real, 526–527, 530
   value added, 525
Growth, 632
   factors contributing to, 627
   money supply, 638–639
   output, 627
   price-level, 637–640
   productivity, 630–631, 633
   aggregate demand, 638
Growth rate, 629
Gutfeld, R., 485

Hall, Robert E., 399
Hamilton, Lee, 730
Happiness, 625
Hardin, Garrett, 489
Hargraves, Monica, 727
Harrington, Michael, 182
Harrison, Bennett, 919
Hart, Gary, 919
Hayek, Friedrich, 981
Haynes, Stephen, 908
Herfindahl-Hirschman Index, 314–15, 336–337
Heterogeneous product, 283–284
Hiring rate, 816
Historical cost, *see* Sunk Cost
Hit and run entry, 325
Homogeneous product, 282–284, 313–14
   and perfect competition, 250
Hong Kong, 999
Hoover, Herbert, 860
Houthakker, H. S., 161
Huddle, Donald, 597
Hyperinflation, 797
Hypothesis, 17

Ignorance, rational, 138
Immigration, Illegal, 596
Immigration Reform and Control Act, 596
Implicit costs, 202–205
Imports, 4, 524, 578, 954
Incentives, 3, 981

Income, *see also*, Personal distribution of income
   and earnings capacity, 451–452
   as a measure of well-being, 447–448
   disposable, 558, 561, 564
   family, 444
   in-Kind, 457
   interest, 516
   labor, 516
   lifetime, 448–449
   long-run, 564
   long-run expected, 563
   national, 525, 534
   per capita, 34, 450–53
   rental, 516
Income elasticity of demand, 164
Income effect, 178–179, 190–191, 612, 762, 884
Income Inequality, 445–455
   and inherited wealth, 452–453
   reasons for, 450–454
Income mobility, 448–449
Income maintenance programs, 826
Income redistribution, 454–455, 462–466
   and economic efficiency, 454
   and incentives, 454–455
   and the equity-efficiency trade-off, 454
Increasing cost industry, 263–264
Indifference curve, 186–186
Indifference curve map, 186
Individual Retirement Acounts, 438
Industrial union, *see* Union(s)
Industries, import-competing, 932
Industry, 195–197
Infant-industry argument, 938
Inferior goods, 61
Inflation, 4, 545, 639
   and interest rates, 439
   cost-push, 679
   demand-pull, 679
   instability of, 545
Inflation expections effect, 763
Inflation rate, real, 695
Information, 889
   asymmetric, 47
   imperfect, 275–278
Information costs, 180–181
Information problem, 922
Infrastructure, Core, 600–601, 626, 631
Innovation, financial, 691, 700, 702, 705, 891
   Government, 630
Inputs, 2, 65
   factor, 523
   real resource, 538
Instability, economic, 667
Interest, compound, 428
   market rate of, *see* Interest rate
Interest Rate, 552, 762, 698, 742–746, 759, 883
   and inflation, 439
   and investment, 428–431, 436–440
   as a return to capital, 438
   equilibrium, 437–438
   expected real, 572, 748, 967–968
   nominal, 436, 758–759
   prime, 439

   pure, 745
   real, 436, 758–59
   determination of, 753
Interest rate effect, indirect, 581, 700
Intermediation, 710
Internal rate of return, 429–431
International competitiveness, 921
International Monetary Fund (IMF), 956
International price ratio effect, 581–582
International reserve currency, 749
Intervention, 962
Investment, 13, 426–438, 440, 523, 655, 777, 868
   benefits of, 431–435
   financial, 570
   government budget, 632 570 630
   gross, 571
   instability of, 575–578, 835–37
   inventory, 576
   net, 571
Investment tax credits, 575, 909
Invisible hand, 123, 273
Involuntary unemployment, *see* Unemployment
In-kind transfers, 447–448, 457
Isocost line, 244–246
Isoquant, 243–244
Isoquant map, 244

James, G.W., 348, 350
Japan, 948
Jevons, William Stanley, 600
Job Training Partnership Act, 463
Johnson administration, 663, 791
Johnson, Lyndon B., 182, 876, 880, 909
Johnson, Paul, 989
Jordan, Jerry, 726
Jorgenson, Dale W., 630

Kahn, Alfred, 342-3
Kane, Edward J., 737
Kennedy administration, 662
Kendrick, John W., 627-628, 921
Kennedy, John F., 909
Keynes, John Maynard, 2, 558, 578, 658, 790
Keynes, John Maynard, 835, 868, 888
Kindleberger, Charles, 940
King, G. A., 161
Kirkland, Richard, Jr., 990
Keynesian Theory, 870–871
Keynesians, 869
Knowledge, Advances in, 630
Korean War, 908
Kuteinikov, Andrei, 987 991
Kuwait, 600, 667

Labor, unskilled, 383, 597
Labor demand, 383–385, 388, 393
Labor force, 592, 803
Labor force participation rate, 373, 592
Labor market model, 813
Labor Market(s), 382–392, 394–400
   aggregate, 383–385
   and monopsony, 396–398

discrimination in, 394–395
disequilibrium, 392
equilibrium, 383–385, 390–391
occupational segregation in, 395
Labor supply, 404–405, 416, 421
and the income effect, 374
and the substitution effect, 373
Labor union, see Union(s)
and nonequalizing wage differences, 390–391
Labor Union(s), goals of, 413–415
Labor-intensive production, 210
Lag, data, 882
enactment, 903–904
implementation, 904
recognition, 882
Lag in the effect of monetary policy, 870–871
Lags in the effect of money supply changes, 843
Laissez faire, 985
Lange, Oskar, 981
Law of diminishing marginal returns, 217–218, 358
Law of diminishing marginal utility, 173
Lawrence, Robert Z., 935
Layoffs, 822 823
Legal cartel theory of regulation, 339
Legal structure of firms, 197–201
Lenin, Vladimir, 989
Lerner, Abba, 981
Lewis, H. Gregg, 420
Liability, legal, 197
limited, 199–201
unlimited, 197–198
Life-cycle hypothesis, 564
Lilla, Mark, 449
Lindert, Peter, 940
Lipton, David, 994
Liquidity, 688
Liquidity effect, 762, 884
Loans, 743
Local union, see Union(s)
Long run, 67
Long-run average cost, 221–227
and natural monopoly, 307–311
Long-run average cost curve, 231–233, 307
investment, 432
Long-run economic profit, 302–303
Long-run marginal cost, 307–310
Long-run cost minimization, 228–233
Long-run decision, 208–209
Lorenz curve, 445–447
Loss, economic, 253–254
Lundberg, Erik, 998

Mabry, Marcus, 811
Macroeconomics, definition of, 134, 514
open-economy, 967–975
Malthus, Thomas Robert, 18, 600
Marx, Karl, 980
Manufacturing sector, 920
Marginal cost, 221–227, 238–239, 289–90, 302–5
and the firm's supply curve, 256

relationship to average total cost and average fixed cost, 223–224
relationship to marginal product, 223
Marginal physical product, 217–219, 223, 357–60
of capital, 229–230
of labor, 217
Marginal product function, 218–219
Marginal propensity to consume, 658
Marginal product of labor, value of the, 615
Marginal productivity of labor, 593
declining, 594
Marginal propensity to consume, 559
Marginal propensity to save, 560
Marginal rate of technical substitution, 244–246
Marginal resource cost, 360–361
in competitive labor markets, 397–398
in monopsony, 397–398
Marginal revenue, 234–239, 251–54, 285–86, 302–5
and perfectly competitive firm's demand curve 234–235, 251
and resource demand, 357–360
Marginal revenue function, 234–237
Marginal revenue product, 358–363, 383–85, 398–99, 421
Marginal rate of substitution, 186–188
Marginal utility per dollar, 174–179
Market, auction, 675
competitive, 71, 75
credit, 551
customer, 675
efficient, 92
goods and services, 550
labor, 551, 590–98, 603
money, 552
secondary, 723 744
underground, 990
Market concentration, see Concentration ratio
Market demand curve for a resource, 361–363
Market failure, 20, 102, 330–331, 333, 337, 470–71
and information costs, 490–493
Market mechanism, 58, 75, 122–124
Market organization, 602
Market power, 101
Market structure, 201
Market supply curve, 256
Markets, aggregate, 538
Materials balancing, 988
Maturity, 200
Mauskopf, Eileen, 850
Mayer, Thomas, 891 889
McDonald's, 810 966
McKenzie, Richard B., 919
McNees, Stephen, 882
Mean family income, 450–453
Medicaid, and antipoverty policy, 463
Medium of exchange, 101, 552, 684
Medoff, James L., 422
Merger, 322–323, 334–37
conglomerate, 322, 334–37
horizontal, 322, 332 -37
vertical, 322, 334–37

Mises, Ludwig Von, 981
Mill, John Stuart, 931
Miller, G. William, 877
Mishkin, Frederic, 858
Mistake theory, 406–407
Mitchell, J., 272
Mobility, imperfect, 275–278
Mobility costs, 181
Model, circular flow, 538
long-run, 621
Models, 18
Modigliani, Franco, 563
Mondale, Walter, 919
Monetarist theory, 871–875
Monetarists, 868–69
Monetary aggregates, 689
Monetary base, 720–721
Monetary policy, 101, 134, 723–731
countercyclical, 870
expansionary, 663, 671, 877
goals of, 727
power of, 968
restrictive, 654, 878
strategy of, 727
targets of, 729
theory of, 869–875
Monetary transmission mechanism, 868–869, 883
Money, 102, 687, 742
commodity, 686
value of, 102
Money balances, Real, 694
Money demand, 702 705 693 694–695, 967, 970
transactions theory of, 693
Money market deposit accounts, 689
Money market mutual funds, 689 705
Money supply, 725, 970
stable, 702
U.S., 688–692
Money supply growth rule, 889
Monopolistic competition, 283–295
and long-run equilibrium, 287–290
and short-run equilibrium, 284–287
compared to perfect competition, 282–285, 289–291
Monopoly, 201, 284, 303–307
and long-run equilibrium, 306
natural, 307–311
regulation of natural, 309–311, 337
and short-run equilibrium, 304–305
compared to perfect competition, 306–307
regulated, 201
Monopsony, 396–398
and labor unions, 421
Moral hazard, 738
Moore, Geoffrey, 882
Morrison, S. A., 346, 350
Motor Carrier Act, 340–341
Moynihan, Daniel Patrick, 782
Mueller, John, 755
Multiplier, deposit, 719
expenditure, 660–661, 837, 898
money, 718 720
Multiplier effect, 658
Munnell, Alicia, 631
Murray, Charles, 456, 464
Mutual fund, 705

1022 ■ INDEX

Mutual interdependence, 312–318
Mutual saving banks, 691

National defense, 940
National income, 206, 356, 382
National income and product accounts, 534–535
National industrial policy, 919–923
National Labor Relations Act, *see* Wagner Act
Natural Gas Policy Act, 340–342
Natural RGNP, 663
Net national product, 534
Neumann, George R., 935
Newman, Barry, 997, 995
Nixon, Richard, 876, 881
Nordhaus, William D., 601
NOW account, 691
Nonequalizing wage differences, *see* Wage diffences
Nonprice competition, 291, 342–343
Normal goods, 61
Normal profit, 203–205, 252
Normative issue, 20, 34
Norris-LaGuardia Act, 410

Occupational segregation, 395
Offset program, 484
Off-budget items, 792
Oil price shock, 671
Okun, Arthur, 820 821
Oligopoly, 313–325
  compared to perfect competition, 325
Olson, Mancur, 625
Open market operations, 715 723
Open shop, 411
Opportunity Cost, 3, 6–7, 11–14, 39, 41, 44, 59, 65, 180, 202–205, 282, 292, 385, 928
  of improvements in environmental quality, 478
  of investment, 426
Organization of Petroleum Exporting Countries (OPEC), 80, 601
Osterfeld, David, 601
Output, aggregate, 543
Output level, natural, 598–602
Output persistence, 654
Ownership, state, 985

Panzar, John, 325
Paper standard, 888
Par value, 970
Paradox of value, 174
Partial equilibrium analysis, 271–272
Partisan cycle, 908
Partnership, 198
  general, 198
  limited, 198
Patent, 300–301
Peak, business cycle, 544
Perestroika, 991
Perfectly competitive economy, 258
Perfectly competitive market, 250–277
Perfectly competitive markets, and short-run equilibrium, 251–257
  and long-run equilibrium, 258–266

Perfectly elastic demand, and perfectly competitive markets, 233, 251
Permanent income hypothesis, 564
Personal Distribution of income, 382, 444–455
  and marginal productivity theory, 453–454
  and standard of living, 448–449
  and taxes, 447–448
  and transfer payments, 448
  by family characteristics, 450–452
Phelps, Edmund, 664
Physical productivity of capital, 427
Planning, government, 626
  Indicative, 986 997
Plans , One-Year, 988
Poland, 991–995
Policy, countercyclical fiscal, 790, 898
  economic, 661
  fiscal, 134, 772
Policy Rule, 872
  active, 872
  passive, 872
Policy Rules, monetary, 875, 889
Politicians, 138–142
Pollution, 477–486
Pollution control policies, 480–486
Population, 18–19
Porter, Michael, 949
Porter, John, 783
Positive issue, 20
Poverty, 455–466
  and standard of living, 456
  causes of, 458–462
  policies to deal with, 463–466
  income, 456
Present discounted value, 586
Present value, 393–394, 428–30
  net, 586–587
Price, 57
  disequilibrium, 76
  equilibrium, 73, 79
  market, 58, 68, 75, 94
  support, 108–109
Price adjustment, 79
Price ceiling, 105–107
Price discrimination, 311, 333
Price elasticity of demand, *see* Elasticity of demand
Price elasticity of resource demand, 363–366
  coefficient of, 363–364
  determinants of, 364–365
  long run, 365–366
  short run, 364–365
Price elasticity of resource supply, 367–373
Price equalization, 931
Price floor, 107–109
Price index (PI), 528–530
Price leadership, 319–320
Price level, average, 528
  expected, 620 595 590
  general, 528
Price searching firm, 235–239, 284–85, 303, 314
Price taking firm, 234–235, 237–238, 250–51, 283–84

Price Taking Firm, and resource demand, 360–361
Price(s), absolute, 517
  aggregate, 637
  base year, 528
  energy, 630–31, 664
  input, 68, 79
  relative, 178–179, 517, 522
Price-level, stable, 4
Primary market, 200–201
Prime rate, *see* Interest rate
Prisoner's dilemma, 316–317
Privatization, 992–993
Problems, economic, 4–5, 123
Producer surplus, 100, 306–307, 934
Product differentiation, 283–284, 288–289, 292–293, 313–14
  and effects on collusion, 321
  imagined, 292–293
  real, 292–293
Production, 517
  domestic, 524
  factors of, 2
Production function, 216–223
  and resource demand, 357–358
Production plan, 981
Production possibilities frontier, 7, 10, 12–13
Productive efficiency, 216
Productivity, and investment, 431–435
  growth rate of, 434–435
  labor, 920
  marginal, 982
Profit, 65, 202–207
  accounting, 203–205
  economic, 203–205, 251–52
  normal, 203–205, 252, 259, 262, 268, 270–71
  normal, *see also* Zero economic profit
  zero economic, 203–4, 252–3, 259–61, 286, 288, 305
Profit maximization, 207–210, 237–39
  and monopolistic competition, 284–288
  and monopoly, 304–306
  and oligopoly, 315–321, 323
  and perfectly competitive markets, 251
  for the price-searching firm, 238–239
  for the price-taking firm, 237–238
Property rights, 101–134, 331, 333, 470–73, 489
Protectionism, 940
Ptolemy, 17
Public choice theory, 135–142
  and union behavior, 414–415
Public enterprise, 331–333
Public good(s), 130–31, 470, 486–489
  and nonexcludability, 486–488
  and nonrivalry, 486–488
  and the exchange of labor, 404
  quasi-public, 486
  policy prescriptions, 488–489
Purchasing power parity, 961–962

Quantity, demanded, 60, 76
  supplied, 76
Quantity theory of money, 639, 842
Quit rate, 816

Quota, 139–40, 860, 942–943 936–938

Rate of return regulation, 309–311
Rate of return, real, 572
Rate of return on capital, after tax, 632
Rate of return on investment, 572
Rational expectations, , 844
Rational expectations hypothesis, 653
Rationality, 3
Rationing, by queue, 57
Rationing mechanism, 57, 81
Reagan, Ronald, 139, 666, 676, 910, 941
Real GNP gap, 654
Recession(s), 544
Redistribution, income, 113, 343–46, 984
Regulation, government, 626
　of monopolistically competitive markets, 293–295, 337
　of oligopoly markets, 321–322
Regulatory capture, 140–41, 338
Regulatory forbearance, 738
Reichenstein, William, 887
Rent, 68
Research and development, 631 630
Reserve, excess, 720
Reserve requirement, 726–27
　Reserve requirement ratio, 715
Reserves, bank, 715
　foreign exchange, 964
Resolution Trust Corporation, 738
Resource, 2, 4, 599–600
Resource demand schedule, 356–363
Resource endowment, 16, 34, 41
Resource immobility, *see* Resource mobility
Resource market, 356
Resource market, equilibrium, 374–376
Resource mobility, 250, 262, 265, 275, 282–84, 292, 300–306, 314, 325, 368–69
　and wage differences, 389–392
Resource supply curve, 367–372
　and resource mobility, 368–369
　long run, 369–373
　short run, 367–369
Resources, idle, 12
　scarce, 34
　unemployed, 12
Retained earnings, 200, 752
Retention rate, 816
Revenue, 65
　average, 234–236, 251–52
　marginal, 234–239, 251–54, 285–86, 302–5
　total, 234–239, 251–54
Revenue requirement, 309–310
Rhoads, Steven E., 14
Ricardian Equivalence, 788, 919
Ricardo, David, 788, 928, 931
Right to Work Legislation, 411
Risk, 101
　and interest rates, 439
　default, 743 745
Risk premium, 745
Robinson-Patman Act, 334
Rohatyn, Felix, 919, 974

Romer, Christina, 836-837
Rosewicz, B., 485
Rubinfien, Elizabeth, 990
Rule for profit maximization, 238–239
Rule of Reason, 334
Rydenfelt, Sven, 989

Sachs, Jeffrey, 992, 994
Sacks, Stephen, 996
Salop, S. C. , 336
Saving, 750–51, 775
Saving and loan crisis, 736–739
Saving function, 560
Saving rate, national, 634
Savings, foreign, 755
Sawhill, Isabel V., 457, 465
Say, Jean Baptiste, 542
Scab Labor, 418
Scarcity, 6, 10, 56
Schwartz, Jacobson, 640
Schwartz, Anna J., 856 882
Science, 16
Screening, 821
Scully, Gerald W., 602
Search theory, 815–820
Sector, financial, 540
　foreign, 542
　government, 542
Securities market, 201
Security, 201
Senile-industry argument, 939
Shakeouts, 289
Shepard, William G., 339
Sherman Antitrust Act, 333–334
Shock, macroeconomic, 603
Short run, 67
Shortage, 73, 81, 103
Short-run cost functions, *see* Cost curve(s)
Short-run decision, 208–209
Shutdown point, 254
Simon, Julian L, 596
Smith, Lee, 949
Smith, Adam, 17, 124-125, 273, 941
Smoot-Hawley Tariff Act, 860
Social Security, 775 782
Socialism, 980–985
　market, 981
Socialists, Utopian, 980
Sole proprietorship, 197–198
Solidarity, 992 994
Soskin, Michael J., 628
Soviet Union, 101, 692, 966, 988–91
Specialization, 43, 48, 102, 123–124
Special-interest group, 139–140
Speculation, 84
Spending, 517
Spillover Effect, and unions, 126, 416, 420
Spillovers, *see* Externalities
Stability, economic, 101, 134
Stabilization policy, 667, 862–63
Stabilizer, automatic, 910 904–905
Stalin, Josef, 989
Standard of value, 687
Stigler, George, 16, 338
Stock, shares of, 200–201, 742
Stock market, 700, 860
Stockholders, 200

Stone, Joe A., 908
Store of value, 687
Stout, Hilary, 814
Strike, 405–407
Stuart, Robert C., 996
Subsidies, and external benefits, 477
Substitutes, 61
Substitution effect, 178–179, 190–191, 612–13
Substitution in consumption, 365
Substitution in production, 365
Suits, D. B., 158
Summers, Lawrence H., 807
Sunk cost(s), 209–210, 254–55, 325
Supplemental Security Income Program, 463–466
Supply, aggregate, 624 603–609
　change in, 76, 79–83
　excess, 73
　labor, 404–5, 416, 421, 558, 632, 802–3
　law of,
　of labor, *see* Labor Supply
Supply curve and marginal cost, 256
　for environmental quality, 479
　for the perfectly competitive firm, 256
　market, 70
Supply of a currency, 958–959
Supply shock, 661, 892
Supply theory, Labor, 612–614
Surplus, 75, 79, 103
Surplus, budget, 542, 633
Sweden, 998 1000

Taft-Hartley Act, 411
Target, monetary policy, 883
Tariff, 936–942
Tastes, consumer, 92
Taylor, Lester D., 161
Tax, capital-gains, 902
　corporate profits, 777
　income, 777, 863, 898–900, 909
　individual income, 776
　loopholes, 115
　windfall profits, 80
Tax credits, investment, 633, 778
Tax Equity and Fiscal Responsibility Act of 1982, 633
Tax rate, average, 777
　marginal, 776–779
Tax Reform Act of 1986, 634
Tax rates, marginal income, 633
Taxes, 770, 778
　and external costs, 476
　indirect business, 526
　payroll, 910
　temporary changes, 570–571
Technology, 15, 68, 601, 626
　change in, in perfectly competitive market, 268–270
Term structure, 745
Term to maturity, 745
Theories, 17
Theory of contestable markets, 324–325, 336
Thoreau, Henry David, 38
Threat effect, 416, 420
Threshold effect, 664

Thurow, Lester, 919
Time preference, 746
Time value of money, 428
Time-inconsistency problem, 873
Tonge, Peter, 481
Total cost, 251–253
    of production, 219–221
Total physical product, 357–358
Total revenue, 234–239, 251–54
Trade, 34
    balance of, 548
    free, 44–45
    gains from, 931–934
    indirect, 685
    international, 40, 860
    mutually beneficial, 16
    restriction of, 49
    terms of, 45, 930, 936
    voluntary, 37, 58
Trade balance, 944
Trade barriers, and unions' goals, 417
Trade deficit, 944
Trade restrictions, 272
Trade surplus, 944
Trade union, *see* Union(s)
Tranfers, unilateral, 954
Transactions costs, 180–183, 471–73
Transfer payments, 516, 524, 770, 773, 775, 863, 899
Transferable discharge permit, 483–484
Trough, 544
Truman, Harry S., 908-909
Tufte, Edward R., 907
Trust, 333
Turning points, business cycle, 882

Unemployment, 4, 382, 384, 802–3
    cyclical, 606, 809, 825–26
    flow model of, 804
    frequency of, 805
    frictional, 808, 825–26
    involuntary, 416
    natural rate of, 810–812, 880
    structural, 809, 826–27
    voluntary, 416
Unemployment rate, 547, 802, 805
Unenmployment policy, 825–827
Union Shop, 411
Union(s), and economic welfare, 421–422
    craft, 404, 406
    industrial, 404–406
    labor, 404–420
    local, 408–409
    national, 408–409
    trade, *see* Labor unions
Utility, 37, 170–178
    marginal, 171–176
    total, 171–173, 176
Utility maximization, 170–178
    rule for, 176

Values, imputed, 524
Variable cost, 219–221, 253–54
Velocity of money, 842, 871, 889–91
Vietnam war, 662, 881
Volcker, Paul, 878
Volume changes, 630
Voluntary import restrictions, 938
Voluntary unemployment, *see* Unemployment
Voters, 136–137

Wage, Reservation, 390, 816, 818
Wage differences, disequilibrium, 392
    equalizing, 386–388
    nonequalizing, 389–391
Wage rigidity, 822 823
Wage rate, 551
    equilibrium, 551
    nominal, 551
    Expected real, 590
Wage subsidies, 935
Wages, Sticky, 603, 646–647
Wage(s), 68, 382–392, 394–400
    and earnings premiums, 387–388
    and unions' goals, 413–414
    effects of unions on, 415–415, 420
    equilibrium in a competitive labor market, 397–398
    equilibrium in a monopsony labor market, 397–398
    minimum, 418–419
    nominal, 385, 590
    real, 385, 607
    reservation, 390
Wage-price controls, 910
Wagner Act, 410–411
Walesa, Lech, 992
Wealth, 917
    secondary, 625
Wealth effect, Direct, 581
Weisman, Katherine, 457
Welfare, social, 526
Welfare state, 1000 998
Wheeler-Lea Act, 334
White, J. B., 272
Willig, Robert, 325
Winston, C., 346,350
Wittman, Donald, 139
Workers, discouraged, 805
Workfare, 458–459
Wright, Jim, 141
Wurtz, Richard E., 861

Yellow-Dog Contract, 410
Yugoslavia, 996–997
Youngson, A. J., 999

Zero economic profit, *see* Economic profit

TABLE 3

Miscellaneous macroeconomic statistics (billions of dollars, except as noted)

Year or Quarter	Surplus or Deficit (−), National Income and Product Accounts		Money Stock		Unemployment Rate, All Workers (Percent)	Average Hourly Earnings Total Private Business	
	Total Government	Federal Government	M1	M2		Current Dollars	1982 Dollars
1929	1.0	1.2					
1933	−1.4	−1.3					
1939	−2.2	−2.2					
1940	−.7	−1.3					
1941	−3.8	−5.1					
1942	−31.4	−33.1					
1943	−44.2	−46.6					
1944	−51.8	−54.5					
1945	−39.5	−42.1					
1946	5.4	3.5					
1947	14.4	13.4					$1.131	$4.875
1948	8.4	8.3				1.225	4.900
1949	−3.4	−2.6				1.275	5.141
1950	8.0	9.2			5.2	1.335	5.340
1951	6.1	6.5			3.2	1.45	5.39
1952	−3.8	−3.7			2.9	1.52	5.51
1953	−7.0	−7.1			2.8	1.61	5.79
1954	−7.1	−6.0			5.4	1.65	5.91
1955	3.1	4.4			4.3	1.71	6.15
1956	5.2	6.1			4.0	1.80	6.38
1957	.9	2.3			4.2	1.89	6.47
1958	−12.6	−10.3			6.6	1.95	6.50
1959	−1.6	−1.1	140.0	297.8	5.3	2.02	6.69
1960	3.1	3.0	140.7	312.4	5.4	2.09	6.79
1961	−4.3	−3.9	145.2	335.5	6.5	2.14	6.88
1962	−3.8	−4.2	147.9	362.7	5.4	2.22	7.07
1963	.7	.3	153.4	393.3	5.5	2.28	7.17
1964	−2.3	−3.3	160.4	424.8	5.0	2.36	7.33
1965	.5	.5	167.9	459.4	4.4	2.46	7.52
1966	−1.3	−1.8	172.1	480.0	3.7	2.56	7.62
1967	−14.2	−13.2	183.3	524.4	3.7	2.68	7.72
1968	−6.0	−6.0	197.5	566.4	3.5	2.85	7.89
1969	9.9	8.4	204.0	589.6	3.4	3.04	7.98
1970	−10.6	−12.4	214.5	628.1	4.8	3.23	8.03
1971	−19.5	−22.0	228.4	712.7	5.8	3.45	8.21
1972	−3.4	−16.8	249.3	805.2	5.5	3.70	8.53
1973	7.9	−5.6	262.9	861.0	4.8	3.94	8.55
1974	−4.3	−11.6	274.4	908.6	5.5	4.24	8.28
1975	−64.9	−69.4	287.6	1,023.3	8.3	4.53	8.12
1976	−38.4	−53.5	306.4	1,163.7	7.6	4.86	8.24
1977	−19.1	−46.0	331.3	1,286.7	6.9	5.25	8.36
1978	−.4	−29.3	358.5	1,389.0	6.0	5.69	8.40
1979	11.5	−16.1	382.9	1,497.1	5.8	6.16	8.17
1980	−34.5	−61.3	408.9	1,629.9	7.0	6.66	7.78
1981	−29.7	−63.8	436.5	1,793.5	7.5	7.25	7.69
1982	−110.8	−145.9	474.5	1,963.1	9.5	7.68	7.68
1983	−128.6	−176.0	521.2	2,186.5	9.5	8.02	7.79
1984	−105.0	−169.6	552.1	2,371.6	7.4	8.32	7.80
1985	−131.8	−196.9	620.1	2,570.6	7.1	8.57	7.77
1986	−144.1	−206.9	724.7	2,814.2	6.9	8.76	7.81
1987	−107.1	−158.2	750.4	2,913.2	6.1	8.98	7.73
1988	−95.3	−141.7	787.5	3,072.4	5.4	9.28	7.69
1989	−87.8	−134.3	794.8	3,221.6	5.2	9.66	7.64
1990	−126.0	−161.3	825.5	3,323.3	5.4	10.03	7.54

Source: *Economic Report of the President, 1991,* Tables B-39, B-44, B-67, and B-79.